The Making of American Liberal Theology: Idealism, Realism, and Modernity

Books by Gary Dorrien

Logic and Consciousness: The Dialectics of Mind

The Democratic Socialist Vision

Reconstructing the Common Good: Theology and the Social Order

*The Neoconservative Mind: Politics, Culture,
and the War of Ideology*

Soul in Society: The Making and Renewal of Social Christianity

The Word as True Myth: Interpreting Modern Theology

The Remaking of Evangelical Theology

The Barthian Revolt in Modern Theology

*The Making of American Liberal Theology:
Imagining Progressive Religion, 1805–1900*

*The Making of American Liberal Theology: Idealism, Realism,
and Modernity, 1900–1950*

THE MAKING OF AMERICAN LIBERAL THEOLOGY: IDEALISM, REALISM, AND MODERNITY

1900–1950

Gary Dorrien

Westminster John Knox Press
LOUISVILLE • LONDON

Book design by Sharon Adams
Cover design by Night & Day Design

First edition
Published by Westminster John Knox Press
Louisville, Kentucky

This book is printed on acid-free paper that meets the American National Standards Institute Z39.48 standard.♾

PRINTED IN THE UNITED STATES OF AMERICA

03 04 05 06 07 08 09 10 11 12 — 10 9 8 7 6 5 4 3 2 1

Library of Congress Cataloging-in-Publication Data is on file at the Library of Congress, Washington, D.C.

ISBN 0-664-22355-9

For my Fair Sara—
Beloved daughter and shining jewel

THE MAKING OF AMERICAN LIBERAL THEOLOGY:
IDEALISM, REALISM, AND MODERNITY,
1900–1950
Gary Dorrien

Contents

Acknowledgments

For the rights of access to and permission to quote from the unpublished letters and papers of Edgar S. Brightman, grateful acknowledgment is made to the Brightman Collection, Department of Special Collections, Boston University, Boston, Massachusetts, with special thanks to Sean D. Noël, Assistant Director for Public Service; for the unpublished letters and papers of William Adams Brown and Harry Emerson Fosdick, grateful acknowledgment is made to the Brown and Fosdick Collections, Department of Special Collections, Burke Library, Union Theological Seminary, New York, New York, with special thanks to Archivist Claire McCurdy; for the unpublished letters and papers of George Burman Foster and Shailer Mathews, grateful acknowledgment is made to the Special Collections Research Center, Joseph Regenstein Library, University of Chicago, Chicago, Illinois, with special thanks to Alice Schreyer, Director of the Special Collections Research Center, and Daniel Meyer, Associate Director; for the unpublished letters and papers of Georgia Harkness, grateful acknowledgment is made to the Brightman Collection, Department of Special Collections, Boston University, and the United Library of Garrett-Evangelical/Seabury-Western Seminaries, Evanston, Illinois, with special thanks to David Himrod, United Library Reference Librarian; for the unpublished letters and papers of Henry Churchill King, grateful acknowledgment is made to the King Collection, Oberlin College Archives, Oberlin, Ohio, with special thanks to Archivist Roland M. Baumann; for the unpublished letters and papers of Albert C. Knudson, grateful acknowledgment is made to the Knudson Papers, Department of Library Research Collections, Boston University School of Theology, Boston, Massachusetts, with special thanks to Dawn Piscitello, Research Collections Librarian; for the unpublished letters and papers of Reinhold Niebuhr, grateful acknowledgment is made to the Manuscript Division, Library of Congress, Washington, D.C., with special thanks to Archivist Fred Bauman and the Columbia University Oral History Research Collection, Columbia University, New York, New York, with special thanks to Associate Director Jessica Wiederhorn; for the unpublished letters and papers of Walter Rauschenbusch, grateful acknowledgment is made to the Rauschenbusch Family Papers, American Baptist–Samuel Colgate Historical Library of the American Baptist Historical Society, Colgate-Rochester/Crozer Divinity School, Rochester, New York, with special thanks to Library Director Stuart W. Campbell and Assistant to the Director Nancy Blostein; for the unpublished letters and papers of Vida Scudder, grateful acknowledgment is made to the Margaret Clapp Library, Archives of Wellesley College, Wellesley, Massachusetts, with special thanks to Archivist Wilma R. Slaight.

For the photographs of Edward Scribner Ames, Shirley Jackson Case, George Burman Foster, Shailer Mathews, Gerald Birney Smith, Paul Tillich, Henry Nelson Wieman, and Swift Hall of the University of Chicago Divinity School, grateful acknowledgment is made to the Special Collections Research Center, Joseph Regenstein Library, University of Chicago, Chicago, Illinois, with special thanks to Director Alice Schreyer and Head of Reader Services Jay Satterfield and Reader Services Supervisor Debra Levine; for the photograph of John C. Bennett, grateful acknowledgment is made to John M. Bennett with thanks to Robert Dewey; for the photographs of Edgar S. Brightman, Albert C. Knudson, Francis J. McConnell, and Howard Thurman grateful acknowledgment is made to the Department of Special Collections, Boston University, Boston, Massachusetts, with special thanks to Assistant Director for Public Service Sean D. Noël; for the photograph of Boston University School of Theology, grateful acknowledgment is made to Boston University Photo Services, with special thanks to Harry Breger, Graphic Designer, Boston University Publications Production; for the photographs of Robert L. Calhoun, Douglas Clyde Macintosh, and H. Richard Niebuhr, grateful acknowledgment is made to the Department of Special Collections, Yale University Divinity School Library, New Haven, Connecticut, with special thanks to Research Services Librarian and Curator of the Day Missions Collection Martha Lund Smalley; for the photograph of Henry Churchill King, grateful acknowledgment is made to the Oberlin College Archives, Oberlin, Ohio, with special thanks to Administrative Secretary Tamara L. Martin; for the photograph of William Adams Brown, grateful acknowledgment is made to Sally B. Brown (Mrs. Thatcher M. Brown III); for the photograph of Harry Emerson Fosdick, grateful acknowledgment is made to the Riverside Archives, Riverside Church, New York, New York, with special thanks to Director of the Critical History Project Sheila Gillams and Associate Archivist Victor K. Jordan; for the photograph of Georgia Harkness, grateful acknowledgment is made to the United Library, Garrett-Evangelical/Seabury-Western Seminaries, Evanston, Illinois, with special thanks to Reference Librarian David Himrod; for the photograph of Rufus M. Jones, grateful acknowledgment is made to the Department of Special Collections, Haverford College Library, Haverford, Pennsylvania, with special thanks to student assistant Cara Furman; for the photograph of Benjamin E. Mays, grateful acknowledgment is made to Moorland-Spingarn Research Center, Howard University, Washington, D.C., with special thanks to Curator Joellen

El Bashir; for the photograph of Charles Clayton Morrison, grateful acknowledgment is made to the *Christian Century,* with special thanks to Heidi Baumgaertner, Advertising Manager; for the photograph of Reinhold Niebuhr, grateful acknowledgment is made to Christopher Niebuhr; for the photograph of Walter Rauschenbusch, grateful acknowledgment is made to the American Baptist–Samuel Colgate Historical Society, Colgate-Rochester/Crozer Divinity School, Rochester, New York, with special thanks to Library Director Stuart W. Campbell; for the portrait of Vida Scudder, painted by Charles Hopkinson, grateful acknowledgment is made to the Wellesley College Archives, Margaret Clapp Library, Wellesley, Massachusetts, with special thanks to Archivist Wilma R. Slaight; for the photograph of Henry P. Van Dusen, grateful acknowledgment is made to Hugh Van Dusen; for the photograph of Union Theological Seminary, grateful acknowledgment is made to the Burke Library Archives, Union Theological Seminary, with special thanks to Joann Anand, Director of Publications/Communications. The photograph of William Newton Clarke belongs to the public domain.

I am deeply grateful to a host of expert readers and respondents whose careful reviews of various parts of this manuscript, sometimes as respondents at academic conferences, have greatly strengthened it. A first group in this category includes Rufus Burrow Jr., Susan Hill Lindley, the late George Pickering, Joe Pickle, Roger Olson, and Edgar A. Towne. A second group, commissioned by the publisher, provided invaluably detailed assessments of the entire manuscript; they are John B. Cobb Jr., Christopher Evans, Langdon Gilkey, and Jerome A. Stone. To several organizations and institutions I am grateful for the opportunity to present parts of this manuscript at conferences and symposia; they include the Winslow Lectureship of Allegheny College, the American Academy of Religion, the American Theological Society, the William Frederick Allen Lectureship of the Bayview Society, the Episcopal Diocese of Western Michigan, the Evangelical Lutheran Church of America Institute for Mission, the Highlands Institute for American Religious and Philosophical Thought, the Marion Dunsmore Lectureship of Kalamazoo College, and *Res Publica.*

As always I am grateful for the friendship and skill of my editors at Westminster John Knox Press, editor Stephanie Egnotovich and project editor Daniel Braden; and also to copyeditor Hermann Weinlick and indexer Diana Witt. Among my numerous colleagues at Kalamazoo College, I will restrict myself this time to mentioning only three, whose friendship belongs to a special category: philosopher Christopher Latiolais, President James F. Jones Jr., and French scholar Janet Solberg. And above all, for the gift of unstinted assistance on all manner of bibliographical tasks, and more importantly for the gift of friendship, I am grateful to Becca Kutz-Marks, Associate Chaplain and Assistant to the Dean of Stetson Chapel at Kalamazoo College.

William Newton Clarke

William Adams Brown

Henry Churchill King

Charles Clayton Morrison

Walter Rauschenbusch

Vida Scudder

George Burman Foster

Shailer Mathews

Shirley Jackson Case   Edward Scribner Ames

Douglas Clyde Macintosh   Gerald Birney Smith

Henry Nelson Wieman

Francis J. McConnell

Edgar S. Brightman

Albert C. Knudson

Harry Emerson Fosdick

Rufus Jones

Georgia Harkness

Benjamin E. Mays

Reinhold Niebuhr

John C. Bennett   Paul Tillich

H. Richard Niebuhr

Henry P. Van Dusen

Robert L. Calhoun

Howard Thurman

Swift-Hall, University of Chicago
Divinity School

Union Theological Seminary

Boston University
School of Theology

Introduction

In the twentieth century the idea of a liberal approach to Christianity became the founding idea of a new theological establishment. This book, the second of a three-volume interpretation of American theological liberalism, interprets the story of American liberal theology during the years of its early and middle twentieth century heyday and chastening.

The essential idea of liberal theology is that all claims to truth, in theology as in other disciplines, must be made on the basis of reason and experience, not by appeal to external authority. Christian scripture may be recognized as spiritually authoritative within Christian experience, but its word does not settle or establish truth claims about matters of fact. In the nineteenth century this idea was imagined and developed by a relative handful of American religious thinkers, until the 1880s, when it became a movement. The liberal theology movement was led by pastors, but, linked with a rising Progressivism in American politics and religion, it gained a foothold in prominent American divinity schools and seminaries. In the early twentieth century it became a field-dominating movement that redefined the religious teaching and social ambitions of mainstream American Protestantism. The second-generation liberals who took over America's elite divinity schools and seminaries in the twentieth century regarded themselves as founders of a new age, but their sweeping optimism and success set them up for a hard fall, and they were slow to recognize that their appeal to the "best of modern knowledge" often turned academic and cultural fashions into new external authorities.

THEMES AND FIGURES

American liberal theology entered the twentieth century with youthful optimism. Trained in the methods and ideas of Ritschlian-school German theology, the American theologians who came of age at the turn of the century launched their careers at the moment that American theological education was ready for them. Theologically, the old orthodoxies of traditional American Protestantism had been dethroned. Socially, the foundations of what came to be called the social gospel movement were in place. Institutionally, the field of theological scholarship was shifting to a new primary home, the university-related divinity school. The new theologians understood that they were beneficiaries of these transformations. In 1901 Oberlin College theologian Henry Churchill King opened his first book by declaring, "A new constructive period in theology, it may well be believed, is at hand."[1] The Christian century, later called the American century, had begun.

The Progressive-era liberals believed that God was immanent in the evolutionary processes of nature and modern cultural development. They accepted the Enlightenment dictum that no credible truth claim can be settled or based upon an appeal to external authority. Most of them embraced an idealistic theology of social salvation that was novel in Christian history. In the early nineteenth century the center of American theological education had passed from the denominational college to the graduate seminary; at the end of the century it began to pass to divinity schools allied with research-oriented universities. Prominent biblical theologian Charles A. Briggs remarked of the latter transition in 1897, "We have only recently entered upon the third stage, and theological education in the future will advance in university lines."[2]

Briggs's ambition for his employer, Union Theological Seminary, was that it would become a model "theological university." Union Seminary never quite fulfilled this ambition, mainly because it remained independent from Columbia University and failed to acquire the requisite institutional resources. Theologically, it also moved too far to the left to suit Briggs, despite his notoriety as a modernizer. In the first three decades of the twentieth century, however, Union Seminary played a leading role in the creation of a field-dominating liberal theology movement. Its only rival as a theological powerhouse was the newly founded University of Chicago Divinity School, which exemplified the "theological university" model and developed a distinctively pragmatic, empiricist, naturalistic approach to theology. A third academic institution, Boston University School of Theology, made a bid for top-tier status on the strength of its advocacy of an idealist metaphysical philosophy pioneered by nineteenth-century Boston University philosopher Borden Parker Bowne.

These three institutions anchored the liberal theology movement during its twentieth-century heyday and kept it alive during its years of reproach. Union Theological Seminary was a bastion of gospel-centered "evangelical" liberalism; the University of Chicago Divinity School was the center of a naturalistic-empiricist approach to religion that was often called "modernist" liberalism; the Boston University School of Theology combined a gospel-centered theology with a distinctive philosophy of metaphysical personalism. American theological liberalism was more variegated and complex than these influential schools, however. The evangelical, modernist, and personalist approaches all produced novel off-shoots; mystical and catholic-centered liberalisms also competed for attention; Unitarian thinkers continued to identify with liberal theology, though usually from a post-Christian humanistic standpoint; and in the 1930s, Union Theological Seminary became the center of a neoliberal alternative while Union's presidents and much of its faculty remained identified with old-style evangelical liberalism.

For all of its differences in style, method, and content, however, the liberal theology movement was distinguished by its commonalities. In the first volume of this work, *The Making of American Liberal Theology: Imagining Progressive Religion,* I defined liberal theology primarily by its original character as a mediating Christian movement. The founders of American liberal theology sought to create a third way between the authority-based Christian orthodoxies of their time and a rising tide of rationalistic deism and atheism. They created this third way by reconceptualizing the meaning of traditional Christian teaching in the light of modern knowledge and modern ethical values. Most liberal theologians were Victorian romanticists who conceived good religion as the triumph of cultivated spirit over nature, though in the twentieth century American liberal theology produced a naturalistic-empirical tradition that spurned all forms of nature/spirit dualism. In both cases, liberal theology was reformist in spirit and substance, not revolutionary. Fundamentally it is the idea of a modern Christianity not based on external authority. Specifically, liberal theology is defined by its openness to the verdicts of modern intellectual inquiry, especially historical criticism and the natural sciences; its commitment to the authority of individual reason and experience; its conception of Christianity as an ethical way of life; its favoring of moral concepts of atonement; and its commitment to make Christianity credible and socially relevant to contemporary people.

Though many scholars have written about American theological liberalism, this is the first comprehensive interpretation of the subject. Though many have analyzed the development of liberal theology in the early and middle twentieth century, mine is also the first work to treat the "neoliberal" theologies of Reinhold Niebuhr, John C. Bennett, and Paul Tillich as belonging to the liberal tradition. The latter interpretion is related to the particular definition of liberal theology that I assume throughout this work. As I argued in volume one and elaborate in this book, much of the scholarly literature overidentifies American theological liberalism with factors that were peculiar to its period of optimistic ascendancy between 1885 and 1917. Liberal theology existed long before 1885, and it remains an important ongoing tradition in forms that bear little relation to the social gospel belief that Christian idealism is building the kingdom of God. Moreover, the liberal character of the Niebuhrian-Tillichian alternative becomes clearer when the optimistic evolutionism and immanentalism of the early social gospel are not defined as essential to liberal theology.[3]

The problem of selection was not very difficult for me in the first volume of this work, since *Imagining Progressive Religion* dealt with obvious founders and the mere beginnings of a social and intellectual movement. This volume deals with a field-dominating movement, however, which presents more difficult problems of selection. Because this is a history of American liberal theology, not of American religious liberalism, on the whole I have selected theologians over ethicists, religious philosophers, biblical scholars, and other kinds of religious thinkers, but not without significant exceptions.

This book discusses numerous thinkers, some of them extensively, who are not featured in the book's organizational scheme. Some are Continental theologians and philosophers who importantly influenced the development of American liberal theology, especially Immanuel Kant, G. W. F. Hegel, Friedrich Schleiermacher, Albrecht Ritschl, Adolf von Harnack, Wilhelm Herrmann, Auguste Sabatier, Ernst Troeltsch, Johannes Weiss, Rudolf Otto, Karl Barth, and Martin Heidegger. Others are English theologians and philosophers, notably Frederick Denison Maurice, Alfred North Whitehead (who became an American in later life), and William Temple. Others are American philosophers who directly influenced American liberal theology, especially William James, William Ernest Hocking, Josiah Royce, John Dewey, Borden Parker Bowne (who was featured in volume one), and Charles Hartshorne (who will be featured in volume three). A final group that is discussed but not featured in the present book consists of various liberal American religious thinkers: religious philosopher John Wright Buckham, theologian Robert L. Calhoun, religious educationist George Albert Coe, seminary president Henry Sloane Coffin, social gospel economist Richard Ely, religious philosopher Ralph T. Flewelling, theologian Frank Hugh Foster, biblical scholar Francis Ernest Charles Gigot, university president and biblical scholar William Rainey Harper, comparative religionist A. Eustace Haydon, theologian Walter Marshall Horton, religious philosopher Eugene Lyman, *Christian Century* editor Charles Clayton Morrison, social gospel pastor Justin Wroe Nixon, theologian Harris Franklin Rall, and social ethicist Harry F. Ward.

Though volume one emphasized the Unitarian roots of American liberal theology, and though Unitarian ethicist Francis G. Peabody made notable contributions to the social gospel, American Unitarianism took a humanistic, arguably post-Christian turn in the late nineteenth century that arrested its theological creativity. It produced no important theologians in the twentieth century, and even its dominant religious-humanist perspective was best expressed by thinkers outside the Unitarian tradition, such as George Burman Foster, Edward Scribner

Ames, and Henry Nelson Wieman, who are featured in this book. The third volume of this work will feature Unitarian-Universalist theologian James Luther Adams. Moreover, though the narrative frame of this book extends a few years beyond the beginning of the third phases of the Boston-centered personalist school and the Chicago-centered tradition of naturalistic empiricism, my treatment of theologians L. Harold De Wolf, Walter G. Muelder, S. Paul Schilling, Nels F. S. Ferré, Bernard M. Loomer, and Bernard E. Meland must wait until the next volume, aside from brief discussions in chapters four, five, and eight.

The Making of American Liberal Theology: Idealism, Realism, and Modernity emphasizes theologians who made a substantial public impact on twentieth-century American theology as representatives of a major school of thought. It also gives extensive attention to several thinkers who represent notable minority perspectives or constituencies in the liberal theology movement. It begins with the making of a new theological establishment in a new century, represented by the movement's first systematizer, Colgate theologian William Newton Clarke, and the movement-building theologies and public careers of Union Seminary theologian William Adams Brown and Oberlin College theologian Henry Churchill King. Symmetry might have called for exclusive attention to Union Seminary theologians in this chapter, but Union merely championed the gospel-centered (usually Ritschlian) approach to theology, it did not dominate this perspective in the manner of Chicago-school empiricism or Boston-school personalism. Befitting the importance of the German Ritschlian tradition in American liberal theology, my first chapter contains a detailed analysis of the Ritschlian school. Theologically, Clarke, Brown, and King played major roles in establishing gospel-centered liberalism as the dominant theology of American Protestantism during the early twentieth century, and King also shows the influence of personalist idealism beyond its base at Boston University. As public figures and church leaders, Brown and King epitomized the responsible, assuring face of American liberal theology in its takeover phase.

Liberal theology and the social gospel were not exactly the same thing—there were liberal theologians who were not social gospelers and social gospelers who were not theologically liberal—but for the most part they blended together as a unity. The social gospel movement was so influential in early-twentieth-century American Protestantism that it cannot be confined to a single chapter; most of the thinkers discussed in this book were social gospelers of some kind, and thus every chapter deals to some extent with the theology and ethics of the social gospel. But the greatest figure of early-twentieth-century Protestantism was chiefly a product of the social gospel, Rochester Theological Seminary theologian Walter Rauschenbusch, and like his lesser-known counterpart in chapter two, he was an advocate of the movement's socialist flank. An electrifying writer, Rauschenbusch made the social gospel daring, inspiring, and unavoidable. He changed American Protestantism in a few years' time, yet his stature in American Christianity and the social gospel movement is anomalous. Theologically he belonged to the Ritschlian mainstream of the movement, but ideologically he belonged to its socialist left wing, a fact that has confused generations of students about the politics of the social gospel. Rauschenbusch deserves his standing as the symbol and champion of American social Christianity, and he was outflanked to his left by some Christian socialists, but his commitment to democratic revolutionary socialism put him outside the mainstream of social gospel opinion.

Wellesley College English professor Vida Scudder belonged to Rauschenbusch's socialist wing from the opposite end of the ecclesiastical spectrum. Like several of the movement's major figures, Rauschenbusch was a Baptist who took pride in his repudiation of most things Catholic. He used the term "priestly religion" as an epithet, blasted the Vatican's opposition to liberalism and democracy and, like most of the social gospelers, saw nothing worth appropriating in Catholic sacramentalism. Scudder's prolific writing and activism offered a rare break from the strenuously Protestant tone of the mainstream social gospel movement; moreover, she made the case for an Anglo-Catholic social gospel from the even rarer perspective of a woman. Writing for the *Christian Century* and other liberal Protestant organs, Scudder stuck out from the causes and groups that she adopted, and thus diversified liberal Protestant theology and activism. In this book she represents minority perspectives that remained decidedly minority in her time, though some of her commitments, notably pacifism and settlement-house work, were mainstream social gospel causes. As a pacifist she exemplified the liberal idealism of her time; in her politics she struggled with the contradictions between pacifism and revolutionary socialism; as a woman and Catholic liberal she prefigured important later developments in liberal theology.

Like the social gospel, the Chicago school looms too large in the history of American liberal theology to be reducible to a single chapter, especially because it began in the early 1890s with the founding of the University of Chicago. My account of the history and method of Chicago theology is both genetic and thematic. It examines the intellectual development of the school's founding religious thinkers, George Burman Foster, Shailer Mathews, and Shirley Jackson Case, within the context of the developing Chicago school, and then examines the working out of the Chicago school's empiricist commitments in the theologies of Edward Scribner Ames, Douglas Clyde Macintosh (who studied under Foster and taught at Yale), Gerald Birney Smith, and Henry Nelson Wieman.

The Chicago schoolers began theologically as Ritschlian-style empiricists who blended the religious languages of moral value and gospel revelation, but under the influence of American philosophical pragmatism and naturalistic empiricism they developed a distinctively American approach to theology that claimed a strictly scientific methodological basis. In its first phase, as exemplified by the writings of Mathews and Case, the Chicago school took a predominantly socio-historical approach to religion, though Foster cautioned against the religious limitations of historicism. In its second phase, which was launched by Wieman in the late 1920s, the school played down its historicist commitments and its emphasis on religious experience in favor of a dehistoricized empirical focus on experience as a whole. In both of its early phases, the Chicago school championed the possibility of a scientific, pragmatic, naturalistic, and thoroughly "modernist" approach to theology; it spoke the social scientific language of process, pattern, evidence, and function; and it conceived God as the highest expression of human ideals. The latter claim marked a key difference between the thoroughgoing modernism championed by Chicago schoolers and other liberals of their type and the milder modernisms of the Ritschlian, personalist, and mystical variants of liberal theology. Though the Chicago schoolers occasionally equivocated about whether God should be conceived as a cosmic reality, for the most part they defined God as an analogical expression for an idealized conception of the universe. Significantly, their most radical and notorious figure, Foster, was also the one who struggled most deeply with the question whether a purely functionalist approach to religious truth is religiously adequate.

In the 1920s, the version of Chicago-school theology that seemed to stand the best chance of redirecting American liberal theology was that of Macintosh, who forged his distinctive position after moving to Yale. Emphasizing the apologetic importance of epistemological realism, he championed the Chicago-school belief that in order to regain its intellectual prestige in the modern world, theology needed to become a form of empirical science. Liberal theology was too subjective by virtue of its neo-Kantian and romanticist elements, he argued; though committed to historical criticism, he added that thoroughgoing historicism wasn't the answer to the problem of subjectivism, either. At the same time Macintosh rejected the nonsupernaturalism of his teachers; Foster's zigzagging on the knowable metaphysical reality of God was a cautionary specter to him. Macintosh's constructive theologizing was a judgment on the religious bankruptcy of Chicago-school theism. In his own way, Wieman made a similar judgment after he joined the Chicago faculty in the late 1920s. Wieman launched the second phase of Chicago theology by defining God as the really existing "Something" on which human life and the flourishing of the good are dependent. For many Chicago divinity students, this became the liberal answer to an ascendant Barthian neo-orthodoxy. By conceiving God as a structured event and theology as the analysis of the total event of religious experience, Wieman made Chicago theology more religious, less historicist, and more stringently empirical at the same time.

The second phases of the Chicago empiricist and Boston personalist theologies overlapped by more than twenty years—Wieman taught at Chicago from 1927 to 1947—but they originated very differently. In its first generation Chicago-school theology was a collective enterprise that pooled the intellectual labors of Foster, Mathews, Ames, Smith, Shirley Jackson Case, Albert Eustace Haydon, and others; its redirection in the late 1920s was inspired by a single thinker, Henry Nelson Wieman. The school of personalist idealism centered at Boston University developed in exactly the opposite fashion. It was founded by a single theorist, philosopher Borden Parker Bowne, who died in 1910 and whose thinking was examined in the first volume of this work. It was carried on and reinterpreted by a productive generation of disciples led by Methodist bishop Francis J. McConnell, Boston University philosopher Edgar S. Brightman, and

Boston University School of Theology dean and theologian Albert C. Knudson, all of whom earned their doctorates under Bowne.

The second generation of Boston personalists inherited and transmitted the liberal movement's most coherent synthesis of philosophical and theological thought. They also made important modifications of Bowne's thinking, especially in Brightman's theorizing about personality, divine temporality, and divine finitude, McConnell's emphasis on social justice issues, and Knudson's emphasis on religious apriorism. Through his writings and leadership of the American Philosophical Association, Brightman elevated the prestige of personalist theory among philosophers; through his writings and church leadership, McConnell legitimized personalist theology in the Methodist church and won a large popular audience; through his writings and seminary leadership, Knudson turned Boston personalism into a major theological school.

The personalists taught that personality is the primary metaphysical reality and that theology must take the risk of making metaphysical claims; some of them followed Bowne in contending that, logically speaking, only mind is real. Their tradition transcended its center at Boston University. McConnell had a national ministry; Bowne disciple Ralph Tyler Flewelling and his journal, *The Personalist,* anchored an influential personalist school in California; more importantly, numerous religious thinkers who were not disciples of Bowne or Brightman incorporated personalist arguments into their thinking, notably William Newton Clarke, Henry Churchill King, and Harry Emerson Fosdick.[4] By embedding their idealism in a coherent metaphysical system, the personalists provided philosophical ballast for the common liberal claim that spirit or personality has primacy over the things of sense. Their success in this enterprise ensured third and fourth generations of personalist theology, but the high tide of Boston personalism was its second generation. Led by McConnell, Brightman, and Knudson, the Boston personalists kept alive a vital tradition of liberal theology and fed the wellsprings of other liberal theologies during the years of liberal disfavor.

Personalist philosophy and theology taught that personality (experience) is the key to reality and that life (experience) is the test of truth. Though Bowne's disciples theorized the former claim with a metaphysical seriousness that was distinctive to their school, virtually all liberal theologians accepted the empiricist dictum that critically interpreted experience is the test of truth. For the Ritschlians who founded the social gospel and personalist movements, as for the Chicago modernists who judged that Ritschlian theology was insufficiently empiricist, it was a fundamental axiom that knowledge is the comprehension of experience. But what does it mean to make experience the test of truth? How should theology evaluate experience? Which experiences deserve to be valorized? Each theological school brought its distinctive interpretive frameworks to these questions, but some of the liberal movement's most compelling responses to them were offered by its practical interpreters and popularizers.

Liberal theology in the twentieth century was a decidedly academic enterprise. In the nineteenth century most liberal theologians were white, male, middle-class pastors. In the twentieth century most of them were still white, male, and middle class, but not all; on the other hand, nearly all of the movement's leading thinkers were academics. Even its leading practical interpreters and popularizers were academics, though not professional theologians: a famous preacher and seminary professor of homiletics, Harry Emerson Fosdick; a popular spiritual writer and practical theologian, Georgia Harkness; an ecumenical leader and the president of Morehouse College, Benjamin E. Mays; an advocate and interpreter of mystical experience, Rufus M. Jones.

I have selected these figures both to represent the varieties of practical theology in American theological liberalism and to underscore the movement's fundamental commonalities; in Jones's case, I am also representing the possibility of a mystical alternative to the evangelical liberal, naturalistic-empiricist, and personalist schools of thought. Fosdick was the movement's greatest public figure and the symbol of its sensibility. He reached a mass audience every week as a radio network preacher, wrote books that nurtured thousands in the therapeutic religion of personality, and represented the mainstream of liberal Protestant thinking on nearly every issue of his time. Harkness earned her doctorate in philosophy under Brightman at Boston University, wrote prolifically on issues in religion and the spiritual life, and was a trailblazing advocate of women's ordination and the rights of women in church and academic life. Mays earned his doctorate at the University of Chicago Divinity School, wrote a pioneering work on the African American experience of God, and became the first African American to serve as a vice president of the Federal Council of Churches. Jones was a modernizing leader in the Society of Friends, wrote many books on the history, theory, and practice of mysticism, blended the discourses of Quaker mysticism and liberal theology, and significantly influenced Fosdick, Harkness, and Howard Thurman. All of them were theologians of the way of Christ and the authority of spiritual experience; through their writings, liberal theology made spiritual sense to a vast audience.

Conventional interpretations of American liberal theology define the field in Progressive-era terms and treat Reinhold Niebuhr as the herald of an antiliberal reaction usually called neo-orthodoxy. In this reading, Niebuhr plays a large role in the history of American liberal Christianity, but mostly as an outside debunker. It follows on this reading that Niebuhr's friend and comrade, John C. Bennett, belongs to the sprawling category of neo-orthodoxy, despite his plainly liberal leanings, and that Paul Tillich, who never aspired to orthodoxy on any topic, was also a neo-orthodox outsider to the liberal tradition.

By contrast, my reading does not view evolutionary Progressivism as fundamentally constitutive of liberal theology. Evolutionary theory was a consuming, life-and-death issue for liberal theology in the 1880s and 1890s, as I emphasized in volume one, but by 1920 it was taken for granted and far from consuming, except as something to be defended from fundamentalist attacks. My reading also accentuates the common liberal commitments of Niebuhr, Bennett, and Tillich, even as it describes their powerful critiques of liberal idealism and rationalism and emphasizes the key differences between Niebuhr and Tillich. In their positions on authority, method, and various doctrines, and in the spirit of their thinking, Niebuhr, Bennett, and Tillich belonged to the liberal tradition, even as they insisted that liberal theology was wrong to sacralize idealism, wrong to regard reason as inherently redemptive, and wrong to suppose that good religion must extinguish its mythical impulses. My point is not to deny that there was such a thing as neo-orthodoxy, however badly named, in twentieth-century theology. There was, indeed, a powerful neo-Reformationist movement that sought to create a third way in theology by reconfiguring the Reformationist dialectic of Word and Spirit as the basis of Christian claims. My argument is that Niebuhr, Bennett, and Tillich belonged more fully to liberal theology than to neo-orthodoxy, and that through their criticism and constructive theorizing they created new forms of liberal theology.

This interpretive issue affects the entire question of how the past seventy-five years of American theological liberalism should be understood. If liberal theology is defined as Progressivist idealism and evolutionary immanentalism, and if the Niebuhrian revolt is viewed wholly as an attack on liberalism from an alternative theological standpoint, then theological liberalism has barely existed in the United States since World War II; only fragments of it remain today. On my reading, however, liberal theology remained a significant theological tradition in the 1940s and 1950s, first because it boasted such thinkers as Knudson, Wieman, Fosdick, Harkness, Howard Thurman, L. Harold DeWolf, and Bernard E. Meland, and second because the towering theologians of mid-century America—Niebuhr and Tillich—creatively renewed the liberal tradition through their critical and reconstructive engagements with it. Though Tillich identified with his German philosophical heritage, not with any American tradition, his impact on American liberal theology was immense during his lifetime, and, like Niebuhr's, it remained a creative (albeit diminished) force in later twentieth-century theology. If one does not treat Niebuhr and Tillich as participants in the American tradition of liberal theology, it is hard to make sense of their enduring influence on this tradition, much of it through the work of liberals such as Langdon Gilkey, F. W. Dillistone, Robert Scharlemann, and John Dillenberger.

The closing chapter of this book analyzes the points of difference and commonality among the early- and middle-twentieth-century liberal theologies, and it ends with the spiritual vision of a prophetic mystic who endured, Howard Thurman. In his lyrical voice, the liberal idea of the religion of Jesus and the mystical vision of spiritual unity were preached from the standpoint of America's oppressed people of color.

MODERNISMS

Liberal theology is the child of two heritages. From its Enlightenment-modernist heritage it has upheld the authority of modern knowledge, emphasized the continuity between reason and revelation, championed the values of tolerance, humanistic individualism, and democracy, and, for the most part, distrusted metaphysical claims. From its evangelical heritage it has affirmed the authority of Christian experience, upheld the divinity and sovereignty of Christ, preached the need of personal salvation, and emphasized the importance of Christian missions. In the nineteenth century the founders of German and American theological liberalism—notably Friedrich Schleiermacher, Isaak A. Dorner, William Ellery Channing, and Horace Bushnell—set influential examples for their tradition by creatively fusing modernist and evangelical commitments. In most of its forms since that time, liberal theology has been a tradition that holds together the principles and values of both of its primary heritages.

As liberal theology developed in the nineteenth and, especially, twentieth centuries, however, theologians increasingly debated the value of sustaining a balance between its Enlightenment-modernist and evangelical elements. The evangelical/modernist distinction, which dominates much of the scholarly literature in the field, is a product of these debates. This distinction, as it is usually construed, breaks the field into an "evangelical" tendency that centers upon gospel norms such as the divinity and sovereignty of Christ and a "modernist" tendency that replaces gospel norms with a modern worldview. Another way of formulating the difference, which is compatible with the first way but also distinguishable from it, focuses upon the two fundamentally different ways of conceiving divine reality in liberal theology. The "evangelical" or transcendentalist tendency conceives God as being transcendent to history and possessing power over nonbeing, while the naturalistic "modernist" stream of liberal theology rejects the spirit/nature dualism of evangelical and romanticist liberalism and contends that God's dwelling place is wholly within history.

This way of categorizing the field is problematic on several counts. "Gospel norm" is a slippery concept because, in liberal theology, biblical teaching is authoritative only as it is received as authoritative in human experience. The terms "evangelical" and "modernist" are even more problematic, and if one defines the distinction between them as involving more than one factor, some thinkers have to be assigned to the evangelical side on some issues and the modernist side on others. For example, Douglas Clyde Macintosh is usually categorized as a modernist, yet he believed in a personal transcendent God and fervently appealed to the spirit and way of Christ; similarly, Paul Tillich and Edgar Brightman are usually categorized as evangelicals, yet their religious philosophies were shorter than Macintosh's on evangelical motifs. Additionally, mystical liberals such as Rufus Jones and Howard Thurman certainly belong to the pietistic-transcendentalist stream of liberal theology, but the term "evangelical" does not fit them at all. Moreover, in the later twentieth century the word "evangelical" became almost wholly associated in the United States with conservative or fundamentalist forms of Protestantism.

More importantly, "modernist" is also problematic, because all American theological liberals were modernists of some kind, nearly all of them retained some normative claim about the divinity of Christ or the saving power of the Christian message, and not all "modernists" rejected the gospel-centered approach for modernist reasons. Liberal Christian Platonism belongs to the gospel-displacing "modernist" category, for example, yet its basis has little to do with modern science or modern philosophy. It is an exaggeration to view "evangelical" liberals as holding out for sacred things and "modernist" liberals as disavowing sacred things in favor of the secular, for liberal theology as a whole was defined by its refusal to place the sacred and secular in unreconcilable opposition. To the liberal theologians, this was what it meant to be modern, and the "modernist impulse" was common to them. Historically, liberal theology sought to hold together the intellectual and spiritual motifs of Enlightenment modernism and evangelical religion, but this nearly essential characteristic of liberal theology has been obscured by the interpretive emphasis of works such as Kenneth Cauthen's *The Impact of Religious Liberalism,* which organizes its entire discussion around the evangelical/modernist distinction. Much of the literature on liberal theology ignores the problems with this distinction and employs a procrustean overuse of it.[5]

Yet the idea behind the evangelical/modernist distinction, if employed judiciously, remains important to the understanding of twentieth-century American liberal theology. Contrary to William Hutchison and Francis Schüssler Fiorenza, who dispense entirely with this distinction, there is an important delineation to be made between liberals who assert the centrality and necessity of particular religious norms and those who claim that no particular norms from the past should be binding for modern Christian belief. Certainly the theologians of the American liberal era believed that much was at stake in the differences between them. The gospel-centered liberals included William Newton Clarke, William Adams Brown, Walter Rauschenbusch, Vida Scudder, Albert Knudson, Francis McConnell, Harry Emerson Fosdick, and Georgia Harkness. The more thoroughly naturalistic "modernists" included the Chicago-school theologians— George Burman Foster, Shailer Mathews, Shirley Jackson Case, Douglas Clyde Macintosh, Gerald Birney Smith, and Henry Nelson Wieman—and various others such as Bangor Seminary theologian Levi Leonard Paine, Cornell University biblical scholar Nathaniel Schmidt, Oberlin theologian Frank Hugh Foster, and, in his early career, Yale theologian Robert Calhoun. The evangelical/modernist distinction identifies the crucial change that occurred (in opposite directions) in the mid-career thinking of Calhoun and Mathews: Calhoun converted to the view that special revelation is absolutely necessary for theology, while Mathews gradually relinquished the evangelical aspects of his theology.[6]

The differences between these rival tendencies in American liberal theology were debated long before each side settled on its names. In 1905, Foster's *The Finality of the Christian Religion* called for a thoroughly modern alternative to the religiously compromised empiricism of the Ritschlian school and the social gospel. In 1910, Smith contended that the Ritschlian liberalism of his teacher, William Adams Brown, was insufficiently modern because it appealed to founding religious norms derived from the Christian past. In 1926, personal-idealist theologian Daniel Sommer Robinson contended in *The God of the Liberal Chris-*

tian that liberal theology was fundamentally divided between its "new theists," who sustained the Schleiermacherian-Hegelian-Ritschlian tradition of progressive theology, and its "social theologians," who opted for a thoroughgoing religious naturalism and pragmatism. The new theists were philosophical idealists who believed in a cosmic, personal God, while the social theologians were philosophical naturalists and pragmatists who conceived God as the ideal society or expression of humanity's highest ideals. Put differently, Robinson explained, "the new theists emphasize the importance of an idealistic metaphysics, and strive to develop and to extend the Schleiermacher-Jamesian method, but the social theologians claim to abandon metaphysical method in the interest of the genetic method of social psychology, although in reality they adopt both the logical and the metaphysical tenets of pragmatism."[7]

Allowing for Robinson's partisan spirit, he made a good case for the importance of this distinction, though his names for it were problematic. He overstated William James's kinship with the personalistic idealists, and he mistakenly reduced the prevailing division in liberal theology to a single issue. The Ritschlian social gospelers were "social theologians" too, and the Chicago modernists might just as well have been called "new theists." Moreover, Robinson shortchanged the importance of liberal disagreements over the questions of religious norms and historical continuity. One measure of Robinson's interpretive perceptiveness, however, is that sixty years after *The God of the Liberal Christian* was published, pragmatic-historicist theologian William Dean made the same argument in describing current liberal theology. Dean's finely reasoned *American Religious Empiricism* (1986) maintained that liberal theology is fundamentally divided between those who appeal to a transhistorical realm of spirit and those who conceive God as the concrete reality of historical process. Dean called the former group "pietistic liberals" and the latter group "empirical liberals."[8]

Dean's renaming of the transcendental/naturalist debate in liberal theology has the advantage of avoiding the problematic terms "evangelical" and "modernist," which, in the decades following Robinson's analysis, became defining categories in liberal theology. But, like Robinson, Dean fixates on one issue, and his categories have some of the same problems as the prevailing ones. As an historical phenomenon, "pietism" is only slightly less circumscribed and connotatively overloaded than "evangelical," and it does not describe all liberals who believe in a spiritual realm. Historically, the Ritschlian stream of liberal theology was pietist of a sort, but the transcendentalist wing of liberal theology includes other theological traditions, and, of course, one of Ritschl's chief works was the devastating three-volume *History of Pietism,* which blasted the pietist tradition as a Protestant spin on the Catholic paganization of the gospel. More importantly, neither of the dominant liberal traditions holds an exclusive claim to empiricism. From Schleiermacher and Ritschl to the present day, liberals on the "transhistorical spirit" side of the field have claimed to practice an empirical approach to religion by virtue of their emphasis on, and study of, religious experience. The naturalistic-modernist stream of American theology thus holds no more exclusive claim over the term "empirical" than it holds over "modernist"; in both cases, the difference is a matter of emphasis and extent. The naturalistic tradition is more thorough-going in its empiricism and modernism than other traditions.

From 1910 to 1930, the zenith of American liberal theology, American liberals described themselves and their basic differences in various ways. The existence of rival orientations was clearer to them than the names that should be given to these orientations. Theologians from both camps called themselves "evangelicals" and "modernists," and some in both camps disliked the designation "liberal." The first American liberal Protestant to embrace the name "modernist," Newman Smyth, appropriated the term in 1908 as a way of declaring solidarity with the battered liberal side of the Roman Catholic controversy over modernism. Smyth's "progressive orthodoxy" was more liberal than Catholic modernism, but it was conservative compared to the Chicago school. Another evangelical leader, William Adams Brown, insisted on his right to the modernist name despite his strong disagreements with Chicago liberalism. On the other hand, but similarly, Mathews argued for many years that modernist theology needed to retain the language and spirit of personal religion that it inherited from Protestant evangelicalism.[9]

Mathews confused the issue as much as anyone. The perspective that came to be called "modernist" theology, including his own later theology, minimized or negated the evangelical aspects of liberal theology. It was *liberal* theology that derived from and sought to sustain the dual heritages of gospel-centered evangelicalism and Enlightenment-modernist Progressivism, but Mathews reserved the term "liberal" for Unitarians and religious humanists. For many years he warned against the spiritually deracinated humanism of "liberal" theology, while emphasizing that genuinely modern theology represented a qualitative break from classical Christianity. His favored self-description was "modernist." Due to his influence especially, this term came to be identified with the naturalistic, empirical, pragmatic theology advocated by the Chicago school, though Mathews was the last Chicago schooler to adopt a thoroughgoing modernism in his language and method, and he never stopped thinking of himself as some kind of evangelical. In his last years he also relented and called himself a liberal; the grammar of contemporary theology had stabilized, and the crisis of liberal theology evoked his feeling of solidarity.

This book emphasizes that there are more than two kinds of liberal theology, and that not all liberal theologies are fundamentally defined by the position that they take on the evangelical/transcendentalist versus modernist/naturalist issue. At the same time, this has been the fundamentally defining issue for most of the field, which reduces to two questions: Is it possible for a modern theology to be based on material religious norms from the past? And is God transcendent to, or located wholly within, the historical realm? Since the early twentieth century, so-called "evangelical" liberals have claimed an essential continuity with the historic Christian tradition, while "modernist" liberals have emphasized the discontinuities between the modern and premodern contexts. "Evangelical" liberals have reclaimed the figure or gospel of Christ as the basis of their religious thinking, while "modernist" liberals have argued that Christian teaching must be reconceptualized in the form of a modern philosophical and/or scientific worldview that satisfies modern tests of credible belief. While both positions have emphasized that the religious subject is historical and that God is immanent within creation and history, they have disagreed on whether the religious object, God, exists beyond history. Similarly, "evangelical" liberals have retained a variable notion of the person or message of Christ as a theology-founding historical revelation, while "modernist" liberals have countered that revelation is not a credible basis of belief and that no version of gospel truth is immune from the acids of criticism.

Both of these broad theological tendencies have rejected the either/or of reason or revelation. Just as liberals insisted upon the unity of the sacred and secular, they viewed the compatibility of revelation and reason as a core liberal principle. For this reason especially, the distinction between pietistic "evangelical" liberalism and naturalistic "modernist" liberalism must be used carefully, always with caveats, and not overworked. A good deal of scholarship on liberal theology implies that evangelical liberals based their truth claims exclusively on revelation, while modernists relied solely upon reason. In fact, both of these possibilities have a logic and a history. There is such a thing as a strictly revelationist liberalism: Nineteenth-century pietist liberalism was sometimes exclusively revelationist, Wilhelm Herrmann's later existential Ritschlianism appealed solely to the experience of revelation, and in the World War I period when he wrote his first edition *Epistle to the Romans,* Karl Barth advocated a revelationist theology within a liberal framework. Moreover, some modernist liberal theologians have eschewed all claims to special or general revelation.

But most American liberal theologies have been "evangelical" *and* "modernist" to some degree. Liberal theologians have argued that reason and revelation are both important for theology and that they go together. Much of the liberal tradition has upheld the ideal of maintaining a balance between liberal theology's evangelical and modernist poles. American Ritschlians such as Brown and King did not believe that their gospel faith excluded them in any way from claiming the mantle of modernism; they were committed to a both/and model of liberal theology.

"On the other hand" prevails in this case, however, because a significant wing of the liberal movement decidedly favored its Enlightenment-modernist heritage over its evangelical heritage. H. Richard Niebuhr later claimed that this was true of liberal theology as a whole. In the years just before and during World War I (1914–18), Ritschlians such as King, Brown, and Rauschenbusch worried that naturalistic liberals were taking modernization too far at the expense of the gospel message. In the 1920s and 1930s, a sense of rivalry hardened between the guardians of these two positions at Union Theological Seminary and the University of Chicago Divinity School; at Union the chief guardians were Brown, Henry Sloane Coffin, and Henry P. Van Dusen. Though the Chicago school did not disown the compatibility principle, it did give up the Ritschlian ideal of equal emphasis. Ritschlians and other gospel-centered liberals argued that their understandings of the historicity and divinity of Christ passed the tests of modern critical inquiry and that their theology sustained continuity with the historic mainstream of the Christian tradition. Modernist liberals countered that modern criticism cannot be counted upon to validate any claim about a gospel norm and that truly modern theology is something new.

In light of the fact that all American liberals have been modernists, and that "evangelical" has an illiberal connotation in American society, one might wish that American liberal theologians had found better names for their contending factions. But the alternatives offered by Robinson and Dean share similar drawbacks, and not because they chose poorly. There are no categories that perfectly name the differences at issue, and the terms "evangelical" and "modernist" were selected by chief partisans. In the former case, the name was insisted upon. To gospel-centered partisans such as Brown, Coffin, Van Dusen, and Georgia Harkness, the term "evangelical" was too precious to relinquish. It was a banner word, and to some "evangelical liberals" today it retains this significance, though others would prefer to be called something else. Even Mathews and Foster prized this name long after their theologies left it behind.

On the other side, no single term accurately describes or distinguishes the intellectual tradition that Mathews, Foster, Case, Ames, Smith, Wieman, Edwin Aubrey, and others developed at the University of Chicago, that Macintosh pioneered at Yale, and that Levi Paine and Frank Hugh Foster advanced. The second- and third-generation Chicago schoolers tended to prefer the name "empiricist" over "modernist," but no single term captures the distinctive commitments of this tradition, and "empiricist" and "modernist" are both claimed by other perspectives. I shall therefore favor the somewhat awkward monikers of "naturalistic-empirical liberalism" and "naturalistic-empirical modernism" when referring to this tradition, while reserving the right to employ the term "modernist" as a shorthand designation. With all of its problems, "modernist" is no less satisfactory than the single-term alternatives, and it has decades of use in its favor. It also marks the relation of early Chicago-style liberalism to later postmodern philosophy and cultural criticism.

Much of the scholarly literature on liberal Protestantism adds to this confusion by exaggerating the twentieth-century novelty of the modernist option. Lloyd Averill's generally excellent book, for example, *American Theology in the Liberal Tradition,* asserts that liberal Protestantism had no modernist tradition until it began to lose its credibility during the period of World War I. He claims that "no major figure of the liberal movement before 1917 qualifies for designation as a modernist." Cauthen's *The Impact of American Religious Liberalism* similarly describes modernist liberal theology as a twentieth-century phenomenon.[10]

I believe that this scholarly convention, also, is not quite right. All American liberal theology has been modernist, but even in the connotatively narrow sense of the term employed by Averill and Cauthen, which refers to the displacement of gospel norms by a modern worldview, a good deal of nineteenth-century American and European liberal theology was modernist. Various American Unitarians and Transcendentalists make good examples, notably Theodore Parker, who famously repudiated "that puerile distinction between Reason and Revelation" while calling for a "real Christianity" that liberated modern people "from all personal and finite authority." Parker rejected all appeals to historical revelation, insisting that Christian truth has nothing to do with the historicity of claims by or about Jesus. His ideal was a modern construct, Absolute Religion, which he described as thoroughly rational and universalist.[11]

Other nineteenth-century religious currents with less-disputed claims to the Christian name also produced forms of liberal theology that qualify as modernist. In Germany, the neo-Hegelian historical theologian and founder of Tübingen-school historiocriticism, Ferdinand Christian Baur, was a forerunner of the kind of modernizing criticism that subjected revelatory claims to historical tests and then translated the "inner meaning" of these claims into the language of modern philosophy.[12] One of his students, David Friedrich Strauss, was a notable modernizer; in his early career Strauss argued that Hegelian philosophy, properly understood, provides a better basis for Christian belief than the gospel narrative.[13] Another of Baur's students, Albrecht Ritschl, rehabilitated the gospel-centered stream of liberal theology, but in the generation that followed Baur's death in 1860, the Ritschlian movement's internal debates over the logic of historical criticism gave rise to a school of liberal religious thinking that promoted an explicitly modernist and historicist approach to Christianity.

This was the *Religionsgeschichtliche Schule,* which began as a Göttingen-centered offshoot of the Ritschlian movement in the 1880s. Led by German scholars Hermann Gunkel, William Wrede, Ernst Troeltsch, Wilhelm Bousset, and Johannes Weiss, the history of religions school taught that religions must be understood according to criteria that do not belong to or derive from any particular religious tradition. They argued that all religious traditions are rooted in cult and liturgy, not theology, and that most religious traditions are syncretistic patchworks of various sources and traditions. Their leading theologian, Troeltsch, pressed hard on the claim that Christian teaching in particular is a patchwork of mythical and eschatological motifs.[14] By the mid-1890s, the church-oriented Ritschlians and the insurgent *Religionsgeschichtliche* group were locked in a struggle for control of the German theology establishment.[15] The rise of an aggressively historicist school of religious interpretation established the possibility of a modernist alternative to Ritschlian-school evangelicalism well before the outbreak of World War I.

This was a mostly German phenomenon, but at the turn of the century the Chicago schoolers opted for the history of religions side of the argument, in their case from a pragmatic-naturalistic standpoint. Moreover, during the same generation that a rising history of religions movement charged that Ritschlian historicism was compromised by its religious commitments, another kind of theological modernism, also rooted in German idealism, gained a prominent standing within British and American philosophy departments. This was the neo-Hegelian approach to religion, which argued that the truthful aspects of Christianity are attainable only by translating the pictorial, mythical thinking of scriptural narrative and religion into the concepts of an idealistic metaphysical system.

Though Hegel and the early German Hegelian school of theology were generally reluctant to question the historical basis of Christianity, and though Hegel occasionally attributed personality to the Absolute, later nineteenth-century streams of German, English, and American Hegelianism were often different on both counts. German neo-Hegelian theologians A. E. Biedermann and Otto Pfleiderer kept up with developments in biblical criticism; English neo-Hegelian philosophers F. H. Bradley and Bernard Bosanquet denied personality to the Absolute; American neo-Hegelian philosopher Josiah Royce struggled with "the problem of Christianity" while ascribing personality to the Absolute; more importantly, the logic of Hegelianism was decidedly modernist regardless of the Hegelian debates on these issues. The point is not that any kind of metaphysical position leads to this result, for most Christian orthodoxies have been tied to some metaphysical position, and among liberal Protestant thinkers of the early twentieth century, several were metaphysically oriented evangelicals, notably Bowne, Knudson, William Ernest Hocking, and Eugene Lyman. What made Hegelianism distinctively modernist was its defining insistence that the mythical picture-language and ideas of early Christianity must give way to the processive-idealistic concepts of Hegelian philosophy. Hegelian variations on this theme gave ballast to a generation of Christian liberals that made "modernism" an article of faith.[16]

It is therefore an exaggeration to claim that the modernist tendency belongs entirely to the crisis of liberal theology that began with World War I. Theological modernism in the narrow sense of the term is not limited to the postwar world or even to the twentieth century. At the same time, it is true and religiously significant that throughout its heyday, liberal Protestantism was a gospel-centered tradition that fused its evangelical and Enlightenment-modernist heritages. Ritschl taught that the basis of Christianity is the collective experience of value inspired by Jesus. Harnack taught that the basis of Christianity is the historically reconstructed person of Jesus and his message of divine fatherhood and human brotherhood. In his 1890s debates with French theologian Auguste Sabatier, which foreshadowed the entire twentieth-century debate over "evangelical" and "modernist" liberalism, Harnack insisted that liberal theology is continuous with the faith of the Protestant Reformation. In a similar vein, with greater ambition, Walter Rauschenbusch and the social gospel movement claimed to recover the ethic and spirit of the kingdom heralded by Jesus.

These claims made liberal theology religiously attractive to vast numbers of pastors and churchgoers during the Progressive era. Evangelical liberalism began to lose its religious cogency in the early twentieth century after its defining religious claims were subjected to withering historical criticism. Critics such as Johannes Weiss and Albert Schweitzer charged that the Jesus of liberal Protestantism was definitely not the Jesus of history. A significant assortment of liberal theologians adopted "modernist" strategies in response. Mathews, Foster, Macintosh, Ames and others variously gave up the liberal Jesus as the basis of faith, while promoting substitutes derived from modern cultural values and reason. To their great dismay, after World War I they witnessed the ascendancy of a theological movement that dismissed their reverent respect for modern culture.

The dialectical theology movement repudiated modern culture as a basis or criterion of faith, and liberal theology as a whole resisted the Barthians on this count. In 1923, Harnack plaintively asked Barth if Christianity did not have a stake in preserving the culture of Kant and Goethe; Barth assured him that genuine Christianity takes no interest in the question. For years liberals called Barth a philistine, an irrationalist, a sophisticated reactionary, and worse things in reply, but by the mid-1930s, following Fosdick's lead, American evangelical liberals began to concede that Barth and Niebuhr were not completely wrong about the cultural captivity of liberal theology. Liberal theology was still the only approach that made sense, they insisted, but it had gone too far in accommodating modern secular culture. Across the spectrum of liberal theology, they allowed, and especially at Chicago, theologians had preached a religion of culture that overly identified Christianity with the spirit of the Progressivist age.[17]

But the Chicago theologians were more sparing in their concessions. Liberal theology could be faulted for being too Kantian and subjective, they believed, and it was inclined to flights of idealistic fancy, but there was no such thing as being too modern. To the extent that the Chicago school changed in response to a changing culture in the 1930s—adopting Henry Nelson Wieman's narrow empiricism and theological realism—it changed in the name of making liberal theology more deeply modernist, not less. As long as "modern" meant empirical and scientific, and theology aspired to modernity, there was nothing to apologize for. Though the cultural tide had turned against the language of evolutionary process, functional patterns, value theory, and cultural progress, this was the language of genuinely modern theology. In the name of rationality and the enduring achievements of modernity, Chicago-school liberalism thus sailed against the cultural tide.

American liberal Protestant theology carried on this inheritance and was marginalized by it for most of the twentieth century. Against the grain of an ascending American "neo-orthodoxy" that played down its liberal elements, liberals such as Fosdick, Knudson, McConnell, Harkness, Charles Clayton Morrison, Henry Van Dusen, Henry Sloane Coffin, Justin Wroe Nixon, and Eugene Lyman endeavored in the 1930s and 1940s to keep alive the gospel-centered faith of liberal social Christianity. Pioneering a therapeutic religion that retreated considerably from the world-saving rhetoric of the social gospelers, Fosdick attracted a huge national audience, while Morrison influenced an important clerical audience as editor of the *Christian Century*.[18] The modernist liberals lacked a figure of Fosdick's star power, but Mathews was a major figure for forty years, Macintosh was the leading liberal theologian of the 1920s, and the University of Chicago Divinity School justly regarded itself as the movement's flagship after Niebuhr and Tillich blurred Union's liberal identity.

The Chicago schoolers aptly called their institution "the mother of modernism." Though they repeated the liberal slogan that reason and revelation go together, during their first and second generations they found less and less reason to appeal to revelation at all. In this they differed from their gospel-centered liberal colleagues, and even from mystics like Rufus Jones and Howard Thurman, but all the American liberals agreed that the project of twentieth-century theology was to make Christianity modern.

1.

Creating a New Mainstream

William Adams Brown, William Newton Clarke,
Henry Churchill King, and the Ritschlian Gospel

The young academics who joined the faculty of Union Theological Seminary in the late nineteenth and early twentieth centuries were interested in the possibilities of a gospel-oriented and explicitly modern Protestantism. Hired under Union presidents Thomas S. Hastings and Charles Cuthbert Hall, they included church historian Arthur C. McGiffert, theologian William Adams Brown, social ethicist Thomas C. Hall, Old Testament scholar Julius A. Bewer, and homiletics teacher Henry Sloane Coffin. A bit later, under the presidency of Francis Brown, they were joined by religious educationist George Albert Coe, history of religionist Robert Ernest Hume, homiletics teacher Harry Emerson Fosdick, and biblical scholar Frederick J. Foakes Jackson. On the strength of their teaching and scholarship, these second-generation liberals, the successors of Charles Briggs at Union Seminary, turned Union into a chief bastion of the liberal theology movement.[1]

Theologically they advocated evangelical liberalism, biblical criticism, ecumenical cooperation, interreligious understanding, and the social gospel; socially they epitomized the mannered niceness of late-Victorian Protestantism. McGiffert and Brown exemplified the new liberalism at Union, which appalled Charles Briggs in its willingness to subject cherished aspects of the gospel narratives to criticism. Significantly, both were protégés of Adolf von Harnack. As a church historian and Union's eighth president, McGiffert upheld the seminary's dual commitment to critical scholarship and faith-based Christian mission. As a prolific theologian and servant of the church, Brown defined the Ritschlian basis of Union theological liberalism and burnished the seminary's image as a church-friendly institution. Union Seminary resisted the radical historicist offshoots of Ritschlian theology but, guided by its defining theologian, it showed how to appropriate the gospel-centered historicism of Albrecht Ritschl and his German theological disciples to the American context.[2]

BOUND FOR UNION: THE MAKING OF AN ESTABLISHMENT LIBERAL

By his middle and last names, William Adams Brown was born to privilege and Union Theological Seminary. His mother, Mary Elizabeth Adams Brown, counted Henry Adams and two American presidents in her family tree. Her father, William Adams, was a prominent Madison Square pastor and New School General Assembly moderator who pushed through, with Union Seminary theologian Henry Boynton Smith, the reunion of the Old School and New School Presbyterian churches in 1869. A founder and longtime director of Union Seminary, William Adams resigned his pastorate in 1873 to become Union's third president. He also taught as Brown Professor of Sacred Rhetoric, in a chair endowed by his close friend, James Brown, the seminary's largest contributor. James Brown was a prominent Wall Street banker and founder of the famous banking firm, Brown Brothers & Company (later Brown Brothers Harriman & Company). His son, John Crosby Brown, who had hopes of a ministerial career, entered the family business after the deaths of two elder brothers and eventually headed the firm. John Crosby Brown served as a board director of Union Seminary for more than forty years. He became vice president of the board of directors in 1883, supported Charles Briggs during his heresy trials of the 1890s, endorsed the dissociation of Union from the Presbyterian church during the Briggs crisis, and became board president in 1898, six years after his son, William Adams Brown, began his teaching career at Union.[3]

The Browns and Adamses were devout Presbyterians, though young William was sent to an Episcopal boarding school in New Hampshire. His paternal grandfather owned three sprawling homes in New York City; Brown spent his contented youthful summers at Brighthurst, on the summit of Orange Mountain, where his parents and maternal grandfather owned summer mansions. The amenities at Brighthurst included a stable and horses, a golf course, prize-earning greenhouses, and magnificent vistas. Brown's late-life memoir contained occasional hints of a downside. Aside from noting that his father was highly intelligent and quietly pious, he confessed that he was unable to say anything personal about his father. Of his mother, Mary Elizabeth Brown, he emphasized her indomitable will, her extreme emotionalism, and the fact that she spent most of her life on the sofa, entertaining numerous doctors, "who found her a fascinating patient." By temperament and conviction, as well as by virtue of her father's New School sermonizing, Mary Elizabeth Brown favored the warm-blooded religion of evangelical revivalism. Her husband's piety, by contrast, was quietly earnest, scholarly, and liberal-leaning.[4]

Brown oscillated between them as a youth. On one occasion his mother took him to Northfield, Massachusetts, to hear the revival preaching of Dwight Moody, Reuben A. Torrey, and other evangelists. Moody and Torrey were both premillennialists, but Moody's ruling theme was personal religion, while Torrey epitomized the literalistic militancy of what came to be called Protestant fundamentalism. Brown preferred Moody's warm-hearted personal religion, and for years afterward he listened to revival preachers, getting his reward as a college student in the artful sermons of Henry Drummond. A Scottish geologist, theological writer, and preacher, Drummond conducted geological research in Central Africa and preached revival missions with Moody in Ireland, England, and the United States. Moody called him the most Christlike man he ever met, and Brown concurred, praising Drummond's combination of learning and piety. Drummond's evangelical evolutionist classic, *Natural Law in the Spiritual World,* interpreted spiritual reality according to the principle of natural-order continuity. From Drummond's example Brown took the assurance that gospel-centered faith can be cool-tempered and rational. He also adopted Drummond's contention that American higher education was making a terrible mistake by separating its colleges and seminaries: "He felt that the theologues, as older men with more mature religious experience, had something to give to their young fellowstudents which would be of benefit to both." Inspired by Drummond's example, Brown resolved that his own religion was closer to the quietly reflective pietism of his father than to his mother's revivalism.[5]

He drifted through Yale College with respectable grades and little inspiration: "We had lessons given and we learnt them. We had recitations and we were marked for them. We were granted cuts and we took them." Intellectually he awakened during his year of graduate study at Yale. Brown wanted to study philosophy, but Yale philosopher George T. Ladd was unbearably dull, so he chose the only riveting lecturer he could find, libertarian William Graham Sumner. A laissez-faire economist and pioneering sociologist, Sumner was an eccentric, cheeky, opinionated classroom performer who shamelessly propagandized on behalf of Social Darwinist ideology. He refused to teach women, railed against government, and exhorted his well-born male students against progressive causes. Like many of his classmates, Brown converted to libertarianism; later he judged that the real world was a wiser teacher, though he continued to admire Sumner's intellectual energy and courage.[6]

In 1887 he enrolled at his father's seminary, where he studied under the guardians of an expiring mediation-theology establishment. Brown's teachers at Union included church historian Philip Schaff ("it bored him to listen to students"), biblical theologian Charles Briggs ("a pall seemed to fall upon him— nothing could be drier than his method of teaching"), President Thomas

Hastings ("who taught us how to parse sentences, how to fold manuscripts, and how to choose a wife"), church historian George Prentiss ("a kindly soul" whom the students liked, but did not respect or take seriously), and theologian W. G. T. Shedd ("he told his class that he believed that there had been no significant contribution to theology since the seventeenth century, and he certainly acted on that belief"). On the other hand, he liked and respected Old Testament scholar Francis Brown, "a great soul . . . from [whom] we learnt what exact scholarship meant," and he benefited greatly from philosopher Nicholas Murray Butler's Columbia University seminar on Kant's *Critique of Pure Reason.* Then, to become an exacting scholar himself, Brown enrolled at the University of Berlin to study under Adolf von Harnack.[7]

THE RITSCHLIAN TURN: RITSCHL, HARNACK, AND BROWN

In 1890, at the age of thirty-eight, Harnack was already a legendary figure. His major multivolume work, *History of Ancient Christian Literature,* revealed little-known sources of early church history; his monumental seven-volume *History of Dogma* was completed; among other projects, he served as editor of the prestigious journal *Theologische Literaturzeitung.* Harnack's subsequent projects included seven volumes of New Testament studies; a major work, *The Mission and Expansion of Christianity in the First Three Centuries,* which contained his own carefully drawn maps; and four volumes of speeches and essays. In addition, he served variously as president of the Evangelisch-Sozialer Kongress, rector of the University of Berlin, director general of the Royal Library, and president of the Kaiser Wilhelm Gesellschaft. As an interpreter of church history, he argued that the hellenization and bureaucratization of the ante-Nicene church seriously distorted the spirit and gospel message of original Christianity, a view that put him at odds with the Prussian state church. Church officials objected to his claims that Jesus did not institute baptism in the name of the Trinity, that Ephesians and the Gospel of John were not apostolic, and that the virgin birth and ascension of Christ were not historical. Harnack's appointment at Berlin in 1888 was approved by Chancellor Bismarck and Emperor Wilhelm II against vehement church opposition. Theologically, he was a liberal Ritschlian who declared early in his career that "the future of Protestantism as a religion and spiritual power lies in the direction which Ritschl has indicated." Harnack and his generation of German Ritschlians trained a stream of American liberals to do likewise.[8]

The founder of Ritschlian theology, Albrecht Ritschl, was an unlikely progressive movement leader. He was the son of a conservative Prussian Protestant bishop and an ardent defender of the Prussian Union Church (the state church that united the Lutheran and Reformed churches). Trained in historical criticism by F. C. Baur at Tübingen, Ritschl taught at Bonn from 1846 to 1864 and then at Göttingen for twenty-five years. He had a strong and mostly conservative social conscience, with a reformist tinge. He emphasized the centrality of the kingdom of God in Christianity; more provocatively, he interpreted the kingdom in ethical terms. Unlike many American social gospelers who later adopted Ritschlian school theology, however, his chief ethical concern was the preservation of the existing social order. Ritschl worried that modern individualism, rationalism, and science were eroding the moral authority and social cohesion of the state, including its religion. Secularism was an appalling specter to him; in the age of Darwin, so was the spectacle of a heightening conflict between religion and science. Ritschlian theology was an answer to both problems.[9]

This answer was influenced by Kant's proposal to expunge metaphysics from theology and, especially, Kant's moral interpretation of Christianity. Ritschl argued that science explains matters of fact but religion is about values. Science describes the way things are, or appear to be, but theology is about the way things should be. Put differently, science uses disinterested pure reason to account for the way that things are, but religious knowledge is never disinterested; religion speaks in the form of value judgments, and the purpose of religious language is to describe the way things should be. As Ritschl explained in his dogmatics, *The Christian Doctrine of Justification and Reconciliation* (1874), religion is about the moral worth and depth of things: "Religious knowledge moves in independent value-judgments, which relate to man's attitude to the world, and call forth feelings of pleasure and pain, in which man either enjoys the dominion over the world vouchsafed him by God, or feels grievously the lack of God's help to that end." It followed for Ritschl that the goal of true religion, the kingdom of God, is the attainment of the highest possible personal and social good.[10]

The Ritschlian strategy was a variation on the liberal quest of a secure home for religion. Kant sought to reestablish the basis of Christianity in moral reason; Hegel developed a philosophy of Absolute Spirit in which the Christian idea was presented as the highest form of religious truth; Schleiermacher located the essence of religion in religious "feeling" *(Gefühl)* or intuition. Ritschl blended the approaches of Kant and Schleiermacher while judging that the kinds of liberal theology inspired by them gave insufficient attention to the kingdom of God and the social meaning of Christianity. Crucial to the Ritschlian program was its claim that the content of the good sought by Christianity cannot be gleaned from an infallible text or doctrine, but must be derived from the "apostolic circle of ideas" as established by historical critical research. The key purpose of historical theology is not to establish what Jesus really said or did, Ritschl argued; it is rather to establish the collective Christian experience of value inspired by Jesus. "It would be a mistaken purism were anyone, in this respect, to prefer the less developed statements of Jesus to the forms of apostolic thought," he contended. As the highest form of true religion, Christianity is concerned essentially with value; historical criticism discloses that the essence of Christianity is the kingdom of God as valued by the Christian community.[11]

Ritschl stressed that the kingdom is valued as absolute only by those who follow Jesus. It followed that the significance or truth of Christianity cannot be grasped from outside the Christian community, even with the tools of historical criticism. Christian truth can be comprehended only within the inner history of the church's life and practices, he argued. That is, only an inside historical criticism yields genuine Christian knowledge, for the value of the kingdom is a matter of knowledge only within the inner history of the church's historical life. From this perspective, Jesus is knowable as the embodiment of humanity's highest ideal; he is the redeemer of humankind who incarnates and inaugurates the realization of the kingdom. Nineteenth-century American theological liberalism in its Emersonian and Bushnellian streams was shaped by the claims of Schleiermacher and Samuel Taylor Coleridge that Christianity is not a doctrine, but a life, the life of true religious experience. The Ritschlian idea was a variation on this theme. Ritschl taught that Christianity is not a doctrine, but a living movement. It is the forward-moving and communal faith of those who know Christ as redeemer and live out his ethic of the kingdom.[12]

This strategy seized the field of German theology in the last quarter of the nineteenth century. Unlike many of the mediating and liberal theologies inspired by Hegel, Schleiermacher, and Coleridge, Ritschl's moralistic historicism recovered much of the language of biblical faith and urged the church to carry out a social mission of reform and renewal. His theological adoption of the Kantian disjunction between pure and practical reason gave the Ritschlian school immunity from conflicts with modern science. Moreover, by replacing all forms of metaphysical reasoning in theology with a combination of historical and moral-religious argument (a project that Ritschlian theologian Wilhelm Herrmann carried out more thoroughly than Ritschl) the Ritschlian approach made an appealing claim to a recovery of original gospel faith. Ritschlian school historicism made a plausible claim to have recovered the religion of Jesus, or at least the gospel of apostolic Christianity. For these reasons, the Ritschlians, especially Herrmann, Julius Kaftan, and Harnack, dominated German theology in the late nineteenth and early twentieth centuries.[13]

Together they set one of the rare examples of a theological school outshining its founder. Harnack's famous bestseller of 1900, *What Is Christianity?* expressed the faith and self-confidence of the Ritschlian movement at the height of its influence. It also showed Harnack's tendency to reduce the Ritschlian approach to religious individualism. Christianity is a religion, he observed, and religion pertains fundamentally to the existing human self. True religion is always concerned with the fundamental human problems of individual living, suffering, meaning, and death. It followed for Harnack that Christianity is the highest form of religion because Christianity "is something simple and sublime, it means one thing and one thing only: Eternal life in the midst of time, by the strength and under the eyes of God." And what is the basis of Christianity? Harnack replied that the answer is both simple and exhaustive: "Jesus Christ and his Gospel."[14]

This answer was exhaustive because it included the history of Christianity as a whole. In the spirit of Schleiermacher and Coleridge, but with Ritschl's emphasis on historical consciousness, Harnack affirmed that Christianity is not fundamentally a doctrine or even an ethic, but a life, "again and again kindled afresh, and now burning with a flame of its own." To grasp the reality or truth of this living object, one must pay attention to its history: "Just as we cannot obtain a complete knowledge of a tree without regarding not only its root and its stem but also the bark, its branches, and the way in which it blooms, so we cannot form any right estimate of the Christian religion unless we take our stand upon a comprehensive induction that shall cover all the facts of its history." This Ritschlian conviction animated Harnack's massive historical scholarship. In response to Cardinal Manning's dictum that the church must overcome history by dogma, he countered that the very opposite is true: only through historical criticism can dogma be purified. The vocation of the modern theologian is precisely to "break the power of the traditions" that had fossilized Christianity into something alien to the gospel of Jesus.[15]

Brown marveled at his teacher and luxuriated in his lectures. He also listened to Harnack's colleagues—especially Friedrich Paulsen on the history of philosophy, Julius Kaftan and Otto Pfleiderer on theology, August Dillmann on the Old Testament, and Bernard Weiss on the New Testament—but none compared to Harnack. Kaftan told him that the work of theology is "to hammer out formulae." Brown judged that Harnack made a higher art of theology and teaching. "To me Harnack gave what I most needed at that time, the vision of what a teacher of religion should be—a man of conviction, disciplined by knowledge and tempered with sympathy." He couldn't get enough of Harnack's teaching: "I have heard many great lecturers, but Harnack was the only man I could hear for two hours a day for six days in the week, for two years, and at the end, look forward as eagerly to the last lecture as to the first. There was a freshness about his mind, an ability to see things in proportion, that I have never found equalled in any other teacher."[16]

To Brown's perception, Harnack possessed in abundance the two essential qualities of a great historical theologian: a fervent religious spirit and the imaginative power to enter the vision and circumstances of other people. The latter attribute distinguished Harnack from Ritschl. "In theology he was a Ritschlian, and that meant one who approached the problems of religion from the ethical rather than from the metaphysical angle," Brown observed. "To him, as to Ritschl, the person of Jesus Christ was the central fact of history and all that went before and all that came after was to be interpreted in the light of that creative personality." But Harnack also had a power of sympathy that enabled him to appreciate and vivify historical figures, movements, and ideas far removed from his own. "Comparing Ritschl's best known book with Harnack's, you felt the difference between an anatomist's model and the living man whose skeleton was being studied," Brown observed. "To Ritschl, the thing that mattered was ideas. One theory battled with another, and the more disembodied they were the better. But to Harnack theory presented itself as the convictions of living men fighting their battle for a place in the world, and he made you understand what they felt as well as what they did." Years later, when Harnack made his only trip to the

United States, Brown served as his host. Later still, their friendship survived World War I, though Harnack wrote the Emperor's call to war in 1914 and subsequently endorsed the German invasion of Belgium. His American friend later reflected in Harnack's defense, "It must be remembered that he had been born in Russia and believed that the Russian terror was a very real menace."[17]

CREATING AN AMERICAN RITSCHLIANISM

Brown returned from Berlin in 1892 on the eve of Charles Briggs's first trial for heresy in the Presbyterian church. Still lacking a doctorate, he expected to enter the ministry, but Philip Schaff asked Union Seminary to relieve him of students, and thus Brown began his career as Schaff's assistant in church history. This position made Brown available to rescue the seminary's star-crossed search for a new systematic theologian. After W. G. T. Shedd retired in 1890, Union offered his position to Bangor Seminary theologian Lewis Stearns, but Stearns turned it down, mainly because he dreaded the prospect of converting from Congregationalism to Presbyterianism. Union proceeded to give the position to prominent Brooklyn pastor Henry Jackson Van Dyke, who was sixty-nine years old, but he died of a heart attack a month later. Opting for a younger man, Union turned next to one of its own graduates, a pastor named John H. Worcester Jr., but he taught for only a few months before falling ill and expiring. In the meantime, Philip Schaff retired, leaving Union with two open chairs. Arthur McGiffert, then teaching at Lane Theological Seminary, was Union's choice for its history chair. That left Brown without a position. Union asked him if he would be willing to switch to theology, taking Shedd's faculty slot. Making a stronger statement than it fully intended, Union Seminary replaced Schaff and Shedd with Harnack's chief American disciples.[18]

Brown later insisted that Union's proposition to him was "a cruel one to put to so young a man." Though it launched his theological career, the offer exposed his vulnerability and lack of theological training. "Systematic Theology was the storm center of the Seminary curriculum, the one chair by which the orthodoxy of the institution was to be tested," he recalled. "I was a young man, entirely unknown to the Church, and was, moreover, wholly without experience in this particular field." His vocational crisis was compounded by his judgment that the field had no text worth using. The systems of Shedd and Hodge were available, "but the type of theology taught in these systems was quite impossible for one who had been inoculated with the virus of Briggs and Francis Brown." A translated edition of Isaak Dorner's dogmatics was available, but the presuppositions and method of this system were equally problematic to a Ritschlian. Dorner was the model theologian to Briggs, Newman Smyth, and other American liberals of their generation. His neo-Schleiermacherian "mediating theology" inspired the American progressive orthodox theologies of the 1870s and 1880s. From a Ritschlian standpoint, however, Dorner-style mediating theology belonged to a

bygone era. The mediationist tradition had a liberal spirit and a partially historical consciousness, but methodologically it was controlled by its philosophical
idealism. To Brown, it therefore shared two of the fatal defects of Shedd/Hodge–
type orthodoxy: It was overdetermined by a philosophical system and deficient
in modern historical consciousness.[19]

Brown would have liked to use Ritschl's dogmatics, but an English edition was
years away. His only option was rather daunting. In a field for which he was academically unprepared, he resolved to develop his own texts. Brown's major contributions to liberal theology as a systematic discipline were thus conceived in the
early years of his academic career, by pedagogical necessity. From the beginning
he was a perceptive teacher, as University of Chicago theologian Gerald Birney
Smith later attested; Smith became a theologian under Brown's influence. In his
early career Brown wrote two books, *The Essence of Christianity* (1902) and *Christian Theology in Outline* (1906), that became classic systematic statements of the
new theology. Yet for the rest of his life Brown insisted that he could not imagine why Union had turned him into a theologian or why he had consented to it.

Brown was less concerned about what he should teach than about how he
should do it. "As to the first I had no doubt," he later recalled. "My years in Germany with Harnack had settled that question for me. I was to find a theology
which could be preached as a gospel, to put in what that required and to leave
out everything else." Harnack taught that Christianity is based on the person and
gospel of Jesus and nothing else. Historical criticism yields the apostolic gospel
in its original simplicity and beauty. It looks for this gospel in the theologies of
the past, but it refuses to adopt any of them wholeheartedly. "I did not believe
that any school of theologians had the monopoly of truth, yet I believed that it
was with truth that the theologian was concerned," Brown explained. The constructive task of the critically informed theologian is "to penetrate to the deeper
meaning that was common to all." Good theology uses historical criticism to
uplift and affirm the true gospel that all Christian theologies fallibly contain. If
Christianity is universally true, he reasoned, "there must be a central gospel running through all its varying formulations."[20]

In 1898 Brown was installed as the Roosevelt Professor of Systematic Theology at Union. His inaugural lecture described the essence of Christianity in statements that closely approximated the ideas and cadences of Harnack and
Herrmann, proposing that the "vitalizing principle of Christian theology" is the
person of Christ. Theology invariably mediates between the old and the new, he
observed; for the theologian, as for every Christian, the key question is whether
there is any sure point of contact between the faith of the past and the life of the
present. Herrmann contended that each believer possesses such a point of contact in the personality or "inner life" of Jesus. Brown called it "the historic personality of Jesus Christ." In the person of Christ, he explained, God entered
humanity in self-imparting love. This is not merely a doctrine, but a historical
and living reality. What matters is not to accept the doctrine as an authoritative
proposition, but to experience God's mercy and love through the saving effects

of God's revelation in Christ. Jesus Christ is the window through which we see the heart of God. "Are the doctrines which form the subject-matter of our science dogmas to be received on authority, irrespective of their contents; or are they living convictions, born of experience, and maintaining themselves in spite of all opposition because of the response which they awake in the hearts and consciences of men?" Arguing for the latter verdict, Brown urged that the very purpose of theology is to make "this connection with experience."[21]

Therefore a new theology was needed. Modern Christianity needed to recover the life and power of the gospel by refounding its proclamation on the radiant and self-sacrificing figure of Jesus. "The new school raises the old cry, 'Back to Christ,'" Brown declared. "Let no theology call itself Christian which has not its center and source in Him." This was the core religious appeal of Ritschlian liberalism. Because he believed, like Harnack, that "Jesus and his gospel" were immune from legitimate biblical criticism, Brown was prepared, like his teacher, to let historical criticism trim away various appendages to the gospel narrative. He shared Harnack's judgment that Ritschl went too far in setting the Jesus of the Gospels against the Christ of the church's creeds. Ritschl believed that the hellenized theology of fourth-century Christian orthodoxy was alien to Jesus. Just as Harnack was a bit more conservative than Ritschl in affirming the Christian legitimacy of Nicene Christianity, Brown was slightly more conservative than Harnack. "I had learnt from Harnack to think of the historic creeds as the natural language in which men of a speculative age had expressed a conviction, which I shared with them, namely, that God was in Christ reconciling the world unto Himself," he explained. Encouraged by this essentially Ritschlian counsel, he accepted Harnack's claim that a hellenizing church obscured the gospel in a haze of Neoplatonist speculation, but with a lighter touch. Brown emphasized that the church obscured the gospel without losing it. He employed historical criticism to affirm, not to refute. It was just as important to him to affirm that historic Christianity possessed the gospel as to pass judgment on theologies he could not accept.[22]

And how should modern theology be taught? The problem of the classroom proved more vexing to him than the essential content of the faith. Brown had enjoyed teaching church history, which he conceived as academic storytelling, but theology was more complex and difficult than storytelling. Beyond its historical component, theology required exegesis, dogma, and synthetic reflection. For this reason it also seemed to require special classroom skills. Brown realized that he fell short in the latter area. His students had genuine affection for him—they called him "Billy Dog"—but they moaned about his stiff and boring style of speaking. It didn't help that McGiffert was a scintillating classroom performer. More troublesome yet, for Brown, was the fact that he lacked an acceptable text. How was he supposed to teach theology before a suitable text could be assembled? He tried various experiments before finding a method that worked. It was essentially the same method by which Karl Barth later composed his *Church Dogmatics*. At the outset of each class, Brown presented a few carefully formulated paragraphs that provided the basis for commentary and class discussion. These opening paragraphs constituted the course's text, which eventually became his classic textbook *Christian Theology in Outline.*

An equally significant breakthrough occurred when one of his students, formerly of Colgate University, loaned him a typewritten manuscript of William Newton Clarke's theology lectures at Colgate. Brown later recalled that the student acted at Clarke's request. Reading Clarke's lectures, Brown found a kindred spirit, one who shared his theological perspective and who was dealing with the same pedagogical problems. He wrote to Clarke that he was grateful and delighted to possess his lectures; Clarke replied, "I cannot tell you how glad I am that you have found my notes suggestive and helpful, or how free you are to make all the use of them that you may desire. I hereby place at your service all the good there may be in my pages. It would be a pity if one teacher could not help another." In person, Clarke proved to be equally gracious, open, and friendly; he and Brown became close friends, and in 1896, before either of them had published his dogmatics, Clarke elaborated on his feelings about collegiality and collaboration: "Moral copyright in theology is a hard thing to get hold of, and I make small claim to it." In that spirit, Clarke and Brown, both of whom had become theologians by accident, produced the major dogmatic textbooks of the liberal theology movement.[23]

THE LIBERAL GOSPEL:
WILLIAM NEWTON CLARKE

The first systematic theologian of the American liberal theology movement epitomized the movement's warm evangelical piety and its excitement at breaking into the sunlight of a new theological era. Otherwise, William Newton Clarke was an anomaly. Though he became the movement's first systematic theologian, he came very late, and by accident, to the field of theology. Though his theology fit the main arguments and emphases of the Ritschlian school, he was not well read in German theology and made no direct use of it. Though he made a significant impact on the generation of Brown and Henry Churchill King, he did not belong to it. Clarke was fifty-two years old when he and Brown became friends in 1893, yet they shared the circumstance of being new to a field that lacked an acceptable textbook.

Clarke was a person of one book. His thinking revolved around, and was suffused by, scriptural narrative and teaching; thus his theological development was identical to his evolving understanding of the Bible. He titled his memoir *Sixty Years with the Bible* and reflected in it: "I am one of the men who have lived through the crisis of the Nineteenth Century, and experienced the change which that century has wrought. I began, as a child must begin, with viewing the Bible in the manner of my father's day, but am ending with a view that was never possible until the large work of the Nineteenth Century upon the Bible had been done." His late-career liberalism scandalized old friends and parishioners, though in later life he also realized that he seemed conservative to much of the liberal theology movement. To both groups he testified: "I know that I have followed my light, and passed through the revolution to which my generation was born, and have never come into danger of losing my faith in God and Jesus Christ. If a man may say it of himself, I have passed without ruin over what many deem to be a very dangerous way—nay, over a road that truly has its perils, not to be forgotten or despised."[24]

He was born in 1841 in Cazenovia, New York, to William and Urania Clarke. His father was a pietistic Baptist pastor of little formal education who possessed, in his son's fond recollection, a personality "of sweet reasonableness." The father was conventionally orthodox in his preaching and revered the Bible, but according to his son he was not a fundamentalist: "I suppose he must have had some theory of inspiration, but he never made the value of the Bible depend on it. He had no need of the theory, for he was building upon the reality." The latter sentence perfectly described the later William Newton Clarke. Less fondly, he recalled that his mother's intense religiosity scarred her children emotionally, because much of it was founded on the legalistic portions of the Old Testament: "She was in unconscious bondage because the Bible brought her the spirit of Judaism as well as the Christian faith." For many years Clarke struggled with conflicted feelings about biblical legalism. He liked the antilegalistic themes of Jesus and Paul, but felt obligated to accept the entire Bible as God's revealed Word and thus had no answer for parishioners who shared his mother's outlook. After he became a liberal, in the late 1880s, one of his crowning arguments on behalf of higher criticism was that it restored the prophetic religion of Moses, Amos, Isaiah, and Jesus to its rightful centrality and showed that biblical legalism is a postexilic, priestly distortion.[25]

Clarke was a diligent and deeply pious student. He enrolled at Madison University (later Colgate University) in 1858, graduated three years later, and enrolled immediately at Hamilton Theological Seminary, skipping the Civil War on account of poor health and his impatient desire to learn the Greek New Testament. Biblical scholar Hezekiah Harvey fed his immense appetite for language training and exegesis at Hamilton, while Ebenezer Dodge, a philosophical theologian trained by the German mediationists August Tholuck and Isaak August Dorner, taught theology. Clarke later recalled that Dodge ranged more widely than Harvey, thought more independently, and had a mystical streak; Clarke strongly preferred Harvey: "One was searching in the Bible to discover the truth of God; the other was using truth that he had found there or anywhere else, in the broad excursions of a reverently exploring spirit." To the extent that Clarke had a philosophy, he took common-sense realism for granted, and he was annoyed by Dodge's religious philosophizing. He complained that Dodge's theology wasn't biblical enough, he didn't build or even buttress his arguments on biblical proof texts. Though Clarke never believed in the verbal inspiration of scripture, he entered the ministry as a fervent biblicist.[26]

He served Baptist pastorates in Keene, New Hampshire; Newton Center, Massachusetts (where he married Emily A. Smith); and Montreal, Quebec, until 1883, when he joined the faculty of the Baptist Theological School in Toronto as a professor of New Testament Interpretation. For twenty years Clarke preached well-crafted, rigorously exegetical sermons while accommodating his belief system to evolutionary theory and the "lives of Jesus" literature of the 1870s. Typically his thinking was more affected by interpretive arguments about the advent and atonement of Christ than about evolution. In the 1870s Clarke judged that the premillennialist and postmillennialist interpretations of the second coming of Christ have an ample scriptural basis and are mutually exclusive. No matter which of these doctrines is the true one, he reflected, the other one has to be false; yet evangelical orthodoxy taught that one is always obliged to accept scriptural teaching. Moreover, the Gospel writers present Jesus as teaching that his second coming would occur in the lifetimes of his disciples. "Certainly they were in error on that point," he later observed. Increasingly he absorbed the fact that he could not accept all biblical teaching even if he tried to do so.[27]

The doctrine of Christ's atonement pushed him further toward liberal theology, which did not yet exist as a movement in American theology. Clarke began to rethink atonement doctrine seriously in the late 1870s after he realized that he didn't understand what it means to say that Christ died as the propitiation for sin. A decade earlier, however, after Horace Bushnell published *The Vicarious Sacrifice,* Clarke took his first pass at rethinking Christ's atonement. His wife Emily later recalled that he couldn't get through Bushnell's book. Clarke always had time and patience for exegesis, but not theology; Emily Clarke offered: "In his busy and weary life he had not found opportunity to do it justice." Ten years later Clarke gave Bushnell's book a second try. This time, Emily Clarke recalled, "He looked at the argument candidly from the author's point of view and felt the power of the book without assenting to it. The genius and personality of the author impressed him more than his teaching, yet Clarke could never afterward see the doctrine of the atonement in precisely the same light as before."[28]

Bushnell blasted the classical objectivist theories of atonement as morally repugnant; he argued that the New Testament metaphors of the altar are completely distorted when they are interpreted literally as legalistic ransom or substitution; and his constructive argument refashioned moral influence theory to account for the objective aspects of Christ's sacrifice. Gradually these arguments went to work on Clarke's moral feelings and exegetical imagination, leading him to the verdict that substitutionary atonement theory violates the Christian belief in God's moral character by making the appeasement of God's wrath the object of atonement. In the spirit of Bushnell, Clarke resolved that he could no longer preach a doctrine that contradicts "the ethical and spiritual principles that the revelation of Christ gives me to be the guides of my inquiry." Emily Clarke later reflected that if her husband had known Horace Bushnell, they would have loved each other. Bushnell was forceful, confident, and actively involved in secular and religious causes, she observed, while her husband was quiet, shy, "distrustful of himself," contemplative, and limited by poor health; yet spiritually they were much alike. If Clarke had known Bushnell, he might have become a Bushnellian: "As it was, he was never the disciple of any man."[29]

In the early 1880s Clarke authored his first book and took his first pass at academic life; in the late 1880s he embraced higher criticism. The book was a commentary on the Gospel of Mark, written for the American Baptist Publication Society. On the lightning-rod issue of biblical inspiration, Clarke wrote that Scripture is inspired in the way it is inspired, "not as we may think it ought to be inspired." His publisher eliminated this statement as being too radical for the Baptist church. On Jesus's eschatological discourse in Mark 13, Clarke assumed that he needed to show that Jesus' prediction of an imminent advent had been fulfilled in some way, so he argued that it occured in the destruction of Jerusalem. This resort satisfied no one, some Baptists denounced it as heretical, and the Baptist Publication Society rushed out a second edition that contained an appendix titled "An Additional View"; characteristically, Clarke accepted the addition with "no objection whatever."[30]

An accumulation of pastoral and scholarly issues drew him into the liberal camp, just as liberal theology was becoming a movement. In each of his congregations Clarke struggled anew with the Pauline injunction that women must keep silent in church, until the strong-minded women of Olivet Baptist Church of Montreal convinced him that Paul's injunction had nothing to do with them. During the four years that he taught at the Baptist Theological School in Toronto—various adjustments of belief aside—Clarke was still an orthodox evangelical. In 1887, however, just after the Baptists of Hamilton, New York, lured him back to Hamilton to serve as a pastor, he began to think about the larger implications of biblical criticism.

An avid student of textual criticism, Clarke had long since made his peace with higher critical judgments about the authorship and historical settings of various biblical books, but he came slowly to the view of higher criticism as a privileged, comprehensive method of interpreting the Bible. He studied the writings of Julius Wellhausen and other German biblical scholars, read the debate between young William Rainey Harper of Yale and orthodox stalwart William Henry Green of Princeton, and read "words of quietness" by American scholars who counseled that nothing crucial was at stake in the current debates over historical criticism. The false assurances of the latter group emboldened Clarke to face up to the revolution in biblical scholarship: "I plainly saw that the Bible would not come out of this crucible as it went in. From the generally accepted views there would certainly be great changes. No one could tell beforehand what they would be, but it was not to be supposed for a moment that the popular conceptions of the Bible, inherited from the Jews and from uncritical Christian ages, would all stand the test of critical investigation. Many of them would have to yield to new conceptions. The coming of great changes was as certain as the coming of the future, if this work went on."[31]

His rule for exegesis and preaching had been that the Bible should be allowed to mean whatever it does mean. Now he resolved that to be true to this principle, he had to consent "to let it be whatever it is." It was not for him or the church to presume the character of scripture, any more than he or the church should dictate its meaning on dogmatic or other grounds: "I must leave these to be determined for me by the facts, and must do my utmost to ascertain the facts. If they prove to be other than I thought, it is I, not they, that must change, and to make the needful change must be my first desire." The Bible does not claim inerrancy or perfection of any kind for itself, Clarke reasoned; it is simply itself, asking for no special privileges and declaring no doctrine about itself. For years he had agonized over God's command to exterminate the Canaanites, the imprecatory psalms that celebrated the slaying of children, and the fact that "God seemed to be contradicting himself" about the status of the law. Now Clarke enthused that most of the Bible's moral problems vanish when one approaches scripture comprehensively from the higher critical perspective: "With what delight and satisfaction then did I welcome the message of the higher criticism! I was now led to see that the central thing in the religion of the Old Testament was not the law but the prophets and their teaching; and the prophets held forth essentially the same religion of spiritual inwardness and sincerity that Jesus preached."[32]

Gradually he settled on the view that the worst heretics are those who chain Christianity to outmoded thought forms. In that spirit he expected to launch a new phase of his ministry in his college and seminary hometown. Though afflicted with a bad leg and a weak constitution, he was known for his vibrant spirit and loved the work of parish ministry, especially preaching. In his last sermon in Montreal he roared with thanksgiving, "The pulpit has been to me as a throne!" But in the first week of 1890, Ebenezer Dodge suddenly died. Clarke had long since repented his poor opinion of his former theology professor. Now he was called to succeed him—at first, temporarily, and by June, permanently— as Colgate University's J. J. Joslin Professor of Christian Theology. He later recalled, "My favorite work had always been biblical, and I had never looked forward to teaching theology, or desired it, or dreamed than anyone would ever wish me to do it, or imagined that I could ever assent if I were asked."[33]

Clarke's immediate problem was even more practical than his lack of intellectual preparation: he had no usable text. Dodge had used a privately printed edition of his own textbook, but at the time of his death only a few copies remained. Clarke resolved that he had to write his own book, because "theology was coming into a new period [and] all the older textbooks were framed upon a method of using the Bible that I could not employ." In the modern period, he reasoned, good theology still needs to be soaked in scripture, but it must not employ scripture as a storehouse of infallible propositions or proof texts. Faced with a pedagogical emergency, he wrote a first-draft textbook in the summer of 1890 that contained successive sections on the doctrines of God, "man," sin, Christ, the Holy Spirit, and eschatology. In the succeeding four years he revised and enlarged the book four times, and in 1894 he had it privately printed.[34]

Since Clarke had never bothered to read much theology, he made no references to theologians. In 1897 he secured an American publisher, Charles Scribner's Sons, which sent the manuscript to Thomas Clark, head of the Edinburgh publishing house T. & T. Clark. Clark told William Adams Brown that he was inclined not to publish the book, "for the public have been fed up on theology." Brown persuaded him to give Clarke's book a chance, and *An Outline of Christian Theology* (1898) became a religious bestseller on both sides of the Atlantic. The book's American edition went through fifteen editions in its first eight years and five more editions before World War I. Brown rejoiced in his friend's success and judged that it cleared a path for his own developing theology.[35]

An Outline of Christian Theology emphasized the ethical and loving character of God revealed in Christ and the openness of Christian theology to modern criticism. The book was written with a warmly personal, felicitous, forward-looking spirit that drew readers to Clarke personally and that calmed their fears about liberal theology. Characteristically he proclaimed that theology must "never stand still while the divine life of the Church is moving forward." The ongoing movement of God's Spirit makes the writing of new theologies an imperative work of the church, he declared: "Progressive experience makes an ever growing Church, and out of the ever growing life of the Church comes an ever growing theology, with the indwelling Spirit of God as the guide of its progress."[36]

The implication that followed connected him to the liberal-romanticist tradition of Samuel Taylor Coleridge, Horace Bushnell, Henry Ward Beecher, and Theodore Munger, though Clarke cited none of them: "Christianity is not a book-religion, but a life-religion. It centres in a person, and consists in a life, and Scriptures are its servant, not its source. To treat it, in proclaiming it or defending it, as a book-religion is to resign one of its best points of advantage." Clarke had a doctrine of biblical inspiration—"the divine element in the Scriptures will never be disproved," he assured—but he dismissed the doctrine of verbal inspiration, explaining that inspiration applies to persons, not to documents. The biblical writers were spiritually inspired, not their writing: "Inspiration is exaltation, quickening of ability, stimulation of spiritual power; it is uplifting and enlargement of capacity for perception, comprehension, and utterance."[37]

This emphasis on true religion as life-inspiration was Clarke's trump against historical refutation, though he did not wield it in the romanticist fashion of denigrating history. Because Christianity is "founded in history," he observed, Christian thinkers are not free "to claim exemption from the laws of historical evidence." *An Outline of Christian Theology* was rather light on historical-critical analysis—the principle of being open to historical criticism was more important to Clarke than any particular use of it—but he strongly affirmed that because Christianity is a historical religion, theology requires the best historical knowledge that can be attained about the founding and development of Christ's kingdom. "If Christ has come, his true character and power will be known, on such evidence as certifies other great facts in history," Clarke reasoned. Since there can be no doubt of Christ's living power, there is no reason for Christians to oppose a "candid and fearless inquiry into the real nature of the Scriptures." The reality of Christ's living power is the essential thing in Christianity, and it will endure "whatever may prove to be the manner in which the record of its founding has been written."[38]

"Whatever may prove" was a key to Clarke's appeal and the long career of his book in American theology classrooms. Modern scholarship was just beginning to determine the relative historicity of the biblical record, he counseled, and no one could say what it would determine about the founding of Christianity. A new Christian mainstream needed to welcome the historical-critical enterprise as a Christian project. Biblical criticism brought modern Christianity closer to the real Jesus of history, and its deconstructive aspects were not to be feared, for even "the annihilation of the Scriptures would not abolish the saving power of Christ."[39]

Clarke's theism accented the nature of God as personal spirit, the character of God as perfectly good, the relation of God to all things, and the loving motive of God. "God is the personal spirit, perfectly good, who in holy love creates, sustains, and orders all," he affirmed. Personality is a spiritual phenomenon, and the essential powers of spirit are thinking, feeling, and willing. Human beings know that spirit is real because they know themselves as spiritual beings through the experience of self-consciousness, and God is the personal ground and perfection of spiritual reality that thinks, feels, and wills in perfect completion. Human beings are compelled to define personality out of their experience of themselves as spiritual beings possessed of moral conscience, Clarke argued, but this understanding is never more than a glimpse of the real, for only God is completely personal and perfectly good. Thus, without denying that God is infinite and absolute, Clarke preferred the language of Christian personalism in speaking of God. The idea of personality is intrinsic to Christian theism by virtue of its spiritual and relational character, he reasoned; but the ideas of infinity and absoluteness are philosophical and reached by inference, do not view God in God's relations, and make God "vague and unreal" to the imagination. Clarke preferred the loving and holy God of biblical faith, whose holiness is "the glorious fulness of God's moral excellence."[40]

On the relation of body and soul, Clarke rejected the "immediate creation" theory that each soul is created by God's direct action in favor of the traducianist position that the entire being of an individual is derived by natural process from the being of the individual's parents. Body and soul go together in the creation of human beings. On the question of the origin of sin, Clarke pleaded that it should be enough for theology to say that moral evil entered history and the human condition through the acceptance of evil by free-willed human beings. An Outline of Christian Theology characterized sin as "badness" that chooses the reprehensible; as the abnormal choice of that which contradicts the life of virtue and love for which human beings were created; and as deviation from the proper standard of moral duty. Sin always involves condemnable moral choice, Clarke argued; it is not merely the domination of animal impulses over spirit or the unavoidable by-product of growth, and it cannot be imputed to the sinner's offspring. His chief examples of sin were greed, dishonesty, cruelty, drunkenness, profanity, adultery, moral shallowness, and petty selfishness. Summarizing these characterizations, Clarke defined sin as "the placing of self-will or selfishness above the claims of love and duty." Sin is the morally deviant choice of that which is condemnable because of what it is; it replaces the divine law with the law of selfishness.[41]

Clarke's account of salvation was equally evangelical: There is no salvation from sin without repentance of it, and there is no God known to Christianity that is not always righteous and loving. The love of God was Clarke's last word on this subject, but he did not speak it in a way that diminished God's hatred of sin: "God's nature requires him to hold, and he does hold, the attitude of perfect righteousness toward sin and toward sinners, and at the same time the attitude of perfect love toward his creatures, reaching out in divine helpfulness. He never swerves from holiness, or is unfaithful to love." God hates nothing that God has made; at the same time, God's perfect righteousness cannot be reconciled to the existence of sin. Therefore God is determined to abolish moral evil, Clarke contended; this is the redemptive hope of the gospel: "All his love for men cannot alter his hatred of their sin, and all the sin of the world cannot turn him aside from loving men, though with a disapproving love that corresponds in its sadness and severity to their ill-desert. He loves them, but cannot do for them all that he would; he cannot take them as they are into free friendship with himself."[42]

Clarke's Christology was typically liberal in its emphasis on the incarnational redemption of Christ. Christianity is essentially a religion of salvation, he contended, and the mission of Christ was to redeem the world in a saving process that includes Christ's divine life, death, resurrection, and the advent of the kingdom of God: "Christ is the gift of the heart of God, who desires to save the world. He comes to make known to men the true God, to infuse spirituality into their being, and thus to give them eternal life." On the stories of Christ's virginal conception, miracles, and resurrection, he argued that such matters are secondary to the question of Christ's divinity, and that the ground for making a judgment about Christ's divinity is the spiritual force of the gospel picture of Jesus, not historical proofs of miracle stories. Clarke affirmed the virgin birth and miracle stories on religious grounds while leaving room for various critical doubts about them; on the resurrection he made a stronger case for historical probability, arguing that the resurrection appearances are the best explanation of the fact that "Christianity sprang up almost in a day, a religion of holy power and spiritual renovation."[43]

He persistently cautioned, however, that all such particulars support the gospel faith; they do not establish it. That which establishes is Christ's divinity and saving mission. The echoes of Schleiermacher were strong in his Christology. To say that Christ is divine is not to claim that Jesus possessed the eternal consciousness of God, Clarke argued, for the divine consciousness in Jesus "was necessarily the consciousness of divinity within human limits." For Clarke, the idea of Christ's divinity was that Jesus possessed the divine consciousness to the fullest extent that such a thing is possible. The spiritual nature of Jesus was divine, but his life experience and embodiment were human: "The fact that that spirit was living within human limitations, spiritual as well as physical, rendered the personality human."[44]

He recommended the attitude of the New Testament toward the saving work of Christ. The New Testament writings are saturated with the conviction that Christ saved the world and reconciled sinners to God, Clarke explained; on the other hand, the "various thoughts of various apostles and apostolic men" concerning the nature of Christ's saving work do not present or constitute a uniform theory of salvation. Moreover, some of the New Testament's language about atonement is outmoded, reflecting the assumptions and thought forms of priestly Hebrew ritualism. Scripture affirms truly that Christ bore the sins of the world, Clarke observed, but this does not mean that Christ bore God's righteous punishment of sin, for only sinners can bear the punishment of their sin. God bears the sins of the world by enduring and suffering them as Christ did in his saving work: "All that the pure One must feel in contact with evil he is made to endure, and upon him is laid all the burden of endeavor against it that a Saviour-God can bear. The sinful world never suspects that it is keeping God in this position, and laying upon him a burden vaster than man can possibly conceive, yet it is plainly true. Sin burdens God."[45]

Jesus is the "meeting-point" between God and sinful humanity. Through Christ's saving life, death, and resurrection, Clarke proclaimed, God reveals God's holiness and outpouring love: "Christ stands in the midst of our humanity, near, knowable, lovable, accessible, where his humanness brings near to us the divine character to which we need to be conformed." What sinners need is not a forensic word of substitutionary cancellation that does not cancel the fact or consequences of sin; what they need is to be saved from the bondage of sinning. People are saved by becoming like Christ, with the help of God's Holy Spirit. There is no salvation apart from this transformation of spiritual character. Salvation is union with Christ and living in Christ's Spirit: "The cross represents the deepest point to which God went in seeking to save, but not the farthest point. After Christ came the Holy Spirit; and God's action of love is continued in the work of the Holy Spirit, and in the entire endeavor to bring men into moral unity with Christ. The same love that endured the cross now calls men to Christ, and seeks to transform them into his likeness by joining them to him in spiritual union."[46]

An Outline of Christian Theology was strong on the moral character of salvation and the personal, practical nature of Christian faith, though it kept a leash on Clarke's progressivist politics. His friends included Walter Rauschenbusch and other social gospelers, and he belonged to Rauschenbusch's (Northern Baptist) Brotherhood of the Kingdom fellowship group. His book expressed the theology behind the social gospel idea of social salvation, and it contained occasional glosses on the social gospel. Clarke counseled that the second coming of Christ should not be understood as an event, even a future event: "It is a process that includes innumerable events, a perpetual advance of Christ in the activity of his kingdom." But the work of writing a systematic theology of social salvation had to wait for Rauschenbusch; Clarke was a forerunner.[47]

At the turn of the century, he had the field of liberal dogmatics to himself. Methodist bishop Edward G. Andrews spoke for many in praising Clarke's "combination of freedom and conservatism, of clear intellectual processes with the sweetness and fervor of devoutness, of strength of material with grace and form." Having found his theological vocation late in life, and quite by accident, Clarke flourished in his closing years, which coincided with the ascension of liberal theology to establishment status. In 1899 he published a primer on Christian faith, *What Shall We Think of Christianity?* which convinced Douglas Clyde Macintosh to remain a Christian and become a theologian. In 1905 Clarke gave the Nathaniel William Taylor Lectures at Yale Divinity School, which were published as *The Use of the Scriptures in Theology*. Clarke's rising eminence gave him the liberty to say certain things with a sharper edge. Commenting on the doctrine of plenary inspiration, he pronounced that "an intelligent reading of the Bible is enough to scatter the theory to the winds." His explanation of the doctrine's persistence was newly pointed: "We can account for the doctrine only by remembering that the Bible is in a way the least intelligently read of books."[48]

Feeling that he had more to say about God than his 120-page textbook section had allowed, Clarke wrote a book in his closing years which argued that Christian thinking about God must keep up with developments in modern thought. "The Christian view of God came from Jesus not as finished once for all, but as a living, growing thing," he observed. "It claims to be truth, truth in the midst of truth, truth supreme, and like other truth it must be apprehended as men are able. It must now fit in with other truth, just as it fitted in with truth known in other periods."[49] Inspired by a soaring social gospel movement, he also published a book titled *The Ideal of Jesus* that confirmed his identification with the social gospel: "A revolutionary work that shall bring the Christian ideal to successful expression in the common life is to be expected in the world of God. His kingdom is yet to come far more completely." More boldly for a shy, sensitive theologian, but in tune with the spirit of 1911, Clarke declared that it was the moral duty of Christians "to make progressive change in the social organism just as fast as we can; whether a convulsion is coming or not, this is the method that is now in operation, with the sanction of all that is good."[50]

He claimed not to regret that he spent most of his life doing plodding exegesis for sermons before discovering his theological vocation. Clarke's wife felt some regret for him: "To sit at his table pondering and judging as to the correct reading and exact meaning of single texts and longer passages of Scripture was not the occupation best suited to his naturally constructive, swiftly working mind." Yet Emily Clarke allowed that her husband's many years of exegetical labor prepared him for "the crowning work of his life." Though slow to find his theological calling, he also found it exactly in time for maximum influence. Emily Clarke explained: "His books were widely read, not only by students and masters in theology, but by many other thoughtful men and women, for whom he had bridged the chasm between the past and the present, and had made the Christian faith possible in a time of doubt and transition."[51]

Clarke's saintly sincerity inspired deep affection and appreciation from his friends and readers. After he died in 1912, Walter Rauschenbusch testified: "He will be a dear, warm memory all our life, one of the high peaks in our horizon of life. Such a sincere, genuine, beautiful human soul!" Douglas Clyde Macintosh called him "our most humane theologian." Henry H. Peabody noted that Clarke's mild and kindly spirit was capable of raging against moral evil: "He had at times a Pauline wrath." Clarke's leading protégé, Harry Emerson Fosdick, recalled that "he was a teacher of the old school—God give us more of them!—who gave his classes his personality and breathed his spirit into them."[52]

Unsurpassed in his affection and appreciation of Clarke was William Adams Brown, who loved the "singular serenity" of his writing and personality and his emphasis that revelation is the manifestation of spirit to spirit, not the imparta- tion of revealed propositions. Recalling his first impression of *An Outline of Christian Theology,* Brown remarked, "The author was evidently one who had communed deeply with Jesus, and had drawn from his communion convictions which had so laid hold upon his spirit as to demand utterance. He believed that the gospel of Christ was a message which the world had not yet outgrown, and it was his endeavor to justify this faith by showing its adaptation to the present needs and problems of men." The moment was ripe for a liberal dogmatics at the end of the nineteenth century, Brown recalled: "Many who had broken intel- lectually with the doctrinal statements of the past still felt themselves at home emotionally in the religious values which they sought to express, and they wel- comed this new statement of old truths because it made it possible for them to preserve their continuity with the Christian past, without the sacrifice of intel- lectual consistency."[53]

Clarke's textbook helped Brown find his way as a teacher of theology, and they shared essentially the same theology and spiritual sensibility, but there were sig- nificant differences between the two theologians. Brown's thinking was more his- torical, academic, and oriented toward trends in modern theology, especially contemporary German theology. When theological colleagues like Macintosh pressed Clarke on his relation to the Ritschlian school, he acknowledged that his arguments were very similar to those of Ritschlians like Brown and Harnack. However, he insisted that he had worked out his theological position indepen- dently of modern theologians, and even his later works did not cite them. For Clarke it was enough to say that the Bible provides knowledge of Jesus and that Jesus gives us knowledge of God; a bit more programmatically, he argued that God is the center of Christian theology, that the spirit of Jesus is the organizing principle of theology, and that theology has "congenial truth from within the Bible and from without for its material." Clarke's writings never unpacked that "from without." Though he proclaimed that theology must keep up with mod- ern philosophy, science, and the social sciences, he did not engage these disci- plines, he made little direct use of higher criticism, and he ignored modern theologians. He also said very little about the church, though in the early twen- tieth century that was a common liberal shortcoming.[54]

Clarke's writing style was considerably more pungent and felicitous than Brown's. On occasion he tried to help Brown acquire a more vivid style, cautioning especially against winding, colorless sentences that began with the word "while." Brown was less quotable than his friend, but the accumulative impact of his writing and career were greater. In 1902 Brown published his first book, *The Essence of Christianity*, which was his doctoral dissertation; in 1906 he published his textbook, *Christian Theology in Outline*, which was closely modeled on Clarke's. After these books were published, Clarke rejoiced that American theological liberalism was surely finding its own voice.[55]

AMERICAN RITSCHLIANISM: KANT, SCHLEIERMACHER, RITSCHL, AND HARNACK

The Essence of Christianity made a strong case for a decidedly Ritschlian voice. Brown explained the meaning of modern theology in a narrative of progress that ended with Harnack and other Ritschlians. The book owed its ample scholarly apparatus to its origin as a dissertation. Despite having avoided philosophy when he studied at Yale, Brown appealed to his alma mater for advanced standing in its philosophy program after Union made him a theology professor. Yale obliged him, and later granted him a doctorate on the strength of his first book. Focusing on the theme of the essential nature of Christianity, he took a brief pass at patristic and classical literature before turning to modern theology. His rendering of the essence of Christianity in modern theology made a case for a blend of Schleiermacher and Ritschl on Ritschlian terms. Brown refused to choose between neo-Kantian religious experientialism and neo-Kantian religious historicism. *The Essence of Christianity* issued a call for an American Ritschlian theology and explained why the schools of Schleiermacher and Ritschl belonged together.

In his reading, Ritschl was an ethical reformer and theological savior of the school of Schleiermacher. The key to the triumph of the Ritschlian school, he argued, was that it took theology back to the approach first theorized by Schleiermacher, who interpreted Christianity as a historical phenomenon from the standpoint of church-informed Christian experience. For Schleiermacher and Ritschl alike, he explained, theology was a positive science that sought to explicate what it found in the subject matter given to it. Every science has a posited subject matter; in the case of theological science, that which is given is religious experience. In Brown's rendering, Ritschl understood that he derived his approach to theology from Schleiermacher: "His only quarrel with Schleiermacher is over the fact that the latter has not always been true to his own premises." Schleiermacher claimed to interpret Christianity as a *historical* phenomenon from the standpoint of *communal, church-informed* Christian experience, but his theology never attained the quality of objectivity that inhered in this starting point. Speaking for Ritschl and, implicitly, himself, Brown observed that Schleiermacher's thinking was pervaded by a taint of individualistic subjectivism, "which is repugnant to the younger theologian." The historic achievement of Ritschl, in this reading, was to rescue the total structure of Schleiermacher's theological method from its originator and his school.[56]

The mediating theologians who dominated German theology in the mid-nineteenth century were church-friendly revisionists and synthesizers in the schools of Schleiermacher and Hegel who sought to establish a theological third way between traditional authority-based orthodoxies and an ascending deistic or atheistic rationalism. This was the defining impulse of theological liberalism. From Brown's perspective, however, the mediating tradition was flawed by its philosophical foundationalism. All of the mediating theologians were committed to some form of philosophical idealism. Some of them were Hegelians, such as Philipp K. Marheineke, Karl Rosenkranz, Karl Daub, and Carl Friedrich Göschel, who developed a theology out of Hegel's philosophy of Absolute Idealism. Hegel theorized a logical process by which the meanings of representations were taken up into the "Concept" through the dialectical movement of Spirit. Because the concepts of the mind are universals, he reasoned, there is no rational basis for dichotomizing between subject and object or form and content. The world exists only as the externalization of self-consciousness, and self-consciousness exists only as a recognized shape of this world as Spirit. Spirit empties itself into the world of sensuous particularity and thereby "creates" the world as an experience of itself.[57]

The Hegelian theologians developed the religious implications of Hegel's project of conceiving the world as Spirit-created reality known totally as Spirit. Brown's one-dimensional "thesis-antithesis-synthesis" rendering of Hegelian logic failed to grasp its triadic structure as a dialectic of three simultaneous cases of reduplicated relation, but he correctly described the work of Hegelian theology as philosophical translation of the pictorial ideas of religious imagination (Vorstellungen) into the forms of pure thought (Begriffe). He also emphasized perceptively that unlike various competing philosophical idealisms, the Absolute of Hegelian idealism is concrete. Hegel conceptualized the world of concrete finite experience as a moment in God's consciousness, not as existing outside of God. Put differently, unlike some of his "right-Hegelian" followers, notably Göschel and Kasimir Conradi, Hegel did not interpret God as hypostatized apart from the world.[58]

Brown gave short shrift to full-fledged Hegelian theology. He allowed that a few Tübingen-school historical critics were Hegelians, especially Ferdinand Christian Baur and David Friedrich Strauss (though in fact, Baur was not a rigorously Hegelian thinker, and in his early career Strauss was theologically to Hegel's left and in his later career renounced Hegelianism and Christianity). Brown noted more accurately that Marheinecke and Daub exercised some influence in German theology and that, more recently, A. E. Biedermann had published the most positive and impressive theological system produced by the Hegelian school. He also gave a respectful nod to the neo-Hegelian philosophical theologies of the Scottish Caird brothers, John and Edward Caird. But *The Essence of Christianity* was geared to the implications of modern theology for

American theology, and full-fledged Hegelianism had little following in American theology. Brown implied that the finer points of in-house Hegelian debate were therefore not significant to the American theological scene.[59]

The neo-Schleiermacherian–neo-Hegelian mediating school was another matter. The kind of German mediating theology pioneered by Isaak Dorner had a history in American theology by virtue of its influence on Union Seminary theologian Henry Boynton Smith and a succession of Gilded Age American liberals. In Germany and other countries influenced by trends in German theology, the major mediationist thinkers were Dorner, August Neander, Carl Immanuel Nitsch, Willibald Beyschlag, Johannes von Hofmann, Johann Peter Lange, Carl Ullmann, and Danish bishop H. L. Martensen. Most of them fused Schleiermacher's religion of consciousness with Hegel's metaphysical idealism, often in ways that favored Schleiermacher. Some mediating theologians wedded Schleiermacher to the transcendental idealism of F. W. J. Schelling; Heidelberg theologian Richard Rothe and Leipzig philosophical theologian Christian Hermann Weisse were prominent examples. Brown appreciated that the mediating tradition played a creative role in modern theology, but he objected that even in its most attractive forms, it sacralized some type of philosophical idealism. The mediating theologians invariably allowed the a priori principle of a philosophical system to overpower the scientific character of Schleiermacher's theological method. Dorner's Hegelian dialecticism was typical. He began with a general definition of religion, broke this idea into two antithetic elements, and then conceptualized Christianity as the "absolute religion" that synthesized the opposing religious elements. This approach to Christian truth is quintessentially Hegelian, Brown observed; in Brown's conviction, it was also profoundly misguided.[60]

It was Ritschl who reclaimed and improved the genuine school of Schleiermacher. "In Ritschl we see the effort to reinstate Christianity upon the unique pedestal from which it has been cast down, without the aid of the principles used by Hegel, and by an appeal to considerations the force of which the positivist himself must recognize," Brown declared. "Instead of seeing in Christianity with Hegel the crown of a religion of nature more or less manifesting itself wherever the religious life exists at all, he calls attention to the uniqueness of Christianity as a phenomenon without parallel." Ritschl brought theology back to its correct point of departure, which is the Christ-experience of a living, distinctive, historical community of faith. Christianity is thoroughly historical, Brown admonished, and history cannot be written solely from an a priori principle. Unlike idealistic philosophy of history, actual history takes irregular twists and turns that look nothing like an orderly philosophical system. In Brown's rendering, good Ritschlians believed so deeply in the historical character of their subject that they renounced even the Kantian *Ding an sich*.[61]

Brown took for granted the basic Kantianism of the Ritschlian school. Ritschlian theology took its theoretical bearings from Kant's distinction between pure and practical reason, his assignment of morality to practical reason, and his view of religion as essentially ethical. Brown cautioned, however, that Kant's belief in the existence of noumenal things-in-themselves belonged to another category. This was the category of misguided speculation, for it was precisely Kant's notion of an unknowable *Ding an sich* that fueled a speculative explosion of new metaphysical systems. Inspired by Kant's dualism of known and unknown worlds, but in opposition to it, Hegel concocted an idealistic system from the conjecture that the world exists as the externalization of consciousness. The Hegelians and Schelling-school idealists thus inspired themselves to speak of an evolution of the Infinite, a coming to consciousness of the Absolute, a self-realization of God, and a manifestation of the divine to the human.

The affinities between the latter phrases and traditional Incarnation language gave no pause to Brown. He countered that all of these phrases amounted to meaningless word-spinning. They referred to "figments of the mind, mere imaginations unworthy of the name of reality." Finitude and infinity are mutually exclusive, he reasoned; infinity begins where finitude ends. Good Ritschlian theology respected the early church's right to express its faith in neo-Platonist forms, just as it respected the gospel spirit in Dorner's neo-Hegelianism, but the Ritschlian school insistently favored the real world over figments of the mind. Ritschlianism represented the triumph of empiricism in theology: "Experience, limited and phenomenal though it be—this is the true reality, and the only reality."[62]

To his mind, this was the crucial Ritschlian achievement: the Ritschlian school made theology real again; it recovered reality. It eschewed the vain metaphysical pursuit of transcendental realities and confined its claims to the sensible world of experience. It took seriously the empirical criterion of meaning upheld by scientific positivists but corrected the typical positivist prejudice against religion. "The characteristic note of the Ritschlian theology is to be found in the union of a strong apologetic purpose, with a scientific spirit equally uncompromising," Brown remarked. A half-century of idle speculation in German theology, rarely appropriated in America, was brought to an end by Ritschl's gospel-oriented historicism: "In Ritschl German theology returns to the path which had been marked out for it by Schleiermacher, but from which it had been diverted for the time by the more ambitious programme of the Hegelian speculation."[63]

Brown maintained that Ritschlian theology marked a return to Schleiermacher's experientialism and a significant improvement on it. Ritschl agreed with Schleiermacher that theology is always rooted in experience, but unlike Schleiermacher, he emphasized the ethical character of Christian experience and the distinctive sociohistorical factors that called it forth. "Ritschl is at one with Schleiermacher in insisting that all theology has to do with subjective experiences," Brown explained. "But he differs from him in the energy with which he emphasizes the fact that the Christian experience is called forth by a certain definite object, and the clearness with which he tries to define the nature of that object." For Schleiermacher religion was essentially feeling; for Hegel it was a form of knowledge; for Ritschl it was essentially a form of moral power. Ritschlian theology accented God's active care for humanity and the moral power over the world that Christians gain through their experience of God.[64]

The latter view was distinctively Christian, Brown observed; more precisely, Ritschl's conception of religion was based on a specifically Christian approach to it. Schleiermacher and Hegel constructed a general definition of religion on the basis of a purportedly universal religious experience; they took for granted that Christianity must be conceptualized as an example of religion before its status as the highest religion can be claimed. Ritschl countered that the way to find out the nature of true religion is to study Christianity. It is not as a species of a genus called "religion" that Christianity is true, he contended. Though he allowed that a general conception of religion can have regulative value as a standard of comparison to Christianity, Ritschl denied that any general idea of religion has constitutive value as a criterion or measure of religious truth. To deduce the meaning of Christian truth from any general conception of religion, he admonished, "even for a moment," is to violate the integrity of the gospel witness. Instead of claiming that Christianity is the highest example of a preconceived notion of religion, theology must affirm that Christianity belongs to a class by itself and is not comprehensible or truthfully represented as an example of a preconceived category.[65]

It followed for Ritschl that the fundamental and determinative project of Christian theology is to identify the historical reality that calls forth specifically Christian experience. His famous simile of the ellipse established the framework for the Ritschlian answer. Christianity is not like a circle, which can be described from a single center, Ritschl argued; it is more like an ellipse, which is determined from two foci. One focal point is the religious conception of redemption; the other is the ethical conception of the kingdom of God. Christ is made known to his followers as the redeemer, but the center of the redeemer's teaching and the moral end of his existence is the kingdom of God: "Now it is true that in Christianity everything is 'related' to the moral organisation of humanity through love-prompted action; but at the same time everything is also 'related' to redemption through Jesus, to spiritual redemption, i.e., to that freedom from guilt and over the world which is to be won through the realised Fatherhood of God." The moral end of individual existence is freedom in God, just as the final end of all existence is the kingdom of God. Ritschl cautioned that this does not mean that redemption is the basis of Christian theology while the kingdom is the basis of Christian ethics. Genuine Christianity is always mutually relational; the religious and ethical dimensions of the Christian movement perpetually interact and advance through history.[66]

This criterion yielded his definition of Christianity: "Christianity, then, is the monotheistic, completely spiritual, and ethical religion, which, based on the life of its Author as Redeemer and as Founder of the Kingdom of God, consists in the freedom of the children of God, involves the impulse to conduct from the motive of love, which aims at the moral organisation of mankind, and grounds blessedness on the relationship of sonship to God, as well as on the Kingdom of God." Like Schleiermacher and Coleridge, Ritschl believed that Christianity is essentially a life, not a doctrine, but he refused to subordinate the socioethical and historical aspects of this life to secondary importance. To him, Christianity was irreducibly the forward-moving and communal faith of those who know Christ as redeemer and live out his ethic of the kingdom. "We know nothing of a self-existence of the soul, of a self-enclosed life of the spirit above or behind those functions in which it is active, living, and present to itself as a being of special worth," he declared. Christian knowledge is thoroughly historical. It knows nothing about God's ontological interrelations or the attributes of the soul, but it knows with faithful certainty that God is redemptively and ethically active in history.[67]

As much as possible, Brown read Ritschl as the restorer of Schleiermacher's theological method; where they differed, he favored Ritschl. Ritschl argued that Schleiermacher made society secondary because his approach to religion was essentially mystical. Schleiermacher had little conception of social salvation, but for Ritschl and Brown, salvation was inseparably personal and social. Brown explained that Schleiermacher was a monist "who sees God in everything, to whom evil is something relative, subsidiary, passing," but Ritschl was a dualist, "face to face with the fact of present evil, to whom unity is an ideal still to be realized, a task still to be achieved." Schleiermacher conceived Christ as the exemplar of a general religious ideal, but Ritschl viewed Christ as a distinctive source of power, "the beginning of a new line of development" linked historically only to the faith of Israel. The latter subject brought out the final important difference between them, though Brown unfortunately failed to note that it was also an important difference between Ritschl and Harnack. Schleiermacher and Harnack exaggerated the differences between the Old and New Testaments, while Ritschl emphasized and affirmed the Jewish basis of Christianity. To Schleiermacher, Hebrew religion was hopelessly primitive and exclusivist; his dogmatics asserted that the best aspects of Christianity came from non-Jewish sources and that "whatever is most definitely Jewish has least value." Harnack said the same thing with nicer words, but Ritschl insisted that genuine Christianity is deeply Jewish. The most grievous error of historic Christianity was its "Catholicizing" denigration of Hebrew religion, he argued. Christianity at its best is an outgrowth of biblical Hebrew faith, for genuine Christianity represents "a culmination of the monotheistic, spiritual, and teleological religion of the Bible."[68]

This account of the personal and social meaning of Christianity was inspiriting to the liberal generation that took over America's elite seminaries and divinity schools. Ritschl's emphasis on the practical, historical, ethical mission of Christianity appealed to American religious thinkers who had little taste for metaphysical speculation and who sought a theological rationale for an ascending social gospel movement. In pragmatic America, the empirical orientation of Ritschlian theology was crucial to its influence. Equally important was the Ritschlian distinction between the essence of Christianity and its disposable secondary elements. Harnack called it the difference between the "kernel" and "husk" of Christianity. He assured that historical criticism was an aid to good theology because it stripped away the disposable husk of Christianity and brought forth its gospel kernel. This distinction was invaluable to a theological generation that struggled to cope with serious challenges from modern science, Enlightenment

philosophy, and an increasingly secular culture. Though Ritschl made little use of
biblical criticism in his own work, his followers employed the essence/accidents
distinction while making heavy use of biblical criticism.[69]

Brown noted the ironies of the Ritschlian ascendancy. The Ritschlian school
dominated contemporary theology despite its founder's lack of personal magnetism, his unattractive style of writing, and the widely varying theologies of his
successors. In 1902, the movement included such influential German theologians as Harnack, Wilhelm Herrmann, Max Wilhelm, T. Reischle, H. Schultz,
W. Bornemann, Wilhelm Bender, Otto Ritschl, Johannes Weiss, H. H. Wendt,
Theodor Häring, Martin Rade, Paul Drews, Ferdinand Kattenbusch, Immanuel
Nitzsch, and Friedrich Loofs. At the extremes it ranged from a doctrine-oriented
supernaturalist, Julius Kaftan, to a history of religions historicist and antisuper-
naturalist, Ernst Troeltsch. The Ritschlian school produced a host of theologies
and vigorously debated Ritschl's ideas, but it held one characteristic in common
that was crucial to Brown's argument: the difference between the variably defined
essence of Christianity and its secondary aspects. Brown called for an explicitly
Ritschlian school of American theology on this basis: "Nowhere, it may be said
with confidence, has the problem which now engages us received more constant
and persistent attention than at the hands of those whose first impulse to theological study has been received from Ritschl."[70]

He allied himself with his famous teacher, though Brown stopped short of
explaining how sharply Harnack wielded the blade of historical criticism. Harnack emphasized the distinctive literary character of the Gospels and the historical chasm between the world of the New Testament and the modern world. He
judged that while the Gospels were "not altogether useless" as sources of critical
history, the crucial fact about them was their unique literary nature as Jewish-
Christian testimonies of faith. The Gospels are a unique "species of literary art"
that were composed for the work of evangelization by the last generational representatives of early Jewish Christianity, he explained. They contain the essence
of Christianity, but they also contain layers of material that have no essential relation to Christianity. Harnack urged that the essence of Christianity consists of
its "timeless essential elements," not its historical appendages. He regarded the
New Testament infancy narratives as purely mythical; he taught that all biblical
stories that featured angels, devils, nature miracles, and foretellings of the apoc-
alypse are mythical; he judged that statements such as "I am the Son of God" are
not gospel statements, but additions to the gospel; and he sharply distinguished
the "kernel" of Easter testimony from its apologetic-theological "husk." The former is the conviction that Christ has gained victory over death; the latter is any
testimony, narrative, or apologetic that seeks to substantiate or codify the Easter
faith, including the New Testament resurrection narratives. Harnack also shared
Schleiermacher's deprecatory view of Hebrew religion, a fact that Brown passed
over without remark.[71]

Without spelling out Harnack's specific positions on these issues, Brown
lauded his teacher's recent work as the fulfillment of the Ritschlian ideal. In Har-

nack's work, he enthused, modern theology ascended to a new level of clarity, scholarly rigor, and spiritual wisdom. Harnack's bestselling primer *What Is Christianity?* was the best account "of the results of modern critical study which has yet appeared." This epochal book expressed the timeless meaning of Christianity and summarized the modern critical picture of Jesus and Christianity. Brown observed that it also advanced the "moralization of religion" that Ritschl inaugurated. Historical criticism was still controversial in America, he allowed; even in Germany a few theologians still doubted that historical criticism was bringing the modern church closer to Jesus and authentic Christianity. Mediating theologian Martin Kähler was a prominent example of the latter phenomenon. Kähler argued that the modern historicist desire to get to the "real Jesus" behind the Gospel sources was "a blind alley," because the Gospels are testimonies of faith without remainder. The only "real Jesus" that can be found or known is the "historic Christ" confessed by faith in the Gospels, he insisted. The New Testament Christ is the only Christ that we know anything about.[72]

Kähler invoked the historic Christ as an alternative to the liberal distinction between the Jesus of history and the Christ of faith. The Ritschlian rootage of this concept was problematic for Brown, who thus failed to acknowledge it. He might have noted that Kähler borrowed the idea of the historic Christ from Ritschl and that his employment of it was nearly as muddled as Ritschl's. For Kähler, as for Ritschl, the historic Christ was "the Christ who has exercised an influence in history, with whom millions have communed in childlike faith, and with whom the great witnesses of faith have been in communion." For both theologians, the object of genuine Christian faith and scholarship was Christ in the total historic impression of his person. Neither thinker defined this concept clearly enough to give it a precise meaning or address the problem of its subjectivism. Ritschl was especially evasive on this topic. He carefully hedged on the question whether the historic Christ was the Christ of the Gospels, or the Jesus of modern criticism, or perhaps, as Brown suggested, something in between.[73]

Employing the same ambiguous concept, Kähler opted for one horn of Ritschl's dilemma. He rejected the modern quest of the historical Jesus and contended that Christianity is solely based on the historic influence of Jesus upon his disciples. In the process of defending this argument against a dominant liberal German scholarship guild, he bequeathed to modern theology a rich fund of concepts that were later adopted by Karl Barth, Emil Brunner, Rudolf Bultmann, Friedrich Gogarten, and the neo-orthodox movement. These concepts included Kähler's distinction between history as the objective dead past *(Historie)* and history as the significant or "historic" past *(Geschichte)*, which he employed to elucidate his claim that the only possible basis of Christian faith is the historic biblical Christ and not the historical Jesus. To describe what it was that the early Christians proclaimed about Jesus, Kähler appropriated an ancient Greek word, *kerygma,* that gained a sizable role in twentieth-century theology. He taught that the preaching of the original gospel kerygma was directly related to *Geschichte,* but only indirectly to *Historie.*[74]

Kähler's challenge to theological liberalism was subtle, conceptually loaded, and rooted in Ritschlian ideas, if not the Ritschlian school. It made a serious albeit problematic claim to explicate the basis of Christianity in the historic Christ, but not in Brown's book. Brown abruptly dismissed Kähler's position, declaring that his argument was "superficial" and that Kähler had no part in the genuine Ritschlian movement. The liberal quest of the historical Jesus was a valuable aid to faith, Brown assured. Modern biblical criticism was bringing the modern church closer to Jesus and early Christianity. On the basis of critical scholarship, modern theology was restoring the humanity of Christ to its rightful place in the church's thinking and preaching: "Through the mists of dogma and of tradition under which He has so long been hidden, the gracious figure of the Man of Galilee begins again to be seen."[75]

By learning more about the world of Jesus, Brown assured, we learn more about Jesus. More importantly, we gain a better understanding of his gospel: "The Fatherhood of God, the brotherhood of man, the worth of the individual human soul, greatness through service, salvation through sacrifice, the kingdom of God as the goal of humanity,—these truths, so inexhaustible in their richness and freshness, are seen to be His peculiar contribution to the religious thought of the race." Most importantly, he concluded, we gain a better understanding of Christ's character: "The Gospel and the character of Jesus belong together. He could speak of God as He did because he had had experience of God in His own soul, and knew whereof He affirmed. He could transform the Jewish ideal of earthly glory and dominion into the Christian kingdom of service because He had learned in His own life that the things which are unseen are eternal."[76]

On the strength of this Harnackian gospel, Brown called for an American Christianity that endorsed the current trend of religious progress: "It must be able to show that the ideals which it reveals, the motives to which it appeals, and the forces which it sets in motion, are such as to promote that type of the religious life toward which, so far as we are able to judge, religious progress is tending." At the high tide of the Ritschlian-school domination of Continental theology, he appealed for an up-to-date American Christianity: "We need to put away all party spirit; all pride of sect, or name, or opinion; that in all the churches, as among those who stand outside of all, we may find the men who have been touched by the spirit of Jesus, and in the forms natural to their day and place, strive to realize the ends for which He gave His life. When we have done this, we shall have found the essence of Christianity."[77]

CHRISTIANIZING THEOLOGY AND THE WORLD

This vision of a Christ-centered ecumenical Christendom fueled Brown's writing and preaching throughout his forty-four-year career at Union Theological Seminary. He held the Roosevelt chair of systematic theology for thirty-two years before moving in 1930 to a research professorship of applied Christianity, which he held for the last six years of his teaching career. His influence as a builder and leader of the American liberal Protestant establishment was exercised mainly as a teacher, church leader, ecumenist, and theological popularizer, not as a scholar or constructive theologian. *The Essence of Christianity* was Brown's only scholarly work. It stayed in print for over forty years and shaped much of the development of American evangelical liberalism during its heyday.

It was also his breakthrough book, which gave it a special status in his affection. Lodged between rows of family photographs and the report card of Brown's son, another John Crosby Brown, the Brown family album inserted a coming-of-age book review published by the *Church Economist:* "The chair of Systematic Theology in Union Seminary, New York, has been made famous by former occupants. Henry B. Smith and William G. T. Shedd have left their impress on the minds of the thinkers of the Protestant world. It is no light thing that a young man, unknown to the great majority of religious workers, placed in the position of professor to supply a pressing need, should so clearly justify the choice by producing such a volume as this." *The Essence of Christianity* was the first installment of Brown's attempt to justify his position; his textbook, *Christian Theology in Outline* (1906), was the second. For the next three decades the latter book shared with Clarke's *Outline of Christian Theology* the distinction of being the chief classroom text of modern American theology; in essence, the two textbooks were variants of the same book. All of Brown's subsequent books aimed at a wider audience.[78]

His early work contributed greatly to the reshaping of American theology as an academic discipline, but Brown's passion was the life of the church in a world that needed to be transformed by liberal Christianity, not by the finer points of theology. His later books often explained in the prefaces that he left the scholarly arguments and details to others. In his early career, and considerably under his influence, the liberal theology movement surged into academe, but to Brown the essential mission of Christian higher education was the renewal of church and society. He embraced the social gospel mission of Christianizing the church, America, and the world, usually in that order. His later books were thus addressed to seminarians, pastors, and lay readers, not to academics. A few were products of his theology classroom; some were sermon collections; several dealt with personal religion; all were devoted to building a new Christendom out of the energy and faith of the liberal social gospel.

Born to privilege and comfortable in it, Brown was never a radical, but he recognized that the Ritschlian social gospel in America had to be more democratic and progressive than the bourgeois, state-church social Christianity of Ritschl and Harnack. In his early career, he identified increasingly with a burgeoning American social gospel movement; in his prime, he played a key role in making the social gospel a mainstream Protestant phenomenon. The latter accomplishment included his substantial role in turning Union Seminary into a social gospel institution. The chief theological works of his later career—*The Christian Hope, Beliefs That Matter,* and *Pathways to Certainty*—sought to reassure lay readers of the credibility of Christian belief. Much of his writing reflected his abiding interest in what he called "applied Christianity," especially such works as *Is Christianity Practicable?, The Church in America, Imperialistic Religion and the Religion of Democracy*, and *A Creed for Free Men*. Brown practiced ecumenical social Christianity even more than he wrote about it. He served on various committees and commissions pertaining to social service, trade unionism, foreign missions, and Christian education and was deeply involved in several streams of the ecumenical movement. His service to the Presbyterian church included many years of work on the Board of Home Missions, the Committee on Church and Labor, and the Social Service Committee. He was a cofounder of the Labor Temple in the East Village section of Manhattan and the American Parish on Manhattan's Upper East Side. His ecumenical work included leading roles in the 1925 and 1937 Universal Christian Conferences on Life and Work, as well as active involvement in the Geneva-based Universal Christian Council and the World Alliance for International Friendship. He also worked for many years in the settlement house movement, serving for a time as president of the Union Settlement Association, gave thirteen years to the Yale Corporation as a board member, and performed various administrative functions at Union Seminary and Yale University.[79]

Above all, he taught Ritschlian-school theology to a generation that took for granted the triumph of the liberal theology and social gospel movements. A number of his students became leading theologians, including Gerald Birney Smith, Walter Marshall Horton, John C. Bennett, Marion J. Bradshaw, Henry P. Van Dusen, and Harry Emerson Fosdick. Though he wrote prolifically and gave much of his time and energy to social causes, Brown regarded classroom teaching as his chief vocation. His classroom textbook and lectures schooled a generation of American theologians and pastors in the concepts of an ongoing Ritschlian theological tradition.

Christian Theology in Outline taught that knowledge of God rests on experience, that God is revealed immanently through the moral and spiritual excellence of Christ, and that the Trinity is best understood as an interpretation of the Christian experience of God revealed as Absolute, self-revealing, and self-imparting. As Brown observed, the Ritschlian school generally demoted the doctrine of the Trinity to secondary status and rejected all theologies that claimed knowledge of God's immanent triunity or trinity of essence. Clarke shared this basic predisposition, though he offered a "tentative" argument for viewing God as "the eternal heart of love," Christ as "the rational expression of the eternal heart," and the Holy Spirit as the "accomplisher of the work of both." Clarke's position steered between the tritheistic-leaning essentialism that views the Trinity as one Godhead with three personalities and the Sabellian trinity of manifestation that posits one God expressed in three modes. Very modestly, claiming only that "it may perhaps commend itself as true," Clarke argued that God's triunity might be viewed as three coinhering elements in the divine self-consciousness on which God's three self-manifestations are founded: "One person exists in three modes, which are essential to his one personality. This is a real Triunity; in one sense God is three, while in another sense, just as truly, he is one."[80]

Brown took a similar tack more aggressively. If God is truly immanent in reality, as all good liberals attest, there is no basis for distinguishing between the models of God's triune essence and manifestation: "We believe that God is to be sought not without but within his world, and that the only way in which it is possible for us to know God as he is in himself is by unfolding the significance of the revelation through which it is made known to men." It followed that liberal theology should reject the traditional antithesis between the trinities of essence and manifestation, he argued: "The self-revealing God is the real God—the only God we either can or need to know." The economic Trinity that is known is the unknown immanent Trinity. Put differently, the God who is revealed in triune manifestation *is* the Trinity of essence. Whatever can be known about God's self-revealing and self-imparting manifestations is what we also know about God's inner being. In this way, which was typical of his approach, Brown took an essentially Ritschlian standpoint while revising it at points on which Ritschl estranged himself from classical Christianity.[81]

His theology of sin and redemption used a similar strategy. It was thoroughly progressive in the Ritschlian mode, but, like Clarke, Brown retained aspects of evangelical orthodoxy that many progressives discarded. Like virtually all theological liberals of the Victorian age, Brown conceptualized the fundamental problem of human life in terms of the conflict between spirit and nature. Like most theological liberals after 1880, he gave religious meaning to evolution by interpreting divine reality as a creative personalizing factor in the evolutionary process. Human beings are dually constituted as creatures of nature and children of God, he taught. We are finite spirits created in the image of the divine Spirit, but we are also evolutionary products of the lower organic forms of natural existence. It followed for virtually all liberals that sin is the residue and expression of the bestial impulses of humankind's animal nature. Nineteenth- and early-twentieth-century liberal theology was persistently Victorian in its diagnosis of the fundamental problem of human life and the role of religion in addressing it. Brown expressed this sensibility exactly: "Progress takes place through the gradual emergence of the spiritual in man, and its growing victory over the animal; and the sense of sin is the consciousness which accompanies the process. So defined, sin is a necessary stage in the evolution of humanity,—an essential element in God's training of mankind for higher things."[82]

Unlike much of what came to be called progressive theology, however, Brown did not rest with the concept of sin as residual animal nature. Liberal Victorianism explained much about the phenomenon of sin as the lack or perversion of a good, but it did not explain moral evil. Put differently, Brown observed that sin is known to consciousness not merely as the failure to attain the good, but often as the willful choice of evil. To sin is not simply to act out of one's animal nature, but often, to join the company of the wicked who actively and consciously oppose the good. Brown thus agreed with Clarke's emphasis on sin as badness, the willfully selfish choice of that which is reprehensible, but he pressed harder on the problem of its origin. The existence of moral evil is plainly evident to consciousness, Brown asserted, but how should theology account for its existence?

Traditional Christian mythology tried to explain it with a devil theory, while various theological traditions influenced by Augustine looked for an explanation in the theory of metaphysical freedom. The latter theory proposed that the human capacity to commit evil is a divinely given power of choice that cannot be explained by its antecedents. To Brown, devil theories belonged to the Dark Ages, and the theory of metaphysical freedom was no explanation at all, but merely the abandonment of seeking one: "Bare will, apart from nature and environment, can as little create evil as these alone apart from will. Such an abrupt change as is posited in the theological doctrine of the fall is psychologically inconceivable. It makes man mightier than God, since in a single instant of time he has been able to accomplish what all the centuries of divine activity have been unable to undo."[83]

We cannot say how it is that moral evil exists, but we must not deny that it does. Brown judged that each of the three prevailing theories fallibly expressed some aspect of a mystery that defies explanation. Evolutionary theory rightly explained a good deal of destructive behavior as a conflict between humanity's bestial and spiritual natures; metaphysical dualism was right to deny the adequacy of any individualistic or social explanation; Augustinian theologies were right to deny that animal nature and social environment add up to a sufficient answer. "In the secret places of the human spirit takes place the strange change by which the non-moral is transformed into the immoral," Brown remarked. "We face here a mystery which we cannot explain, yet may not deny. It is the mystery of all beginnings, neither greater nor less." A good deal of liberal theology in the succeeding generation gave a poorer answer than this modest conclusion.[84]

If the universal human problem is the conflict between nature and spirit and the inexplicable choice of moral evil that alienates humankind from God, it followed that salvation must be about the victory of spirit and righteousness. Here again, in his rethinking of the meaning of salvation, Brown took an essentially liberal Ritschlian approach while seeking to maintain contact with traditional orthodoxy. Since much of the problem is rooted in the conflict between humanity's destructive animal nature and the creative impulses of its God-given spiritual nature, he reasoned, much of the solution lay in the training and edification of the human spirit. Brown favored Horace Bushnell on this theme. Citing Bushnell's *Christian Nurture,* he remarked that growth in spiritual consciousness requires a gradual development of the sense of sin, "and should be accompanied always by a corresponding insight into the grace of God, which robs the discovery of its terrors by pointing out at the same time the way in which sin may be overcome." For Brown, as for Schleiermacher, salvation in Christ was bound up with the promise of the triumph of spirit over nature as mediated by the example and teaching of Jesus. Under the influence of Jesus, whom Schleiermacher described as the perfectly God-conscious redeemer, human beings are delivered from the destructive impulses of their animal nature and the perverse moral choices of their mysteriously fallen will. Salvation is the triumph of one's moral and spiritual personality over nature through the mediating influence of Christ. In Brown's words, "It leads to the subordination of the desire for individual gratification to the wider aim which finds self realized through service of one's fellows, and has as its fruit the joy which is the invariable accompaniment of self-forgetfulness in a worthy cause."[85]

Unlike some liberal theologies, but like Clarke's theology, this definition still carefully distinguished between the "it" and its "fruit." By the turn of the century, Brown was unsettled by the liberal tendency to blur the distinction between justification and sanctification. Despite Ritschl's insistence on the twofold character of salvation, the Ritschlian school typically treated justification and sanctification as different words for the same process of moral transformation. Brown admonished that these transformations are not the same thing, however. Justification is temporally prior to sanctification and refers to the religious process of reconciliation with God; sanctification is the fruit of justification and refers to the transformation of moral character toward the ideal of Christ. "The religious experience of acceptance with God is not the same as the ethical experience of the realization of the moral ideal; nor is it necessary to wait for the latter in order to enjoy the former," he asserted. "The true relationship is rather the reverse. It is the religious experience of acceptance and forgiveness which makes possible the realization of the ethical ideal." Human beings cannot save themselves or society by their idealism or moral sincerity alone. They must repent of their sin and come to Christ apart from all hope of self-righteousness. This is the abiding Christian truth that the Reformers recovered at great cost. To Brown, liberal theology gained nothing if it abandoned the Reformers at this point. The purpose of liberal theology was to recover "Jesus and his gospel" in their sublime simplicity, not to water them down to a religion of works righteousness.[86]

Christian Theology in Outline was perfectly calibrated for its purpose and generation. It was traditional enough to be assuringly Christian, but sufficiently revisionist and progressive to speak for the liberal movement's evangelical mainstream for more than thirty years. Brown took an essentially Harnackian line on theological issues, but, like Clarke, for the most part he avoided precise judgments on higher critical issues. He was sympathetic to the social gospel, but, like Clarke, his affirmation of social salvation was muted. Social salvation was not yet a unifying liberal theme. At the same time, on the key interpretive issue that later proved to be troubling for the social gospel, Brown invoked the kernel/husk dichotomy rather too glibly.

The question was whether the historical Jesus was an apocalypticist. Beginning with the pioneering work of Otto Schmoller, Ernst Issel, and Johannes Weiss in the early 1890s, German biblical scholarship was moving toward the view that Jesus accepted and proclaimed the Jewish apocalypticism of his time.[87] Some liberals coped with this trend by claiming that the gospel pericopes of an apocalyptical nature (such as Mark 13:1–37) owed more to the worldview of the early church than to the teaching of Jesus. Walter Rauschenbusch gave vivid expression to this argument, and Clarke employed a version of it, arguing that Jesus proclaimed the coming of the kingdom, that the disciples misconstrued the promise of the kingdom in imminent-apocalyptic terms, and that Jesus's prophecy was fulfilled in the destruction of Jerusalem and in Christ's spiritual coming in the Holy Spirit. Christ's kingdom was "more spiritual and inward" that his disciples understood, Clarke explained, and it is rightly understood as a process, not an event. On the negative side, the temple was destroyed, as Jesus predicted; on the positive side, the reign of Christ's kingdom began with the pouring out of God's Holy Spirit of power. The coming of the kingdom promised by Christ is a perpetual advent, "in which Christ comes ever more fully into the life of the world."[88]

Brown was more cautious on the historical problem, partly because he was more keenly aware and respectful of the current scholarly trend. By the time that his textbook was published, American scholars were beginning to accept the apocalyptic thesis. He advised that it was "entirely likely" that Jesus fully shared the apocalypticism of the early church, though Jesus surely did not predict the end of the world in a way that contradicted "the spiritual nature and universal scope of his Gospel." More important for theology, Brown instructed, was the overriding question of interpretive appropriation that all such issues posed and that the problem of apocalyptic raised with particular force. This was the "kernel or husk" question taught by Harnack. As applied to the apocalyptical aspects of the teaching of Jesus, Harnack judged that however extensive these aspects may have been, they belong to the husk of the gospel, not its kernel. In matters of interpretive appropriation, Jesus must always be understood according to that which made him stand out from his religious and historical context, not in terms of what he shared with it. His teaching that the kingdom of God was at war with the kingdom of the devil was a notable example of the latter kind of belief. Harnack doubted that Jesus was a full-blown apocalypticist, but he never doubted that Jesus viewed the world as a theater of God's spiritual warfare with Satan. The interpretive principle applied in both cases. Devils and apocalyptic both belong to the husk. Brown put it this way: "It is not in the inherited imagery, but in that which is new and revolutionary in his teaching that we are to find his distinctive message. Our task is to take this new message and to express it in the terms of our own thought even as the men of an earlier generation did in theirs."[89]

With these two sentences he dismissed a more serious problem for the liberal social gospel than his dogmatics allowed. Brown's career extended far enough beyond the heyday of the social gospel for him to acknowledge the point. In his last book, long after the scholarly tide in biblical criticism turned against him, he defended "the liberal portrait of Jesus" and predicted that "the best scholarship" would someday return to the social gospel picture of Jesus as a this-worldly ethical teacher and prophet. At the same time, he allowed that when biblical scholarship took this turn, it would have to do so in a way that was less one-sided than the picture promoted by social gospel liberalism. "I can remember as if it were yesterday what it meant to us to turn from the Christ of the creeds to the simple human figure whom the Gospels present," he recalled fondly. "In Jesus we found not simply an example we could imitate, not simply a master we could obey, but a leader whom we could follow." But the inspiring ethical figure of liberal preaching was too simple, he acknowledged: "There are other elements in the record of which it does not take adequate account." Chief among these elements was the deeply eschatological mentality of intertestamental Judaism.[90]

Brown and his social gospel comrades had a very different mentality in the early twentieth century. They lived in a world that seemed to be getting more and more democratic, progressive, manageable, exciting, and Christian. America was growing as a world power; the American idea was being democratized by a host of reform movements; modern science was breaking the power of nature and disease; modern Christianity was recovering the kingdom-building ethic of true religion. The social gospelers used the words "Christianize" and "democratize" interchangeably. They found their inspiration and hope in a burgeoning progressive Christianity that vowed to Christianize America and Americanize the world. In the idealism and institutional gains of this movement they also found their protection from an aggressive multidenominational backlash.

The backlash that came to be called the fundamentalist movement was especially strong in the Presbyterian and Baptist denominations. By virtue of his status as a prominent Presbyterian theologian at a seminary that catered mainly to Presbyterians, Brown was a chief target of fundamentalists who espoused the doctrine of biblical inerrancy and a literal understanding of such doctrines as the substitutionary atonement and second coming of Christ. In the years just before the outbreak of World War I, a newly mobilized fundamentalist movement made him and Union Seminary the objects of renewed controversy in the northern Presbyterian church. Fundamentalist leaders attacked Union's commitment to liberal theology and the social gospel as a novel species of apostasy. At the 1910 General Assembly, they pushed through a five-point declaration of "fundamental" Christian doctrines that began with the inerrancy of scripture. The same year, Brown gave them a fresh example of seminary-endorsed apostasy with his Harvard University lecture on "The Old Theology and the New."[91]

MODERNISM IN THEOLOGY

"The Old Theology and the New" contained nothing new for Brown. It traced the new theology to Schleiermacher and Coleridge and described revelation as spiritual illumination, not propositional disclosure. It defined sin as "the survival of the animal in man, his failure to rise to the higher capacities within him," not a foreign intruder suddenly rupturing nature from without. It referred to Christ as "God in man . . . the type to which all mankind is ultimately destined to conform." It described God as the immanent law of the universe, "an ever-present spirit guiding all that happens to a wise and holy end." It proposed that nature and the supernatural are different aspects of the same reality, not two different kinds of reality: "Nature expresses the law in the process, the supernatural the end to which it tends. Nature has to do with cause, the supernatural with meaning and value." It noted that the dichotomy between the religious and the secular, so prominent in the old theology, "has been wiped out in the new."[92]

By 1910 these were staple themes of mainstream liberal theology. Brown sought to reconceptualize the supernatural for liberal theology, not discard it as mythological. His position affirmed the personal authority of Christ, the personal reality of God, the fallen condition of humanity, and the reality of moral evil, though his lecture did not emphasize these points. He might have avoided a firestorm of criticism by doing so. Styled like a manifesto, and lacking his typical caveats and nuances, Brown's Harvard speech enraged Presbyterian conservatives. For three years they accused him of heresy, some in the form of presbytery overtures to the Presbyterian General Assembly, and in 1913 one accuser denounced him from the floor of General Assembly as a "Hindu Pantheist" who denied the personality of God.[93]

The latter attack deeply wounded Brown's feelings. He later recalled that "the building rocked with applause" as his accuser "demanded that the Church put a stop, once and for all, to this intolerable violation, not only of orthodoxy, but of decency." That night, traumatized by the experience, Brown shook and moaned in his bed all night long, "the most wretched of my life." The General Assembly of 1913 was high on atmospheric fundamentalist hostility—comparable to that of the Assembly that condemned Charles Briggs for heresy in 1893—and Brown was scorched by it.[94]

But theologically and ecclesiastically, 1913 was far removed from 1893. The social gospel movement was at the height of its influence, liberals held most of the theology chairs at elite seminaries and divinity schools, and Brown was a widely admired theologian and church leader. His institution was also much less vulnerable than it had been during the Briggs trials. Union Seminary was flush with students, especially from the Presbyterian church; its ecumenism was firmly established; its newly launched capital campaign was seeking the astronomical sum of $2,160,000, and its reputation as a center of cutting-edge Christian scholarship was unsurpassed in the United States. In the moment of its flowering as a forthrightly progressive institution, Union had no reason to minimize the facts or cower before the fundamentalist backlash.

Anticipating an opportunity to defend himself, Brown composed a formal speech. To his chagrin, he was prevented from addressing the General Assembly, but his friend and former teacher, Union Seminary president Francis Brown, was not silenced. The following day, and again the following year, Francis Brown delivered rousing defenses of his seminary and its theological leader that effectively ended the presbytery campaigns against both. Many years later, Brown disclosed what he would have said in 1913 if he had been allowed to speak. His closing words struck a note of self-righteousness that was out of character for him but reflected his rage at being counted a heretic: "Not everyone that saith unto me 'Lord, Lord' shall enter into the Kingdom, but he that doeth the will of my Father which is in Heaven."[95]

Brown's years of battle with fundamentalists burnished his reputation as a leader of the liberal theology movement. Though it grieved him deeply to be accused of apostasy, he was otherwise comfortable with his position in the movement's Ritschlian mainstream. In 1910 the *American Journal of Theology* cast him as the moderate in a forum on the task and method of theology. Princeton Theological Seminary theologian Benjamin B. Warfield defended the conservative evangelical position; Gerald Birney Smith made a case for Chicago-style modernism; Brown contended that external authority proves nothing in theology and that Christianity is "the final and perfect religion for man."[96]

His argument about authority dismissed the old orthodoxy, while his argument about Christianity upheld a liberal position that was under attack in the movement's left-liberal flank. Brown contended that the finality of Christianity is proved by its unparalleled effects in personal and social religion. To claim that Christianity holds a unique authority is not to claim any infallible doctrine, he explained, "but that through all its many changes it has continued to meet the needs of the human heart as no other institution has done." For Brown, as for the Ritschlian mainstream, theology had two fundamental tasks: to express the Christian gospel in a way that maintained continuity with the historic Christian tradition and to express the gospel in a way that remained "in living touch with the present."[97] Smith described him accurately as the kind of thinker who tried "to mediate as smoothly as possible the transition from the method of authority to that of interpreting Christian experience."[98]

Smith respected his former teacher, but this description was not a compliment at the University of Chicago Divinity School, where smooth transitions were no longer valorized. Increasingly the Chicago theologians emphasized the chasm between the biblical and modern worlds. In Europe liberal theology divided between Harnack, who claimed that modern Protestantism was essentially continuous with the religion of the Reformation, and French theologian Auguste Sabatier, who claimed that the modern "religion of spirit" was essentially different from the Reformationist "religion of authority." With an increasingly either/or spirit, the Chicago schoolers sided with Sabatier. They wedded the case for liberal Christianity to current forms of American pragmatism, humanism, and radical empiricism.[99]

Smith eschewed the first of Brown's fundamental tasks. What matters in theology is solely whether a belief is practically effective and rationally credible at the present time, he admonished, not "whether the solutions demanded by present problems do or do not correspond with the doctrine of some former age." Theology might draw interpretive insights from the past, but a truly critical theology ascribes no normative status to any tradition. The only norms are modern relevance and credibility.[100] Instead of translating Ritschlian evangelicalism to the American scene, the Chicago modernists increasingly identified with the Göttingen-centered former Ritschlians who launched the *Religionsgeschichtliche*

Schule. They followed Ernst Troeltsch in approaching all religions, including Christianity, by the same outside historicist criterion. With the rise of a strongly naturalistic-modernist school of theology, a weighty segment of American theological liberalism began to hedge its claim that historical criticism always yields the Christ of faith.

For years Brown puzzled over his relation to the Harnack-Sabatier argument while insisting on his equal right to the mantles of liberalism and modernism. To him, the essence of modernity was its commitment to enlightening, verifiable progress. In the name of Christian-inspired moral progress, he resisted the humanistic drift of Chicago-style theology; at the same time, he recognized that Sabatier and the Chicago school made compelling arguments about the novelty of modern theology. Like Harnack, he wanted to affirm his continuity with Luther and Calvin; at the same time, he judged that the differences between the religions of external authority and the modern religion of spirit were nearly as categorical as Sabatier maintained. The authority issue marked an essential discontinuity between modern and Reformationist Protestantism. Characteristically, he settled on a middle position between Harnack and Sabatier. With Harnack, he argued that modern and Reformationist religion were fundamentally linked by the principle of the direct approach of the individual to God, in opposition to the principle of ecclesiastical authority. With Sabatier, he affirmed that modern Protestantism had created a new historic form of Christianity by rejecting the principle of external authority; modern Protestantism represented a "new Reformation" that did not rely on the infallibility of a sacred text.[101]

The Chicago theologians played up the modern American origins of their pragmatism, but Brown insisted that Ritschlian theology was no less pragmatic or empirical. As a good Ritschlian, he grounded theological claims solely in the sphere of practical reason and expressed his faith in the language of contemporary philosophical pragmatism. There are two kinds of certainty, he argued: "The certainty which is the aim of the exact sciences and the certainty which is attainable in common life." Theological certainty is strictly of the second kind: "It is a certainty that invites to experiment and is confirmed by its results." Just as the mistakes of science are corrected only by more science, the misconceptions of religion are corrected only by better religion. Brown rendered modern science as the story of the "gradual emergence and progressive verification" of certain primary convictions concerning the nature of the natural world that survived the process of scientific testing. Likewise, the history of religion was the story of the emergence and progressive verification of "certain permanent convictions concerning God and man's way of knowing him."[102] For Brown, the language of assurance and certainty was second nature, but always on modernist grounds: "I am a Modernist, and as such I am committed to follow the scientific method to its limit wherever it shall take me."[103]

He lived to witness the declining years of the social gospel movement and the attacks of his Union Seminary colleague, Reinhold Niebuhr, against it, and he acknowledged that liberal theology sometimes underestimated human evil and reduced the divine mystery to human idealism. But Brown never relinquished his controlling convictions about the progressive realization of science and true religion in the ongoing progress of modern culture. He never doubted that modern Protestant theology represented the history "of the progressive stages in the adjustment of religious faith to the new world made familiar to us by modern science."[104] He experienced World War I and the subsequent decline of the social gospel movement as a challenge to his moral optimism, not as a refutation of it. Like most liberal Protestant leaders, including Shailer Mathews, Henry Churchill King, Washington Gladden, Shirley Jackson Case, Eugene Lyman, Henry Sloane Coffin, George Albert Coe, and Arthur C. McGiffert, Brown opposed the war during the years that preceded his country's intervention, advocating American neutrality and military unpreparedness.

After the United States intervened in the war, he embraced Woodrow Wilson's idealistic reasons for doing so, like most of his colleagues, while worrying about the loss of virtue that came with it. "War which elevates, hardens," he cautioned. "We face that searing, devastating fact. We must not blind our eyes to it. It is there, and we must deal with it." Even while carrying out the cruel business of making war, American Christianity needed to sustain the social gospel faith that "this new world can be made over again into a family of the Spirit." Toward that end he played a major role in organizing the General War-Time Commission of the Churches, an international agency of the Federal Council of Churches of Christ in America.[105]

The Federal Council of Churches, founded in 1908, had floundered during its early years, uncertain of its ecumenical mission and plagued by weak grassroots support. It became an important institution in American religion largely as a function of its wartime service. Under the leadership of Brown (who served as executive secretary), Presbyterian missions administrator Robert E. Speer (who served as chair), and Massachusetts Episcopal bishop William Lawrence, the General War-Time Commission secured chaplains for the armed services, coordinated the activities of various denominations in lending aid to the war effort, developed programs for workers in munitions plants, and served as a central interdominational clearinghouse of information and support work. After the war it was succeeded by the Committee on the War and the Religious Outlook, another Federal Council project chaired by Brown, which studied the tasks of postwar reconstruction. Having played a key role in turning the Federal Council into a valuable emergency service organization, Brown gave more than twenty additional years to making it an effective ecumenical agency. He organized and for many years chaired its Department of Research and Education, a central bureau for the ecumenical movement's ongoing study of contemporary social problems.[106]

He played equally prominent roles in the creation of the international ecumenical movement. Brown was a chief organizer and theological leader of the two conference-movements that produced the World Council of Churches. In the early 1920s he joined Swedish archbishop Nathan Söderblom and a handful of other Protestant leaders in organizing the Universal Christian Conference on Life and Work, which was held in Stockholm in 1925. Brown chaired the Stockholm conference's Commission on Christian Education and for many years served as president of the Life and Work movement. A second Life and Work conference was held at Oxford in 1937. Brown also played major organizing and theological roles in the movement's Faith and Order track, which held World Conferences at Lausanne in 1927 and Edinburgh in 1937. At Lausanne he chaired the Commission on the Church; at the Edinburgh conference, a proposal for the formation of the World Council of Churches was formally adopted. The fruit of his many years of international ecumenical activism was the founding of the World Council in 1948. Though he did not live to see its founding, the creation of a world ecumenical Christian fellowship of churches owed more to Brown's leadership than to that of any other American.[107]

As much as any American of his generation, he epitomized the spirit of mainstream American liberal Protestantism during its social gospel heyday. Persistently he explained that the Ritschlian understanding of Christianity does not invest Christian doctrine with authority or embrace the letter of Christ's teaching or even imitate Christ's conduct. To be a Christian, he insisted, is to yield oneself to the Spirit of Christ, "and under the guidance of that spirit do one's own thinking and follow one's own conscience wherever that might lead."[108] The Christian is normatively connected to the great tradition of Christ-followers who asked themselves what it means to follow Christ in their situation, he affirmed; at the same time, the tests of sound theology and discipleship are strictly modern. The question of what it means to be a Christian in the modern world can be answered only by modern criteria of relevance and credibility, seeking the Spirit of Christ with the tools of modern knowledge and religious discernment. Brown's strength as a theological leader derived, in part, from his confidence that modern scholarship at its best can always be counted upon to yield the Christ of faith.

RELIGION AS PERSONAL RELATION:
HENRY CHURCHILL KING

The figure most like Brown as a theologian and church leader was his Ritschlian Congregationalist contemporary, Henry Churchill King. Like Brown and Clarke, King spoke for the evangelical mainstream of the liberal theology movement. Like Brown, he drank deeply from the well of the Ritschlian school and adapted its themes to the American situation. Like Brown, he was a prominent church leader who performed on a larger stage than the world of academic theology. Like Brown, he launched his public theological career just after the turn of the century, during the same period that Charles Clayton Morrison tellingly renamed his magazine *The Christian Century.* Like Brown and Morrison, King believed that the mission of American Protestantism was not merely to make Christians of all Americans, but to Christianize America.[109] King's case for this project was distinctive; for a sizable Protestant audience, he played all the right chords. Philosophically he appropriated the personalist idealism of Rudolf Hermann Lotze and Borden Parker Bowne. Theologically he appropriated the existential Ritschlianism of Wilhelm Herrmann. With his development into an important liberal theologian, Oberlin College became a pillar of the liberal theology movement and set an example followed by church-related colleges across the country.

The school in which King began his teaching career in 1884 had a rich religious legacy. Founded in 1833 by Congregational abolitionist John J. Shipherd, Oberlin College was from 1835 to 1858 the home of famed evangelist Charles Finney, the school's first theologian and second president. Under Finney's influence the college housed a remarkable blend of evangelical radicalisms from the Congregationalist and Wesleyan traditions, especially abolitionist, antimilitarist, and egalitarian commitments. Structurally it consisted of three schools, the (preparatory) Academy, the College of Arts and Sciences, and the Theological Seminary; Oberlin incorporated its later-distinguished Conservatory of Music in 1867. The postmillennialist kingdom-building passions of Oberlin College cooled after the Civil War, but under the guidance of its third president, James Harris Fairchild, the school retained its evangelical pietism. Fairchild was a member of the college's second graduating class; his only graduate degree was earned at Oberlin Seminary. As a professor of theology and moral philosophy, he continued Finney's sturdy evangelicalism and his emphasis on the morally regenerative power of the gospel, though in a calmer spirit. Oberlin made no pretense of rivaling Andover Seminary as a guardian of Reformed orthodoxy—Andover theologian Edward Park looked down on Finney's perfectionism—but in the 1880s, after Park retired, and the Andover faculty turned liberal, and a bitter churchwide controversy ensued, Oberlin Seminary resolved to take up the foresaken cause of Congregational orthodoxy. Oberlin acquired Park's esteemed journal, *Bibliotheca Sacra,* and sternly censured the liberal novelties of Andover Seminary. For several years the journal's new editors—Oberlin professors George Frederick Wright, William G. Ballantine, and Frank Hugh Foster—resumed the old Andover attacks on theological liberalism, until modern theology spread to Oberlin.[110]

King was a product and favorite son of Oberlin. His father, Henry Jarvis King, was an Oberlin graduate who served for nearly twenty years as secretary-treasurer of Hillsdale College. The younger King began his college career at Hillsdale but transferred to Oberlin after his father became a U.S. Indian agent in Minnesota. As a student at Oberlin, King acquired the attention and favor of President Fairchild. The two formed a bond that shaped King's entire career. Upon completing his undergraduate and seminary training at Oberlin, King moved to Harvard in 1882 to prepare for a promised faculty career at Oberlin. Fairchild would have sent him to Andover Seminary, but Andover turned liberal in the early 1880s. Harvard was even more liberal, but at least it was prestigious and comparatively cosmopolitan; Fairchild reasoned that King needed an antidote to Midwest provincialism.

King appreciated the wisdom of this judgment; Harvard provided the broadening educational opportunities that he needed. At the same time he keenly missed the nurturing guidance of his Oberlin teachers. Harvard Divinity School, especially, put him off. Neglected for many years, the Divinity School was in a rebuilding mode under Harvard president Charles Eliot, who told prospective donors that it needed to transcend its Unitarian identity and become a university school of theology. By 1882 the Divinity School had taken a few steps in this academic and ecumenical direction, but King was not impressed. "The ultra-liberal position of the Divinity School, I may say just here, seems to me to make next to impossible any harmony of beliefs among the students at any rate, and I judge also among the professors," he wrote to Fairchild. "As a consequence, no man trusts any other, and the bi-weekly conference (a supposed sort of an imitation of a prayer meeting) becomes a kind of debating society." He especially disliked the noncommittal liberalism of Harvard professors: "They are very ready to tell you all the different views except their own." King had better experiences in philosophy and mathematics courses, but his second year at Harvard was marked by illness, apparently from overwork, and he was forced to drop his studies.[111]

On that unsettling note he returned to Oberlin in 1884, beginning his teaching career as a mathematics instructor. He taught mathematics for six years before switching to philosophy in 1890; the following year he moved to philosophy and theology. In the meantime Fairchild retired as president and began to contemplate his retirement from the school's chair of theology. King was the obvious choice for the theology chair, but Fairchild and the new Oberlin president, Old Testament scholar William G. Ballantine, recognized that his training for it was deficient. Oberlin therefore sent its most promising faculty leader to the University of Berlin in 1893 to acquire a state-of-the-art theological education.

King studied church history under Adolf von Harnack, theology under Julius Kaftan, theological ethics under Otto Pfleiderer, and epistemology under Wilhelm Dilthey. Financial problems at Oberlin cut his sabbatical in half, to one year, but that was long enough to change his life. Like Brown, he was enthralled by Harnack; King became a Ritschlian and adopted most of Harnack's historical conclusions. Seeking to ground himself in Harnack's theological tradition, he studied Ritschl, various Ritschlians, and Ritschl's favorite philosopher, Rudolf Hermann Lotze; the latter influence was crucial for him. Lotze was Ritschl's former colleague at Göttingen and a religion-friendly proponent of personalist idealism. One of his protégés was Boston University religious philosopher Borden Parker Bowne.

Lotze's post-Hegelian idealism was congruent with the personalist dimension of Ritschlian theology. He taught that mechanism is subordinate to consciousness and that personality is the ultimate reality. At Boston University, Bowne was already developing the implications of Lotzean idealism for American liberal Protestant theology. In 1894, upon returning to Oberlin as a Harnack-quoting Ritschlian and theological personalist, King devoted himself to a similar project. In collaboration with New Testament scholar E. I. Bosworth and, more surprisingly, with Ballantine, who increasingly accepted higher critical scholarship, he nurtured a liberal turn at Oberlin. In 1897 he accepted the school's chair of theology; the following year, Oberlin invited the chief organizer of the 1892 World Parliament of Religions, John Henry Barrows, to be the college's fifth president. Three years later King published his landmark first book, *Reconstruction in Theology*, which proposed to speak for an ascending liberal theology movement.[112]

His opening sentences announced the dawning of a new theological epoch. King's focus and tone were explicitly movement-oriented: "This book has been written with the earnest desire and hope that it may contribute something toward the forwarding of a movement already going on—a really spiritual reconstruction of theology in terms that should bring it home to our own day." The book embraced its time with a hopeful, friendly, pastoral spirit. Its key phrases were "progressive revelation," "emergent evolution," "sacredness of the person," and, especially, "personal relation." Theology is obliged to "make real" the abiding truths of Christianity, he urged. It cannot be real without "sympathetic knowledge" of its own age, and every age must be its own interpreter. To be modern in theology is to recognize that the age of great theological systems has passed. This is not because "the great truths do not abide," King assured, but because modern consciousness is open-ended, progressive, and pluralistic. The modern spirit recognizes the partial nature of all perspectives and the "many-sidedness of truth." King observed that modern theology was like modern philosophy. It did not expect to find or produce a last word or definitive system. As in philosophy, however, there was a definite best way to make theology real. This was to rethink all of its basic claims in terms of personal relations.[113]

Reconstruction in Theology made a case for a moderately liberal acceptance of biblical criticism, evolution, and the modern spirit. It quoted Lotze repeatedly on the ultimacy of spiritual consciousness and the need to unify "the mechanical and ideal views of the world." It embraced evolutionary theory as a description of the method, plan, and telos of God's immanent agency in the universe. It praised higher criticism for destroying "proof-text" biblicism and for highlighting the progressivity of God's revelation in Scripture, though King wrongly judged that in biblical scholarship "the tendency to extreme and minute analysis has well-nigh reached its climax." In the spirit of modern science, he paid no respect to the distinction between sacred and secular things, but in the spirit of Lotze and Bowne, he held out strongly for the sacredness of persons. Human beings live in the world but do not belong to it, he explained. For him this maxim was the key to Christology, for "the revelation of God in Christ is beyond all else personal, and only personal."[114]

King had no premonition of Albert Schweitzer. The apocalytic turn in recent German biblical scholarship made no impression on his view of the quest of the historical Jesus, which was straightforwardly positive. "The simple truth is that we stand face to face with the historical Christ," he enthused in 1902. "It is a most significant fact that every single great life of Christ since the Gospels is the product of the last sixty-five years." Neither did he keep up with the thinking of his favorite contemporary theologian, Wilhelm Herrmann. King embraced

Herrmann's existential appeal to the "inner life of Jesus," but he supported this strategy with apologetic arguments that Herrmann increasingly disdained. Herrmann taught that while historical criticism is necessary and useful to theology, it has no role in providing or confirming the basis of faith. The ascendance of Troeltschian *Religionsgeschichtliche* criticism drove Herrmann to a purely existential position, but King retained the enthusiasm of an unchastened Ritschlian historicism. He portrayed the liberal quest of the historical Jesus as an event of epochal spiritual significance that restored the living Christ to the center of Christianity and enhanced modern knowledge of "the real Jesus." Echoing a chief Herrmannian theme, he did caution that the point was not to repristinate the language and thought forms of Jesus' time. By stripping away the layers of church theology and folklore that obscured the Gospel portraits of Jesus, he explained, modern Christians were able to grasp the spirit of the living person of Christ. Instead of trying to speak about Christ in the manner of the apostles, "we would much better try to speak as we believe they would speak now."[115]

His account of what this meant was straight from Herrmann: speaking of Christ as the supreme revelation of God, taking over Christ's conception of God as personal Father as "the really ruling conception" of theology, an emphasis on "the real character of the man Jesus," the scriptural assertion that whoever sees Christ sees the Father, and an emphasis on the practical lordship of Christ. He stressed the last theme above all. King loved Harnack's reflection that we are most likely to be saved by the personality of Christ when we are most afflicted with despair at not finding God in this dismal world.[116] He loved even more what he called "these golden words of Herrmann," which he often quoted: "The childlike spirit can only arise within us when our experience is the same as a child's; in other words, when we meet with a personal life which compels us to trust it without reserve. Only the person of Jesus can arouse such trust in a man who has awakened to moral self-consciousness. If such a man surrenders himself to anything or any one else, he throws away not only his trust, but himself."[117]

Both of King's major works revolved around this quotation. *Reconstruction in Theology* asserted that Herrmann's personalistic christocentrism contained the kernel of an abiding faith that met the test of real-life concreteness. It was a personal faith at its core, but in King's rendering, it had a definite moral and social trajectory. Compared to past orthodoxies, modern liberal Protestantism at its best was closer to the spirit of Christ: it was more personal and reverent of personality, more biblical in its fidelity to the central scriptural claims, more historical in its concern to learn how God has actually acted in history, more practical in its single-minded focus on life and living, more ethical in its understanding of God's moral character and the moral meaning of Christianity, more social for all of the foregoing reasons. In 1902, King did not yet speak of building Christ's kingdom on earth; Walter Rauschenbusch's electrifying *Christianity and the Social Crisis* was still a few years away. But King did affirm that no contemporary theologian could be excused from exploring the relation of theology to the distinctive social consciousness of modern liberal Christianity.[118]

His second major work, *Theology and the Social Consciousness,* proposed that the social Christian consciousness of recent vintage was "at bottom only a true sense of the fully personal." He leaned on Lotze, Ritschl, and Bowne for the argument. Lotze retained a form of the Kantian thing-in-itself in his claim that the "substance" of anything, even one's soul, is unknowable. Ritschl applied the reasoning of Kant and Lotze to theology, teaching that Christ has the *value* of God for us because in Christ we encounter God's attributes of holiness, sacrificial love, and the like. King followed the same logic in teaching that the "essence" of anything consists in the purpose for which it exists. The discipline of theology, for example, is "simply the thoughtful, comprehensive, and unified expression of what religion means to us." The theologian is "a believer in the supremacy of spiritual interests." King proposed that to think this starting point through is to reconceptualize theology in terms of reverence for personality.[119]

The latter phrase acquired nearly the status of a God-concept in his thinking: "Reverence for personality—the steadily deepening sense that every person has a value not to be measured in anything else, and is in himself sacred to God and man—this it is which marks unmistakably every step in the progress of the individual and the race. Without it, whatever the other marks of civilization, you have only tyranny and slavery; with it, though every trace of luxury and scientific invention be lacking, you have the perfection of human relations." Personality requires the possession of reflective intelligence, conscience, and free will, he argued, but it is not reducible to these faculties. Personality also requires a specific content, the elements of social consciousness: "the sense of like-mindedness, of mutual influence, of the value and sacredness of the person, of obligation, and of love." For a person to be "fully personal," King argued, all these qualities must exist and flourish inseparably with their implied ethical demands. With this idealistic definition of personality in place, King made a case for the necessity and moral meaning of religion.[120]

King's necessity argument leaned on Bowne. In his Lotzean-influenced *Theory of Thought and Knowledge,* Bowne contended that the correct philosophical antithesis is between mechanical and volitional causality, not between purpose and causation. Building on this claim, King observed that the demands of an adequate theory of causality seem "to lead us up inevitably to purpose in God." Bowne turned David Hume's question about causality to the advantage of philosophical theism. If science cannot find or account for causality in the phenomenal realm, he argued, philosophy must look for it "in a power beyond the phenomenal which incessantly posits and continues that order according to rule." King concurred that the ultimate metaphysical ground of reciprocal actions must be traced to the unity of God's immanent will: "The social consciousness, therefore, so far as it is an expression of the possibility and inevitableness of our mutual influence, is a reflection of the immanence of the one God in the unity and consistency of his life."[121]

Just as he appealed to historical-critical arguments that supported his Herrmannian Christology, King appealed to metaphysical arguments that supported his personalist theism. He was too good a Ritschlian to make his case stand or fall with these arguments, however. As a Ritschlian, the moral argument was his centerpiece; the rest was window dressing and support structure. To the extent that the social consciousness is ethical, he observed, "it can have no final explanation in the metaphysical, considered as a mere matter of fact." In the crucial chapter of *Theology and the Social Consciousness,* titled "The Thorough Ethicizing of Religion," King declared that through the pressure of its ethical demands, the social consciousness "positively thrusts upon every religious man, who believes in it, the problem of the thorough ethicizing of religion." The Ritschlian school taught that faith gives rise to knowledge in the realm of practical (moral) reason. King urged that if the modern social consciousness is correct in valorizing the sacredness of the person, "then religion must be clearly seen to hold this conviction, or lose its connection with what is most real and vital to us." There is no such thing as individual salvation, he admonished: "We are 'saved,' we come into the real religious life, only in the proportion in which we have really learned to love."[122]

According to 1 John 4:7, whoever loves is begotten of God and knows God. Religion is about sharing the life of God. By this criterion, King suggested, the Apostles' Creed compares poorly to the New Testament, because it excludes the ethical: "It has nothing to say, except by rather distant implication, of the character of God, of the character of Christ, or of the character of men." King's alternative was vigorously Ritschlian. If Christianity is to be real to modern, socially attuned people, he declared, "there must be a real revelation of a real God in the real world, in actual human history, not an imaginary God, nor a dream God, nor a God of mystic contemplation." The church should not ask people to try to believe something. Rather, it should encourage people to put themselves in the presence of Christ, "the greatest and realest of the facts of history, and let that fact make its own legitimate impression, work its own natural work; that fact alone, of all the facts of history, gives you full and ample warrant for your own being."[123]

SPEAKING FOR LIBERAL PROTESTANTISM

With his second, forthright, influential work of theological self-expression, King appeared to be coming of age as a major liberal thinker. His attractive style and broadly Ritschlian personalism made him well suited to develop the theological basis of his movement's moderately liberal mainstream. Shortly after *Theology and the Social Consciousness* was published, however, he was elected president of Oberlin College. Barrows had died of pneumonia after four years of intense fundraising that lifted the college from financial peril. King summarized his own credo in his eulogy for Barrows: "If, as I devoutly believe, and suppose Christ to teach, the problem of life is the problem of friendship; if to learn to live is to learn to love; if persons are the most indubitable and the most important of facts; if love is the one all-inclusive virtue, as Oberlin has always taught, and the one abiding thing in the universe of God, then surely Oberlin has a rich heritage in the memory of this truly loving man."[124]

By then the college community had grown accustomed to having King speak for it. In 1901 he had declined two presidencies—one at Chicago Theological Seminary—and been appointed dean of Oberlin College. In May of 1903 he was inaugurated as Oberlin's sixth president; social gospel luminary Washington Gladden gave the ceremonial invocation. Upon assuming the presidency, King gave up his work as a constructive theologian; the liberal theology movement gained an effective public spokesperson, public moralist, and institutional leader but lost a promising theologian. Most of his later career was devoted to the upbuilding of an institution. Nearly all of his later writing was geared to his administrative and public roles as a mainline American Protestant leader. Politically he aligned himself with a burgeoning social gospel movement and the nationalist-internationalist progressivism of Herbert Croly's *New Republic* magazine. He approvingly quoted Croly's claim that democracy "cannot be disentangled from an aspiration toward human perfectibility." He lectured widely on the need to Christianize Croly's progressive democratic vision. While conceding that the world had never seen "a genuinely Christian democracy," King sermonized that "America may not set before herself any lesser goal." As an increasingly respected public moralist, he called for an ongoing moral renewal of democracy and a democratic transformation of morality: "A true democracy must be permeated through and through with the spirit of reverence for every personality; and this requires both a clear-sighted and tireless, unselfish leadership, and some response to an unselfish and reverent standard of conduct on the part of all citizens."[125]

All of his later-career public sermonizing and social advocacy were held together by his belief in the principle of personality. For King, reverence for personality was the ruling principle of religion and ethics at their best, "the truest and highest test of either an individual or a civilization." Throughout history, even unconsciously, it was the guiding principle of all human progress. To hold personality in reverence is to respect the liberty and inner worth of all persons, he exhorted. At the high tide of American Progressivism, King struggled with the imperialist side of American progress. He celebrated the expansion of Western democracy, individualism, and Protestantism throughout the world but sharply regretted that these regenerative aspects of Western culture nearly always entered foreign lands on the coattails of Western coercion and economic exploitation. In East Asia, he observed, Western civilization intervened "for commercial reasons, and in almost all cases practically by force." It took shape as "a merely commercial interest [that] was quite too liable to become simply selfish exploitation of the less advanced peoples." King lamented that capitalist violence and exploitation established a poor basis for democracy, let alone cooperative relations between the imperial powers and their colonial subjects: "It was not a persuasive introduction to a civilization having a really moral basis."[126]

Like Washington Gladden, Shailer Mathews, and other liberal-oriented social gospelers, he called the churches to claim the entire world as a mission field for democracy, political liberalism, and progressive Christianity. While wishing that the capitalists and colonizers had been preceded into foreign lands by progressive-minded missionaries, King cautioned that reality was another story. He grieved as well that many missionaries were fundamentalists. The ethic of modern Christianity is inherently outward moving, modernized, idealistic, and transformative, he proclaimed. The fact that much of the world had already been colonized by the economic and state power of the West made it doubly imperative for the social gospel movement to internationalize its social vision. Like most liberal Protestant leaders, he actively campaigned against military preparedness in the early years of World War I, though King made his peace with American intervention more readily than some, virtually in lockstep with President Wilson's actions and his reasons for them.[127]

During the war, he worked in Paris as director of the YMCA Religious Work Division and served as chair of the Federal Council of Churches' Committee on the War and the Religious Outlook. After the war he was appointed by President Wilson to serve as cochair (with Charles R. Crane, later U.S. ambassador to China) of the Inter-Allied Commission to Syria, which was part of the postarmistice Commission to Negotiate Peace. This assignment gave King a heavy share of responsibility for making the first official proposals on how the victors of World War I should manage the breakup of the Ottoman Empire. Under the assumption that the United States would enter the League of Nations, the King-Crane Report recommended the establishment of a League-appointed, temporary mandatory for Syria, preferably the United States. It argued that Great Britain should be assigned mandatory power over Mesopotamia and that the victorious powers should not support the formation of a Zionist state. King and Crane maintained that any struggle for a new Israel would infringe the rights of Palestinians and ignite unacceptable levels of violence on all sides. For these reasons their commission's report approved only limited Jewish immigration to Palestine. Regarding Turkey, they recommended separate American mandates for Armenia, an international Constantinopolitan state, and a continued Turkish state in Anatolia; for the rest of Asia Minor they recommended a general American mandate. King was unblushing in his Wilsonian ambitions for his country. He observed that America entered the war "with the ardent faith and hope that a more democratic world might result." Was America serious about making the world safe for democracy? Were Americans willing to make good on the promises and purposes of the war? King declared: "Here in Turkey is an unrivalled opportunity to try these purposes out, for the good not only of a single people, but of the entire world."[128]

The King-Crane Report was delivered to the Paris Peace Conference on August 28, 1919, and to the White House the following month. There is no evidence that President Wilson, who had collapsed after the peace conference, ever read it. While Wilson faded to his death, the United States spurned the League of Nations, and Warren Harding gained the presidency on a promise to "return to normalcy," King spoke out for the Wilsonian dream of international cooperation. He described the League of Nations as a precious vehicle of the "divine" hope of world peace and cooperation. Otherwise he rededicated himself to building up Oberlin College. Returning to Oberlin with the prestige of a world figure, he was welcomed accordingly, with an inauguration-like reception. Under his stewardship, Oberlin launched an ambitious development campaign in 1923 and subsequently raised its standing as a nationally recognized institution. Upon relinquishing his teaching position in 1925, he observed that his theology chair had been filled by only three people in the college's history. Not coincidentally, all were longtime Oberlin presidents: Charles Finney served as professor of systematic theology from 1835 to 1858, Fairchild from 1859 to 1897, and King from 1897 to 1925. King passed it to Walter Marshall Horton, who sustained Oberlin's theological prestige.[129]

Frank Hugh Foster later reflected that King's geniality, personal integrity, and deep piety made it possible for Oberlin to turn theologically liberal with little controversy. These were key factors, to be sure, but there were larger ones. Oberlin's liberal turn was a reflection of powerful socioeconomic and intellectual trends in American life. An expanding middle-class economy and the ascendance of a new educational powerhouse, the research university, changed the reward structure of American higher education. Oberlin College ardently sought professional prestige in an educational establishment that rewarded openness to modernity, an ethos of cultural and intellectual cosmopolitanism, up-to-date facilities, and distinguished faculty appointments. The college's leaders sought to show that church-related liberal arts colleges could make themselves worthy of respect in a modernizing new century.

At every step of his early and middle career, King was cultivated to bring Oberlin into the twentieth century. Upon being sent to study in Berlin, he embraced Harnackian liberalism with no fear of losing his position. Moreover, having inherited an Oberlin tradition that emphasized the morally regenerative power of the gospel and the benevolent moral nature of God, he was able to claim with sufficient plausibility that he was merely updating Oberlin theology. Foster was surely correct, however, that King's personal qualities were crucial to the relative ease with which Oberlin made the transition. Foster and King joined the college's faculty in the same year. Though he regretted that King chose the path of worldly power and responsibility over the higher calling of theory, and though his own theology in his later career veered sharply to the left of King's, Foster appreciated that King was distinctly suited to speak for liberal theology in the public realm. Widely respected for his piety and moral seriousness, King unfailingly insisted that modern social Christianity was a recovery of the spirit of the apostolic faith in modern forms of expression. The liberal social gospel, he believed, was a continuation of genuine Christianity, not a deviation from it.[130]

This claim was a staple of Protestant rhetoric wherever liberal theology took root. It flourished in the heyday of the American social gospel movement. In the nineteenth century it was invoked by Unitarians and Bushnellians well before scriptural higher criticism became part of the presuppositional matrix of

American theological liberalism. Later it was invoked by Charles A. Briggs and other American scholars who defended the legitimacy of higher critical methodologies. It was virtually built into the rationale for the quest of the historical Jesus. American theological scholarship lagged behind German scholarship for decades after it resolved to catch up, but in both cases, the quest of the historical Jesus was defended as a scientific and essentially evangelical search for the true teaching and person of Jesus. Even the Chicago schoolers routinely assured that historical criticism yields the Christ of faith or, at least, the Jesus who deserves to be the basis of faith. In the early years of the twentieth century, however, the Chicago school began to develop another kind of liberal theology.

2.

Thy Kingdom Come

*Walter Rauschenbusch, Vida Scudder,
and the Social(ist) Gospel*

The social gospel was something new in Christian history. It propounded a novel theology of social salvation and envisioned a Christianized economy of cooperation and fellowship. Led by Washington Gladden and Richard Ely, the early social gospel movement was decidedly reformist and idealistic, not revolutionary. Gladden repeatedly assured that the socializing spirit of modern liberal Christianity did not lead to socialist politics. He also took for granted that the novelty of the social gospel was a good thing. In its second generation, however, the social gospel attracted a handful of key leaders who differed from Gladden on both counts. They worried about the movement's religious novelty, but they also spurned the movement's fear of socialism. Walter Rauschenbusch insisted that the social gospel was "neither alien nor novel"; Vida Scudder contended that the "great tradition" of Catholic sacramentalism offered a better home for modern social Christianity than the deracinated individualism of the Protestant churches; Rauschenbusch and Scudder both wanted the church to be the spiritual leaven of a world-transforming socialist movement. The dream of Christian socialism received its classic American expression through their writings and speeches. For most of Rauschenbusch's career and the first part of Scudder's, their vision of a Christ-infused cooperative commonwealth did not appear to be so wild a dream.

TO SEE THE KINGDOM:
WALTER RAUSCHENBUSCH

The history of Protestant theology carries more than its share of oedipal weight, mainly because many Protestant theologians have been the sons of formidable Protestant pastors and theologians. In some cases the oedipal drama is unavoidable as a clue to the thinking of the theologian. Friedrich Schleiermacher, Albrecht Ritschl, Karl Barth, and Henry Ward Beecher offer notable examples; Walter Rauschenbusch is another. His father, August Rauschenbusch, was born to a prominent Westphalian German family that claimed five successive generations of university-trained Lutheran pastors; August extended this unbroken family line to six generations. Born in 1816, he entered Berlin University in 1834, a few months after Schleiermacher's death, and struggled with the theological liberalism of his teachers. In biblical studies he preferred the conservative Ernst Hengstenberg over Berlin's practitioners of higher criticism; his favorite teacher was the mediating theologian and eminent church historian August Neander. Near the end of his studies at Berlin, August Rauschenbusch suffered a nervous breakdown. His personality was brittle and overwrought to begin with, and it coped poorly with his university-induced crisis of faith. He took an extended break from school, rested, took health travels throughout Germany and Austria, and transferred to Bonn, where the conservative-mediationist theology of Carl Immanuel Nitzsch had a tonic effect.[1]

August Rauschenbusch's recuperation was aided by neopietist revival preaching, which shaped his own preaching after he became a pastor. For four years he pastored his father's former church in Altena, where he campaigned for foreign missions and temperance and preached the need of revival. As a church pastor he felt the call of his own mission preaching, and thus in 1846 August headed off to the mission fields of the United States. His call was to German immigrant mission work, mostly to settlements on the Missouri frontier. Bravely he opposed the existence of slavery in his adopted country. August Rauschenbusch moved to New York City upon accepting the directorship of the American Tract Society's national program for German immigrants; in this capacity his contact with German Baptists prompted a second conversion. His Baptist friends claimed that on the question of infant baptism, they had the New Testament on their side, and in 1850, after studying the issue intently, he judged that they were right. To the chagrin of his thoroughly Lutheran family, he was baptized by immersion in the Mississippi River and later returned to the Missouri frontier as a Baptist missionary. Many years afterward his admiring son Walter wrote of August's baptism, "It was a step that cost him dear; it cut his family to the quick; it completely alienated many of his friends; it rendered his entire future uncertain; but he followed the truth."[2]

August Rauschenbusch was headstrong, intelligent, highly irritable, religiously zealous, a gifted teacher, and, to his family, prone to self-pitying meanness. His nervous bullying made him a bad husband and, at best, a difficult father. Though corroborating evidence is lacking, the biographer who knew Walter Rauschenbusch personally claimed that August was also a drunk, his temperance sermons notwithstanding. Rejected by his first love, on the rebound he married one of his confirmation students from Altena, then regretted his impulsiveness. With Caroline Rump Rauschenbusch he fathered four children; Walter was the third. Twelve years older than his wife, August had little in common with her and imagined himself to be a much better Christian than she; sometimes he denied that she was a Christian. Some of his letters paint a chilling picture of contempt. On one occasion he asked his sister to join him in praying for Caroline's death: "I ask God to liberate my children and me from her by removing her from this earth." He reported that at times his terrible marital sufferings caused him to wish for his own death, "but then I think that I must live in order to protect my children from their evil mother."[3]

In 1858 August and Caroline Rauschenbusch lost a sixteen-month-old son to dysentery; the same year August began his career as a professor in the German Department at Rochester Theological Seminary; three years later Walter was born. Seminary president Augustus Hopkins Strong privately commented on his colleague's marriage: "Poor Mrs. Rauschenbusch learned early that absolute submission was the only way of peace. This submission was not natural to her. There grew up a shocking alienation between them." Although he wrote extensively about his father in later life, Walter carefully refrained from commenting on his bullying manner and bad temper. The family drama peeks through in only a few of his letters. On one occasion, interceding on his mother's behalf, he wrote to his father from Germany, "You cannot imagine how the quarrels at home have oppressed us children."[4]

Walter spent much of his youth sympathizing with his mother and trying to please his father. August Rauschenbusch's fervent piety and demanding academic expectations pervaded the life of his family, even during lengthy periods of separation. As the family's only surviving son, Walter was the focal point of his father's ambitions, a fact that he mostly appreciated. "He was a man of the old school and not to be trifled with," Walter later recalled. "But I never doubted his love and care for me." Rauschenbusch especially appreciated that his father "educated me by sharing his own interests with me." It was very important to August Rauschenbusch that his children become Christians and that they not become Americanized. He was proud of his cultured German identity and sought to pass it on to his children. He was also anxious to arrange lengthy separations from his wife. Walter thus spent four years of his early childhood in Germany, in the company of his mother and sisters; for three years they lived in Barmen. By the age of eight he was equally fluent in English and German, and at home in both the United States and Germany, just as his father desired.[5]

As a teenager he studied for three years at the Rochester Free Academy; he also took a reprieve from pleasing his father. For several years Walter rebelled against his family's churchly moralism, hanging out with rough characters and taking up swearing. Undoubtedly the contradictions between his parents' outward piety and their bitter feuding at home worked on his psyche. On one occasion Walter was whipped by his father for spreading unbelief at Sunday school; his mother had to prevent him from running away from home. Youthful rebellion did not suit Walter Rauschenbusch, however, and at the age of seventeen he returned to Jesus. He later recalled that he felt the stirring of young manhood and worldly ambition. "What I said to myself was, 'I want to become a man; I want to be respected; and if I go on like this, I cannot have the respect of men.' This was my way of saying, 'I am out in the far country, and I want to get home to my country, and I don't want to tend the hogs any longer.' And so I came to my Father, and I began to pray for help and got it. And I got my own religious experience."[6]

In later years Rauschenbusch remembered this event with deep gratitude and some embarrassment. His conversion experience was "a very true one," he reflected, "although I have no doubt there was a great deal in it that was foolish, that I had to get away from, and that was untrue." The egotistical and opportunistic aspects of his conversion were unsettling to him, but this fact did not negate his gratitude for the gracious effects of the experience: "Such as it was, it was of everlasting value to me. It turned me permanently, and I thank God with all my heart for it. It was a tender, mysterious experience. It influenced my soul down to its depths. Yet, there was a great deal in it that was not really true."[7]

August Rauschenbusch agreed that his son should not spend his life tending hogs. After Walter's graduation from high school his father sent him back to Germany for four years of classical education. Enrolling at the Evangelische Gymnasium zu Gütersloh, a private secondary school in Westphalia, Walter mastered Greek and Latin, learned French and Hebrew, and won the school's top prize. "I am full of it, modesty or no modesty," he exulted to Munson Ford, his friend and former classmate at the Rochester Free Academy. "I am Primus Omnium of the Gymnasium, that is, the first man of the establishment." In other words, "I am blooming like a wild rose."[8]

Later he clarified that he was blooming intellectually, not sexually. Rauschenbusch graduated in 1883 and for three months got a taste of university lecturing in Berlin, Leipzig, Halle, Greifswald, and Erlangen. From Berlin he reported to Ford, "I look all green when a girl only looks at me, which you probably know is the most violent kind of blushing. It is true, now I am in the capital of the empire, it ought to be different, but on the one hand my natural timidity forbids me to obtrude myself and on the other hand the young ladies, who obtrude themselves on me (and their name is legion here) repulse me." Sticking to his father's lecture-tour agenda, he imagined himself as a church historian. After Ford urged him to choose farming over a profession, Rauschenbusch gently told his friend that he was too conceited and ambitious to be a farmer. He aspired to be a kinder version of his orthodox, academic father. The Gütersloh Gymnasium was conservative, his father's religious influence upon him was commanding, and Rauschenbusch knew the past century of German liberal theology only as something to be dreaded. He took for granted that he would take his theological training at his father's seminary. The only question was whether he should complete college first.[9]

Rochester Seminary accepted Rauschenbusch's Gütersloh program as the equivalent of a college education, but he worried that his classical training left gaps in his knowledge, especially the social sciences. He also didn't want to be the first Rauschenbusch since the seventeenth century to enter the ministry without a university degree. Taking these concerns seriously, August Rauschenbusch advised his son to complete the University of Rochester's final-year courses before he enrolled at the seminary. Walter countered that he was ready to pursue both degrees at the same time. The University of Rochester was still proudly Baptist in 1883, and the president was a family friend. Rauschenbusch took on a double load of classes, though his college instructors graded him in only one course. To them he seemed already beyond college; one student later recalled that he "became an object of scholarly awe to the rest of us." One of his teachers, physiologist Harrison E. Webster, became a cherished friend. Webster assured Rauschenbusch that Darwinian evolution could be harmonized with Christianity; he gave "breezy and geniusy" lectures about cell structure, brachiopods, and the riddles of life; and on the side he commended Henry George's "single tax" populism to Rauschenbusch.[10]

The social Christian movement was in its infancy when Rauschenbusch attended seminary. Washington Gladden, Richard Ely, and Josiah Strong were just beginning to create social gospel organizations and make names for themselves. The absorbing questions for Rauschenbusch were vocational and critical, not social. To what kind of pastoral or missionary work was he called? How should he deal with higher criticism of the Bible? Theologically, all of Rochester Seminary's faculty were either conservative or very conservative. Evangelical icon and seminary president Augustus Hopkins Strong, who taught theology, taught a slightly updated version of Baptist Calvinist scholasticism; Old Testament scholar Howard Osgood held out for an aggressively fundamentalist view of scriptural inspiration and infallibility; the seminary's least conservative professor, New Testament scholar William Arnold Stevens, earned his reputation as a liberal by rejecting fundamentalist inerrancy theory. Stevens taught that scripture is an inspired *record* of divine revelation, not revelation itself. His first-year course pointed out various discrepancies in the Gospel narratives, which was not what Walter Rauschenbusch expected to learn at seminary. Stevens inspired Rauschenbusch and eventually persuaded him. While resisting some of his teacher's mildly critical conclusions, Rauschenbusch increasingly tacked in Stevens's direction and gave up the doctrine of biblical infallibility.

He took what encouragements he could find at Rochester Seminary for the project of progressive orthodoxy. Church historian Benjamin True brought to life the incarnationalist historicism of August Neander, which impressed Rauschenbusch with its concept of Christ as a divine power entering and progressively transforming history. Homiletics professor Thomas Harwood Pattison encouraged Rauschenbusch to study the life and sermons of liberal Anglican

Frederick W. Robertson. Though he played a careful hand for the most part, avoiding direct disagreements with his father, by his last year of seminary Rauschenbusch was ready to stand up to Augustus Strong. Strong's *Lectures on Theology* (1876) defined Baptist orthodoxy for his generation until it was superseded by his *Systematic Theology* (1886). On atonement theory Strong contended that because genuinely Christian doctrine is objective and substitutionary, Horace Bushnell's atonement theology was sub-Christian.[11]

In a paper Rauschenbusch made a case for Bushnell's view "that Christ's death is not a sacrifice to appease the wrath of an angry God against sinful men, but a sacrifice to reconcile the hearts of sinful men to their loving God." Substitutionary atonement theory was not taught by Jesus, he observed; it turns salvation into an abstract Trinitarian transaction and teaches a morally repugnant conception of divine justice. Bushnell's theory, on the other hand, was gospel-centered, intelligible to human experience, and morally uplifting. In the manner of Bushnell's later theology, Rauschenbusch did not deny that atonement has an objective element: "We only claim that with our present spiritual insight a knowledge of such an effect is not necessary to our peace and assurance of forgiveness." Strong was alarmed by Rauschenbusch's paper, admonishing his senior-class theology students that the doctrine of objective substitutionary atonement was orthodox and Horace Bushnell was not. Rauschenbusch later recalled: "This paper was written with a good deal of heat and was felt by Dr. Strong to be subversive of Scriptural authority. He spent several lectures after it going over the ground."[12]

Rauschenbusch quietly held his ground that biblical statements are not true merely because they appear in the Bible. Like any other statements, he maintained, biblical statements are true only if they appeal to us as true in their own right. This was a signature theme of his favorite religious writers. As a seminarian Rauschenbusch compiled a notebook of favorite spiritual sayings that eventually grew to over fifty pages; his chief oracles were Anglican liberals Frederick W. Robertson, Samuel Taylor Coleridge, and Phillips Brooks, poets Robert Browning, William Wordsworth, and Coleridge, neopietist leader Friedrich August Tholuck, and religious philosopher Blaise Pascal. Rauschenbusch identified especially with Robertson's ethical conception of the way of the cross and his personal example of shedding an inherited conservative religion. Like Robertson, he found that the gospel became real to him in a new way after he preached a liberal version of the way of the cross to working-class churchpeople. In Rauschenbusch's case, the churchpeople were Baptists of a struggling congregation in Louisville, Kentucky, where he undertook two summer pastorates.

"I began with the determination to raise the spiritual standard of every Christian among them," he told Munson Ford of his first summer in Louisville. Working from door to door, he sought to "awaken in their hearts the love of Christ as the only sure cure for their love of self and sin." This experience convinced Rauschenbusch that parish ministry, not academe, offered the best outlet for his religious idealism. "It is now no longer my fond hope to be a learned theologian and write big books. I want to be a pastor, powerful with men, preaching to them

Christ as the man in whom their affections and energies can find the satisfaction for which mankind is groaning." Ford had settled for a job as an assistant book-keeper; Rauschenbusch admonished him that mere machines can add and sub-tract: "I fear the sing-song of the day-book will be the lullaby to your finer capacity." There was nothing of the "higher life of man" in bookkeeping; as for himself, he aspired to be a ministerial captain in "the onward marching army of our people."[13]

Having discarded the belief that Christ's saving death is imputed to believers, Rauschenbusch exulted that the way of the cross was newly meaningful to him: "I am just beginning to believe in the Gospel of the Lord Jesus Christ, not exactly in the shape in which the average person proclaims it as the infallible truth of the Most High, but in a shape that suits my needs, that I have gradually constructed for myself in studying the person and teaching of Christ, and which is still in rapid progress of construction." He was ready to "do hard work for God," living literally by the teaching and spirit of Jesus. Toward this end he was still avoiding romantic entanglements: "On the whole I find myself better without." In later years he recalled that he was consumed by the notion "that I ought to follow Jesus Christ in my personal life, and live over again his life, and die over again his death."[14]

Rauschenbusch's liberal turn had little sense of a social dimension; it was also socially isolating. He was lonely in seminary. Having stayed in school to a comparatively advanced age—"He kept me at school till I was twenty-four," Rauschenbusch later wrote of his father—he was left alone in Rochester after his best friends moved away and his sisters, Frida and Emma, both married and departed. Frida's husband was a professor at Hamburg Seminary in Germany; Emma's husband was a missionary in Telugus, India. Though Walter embraced his father's vocational dream for him—to minister to the German Baptist com-munity—his relations with his parents were tense and, at best, polite. August and Caroline Rauschenbusch were dismayed by their son's liberal turn. They regarded the influence of Webster and Stevens upon him as a threat to his ministerial career and, more seriously, his faith. "I am struggling through this last term as well as I can," Rauschenbusch told Ford, eager to begin his parish career. After Walter was called to the Second German Baptist Church of New York City, August correctly surmised that his son was sufficiently discreet to get past the Baptist ordination exam, but Caroline worried that her son's liberal leanings would disqualify him for ordination. Rauschenbusch told his parents, "I believe in the gospel of Jesus Christ with all my heart. What this gospel is, everyone has to decide for himself, in the face of his God." This was the kind of assurance that set them on edge; Rauschenbusch tried a bold analogy. On the strength of personal conviction, he reminded them, they had left "the great and venerable Lutheran Church" to join the lowly Baptist movement. This was exactly what he was doing now. He did not worry about Baptist church councils; he wanted only to be true to his read-ing of Scripture and the dictates of his conscience.[15]

The Second German Baptist Church of New York City was located on West Forty-fifth Street near Tenth Avenue on Manhattan's West Side. It bordered the northern edge of the notorious gang-ruled district known as Hell's Kitchen and was only a few blocks west of the Tenderloin district, where gambling and prostitution flourished. The church was barely functional when Rauschenbusch arrived. It numbered approximately 125 members, most of them factory-laboring German immigrants, and its building was ugly, run-down, and depressing, like its neighborhood. "There are many little splits and much big discouragement," Rauschenbusch reported. "The church has had bad experiences with my predecessors who have left an unsavory reputation behind them." Rauschenbusch took all of this as a challenge to his Christ-following idealism. He would share the conditions of his impoverished German-American brothers and sisters and bring the saving word of Christ to them. While lacking any concept of the church as an instrument of social justice—"My idea then was to save souls, in the ordinarily accepted religious sense"—his preaching was fueled from the beginning by his determination to live according to the way and spirit of Jesus and by his Neander-influenced idea of Christianity as the expansion of Christ's incarnation in history. Rauschenbusch conceived the Christian life as a corporate kingdom-building journey from sin to salvation; his theology was historical and postmillennialist before it became socialist. From the outset of his ministry he preached that the church exists to hasten and participate in the coming of God's kingdom. The ethical meaning of the gospel is that Christians are called to insinuate God's love and justice into the world.[16]

As a pastor Rauschenbusch was diligent, faithful, and inspiring. His sermonizing and energetic care gave an emotional lift to his long-dispirited congregation. Under his leadership, and with the generous assistance of John D. Rockefeller—who took a kindly interest in August Rauschenbusch's promising Baptist son—the church built an impressive new building a few blocks away, on West Forty-third Street near Ninth Avenue. Rauschenbusch was proud of this accomplishment while fretting that the congregation's new sanctuary might be too nice for its spiritual good. By the time that the new building was dedicated in March 1890, he was well acquainted with ambivalent feelings on other matters, as well as feelings of distraction, frustration, and wounding disappointment. A few weeks after his pastorate began, he was nearly offered the presidency of Telugu Theological Seminary in India, until a bad recommendation from Howard Osgood killed his candidacy; Osgood warned that his former student had liberal leanings. Rauschenbusch was conflicted about seeking the position. He felt strongly committed to his West Side congregation, and he had health concerns. During his last year of seminary his hearing diminished; after he arrived in New York, it worsened dramatically. Rauschenbusch sought medical treatment and was told that he suffered from a neurological defect. While undergoing treatments that failed to improve his hearing, he worried that he could not be a pastor if he went deaf.[17]

He also worried that his parents' marriage was finished. In 1888 August Rauschenbusch retired from teaching, and Rochester Seminary offered his German Department position to Walter. Because his work in New York City was just beginning, he declined it with flattered gratitude. August gave himself a retirement gift by returning to Germany without his wife. On the pretext that Walter could use some household help, August deposited Caroline with her son just before he sailed from New York. His good-bye consisted of a handshake; afterwards Walter found his mother convulsed in tears. For two years they shared an apartment as August brushed off the admonishments of scandalized Baptist friends. Walter and his mother coped with the situation gamely, though there were strains between them. In 1890, strengthened by the assurance that his daughter Frida would look out for Caroline, August Rauschenbusch allowed his wife to join him in Hamburg, where they lived more agreeably until August's death in 1899. Walter revered his father as the trailblazing German-American Baptist of his generation who set the standard for German Baptist education. He internalized his father's ambitions for his ministerial and, later, academic career, and its locus in the German Baptist community. But he became a determinately different kind of husband and father and preached a transformationist social gospel that his father barely recognized. In his introduction to the half-autobiography, half-biography of August Rauschenbusch that Walter completed after his father's death, he allowed that his father was known to be stern and even harsh with students and various acquaintances. A heavy veil was cast over the family drama, however. The loyal son would not tarnish the memory of his father, hurt the feelings of relatives, or deprive German-American Baptists of their favored hero.[18]

Under these trying personal circumstances Walter Rauschenbusch found his way to the social gospel. He embraced his father's missionary ambitions, but not his father's authority-religion. He became shy and acquainted with loneliness, yet committed himself to an outward-reaching religion of social transformation. He went deaf but did not leave the ministry. Rauschenbusch bore his loss of hearing bravely and adeptly, though without the saving grace of learning to laugh at it. In the course of coping with his deafness, his gregarious personality became shy, sensitive, and somewhat lonely. Yet at the same time, buoyed by a happy marriage, a cadre of like-minded friends, and an upsurge of social idealism outside the churches, he dared to imagine the church as an agent of social transformation and the nations of Europe and North America as cooperative socialist commonwealths.

ASKING THE SOCIAL QUESTION

Rauschenbusch's piety was firmly evangelical-pietist when he entered the ministry, and in a crucial sense it remained so for the rest of his life. He was fond of exhorting colleagues and parishioners to make time "to be in the Master's presence." He admired Dwight Moody's revival preaching and closely studied his personal collection of Moody's sermons. In 1888, for spiritual refreshment, he attended Moody's ten-day revival conference in Northfield, Massachusetts. Afterward he teamed with Moody's song leader and gospel hymn composer, Ira

D. Sankey, to publish a German-language edition of Sankey's *Gospel Hymns No. 5*. This hymnal, *Evangeliums-Lieder*, was published in 1889 and sold very well. Rauschenbusch translated half of the book's 218 hymns, which included such evangelical standards as "I Need Thee Every Hour" and "What a Friend We Have in Jesus." In later years he and Sankey published several German-language hymnals, causing later generations of students to wonder how the author of *Christianity and the Social Crisis* could have produced the Old Religion's songbooks.[19]

Part of him resisted the question. Rauschenbusch wanted to believe that the Jesus of kingdom-building postmillennial Christianity was the Jesus of revival Christianity at its best. He had barely grasped that a social crisis existed before he began to relate the ethic of Jesus to it. In later years it bothered him greatly that he had to come to the social gospel from outside the church, for the church was the entrenched enemy of social idealism. "This is one of the saddest things that I can say, but I cannot get it out of my mind," he reflected in 1913. "The church held down the social interest in me. It contradicted it; it opposed it; it held it down as far as it could; and when it was a question about giving me position or preferment, the fact that I was interested in the workingman was actually against me."[20] He came to New York with "no idea of social questions," he recalled elsewhere. To the downtrodden immigrants of Forty-fifth Street he brought the pious maxims of his inherited evangelicalism, and "discovered that they didn't fit." Rauschenbusch was driven to what he called "social ideas" by the misery of his congregants and neighbors. "The world is hard and without feeling," he wrote to his cousin Maria Döring. "Here I see so much of this that my heart bleeds for the victims."[21]

His congregants lived in squalid five-story tenements that pressed more than twenty families into each building. His heart broke at the malnutrition and diseases of the children, and their funerals: "Oh, the children's funerals! They gripped my heart—that was one of the things I always went away thinking about—why did the children have to die?" Friends and clerical colleagues admonished him that pastors were supposed to save souls, not waste their time and vocation on social work. A young missionary on his way to an early death in Africa "implored me almost with tears to dismiss these social questions and give myself to 'Christian work.'" These appeals were painfully upsetting to Rauschenbusch, but not convincing: "All our inherited ideas, all theological literature, all the practices of church life, seemed to be against us." He replied that his "social work" ministry was surely the work of Christ. "I went ahead, although I had to set myself against all that I had previously been taught. I had to go back to the Bible to find out whether I or my friends were right." This process of discernment took years, but the social crisis was immediate. For Rauschenbusch, politics became unavoidable. If people suffered because of politics and economics, then authentic kingdom preaching had to deal with politics and economics. He found his first guides to "social ideas" in the economic journalist Henry George, who ran for mayor of New York in 1886, and Richard Ely, the founding economist of the social gospel.[22]

Henry George was a high school dropout whose Damascus-road moment occurred at the age of thirty. Walking the streets of New York in 1869, he was overwhelmed by the contrast between the comforts of the city's upper class and the degradation of its poor. He resolved to devote his life to reforming the system that produced such extremes of wealth and poverty. Ten years later in his major work, *Progress and Poverty,* he argued that the state should impose a "single tax" on the unearned increment in the value of land. As long as land values increased, he observed, those who worked the land were forced to pay more and more for the right to work. The most ethical and practical way to break the cycle of structural impoverishment was to appropriate the unearned increment in the value of land by taxing it. The tax would free up land presently held for speculation, stimulate construction, create new housing and jobs, and drive down the cost of rent, while the proceeds of the tax would fund government programs designed to help the needy.[23]

In October 1886, five months after Rauschenbusch moved to New York, George launched his campaign for mayor as the candidate of a reformist coalition of trade unionists and socialists. Rauschenbusch attended a rally for George at Cooper Union at which Father Edward McGlynn, an ardent George supporter and Catholic priest, excited the crowd by exhorting, "Thy kingdom come! Thy will be done on earth." Rauschenbusch was deeply stirred. The George campaign had Christian support, and it was about the right issues. While steering clear of socialism, it claimed that the existence of poverty and unearned wealth were structurally linked in the existing system. A progressive interventionist government was needed to reform capitalism. Rauschenbusch supported George's candidacy and devoured his writings; later he defended his right to preach George's ideas from the pulpit, telling a parishioner: "The time will probably come when the truth now perceived by a few who have economic training will penetrate our laws and the average moral judgment of society, and then the private appropriation of that increase in real estate value will seem just as outrageous as other forms of income which were once highly respectable and are now felonies before the law." To his disappointment, George's policy proposal stirred little interest among workers, and Rauschenbusch later judged that the social crisis of modern capitalism had structural aspects that the "single tax" did not address. Yet for the rest of his career he drew on George's analysis, supported the single tax as one means of preventing the accumulation of unearned wealth, and expressed gratitude for the inspiring impact of George's activism: "I owe my own first awakening to the world of social problems to the agitation of Henry George in 1886 and wish here to record my lifelong debt to this single-minded apostle of a great truth."[24]

George inspired Rauschsenbusch to become a student of the social question; Richard Ely was the key thinker that he studied; Leighton Williams was the mutual friend who introduced him to Ely. Shortly after he arrived in New York Rauschenbusch became a friend of Williams, who had recently succeeded his father, respected minister William R. Williams, as pastor of the midtown Amity Baptist Church. The Williamses were wealthy and well connected, but devoted to reform causes; the younger Williams was working in Henry George's mayoral campaign when he met Rauschenbusch. A graduate of Columbia University, Union Theological Seminary, and Columbia Law School, he was on track to become a prominent lawyer until his father's pending retirement gave him second thoughts. Williams gave up his promising legal career to carry on his father's pastoral work. At Columbia one of his classmates and friends was Richard Ely, whose subsequent training in political economics made him distinctively suited to influence the social gospel movement. Schooled in the historical approach to economics pioneered by German social theorists Karl Knies, Wilhelm Roscher, Adolf Wagner, and Bruno Hildebrand, Ely earned a doctorate under Knies's direction at Heidelberg and subsequently accepted a teaching position in political economy at Johns Hopkins University. Economically he embraced Knies's historicism, which rejected the prevailing notion of economics as a science of immutable universal laws; Knies and Ely emphasized the sociohistorical variability of economic systems. Religiously Ely was an Episcopal layman, converted from conservative Presbyterianism, who was strongly influenced by the Christian socialism of English Anglican theologian Frederick Denison Maurice.[25]

The ascendance of social Darwinist trends in American politics and social sciences gave Ely plenty to oppose. Hired by Johns Hopkins in 1881, he showed his political colors in 1884 with an anti–social Darwinist book titled *The Past and Present of Political Economy;* the following year he founded the American Economic Association. Both were protests against the ideology of laissez-faire individualism. Against the notion that economics is a science of universal laws, Ely argued that economies are shaped by particular cultural, historical, and political factors and that some forms of government intervention produce better economies than unregulated or poorly regulated economies. Against the antigovernment dictums of libertarians and social Darwinists, he argued that the state is an "indispensable" agent of social progress, especially in its roles as the guardian of legal trade and guarantor of justice for the poor. His cofounders of the American Economic Association included economist John Bates Clark and social gospelers Washington Gladden and Lyman Abbott.[26]

Ely's politics were reformist, trade unionist, moralistic, and mildly socialist. He supported private ownership as a rule but made exceptions of the gas and water utilities and all other natural monopolies, for which he prescribed government ownership. To him the modern trade union was the second most important force for social progress in the world; its promise was trumped only by the church. "It must be recognized that extreme individualism is immoral," he admonished in *The Labor Movement in America.* "The absolute ideal was given two thousand years ago by Christ, who established the most perfect system of ethics the world has ever known." Prolific in the cause of awakening the social conscience of the church, Ely wrote and lectured constantly and developed new organizations such as the Chautauqua Society's American Institute of Christian Sociology. In 1888 he told a group of Baptist ministers that the church had thus far preached only a "one-sided half-gospel" of individual salvation; it was time for the church to recover the social righteousness of Jesus. Rauschenbusch was in the audience; he had found his mentor. Ely was the movement's first academic heavyweight; with inspiring conviction he exhorted Rauschenbusch and other Protestant pastors that to follow Christ in the modern age is to struggle for righteousness and justice in all realms of society. Before long Rauschenbusch was calling him "a personal friend of mine, a simple and serious man, a convinced Christian and one of the top experts on national economy."[27]

In December 1887, eighteen months after he arrived in New York, Rauschenbusch began to write and lecture on behalf of social reform. He told the East Side Literary Society of Rochester: "Dear friends, there is a social question. No one can doubt it, in whose ears are ringing the wails of the mangled and the crushed, who are borne along on the pent-up torrent of life. Woe to the man who stands afar off and says, 'Peace, peace,' when there is no peace." In his first article on social reform he asked readers to look "beneath the glitter" of modern society to see the terrible misery underneath; his example was an imaginary "bullet-headed tailor" whose employer would not permit him to care for his dying daughter: "And so he has to sew away and let his little girl die three blocks off. When he gets home he can sob over her corpse; what more does he want? Exceptional case, you think. Not a bit of it. It's the drop on the crest of the wave." Two cases later Rauschenbusch stopped in mid-sentence: "Got to go, eh? Bored you, didn't I? Yes, guess I am something of a crank on these things." But if people only looked beneath the glitter of their booming society, he believed, they wouldn't think so highly of the country that America was becoming.[28]

Rauschenbusch found a kindred spirit in Leighton Williams, whose Amity Baptist Church was only a few blocks away on West Fifty-fourth Street; he found another in scholarly Nathaniel Schmidt, pastor of the First Swedish Baptist Church on East Twentieth Street, who was fresh out of Madison Theological Seminary in Hamilton, New York. Quickly the young pastors became a threesome, meeting every week for discussion and prayer. On Sunday afternoons they held communion services that strengthened their sense of spiritual fellowship. Theologically they were very similar; more surprising to them was the bond of friendship that they found in their social concerns. Though Schmidt's pastoral stint was brief—he returned to Madison Seminary as a professor of Semitic languages and biblical Greek in September 1888—his departure from New York did not diminish the ties of friendship and spiritual feeling that bound them to each other. It merely prompted them to become avid correspondents and arrange frequent reunions, often at Williams's summer home near Marlborough, where they resolved to think of themselves as a true "society of Jesus." This was the seed of a formalized fellowship that came to be called the Brotherhood of the Kingdom.[29]

The three ministers were eager to crystallize and disseminate their views. Together they drafted chapters for a book on the social meaning of the gospel, which they never completed. Williams acted as the group's mentor; Rauschenbusch did most of the writing; Schmidt contributed some writing and a heavy editorial hand. For the next twenty years they wrote collaboratively in this manner.

Rauschenbusch later reported that during his early ministry he had six books in his head: five were scholarly, one was dangerous. He tried to write the dangerous one, and resolved on three separate occasions to complete it, but "each time I was compelled to stop in the middle on account of work. When I went back to my book, I found each time I had out-grown the book." Meanwhile he poured out sharply written, sometimes cheeky articles for a monthy newspaper, *For the Right*, that he and Williams launched in 1889 with the help of business manager J. F. Raymond (a Harlem Baptist minister) and managing editor Elizabeth Post. Pitching the paper to a working-class readership, Rauschenbusch and Williams had ambitious hopes: "We desire to make this paper a 'people's paper': one that shall express their best sentiments, their highest thoughts, their truest aspiration, and their sincerest opinions on all matters of a practical, social, literary, or religious significance." *For the Right* was certainly this wide-ranging, though rarely this lofty. It was practical, reformist, and often homespun in its style and content; it was also unsparingly opinionated.[30]

The paper was launched during the very period that Rauschenbusch came to identify with an ascending socialist movement. Shortly after he moved to New York, his cousin Maria Döring sent him a biography of Frederick Denison Maurice, which Rauschenbusch consumed. He shared Williams's admiration of Maurice. Three years later, in May 1889, Rauschenbusch and Williams made contact with the Society of Christian Socialists, which had been founded the previous month by a Boston Episcopal priest, W. D. P. Bliss. Bliss favored the English Fabian school of socialism, which vested its social hopes in the gradually developing collectivism of modern society. His organization endorsed no particular brand of socialism, but it was decidedly cool to Marxist radicalism, and religiously it was ecumenical. The group's president was O. P. Gifford, a Baptist minister and friend of Williams and Rauschenbusch. In its founding statement of principles, the Society of Christian Socialists declared its belief that "the teachings of Jesus Christ lead directly to some specific form or forms of socialism." *For the Right* was founded only a few months after Rauschenbusch resolved that he, too, was a Christian socialist, though not in a party sense of the term. The editors promised that their paper would serve no party interest or ideology; at the same time they exempted Christian socialism from these categories. By their reckoning Christian socialism was broad-minded, wholesome, and ecumenical; it was also their perspective: "To apply the ethical principles of Jesus Christ so that our industrial relationships may be humanized, our economic system moralized, justice pervade legislation, and the State grown into a true commonwealth—we band together as Christian Socialists."[31]

Rauschenbusch was a rich source of opinions for the paper. He advocated an eight-hour workday, socialization of the railroads, municipal ownership of utilities, a city-owned underground transit system, the single tax, separation of church and state, government regulation of trusts and monopolies, ballot reform, and workplace safety. He also wrote about technology, strikes, labor and capital relations, good government, free trade, personal ethics, individualism, and the kingdom of God. Persistently he counseled that personal salvation and social salvation go together. "One of the peculiarities which distinguishes *For the Right* from many other papers akin to it, is that it stands for a combination of personal regeneration and social reform," he observed. The churches claimed that regenerated individuals create good societies, but Rauschenbusch noted that revivals were common in the Old South—where regenerated white Christians treated black people as chattel. Secular reformers claimed that a just social order would abolish individual selfishness and cruelty, but Rauschenbusch begged to differ: "Mankind rolling in material wealth with no moral earnestness and spiritual elevation would only be something worse than swine champing in a full trough or maggots burrowing in a carcass." *For the Right* believed in God, he countered; therefore it also believed in God's moral law, in which personal and social salvation are correlated. To be saved is to obey God's law solely because one loves it: "Only if the number of such God conquered souls is great and increasing in any nation will the progress of the nation in material wealth be of real benefit to the people!"[32]

For the Right lasted eighteen months, folding in March 1891 during the same week that Rauschenbusch departed for a sabbatical in Germany and England. The paper never connected with its targeted readership. It found an appreciative audience among a small group of middle-class Protestants but inspired few working-class readers. It was too radical for most of its desired audience and too Christian for disaffected workers who were already radicalized. The editors' earnest moralizing fell flat, some of their articles were patronizing (Rauschenbusch resorted to children's stories on several occasions), and they never found a clear focus. By 1891 their seed money ran out, and Rauschenbusch was ready to resign his pastorate. The surflike roar in his ears had not abated. He was nearly deaf and felt unable to continue as a minister. Augustus Strong renewed his offer of a teaching position at Rochester Seminary, but Rauschenbusch doubted that he could teach, either. He proposed to resign from his pastorate, go abroad for a year of study, and then begin a literary career. His congregation pleaded with him to take a paid sabbatical instead. Gratefully Rauschenbusch accepted their generous offer and sailed to Europe, in search of a medical cure, and in search of a deeper grounding in Christian socialism.

THE KINGDOM AS POLITICAL THEOLOGY

In the company of his sister Emma, who longed for Europe after five hard years in the mission fields of India and two years of study at Wellesley College, Rauschenbusch traveled first to England. As a German-American youth he had been raised to regard England as an expansionist bully; as a young man he found now that England appealed to his imagination as the land of Maurice-style Christian socialism and gradualist Fabian socialism. Walter and Emma traveled first to Liverpool, which they found appallingly dirty and miserable. They proceeded to

Birmingham, where Walter found his reward, and then to London, where Emma found hers. In London Emma learned of the eighteenth-century feminist Mary Wollstonecraft, on whom she later wrote a doctoral dissertation at the University of Bern. Her brother rejoiced at finding a model of municipal socialism in Birmingham. To Rauschenbusch, Birmingham proved that vigorous reformist governance could make all the difference in coping with the ravages of industrialization. Birmingham had been a typical outpost of industrialized urban misery in the mid-nineteenth century. Two decades later it was a clean, attractive, and egalitarian city with socialized gas and water systems, renovated slums, ample public parks and libraries, female suffrage in local elections, and free meals for schoolchildren. Rauschenbusch hoped that he was seeing a preview of American urban life. He wrote that new American cities should "do by foresight what Birmingham did by hindsight."[33]

He showed less interest in current Anglican Socialism. Rauschenbusch's enthusaism for the Anglican tradition of Christian socialism cooled upon reflection and a bit of sightseeing; he made no effort to contact Anglican Socialist leaders. The liturgical sensibility of Anglican Socialism was too Catholic for his taste. Theologically, like Anglicanism generally, the Anglican Socialist schools were centered on the incarnation and the sacraments, not the ethic of the kingdom, and they were comfortable with their privileges. Maurice's state church disciples took little interest in ecumenical cooperation. Of the three major Christian socialist organizations in England, only the Christian Socialist Society admitted Nonconformists; the Guild of Saint Matthew and the Christian Social Union were open to Anglicans only. Rauschenbusch's distaste for the priestly sacramentalism of Anglican piety came to a head during a visit to Westminster Abbey.

"I walked into Westminster Abbey when they were consecrating three bishops," he recalled, perhaps a few weeks afterward. "Over the heads of the congregation I caught a glimpse of a solemn procession in the nave, garments, robes, gilt crucifixes. I returned an hour later; they were still consecrating the bishops. I went off for lunch and came back; the bishops were still on the make. Now, how can we more readily imagine Jesus, in an archbishop's robe bowing, kneeling, marching, wheeling, and all that to get a man fit to be a successor of the apostles and to draw a salary—or on the tail of a cart talking to the multitude on the social question? Which would seem to him more important for the Kingdom of God on earth?"[34]

These words, so typical of his Baptist-socialist outlook, may have been written in Germany, where Walter and Emma visited their parents and their sister Frida. Walter painfully observed that his parents were still consumed by marital bitterness; at the same time he struggled to make peace between Emma and her father, who were nearly equally estranged. Harder yet to bear was Walter's failure to find a cure for his deafness. By mid-August he realized that his condition was hopeless; he would have to live with being deaf, a condition he described as physical loneliness. His letters to Williams were so despairing that Williams felt obliged to assure him that his congregation still wanted him back. "God is better to us than our fears," Williams assured. Rauschenbusch had days when he doubted this assurance, but through the worst of them he labored over his "dangerous book"—the massive manuscript on the social meaning of Christianity. This was at least his second major pass at writing the book, which he continued to revise for six years. As his learning proceeded, so did his need to rewrite the book. He titled it *Revolutionary Christianity* and crammed it with his new learning in biblical criticism, Christian history, and social analysis. Parts of the book ended up in his blockbuster coming-out volume, *Christianity and the Social Crisis,* which Rauschenbusch published sixteen years later, and parts of it were published as separate essays. Much of it was lost to readers until American ethicist Max Stackhouse discovered in the 1960s in the archives of the American Baptist Historical Society a misfiled manuscript that he published as *The Righteousness of the Kingdom;* other manuscripts were lost.[35]

In Germany Rauschenbusch found the key to his theology and his life. This was the coming of the kingdom on earth, which was not a new theme for him, but which he for the first time grasped in its centrality and symphonic totality. Previously he was content to repeat the Ritschlian image of Christianity as an ellipse with two centers: eternal life as the goal of individual existence and the kingdom of God as the goal of humanity. But in Germany it occurred to Rauschenbusch that the kingdom was not merely a major part of Jesus's teaching; it was the controlling center. *Revolutionary Christianity* proposed that Christianity is revolutionary in its nature because the ethic and example of Jesus are revolutionary. What was missing in historical Christianity was the very core of Jesus's teaching and meaning: "What, now, is the aim of this revolutionary movement inaugurated by Jesus? What word is inscribed on the banner he raised? The Kingdom of God! About that his thoughts circle like a host of planets 'round a central sun." Because Jesus proclaimed and initiated the kingdom, he reasoned, the church is supposed to be a new kind of community that transforms the world by the power of Christ's kingdom-bringing Spirit. The mission of the church is not merely to save people's souls for the heavenly world to come, but "to overcome the spirit dominant in the world and thus penetrate and transform the world."[36]

Rauschenbusch's realization of the centrality of the kingdom brought a new coherence to his thinking. Though he continued to struggle with his manuscript, realizing continually that his scholarship lagged behind his insights, his controlling insight was in place. He stopped struggling with the question of how to fit his new, Christ-following social consciousness into his old Christianity, "my old religion." He later recalled:

> And then the idea of the kingdom of God offered itself as the real solution for that problem. Here was a religious conception that embraced it all. Here was something so big that absolutely nothing that interested me was excluded from it. Was it a matter of personal religion? Why, the kingdom of God begins with that! The powers of the kingdom of God well up in the individual soul; that is where they are born, and that is where the starting point necessarily must be.

> Was it a matter of world-wide mission? Why, that is the kingdom of
> God, isn't it—carrying it out to the boundaries of the earth. Was it a
> matter of getting justice for the workingman? Is not justice part of
> the kingdom of God? Does not the kingdom of God simply consist
> of this—that God's will shall be done on earth, even as it is now in
> heaven? And so, wherever I touched, there was the kingdom of God.
> That was the brilliancy, the splendor of that conception—it touches
> everything with religion. It carries God into everything that you do,
> and there is nothing else that does it in the same way.[37]

It was not a question of fitting the ethic of the kingdom into the old Christianity. The kingdom is the heart of Christianity, he reasoned; it is a social reality that pervades all humanity and nature. It is always working toward the realized
life of God. Rauschenbusch never failed to sound an evangelical note in proclaiming the kingdom faith, however. The kingdom stands at the center of Christianity, he asserted, not merely on account of its symphonic beauty or because of
the ethical work that it does, but because "you have the authority of the Lord
Jesus Christ in it." The kingdom is Jesus's Word and idea. For years after the name
"social gospel" came into vogue, Rauschenbusch had mixed feelings about it; the
name seemed redundant to him. He hated to concede that any nonsocial faith
deserved to be called a form of the Christian gospel. The kingdom of God "cannot be lived out by you alone," he exhorted. "You have to live it out with me, and
with that brother sitting next to you. We together have to work it out. It is a matter of community life. The perfect community of men—that would be the kingdom of God! With God above them; with their brother next to them—clasping
hands in fraternity, doing the work of justice—that is the kingdom of God!"[38]

Rauschenbusch and Williams were wily organizers and movement activists.
They attended the 1887 convention of Josiah Strong's Evangelical Alliance in
Washington, D.C., attended by nearly fifteen hundred delegates, which gave
them a sense of belonging to a movement. The following year they infiltrated the
Baptist Congress, winning the office of secretary for Williams and gaining a crucial forum for their social Christian views. A year later they made contact with
Bliss's fledgling Society of Christian Socialists and worked on various neighborhood projects financed by Williams's mother. When Rauschenbusch returned to
New York in 1892, he and Williams expanded these projects, which came to
include a deaconess home, an association for working women, an institute for
working men, and a theological school. Rauschenbusch's congregation welcomed
him warmly, while recognizing that his deafness was vocationally limiting. They
dealt with the latter problem by transferring some of his pastoral duties to the
cleric who had filled in for him. Rauschenbusch was gratified and delighted to
be granted an assistant; it meant that he could pursue his wider ministry.

In 1892 Williams published a slender book titled *The Baptist Position: Its
Experimental Basis,* which argued that the church's best antidote to modern criticism and disbelief is the faith that the Holy Spirit is at work building the kingdom of God. God's Spirit is the authenticating authority for faith, not the words

of Scripture or the dogmas of the church. The same year Rauschenbusch delivered a kingdom-focused version of this message to the Baptist Congress, his first address to a national convention. The idea of the kingdom captures "the whole aim of Christ," he declared: "In that ideal is embraced the sanctification of all life, the regeneration of humanity, and the reformation of all social institutions." When this position proved to be too radical-sounding for most Baptist Congress delegates, Rauschenbusch and Williams joined with Philadelphia pastor Samuel Zane Batten to organize a progressive caucus within the Congress. The following year this caucus became the Brotherhood of the Kingdom.[39]

The Brotherhood became Rauschenbusch's spiritual home. Its original members included Batten, Williams, Rauschenbusch, Schmidt, Philadelphia pastor George Dana Boardman, Hamilton theologian William Newton Clarke, and a half-dozen others. Like Rauschenbusch's original "society of Jesus," it pledged to exemplify the life and spirit of Jesus; like the Fabian Socialists whom some of the Brotherhood Baptists admired, they were skilled pamphleteers. While disagreeing about socialism and women's suffrage, and even disagreeing, at first, about allowing non-Baptists to join, the Brotherhood Baptists held in common the idea of a Christ-following kingdom ideal: "Obeying the thought of our Master, and trusting in the power and guidance of the Spirit, we form ourselves into a Brotherhood of the Kingdom, in order to re-establish this idea in the thought of the church, and to assist in its practical realization in the life of the world." By 1894 Rauschenbusch's view of the membership issue prevailed, and the Brotherhood of the Kingdom opened its fellowship to women and non-Baptists.[40]

To him it made no sense to limit a kingdom fellowship to Baptists or men or clerics, for the kingdom faith was the antithesis of sectarian exclusion. In 1893 he reflected: "We saw the Church of Christ divided by selfishness; every denomination intent on its own progress, often at the expense of the progress of the Kingdom; churches and pastors absorbed in their own affairs and jealous of one another; external forms of worship and church polity magnified and the spirit neglected; the people estranged from the church and the church indifferent to the movements of the people; aberrations from creeds severely censured, and aberrations from the Christian spirit of self-sacrifice tolerated." This was what the Brotherhood of the Kingdom opposed in the body of Christ. Formally it focused on what it called "the drink evil," "the social evil," and "the next steps in social reform"; Rauschenbusch urged that the key to the vitality or corruption of Christianity in any age is how it represents the kingdom: "It grew clear to us that many of these evils have their root in the wrongful abandonment or the perversion of the great aim of Christ: the Kingdom of God. As the idea of the Kingdom is the key to the teachings and work of Christ, so its abandonment or misconstruction is the key to the false or one-sided conceptions of Christianity and our halting realization of it."[41]

A year later he wrote his most important Brotherhood tract, which set forth his conception of the kingdom as a five-dimensional spiritual reality. Rauschenbusch was not always careful to affirm that the kingdom of Christ is more than the building of God's cooperative commonwealth on earth, but in the pamphlet that proposed to set the matter straight, he was very careful. The most common concept of the kingdom of God was the kingdom of heaven, he observed. Christians commonly thought of the kingdom as the heavenly hope of life after death. A smaller group in Christian history, Christians of a mystical mind, were inclined to conceive the kingdom in terms of the inner life of the Spirit. Their favorite scripture passage was Luke 17:21: "The kingdom of God is within you." A third group of Christians, often priestly, sometimes possessing ecclesiastical power, employed the words "kingdom" and "church" interchangeably. To the ecclesiastical mind, Rauschenbusch explained, the kingdom is coterminous with the church, because the church encompasses the totality of divine action in the world. A fourth group in Christian history, newly aroused in the nineteenth century, identified the kingdom with the second coming of Christ. Those who restricted the kingdom to this meaning tended to be premillennialists, he noted; they reduced the hope of Christ's kingdom to the literal millennial reign of Christ that is to be established after his physical return to the earth. The last group, also newly aroused in recent times, was inclined to conceive the kingdom as "kingdom-building" work beyond the existing work of the church. Some were missionaries and social-oriented pastors who called for new fields of Christian action; others reduced the work of the kingdom to social work alone.[42]

Rauschenbusch urged that all these views lay claim to a vital piece of the kingdom idea; the problem was that each of them tended to reduce the kingdom to only one or two of its constitutive elements. The true kingdom of God "stands for the sum of all divine and righteous forces on earth," he contended. "It is a synthesis combining all the conceptions mentioned above."[43] Elsewhere he expressed the upshot more vividly: "It is strange, and yet it seems true, that the leading conception in the teaching of Jesus, at once its historical basis, its logical center, its ethical aim, and its religious impulse, has almost dropped out of the Christian vocabulary." The Christian memory of what it means to pray "Thy kingdom come" had been "so pruned and so tangled up" by secondary meanings that the revolutionary thrust of Christ's petition had been lost. The idea of the kingdom as heaven is a biblical truth, he acknowledged, as is the idea of the kingdom as a reality of the individual spiritual life. Moreover, the idea of the kingdom as the collective body of Christ is "a tremendous truth"—one that Americans typically ignored, "because they understand nothing but individualism."[44]

But none of these ideas makes up Christ's full idea of the kingdom of God, he urged: "When taken as parts of that larger idea, and recognized in their relation to it, they are good and indispensable. When taken as a substitute for it, they work mischief." Rauschenbusch posited two further dimensions of the biblical idea of the kingdom: the apocalyptic aspect of the kingdom hope and the kingdom as an ongoing ethical project. These ideas are counterposed to each other, he explained, and both have to do with the hope of the kingdom as futural expectation in human history. Unlike most liberal theologians, Rauschenbusch gave the premillennialists their due on the former pole. Part of what it means to pray "Thy kingdom come," he allowed, is to faithfully anticipate Christ's second coming. Modernized Christians and non-Christians tended to sneer at the fundamentalist fixation on the second coming of Jesus. While agreeing that premillennialist literalism was often ignorant and reactionary, Rauschenbusch told liberals to stop sneering, for the (later-named) fundamentalists grasped a neglected aspect of the kingdom idea: "They have it in a bizarre form often, but they have it." The kingdom idea includes the idea of the end of history by an apocalyptic divine act. By Rauschenbusch's reading, the champions of the other pole of the kingdom hope were the socialists. Though their struggle for the kingdom of God was often conducted "with God left out," he acknowledged, "yet that fractional part of the idea of the kingdom which they have got casts a halo about their aims, and puts a religious enthusiasm into their propaganda." To Rauschenbusch it was shameful and undisputably a fact that atheistic socialists took the ethical content of biblical prophesy more seriously than the Christian church. The socialists were keepers of the biblical dream that society should be organized for the sake of all its people. Rauschenbusch called the church back to the prophetic vision of social justice and community that modern parlance called "socialist."[45]

In the very years that a rising *Religionsgeschichtliche Schule* in Germany began to challenge the liberal picture of Jesus, Rauschenbusch's early 1890s articles on the meaning of the kingdom defined his core theological outlook and that of his kingdom-claiming comrades. He felt certain of his starting point; by his lights it was the best understanding of the kingdom because of its comprehensive wholeness. The kingdom is not only in heaven but also on earth, he asserted; while it begins in the depths of the human heart, it is not meant to stay there; while the church is an instrument for the advancement of the kingdom, it does not embrace all the forces of the kingdom; though the perfection of the kingdom may be reserved for a future epoch, the kingdom exists and is being developed in the here and now. The project of the Brotherhood and the Christian church was to recover the organic vision of the kingdom that history broke into otherworldly, mystical, ecclesiastical, millennialist, and socialist fragments. Rauschenbusch's shorthand for the kingdom was "the sum of all divine and righteous forces on earth." The sin of the church was to settle for less than the kingdom, he charged. The error of the socialist movement was to struggle for the kingdom without God. While cautioning that certain socialist schemes contained "a real menace to individual liberty," Rauschenbusch proposed to wed the Christian and socialist movements, "bringing them into their just and natural relation to each other, infusing the exalted fervor and power of religion into the social movement, and helping religion to find its ethical outcome in the transformation of social conditions."[46]

GERMAN AMERICA AND THE WIDER KINGDOM

In 1889 Rauschenbusch met Pauline Rother, a Milwaukee schoolteacher, while he attended a German Baptist convention in Milwaukee. They met again the following year, corresponded for two years, and were married in 1893. Rauschenbusch told his seminary classmates, "I have surrendered to our friends, the enemy. I went out West, came, saw, and was conquered. Her name is Pauline."[47] Their marriage became a sustained love affair, mutually supportive, affectionate, and admiring, which produced five children. Pauline Rauschenbusch was devoted to her husband and strongly supportive of his activist calling. She often made home visits with him, and in a variety of personal and practical ways, she helped him cope with his deafness. Rauschenbusch marveled at her love for him; expressions of gratitude and love passed easily between them throughout their marriage. Four years after their wedding Rochester Seminary called again, offering Rauschenbusch a position in the German Department; this time he was ready to become an academic. He reasoned that his deafness would be less of a handicap in the classroom than in the ministry, that Pauline would like Rochester more than New York, and that Rochester Seminary was shedding its rigid conservatism. On the last subject, a liberal tilt in Augustus Strong's recent work was his main source of encouragement.

Rauschenbusch was less than confident that theological progressives were winning the battle for America's seminaries. Though liberals and social gospelers were gaining key appointments at leading seminaries and divinity schools, the liberal march through the schools set off backlash movements in every denomination. The Northern Baptist backlash hit close to home. In 1896 Nathaniel Schmidt was fired from his teaching position at Colgate University's Hamilton Theological Seminary, essentially for using higher criticism in his Scripture scholarship. Rauschenbusch blasted the dismissal of his friend (who soon found higher-prestige employment at Cornell), but he played a careful hand in describing himself. While implying that he was not as liberally inclined as Schmidt, Rauschenbusch defended the religious legitimacy of Schmidt's position. In a letter to Baptist church leaders he wrote: "Even if some of us do not belong to it ourselves, we assert the right of a liberal wing of the Baptist denomination to exist and to contribute its share to our development. We assert that the critical investigation of the Bible is the proper function for a theological professor, if exercised with wisdom and spiritual insight, and without such wisdom and insight the most conservative attitude may be just as deleterious as the most radical." This protest stopped just short of jeopardizing Rauschenbusch's own prospects for a seminary appointment. A year later his appointment at Rochester Seminary was briefly held up by trustee anxieties about his socialism; Rauschenbusch had to assure John D. Rockefeller and a second seminary trustee that his socialism was critical, mild, and gradualist. He won a position in the department that his father had created, but not before taking a dose of humiliation.[48]

To German Baptist leaders he remained, above all, the son of August Rauschenbusch and a gifted advocate of his cause. August Rauschenbusch's German Department was a showcase institution for Rochester Seminary; no American seminary or denomination could boast of a more ambitious attempt to keep alive the ideal of a nonassimilated non-English speaking Protestantism with high academic standards. Most German Baptist leaders had no sympathy for Rauschenbusch's socialism or his liberal theological leanings. By temperament and conviction they—especially the German-Russian immigrants—espoused a religion of otherworldly sectarianism. As long as Rauschenbusch labored in the cause of his father, however, the German Baptists were prepared to tolerate his politics and theology. For them, as for August Rauschenbusch, the cause of German-American Protestantism was consuming. Many German Baptist leaders were not shy in expressing the view that northern European immigrants made the best Americans and Christians and that German immigrants were the best Americans and Christians of all. America's openness to immigrants from southern and eastern Europe made them anxious; vehemently the German Baptist leaders drew the line at admitting non-Europeans. They worried that America's republican democratic experiment would fail if the United States opened itself to people from backward parts of the world.[49]

In his early pastoral career Rauschenbusch took a principled stand against these prejudices. He strongly supported open immigration, denounced racist arguments for immigration restrictions, and told the Baptist Congress that America should be open to all who come to it, "for I believe God made it for all." Two years before he was appointed to Rochester Seminary's German Department faculty, however, he repaired his credentials as a German Baptist leader by writing an ugly fundraising letter for the German Department. "Is the American stock so fertile that it will people this continent alone?" he asked. Not content to make a pitch for German immigrants, Rauschenbusch played to the racial fears of potential German Department donors: "Are the whites of this continent so sure of their possession against the blacks of the South and the seething yellow flocks beyond the Pacific that they need no reinforcement of men of their own blood while yet it is time?"[50]

Two years later he toned down the racism but made essentially the same appeal in another fundraising pamphlet for the German Department. The Germans "are of the same stock as the English, readily assimilated, and a splendid source of strength for America, physically, intellectually, and morally," he boasted. Neither of these fundraising appeals were publicly signed; only insiders knew that it was Rauschenbusch who stooped to racist demagoguery to raise money for the German Department. In 1902, however, Rauschenbusch stood before a commencement assembly at the German Department's fiftieth anniversary celebration and said the same thing. Linking the "princely stock" Teutons to America's Anglo-Saxon forebears, he claimed that the English, Germans, and Americans belonged to a single Teutonic racial stock that created and sustained modern civilization at its best. The civilizational achievements of America's Teutonic race were imperiled by "alien strains" arriving from places like France, Spain, the Slavic lands, Bohemia, Poland, and the Russian Jewish territories, he warned: "Let the Teutons of the old home, the Teutons of the island and the Teutons of the farther continent look each other in the face and stand shoulder to shoulder in whatever mission for the world God has in store for us."[51]

Having championed a generous and enlightened view of immigration in the past, Rauschenbusch surely knew what was wrong with his subsequent tack. His alarm at the declining number of immigrants from Germany reduced him to making prejudiced appeals to promote his group. In addition, he genuinely worried that immigrants from authoritarian cultures posed a threat to America's fragile experiment in democracy. In his usage, "Teutonic" was a cultural signifier more than a literally racial one; it referred to a cultural tradition that was favorable to democratic values and institutions. He meant to promote democratic ends; moreover, on various occasions he lauded the United States for giving all races equality under the law. Under the pressure of his ethnic and prodemocracy concerns, however, he claimed that immigrants from some racial groups were more equal than others, an odious claim that also undermined his own argument for the universality of democratic rights and values. Despite his general inclination to resist the prevalent racism of his culture, he resorted to racist tactics in the service of his ethnic group.

Rauschenbusch's concern to carry on his father's legacy to German-American Baptists absorbed his early academic career. Faced with a declining number of German immigrants and serious questions about the viability of maintaining separate German institutions in the American Baptist church, German Baptist leaders looked to August Rauschenbusch's son for leadership. By patrimony and training he seemed ideally suited for the task. Rauschenbusch was intimately acquainted with the languages and cultures of Germany and the United States, he praised the civilizational virtues of German-Americans, and he accepted the burden of explaining Germany's new expansionist militancy to wary Americans.

The new German imperialism was no more fearful or unwarranted than the old English imperialism that Americans half-admired, he assured. In 1899 he observed that "wherever Germany goes, she finds England there before her. . . . Is it strange or ridiculous that the Continental Teutons, now that they have at last found their organic unity, should seek to do what the insular Teutons have been doing for ages?" His concern to allay American fears about Germany sparked a new personal interest in international politics in the mid-1890s; later this interest was heightened by his country's leap onto the world stage. Rauschenbusch's Thanksgiving Day sermon of 1898 found great national and religious meaning in the Spanish-American War. "It has been a great year in the history of our Nation," he enthused. "This year 1898 will be one of the mountain ranges in the geography of times, a great watershed from which the rivers begin to flow toward new and distant oceans." Like many social gospelers, he praised America's victory as a world-resounding triumph for democracy and progress. The war pitted the cause of Protestantism, America, and freedom against the corrupt authority-religion of Catholic Spain, he pronounced. He hated war, but he gave thanks for this one; he looked forward to the eschatological day of peace, but in the meantime, "I do not rule God out of war." Rauschenbusch never renounced his Protestant chauvinism, but his war-boosting jingoism later embarrassed him greatly.[52]

He gave five years to the German Department. During the school year he taught English and American literature, physiology, physics, civil government, political economy, astronomy, zoology, and a cluster of courses on the New Testament; during vacations he raised money for the German Department on lengthy speaking tours. It was an exhausting regimen that left little time for his wider concerns. Increasingly he resented the demands of carrying on his father's work, especially after his father died in 1899. The German-American community was unhospitable to the social gospel, the demands of maintaining August Rauschenbusch's legacy were withering, and English-speaking America showed no interest in a three-way marriage of "Teutonic" nations. In 1902 Pauline remarked that while Rauschenbusch could certainly get along without the German Department, the German Department could not get along without him. This was an argument for staying put, which Rauschenbusch accepted as such. He wanted deeply not to offend his German Baptist constituency. But a few months later, with the death of his former teacher, Benjamin True, the seminary's English Department position in church history became available. Augustus Strong told Rauschenbusch that it was time for him to serve the wider kingdom of God; Rauschenbusch gratefully agreed. Thus it was as a church historian that he wrote the classic works of the social gospel movement.[53]

As a German Department functionary he was short on time and a favorable audience for advocating the social gospel, though Rauschenbusch managed occasional articles and lectures on his favorite topics. At the turning point of his career he hoped for a sabbatical leave to make himself competent in church history, but the seminary made him wait five years. He had to learn a new field as he taught it and thus found himself squeezed again for time. But Rauschenbusch found a way to make his job preparation serve his social gospel vocation. He felt acutely the historical implausibility of his movement's position. If he and Gladden were right about the kingdom basis of Christianity, why was social Christianity so novel? Why had no one preached the social gospel version of the gospel until very recently?

Rauschenbusch approached his courses and his movement-writing with these questions in mind. He made the unlikely field of church history an ally of the social gospel. He often spoke at civic groups and churches, launched a local chapter of the Brotherhood of the Kingdom, and supported efforts to organize a Federal Council of Churches. He gently counseled his Marlborough-centered friends that the proposed Federal Council might be a worthy successor organization to the Brotherhood of the Kingdom. And he returned to his ambition of writing a big, dangerous book. Though chastened by his failure to turn *Revolutionary Christianity* into a polished work, Rauschenbusch incorporated various parts of his previous writings into a mostly new work on the modern social meaning of the gospel of Jesus. Though he made note of recent scholarly works that played up the apocalyptic aspects of the teaching of Jesus and the early church, he gave no sign of doubting the cornerstone of his position. Jesus and his kingdom was the starting point. The first part of *Christianity and the Social Crisis* described the essential purpose of prophetic biblical religion as the transformation of human society into the kingdom of God; the second part explained why the Christian church has never carried out this mission; the third part urged that it was not too late for the church to follow Jesus. The second part was the key to the book, as Rauschenbusch knew, though he feared that the third part would get him fired. He leaned on Harnack, citing him eight times, for parts of his answer to the book's central question, while maintaining that no one had given a satisfactory answer to it. Rauschenbusch implied, but was too modest to say, "no one until now."[54]

By 1907 *Christianity and the Social Crisis* was ready for publication. Characteristically it was dedicated "to the women who have loved me": his mother, his sisters Frida and Emma, his wife Pauline, and his daughters Winifred and Elizabeth; underneath it was inscribed: "Thy kingdom come! Thy will be done on earth!" Just before the book was published, Rauschenbusch finally took his German sabbatical. Though he excelled as a teacher and was held in great affection by students and colleagues, he feared that his book's blazing socialism would jeopardize his seminary position. This fear had a specific basis, for Strong's flirtation with liberal theology had ended; Strong finished his career by returning to the theological right. In Germany Rauschenbusch met Harnack and *Die Christliche Welt* editor Martin Rade, who introduced him to other Ritschlian social gospelers in their orbit. Rauschenbusch's feeling of kinship with the Ritschlian school deepened significantly as a result of these contacts, though he never quite identified with it. By the time that he returned from his sabbatical, he was too big to be censured or fired at Rochester Seminary. *Christianity and the Social Crisis* electrified a social-turning liberal theology movement and made Rauschenbusch famous.[55]

THE SOCIAL CRISIS AND THE SOCIAL GOSPEL

Revolutionary Christianity had patches of labored writing and clumsy connections, but all was smooth and sparkling in *Christianity and the Social Crisis*. The book enthralled readers with its graceful flow of short, clear sentences, its charming metaphors, and its vigorously paced argument. It was filled with sharp moral judgments, especially against priestly religion and social oppression, but the book showed a tender heart for individuals of all kinds. Rauschenbusch professed that he wrote "with malice toward none and with charity for all." He also wrote to discharge a debt to the humble congregation that he had served for eleven years. "I shared their life as well as I then knew, and used up the early strength of my life in their service," he reflected. "In recent years my work has been turned into other channels, but I have never ceased to feel that I owe help to the plain people who were my friends." His evident good will opened many readers to take him seriously.[56]

His basic argument was that prophetic religion is the "beating heart" of Scripture, that the prophetic spirit "rose from the dead" in Jesus and the early church, and that Christianity is supposed to be a prophetic Christ-following religion of the kingdom. Most religions are priestly and power-worshiping, Rauschenbusch observed. Religion typically seeks to reconcile human beings, through ritual, with the powers of nature or force or wealth. But prophetic biblical religion eschews the worship of power, it condemns the evils of injustice and oppression, and it insists that "ethical conduct is the supreme and sufficient religious act." The prophets insisted that God desires goodness and justice, not sacrifices. They were public figures, interested in public affairs, who sympathized persistently with "the side of the poorer classes." Rauschenbusch noted that the false prophets described in Scripture often were not particularly bad men; they were mouthpieces of "average popular opinion" who drew their inspiration from common patriotism and a desire to get along. The prophets were the ones who dared to speak God's moral and justice-seeking word against the complacency, indifference, and selfishness of the ruling order. They had no concept of a merely personal religion and denounced religious practices that ignored or sacralized injustice. "Those who hold that the flower of religion can be raised only in flower-pots will have to make their reckoning with the prophets of Israel," he remarked. "If any one holds that religion is essentially ritual and sacramental; or that it is purely personal; or that God is on the side of the rich; or that social interest is likely to lead preachers astray; he must prove his case with his eye on the Hebrew prophets, and the burden of proof is with him."[57]

He conceived Jesus as a prophet of the kingdom of God who "realized the life of God in the soul of man and the life of man in the love of God." This liberal formula—"the real secret of his life"—smacked of the modernist self-projections that Albert Schweitzer skewered the year before in *The Quest of the Historical Jesus,* but Rauschenbusch cautioned that Jesus was not a modern figure. Jesus knew "how to live a religious life," and his teaching was fired by the prophetic passion for justice, but he was not a social reformer of the modern type: "Sociology and political economy were just as far outside of his range of thought as organic chemistry or the geography of America." To comprehend the social aims of Jesus, he instructed, we must interpret Jesus in relation to his historical context, in which the most pertinent factors were the subjection of Jews under Roman tyranny and the resulting prevalence of apocalyptic expectations. The popular hope was for a "divine catastrophe" that smashed the power of Rome and raised Israel to new life. This is what the Jews of Jesus' time called the kingdom of God. Rauschenbusch acknowledged that Jesus evoked and drew upon this common understanding of the kingdom. Jesus shared the Jewish revulsion at Roman tyranny, he believed that the coming kingdom was to be God's creation—"it was not to be set up by man-made evolution"—and he believed in a divine consummation at the end of history.[58]

But the crucial factors were the things that he did not share in common with his time. This was Harnack's principle, which Rauschenbusch invoked without mentioning Harnack. The more that Jesus came to believe in the spiritual and moral blessings of God's kingdom and in the power of these blessings to reshape human life, Rauschenbusch argued, "the more would the final act of consummation recede in importance and the present facts and processes grow more concrete and important to his mind." John the Baptist proclaimed that the kingdom was almost here; Jesus announced that it was already here or, at least, that its kernel was already here. This was the essence of his novel and transcendent faith. Those who claimed that Jesus conceived the kingdom as a purely catastrophic-eschatological reality had some scriptural texts on their side, Rauschenbusch allowed, but there are other texts that support a social, comprehensive, and developmental understanding of the kingdom. The parables of Jesus are nearly always polemical in intent, he observed; Jesus told parables to subvert the commonplace worldview of his listeners. In the cases of the synoptic parables of the sower, the tares, the net, the mustard seed, and leaven, Jesus replaced a catastrophic-apocalyptic idea of the kingdom with a developmental, realistic idea. The parables were protests against the worldview of late Jewish apocalypticism, not products of it. Jesus was sociable, made ethics the test of religion, said that the kingdom is already here, and compared the kingdom to the germinating and growing processes of natural life.[59]

Then how were the apocalyptical aspects of the Synoptic Gospels to be explained? What was one to say to American social gospeler Shailer Mathews, who had recently given up the typical liberal reading of Jesus, or to Albert Schweitzer or Johannes Weiss? Rauschenbusch referred several times to Mathews's turning-point work on Jewish messianism, never in direct disagreement. He was prepared to concede a great deal about the worldview of Jesus' Jewish contemporaries and later Christian followers. We know that first-century Judaism was apocalyptical and that the early church was apocalyptical, Rauschenbusch acknowledged; we can even allow that Jesus was strongly influenced by these beliefs. But to Rauschenbusch these were not compelling reasons to smash the ethical and developmental core of Jesus's teaching with an apocalyptic sledgehammer. Weiss and Schweitzer treated Mark 13 as a master text of apocalyptic smashing; Rauschenbusch replied that Mark 13 sounded more like the early church than like Jesus. "We must allow that it is wholly probable that the Church which told and retold the sayings of Jesus insensibly moulded them by its own ideas and hopes," he argued. The Jewish kingdom hope was apocalyptical, Jesus clearly failed to wean his disciples from it, this was the form of the kingdom hope "most congenial to cruder minds," and it fit the needs of the early church in its fervid impatience with the world. Rauschenbusch concluded: "It is thus exceedingly probable that the Church spilled a little of the lurid colors of its own apocalypticism over the loftier conceptions of its Master, and when we read his sayings to-day, we must allow for that and be on the watch against it."[60]

The notion that the gospel has a social meaning had been recovered only recently. Rauschenbusch feared that if the Weiss-Schweitzer reading of Jesus carried the day, or at least the field of theology, the importance of the gospel's moral commands would be forgotten again. He conceded as much as he could without giving up the liberal Jesus. Jesus shared the substance of an apocalyptical expectation with his community, "but by his profounder insight and his loftier faith he elevated and transformed the common hope." Jesus rejected violence of all kinds, including the immanent-apocalyptical violence of God, Rauschenbusch argued: "He postponed the divine catastrophe of judgment to the dim distance and put the emphasis on the growth of the new life that was now going on." Thus did the provincial Jewish hope of the kingdom by divine violence become "a human hope with universal scope," to be carried out by those who build the kingdom of the good.[61]

Rauschenbusch pressed hard on the point that the latter is not what happened. Early Christianity was too pervaded by apocalyptic dreams to conceive the kingdom as a worldly social hope; moreover, early Christianity was too repressed by a dominating external power to think otherwise. Rauschenbusch made no claim that Paul or the apostles had a social conscience. "Paul held no antislavery meetings, and Peter made no protest against the organized grafting in the Roman system of tax-farming," he allowed. "Of course they did not. Even the most ardent Christian socialist of our day would have stepped very softly if he had been in their place." Paul dealt with the slavery issue by telling slaves to do their duty, to disregard the unfairness of slavery, and to hold fast to their equality in Christ; Rauschenbusch commented, "This is sublime, but it is too rare an atmosphere for the mass of men." He played up the sociohistorical gulf between the ancient and modern worlds. Paul lived under a hostile government, he observed; like all Christians of his time he believed that the world is pervaded by demons; and he lived in the hope of an imminent end of the world. By contrast, Americans live in freedom under their own government, don't believe in demons, and know that Pauline Christianity was the beginning of Christianity, not its end: "Yet it still passes as a clinching argument for Christian indifference to social questions that Paul never started a good government campaign."[62]

The cause of the kingdom took a further beating, by his account, after Christianity became thoroughly Hellenistic. Hellenistic Christianity was ascetic, emphasized the dualism of spirit and matter, fixated on salvation as the eternal life of an individual soul, and accommodated a priestly, hierarchical, ecclesiastical notion of the church. All of this was a disaster for the Christian parts of Christianity, Rauschenbusch charged: "As the eternal life came to the front in Christian hope, the kingdom of God receded to the background, and with it went much of the social potency of Christianity. The kingdom of God was a social and collective hope and it was for this earth. The eternal life was an individualistic hope, and it was not for this earth. The kingdom of God involved the social transformation of humanity. The hope of eternal life, as it was then held, was the desire to escape from this world and be done with it. The kingdom was a revolutionary idea; eternal life was an ascetic idea." Rauschenbusch saw some redeeming features in the monastic movement, but not enough. Monasticism heightened the ascetical aspects of Christianity; moreover, the socialist elements retained by monastic leaders and other church fathers were wrong-headed. "They never proposed a communistic production of more wealth, but only called on men to share what wealth they had," he explained. "If all had obeyed them, the productive capital of society would have been turned in for consumption, and society would have eaten its own head off."[63]

Rauschenbusch made no brief against Constantinianism; in its short-term politics the social gospel was a theology of the state. By his rendering, the church's reversal of political fortunes in the fourth century was a potential breakthrough for the kingdom. When the empire was Christianized, he explained, at least the church gave up its anti-Christian superstition that society and the state are pervaded by demons. "But this primitive pessimism was not supplanted by any true conception of this world as the very place in which the kingdom of God was to be built up by making all natural relations normal and holy." Medieval Christianity locked its best people in monasteries and thereby turned the laws of heredity "against the moral progress of the race." It made the church a stand-in for the kingdom and thus besmirched the kingdom with the church's evils. The true kingdom of God is about the moral and spiritual uplifting of humanity, Rauschenbusch exhorted; it can "never be advanced by cruelty and trickery." By his lights the Reformation effected a partial recovery of the gospel faith, but not much of its kingdom ethic. This was the work of modern social Christianity. "We need a combination between the faith of Jesus in the need and the possibility of the kingdom of God, and the modern comprehension of the organic development of human society," he declared. The mission of the social gospel was to complete the regenerative work of the Reformation by recovering the lost kingdom ideal of Jesus.[64]

Christianity and the Social Crisis was short on the socioeconomic specifics of Rauschenbusch's politics, but long on the need for an alternative to capitalist civilization. While paying little attention to the problems and varieties of socialism, it urged the church to fuse an alliance with the socialist movement. In 1901 Rauschenbusch gave a speech to the Rochester Labor Lyceum that distinguished between his own practical, gradualist, Christian Socialism and the various dogmatic socialisms that spurned moral reason. He accepted most of the Marxist critique of capitalism; at the same time he opposed the dogmatic mindset and materialistic philosophy that Marx bequeathed to socialism. His project was to reclaim the Christian, moral, democratic heart of socialism. *Christianity and the Social Crisis* was a bid for a positive example of how Christian Socialists should proceed. It abounded in the language of crisis and collapsing civilizations while acknowledging that the cry of crisis had become a weariness in modern literature: "Every age and every year are fraught with destiny."[65]

Rauschenbusch accented the crisis of his time and country because his country was inclined to regard itself as an exception. Persistently he warned that the crisis of capitalist civilization was not merely a European problem; with a touch of admonition he warned that America was falling behind England and Germany in dealing with it. American capitalism was no less predatory and rapacious than its European variants, and American cities were no less racked by poverty, malnutrition, and disease: "The tenement districts of our great cities are miasmatic swamps of bad air, and just as swamps teem with fungous growths, so the bacilli of tuberculosis multiply on the rotting lungs of the underfed and densely housed multitudes." In England, he noted, the death rates in former slum areas were declining as a result of slum clearance programs and sanitation reforms, but America had no socialist movement to speak of and therefore had no prevention programs. Rauschenbusch's judgment on the difference was withering: "The preventible decimation of the people is social murder."[66]

America's refusal to provide for its working-class laborers and its poor contrasted with Germany, as well, where "socialism" was not a scare-word. Germany was short on democracy, but not short on social decency. "In Germany they have a socialist system of insurance for old age," he observed. Rauschenbusch surmised that this was a chief reason why German immigration to the United States had slowed to a trickle. Why leave a country that provides security for one's old age to live in a country that provides none? "We are not even thinking of such an institution in America," he remarked. "Fear and insecurity weigh upon our people increasingly, and break down their nerves, their mental buoyancy, and their character." He scorched the capitalist system for turning its laborers into expendable hirelings bonded to mass-production machines: "This constant insecurity and fear pervading the entire condition of the working people is like a corrosive chemical that disintegrates their self-respect." There is great dignity and satisfaction in unalienated work, he reflected, but "for an old man after a lifetime of honest work to have nothing, to amount to nothing, to be turned off as useless, and to eat the bread of dependence, is a pitiable humiliation."[67]

What was needed was a politics of the cooperative commonwealth that steered America in the direction of democratic socialism. Rauschenbusch urged that the best way to get it was to improve and inspire the socialist movement by making socialism Christian. "The modern socialist movement is really the first intelligent, concerted, and continuous effort to reshape society in accordance with the laws of social development," he believed. At the same time, modern Christianity was moving in a socialist direction. "The current of modern religion does not run away from the world, but toward it. . . . To us salvation means victory over sin rather than escape from hell." In the social sphere, he argued, to live in sin is to live by the law of predatory competition; to be saved is to live by the law and spirit of cooperation: "Every joint-stock company, trust, or labor union organized, every extension of government interference or government ownership, is a surrender of the competitive principle and a halting step toward cooperation." This gradualistic principle was the linchpin of English Fabian Socialism, though most of the Fabians were nationalizers. They argued that every act of collectivization marked progress toward the "rationalization" of society, which they identified with centralized economic planning. Without referring to the different schools of socialism, Rauschenbusch suffused the Fabian principle with Christian sentiments while leaning politically toward the syndicalist emphasis on decentralized forms of socialization. He shared syndicalist misgivings toward centralized government ownership. Cooperative and decentralized social forms of ownership can work economically, he assured; more importantly, they do not militate against community and personal virtue: "If money dominates, the ideal cannot dominate. If we serve mammon, we cannot serve the Christ."[68]

The crisis of capitalist civilization was an opportunity to recover the lost kingdom ideal of Jesus. If production could be organized on a cooperative basis, if
distribution could be organized by principles of justice, if workers could be
treated as valuable ends and not as dispensable means to a commercial end, if parasitic wealth and predatory commerce could be abolished . . . : Rauschenbusch's
fantasy of "ifs" went on for a half-page. If all these things could be effected in our
time, he dreamed, "then there might be a chance to live such a life of gentleness
and brotherly kindness and tranquillity of heart as Jesus desired for men. It may
be that the cooperative Commonwealth would give us the first chance in history
to live a really Christian life without retiring from the world, and would make
the Sermon on the Mount a philosophy of life feasible for all who care to try."[69]

That was the idealistic dream of the kingdom come, but Rauschenbusch
warned that nothing close to it can be effected by idealism alone. He was sentimental, to be sure, and he admonished trade unionists and socialists against a
merely class-interested politics. The moral vision of the kingdom was always paramount for him. He got as much mileage as he could from moral idealism, and
he tried to make socialism less frightening to middle-class readers. In the closing
pages of his 420-page manifesto he observed that the three institutions closest to
the hearts of ordinary Americans—the home, school, and church—were all
socialistic as forms of organization. Individualism is neither warm nor saving, he
argued; it is the social impulse that redeems life and makes it good. For this reason, "there cannot really be any doubt that the spirit of Christianity has more
affinity for a social system based on solidarity and human fraternity than for one
based on selfishness and mutual antagonism." It followed that "one of the greatest services which Christianity could render to humanity in the throes of the present transition would be to aid those social forces which are making for the
increase of communism."[70]

In 1907 "communism" was interchangeable with "communalism" or socialism, at least in Rauschenbusch's usage. Lacking any anticipation of Bolshevik
totalitarianism, his rhetoric was innocent. But Rauschenbusch was not naive
about the power of middle-class moralism. He did not claim that moral idealism
alone could create a good society. "We must not blink the fact that the idealists
alone have never carried through any great social change," he admonished. "In
vain they dash their fair ideas against the solid granite of human selfishness." The
possessing classes rule by force and cunning and long-standing monopoly power,
he observed: "They control nearly all property. The law is on their side, for they
have made it. They control the machinery of government and can use force under
the form of law." For these reasons, the capitalist and aristocratic classes were
nearly impervious to moral truth. Rauschenbusch counted it a good thing to be
on the side of moral truth, but he warned that being morally right is not enough:
"For a definite historical victory a given truth must depend on the class which
makes that truth its own and fights for it."[71]

His negative example was the German Peasant Revolt of 1525. The Anabaptist peasants struggled in a good cause, he recalled; they were deeply Christian

and their demands were noble and just, but they were crushed in streams of blood. They lacked the organized power to win their rights. Rauschenbusch's verdict placed him on the left edge of his movement: "If there is no such army to fight its cause, the truth will drive individuals to a comparatively fruitless martyrdom and will continue to hover over humanity as a disembodied ideal." The class struggle must be taken seriously on its own terms, he exhorted. Essentially it was a "war of conflicting interests." No ruling class has ever given up its privileges out of altruism and no proletarian class will ever make social gains without fighting for them. Rauschenbusch admonished: "Christian idealists must not make the mistake of trying to hold the working class down to the use of moral suasion only, or be repelled when they hear the brute note of selfishness and anger. The class struggle is bound to be transferred to the field of politics in our country in some form. It would be folly if the working class failed to use the leverage which their political power gives them." A generation later, this is exactly what Reinhold Niebuhr maintained in bidding farewell to an idealistic social gospel movement.[72]

Rauschenbusch ended with a flourish. His trump argument was the necessity of struggling for an ideal that cannot be fully attained. "We shall never have a perfect social life, yet we must seek it with faith," he urged. Human beings will never create a perfect commonwealth, yet they cannot find out how much of the cooperative ideal can be attained without struggling for the whole thing. Those who cynically spurn the struggle for the ideal preempt the possibility of making attainable gains toward it: "At best there is always an approximation to a perfect social order. The kingdom of God is always but coming. But every approximation to it is worth while."[73]

THE SOCIAL GOSPEL ASCENDING

Christianity and the Social Crisis was skillfully fashioned and perfectly timed. It sold fifty thousand copies, going through thirteen printings in five years, and boosted the social Christian movement to new heights of recognition and influence. As a work of social Christianity it stood on the shoulders of such works as Washington Gladden's *Applied Christianity,* Josiah Strong's *Our Country,* George D. Herron's *The Larger Christ,* Shailer Mathews's *The Social Teaching of Jesus,* and Francis G. Peabody's *Jesus Christ and the Social Question,* but as a work of creative political theology it set a new standard.[74] Nothing like its sprawling conflation of historical, theological, and political arguments had been published before. The book's bold arguments inspired social gospel leaders to be more daring in their religious and political claims. To a churchly religious establishment Rauschenbusch warned that "if the Church tries to confine itself to theology and the Bible, and refuses its larger mission to humanity, its theology will gradually become mythology and its Bible a closed book." Institutions like Union Theological Seminary became vanguards of social Christianity in response to this challenge; the book influenced hundreds of seminarians and inspired numerous progressive activists to train for the ministry. Rauschenbusch's advocacy of socialism legitimized the socialist wing of liberal Protestantism and cleared a space for radical socialists to his left, such as George Herron. Though criticized by some, including Chicago sociologist Albion Small, for failing to delineate its brand of socialism, *Christianity and the Social Crisis* gave ballast to the call of a rising Progressivist movement to employ state power as a means to control capitalism and promote equality. Rauschenbusch later reflected that the book's fortuitous timing allowed it to become "an expression of what thousands were feeling." It also emboldened many to imagine new possibilities.[75]

Augustus Strong thought the book overly indulgent toward underdogs—"the underdog sometimes deserves a pounding," he opined—but he quickly perceived the historic dimensions of Rauschenbusch's achievement. *Christianity and the Social Crisis* was an epochal work, he judged; it compared favorably to Henry George's *Progress and Poverty* and was likely to have greater influence. Already beloved at Rochester Seminary, Rauschenbusch became an object of pride to Rochester colleagues, students, and the seminary's president after his book became a national sensation. He returned from his German sabbatical to find himself cast as a major movement leader and religious celebrity. His return occurred in time to assist and applaud the founding of the Federal Council of Churches in December 1908 and the promulgation of the Methodist Social Creed during the same year. Three years later Strong retired from Rochester Seminary after serving as its president and theology chair for forty years; by the following year the seminary moved decidedly in the liberal direction of the heralded Rauschenbusch. When Clarence Barbour was inaugurated as the seminary's president in 1915, the featured speakers were liberal paragons Henry Churchill King and Shailer Mathews, and Rauschenbusch gave the invocation. He marveled at the pace of social change around him while he struggled to meet the demands of his national prominence. Speaking requests poured in from organizations throughout the country. Rauschenbusch gave as many speeches as he could, but rejected more requests than he accepted, and gave fewer speeches in the Rochester area than in the years before he was famous.[76]

The Federal Council of Churches was the fulfillment of a nineteenth-century American Protestant dream. Realizing that the cause of Christianizing the American frontier, and ultimately the world, was beyond the scope of any denomination, nineteenth-century evangelicals founded the American Board of Commissioners for Foreign Missions (1810), the American Bible Society (1816), the American Sunday School Union (1824), and the American Home Missionary Society (1826). New forms of interdenominational cooperation were established in the 1850s and flourished after the Civil War; they included the Young Men's Christian Association and the Young Women's Christian Association (originally called the American Ladies' Christian Association). These organizations, like the World Student Christian Federation (1895), were service-oriented and mostly youth-focused. Along with the still-productive American Home Missionary Society, they cultivated a generation of ecumenically minded social gospelers. In 1908 this generation of Christian missioners culminated a century of interdenominational cooperation by forming the Federal Council of Churches, which represented thirty-three denominations. Its key leaders were ardent social gospelers: Washington Gladden, Josiah Strong, Shailer Mathews, William Adams Brown, Harry F. Ward, Charles Stelzle, Frank Mason North, Graham Taylor, and Walter Rauschenbusch. The early Federal Council functioned, in effect, as a kind of laboratory for social gospel ideas that infiltrated the churches and seminaries. It placed divisive Christian doctrines off-limits and sought to advance common social goals, especially through its Committee on the Church and the Labor Problem. Chaired by Frank Mason North, this committee composed a Social Creed, closely modeled on the Methodist Social Creed of 1908, which the Federal Council of Churches endorsed the same year. The Methodist Social Creed was written by Ward and North, and Rauschenbusch had a hand in drafting its Federal Council of Churches version. It called for "equal rights and complete justice for all men in all stations of life," the abolition of child labor, the right to safe working conditions, special provisions for the safety of female workers, a living wage in every industry, the abatement of poverty, old age insurance, a more equitable distribution of wealth, and other reforms.[77]

Rauschenbusch could see the kingdom coming. Sensitive to the charge that social Christianity reduced Christianity to socialist politics, he looked for ways to show that the social gospel was rooted in personal piety. His prayers were the best evidence of his personal faith. In addition to his personal devotions, Rauschenbusch wrote prayers for worship services, for conferences and Brotherhood retreats, and for his seminary classes. He published several of them in *The American Magazine*, a popular monthly that was newly open to social gospel ideas. In 1910 these prayers and others were published as a book by Pilgrim Press under the title *For God and the People: Prayers of the Social Awakening*. The book revealed to many readers the possibility of real-life, socially engaged prayer; for some it was the reassuring word they needed to become social gospelers. Certainly the author of these affecting prayers could not be totally politicized. Rauschenbusch offered petitionary prayers for a wide variety of occasions, grouped according to subject and time of day. He often gave thanks for the glory and love of God: "O Thou great Father of us all, we rejoice that at last we know thee. All our soul within us is glad because we need no longer cringe before thee as slaves of holy fear, seeking to appease thine anger by sacrifice and self-inflicted pain, but may come like little children, trustful and happy, to the God of love." His evening prayers were especially moving; at the end he wrote: "O Thou who art the light of my soul, I thank Thee for the incomparable joy of listening to Thy voice within, and I know that no word of Thine shall return void, however brokenly uttered."[78]

For God and the People gave Rauschenbusch a singular delight, both in its writing and in the warm-hearted reactions that it received. Josiah Strong enthused that "your volume is filled with the spirit of the Master, and apart from the Scriptures themselves, I have never read anything that so aroused in me the devotional spirit." Rauschenbusch was generous with gift copies, and later convinced his publisher to shorten the book's title to the user-friendly *Prayers of the Social Awakening*. Seeking to give readers additional windows on his personal faith, he published two brief books with Pilgrim Press. *Unto Me* (1912) was addressed to social workers; *Dare We Be Christians?* (1914) addressed its title question in a popular style; neither book attracted much of a readership. From his heavy load of public lecturing, however, Rauschenbusch knew what many readers wanted from him, for he heard the same questions from audiences across the country. In *Christianity and the Social Crisis* he advocated democratic socialism but did not explain what it was; the book ended with an 80-page chapter titled "What to Do" but gave little practical guidance. These were the issues that absorbed his attention in the wake of his unexpected fame. His publisher, Macmillan, wanted a sequel to *Christianity and the Social Crisis*. Rauschenbusch labored anxiously over the sequel, even after he delivered most of it in two prestigious lectureships. His labors produced his sharpest and most impressive work, which he provocatively titled *Christianizing the Social Order*.[79]

CHRISTIANIZING THE AMERICAN ORDER

It was the high tide of American socialism, Christian or otherwise. *Christianizing the Social Order* appeared in November 1912—the same month that Theodore Roosevelt, Woodrow Wilson, and Eugene Debs competed for the votes of progressives in the U.S. presidential election. Incredibly for a socialist, Debs won almost one million of them—nearly six percent of the electorate. Rauschenbusch confessed at the outset that when he published *Christianity and the Social Crisis*, he expected to write no more books on the social question. He had filled his manifesto with everything that he had to say on the subject. So he took a sabbatical in Germany to study Christian history, his professional field. "But meanwhile the social awakening of our nation had set in like an equinoctial gale in March, and when I came home, I found myself caught in the tail of the storm," he recalled. "*Christianity and the Social Crisis* had won popular approval far beyond my boldest hopes, and the friends of the book drew me, in spite of myself, into the public discussion of social questions."[80]

He posed as the reluctant movement leader. Rauschenbusch apologized for burdening the public with another large tome on social Christianity. But then he took it back: "The subject of the book needs no such apology as is implied in the foregoing statements. If there is any bigger or more pressing subject for the mind of a Christian man to handle, I do not know of it." For years he had believed and enthused that the world was getting better. The premillennialists astonished him chiefly because they refused to recognize that the world was improving. *Christianizing the Social Order* was written at the high point of Rauschenbusch's optimism that America could be won for Christ, democracy, and the cooperative commonwealth. He recalled that before 1900 he belonged to a handful of socially concerned ministers who shouted in the wilderness: "It was always a happy surprise when we found a new man who had seen the light. We used to form a kind of flying wedge to support a man who was preparing to attack a ministers' conference with the social Gospel." But now the social gospel was sweeping the ministers' conferences. A third great awakening was occuring in American life, but this one recovered the social spirit and kingdom goal of Jesus.[81]

Christianizing the Social Order reworked familiar Rauschenbusch themes, sometimes with heightened claims. The kingdom of God was not only "the lost social ideal of Christendom," but also "the first and the most essential dogma of the Christian faith." The sixteenth-century Reformation was a revival of Pauline theology, but "the present-day Reformation is a revival of the spirit and aims of Jesus himself." That Jesus retained some of the unfortunate thought forms of his background should be expected, Rauschenbusch counseled. The crucial thing is the spirit and trajectory of Jesus' religion, not the list of dogmas that he retained from his religious inheritance. We should not ask, "What did Jesus think?" The appropriate question is "In what direction were his thoughts working?" Rauschenbusch explained that we follow Jesus by following "the line of his movement," not by pretending to embrace every aspect of his worldview. He brushed off the problem of apocalypticism on this basis: "I know that this charge will pain some devout Christian minds whom I would not willingly hurt, but in the interest of the very hope for which they stand I have to say that the idea of the Kingdom of God must slough off apocalypticism if it is to become the religious property of the modern world." Those who vested their hope in "salvation by catastrophe" needed to historicize the kingdom hope of the early church and update their own. Religiously, they needed to grow up: "They must outgrow the diabolism and demonism with which Judaism was infected in Persia and face the stern facts of racial sin. They must break with the artificial schemes and the determinism of an unhistorical age and use modern resources to understand the way God works out retribution and salvation in human affairs."[82]

Revisiting his theme of the eclipse of the kingdom ideal in Christian history, Rauschenbusch took a longer look at the limitations of the Reformation. "The great battle of the Protestant Reformation did not turn on the establishment of the Kingdom of God on earth, but on the question of how a man could be justified before God and save his soul now and hereafter," he observed. "The theology of the Reformation was not modeled on the teachings of Jesus, in which the Kingdom is central, but on the doctrinal system of Paul. It was a discussion of old Catholic problems from new points of view." Luther and Calvin had little feeling for the kingdom, they didn't like the book of Revelation, and they possessed precious little democratic spirit. The Reformation broke the Catholic church's imprisonment of the kingdom idea, but not for the sake of the kingdom's true meaning. It took modern social idealism and modern historical criticism to recover Jesus and his kingdom, Rauschenbusch declared: "The eclipse of the Kingdom idea was an eclipse of Jesus. We had listened too much to voices talking about him, and not enough to his own voice. Now his own thoughts in their lifelike simplicity and open-air fragrance have become a fresh religious possession, and when we listen to Jesus, we cannot help thinking about the Kingdom of God."[83]

The evangelical and modernist impulses were equally crucial. "For four centuries theology has been simultaneously modernizing itself and working backward toward Christ," Rauschenbusch remarked. The Reformation worked back to Paul; with the aid of historical critical tools, modern theology worked back to Jesus; at the same time modern theology accommodated the master concept of modern thought, evolution. The modern rethinking of the kingdom is rooted in evolutionary theory, he observed. It was evolution that prepared Christians to understand the world as the reign of God toward which all creation is moving: "Translate the evolutionary theories into religious faith, and you have the doctrine of the Kingdom of God." Rauschenbusch's version of this faith was closer to Hegel than to Darwin. Conceiving history as "the sacred workshop of God," he enthused that like modern philosophy at its best, modern theology "realizes spirit behind all reality." History is the unfolding of an immanent divine purpose that works "toward the commonwealth of spiritual liberty and righteousness," he argued. When we cooperate with God in God's expressive revelation in history, we "realize" God: "Religion is insuppressible."[84]

Even at the high tide of the social gospel, *Christianizing the Social Order* was a provocative title. Rauschenbusch appreciated that rhetoric about "Christianizing" society, though long-established in liberal theology, remained unsettling to many. He assured that he had no theocratic hankerings. To speak of Christianizing the social order has nothing to do with putting Christ's name in the U.S. Constitution or otherwise breaching the American wall between church and state, he argued. The social gospelers wanted social and cultural transformation, not a state religion: "Christianizing the social order means bringing it into harmony with the ethical convictions which we identify with Christ."[85]

This did not mean that the moral values of Christ are exclusive to Christianity. For Rauschenbusch it was very important to affirm the opposite. Christianity is historically particular, he reasoned, but the moral values of Christianity are universal. The moral values of Christianity are shared by all people of goodwill, regardless of religious creed or lack of one; these values define the universal content of goodwill. At the same time, he believed, it is appropriate to identify the ethical ideal with Christ, for Christ is its ultimate exemplar. The moral values of freedom, sacrificial love, compassion, justice, humility, fraternity, and equality find their highest expression in the life, teaching, and spirit of Jesus. Rauschenbusch understood that this argument did not absolve him of the appearance of exclusivism. He knew that some Christian and non-Christian allies of the social Christian movement preferred to dispense with specifically Christian claims in favor of an exclusively liberal-Enlightenment rhetoric of moral value. To him this form of exclusivism was more objectionable than the liberal-Christian strategy it sought to replace. Though he acknowledged that his aim of Christianizing society could be described just as accurately as "moralizing" the social order, Rauschenbusch petitioned his allies to accept "Christianizing" rhetoric as legitimate. It is better to use the name of Christ "for the undertaking which he initiated for us" than to avoid speaking of Christ, he argued. The social gospel movement had more to lose than to gain by replacing the name of Christ with common-denominator moral language: "To say that we want to moralize the social order would be both vague and powerless to most men. To say that we want to christianize it is both concrete and compelling."[86]

While holding out for "Christianize" as a trump term, Rauschenbusch used the words "Christianize," "moralize," "humanize," and "democratize" interchangeably. "Christianizing means humanizing in the highest sense," he asserted. *Christianizing the Social Order* maintained that most of America's social order was already Christianized. An unchristian social order makes good people do bad things, he instructed; a Christian social order makes bad people do good things. By his account, American society in 1912 was semi-Christian. America's families, churches, politics, and educational systems were Christian for the most part, but these moral gains were threatened by an economic system that militated against America's democratizing Christian spirit. In a Christianized society, he argued, democracy is the test of legitimate authority. Most Americans took for granted that only democratic social structures and democratic forms of political authority are legitimate. Rauschenbusch gave special attention to the Christianization of American families and churches, which were intimately linked.[87]

In his view, the premodern family and the premodern Christian church were both despotic and exploitative. As an institution the church was reactionary, coercive, and politically cunning; as a moral power it conspired with society in condemning females to subservience. But the democratizing spirit of the modern age has raised the legal status of women nearly to the point of equality with men, Rauschenbusch observed. He looked forward to the next stage of women's progress: "The suffrage will abolish one of the last remnants of patriarchal autocracy by giving woman a direct relation to the political organism of society, instead of allowing man to exercise her political rights for her." Meanwhile the churches were learning that coercion has the same relation to true religion that rape has to love, he argued. Christianized by their loss of temporal authority and unearned wealth, the churches did not welcome their salvation; they had to be converted to the good against their will. By Rauschenbusch's reading, the churches that had less to lose got there first, especially the democratic churches of the Anabaptist, Congregational, and Baptist traditions. He did not claim that any church was fully Christianized as yet; for one thing, even in modern times many churches took reactionary positions on "the public activities and the emancipation of women."[88]

Rauschenbusch was a good enough Victorian to feel substantial inner conflict on the place of women. Though he supported the right of women to equal rights in society, he wanted wives and mothers to stay home and take care of their families. Though he supported the right of women to higher education, it disturbed him greatly that most college-educated women of his generation remained unmarried. Repeatedly he urged his reading and lecture audiences not to erode the (late Victorian) middle-class ideal of family life in the name of individual progress for women. To his thinking, what made the middle-class family ideal was precisely that it allowed women not to work outside the home. Rauschenbusch's tender feelings for the domestic cult of true womanhood inspired some of his most florid passages. "The health of society rests on the welfare of the home," he declared in *Christianity and the Social Crisis.* "What, then, will be the outcome if the unmarried multiply; if homes remain childless; if families are homeless; if girls do not know housework; and if men come to distrust the purity of women?" That was a vision of barbarism to Rauschenbusch. He spurned the "optimists" who treated the entrance of increasing numbers of women into the workforce as a sign of progress. This trend destroyed families and abused women, he insisted: "It is not choice, but grim necessity, that drives woman into new ways of getting bread and clothing." Breaking the link between socialism and the kind of feminism that he dreaded, Rauschenbusch blamed capitalism for the latter development. *Christianizing the Social Order* charged that it was capitalism that emptied the home of its nurturing wives and mothers.[89]

Christian socialism was the wholesome alternative. It lifted women to the level of equality that they deserved, while supporting the mother-nurtured family as the key to a healthy society. This crucial balancing act was a job distinctively suited for Christian socialism, Rauschenbusch believed. Just as modern Christianity needed the socialist passion for justice to fulfill the social ideals of the gospel, the socialist movement needed the spiritual and moral conscience of Christianity to be saved from crude materialism, especially on the subject of family values. Though most social gospelers stopped short of wrapping socialism in the banner of family values, they shared Rauschenbusch's conflicted and qualified support of the women's movement. Like him, they were anxious to be counted as advocates of the rights of women; at the same time they worried that modern feminism was eroding family values. As long as the suffrage movement did not promote cultural barbarism, feminism was a good thing. As long as it cherished Victorian womanhood, the women's movement was a justice-making product of the same progressive movement that increasingly brought American churches into the orbit of the spirit of Jesus.

Rauschenbusch was equally conflicted about the state of America's churches, but his buoyancy about the churches' democratizing trend won out. "The church has become a Christian," he enthused. In the modern age, the church was still hated wherever it suppressed popular movements for freedom and equality—Rauschenbusch knew a number of anticlerical socialists—but it was loved "where it is a cooperative organization, resting on a basis of liberty and equality, held together by good will, and serving the highest ends known to the people." Just as the American family was Christianized by giving up patriarchal privilege and domination, "the Church was Christianized by unlearning despotism and exploitation, and coming under the law of love and service." Similar arguments applied to education and politics. In a predemocratic society, education is the privilege of the few; in a democracy it is the right of all. "Democracy stands for the cooperative idea applied to politics," Rauschenbusch asserted. Though democracy is not quite the same thing as Christianity, he allowed, "in politics democracy is the expression and method of the Christian spirit." By this criterion America was nearly Christianized.[90]

The holdout was the economic system, "the unregenerate section of our social order." Rauschenbusch cautioned that the problem was systemic, not personal. He doubted that capitalists as individuals were less moral than others. The defining evil of capitalism was that it made even good people do bad things. The predatory, antisocial spirit of capitalism is inimical to Christianity, he judged, yet Christian moralists timidly avoided the subject: "We have been neglecting the Doctrine of Sin in our theology." By his account this neglect was an especially Protestant problem. In Catholicism the dominant power was the dogmatic mythology of a priestly class; in Protestantism it was the financial and cultural power of a ruling capitalist class. But the tests of Christian morality apply to the economic sphere no less than to other spheres, Rauschenbusch insisted: "Does it make it fairly easy to do right and hard to do wrong? Does it call men upward or tempt them downward? Does it reward or penalize fraternal action? Does it furnish the material basis for the Reign of God on earth?"[91]

Rauschenbusch answered that capitalism is essentially corrupting. The commodifying spirit of capitalism, which extends to every sector of society, degrades every profession that it touches, he warned, and turns impressionable people into small-minded consumers. It thus threatened to undermine the social gains of recent decades in all other spheres of American society. Anticipating by sixty years Daniel Bell's "cultural contradictions of capitalism" thesis, Rauschenbusch argued that capitalism was "sapping its own foundations" by degrading the cultural capital on which America's economic success depended. "Religious frugality laid the foundations for capitalism and put civilization on its legs financially," he explained. "Now capitalism is disintegrating that virtue in the descendants of the Calvinists and persuading them to buy the baubles that capital may make profit."[92] Rauschenbusch allowed that the learned professions were not as commercialized as the rest of American society, but he warned that the "rising tide of capitalistic profit making" was steadily eroding even this class of exceptions. The law was the most commercialized profession thus far, he judged, which was the same thing as saying it was the most corrupt: "'Commercializing a profession' always means degrading it. Of the learned professions the Law is farthest gone. The most lucrative practice is the service of corporations, and they need the lawyer to protect their interests against the claims of the public." The parts of American society that still support Christian values are the parts that have not been corrupted by American capitalism, Rauschenbusch believed. It was still possible to identify sectors of American life in which democracy was valued, the personal virtues were not assaulted, and the public good was a paramount concern. But wherever it prevailed, the logic of capital effected "a surrender of the human point of view, a relaxing of the sense of duty, and a willingness to betray the public—if it pays."[93]

Rauschenbusch did not believe that the law of profit in capitalist economics was the key problem. Neither did he believe that liberal reformism could tame the capitalist beast. Under the pressure of reformist movements, he allowed, the American state made the beast more tolerable "by pulling a few of the teeth and shortening the tether of greed." But these actions merely turned American capitalism against the Christianized sectors of American society, "invading the regenerate portions of the social order, paralyzing their activities, breaking down the respect for the higher values, desecrating the holy, and invading God's country." Rauschenbusch counseled that this situation could not be remedied by pulling a few more teeth. The fundamental problem was structural: the autocratic power "unrestrained by democratic checks" that capitalism gives to owners and managers. In his view, profit had a sound moral basis to the extent that it represented a fair return on one's useful labor and service. Even the wage system could be justified, he believed, where free land was available, or a certain kind of labor was scarce, or an employer was especially generous. But these situations are not the rule in capitalist America, he warned; the rule was that crowded labor markets and the capitalist control of the instruments of production allowed capitalists to make unearned profits off the exploited labors of the weak. Rauschenbusch called it "a tribute collected by power."[94]

The root problem was that workers have no property rights under capitalism. A modern American worker is a rights-bearing citizen in the political sphere, Rauschenbusch observed, but in the economic sphere the same worker "has only himself." One can give forty years of labor to a factory and still possess no more rights over property than a medieval serf. The property with which industrial workers labor is too expensive for them to own, yet most industrial property is financed by the savings of working people through their banks and insurance companies. "But therewith the money passes out of the control of the owners," he remarked. "What a man deposits today may be used next week to pay Pinkertons who will do things he abominates." It followed for Rauschenbusch that the fundamental challenge of Christian socialism in the social sphere was to democratize the process of investment. "Political democracy without economic democracy is an uncashed promissory note, a pot with the roast, a form without substance," he declared. "But in so far as democracy has become effective, it has quickened everything it has touched." Democracy is needed in the economic sphere for the same reasons that it is needed elsewhere in society. It promotes freedom and equality, legitimates the necessary exercise of authority, and serves as a brake on the will to power of the privileged classes.[95]

Economic democracy is not about the elimination of property rights, Rauschenbusch cautioned; it is about the expansion of property rights under new forms. He took for granted that those who possess economic power inevitably attain political power over the legislative process. Under capitalism, he observed, the capitalist class inevitably writes its own interests into the law; under a fully realized democracy, the nation's property laws would serve the interests of the public as a whole. Rauschenbusch's conception of fully realized economic democracy was a patchwork of themes from various socialist and reformist traditions that did not always fit together. He could be sloppy in failing to distinguish among direct workers' ownership, mixed forms of cooperative ownership, and public ownership of production. He offered no help in delineating among various schools of socialism. Though he opposed centralized collectivism and accepted the necessity of the market in a democratic society, he often claimed that in a socialist society prices would be based entirely on service rendered. Economic democracy runs straight from the farm to the kitchen, he promised: "It means the power to cut all monopoly prices out of business and to base prices solely on service rendered." He thus retained the utopian Marxist vision of a cooperative society while assuming—as Marx did not—that markets cannot be abolished in a free society.[96]

Rauschenbusch's weakness for idealistic rhetoric caused him to exaggerate the extent to which economic democracy could replace economic competition. He thought that economic democracy would ensure the elimination of the middleperson's profits. While he rejected Marx's materialistic determinism and his contempt for liberal democracy, he accepted the Marxist theories of surplus value and the class struggle. He argued that the good parts of Marxism could be saved by extending the democratizing logic of liberal democracy into the economic sphere. For all of his idealistic rhetoric and his unassimilated borrowings from Marx, however, Rauschenbusch wisely urged that the mix of ownership modes in a democracy must always be a matter of contextual judgment. The blueprint dogmatism of the Marxist tradition was alien to him. John Stuart Mill's vision of decentralized socialism fit Rauschenbusch better, as did Mill's claim that the logic of liberal democracy leads to democratic socialism. Mill's *Principles of Political Economy* envisioned workers "collectively owning the capital with which they carry on their operations, and working under managers elected and removable by themselves." *Christianizing the Social Order* embraced this vision of pluralistic democratic socialism, claiming that only socialism could compete with militarism as a unifying social force in American life.[97]

Rauschenbusch tried to be optimistic that Americans were up to it. He knew that liberalism was too weak to compete with the spirit of capitalism or the spirit of nationalistic militarism. He tried to believe that Christianity linked with socialism could overcome America's assiduously cultivated egocentrism. "Capitalism has overdeveloped the selfish instincts in us all and left the capacity of devotion to larger ends shrunken and atrophied," he lamented. He worried that Americans lifted themselves to a sense of common purpose only when they went to war. He worried that the habits of cooperation would be hardest to learn in a culture that celebrated isolation, self-preoccupation, acquisitiveness, and will to power. He worried that reformers would settle for liberalism. "We fritter away precious time by dallying at the half-way house of mere public supervision and control," he protested. "We must come to public ownership some time, and any one whose thinking parts are in order ought to see it by this time."[98]

In 1912, however, Rauschenbusch believed that he was witnessing the beginning of a new epoch in American life. The human race took centuries to consoli-
date the patriarchal family, the village commune, and the modern state, he
recalled. The task of building a cooperative commonwealth would be considerably more daunting, especially in a country that prized its individualism: "But if
any one thinks it is beyond the possibilities of human nature, let him rub his eyes
and look around him." The cultural problem was less daunting if one did not conceive socialism as one specific thing. There are as many kinds of democracy as there
are democratic nations, Rauschenbusch observed. Democratic socialism needed
to be no less pluralistic. Just as he argued for a democratic and morally inclusive
understanding of the social gospel's Christianizing project, he insisted that democracy is inherently inclusive, pluralistic, and nonchauvinist. "I disavow any notion
that all the world henceforth is to be made after one ready-made pattern and
labeled 'Christian,'" he declared. Every civilized nation was, by now, a democracy
of some kind, he reflected, but democracy adapts well to cultural diversity: "There
is unity of movement, and yet endless diversity of life." If democratic socialism
was to get a hearing in the United States, it had to become American.[99]

Rauschenbusch held out the same hope for socialism that he held out for
Christianity: that it would become more truly itself. He was well aware, he told
Harvard social gospeler Francis G. Peabody, that most socialists wanted nothing
to do with Christianity. But if modern Christians could hope for the Christianization of China, why was it ridiculous to hope for the Christianization of a Western political movement that got its inspiration from Christianity? "The Socialists
are hopeless about the social regeneration of the Church," Rauschenbusch
observed. "Yet it has come faster than I dared to hope. At any rate I am not going
to tell the Socialists that I expect them to remain atheists. I shall tell them that
they are now religious in spite of themselves and that an increased approach to
religion is inevitable as they emerge from the age of polemics and dogmatism."[100]

Christianizing the Social Order dispensed with the cautionary words about the
class struggle that ended *Christianity and the Social Crisis*. The social gospel movement was soaring, churches were scrambling to get on the right side of the social
question, and politicians were competing for the mantle of Progressivism.
Rauschenbusch dared to hope that idealism might prevail without a class war
after all. He counseled liberals and progressives to own up to the socialism in their
creed: "Every reformer is charged with socialism, because no constructive reform
is possible without taking a leaf from the book of socialism." He urged that it was
better to wear the label as a badge of honor than to cower from it. He was sensitive to the charge that his long discussions of political economy marked a falling
away from "the high religious ground" that is proper to Christian thought.
Rauschenbusch replied that all 476 pages of *Christianizing the Social Order* were
religious. The book's sole concern was the kingdom of God and its salvation. The
social gospel is primarily a call for a revival of religion and a Christian transformation of society, he pledged: "We do not want less religion; we want more; but
it must be a religion that gets its orientation from the Kingdom of God. To con-

centrate our efforts on personal salvation, as orthodoxy has done, or on soul culture, as liberalism has done, comes close to refined selfishness. All of us who have been trained in egotistic religion need a conversion to Christian Christianity, even if we are bishops or theological professors. Seek ye first the Kingdom of God and God's righteousness, and the salvation of your souls will be added to you."[101]

WORLD WAR I AND THE SOCIAL GOSPEL

The heyday of the social gospel movement lasted about seven years, from 1907 to 1914, the same years in which Rauschenbusch enjoyed his fame. Though he suffered "a sort of compressed anxiety" anticipating the reaction to *Christianizing the Social Order*, for a brief time he tapped the zeitgeist again. The book was widely reviewed and sold well; brimming with idealism, it kept a vow of silence on the aspects of German politics that Rauschenbusch fretted over, while saying many hopeful things about German reform legislation and German socialism. After Germany went to war, Rauschenbusch was among the first to recognize that the animating spirit of his book belonged to a bygone era.[102]

For ten years he worried about Germany's military buildup and the hostile relations between Germany and England. A return visit to Germany in 1910 heightened his foreboding. On various occasions he warned that even civilized nations can be driven to war by appeals to nationalist pride and greed. In January 1914 he cautioned a lecture audience in New York that historic opportunities rarely last for more than a few years. He could feel the passing of the social gospel moment. After Europe plunged into war, Rauschenbusch felt the threat of its carnage very personally. He feared for Westphalian relatives and friends who fought for Germany, and for his widowed sister Frida and her daughters in Germany. From several of them, including Frida, he received pro-German letters that defended the Kaiser's invasion of Belgium and France. Above all, he feared that the United States might intervene in the war and that his three teenage sons would be called to fight.[103]

Rauschenbusch was not an absolute pacifist. In 1898 he celebrated America's victory in the Spanish-American War; on various occasions he praised the Puritan Revolution, which produced "the ablest ruler England has ever had" (Oliver Cromwell); the American Revolutionary War, because it gave birth to American democracy; and the American Civil War, because it abolished slavery. But he insisted that most wars have nothing to do with creating democracy or liberating enslaved masses, and in the years that built up to world war in Europe, his revulsion for war deepened. Most wars are fought for conquest and exploitation, he emphasized. *Christianizing the Social Order* judged that wars are nearly always fueled by private interests; *For God and the People* lamented that "ever the pride of kings and the covetousness of the strong has driven peaceful nations to slaughter." That was his feeling when Europe plunged into war in August 1914. Rauschenbusch's students and colleagues noticed an immediate change in him.

His sparkling optimism and humor vanished as he battled a deep sadness, admitting to *The Congregationalist* that he felt overcome by "profound grief and depression of spirit." As a symbol of mourning he began to wear a piece of black crepe on his lapel. He appealed to American Baptists to aid afflicted Baptists on both sides of the war, and he spoke out against American intervention.[104]

It pained him that American public opinion favored England. Rauschenbusch loved Germany only a little less than he loved the United States. In 1902 he reflected that he was deeply bonded to both nations. "My cradle stood on American soil, but my mother's cradle-song was German as her heart," he told a commencement crowd. "Will you blame me if I love both countries and defend each in turn? The intellectual life of America and Germany cross in my thinking like warp and woof, and what better service can I render my country than by offering that blended life as my contribution to true vision?" The war immediately tested this calling, as anti-German feeling inflamed American society. "I was stunned and overwhelmed by it," Rauschenbusch later recalled. "Was it just and fair?" In October 1914 he countered a flood of anti-German press reports and editorials by calling Americans to be fair to Germany. Germany was no more militaristic than its neighbors and no more imperialist than England, he asserted. Though the Germans committed atrocities in Belgium and France, war always breeds atrocities. There were no stories of English atrocities as yet, he observed, only because no fighting had taken place in Germany. The following year Rauschenbusch protested against America's policy of selling armaments to the Allied powers and called for a government prohibition of all arms shipments.[105]

His plea for fairness and neutrality was greeted with chilling hostility; his opposition to American arms shipments provoked a firestorm of outrage. Most social gospelers shared Rauschenbusch's view that the United States should not send troops to Europe, but it was another matter to oppose Allied arms shipments and claim that Germany was no worse than England. Rauschenbusch's patriotism was maligned by numerous preachers and editorialists, his summer cottage in Ontario was repeatedly vandalized, and many of his friends and followers distanced themselves from him. After one of his lecture invitations was rescinded, a newspaper headlined, "Methodists Do Not Want to Hear Pro-German Divine." Longtime friends refused to attend his services and lectures. Others remained civil toward him, but cool; Rauschenbusch took their discreet silence as a rebuke.[106]

To friends he protested that his antimilitarism was a Christian conviction, not a recent phenomenon, and that he did not favor Germany over the United States: "I have been a Christian supporter of the peace idea for some years. During the Spanish-American War I took the average attitude and voiced it effectively. But shortly afterward the peace movement got a strong grip on me." It grieved him to read that he was motivated by a "disloyal preference" for Germany: "I have always expressed strongly my preference for America."[107] As America's involvement in the war grew deeper and the charges of disloyalty rang in his ears, Rauschenbusch withdrew from the public debate over the war. He agonized over the militarization of his country and church. "It was hard enough to combine

Christianity and capitalistic business," he remarked. "Now we are asked to combine Christianity and war." He told a friend that the spirits of Martin Luther and Oliver Cromwell were alien to him; they despised the lower classes and "cheerfully" supported mass killing, but he could not combine Christianity and war without losing his faith: "Don't ask me to combine religion and the war spirit. I don't want to lose my religion; it's all I've got."[108]

Brown University president W. A. P. Faunce was among the friends who pressed Rauschenbusch to justify his position and his withdrawal from public debate. Rauschenbusch told him that the spirit of Christ is incompatible with militarism and that the "bitterly anti-German" mood of America compelled him to suffer in silence: "I was not only sure to anger friends and colleagues and interfere with my work and happiness, but was sure to injure any cause I talked for." There was a further reason that he quietly opposed the war, he confided: "My sense of honor recoiled from putting my knife into the land of my father, where my father and mother are buried, at a time when all men are down on it." He could not join Americans in hoping that Germany would become the prey of Russia and England, he added; moreover, "I am still a socialist, and see the real causes of war in the exploiting classes and nations. I am still a Christian, and in the midst of war have written an exposition of the social principles of Jesus, in which few Christians believe. I am more than ever a pacifist."[109]

To Washington Gladden he warned that an idealistic victory was the greatest illusion of all. The Allied powers were deceiving themselves and others about why they were fighting: "Their entire scheme of morality is based on the premise of a successful democratic termination. But under the table they will be making very different deals." To Episcopal social gospeler Algerman Crapsey he admitted, "I am glad I shall not live forever. I am afraid of those who want to drag our country in to satisfy their partisan hate, or because they think universal peace will result from the victory of the allies." In 1916 he joined the newly founded pacifist Fellowship of Reconciliation, telling Sharpe that he was delighted to find people more radical than himself.[110]

His last two books fought off his deepening sorrow and depression. In 1914 Rauschenbusch cut back on his grueling lecture schedule, which had kept him from writing major works that he had in mind, especially a book on social salvation. In 1915 he turned to a project requested by the Sunday School Council of Evangelical Denominations: a fourth-year textbook on the social teaching of Jesus, to be published in the Sunday School Council series, "College Voluntary Study Courses." Rauschenbusch was eager to reach young people with his version of the gospel message. His brief social gospel primer, *The Social Principles of Jesus,* was published in 1916 and sold more than 27,000 copies in its first two years. In it Rauschenbusch summarized the teachings of Jesus on poverty, property, compassion, violence, justice, and the kingdom of God, declaring that the kingdom "is a real thing, now in operation." The kingdom is within us and among us, he assured: "It overlaps and interpenetrates all existing organizations, raising them to a higher level when they are good, resisting them when they are

evil, quietly revolutionizing the old social order and changing it into the new."
At times the kingdom suffers terrible reversals, he allowed—"we are in the midst
of one now." But God has sufficient power to wring victory out of the wrecks of
defeat: "The Kingdom of God is always coming; you can never lay your hand on
it and say, 'It is here.' But such fragmentary realizations of it as we have, alone
make life worth living."[111]

That was also the tone of his final work, *A Theology for the Social Gospel,* published in 1917. From certain appearances, the social gospel movement was still
doing very well. Many Protestant leaders were enthused by America's wartime
solidarity and sense of moral purpose; they believed that America entered the war
for idealistic reasons. Having finally joined the Allies in their struggle against
German tyranny, America was making the world safe for democracy. One of their
own, Woodrow Wilson, was leading America's venture in democratic globalism.
To social gospel leaders such as William Adams Brown, Henry Churchill King,
Shailer Mathews, Lyman Abbott, and many others, Wilson's military intervention was an example of social gospel idealism. Rauschenbusch countered that it
was nothing of the kind. To him the real social gospel movement was paralyzed
and dispirited, if not disintegrating. It survived only on the hope that genuine
social Christianity could be revived after the war was over. *A Theology for the
Social Gospel* gave voice to this rather desperate hope: "The Great War has
dwarfed and submerged all other issues, including our social problems," he wrote.
"But in fact the war is the most acute and tremendous social problem of all."[112]

He called for a larger social gospel vision that dealt with international issues.
"Before the War the social gospel dealt with social classes; to-day it is being translated into international terms," Rauschenbusch observed. The social gospel that
was needed would address not only national inequality, injustice, and immorality but also nationalism, militarism, imperialism, and global interdependence.
The war caused many people to dispense with Christianity altogether, Rauschenbusch allowed, but in due time the social gospel would be internationalized by
those "whose Christianity has not been ditched by the catastrophe." In his view
the war was caused by the same greed and arrogance that created unjust conditions within modern nations: "The social problem and the war problem are fundamentally one problem, and the social gospel faces both. After the War the social
gospel will 'come back' with pent-up energy and clearer knowledge."[113]

Rauschenbusch struggled to believe this assurance, claiming that "the era of
prophetic and democratic Christianity has just begun." Since this was not the
moment to Christianize the social order, he proposed to strengthen the social
Christian movement by offering a social gospel theology. The Taylor Lectures at
Yale gave him a forum and a schedule of deadlines to pursue this project. *A Theology for the Social Gospel* reworked familiar Rauschenbuschian themes on the
teaching of Jesus, the primacy of the kingdom, and the eclipse of the kingdom
ideal in Christian history: "We shall not get away again from the central proposition of Harnack's History of Dogma, that the development of Catholic dogma
was the process of the Hellenization of Christianity; in other words, that alien

influences streamed into the religion of Jesus Christ and created a theology which he never taught nor intended." The social gospel movement is new, Rauschenbusch allowed, but the social gospel is not new at all. It is "the oldest gospel of all," neither alien nor novel. Christianity will perish if the church tries to restore the old theology, he warned; but if the church holds fast to the gospel of Jesus in the idioms of modern thought, the future can still belong to Christ and his kingdom ideal.[114]

What was new and significant in his last work was its emphasis on sin, especially his neo-Ritschlian concept of the "kingdom of evil." Rauschenbusch wearied of reviewers who found his writings weak on sin, though the worst on this theme was yet to come. He granted that some social gospelers deserved to be criticized on this count. The social gospel emphasis on social environment has a tendency to unload personal responsibility for sin, he allowed, "and human nature is quick to seize the chance." On the other hand, traditional orthodoxy did the same thing with its doctrines of original sin and the divine decrees. The old theology prattled endlessly about sin, Rauschenbusch observed, but it placed responsibility for sin on Adam, the devil, and predestination. More importantly, the old orthodoxy obsessed over small legalisms pertaining to personal habits while it ignored massive social evils that oppressed millions of victims. *Christianity and the Social Crisis* observed that very few Christians perceived the evil of holding land idle for speculation in cities in which people choked to death for lack of decent air to breath. *A Theology for the Social Gospel* put the point more sharply. In Christian nations for century upon century, the great majorities of peasants and workers suffered the ravages of exploitation, war, and repression, "sucked dry by the parasitic classes of society," Rauschenbusch recalled: "Yet what traces are there in traditional theology that the minds of old-line theologians were awake to these magnificent manifestations of the wickedness of the human heart?" *A Theology for the Social Gospel* proposed to show what it meant to take evil seriously.[115]

"It would be unfair to blame theology for the fact that our race is still submerged under despotic government, under war and militarism, under landlordism, and under predatory industry and finance," Rauschenbusch allowed. "But we can justly blame it for the fact that the Christian Church even now has hardly any realization that these things are large-scale sins." As the keeper of Christ's kingdom ideal, the social gospel recovered the moral idealism of Christianity; at the same time, for the same reason, it was also the church's accusing conscience. It conceived the essence of sin as selfishness, but with crucial differences from orthodoxy. Jesus never mentioned the sin of Adam, but he repeatedly denounced the active sources of sin in his own time. The old orthodoxy was right to assert the biological transmission of evil on the basis of the solidarity of the human race—Rauschenbusch believed in original sin—but it erred in fixing on all human beings a uniform corruption: "If our will is so completely depraved, where do we get the freedom on which alone responsibility can be based? If a child is by nature set on evil, hostile to God, and a child of the devil, what is the use of education?" Because it pressed an unreal doctrine of uniform corruption, the old orthodoxy overlooked the fact that sin is also transmitted through social tradition and institutions. Rauschenbusch exhorted that the latter channel is at least as important as original sin and is more amenable to moral correction: "Original sin deals with dumb forces of nature; social tradition is ethical and may be affected by conscious social action."[116]

He appealed to Schleiermacher and Ritschl as kindred theorists of the solidaristic character of sin; they emphasized the centrality of the religious consciousness of solidarity, he observed. On this ground they argued that sin has a hereditary racial unity. Ritschl's correlation of a solidaristic conception of sin with a sociohistorical doctrine of salvation was the basis of his theological system. Rauschenbusch embraced Schleiermacher's principle that sin is something wholly common, "in each the work of all and in all the work of each."[117] With Schleiermacher and Ritschl, he argued, the social gospel must recognize the supernatural power of evil and the social reality of original sin. Human beings are bonded to each other in their bondage to sin, but this bondage is not uniform essential depravity. Some people are more sinful than others; some traditions bear greater moral guilt than others. By exaggerating the biological transmission of evil as uniform depravity, traditional Christianity overlooked the equally destructive means by which evil is transmitted through social tradition. Rauschenbusch admonished that this failing has reactionary consequences, because it undercuts the theological basis of moral efforts to resist the spread of evil. It is through socialization, not through heredity, that such evils as drug addiction, social cruelty, perversity, racism, and ethnic feuds are transmitted from one generation to the next: "When negroes are hunted from a Northern city like beasts, or when a Southern city degrades the whole nation by turning the savage inhumanity of a mob into a public festivity, we are continuing to sin because our fathers created the conditions of sin by the African slave trade and by the unearned wealth they gathered from slave labour for generations."[118]

He called the sum of these evils the kingdom of evil. The concept of a kingdom of evil is very old, Rauschenbusch reflected, but he meant something a bit different in retrieving the name. Ancient and medieval Christianity believed in demons. The "kingdom of evil" for traditional Christianity was a kingdom of evil spirits headed by Satan. But modern people do not believe in demons, he noted, and Satan has become nearly as unreal: "A vital belief in demon powers is not forthcoming in modern life." Rauschenbusch was fully modern on this count; he felt no nostalgia for devil mythology. His conception of the kingdom of evil was social and historical. What disturbed him was the prospect of a modern Christianity that also didn't believe in the reality of evil or that conceived evil only as "disjointed" events. He countered that evil is real, powerful, organic, and solidaristic in modern life. All people are bound together in the condition of bearing the yoke of evil and suffering, but only the social gospel makes sense of this fact: "The social gospel is the only influence which can renew the idea of the Kingdom of Evil in modern minds, because it alone has an adequate sense of solidarity and a sufficient grasp of the historical and social realities of sin. In this modern form the conception would offer religious values similar to those of the old idea, but would not make such drafts on our credulity, and would not invite such unchristian superstitions and phantasms of fear."[119]

A Theology for the Social Gospel urged that it was not enough to democratize politics, the church, or even economics; modern Christianity needed to complete the task of democratizing God. The kingdom of God is a democratizing historical force, not merely an ideal, Rauschenbusch asserted: "It is a vital and organizing energy now at work in humanity." If the kingdom of God is thoroughly democratizing in its ethical and spiritual character, he reasoned, so must be the God of the kingdom. God is the loving Creator whose nature we share, not the feudal monarch of classical theology: "The worst form of leaving the naked unclothed, the hungry unfed, and the prisoners uncomforted, is to leave men under a despotic conception of God and the universe." The saving work of humanizing God began with Jesus: "When he took God by the hand and called him 'our Father,' he democratized the conception of God. He disconnected the idea from the coercive and predatory State, and transferred it to the realm of family life, the chief social embodiment of solidarity and love." In this way, Rauschenbusch claimed, Jesus did not save humanity only; by humanizing the character and representation of God, "he saved God." Jesus made it possible for faithful people to actually love God.[120]

For centuries the church was not ready for a saved God, for the church nearly always reflects the values of its culture. Rauschenbusch believed that in the age of democracy, however, the church had an opportunity to reclaim the God of Jesus: "It is not enough for theology to eliminate this or that autocratic trait. Its God must join the social movement. The real God has been in it long ago." The old religion of authority was based on the idea of God as a fearsome monarch, but democracy and good religion correlate with the religious belief that God "is immanent in humanity." The God of the heavenly monarchy needed vice-regents and popes and kings to manage his kingdom, but the indwelling, democratic God lives and moves in the lives of human beings, acting directly upon them. Rauschenbusch explained: "A God who strives within our striving, who kindles his flame in our intellect, sends the impact of his energy to make our will restless for righteousness, floods our subconscious mind with dreams and longings, and always urges the race on toward a higher combination of freedom and solidarity—that would be a God with whom democratic and religious men could hold converse as their chief fellow-worker, the source of their energies, the ground of their hopes."[121]

FROM TIME INTO ETERNITY:
THE GATE TO GOD

The war shadowed every line of his last book. *A Theology for the Social Gospel* was written during the spring of 1917 while America prepared for war. Rauschenbusch put it more precisely, that America was preparing "to invade another continent for the purpose of overthrowing the German government." He did not deny that the German government was as bad as President Wilson claimed; he denied that Germany was worse than its enemies. Germany was cunning, greedy, bullying, and imperialistic, he agreed, but so was England; for that matter, so were most nations of the past and present. The real enemy of the United States was war, not Germany. For years Rauschenbusch offended American readers by refusing to characterize the German invasion of Belgium as anything more than a terrible "blunder." In his view, Germany's war-launching aggression did not alter Europe's equivalence of evil. After the United States sent troops to Europe, Rochester Seminary and its friends waited anxiously for his public profession of support. Seminary president Clarence Barbour declared his school's absolute loyalty to the American cause, which the seminary displayed by flying two American flags; the second was located outside the German Department.[122]

Rauschenbusch shared the absolute loyalty of his colleagues to the United States, though, unlike them, he did not accept that loyalty required his approval of America's intervention. For more than a year he fended off appeals from personal friends and friends of the seminary to endorse his country's war policy. At the same time he worried that the timing was wrong for his last book. He doubted that *A Theology for the Social Gospel* could get a fair hearing during wartime. He dreaded the prospect of patriotic abuse. Should he hold back on publication until the war was over? As it was, his publisher's urgings prevailed; the book was published in November 1917 and received little attention of any kind. Americans were so absorbed by the war that the social gospel commanded attention only in its war-boosting forms. The book sold poorly and Rauschenbusch took solace in favorable reviews by Chicago theologian Gerald Birney Smith, *Christian Century* editor Charles Clayton Morrison, and his close friend Episcopal pastor James Thomas. The book was dedicated with glowing "reverence and gratitude" to Augustus Hopkins Strong, who privately praised its social conscience while regretting that Rauschenbusch failed to affirm the transcendence and righteousness of God, the deity of Christ, and the authority of Scripture. Strong's hope of an orthodox social Christianity faded; the social gospel belonged to theological liberals like Morrison and Shailer Mathews, just as the fundamentalists claimed.[123]

In his last years a burgeoning fundamentalist movement added to Rauschenbusch's personal misery. William B. Riley, a Baptist cofounder of the World's Christian Fundamentals Association, denounced him as a modernizing liberal; other fundamentalist leaders called him worse things. One reason that Rauschenbusch avoided personal criticism in his writings was that he was easily wounded by criticism or perceived slights. Especially sensitive to attacks on his faith, he told Riley, probably without exaggeration, "When you charge me with 'denying the Lord that bought me' you hurt me just as if you charged me with being false to my wife or cruel to my children." The ascendancy of an organized fundamentalist movement in Rauschenbusch's last years gave him ample heartache, compounding the torment that the war wreaked upon him. The bitter criticism that he received from church conservatives and church war-boosters wounded all five of his children, who later carried on his passion for social justice, but not his love of the church.[124]

In the same month that *A Theology for the Social Gospel* was published, Rauschenbusch began to feel desperately tired. He experienced convulsions, numbness, and other ailments, and he was diagnosed with "pernicious anemia." Rauschenbusch surmised that he was exhausted and violently depressed. He canceled his outside lectures, explaining, "I have overworked," but he kept teaching until March 1918. To Clarence Barbour he reported in February, "I am not getting better." He had no strength, he couldn't type, and his legs were stiff. Sensing that he was dying, he wrote several final statements. One was a set of instructions that expressed his willingness to accept his early death as God's will: "Since 1914 the world is full of hate, and I cannot expect to be happy again in my lifetime."[125]

Another statement, carefully crafted, tried to reconcile Rauchenbusch to his country and take wartime pressure off Rochester Seminary without violating his pacifist conscience. In response to a query from Cornelius Woelfkin, pastor of Fifth Avenue Baptist Church in New York City, Rauschenbusch drafted a public letter that nearly expressed hope for an Allied victory. He described Germany as "the champion of two hateful remnants of the past, autocracy and war," and observed that the "Russian, Austrian and Prussian governments have long been the chief reactionary and anti-democratic forces of European politics." Though he hated war above all, "I heartily hope that out of all this suffering will come the downfall of all autocratic government in the central empires." He warned that if the Central Powers were to win the war, they would "doubtless fasten this philosophy of imperialism and militarism on the world. I should regard this as a terrible calamity to the world, and have always feared a German triumph." From the beginning he had felt that a German victory would be "a terrible calamity to the world."[126]

His position had not really changed, but he had muted his criticism of Germany throughout the war. Had he made his deathbed statement two years earlier, Rauschenbusch might have spared himself much of the hate mail that so deeply wounded him. At the end of his letter he took a further half-step in the direction that friends and colleagues had long pleaded for: He informed Woelfkin that, with his approval, his son Hilmar was serving an American ambulance section near the front in France. "We best realize some things through our children," he remarked. Even Dores Sharpe wasn't sure what that meant. Though the letter said less than Rochester Seminary wanted, Barbour eagerly publicized it. Though he never quite endorsed America's intervention, Rauschenbusch could not die estranged from his friends and country.[127]

In May, Lemuel Call Barnes of the American Baptist Home Mission Society asked for a greeting that he might read to an upcoming conference on personal religion and evangelism. Rauschenbusch wrote to Barnes, "My life would seem an empty shell if my personal religion were left out of it." While recalling that his later life had been "very lonely" from deafness and often tormented by attacks from conservatives, "I have been upheld by the comforts of God. Jesus has been to me the inexhaustible source of fresh impulse, life, and courage."[128] In the same mood, probably during the same weeks that he wrote his prose version to Barnes, Rauschenbusch expressed his mystical core in poetic form:

> In the castle of my soul
> Is a little postern gate,
> Whereat, when I enter,
> I am in the presence of God.
> In a moment, in the turning of a thought,
> I am where God is.
> This is a fact.
>
> This world of ours has length and breadth,
> A superficial and horizontal world.
> When I am with God
> I look deep down and high up.
> And all is changed.
>
> The world of men is made of jangling noises.
> With God it is a great silence.
> But that silence is a melody
> Sweet as the contentment of love,
> Thrilling as a touch of flame.
>
> In this world my days are few
> And full of trouble.
> I strive and have not;
> I seek and find not;
> I ask and learn not.
> Its joys are so fleeting,
> Its pains are so enduring,
> I am in doubt if life be worth living.
>
> When I enter into God,
> All life has a meaning.
> Without asking I know;
> My desires are even now fulfilled,
> My fever is gone
> In the great quiet of God.
> My troubles are but pebbles on the road,
> My joys are like the everlasting hills.
> So it is when I step through the gate of prayer
> From time into eternity.
>
> So it is when my soul steps through the postern gate
> Into the presence of God.
> Big things become small, and small things become great.
> The near becomes far, and the future is near.
> The lowly and despised is shot through with glory,
> And most of human power and greatness

> Seems as full of infernal iniquities
> As a carcass is full of maggots.
> God is the substance of all revolutions;
> When I am in him, I am in the Kingdom of God
> And in the Fatherland of my Soul.[129]

He died of colon cancer on July 25, 1918, during the last months of World War I, at the age of 56. Rauschenbusch experienced profound sorrow and depression in his last years, but his friend Dores Sharpe rightly cautioned against the often-repeated claim that he died with a broken heart. Rauschenbusch had enormous faith and moral courage. Bruised by cold paternal treatment in his youth, he poured himself out in pursuit of his vision of society as a nurturing, cooperative family. For him, the "energy of God realizing itself in human life"—the kingdom of God—was a powerful force in all its senses throughout his adult life. It was also, in its germ, a paternal inheritance. Near the end of his life he recalled that "my father by choice tied up his life with poor and comparatively ignorant people" and that, by personal choice, he had followed his father's path. "I learned to put my message in simple words, and to adjust myself to the viewpoint of extremely conservative people." In later life he wrote books on theology, he reflected, but for the most part they were not written for academics; they were written "for the thousands of ministers and laymen who have spent a good part of their life within the old theology and yet feel the draw of the new."[130]

Though Rauschenbusch despaired that the war destroyed the promise of the social gospel movement, the common scholarly tendency to confine the movement to the period 1885–1918 is mistaken. To be sure, the war put an end to the ambitious movement-buoyancy days of the social gospel. In the year that the war finally ended, the movement lost its greatest leaders, Gladden and Rauschenbusch. Those who championed the social gospel in the 1920s had to function in a comparatively barren cultural environment.

Social gospel leaders such as Shailer Mathews, Charles Macfarland, Kirby Page, Sherwood Eddy, Harry Emerson Fosdick, George Albert Coe, Charles Clayton Morrison, Harry F. Ward, Justin Wroe Nixon, and Francis J. McConnell tried to revive the social gospel in the generation after Gladden and Rauschenbusch. Forced to fight rearguard battles for control of the mainline denominations against a militant fundamentalist backlash, they tried to accentuate the positive. Social Christianity was not merely antifundamentalist, they argued; it stood for good things. It stood for peace, social justice, cooperative relations, healthy families, international order, and the spirit of Jesus. In the seminaries they got a respectful hearing. A peace-oriented version of the social gospel had a strong influence in the liberal Protestant seminaries and divinity schools of the 1920s and early 1930s. It fueled a sprawling network of denominational peace fellowships and social justice ministries, inspired a burgeoning antiwar movement, provided a theological basis for much of the ascending ecumenical movement, and in one way or another influenced the thinking of virtually every prominent liberal theologian of the time.[131]

But Americans in the 1920s were tired of social crusades, both foreign and domestic. They rejected the League of Nations and vowed to "return to normalcy." They accepted female suffrage and rebelled against Prohibition—the passage of which ended the two great social movements of the late nineteenth century. With the partial exception of the ecumenical movement—which was a project of clerics and academics—the only social gospel cause that attracted popular interest was the peace issue. Many mainline Protestants repented of their wartime jingoism. They pledged not to support the war business again. Reduced to this cause, the social gospelers who lived beyond World War I did what they could to redeem Walter Rauschenbusch's vision of a good society. One of the most interesting among them was Episcopal socialist and Wellesley College English professor Vida Scudder.[132]

VIDA SCUDDER: ENGLISH IDEALISM
AS ANGLICAN SOCIALISM

Though closely allied to Rauschenbusch's version of the social gospel and influenced by it, Vida Scudder was shaped more deeply by the Anglican socialist tradition to which he cooled. Though she was throughout her life a female trailblazer who treasured her opportunity to educate women at a prominent women's college, her interest in feminism paled next to her absorbing concerns. Born in India in 1861 (the same year as Rauschenbusch), Vida Scudder was the only child of a Congregational missionary who drowned while she was an infant. Her father's copy of the Bhagavad Gita became a precious inheritance; she studied the book fervently throughout her life. Her given name was Julia, but when her mother returned to her parents' home in Auburndale, Massachusetts, there were already two Aunt Julias in the house. Thus she was called Vida, short for Davida, the feminine form of her father's name. Deeply attached to her mother, Harriet Louisa Dutton Scudder, with whom she lived (college years aside) throughout her mother's subsequent life, Vida Scudder later recalled that her mother's well-to-do family cared more about grammar and pronunciation than about wealth. Vida's love of literature was a family inheritance from both sides. At the age of six, after her grandparents died, she and her mother moved to Rome. This was a formative experience; she later recalled that her four years of exposure to Italian culture "determined what sort of person I should be." She was a person devoted to beauty and the glory of Europe's Catholic past. Though she had no friends in Europe, she never felt lonely there—"I loved being alive." Though she made many friends in her subsequent American life, she always felt lonely in America and yearned for the Catholic culture of the Old World.[133]

Upon returning to the United States in 1871, Scudder took consolation and enjoyment chiefly from an extended family of aunts, uncles, and cousins. Her relatives from both of her family lines were literate, warm-hearted, generally well off, and self-effacing. Their modesty was a bit exasperating to her; Scudder's favorite relative, her Aunt Jeanie, was the only headstrong personality in the bunch. Scudder took her schooling at a private girls' school, spent another year with her mother and Aunt Julia in Europe, studied for two years at the Girls' Latin School of Boston, and then enrolled at Smith College.

Her coming-of-age years had two turning points. The first was her mother's conversion to the Episcopal Church in 1875. Harriet Dutton Scudder and her daughter attended Anglican churches during their years in Europe. Upon returning to Boston and being exposed to the eloquent preaching of Phillips Brooks at Trinity Church, Scudder's mother yielded what remained of her Puritan Congregationalist loyalty. She joined Trinity Church, identified with Brooks's broad-church Anglican theology, and studied the writings of Frederick Denison Maurice. At the same time, one of the aunts closest to Scudder migrated to the Anglo-Catholic wing of the Anglican communion. Scudder was intrigued by her Aunt Eliza Scudder's regime of retreats and Marian devotions and Communion services. It occurred to her that someday she might have to go all the way to Anglo-Catholicism or even to the Catholic Church, but she followed her mother into a broad-church Anglicanism that leaned toward the Anglo-Catholic side. She later recalled that upon immersing her spiritual life in the sacramental piety and practices of the Episcopal Church, she found herself breathing the air that she craved.[134]

She was slow to perceive the good fortune of her schooling. The Girls' Latin School was newly founded when Scudder entered its first class in 1878; two years later, when she began college, Smith College was five years old. Scudder proceeded through both schools in a desultory mood. At the Latin School she was put off by her working-class classmates, who came from the rough streets of Boston's South End and who seemed like little children to her, despite their greater aptitude for Latin and Greek: "Most had come through the Public School system; they were unsophisticated, they had no contact with the society buds with whom my former school life had been cast." In certain respects Smith College was worse yet. Scudder's classmates were closer to her social class and tastes, but Smith was barely more than a finishing school in 1880. At least the Latin School challenged her with machine-like classroom drills; Smith was a vacation from hard work, "pretty dull for a clever girl." Scudder responded by sloughing off. Though she aspired to higher achievements—as an adolescent she fantasized about sneaking into Harvard disguised as a boy—she needed to be challenged. She was too bored to become an autodidact, and she felt plagued by a haunting sense of unreality. Discussions at her family table were more interesting than anything at Smith. "Though I felt less disillusion at Smith than in the Latin School, I was still unconsciously a little intellectual snob," she later recalled. Only later did she reflect on the privileges and fortunate timing that prepared her to become one of the first women to attend Oxford University.[135]

Her second turning point occurred at Oxford. In 1884 Scudder graduated from Smith and in the company of her mother headed for graduate study at Oxford. By then, with the enthusiasm of grateful converts, both Scudders were deeply grounded in their cultured Anglicanism. They identified with Maurice's broad-church sensibility, his sacramentalist incarnationalism, and his liberal atonement theology, while ignoring his socialism. Politics and economics were profane to them; they were devotees of Victorian higher things. Scudder entered Oxford with a strong sense of herself as a person who was religious, but not a conservative. Unlike most theological liberals of her generation, she had no Calvinist or evangelical background to give up. "The gracious teaching of Phillips Brooks, and the thought of F. D. Maurice, so dear to my mother, had saved me," she later recalled. "To this day, some antagonists of traditional faith and super-natural religion seem to me to be fighting windmills." Scudder gave no quarter to biblical literalism, hellfire, demons, substitutionary atonement, or other sta-ples of unenlightened orthodoxy; at the same time, skeptical unbelief seemed pointless and cold to her: "The hard literalism which repelled so many from orthodoxy never touched my mind, even to be refuted; I was, moreover, intensely aware of the sterility of skepticism." In that secure state of mind she enrolled at Oxford along with her friend Clara French. Oxford had only recently extended study privileges to women; Scudder and French were the first American women to take advantage of them.[136]

The first lecturer that she heard, legendary art critic John Ruskin, changed her life. Scudder had read Ruskin's criticism for years; she adored his descriptions of sunsets and Venetian palaces; and owed to Ruskin especially her appreciation of painting, architecture, and what she called the "portals of the temple of beauty." After a distinguished career at Oxford, but before his career should have ended, Ruskin was giving his last lectures. Scudder approached him with a wary eye; something had gone terribly wrong in her hero's life. She later explained that like all her well-bred friends and relatives, she disapproved of the ideological turn that his idealism had taken. Ruskin had forsaken the higher things for political eco-nomics. His recent books blathered about wage rates, modes of production, and similar dismal fare, and he had apparently become some kind of socialist. Scud-der shook her head; Ruskin was wasting his spirit on issues that should have been beneath him. He had become an embarrassment. She did not mention, years later, that he had also begun to lose his mind, that he experienced periods of out-right lunacy in subsequent years, and that he outraged Victorian England in 1884 by using an engraving of a pig to represent the spirit of Protestantism. Ruskin's image of the Catholic spirit was Carpaccio's dreamily beautiful St. Ursula.[137]

But in Ruskin's presence, listening to his lectures, Scudder quickly felt ashamed of her disdain for his socialism. Ruskin's moral intensity, especially his profound and impassioned concern for the poor, made a riveting impression on her. Some of his personal asides were mournful invectives, she later recalled; oth-ers were amusing remarks that softened the invectives; some took the form of searching questions, "gently put to the puzzled and half conscience-stricken audi-ence." Ruskin made her question for the first time whether art or political econ-omy can be wisely considered apart from the commands of righteousness. He pressed for a verdict: "Could art flourish as the monopoly of the privileged? Is it delicate, is it courteous, is it Christian, is it even just, to rejoice in descriptions of nature or contemplation of art, while throngs of those to whom we owe our fine sensibilities and the leisure to enjoy them are shut off from art and nature alike?" A morally healthy nation cares about its poor, Ruskin insisted; that is the basic prerequisite of national moral health. Inspired and chastened at the same time, Scudder had the sensation of being awakened to the real world: "Something within me stirred, responded, awoke." It impressed her greatly that for Ruskin every line of thought was a path of access to the real-life struggles of human beings. With feelings of "eagerness and reverence" she read his attack on laissez-faire capitalism, *Unto This Last;* with conviction of sin she renounced her class snobbery and stopped ignoring the socialism of her favorite theologian, Maurice.[138] An "intolerable stabbing pain" of guilt forced her to realize "for the first time the plethora of privilege in which my lot had been cast." Scudder vowed to give the rest of her life to serving the needs of the poor. She joined the street meetings of the Salvation Army, driven by a "desperate wish to do violence to myself." For the rest of her life she felt acutely the stabbing guilt of her privileges.[139]

"It was at Oxford that I woke up to the realities of modern civilization, and decided that I did not like them," she wrote in her memoir. Lacking any ambition for a doctorate and feeling that she needed a break—"I always needed long spaces of repose and inaction if I were to reap my harvests"—Scudder returned to Boston after one term of study, now as a Ruskinian idealist. For two years she wrote, read, and floundered. Her articles were rejected as immature by magazine editors, her mother was flummoxed by her radical turn, and she worried about lapsing back into dreamland. Scudder's reading concentrated on authors who stoked her social passion, especially Ruskin, Leo Tolstoy, Thomas Carlyle, Matthew Arnold, Percy Shelley, and Thomas More. To keep her social passion alive and real, she needed to belong to something besides her mother's family and church. She needed a vocation and a network of socially concerned organizations. Wellesley College became part of the solution in 1887. While fretting that Wellesley, only twelve years old at the time, was not ready for her politics, Scudder joined its faculty of English literature. She found another home in 1889 by joining the Society of the Companions of the Holy Cross, a justice-oriented spiritual fellowship of Anglican women. The same year, while graduating to Marx and the Fabian Socialists in her reading, she found another formative association by becoming a charter member of W. D. P. Bliss's Society of Christian Socialists. In the company of radical Christian reformers at Bliss's Church of the Carpenter in Boston, Scudder got her first dose of political activism. Her coming-out article for Bliss's periodical, *The Dawn,* was titled "The Socialism of Christ." It argued that meeting the needs of the body is part of the work of saving souls, for bodies and souls are complementary. The following year Scudder exhorted the Society of Christian Socialists that socialism stood for more than a better economic order; the hope of socialism was that a better economic order might allow people to act out of their better nature.[140]

"We are all talking about socialism to-day," she observed. Activists spoke constantly about the methods, abstract principles, and machinery of socialism, "but there is just one thing we do not talk much about, and that is, supposing the socialistic state a fact, supposing we arrive, what sort of men and women shall we be when we get there?" Scudder admonished that the main issue between social-ism and capitalist individualism was vital, not technical. History is made by those who see truly because they see simply, she reasoned; those who perceive a great principle in the confused disorder of life are those who glow with moral passion. Luther, not Erasmus, is remembered as the great hero of the Reformation. This was not an argument for utopianism, however. Scudder judged that the utopias imagined by utopian socialists are always dreary, painfully dull, and lacking in color and moral passion. Edward Bellamy's *Looking Backward* was popular at the time, but Scudder found it dismal in its smug materialism and philistine com-forts: "I confess that the life which *Looking Backward* describes for us does not attract me in the least."[141]

The better socialist ideal is closer to ordinary middle-class life than the dreams of utopians, she believed; it is also closer to the ideal of the Gospels. This ideal is to be liberated from sordid cares, yet also freed from choking riches. Scudder judged that the rich and poor classes alike are never creative or free, because the rich are stifled by overabundance and the poor are starved by material want and oppression. The great reformers always spring from the middle class. It followed for her that good socialism had nothing to do with bureaucratic utopias that cre-ate an "infesting horde of deadbeats." The goal of socialism was "the uplift of the struggle of humanity to a higher plane, the removal of certain external clogs and shackles that bind down to the earth the free spirit of man." Socialism is not about the elimination of private property, she assured; only utopians want to live in that unreal world. Socialism is about the uplift of humanity through collective own-ership of the means of production and the redistribution of material wealth on the basis of need. The great promise of socialism is that literal obedience to the commands of Christ would become possible: "It would enable men to 'take no thought for the morrow,' for it would remove from them the necessity of con-stant thought for what they shall eat, what they shall drink, and wherewithal they shall be clothed." Socialism proposed to set free the creative human soul by deliv-ering human beings from the grubby struggle for survival.[142]

Scudder was a popular teacher almost from the beginning of her career. Her socialist views were often thinly veiled in class, which gave heartburn to Welles-ley administrators. Her organizing was equally provocative. Early in her career she settled into a five-track orbit of teaching, settlement-house work, literary-critical scholarship, political activism, and spiritual practice and reflection. Inde-pendently from Jane Addams and Ellen Starr in Chicago, of whom she learned only belatedly, Scudder was the chief founder and organizer of the College Set-tlements Association, which launched settlement houses in New York City, Philadelphia, and Boston. Under her leadership the first settlement was estab-lished in New York in 1889, two weeks before Addams and Starr opened Hull House in Chicago.

The settlement house pioneers had different ideas about the essential purpose of their movement. Addams emphasized education and community development; Robert Woods and other social scientists conceived the settlements as social science laboratories; Scudder believed that the settlement movement should advocate "a purely spiritual ideal" that approximated the compassionate and sacrificial way of Christ. More emphatically than Addams, she wanted the settlements to be "centers of revelation," not merely centers of social work and self-education; emphatically against the academics, she insisted that the settlement houses needed to be more than social science laboratories for the advancement of social science. By 1892 the college activists constituted one wing of a thriving settlement movement. That year the movement's pioneers met in Plymouth, Massachusetts, to compare notes and respond to criticism.

Scudder resisted the desires of various activists to professionalize the movement; to her mind, its lack of professional standards was a strength. The settlements attracted young women who wanted to live simply, educate themselves, and give aid to people less fortunate than themselves, she observed; these women wanted "not improvement in method but regeneration in life." To Scudder's mind, the settlement workers exemplified the moral ideal of combining social activism and self-sacrifice; they offered a model of righteous living "by the simple process of refusing to receive more than a just share of the world's goods."[143] In later years she allowed that the settlement movement was fueled by the guilt feelings and noblesse oblige of privileged women, and she had mixed feelings about the professionalization of social work, but she defended the movement's early religious idealism and its concern to promote social justice. For many years she gave her voice and time to the settlement cause, writing on behalf of the movement's ideals and spending her vacations in settlement houses.[144]

All her causes were heavily chronicled by virtue of her participation in them; Scudder wrote prolifically about settlements, socialism, spirituality, saints, education, and church affairs, while giving pride of place to literary criticism.[145] Her major works grew out of her courses, which reflected her social commitments. An early reader on Ruskin opined that Ruskin and Tolstoy, in that order, expounded nineteenth-century thought at its best. Ruskin was less extreme and less literal than Tolstoy, she explained; he was more "balanced and broad in his ideals," and his work was both inspiring and practical: "The best results of his life are written in the souls he has awakened to the love of beauty and the vision of the right."[146] That was Scudder's ambition for her own scholarly work. Her major work, *The Life of the Spirit in the Modern English Poets* (1895), portrayed Shelley, Wordsworth, Tennyson, and Browning as precursors of Fabian-style evolutionary socialism. England's greatest modern poets were champions of progress, growth, and development, she argued; Scudder read even the later Wordsworth as an exemplar of the democratic spirit. While allowing that the nineteenth-century poets were shaky as theologians—Coleridge alone was a strong Christian—she noted that the later Victorians were haunted by Christian visions of sin and that some of them were sublime visionaries of immortality, conceived as "the reconciliation of peace with desire, of a perfect development with a spiritual ideal." From Shelley and Wordsworth to Tennyson and Browning, she argued, modern English poetry gradually recovered its faith in a Universal Spirit. At its best this tradition was a pilgrimage from modern pantheism to a new Christianity. Put differently, after long searchings, "the Witness of the Spirit was to the Father and the Son."[147]

The Life of the Spirit in the Modern English Poets featured Scudder's sociopolitical interests in its early chapters, but gave way to a religious argument about the putative trend toward Christian spirituality in late Victorian poetry. The year after its publication she made a bolder move, launching a course on "Social Ideals in English Letters" that unabashedly read her social concerns into the core of her academic discipline. Wellesley administrators shuddered at the course, and Scudder's departmental colleagues were cool to it, but her students embraced it avidly. Very selectively she tracked the history of English literature from the fourteenth to the nineteenth centuries, beginning with William Langland's fourteenth-century vision of Christian socialism. Scudder's book version was published in 1898. *Social Ideals in English Letters* featured More's *Utopia* and Jonathan Swift's satires; this time she gave short shrift to poetry; in her telling the great awakening in English literature began with Carlyle's *Sartor Resartus* and reached its high point in Ruskin's *Unto This Last*.

For centuries English literature was primarily concerned with the individual, she argued, but the tradition of English letters contained a saving thread of social concern that exploded into a field-overtaking movement in the nineteenth century. Charles Dickens and William Thackeray depicted the inequalities between the social classes but made no attempt to account for their structural causes; George Eliot took the survey-narrative approach of Dickens a step further, but only a step. Straining hard to fashion Matthew Arnold as a democratizer, Scudder read the mid-century Victorians Carlyle, Ruskin, and Arnold as pathbreaking advocates of democratizing progress. Even the best of the Victorians were inconsistent in their advocacy of democracy, she allowed, but they were essentially modern and progressive. Their writings were best described as "literature of the Privileged hailing the Underprivileged as masters of the future." In Scudder's telling, the inconsistencies of her heroes merely pointed out the need for a "synthesis of forces" that redeemed the best hopes of Victorian England. She ended with a challenge to her students and readers: "Will that synthesis be the social democracy of the future? Will it be the socialist state?"[148]

Social Ideals in English Letters was Scudder's signature work. In later years she called it her "most original and significant contribution" to English literature. To her mind it was "the permanent link between my social concern and my love of letters." As a course it was also her most controversial venture. Scudder's department refused to list the course the first time that she taught it; later it was banned by the administration for two years. Pedagogically, she realized, she skated on thin ice: "But I know that the ice never broke." Scudder insisted that she was not an ideologue as a teacher. She "recoiled" from propaganda in the classroom, and she disapproved of "a dear radical colleague" who dragged the *Communist Manifesto* into her astronomy lectures. Scudder compensated for her perceived propagandizing by including conservatives on her reading list. She taught them "with special gusto" she claimed, especially Edmund Burke, who provided "valuable pedagogic material." On this ground she judged herself to be innocent of partisan propagandizing. Asked to teach "Social Ideals in English Letters" under the auspices of the sociology department, Scudder refused; she believed that a women's college English department should have room for a socialist take on the canon. "I got into trouble," she later reflected, "but my conscience is clear."[149]

She got into trouble by offending conservative alumnae and parents, instigating a faculty protest against Wellesley's acceptance of "tainted money" from Standard Oil in 1896, and giving a forceful pro-union speech at the Lawrence, Massachusetts, "bread and roses" strike of 1912. Scudder's objection to Rockefeller money nearly ended her career, until she backed down. She was saved from professional martyrdom only by the admonishment of reformer Henry Demarest Lloyd, who was famous for exposing the ruthless tactics of Standard Oil. Lloyd told Scudder that her protests against accepting money from Rockefeller were too personal and self-righteous, and that moral exhibitionism did not build serious social movements.[150] From 1901 to 1904 she experienced a devastating nervous breakdown, largely the result of emotional exhaustion; Scudder's therapy included the cultivation of new personal interests in the lives of Francis of Assisi and Catherine of Siena. In 1912, after her speech at Lawrence ignited another campus uproar against her, she opted for professional martyrdom. For years Scudder had "hated" her salary while rationalizing that earning money was at least more respectable than inheriting it. Her main consolation was that her courses radicalized some of her students. But the fallout from her Lawrence speech was unbearable for her. Scudder's feelings were still deeply wounded from the Standard Oil controversy, and this time she told Wellesley's board of trustees that she was ready to resign. She maintained her innocence of propagandizing in the classroom, while allowing that, in treating the authors who led her to socialism, "I suppose I inevitably interpret them from my own point of view." Wellesley administrators declined to accept her resignation, but they cancelled her course on social idealism in English literature.[151]

Scudder chafed at her limitations and compromises. Writing to Rauschenbusch, she asked him, "Do you speak out to your students? I can't to mine." Bitterly she complained to him that by canceling her best course, the Wellesley administration had suppressed her right to address crucial issues. "I shall make a fight to have it restored next year. It's a good course!" she vowed, not realizing that Walter and Pauline Rauschenbusch had accepted money from John and Laura Rockefeller for years. Scudder wanted to leave Wellesley on moral principle but admitted that the thought of actually doing it gave her "a shivering dread of severance from pleasant ways."[152]

At Lawrence she attended strike meetings, visited striking workers in their homes, and in one speech to a meeting invoked the words of Jesus: "Blessed are they who suffer for justice's sake." She reported that it moved her deeply to see people of different languages and "alien cultures" work together in a common justice-seeking purpose. The Lawrence strike gave Scudder a glimpse of a future "when in America those of differing races shall be indeed of one heart, one mind, one soul." She spoke for thousands, she assured, in declaring that "I would rather never again wear a thread of woolen than know my garments had been woven at cost of such misery as I have seen and known past the shadow of doubt to have existed in this town." The latter words gave particular offense to editorialists, who raged against her for months. Scudder found certainty in her socialist convictions barely in time for this onslaught. For twenty years she waved the red flag while harboring private doubts that socialism was possible and true. By the time that the Lawrence strike made her notorious, she was ready to defend Christian socialism, if not her job. "I fought my way to my little red card through all these difficulties," she told Rauschenbusch. Rauschenbusch never quite joined the Socialist Party, but Scudder got her red card in 1911.[153]

THEORIZING CATHOLIC-STYLE CHRISTIAN SOCIALISM

Earnestly she exhorted Rauschenbusch to get over his personal qualms about the socialist movement's dogmatic anti-Christian elements. "I never regret having joined the Socialist party," she told him in 1912. "I am sure that it is immensely important for people of our type to be *within* the political movement, both in order to preserve it so far as possible from that hard dogmatism of which you speak (& it *can* be preserved if sufficient numbers of persons with religious tradition get into it) *and* to vindicate the honor of Christianity." It was precisely people of their type whom the socialist movement needed if it was to be spared of its spiritually desolate materialism and dogmatism, she believed. Christians like Rauschenbusch and herself could Christianize the socialist movement: "Nothing but party-membership convinces these men that one is in earnest. I covet you for the party!" While discounting her own practical value to the party, Scudder urged Rauschenbusch that his could be immense: "It would draw many, and we could get a political socialism of a better type. After all, the thing has got to get out into the political arena, you know. It can't stay a tendency or a theory." Scudder characterized Rauschenbusch's position as "Get more decent and we'll join you perhaps." Her alternative was "The initiative is ours to make."[154]

With equal fervor she implored Rauschenbusch to give up his anti-Catholic prejudices. "You make me cross, in *Christianity and the Social Crisis,* when you inveigh against priestcraft and the ecclesiastical animus," Scudder declared. "I grant all that to be on the surface very different from the gospels, but I hold it to be implicit in them, and in all sound psychological development of the religious life through history. I know many people who can hardly receive your splendid teaching because your anti-Catholic animus so distresses them."[155] Rauschenbusch's anti-Catholic proof text was Matthew 23:1–39: Jesus railing against the religious hypocrisy of the scribes and Pharisees. Scudder admonished him that

Matthew 23 is not the entire gospel: "There is also John 6. All heresies mean partial emphases, and I hate to have you a heretic. Christianity in all its synthetic glory of the mystical and the social, blended in the sacramental, is none too big for us."[156]

Despite the Vatican's condemnations of socialism and the socialist diatribes against religion, Scudder believed that Catholic socialism was the hope of the world and the worldly hope of the church. What was needed was a transformationist social movement that refused to settle for moral idealism or economistic class analysis alone: "One can read his history either with the economic determinist or with the idealist. I want to read mine with both. This is hard to do just now, but it is not impossible." Just as Thomas Aquinas transformed Christian theology by reinterpreting it along Aristotelian lines, Scudder proposed that modern Christianity needed to be reinterpreted along Marxian lines.[157] This was a project better suited to the Anglican and Roman Catholic churches than to the Protestant churches, she reasoned. Individualism is intrinsic to Protestantism, but the high sacramental churches were holistic and solidaristic. Moreover, the game of identifying the true "essence" of Christianity, though played by others, was a quintessentially liberal Protestant enterprise. Scudder despaired of kernel-and-husk strategies: "Must we not rather find that distinctive strength in the help the religion affords our whole thinking and feeling being to relate itself to the eternal? So the great saints have thought; they ought to know better than we."[158]

Liberal Protestantism was prone to minimize or disregard the doctrine of the Trinity, but Scudder commended Catholic tradition for holding to an implicitly social conception of the divine nature. In light of William James's recent call for a pluralistic philosophy, she reflected that the old doctrine of the Trinity looked increasingly compelling: "Why should not what he means find satisfaction in that Christian thought of the Final Mystery in which not only diverse aspects of One Being, but also centres of consciousness diversely related to the universe even while inter-dependent, are dimly discerned?" To a generation that possessed a growing sense of multiplicity in unity, she believed, the pale deism and unitarianism of the old progressive theologies were thoroughly bankrupt. But a Christian socialism that retained Catholic ways of speaking and spiritual practice had much to say to modern people.[159]

In 1912, the banner year of social gospel socialism, Scudder sought to show that socialism and Christianity are compatible not only in their pink-idealistic forms, but at their cores. *Socialism and Character* bade farewell to "timid platitudes concerning brotherhood and democracy." It called all Christians, socialists, and especially Christian socialists to the hard work of "moral preparation for a New Order." In the same year that Rauschenbusch pronounced that most of America's social order was already democratized, Scudder judged that "our democratic faith seldom penetrates below the surface of our theories or actions." She was unfazed by the objection that full-scale democratic socialism would require a transformation of human nature before it could succeed, for this was exactly what she called for. She was a "class-conscious, revolutionary socialist," she reported, yet she was also the kind of socialist for whom "the spiritual harvest, the fruits of character, are the only result worth noting in any economic order." Ruskin had asked whether it is possible for manufacturers to care about "the manufacture of souls of a good quality" and whether socialism was the system that could effect such a transformation; *Socialism and Character* argued that these were the right questions, and the answer to both was yes.[160]

To Scudder, moral idealism was indispensable, but insufficient. Charles Dickens and Victor Hugo raised the moral consciousness of many, but they believed that "all the world needed to set it right was a lavish application of sentiment." Fired by a similar moral idealism, Carlyle and Ruskin envisioned an organized feudalism with socialistic features, but the democratic revolution left them looking rather quaint. *Socialism and Character* lifted Tolstoy above Ruskin as the greatest figure of the nineteenth century—"the only spiritual leader of our day who can be said to have attained international importance"—but judged that Tolstoy's practical legacy was the same as Ruskin's. It was the prescription of "the simplification of wants and the return to manual labor." Scudder averred that the early Anglican Socialists, Maurice and Charles Kingsley, had a better insight, though only a trickle of a legacy. They perceived that the industrial system had to be structurally transformed, though Maurice and Kingsley were "blundering and bourgeois" in pursuing socialism. Early Christian socialism was no match for the analytical power of Karl Marx, who provided the ideas with which socialists and conservatives of all kinds were forced to grapple.[161]

Scudder took Marx seriously on the class struggle, the labor theory of value, and the need to socialize the means of production; she argued that Marx was right about bourgeois moralism but wrong to deride moral reason as a whole; she sympathized with Marx's reasons for not taking Christian socialism seriously, but argued that a truly revolutionary Christianity was in the making. While identifying with Rauschenbusch's wing of the social gospel movement, Scudder positioned herself to Rauschenbusch's ideological left. Apparently forgetting the last chapter of *Christianity and the Social Crisis,* she claimed that Rauschenbusch held the doctrines of economic determinism and the class struggle "in horror." Though she exaggerated Rauschenbusch's unwillingness to face up to the class struggle and the limitations of moral idealism, Scudder was clearly more hard-edged on these matters than her Baptist comrade. While allowing that the theory of the class struggle was "gravely disturbing" at best and "dangerous and misleading" in its cruder forms, she urged that it had to be taken seriously if economic oppression was to end. Socialism, she argued, is essentially a movement of the downtrodden working class, "and those who adhere to it should recognize that in the designs of Providence the time has come for the class that, though disinherited, yet serves human need in most essential ways, to be the leaders of the whole race toward substantial freedom."[162]

The time had come for the church and all people of good will to join the socialist movement. Socialism had distinctive moral credentials, Scudder believed; it was the first movement in history "to look beyond its own corporate aim." She explained that genuine socialism was unfailingly universalist in its spirit and aims. It struggled even for the good of its enemies: "It is inspired by a passion of good will for all men, and never loses sight of a universal goal." For many critics, this theme raised the question of alien loyalty. *New Republic* editor and liberal nationalist Herbert Croly worried that socialism was hostile to the national principle. Scudder replied that socialists were perfectly capable of being faithful to their nation while holding to a higher loyalty. It is right and good that socialists exalt the good of humanity over their patriotic loyalties, she contended; at the same time, "Patriotism has deep roots, and socialists are men." American nationalism had nothing to fear from a rising Socialist movement.[163]

Scudder ended *Socialism and Character* with a variation on this theme. Like Rauschenbusch, she recognized that the kingdom of God cannot be fully realized in history. The kingdom is to be consummated in eternity, not in time, she affirmed. Christians are called to struggle for a redeemed social order that always lies beyond their horizon. What was interesting to her about this eschatological principle was that the socialist movement had its own version of it. A socialist order cannot be built without extensive government action, she observed, yet the literature of socialism was filled with images of stateless utopias. The deepest political impulse of the socialist imagination is the anarchist dream of a transformed state that votes itself out of existence. Instinctive harmony should control all human relations; when the revolution comes, governments will no longer be needed. "We can hardly evoke the picture without a shrug and a sigh," Scudder remarked. "But the philosophical anarchist can. It is conceivable that he reads to a greater depth than we the ultimate hope in the Mind of Jesus." Christian socialism served several loyalties while holding its kingdom hope above all others.[164]

"I suppose it was a queer book," Scudder later reflected. "I am sure it was premature."[165] Her proposal to unite Marxism and Christianity attracted little interest at the high tide of social gospel optimism. *Socialism and Character* was too hard-edged in its politics and too loaded with literary allusions to win the attention of Rauschenbusch's audience. It found few readers and attained nowhere near the notice gained by *Christianizing the Social Order*. In the decades that followed the outbreak of World War I, however, Scudder reflected and influenced the winding pilgrimage of her movement. Her response to the war was closer to the mainstream of the social gospel movement than Rauschenbusch's, her subsequent turn to pacifism was even more representative of a generational trend, and in the 1930s, though they rarely quoted her, a new generation of Christian thinkers took up her "queer" project of blending Marxism with a modernized orthodox version of Christianity.

Scudder did not share the anguish and shock felt by most liberals when the war began. To her the war was horrifying, but not disillusioning. She was radical enough in her rejection of modern civilization not to feel wounded by its implosion. "I felt the social order in which we moved to be poisoned at the roots, beneath its smooth suave surface," she later explained. "And my sad impatience, which smoldered and burned in the depths of my consciousness, experienced a terrible sensation something like relief, when the great explosion came." At least the conceits of the ruling groups were finally discredited. Scudder kept making the case for Christian socialism, often with barely a passing reference to the war. Steeped as she was in Tolstoy and the Gospels, she thought of herself as some kind of pacifist, but she rejected the absolute pacifism of her closest friends. Moreover, unlike most Americans, she did not swallow the media line against Germany. England and Russia were as selfish and imperialistic as Germany, she believed. Scudder even took a skeptical view of America's early determination not to directly join the fighting. Though she took the typical social gospel line on intervention, she suspected that America's pre-1917 reasons for staying out of the fighting were less than moral. She faulted her pacifist friends for failing to connect the war to the social and economic factors that produce wars, and on one occasion before America entered the war, she made an explicitly nonpacifist appeal for a chastened, "less materialized" postwar socialism. As passionately as she believed in anything, Scudder believed in chivalry. The world is a battlefield, she reasoned, and the weak must be defended against their oppressors. To her, the Bhagavad Gita trumped Tolstoy and the Sermon on the Mount on the spirituality of armed resistance.[166]

Thus she was ready, in her own way, for Wilson's call to arms in 1917. By then Scudder was not really alone in her view of the war—Jane Addams's recently founded Women's International League for Peace and Freedom took essentially the same position, as did most social gospelers—but she felt alone. "I had a desperate and tragic sense of playing a lone hand," she later recalled. "When the time came for my own country to make her decision, I could not regret her choice; so sure was I that she would have held aloof through her meaner rather than her finer motives."[167] She did not kid herself that ordinary Americans had better motives than America's leaders; if anything, she believed, the reverse was the case. As a self-defense addressed to her pacifist friends, she wrote an article for *The Yale Review* that disputed the implicit materialism of pacifist thinking.

Scudder's witnesses were Socrates, Krishna, and Jesus. Socrates assured his friends that he would evade them no matter how they buried his corpse; in the epic poem of the Bhagavad Gita, Krishna admonished the pacifist-turning warrior prince Arguna that he could not really *kill* anyone; Jesus taught that those who kill the body do not hold ultimate power. Scudder observed that pacifists usually appeal to the sacredness of life as a trump against war. In this argument, taking a human life is the supreme wrong because it destroys personality. Wars are fought over ideas, but they kill persons in the process, and persons are more sacred than ideas. Scudder countered: "Now, one may grant the major premise, the supreme sanctity of persons, yet reject the syllogism. For surely that syllogism ignores all larger thought of human development; it throws immortality out of the running." It troubled her that "some very religious people, Quakers and others" commonly appealed to this kind of argument: "It suggests that no one believes any longer in eternal life."[168]

Scudder believed fervently in eternal life and a personal God. It troubled her that liberal Christians often moved quickly from not taking Christian dogma literally to not taking it seriously at all. She regarded her Catholic-style Anglicanism as a brake on this tendency. "Yearly my respect grew for Catholic theology," she later recalled. "I was no literalist; the Latin term for the creed, *Symbolum,* has always been a comfort to me; but the Christian 'Symbol' reflected deeper as well as wider experience than any other of which I was cognizant." Her article "The Doubting Pacifist" called Americans to join the war "confident of the justice of our cause." It was otherwise short on certainties, aside from Scudder's admonition that the war question must never be viewed in isolation from the question of social justice.[169]

Throughout her life she zigged and zagged on the war question. For much of World War I and its generational aftermath, her views on the war question closely resembled those of Charles Clayton Morrison's *Christian Century,* which evolved during the war years from a Disciples of Christ denominational magazine into the flagship magazine of mainline social gospel Protestantism. Morrison was not a strict pacifist—he rated some ideals higher than life—but the *Christian Century* initially opposed the war as having no moral issue worth fighting for and condemned the war as a horrible madness. In 1917 the *Century* reluctantly concluded that intervention had become unavoidable for America and its Christian leader. Wilson had kept America out of the war for as long as Christian conscience could allow, Morrison reasoned. He shared Wilson's hope that the war could be fought to extend democracy and ensure international peace. Like many social gospelers, he was bitterly disappointed when the victors of the war vengefully punished Germany at Versailles. The *Christian Century* cried betrayal after Wilson signed the Treaty of Versailles. It blasted the victors' peace terms as "unjust and vicious." Though he took some hope in Versailles's proposed League of Nations, Morrison worried that the League would be fatally flawed by its connection to the treaty.[170]

A significant shift in the sensibility and chief concerns of the social gospel began. The social gospelers resolved that war was the problem, not merely a symptom of the problem. Most of them gave top priority to the abolition of war; many of them, especially Morrison, gave Prohibition a close second place; most of the latter group otherwise cut back on the socioeconomic content of the social gospel; Scudder followed the postwar pendulum swing toward pacifism, but not at the expense of her socialist convictions. The way the war ended was disillusioning to the social gospelers, and the way that Americans reacted to the end of the war was equally chastening. After the war Americans rejected the League of Nations and resolved to "return to normalcy" by electing Warren G. Harding to the presidency. They lost their tolerance for social crusades of any kind, especially the moralistic and missionary enthusiasms of social gospel Protestantism. Most social gospelers trimmed their sails in response. To the *Christian Century,* it was enough to campaign for the abolition of war and the necessity of Prohibition; everything else political was secondary. Scudder shared the *Christian Century's* view of the war and contributed to the social gospel movement's subsequent privileging of the war issue. At the same time, though her life slowed down in the 1920s, she reminded

social gospelers of their bolder prewar dreams. She resisted her movement's rele-
gation of the of the cause of social justice to secondary status.[171]

Her reasons for slowing down were personal and political, beginning with the
death of her mother in 1920. Scudder later recalled that until the age of thirty
she wanted desperately to fall in love and become married.[172] After no partner
emerged, she grew comfortable in her circle of relatives, close friends, spiritual
associates, and political comrades. With the death of her mother, she felt a deepening need for silence and prayerful solitude. In the spirit of Rauschenbusch she
insisted that personal spirituality and serious social activism should go together;
like Rauschenbusch she also refused to let the social gospel give up on socialism.
But her religious life was grounded in the spiritual practices and texts of the
church's liturgical cycle. Scudder's first postwar book, *Social Teachings of the Christian Year,* reflected on the social meanings of the liturgical seasons. The seasons
from Advent to Trinity focus on doctrine, she allowed, but even in these seasons
the lectionary Gospels and Epistles "are ethical in their very fibre." Moreover,
after Trinity the ethical questions come to the fore. The liturgical cycle places the
apprehension of divine mysteries before socioethical questions, but it is never
short on the latter.[173]

Social Teachings of the Christian Year clung to the optimism of the prewar social
gospel. "A new world-order is surely on the way," Scudder assured. "Democracy
is reaching out from the political to the industrial sphere; the old class-alignments
are doomed to vanish; large types of wealth and large sections of industry are to
be socialized." These words were written in September 1920; Scudder refused to
believe that the war had derailed the West's march toward economic democracy.
The future still belonged to democratic socialism. "This socialized democracy may
be coming sooner than we think," she claimed.[174] But 1920s America was a hard
place to sustain the belief that the social democratic revolution was coming. Gradually Scudder perceived that the cause of democratic socialism was going nowhere
in her country. In response she tried out the language of the faithful remnant,
praising the new peace fellowships and social justice ministries of the mainline
denominations. The Episcopal Church's League of Industrial Democacy was a
notable example. "Here is a fellowship vibrating with the spirit of the religious pioneers of old," she enthused. This "small but valiant organization" sailed against the
selfish spirit of the time, holding out for the cooperative ideals of the radical social
gospel. Scudder reflected elsewhere that the "simple compunction" of faithful remnants is indispensable to progressive movements; every progressive movement
needs the intuitive sense of justice that prophetic minorities stubbornly profess.
"These are fine feelings; the Franciscans knew them," she remarked. At the same
time she worried that prophetic grouplets do not build just societies: "It is doubtful whether such impulses will ever reconcile people to any considerable extent
with leveling movements; compunction and the instinct for sacrifice [have] never
yet affected change on a large scale. They belong to the remnant."[175]

To her mind the 1920s amounted to a colossal waste. "Those ten exhausted
years were the most discouraged I have known," she later reflected. "It was not

easy to watch the surging flood of disillusion which threatened to submerge the idealism and drown the hopes of the world." Neither could she bear to witness the destruction and abandonment of hard-gained political reforms. She thought of herself as a "doggedly loyal" social gospeler of the radical school, though now she was lonely, often dispirited, and withdrawn from active politics. Throughout her adult life Scudder struggled with the tensions between her ascetic medievalist spirituality and her socialist utopianism. By the time that she retired from teaching in 1927, her asceticism was the stronger inner force. Politically she took encouragement only from the Bolshevik revolution in Russia, which she called "the one thrill of hope the world spectacle afforded." In her private oratory she placed a red flag beside the crucifix; at mealtime she prayed, "We have food, others have none; God bless the Revolution!" Scudder's alienation from the modern world heightened her revolutionary feelings while confining her increasingly to her oratory. "Revolutionary music sounded in my ears," she later recalled. "Middle-class or bourgeois initiative ceased for the time being to interest me; I definitely saw the revolt of the proletariat as the spear-head in social change."[176]

Yet she also encouraged and applauded a rising pacifist movement in the churches. In the late 1920s and early 1930s, most of America's mainline Protestant churches pledged with varying degrees of militancy never to endorse another war. The single activist issue on which a reeling social gospel movement found common ground with an isolationist majority culture was the war question. The revolution notwithstanding, Scudder sided with an ascending pacifist current. In 1931 she enthused that the day was fast approaching when conscientious objectors to war would be able to invoke "the support of the whole church of Christ." She did not explain how this enthusiasm squared with her Marxism. "My attitude was confused," she later recalled. "To intensify simultaneously Marxist revolutionary ardor and pacifist conviction was a little difficult. To reject war between nations was all very well, but one would have loved to die on a barricade." Scudder was a pacifist and a Marxian revolutionist for essentially the same reasons: Both commitments were absolutist positions that stood against the prevailing system. Neither impulse had any patience with gradualist political reforms. As forms of moral absolutism they linked together in what she called "a truce in my mind."[177] The reformist politics of the social gospel had failed. A harder-edged religion was needed to replace the sentimental humanism of liberal Christianity. Though confused in her attitude, Scudder was not alone in it. Young Reinhold Niebuhr wrestled with the same conflicting impulses in the early 1930s. Nearly alone among her liberal friends, Scudder appreciated the genius of Niebuhr's liberal-blasting *Moral Man and Immoral Society* of 1932, but she judged that Niebuhr's vision was too Protestant to be saving. She would not follow Niebuhr into dialectical individualism, for she belonged to a more encompassing spiritual home that did not recognize its redemptive capacities.

Her love of the church and its spiritual disciplines saved her from an alienated later life. In the mid-1930s Scudder pondered the fact that she believed in the saving grace of the existing church more than the church believed in it.

"Organized Christianity desperately needs to recognize the social dynamic it possesses simply by virtue of its corporate existence," she remarked in 1934. Niebuhr's field-shaking work made her point, albeit negatively. His writing burned with the same justice-seeking passion as her own, and he shared her impatience with the conceits and illusions of middle-class idealism. He argued that human groups never willingly subordinate their interests to the interest of others. Morality is for individuals, Niebuhr contended; all human groups are sustained by powers of self-interest and collective egotism that are not amenable to moral correction. To a point, Scudder recognized a kindred spirit in Niebuhr's Marxist Christianity, but she recoiled from his lonely religion. *Moral Man and Immoral Society,* "a brilliant work much discussed of late," was "defeatist" in its tone and argument, she contended. The book was earnestly argued "and very Protestant." To her mind, Niebuhr's defeatism was linked to his Protestantism.[178]

Scudder exclaimed, "Never once does Niebuhr allude to a corporate Church as a possible instrument of social redemption!" Like many Protestants, Niebuhr had a merely sociological understanding of the church. While skewering the sentimental social gospel notion that Christianity might defeat the selfish forces that drive human destiny, he treated the church as a typical self-interested organization. Scudder countered that the church thus described is not the church of Christ at all. The existing church often does behave with the same self-regarding will to power as other groups, she allowed, but whenever the church behaves in this way, "she crucifies her Lord." The church of Christ is called to follow the sacrificial way of Christ, not the self-seeking way of the world. "Unless the life within her supersedes both in her individual members and in her corporate action all passions transferred from the natural and secular order, she is no reality at all, she is only a phantom," Scudder asserted. "For what differentiates her from all other groups is precisely this, that she lives to die. Her *raison d'être* is sacrifice, her center is the Cross."[179]

To the extent that an actually Christian church exists in the world, it insinuates a saving presence by the law of its being. And because the Spirit of Christ is the church's energizing force, Scudder argued, the church possesses "a social dynamic strong enough to overcome all other forces and to release love in every human activity." By implication, any lesser conception or representation of the church was sub-Christian. To Scudder, the church described by Niebuhr was a collection of "half-hearted individuals leading a divided existence." But what if the church renounced self-interest and followed the way of Christ? What if the church, actuated by the Spirit of Christ and the law of love, were to exemplify "the potent force of mass movement?" On the occasions that they laid claim to this religious hope, the Protestant social gospelers fell back on their evangelical roots; even liberal Protestants conceived social salvation in terms not far removed from the revival meeting. Personal regeneration leads to social regeneration. Scudder replied that the social gospel needed a stronger dose of Anglo-Catholic ecclesiology. Even in its social gospel and Niebuhrian forms, she observed, modern Protestantism recycled a bootstrap theory of salvation: "The Catholic knows better; and the Church which clings to the awful truth of the Real Presence has a triumphant clarity of social faith which no subjective or individualist type of religion can compass." To Scudder it was no coincidence that the gloomiest modern theologians—Niebuhr and the Barthians—were anti-sacramentalists. If modern Christianity were to raise up a Christian community that took seriously its self-description as the body of Christ, she exhorted, "we might be able to take a less gloomy view of the future."[180]

In that hope Scudder rested and prophesied. She zigged and zagged a bit more on the war question, inching away from pacifism in the later 1930s, then returning to a pacifist position as World War II approached. The rise of fascist movements in Germany and Italy tempered her enthusiasm for centralized government ownership; in later life Scudder called for a decentralized socialism that relied as much on the trade union and cooperativist movements as on state-socialist nationalization strategies. Her pacifist impulse was bound up with her Christian identity, which eventually prevailed over her enthusiasm for class warfare. Scudder agreed with Niebuhr that authentic Christianity is intrinsically paradoxical in its theology and ethical character, but she construed the ethical paradox of the cross very differently from Niebuhr. A few weeks before her country went to war again in 1941, she explained that a Christian "cannot see the Cross as Reinhold Niebuhr does, at the edge of history, a sad estray from eternity into the world of time." Niebuhr's dialectic of the cross did not take the cross seriously as a factor in history, she charged. The cross is either the key to history or, as in Niebuhr's case, something negligible to real-world social issues. To the Christian, Scudder exhorted, the cross of Christ must be "the very centre of history, the source of all abiding progress, the only banner under which Mercy and Truth can meet together, and Righteousness and Peace achieve their miraculous embrace." On that basis she held out for the hope of the radical social gospel.[181]

THE SOCIAL GOSPEL AND THE KINGDOM CULTUS

The social gospel was rarely as radical as its signature proclamations. On the whole, the movement was sentimental and moralistic, just as Reinhold Niebuhr claimed; its various causes were compromised by its middle-class interests and its late-Victorian sensibility; and it overidentified the kingdom of God with democracy. Though Rauschenbusch was a stronger socialist and a more chastened believer in the reality of evil than much of the literature about him claims, he shared his movement's signature faults. Like his movement he spoke the language of triumphalist missionary religion, gave tepid support to the cause of women's suffrage, and indulged in Anglo-Saxonist chauvinism. About America's mistreatment of blacks he had little to say. Four years before his death he explained, "For years, the problem of the two races in the South has seemed to me so tragic, so insoluble, that I have never yet ventured to discuss it in public."[182]

To his understanding and experience racial injustice was overwhelmingly a southern problem. In 1900 nearly 90 percent of American blacks still lived in the

South; in Rochester barely 600 of the city's 162,000 residents were black, and Rauschenbusch had precious little acquaintance with them. To his credit, his frequent use of the word "race" was usually solidaristic, denoting the human race. Moreover, his writings occasionally condemned racial prejudice. *Christianizing the Social Order* asserted that in Jesus "we encounter the spirit that smites race pride and prejudice in the name of humanity; and that refuses to accept even from religion any obligation to hold ourselves apart from our fellows." *Dare We Be Christians?* declared that true Christianity makes no distinction of "religion, race, color or previous condition of servitude" and that it stands "for the solidarity of the race in its weakness and strength, its defects and conquests, its sin and salvation." Rauschenbusch spoke a bit more expansively about racial justice in his last years, but the subject remained marginal to his thinking and vision. Some social gospel leaders were stronger advocates of racial justice—especially through their involvement in the education programs of the American Missionary Society—but on the whole, Rauschenbusch was typical. He and his northern middle-class comrades felt guilty about America's treatment of blacks without doing or even saying much about it. They accepted the 1896 ruling of the Supreme Court in *Plessy v. Ferguson* that "separate but equal" segregation was consistent with the Fourteenth Amendment's guarantee of equal protection under the law. Like Rauschenbusch, many social gospel leaders had too little acquaintance with blacks and too little knowledge of African American history to bring racial justice into the purview of social Christianity.[183]

Scudder said as much in reflecting on her settlement house experiences. In 1890 and 1891 she spent her Christmas vacations at the New York settlement on Rivington Street; in 1892 she spent six weeks at the new Philadelphia house on Christian Street. "I had wanted to escape from my class prison; and I did," she later recalled. More sharply than most social gospelers, Scudder perceived that she would not get very far as an advocate of social change if her class privileges remained unchallenged. Her attempts to share the lives of the poor, however, were chastening to her. She recognized the limitations of the settlement movement's work, especially as it confronted cultural differences of race and class. The Philadelphia settlement, she recalled, "was in a rough negro quarter." It was not long before her perplexity and conflicted feelings drove her to question what it was that she proposed to do for her neighbors: "What we young women had to offer was not quite what was needed there." Neither did her brief experiences of living and working with poor urban blacks make much of a difference in her conception of social Christianity. Though outspoken on many topics, Scudder had little more to say about racial justice than Rauschenbusch.[184]

In crucial respects she did not share the faults commonly attributed to the social gospel movement by generations of Niebuhrians, liberationists, and other academic critics. Scudder never failed to take seriously the reality of the class struggle. She kept her moral idealism on a leash and, with select exceptions, did not tailor Christian teaching to fit the values of modern culture. Her judgments on modern culture were as disapproving as those of Niebuhr and Barth. The postwar social gospel movement would not have done better by adopting her politics, however. For twenty years she flirted with communism, insisting that the Soviet revolution marked a great leap forward for humanity. She embraced a morally absolutist pacifism but also embraced the expansionist aims of the armed Communist movement. She came very late to the realization that Soviet communism was not a Russian version of her socialist hope. The ongoing defeat of that hope in the 1920s and early 1930s made her lonely and extremely frustrated. Her saving grace, which she heartily recommended to the social gospel movement, was her rootage in the spiritual disciplines and piety of Anglican sacramentalism.

In 1933 Charles Clayton Morrison reflected that the basic problem of the social gospel was that it neither possessed nor engendered a comprehensive Christian cultus. On one level the movement was a spectacular success, he observed. Contrary to the feelings of many social gospel leaders, the 1920s were not a wasted decade, for during this period the social gospel became deeply entrenched institutionally in the mainline denominations. Social Christianity in the 1920s spawned a profusion of peace fellowships, social justice agencies, and mission programs. Its theology took over the modern theological curriculum in which a generation of mainline pastors were educated. "The social conception of Christianity commands the sympathy, if not the adherence, of practically the entire Protestant ministry," Morrison noted. "One cannot name a northern Methodist, Baptist, or Presbyterian seminary, or a Congregational or Disciples seminary, in which the Social Gospel is not taken for granted."[185]

The Lutheran seminaries were exceptions, and Morrison allowed that although the picture was more ambiguous among mainline seminaries in the South, even in the southern seminaries social Christianity was the strongest voice. As the editor of liberal Protestantism's flagship magazine, Morrison was well placed to evaluate social Christianity. As an advocate of the social gospel, he believed that the triumph of social Christian thinking in the mainline churches marked an epochal recovery of the original Christian spirit and hope. To him, as for Rauschenbusch and Scudder, the social gospel was a recovery of the spirit of Jesus and thus a rediscovery of the biblical ethic of the kingdom. "When our eyes look at Jesus they do not see the Figure which Origen saw, or Augustine, or Aquinas, or Luther, or Calvin, or Wesley," Morrison wrote. "It is our new acquaintance with him that has revolutionized our gospel and given us the gospel of the Kingdom of God which was the dominant concept and passion of his life."[186]

The social gospel idea of the kingdom was at the same time the oldest idea in Christianity and a fresh discovery. The problem was that this idea preceded and somewhat contradicted the idea of the church. Modern Christianity proposed to do something that had never been done before, Morrison explained. Early Christianity possessed the kingdom ideal without an established church; patristic Christianity obscured the kingdom ideal in the process of building an institutional church; the modern social gospel tried to reclaim the kingdom ideal *within* the established church. The social gospelers proposed to infuse the radical spirit of Christ into a religious institution. They tried to fit the early Christian idea of the kingdom into the existing church cultus. But this cultus—the total theological, ethical, liturgical, and cultural expression of the faith—was not designed to live in the spirit of the kingdom, Morrison argued. The idea that the church is supposed to exist for the sake of the kingdom is distinctly modern. It is not a teaching of Jesus, for Jesus made no place for the church in his teaching. "His words throw no direct light on the relation of an organized Church to the Kingdom of which he spoke so frequently," Morrison observed.[187]

To his perception, this fact explained a great deal about the current problems of the social gospel: "In our time we are trying to restore the concept of the Kingdom to a place in our thought and purpose like that which it occupied in Christ's thought and purpose, and we find that the major problem which we confront arises from the fact that the Christian cultus, fashioned under the influence of a conception of Christianity which in modern thought has undergone profound modification, is not congenial to the social gospel. The old cultus is not adapted to the new gospel." Rauschenbusch believed that the democratized denominations deriving from the Anabaptist and Puritan movements had a natural advantage in the task of remaking the church in the image of Christ's kingdom; Scudder believed that the organic sacramental consciousness of the Anglican and Catholic traditions was better suited to this end; though Morrison sided with Rauschenbusch, he argued that no Christian denomination had shown as yet how to infuse an institutional church with the spirit of the kingdom. His proof was that social Christianity was almost entirely a clerical phenomenon thus far.[188]

"The amazing spread of the social gospel among the clergy is paralleled by its failure to make any significant progress among the laity," Morrison observed. A recent interdenominational gathering of Ohio pastors exemplified his point. This convocation of six hundred pastors condemned "the whole war system" and called for a new egalitarian economic order "by means of cooperative industry, government regulation or government ownership." Morrison noted in 1933 that such conferences were commonplace, but they rarely affected the ways that churches worshiped on Sunday morning. The pastors who called for a cooperative commonwealth at weekday conferences usually resorted to tamer fare with their congregations. They knew that their social idealism, which was well received at clergy conferences, would receive rougher treatment in the congregations that paid their salaries. "These men regard the reconstruction of the social order as of the very essence of the Christian gospel," Morrison remarked. "But they find it impossible to introduce into their pulpits and their parish work anything more than the faintest suggestion of the social idealism which burns in their hearts."[189]

Many pastors kept their true beliefs to themselves and thus grew alienated from their work.[190] Others revealed enough of their theological, ethical, and political thinking to earn the enmity of conservatives and lose their positions. Some pastors preached the social gospel and won their congregations to it. Morrison worried at length about the first two groups, but he cautioned that even the third group was problematic. It restricted the social gospel to sermons and the activism of social Christian agencies. The cultus of a church includes its worship, its theology, its organizational structure, and its ethical standards, Morrison explained, but in the cultus of modern Protestantism, the social gospel was confined cultically to the sermon. At best, it was a preacher's gospel. "It has not been the church's gospel," he judged. "The laity have little share in it. They do not know how central and dominant it is in the thinking of their ministers. They only get enough of it to be irritated by it." The upshot was that social Christianity seemed to be lacking in religion. Confined to the sermon and the activism of activists, it gave the appearance of a secular diversion: "He is preaching politics, they say, or science, or economics, or internationalism; we want our preacher to talk about religion!"[191]

Morrison sympathized with this reaction. He agreed that the typical discourse of social Christianity was overly secularized. It talked politics from the pulpit. What was needed, he argued, was to make social Christianity religious: "And to make it religious it must be given an organic place in the liturgy of communal worship, so that it shall not be merely the individual utterance of a preacher but the confessional utterance of the worshiping congregation itself." The social gospel cannot carry sufficient religious power if it is merely preached, he warned. It must be incorporated into other dimensions of the church's cultus. Many pastors read Rauschenbusch only as source material for sermons, but this was not nearly enough. Social Christianity needed to appropriate not only Rauschenbusch's sermon material, Morrison urged, but also his systematic theology, his interest in hymnody, his deep concern with prayer, his desire for new liturgical forms, his commitment to the democratization of church structures, and his vision of the church as a transforming moral community. Rauschenbusch understood that a kingdom-oriented church requires a transfigured cultus: "His hopeful eyes saw new hymns, new prayers, new denominational activities expressive of social idealism as signs of the awakening of the whole church." Rauschenbusch epitomized the kind of culture-transforming spirit that modern Christianity needed.[192]

Morrison acknowledged the irony in this claim. To argue that Christianity needed a new kingdom-oriented cultus was to emphasize the importance of the priestly function. He cast Rauschenbusch as the exemplar of prophetic *and* priestly religion, notwithstanding the fact that Rauschenbusch's writings were filled with hostility toward priestly religion. Rauschenbusch repeatedly contrasted the ethical, justice-making character of prophetic faith to the corrupting ceremonialism of priestly religion. In his vocabulary, *priestly* and *priestcraft* were always epithets. Though he had friendly relations with various priests, in his writings the priest was always the functionary of decadent authority religion. But Rauschenbusch was also a priest, Morrison observed. His prayers and hymn collections were priestly efforts, and his last book, *A Theology of the Social Gospel*, was more priestly than prophetic. He failed to see these efforts as priestly work because he failed to recognize the constructive aspect of priestly religion. Morrison judged that contemporary social Christianity was paying a large price for this failure. The social gospel was intrinsically a Protestant project, he believed—Morrison's anti-Catholic chauvinism was unyielding—but it could not afford the typical Protestant prejudice that all priestly religion is bad.[193]

Morrison pleaded for the recognition that biblical religion is both priestly and prophetic. Like Scudder he perceived that liberal Protestantism was religiously too thin to sustain the kingdom hope of the gospel; unlike Scudder he believed that only a new cultus could sustain a kingdom-oriented church. The social gospel was not alien, but it had to be new. When the social gospel was very near the end of its run as a dominant religious perspective, Morrison exhorted that it needed a major overhaul and a more ambitious objective. The liberal churches were socially compromised by their establishment status, he argued; more importantly, partly for the same reason, they were also spiritually weak. The culturally transforming Christianity that was needed would live more dangerously than the socially accommodated churches of modern Protestantism. It would also live with deeper spiritual conviction. Morrison shrewdly perceived much of what was wrong with an ailing social gospel movement, but it was Niebuhr, not the *Christian Century*, that pushed liberal Protestantism in a new direction.[194]

3.

Post-Ritschlian Religion

George Burman Foster, Shailer Mathews, Shirley Jackson Case, and the Chicago School of Theology

The decision to move from a gospel-centered Ritschlianism to an essentially modernist-centered naturalistic empiricism was made first in American theology at Chicago. It was pioneered by two Baptists, of strikingly different temperaments. Shailer Mathews and George Burman Foster began their careers in the orbits of Ritschlian historicism and left-Ritschlian personalism, respectively. They joined the University of Chicago Divinity School only a few years after its founding, but they belonged to the second generation of the school's faculty. A decade after they arrived in Chicago, they set the Chicago school of theology on a decidedly post-Ritschlian trajectory.

Over time, Mathews became the larger figure. A prolific theologian, church leader, and dean of the divinity school, he led the liberal theology movement and, with his colleague Shirley Jackson Case, developed the distinctive Chicago version of socio-historical interpretation. Mathews epitomized the ethos of Chicago theological modernism, while Foster has been largely forgotten. In the early years of the Chicago school, however, the faculty star was Foster. Renowned as the university's celebrity intellectual in the years after John Dewey left Chicago, he was a daring religious thinker and captivating public speaker and teacher. Foster was not the first lightning rod of controversy on the Chicago faculty, a distinction that belonged to the university's legendary founding president, William Rainey Harper. To Harper's distress, however, Foster exceeded him as the university's object of controversy, setting into motion a religious legacy that was not quite what Harper had in mind for his university.

HARPER'S UNIVERSITY:
THEOLOGY IN A MODERN SPIRIT

The University of Chicago was the product of John D. Rockefeller's money, Midwest Baptist anxieties about falling behind other denominations, and William Rainey Harper's vision of a modern Baptist university. The last factor was crucial to the kind of university it became. Harper was a Yale-trained professor of ancient languages and a phenomenally enterprising administrator, organizer, and advocate of popular religious education. His zeal for critically informed religious education was a by-product of two conversions. Harper earned his doctorate at the age of eighteen in 1875, a year before America's first research university, Johns Hopkins University, opened its doors. Had he been slightly less precocious, he might have proceeded from Yale to Johns Hopkins and missed his Baptist career. As it was, he began his teaching career at a Baptist college, Denison University, where he underwent a conversion experience and joined the Baptist church.[1]

In the afterglow of his conversion Harper held out against biblical criticism. He moved to the Baptist Union Theological Seminary of Morgan Park, Illinois in 1879, where he taught Hebrew and expounded a moderately conservative opposition to higher critical scholarship. His enterprising spirit quickly showed through. In 1880 he established one of the country's first correspondence schools, the Correspondence School of Hebrew, which popularized Old Testament and Hebrew-language studies with remarkable success. The school quickly enrolled over three hundred students, and by 1883, when it was renamed the American Institute of Hebrew, its staff included seventy professors of Hebrew and Old Testament. In the early 1880s Harper began his long association with the Chautauqua Society, teaching summer courses; during the same period he came to the judgment that the best biblical scholarship was being done by scholars who used the tools of higher criticism. This was his second conversion. Harper not only accepted that higher critical study was methodologically legitimate; he resolved that biblical criticism could be a crucial aid to faith and religious education. In 1886, to the sharp disappointment of Chicago Baptists, he joined the faculty of Yale University, where he became an outspoken advocate of biblical criticism.[2]

Harper's passion was biblical literacy. He believed that lay biblical study was the key to the regeneration of American life and culture, and he viewed his academic career as an extension of his mission to make Americans biblically literate. To this end he assumed the directorship of the national curriculum section of the Chautauqua Society; more ambitiously, in agreement with Rochester Theological Seminary theologian Augustus H. Strong, he urged that the Baptist church needed to establish a new showcase university. Strong wanted the Baptist showcase to be, like himself, both firmly conservative and located in the state of New York. Harper countered that it had to advocate biblical criticism and a modern scientific spirit. In 1891 a group of Baptists allied with John D. Rockefeller lured Harper back to Chicago to create the University of Chicago.

This was to be the second University of Chicago; it was also the second time that this group tried to enlist Harper. In 1886 a Baptist institution called the University of Chicago went out of business, crushed by unsustainable debt. Harper declined an eleventh-hour appeal from Rockefeller, Morgan Park seminary financial secretary Thomas W. Goodspeed, and a group of university officials to assume the presidency. These local Baptists and Rockefeller were anxious about the state of Baptist education in the Midwest. Baptists outnumbered other Protestants in Chicago, but in the field of education the denominaton had fallen behind the Methodists (who founded Northwestern University and Garrett Biblical Institute in the 1850s), the Congregationalists (who founded Chicago Theological Seminary in 1855), and the Presbyterians (who moved their Indiana seminary to Chicago in 1859, later renaming it McCormick Theological Seminary). The Baptists had the Baptist Union Theological Seminary of Morgan Park, but it was financially strapped and its viability was tied to the fortunes of the first University of Chicago. The year 1886 had been grim for the Chicago Baptists: Harper declined the presidency of their failing university, the university folded, and Harper left Morgan Park to teach at Yale.[3]

Now, five years later, he was returning to create a new university, at the age of thirty-two, armed with enough Rockefeller money to recruit an impressive faculty. Harper designed a full-scale university consisting of four undergraduate colleges, a nonprofessional graduate school, and graduate schools of divinity, law, medicine, engineering, pedagogy, fine arts, and music. He established the Divinity School first. Most of the faculty belonged to the colleges of the Arts, Literature, and Science, but to Harper and his backers, the Divinity School was the key to everything else. He accepted the position of founding president on the condition that the new university would absorb Morgan Park seminary, the new Divinity School would be an organic part of the university, university chairs in Hebrew and Old Testament would be established, and he would serve as head professor of Hebrew and Old Testament in addition to his presidential duties. Though he failed to breach the senior ranks of Harvard or Johns Hopkins, Harper lured a distinguished faculty to Chicago. His prize recruits included Freiburg historian Hermann von Holst, Yale linguist William I. Knapp, two college presidents (geologist Thomas C. Chamberlin and sociologist Albion W. Small), Newton Theological Institute New Testament scholar Ernest DeWitt Burton, and half the faculty of Clark University. "Harper's University," inevitably called "Harper's Bazaar," opened its doors in October 1892. Its gray Gothic towers were erected on the same strip of land—the Midway Plaisance—that housed the gigantic Ferris wheel and other attractions of the 1893 World's Columbian Exposition. In

1895 Harper explained himself to the president of Vassar College: "You understand that my special business in the world is stirring up people on the English Bible. The University of Chicago is entirely a second hand matter."[4]

His idea of what American theological education needed to become had distinguished company. In 1883, Harvard University president Charles W. Eliot observed that modern life had transformed the sociocultural environment in which Protestant ministers carried out their work. Fewer college graduates were entering the ministry than in previous generations, other professions had better training standards and higher prestige, and the best students rarely entered the ministry. Eliot warned that theological education compared poorly to the natural sciences, which had recently gained considerable esteem in American society. Scientific education was widely respected for the rigorous methods by which it pursued truth. On the whole, he remarked, modern education was becoming more rigorous, honest, and objective by virtue of its turn to scientific method, but the seminaries were turning out "young men of small mental capacity and flaccid physical or moral fibre."[5]

Eliot judged that the deteriorating prestige of theology was tied to its backwater image. American theological education remained overwelmingly authoritarian and provincial in a society that was increasingly democratic in its politics and scientific in its approach to knowledge. Most seminaries had low academic standards, cherished their claims to denominational orthodoxy, and were located in isolated rural areas. Eliot warned that this was a prescription for diminishing public prestige. In modern society "even the ignorant have learned to despise the process of searching for proofs of a foregone conclusion." If church leaders wanted to regain the respect of academe and the educated public, he admonished, they needed to reinvent theological education. They had to create institutions that pursued religious truth with the same scientific spirit and methods that prevailed in other disciplines. They had to raise their academic standards, encourage specialized research, and respect academic freedom. These were cosmopolitan ideals, Eliot emphasized. Backwater seminaries were not likely to develop or appreciate the critical approach to theology that was needed: "This academic freedom is much more likely to be obtained in universities, and in cities which are large enough to be centres of diversified intellectual activity, than it is in isolated denominational seminaries." If theology had a future worth having, it belonged to the divinity schools of America's research universities.[6]

Harper agreed on every point. In the 1880s Eliot nudged Harvard Divinity School in the direction of his vision of university theology; a decade later Union Theological Seminary and Yale Divinity School committed themselves to what Charles Briggs called the "theological university" model. Harper had the advantage of beginning at the very moment of the liberal ascendancy in American theology. Though he built the Divinity School on an existing Baptist seminary, he infused it with ambitious liberal theologians. His interest in theological education was deeper and broader than Eliot's by virtue of his theological training and personal commitments. Eliot's interest in theological education was essentially professional; he was preoccupied with the question of how ministers should be trained to meet the demands of the modern world. Harper shared this concern, but to him the discipline of theology was integrally related to other academic disciplines and to society as a whole, which caused him to give more attention than did Eliot to curricular issues.

Harper conceived the role of the university in modern society in the categories of Hebrew religion. Upon moving to Chicago he brought with him the American Institute of Hebrew, renamed the American Institute of Sacred Literature, which eventually formed the heart of Chicago's University Extension department. To Harper, the university was the prophet, priest, and sage of modern democracy. Like the prophet, the university sought the truth and stood by it without compromise; like the priest, the university was a caretaker of the soul and the social order; like the sages of Hebrew Scripture, the university was the repository of society's wisdom. Explaining his categories, he mused in 1905, "The thoughts and forms of thought of the ancient Hebrews have made deep impressions on my mind."[7]

Like the liberal theology movement as a whole, Harper habitually blended biblical and modernist motifs. In 1899 he reflected that his thinking about theological education was guided by the principles that theology needed to incorporate the "assured results" of modern knowledge, especially modern psychology and pedagogy, and that it had to accommodate "the modern democratic situation." Harper reasoned that ministers acquired their social authority from their practical ministerial efficiency, not from a handed-down body of doctrines. It followed that if ministers wanted to retain or enhance their authority in modern society, they needed to be educated in "the modern spirit of science." The modern seminary was not a place where students should be expected to accept received opinions, he declared: "It is rather a place in which men shall be taught to think."[8]

Having incorporated the old Morgan Park seminary into the new university divinity school, Harper had to bide his time with the Divinity School. Morgan Park divines Galusha Anderson, Eri Baker Hulbert, and George W. Northrup were appointed as head professors, with Hulbert serving as dean until 1907. Most of the remaining divinity appointments were filled by Morgan Park faculty. The Morgan Park Baptists were sufficiently forward-looking to launch Harper's University, but there were no prominent scholars among them. They were transitional figures, rooted theologically in mid-century evangelical Calvinism, who mediated their institution's passage to a modernist form of evangelicalism. Divinity School alumni, short on cultural sensitivity, later dubbed them "the Aborigines."[9]

In the early years of the Divinity School, Ernest DeWitt Burton headed the New Testament department, and Harper chaired and taught in the Old Testament department. Harper prized his opportunities to make new Divinity School appointments. He pursued Foster before the university existed; more than four years later, in April 1895, he lured Foster away from McMaster University. Mathews had arrived in Chicago the previous fall. In 1897, energized by these appointments, the Divinity School faculty launched its flagship journal, the *American Journal of Theology*, which announced on its opening page, "Theology needs above all things else the application of thorough scientific methods. The editors will admit only articles which are of this character." Harper believed that Foster epitomized his ideal of modern theology. In 1895 he enthused that Foster was "the greatest living thinker in his line." There is no evidence that Harper ever changed his mind about Foster's brilliance, but he had ample cause to regret Foster's proclivity for controversy. In his own field, as well, Harper's legacy at Chicago turned out to be quite different from what he had in mind. Harper was devoted to the German higher-critical concept of biblical scholarship, which emphasized grammar, lexicography, textual criticism, source criticism, and exegesis, but the Chicago Schoolers pioneered a sociohistorical variant of the German history of religions approach that emphasized the social and cultural environment in which biblical religion took shape.[10]

GEORGE BURMAN FOSTER
AND THE MAKING OF CHICAGO MODERNISM

Born in 1858 to Alderson, West Virginia, mountain farmers, George Burman Foster was a poignant, tragic, arresting figure who coped throughout his life with the premature deaths of loved ones. His mother died when he was five years old; Foster's grieving father placed Foster with his paternal grandparents while he went off to fight in the Civil War. The family reassembled after the war with a stepmother in charge of the home. As a youth Foster consumed books, in Lincolnesque fashion, before an open fire. He attended Shelton College in Saint Albans, West Virginia, for three years, was ordained to the Baptist ministry in 1879, and earned two degrees from West Virginia University in 1884. In his early preaching career he conducted several successful revivals. In 1884 Foster enrolled at Rochester Theological Seminary, where Augustus Hopkins Strong was a dominant faculty presence; one of his classmates was Walter Rauschenbusch. Foster's classmates later disagreed about Strong's influence over him during his student days, some claiming that Foster accepted Strong's theological conservatism without equivocation, others remembering that his liberal leanings began during seminary. In his decidedly liberal adulthood Foster described his teacher as intellectually impressive and theologically impossible.[11]

After graduating from Rochester Seminary in 1887, he served a pastorate at First Baptist Church in Saratoga Springs, New York, for four years. Foster was too absorbed by theory to flourish in the ministry; colleagues later recalled that he was apparently incapable of not thinking intensely about intellectual problems all the time. In 1890, before Harper formally accepted the position of founding president, he urged Foster to study in Germany for a year as preparation for a faculty position at the new University of Chicago. Foster fretted that Harper's proposal was financially unfeasible, but the following year he found academic refuge at McMaster University in Toronto, which appointed him to its chair in philosophy. McMaster promptly sent him to Göttingen and Berlin for a year of graduate training, where Foster's Ritschlian leanings were cultivated. Though little is known about his German sabbatical, his subsequent references to Julius Kaftan suggest that he heard Kaftan lecture at Berlin. Foster's early writings, which began after he moved to Chicago, took for granted that theological orthodoxy was discredited and often cited Kaftan's dogmatics. He taught at McMaster for three years before yielding to the offer of a lesser salary from Harper, who persuaded the McMaster Baptists to give up their most promising teacher.[12]

Foster was a seeker and prober, tender-hearted, restless, and generous toward opponents. His lectures and personal relations were marked by a distinctly vulnerable intensity. His wife Mary, whose father was one of Foster's professors at West Virginia University, apparently suffered from neurasthania, and all five of their children were afflicted with poor health. A gloom of illness pervaded the Foster household, punctuated by periodic tragedies. Foster's oldest child drowned shortly before he was to enter college; his favorite child died shortly before her wedding; another son was lost during World War I; his remaining son and daughter struggled against severe depression throughout their lives. Mathews later recalled that the first of these tragedies occurred just before he met Foster for the first time, and that he was deeply moved by Foster's moral courage: "Professor Foster was one of the noblest and bravest souls I ever knew. He faced misfortunes with courage which was sublime."[13]

Foster's vulnerable intensity reflected his inner suffering and made him an unforgettable teacher with charismatic appeal on the lecture platform. Even his scholarly writing contained glimpses of it. In 1909 he introduced himself to a Baptist conference in New York City as "a man who has suffered as keen spiritual anguish for twenty-five years as one could well suffer, and maintain his sanity and health, in brooding and living through these great problems, and I am wondering whether or not a great change is not coming to us." Craggy and unkempt in personal appearance, he possessed a deep West Virginia drawl and was prone to startling tangents. His writings—disorderly, relentlessly headlong, and impossible to outline, yet highly engaging—presented Foster as a student of the great questions. From the beginning of his Chicago career he denounced the presumption of infallibility in religion, calling for "the complete rejection of the false principle of authority." Modern theology amounted to a new Reformation, he urged, "the completion of Luther's Reformation, the disengagement of our Protestantism from the remainders of Roman Catholicism." To his left-Ritschlian early thinking, only the "true religion" of individual spiritual freedom had any sovereign right in the kingdom of religion.[14]

Foster struggled thoughout his life to settle upon his personal beliefs, but he was never one to hedge or equivocate. In his early career he took leave of classical Trinitarianism and Christology, judging that these doctrines were inextricably imbedded in ontological categories that belong to the worldview of authority-religion. In their place he emphasized religious consciousness, especially the religious consciousness of Jesus, which he described as "a feeling of the abiding nearness of God; the filial consciousness that knows nothing distant, strange, unfamiliar, unhomelike in his father; the jubilant certainty that God has completely disclosed his heart to him." With Schleiermacher, he asserted that religious experience is the ground of religious truth; with a Ritschlian image, he argued that Jesus knew God intimately as both king and father "not like the two foci of an ellipse, but the center of a circle." In the exemplary religious experience of Jesus, he explained, "kingliness is ethicized by fatherliness, and fatherliness is energized by kingliness." God is awesome and glorious, but always awesome and glorious in ethical loving.[15]

By eschewing ontological theologizing, Foster sought to avoid the debates over Arianism and Trinitarianism that trapped William Ellery Channing and other nineteenth-century Unitarians. He soon discovered that he had no hope of avoiding disagreeable debates or the charge of Unitarianism. He contended that while it is improper to say that "Jesus is God," it is not improper to speak of Jesus as the supreme and saving revelation of God. We know that God is ethical and loving because we know Jesus, Foster argued. Put differently, in a formulation that he invoked repeatedly, "instead of saying that Jesus is as good as God is, it is nearer the point of the gospel to say that God is as good as Jesus is."[16] Foster told his students that this claim was the key to Christianity and everything else: "The essential thing in the Christian faith in Jesus is that God is as good as Jesus is, even though appearances may sometimes be to the contrary. If we can stick to this in all the grind and torture and darkness of this world, we can live in hope and die without despair." His spiritual voluntarism was expressed personally. At the heart of things there is a will that is as good and loving as the will of Jesus, he affirmed. Armed with this faith, "I can bury my child, I can pass through invalidism, lose my fortune, be maligned, and die forgotten before I die."[17] This was Foster's version of the Ritschlian essence of Christianity. It was also his answer to those who charged that he denied the divinity of Christ: "God is like Jesus—this is the gospel."[18]

This answer struck his many conservative critics as mere Ebionism or even modern humanism; many of his later humanist followers agreed. Throughout his career Foster was routinely called a Unitarian, sometimes by friends. From the beginning of his Chicago career to its end, he made Unitarian/humanist-like statements while insisting that he was a good Baptist. A certain double-mindedness made him prone to offend and confuse opponents and friends alike. Foster said that he did not deny the divinity of Christ, but he also made statements that lurched to the very edge of Ebionism. In 1898 he asserted that while the old theology put Jesus over against humanity, "we must now put him in the human category entirely." To identify Christ entirely with humanity does not necessarily negate all claims about his divinity, he assured, for "the question of the divinity of Jesus will depend upon one's philosophy, and will correspond with one's evaluation of man, the difference being one of degree only." The pertinent issue in his rendering was the question of the divinity of the human spirit. Foster explained that the ideally human is higher than the messianic. We have no knowledge of anything that is more divine than the "essentially and ideally human," he contended: "Once, people made little of man, in order to make much of God. Now we make much of man, in order to make much of God."[19]

When critics alleged that he denied the divinity of Christ, Foster affected wounded incredulity; when they called him a Unitarian, he protested that his position was "so far from Unitarianism that I much prefer traditional orthodoxy to this type of rationalism." He seemed to delight in tweaking church audiences, though he disclaimed any desire to unsettle the faith of pious traditionalists. At church conferences he often sparred with conservatives and routinely offended them; repeatedly they protested that he had no business teaching theology at a Baptist institution. Foster insisted that one cannot be modern and still accept the dualistic supernaturalist worldview of the Bible; on eschatology, for example, he stated, "Immanent values of present human life are in conflict with transcendent eschatology, and that is the end of that matter too."[20]

The Divinity School would have attracted ample conservative opposition without Foster; with him, controversy became a way of life. In 1897 Baptist conservative J. V. Read blasted the Chicago Schoolers for teaching "that the Bible is a mass of traditions, redactions, idealized history, fiction, allegory, etc., wanting in historical and predictive elements." Addressing Divinity School dean Hulbert, Read protested that Chicago liberalism denigrated the integrity of Scripture: "You, of course, know that this is the position of Briggs, Smith, Driver, Harper, and their allies. To this position of disbelief in the truthfulness of God's Word, the destructive critics are bending their energies, with arrogant dogmatism, to drive the timid and unlearned, as did Satan in Gen. 3:4." Though Mathews boasted that Chicago seminarians were deeply pious and liberal, some divinity students rebelled against their teachers. In 1900 one of them blasted Mathews's "suppression of the truth" and his "irreverent thrusts at the narratives of the Evangelists . . . making out Luke and John liars when it suited a theory to do so . . . the little German theory of higher criticism." Wincing at this protest, Mathews told Foster that the two of them were linked as Christian brothers in an often misunderstood but Christly cause: "I trust that we shall be able to keep turning our left cheek and then our right cheek, and then our left cheek, and then our right cheek, and then our left cheek and then our right cheek, and then our left cheek and then our right cheek, as long as the Gospel would wish us so to do."[21]

The Chicago theologians took for granted that modern scholarship was upsetting to many church people; Mathews lamented that "it is one of the most difficult questions in the world how to swing the laymen, whose views on theology are based on essential literalistic scripture." But Foster surpassed his colleagues at provoking church conservatives and moderates, which rankled his colleagues, including Matthews, on numerous occasions. Drawing on the recollections of Foster's contemporaries, Bernard Meland later wrote that Foster's speaking appearances were "generally awaited either with apprehension or with a certain amount of demonic glee, anticipating some dire disclosure that might erupt into controversy." Harper grew especially perturbed at his manner of drawing attention to the

Divinity School. In 1903 Foster gave an address at the Divinity School on "The Ethics of Doctrinal Reform" that galled Harper. "When he used the term 'modern man' in many instances he contrasted it with the Christian man; in every case he put the word 'we' after it," Harper complained. Nothing was more important to Harper than his sense of himself as being both Christian *and* modern. He resented Foster's apparent insinuation that one might have to choose: "I do not believe that Foster himself meant what he said. The statements were entirely misleading and confusing."[22]

In public, Harper defended Foster and the Divinity School from a rising chorus of complaints. He insisted that Foster was a good Baptist and that the Divinity School was a faithfully Baptist institution. Privately, he fretted that he could not win both arguments in the Baptist church. Harper admired Foster and wanted to keep him at the university, but he had to get him out of the Divinity School. He also expressed the desire to appoint a certain theologian named "Clarke" to the Divinity School faculty; this was undoubtedly William Newton Clarke, who was sixty years old at the time and not in good health. Foster strongly opposed the appointment; Clarke was too old for the position and theologically outdated, and the appointment would reflect badly on himself. As for himself, Foster proposed a graceful exit: Why not appoint him to the university chair in the philosophy of religion? Two years later Harper pitched the latter option to his friends, Mr. and Mrs. John R. Stetson, whose financial help he needed: "Dr. Foster is one of the best men I have ever known, but he keeps putting his foot into trouble as rapidly as any man I have ever known. We have stood by him bravely, but he seems to have no thought that people must be educated before they can enjoy or appreciate or even approve his position."[23]

Harper sought to defuse the volatile church politics of the Foster situation. First, he appointed Shailer Mathews to the Divinity School's chair of Systematic Theology and dropped the idea of hiring Clarke. The university's trustees and its Baptist-dominated Advisory Committee of 100 expressed their relief; Mathews prided himself on his good relations with church conservatives. The next step was the removal of Foster from the Divinity School. With great anxiety, Harper scheduled a meeting with the university's governing Advisory Committee to determine Foster's future at the university. Harper apparently realized that there was some sentiment to get rid of Foster altogether. He defended Foster's right to teach as an expression of academic freedom; at the same time he recommended that Foster be transferred to the Department of Comparative Religion. On the day after he met with the Advisory Committee, Harper was supposed to meet with Foster. Foster begged off at the last minute, however, pleading that he was too emotionally "unstrung" to keep the appointment; he feared that he would say "harsh words" if they faced each other, and he admonished Harper in a note "to stop keying the Div. School to *Mileau.*" Foster was taking back his own proposal; he didn't want to leave the Divinity School. He had no objection to Mathews's transfer and promotion, but as for himself, he didn't want to be cut off from the churches and divinity students.[24]

Harper responded that the politics of the situation was not a secondary matter. He also suggested that his own poor health was a factor; Harper was battling cancer. In February 1905, Foster was officially informed that the Board of Trustees had transferred him to the Department of Comparative Religion as Professor of the Philosophy of Religion. He tried to take it well, thanking Dean Hulbert for his personal kindness throughout the ordeal. His note to Hulbert ended: "Suffering from a temporary collapse myself, Mrs. Foster is writing this line for me. Trusting that your illness may after all prove to be not so serious, and assuring you of our great appreciation and esteem we remain . . ."[25] Foster moved to the Department of Comparative Religion, which was housed in the school of Arts and Literature, but nearly all of his students continued to come from the Divinity School. The following January his life turned another corner when his sensational first book, *The Finality of the Christian Religion*, was published during the same month that Harper, at the age of forty-nine, succumbed to cancer.

The coincidence was doubly unhappy for Foster. For ten years Harper had been the university's main lightning rod for criticism; at the same time he had defended Foster and safeguarded Foster's standing at the university, if not the Divinity School. Now, at the very moment when he lost his protector, Foster's book made him the center of intense controversy. For 518 pages he poured out complicated, ponderous arguments that tracked back and forth across Christian history, modern biblical scholarship, and German theology and philosophy. The book rippled with provocative assertions that showed little of the mannered sense of audience possessed by Brown, King, and Mathews. Mathews later recalled that Foster "was a wonderful spirit but lacked persuasiveness," for he spoke and wrote in a way that "was apt to be irritating even to those who agreed with him."[26]

THEOLOGY BEYOND RITSCHL AND TROELTSCH

The outrage in response to Foster's book set a new standard for complaints against Chicago modernism. It sorely tested the adherence of American Baptists to the principles of academic freedom, the liberty of individual conscience, and the independence of Baptist-related educational institutions. *The Finality of the Christian Religion* is one of the most controversial volumes ever published by the University of Chicago Press. The mere fact that it was published by a Baptist-affiliated institution served as a provocation and symbol to church conservatives for decades afterward. Shortly after its publication, the *Baptist Alliance* announced in a headline that the book aroused many ministers and was "Severely Criticized from Many Pulpits." The *Chicago Tribune* offered a more detailed headline: "Learned Critic Rips Theology . . . Startling Book Written by Professor in University Divinity School . . . Assails Canon of Bible . . . Declares Miracles Incredible and Says Proof of Resurrection Is Lacking." *Interior* editor Nolan R. Best assured Mathews that he was not prejudiced against the Divinity School, but "I should have to confess considerable prejudice against Dr. Foster." Another local editorialist summarized the incredulity of many pastors: "Is there no place in which to assail Christianity but a divinity school? Is there no one to write infidel books except the professors of Christian theology? Is a theological seminary an appropriate place for a general massacre of Christian doctrine?" Foster was censured by the Baptist Ministers Conference for denying essential Christian teaching; he was undoubtedly saved from even greater notoriety by the difficulty of his prose. From his perspective, however, the book was barely radical at all. He told Mathews that it represented "the maximum of Christianity that could be retained by the modern mind."[27]

His web of essential convictions was familiar enough. Like all theological liberals, Foster looked for a third way between the old supernaturalism and the new mechanistic naturalism. Like Bowne and King, he embraced the core of Lotzean personalist philosophy and equated true religion with the dynamism and ethics of personality. Like all theological liberals of his generation, he claimed to recover the religion of Jesus from the oppressive superstructure of historic Christianity. But in Foster's case, all of these claims were advanced with a harder-edged critical thrust and accompanied by a host of sweeping negations. He put his religious doubts on display and denied that many traditional beliefs were worth struggling over. Instead of calling for a liberalized understanding of inspiration or atonement, he dismissed these doctrines as impossible, fantastical, and outdated. Traditional atonement theory was beyond the pale for him. At the same time, unlike many liberals, he did not compensate by emphasizing the divinity of Jesus. Foster's christological affirmations fell short of Arianism. He dispensed substantial sections of the Gospels to the categories of myth and church theology. In the tradition of David Friedrich Strauss and Ernst Troeltsch, he showed that the most effective critique of dogma is its history.

The Finality of the Christian Religion smacked of Hegel and Troeltsch in more than its title. Though he spurned Hegel's metaphysical reinterpretation of the Trinity and incarnation, Foster embraced Hegel's dictum that nothing comes into the world fully developed. With qualified assent, he accepted the Troeltschian comparativist approach to religion. Foster judged that the history-of-religions method was useful, illuminating, and by itself insufficient. It could not be the sole measure of religious truth because it excluded the understanding of any religion on its own terms. Mistakenly, Foster implied that Troeltsch restricted theology to comparativist historicism; in any case, he objected that this method "has its limits precisely at the points where the divinatory creative word or the value-judgment of the investigator becomes necessary in order to the vivification of the material which as been aggregated in an objectively critical way." The history of religionists attached themselves too closely to mathematics and natural science in their study of human historical phenomena, he believed; as a result they failed to do justice "to the *whole* of the human, and hence to the Christianly human." Foster countered that good religious thinking had to be more flexible and use the comparativist method without restricting itself to the limitations of history-of-religions objectivism.[28]

His own approach made a fundamental distinction between the "religion of authority" and the "religion of the spirit." Auguste Sabatier's *Religions of Authority and the Religion of the Spirit* was published in 1904; Foster noted that he developed these categories before Sabatier (independently) made essentially the same argument. Like Sabatier, he began with a review and critique of authority-based religion before moving to an account of Christianity as a religion of the spirit. "The retirement of Christianity as authority-religion is the negative side of the work of a return to a religion of Jesus, which was the religion of freedom, of the spirit," he argued. For Jesus, the ultimate test of truth was "neither authority nor speculation, but experience." Life itself, living, was the criterion of life for the Jesus of history. "Nothing is farther from the truth than to say that he grounded his glad message of the kingdom of God on external authority," Foster insisted. "Nothing so little corresponds to his procedure as a compulsory dogma. Jesus' grounds of faith are all without exception of a moral kind."[29]

The basic argument was left-Ritschlian, but Foster refused to reconceptualize old dogmas in "value" terms. He likened himself to Strauss in denying that he meant to disturb the faith or contentment of any person. The basic problem, as Strauss observed in *The Old Faith and the New,* was that Christian belief was already in a state of crisis. Like Strauss, Foster felt obliged to find a new basis of faith. He further admonished that "there are historical situations, and the present is one of them, when an unsettled faith is not an unmitigated evil." Foster could be disarmingly personal on the latter theme. He invited readers to reflect on their own experiences of walking, like himself, "with bleeding feet, the same *via dolorosa* tomorrow and the day after. It is a pathetic and tragic, or inspiring and illuminating, spectacle, according as one looks at it." Whether pathetic or inspiring, he refused to preach orthodoxy under the mask of liberalism or liberalism under the mask of orthodoxy. America's elite divinity schools taught liberal theology, he allowed, but authority religion still ruled "in all our denominations in some parts of the country, and in some of our denominations in all parts of the country." The mythical Christ of the church still supplanted "the real Jesus of history, whose spirit alone is the life of our spirit." Foster inveighed against the common notion that Christianity is a historical religion; this idea is true only in the superficial sense that Christianity has a history, he contended. In its depths Christianity is a religion of spirit and personality, not redemptive facts (*Heilsthatsachen*): "It is not a religion of facts, but of values; and values are timeless; that is, Christianity is an eternal religion which is *in,* but not *of,* the historical."[30]

He thus made no attempt to redeem various doctrines precious to authority Christianity. The inspiration of Scripture was a prime example:

> Verbal inspiration was first limited to sayings introduced as "Word of God," then completely given up; inspiration was next conceived as a positive divine guidance in the writing-down of what was supernaturally revealed; then it was changed to a mere negative protection from error; then, next, the inerrancy of the Scripture itself was surrendered bit by bit—limited at first to the redemptively necessary doctrines,

then to their essentially religious content; finally, the personal inerrancy of the biblical authors was reduced to the inerrancy of Jesus, and that of the latter, again, limited to the region of religious truth.

Modern liberals and moderates usually tried to save the doctrine of inspiration by speaking of "plenary inspiration" or the "divine-human character" of scripture, but Foster swept the house of authority clean. The point of the old inspiration doctrines was to secure a divine and absolute text, he observed. It gained theology nothing to claim that the Bible is sort-of inspired, for the Bible is either divine and absolute or it is not. Foster admonished that reason and experience come down on the latter side: "'Inspiration' of the Book is untrue historically and impossible psychologically."[31]

Apologetic appeals to biblical miracles got a similar treatment. Augustus Hopkins Strong analogized that just as Jesus turned water into wine in ancient Palestine, he was currently turning the moisture of the earth into vineyard grapes all over the world. Another conservative apologist suggested that the virgin birth may have been an extreme instance of parthenogenesis. Foster replied that any educated person "who now affirms his faith in such stories as actual facts can hardly know what *intellectual* honesty means." His employment of rationalist criticism was of a piece with his use of history-of-religions methodology. Rationalist criticism has "little religious value," Foster judged; moreover, scientific rationalists were wrong to dismiss all miracle stories as impossible. At the same time, Enlightenment rationalism did have the value of working "as a disintegrating solvent upon the static finalities of the church." Science has very little capacity to judge religious faith, he explained, but it refutes factual nonsense. Because it routinely confused questions about facts—which are matters of knowledge subject to the canons of scientific evidence—with the "timeless character" of religious faith, traditional Christianity had a sorry record of conflicts with science: "Whoever substitutes an historical fact for such object of faith externalizes faith, holds religion down to a stage which has been overcome in the world-historical movement, and complicates religion in insoluble contradiction with all the rest of our life."[32]

He did not enlist the apostle Paul as an ally of this view. By Foster's reading, Paul was clearly an advocate of authority religion. He especially recoiled at Paul's claim in 1 Corinthians 15:14 that Christian faith is vain apart from belief in Christ's resurrection:

> Is it, indeed, necessary that we build our salvation on this occurrence? Is there no other foundation of salvation? Are not the truths of our faith, God's love and grace, his commandments and kingdom, reliable in and of themselves? Do they need a visible authentication? Are we not children of God if we say with love and confidence, Abba Father? Do we not have forgiveness of our sins if we are penitent, and believingly seek his grace? Is Jesus not our reconciler if his Spirit dwells in us and fills us with the peace of God? Is our faith in eternal life vain and baseless if Jesus be not bodily risen, and did not show

himself for a certain length of time to his disciples? What of Old Testament worthies who of course did not believe in the bodily resurrection of Jesus? Of John the Baptist?

Repeatedly he insinuated that the religion of Paul was not the religion of Jesus. For this reason, if for no other, he claimed, Christianity does not have to be Pauline. "We need not fear its collapse if an idea which, in initial Christianity, became the means of its historical unfolding, proves to be transitory and alien to the essentials of Christianity." Paul's claim about the necessity of the resurrection was plausible as historical interpretation, but not as normative theology. Foster declared, "Faith in the divine truth of Christianity is not founded on the bodily resurrection of Jesus, as is the case in authority-religion, but on its new content, the world of love and grace."[33]

The foundational either/or was the question of personality. Foster took the personalist option exclusively, without recourse to apologetic support systems or orthodox stopgaps. "The very peculiarity of Christianity is that it exalts psychic internality to a self-dependent world, and makes this world the center of all reality," he asserted. "If this internality is, not the goal, but the secondary by-product, of cosmic process, the ground is taken away from under Christianity. Hence the controversy over personality becomes a matter of life and death for Christianity." Christianity neither needs nor possesses any other basis; like Borden Parker Bowne, Foster argued that the question of personality is fundamental to Christian theology. The enemies of good theology were authority religion and the various ideologies of impersonalism, not always in that order. Foster spurned Bowne's emphatic incarnationalism, however, and more clearly than Bowne (whose soul language still smacked of substantialist glue), Foster emphatically broke with any notion of the soul as a material or spiritual substance. Traditional Christianity conceived religion as a communion between the soul (a personal substance) and God (another personal substance), he explained, but modern critical consciousness is processive and immanental in its understanding of reality. By Foster's lights, genuinely modern theology was Hegelian and Darwinian. It conceptualized divine reality as a process of becoming and the soul as a progressive synthesis of experience. The soul is not an eternal subtance, he admonished, but "a passing moment in the dialectic process of reality, a fleeting thought of the Thought."[34]

He traced the root of authority religion to this point. Foster was sufficiently committed to an "original gospel" argument to claim Jesus for his side. He argued that the reason why the religion of Jesus "soon took its place among the authority-religions of the old world, why it lost its original path and supported itself on external authority," was that the Christian church subsumed reality under the category of substance. A Platonizing, increasingly institutionalized church supposed that matter, the soul, and God are static substances. This is the core of authority religion, Foster instructed. If the God of Jesus Christ is a static substance, then God is final and absolute, like orthodox Christianity. Orthodoxy and rationalism alike assumed a static world picture. Foster urged that the spirit of Jesus and the modern spirit were very different from this picture: "Let it be repeated—what a great, world-historical change has taken place! The Platonic, medieval, rationalistic world of the static—the Hegelian, Darwinian world of process, becoming, evolution—how great the contrast!"[35]

The static world of Plato, traditional Christianity, and scientistic rationalism was already overthrown. The challenge for Christianity was to catch up to the modern world. Foster tried to be optimistic that a truly modern, progressive Christianity was a possibility. He repeated Bowne's strictures against impersonalism and heightened his critique of religious conservatism. He embraced Hermann Lotze's personalist-idealist thesis that the mission of mechanistic explanation is "absolutely universal" in its extent and "completely subordinate" in its significance. Foster exhorted that the life of the spirit "is not a mere *plus* of nature, but the beginning of a new order; a new kind of reality is manifest in it." He admonished that genuine piety is never content with facts, doctrines, or moral rules: "Piety seeks the deep in things. It is drawn toward the Hidden, the Understood, the Mysterious. It is more than humility, it is adoration; and adoration is the experience of mystery." With a sharper edge, Foster warned that it was not enough to reduce the hope of Christianity to progressive morality.[36]

He feared that much of modern liberal Protestantism was making the latter mistake. While pressing this argument, a year before Albert Schweitzer's apocalyptic thunderbolt, Foster showed that he was up to date in his reading of New Testament scholarship. In the 1890s the *American Journal of Theology* ignored the apocalyptic trend in biblical scholarship pioneered by German scholars Otto Schmoller, Ernst Issel, Johannes Weiss, and Wilhelm Bousset. Shailer Mathews broke this silence in *The Social Teaching of Jesus* (1897), but, like American liberals as a whole, he resisted the apocalyptic reading of the Gospel kingdom sayings. Mathews taught that when Jesus referred to the kingdom of God, he meant "an ideal (though progressively approximated) social order in which the relation of men to God is that of sons, and (therefore) to each other, that of brothers." The "brotherhood of man" was a favorite liberal description of the kingdom of God; Mathews often called it "the goal of social evolution." By the turn of the century, however, Mathews began to make concessions to the trend of German scholarship; by 1905 he converted to it. There were serious differences between the kingdom-building rhetoric of the social gospel and Jesus' understanding of the kingdom, he admonished. In his book *The Messianic Hope in the New Testament* he explained that for Jesus the kingdom was a vertically imposed disruption of the social order, not a process of social evolution.[37]

Foster invoked this scholarly turn against the social gospelers without assimilating it to the rest of his argument. He warned that Christianity had no future as a mere society of ethical culture or political reform. He judged that the story of a lost faith was epitomized in the popular phrase "practical Christianity." He worried that the social gospelers were proving the point. "An effort was made to derive a social program from the Bible," Foster recalled. "The effort was impracticable." The social gospelers fell back on the claim that scripture furnishes the spirit and essential principles of a good society. By the turn of the century, however, biblical scholars were shredding the latter resort. Foster observed, "Biblical scholarship seems to have settled down to the conclusion that Jesus, in common with the entire primitive Christianity, expected the immediate advent of the kingdom of God. His idea of the kingdom of God was not that of modern philosophy—*e.g.,* the Kantian idea; nor of modern theology, especially of the Ritschlian type, which is also Kantian." The social gospelers had barely kindled their enthusiasm for the historical Jesus when "the hour struck for the knowledge that the historical Jesus was much farther from us and much stranger to us than we had believed, and that we could not count upon him off-hand to play a leading part in our social program." The ethic of Jesus was about compassion, purity, inner disposition, and personality, he explained—still evading the point as applied to his own Jesus—but the social gospel needed an ethic of social justice and world politics. "His is good; but we need the other: hence the problem of the possibility of Christianity in the modern world."[38]

Foster had no answer, but he could see the problem. Modern theology was stuck in a crisis of belief. The purpose of modern theology was to respond to modern doubt, but modern theology inspired fresh doubt at every turn. "First verbal inspiration passed away, then the christological dogma, then the traditional portrait of the gospels." For a time the Gospel ethic remained intact, he reflected; the summit of the Sermon on the Mount seemed to reach to heaven. "But the waves of doubt climbed higher and higher until they overflowed it. This was the way of doubt." Foster believed that the Ritschlian school was still producing the best theology. The problem was that "Ritschlianism is ethically oriented through and through." This was the problem of liberal Protestantism. It settled for moral progress and rested in its negations. It sowed religious doubt and gave little evidence of a positive religious message.[39]

Without citing either Bowne or King, Foster reached for their answer to the problem. The good news of modern Christianity should be its resounding belief in personality, the life of the spirit, he exhorted. If liberal Protestantism gave a pale witness to this gospel, the problem was with modern liberal Protestantism, not the gospel. Foster noted that Friedrich Nietzsche was never boring: "Nietzsche thundered in the interest of *personality.* He ridiculed science as folly, denied every objective norm, preached the right of passion as against logic, instinct as against *Dressur,* the wilderness as against the schoolroom, heroism as against utility-morals, greatness as against philistinism, and the intoxicating poesy of life as against its regulation." Nietzsche was wrong about various things, but on all of his main themes, "barring the exaggerations of the poet, he was right fundamentally. We have cause to thank Nietzsche." The fact that Nietzsche hated Christianity should not prevent Christians from being inspired by him, Foster suggested: "He broke down ramparts against which we were too weak. He would give back the deep again to man and awaken a great yearning. Yearning is combined with a knowledge of a defect, and the kingdom of heaven belongs to the spiritually poor."[40]

The true mission of Christianity is the true mission of humankind, Foster exhorted. It is for men and women to become personality. "But it is only as an unconditionally worthful member of an unconditionally worthful reality that he becomes personality." Foster's theme was King's, set free from King's tameness. The more personal that an individual becomes, "the more he seeks society; and the more society realizes its own essence, the more does it promote the growth of personality." It is through change, process, becoming that we find the possibility of truth and goodness, Foster enthused, "the possibility of personality in which there is an eternal and absolute moment." Development and personality go together as means and end. Supernaturalism excludes development and naturalism excludes personality; true religion embraces both. Rightly understood, he assured, the religion of Jesus is the best example of true religion.[41]

Foster admonished that historical criticism is very limited in aiding the latter understanding. "Little by little we are coming to see that the *content* of religious faith is exposed to no peril from historical criticism," he asserted. "Criticism has compelled us to withdraw our faith from false objects, and to concentrate it upon its true object. And the object of faith is not the Bible with which historical criticism deals, but rather the spirit of the gospel." Most of the reasonable questions about Jesus cannot be answered, he observed. Having claimed to know that the Jesus of history did not support authority religion, Foster ended on a more cautionary note: "Did Jesus do this or that, go here or there, say this or that? Where was he born; when did he die; how long did he live; what was the length of his ministry? As a matter of fact, we do not surely know. But nothing concerning him of which critical inquiry can make us uncertain is an object of religious faith. The spirit and ideals and forces and value of that life—*these* are what faith needs; but these are known only by being experienced, and not by literary and historical criticism."[42]

JESUS AND THE RELIGION OF SPIRIT

The Finality of the Christian Religion was the first theological blockbuster by a member of the Chicago school. It contained enough of Troeltsch and Hegel to foreshadow much of the school's future, though its Nietzschean spirit belonged distinctively to Foster. The book sustained a vigorous conversation with prominent critical historians, especially Hermann Gunkel, Wilhelm Bousset, Paul Wernle, and Otto Pfleiderer. Like generations of Chicago schoolers to come, it affirmed that theologians need to compare Christianity objectively with other religions and that historical-religions analysis is indispensable to the understanding of Christian history. Foster appreciated the historical-religions deconstruction of messianic theology, especially the "sophistical exegetical fantasy" that supported messianic interpretations of the Old Testament. He believed that the Jesus of history could be reached only by stripping off the adornments of messianic late Judaism and early Christianity. At the same time, he was sharply critical of the pictures of Jesus that emerged from the *Religionsgeschichtliche Schule*. He complained that if one fully accepted these accounts, "one would conclude that Israel was the only sterile race ethico-religiously, having borrowed all from other peoples, and that Jesus was the only man to whom spontaneity and originality had been denied." The historical-religions school was biased against individuality and personality, he implied, but personality is what matters. The strength of the history-of-religions school was its weakness. Troeltsch's colleagues unveiled the considerable syncretism of early Christianity and then exaggerated it. In Foster's reading, what was needed was an historical critical scholarship that highlighted not only the commonalities, but especially the differences between Jesus and other figures.[43]

Like much of the Chicago school after him, Foster insisted that his commitments to rationalist criticism, historical consciousness, and philosophical idealism did not conflict with his central focus on the life and ideals of Jesus. Ideas are important, he allowed, but the salvation that we need is not a matter of acquiring the right ideas. It is a matter of being delivered from bad will, "the evil state of the heart." It followed that "sound personalities" are more important to the process of redemption than right doctrine: "As fire kindles fire, and not some theory about the nature of flame, so persons save persons." Revelation is the "content of holy personalities" who save us by their *ideals,* not their ideas.[44]

To Foster, Jesus was unique as the ultimate exemplar of this saving process. "It was not belief in angels, in spirits, and in the hereafter that constituted his peculiarity and his power. It was not his working of miracles, nor his belief in demons; he knew that he was not sent to do miracles, and his belief in demons he shared with his times." Neither was it his announcement of the imminent kingdom of God, or his ostensible claim to be the Messiah, or his supposed claim to be the Son of God, or his moral code that constituted his uniqueness, for all these claims had ample precedent, and the first three were loaded with historicity problems. What was unique about Jesus was *himself* and his spiritual power to renew the lives of others. At the outer edge of this claim, Foster contended that "the unity, wholeness, spirituality, and simplicity of his moral thoughts, as well as the freshness, liveliness, and beauty of their presentation, were new," though he respectfully noted that "certain modern Jewish scholars" disputed this attribution.[45]

The heart of his claim was more personal; it was a page from Herrmann. "What was certainly new was the disposition and self-consciousness of Jesus," Foster argued. "From these there gradually sprang up in his soul a value judgment that was new also, namely, that not *things,* not even *sacred* things, but that *persons only,* are worthful. Faith in the infinite worth of the human personality in the sight of God—if there was anything new in the thought of Jesus, it was this." To a Christian, Foster contended, Jesus of Nazareth was and is the unique expression of God's personal life. This was the true meaning of the incarnational dogmas that Christianity mistakenly heaped upon Jesus: "The Christian is one who knows God in the man Jesus, one for whom Jesus is the personality which determines his relation to God."[46]

Foster realized that his constructive claims were thin and sketchy at best. What exactly did it mean to uphold "the spirit and ideals and forces and value" of Jesus?

Why was it important to claim that Jesus uniquely expressed the personal life of God? What would a fully modernist theological personalism look like? More precisely, what was the constructive theological expression that came from the left-Ritschlian position outlined in *The Finality of the Christian Religion*? He promised that the answer was forthcoming. Having rejected authority religion and scientistic naturalism, and having surveyed the problems of modern theology, Foster resolved to provide a constructive theological account of the religion of spirit in an American voice. He felt keenly the need to *do* some exemplary theologizing rather than merely describe theology's problems. His first book provided the central question of this project, his version of Troeltsch's essential question: "Is, now, the conviction of the finality of the Christian religion tenable in this new world of ours, where the fixed has yielded to flux, being to becoming, absoluteness to relativity, force to ideals? Having seen that Christianity is no longer absolute as a religion of authority in a world of static entities, can it be shown that it is absolute as a religion of ideals in a world of evolution and immanence? That is the great problem."[47]

But Foster never published his constructive theology. He drafted a manuscript, apparently revised it for several years, and then abandoned it. He told colleagues that the ascendancy of philosophical pragmatism subverted the religious sense of the world that pervaded his first book. In addition, he was a professor of theology when he wrote *The Finality of the Christian Religion;* now he was out of the Divinity School. Having celebrated the Hegelian-Darwinian modern world of immanence and becoming, Foster was unnerved, on second reflection, by the seriousness of the pragmatist rejection of absolutes. Many of his colleagues were philosophical pragmatists; a pragmatic-empiricist school of thinking clustered around John Dewey had germinated at Chicago in the mid-1890s. In 1907 Foster published an article that explained why he was not (yet) a pragmatist: "In my opinion the most serious question of the hour is whether religion stands or falls with the affirmation or denial of cognitive function of the ideas which faith possesses." For him, this was a personal question. Was he prepared to defend the objective validity of the idea of God? If not, was he prepared to rethink his entire religious philosophy? Did he have sufficient reason not to move all the way to the philosophical pragmatism of Dewey and William James? Since his own account of Christian truth was based on the personal effects of personality and ideals, why not embrace pragmatism as the best philosophical aid to religious thinking? Having declared, in praise of Nietzsche, that "a God outside the cosmos is dead," did he really believe that his ideas of God and religious ideals possessed an ontological foundation?[48]

PRAGMATISM AND RELIGIOUS TRUTH

Foster wavered back and forth on the last question for the rest of his life. He answered the former questions in 1908, but never gave his heart and mind to the answer, hence the wavering. His philosophical conversion, announced in a

1908 Berkeley lecture series, was published the following year as *The Function of Religion in Man's Struggle for Existence*. In the preface he declared that he was determined to cleave "to the sunnier side of doubt." He hoped for "light and warmth enough to keep us from freezing in the dark." Thereafter he reported that he had become a radical empiricist and pragmatic functionalist. There is no such thing as a priori knowledge, he asserted; the idea of knowledge as something that is independent of experience is a phantom. All truly modern thinking, including modern religious thinking, begins at that point. For all their greatness, Kant and Schleiermacher failed this fundamental test. Kant conceived God as the a priori necessity of moral conduct; Schleiermacher conceived God as the necessity of the feeling of dependence. Foster countered that modern scientific consciousness knows no a prioris that have not come to be. All categories have a natural history, like everything else; all things are products of the flow of experience. The validity of a category of any kind, including a religious category, is not rightly determined by referring to some hypothetical cause, but rather by observing its value to the life of the human spirit.[49]

It followed that religion is best understood as a useful instrument by which the human organism adapts to its environment. Foster explained, "A man creates whatever concepts and principles he may need in order to make himself master of the phenomena of his environment. To the same end were the gods created." This modern perception is not necessarily hostile to religion, he assured, for religion is not fundamentally about the existence of an a priori God-idea. Religion is about "those inner motives of will and feeling in the service of which the God-idea is created." A person's religiousness is not that she has a God; her religiousness is her God-making capacity. In this sense, Foster noted, Nietzsche was correct that "God"—the God of traditional church theology—is dead. Modern consciousness would not have created the Trinity-God of classical Christianity, any more than it would have created the Messiah figure of early Christian preaching or the "fully God and fully man" Christ of Chalcedonian Christology. The very notion of religion as a vessel of metaphysical truth has to be discarded, Foster asserted: "The man of today must think of religion as a necessary creation of human nature and evaluate it from that point of view, or else be excused from further interest in the old problems of God and freedom and immortality."[50]

He appreciated that this verdict was hard to distinguish from the Ludwig Feuerbach/Karl Marx tradition of religion debunkers who dismissed religion as illusory wish fulfillment. Foster countered that wish fulfillment is not necessarily an illusion. The religious consciousness is probably no more illusory than other forms of consciousness, he reasoned; in any case, the tests are pragmatic. For the most part, it was his experience that "the fear of illusion is the bitter fruit of speculation dissociated from life, and not the practical outcome of really living in religion. Indeed, the man who *really lives in* religion, deriving the strength and recuperation and meaning of his life therefrom, will not be haunted by this dread of illusion." Citing William James for support, Foster urged that the serious test of truth in religion, as in everything else, is what works. "God" is a good idea if this idea of the good promotes the attainment of all that is true, good, and beautiful. In Foster's words: "The word God is a symbol to designate the universe in its ideal-achieving capacity. It is the expression of our appreciation of existence, when our feelings are so excited as to assign worth to existence. But all our highest ideas are but figurative expressions. Even the concept of a personal God has symbolic validity only."[51]

Foster's Christology was ready-made for this philosophical conversion. He made a typically two-handed argument. On the one hand, he showed how a left-Ritschlian theology could say everything that it wanted to affirm about the religion of Jesus from a pragmatic-functionalist standpoint. On the other hand, he made a clean break from Ritschlian attempts to claim that Christianity is the absolute or final religion. With quotations from Bousset and himself, though with a sharper concern this time not to overstate the case for Jesus as a unique figure, he claimed the spirit of Jesus for modern religious pragmatism. For modern religionists, as for Jesus, he exhorted, religion was essentially a creative activity of the human spirit. Religion expresses the pillar of fire in the human race; for as long as human beings are human, it will continue to do so. At the same time Foster made it clear that he was finished with the Ritschlian project of claiming absoluteness for Christianity:

> We can never be satisfied with this Jesus religion as a finality. We must pass on from faith in man to faith in a new eternal Messiah—*our* Messiah, a creation of the spirit of modern humanity, "becoming flesh" in all human souls, born anew in every child, in order to celebrate his resurrection of truth and love, of justice and freedom. And this Messiah will be to us—what he really was to every people that created or adopted him—our Ideal.[52]

Religion is always about faith and conviction, he urged, not about sight. Religious pragmatism is simply honest about this fact. Though he allowed that modern people are entitled to assume that existence as a whole "has an ideal-achieving capacity," Foster cautioned that we cannot *know* that the world exists for the sake of ideals. The latter is a question for faith. In faith, he still trusted that "reality is on the side of the achievement of ideals such as ours," but he noted that something unforeseen could happen in the future to affect religion: "The menace to the future of religion lies in the religion of the future."[53]

This road led beyond liberal Christianity, though Foster regarded his new position as the next logical phase of liberal Christianity. By linking his post-Ritschlian theology to philosophical pragmatism, he identified himself with an emerging Chicago tradition. The foundations of Chicago-School pragmatism were laid between 1894 and 1904 by a group led by John Dewey, sociologist George Herbert Mead, psychologist James Rowland Angell, and philosopher James Hayden Tufts. Other prominent Chicago School pragmatists included philosopher Addison Webster Moore, psychologist Harvey Carr, psychology of religionist Edward Scribner Ames, and Divinity School theologian Gerald Birney Smith. Except for Tufts, who was a close friend of Foster's, the founding four-some had little interest in religion. At its core the Chicago School reflected Dewey's humanism. Among Foster's closest colleagues at Chicago, however, several were pragmatic empiricists who had strong religious interests. Tufts, Ames and Smith believed that nonreligious pragmatism was short-sighted and impoverishing; on this theme, the key figure was Ames.[54]

Ames was an early product of the Chicago School who earned his doctorate under Tufts and Mead in 1896. While teaching in Chicago's philosophy department, he essentially created the field of functionalist psychology of religion, all the while serving as pastor of nearby Hyde Park Church (Disciples of Christ) and founder of the university-based Disciples Divinity House. He later chaired Chicago's philosophy department for many years. At the time of Foster's philosophical conversion, Ames was completing a major work, *The Psychology of Religious Experience*, which used the tools of pragmatic-functionalist analysis to interpret religion as a social, evolutionary, utility-driven historical phenomenon. His teaching in the psychology of religion had already produced accomplished disciples such as Irving King and Frederick G. Henke. Ames taught his students and church followers to think of God as a functional concept that develops out of the social psychology and history of a people.[55] The example that he set for local theologues was attractive in the environment of Chicago pragmatism. Mathews was committed by his training and interests to a naturalistic, sociohistorical approach to religion; under local influence, Smith migrated from left-Ritschlianism to naturalistic religious empiricism; in 1908, sociohistorical empiricist Shirley Jackson Case joined the Divinity School faculty; during the same period, Foster joined a growing pragmatic-empiricist caucus at Chicago; under Foster's influence, comparative religionist A. Eustace Haydon later became a leading member of a pragmatic-functionalist faculty core at the Divinity School.[56]

Foster's post-Ritschlian pragmatist turn was too much for local Baptists. His book aroused weeks of passionate debate about his right to the Baptist name and provided fuel for what came to be called the fundamentalist movement. Called to appear before a ministers' meeting in 1909 to explain his understanding of the deity of Christ, he replied by letter that he refused to submit to any sort of inquisition. Foster was bitterly accused of heresy and infidelism. Conservative Baptist church leaders Johnston Myers, W. A. Matthews, C. F. Tolman, and Amzi C. Dixon condemned him repeatedly; Myers sermonized that "no man has the right to deny Jesus Christ." Foster's defenders appealed to academic freedom and the Baptist principle of the liberty of conscience. Though he made serious attempts to explain his position, Foster could not resist fanning the flames with cheeky remarks to reporters. He also preached regularly at a local Unitarian church. For two months the controversy garnered daily coverage in at least nine Chicago newspapers. After weeks of bitter polemics and several cycles of motions and resolutions, the Baptist Ministers Conference voted 39–9 to "eject" him from the fellowship of the Baptist ministry. This was a purely symbolic excommunication, since, under Baptist polity, only Foster's congregation possessed the authority to expel him. He refused to demit from the Baptist ministry, insisted that he was still a good Baptist, and was deeply grateful when his congregation, the Hyde Park Baptist Church, rejected the Conference's order to "disfellowship" him. For the rest of his life he remained on the roll of ministers of the Chicago Baptist Association. Foster was painfully aware that in the minds of many local clergy, however, he remained neither a minister nor a Baptist.[57]

The controversy over his theology played an indirect role in the schism within the state Baptist convention that led to the founding of Northern Baptist Theological Seminary in 1913. More broadly, it also played a role in the mobilization of fundamentalism as a mass movement. Amzi C. Dixon, pastor of the Moody Memorial Church in Chicago, was a strident opponent of modernizing apostasy in the churches. At the height of the Foster controversy he gave an anti-Foster lecture at the Baptist Temple Auditorium in Los Angeles that greatly impressed millionaire layperson Lyman Stewart. Stewart and his brother, Milton Stewart, enlisted Dixon to produce a multivolume defense of traditional Protestantism that was pitched (and generously distributed) to a mass audience. Lyman Stewart later recalled to Dixon that their movement-launching twelve-volume series, *The Fundamentals,* owed its birth to Dixon's lecture against "one of those infidel professors in Chicago University."[58]

Foster took pride that his work pressed the Protestant churches to choose sides between theological modernism and traditional authority religion. He was fond of speaking of doubt or the critical spirit as the "purgative side" of faith. He took satisfaction in his influence on various left-Ritschlian, personalist idealist, pragmatic empiricist, critical realist, and religious humanist thinkers. By his lights, he was a good Baptist. He wanted to help modern Christianity become thoroughly modern without relinquishing Jesus. "Never in my life have I denied the divineness of Jesus Christ; but that the doctrine thereof has to be restated and revalued in terms of modern thinking," he insisted in 1909. "Jesus is the best that we know, human or divine." Foster clung to his post-Ritschlian Ebionism as the basis of a genuinely modern Christianity. The serious question for Christianity is not whether Jesus is as good as God is, he maintained, "but whether God is as good as Jesus is." The best that we know must be the divine; the predicate attaches worthily to no other object: "I repeat my assertion: I am a typical, loyal, old-fashioned Baptist; believing and trusting in the grace of God—that God whom Jesus reveals—and in the necessity of the inner renewal of the heart of us sinners by the Divine Spirit, if we are to be saved from sin at all."[59]

But Foster struggled mightily with his religious doubts, openly and without apology. His vulnerability and distinct double-mindedness invited ridicule even from people who were more or less in his corner. Harry Pratt Judson, president of the Northern Baptist Convention and Harper's successor as president of the University of Chicago, was one of them. In August 1909, after the Foster controversy began to fade, Judson gave this account of it to Ernest DeWitt Burton, who had returned from traveling in east Asia: "Our Professor Foster has been causing more or less hubbub during the last few months. He wrote a book which some of the brethren regard as the sum of all villainies. I doubt myself whether many people understand what it means anyway. However, that being the case, anybody is at liberty to understand what he pleases from it. Possibly Mr. Foster himself understands it, although I regard that as a rather dubious proposition." Judson took a managerial-liberal approach to his Foster problem. He tolerated Foster's iconoclasm while doubting that he was worth the trouble that he caused for the university or the Baptist church. Foster lived with the awareness that he stirred the same reaction in some of his colleagues, though some of them fell considerably short of his spiritual intensity.[60]

At the moment of his ostensible conversion to pragmatic empiricism he warned that Christianity was "in the most grievous crisis of its history." As always, the historic crisis of Christianity was personal to him. He reflected that the crisis was "the quiet, bitter struggle which serious men are fighting out in their own souls." It was "the dying of the old faith which Western Christendom is experiencing." Foster tried to speak for the sunny side of doubt: "My contention still is that religion is a necessary factor in the struggle for life."[61]

But does faith have an object besides itself? Is faith merely faith in faith? Are people actually saved by the psychologically useful *idea* of God? Foster's personal experience contradicted his theorizing about it. Mathews later recalled that he and Foster first met during Foster's days of mourning over the drowning of his son: "He was suffering deeply and cried out, 'There must be a God somewhere in the universe.'" Mathews believed that Foster never relinquished that conviction. He recounted a similar conversation that occurred during Foster's later, pragmatist phase. The encounter occurred just after Foster finished giving a lecture on pragmatism. In Mathews's account, Foster confessed to him what he really believed, or at least deeply felt: "I remember his calling out in his penetrating voice, 'Mathews, we need a God, a real God, a God to whom we can pray for rain.'"[62]

The *Titanic* disaster of 1912 evoked the same sentiment in him. In the wake of the ship's catastrophe on its first voyage, Foster wrote an article for the *Chicago Tribune* that stood his recent book on its head. "We foolish men make conditions and prescribe to God how he must behave, if we are to believe in him," he observed. "So long as this is our attitude we are still far from the real God. We have a catechism God, not the living God; shadow of God, not God himself. From such a point of view God is an idol." He reflected that idolators make their own gods and are subsequently disillusioned by them, for the god of one's own making is a nonentity. Foster declared, "It is a different way that leads to the real and living God." This was the way of experience, "the experience of yearning and love, of seeking and trusting, of ever new discovery and ever deeper intimacy. Already our childish souls found God, without stipulations and calculations. God greeted us as the sun greets us." Foster was moved by the piety of the victims who sang "Nearer, My God, to Thee" as the *Titanic* went down. He judged that the disaster would produce atheists only among cynical outsiders, not among those who lost their loved ones: "It is a most superficial assumption that men would be nearer to God if the world were less offensive. Faith arises out of the tension between the world around us and the Eternity within us. The stream of life wells up from the deepest need. God rules in the riddle, in the tension; the ever-living, ever-loving is at work there."[63]

Foster was blessed with appreciative disciples and doctoral students; A. Eustace Haydon, John Dietrich, Curtis Reese, and Douglas Clyde Macintosh were prominent among them. In 1912 Macintosh, a young professor at Yale, was just beginning to develop his distinctive form of empiricist theological realism. Upon reading his teacher's article, he asked Foster the obvious question: had he changed again? Foster replied, "Yes, I have passed through the slough of epistemological subjectivity, and see more clearly and hold more firmly the objective and social reality of religion. Still, I think that dualism is dead, that our choice is between monism and pluralism—or some new adjustment of the two. But a real God, a real man, a real world—our need of these is too imperious to give them up."[64]

Genuine religion holds fast to God, he believed, not merely the useful idea of God. For several years Foster emphasized the difference. He told the Baptist Congress of 1912 that the question of God's ontological existence is fundamental to everything else: "The question of the truth of our belief in God, even more than the question of the historicity of Jesus and the knowability of his own gospel, is the real crisis of the modern world." He noted that an unnamed American psychologist (it was Ames) described God as being like Uncle Sam. Foster countered, "But Uncle Sam is not a being for himself, he is a being for the American people; he did not make them, they made him; he has no feeling or consciousness for them, they have feeling and consciousness for him. And if the American people were to disappear, Uncle Sam would disappear." While cautioning that he did not deny the truth of the Uncle Sam analogy as a functional description, he sharply denied its adequacy as an account of religious truth. He quoted Macintosh's recent dissertation on the need of an explicitly ontological philosophical theology: "Theology, instead of fading away into mere psychology of religion, must boldly take up the ontological-metaphysical task. Theology must, if religion is not to suffer seriously, undertake to build into the very fiber of its tissues a philosophy of reality." Foster agreed with his protégé. Instead of reducing itself to the level of phenomenology or psychology, Foster urged, theology needed to deal with "the meaning and value and truth of our Christian belief in God and immortality." The intellectual task was daunting, "but it cannot be surrendered without inflicting irreparable injury on the life of the human spirit."[65]

For four years he exhorted pastors and religious thinkers to hold fast to God's real existence and presence. "Men are suffering far more from the loss of God and of the moral imperative than from the lack of bread and work, of recreation and amusement," he declared in 1916. "What can silence the voice of the heart's pain?" Foster never bridged the Ritschlian divide between knowledge and faith; his persistent use of heart language was a clue. Sometimes he blared the difference: "Briefly expressed, religion experiences, science calculates; religion creates, science discovers; religion ventures, science weighs. Science avails itself of concepts and categories and laws; religion, of symbols and pictures and parables." In 1916 he told Macintosh that he believed as strongly as ever in the need of a metaphysical justification of the idea of a real God, "but I don't quite see how to do it."[66]

Then he fell back into the slough of epistemological subjectivism. World War I troubled him deeply, especially after the United States intervened. In February 1918 Foster's son Harrison died of pneumonia in a Texas army camp. A grieving Foster reported to Macintosh that he had lost his "brilliant soldier boy, Harrison." By then he had stopped speaking of God's real existence. Classroom notes taken by his graduate students indicate that by the spring of 1917, Foster had returned to speaking of God strictly as the personification of human ideals. He taught that God is more like Uncle Sam, who depends upon the people for whom he functions, than like George Washington, who was the Father of his country. All that we can say about God is that God's reality is functional, he contended, for "that is the only kind of reality we know." Foster reflected that in the modern world, society is the final interpreter and judge of humankind. But is society always right? Doesn't humankind need a supersocial? The latter question haunted his last book, a sympathetic meditation on Nietzsche. "Back of everything else is the everlasting, heartbreaking question whether the root of this tumultuous, torturing universe is force or love," he wrote. "Is force primary and love a mere transitory product? That is the question of questions, the doubt of doubts. And the answer to that question must determine who is to be master of the world, Nietzsche or Christ!"[67]

In his heart, Foster held fast to the left-liberal Jesus, whom the Ritschlians and Amesian pragmatists invoked more or less in common. Philosophically, he returned to Ames and the religion of pragmatism. This time he may have stepped beyond Ames's churchly pragmatism, however, at least with one foot. On various occasions in the last two years of his life Foster urged that modern Christianity needed to create a better God; on other occasions he claimed that the idea of God belonged to a bygone age. "We are ethically required to make a better God," he urged his students. "We must not pass into godlessness, but we must find a new God-idea which shall be as efficacious as the old idea was." Out of the other side of his mouth, a few months before his death, Foster asserted on several occasions that the modern world had outgrown its need for a God-idea.[68]

In 1918 he gave the Dudleian Lecture at Harvard in the company of one of his closest friends, Harvard Divinity School dean William Wallace Fenn. Foster took a purely pragmatic-functionalist approach to religion, tracing the movement of religious thought from the idea of an objective-revealing God to the idea that humans project a God-idea for their use. His subject was "the long process of transition from revelation without religion to religion without revelation." For centuries humanity was dependent upon God for everything, he reflected; during the Enlightenment, rationalist philosophers appealed to God as the ground of intellectual certitude; more recently, moral theologians influenced by Kant appealed to God as the ground of virtuous human will. Foster announced that modern culture had arrived at a posttheistic stage in which humanity took possession of the powers of agency and creativity that it formerly projected unto

God: "At length the dualism of God and the world was overcome. Little by little, the creative and preservative and gubernatorial activities were alienated from God and integrated upon the world. The world now did for itself what God once did for it." The last refuge of theology was the God of immanence, he observed, but what exactly does it mean to claim that the world is God's body? "If God does what the world does, the reality of the world is gone; if the world now does what God was once supposed to do, the reality of God is gone."[69]

Two months before his death, Foster confirmed to Ames that he had moved to what he called a "humanistic naturalism." He explained: "Religion is loyalty to the values of human life—only this and nothing more. The source of these values is the human will to live and to create. These values are self-justifying and self-supporting, therefore supernatural sanction and support are superfluous. Hence the present passing of theism, not violently, but slowly, quietly, because it is outgrown."[70] His review of Ames's *The New Orthodoxy* contained a clue to this judgment: "By and by, when your children have died and your life is almost gone, and you seem to have done almost nothing, is there anything that can give you heart and hope? Or is it the condition of nobility in man that the All should be against him? If there were a foregone assurance of victory, what kind of man would that give?" Foster's verdict at the end of the war, and the end of his life, was that "we are witnessing the passing of theistic supernaturalism." The world was outgrowing theism "in a gentle and steady way."[71]

CHICAGO CURRENTS AND THE LEGACY OF FOSTER

Foster's legacy was nearly as curious and ironic as his career. He had a powerful impact on his students, his friends, and a sizable public audience. Fenn spoke for many friends and students in calling him "the most profoundly, purely, genuinely, religious man that I ever knew." Religion was not a part of Foster's nature, Fenn observed; "it was his nature, in its wholeness." Foster regularly opened his classes with intense, evocative prayers that seemed to invite students into his interior spiritual struggle. Chicago colleague J. M. Powis Smith believed that "no one could come into close contact with him for any length of time without yielding to the charm of his personality." Foster was brilliant, childlike, and instinctively kindly, Smith recalled; he was also "an out-and-outer in everything." Macintosh reflected that his teacher was able, "as few are, to lead the afflicted and perplexed to the sources of spiritual strength." In his experience, Foster was "humane and sympathetic toward every fellow-sufferer," and a gifted teacher without peer: "He knew what religion was, for it was his daily life." Perhaps most instructive in explaining the force of his impression on many students, Macintosh recalled that Foster "could take more daring excursions into the realms of doubt than would have been spiritually safe for a less deeply religious man."[72]

This quality of restless vulnerability was the key to Foster's considerable public impact. He eschewed the mannered correctness of liberal leaders like King and

Mathews. His writings and lectures were interesting, daring, and, his denials notwithstanding, usually designed to provoke. He had a knack for taking the next step that weaker souls might have been thinking about but were afraid to express. After Dewey left Chicago in 1905, Foster was unrivaled as the faculty's public celebrity. On a faculty that was unusually adept at bridging the gap between town and gown—the pragmatists were good organizers—Foster stood out. He was a highly sought after speaker to all manner of church groups, social causes, and civic associations throughout his career. In 1917 he debated superlawyer Clarence Darrow at the Garrick Theatre on the question "Is Life Worth Living?" (Foster argued the affirmative.) Later he debated Darrow at the Cort Theatre on the freedom of the human will. Foster and Darrow became good friends; Darrow described him as the most intellectual person he ever met. In November 1918 Foster caught a chill while conducting the funeral of his friend President Van Hise of the University of Wisconsin; he died the following month, saying to his wife at the end, "Tell them I am still captain of my soul."[73]

As a religious thinker he variously developed or set into motion most of the currents of thought that distinguished Chicago theological liberalism. Foster's personalism, widely shared in his early career, faded away in later Chicago theologies, though Mathews retained a version of it. His conversion to functionalist-pragmatic analysis helped to establish a post-Ritschlian center of gravity at the Divinity School that persisted for decades, and he shared the naturalism of the entire Chicago school. His vigorously liberal use of historical criticism established a strong Chicago tradition, as did his advocacy of a left-Ritschlian theology of the spirit of Jesus, though the latter gospel faded in subsequent Chicago theology. His protégé, Macintosh, rejected much of Foster's metaphysics and epistemology, but like most Chicago schoolers, he embraced Foster's relativizing appeal to historical consciousness. Foster told his students that the essence of Christianity cannot be something that belongs exclusively to the past. This principle, rooted in the theologies of Schleiermacher and Ritschl, became a Chicago trademark. Macintosh insisted that it was "preposterous" to suppose "that a mere change in one's historical opinions, honestly arrived at, could necessarily make one cease to be a Christian, if his Christianity were a matter of his own religious experience."[74]

In 1905 Macintosh was a student in Foster's classes on Christian dogmatics and ethics; in 1921 Macintosh published his teacher's lectures, which had changed his life. He regretted that Foster never delivered them again, and he published them in the hope that they would inspire others in the same way. But Foster's legacy was already fading at Chicago and the rest of American theology. His books went out of print, philosophical personalism became the property of a more conventionally liberal school, and the Chicago school of theology came to be identified with other figures, especially Mathews, Ames, Smith, Case, and, later, Henry Nelson Wieman. The pragmatic-empiricist option prevailed at Chicago. Mathews, Ames, Smith, and Case developed functionalist approaches to religion that emphasized sociohistorical analysis and pragmatic philosophy; in the 1930s Wieman took Chicago theology in an ahistorical, stringently empiricist direction;

still later, Bernard E. Meland and Bernard Loomer fused the language of Chicago empiricism to Whiteheadian process metaphysics. Foster had an intellectual relationship to nearly all of these developments, but he became a dimly remembered figure in American theology as Wieman and Meland struggled to keep liberal theology alive in an unsympathetic time.[75]

Foster's writings had a shorter life span than many lesser works in the field. His rollicking, argumentative, sometimes emotional magnum opus did not wear well. *The Finality of the Christian Religion* was quickly dated because of its preoccupation with current debates and because of a certain verbal prolixity that contrasted with the chastened prose of American pragmatism. Its academic reputation was not helped by his nearly immediate announcement that the book was philosophically out of date. His major work deserved stronger advocacy and constructive development. Thereafter his writings were easily quoted against each other. Foster had an extraordinarily sympathetic imagination. He was adept at entering and appropriating the intellectual visions of diverse thinkers. This quality was perhaps his chief intellectual virtue and a major strength of his work. At the same time, in his case, his capacity for multiperspectival reflection clearly impeded his attempts to achieve intellectual definition.

Though forgotten by most of the field, Foster was remembered by a trickle of mainline Protestants who claimed him for liberal Christianity and a larger current of Unitarians and religious naturalists who claimed him as a founder of modern nontheistic religious humanism. Macintosh, Mathews, and Edgar A. Towne argued in different ways for the former reading; Charles Harvey Arnold, Larry R. Axel, Alan Gragg, and Creighton Peden contended for the latter view.[76] Both sides of this debate have ample proof texts and biographical clues to cite. Foster made post-Christian claims on various occasions while continuing to identify with liberal Christianity. In the last months of his life he explicitly proclaimed the end of theism, but he also pastored a Unitarian church on the side and never renounced his Christian identity or Baptist membership.

My view is that he should be assessed on the basis of his entire career, which was double-minded and persistently conflicted. Darrow believed that Foster finally settled on a definite position—nontheistic humanism—in the closing weeks of his life.[77] Foster may have claimed as much to Darrow, but a settled conviction in his case was unlikely. Foster never gave up the liberal Jesus—at least in the sense of a post-Ritschlian ideal—and he insisted that liberals of his kind belonged in the church. At the same time, he fell in and out of belief in the reality and knowability of God. He was too influenced by Darwin, Strauss, Nietzsche, and Dewey to speak in Bowne's assured tones about the existence of divine personality, but he was too fervently religious to be satisfied with any form of secular reason. Thus he spent his entire intellectual career never quite belonging anywhere. He wanted to believe in something that antimetaphysical modern pragmatism could not secure, but he found pragmatist religion religiously wanting. His interesting, pathbreaking, headstrong works demonstrated the virtues of religious relativism and its limitations. In the decades that followed his death,

Foster was claimed as a forerunner by nontheistic religious humanists; a bit closer to his conflicted theological identity, he was also claimed by a handful of vaguely theistic Unitarians as a forerunner of their brand of religious humanism.

Macintosh observed that Foster's conflicts were always cognitive, never affective. In his feeling, Macintosh explained, Foster remained a steadfast liberal Christian, though he appears to have become "alienated from theistic ways of thinking" at the end of his life. This was the closest that Macintosh came to capturing the paradox of Foster. From the vantage point of closer personal acquaintance, William Wallace Fenn cautioned against the inclination to assign a definite position to Foster, noting that his friend was an unusual kind of thinker. Foster never moved straight to his point or position, Fenn recalled: "It was his habit to throw himself heartily into a new idea, trying to discover all that could be said for it, to see how far it could be carried, and what would be its consequences if it should be accepted, yet in all this his own judgment was often held in suspense. The result was that he often seemed to hold opinions concerning which he had not made up his mind, and, therefore, was often misunderstood."[78]

This manner of thinking did not make a good fit with the confident liberal empiricism that ruled the Chicago school during and after Foster's career. Foster wavered for years on whether he could be a good empiricist. The manner of thinking that Fenn described, however, has a good deal in common with contemporary postmodern consciousness. In his own way, like postmodern thinking today, Foster's work was pluralistic, multivocal, multiperspectival, and featured a conflicted sense of identity. Fenn recalled that for years he mistakenly thought that Foster was a straightforward James-style pragmatist in his theory of knowledge. It surprised him greatly when Foster assured him that he was not a philosophical pragmatist. "Remembering this, I dare not say that Foster was so much of a 'Humanist' as he appeared to be. He died with pilgrim staff in hand and nobody can tell what would have been the final resting-place of his thought, if, indeed, it had ever found one."[79]

The Chicago school of theological liberalism grew out of such fertile, contradictory, and profuse beginnings. It became a major school, however, by tacking in the direction of Foster's initially less-promising colleague.

SHAILER MATHEWS'S ROAD TO CHICAGO

Shailer Mathews came to Chicago with no indication of Foster-like brilliance. He had little training and no particular interest in the field of theology; barely a few months before his arrival he thought of himself as a prospective sociologist. Like many theological leaders of his generation, Mathews undertook his graduate training at the University of Berlin, but he avoided Harnack and all other religious thinkers. He later judged that his training in secular historical criticism was an ideal preparation for the kind of theology that he developed, on which the Chicago School was forged.

His personal background was thoroughly middle class, mid-Victorian, and evangelical. Mathews was born in Portland, Maine in 1863. His father was a Baptist deacon and storeowner who ran a wholesale tea and flour business; through his mother he descended from several generations of teachers and ministers; his local Baptist pastor was his maternal grandfather. He later recalled that evangelical Protestantism pervaded the simple, secure, wholesome atmosphere of his Portland boyhood world. New England Protestants did not doubt that the world was in God's hands; to his perception, New England Congregationalists and Baptists understood God's plan of salvation quite precisely. Theological debate was limited to the question whether Christ's death was vicarious or substitutionary; all other questions of theology were settled; church leaders took for granted that only Unitarians bothered to read German theology. Mathews reflected that they worried a bit more about Darwin and Huxley, but not very much more: "There were no serious doubts and, thanks to wise family discipline, no serious temptations. It was a healthy life in which religion was a natural element. God could be trusted to order the affairs, especially the business and health, of Christians. Sickness and misfortune were His discipline. God was very real."[80]

In that frame of mind he attended Colby College, taking for granted that he would become a minister. Mathews's late-life recollections of his upbringing and education were affectionate, slightly condescending and persistently wry: "We had no serious anxieties about the social order. Indeed I do not remember that we knew there was a social order. We knew God had been good to New England." At Colby he came under the influence of a charismatic professor of history, political economy, and elocution, Albion W. Small, who introduced him to the concept of the social order. Later famed as a founder of American sociology, Small was a disciple of the German historical school of economics led by Adolf Wagner and Gustav Schmoller, which taught that social orders are social constructions, not products of immutable natural laws. Mathews studied evolution at Colby with a biology professor who told him that if science refuted any Christian belief, Christianity had to be modified at that point. "I can still feel the shock which such a statement gave me," he recalled fifty years later. "But I am inclined to think that it was the beginning of what independent thinking I may have done."[81]

After college he enrolled at Newton Theological Institution "as a matter of course." His parents expected him to become a minister, and he was anxious to please his parents. Mathews had no other sense of a ministerial calling. He later recalled that he also had "no questions to be answered and no serious doubts to be settled." The Newton curriculum revolved around Bible study with theology as a form of biblical exposition; higher criticism was mentioned only as something to be avoided. Mathews heard very little about the ongoing controversy at Andover Seminary, except that Andover's liberal turn threatened to "cut the nerve of missions." He was only vaguely aware of the ongoing debate between young William Rainey Harper and Princeton Seminary conservative William H. Green over the composition of the Pentateuch. Harper's enthusiasm for Hebrew language study made a greater impact on the Newton campus; more importantly for Mathews, he became friends with young New Testament scholar Ernest DeWitt Burton, whose courses at Newton extended the discipline of lexicography to biblical exegesis.[82]

Mathews stifled a growing theological restlessness during his seminary years. His courses raised perplexing questions on occasion, but Newton was designed to cultivate religious conformity in future ministers and missionaries, not produce critical scholars. He puzzled over the question of how the teachings of Jesus and Paul could be said to have divine authority if they were both influenced by rabbinic traditions. In the summer before his senior year of seminary he got his only taste of the pastorate, serving a small congregation on the eastern frontier of Maine. By the end of the summer Mathews knew that he didn't want to be a pastor. He seriously considered the mission field, but was offered a position as a teacher of rhetoric and elocution at Colby College.

Albion Small had tired of the drudgery of teaching elocution, while Mathews resolved not to pursue further study in theology. For two years he taught rhetoric and public speaking, and also filled in for an ailing Burton at Newton. In 1888, after Small was elected president of Colby College, he announced that he would teach only in a field called "sociology" and that Mathews would be transferred to Small's former position in the department of History and Political Economy. Mathews had never heard of sociology and was ill-prepared to teach history and political economy. In 1890, in order to train him in this field, Small sent him, newly married, to Berlin where Mathews studied under Hans Delbrück, Ignaz Jastrow, and Adolf Wagner. This was the key intellectual experience of his life. Delbrück and Jastrow were close associates of the eminent historian Leopold von Ranke; from them, Mathews learned the methods and embraced the disciplinary self-understanding of Ranke's objectivistic historiography, which claimed to recover the past "as it was." Equally formative for Mathews was the social reformism of Small's teacher, Wagner, whom Mathews called "the prophet of scientific economics." For the rest of his life Mathews championed the reform-oriented, gradualist, early welfare-state approach to political economy that he learned from Small and Wagner. Had he attended Harnack's lectures, he might have encountered William Adams Brown or Walter Rauschenbusch, but theology was far from his mind. Long afterward he reflected that this was a good thing: "I have never regretted the fact that I learned historical method in a field where there were no temptations to apologetics." For him it was better to learn historical criticism without having to worry about its implications for religion: "One could learn objective historical research without concern as to its results."[83]

The scientific approach to history was Mathews's touchstone; thereafter he took for granted that serious thinking in any discipline must be scientific. He returned to Colby as a convinced historicist and social reformist, with a worldly edge. In Berlin, Mathews debated history in beer halls and went to parties on Sunday afternoons. The churchly puritanical culture of Maine lost some of its authority for him after that experience. Mathews belonged to the transitionary generation of social gospel leaders, virtually all of whom were late-Victorians who employed the word "civilization" as a near God-term. The social gospelers fervently preached the overcoming of humankind's lower nature with its higher qualities of spirit, but they also criticized the repressive legalism of the old evangelicalism. Mathews exemplified the type. He retained his Victorian moralism after he returned to the United States, but like other social gospelers, he loosened the moral restraints of the old religion and relativized its religious sanctions. In Germany, he luxuriated in his professors' intellectual freedom; it delighted Mathews that they felt free to examine the validity of received dogmas. He also found Berlin's open culture exhilarating. Having breathed the atmosphere of life in and around the University of Berlin, he later recalled, it was possible for him to resume the lifestyle of late-Victorian New England but not to believe in its moral infallibility.[84]

For three years after his German sabbatical he taught history and political economy at Colby. By returning to Colby, Mathews had gone home, but Maine no longer felt like home to him. He was bored and restless at his isolated alma mater. Politically he found a kindred spirit in Richard Ely, whose training in German historical economics and social-welfare policy was similar to his own, and who was then creating the social gospel movement, along with Washington Gladden and Josiah Strong.[85] Mathews pined to be involved, like them, in the great issues of the day. As the youngest member on the faculty, newly enlightened, he clashed with older faculty colleagues. "I was impatient of the conservatism of the older members and I became aggressive," he later recalled. Indirectly, William Rainey Harper came to his rescue. Harper lured Albion Small from Colby in 1892 to establish the University of Chicago's department of sociology. With the promise that he would soon have a position for Mathews at the university, Small told him to start studying sociology. Mathews started reading Herbert Spencer, but before the sociology position materialized, Ernest DeWitt Burton offered him a position as a professor of New Testament History at the Divinity School. His old teacher and friend at Newton had been the Divinity School's first outside appointment.[86]

Mathews hesitated, although he was flattered by the offer, eager to join Small and Burton as a colleague, and eager to get out of Maine. "There is no incentive to ambition in such surroundings," he later explained. Colby seemed hopelessly provincial to him, cut off from the main currents of modern thought and social reform: "I was isolated in a world in which I had been born." But the downside was sizable; Mathews had no desire to teach at a theological school and possessed no training in New Testament history. He had already declined a similar position at Newton Theological Institution. He would again have to start over in a new field, this time in a field he thought he had left behind. "I had never worked in the field proposed and knew nothing about it," he later recalled, only slightly exaggerating the poverty of his seminary education. He was inclined to wait for the sociology position, though he had unsettled feelings about that option as well. He hadn't liked Chicago when he visited the Columbian Exposition in 1893. Chicago was raw, diverse, and bustling, and Mathews and his wife were still New Englanders.[87]

But Burton swept away Mathews's misgivings. America needed a new research university like the one that Harper was building, he exhorted; moreover, Mathews's training in historical criticism was adaptable to the field of New Testament history. "I caught his enthusiasm for a university in the making," Mathews later recalled. "My inherited interest in religion took form in an ambition to have a part in extending its frontiers. A new age was in the making and religion was needed in social change." This was a decidedly modern rationale for a theological career, but it perfectly suited the needs of William Rainey Harper and his divinity school.[88]

JESUS AND THE MODERN GOSPEL

The University of Chicago was a crude operation in 1894. Its scattered buildings had unfinished brick ends; the athletic field was a section of open prairie; the gymnasium was a temporary one-story building that also housed the university press and the library. To Mathews, however, the spirited atmosphere of Harper's experiment made up for a host of material shortcomings. He quickly began to echo Harper by means of his various editorial and institutional tasks and as a speaker on the Chautauqua lecture circuit. From the beginning he was sensitive to the peculiarities of academic freedom in a university divinity school. On the one hand, the Divinity School prized its intellectual freedom and independence; on the other hand, unlike the chemistry and biology departments, it was connected to a specific denomination and a particular theological movement. Early in his career, in contrast to Foster, Mathews acquired a reputation as a skillful arbiter of this dual identity. Though he allowed that it was tempting to opt one way or the other, he argued that the Divinity School needed to assert its identity as an independent research institution while remaining a church-related professional training school. The best option was to hold fast to both identities, under the authority of modern knowledge in both cases. Less than a year after Mathews arrived in Chicago, Harper sent him on a six-week tour of Southern colleges to publicize the university's innovative year-round quarter system. At the same time Mathews launched a series of articles on "Christian sociology" for Albion Small's *American Journal of Sociology.* Because religion was needed as an agent of social change in the coming new age, he unveiled the hidden social gospel of Jesus. These articles were republished in 1897 as his first book, *The Social Teaching of Jesus,* which became a social gospel classic.[89]

The Social Teaching of Jesus announced that modern Christian sociology was "rerunning the career of Christian theology." There is such a thing as a social-scientific understanding of Christianity, Mathews declared, though it was rarely pursued: "There is but one way to the apprehension of the teachings of Jesus, whether religious or social, and that is the patient study of the gospels with the aid of all modern critical and exegetical methods." This was what he called Christian sociology: the use of modern social science to explicate the objective contemporary meaning of Christianity. Mathews cautioned that religious thinkers were prone to ignore scientific evidence in making their claims. This problem was not confined to authority-citing conservatives; liberals were more inclined to face up to the challenge of historical relativity, but they had a pronounced tendency to read their own beliefs into the thinking of Jesus. Mathews admonished that liberal Christians needed to recognize that the first century was not like the nineteenth century. The Jesus of history was a product of first-century Judaism, not of Greek syllogisms or German philosophy.[90]

The Social Teaching of Jesus was quick to make liberal assurances, however. Mathews immediately asserted that a scientific reading of the Gospels yielded a picture of Jesus that approximated the picture of modern social Christianity: "Were one to come to the words of Jesus unbiassed by traditional interpretations, the impression would be inevitable that the goal of his efforts was the establishment of an ideal society quite as much as the production of an ideal individual." In this crucial respect, he claimed, the first century was "surprisingly like the nineteenth." Good theology was based on scientific scholarship, not personal desires, but in this fortunate case, science and desire agreed. The historical Jesus yielded by scientific scholarship was essentially the Jesus of modern liberal Protestantism.[91]

Like his American liberal colleagues, Mathews resisted the apocalyptic trend of recent German scholarship, especially the German history of religions school. Unlike his American colleagues, who in the 1890s ignored Johannes Weiss, Mathews tried to deal with Weiss. He made marginal concessions to Weiss's interpretation of Jesus and early Christianity while judging that his overall argument was implausible. The "total impression" of Jesus' kingdom sayings was "not that of a postmortem or postcatastrophic condition," Mathews argued. Jesus announced the coming of the kingdom at the outset of his ministry (Mark 1:15), he declared the current fulfillment of the glowing promises of Isaiah (Luke 4:17–21), he declared that the kingdom was present among those gathered (Luke 17:20), and he taught that the kingdom in the person of its members was already the "good seed" in the field (Matt. 13:24–43). Mathews urged that these were the core elements of Jesus' kingdom preaching: "It is impossible in the light of them all and of other sayings of Jesus to believe that he occupied an exclusively eschatological point of view."[92]

To Jesus, the kingdom was an ideal social order, progressively approximated through historical process, in which the loving fatherhood of God and the brotherly fellowship of humanity were affirmed. Mathews ascribed to Jesus the view that the achievement of a perfect society was a "natural possibility." He commended Jesus' audacity in assuming that the apostles would bring about the "indefinite expansion" of the kingdom. This act of faith was equaled, he wrote, "only by the superb optimism that saw possibilities of infinite good in humanity." The possibilities of good would be realized when human beings accepted God's love for them, as mediated to them and inspired by the example of Jesus. Jesus was not a political thinker, Mathews cautioned; for that reason there is no such thing as a divinely sanctioned politics or Christian ideology. But there is such a thing as a Christian government: "A government is Christian, not because it is of this or that form, but because it is attempting to realize the principles of fraternity and love that underlie the entire social teachings of Jesus." Jesus believed that the possibilities of human good are infinite because human beings are creatures of a loving God. The kingdom of God is precisely the mobilization and fulfillment of these possibilities.[93]

This remained the essence of the social gospel to many Christians long after Mathews allowed that it was not quite the gospel of the historical Jesus. *The Social Teaching of Jesus* was the first book of its kind in English. For twenty years it was the chief textbook of the social gospel movement; for many years afterward the book (in its revised edition) was second only to Rauschenbusch's *Theology for the Social Gospel* as a movement primer. In its first generation it provided scholarly ballast for the picture of Jesus offered in Charles Sheldon's epochal bestselling novel *In His Steps*, which taught millions of Christians to ask in every situation, "What would Jesus do?" Much of the social gospel progeny inspired by Sheldon and Mathews exceeded even their high standards of sentimentality. Mathews's primer remained in print until 1928, when he replaced it with an updated revision titled *Jesus on Social Institutions*. Some of the core concerns of his first book remained central to his thinking for the rest of his career; *Jesus on Social Institutions* recycled sizable sections of his first life of Jesus.[94]

Virtually from the time of its publication, however, Mathews was unsettled by the book's special pleading. He was the first American to judge that his response to Weiss was not convincing. Like other American liberals, he resisted Weiss's argument for social ethical reasons, but this motive conflicted with his scientific claims. If the only worthy basis for theology was modern scientific knowledge, and the best modern scholars were moving in Weiss's direction, how could he hold out against them?

Mathews struggled with this question for eight years. His rethinking occurred against the background of the breakup of the Ritschlian school. By the turn of the century, the leading Ritschlian dogmatic theologians and their followers were estranged from an ascending *Religionsgeschichtliche* offshoot of the Ritschlian school. Julius Kaftan and Theodore Häring developed systematic theologies that sought to translate traditional Christian beliefs into forms of thought suitable to modern philosophy and culture; Wilhelm Herrmann's existential Ritschlianism appealed to the believer's experience of the "inner life of Jesus"; various Ritschlians blended aspects of these approaches. Led by Ernst Troeltsch, the historicists countered that no dogma, religious principle, or experience deserves to be privileged over history. It was not enough to translate Christian beliefs into modern forms of expression; first the beliefs have to be interrogated for their historical credibility and analyzed through the use of an objective history-of-religions method. By 1897 the church-oriented Ritschlians and the insurgent *Religionsgeschichtliche* group were factional rivals, as Gustav Ecke documented in his book, *Die theologische Schule Albrecht Ritschls*.[95]

The emerging Chicago school differed from most American liberal theologians in favoring the historicist side of this argument. Foster's radicalism placed him closer to Troeltsch than to the church-oriented dogmatists, though he agreed with Herrmann and Kaftan that history establishes nothing in religion; Mathews went farther than Foster in privileging historical method, arguing that historical criticism must be deconstructive and religiously reconstructive. For Mathews and a succession of Chicago schoolers, theology had no credible basis if it was not historically realist in spirit and governed by historical-critical conclusions. They rejected Foster's claim that critical history cannot touch the real subject matter of religion; to both Mathews and Shirley Jackson Case, historical method was uniquely suited to establish beliefs. *The Social Teaching of Jesus* cited Weiss against Kaftan and Herrmann, implying that at least Weiss's eschatological understanding of the kingdom was grounded in historical-critical exegesis. Thereafter Mathews took up a sustained argument with Weiss in which he gradually relinquished his entire opposition to the eschatological thesis. For five years, while increasingly yielding to Weiss's essential argument, he insisted that the social meaning of the kingdom was more important to Jesus and early Christianity than its eschatological meaning. For three years after that he drew the line at equality, claiming that the social and eschatological meanings were equally important to Jesus and early Christianity.[96]

Mathews struggled mightily with the messianism of Paul. Though he allowed that Paul's understanding of the kingdom was strongly eschatological, he argued that for Paul the kingdom was also a socioethical project. In 1903 he took a further step in Weiss's direction, concluding that "the precisely Messianic work of Jesus was in the future and formed the substance of the hope of the church." Weiss argued that the New Testament writers viewed the period of the church as a brief historical interim; Mathews conceded that this critical judgment was essentially correct. He comforted himself with a Harnackian kernel/husk distinction between the substance of messianism and its cultural framework. The substance was eternal life, which had already begun in the work of Christ's Spirit as "a first installment of the life of the coming kingdom"; the disposable framework was the early church's understanding of history and the world.[97]

Mathews inched his way to Weiss's reading of the New Testament by assuring that the eschatological sayings of Jesus embodied ethical teachings. This was a self-assurance, for he shared the social gospel anxiety that the recent scholarly emphasis on eschatology threatened to truncate the recent gains of social Christianity. Mathews fervently believed that the ethical demands of the gospel were more important than the apocalyptic mentality of Jesus and the early Christians. For five years he argued that Jesus and the early church shared this predisposition. For Jesus and early Christianity, he contended, the eschatological meaning of the kingdom was subordinate to its kingdom-building social meaning. From this position he retreated to the claim, in 1903, that the eschatological and social meanings of the kingdom were equally valued by Jesus and early Christianity. Then he gave up the cause of saving Jesus from full-blown eschatology and announced his surrender in *The Messianic Hope in the New Testament,* published in 1905. A year before Albert Schweitzer's *Von Reimarus zu Wrede* scorched the liberal lives-of-Jesus tradition, Mathews concluded that modern Protestantism had to make its peace with the eschatological turn in biblical scholarship. The social understanding of the kingdom had done good work for liberal Christianity, but as a claim about the teaching of Jesus and early Christianity, it was simply wrong. In Mathews's words, the understanding of the kingdom propounded in *The Social Teaching of Jesus* and like-minded works "is not the proper point of departure for a study of the social teachings with which the gospels abound."[98]

The Messianic Hope in the New Testament contended that the teaching of Jesus and early Christianity was pervaded by the expectation of an imminent world-sundering act of God. The ethical aspects of the gospel were clearly subordinate to this expectation, Mathews argued. Since the apostles clearly believed in the kingdom as an imminent eschatological intervention from above, the inference was unavoidable that "Jesus' teaching must also have contained and emphasized the eschatological hope." Mathews moved beyond his earlier argument that Jesus was merely influenced by the apocalyptic messianism of the Pharisees; now he claimed that, rather, "the extant sayings of Jesus show beyond doubt his acceptance of pharasaic eschatological messianism."[99]

Mathews drew the line at pure apocalypticism. He never accepted the post-Schweitzerian picture of Jesus as a deluded apocalyptic prophet who lacked any this-worldly ethical concerns. Neither did he believe that Jesus' worldview was entirely a patchwork of local traditions. Jesus was an original thinker, he affirmed; spiritually and ethically, Jesus "broke utterly" with Pharisaism as a system; in other respects he creatively blended themes of his own with the worldview of Pharisaic messianism. But Mathews judged that nearly all of the constitutive elements of Pharisaic apocalyptic messianism were integral to the teaching of Jesus. Modern Christianity could not evade the fact that Weiss's historical reconstruction was basically correct: the Gospels contained apocalyptical elements that pervaded early Christian consciousness and reflected the heart of Jesus' own teaching. For Jesus, the kingdom was primarily an eschatological reality: "Any strict definition of the kingdom of God must be eschatological. With Jesus as with his contemporaries, the kingdom was yet to come. Its appearance would be the result of no social evolution, but sudden, as the gift of God; men could not hasten its coming; they could only prepare for membership in it."[100]

The Messianic Hope in the New Testament was the most deeply scholarly work of Mathews's career. He wrestled with biblical texts on his own and appealed to a host of German authorities. The book exemplified its theme that, like it or not, the turn in recent critical scholarship had to be taken seriously. "The theologian must be a historian," he exhorted. "There must be, first, a precise interpretation of the Gospel as it stands in the New Testament, in its own terms and from its own point of view." Serious modern theology therefore had to take instruction from a new cast of biblical scholars. Mathews's chief scholarly authorities in *The Social Teaching of Jesus* were two German liberals, H. H. Wendt and Willibald

Beyschlag, and the Anglo-Austrian evangelical Alfred Edersheim; by 1905 he was telling American liberals to deal instead with the Troeltschian historicists, especially Weiss, Wilhelm Bousset, and Paul Wernle. A year later everyone had to deal with Schweitzer. With devastating polemical force, Schweitzer affirmed Weiss's essential argument and skewered the nineteenth century's liberal depictions of Jesus. He showed that virtually all of the past century's critical questers of the historical Jesus had projected nineteenth-century liberal values onto Jesus. In his haunting analogy, they had looked into a well in search of Jesus and seen their own image.[101]

MATHEWS AND SHIRLEY JACKSON CASE: HISTORICISM AND SOCIAL PROCESS

The Messianic Hope in the New Testament marked the turning point for Mathews. He gave up the kingdom-building liberal Jesus, took Foster's place as a theologian at the Divinity School, and set out to devise a new theological basis for the liberal social gospel. His constant whirlwind of Harperesque projects and ambitions somehow accelerated after Harper's death. Mathews was the evangelist of Chicago theological liberalism. Throughout his Chicago career he crammed his calendar with academic, civic, and ecclesiastical lecture appearances, especially for the American Institute of Sacred Literature and Chautauqua lecture circuits. In 1903, at Harper's behest, he had assumed editorial responsibility for a weekly newspaper called *Christendom,* which was modeled on *The Outlook* and *The Independent.* Founded as a successor to the *American Weekly* by a Harper-headed business group that did not share Harper's and Mathews's religious ambitions, *Christendom* lasted only a few months, to Harper's chagrin. It was succeeded, however, by a monthly magazine called *The World Today,* for which Mathews continued as editor. For eight years he spent his afternoons in the Chicago Loop, running a mass-circulation periodical that gave a lightly religious spin on political and social trends. To his mind, *The World Today* provided a valuable point of contact between social gospel idealism and real-world politics.[102]

In 1908 Mathews succeeded Eri Baker Hulbert as dean of the Divinity School, a position that he held for twenty-five years; the same year he also welcomed to the Divinity School faculty Shirley Jackson Case, who had recently completed his doctorate in New Testament studies at Yale under Benjamin W. Bacon and Frank Chamberlin Porter. In Case, Mathews found a colleague whose historical and sociological commitments blended fortuitously with his own. Though he lacked Mathews's churchly piety, Case's long career at Chicago otherwise paralleled and complemented Mathews's to a remarkable degree. Together they developed the Chicago school's distinctive sociohistorical method of interpretation, arguing that the best way to understand any religion is to study the historical milieu and process in which it has developed. Case began his career at Chicago as a professor of New Testament interpretation, but for much of his career, beginning in 1917, he doubled as Professor of Early Church History. In 1933, when Mathews stepped down as dean of the Divinity School, Case succeeded him in that position. Born into a liberal Christian home and grounded in German and American historicism, Case had a strong belief in the relevance of historical scholarship for modern Christianity, and an aversion to theology, philosophy, and displays of piety. Lacking Mathews's vast array of civic, ecclesiastical, and administrative commitments, for most of his career he was able to concentrate more singularly than Mathews on the application of their distinctive brand of historical interpretation.[103]

Upon taking on the deanship of the Divinity School, Mathews gave himself even more unreservedly to editorial ventures and the lecture circuit. In 1912 he assumed the editorship of *The Biblical World,* a Harper-founded Divinity School organ that popularized trends in biblical study; the following year he launched a twelve-volume textbook series titled the *Woman's Citizen's Library,* which sought to prepare American women for their exercise of political responsibility. On top of these commitments he was active in Jane Addams's settlement-house movement and helped to establish the Voter's Clearing House, which screened candidates for the Chicago Republican primaries. With Harper, George Albert Coe, and others, in 1903 he cofounded the Religious Education Association, which applied Deweyan Pragmatism and social gospel liberalism to religious education. In 1907 he helped create the Northern Baptist Convention, which he served as president in 1915 and 1916. For more than twenty years Mathews served as director of religious work for the Chautauqua Society; from 1912 to 1916 he was president of the Federal Council of Churches of Christ in America; between 1908 and 1915 he was president of the Chicago Council of City Missions; from 1910 to 1919 he served as president of the Baptist Executive Council of Chicago.[104]

Meanwhile, before breakfast and at odd moments during his travels, he wrote theology. Asked if he had read a certain book, Mathews snapped impatiently, "We don't read books, we write them." Characteristically, *The Messianic Hope in the New Testament* assured that all was not lost for liberal social Christianity. There was a great need for theology, Mathews instructed, but the liberal theology that was needed had to be "at once critical, experiential, historical, revering Jesus as the divine Way rather than the divine End." Theology had to take seriously the picture of early Christianity unveiled by modern scholarship: early Christianity was pervaded by an apocalyptic consciousness that was profoundly different from the scientific consciousness of the modern social mind. Mathews urged that both sides of this fact were crucial. The gospel idea of the kingdom was primarily eschatological; modern theology could not credibly maintain otherwise. But apocalyptic thinking was alien to the modern social mind; no modern theology could pretend otherwise. What was needed was a theological strategy that faced the historical truth, affirmed its own modern character, and reinterpreted the primitive elements of Christianity in modern terms. The strategy that Mathews eventually settled upon employed the concept of "social process" as a sociohistorical bridge between the ancient and modern worlds. Building upon a sketch of the French

Revolution that he wrote for the Chautauqua Society, he interpreted Christianity as a social movement inspired by its loyalty to Jesus. For many years he employed "loyalty to Jesus" as a banner phrase alternative to the traditional notion of the authority of Jesus. His first attempt to negotiate the ancient-modern chasm invoked the "eternal element" in Christianity that transcended its relative historical elements: "Not an interpretive concept born of an abandoned cosmology and a persistently political conception of God, but the eternal life born of God through the mediation of faith in Jesus as his revelation—that is the eternal element in Christianity."[105]

That was Harnack's strategy. Mathews dropped similarly Harnackian statements into sermons and lectures for the rest of his life. In the same way, though he criticized Rauschenbusch and other social gospelers for speaking of Christ's kingdom as a socioethical project, his own writings occasionally spoke of the kingdom as an ongoing social project without any qualifying historical asides. This contradiction has two explanations. The first is that Mathews was extraordinarily busy during the heyday of the social gospel movement; the second is that he could not resist the rhetorical appeal of social gospel kingdom language during the movement's heyday. Mathews recycled material from his stock lectures and essays throughout his career. Some of the "kingdom" sayings in his mid-career writings derived from pre-1905 essays and lectures that he recycled without editorial correction; in other cases, he made fresh resort to kingdom-building imagery. This language had ample rhetorical power in the prewar Progressive era; Mathews continued to feel it as part of his personal faith. For the most part, however, he employed an alternative social Christian rhetoric that passed his tests for historical and modernist credibility. His writings minimized "kingdom" language, emphasized the sociohistorical chasm between early and modern Christianity, and bridged the chasm by appealing to the modern sociohistorical concept of "social process."[106]

Jesus and the apostles had no concept of the kingdom as an ongoing historical project, Mathews explained, but history shows that nonetheless the kingdom is transformative in social process. He found modern history to be especially revealing. Through the faithful witness of modern social Christianity, society was being transformed by the kingdom in a way that closely appoximated social gospel rhetoric about it. Mathews reasoned that the language of the social gospel was therefore misleading and true at the same time. It was misleading as a characterization of the kingdom faith of early Christianity, but it was true as a description of its own Spirit-moved religious witness. The social gospel movement was building the kingdom by Christianizing society. It was transforming the social order with the principles of the gospel as a preparation for the consummation of the kingdom. When he spoke carefully, Mathews used "social process" as a signifier for the kingdom faith; on other occasions he spoke of Christ's kingdom as an ongoing historical project. The difference was important to him, but not as important as the truism proclaimed in both cases: that modern Christianity grafted the ideals of Jesus into the ongoing social process as history moved toward its consummation as the kingdom of God.[107]

Mathews often sounded an evangelical note upon warming to this theme. He became a theologian because morality without religion has no inspiriting power, and religion was needed in social change. But as a theologian he warned that religion has no inspiriting power if it lacks a revitalizing personal faith. Liberal Protestantism needed to learn this lesson from the history of Unitarianism and the various ethical societies, he admonished: "The so-called liberal movement, while justly criticizing evangelicalism in the old, crude, popular sense, has too often confused religion with ethical culture." Mathews worried that liberal Protestantism was taking the Unitarian path. He countered that genuine Christianity is personal, vital, and regenerative. It speaks of sin and redemption as personal and social realities. It takes seriously the fallen condition of humanity and the biblical promise of salvation and a coming new creation. Mathews allowed that his preaching on these themes sounded more evangelical "than that which has been considered progressive orthodoxy of the past generation."[108]

The language of sin and eschatology sounds reactionary to modern ears, he admitted, but any religion that does not speak of sin and salvation soon reduces to enervated ethical culturalism. Moreover, though kingdom language was admittedly problematic for modern people, it was also the key that opened the gospel to them. Mathews explained that Christianity was born in messianism and it remained true only as a form of messianism. It was through their messianic expectation that the early Christians expressed their conviction of God's presence in history and their sense of the differences between the ways of righteousness and unrighteousness. Modern social Christianity needed to be a quite different way of expressing the same faith. To Henry Churchill King, who worried that he was going too far in establishing a modernist basis for Christian belief, Mathews reflected, "I think in a pretty large sense I am a pragmatist." His theology was shaped by the empirical facts of science and history, including the evidence that some kinds of religious belief produce greater moral and spiritual health than others: "I am trying to get at the facts which are true for any man and to combine them under conceptions which are recognized generally as true," he told King. "My conception of the various doctrines is that they are genetically the outcome of this process."[109]

Mathews believed that Rauschenbusch failed to face up to the historical truth about early Christianity and that he overcompensated for the backward-sounding impression of eschatology language. Wanting to believe that his ethic of the kingdom linked him to Jesus, Rauschenbusch gave in to the allure of his own social gospel rhetoric. On other counts, as well, Mathews and Rauschenbusch were different kinds of social gospelers. Rauschenbusch was a political radical and high-voltage prose stylist who condemned capitalism as unregenerate, supported the ascending trade-union movement, and blasted his opponents. Mathews was a political liberal and gradualistic reformer who urged that "non-combativeness is good strategy in religion." The classic literature of the social gospel movement was written by Rauschenbusch, who came to be seen, rightly, as the movement's greatest figure, but during Rauschenbusch's lifetime,

Mathews was its more representative figure. Rauschenbusch was inspiring and challenging to social gospel pastors, but also dangerous. He called for a socialist transformation of the economy and opposed America's intervention in World War I after most social gospelers rallied to President Wilson's call to make the world safe for democracy.[110]

Mathews was never dangerous. Generationally he succeeded Washington Gladden as the champion of a mainstream idealistic Protestantism that spoke the language of moral progress, cooperation, and peace, though he dropped Gladden's strong interest in trade unionism. He urged that a modernist/fundamentalist schism could be avoided in the Baptist church "if we refuse to get into a fight about it," and he often counseled that Christians should forget about class. In his politics he epitomized the middle-class moral idealism of the mainstream social gospel. He was an ardent peace activist, but not a pacifist; he advocated female suffrage and racial integration but had relatively little contact with American blacks; he supported structural social change in the direction of equality if it proceeded from a gradual social process fueled by the moral regeneration of individuals, but he firmly resisted the socialist wing of the social gospel movement. Christianity and socialism were different kinds of social movements, he contended. While socialism expected society to make good individuals, Christianity expected good individuals to make a good society. "Christianity assumes that it is impossible to have a good social order composed of bad men," he explained. For this reason, Christianity was better suited to produce "permanent social betterment" than socialism. It resisted the explicit economism of the socialist claim that a good society could be attained by creating a just economic order. Mathews countered that the Christian movement was more attentive to moral, intellectual, aesthetic, and religious factors. Modern liberal Christianity did not so much oppose socialism as insist that a good society could be created "only by producing religiously regenerate lives."[111]

His primer on the essence of the social gospel began with the latter claim. "Jesus has no social gospel for bad people," he declared in *The Social Gospel*. "His ideals presuppose goodness." While assuring that the church of Christ is obliged by the social implications of Christ's ideals to promote fairness, cooperation, fellowship, and peace, Mathews admonished that these ideals are unattainable without morally transformed hearts. The ethic of Jesus presupposes transformation. In moral language: "The teaching of Jesus is not for bad people—for those who are not possessed of a spirit like that of Jesus."[112] Faced with an upswing of socialist sentiment in the social gospel movement, Mathews admonished that regenerated individuals create good social structures, not the other way around. He recognized Rauschenbusch's essential evangelicalism, but worried that Christian socialism was often short on evangelical conviction. For Mathews, as for the evangelical liberal tradition of Harnack, Brown, King, and Rauschenbusch, the gospel was a message "that seeks to transform human lives into conformity with the ideals of Jesus by bringing them into regenerating relations with God."[113] He proclaimed that the "very heart of the Social Gospel" is the faith that Jesus can save the world by transforming it into the kingdom of God.[114]

Christianity is essentially a movement, not a doctrine. From the standpoint of this movement, Mathews explained, Jesus is the symbol and agent of spiritual regeneration. He is the Christian's moral example of how to live; more than that, he is the datum for religious induction as truly as Darwin's earthworms were his data for the explanation of the laws of evolution, for in Jesus "we have demonstrated the power of that spiritual life to triumph over sin and death." But Jesus is not merely the moral example and datum of Christianity, Mathews observed; he is also its founder. The Jesus movement was born out of love for the Jesus of history and was transformed "into religious faith in him as more than a person *in* history." In the historical experience of the Christian movement, "the Jesus of history became the Christ of experience." Mathews became a theologian under the strength of his conviction that the transforming spirit of Christ is unrivaled as a source of moral regeneration in Western history. He remained a theologian under the conviction that it remained unrivaled under modernity: "The real significance of the historical Jesus lies in the fact that in him the Spiritual Life for which humanity has searched was perfectly brought in terms of time and human relationships." Regeneration is a possibility for individuals and for society because the Spirit of Christ is a real spiritual power.[115]

Mathews was serious in urging that liberal Protestantism had to retain its evangelical core. He spoke against the liberal tendency, increasingly evident at this Divinity School, to replace the centrality of the gospel story with a story about modern progress or enlightenment. He insisted that liberal theology could have it both ways, and that it needed to. It needed to be firmly evangelical and thoroughly modern at the same time. Unlike Brown and Rauschenbusch, however, who kept their balance in this respect, Mathews became the kind of liberal that he warned against. His prewar writings raised the issue repeatedly and gave signs of a tendency to subordinate the gospel message to a modernist theology of social process; in the 1920s he insisted that he was still an evangelical modernist, though his writings strongly tilted to the post-evangelical side; in his later career and in the Chicago school his naturalistic empiricism prevailed.

From the beginning, the Chicago school resolved to take empiricism and naturalism more seriously than earlier types of theological liberalism. All the Chicago schoolers were empiricists, naturalists, and pragmatists, but they differed over the promise of historical interpretation for liberal theology. Foster used history-of-religions scholarship, but he also criticized the religious limitations of historicism; Case was a straightforward sociohistoricist who insisted that history is the golden key to unlocking whatever is worth knowing about religion. In the 1930s, after Henry Nelson Wieman became the dominant theological figure at Chicago, Chicago empiricism took a decidedly ahistorical turn.

For thirty years Case advocated against all kinds of ahistoricism, including the kind that came to prevail at the Divinity School during his years as its dean.

Persistently he argued that history is the irreducible basis of religion and that, rightly pursued, the historical approach to Christianity must attend to something more fundamental than the history of church councils and doctrines. Church councils, doctrines, rituals, and the like are important to the understanding of Christianity, he affirmed, but they are vital mainly as clues to Christian experience. To understand Christianity is to grasp the history of the religious experiences of Christians. Religion is irreducibly social and historical; so-called "Christianity" is nothing apart from "the actual life-process of the Christian society in its totality from its earliest beginnings down to the present moment." Christianity is an ongoing movement of historical subjects; it cannot be understood apart from the social and historical circumstances in which it developed and continues to evolve. Case explained: "The history of Christianity is the story of religious living on the part of real people who from the first to the last have constituted the membership of the Christian movement."[116]

For Case and Mathews, the point was not merely to recover the social and historical character of Christianity; to a considerable extent, the Ritschlian school had done that. Case and Mathews pressed the more radically social thesis that Christianity is nothing but the name for a particular phase of social existence. It is a problem of social adjustment that is best understood as the sociohistorical experience of Christian communities. In an influential theological encyclopedia edited by Gerald Birney Smith in 1916, Mathews explained that "generic religion never existed apart from religions, and religions never existed except as interests and institutions of real people." Religion is nothing in itself; it possesses no independent or metaphysical existence; it is social and historical without remainder. Therefore, Mathews urged, "It is only from a strictly social point of view that either religion or religions will in any measure be properly understood." In the same volume Case put it this way:

> The beliefs which different Christians held, the forms they employed in worship, and the decrees they enacted for the conduct of the ideal life must all receive due attention, but the true historian will ever remember that his work is not completed when he has merely catalogued and evaluated these products of early Christian living. His ultimate task is to interpret the great complex of actual life out of which these things came and of which they formed an integral part. Thus Christianity must be conceived as thoroughly vital and developmental in nature.[117]

Steadily, prolifically, with no turns of mind or purpose, Case's books and articles maintained that the appropriate test of religious truth is functional significance, not the source from which religious ideas or practices derive. He proclaimed himself determined "to know nothing among theologies save the beliefs and quests of real people." The program of retreat is bad strategy in religion, he counseled; no dogma can secure a vital liberal religion, including the dogma of inner religious certainty: "When asked what the Christian of today should believe, I can only reply, 'What he thinks he ought to believe in the light of his own experience and knowledge.' I feel impelled to help him enlarge his experience and increase his knowledge, but I should be untrue to my principles if I sought to superimpose upon him any system of dogma of my own making."[118] Case's scholarship emphasized that early Christianity appropriated myths, liturgical practices, and other motifs from a wide variety of pagan sources and that the early church's existence in a Hellenistic culture caused it to hellenize the Jewish concept of messianic deliverance. Similarly, he instructed, every age reinterprets religion according to its own socially generated master concepts. The meaning that such terms as "God" and "atonement" had for Christians in the past can be perceived only by reconstructing the social settings in which these terms were employed, and they can have meaning for modern people only if they are translated into modern concepts: "In the last analysis Christianity is, always has been and always will be, a way of religious living in a complex and changing world. It ever remains a quest rather than a finished attainment."[119]

By the time of World War I, Mathews wrote decidedly in this tone and perspective. Though his work remained stronger on evangelical feeling than Case's, and Case confined himself more narrowly than Mathews to historical scholarship, their positions on sociohistorical interpretation were virtually identical. Mathews offered his seminal case for it—and the rationale for his mid-career religious trajectory—in 1915, in a seven-chapter essay titled "Theology and the Social Mind." The "social mind" was a sociological concept that Mathews probably borrowed from Lester Ward's *Dynamic Sociology.* He defined it as a "more or less general community of conscious states, processes, ideas, interests, and ambitions which to a greater or less degree repeats itself in the experience of individuals belonging to the group characterized by the community of consciousness." In Christian history, Mathews observed, the self-understanding of the Christian movement has been shaped and defined successively by the Semitic, the Greco-Roman, the imperialist, the feudal, the nationalistic, the bourgeois, and the modern democratic social minds. Each social mind generates from its own experience the conceptions that fulfill current religious needs. For Mathews, as for Case, this was the crucial sociocultural phenomenon that made historical progress possible. Hellenistic Christianity needed to be assured that true salvation is mediated through Christ; it therefore produced the logos and Neoplatonist essence theologies of Nicene and Chalcedonian orthodoxy. In the midst of the chaos and social breakdown of the Middle Ages, the Christian movement needed a theology of divine sovereignty; thus the authoritarian theologies of the imperialist and feudal social minds were created.[120]

The bourgeois social mind made enormous progress in certain areas, Mathews judged, but not in theology. The premodern bourgeoisie created capitalist economics, the middle class, and Whig liberalism, but theologically it remained in the Middle Ages, fixated on the individual's need of salvation in heaven: "It was essentially eschatological in its conception of salvation, and viewed with no small uneasiness such men as [Frederick Denison] Maurice and the Christian socialists who were not ready to make of the gospel a message of mere 'other-worldliness.'

It was natural, therefore, for this commercially minded self-centered community to find satisfaction for its religious needs in the extension of commercial principles to religion." To Mathews, that explained American revivalism and the other authority religions of the nineteenth century. Nineteenth-century evangelicalism had a social conscience, especially regarding slavery and prison reform, but because the evangelicals failed to take up the cause of democratizing privilege in industrial society, their conception of salvation made no advance beyond the heaven-salvationism of the Middle Ages. Bourgeois religion was fixated on rescuing individuals from the world; it had no conception of the transformation of character "through the individual's participation in God's activity conditioned by a thoroughgoing extension of Christ's principle of love to social structures."[121]

Only modern people understood salvation as democratic social regeneration. The social gospel conception of redemption as social salvation was the defining theological expression of the modern social mind, which Mathews defined as essentially democratic and scientific. While allowing that capitalism also played a sizable role in the modern world, he contended that its creative period had long passed and that capitalism was incapable of producing a progressive theology. "The religious interests of capitalism are in the very nature of the case allied with those of imperialism and supramundane salvation," he judged. "As a system it has frankly undertaken the worship of Mammon and it is by no means ashamed." The ethos of capitalism was antisocial and materialistic; as a system it was therefore content "to preserve the theology born of imperialism and feudalism."[122]

Mathews urged that the truly modern elements of the modern social mind were its commitments to democracy and scientific truth. He conceived modern democracy as a "counter-movement to capitalism" from which progressive religious impulses flowed. In 1915, he allowed, these impulses were "only beginning to express themselves in the religious world." Roman Catholicism was inherently undemocratic; Protestantism was mostly bourgeois; authoritarianism was the norm in religion; the social gospel movement was barely a generation old. Moreover, the growing class consciousness of modern democracy was not necessarily a good thing, Mathews cautioned, for the socialists were training it into class hatred. But socialism was not the only expression of the modern social mind: "The significant thing is that the bourgeois class itself is rapidly being leavened by democratic ideals of social service." By his lights, middle-class idealism was the hope of the world in the sphere of politics. It democratized privilege in a peaceable spirit. It replaced the predatory ethos of capitalism with its own cooperative ideals. Theologically it found expression in the social gospel movement.[123]

Every creative age is alike, Mathews observed. Creative ages make progress in religion by changing to meet the needs of their time. He cautioned that the creative task of modern theology was more daunting than that faced by the Nicene fathers, because the Nicene fathers were able to carry on the Semitic conception of divine sovereignty. This worldview was out for modern people; it represented "impossible cosmology on the one side and autocratic monarchy on the other." Yet the deeper lesson of Christian history was hopeful, he exhorted. The hope of social process was that every social mind produces conceptions out of its own experience that speak to its distinctive needs. "In our modern world we shall find that Christianity furnishes satisfaction for the universal need of a religion that shall not only save individuals but society in accordance with the laws of the universe," Mathews assured. "Our task is indeed great, but the history of the evolution of Christianity gives us courage." What was needed was a theology of social process that kept up with the spirit of the age.[124]

THE MISSIONARY SPIRIT, WORLD WAR I, AND THE MODERNIST TURN

The war in Europe cast a dark shadow over these hopeful words. Though Mathews was deeply involved at the time in the movement to keep the United States out of the war, his call for a theology of the modern social mind made no reference to the war. "Theology and the Social Mind" called for a theology of the present age, but the age of its own progressive missionary idealism was nearly over. For thirty years the social gospelers had called for a Christian movement that took literally the gospel command to save the world. The social gospel was nothing if not a missionary faith. In its prewar high tide the social gospel movement routinely called for the Christianization of America and the world, though, like Henry Churchill King, Mathews worried that American Christianizing usually took a backseat to American commercializing. "In too many cases the appearance of the missionary of God has been accompanied by the missionary of Mammon, and Western civilization with all its imperfections has appeared in Eastern lands," he lamented in 1914. "The missionary, whatever his regrets, in too many cases has accepted this incursion of industrialism as a matter of course and has not been able, even if he has undertaken the task, to extend the Christian ideals into the larger forces that are reshaping the social order of the entire world."[125]

The theological task of modern Christianity was to develop a theology of the modern social mind; its social-ethical task was to wage a world-embracing struggle for the world. The entire history of Christianity was a prelude to this challenge. "The greatest problem which faces the world at the present time is not as to whether the Western civilization will conquer the world," Mathews declared. Western civilization had already settled that question. "The real problem is whether Christianity will conquer civilization." Could liberal Protestantism Christianize the world-conquering civilization of the West? Could it "socialize the spirit of Jesus" and put an end to war? Could it spread the values of democracy and democratize the privileges of the West? Could it infuse science and education with spiritual idealism and replace the predatory spirit of capitalism with the spirit of cooperation? To the social gospelers, these were the real questions, which reduced to a single question. Since the West was taking over the world in any case, could modern Christianity turn this overtaking into a blessing instead of a curse?[126]

The social gospelers understood, at first, that these questions would be off the table if America went to war. "We were engaged in making a new world," Mathews later recalled. "It was a thrilling hope. And then came the war. The power of Christianity to prevent violence was seen to be negligible. The Kingdom of God disappeared in the smoke and poison gas and treaties of a civilization that was anything but swayed by the principles of Jesus." It was telling, to him, that theological conservatives were barely affected by the catastrophe of World War I. Mathews did not necessarily mean that conservatives were morally callous; he did mean that the war caused them no spiritual or intellectual disillusionment. The war inflicted no damage to religious orthodoxy, "because orthodoxy had embodied in itself the very political principles which had led to the war." The God of orthodoxy had sacralized the wars of Canaan, but to the social gospelers, the war was a siren from hell that threatened all their hopes and cherished beliefs. Mathews joined Andrew Carnegie's war-resisting Church Peace Union upon its founding in 1914, which quickly spawned the World Alliance for International Friendship through the Churches. As president of the Federal Council of Churches he campaigned against military preparation and argued the case for American neutrality. In 1916 he played a leading role in the founding of the League to Enforce Peace, which called for the establishment of a multinational league to prevent war. At the group's banquet on May 27, 1916, President Wilson issued his first declaration of support for the idea of a league of nations.[127]

Like most liberal Protestant leaders, however, Mathews fell in line as soon as America entered the war in April 1917. Opposition to his country's intervention was not a serious possibility for him, especially after Wilson made it a moral crusade. The cause of the League of Nations became part of this crusade, which sealed Mathews's resolve to secure moral support and even enthusiasm for the war. Some liberal Protestant leaders took a critically loyalist approach to their country's intervention, supporting it merely as the lesser of two evils. For the most part, Washington Gladden, though he did some Wilsonian war-boosting, was one of them; others included Union Seminary professors William Adams Brown, Eugene Lyman, and Henry Sloane Coffin, and Union Seminary president A. C. McGiffert. The critical loyalists tried to restrain America's rising tone of self-righteousness and vengeance and insisted that the church should have no part in glorifying war or demonizing America's enemies; some of them refused to enlist Christianity as a source of support for the war.[128]

Mathews and Henry Churchill King became leaders of a more ardent group. Though not as militaristic as Lyman Abbott or Harry Emerson Fosdick, they used their standing as church leaders to build moral enthusiasm for the war. Virtually all liberal Protestant leaders spoke against extremism and vengeance, but to Mathews and King, critical loyalism was not enough. Mathews gave scores of patriotic speeches across the country that draped the war in the causes of democratic and Christian progress. He dropped his classes (while remaining Divinity School dean) to become Martin A. Ryerson's Executive Secretary of War Savings for the state of Illinois. This campaign was tremendously successful, selling approximately $100 million worth of wartime certificates. The entire wartime experience was exhilarating to him; Mathews later recalled that after he returned to the classroom, academic life seemed boring by comparison. He recovered his interest in theology only upon reflecting that dogma is the religious aspect of group solidarity.[129]

He experienced his country's wartime solidarity as a profoundly religious phenomenon. In the early months of the war, flush with nationalist enthusiasm, German theologians devised what they called a "war experience" theology (which set Karl Barth on a contrary theological path). Three years later Mathews, showing the same vulnerability of liberal theology to nationalism and cultural idolatry, sacralized the war from the American side. He urged that there is a deep kinship between religion and patriotism. The war made Americans remember that American liberty was more precious and more Christian than the "new god, Teutonic Efficiency." Americans had nearly forgotten their patriotic songs and rites of allegiance to their flag and nation, but these practices were splendidly renewed as "tests of loyalty to a land that rises in splendid personality." America was not merely a collection of individual persons, Mathews enthused; the war revealed that America was "a glorious super-person, possessed of virtues, power, ideals, daring, and sacrifice." His enthusiasm for super-America swept away any lingering feelings of solidarity with American socialists. Mathews condemned the Socialist Party's opposition to the war and provided a nasty explanation of it. He claimed that American Socialists opposed the war not because they were Socialists or opposed to war, but because they were Germans: "Masquerading as opposition to war itself, nationalistic tendencies in Germany have reexpressed themselves among German socialists in the United States. Organized socialism in America has turned itself into anti-Americanism, condemning a war of national self-protection and pleading for peace in speech self-betrayed by its German accent." The relevant issue was alien disloyalty, not ideology, he assured: "The bolsheviki may be sincere; the German socialist is disloyal."[130]

Mathews offered no attempt to explain why non-Germanic Socialist leaders like Eugene Debs opposed the war; neither did he assure that his ugly attacks on war-resisting German-American Socialists excluded the likes of Walter Rauschenbusch. He played up the contrast between the patriotic war-boosting of the churches and the alien disloyalty of the war-resisters. In America's days of trial, he enthused, the churches strengthened the hearts of patriots, liberated patriotism from vengeance, and furnished moral enthusiasm for the war effort. By his reading, the American war effort deserved Christian support, not merely because it sought to save democracy, but because it continued a seventy-year national tradition of following ideals "which are worthy of a Christian people." In his rendering, modern American history was a narrative of freedom and other-regarding benevolence. The Civil War abolished slavery; the Spanish-American war was fought to set Cuba free; America's colonization of the Philippines brought education and democracy to the Filipinos; thanks to the United States, the Western hemisphere was saved from "European spoilation." Mathews was not as jingoistic as social gospeler Lyman Abbott on this theme; he allowed that America was guilty of its share of blunders and crudities. Like most of the social gospelers, however, he regarded his country as the world's redeemer nation. He took for granted that America was endowed with unique moral health and the burden of a world-embracing moral responsibility. Its mission was "not only to make the world safe for democracy, but to make democracy safe for the world." Both were Christian-izing projects.[131]

Some war-boosting liberal Protestant leaders had second thoughts after the war ended, especially after the Treaty of Versailles and America's refusal to join the League of Nations negated their conception of the war's purpose. Fosdick and Reinhold Niebuhr were prominent examples. Rarely prone to self-doubt, and never on an issue of this kind, Mathews did not join them. While allowing that he was "not untouched by war psychology" after America entered the war, he expressed no regrets. He recalled that in his speeches, "I never used such mur-derous eloquence as did some of my clerical friends." From his standpoint the cause was just, and his reaction to it was inevitable, given the mood of the times. With a rare self-revealing aside, Mathews added that he delivered his most jin-goistic statements just after his son was shipped to the front in France. "I saw in the war a conflict of two conceptions of society," he reflected. "It was tragic that they should be forced to arms, but I hoped that the new national feelings and the misery which war caused might lead nations to see the futility of war and estab-lish relations which would lead to international morality." Mathews spent much of his later life working to express this hope through his activism in a variety of peace organizations. The social gospel movement of the 1920s elevated "the war problem" above all others. But the "new national feelings" that inspired him dur-ing the war did not energize a new generation of social gospel idealism afterward. Aside from its antiwar activism, the social gospel went into eclipse.[132]

World War I shattered the cultural optimism and liberal hopes of European progressives. Having experienced the war very differently, Americans did not endure the epoch-ending sense of cultural crisis and disillusionment that pro-duced the Barthian revolt against theological liberalism in Europe. The United States emerged from the war with enhanced international prestige and a height-ened international profile. Having dreamed for the past generation of a new world order of mutually cooperating states, the social gospelers wanted to use their country's enhanced standing to promote the League of Nations, world democracy, and an international pact to "outlaw" war. The peace organizations that Mathews cofounded were devoted to the strategy of collective security as an alternative to war. In the aftermath of the war, American progressives won two historic victories, one of them fateful: women gained the right to vote, and Pro-hibition went into effect. During the same weeks that Prohibition went into effect, however, the U.S. Senate rejected America's entry into the League of Nations. Americans chose to "return to normalcy." They were tired of crusades for world democracy; they soon grew tired, as well, of the great progressive reli-gious experiment in national morality called Prohibition.

The social gospelers of the 1920s were forced to operate in a very different political culture from the one that allowed Rauschenbusch's fame, and they trimmed their sails in response. They were not routed from the field by an alternative theology, as in Europe, but they were forced to admit that they had been overly optimistic about the prospects of applying biblical teaching to the social order. Mathews later recalled that "it became fashionable, despite obvious facts, to disparage the social gospel and to turn from moral endeavor to worship and mysticism." Even liberal theologians denigrated the intellectual aspects of religion; even ardent social gospelers became more inward-looking and reflective in this environment. They sought less to transform society than to defend their faith. They had ample cause to be defensive, for in the early 1920s, mainline American Protestantism was rocked by controversies between modernists and fundamentalists.[133]

DEFENDING THE FAITH OF MODERNISM

Though he prided himself on his churchmanly tact, Mathews was a lightning rod for fundamentalists. His prominence was a provocation to them: how could he hold the highest church leadership positions while plainly denying all of the fundamentals? In 1917 he and Case stirred the outrage of premillennialists by pamphleteering against the notion that Christians should believe in the literal second coming of Jesus.[134] Fueled by a wartime resurgence of premillennialism and the development of a transdenominational antimodernist movement, fundamentalist activism surged after the war. By 1920 the northern Baptist and Presbyterian churches were seriously threatened by the possibility of fundamentalist takeovers. For fundamentalists Mathews was the leading example—until Fosdick in the mid-1920s challenged him for the honor—of what had gone wrong in the churches. Prominent New York City Baptist pastor I. M. Haldeman blasted what he called "Professor Shailer Mathews' burlesque on the Second Coming of Our Lord," while popular fundamentalist author John Horsch spotlighted the entire Chicago school as purveyors of "the immorality of theological counterfeiting."[135]

In 1924 Mathews replied with his theological manifesto, *The Faith of Modernism*. Like all manifestos, it was a period piece; in this case, the controversy that defined it was already roaring. Fosdick's sermon of 1922, "Shall the Fundamentalists Win?" launched the climactic battle of the thirty-year struggle between liberals and the recently renamed "fundamentalists." Fosdick's widely reprinted sermon plainly described his liberal beliefs and raised the specter of a fundamentalist takeover of the churches. The following year, Princeton Seminary conservative J. Gresham Machen famously argued in *Christianity and Liberalism* that modernist religion was not a "liberal" form of Christianity but an alternative religion.[136] Mathews's book finished off the defining trilogy of the modernist-fundamentalist controversy, a year before the controversy reached its climax in the Scopes evolution trial in Dayton, Tennessee. For Mathews, the pressing need of the moment was to assert the necessity of modernism and its ideally Christian character.

Like Fosdick, he took a third-way posture. Though Fosdick and Mathews were often condemned as radical church-splitters, both of them were broad-church Baptists. They claimed to stand for a "third way" between contending factional forces. Their third way was the way of holding the denominations together against church-splitters on both sides; both of them argued against a growing sectarian mentality on the right and a smaller number of schism enthusiasts on the left. Mathews believed that his modernism was an aid to the cause of broad-church viability. Though fundamentalists tended to use the word "modernist" as a synonym for "ultraliberal," as in "ultraliberal Chicago modernism," Mathews employed the term differently. He viewed theological "modernism" as a tradition-friendly improvement on the liberal tendency to cut itself off from the permanent elements of Christianity. To his mind, American Unitarianism represented the working out of the purely liberal idea of Christianity. Modernist theology was a different kind of liberalism. It maintained the constant factors of Christianity while it continually redefined the meaning of Christian faith. In *The Faith of Modernism* he spelled out what he meant.

The "social mind" concept formed the heart of his argument, which Mathews updated to the cultural circumstances of the mid-1920s. He observed that every creative age gives birth to a new social mind, and the modern age was nothing if not creative. But the modern age had not yet learned how to use its new power, wealth, knowledge, ideals, and freedom. The dangers of progress were serious, he cautioned. They included a host of reactionary backlashes, such as those that produced World War I and the fundamentalist movement. Mathews attributed the mindless hedonism of the Roaring Twenties to the cultural ravages of the war, which made people cynical about the future and self-obsessed: "Distrusting the future, men seek to enjoy the present. Nations with millions of their children starving abound in those who are feasting. Distrust of spiritual values has given rise to pagan enjoyment of animal life." *The Faith of Modernism* called for a renewal of outward-reaching care and cultural progress in a society that showed signs of having lost its way morally, proposing that only a renewed social Christianity could redeem that hope.[137]

The modern social mind constituted an advance on previous social minds by virtue of its commitments to democracy and science, Mathews observed, but these forces were not saving by themselves. There is such a thing as bad democracy, he implied; good democracy requires goodwill and sound knowledge. Moreover, though science gave immense new powers to modern civilization, it was an open question whether the postwar West would use its power wisely and ethically. Mathews warned that lacking a regenerative religious influence, the West was sure to use its power badly. Humanity is not good enough for its new powers, he explained. Human beings are selfish and vain, as postwar America amply demonstrated. To convert modern democracy and science into powers for good, humanity had to be regenerated by a redemptive spiritual power. The modern social gospel was needed more than ever, but just when the culturally regen-erative power of the social gospel was needed more desperately than ever, what were the churches arguing about?

Mathews's summary spared no sarcastic disapproval: "The world needs new control of nature and society and is told that the Bible is verbally inerrant. It needs a means of composing class strife, and is told to believe in the substitutionary atonement. It needs a spirit of love and justice and is told that love without ortho-doxy will not save from hell. It needs international peace and sees the champions of peace incapable of fellowship even at the table of their Lord. It needs to find God in the processes of nature and is told that he who believes in evolution can-not believe in God. It needs faith in the divine presence in human affairs and is told it must accept the virgin birth of Jesus Christ. It needs hope for a better world order and is told to await the speedy return of Jesus Christ from heaven to destroy sinners, cleanse the world by fire, and establish an ideal society composed of those whose bodies have been raised from the sea and the earth." This was a provoca-tive rendering of current church debates over "the fundamentals." Dogmatic Christianity was untrue and irrelevant; in his uncharacteristically in-your-face protest, Mathews strongly implied that it was also stupid.[138]

The mainline churches were trapped in stupid debates over outmoded literal dogmas while the world went to hell. Mathews assured that the fire of the social gospel still burned in the churches, however: "War is being denounced. Social service is broadcasting Christian love. Economic justice is being promised. Denominations are seeking to cooperate in service to men irrespective of race or attainment." The struggle in the churches was a struggle for the world. Mathews urged that modern Christianity, which had "its own intellectual expression and method, its own uplift and revelation," could save the world if it prevailed in the churches. "There are two social minds at work in our world," he observed. "The one seeks to reassert the past; the other seeks by new methods to gain efficiency." The first was a futile reaction against modernity, but the second could not suc-ceed without progressive Christian guidance and support.[139]

Mathews pressed the point that dogmatism and modernism are products of separate social minds. In *The Faith of Modernism* he took a brief pass at stating the point negatively with reference to liberalism. It is possible for certain kinds of liberalism to contend with theological conservatism on the same plane, he observed, for some liberals are merely countertypes of their conservative oppo-nents. Some liberals are merely dogmatic, resting in their negations. Mathews gave his usual cautionary example, American Unitarianism. In his reading, despite its outspoken opposition to dogmatic and confessionalist theologies, the Unitarian tradition remained essentially dogmatic. Unitarians and orthodox the-ologians shared a creedal mentality and expounded their positions "on the same plane of theological rationalism." Though short on beliefs of their own, Unitar-ians identified themselves by the things they did not believe. Mathews remarked, "With all due respect for the influence of Liberalism in clarifying religious thought, its origin and interest tend toward the emphasis of intellectual belief and the criticism and repudiation of doctrines *per se.*" There is such a thing as liberal fundamentalism, he implied; modernist theology was something categorically different.[140]

The key to the difference was its scientific character. Mathews argued that modernism was not a new theology or philosophy. It was essentially a method, not a creed. As a theological strategy, modernism was an empiricist approach to Christianity that operated within the received tradition of Christianity. Every science holds a presumption in favor of the object that it studies, he explained. In his definition, modernism was "the use of the methods of modern science to find, state and use the permanent and central values of inherited orthodoxy in meeting the needs of the modern world." More specifically, it was "the use of scientific, historical, social method in understanding and applying evangelical Christianity to the needs of living persons." Modernism had no confessions, it did not vote in conventions, and it did not enforce beliefs by coercion. It established beliefs only through the application of empirical methods and it relinquished its beliefs whenever they were falsified by scientific investigation. The Christian movement is essentially formative for modern Christianity, Mathews affirmed, but the way that the Christian community shapes modern Christianity is very different from its function in dogmatic Christianity. Dogmatic Christianity is based on doctrinal conformity through group authority; modern Christianity begins with the religious movement that gave rise to doctrine and interprets this movement through the use of critical methodologies. Modernists are Christians "who accept the results of scientific research as data with which to think religiously."[141]

The Faith of Modernism was a transitional work. Mathews tried to have it both ways. Though he granted sole intellectual authority to the natural and social sciences, he persisted in his claim to the evangelical tradition. He argued that modernism is the true form of evangelical Christianity because it focuses upon Jesus himself, rather than upon the church's later dogmas about Christ. He cautioned against any modernist inclination to cut loose from the evangelical tradition: "The place of evangelical Christianity in social and ethical life, the aid it gives to millions of human hearts, the moral impetus it has given social reforms, forbid treating Christianity as an unborn child of human thought." Mathews shuddered at the thought of doing theology in a deracinated academic vacuum. For the rest of his life he claimed to belong to evangelical Protestantism.[142]

But the tension that pervaded *The Faith of Modernism* was not creative or sustainable for him during the waning of liberal enthusiasm and in his academic environment. Mathews wanted the mantle of evangelicalism while claiming no normative authority for the gospel. He asserted the priority of method over belief while assuring that the heart of Christian belief can be secured by the natural and social sciences. He did not explain how he knew that science can be counted upon to confirm Christianity. Neither did he acknowledge that his naturalistic empiricism was another system of belief, though he ended the book with a credo, modeled on the Apostles' Creed, that began, "I believe in God, immanent in the forces and processes of nature, revealed in Jesus Christ and human history as Love." Though he imagined that modernist Christianity might find its future home in service organizations, not in churches, Mathews professed that he could not imagine a world in which youth were not trained in the Christian way of life or in which people did not associate themselves for worship and cooperation in the way of Christ.[143]

Liberal theology was the child of Enlightenment-modernist and evangelical heritages; for the most part, the liberal ideal was to fuse the rationalist, scientific, democratic, and humanist values of its Enlightenment-modernist heritage with the gospel norms of its evangelical heritage. Mathews still insisted that this was his ideal, but the balance decidedly tipped away from gospel norms in *The Faith of Modernism.* It was a vigorously post-Ritschlian work, and not only because Mathews rejected Ritschl's neo-Kantian disjunction between pure and practical reason. At Chicago, Mathews was surrounded by thinkers who interpreted Christianity in the American spirit of William James and John Dewey and who made no secret of favoring their Enlightenment-modernist heritage over the special pleading of their evangelical heritage. In the succeeding phase of the Chicago school, launched by Wieman in the late 1920s, even the language of heritages was abandoned in favor of a more narrow empiricism. Mathews facilitated and reinforced the latter turn by increasingly relinquishing the language of salvation and revelation.

For years he warned against the spiritual consequences of taking the modernist option exclusively. "Social evolution is a splendid term, but it leaves the heart empty," he cautioned. *The Faith of Modernism* repeated the sentiment while emphasizing the language of social evolution. Thereafter his writings opted decidedly for the religion of naturalistic process.[144] Mathews's evangelical self made occasional appearances in his later sermons and lectures, but the major writings of his later career were cast in the social scientific language of process, pattern, and function, beginning with a symposium on the contributions of science to religion and a second look at his first book.

In the mid-1920s Mathews resolved to replace *The Social Teaching of Jesus* with an updated revision titled *Jesus on Social Institutions.* His first life of Jesus had appropriated liberal nineteenth-century biblical scholarship; his second appropriated twentieth-century biblical scholarship and, especially, contemporary social psychology. The Chicago theologians were determined to show that a worthwhile life of Jesus could still be written after Weiss and Schweitzer. Case's *Jesus: A New Biography* (1927) emphasized the sociohistorical context in which Jesus lived, insisting that Jesus can be understood if Nazareth can be understood. Case declared, "To visualize in concrete fashion the social setting in which he did his work will carry one a long way toward a genuine understanding of the tasks that confronted him and the line of conduct he chose to adopt." Jesus would not have attracted disciples or created enemies if he had talked about things that were remote from the common concerns of people of his time, Case reasoned. Mathews's version of the same project argued that Jesus sublimated the revolutionary expectations of his followers by appropriating the messianic elements of their prevailing culture. Though much of the book's original exposition remained intact, its focus shifted from the kingdom of God proclaimed by Jesus to the effect of Jesus on the social process. *Jesus on Social Institutions* emphasized the sociohistorical chasm between the world of Jesus and the modern world. In the profoundly different world of 1928, Mathews observed, people still look to Jesus for guidance: "But the one whom they seek is not the documentary problem of criticism, the synthetic myth of archaeology, the personalized covenant of dogmatic theology, the gentlemanly martyr of romantic liberalism. The one real Jesus is the Jesus of history and the Jesus *in* history. And he is more than the Jesus of the gospels."[145]

THE GOD OF SOCIAL PROCESS

The burden of Mathews's later career, like that of the Chicago school, was to make theology as scientific as possible. Liberal theology in its Schleiermacherian and Ritschlian streams gave science its due while contending that science has little to offer to the constructive work of theology. The Chicago school renounced this Kantian bargain with scientific reason, but for a different reason than the one propounded in idealist and organicist theologies. Personalists, neo-Hegelians, and Whiteheadians charged that liberal theology was impoverished by its metaphysical agnosticism. Macintosh made the same argument against the Kantian basis of Ritschlian theology, in his case as an argument for epistemological realism, but for the most part the Chicago schoolers pressed their case on a practical level, not on the level of epistemological theory. For them, especially for Mathews, the problem of liberal theology was that its Kantian presuppositions kept it from being taken seriously in an increasingly scientific culture.

The Chicago school had a stronger consensus on what it was against than on what it was for. It was against authority religion, supernaturalism, philosophical idealism, and liberal subjectivism; it was for making theology credible in a scientific age by embracing naturalism and scientific tests of seriousness. Philosophically, Ames was a nonmetaphysical pragmatist; Smith leaned toward pragmatism, and in his later life, developed an interest in nature mysticism; Case was a pragmatic historicist; Wieman was committed to epistemological realism, ahistorical empiricism, and process philosophy. Like Smith, Mathews avoided precise epistemological and metaphysical position taking, but he assumed the existence of a pretheoretical world of facts. Implicitly he conceded that Kant's dichotomy between pure and practical reason paid dividends to theology in the generations of Schleiermacher and Ritschl; explicitly he judged that theology suffered from it in the long run. While conceding that there is undoubtedly a crucial difference between knowing something scientifically and acting morally in accordance with knowledge, Mathews urged that reality is a singular whole. Religion and morality are part of the only universe that exists. A person has to be religious in the same real world that science investigates, and religious faith is either consistent with reality or mistaken. For that reason, Mathews judged, the Kantian strategy could not sustain theology in the long run. Knowledge and values belong to the same singular reality: "Sooner or later, by a sort of osmotic pressure, one belief has permeated the other."[146]

In 1924 Mathews published a symposium on the contributions of science to religion. Thirteen scientists wrote chapters on aspects of current scientific research, while he wrote the book's chapters on religion. This project gave him the agenda for his later career. Mathews urged that the essential question of theology has a factual answer and that scientific empiricism is the only way to attain the answer. The question was: "Is religion legitimate? Is it an expression of life itself, rationally consistent with such knowledge of reality as we have?" Mathews believed that modern science was giving "new content" to the modern conception of God, though he allowed that empirical method cannot prove the existence of God. More promising to him was the proof-making capacity that science brings to the study of religion. Though limited in what it could do with God, science could do a great deal with religion. Particular religious worldviews either conform to what is known about reality or they do not. It followed for Mathews that the functions of religion could be studied as techniques for gaining support from their social environments.[147]

Chicago theological empiricism in the later 1920s was distinctive, but part of a realist trend in American theology. As a divinity school dean, Mathews rued the lack of respect for theology by his colleagues in the natural and social sciences. The academy dismissed conservative theology as stupid and liberal theology as too subjective to be taken seriously; Mathews noted that this attitude was spreading to the wider culture. "Humanity is pragmatic," he cautioned. "The really critical moment for a religion is when it is challenged by a new social mind to give reasons for its existence." To his perception, that moment had arrived for modern Christianity. Christianity was losing its cultural prestige, not because modern Christians were unfaithful, but because modern theology lacked intellectual respectability. "When a religion ceases to be intellectually respectable it is senile," Mathews warned. By seeking to repair the intellectual reputation of theology, he and his colleagues were actually endeavoring to give new life to Christianity as a whole.[148]

His linchpin was the concept of a "social pattern." Mathews analogized that patterns have the same relation to thought that axioms have to mathematics. His book, *The Atonement and the Social Process*, explained that a pattern "is a social institution or practice used to give content and intelligibility to otherwise unrationalized beliefs." By this definition, he reasoned, all Christian doctrines are social patterns. All Christian doctrines originate in the impulse to make something intelligible by analogizing something within the unintelligible object to something that is securely understood. All doctrines begin as metaphors and develop into patterns from which corollaries can be drawn. Christian doctrines about the meaning of the death of Christ, for example, are patterned expressions of the successive social minds of Christian history. Distinguishing between the religious function of atonement theory and the various social patterns through which this function has been conceptualized in Christian history, Mathews showed that "atonement" bore different meanings as it was conceptualized in messianic, sacrificial, imperial, feudal, monarchical, and modern social patterns. The mission of a savior is to save, but from what? The answer is historically relative in Christianity, he maintained, but not absolutely relative. The patterns of patristic and classical atonement theory are now outmoded, but all of them contain the feature that modern thinking about Christ's saving work emphasizes: that the God known in and through the experience of Jesus is revealed to be cooperative goodwill.[149]

Christ's saving experience of God as cooperative goodwill exemplifies the method of cosmic activity in the field of personality. Empirically, Mathews explained, Christianity is about Christ's saving process of activity, which is the same process that is disclosed in the fields of natural and social science: "Progress toward fuller assimilation of personality-producing forces involves the abandonment of that which is already accomplished. Man exchanges comfort for moral development and life itself for the life of the spirit. From such a point of view the death of Christ is not to be described as satisfaction of dignity or justice, but as an exponent of the forces inherent in the process through whose aid the loss of that which is good conditions the gain of that which is better—a personality more individual, less dependent upon its earlier stages and more appropriative of the personality-evolving activity of God." Schleiermacher and Theodore Munger said it better, but with the aid of social science tools that they lacked, Mathews conceptualized Christian redemption as healthy readjustment to "personality-evolving forces of the cosmic process."[150]

The Atonement and the Social Process explicated the social-scientific way to God through the experience of Jesus; in *The Growth of the Idea of God* Mathews applied the same method to the ultimate object of religious language. He accepted that the litmus test of theological empiricism is how it negotiates its limitations in addressing the Kantian transcendentals, especially God. In his opening pages, he ruled out the metaphysical God: "To argue that God exists is to argue that something behind experience corresponding to an already accepted definition exists," he observed, describing the problem of divine predication. To argue that God must exist is to presuppose some particular meaning for the word *God*. But this procedure begs the crucial questions: What would God be if God existed? Where did the idea of God come from? These are serious questions, Mathews counseled, but only sociohistorical science can provide serious answers to them.[151]

"The history of religious thought is really the history of patterns derived from social experience by which religious behavior is shown to be rational," he asserted. "A pattern, let us say, like the sovereignty of God, varies as the experience of sovereignty in social life varies." Mathews's pattern was the Enlightenment progress narrative. Tracing the history of Western religion, he drew a straight line of progress from "primitive" polytheism to biblical monotheism to classical theism to the rise of modern pantheist, panentheist, and naturalistic conceptions of divine reality. The best conception of God is the one that fits the account of reality given in modern science, he urged. Mathews staked his constructive claim on a naturalistic empiricism that left room for a religious explanation of personality. The process of evolution brought humanity into being, he reasoned, "but if that be the case, there must be activities within the cosmos sufficient to account for the evolution of the human species with its personal qualities." His naturalism ruled out all appeals to supernatural being or agency, but it did not exclude a religious explanation of consciousness. "There must be personality-evolving activities in the cosmos," he argued. Human beings would not exist without them. Human consciousness would not have survived the ravages of time and environment apart from the existence of ongoing personality-evolving activities of the cosmos: "That is the law of life itself."[152]

The lesson of his work on atonement thinking applied to God: "The patterns may change but the search for adjustment is as imperative as life itself." The religious relation does not disappear merely because outmoded patterns prove to be outmoded, he reasoned: "To realize that the traditional conception of God as sovereign or trinity is no longer tenable is not to say that the reciprocal relationship of men with the personality-producing activity of the universe is [at] an end. It simply means that in religion, as in physics, we must adopt new patterns by which cosmic relations can be rationalized and better established." Without invoking the name, Mathews presented his theistic naturalism as a culminating Hegelian moment in religious thought. The meaning of past religious patterns is revealed by the modern achievement of an empirically credible understanding of God, he argued. All of them stand for and point to conceptions of the personality-enhancing reality of the cosmos.[153]

Mathews cautioned that this was not an ontological claim. Atheism and classical theism both assume that God is an ontological term; modern theological empiricism interpreted *God* as an instrumental notion expressing "an experienced relationship with an objective environment, which is an element of a dynamic relation in which we are also elements." God is an interpretive pattern. In the case of Mathews's favored pattern, God was a name for the personality-evolving reality of the cosmos. As long as one bears in mind that God is an instrumental pattern, he reasoned, it is legitimate to use such personal metaphors as Father or Almighty in speaking of divine reality: "For God is our conception, born of social experience, of the personality-evolving and personally response elements of our cosmic environment with which we are organically related." Even the best conceptions of God are pragmatic and provisional, but they have a cosmic dimension and they are necessarily personal, like the personal agents who create them. These conceptions have a cosmic nature because the underlying reality experienced by the knower is prior to any knower's experience; their personal character is illustrated by the fact that the same argument does not apply to demonic power. Mathews explained that the notion of a personal Satan is not religious in the normative sense, for it is not functional to the process of personal adjustment to reality. "Satan" is the personification of impersonal activity, but the impersonal is precisely that which must not be personified. Impersonal forces negate personality, reversing the creative process: "Our idea of God is our conception of personality-producing activity within our environment, but there is nothing except poetic personification of impersonal forces in the concept of Satan."[154]

Mathews took for granted a commonsense realist epistemology while disclaiming any interest in epistemology and metaphysics. He spurned Hegelian and Jamesian arguments about the nature of reality. He refused to indulge metaphysical discussion about whether the universe is pluralistic or monistic, or whether God is finite or infinite. Empirical method deals with concreteness, he admonished, not abstractions. At the same time he cautioned that to speak of God as personality-producing activity is not to conceive of a distinguishable force, like electricity. Mathews reasoned that God is an empirically knowable process in which the potencies of ultimate reality find expression in emergent reality, especially human consciousness. Religion is cooperation with the universe and its evolution. Process is not identical with progress, for there is such a thing as devolution: "But whoever accepts the findings of science as to the genetic relations which explain a sometimes imperfectly traced process, gains a new perception of religion as something more than an inheritance of ancestral fears." By his reckoning, modern religion marked a sizable advance on Paul and Luther. The patterns of biblical and classical Christianity were all political, conceiving God as a sovereign and religion as transcendentalized politics. The pattern of Mathews's modern naturalistic theism was biological: "As an organism seeks the development of life through relationship with an environment which has conditioned its development, so men seek relationship with the cosmic activities on which they more or less intelligently find themselves dependent. If the flower in the crannied wall is to picture what these relations are, it must be left in the crannied wall."[155]

Mathews found this theology inspiring. It retained a whisper of the evangelical social gospel that he still loved, but now it was expressed in a form that deserved to be called knowledge. "It is hard to see how anyone can fail to feel the worth of such a basis for morals," he declared. "It is realism, not legalism."[156] In his last book, written during the first year of World War II, he acknowledged that many people undoubtedly did not find his thinking religiously inspiring. He replied that traditional Christianity had not prevented another catastrophic world war and that many people were not inspired by "the anthropomorphisms and group practices" of the old religion. "To turn to a sovereign God when humanity is weak will always be a souce of comfort for those who are defeated," he allowed. That was his take on the ascendance of neo-orthodox dialecticism; to Mathews, neo-orthodoxy was a smoke-and-mirrors refuge, barely an improvement on the old supernaturalism. The God of naturalistic theism was a stronger help than the neo-orthodox God of hidden holy mystery: "He is not lost in the shadows of a dialectic that declares him to be undefinable. He represents no absentee sovereignty, nor a personality who may be swayed by human petition or held responsible for human wrongdoing. His will is not mysterious, but a sym-

bol of an orderly process in the universe with which man must establish reciprocal adjustment if personal welfare is to be advanced."[157]

Mathews was sensitive to the irony of his later years. He had spent his entire
career trying to assimilate Christianity to the spirit of his age, only to have in his
later years, the spirit of the age turn against him. To a generation that endured,
in its youth, the horrors of World War I and that presently confronted the ravages of the Great Depression and another world war, Mathews's rhetoric of social
process and enlightenment came to sound quainter than the biblical language of
sin, redemption, and transcendence. He struggled to comprehend the Barthians
and Niebuhrians who claimed to represent an alternative to theological liberalism. "Those of us who are unrepentant liberals are sometimes bewildered at the
criticism of those who we thought were our fellows," he wrote in 1936, holding
Reinhold Niebuhr especially in mind. "And we are quite as much confused about
their claim to have a new orthodoxy." Protestant orthodoxy is a perfectly definite
concept, he observed; it includes a long list of literal beliefs that no Barthian swallowed. So what was the point of all the current noise about "the new orthodoxy"
and the "death of liberalism"?[158]

Keeping Niebuhr foremost in mind, without mentioning his name, Mathews
observed that the new dialectical theology was an essentially liberal movement
that sought to clear the field for itself by blasting its liberal fathers. The Barthians took various liberal gains in theology for granted, he observed, but at the same
time they criticized liberal theology for being liberal. Politically they veered to the
left; theologically they veered selectively to the right. Against the democratic
individualism and reformism of liberal theology, the Barthians and Niebuhrians
supported socialist collectivism. Against the cultured modernism of liberal theology, they reclaimed (or at least refashioned) the traditional doctrines of human
depravity and divine transcendence. Mathews dissented on both counts; "Forward to Moscow and back to sin" was not a good slogan for Christianity in 1936.
The collectivistic impulse of socialism was dangerously antiliberal, he warned;
moreover, dialectic was equally dangerous for theology, because it severed the
connection between the world of God and the known world.[159]

Mathews urged that democratic individualism was better than socialism and
"historical-mindedness" was more trustworthy than theological dialecticism.
"Few idealists have been able to resist the temptation to rely upon coercion when
once they have got possession of political power," he warned. "The great terror-
ists have been idealists. It is altogether too easy for men to let a good end justify
a bad means." With regard to the supposed failure and faithlessness of liberal theology, he countered that the dialecticists grievously misrepresented the liberal
view of sin: "The charge that liberals have been indifferent to sin grows out of a
dialectical rather than a factual reading of the literature of liberalism. It is born
of the thought now regnant in the fascism and Marxism of the continent of
Europe—that the individual gets his value through subjection to some group and
that the hope of social progress lies in group coercion." Mathews allowed that
liberals may have been too optimistic about human nature; he granted that the

early social gospel movement wrote self-projecting nonsense about Jesus; but he stoutly denied that the social gospel failed to take sin seriously: "I do not see how anyone can read the literature which those of us who pioneered the social gospel produced, and claim that we are indifferent to sin." What were they talking about? The social gospel was all about struggling against personal and social sin![160]

His thinking about sin was, in fact, thin and uncomprehending, as Niebuhr exposed. On the other hand, his thinking about political options was wiser than Niebuhr's in the 1930s, which says something about the wisdom of the social gospel movement that Mathews represented. For all of the critical pounding that it took for decades, the social gospel movement was better in its cooperativism, individualism, and reformism than the ideologies of its conservative and radical critics. Liberal social gospelers like Mathews held out for social insurance, public works employment, an expanded cooperative sector, and a more progressive income tax while Niebuhr claimed that these were nothing but Band-aids to make middle-class moralists feel better. Mathews confessed various doubts and failures of the liberal theology and social gospel movements, but he vowed that he would never confess "that we have lost faith in a God discoverable in the universe and human history, or that we adopt the corollary of pessimism—that mass coercion is superior to love implemented by intelligence." He would not back off from core convictions or apologize for them. He prayed that the Barthians and Niebuhrians would rediscover their own liberalism before they destroyed the gains of liberal theology.[161]

Mathews acutely understood in his later years that his kind of religious liberalism had been marginalized. He never doubted that World War I had been necessary or that America's intervention served the cause of democracy and progress, but when he sought to explain the unraveling of his generation's religious and social achievements in the 1920s and 1930s, he had no doubt that the war was to blame. In 1936 he reflected: "The natural course of all reconstructive processes has been disarranged by the Great War and those who are now entering middle age have grown up in an age of disillusionment and struggle. Their confidence in democracy has been rudely shaken. The inability of individuals to withstand group pressure has induced among some theologians an almost psychopathic attitude of pessimism and the elevation of crisis above process."[162]

Thus did Mathews, the symbol of modernist Christianity and social gospel moralism, concede his movement's overthrow by its children, who exalted crisis, pessimism, and power over love and cooperation. On his hopeful days, he hoped that the liberal Christians and their disillusioned orphans might stop quarreling over ways of proving things they all believed. The rest of the time he knew that the heyday of social Christian modernism was over. The Barthians were like premillennialists—they really believed that God is wholly other and that history is the footprint of God's wrath. On that impression, the Chicago schoolers stopped granting the liberal name to the Barthians and Niebuhrians.

By his reckoning, social gospel modernism was never defeated by a superior argument; it was merely pushed aside by a rhetorically overpowering offshoot of liberal theology that retreated from the fondest hopes of modernity and the social gospel. After decades of fame and prominence, he grasped that his Chicago successors, if they remained true to their intellectual heritage, would be lonelier in it. Those who kept the Chicago tradition alive in the 1940s and 1950s preferred Mathews's later works over his evangelical-leaning earlier writings. The Chicago school remained highly vital, intellectually vigorous, and small on that account. Mathews was seriously dated by the end of his career. His books did not wear well beyond his generation; even at Chicago his writings were valued more for their methodological clues than for their constructive theological ideas. His enduring legacy was his devotion to social scientific method, which had the effect of making sociohistorical criticism his chief article of faith. The Chicago school built an impressive legacy on the empirical dimension of that faith, but in the 1930s the Chicago theologians dropped historicism almost completely, even as the quintessential Chicago historicist, Shirley Jackson Case, succeeded his friend and comrade as dean.[163]

4.

In the Spirit of William James

Edward Scribner Ames, Douglas Clyde Macintosh,
Gerald Birney Smith, Henry Nelson Wieman,
and Chicago School Empiricism

"Empirical theology" is an idea with oxymoronic connotations. In the broad sense of the term, empiricism is a method of inquiry that bases its claims to knowledge on the datum of experience. By this definition, most of the liberal theology tradition qualifies as empirical, beginning with Schleiermacher's refounding of theology on the datum of religious consciousness. The American religious thinkers who proposed that there can be such a thing as empirical theology, however, adopted a more exacting concept of empiricism. They swept aside the transcendental a prioris of Kant and Schleiermacher, identified with the tradition of sense-experience empiricism represented by Locke and Hume, and embraced William James's "radical empiricist" reformulation of the Lockean tradition. In James's sense of the term "empiricism," the Chicago schoolers proposed to reinvent modern religious thinking as an empirical science, notwithstanding the oxymoronic connotations of "empirical theology."

Some Chicago theologians, especially Shailer Mathews, Douglas Clyde Macintosh, and Henry Nelson Wieman, sought to make theology as scientific as chemistry, or at least sociology; others, such as George Burman Foster and, in his last years, Gerald Birney Smith, zigged and zagged on how theology should go about making itself as modern as possible; still others, such as Edward Scribner

Ames, Shirley Jackson Case, and A. Eustace Haydon, made their case for liberal religion with little or no interest in theology; all of them drank deeply from the well of Jamesian empiricism and pragmatism. In the school's first generation, Mathews, Case, and Smith made "Chicago theology" synonymous with the sociohistorical approach to religion, though Foster cautioned about the religious limitations of historicism. Meanwhile Ames concentrated on the psychological, sociological, and pragmatic meaning of liberal religion, and in 1919 Yale theologian Macintosh wrote the first programmatic example of what came to be called "empirical theology." In the late 1920s the Chicago school moved in the explicitly empiricist direction of its disciple, Macintosh, but without his warm piety or personal theism. Wieman launched the second phase of Chicago theology by making it more philosophical, less historical, more stringently empirical, and more distantly removed than ever from its Ritschlian roots.

The Chicago school was rooted in nineteenth-century liberal theology, historical criticism, post-Kantian personalist idealism, Darwinism, history-of-religions comparativism, and, in the case of Foster, Nietzschean existentialism. It inherited a moderate empiricism from several of these traditions, but its distinctive quality was the radically empiricist spirit of William James and John Dewey. Most of the early American Unitarians were Lockeans in epistemology, and even the Unitarian leader who was not, William Ellery Channing, took a Lockean evidentialist approach to apologetics. Channing opened the way to a different kind of appeal to religious experience—the way of self-authenticating religious feeling—which Theodore Parker and the Emersonian Transcendentalists advanced in the mid-nineteenth century. A similar appeal to religious feeling was advanced by the forerunners of American Ritschlian theology, especially Horace Bushnell, Newman Smyth, and William Newton Clarke. The founding Chicago schoolers, Foster and Mathews, were Ritschlian liberals who began with the typical quasi-empiricism of this tradition. In the manner of Schleiermacher, they appealed to the subjective element in religious experience as the basis of Christian knowledge; in the manner of Ritschl and a host of contemporary Ritschlians, they emphasized that Christianity is a social movement, not a doctrine.

It was this sociohistorical dimension of the Ritschlian gospel that facilitated the transformation of Chicago Ritschlianism into forms of radical empiricist theology. Liberal theology began as a romanticist tradition that emphasized individual experiences of sensed things; the Ritschlian school recovered the relational character of Christianity as a socioethical and historical movement; the Chicago Ritschlians and, subsequently, post-Ritschlians moved from a blend of Schleiermacherian subjectivism and Ritschlian historicism to an empiricist emphasis on sense data and relationships. Put differently, the Chicago school of theology turned the focus of theology to the empirical study of experiences within relationships, and it studied not merely religious experience, but experience as a whole. Following William James, the Chicago theologians taught that radical empiricism is distinguished by its focus on the relationality of experience. Genuine religious knowledge is not a product of religious experience, they contended;

it is rather a product of disciplined empirical reflection on experience, especially the experience of external relations. We attain knowledge of objects by observing and making inferences about what they do. Ontologically, unlike Macintosh, the Chicago schoolers were thoroughgoing religious naturalists; epistemologically, like Macintosh, they affirmed the primacy of perception and the pragmatic criterion of truth. In the name of making the study of religion modern, they forged an impressive theological school that proved to be long on programmatic works, a bit short on constructive theology, and instructively discordant about what it means to be theologically objective.

WILLIAM JAMES AND THE PHILOSOPHY OF PRAGMATIC EMPIRICISM

Until Wieman arrived at Chicago, the Chicago theologians were ambivalent about philosophy, and even Wieman later resolved to keep his philosophical commitments to a minimum. In both cases the Chicago theologians asked themselves why they should need a philosophy if they were good empiricists. Didn't philosophy just get in the way of finding the (scientific) truth?

Under the influence of John Dewey, however, the early Chicago-school theologians judged that there was one kind of philosophy that facilitated the quest for truth, by spelling out the philosophical implications of empiricism. This was the pragmatic empiricism of Dewey and William James, which was not only the best philosophy of the time, but which held the key to making theology truly modern.

It helped that James was sympathetic to religion. William James began his academic career at Harvard in 1872 as an instructor in physiology; four years later he moved to the psychology department; in 1880, following the trajectory of his intellectual interests, he moved again, to the philosophy department; in 1890 he published his major work, the two-volume *Principles of Psychology*, which contained, in germinal form, most of the keynote ideas of his later philosophy. Over the next twenty years, while the Chicago schools of pragmatic philosophy and theology came into being, James worked out his many-sided, inventive case for philosophical pragmatism and radical empiricism. Appropriating Charles Sanders Peirce's conception of beliefs as rules for action, he defined pragmatism as a functional method and theory of meaning and truth, "the attitude of looking away from first things, principles, 'categories,' supposed necessities; and of looking towards last things, fruits, consequences, facts." Pragmatism was not a form of antirealism, in his conception. James took the reality of the external world for granted; in his words, he "carefully posited 'reality' *ab initio*," and remained an epistemological realist while contending that ideas must be judged by their factual consequences. "Realities are not *true,* they *are;* and beliefs are true *of* them," he contended. At the same time, from a pragmatist standpoint the truth of an idea is not a static property inherent in it; truth *happens* to ideas. Ideas become true through events. The truth of an event "*is* in fact an event, a process:

the process namely of its verifying itself, its veri-*fication,*" James explained. "Its validity is the process of its valid-*ation.*" Even the words "verification" and "validation" signify particular practical consequences, for the tests of truth are always practical. Ideas are tools that people design to make sense of the world into which they are thrown.[1]

While giving credit to Peirce, James refrained from grounding pragmatism in Peirce's logical system of categories. Though novel and controversial, he allowed, "pragmatism" was at root "a new name for some old ways of thinking." His empiricism belonged to a more settled intellectual tradition with which James consciously identified; at the same time, he argued that classical empiricism was crucially misguided. The empiricist tradition of Locke, Hume, and John Stuart Mill focused its analytic gaze on atomistic units of experience, positing a world of disjunctive relations. James objected that this framework and procedure missed the most important feature of experience, which is its flowing, immediate continuity. Life is a continuous flux or stream of experiences without distinct boundaries, he reflected: "In the same act by which I feel that this passing minute is a new pulse of my life, I feel that the old life continues into it, and the feeling of continuance in no wise jars upon the simultaneous feeling of a novelty."[2]

James reasoned that because life flows together and onward in a stream of experiences that are continually overlapping, the relations that exist between things are as real and as directly experienced as the things themselves. The relations that connect experiences are themselves experienced relations. This was the root of the difference between classical and radical empiricism as he conceived them. Radical empiricism was radical by virtue of its emphasis on the relationality of experience. "Radical empiricism takes conjunctive relations at their face value, holding them to be as real as the terms united by them," he proposed. "The world it represents as a collection, some parts of which are conjuctively and others disjunctively related." Some experiences are confluent, others are coterminous; some experiences are of likeness, or nearness, or simultaneity; others are of on-ness, or for-ness, or with-ness. In every case these relations are real as we actually experience them, James contended.[3] Radical empiricism affirmed the reality of immediate experience and the reality of things in all their plurality and diverse relations. Against the reality-devouring idealism of Hegel and other forms of philosophical monism, James insisted that "a real place must be found for every kind of thing experienced."[4] Monistic philosophies are principle-oriented and universalistic, he explained; they argue from wholes to parts. Empiricism is fact-oriented and particularistic; it argues from parts to wholes, remanding individual knowers to sensation.[5] James called his philosophy empirical "because it is contented to regard its most assured conclusions concerning matters of fact as hypotheses liable to modification in the course of future experience." He called it *radical* empiricism because it featured a plurality-affirming relational theory that treated the monist principle as a mere hypothesis.[6]

In James's usage, pragmatism and radical empiricism were closely related as functional methods, though he emphasized that they were logically distinct as theoretical positions. Each position stood on its own feet as a doctrine. It is possible to be a pragmatist without being a radical empiricist, he affirmed, and it is possible to be a radical empiricist without being a pragmatist. A person can subscribe to the pragmatist theory of meaning without basing it on James's theory of relations, or one can accept his radical relationism without adopting a pragmatic theory of meaning. In his last years James treated radical empiricism as the more important of the two doctrines, while stoutly defending pragmatism from a firestorm of criticism. A year before his death, in 1909, he argued in *The Meaning of Truth* that pragmatism is the best method of determining the meaning of empirical experience. The two doctrines work and belong together, he contended; pragmatism is an indispensable means to the radical empiricist salvation of philosophy and religion. In James's words, "It seems to me that the establishment of the pragmatist theory of truth is a step of first-rate importance in making radical empiricism prevail."[7]

To James, radical empiricism consisted of a postulate, a statement of fact, and a generalized conclusion. The postulate was that philosophers should debate only about things that are definable in terms drawn from experience. The statement of fact was that all relations between things, whether conjunctive or disjunctive, are equally matters of direct particular experience as the things themselves. The generalized conclusion was that parts of experience hold together by relations that are themselves parts of experience. James explained: "The directly apprehended universe needs, in short, no extraneous trans-empirical connective support, but possesses in its own right a concatenated or continuous structure." In his view, the chief obstacle to radical empiricism was the deeply rooted and mistaken rationalist belief that experience as immediately given has no conjunctive structure. Neo-Hegelian philosophers such as F. H. Bradley and J. E. McTaggart, and, closer to home, James's Harvard colleague Josiah Royce all viewed experience as disjunctive, torn apart from reason and truth. They disclosed the hidden wholeness of things by interpreting the world's separate things as shapes of Spirit. "To make one world out of this separateness, a higher unifying agency must be there," James observed. "In the prevalent idealism this agency is represented as the absolute all-witness which 'relates' things together by throwing 'categories' over them like a net." Philosophical idealism reunited "parts of reality in pairs," such as subject and object, knower and known, thought and being, reason and experience, through its dialectics of the truth relation. James countered that the truth relation has a definite content and that everything in this relation is experienceable. Though it grieved him that many readers interpreted his empiricism as a brief for philosophical materialism, he insisted that the whole nature of the truth relation can be told in positive terms. In order to be true, ideas must "work" functionally, and they do.[8]

His deep interest in religion was a function of his respect for its practical power. James did not believe in the infinite, personal God of Christianity or the deity of Christ, and thus did not count himself a Christian. At the same time he possessed a deeply religious sensibility, decidedly of a liberal Protestant kind, and he respected the experience of intelligent religious believers. For James the great problem of modern philosophy and of modern life was to reclaim personality from the impersonal world of chance depicted by science. He viewed religion as a still-significant way of claiming the personal standpoint. The book that offered his first defense of pragmatism was his first explicitly philosophical work, *The Will to Believe and Other Essays in Popular Philosophy* (1897). Significantly, it was a book about religion. Responding to W. K. Clifford's essay "The Ethics of Belief," which asserted the immorality of believing anything on insufficient evidence, James offered a pragmatic-empiricist case for believing in God and moral truth. *The Will to Believe* asserted that the most important questions in life cannot be settled on purely intellectual grounds. The existence of certain truths is brought about only by the human desire for them. There are cases "where a fact cannot come at all unless a preliminary faith exists in its coming," James observed. He pressed the point that this was an empirical truism; Clifford's seemingly staunch empiricism was insufficiently empiricist: "And where faith in fact can help create the fact, that would be an insane logic which should say that faith running ahead of scientific evidence is the 'lowest kind of immorality' in which a thinking being can fall."[9]

James did not deny the reality of objective knowledge. "In our dealings with objective nature we obviously are recorders, not makers, of the truth," he assured. "Throughout the breadth of physical nature facts are what they are quite independently of us, and seldom is there any such hurry about them that the risks of being duped by believing a premature theory need be faced." Subjective preferences do not affect the movement of the stars or the facts of history, he reasoned. The world is real and so is our knowledge about it. On the other hand, there are other domains of knowing in which subjective preferences are plainly truth-creative. James asserted the latter fact in an 1879 essay, "The Sentiment of Rationality," that he appended to *The Will to Believe*. Reflecting on the reality of religious and moral truths, he wrote: "There are then cases where faith creates its own verification. Believe, and you shall be right, for you shall save yourself; doubt, and you shall again be right, for you shall perish. The only difference is that to believe is greatly to your advantage." James himself was not a believer, but he wished for deeper religious experiences than he experienced, and he respected the role that religion played in helping people find personal meaning in a meaningless world.[10]

These sentiments were famously displayed in his subsequent major work, *The Varieties of Religious Experience* (1902), which was brilliantly pluralistic and impossibly narrow at the same time. James had no interest in the communal or institutional aspects of religion. To him, all institutional religion was secondhand. Despite his interest in the practical power of religion, he failed to see the practical power of its communal and liturgical functions; despite his socioethical concerns, he gave a privatistic rendering of the social meaning of Christianity. Institutionalized churches live on secondhand tradition, he asserted, "but the *founders* of every church owed their power originally—to the fact of their direct personal communion with the divine—so personal religion should still seem the primordial thing." For this defining prejudice the champion of empirical method offered no empirical evidence at all and ignored the otherwise Jamesian truism that there is no such thing as unmediated experience. He defined religion as "the feelings, acts, and experiences of individual men in their solitude, so far as they apprehend themselves to stand in relation to whatever they may consider the divine." Wrongly, this definition implied that there is such a thing as "religion" that is experienced most profoundly by inspired individuals apart from the language uses and ritual practices of historical communities.[11]

With all of its blinders, however, *The Varieties of Religious Experience* made an absorbing case for the practical value of personal faith, showing special feeling for saintly mysticism. With psychological insight informed by personal experience, James distinguished between the sensibilities of "once-born" and "twice-born" believers. The once-born soul is healthy-minded and optimistic, he argued; once-born people experience grace and nature as a unity and require no dramatic conversion experience to be religious. Twice-born religion, on the other hand, is the faith of the great spiritual movements. It is the religion of the sin-sick soul epitomized by Augustine's *Confessions* and enshrined in classical Western theologies, which effects unity in a divided will through conversion. James knew the melancholic background of twice-born religion from personal experience; he struggled for many years from panic attacks and the chronically joyless anxiety that he called "anhedonia." Relatedly, he acknowledged that *The Varieties of Religious Experience* was too subjectve in subject matter and approach to qualify as scientific research. The book's objectivity was sufficiently debatable to inspire decades of scholarly disagreement about its biographical nature.[12] If short on empirical objectivity, however, *The Varieties of Religious Experience* was pervaded by James's distinctive capacity for intellectual sympathy and the open-ended, curious, results-oriented spirit of his pragmatism. It also prefigured his equally famous distinction in *Pragmatism* between "tender-minded" thinking, which he described as rationalistic, intellectualistic, idealistic, optimistic, religious, free-willist, monistic, and dogmatical, and "tough-minded" thinking, which he contrasted as empiricist, sensationalistic, materialistic, pessimistic, irreligious, fatalistic, pluralistic, and skeptical.[13]

James's mind was a mixture of these types. He was emphatically empiricist and pluralistic, but he also had a vaguely mystical religious temperament and tried to be optimistic. James interpreter Richard M. Gale aptly characterizes him as a "divided self" whose Promethean empiricism conflicted with a mystical longing for intimacy with other selves and even union with a higher Self. The Promethean James debunked spiritual concepts of consciousness, but the mystical James described reality as a panpsychic continuum of consciousness and conducted research on psychic phenomena. Near the end of *The Varieties of Religious Experience,* James gave haunting expression to this struggle of his soul.[14]

He observed that the story of religion is an important chapter in the history of human egoism, because religion is always about the anxieties of human subjects. The function of religion is to assure individuals that sacred reality meets them on the basis of their personal concerns. James took this function very seriously, while admonishing that science negates the personal point of view. Religion ascribes a meaning to life, while science demonstrates that the world is ruled by chance, not purpose: "Though the scientist may individually nourish a religion, and be a theist in his irresponsible hours, the days are over when it could be said that for Science herself the heavens declare the glory of God and the firmament showeth his handiwork." The material universe is a product of time and chance. It does not feel, it has no meaning, and it has little future. "The Darwinian notion of chance production, and subsequent destruction, speedy or deferred, applies to the largest as well as the smallest facts," James remarked. "It is impossible, in the present temper of the scientific imagination, to find in the drifting of the cosmic atoms, whether they work on the universal or on the particular scale, anything but a kind of aimless weather, doing and undoing, achieving no proper history, and leaving no result."[15]

Nature is self-destructive; it possesses no ultimate tendency "with which it is possible to feel a sympathy." James reflected that before the age of Darwin it was possible for an educated person to be impressed by classic natural theology. Now the old scholastics and theological rationalists seemed "quite grotesque," because they pictured a God "who conformed the largest things of nature to the paltriest of our private wants." Science cannot accommodate the God of personal concerns, he judged: "The God whom science recognizes must be a God of universal laws exclusively, a God who does a wholesale, not a retail business." Whatever reality that God may have, "he cannot accommodate his processes to the convenience of individuals." Individuals are like the bubbles on the foam of a storming sea, James analogized; they are "floating episodes, made and unmade by the forces of the wind and water." Clifford called them mere epiphenomena, and James agreed: "their destinies weigh nothing and determine nothing in the world's irremedial currents of events."[16]

This was the verdict of tough-minded materialistic empiricism. James scratched for immanent meanings in all his books while keeping firmly in view the world-picture of Darwinian science. The world is not an orderly creation but an accidental product of chance; only by chance do we exist and know that we exist. The latter fact—that we know, by chance, that we exist—was the root of James's conception of true religion as firsthand personal faith. What was needed in the modern world was to reclaim personality from the impersonality of the contingent world described by science. James reasoned that religion was most vital and real as inspired personal faith. Religion offered the most typical and, socially, the most important example of people reclaiming their humanity in the face of outer meaninglessness. Religion occupies itself with personal destinies, James explained, in contact with "the only absolute realities which we know." On that ground, against the grain of modern sociological theory, he insisted that religion "must necessarily play an eternal part in human history." Certain forms of institutional religion were bound to fade away in an increasingly secular modern culture, but the religious impulse itself was constitutively human and humanizing.[17]

James read enough liberal Protestant theology to feel his blood relation to it. Upon sending a copy of *The Varieties of Religious Experience* to social gospeler and Harvard colleague Francis G. Peabody, James wrote insightfully, "You will class me a Methodist, *minus* a Savior." His pietistic humanism was minus a few other traditional Christian beliefs. James never quite decided whether he believed in God, but he was quite certain about the God in which he did not believe. He disliked the idea that God created the universe, because this idea separates the human subject from the deepest reality of life and turns humanity into an afterthought. By his reckoning it also had the effect, in orthodox Christianity, of making God a completely self-sufficient entity. James protested that traditional Christianity was so jealous of God's glory that it turned God into an idol of impassible separateness and isolation: "Page upon page in scholastic books go to prove that God is in no sense implicated by his creative act, or involved in his creation."[18]

He sought to save modern theologians from wasting their time on the metaphysical attributes of God: "I cannot conceive of its being of the smallest consequence to us religiously that any one of them should be true. Pray, what specific act can I perform in order to adapt myself the better to God's simplicity? Or how does it assist me to plan my behavior, to know that his happiness is absolutely complete?" The God of absolute being portrayed in classical theology struck him as a "metaphysical monster." From the standpoint of practical religion, he judged, this idea of divine reality was "an absolutely worthless invention of the scholarly mind."[19] In the name of practical religion, James did a bit of metaphysical spinning of his own. It cannot be known whether God exists, he believed, but if God does exist, then God must be finite. The God of infinite being is a monster who denies the human subject its rightful powers: "If there be a God, he is no absolute all-experiencer, but simply the experiencer of actual conscious span."[20]

James's Harvard colleague George Santayana once remarked that James was not really a religious believer: "he merely believed in the right of believing that you might be right if you believed."[21] James explained himself more poignantly, if elusively, in a letter to psychologist James Leuba: "My personal position is simple. I have no living sense of commerce with a God. I envy those who have, for I know that the addition of such a sense would help me greatly. The divine, for my active life, is limited to impersonal and abstract concepts which, as ideals, interest and determine me, but do so but faintly in comparison with what a feeling of God might effect, if I had one." James allowed that this feeling, or its lack, was largely a question of intensity, "but a shade of intensity may make one's whole centre of moral energy shift." While lacking in living experience of God, he reflected, "yet there is *something in me* which *makes response* when I hear utterances from that quarter made by others. I recognize the deeper voice. Something tells me:— *'thither lies truth'*—and I am sure it is not old theistic prejudices of infancy." In his case, the youthful background was Christian with a strong dose of Swedenborgianism, but he had moved well beyond Christianity. The deeper voice was known to Christianity but not exclusive to it. James called it "my mystical *germ.*" He believed that this germ was common to religious people of all kinds; for them and for himself, he also believed that it was sufficiently strong to withstand atheistic criticism.[22]

His relations with liberal Protestant theologians fit this outlook. James carried on a friendly crosstown rivalry with Borden Parker Bowne throughout his philosophical career. Though he chided Bowne for his tone of metaphysical certainty, he counted Bowne's personalist Christian idealism as an ally in the battle against all forms of philosophical monism. He was equally friendly with his former student, liberal Congregationalist pastor and theologian George A. Gordon, whose books he read with appreciation. To Bowne and Gordon he emphasized the deep kinship, as he saw it, between liberal theology and pragmatic empiricism. Near the end of his life James enthused to Gordon that his philosophical reputation appeared to be gaining stature. *Pragmatism* inspired an uproar of ridicule and praise; James recognized that both reactions aided his cause. The volatile reaction to the book boosted his reputation and won him a larger audience: "I seem to be getting 'recognized' as I never was before, and feel in consequence as if my place in the world was warmer." He told Gordon that from his standpoint, the two of them were doing the same work, building up the kingdom of God, "you more openly and immediately, I more subterraneanly and remotely, but I believe we are converging upon the same thing ultimately."[23]

Two years later, in his famous lectures at Oxford on intellectual pluralism, James urged that empirical philosophy was potentially the salvation of religion and philosophy. Monism still ruled the day in philosophy, he observed, because philosophers preferred elegant logical solutions to the real world, and because they feared, like much of the public, "that the only solidly grounded basis for religion was along those lines." James countered that religious ideals are better secured by an open-minded philosophical empiricism that tracks the flow of experience. Empiricism approaches the only reality that has any meaning, he argued; it respects the human experience of plurality and different kinds of unity in a world of flux and sensation: "The essence of life is its continuously changing character; but our concepts are all discontinuous and fixed." James scorned the sheer unreality of nonempirical philosophies and theologies. The concepts of speculative philosophy are not parts of reality, he objected; they are merely suppositions about it, "notes taken by ourselves." They hold reality no better than a net holds water. Empiricism is the alternative to abstract "cut out and fix" concepts. Though empirical method was commonly regarded as a threat to religion, he believed that it held the potential to become the indispensable friend of true religion: "Let empiricism once become associated with religion, as hitherto, through some strange misunderstanding, it has been associated with irreligion, and I believe that a new era of religion as well as philosophy will be ready to begin."[24]

The Chicago schools of social philosophy and theology took these words very seriously. James was born to high culture, wealth, and Harvard, but some of his leading disciples came from humble backgrounds. Edward Scribner Ames, a product of the early Chicago school, was a key example. A Disciples of Christ pastor who turned his church into a laboratory of Jamesian progressive religion, he made his fame as a pastor who doubled as a University of Chicago psychologist and philosopher. To the Chicago theologians and the larger Chicago school that included them, Ames's ministry and intellectual career offered impressive evidence that radical empiricism offered a preachable gospel, if not a new theology.

EDWARD SCRIBNER AMES
AND THE GOSPEL OF PRAGMATIC EMPIRICISM

Edward Scribner Ames was a product of midwest Campbellite piety and Midwest American practicality. Born in Eau Claire, Wisconsin, he moved with his family nine times during his early childhood and adolescence. His father, Lucius Bowles Ames, was a Calvinist pastor in West Rupert, Vermont, before he embraced the creedless freedom of Alexander Campbell's new Disciples movement. After moving to Wisconsin at the end of the Civil War, Lucius and Adaline Scribner Ames moved from one small town to another in Michigan, Illinois, and Iowa, where he pastored small Disciples churches and struggled to sustain a subsistence living. All of Lucius Ames's pastorates were in hard-pressed new congregations; the family's longest stay in any of them was four years. Ames later recalled that his devout father trusted in God's providential care and his devout mother coped heroically with her family's threadbare existence. Ames spent his early childhood on a fruit farm in Benton Harbor, Michigan; his happiest years were in Toulon, Illinois, where his father served one pastorate and later returned for a second; in 1885, when Ames turned fifteen, his father moved the family to Des Moines to enable the two youngest children to attend Drake University.

Drake was a Disciples college, founded four years earlier. It had no library to speak of and no intellectual aspirations, but Ames learned enough in college to be dissatisfied with his education. He later recalled that he possessed the kind of boldness that is peculiar to timid people: "Being diffident and fearful of the world, I constantly craved such discipline and advantages as would give the sense of being able to cope with other men and play my part with them." Achievement-oriented, craving further education, and anxious about his future, he was ordained to the Disciples ministry, but was discouraged by Disciples' leaders from attending seminary; the concept of seminary education was beyond their experience. Ames wanted to study at a solidly Christian seminary; more importantly, he wanted as much prestige as possible. To his mind, the former consideration ruled out Harvard, so he went to Yale Divinity School.[25]

He arrived in New Haven just after William Rainey Harper departed to found the University of Chicago; one year proved to be enough for Ames, for Yale Divinity School was not much of a seminary in the early 1890s. He entered with advanced standing, mostly because he was already an ordained pastor, and he quickly judged that the divinity school compared poorly to three local pulpits and Yale's philosophy department as a source of intellectual stimulation. For the rest of his life Ames assured parishioners that theology is boring. Though he snored through his theology courses, he found inspiration in the eloquent liberal preaching of Theodore Munger and Newman Smyth, who pastored the campus's side-by-side Congregational churches, and in the sermons of distinguished visiting preachers at Battell Chapel, notably Lyman Abbott, George Gordon, Phillips Brooks, and Henry Van Dyke. Religiously, these preachers attracted Ames to liberal Christianity and convinced him that the "new theology" was genuinely Christian; intellectually he converted to liberal Christianity after taking a course in the philosophy of religion taught by Yale philosophical idealist George T. Ladd. Ladd taught philosophy of religion from an historical-critical standpoint, using German theologian Otto Pfleiderer's *The Philosophy of Religion on the Basis of its History* as his text. Ames later recalled that Pfleiderer's book "displaced in my mind the idea of a supernatural, miraculously inspired religion, providing instead the more interesting and fruitful notion of a religion growing up with the life of a people and being modified by their changing experiences." Ames was enthralled by the possibility of interpreting Christianity as a product of Semitic history; the fact that he learned this lesson in a philosophy course convinced him that "many problems in theology are dealt with more fully and freely in philosophy." Later he judged that psychology also offers more to the understanding of religion than theology.[26]

With little emotional strain he relinquished the theologically conservative aspects of his Disciples background. Though Disciples preaching was typically supernaturalist and evangelical, he reasoned that the noncreedal spirit of the Disciples movement was well suited to accommodate modern criticism. Upon graduating from Yale Divinity School, he wanted to study philosophy at Harvard with William James, but James took a sabbatical in 1892. Ames interviewed Josiah Royce, who stressed the importance of higher mathematics and German idealism as foundational for graduate work in philosophy. Royce's metaphysical interests were alien to him, as were those of Royce's younger colleague at Harvard, George Santayana. Ames later reflected that Santayana's speculative cast of mind would not have suited his own Midwestern practicality. Since James was unavailable and Ames had no desire to study metaphysics, he returned to Yale for graduate studies in philosophy, where he studied Kant, Pfleiderer, James, and Arthur Schopenhauer under Ladd's direction.[27]

This canon showed through in his thinking for the rest of his career. Ames took as much from Schopenhauer as from Kant or Pfleiderer. "He not only challenged all my traditional beliefs but attacked the very foundations of all moral and religious values," he later recalled. Schopenhauer's voluntarism was convincing to him; Schopenhauer's pessimism was both chastening and, in a devil's-advocate way, exciting: "He denied that it is a rational world and cited a surprising amount of evidence in support of his dark thought. Dreams of happiness and of ideal hopes are illusions." For the rest of his life Ames tried to be the kind of liberal who kept in mind Schopenhauer's chastening truism that we cannot catch any experience; every experience becomes a thing of the past as soon as we try to seize it: "Men are never satisfied, their hungers are never satiated, and time engulfs their finest achievements. Every person is beset by inordinate ambition, by unfathomable selfishness, and by fears of illness, misfortune and death." Like most liberals, Ames took for granted the Victorian idea of religion as a spiritual antidote to humankind's lower nature. "As I see the religion of Jesus, it makes the love of life central," he asserted. Religion calls for the triumph of spirit over the heart's "bottomless abyss of desire and longing." With Schopenhauer he judged that will transcends intellect and that all human impulses, desires, sentiments, and choices are contained in the will. To a lesser degree he even accepted Schopenhauer's realism about the bitter sadness of nature. But Schopenhauer held that the will is capricious, irrational, and essentially at war with itself; this was the root of his pessimism. To Ames, as to the social gospelers, pessimism was the enemy; it was the spiritual abyss that religion struggled against. Ames took his psychological voluntarism from a more balanced philosopher, William James.[28]

James's newly published major work, *The Principles of Psychology*, removed all metaphysical notions from psychological theory and proposed to base psychology on the living stream of everyday experience. James called his model "psychology without a soul," which offended many religious leaders and philosophers, but not Ames. He later recalled that for all empirically minded thinkers of his generation, James's psychological theorizing set a new standard of thinking about the self: "It directed attention to the concrete nature of the self, to the force of human habits, and to new interpretations of the emotions and the will. In place of the traditional mysteries of man's inner life, it made clear the growth of ideas through the functioning of the sense organs and the brain, in relation to things and events of the environment. The wonders of memory and imagination were put into terms of imagery derived from sense perception and the operation of the laws of the association of ideas." James grounded psychology on things that can be identified and measured. To Ames, James made psychology real and provided "definite handles by which to take hold of the task of developing and reconstructing all human idealisms." More importantly, he provided a model of courageous, independent, empirical thinking. "His breath-taking, innovating assertions and assumptions filled me with amazement," Ames later recalled. Following James's example, he vowed to discard the claims of all external authorities and attain his truths from the flow of empirical experience. From James he got his first sense of a vocational calling. James made psychology scientific; what the field of religion needed were ministers and academics who appropriated James's style of empirical thinking for the cultivation of religious behavior.[29]

This intuition was vigorously confirmed at the University of Chicago, where Ames completed the last year of his doctoral program under a fellowship provided by Harper, whose friend, Sanford Scribner, was Ames's uncle and a member of the Divinity School's board of trustees. An empirically minded coterie of academics centered around James Hayden Tufts, George Herbert Mead, Addison W. Moore, and John Dewey was just beginning to develop at Chicago; James later dubbed it "the Chicago school." To Ames, the Chicago school was a godsend. It confirmed his intuitions about the work of philosophy and the superiority of Jamesian psychology. It replaced the idealist theorizing of Ladd, Royce, the British Hegelians, and the rest of the Anglo-American philosophical establishment with testable real-world data. Under Tufts's direction, he studied Locke's *Essay on the Human Understanding,* which confirmed his identification with empiricist philosophy and, to his surprise, Disciples religion. Ames learned that Alexander Campbell's favorite philosopher was John Locke. Like the Campbellite Disciples movement, Locke believed in the reasonableness of Christianity; like the Disciples, he taught that only one article of faith—the confession of Christ as Lord—is essential to Christianity and the hope of Christian union; like the Disciples, Locke rejected theological metaphysics, the doctrine of innate human depravity, and revivalistic emotionalism. For Locke, as for the Disciples tradition at its best, the tests of worthy belief and action were rational, empirical, and practical. This was the faith that Ames set out to teach and preach after completing his doctorate at Chicago in 1895; at his oral examination he met John Dewey. Of all the Chicago theologians, Ames was the one who remained closest to Dewey's philosophical position.[30]

Ames taught briefly as a privatdocent at Chicago before moving to Butler College, a Disciples school near Indianapolis, where he taught philosophy and education. He gave three years to Butler and then returned to Chicago in 1900 to assume the pastorate of the Hyde Park Church, a six-year-old Disciples congregation located near the university. Against the example of his father, he remained in this pastorate for forty years. He also became a major figure at the University of Chicago. Returning to the Chicago faculty as a part-time assistant instructor in the philosophy department, Ames quickly gained a significant following in a new field, the psychology of religion. While teaching on a part-time basis, he eventually became chair of the department, and his congregation expanded and thrived. The Disciples movement in Chicago boasted a vigorous community of intellectuals that included Herbert L. Willett, Errett Gates, W. E. Garrison, William Clayton Bower, and Charles Clayton Morrison. Willett was a Disciples pastor, cofounder of the campus-based Disciples Divinity House, and editor of the Disciples' magazine *The Christian Oracle.* In 1900 Morrison bought *The Christian Oracle* and renamed it *The Christian Century.* Aside from his Deweyite friends, this group was Ames's home base. He wrote frequently for *The Christian Century,* supported its development into the flagship journal of mainline American Protestantism, cofounded the Campbell Institute as a base of Disciples scholarship, and served for eighteen years as dean of Disciples Divinity House, where he profoundly influenced a generation of Chicago seminarians, ministers, academics, and church administrators.[31]

"My experience as a student and as a teacher of philosophy had brought me to regard religion as a natural growth in human life, and as subject generally to slow and unconscious changes in the prevailing culture," he later reflected. Religion needed to keep up with the prevailing culture. The natural sciences were flourishing, the social sciences were beginning to acquire a solid base of knowledge, and

Chicago was rife with interesting social-science experiments, such as Dewey's Laboratory School and Jane Addams's Hull House. Like Shailer Mathews, Ames resolved that it was crucial for America and Christianity that religion not be left behind.[32] Social gospel modernism was taking off as a church movement, but the churches remained overwhelmingly behind the cultural curve as a whole. As a pastor he preached a straightforwardly liberal religion to a congregation that supported the social gospel and practiced ecumenism. As an academic he applied the functional psychology of William James and James R. Angell to the understanding of religious experience. Consciousness is a biological phenomenon that must be understood with reference to its function in the total life process, he taught; activity is the inmost nature of the will; religious ideas and feelings are always secondary by-products of the choices and power of will. On the strength of these themes, Ames became an academic pioneer of religious psychology, along with James, George Albert Coe, and Edwin D. Starbuck.[33]

He began his early major work, *The Psychology of Religious Experience*, with a Jamesian description of religion. The prevailing definitions of religion are either narrow or vague, he noted. Kant defined religion as the knowledge of one's duties as divine commands; Schleiermacher defined it as the feeling of absolute dependence; Hegel defined it as the knowledge possessed by the finite mind of its nature as absolute mind. Ames did not cite James's specific definition of religion—"the feelings, acts, and experiences of individual men in their solitude"—which had its own narrowness problems, but he argued that in contrast to the prevailing alternatives, James was broad and concrete. For James, "religion" was a collective name, like "government." It did not signify any specific belief or attribute, but included many practices, beliefs, and sentiments. Religion was a name for the many ways in which people engaged in religious practices. For James, as for Ames, there was no such thing as a single essence of religion. On empiricist grounds, Ames banished "essence" language altogether. He suggested that even such words as idea, image, and concept should be replaced by such words as reacting, associating, attending, feeling, perceiving, reasoning, and the like. Ideas are comprehensible only in the context of their history and by their effects, he explained, expounding a Lockean theme. So-called "ideas" are movements of imagery and feeling. Mental life is the cognitive process of mediating ends and smoothing the way for action. With Hume and James, he believed that just as there is no such thing as an essence of religion, there is no such thing as pure consciousness. Thought is always particular. We never merely think, but always think about something, just as we never merely feel, but feel cold or warmth or pain: "In the same way, consciousness is actually of this or that kind, and there is no more a consciousness in general than a tree in general."[34]

For James, will was, at root, the sustaining of a thought that one has chosen. He once remarked that his first act of free will was to believe in free will. In the spirit of Jamesian voluntarism, Ames insisted that thought is inherently teleological. The process of thinking is fundamentally purposive in its "normal" course, he explained. It is only when thought is abstracted or otherwise ripped out of context that it reduces to mere description or factuality. Like James, Ames valued religion for essentially the same reason that he valued thought. The phenomenon of thinking demonstrates the reality of personality in the impersonal world depicted by science, and religion is about the idealization of personal values. More plainly than James, Ames asserted that the idea of God, "when seriously employed, serves to generalize and to idealize all the values one knows." Ames took the Jamesian argument about God further than James. The God of absolute being has no claim to the idea of God at all, he insisted, for personality is the basis of the God-idea. Personality is active and purposive; it is more than static being: "The character of a person cannot be thought of except in terms of what he does." It followed that the idea of God, rightly understood, "involves in the highest degree the element of will, of purpose and of movement toward great goals."[35]

Ames accepted Jamesian psychology nearly all the way down. His thinking was thoroughly evolutionary and naturalistic, making no recourse to a transcendent God or an immortal soul. The interests and processes of life were enough for him. Religious experience has intellectual and affective elements, he allowed, but all such elements are secondary to and conditioned upon a variety of instinctive activities, such as habit, imitation, or custom, and the interplay among them. Against common intuition and the Romantic stream of liberal theology, he insisted that James's *Principles of Psychology* was right about the derivative character of feeling. Feeling depends upon the activities of the organism. We feel sad because we cry; we feel angry because we lash out; we feel afraid because we tremble. What we call "emotions" are the feelings produced by the bodily changes involved in the activities of crying, lashing out, trembling, and the like. Ames accepted Dewey's correction that the relation of feeling and activity is complicated by the evolutionary inheritance of various organized systems of reaction in the nervous systems of individuals. Dewey observed that conflicting tendencies in the self—flight or fight?—inhibit and hinder each other, producing uncertainty in the execution of any single reaction. This inner tension is experienced as the emotion of fear or courage depending on the course of action that wins out. Ames did not claim that James or Dewey fully comprehended the relation of feeling to action, but he assured that their pragmatic empiricism placed modern thinking about the self on a scientific plane.[36]

THE RELIGION OF LIBERAL PRAGMATISM

Ames and Foster were linked in the development of Chicago theology, but they absorbed pragmatic functionalism very differently. Foster struggled with its religious implications; even when he took an instrumentalist line in his writings, he was unable to stifle a metaphysical conscience. Foster could not ask himself, "Does this belief work for me?" or "Is it in my best interest to hold this belief?" or "Does this belief serve the common good?" without asking himself whether his beliefs about God or the good were metaphysically true. Ames suffered no unsettling disturbances of this kind. He spoke the same straightforwardly liberal-pragmatist language in his sermons as in his academic writings. Because he did not worry, as Foster did, about the things he did not believe, he remained more comfortably at home in liberal Protestantism than Foster. Foster worried that religion is meaningless without a personal God and that pragmatist religion was even more subjective than the Romantic and historicist theologies that it sought to replace; Ames suffered no regrets over the demise of the God of being and was sure that, with science on its side, pragmatic empiricist religion was as objective as religion can get.

As a good social gospeler, he also claimed Scripture for his side. The New Testament construes "belief" as conviction that controls action, he argued. To believe in Jesus, therefore, is "to imitate his example, to enter into sympathy with his purposes, to cooperate with him in establishing the kingdom of heaven on earth." Modern people are not convicted by traditional ways of speaking about the divinity of Christ, Ames observed. This was not due to any loss of appreciation of Christ, which had "grown marvelously" in the age of the social gospel; it was due to a change in the spirit of the age. Traditional theology was scholastic and deductive, but the modern spirit is experimental and ethical: "The inquiry now is not so much how he came into being, but what was his actual life among men, what were his thoughts, his feelings, his volitions." From this vantage point, he reasoned, to ask whether Jesus was divine is like asking whether Shakespeare was a playwright or Kant a philosopher or Newton a mathematician. If any person in history revealed the divine life to the world by his work and influence, surely that figure was Jesus. Ames agreed with Foster that the appropriate way of phrasing the confession of the divinity of Christ is to affirm that God is as good as Jesus.[37]

"It seems to me that empiricism attaches no validity to the old dualism of the natural and supernatural, the human and the divine and that therefore we are not any longer concerned with the 'divinity' of Christ but rather with his goodness and worth," he declared. The modern empirical tests are practical and ethical; even the gods must answer to them: "Have they good hearts, good wills, efficient minds?" Just as the modern mind does not admire kings and royal pomp and the tinsel of heaven, neither does it take interest in a uniquely endowed being who descended from heaven: "We have little interest in the question whether a being with a double nature such as Christ is often represented, could suffer to death upon a Roman cross, but we are tremendously concerned as to whether men with one nature like our own can intelligently and disinterestedly labor and serve for the welfare of our kind here and now." More precisely, the figure of Christ is meaningless to modern people as a message about "the weird magic of a dying god's power," Ames contended, but it is religiously powerful as the revelation of the divine Way of ethical action and self-sacrificing love. Ames observed that the early Jewish-Christian church associated the blood of Christ with the blood of slain lambs on the Jewish altar; in the same way Americans might very well associate the blood of Christ with the blood of Abraham Lincoln. The meanings in both cases are ethical, not ontological.[38]

Ethical pragmatism eschews ontology. "I will confess bluntly that I have lost interest in ontological questions," Ames declared. The most that he sanctioned along this line was the confession that the personality of Jesus reveals the heart of the world in something like the way that a beautiful oak tree makes known the nature of the earth in which it grows. The beauty and strength of the tree are expressions of nature's life; in the same way, an exemplary person is proof of the personal quality of existence. The personality of the world is expressed through the shining humanity of ideal figures, Ames argued: "In this way, with his marvelous moral grandeur and simplicity, Jesus Christ seems to me to be a revelation of the best things we know about the world." By "Jesus Christ" he meant the actual figure disclosed by historical research and the ideal of Christ. The former is reasonably secure as an object of knowledge, Ames judged, but the latter is the prize, for Christianity is religiously true whether Jesus lived or not: "Even if he never lived, we have yet to reckon with the ideal which his name suggests. And the ideal is a fact as stubborn and as obvious as a flesh and blood existence. If the ideal of Christ has grown up either by imposture or by good intention or by an unconscious idealization of virtue, it is nevertheless among the finest things we possess, and is the product of our own life in any case."[39]

Ames wore the liberal label proudly, while reserving the right to define his brand of liberalism. Though often called a Unitarian, he countered that Unitarianism was too negative and dogmatic for him; it lacked the constructive and socializing impulses of good religion. In his view, his liberalism kept ideology to a minimum: "Empiricism starts with facts, with tangible experiences, and cautiously builds upon them," he asserted. "It has great respect for reality, for history, for criticized and classified knowledge. If religion is to be vital and satisfying in this new age, it must also deal with facts of actual experience, discarding superstitions, miracles and magic."[40] But Ames's work was pervaded by the ideology of the modernist social gospel; he called it "the new orthodoxy." The old Christian orthodoxy made claims to absoluteness and finality, he explained; the new orthodoxy renounced these claims, affirmed the principle of free inquiry, and thereby gained concreteness and effective power for modern Christianity. "All who truly dwell in this new world of the natural and the social sciences have certain attitudes and habits of thought in common," he remarked. "These constitute the new orthodoxy of method and spirit."[41]

In the spirit of William James he opted for particular truths in various fields of experience over against metaphysical truth; he affirmed the Jamesian will to believe—"the dominance of the passional, volitional life in the operations of the intellect"—while cautioning that James employed this notion selectively; he embraced James's concept of the self as fluid, shifting, always *in* the flow of experience. Beyond James's limitations and extravagances, he theorized religion as a social process and God as idealized reality. James had little understanding of the social nature of religion, Ames allowed; his conception of religion was individualistic, he "clung wistfully" to the experiences of mystics, and he devoted an extraordinary amount of fruitless effort to psychical research. Ames socialized

James's approach to religion, defining it as "the cherishing of values felt to be most vital to man's life and blessedness, by means of ceremonial dramatization, expressive symbols, and doctrinal beliefs." With echoes of Shailer Mathews's "social minds" schematism, he held that modern religion is devoted to the attainment of knowledge, the development of personality, and the enjoyment of the fullest possible experience. "Religion is in a confused state because its conventional forms are still bound up with the values of the past, with submissive faith, otherworldliness, and the symbols which these have generated," he lamented. The age of the modern social mind was well under way, but mass culture and the popular mind lagged well behind it.[42]

The key to rectifying this cultural lag was redefining the idea of God, not religion. Ames was a nearly pure conceptualist on divine reality. He argued that God is a name for selected aspects or functions of the world, and the key aspect is love. Love is a powerful reality in the world, and whoever experiences love has an experience of God. God is where love is, and only where love is. Wherever love exists, Ames contended, God exists; where love does not exist, God is not present; as love, God is not far from any of us: "This love exists as personal, intelligent, and active in the living world of actual reality. Hence we say that God is reality idealized." Though Ames is usually interpeted as a thoroughgoing functionalist, he pointedly cautioned that the God idea is not merely imagined. Jerome Stone rightly observes that Ames identified God with selected *real* aspects of the world as a brake against complete subjectivism. For Ames, "God as idealized reality" was a selective idea that fastens on certain aspects of the world and not others. "God is the world or life taken in certain of its aspects, in those aspects which are consonant with order, beauty, and expansion," he explained. It is an empirical fact that reality manifests love, "and this empirical fact is the ground for the religious interpretations of reality as God."[43]

God is love; in the same way, God is also order and intelligence. These idealizations are saving and unarguably real, Ames observed; there is no world without them. Yet love, order, and intelligence are finite idealizations; all of them exist in the world, but none of them pervades the world fully or universally. For this reason, he admonished that modern people are "required to be content with a finite God." The only gods that we know are finite. Just as we are constantly pressed to face the fact "that we have either a limited and finite world or no world at all," so must we recognize that we have either a finite God or no God at all. James was right about the unreality of attributing infinity to God. Christians are inclined to make an exception for the Christian God, Ames noted, but the limitations of the Christian God are readily apparent to Buddhists and Muslims, just as the limitations of the Buddhist and Muslim notions of sacred reality are apparent to Christians: "It is a mistake to suppose that religious loyalty, any more than other kinds of loyalty, such as patriotism and romantic love, depends upon demonstrated perfection in the object loved. We admire and love life as we know it, and if we identify God with the degree of order and loveliness which we find, we may also love and reverence him." Though often accused of atheism, Ames rarely took the accusation personally. Genial and optimistic by nature, he handled pious criticism with wry humor. When Charles Harvey Arnold asked him if he was really an atheist, Ames told him playfully, "It depends on what kind of theism I'm atheistic about!"[44]

Persistently he asserted that religion is a practical interest. Religion has the capacity to inspire people to live and let flourish. To critics from the religion-as-illusion school, he gave Foster's answer, that wish fulfillment is not necessarily illusory. Psychologist James H. Leuba pronounced in his book *A Psychological Study of Religion* that God is "not so much known as used" and that God has only subjective existence; Ames disputed only the latter verdict. Use is the very purpose of the God idea, he countered, but the verdict that God is merely subjective applies only to the notion of God as a metaphysical being. It does not apply to the social conception of God as idealized experienced reality, nor does the illusion argument perceive that religion is not necessarily dependent upon metaphysical concepts. Religion can be the occasion and source of its ways of viewing reality. Ames explained that God is like "Alma Mater." The reality to which the term applies is not the image it suggests, much less the word itself, but rather "the reality of a social process belonging to the actual world." Just as Alma Mater designates an association of actual things and people, the word "God" refers, not to a particular person or metaphysical being, but to "the order of nature including man and all the processes of an aspiring social life." In both cases, it is precisely use that defines the concepts. Modern life is pervaded by concepts such as "electricity" and "mind" that are only slightly understood and which have no meaning apart from their use. "Religious experience is no exception," Ames argued. "Its gods are not to be understood apart from that experience, as abstract, isolated entities. They have their being in the action and outreaching of life itself."[45]

To Ames's mind the cultural optimism of the social gospel and the cultural optimism of Jamesian-Deweyian pragmatism blended together. It distressed him that after World War I many social gospelers lost their faith that the world was getting better. Ames kept the faith of social gospel pragmatism. "The modern spirit glories in the vision of an indefinitely great future in which through the same process of growth and renewal by which we live now we may go on to greater and nobler achievements," he insisted.[46] In the 1920s he observed that the emergence of Barthian crisis theology in Europe was a sad by-product of the war. The crisis theologians spurned the wisdom of modern knowledge. They despaired of social science in particular and taught that God should be glorified; Ames countered that "quite a different evaluation of human effort is possible upon an empirical basis." The case for Enlightenment was still very strong, he insisted in 1929; in fact it was overwhelming: "Enlightened men of all nations have more understanding. They assist each other by interchange of scientific knowledge, through trade and personal contacts more than ever before. International treaties have prevented some wars, even if they have not been equal yet to the entire abolition of war. For the fulfilment of the greatest hopes of man, there are elicited not only tireless energy, but also an appreciation of the vast length of time stretching before the race in which to gain such great ends."[47]

Ames embraced all the keynotes of modernist progressivism: optimism, rationalism, humanism, naturalism, evolutionism, historicism, democratic idealism, romanticism, pragmatism, empiricism. For many years he posted a self-description in his church's weekly calendar that read: "This church practices union; has no creed; seeks to make religion as intelligent as science; as appealing as art; as vital as the day's work; as intimate as the home; as inspiring as love."[48] In 1936, while allowing that his position was "now tempered with the qualifying influence of longer experience," he chastised the postwar generation for failing to keep the faith. "Since the war a dark sea of pessimism has swept over the world," he lamented. The new breed of intellectuals usually called themselves "realists," but Ames disputed their right to the term. "The novelists, the poets, the artists, and certain theologians talk about realism as if the only real experiences were drab and bitter," he observed. "They seem to take no account of the fact that sugar is sweet, that the sunshine is warm and healing, that love is comforting and inspiring as well as exacting and jealous." The Barthians and Niebuhrians paraded as prophetic truth tellers, "facing gallantly the stark facts of experience," but Ames smelled cowardice in their purported realism: "I have come to think of them as very tender-minded, if not cowardly souls. They are extremely fearful of being deceived by any claim of good or worth-while values in life, and therefore they take a wholly negative attitude and refuse to act upon their better impulses."[49]

The Barthian and Niebuhrian pessimists and their intellectual kin were timid and squeamish, lacking moral courage; Ames believed they were also hypocrites. They dismissed the achievements of modernity while living nicely off of them: "These realists talk one thing and live another. They seek good jobs, they plan for good food and drink, they strive for recognition among their fellows even if they have to write shocking novels, risqué poems, and pessimistic philosophy to get it. They are really the court jesters of modern life, dressing themselves in fantastic mental garb and making jokes out of the serious affairs of sober people. They create nothing and only laugh at those who are courageous enough to venture some effort for achieving better things." He allowed that much of the classical Christian tradition provided grist for the neo-orthodox mill. The Barthians made a plausible claim to the sin-haunted spirit of Paul, Augustine, Dante, Luther, Calvin, Milton, and Bunyan, though not to the spirit of Jesus. By 1936 Ames was acutely nostalgic for the world of his youth: "A more wholesome and truer view of human nature and society was developing before the world war. What William James called a religion of healthy-mindedness was making rapid headway in various New Thought cults, and was softening the old theological austerities of Protestant churches, when the war plunged the world back into suffering, tragedy and hysteria of fear, and revealed in the roar of blazing cannon and falling bombs the possibilites of human ferocity and brutality." The postwar generation took Barth's refuge in reaction, trusting in a God of wholly other transcendence who cannot be known by human effort.[50]

Ames held out for a different kind of Christianity and a social understanding of religion. Religion has no origin or meaning outside human experience, he admonished. It is within human experience, both the good and the bad, the beautiful and the ugly, the kindly and the cruel, that religion gets its bearings: "War, the inhumanity of man to man, the selfishness, the tragedy of life, are part of the reality, but they are not the whole of it nor the most significant part." The most significant part is the love of life that all people hold by natural possession in some measure and which Jesus possessed in extraordinary measure. "I interpret Jesus as a teacher of practical, matter-of-fact wisdom about successful living," Ames explained. "He seems to me to have believed in the natural man's capacity to distinguish between love and hate, between selfishness and generosity, between the transient, material goods of life and the more enduring things of the mind and heart." Jesus claimed no peculiar authority for his teachings beyond their evident validity in ordinary experience. He submitted his teaching to the test of life and judged religious doctrine by its fruits. Ames believed that the religion of Jesus was "identical with the natural idealism of mankind," yet it remained substantially untried by every Christian church. "No one of them has ever really succeeded in adopting the simple, natural religion of Jesus, with his deep human sympathy, his lofty idealism, his generous patience with sinners, his confidence in love and wisdom, and his trust in the divine quality of man's aspiring life."[51]

What was needed was to insinuate the spirit of Jesus into the thought forms and worldview of scientific modernism. Ames and Mathews shared essentially the same conceptualist view of divine reality, and Ames praised Mathews for showing the way in the field of theology: "We have become familiar with the idea that God is to be identified with 'the personality-evolving activities of the cosmos,'" Ames observed. This way of speaking about God met the religious need of the modern age, because it incorporated "those activities of self-criticism and imagination within man himself by which he strives for the realization of ideals." Mathews spoke of God in a nonanthropomorphic way that made God a real-world partner in the process of redemption. Human beings are responsible for their own salvation in cooperation with the idealizing reality of God. "But this does not lessen the reality of God," Ames assured. "It rather gives to the divine all the reality of the living process of growth in the discovery and realization of our better selves in both our individual life and our concrete social life." God is real as the spirit of a human group, symbolizing its ideals. God is our idea, made for our use, but God is not less real for that fact.[52]

MAKING THEOLOGY OBJECTIVE: DOUGLAS CLYDE MACINTOSH AND THE DIVINE OBJECT

The conceptualism of Ames and Mathews raised a defining question for the Chicago school: Is God language merely representative, or does it refer to a cosmic reality? Is "God" merely the highest expression of human ideals, or is God a cosmic reality to which human beings must be brought into right relation? Before Wieman entered the picture, all the Chicago schoolers spoke of God as the highest expression of human ideals, which evoked Wieman's protest. Otherwise, while sometimes wavering on whether God may be a cosmic reality, they usually contended that in any case, theology should restrict itself to making claims about that which can be known. At most, God is a finite reality within nature, not the infinite and personal deity of classical theism; at the least, God is a projection of human ideals. Foster agonized for many years over the question of God's metaphysical reality and took a negative view at the end of his life; Mathews combined realist and conceptualist motifs, describing God as a real factor in the universe and as a concept that unifies in the mind the personality-producing processes of the universe; A. Eustace Haydon was a non-theistic humanist; Smith did not rule out the possibility of God's cosmic reality, but he did not affirm it either; Ames's thoroughgoing pragmatic functionalism was saved from complete subjectivism only by his emphasis that the God idea idealizes selected aspects of the real world.

To Foster's protégé, Douglas Clyde Macintosh, who achieved a distinguished career at Yale, all of these positions were religiously anemic and subjective. Though he claimed Mathews as a partial ally and did his best to Christianize Foster's reputation after Foster's premature death, Macintosh insisted that his Chicago teachers misconstrued what it means to make theology empirical. The Chicago school was right to criticize the subjectivism of liberal theology, he affirmed; it was right to carry out the logic of historical criticism and right to seek an empirical foundation for Christian claims. The problem was that it undermined all its achievements by failing to ground Christian thinking in a realist epistemology that vigorously construed the object of Christian faith as an objective power. Theological liberalism rightly focuses on religious experience, he argued, but the appropriate point of focusing on religious experience is not to sacralize human ideals. The point is to describe the divine object known through religious experience. Modern Christianity needed a thoroughgoing realism that made theology scientific. Before the name was taken over and substantially redefined by his politicized student, Reinhold Niebuhr, Macintosh made "Christian realism" a trend in American theology. In the late 1920s he also cheered the emergence of a theological realist ally at Chicago, Henry Nelson Wieman, though only to a point.

A Canadian of Scottish descent with a long line of Congregationalist ministers on his mother's side, Macintosh could say, with Schleiermacher, that he was nurtured in the womb of piety. His father was a Baptist deacon; by his recollection, his "exceedingly conscientious" mother was extremely devout; when he was fourteen she told him that if he was a Christian he ought to be sure of it. One could not be a Christian without knowing it. That evening Macintosh responded to an altar call at his church in Breadalbane; he wanted to know that he was a Christian. "I felt no objection to the terms employed," he later recalled. "To find salvation was what I was there for, and 'being saved' to my mind meant becoming a real Christian."[53] Macintosh's orthodoxy was educated out of him a decade later, when he belatedly attended college at McMaster University, but he never ceased being grateful for his conversion experience. Structurally it contained all the elements that he later called "the right religious adjustment": aspiration after a truly Christian life, concentration upon an absolutely good Divine power, expectant waiting, an act of reconciling faith, and a moral resolve to follow God's will. For the rest of his life he insisted that vital Christian living requires an experience of personal salvation. His late-career volume *Personal Religion* put it plainly: "What we need above all is a 'return to religion' by the way of the recovery of an effective personal evangelism, or, better perhaps, through the discovery of a still vitally Christian evangelism and evangelicalism adapted to our times and the peculiar situation which exists today."[54] Macintosh was the kind of liberal who never doubted that conversion is more important to religious life than nurture or critical rationality. Though his friends in the religious education movement looked down on revivalism, he fervently praised the "wholesome" effects of revival preaching, which included his own conversion.

His academic coming of age was delayed by six years of teaching and mission work. After graduating from high school, Macintosh worked briefly on his family's farm, taught for two years in a one-room country school, preached for two years at a small Baptist mission church in western Ontario, and spent several months on the revival trail giving evangelistic sermons. His intellectual guide was the conservative Baptist standard-bearer Augustus H. Strong. At the turn of the century, feeling amply experienced but little educated, he enrolled at McMaster, where he confronted the specters of relativism, modern criticism, and what he later called "intellectual agnosticism." James and Mill soon replaced Strong as his intellectual guides, until he studied Spinoza and post-Enlightenment idealism, whereupon James and Mill were replaced by Spinoza, Kant, Hegel, and Lotze. Macintosh was absorbed from the outset with the problems of knowledge and truth. He worried that modern philosophy cast doubt on the reality of our knowledge of the external world. Reading James and Mill, he struggled not to believe that we know only what we experience and that what we experience is only the content of our own consciousness. For him the problem of empiricism was intellectual uncertainty; he puzzled over the paradox that in the name of truth, the empirical tradition taught agnosticism about knowledge.[55]

Macintosh made his peace with empiricism only after making an unsettling Jamesian bargain with it. He resolved that he would be a *Christian* agnostic. We might not *know* anything independently real, he reasoned, but we can believe something about it; moreover, people are better off having a religion than not having one. The attractive spirit and practical experientialism of William Newton Clarke's *Outline of Christian Theology* assured him that he could embrace empiricism as a philosophy without destroying his religious faith. This was a stopgap, however; Macintosh's philosophical and religious concerns were too deeply metaphysical for him to rest content with pragmatic religion. The pantheists and idealists spoke to his mind and heart as soon as he read them. More or less in succession, he embraced the philosophies of Spinoza, Kant, Hegel, Lotze, and the

British Hegelian T. H. Green. Macintosh discarded the Humean-empiricist picture of the self as a passive recipient of sense impressions. He luxuriated in Spinoza's pantheism and began to think of himself as some kind of Hegelian. The idealists convinced him that the contents of experience become known only by virtue of the mind's constructive activity.

He tried to imagine a post-Kantian synthesis of Spinoza, Hegel, and Lotze; he worried that his religious beliefs were falling apart; he told himself that he was prepared to sacrifice all of his cherished beliefs for the sake of truth. But what is truth? What is the ground of the real? In the spirit of Hegel, Macintosh resolved that rationality must be the touchstone of truth and reality. In order to have the possibility of any real knowledge, the real must be the rational, and the rational the real. He refused to believe anything that did not pass the test of rationality. "This meant, for one thing, that since the laws of nature are laws of reason, no law-violating miracle could be admitted as even possible," he later reflected. "Most of my old sermons were now unpreachable." His old sermons seemed stupid to him, as did the old religion. He was unhappy and exhilarated at the same time. Rebellion did not suit Macintosh; he snarled at the dogmatism of his theological professors, developed some bad habits, gave in to feelings of alienation and loss, and tried to write some new sermons.[56]

Gradually his sermons gained a new vitality along liberal lines. While doubting that Hegel's timeless Absolute is a satisfactory substitute for the personal God of Christianity, or that moral evil should be explained away as metaphysically unreal, Macintosh preached a liberal gospel of philosophical idealism. By the time that he graduated from McMaster, he thought of himself as a post-Kantian Spinozist or neo-Hegelian. By then he believed that he could best serve the cause of rational Christianity as a philosopher, not a pastor. This conviction took him in 1905 to the University of Chicago, where he planned to study for a year under Foster and Dewey before taking his doctorate under James at Harvard. Upon arriving at Chicago, Macintosh was crestfallen to learn that Dewey had just moved to Columbia, but he found a home at the Divinity School.[57]

He was slow to relinquish his absolute idealism in the land of the Midwest empiricists. The language of pragmatism was strange to him; it surprised him that even the theologians spoke it at Chicago. For a time his classmates dubbed him "the Hegelian." Fittingly, as a thinker absorbed by the problem of knowledge, the issue that converted him to the Chicago school was the nature of religious knowledge. Foster's seminar on Ritschlianism pressed hard on the theme that religious claims are fundamentally value judgments. Under the force of Foster's persuasion, Macintosh adopted the Ritschlian understanding of religious knowledge. He reasoned that in most judgments, including virtually all religious claims, the predicate expresses the value that a given reality holds for those by whom the judgment is made. Judgments are instrumental to human purposes as living acts of thought; any reckoning of their validity must take into account their value for life. He later recalled that Foster's vigorous prosecution of this theme made it seem impossible to deny that practical reason offers a stronger ground for religious claims than metaphysical speculation. Macintosh changed again, this time in the direction of his mentor's left-Ritschlian personalism.[58]

But his teachers, Foster and Smith, were moving beyond Ritschlian liberalism, and Macintosh puzzled over how far he should go in following them. In one respect, it was a short step from Ritschlian practical reason to Jamesian pragmatism, and Macintosh thought that he was ready to take it. At the same time, it troubled him that Foster and Smith retained the worst aspect of their Ritschlian backgrounds. While conceding to them that religious claims are value-judgments, Macintosh never accepted their Ritschlian insistence that this verdict precludes metaphysical reasoning in theology. Eliminating metaphysics from theology is neither possible nor desirable, he argued. All religious claims make tacit assumptions about reality, and all of them make statements about a reality of some kind. Every religious claim contains metaphysical elements; even strict Ritschlians mapped the fields of knowledge in ways that made claims about reality. The Ritschlian and post-Ritschlian theologies expounded by his teachers were loaded with claims about realities experienced or believed in. Macintosh wrote his doctoral dissertation, "The Reaction against Metaphysics in Theology," on this topic, admonishing that liberal theology does not make itself stronger or purer by ignoring its metaphysical elements. There is a place for theology in metaphysics and a place for metaphysics in theology, he argued. In a broad sense of the category, he contended, religious claims are not merely practical judgments of value; they are also theoretical judgments of existence. It followed for him that it should be possible to accept the Ritschlian value-judgment theory of religion and still regard theology as a theory of reality. Though he began with larger ambitions for it, Macintosh's dissertation scaled down to the story described in its title. The project of reconstructing Ritschlian value theology as a theory of reality absorbed the rest of his life.[59]

Modern philosophy and modern theology had the same problem, he believed: "how to retain the ethical and religious values for which theistic personal idealism stands, together with the common-sense of realism and the new insights made possible by the functional psychology which is fundamental to the instrumental logic of the most fruitful kind of pragmatism."[60] At theologically conservative McMaster Macintosh had turned into a rebellious rationalist embarrassed by traditional Christianity; at notoriously liberal Chicago he rediscovered his constructive and objectivist impulses. He wore his liberal beliefs in a conservative way. Ordained to the ministry by the Baptists of Western Canada after a lengthy debate over his views on biblical authority, miracles, substitutionary atonement, and the devil, Macintosh taught theology for two years at Brandon College in Manitoba, until Yale Divinity School snatched him for its theology department in 1909. Mathews had expected to hire him, but at the time he was still a doctoral student.

At Yale his new colleagues worried less about his theological liberalism and unfinished dissertation than about his pragmatist leanings. Was he essentially a pragmatist or an intellectualist? Separated from the strong personalities of Foster and Smith, Macintosh began to formulate his answer. He judged that the old intellectualism was correct in its generic notion of truth as correspondence of ideas with reality; it was only within the framework of the correspondence or "identity" theory of truth that he gave place to pragmatism. From this perspective, James and Dewey correctly described the difference that delineates true and false representations of reality in particular judgments; the difference is the sufficiency of representations for practical purposes. Macintosh reasoned that from the standpoint of a realistic intellectualism that accepts pragmatism as a criterion of truth, truth can be regarded as ideal, permanent, and universal while still being accessible and practical. At least some practical purposes are universally valid, he believed. Throughout his career, Macintosh epitomized the kind of theological liberalism that grounds its religious claims in a general theory of knowledge. He assumed that he could not solve the problem of religious knowledge without solving the problem of knowledge as a whole. "From the fall of 1911 to the spring of 1914 a realistic theory was taking shape in my mind," he later recalled. He began his career as a Chicago-product pragmatist who tried to make room in Ritschlian theology for metaphysical questions, but soon this relational emphasis reversed. Instead of making room for metaphysics in a Ritschlian pragmatic theology, he subordinated pragmatism to his metaphysical theory. Influenced by the vitalism and intuitionism of French philosopher Henri Bergson and the mystically oriented idealism of his philosophical colleague at Yale, William Ernst Hocking (who subsequently moved to Harvard), Macintosh increasingly contended that the crucial questions are the metaphysical ones. A second difference from his teachers became equally important; Macintosh embraced the Chicago school's commitment to empirical method, but against its preoccupation with social process, he redirected his own theological empiricism to the religious experiences of ordinary church members. Just as medical science informs and disciplines the work of physicians, he reasoned, theology should take the form of a clinically focused empiricism that aids the work of pastors.[61]

This twofold intellectual turn was strengthened by Foster's emotional response to the *Titanic* disaster. After reading Foster's plaintive article on "The Tragedy of the Titanic," Macintosh wrote to him, "What I think we need is a religious realism, such as I seem to find in your article. The religious subjective idealism which leaves one with only the God-idea as its object is fatal, if taken seriously. Are you interested in the new realism? I am; I think it needs criticism, but I believe it has an important contribution to make to theology which its representatives do not begin to suspect. The hopeful movements in contemporary thought seem to me to be a *scientific* pragmatism, the emphasis on mysticism, the vitalism of recent thinkers (Driesch, Bergson, Eucken, et al.) and the new realism."[62] H. Driesch and Rudolf Eucken were popular vitalistic philosophers; Arthur O. Lovejoy and Ralph Barton Perry were prominent among the new realists; though he respected Hocking, Macintosh's deepening commitment to epistemological realism stopped him from pursuing any interest in mysticism. In 1913 he called for a critical realistic monism that bridged the differences between

Lovejoy's dualistic realism and Perry's Jamesian empiricism.[63] *The Problem of Knowledge,* published two years later, gave an example of what he had in mind.

PERCEIVING KNOWLEDGE
AND RELIGIOUS KNOWLEDGE

The Problem of Knowledge, Macintosh's massive first work, divided the philosophy of knowledge into immediate knowledge (problems in epistemology) and mediate knowledge (problems in logical theory and methodology). It contained three chapters on types of epistemological dualism, five chapters on types of epistemological idealism, four chapters on the new realism, and four chapters on logical theory and method. The book's main sections on epistemology and logical theory ended with constructive statements on the promise of critical monism in these fields. Essentially there are two sets of either/or choices in the theory of knowledge, he argued. An epistemological theory may be either monistic or dualistic, and it may be either realistic or idealistic. Epistemological monism is the view that at the moment of perception the experienced object and the real object are one; epistemological dualism is the view that at the moment of perception the experienced object and the real object are two different things; epistemological realism is the view that real objects exist independently of conscious experience; epistemological idealism is the view that real objects do not exist independently of conscious experience. Macintosh surveyed the varieties of contending theories in the field, paying special attention to versions of epistemological monism that differed from his own, before making a case for his own critical realistic monism. If the reality of knowledge yielded by empirical investigation is to be secured, he argued, what is needed is a critical theory of knowledge that establishes the reality of immediate experience and upholds the objective existence of the world.[64]

Critical realistic monism steered a careful path between his accounting of the fallacies, subjectivisms, and abstractionisms of idealistic philosophy; the fallacies and ultimate intellectual agnosticism of dualistic theories; and the dogmatism and unsolvable riddles of the new realism. Mediating Lovejoy's defense of the reality of mediate knowledge and Perry's rejoinder that there is no knowledge at all without immediate knowledge of reality, Macintosh argued that mediate knowledge is possible and real only because of the prior reality of immediate knowledge. He proposed a theory of knowledge that affirmed, with sufficient critical subtlety on all sides, the certainty of the real world external to consciousness, the qualitative duality of percept and object, and the insights of idealism and pragmatic functionalism into the creative role of the perceiver. Critical realistic epistemological monism was the doctrine "that the object perceived is existentially, or numerically, identical with the real object at the moment of perception, although the real object may have qualities that are not perceived at that moment; and also that this same object may exist when unperceived, *although not necessarily with all the qualities which it possesses when perceived.*"[65]

Macintosh's brand of realistic monism affirmed the certainty of knowledge both in its immediate givenness and in true judgments. With careful allowance for subjective factors, he upheld the partial identity or coincidence of that which is directly experienced and that which is independently real. For the rest of his career he called for metaphysical rethinking in theology, yet pursued little of it. He kept refining his method, backtracking to issues in epistemology and empirical procedure, and developed his theology of moral optimism. On various occasions he tried to clarify his central epistemological claims. "In perception of a physical thing, part of what is independently real would not be immediately perceived, and part of what is immediately perceived would not be independently real; but part of what is independently real would be absolutely the same existence as part of what is immediately perceived," he wrote. "Such a partial identity or coincidence of the immediately perceived and the independently real would be sufficient to make human knowledge of independent reality not only possible but actual."[66]

Sensation is a phenomenon of the subject's creative activity; consciousness is an essentially productive activity; perception occurs in a cognitive complex that always includes concepts. Macintosh conceived perception very broadly, using the term to describe the cognition of such varied objects as change, life, selfhood, imaginative processes, and conception itself. In a broad manner of speaking he argued that all cognition is essentially perceptual. All mediate knowing depends for its existence on the existence of immediate knowing, and thus, as an internal relation to immediate knowing, mediate knowing acquires the status of knowledge "only as a part of the machinery of apperception." Knowing is always conceptual—Macintosh's realism was critical—but knowing is never merely conceptual. Merely conceptual knowing would be epistemologically antirealistic. Macintosh kept his balance and preserved the reality of the world external to consciousness. He viewed conception as cognitive, but limited the cognitive dimension of conception to its interpretive inner relation with perception.[67]

His conception of perception was unusually broad. Macintosh spoke of "perceiving" perceptions and even of "perceiving" concepts, thus making perception nearly synonymous with cognition. Moreover, his expansive understanding of perception did heavy work for his system: it laid the groundwork for his concept of experience and supported his claim that theology should be an empirical science. Macintosh gave his best years to the latter claim. Having surveyed the problem of knowledge in general, he was ready to do some theology. Like Shailer Mathews, who was fond of saying that the proper starting point for theology must be "a relationship with the universe described by the scientist," Macintosh proposed to make modern theology as scientific as chemistry.[68]

His major works pursued this end by describing what happens to people as a result of particular religious experiences. *Theology as an Empirical Science* (1919) offered a programmatic case for a scientifically objectivist theology; *The Reasonableness of Christianity* (1926) proposed that a "gospel of moral optimism" passes the empirical tests of modern reason and meets the religious needs of modern people; several lesser works explored aspects of faith and religious philosophy in a more popular vein; *The Problem of Religious Knowledge* (1940) capped his career by developing a philosophy of religion. In the spirit of Chicago theology, but with an emphasis on the objectivity of divine reality that distinguished him from was his teachers, Macintosh urged that theology needed to become scientific "in the full, modern sense of the word." The old scholasticism was scientific in its devotion to deductive logic, he allowed, and the rationalistic theologies of the eighteenth and nineteenth centuries were scientific in breaking free from the dogmatism of traditional Christianity. Both of these traditions subscribed to serious tests of rational coherence and plausibility, and the Enlightenment liberation from the bondage of external authority marked a huge step forward for theology.[69]

But fully scientific theology was something else. It was concrete, empirical, and inductive. It practiced the scientific method of observation and experiment, of generalization and theoretical explanation. "If theology is to become really scientific it must be by becoming fundamentally empirical," Macintosh declared.[70] Because theology necessarily draws upon faith and knowledge, he did not claim that the entire content of valid Christian theology can be verified empirically. "There is an element of reasonable, practically defensible *faith* and an element of speculative *surmise* in our theological theory, as well as a nucleus of scientifically verified (or at least verifiable) religious *knowledge*."[71] But Macintosh did claim that Christian theology could regain its intellectual credibility only by basing itself on empirically established truths. The challenge of modern theology was to make theology objective. Reprising the argument of his doctoral dissertation, he allowed that theological liberalism had a passing acquaintance with empirical reasoning; Schleiermacher's theology of religious consciousness and Ritschl's theology of moral value both made empirical claims to the data of religious experience. But these theologies were too subjective, he judged; what was needed in theology was to objectivize the empiricism of the Schleiermacherian and Ritschlian schools.

Schleiermacher's experientialism was too subjective to discriminate between rival claims to truth; it could not definitely determine which doctrines correctly express the Christian consciousness or even why Christianity should be chosen over other religions. Macintosh commended the Ritschlian school for seeking to gain some objective control over Schleiermacher's appeal to experience, but he judged that the Ritschlian appeal to history made only marginal progress. The Ritschlians appealed to their pictures of the historical Jesus and their reconstructions of the "kernel" of early Christianity without acknowledging that these claims are highly subjective. They never justified their choice of Christianity over other religions, and thus, for all their modern spirit, they perpetuated "a certain narrow and unscientific dogmatism" in theology. Truly modern theology cannot presume that Christianity is the highest religion, Macintosh contended. Most important from his standpoint was the fact that the Ritschlian school took Kant's metaphysical agnosticism for granted in formulating its doctrine of religious value judgments. "Agnosticism" was a shudder term for Macintosh. If experience has no access to ultimate reality or the Kantian "thing-in-itself," then knowledge is limited to the realm of appearances. Ritschl made a virtue of this predicament by restricting theology to value statements. Macintosh judged that this strategy made theology immune from various forms of outside criticism, but at the cost of making it merely subjective. The Ritschlians distrusted metaphysical reason ostensibly because they wanted to protect the integrity of Christian faith, but their metaphysical agnosticism undermined their ability to explicate or defend Christianity. They failed to secure the objective validity of their religious claims because "with their doctrine of the inaccessibility of ultimate reality, divine or other, to human experience, they have excluded the idea of a scientific verification of religious judgments."[72]

That was the authentication that Macintosh sought for theology. While commending Ernst Troeltsch and the *Religionsgeschichtliche Schule* for at least trying to make theology more objective and universal, he judged that the history-of-religions approach was still woefully subjective. Troeltsch sought to develop a universal theology of religion that would be rational as well as historically and experientially empirical. He affirmed that a credibly rationalized Christianity would have to take the form, ultimately, of a metaphysical system. This was a commendable goal, Macintosh believed, but Troeltsch's thoroughgoing historicism stopped him from getting anywhere, because history is merely probable and relative and establishes nothing with certainty. Troeltsch defended Christianity as the religion best suited for modern Western culture. His historicism was so thoroughgoing that he ruled out the idea of making theology scientific. "He cannot even claim that it is knowledge; strictly speaking, he has to confess to an ultimate agnosticism," Macintosh remarked. "His eclectic approval of Christianity, as valid for our time and place and culture, is symptomatic of the incurable subjectivity which remains in his religious system."[73]

Closer to home, Macintosh judged that religious pragmatism was insufficiently scientific as well. In *The Problem of Knowledge* he criticized James's identification of truth with function, arguing that James wrongly treated all truth as temporary and mutable. Without naming names, *Theology as an Empirical Science* described and rejected Ames's approach to religion. Ames-style pragmatism was capable of producing a theology of postulates, Macintosh allowed, but it could not establish a theology of verified propositions. The pragmatist theologians prescribed belief in whatever promoted the realization of given ideals and claimed a blood relation with social science on this basis; Macintosh found the latter claim weak at best. It is true that all empirical sciences select and systematize their material for designated purposes, he acknowledged, "but the point of importance is that it must be already verified scientific material which is thus selected." Social science is not objective if it does not work with scientifically established data. For theology to become empirical, religious thinkers must not settle for the kind of pragmatism that merely ratifies common sense with a bit of critical panache. Genuinely empirical theology requires "verified theological material" and an instrument that transforms pragmatic common sense into science.[74]

This was the frontier for modern theology. Progressive theology in the eigh-teenth century was rationalistic; progressive theology in the nineteenth century blended romanticist, pietist, socioethical, and historicist elements; the next stage of progress would make theology genuinely scientific. Despite its metaphysical shortcomings, Macintosh reckoned that the pragmatic school of James and Dewey was on the verge of ascending to a science. Pragmatic philosophy attained this status whenever it submitted without equivocation to the test of empirical verification. Macintosh urged that theology could become a science in the same way. When theologians finally embraced the distinction between empirically ver-ified and unverified claims, he declared, "then we shall have alongside of the *novum organum* of inductive logic in general a *novum organum theologicum,* a new instrument for the criticism of religious thought and the discovery of religious truth, which will transform theology from mere religious common sense into an inductive empirical science." Just as Thomas Aquinas transformed the "external-authority religion" of the Middle Ages by using Aristotelian metaphysics, theo-logical empiricism would transform the "undogmatic experience-religion" of modern liberal theology by using the inductive empirical methodology of mod-ern science.[75]

While sharing Ames's vocabulary and ideals, Macintosh's proposal of how to make theology empirical stood Ames on his head. Ames's religious pragmatism eschewed revelation and the very notion of God as a cosmic reality; Macintosh countered that empirical theology is pointless, if not impossible, without revela-tory traces of the divine presence in human life. Every science assumes the exis-tence and knowability of its object, he observed. Chemistry assumes the existence of matter; psychology assumes the existence of states of consciousness; psychol-ogy of religion assumes the existence of religious experience. In the spirit of sci-entific inquiry, and in order to generate verified scientific material in its field, theology is similarly entitled to assume the existence and knowability of its object as a working hypothesis. Macintosh explained, "On the basis of knowledge of God through religious experience, one can scientifically assume *that* God is, although he may have as yet very little knowledge as to *what* God is."[76] His premise was thoroughly liberal; Macintosh took for granted that religious expe-rience is the working material of theology. The purpose of working with religious experience, however, was not to treat experience as the measure of religious value, but to describe the Object known through it. While acknowledging that subjec-tive factors are constitutive to all experience, he believed that theology must attend primarily to that which is apprehended in religious experience, rather than to the dynamics of religious consciousness itself.

"All religious experience is material for the psychology of religion; it has no criterion for distinguishing between true and false religions; it cannot say the first thing about the existence or nature of God," he observed. These were tasks for theology proper. Ames eschewed theology on that count; Macintosh believed that Christian belief without theology fails the test of seriousness. He proposed that theology should be related to psychology of religion in the same way that the physical sciences are related to psychology: "Psychology of religion is simply a department of psychology, and psychology is the science which describes mental activity and experience as such," he reasoned. "Empirical theology, like the physical sciences, would be a science descriptive not of experience but of an object known through experience." The work of empirical theology is not to prove the existence of the object of religious experience, but to study the effects of this working hypothesis upon its human subjects: "Experimental religion has been able to maintain its vitality only as it has been able to point to facts that, for the time being at least, could be regarded as revelation, i.e., as manifestation of the presence of the divine Being, or of the present activity of the divine Power."[77]

Macintosh's theory of religious knowledge was deeply enmeshed in his general theory of knowledge. Just as he defended the objectivity of cognitive referents in *The Problem of Knowledge,* he defended the objectivity of the referent of theological language in his religious writings. While allowing that existence judgments cannot be directly derived from value judgments, he argued that existence judgments can be reasonably postulated on the basis of value judgments for further verification in experience. *The Problem of Religious Knowledge* described religious knowledge as "subjective religious certitude critical enough to become objective certainty." In formal terms: "Religious knowledge includes adequate and adequately critical (i.e., logical) certitude of the validity of ideals or values appreciated as divine (i.e., as worthy of universal human devotion), and a similar certainty (adequate and valid certitude) of the trueness of religious judgments (i.e., judgments about the divineness of reality or value, or about the reality of the divine)." In his rendering, the essential work of empirical theology was to elaborate the laws by which God responds to "the right religious adjustment."[78]

Macintosh defined theological laws as generalizations about the ways that God can be expected to respond to human actions under particular conditions. He conceived these laws as fundamentally volitional; they depended upon the right religious adjustment, which consisted primarily of devotion to values and secondarily of a sense of religious awe. The practice of prayer was a key example. "Experience will show that the indispensable element in prevailing prayer is not a matter of mere words or formal petition, nor of the name or national mythology associated with the deity, whether Jewish, Grecian, Mohommedan, Hindu or Christian," he observed. "It is the character of the religious adjustment that is all-important, and this will be influenced by the belief as to the character and power of the religious Object." Theology rightly presupposes that God's Spirit is everywhere, like electricity, but only those who appropriately prepare themselves to receive it will benefit from it. By Macintosh's reckoning, prayer was an elemental volitional experience; the experiences of regeneration, perseverance, fullness of the Spirit, sanctification, and salvation were more complex volitional experiences; all were primary material for the empirical theology of revelation.[79]

Macintosh's primary source was his own experience in evangelical and liberal Protestantism. Though he criticized the Ritschlians for privileging Christianity, and only one version of it, he did the same thing; his account of "the right religious adjustment" took no instruction from other religious traditions. In this respect he exceeded the standard provincialism of liberal theology, though not by much. For all of their universalist claims and world-embracing historicism, the liberal theologians were fixated on Western liberal Protestantism, even at Chicago. Their idea of "true religion" was their ideal of religion as they knew it. As an advocate of making theology empirical, albeit with this limitation, Macintosh reflected and importantly advanced the ideal of the Chicago school. He led a field-redirecting movement to make the study of religion scientific.

At the height of his movement-leading influence in 1931, and his hope for an object-oriented redirection of liberal theology, Macintosh accented his affinities with Wieman and Mathews. He enlisted Wieman as a contributor to his movement reader, *Religious Realism,* played up the realistic aspects of Mathews's position, and gave a Mathews-like description of the divine object. Like Wieman, Mathews, and James, he placed God within the immanent processes of the cosmos. "There is in the universe a divine-value-producing factor (which we may call God) which works more effectively toward the production of divine values on condition of appreciation of spiritual values, scientific adjustment to the world, and intelligent and friendly cooperation on the part of human persons," he asserted. This was Macintosh's verified concept of God; vast sections of his work read like a laboratory version of Ritschlian value theory. For Macintosh, as for Mathews and Wieman, God was the factor in the universe that works through human values and goodwill to produce divine values.[80]

The fact that religious experience is subjective was a problem for their scientific ambitions. James conceded that his study of religious experience was too subjective to be counted as scientific; Wieman eventually moved away from experiential claims on account of their subjectivity; in different ways, Wieman and Mathews both emphasized structure and process rather than experience; Macintosh held firm that the appeal to experience is indispensable for liberal-empirical theology. He treated the subjectivity of religious experience as a warrant for his system of overbeliefs. Theologians must not back away from the fallible attempt to understand the objective aspects of subjective experiences, he insisted. Because religious experience is unavoidably subjective, the conditions under which theological empiricism operates are unavoidably subjective. At the same time, he argued, empirical theology is objective in a twofold sense. It submits to the scientific test of verification, and its divine referent is an objective reality. In Macintosh's scheme, theology in an empirical mode understood the nature and character of God by studying the effects of theology's hypothesized divine object in human experience. It paid special attention to the experiences of attention to God, surrender to God, dependence on God, moral responsiveness to the divine will, and persistence in religious attitude. Macintosh believed that it could be shown that a certain kind of "religious adjustment" evokes the most gracious and life-giving responses from the divine cause. His name for the kind of faith in which he believed was "the gospel of moral optimism." *The Reasonableness of*

Faith defined moral optimism as "a fundamental attitude of confidence in the cosmos, together with a full sense of man's moral responsibility." Macintosh shared Ames's Jamesian voluntarism. To the person whose will is right, he asserted, the world holds no terrors: "He need have no fear of anything the universe can do to him; no absolute or final disaster can come to him whose will is steadfastly devoted to the true ideal." If a person's will is right, "the Supreme Power on which he is dependent will do whatever else needs to be done."[81]

These assurances were written shortly after Macintosh lost his brother and then his wife to premature deaths. Indirectly, *The Reasonableness of Faith* was a report on his inner sense of divine providence and grace; he experienced a renewal of moral optimism during his days of grieving. It is reasonable to believe in the conservation of values, he argued, and if we judge that the value-conserving factor in life is good and personality-enhancing, we are warranted in surmising that God is good and personal. In this way, a normative theology can be built on empirical foundations. Macintosh's ethical intuitionism held his two-level house together. It was a decidedly late-Victorian ethic, with a near-pacifist edge. "As the moral consciousness develops and the will is brought into a condition of moral health, there is a tendency to transform the original, uncritical, natural optimism into a critical, moral optimism," he observed. The optimistic way of life is the healthiest way to live, once optimism has been chastened by training, suffering, moral concern, and the critical spirit: "It is what the strong good will says must be true. It is the faith of the virile and pure." The creed of moral optimism is thoroughly reasonable and deeply wholesome: "Be normal and be moral. Be healthy in body and mind, be buoyantly optimistic; but take full account of your moral responsibility." Moral optimism is the way of living an ethically wholesome life in persistent devotion to the highest spiritual ends, he preached. It is "the vital core of spiritual religion" and the essence of genuine Christianity. To Macintosh this was the gospel kernel; the rest of Christianity was dispensable husk. The heart of Christianity is the experience of morally optimistic faith in God and the experience of moral salvation through the right religious adjustment: "Anything in traditional Christianity which conflicts with this is rightly to be discarded as nonessential and outgrown."[82]

His list of worn-out beliefs included "any number of ancient creeds," belief in miracles that violated laws of nature, and all doctrines that prescribed particular conclusions about historical events. Macintosh learned from Foster that the essence of a living Christianity cannot belong only to the past. In the manner of his teacher, he found it "preposterous" that any Christian thinker should suppose "that a mere change in one's historical opinions, honestly arrived at, could necessarily make one cease to be a Christian."[83] Though he did not doubt the essential historicity of the gospel story, Macintosh counseled that Christianity is not more or less true to the extent that the gospel story is more or less historical. "An essentially Christian faith in God and an essentially Christian experience of moral salvation through the right religious adjustment are *logically* possible without either Christology or an assured belief in the historicity of Jesus," he contended. The moral ideal of progressive Christian optimism is valid whether it was taught by Jesus or not. Christianity needs no higher certainty than the fact that the gospel of moral optimism is reasonable and verifiable. Macintosh's Christology was the typical liberal claim that the spirit of Jesus provides a clue to the character of God. This clue is primarily moral, he assured: "If one can believe in an essentially Christian morality and Christian optimism, with what the latter involves for belief in God and a future life, he can logically believe enough to enable him to become a Christian and experience the revelation of God in moral salvation."[84]

Macintosh shook his head at the Barthian insistence that theology must be done as the explication of revelation alone. For him it was self-defeating to tell modern people not to begin with their own questions and experience. His regard for mysticism was not much higher, because mysticism is usually associated with ascetic elites and takes expression as philosophical idealism and theological pantheism. Macintosh countered that the best way to faith is afforded by commonplace reason and experience. His faith map began with the common sentiment that there ought to be a God to give spiritual meaning and moral direction to life. This sentiment makes a better starting point than any claim about extraordinary experiences or revelations, he believed. It leads to the consideration that there may be a God, since modern science is compatible with the notion of a rational, indwelling, purposive divine mind at work in nature and history. With Jamesian logic, Macintosh moved to the tentative conclusion that there must be a God if the life of moral optimism is to be affirmed as a valid, reasonable, healthy, and necessary approach to living: "We have a moral right to believe as we must in order to live as we ought." If moral optimism is true, there must be a God. The knowledge that God does exist is gained, he concluded, through the experience of moral-spiritual transformation, in which we learn that the object of religious desire is objectively real.[85]

Macintosh's theory of religious knowledge affirmed the validity of what he called "appreciative perceptions" of divine values. Values are adjectival and always relative to teleological processes, he argued, yet the ends of such processes are values also. The value of a value process is determined in relation to its end, and the value of the end is determined in relation to the process that leads toward it. The "divine" is the ideal in the realm of the spiritual, of which Macintosh predicated human or cosmic reality only as it participates in the quality of ideality. With a nod to Rudolf Otto's *The Idea of the Holy* (1917), he observed that believers are also grasped by the holiness of the divine values that they perceive. His theorizing on the latter theme moved along a similar spiritual and generational wavelength as Otto's description of the *mysterium tremendum*; he and Otto were theorists of the numinous dimension of religious experience. Convinced that the Ritschlian school was in decline, they both believed that liberal theology needed to speak the language of religious objectivity. Macintosh's theory of religious knowledge further claimed that judgments about the existence of God may be made only upon the basis of experimental "adjustments" in life to such values. Theology ascends to the status of a science when it subjects these adjustments to empirical scrutiny, he contended. The results of different adjustments are predicted and verified, revealing an objectively divine power at work in the moral and spiritual transformation of human character.[86]

Religious experience is not confined to religion; it is the total experience of certain values shared by religion. Macintosh granted a place to Ames-style psychology of religion in his program, but he cautioned that psychology of religion gets its data from the subjective side of religious experience. The objective side of religious experience is the domain of empirical theology. Claiming Mathews for the cause of religious realism, he embraced Mathews's admittedly "meager" conception of the divine object. By Mathews's definition of God, he asserted, it is fully warranted to claim that the existence of God is "a known fact," for no one disputes that there are personality-creating activities in the world: "In other words, there is a divinely functioning reality, not to be identified exclusively with the human, and not to be identified with reality as a whole, since not all reality is making for the realization of absolutely valid ideals." What Macintosh called "religious perception" was simply the empirical awareness of this divinely functioning reality; sometimes he called it a "religio-empirical intuition." Convinced that the Barthian appeal to revelation alone was a loser for theology, he urged that theology had to begin with what is concretely known in experience. Modern theology had to attain objectivity and thus make itself real again by entering the path of "gradual constructive procedure."[87]

Macintosh's project heightened the oxymoronic connotations of empirical theology. He raised the standard on what constitutes an empirical argument in theology, but refused to give up personal theism. While allowing that the immortality of the soul cannot be empirically verified, he insisted that belief in immortality is pragmatically important. Good empirical thinking cannot be merely empirical in the narrow sense of the term, he contended; empirical method requires not only intellectual certainty and functional verification, but also a strong dose of valuational intuition if its ethical trajectory is to be morally worthy. Macintosh's emphasis on certainty and verification spoke the language of disinterested empiricism, but his ethical intuitionism was loaded with subjective, ideological, and cultural interests. His theory of religious understanding was a species of ethical intuitionist appreciation, resting on the spiritually and ethically subjective notion of a religious perception of certain values as divine. This notion warmed the coldness of his empiricism, but it also made Macintosh's theology vulnerable to the vicissitudes of cultural change. He sacralized the values of his time and ideology, only to witness the rise of a generation that did not prize the values of his late-Victorian, pietistic, idealistic worldview. For all of his claims to realism, the content of Macintosh's moral optimism appeared quaintly unreal to the Depression-era generation of his students. Macintosh fared no better than Ames or Mathews in coping with this problem; in his later career it eviscerated his influence over the field.

In one respect, however, he began to struggle with the problem before his influence was diminished by it. For many years he struggled to locate the appropriate place of moral optimism in his system. *The Reasonableness of Christianity* construed moral optimism as the basis of right thinking. Macintosh employed the notion apologetically, basing his advocacy of modern Christianity on his case for moral optimism. First he argued for moral optimism, then he argued that God exists. It is reasonable to believe what we need to believe in order to live virtuously, he contended. Confirming a late-career remark of James's, he contended that the Jamesian "will to believe" is better construed as the "right to believe." An idea is undoubtedly true if it is theoretically plausible in the light of modern knowledge and if it appears to be practically necessary for the realization of a good moral purpose.[88]

Macintosh never recanted the Jamesian right to believe. He never tired of explaining that for James, as for himself, the right to believe pertained only to hard cases between two plausible options in which a strong practical difference was at stake. By 1931, however, Macintosh recognized that moral optimism is self-defeating as a form of apologetics. His centerpiece essay in *Religious Realism* presented moral optimism as a step between belief in God as immanent and belief in God as transcendent; his subsequent autobiographical essay for Vergilius Ferm's *Contemporary American Theology* retracted his appeal to moral optimism as the basis of an argument for choosing to be Christian; his last book, *The Problem of Religious Knowledge,* treated moral optimism as a religious intuition that flows from the subjective certitude of an established normative commitment. Macintosh allowed that his early advocacy of the right to believe confused the relation between the logic of Christian experience and the moral good. *The Reasonableness of Christianity* treated moral optimism as the basis of an apologetic argument, but the case for Christian moral optimism was not convincing to those who lacked faith or optimism. It was instructively unpersuasive to a pessimistic younger generation. The power of moral optimism is not its apologetic value, Macintosh concluded. Moral optimism is a fruit of Christian faith, not its basis. The way to gain the faith that engenders moral optimism "is not to try to reason one's self into moral optimism simply, but to *become* a moral optimist by having the Christian religious experience."[89]

This retraction corrected some of Macintosh's thinking about the apologetic limits of the liberal gospel, as well as the relationship between Christian experience and its moral trajectory. It also highlighted the repressed subjectivism of his project. Macintosh's advocacy of moral optimism was an appeal to the functional benefits of a certain attitude; he asserted that people have a right to believe in plausible worldviews that bear good fruit. His retraction took a further step: he admitted that his appeal to a morally optimistic attitude itself presupposed an ample package of subjectively loaded religious experiences and commitments. This was a trait that he shared with Ames and Mathews. While claiming to overcome the subjectivism of their tradition, the empirical theologians reproduced its typical interests and desires. In the name of making theology scientific, they invoked the blessings of science on the politics and morality of middle-class liberal Protestantism. James Alfred Martin Jr. later found in Macintosh's work a showcase example of the empirical theology tendency to fasten upon "certain uncriticized but fundamental value-judgments common to a given tradition and culture."[90]

Like many liberals of his generation, Macintosh seemed oblivious to the latter irony. His ethical intuitionist sense of the good was his anchor; he could not take seriously forms of criticism that challenged it. He was more sensitive to the problem of the relationship between Christianity and the good, which yielded a rare word of praise for the Barthian ascendancy. The Barthians had one thing right, he allowed: they appreciated the dialectics of Christian existence. The problem of the relation between the experience of the good and the Christian experience is a dialectical problem; it required a dialectical approach that paid greater respect than the liberal tradition to the paradoxical aspects of Christianity. Macintosh perceived that this was the source of the power of the Barthian school. The Barthians understood Christianity as a series of sublime paradoxes; otherwise he thought they were disastrously wrong. They overemphasized the transcendence of God and denied God's immanence "to the extent of a pessimistic despair of nature and civilization and an agnostic theory of religious knowledge such as will be driven to seek compensation in dogmatism and a return to an outworn Calvinism or some other such form of theological reaction."[91]

That was a glimpse of the abyss. To Macintosh, pessimism and Christian progress were enemies; a pessimistic theology was a reactionary absurdity. He called the Barthian movement "reactionary irrationalism." He exhorted in the 1930s that it was not too late for liberal theology to create a "new untraditional orthodoxy" that affirmed the modern experience. If this was the modern age, how could modernist theology be outdated? Sadly, Macintosh absorbed the answer of a neo-orthodox-turning field in the late 1930s. He had sought to make liberal theology realistic and scientific, but he made few disciples, and his key ally, Wieman, took a post-Christian turn. His students dropped his scientific presumptions; some of them also dropped his identification with theological liberalism. Having made his mark as a major theologian during the American interim between European crisis theology and the Niebuhrian eruption, Macintosh was a minor figure by the time that he retired in 1942. His influence evaporated with the rise of American neoliberalism and neo-orthodoxy; by mid-century his remaining influence was personal, not intellectual. It came through the students that he gave to modern theology, who took their own paths as religious thinkers. They included Julius Seelye Bixler, Robert Lowry Calhoun, Vergilius Ferm, H. Richard Niebuhr, Reinhold Niebuhr, Filmer S. C. Northrop, and George F. Thomas. Bixler and Calhoun upheld parts of his liberal credo; Northrop and Thomas retained aspects of his philosophical perspective; Ferm carried on his interest in survey-trend writing; Helmut Richard Niebuhr appropriated his commitment to value theory; Reinhold Niebuhr gave new meaning to his favorite theme, religious realism, by blasting the worldview of moral optimism.[92]

In 1937 their festschrift for Macintosh treated him more kindly than his position. They revered him as a teacher and friend; some appreciated his pietism; most respected the sincerity of his pacifist-leaning politics. But by 1937, Macintosh's blend of old-time religion, moral idealism, and experimental ambition seemed triply impossible. Bixler judged that theological empiricism raised more problems than it solved; H. Richard Niebuhr objected that Macintosh-style theology turned values into ideals abstracted from the givenness of religious experience.[93] The revivalist core of Macintosh's religious model was alien to the Depression-era generation of liberal Protestants; it carried backward associations and seemed religiously exclusive; even his closest disciples eschewed the language of the "right religious adjustment." His moral idealism was blasted for its sentimentality and religious reductionism; his ambition of making theology scientific in an experimental sense was widely judged to be misguided. Even if values or value processes are granted to be "facts" in some sense, they are not perceptible objects comparable to the sensory percepts of experimental science. Even if one follows a "right" religious adjustment and gets a "right" response, what does that prove? At a dinner in honor of Macintosh's sixtieth birthday, Reinhold Niebuhr quipped that if another Macintosh festschrift were to be published, it might have to be titled "My Former Students and Other Battlelines." Macintosh replied by quoting George Holmes Howison, a philosopher who shared his situation: "Yes, and no one of them is teaching the truth."[94]

Having contributed more than any theologian to the renewal of American liberal theology in the 1920s and early 1930s, Macintosh saw the field turn against him. In 1932, at the height of his influence as the leader of a realist-turning theological movement, he conducted an eight-round debate in the *Christian Century* with Wieman and Max Carl Otto over the existence of God. Wieman represented the theological left; Otto spoke for humanistic atheism; Macintosh defended theological liberalism on the basis of the reasonableness and attractiveness of moral optimism. He wore his establishment credentials proudly. Macintosh called his approach "hopeful thinking" and "pragmatic faith," and occasionally posed as a rose between two thorns. "If moral optimism be true, *there must be a God*," he assured. "There must be a dependable Power great enough and favorable enough to man to make it possible for man to produce progressively the moral values he must recognize as unconditionally imperative." By the end of the 1930s, however, not even ardent social gospelers claimed to be moral optimists. Liberal theology was attacked for its optimistic sentimentality and idealism, the biblical language of sin and transcendence was exalted, and the agenda of experimental verification was spurned. Macintosh had heirs, but very few that he would have claimed theologically. At Yale, his disciple Randolph Crump Miller kept religious empiricism alive in the field of religious education; at Chicago, the third and fourth generations of empirical theologians remembered him respectfully as the first programmatically empiricist theologian; but Macintosh ended more poorly than he began. In the 1920s he was America's most important theologian; in later life he remained significant only as the teacher of students who turned against him, as the forerunner of an empiricist tradition that was religiously alien to him, and as the forerunner of a realist turn in theology that turned out to be equally alien to him.[95]

Theological empiricism, begun as a Chicago project, for the most part remained one, with offshoots at Chicago-influenced institutions. In his capstone work, *The Problem of Religious Knowledge,* Macintosh emphasized his connection to the Chicago school, especially to Mathews and Wieman. Like Mathews and Wieman he emphasized that theology gets its bearings by intuiting, perceiving, and apprehending the activity of a divine factor in the life process. Unlike Mathews, with his empiricism of religious process, Macintosh defended an empiricism of religious experience, while noting sadly that Wieman seemed to be turning away from the religious aspects of religious experience. Against the dominant trend of the Chicago school, exemplified by the "tentative and sketchy" writings of Gerald Birney Smith and the vigorously assertive writings of Wieman, Macintosh implored that even a rigorously empirical and rational theism should have room for a personal God—"conscious, intelligent, and morally purposive."[96] With Wieman in mind, he admonished elsewhere that God is not merely a process of integration or a system of patterns. Wieman taught that God is a present, potent, operative reality, but not a personal reality. Macintosh recalled that when Wieman's books began to appear in the late 1920s, he welcomed Wieman as a powerful ally, "but it soon began to appear that what Mr. Wieman was proposing was a purely behavioristic theology, leaving no place for Divine Mind, Consciousness, Intelligence or Will, but only for divine behavior." While granting that behaviorist method has its uses in certain disciplines, Macintosh protested that behaviorism is too simplistic to deal with problems in the philosophy of mind. It followed that deity should not be studied on the model of animal behavior, for God is Superhuman Mind. To Macintosh God was a "Superhuman Spiritual Being, an essentially personal cosmic Power, an intelligent loving moral Mind and Will." On that count he gave a pious face to the legacy of Chicago theology; Smith and Wieman gave it a harder face.[97]

GERALD BIRNEY SMITH
AND THE MORALITY OF MODERN KNOWLEDGE

For the first twenty-nine years of the twentieth century the systematic theologian and ethicist of the Chicago school was Gerald Birney Smith. Born in 1868, he was raised in Middlefield, Massachusetts, and educated at Brown University, Union Theological Seminary, and Columbia University. His studies under William Adams Brown were formative in drawing him to the Ritschlian school. Upon graduating from Union in 1898, he won a two-year traveling fellowship from Union that allowed him to study under Wilhelm Herrmann in Marburg, Auguste Sabatier in Paris, and Adolf Harnack in Berlin. By the time he returned to the United States in 1900 to begin his teaching career at the University of Chicago Divinity School, Smith was already skeptical of Harnack's Ritschlian assurances. Like Sabatier, he was impressed by the novelty of the modern age. Like Foster, he had little trouble deciding who was right in the Sabatier-Harnack argument over the continuity of Christian belief. Modern Christianity is not merely an extension of the Reformation principle, he judged; by rejecting the finality of all external authorities, modern theology had begun something new.[98]

Smith respected the Ritschlian school for its creative energy, its ethical interpretation of Christianity, and its critical spirit. His thinking retained the ethical idealism and historicism of Ritschlian theology long after he discarded its evangelical features. "The Ritschlian school has rendered great service in revealing so clearly the fact that scientific acuteness may go hand in hand with religious zeal," he remarked in 1915. "To read and digest such a book as Herrmann's *The Christian's Communion with God* will leave a lasting impression of the dignity and the religious possibilities of keenly critical theological discussion." Unlike the Ritschlian school, however, and unlike even Foster and Sabatier, Smith urged that scientific method holds the key to religious meaning and truth. His model for good theology was the social scientific model of inductive inquiry, and, like Dewey, he played down the theory-laden aspects of science. Social scientists are variously informed by the theories of Comte, Spencer, Marx, and the like when they pursue their investigations, Smith allowed, but good social science grows out of the empirical analysis of the facts of human life. It does not proceed from the need or desire to confirm Comtism or Spencerism or Marxism as a final norm.[99]

In 1910, a year after he became managing editor of the *American Journal of Theology*, Smith pressed this claim against the Ritschlianism of his teacher. In his telling, Brown tried to have it both ways by affirming both the normative authority of modern experience and the authority of Christian tradition. Smith countered that theology cannot serve two masters. Modernity presents a choice, not an additional source for dogmatic affirmations. Theology cannot be modern and still grant normative authority to Christian Scripture or tradition, he declared: "In so far as religious belief which has been inherited from the past is really adequate to the needs of the present, it of course needs no revisions. But the theologian should be equipped with a scientific method of investigation which will enable him to judge whether a given type of theology is actually suited to enlist the most worthy aspirations of men in a given age and environment." Traditional orthodoxies appealed to the Bible, a superhuman Christ, and sometimes church tradition and the pope as courts of authoritative appeal; most liberal theologies appealed to a religious a priori of a Schleiermacherian or Ritschlian type; Smith exhorted that modern theology needed to sweep its house clean of absolutist exceptions to the natural order, lest the theologian "seem like an advocate rather than an investigator." For Smith, as for his Chicago colleagues, modernity required "a significant revision of belief," and the basis of worthy belief was modern knowledge, not doctrinal norms of the past.[100]

He could be rough on Chicago colleagues who fell short of this exacting test. In 1914 Smith observed that Mathews still assumed, like Harnack, that the modern Christian "derives his religious life directly from the New Testament form of Christianity." Smith admonished that Mathews's vestigial evangelicalism was naive; like Harnack, Mathews assumed that the normative truth of Christianity is contained in the New Testament and that historical criticism should be used by modernists as an apologetic tool. Persistently Smith countered that science bows to no outside norms, that "the entire course of Christian history must be taken into account if we are to understand what Christianity really is," and that truly modernist theology has to be strictly scientific. The dominant status of the Ritschlian theology showed "how reluctant the religious world is to part with a method by which experience may be corrected by divine authority," he judged. This reluctance was the chief barrier to the development of a truly modern theology; Smith urged repeatedly that theologians needed to cultivate a sense of appreciation for the "positive character" of scientific method and a spirit of trust in its capacity to engender a new, superior, life-giving theology: "The norm for the construction of theology is no longer to be found in any given statement of faith, or in any isolated section of history, but rather in the immanent principles of growth and life which are to be ascertained by a knowledge of the facts of religion itself. When once this method of theologizing shall have come to prevail, we shall have a means of keeping religious experience and religious doctrine in such close interrelation that the historical changes which take place will be accompanied by an adequately developing theology."[101]

In the modern age of science and democracy, religion needed to inculcate new values, including new ideas about religion. The basic ideas about what it means to be "religious" and how a religion should make truth claims needed to change: "It is of fundamental importance that the student of theology should *learn to feel the religious value of honestly facing the facts.*" Idealogues and fundamentalists worried that science is destructive; Smith countered that "loyalty to the truth is more religious than mere conformity to a prescribed statement." The truth-seeking theologian or biblical scholar abandons the debater's attitude: "He must attempt to take account of all the facts, and must let his conclusions be dictated by these facts." To the scientifically minded religious thinker or scholar, what matters is accuracy in investigation, not doctrinal content. Smith put it bluntly: "While abandonment of a doctrine seems to the believer in authority like radical disloyalty, it is an incidental matter to the historical scholar." This predisposition is the essential precondition of worthwhile theological scholarship, he urged. The tests of serious theology are scientific credibility and practical relevance: "If the student can come to measure the validity of his theologizing, not by its conformity to standards of the past, but by its capacity to meet the questions of the present, he will be in a position to do fruitful work."[102]

Smith's excurses on this theme strongly influenced his colleagues and students, though he produced little constructive work of his own aside from programmatic essays, and in his later career he wavered on the scientific salvation of theology. His writings, which included three authored books and two coauthored books, specialized in essays that surveyed trends in contemporary theology and called for a new empirical theology. For eleven years he served as managing editor of the *American Journal of Theology*; for another nine years he edited the new *Journal of Religion*. These posts heightened his personal role in the growing field of liberal theology and suited his preference for survey writing. Though he contributed substantially to the development of Chicago theology, Smith never attained the public prominence of Foster, Mathews, or Ames. His chief themes were pursued in the work of his protégé, Bernard E. Meland, who later recalled: "G. B. Smith was warmly sympathetic toward people, and exceedingly judicious in weighing a conflict in issues; yet in his criticism of thought, whether of an individual, or a group of thinkers presuming to express a consensus, he could be devastating. With the precision of a physician's scalpel he would cut into an issue or a proposal of thought, laying bare its pretensions and ill-considered notions, or pointing up the thin line of constructive insight that gave promise to its line of inquiry. Students and faculty alike came to depend on his judgment for winnowing out the truth and error of situations in Divinity School life and thought."[103]

For most of his career Smith was the Chicago school's truest believer that science was the salvation of theology, but in the mid-1920s he had second thoughts, just before Wieman heightened the empirical ambitions of Chicago-school theology. In his early years at Chicago, Smith shared Mathews's enthusiasm for the burgeoning field of Christian sociology; inspired by Mathews's collaboration with Albion Small, Smith believed that the future of modern theology rested on its affinities with the new social sciences. Having vested his faith in the alliance between theology and sociology, however, Smith witnessed the subsequent secularization and professionalization of sociology with mounting disappointment; Albion Small's colleagues and successors did not share his religion-friendly concept of sociology as an instrument of social reform. Chicago sociologists W. I. Thomas and Robert E. Park sharply distinguished between social science and social intervention, minimized reformist concerns, emphasized concrete studies of social groups and institutions, and made their field as academically professionalized as possible. By the mid-1920s Smith was resigned to the fact that sociology had gone its own way and that "the procedure of the sciences offers no help to religious adjustment." Increasingly he described religion in vaguely mystical terms. Religion needs to be scientific in its devotion to the facts, he assured, but religious truth cannot be adequately grasped by scientific methods alone, for religion has more in common with poetry and the fine arts than with science. "The inescapable fact which we must face is that the primary interest of the religious leader is not scientific," he instructed. Actual lived religion, even in its liberal forms, is usually about inducing personal attitudes and loyalties, not finding objective truth. While cautioning that religion must concern itself with objective truth, Smith stopped resisting the religious character of religion: "The fact is that religion belongs in the realm of art rather than in the realm of the sciences. Its function is to enable men to feel the beauty and the nobility of high-minded living rather than to analyze the physical and psychical processes of living. Religion *must* employ symbol and poetry and pageantry and music if it is to be religious at all."[104]

This slightly mystical turn to the fine arts and the "higher things" had a future in Chicago school theology—in the work of Bernard Meland—but it was too mushy for Wieman, whose empiricist ambitions left little room for history, let alone poetic feeling. Reviewing Wieman's agenda-setting book *Religious Experience and Scientific Method,* Smith noted that Wieman had no interest in the history of thought and that he denigrated mystical experience as "a state of mental deliquescence." He also charged that Wieman's harmonization of religion and science was simplistic. The creative power of religion depends on the feeling of a reality that science cannot grasp or precisely formulate, Smith argued. To restrict theology to scientific statements about experience and natural process is to divest religion of religious significance: "Must not religion, in order to remain religious at all, aim at symbolic expression rather than at scientific formulation? And if this be true, just how are the symbols to be correlated with scientific formulas?" Though he applauded Wieman's conviction that religion and science need each other, and though he greatly respected Wieman, Smith saw a reflection of his own former one-sidedness in Wieman's aggressive literalism.[105]

Meland later reflected that to the extent Smith pursued a coherent theological agenda, he devoted himself to the question whether the natural universe, as described scientifically, "was hospitable to a religious response and to a doctrine of theism." Smith's last book, *Current Christian Thinking* (1929), gave the provisional answers of his mature thinking, which blended a nature-mystical motif with his customary empiricism. He praised the immanental-idealistic theologies of the previous generation for defusing the conflict between Christianity and evolutionary science, but cautioned that it was no longer convincing to appeal to God as the immanent spirit of life or power of being. "Of great importance is the fact that this idealistically interpreted universe does not seem to have much in common with the conclusions of modern science," he warned. "It is too sentimental, too largely derived from an unproved assumption concerning the character of the God who is asserted to be the principle and the source of all that is." In his judgment, the evolutionary theisms of the prewar Progressive era overpersonalized the universe and lightly passed over the problem of evil. Liberal theologians assured that the world is continually improving and that God is in control of the world's progress. Smith countered that tough-minded Jamesians no longer thought of God as being in control of a progressing world; the staggering evils of World War I refuted the benevolent liberal reconception of providence.[106]

Science no longer bothers to look for religious support, he observed elsewhere: "Modern science is creating a type of culture which stands on its own feet, asking and needing no support from religion." A bit of Foster-like double-mindedness seemed to set into Smith's mind; while judging that religion is more like the fine arts than like science, he continued to assert that theology must become as empirical and naturalistic as science. "The conception of religion as something entirely natural, and as having its proper field of development in this world, has increasingly come to be generally accepted," he observed. This was the drift of the religious education movement, in which Smith and George Albert Coe played leadership roles; it also described the academics who wrote for the *Journal of Religion.* "Theologians are fast ceasing to concern themselves with the problem of discovering an authentic channel by which a supernatural revelation might come to men," Smith declared. "They are rather attempting to understand what religion is, and they generally think of religion as an attempt on man's part to enter into right relations with those forces which will enable him to realize the richest life in this world here and now."[107]

This self-description claimed to speak for all forward-thinking theologians and their students. Smith maintained that "the younger generation today has in general no sense of a supernatural world." Science increasingly explained the only world that exists, and it took nothing from religion as a form of explanation about matters of fact. The vast cosmic process that produced the human bearers of consciousness and creators of religion is explained by science, not religion. Smith argued that the implication of this truism for religion was that religion needed to find its own work. The function of religion is to attain appropriate adjustment to the cosmic process described by science, he proposed. A religion that takes this self-understanding seriously will conceptualize God "as a reality in the process to which right adjustment may be made." At the same time, he admonished, anything that religious thinkers say about God has to be squared with everything that scientists say about the nature of the natural world. Theologians have to be open to the possibility that someday science will leave no room at all for the metaphysical God.[108]

Smith wavered between the latter assertions about God to the end of his career. He spoke of God as a limited cosmic reality, but only tentatively. At the end of his life he believed that theology was at a crossroads: "It would seem that we are on the threshold of an extremely interesting development in theological thinking," he observed, putting it positively. He was sure that religion had a vital future, especially in its mystical forms, because science merely describes what it finds. The human spirit will never settle for a way of knowing that cannot deal with spiritual meanings or moral values, he believed. Smith was certain that some kind of religion was bound to endure on the strength of humanity's mystical sense of the hidden wholeness of things, but he was less sure about God. "Just what conception of God will ultimately emerge from the great experiment we cannot yet tell," he counseled. As the representation of religious ideals, God surely had a future; as a posited object of faith, Smith was doubtful. Many forms of mysticism get along with no god at all, and Smith believed that mystical yearning is the wellspring of religion. His last word was that more empirical studies were needed: "Our religious relationship to what we worship in our cosmic environment must be empirically studied, and our conception of God must be formulated in tentative terms which grow out of that experience, rather than in terms of an a priori philosophy assuming to be final. Men may believe in God without being able to define God."[109]

The last sentence was Smith's theological epitaph. Though precise in his negations, he stayed vague and kept his options open on the constructive side. The work of making Chicago theology precisely constructive was left to his junior colleague, Henry Nelson Wieman, whose appointment to the Divinity School faculty in 1927 marked a turning point in its development. To Wieman's subsequent regret, this turn had a strongly metaphysical cast; to his enduring pride, it was empiricist in a philosophically reflective fashion. With Wieman's appointment the Chicago school entered its second phase, the phase of empirically centered philosophical method.

HENRY NELSON WIEMAN AND THE WRESTLE
OF EMPIRICISM AND METAPHYSICS

American liberal theology was (and remains) double-minded about meta-physics. From its Kantian-rooted Schleiermacherian and Ritschlian streams it inherited an aggressively antimetaphysical rhetoric; in its Hegelian, personalist, and realist streams it spoke in explicitly metaphysical terms; in various mediat-ing forms it tried to restrict metaphysical reason to an important but subordinate role. The gospel-claiming Ritschlians ruled the field for most of the liberal era, yet even the theologies of the Ritschlian school were pervaded by metaphysically loaded claims about personality, value, idealism, and consciousness. Just as their German mediationist forerunners blended Schleiermacherian experientialism and Hegelian idealism in the mid-nineteenth century, American thinkers such as Macintosh, Wieman, Union Seminary religious philosopher Eugene W. Lyman, and the Boston personalists effected their own forms of post-Ritschlian meta-physical theology. They combined an emphasis on religious experience with a strong assertion of the metaphysical competence of reason. At Chicago the latter theme was novel in 1927. The thinker who provoked the Chicago school to make its peace with metaphysical reason was Alfred North Whitehead; the person who first effected that peace was Wieman. Under his influence, the Chicago school came to stand for the proposition that theological empiricism and metaphysics belong together; against Wieman's later turn of mind, the University of Chicago Divinity School became the center of Whiteheadian process theology.

Wieman came to Chicago at the age of forty-three, as a consequence of a Math-ews hunch. In 1926, three years before he completed *Process and Reality,* White-head published a primer on religion titled *Religion in the Making.* The Chicago theologians read the book with considerable irritation. Though Whitehead's early work in the philosophy of mathematics and his recent metaphysical writings gave him a reputation as a genius, his argument was completely unintelligible to them. Mathews confessed: "It is infuriating, and I must say embarrassing as well, to read page after page of relatively familiar words without understanding a single sen-tence." Ames and Case found the book equally impossible; Case wrote it off as an example of meaningless metaphysical word spinning. Smith felt some affinity with the book without being able to explain why. With his usual wry humor, Mathews reflected that it was at least possible that the problem was not with Whitehead: "Whitehead may be telling us something we ought to know about."[110]

That hunch inspired a lecture invitation to Wieman, who was then a little-known philosophy professor at Occidental College and a visiting lecturer at

McCormick Theological Seminary. A native of Missouri and the son of a Presbyterian pastor, Wieman was educated at Park College (his mother's alma mater) and San Francisco Theological Seminary. In college he dabbled with Kant, Leibnitz, and Josiah Royce; in seminary he endured three years of Calvinist orthodoxy via Charles Hodge's dogmatics and Calvin's *Institutes,* both of which struck him as "slightly ridiculous," though he respected Calvin's intellectual seriousness. The legitimacy of biblical criticism was strenuously debated at San Francisco in those years, but Wieman found the arguments boring. Why should anyone care who wrote Isaiah? Largely on the hope of winning a German fellowship, he willed himself through seminary—"it all seemed rather alien and irrelevant"—and in 1910, he was awarded the fellowship. For a year he lecture-toured at Jena and at Heidelberg, where he heard Troeltsch, whose historicism bored him no less than debates over biblical criticism. History has no answers and solves no problems, Wieman judged.[111]

Upon returning to the United States, Wieman married Anna Orr, with whom he lived for twenty years before her death from cancer, and for two years he worked as a Presbyterian pastor before entering the doctoral program in philosophy at Harvard. Wieman knew what he wanted: the true philosophy. He had already decided that Henri Bergson's emphasis on creativity was a crucial insight, though he rejected Bergson's anti-intellectualism. He had also judged that William James's writings were interesting, but superficial: "It always seemed to me that James slipped over and around problems, touching them lightly and entertainingly, making a few brilliant remarks, but never really penetrating them. He always seemed to slip away and pass on just when he should begin to dig down." At Harvard, Wieman found a Jamesian mentor who was not averse to digging, Ralph Barton Perry, and a second mentor who shared his religious interests, W. E. Hocking. He later recalled that he basked in the "great light" of Perry's empiricist clarity and was deeply influenced by Hocking's insights into religious experience: "The fascination and exhilaration of those two years stand out in my memory most vividly." Like Hocking he became a hybrid—trained in philosophy, yet driven by religious questions, and committed to a philosophical approach to religious questions.[112]

He was also slow to make a scholarly mark. For nearly ten years at Occidental College, Wieman pondered his viewpoint on a modest scale, producing a handful of articles, but no books.[113] It took him several years to realize that the idealist option was out for him, and thus, that he had to find an approach to religion different from Hocking's. The formative influences on his thinking were James, Dewey, Bergson, Perry, and Hocking, and in the 1920s the leaders of the new organismic philosophy entered his canon, notably Samuel Alexander, C. Lloyd Morgan, and Alfred North Whitehead. Wieman read Alexander's and Morgan's books on "emergent evolution" and made a close study of Whitehead's ongoing work, especially *Inquiry into the Principles of Natural Knowledge* (1919), *The Concept of Nature* (1920), *The Principle of Relativity* (1922), and *Science and the Modern World* (1925). To the extent that Wieman was known in 1926, he was known as the first American to become conversant with this literature. That year he convinced the Chicago historicists that Whitehead's developing religious philosophy was intelligible and important. In Wieman's telling, Whitehead showed that the existence and nature of God are revealed in the inherent structure of physical nature; he proved that the universe can exist only by virtue of its order, which is aesthetic, loving, and not accidental. Meland later recalled that with Wieman's lecture to the Divinity School's Theology Club, the school entered a new era: "It was as if shuttered windows in one's own household had been swung open, revealing vistas of which one had hitherto been unmindful." Wieman's performance and the appearance of his first book, *Religious Experience and Scientific Method*, won him a new academic home.[114]

The timing was fortuitous for Wieman and the Divinity School. As a field-dominating movement, American liberal theology was at high tide, though embattled, in the mid-1920s. Christian modernists and moderates defeated their fundamentalist rivals for control of the mainline churches; every major Protestant seminary joined the nonfundamentalist side; even Princeton Theological Seminary made its peace with historical criticism in the late 1920s. But it was only from a later standpoint that liberal Protestants realized that they had prevailed against their fundamentalist opponents in the mid-1920s. At the time they felt embattled, and it was an awkward time for their movement.

By 1928 the founders of the social gospel were aging or deceased, the movement's intellectual creativity was eroding, and its evangelical-Ritschlian wing was in retreat against an array of modernist, humanist, and dialectical perspectives. Signs of confusion and inner doubt were plentiful. Theologically the Chicago school was drifting into mere religious humanism, just as the fundamentalists charged; as a movement the social gospel faltered throughout American Protestantism; on both counts Wieman offered a bracing alternative. He shared the modernism and naturalistic empiricism of his new colleagues, but opposed their humanistic leanings, showed little interest in their social concerns, and invested no importance at all in their cherished historicism. Bernard Meland later recalled that Wieman represented "an intriguing combination of familiar and alien elements" to the Chicago schoolers: "He was like them, yet strangely and tantalizingly unlike them." To Wieman's perception, the differences were much more obvious: "I felt strangely out of place and in a very alien intellectual atmosphere, despite the most exceptional kindness shown toward me by almost all the faculty." The Chicago schoolers were committed to sociohistorical research, he recalled, but "all this has always seemed to me irrelevant to the important problem of religious faith, quite harmless but futile in guiding our devotion." To Wieman, the consuming issue was "What is it all about? What was the nature of that reality which men were trying to serve and put themselves into the keeping of, when they went through all these motions? No one seemed to be interested in that question."[115]

Inner doubts notwithstanding, from the beginning he spoke in a voice that was confident, high-minded, and prone to lecture. Wieman vigorously affirmed the reality of God, but not in a way that pretended to sound like traditional Christianity. "I am very sure that religion must plant itself firmly on the data of sense else it will become the plaything of the sentimentalist and nothing more," he declared. Wieman believed that the key issue in religion was the difference between tough-minded and weak-minded thinking; the liberal-conservative debate was secondary. Liberal theology banked on sentiment, shrank from defending its assertion of God's existence, and tried to make itself attractive by appealing to social concerns. To Wieman this strategy was disastrous; it drove the strong and intelligent people away from religion. The serious religious question is the question of God, he admonished; religion is pointless without God, but in the modern age science has negated traditional ways of conceiving divine reality. The opening sentences of Wieman's first book conveyed his agenda and spirit: "Whatever else the word God may mean, it is a term used to designate that Something upon which human life is most dependent for its security, welfare and increasing abundance. That there is such a Something cannot be doubted. The mere fact that human life happens, and continues to happen, proves that this Something, however unknown, does certainly exist."[116]

God is as certain as the external world; Wieman later grew fond of saying that God is as real as a toothache. Liberal theologians like Smith had made everything uncertain, but Wieman admonished that religion and the modern age need certainty above all. While allowing that many conditions converge to sustain human life, he argued that Something must be fundamental to life or essentially constitutive of it. At bottom, there are two possibilities about this Something. Either the universe is a single organic unity that has indivisibly created and sustained human life, or some of the universe's sustaining conditions are more crucial than others. The first view is pantheistic, the second theistic; in either case, Wieman argued, God is the name for the undeniable Something of supreme value in life. Minimally defined, God's existence is a metaphysical deduction, but as a real object of knowledge, God must be studied scientifically, for science is the true method of knowing. Science judges the truth or falsity of metaphysical propositions. Wieman lectured that in the rigorous sense of the term, all *knowledge* is scientific. There is such a thing as prescientific knowledge, he acknowledged; for centuries the human race was knowledgeably acquainted with food before it understood anything about food scientifically. But the goal of any discipline that claims to know anything must be to develop a scientific method that adequately examines its data; acquaintance knowledge must give way to scientific understanding. Because experience is more complex than such phenomena as light, sound, and motion, Wieman reasoned, modern psychology lagged behind modern physics as a science. Because religious experience is notoriously complex, and because theologians had only recently begun to accept the scientific imperative, theology lagged further behind. In the spirit of the Chicago school, but shorn of its historicism and ambivalence toward philosophy, Wieman called for a rigorously empirical theology that moved beyond mere acquaintance knowledge of God.[117]

His rationalism was unyielding. To him the cognitive meaning of religion was consuming and religiously sufficient; Wieman did not lack feeling but stressed that sentimentality is the enemy of religion, "a dry rot that destroys religion at its roots." He appreciated Whitehead's religious intention in speaking of religious experience and the divine order as "aesthetic," but he advised Whitehead to find a better word. He was especially hard on evocative language. While granting an exception to music and poetry, where aesthetic considerations prevail, and another exception to religious worship, which is another form of art, Wieman argued that there is only one proper way to use words. Words should be employed to designate an object, not to evoke a sentiment. It grieved him that most Christian preaching appealed to sentiment. Liberal and conservative theologies alike abounded with evocative references to love, the community of faith, the cross, the Word of God, and the Spirit of Christ, he observed. Wieman protested that "these are dangerous words and should be rarely used." To his mind there was something inherently dishonest about using a word for the sake of the sentiment attached to it. Truthful Christian speaking refers to the proper objects of faith; evocative speaking transfers loyalty from these proper objects to the words that designate them. It followed that to invoke the "fatherhood of God" or the "love of Christ" in an evocative way is to betray Christianity.

Designative language is clear and concrete; evocative language indulges and obscures. In his later career Wieman succumbed to the flat literalism that marked his thinking from the outset, but *Religious Experience and Scientific Truth* contained a theme that saved his argument from this fate: totality or "gestalt." Wieman argued against the notion that empirical religious thinking should cut down its objects to the limits of its own method in order to gain power over them. Religious understanding is not like physics or chemistry, he reasoned, for religion deals with the concrete fact in its totality; unlike the laboratory scientist, the theologian has to be willing to wrestle with obscurity. Religion is loaded with mystery, thus theology cannot avoid it; even the empirically minded theologian cannot avoid it altogether. Wieman was emphatic that serious theology needed to keep mystery talk to a minimum, however. In their wrestling with the obscurity of their object, religious thinkers are obliged to make theological language as designative and rigorously empirical as possible. Religion must "plant itself firmly on the data of sense," he instructed, and the datum is provided by religious experience, the "awareness of the total passage of nature, the undiscriminated event." Instead of paying attention to only a few familiar data, theology needed to study "that total event of nature which enters awareness in the form of the concrete fullness of experience."[118]

In 1927, the year Wieman joined the Chicago faculty, he published *The Wrestle of Religion with Truth* as an example of his ideal. This book put Whiteheadian philosophy on the map of American theology. Wieman spared no terms of rebuke for theologies that played up the difference between reason and faith. In all of its forms, he contended, the irrationalist impulse is disastrous for theology: "It works like a deadly poison both upon intelligence and upon religion. It is one of the great evils of human life." Like Macintosh, Wieman proposed to understand religion scientifically as the process by which human beings seek adjustment to God, but Wieman was not burdened with Macintosh's evangelical vestiges. In his youth he was indifferent to churchly religion and preferred to read poetry on Sunday mornings; in his telling his parents agreed with him that "the church was a good business." He came to his intellectual vocation in a quasimystical experience during his senior year of college, as he watched a sunset across the Missouri River, when the idea suddenly occurred to him that a career in philosophy of religion would be more interesting and fulfilling than journalism. Wieman never passed through an evangelical phase, a phase in which the Bible interested him, or even a Ritschlian phase. He opined to students that the Bible is "a vastly over-rated book" and that "to call it the 'inspired Word of God' and all the rest of the hullabaloo has given it a false prestige." Though his early books retained traces of the idea of God as a reality beyond the reach of empirical enquiry, from the beginning of his career Wieman's working concept of divine reality was deeply naturalistic and nonpersonal. His second book defined God as "this most subtle and intimate complexity of environmental nature which yields the greatest good when right adjustment is made." God may be more than this definition, Wieman allowed, but in the wrestle of religion with truth, it is best to work with the God that is known.[119]

Wieman's tough-minded religious empiricism dispensed with liberal idealism and premodern Christian dogma without remainder. To him, facts were more important than any cherished belief, the world was not a nice place, "and God is not a nice God." The latter conclusion followed from the second. Whitehead noted that religion can be evil as well as good; Wieman stressed that God can be terrible even when God is good. Whitehead's description of religion made a profound impression on Wieman and shaped his argument. Religion is "what the individual does with his own solitariness," Whitehead asserted. The person who is never solitary is not religious. Religion is the transition "from God the void to God the enemy, and from God the enemy to God the companion."[120]

To Wieman, these statements burned the sentimental pietism out of liberal religion. Whitehead's emphasis on solitariness was a needed corrective to politicized religion. True religion is about adjusting to God, Wieman argued, not about achieving human ideals. The idealism of the social gospel substituted a program of superficial social work for the consuming God-centered consciousness of genuine religion. Wieman countered that the object of religious experience is within religious experience, not in the transformation of society. Religion is the art and theory of individual introspection; it involves the adaptation of the whole of life to ultimate facts and thus depends on human agency and the permanent nature of things. Religion begins in the wounding experience of the void; it deepens with the experience of God as the enemy; it matures in the experience of God as the companion of one's living. Wieman played up the necessity of the enemy stage. To those who cling to illusion-cherishing theologies, he observed, God is never the enemy; bad religion is usually sentimental or dogmatic or both. But from a deeper religious standpoint in which God is the ultimate factual character of events to which human beings must adapt, God takes on the character of the enemy before God can be known as one's companion. God is the ultimate fact of life with which human beings must struggle; the struggle of life is painful and sometimes terrifying; when individuals learn to adapt to life in ways that allow them to survive and flourish, they come to know God as their companion.[121]

This was a page from Whitehead. Through the influence of Whitehead and Bergson, Wieman spoke the language of organismic philosophy; his master concepts were concretion, holism, emergence, and especially, creative process. His concept of God was Whitehead's principle of concretion. Tennyson asserted poetically that a little flower in a crannied wall contains the inner reality of God and humanity; Whitehead agreed that everything that exists involves in its existence the totality of all being. Each particular thing in existence is what it is because all the rest of being is what it is. Tennyson's flower "prehends" all being; the universe is "concreted" in the flower; while cautioning that he was not a pantheist, Whitehead described God as the principle of concretion. For Whitehead, Wieman explained, "God" was not simply another name for the existing world in its totality: "On the contrary God is simply this one, sustaining, all-pervading character which the universe displays, the principle of concretion, the constitutive, aesthetic order of all being." For Whitehead, as for Wieman, God was both more and less than the total concrete world of existing things. God is less than the existing world in its totality because God excludes evil; God is more than the world because God transcends the existing world as the power that shapes and pervades the world. Though God cannot transcend all being, Wieman assured, it is meaningful to speak of God as transcendent by virtue of God's creative power over the world of abstract forms.[122]

Metaphysically Wieman plugged hard for Whitehead's organismic vision; very briefly he took a pass at claiming scientific verification for it. The proof was Whitehead's demonstration that every unit of space and time, no matter how small, involves all the rest of space and time. Whitehead showed that materialistic theory is wrong in supposing that small units of space or time or space-time can be securely separated from the rest of space-time. He theorized that every "point-moment" focalizes or "prehends" the totality of space-time. Since everything that exists or will exist or has existed must participate in space-time, he reasoned, the principle of all being entering into each particular thing applies to all existence.[123] In 1929 Whitehead published his systematic elaboration of this insight, and numerous others related to it, *Process and Reality*, which distinguished between the "primordial" and "consequent" natures of divine reality.

In this system, later dubbed process philosophy or "neoclassical metaphysics," God's primordial nature is the total potentiality of all existing entities at all moments of their actualization. Whitehead argued that the life and freedom of each self-actualizing entity is made possible by its participation in God's primordial nature. At the same time, the freedom of each entity makes it possible for all subjective entities to choose evil; each self-actualizing self possesses the power to actualize or negate the life-enhancing aim of God's primordial nature. Whitehead conceived God as luring God's subjects to make other-regarding, life-enhancing choices, always creating new possibilities to choose life. At the same time he insisted that God never infringes the freedom of the moral agent to make choices. The consequent nature of God is the accumulated actualization of whatever choices God's subjects make. God's consequent being is shaped through its process of interrelation with self-actualizing subjects. As the ground in actuality of all possibility, God is the metaphysical reality that unites actuality and possibility.[124]

Wieman made his early name as the first American advocate of this metaphysical vision. The Chicago school of theology took a philosophical turn with his early insistence that Whitehead's organismic worldview was the metaphysical master theory that modern theology needed in order to make sense of its appeals to value, truth, reality, and divine reality. *The Wrestle of Religion with Truth* contended that Whitehead's organismic philosophy was true to religious experience, that it dealt adequately with the problem of evil, that it was up to date in its science, and that its principle of concretion provided the best available concept of God.[125] In subsequent decades the Chicago school produced thinkers who defended these claims. Like Wieman, they directed liberal theology away from its preoccupation with ideals in favor of a religion centered on a divine good that transcends human striving.

But Wieman's heart belonged to empiricism, not metaphysical speculation. The experience of reading Whitehead's *Process and Reality* was unsettling to him; on reflection it became alienating. In a generally positive review he lauded Whitehead's system as "the best possible answer up to date," but he also began to hedge. He was sure that Whiteheadian philosophy would eventually give way to a better system. Undoubtedly there were errors in Whitehead's thinking, though Wieman admitted that he couldn't identify them yet. He did believe that Whitehead's sweeping abstractions and new uses of old words had the misleading effect of seeming to justify classical theism. "There is danger he will be quoted in defense of all sorts of orthodox religious notions that are quite alien to his thought," he cautioned. For the next two years, Wieman's inner doubts went to work on him. Was empiricism necessarily materialist? Did it make any sense to call Whiteheadian philosophy a form of empiricism? For all its grandeur, wasn't Whitehead's system essentially a castle of abstractions? Whitehead dealt exclusively with ideas, building one idea out of another. Wieman accepted that ideas are necessary; even metaphysics is necessary to a point. But ideas should be regarded and used as tools, not as ends, he reflected. Ideas are torches that light the way, not suns and stars that one adores and to which one declares one's commitment. In a chastening estimate, Wieman judged that virtually nothing in Whitehead's system was based on empirical demonstration. The brilliance of *Process and Reality* was not in doubt; it was "the most magnificent achievement of constructive imagination that modern times can show." Notwithstanding its genius, however, the book's argument was also a "wholly groundless" piece of speculation: "There is no evidence whatsoever to support it."[126]

The concept of the consequent nature of God was a major case in point. Wieman allowed that this construct is compelling as a myth or a form of poetic symbolism. It paints an attractive picture. But Whitehead's system was true only as a form of imaginative myth making, he argued. Not to recognize this fact is dangerous, though metaphysical concept spinners never called their systems myths. Not to recognize the imaginative-mythical basis of metaphysical reason is simply to replace an older dogmatism with a new one; to recognize it is to be spared from taking metaphysical speculation too seriously. Wieman judged that Whitehead's system was "infected with error through and through. Such ambitious efforts always are." Wieman resolved to leave Whitehead behind by tracking the flow of experience, though he never left him completely behind. Whitehead taught that duration is actual and factual; that events constitute the ultimate fact beyond which there can be nothing else; that everything that is or can be pertains to events; and that objects are aspects of events. An object is the aspect that an event presents when it interacts with another event. In the language of a simpler materialism, Wieman directly appropriated the Whiteheadian-Bergsonian belief that duration is real. He reformulated the Whiteheadian language of events, his theology remained a religious philosophy of creative process, and his later distinction between "creativity" and "the creative event" was strongly reminiscent of Whitehead's distinction between the primordial and consequent natures of God. By his lights, however, his ambition was more scientific and thus more modest than Whitehead's, because it was more determined to stick to empirical facts.[127]

TRACKING THE SOURCE OF HUMAN GOOD

Wieman's ambition was to discover what God is actually doing in the world, as distinguished from theologies and philosophies that propound favored ideas about how God relates to the world. "What I am chiefly trying to do in the field of religion is to promote a theocentric religion as over against the prevalent anthropocentric," he explained in 1932. "The first requirement of a theocentric religion is that we make the actuality of God himself, and not our ideas about God, the object of our love and devotion. The second requirement is another side of the same thing. It is that we do not allow our wishes and needs to shape our idea of God, but shall shape it solely in the light of objective evidence." To defend a cherished idea about God instead of pursuing God's actuality is to worship one's self, not God, he admonished. "If we allow our idea of God to be shaped by our desires and needs, we are cuddling ourselves, not serving God."[128]

Theology had to become as scientific as possible, because science is the one method by which inquirers subordinate their own desires to objective reality. "By checking the constructs of reason by observation, and directing our observation by the constructs of reason, we gradually acquire an idea of objective reality, and circumvent the thronging urgency of our desires which so persistently hide from us the real nature of objective existence." Wieman denied that he sought to make religion respectable in the modern academy. He had no interest in trying to make religion appealing to others. It was of no concern to him whether his religious thinking was preachable, attractive, or relevant: "My sole concern is to find some way of escaping from the miasma of subjectivism and making contact with sacred reality," he maintained. "The only reason I insist on scientific method in religion, is because I want to deal with the objective, existential God, and not merely ideas."[129]

The Barthian movement was popular because it was dramatic, evocative, and traditional; Barthian theology was extremely preachable. To Wieman it was also a disaster for theology, because the Barthians thumbed their noses at science. Wieman agreed with Barth that most religion is the enemy of truth, that liberal Christianity trusted too much in religion, and that some way of restoring objectivity to theology was necessary. But the Barthians disastrously ignored the only method that gains objective results. "The idea of God which Barth and his followers finally achieve is simply what tradition hands down to them, but which they claim is the direct revelation of God," Wieman observed. "How do they know what is revelation and what is not? How do they know that what they accept as revelation is revelation?" Since they eschewed the only means to real knowledge as inapplicable to Christian truth, the Barthians had no way of knowing what they were talking about. "What they accept as revelation is mere prejudice, unless its truth is sustained by observation and reason," Wieman charged. "The only possible way to achieve a theocentric religion is to relinquish all claim to knowledge of God save that which can be obtained by way of observation and reason."[130]

The Barthians proposed to revive theology by living off the evocative power of Christian symbols. They treated received tradition as revelation, played up the otherworldly and paradoxical aspects of Christianity, and pictured God as personal and transcendent; Wieman countered that all of this was nonsense. The issue of divine personality was crucial to him; it marked a major difference between the critical, modern theocentric religion that he espoused and the various dogmatic and liberal-anthropocentric theologies that he opposed. The claim that God is personal is anthropocentric on its face, he argued. Conservative and liberal Christians alike preached that God must be personal because personality is the highest form of existence that we know and because no communion with God is possible if God is not personal. Most theologians assumed that persons are ontologically real and that the interactions that take place among persons are ontologically abstract. Wieman believed the opposite. With Whitehead he assumed that events are the fundamentally constitutive elements of reality; in the 1930s he pressed hard on the theme that God is not a personality. The latter argument began with an assertion of the inherently social nature of personality. It is only within interactions between individuals that personalities are generated, Wieman observed; personalities develop only to the extent that individuals develop a common body of experience that each of them shares with others. Since personality is absolutely dependent on the relational sharing of experience, and since personality is degraded or otherwise diminished when social interaction is lacking, "it is plain that God cannot be a personality."[131]

A personality can exist only in a society, and no personality can be perfect in an imperfect society. Every personality partakes of not only the good aspects but also the evils of the society to which it belongs; so God must not be personal if God is not to be implicated in evil. Wieman believed that God is an ordered process, a power that brings things to pass. As the ordered process that generates the greatest possible value, God sustains and develops personality, but personality is not the goal or end of this process. God is the means and end of the process, and personality is a necessary means to the actualization of the greatest value, which is God. God is superhuman, Wieman proposed, but not supernatural; God is a present, potent, operative, observable reality, but not a being hypostatized beyond empirical process. More precisely, God is the structure and process that sustains, promotes, and constitutes supreme value in life.[132]

Wieman recognized that to many readers this style of religious thinking was short on inspiring qualities. He counseled that while religion has a place for the glowing words of the language of love, "accurate thinking demands cold, abstract terms." God is not exalted if theologians describe God with evocative weasel words instead of the empirical language of structure and process. Everything intelligible is a structure, and if the God of structure and process awakens no response in the loving heart, "we can only plead that there is a time for love and a time for clear thinking."[133] Elsewhere he affirmed that he was a lover of God who knew the symbols of Christianity as heart knowledge, "but I cannot use them here, because it is disastrous to try to draw logical inferences from a metaphor." Loving symbolization has its place in piety and the rituals of religious ceremony, he argued, but serious religious thinking must be based strictly on sensory observation, experimental behavior, and rational inference. In the modern age God must be conceptualized with adequate concepts if intelligent people are to find their way to houses of worship. Wieman thus wrote apologetics in spite of himself; though he regularly denied any interest in making religion attractive or credible, his writings were pervaded by apologetic concern. "Whether we continue to use the word God is not important; but it is supremely important that we love and adore above all else what is most worthy of such devotion," he exhorted. "That is God." Like everything else in existence, God is a process possessing a distinctive pattern. Put differently, God is the creative interaction among individuals, groups, and ages that "generates and promotes the greatest possible mutuality of good."[134]

Does this mean that God is less than personal? Wieman replied that God is greater than personality, for God is the creative source of mind and personality: "I deny personality to God not by subtraction but by addition." Can people pray to an interaction? Wieman replied that people have done it for centuries, under various concepts of God. Can people love an interaction? Wieman replied that that is precisely what people always love. When one person loves another, he explained, it is the fellowship of the other that is loved. Fellowship is a form of interaction; as the force that generates love, fellowship is the real object of love. "I love humans and hills and trees and houses and landscapes only because they are caught up by this interaction which generates and promotes the rich body of shareable experience," Wieman wrote. Human personalities are socially produced phenomena within events; God is the creative interaction that makes people loving when they are loving. As the growth of meaning and value in the world, God is the actuality that sustains, promotes, and constitutes the supreme good. As such, God is the creative event that, whether named or not, all lovers love above all.[135]

Wieman's religious temperament put him closer to James than Dewey, but he cherished his kinship to Dewey on account of Dewey's stricter empiricism and his interpretation of religion as the actualizing of ideal possibilities. Thus Wieman was anxious to claim Dewey as an ally of his own naturalistic theism. Dewey argued that the search for a single all-inclusive good is doomed to failure; at the same time he espoused a pragmatic concept of God—as the active relation between the ideal and the actual—and described the struggle for continued progress and enlightenment in a vaguely religious way that was congenial to Wieman. Wieman treasured Dewey's statement that "if we could slough off the opinions that have no living relationship to the situations in which we live, the unavowed forces that now work upon us unconsciously but unremittingly, we would have a chance to build minds after their own pattern, and individuals might, in consequence, find themselves in possession of objects to which imagination and emotion would stably attach themselves." To Wieman, this was a deeply religious assertion that reflected his own worldview, Dewey's religious disclaimers notwithstanding. Dewey professed no personal belief in a cosmically real God, but Wieman claimed to formulate the idea of God in a way that made the question of God's existence a dead issue. By his definition, the existence of God was as undeniable as the existence of value and the world; the crucial question was how God should be defined.[136]

Dewey declined his enrollment as a naturalistic theist. He noted that Macintosh and Wieman both departed substantially from traditional Christianity, though Macintosh was at least clear in affirming the being of a God. He doubted that the same could be said of Wieman. From Dewey's perspective, there were two critical problems with the kind of empiricist-claiming liberal theology that Macintosh and Wieman pioneered. The first was that it made universalist claims on provincial grounds; only a modern, Western, liberal Protestant would describe religious "adjustment" in the terms employed by Macintosh and Wieman, he observed; the religious adjustment of a devout Buddhist or Vedantist would yield empirical evidence of a very different kind. The second problem applied especially to Wieman. Wieman charged that Macintosh used God merely as a hypothesis to support and justify human moral idealism; Dewey replied that at least Macintosh used moral idealism as a rational approach to the idea of God's existence. There was at least a kernel of Kantian-like objectivity in this version of moral religion, unlike Wieman's position, which (in Dewey's reading) started with nothing more than the alleged need of human beings for something to love. "Mr. Macintosh wants a cosmic guarantee for our moral idealism and optimism," Dewey remarked. "Mr. Wieman wants an objective counterpart for human love and devotion. Of the two, the latter seems the much more subjective."[137]

Dewey recognized that Wieman made a stronger claim to an objective referent than this. Wieman argued that there is Something objective that generates, supports, and constitutes the good; "God" is this objective Something that we find in our conduct. Dewey replied, "But right here is where the shift in Mr. Wieman's position comes in, a shift between something altogether too universal and inclusive to be identified with any historic religion and conception of God, and something sufficiently exclusive to be linked with, say, some phase of Christian theism." It is one thing to say that people find conditions and forces in existence that sustain the goods of living, Dewey explained; it is quite another thing to claim that these things constitute a single unified object that rightly demands the devotion of all human beings. The first claim is intelligibly empirical, but the second is not. Empirical reason does not find a unified and unifying power that rightfully commands adoration from the fact of human care; there is plenty of evidence for goods, Dewey judged, but no evidence at all for a single universal source of good.[138]

Wieman had to reach beyond empiricism to make the latter claim, and he had to make the latter claim, Dewey believed, because without it his position lacked any vestige of theistic belief. Dewey explained the meaning of Wieman: it was the dilemma of the post-Christian with apologetic concerns who didn't believe in God but who couldn't relinquish the idea of God. The apologetic concerns and the emotional need of God were mutually reinforcing; Wieman tried to buck up his own religion by defending it to others. In a time of transition and disturbance, Dewey reflected, Wieman's apologetic offered a dose of consolation to intelligent modern people who, for personal reasons, could not let go of the word "God." Dewey disclaimed any resolve to take away that consolation. He respected the importance of personal temperament and cultural background; Wieman had a role to play in helping America make the transition to a fully modern, secular, pluralistic democracy. Dewey made clear, however, that the theistic droplet in naturalistic theism was based on emotional needs, not empirical evidence. He did not doubt that Wieman himself was basically a modern person, but he judged that Wieman presented a case of arrested intellectual development, "because in the end he is overmastered by emotional overtones derived from the earlier conception of an exclusive and jealous God."[139]

Dewey's rebuke cut Wieman deeply. He backed off from claiming Dewey as a soul mate, while insisting that his own position drew out the religious implications of Dewey's philosophy. Though Dewey made much of the plurality of meanings and purposes in life, Wieman observed, he did not lack a notion of common value. Dewey had no problems with the language of universality and "unitary object" when he wrote about other subjects. He understood that cultural diversity and unitive value are not necessarily exclusive to each other. Wieman noted that only when Dewey turned to religion did he become an irreducible pluralist. On the subject of value, Dewey espoused exactly the same argument as Wieman: there is such a thing as "greatest value" that lies in whatever unity there is now, or ever can be, among all the conditions, forces, and goods that exist now or in the world's future. This unity requires variety and diversity, and because it is of greatest value, it commands our supreme devotion. Wieman cautioned that he was no pantheist or absolute idealist; he made no claims about the value of the total universe. His claim was the Deweyan contention that our highest devotion is owed to whatever organic unity there is in the universe; his whole argument was grounded in Dewey's except that he explicitly used the language of religion in describing value. For this he drew the scorn of Dewey, who bristled at the prospect of being appropriated by theologians. Dewey had no problem making alliances with religious humanists like Ames, but he drew the line at people who tried to save some semblance of the old God.[140]

Wieman took it personally. "He has almost betrayed the holy cause for which he has given the greater part of his life in devoted service," he charged. Now was no time for the guardians of modern civilization to betray the cause of progress and enlightenment. Whatever future the word "God" may have, Wieman warned, "we cannot without disaster ignore the reality which I am here trying to indicate by means of it." Civilization in 1933 seemed to be disintegrating; Fascism and Communism were ascending; the democracies were reeling from economic turmoil, political crises, and the threat of war. This did not mean that the civilized world had no unitive moral hope, Wieman believed; the hope of saving the world from self-destruction rested precisely on the world's hidden unity of moral value. What was needed to save Western civilization was a full mobilization of right-thinking religious energy. "The present perilous state of our civilization and culture calls for such religious devotion with an urgency that is terrible," Wieman implored. "Our state is perilous because the techniques of efficient doing, which constitute our civilization, have changed and complicated our life so rapidly, that the organizing unity which makes us functional members one of another has not kept up. We must turn with all our powers of devotion and service, sensitivity and intelligence, to this unity in our midst which makes us functional members one of another, and which is capable of growth if we give ourselves to it with sufficient devotion. If we cannot call this functioning unity God, then let us give it another name. But it alone can save us."[141]

The Deweyan pragmatists had the answer, but their secular prejudices kept them from being faithful to it. More than ever, religion was needed in the cause of social progress. Though he insisted that he had no apologetic concerns, Wieman sought to make religion attractive and relevant. He coauthored books on the psychology of religion, American philosophy of religion, and the development of religion, and in 1941 he wrote a Deweyan plea for the renewal of democracy as the answer to the world crisis.[142] Wieman rejected the refrain that the democracies were weak and mortally threatened because they shrank from war in the face of fascist aggression. He countered that they were weak because they allowed their democracy to deteriorate into a cacophony of conflicting interests that lacked any unifying faith or purpose. The democracies were spiraling toward destruction because they lacked "a unifying drive which could mark out a course of action straight and wide and deep, down which the massive might of democratic peoples could pour with purpose clear and sure." They had ample power, "but it was dissipated through channels shallow, crooked, and narrow. Hence their potential might was of no avail. It could not be mobilized and released in action free of inner conflict and cross-purposes. There was blocking within, one interest struggling against another."[143]

Wieman's essential project never changed, though he made various midcourse corrections in pursuing it. Throughout his career he sought to explicate rationally the Something in life that transforms human agents beyond their powers of self-transformation. His question was always, What is the process in life that saves human beings from evil? In his early career he treated mysticism favorably and denigrated social religion; later he downgraded the cognitive value of mystical experience—while still acknowledging a mystical impulse of his own—and developed a stronger social conscience. In his early career he disdained biblical scholarship as antiquarian and history itself as lacking intellectual importance. Wieman never developed any interest in the Bible, and he gave remarkably short shrift to the fact that experience has a history, but his later writings had a stronger sense of the importance of history to religion and its saving process.[144]

Most importantly, in his early career he focused on the nature of the Something that advances and constitutes the supreme good. Though Mathews believed that he and Wieman shared essentially the same project, Wieman judged that Mathews's emphasis on conceptualism was too strong, and in the mid-1930s Wieman vigorously dissuaded Meland from his commitment to an Ames-style conceptualist position. God is an object of immediate experience, Wieman contended, not only conceived by human beings, but also perceived. The view of God as a conceptual symbol does not account for the reality of unities, which are corporate actualities, not simply works of the imagination. The essential work of theology is to discern empirically God's actual creative activity in the world. Collaborating with Wieman as a coauthor in 1936, Meland observed that Wieman's focus on God as a creative factor in the universe helped to explain "the tentative element in Wieman's philosophy. He is committed to no final definition of God, except the minimum statement that God is the supremely worthful for all mankind. Thus his quest for the Supremely Worthful becomes a patient and faithful concern to clarify and enrich its meaning for human devotion."[145]

Wieman's subject was always the growth of meaning in the world; that was his shorthand definition of Supreme Value. His most lucid statement of this project, The Source of Human Good (1946), showed a keener sense of the power of Christian symbols than his earlier works and his later ones. Wieman was not oblivious to the irony of modernist theology, which became the plight of his generation. Having sought to make Christianity relevant to the modern age, the liberal modernizers of his generation became quaint by the time their careers were half-completed. They inherited a theological establishment and lost it; their musty rhetoric of progress and value was no match for Barth and Tillich in the 1940s. Wieman compensated by Christianizing some of his rhetoric in the manner of the liberal social gospel. He made new resort, especially, to the symbols of resurrection and the kingdom of God. The value-increasing growth of meaning that saves the world is an inherently Christian project, he asserted: "The struggle was, and the struggle is, to save man from self-destruction and from internal, disruptive conflict within the individual and within society and, finally, to establish the Kingdom of God. The Kingdom of God is a world so transformed that every part responds with rich delivery of meaning to every other part and supremely to the spirit of man."[146]

The Source of Human Good took a rare, for Wieman, pass at Christology. He described God as the creative matrix and source through which created goods flow; he described Christ as the "creative event" through which the work of salvation was accomplished and remains to be fulfilled: "It was not something Jesus did. It was something that happened when he was present like a catalytic agent. It was as if he was a neutron that started a chain of reaction of creative transformation. Something about this man Jesus broke the atomic exclusiveness of those individuals so that they were deeply and freely receptive and responsive each to the other." The power of creative transformation that is symbolized by the name "Christ" could not have occurred apart from the man Jesus, Wieman affirmed; at the same time, the power was not *in* Jesus: "Rather he was in it. It required many other things besides his own solitary self." The locus of the creative power of Christ was the interactions that the disciples of Jesus had with him and each other. "It transformed their minds, their personalities, their appreciable world, and their community with one another and with all men." This creative power is the source of human good, he affirmed; its most powerful symbols are the death and resurrection of Christ and the kingdom of God.[147]

Wieman described these symbols with an orthodox flourish: "The best in Christianity, put into the form of ancient doctrine, is revelation of God, forgiveness of sin, and salvation of man—these all by way of Jesus Christ." In Christian experience, he reflected, revelation, forgiveness, and salvation blend together into the single complex event of creative transformation. Instead of being dominated by their concern with created goods, transformed people live in the life-giving power of creative good. The saving event of Christ opens the gates of history to the conquering advance of creative good; Wieman called it "the most important happening on this planet since the creation of man."[148]

The Source of Human Good thus contained signs of Wieman's turn to a more gospel-centered liberalism. It was chastening to him that liberals had lost the field to Barth, Tillich, and their kin. He called for a liberal counterattack that employed the symbols of traditional Christianity; at the same time he rationalized that the neo-orthodox ascendancy could be a toxin for theology. In 1947, the year after he left Chicago, Wieman explained that "neo-orthodoxy is a stage through which we had to pass to recover from a situation that might otherwise have been hopeless. It is like the fever of a diseased organism; it is a form of pathology, but if it does not continue too long or go too far it enables the organism to throw off the poison infecting it and thereby return to normal health." Wieman tried to learn what he could from the Barthians and neoliberals, especially Tillich, though he was inclined to lump all of them under the category of antiliberal neo-orthodoxy. He accepted the neo-orthodox judgments that the old liberalism was sentimental, relied on a "promiscuous" appeal to religious experience, and promoted a naive picture of the historical Jesus. He allowed that some of the best theologians of his generation were neo-orthodox. "But the time is shortly coming when we must get rid of it if we can," he exhorted. "A fever may be deadly when it passes beyond the period and intensity of its corrective function."[149]

He seemed to hope that liberalism would make a comeback after World War II. His opening essay in *Religious Liberals Reply* (1947) had the look and feel of a movement primer, like the book as a whole. But the liberals staged no postwar comeback, and Wieman's relation to Christianity drifted into Foster-land. He moved to the outer edge of Christianity for reasons that were implicit in his thinking from the outset. For many years Wieman signaled his willingness to give up the word "God" even as he struggled to win acceptance for his concept of God. In later life he gave up the word, in effect, and his struggle to redefine it. He settled on the conviction that the question of God is unnecessarily distracting to the problem that religion tries to solve. Religion is about ultimate commitment and the ethical imperative of being saved from evil, he argued. Religion does not need "God" to address its problem. Wieman allowed that "God" is relevant to the religious problem if God is conceived as "whatever in truth operates to save man from evil and to the greater good," but this is not how the word is usually employed in religious discussion. The latter fact weighed heavily on him after a long career of attempting to change the ways that modern people think about God. Wieman resigned from Chicago in 1947 in the aftermath of a bruising and messy divorce and finished his teaching career at Southern Illinois University. He also left the Presbyterian church, joined the Unitarians, hedged on his identification with Christianity, and disavowed his longtime preoccupation with signs of divine existence.[150]

With sad disapproval he noted that most Christians and non-Christians alike conceive God as a being. With equal sadness he observed that neo-orthodoxy ruled the field of theology. Wieman perceived and felt his isolation: "I am fully aware that I swim against the current."[151] He lamented that even theologians conceived God according to favored "pictures in the mind."[152] In his view, the essence of neo-orthodoxy was the oxymoron "true myth." The Barthians and Tillichians were sophisticated theologians, he allowed, but their entire enterprise was founded on the impossible notion that certain religious propositions are both mythical and true. They proposed to find cognitive value in the pictorial fictions of myth. Wieman remarked, "They try to use the propositions found in myths to interpret the matters of supreme concern for human living. But a great religious myth, precisely because it is a myth, does not correctly describe the realities by which and for which men may live under its guidance when it is intrinsic to the life of a fellowship and a tradition."[153]

Wieman epitomized the Enlightenment liberal view that Christian teaching cannot be true without being thoroughly demythologized. He allowed that myth can have a religious value, but theologically he was a literalist; myth has no value for thought. Throughout his career he admonished that science is myth-negating and naturalistic; in his later career he downplayed even the importance of believing in a divine presence. Wieman argued that the actual processes of human existence are what matter, not the existence or nature of a divine source. His later writings moved closer to Dewey than those of his Dewey-quoting early career. "I never quite understand what he is saying, but I am generally enthusiastic about it," he confessed of Dewey's work. "I seem always to feel that he is trying to do something that much needs to be done, and his ideas are sufficiently inchoate so that I can almost always make out of them something a little different from what he intended, and nearer to what I think he ought to say." Without lapsing all the way into secular humanism, Wieman moved to a methodological focus on "what operates in human life, and not to a realm beyond human life." His early-career emphasis on the *total* concrete fact gave way to a narrow focus on what can be known in the manner of ordinary experimental science. If God is what God does, Wieman reasoned, and what God does meets the conditions of scientific objectivity, theology is better off focusing on what it knows than upon what is disputed.[154]

This was an argument for a liberal consensus. Wieman believed that the key to the weakness of liberal theology was its lack of agreement "on what is supremely important." Lacking a common sense of purpose and therefore a common commitment, he argued, theological liberalism was bound to lack discipline, power, and persuasiveness.[155] He proposed that the only unity worth having is based on empirically established truths; his own approach to religion offered the unitive and secure foundation that modern theology needed. Wieman knew very well that his role in the field was far from unifying, however, and he tired of defending his right to the Christian name. Contributors to his festschrift raised the issue repeatedly, to which he gave testy, nonanswer replies; he told Randolph Crump Miller that he considered the question to be akin to "children quarreling over who belongs to the most respectable family." Finally, in the volume's closing pages, Wieman stopped ducking the question. The Christian tradition was his chief resource, he acknowledged to Edwin A. Burtt, but he was ambivalent about identifying with it. Culturally and intellectually he considered himself a product of Western Christianity, but "I strongly resent the current practice of appealing to the Christian and Jewish tradition as being the guide of life and identifying this tradition with God rather than seeking what operates in all human life to create, save, and transform."[156] His later writings had a similar problem with God. Speaking of the problem of using the word "God," Wieman observed, "A word becomes very misleading when it has acquired a conventional meaning contrary to what one wishes to discuss."[157]

His later works narrowed to the subject he considered worth discussing. It doesn't really matter whether people believe in the God of creative process or *any* god, Wieman argued; what matters is the reality of creative transformation. Commitment to the supreme good is possible, real, and absolutely needed, whether or not one uses religious language to describe it. At the same time, he maintained, there is such a thing as explicitly religious creative religion. True religion is evidence-supported ultimate commitment; faith is the act of commitment to creative good; revelation is the transforming power that operates in religious fellowship; the world is saved by creative transformation, which was Wieman's stand-in for grace. Notwithstanding his ambiguity about its referent, he continued to affirm the gracious character of creativity. Wieman regarded himself to the end as an opponent of merely idealistic religion. With occasional lapses, he was usually clear in affirming that the world is saved by (God's sovereign) creativity, not by human idealism. He shared with Barth the conviction that idolatry is the defining sin of bad religion and that recognition of the otherness of God is the precondition of nonidolatrous religion. For all that he shared with Ames, he insisted that sin is not merely the impossibility of attaining the highest human ideals and that God is not merely "man lifted to the nth degree of perfection." The spirit of Calvin, highly modernized, reverberated through his writings whenever Wieman warmed to these themes.[158]

WIEMAN AND THE LEGACY OF THEOLOGICAL EMPIRICISM

But what is modernized Calvinism without God? This unpromising question lay behind Wieman's later works. "Increasingly, I am convinced that religious inquiry is misdirected when some presence pervading the total cosmos is sought to solve the religious problem," he declared. "It is even more futile to search for infinite being which transcends the totality of all existence." We have no hope of gaining knowledge of the total cosmos, much less of the infinity that transcends the cosmos: "Consequently, beliefs about these matters are illusions, cherished for their utility in producing desired states of mind." Theology must restrict itself to what can be known scientifically, which is not the universe in its wholeness, but only selected structures in life and the relations between them over which experiential reason holds power. The object of religious inquiry must be "the actual processes of human existence," he insisted, not their hypothesized divine ground. While allowing that creativity may be the manifestation of a transcendent entity, the later Wieman stuck to what can be known, conceiving creativity as the observed character of natural events through time.[159]

Did this verdict not deliver him into the arms of Ames and Dewey? Wieman replied that his project remained essentially unchanged, because it was a theology of creative transformation. Ames-Dewey humanism preached a gospel of self-transformation; people were encouraged to transform themselves by devoting themselves to appropriate ideals. Wieman countered that self-transformation is an illusion: "No man by conscious volition can change the established organization of his personality on those levels which are beyond the reach of his own consciousness. If psychopathology has demonstrated nothing else, it has certainly demonstrated this." People are driven by unconscious propensities that undermine and destroy their own conscious aims. On that basis, Wieman proposed, the proper object of religious inquiry remains the phenomenon of gracelike creative transformation. To be transformed is to be saved from evil and moved toward the good by a creative power that transcends the power of conscious volition. This is what modern theology should study and proclaim, he argued. To call this phenomenon "grace" or attribute it to "God" is to provide no information and solve no problem. What was needed in theology was to attain genuine knowledge about the gracelike power of transformation. How does it operate? Under what conditions does it operate most effectively? A half-century after the death of William James, and forty years after theology succumbed to the toxin of neo-orthodoxy, this remained the agenda of any truly empirical theology.[160]

In Wieman's work the empirical approach to theology was sustained for a generation beyond its demise and received its most rigorous expression. He wanted to be known as the person who showed how to make theology a modern and empirical servant of the Supreme Good, though he did not claim that the good shall triumph. We cannot claim to know that good is stronger than evil or that the ontological status of good is more ultimate than that of evil, he argued, for these claims lack sufficient evidence. But with ample rational warrant, we can commit ourselves to the expansion of the good.[161] In his early career he called this project "theocentric religion," later he called it "creative communication," and in his last years he favored "liberal religion." While defending the integrity of certain forms of God language from Dewey's later criticisms, and while shaking his head at Dewey's signing of the Humanist Manifesto, Wieman minimized his own resort to God language. "The faith of liberal religion reaches beyond all available answers to the actuality operating in human life," he asserted. To Wieman, liberal religion thus defined was the true religion, profoundly at odds with all other world religions. Other religions claim that an individual's essential needs can be satisfied only in a "final state" of atman or nirvana or oneness with God, he observed, but liberal religion counters that salvation is possible for an individual only "in a continuous creativity which reconstructs every state of existence to expand his horizons continuously."[162]

"Expanding horizons" was as poetic an expression as Wieman dared. It stood for the continuous expansion of the range of one's knowledge, control, appreciation of goodness, discernment of evil, self-understanding, and understanding of others. Wieman emphasized that all of these things can be measured; though he modified his concept of sense perception to include things that affect the sensorium, he took pride in the fact that his thinking grew more narrowly empiricist over the course of his long career. But Wieman was never as strictly empiricist as he claimed. His God principle of creative communication was circular and hortatory; it amounted to the claim that expansive communication expands awareness. He hung the weight of his system on this very thin line. Moreover, his theology retained various Whiteheadian concepts under changed names long after he judged that Whiteheadian philosophy lacked a shred of evidence. He retained Whitehead's signature emphasis on the reality of duration and the ultimacy of events, which made even God a structural process, and in the manner of White-head's doctrine of the primordial and consequent natures of God, Wieman distinguished between the structure of creativity (an abstraction) and the creative event as an object of experience. More importantly, his thinking was pervaded by a veiled absolute that caused Ames and Dewey to keep their distance from him. Here the influence of Hocking's religiously tinged idealism was decisive. In the manner of his teacher, Wieman claimed that while evil may be plural, the good is always one. He held out for the metaphysical principle of the singularity of good, notwithstanding empirical evidence that experience knows a plurality of goods and evils.[163]

Wieman exaggerated his liberation from metaphysical reason and his devotion to empirical results; in the name of this exaggeration he adopted a simplistic materialism that eclipsed his early-career emphasis on reality in its totality. His theological successors proved to be more adept at sorting out the relation of metaphysics to empiricism in theology; they also rescued the Chicago school from Wieman's frosty intellectualism. Wieman's legacy was curtailed by his early departure from the Divinity School and the narrow instrumentalism of his position. He retained too much organismic philosophy to satisfy the pragmatists, and he spurned Whitehead too harshly to belong to process theology. He was also too alienated from classical Christianity to be a useful religious thinker to many colleagues in the biblical and historical fields. For years he struggled without success to formulate a concrete concept of the divine creative activity; at the same time he puzzled over his dwindling audience and lack of followers. Upon returning to the Divinity School one fall after summer vacation he was greeted by Christian historian Wilhelm Pauck, who grasped Wieman closely by the shoulder, peered closely into his face, and asked, "Well, Henry, what are you calling it now?"[164]

Liberal theology attained greater help from Whitehead than from Wieman in Wieman's later years. Led by Whiteheadian philosopher Charles Hartshorne and Wieman protégés Bernard M. Loomer, Bernard Meland, and Daniel Day Williams, the Chicago process theologians created an intellectual school that outlasted and outperformed Wieman's version of empirical theology. To most of the process theologians produced by the Chicago school it remained important to affirm that process philosophy is empirical in its focus on the flow of experience within the creative social matrix. In the middle decades of the twentieth century, they kept alive the core elements of old-style theological modernism nearly by themselves. Always they remembered Wieman with personal affection, intellectual appreciation, and a touch of regret at his rationalistic literalism.

Meland regarded Wieman's emphasis on duration as an empirical ground of existence as his greatest contribution to theology; he recalled that when Wieman burst upon the theological scene in the 1920s, he gave the impression of "a theological sport, possibly an oddity, who had broken into the theological conversation." It was Wieman who changed the tenor of Chicago theology during Meland's student years at Chicago. Religious humanists like A. Eustace Hayden and, possibly, Foster had dispensed with God altogether; conceptualists like

Mathews and Ames used "God" analogically as an expression for idealized or personalized conceptions of the universe; Wieman made theological realism respectable again in the eyes of students like Meland and Williams. "To this humanistic faith, Wieman threw down the gauntlet of battle," Williams recalled. "He made the issue sharp, unavoidable, and compelling for us who studied with him in those days." For Ames and Mathews, the issue was to show that Christianity can do more for modern individuals and society than any other view; for Wieman the issue was whether or not God is to be served. While outflanking most of his faculty colleagues as a modernizer, Wieman was also something of a throwback. A generation of Chicago students became theologians in a nearly forgotten sense of the term on the strength of his influence; some were heard to say, "I don't need Barth; Wieman is my Barth."[165]

Even his chief protégés felt keenly his limitations, however. Meland protested that Wieman overdichotomized the self into the religious self that worships God and the academic self that studies God. He argued that Wieman the academic was too confined by his instrumentalism to appreciate or illuminate the object of religious experience. The critique of reason, except by reason itself, had no place in Wieman's theory or method; he lacked any sense or concept of faith as preceding or judging the life of reason. The latter characteristic marked the key difference between Wieman and his main theological successor. Meland felt the deficiency of Wieman's rationalistic empiricism as an account of Christian truth. More explicitly than Meland, Williams judged that Wieman's account of religious knowledge was deficient because his theory of knowledge was inadequate. Having adopted a simplistic positivism in epistemology, he observed, Wieman tried to account for all the cognitive aspects of religious knowledge within the framework of his positivism.[166]

A generation later, three empirical theologians contended that the key to Wieman's theological shortcomings was his ahistoricism. William Dean and Delwin Brown charged that Wieman's claim to the mantle of empiricism was undermined by his disregard for historical concreteness and complexity; a bit closer to Wieman's position, Nancy Frankenberry called for a historically grounded empirical analysis of religious experience that eschewed Wieman's speculations about experiences of "the totality." Dean observed that Wieman's ahistoricism yielded an inadequate anthropology; Frankenberry continued Wieman's focus on religious experience, while correcting his tendency to conceive it as a sui generis phenomenon; Brown argued that even Dean and Frankenberry did not go far enough in historicizing empirical theology. Against Wieman-style empiricism, all of them urged that history is essential to the life and being of human beings, and thus essential for good theology. Because all experience is mediated by language and history, there is no single or general phenomenon called "religious experience." In the spirit of early Chicago sociohistoricism and the commanding language of Gerald Birney Smith, but also in the name of later Chicago process theology, Brown put the implication sharply: "A truly empirical theology must be a sociohistorical theology; it must engage concrete, particular histories." Thus did the protégés of Meland and Loomer try to overcome the sterile feeling and legacy of Chicago's Wieman phase.[167]

Toward a similar end, the theologians of the Chicago school's third generation, especially Williams and Meland, echoed one of the key points made by Yale theologian Robert L. Calhoun in his mid-1930s debate with Wieman. Wieman believed that analogical inferences are too imprecise to qualify as knowledge; he therefore disparaged all analogical reasoning in theology, including the description of God as mind. Calhoun countered that Wieman's theology was distorted and self-contradictory on this account. To speak of God as "mind" is to make a valid analogical inference from the empirical truism that there must be some connection between structure and creative event, Calhoun argued. Some factor must guide the process of life, and there is sound empirical evidence that this factor is purposive. Wieman denied to theology the right of analogical inference, Calhoun observed, yet he employed analogical arguments in making his own claims. Despite his strictures about the limitations of knowledge, he made assertions about total existence on the basis of rather expansive analogical reasoning; moreover, most of his theorizing about interaction was a form of analogical projection based on limited observation. Wieman asserted that because everything that exists is a process and interacts with other things, the terms "process" and "interaction" rightly apply to everything that exists. And how did he come to know about everything that exists? It was certainly not by direct observation, Calhoun remarked: "In such affirmation I must assume, then, that what lies beyond my observation is presumably, in at least certain essential respects, like what I can observe. But this is resort to analogy. And since I can observe at best only an infinitesimal portion of all that has been, is, and will be, any assertion I may make about 'everything that exists' will involve a very bold use of analogy indeed."[168]

Wieman's empirical focus narrowed in the years after his debate with Calhoun, probably not coincidentally, but twenty-five years later Williams pressed Calhoun's critique a step farther. Every meaningful concept of God contains metaphysical presuppositions and hypotheses about God's being, he observed. To speak meaningfully about "God" is to assume something about God's unity and God's relationship to time, space, eternity, and all other beings. Wieman permitted metaphysical language only about claims that can be empirically verified. "But metaphysical structures require something more than scientific empirical validation; they require a method which can deal with the problem of being at the level of utmost generality," Williams objected. The objects of religious concern cannot be caught in the nets of literal tests and propositions. Most of our knowledge across the sciences and humanities falls somewhere between the precisely literal and the merely symbolic. In the case of religion, the primary objects of concern include such metaphysically loaded notions as God, values, and persons. Too much is lost to theology when theologians are restricted to the literalistic mindset of empiricism, Williams judged; the chief casualty is an appropriate concept of divine reality: "When all the metaphysical questions are pushed into the background, then there results something flat and, in the end, superficial about the doctrine of God." Williams admonished Wieman that Whitehead was wiser in recognizing and coping with the inadequacies of language for the expression of experience, especially religious experience. His larger admonition carried beyond Wieman: "Wieman has not taken seriously enough the tradition of Christian thought, in either its theological, biblical, or philosophical aspects."[169]

For the mid-century generation of Chicago empiricists who took Wieman, Ames, Smith, Macintosh, and Mathews seriously, but Whitehead more seriously yet, that was a judgment to ponder. Williams believed that Wieman's constructive position was controlled by a questionable ontology. Process theologian John B. Cobb Jr. concurred that Wieman's position made sense only if one accepted his ontological position that persons are strands within events, that events are the entities fundamentally constitutive of reality, and that persons are separable only by abstraction from events. Christian theology has better ontologies to choose from, Cobb implied. There are philosophies compatible with Christianity that do not commit Christianity to the desultory view that interactions are ontologically real but persons are not. Personalism was a major alternative; Whiteheadian neoclassical metaphysics was another. Both of these religious philosophies did heavy work for liberal theology during its lean years.[170]

5.
The Real Is the Personal
Albert C. Knudson, Francis J. McConnell, Edgar S. Brightman, and the Boston Personalist School

The most coherent school of American liberal theology took its inspiration from the personalistic idealism of a single thinker, Borden Parker Bowne. Not coincidentally, so-called "Boston personalism" acquired school status in the very years that liberal self-confidence began to erode.

Having agreed that credible religious claims cannot be based on external authority, the founders of liberal theology argued variously for ethical conviction, religious experience, and metaphysical reason as the basis of theology. The Kantian school argued that religion has its home in the moral concerns of practical reason; Schleiermacher and his followers urged that precognitive religious experience or intuition is the wellspring of religion; the Hegelian school developed a theology from Hegel's metaphysical philosophy of Absolute Spirit. For over a century liberal theology was usually Kantian or Schleiermacherian or Hegelian, or a blend of Schleiermacher and Hegel (as in German mediating theology), or a blend of Kant, Schleiermacher, and modern historicism (as in the Ritschlian school). For most of the nineteenth century American liberal theology typically appealed to experience or piety, if not to Schleiermacher. In the social gospel era most American progressives took the Ritschlian option, excluding metaphysical reason, or moved through and beyond Ritschlian theology, as in the Chicago school. Though America produced its share of neo-Hegelian philosophers, notably Josiah Royce and W. E. Hocking, the party of Hegel had little theological following in the United States.

The school of personalist idealism centered at Boston University was a synthetic alternative. It affirmed moral intuition *and* religious experience *and* the social gospel *and* metaphysical reason. Hegel was half right, as were Kant, Schleiermacher, Ritschl and the social gospelers. The theological traditions inspired by these thinkers variously affirmed and rejected metaphysical reason; some of them slighted historical consciousness; some of them slighted social ethics. What was needed was a liberal theology that synthesized the best aspects of its rival modern sources. Philosophically and theologically, Borden Parker Bowne showed the way, but even Bowne shortchanged the social meaning of Christianity. His disciples sought to rehabilitate liberal theology along Bowne's distinctively Methodist lines. To them the Ritschlian social gospel was too thin to hold the field, because it banished metaphysical reason. The Chicago school seemed more impoverished to them, while the paradoxical dialectics of a rising American neo-orthodoxy were even worse.

Against these options Bowne's disciples championed his personalistic idealism and added socioethical commitments. They developed a theological school that espoused typical liberal causes and a distinctive metaphysical basis. Persistently the Boston personalists maintained that every theology is only as good as the philosophy behind it. Their philosopher was Boston University idealist Edgar Sheffield Brightman, who studied under Bowne near the end of Bowne's life and earned his doctorate in 1912. Their most prominent link to the church and the social gospel movement was Methodist bishop Francis J. McConnell, who earned his doctorate under Bowne in 1899. Their theologian was Boston University School of Theology dean Albert Cornelius Knudson, who earned his doctorate under Bowne in 1900. Though he came late to his theological calling, it was Knudson, especially, who made Bowne-style personalism a significant theological school.

ALBERT C. KNUDSON:
THE MAKING OF A THEOLOGIAN

Knudson was a product of Midwest Methodist piety and a graduate school conversion. The fourth of nine children, he was born in 1873 in Grandmeadow, Minnesota, where his father Asle was a distinguished and impeccably orthodox Methodist pastor. Both of his parents were immigrants from Norway; their American home life and Asle Knudson's preaching emphasized the centrality of spiritual experience. Knudson later recalled that the sanctificationist Wesleyan piety of his parents was "all very simple, but it was intensely real and vivid." It remained vitally real to him long after he discarded much of his father's theology. "I was allowed to go my own way, and no regret was expressed at my later departure from some of the tenets of the traditional evangelicalism in which I had been brought up," he reflected. "Whatever may have been my father's feelings about the matter, he had an instinctive reverence for the honest convictions of others and was quite willing that I should work out my own intellectual salvation." Like his father, Knudson sustained the belief that good religion is positive, vital, and deeply felt. After several years of struggling to determine what else he believed, he found the answer in Bowne's philosophy classroom.[1]

As an undergraduate at the University of Minnesota Knudson drifted toward the neo-Hegelianism of a favorite teacher, Williston S. Hough, who steered him to Josiah Royce's *The Spirit of Modern Philosophy* and Edward Caird's *The Evolution of Religion*. Knudson felt edified and newly sophisticated upon reading these books. He liked their critiques of commonsense realism and the "new and firm foundation for religion" that he found in them. For a while he regarded himself as a neo-Hegelian—"There seemed to me to be something elevating about it. It lifted one above the sense plane"—but something was missing in the neo-Hegelian religiosity of Royce and Caird. Knudson worried that it was too vague and abstract to provide a basis for one's thinking and belief. A prime example was Caird's conception of a unity implied in subject and object that transcends both subject and object. Caird identified this vague unity with God; Knudson scratched his head: "It left me in a fog, and that was where I found myself at the end of my college course."[2]

Naturalistic materialism was never an option for him; commonsense realism merely scratched the surface; neo-Hegelian idealism seemed edifying but strangely elusive. Philosophically and theologically Knudson was confused. His single certainty was the reality of his personal religious experience: "There I found something of incomparable worth—something that I could preach."[3] On the strength of this conviction he enrolled at the Boston University School of Theology, where he studied Old Testament under Hinkley G. Mitchell, church history under Henry Clay Sheldon, and systematic theology under Olin A. Curtis. Curtis was the faculty's most conservative member; Sheldon was a cautious, theologically moderate, impressively learned scholar; Mitchell was an advocate of the higher-critical approach to scripture. Curtis and Sheldon both began their careers as advocates of a conservative, slightly modernizing "modified orthodoxy," but Curtis moved a bit more in Bowne's direction during the period that Knudson studied under him, and Sheldon moved substantially toward Bowne's position. From Sheldon, Knudson took the assurance that the modern approach to theology does not require a radical break from the past; under Mitchell's influence he converted to the cause of biblical criticism.[4]

Knudson gave his early career to the latter cause, eventually becoming Mitchell's successor at Boston University, but for him the philosophical questions were always deeper and more formative. He finished his seminary program in a state of discontented perplexity; he caught the uncertainty of his theological teachers and longed for a more settled position. He noticed that his teachers looked up to Bowne, even those who disagreed with him. Knudson felt reasonably sure that his moderately liberal theology was right, but what was its philosophical basis? On what basis should he reject naturalism? What was the truth about realism and idealism? "My epistemology and metaphysics were at loose ends," he later recalled. Knudson felt keenly his lack of a philosophical foundation; as a consequence he worried that his theology lacked a stable basis. Thus he spent a year studying philosophy under Borden Parker Bowne.[5]

It was an experience of conversion and fulfillment. Bowne's "magnetic influence" was enthralling to Knudson, who later recalled that to "an almost unprecedented degree he possessed the power of excitation over his students." Edgar S. Brightman later concurred that Bowne's dignified bearing, "his sheer power, his comprehensive grasp of philosophical issues, and his lucid exposition of personalism made him seem almost a superman." Brightman reflected, "Everyone who sat in the classroom where Borden Parker Bowne lectured was conscious of being in the presence of greatness." To Knudson, Bowne was a godsend: "Here at last I found a thinker and a system of thought that matched my own mind. It would be difficult to express the degree of satisfaction that the year brought me. Not only was there the stimulus that came from the keenest, profoundest, and most masterful mind I ever knew, but the content of the teaching met my need as nothing else had done." Knudson found his philosophical foundation: "On the most fundamental questions he expressed himself with a freedom, precision and grace that the present writer has never heard equaled."[6]

Bowne converted his young student to personalist idealism. Knudson's highest compliment for him was "He had a system. . . . He worked out a comprehensive theory of reality and of the intellectual, moral and religious life." In Knudson's rendering, Bowne's system synthesized Descartes, Leibniz, Berkeley, Kant, Hegel, Lotze, and James. Though he sometimes overemphasized Bowne's rationalism at the expense of his Jamesian pragmatist elements, Knudson's rendering of the essential Bowne was exactly right: "First, personality is the key to reality, and second, life is the test of truth."[7] In Bowne's comprehensive theorizing Knudson found the systematic philosophical coherence that he craved. His life turned a corner when he learned to read the history of philosophy in the way that Bowne interpreted it: "What Bowne did for me was first to clarify the field of thought, to mark out its great highways, and to show where each led. Then he laid bare with extraordinary lucidity the grounds of faith, and gave me an insight into the conditions of a sound metaphysic that has guided me in all my subsequent thinking."[8]

For Knudson, the academic year 1896–97 was the year of *Aufklärung*, an illumination: "It brought me a mental relief and an intellectual illumination that may be described as akin to a redemptive experience." Bowne's metaphysical flights were intellectually dazzling, yet his thinking and personality were unfailingly vital and real: "He saw distinctly the true aim of all sound philosophy, and knew with the unerring vision of a seer how best to realize it. To listen to him or to follow him in his books was to see the mists arise from the valleys, and the clouds and the shadows flee away." His influence over Knudson was both intellectual and personal. "It was his whole soul, not merely his intellect, that was a source of light," Knudson later recalled. Bowne lived the truth of personalistic theism as a consuming spiritual passion. Frequently he and Knudson went for long walks through the Fenway in Boston, discussing philosophical problems. Knudson told friends that upon returning from these conversations he often recalled the lines that Wordsworth wrote near Tintern Abbey: "I have felt a presence that disturbs me with the joy of elevated thoughts."[9]

Knudson was the blessed child, for Bowne rarely gave personal time to students. Though riveting in class, he had few words for his students outside class; Brightman heard barely four sentences from him in two years. In the academic year 1897–98 Knudson studied in Germany as a fellow of Boston University. At Jena he studied under Hans Hinrich Wendt, whose two-volume *The Teaching of Jesus* was an influential liberal work. At Berlin he studied under Bernhard Weiss in New Testament, Adolf von Harnack in church history, and Julius Kaftan in systematic theology. Knudson was underwhelmed by the German titans. He appreciated their learning and eminence but found them uninspiring compared to Bowne. While studying in Germany he received a job offer in church history from the Iliff School of Theology, where he taught for two and a half years and married Mathilde Johnson. In 1900 Boston University awarded Knudson a doctorate in philosophy based on his studies with Bowne; the same year he moved to Baker University, where he taught philosophy, biblical studies, church history, sociology, and economics. Bowne quipped that his disciple occupied "not a chair but a whole settee." Two years later Knudson accepted a similar position at Allegheny College in Meadville, Pennsylvania, where he taught for three years while keeping a worried eye on developments at his alma mater.[10]

The School of Theology at Boston University endured its version of the modernist controversy at the turn of the century, where the controversy centered on Hinckley Mitchell. He was a diligent scholar, highly respected by colleagues and students, and a vigorous advocate of the higher-critical approach to Scripture. Knudson revered him. For six years Mitchell struggled to keep his teaching position while fundamentalists claimed that he was theologically unfit to teach at a Methodist seminary. In the prevailing polity of the Methodist Episcopal Church, responsibility for certifying the doctrinal fitness of seminary professors was held by the denomination's Board of Bishops. Mitchell's critics charged that he failed to uphold the authority of the Bible as the word of God; his colleagues, especially Bowne, countered that he was a learned and faithful modern scholar. Mitchell's right to teach was upheld by the School of Theology and by university administrators. In 1905, however, after formal complaints were filed against him, the Board of Bishops refused to confirm his appointment. Some of the bishops acted out of conservative theological conviction; others sought to end a bitter controversy. Together they drove out the school's best Scripture scholar. The Mitchell case eventually struck a blow for academic freedom in the Methodist Episcopal Church, as the church's policy of episcopal confirmation was terminated, but not in time to save Mitchell.

Boston University was forced to look for a successor, one who could carry on Mitchell's scholarly legacy without inflaming his ecclesiastical enemies. Shortly before Knudson was named to the post, Mitchell wrote to him, "The Bishops have put themselves so clearly in the wrong that I am sure they will have to retreat from their position." Knudson wasn't sure what to make of this assertion. Did Mitchell mean that the conservatives were bound to be discredited in the long run? Or was he planning to appeal his firing? Mitchell admitted that it pained him deeply to be dismissed from the School of Theology—"I love the boys." At the same time he informed Knudson that he would not leave the Methodist church "or the boys whom I have helped to train for its service." Not realizing that he was writing to his successor, Mitchell asked Knudson to ask the bishops "whether they really think that one's faith in a universal atonement in Christ depends on the historicity of the first Adam."[11]

Less than three months later Mitchell had occasion to write again to his disciple. With a heavy heart for his beloved teacher, Knudson had accepted the challenge of replacing him. Mitchell's letter was characteristically gracious. "I hasten to congratulate you," he wrote, praising Knudson as "a master of the Bible." He asserted that "I can think of no one whom I would rather see in my place than you." More importantly, he assured Knudson that he would not make life difficult for him. He would speak out against the action of the bishops in deposing him, but he would not ask them to reverse their decision. Now that Knudson had been appointed, the institutional issue was settled: "I hope you will not for a moment think of my retention as possible."[12] With that assurance Knudson welcomed the opportunity to settle into a field of specialization. Assuming the title of Professor of Hebrew and Old Testament Exegesis, he returned to his alma mater in 1906, threw himself into the field of Old Testament studies, and gave fifteen years to this field. As a teacher he was an immediate success; students marveled at his detailed, enthusiastic, masterfully organized lectures. As a teacher and scholar he focused on the problem of how to appropriate the religious values of Scripture to the modern Christian consciousness.

His answer was that Scripture contains the key elements of modern personalist philosophy. Knudson's inaugural lecture as Mitchell's successor declared that the Old Testament is the connecting link between "heathenism" and Christianity, and that Christianity is the consummate religion of rational personality. To study the Old Testament, he asserted, is to trace the process in and beyond Hebrew religion "from superstition to rationality, from sorcery and divination to rational faith, from particularism to universalism, and from nationalism to individualism." The Bible is a narrative of progressive enlightenment; biblical criticism is an indispensable aid to unveiling the Bible's story and message of progress; to affirm the Bible's values of rationality, universality, and personality is to appropriate the biblical witness with the best critical and philosophical tools that we possess. Elsewhere Knudson affirmed evolution and progressive revelation as logically linked truths and he asserted that the Kantian-personalist theory of the activity of mind negates the traditional static view of biblical authority.[13]

In addition to his inaugural lecture, which was published as a book in 1908, Knudson wrote three books in scriptural studies. He made no bid for the attention of biblical scholars. His training in Old Testament was late and rushed; he had a movement sense of his scholarly role; and he taught Scripture from a theological-philosophical standpoint. Mitchell's teaching emphasized historio-critical issues and the finer points of Hebrew; Knudson's teaching emphasized his reading of the moral and religious meaning of Scripture. On that count Knudson's teaching was more interesting to students and less threatening to conservatives. His early books were pitched to pastors and religiously literate laypeople.

In *The Beacon Lights of Prophecy* (1914), Knudson explicated the religious teaching of Amos, Hosea, Isaiah, Jeremiah, Ezekiel, and Deutero-Isaiah with a very light pass at critical issues in the field, though he did maintain, against a dominant liberal trend, that the preexilic prophets were heralds of the coming kingdom of God. The prophets were not merely preachers of repentance, he argued; eschatological consciousness in Israel preceded the age of literary prophecy. Knudson's next book, *The Religious Teaching of the Old Testament* (1918), expanded his topical method of exposition to the entire Old Testament, introducing pastors and laypeople to the doctrinal content of Hebrew religion from a modern standpoint. He accepted the main outlines of the Graf-Wellhausen documentary hypothesis while taking a case-by-case approach to biblical miracles and predictive prophecy. His last book in this series, *The Prophetic Movement in Israel* (1921), returned to his favorite portion of the Old Testament, this time in the form of a Sunday school textbook. The prophetic movement in ancient Israel was predominantly national, not personal, he cautioned; the prophets addressed the Hebrew nation and took for granted that the individual is subordinate to the family, the tribe, and the nation—"It is so with all primitive peoples." At the same time Knudson played up the accents of personal religious experience in Ezekiel, Jeremiah, and Job, especially Jeremiah: "He was the human agent through whom the divine Spirit first revealed the innermost truth and highest form of religious experience."[14]

Knudson tried to give himself to the field in which fate had cast him. Four years after he embarked on his career in Old Testament studies, he gained a sabbatical leave in Berlin to deepen his knowledge of the field. At a farewell party his friends toasted him with compliments; Bowne topped the occasion by declaring that Knudson was at least the equal of any student he had ever taught. Boston Schoolers later remembered the occasion as the passing of a torch. Four days after Knudson's friends bade him farewell, in April 1910, Bowne suffered a stroke in class and died. Knudson received the news in Paris. In a public tribute he mourned, "Boston University—how is she bereft! Her chief light is gone out. . . . I cannot adequately express my sense of personal loss." He declared that it was Bowne, and Bowne alone among philosophers, who met the deepest needs of his time: "And because those needs in their essential nature are not ephemeral, but permanent and to some degree universal, his light is, to my mind, destined to be that which shineth more and more."[15]

The following year Knudson returned from his sabbatical at the same time that Lemuel H. Murlin became the new president of Boston University. Murlin had hired Knudson during his presidency at Baker University; now he urged Knudson to succeed Bowne as Professor of Philosophy. McConnell had already declined to be considered for the post, and Knudson told a colleague, historical theologian George Croft Cell, that the opportunity to become a philosopher had passed him by; he was too old to return to philosophy. To Murlin he pleaded that his years of making himself competent in the field of Old Testament were just beginning to bear fruit; he had to make something of the years that he invested in this field. At the same time Knudson reached an agreement with Murlin that he would succeed Henry Sheldon as Professor of Systematic Theology when Sheldon retired, which would allow several years of preparation.[16]

In 1913 he began to prepare for this transition by teaching a course on "Theological Aspects of Philosophy." Another eight years passed before his theological career could begin. Sheldon taught theology at Boston University until 1921, when Knudson finally became the School of Theology's systematic theologian. Later he regretted that it took so long. "In my student days I formed the purpose of rethinking Christian theology in the light of the philosophy that I had found so significant in my own thought life, and to this purpose I wish I might have devoted myself from the start," he admitted. As a consequence, the school of Bowne was slow to develop. In his lifetime Bowne transformed Boston University, had a large impact on American Methodism, and was easily the major American Christian thinker of his generation, with a significant ecumenical following. Explicitly personalist arguments were commonplace in the decades that preceded and followed Bowne's death. Henry Churchill King and Boston Congregationalist pastor George A. Gordon wrote popular books that described personality as the key to reality and the Christian worldview. Pacific School of Religion religious philosopher John Wright Buckham, a protégé of Gordon's, taught that personality is the fundamental metaphysical reality and that Christianity is founded on the reality of the Supreme Person (God), the developing person ("Man"), and the ideal divine-human person (Jesus Christ). In 1915, Bowne disciple Ralph Tyler Flewelling made a case for the historic importance of Bowne's personalist idealism in relation to other philosophical systems.[17]

But it was only in the 1920s, after Knudson became a theologian, that personalist idealism became a significant theological school and movement. Fortunately his Methodist colleagues laid some of the school's groundwork before he turned to theology, and more fortunately still, they did so as proponents of a thriving social gospel movement.

THE RELIGION OF PERSONALITY:
FRANCIS J. MCCONNELL

The social gospel movement was launched in the late nineteenth century by Congregationalists, Baptists, and Episcopalians, but at the turn of the twentieth century liberal Methodists converted to it, and quickly became the movement's leading denominational force. In 1907, Methodist pastor Harry F. Ward cofounded the Methodist Federation for Social Service, and, the same year, coauthored the famous "Social Creed of the Churches," which was adopted by three Methodist denominations and the newly formed Federal Council of Churches. One of his chief social gospel comrades was Methodist religious educator George Albert Coe, an alumnus of the Boston University School of Theology, who applied Bowne's personalist idealism to the new field of religious education and espoused a socialist-leaning politics that, like Ward's, later drifted to the left. A third Methodist social gospeler, theologian Harris Franklin Rall, earned his doctorate at Halle in 1899 and played an active role in the Methodist Federation for Social Service, which Ward served as executive secretary.

The Methodist social gospelers looked to their movement, not to Bowne, for guidance on social ethics. Bowne was a strong advocate of women's rights, but otherwise his social conscience was sporadic, generally conservative, and subordinate to his individualism. He insisted that groups and institutions consist of nothing but the individuals that compose them, and he could be rough on the downtrodden. Francis McConnell later recalled that Bowne sometimes expressed contempt for the "weak brothers" who impeded humanity's cultural and material progress. "When this happens," Bowne would say, "somebody must step out and knock the weak brother down, to let the human procession move on."

For Coe and McConnell, who embraced Bowne's personalist idealism, this aspect of Bowne's thinking was troublesome; for all of the Methodist social gospelers it was ethically a non-starter. Ward's early books campaigned for progressive social and economic policies; gradually he became a socialist; by the early 1930s he was a militant socialist; and by the late 1930s he was a dogmatic apologist for Soviet Communism. One of his last books was a fellow-travelling embarrassment titled *The Soviet Spirit* (1944). Coe's politics took a similar trajectory, to a lesser extreme, and like Ward, he wielded significant influence in American Protestantism. In 1902 his book *The Religion of a Mature Mind* proclaimed the doctrine of "salvation by education"; the following year, Coe joined John Dewey, William Rainey Harper, and Luther Weigle in founding the Religious Education Assocation; a year later, Coe published *Education in Religion and Morals,* which explicated his (and Dewey's) commitments to science, social reform, practical education, and humanistic religion. Under Coe's influence especially, the Religious Education Association propagated the values of the social gospel in the Protestant churches long after the social gospel movement went into decline. Rall's influence was more conventionally theological, and less bound up with extra-academic institutions. His books promoted a Ritschlian liberalism that was politically milder and theologically closer to the Methodist mainstream than the social gospel radicalisms of Ward and Coe, and which, aside from its non-personalism, was close to McConnell's perspective.[18]

Thus, the Boston school personalist developed their social ethic amidst plenty of Methodist social gospel company. Ward began his teaching career at Boston University School of Theology, and taught social ethics at Union Theological

Seminary from 1918 to 1941; Coe taught at Northwestern University for fifteen years, founded the department of Religious Education and Psychology at Union Theological Seminary in 1909, and resigned from Union in 1922 as a protest against the seminary's refusal to give tenure to his colleague Hugh Hartshorne. He spent the remainder of his academic career at Teachers College, Columbia University. Rall served as professor and president at Iliff School of Theology from 1910 to 1915, and taught theology at Garrett Biblical Institute for twenty-five years. His chief legacy was to stand for the possibility of a liberal, social gospel Methodism that was not rooted in Bowne's personalist idealism. This was an estimable project. The Methodist liberal tradition was stronger for the fact that Rall studied under German Ritschlians, especially Julius Kaftan and Adolf von Harnack, not under Bowne. Liberal Methodism was stronger for not being completely identified with the theorizing of a single school and founder, but for the most part, it was so identified, and the exemplar of Methodist social Christianity was Francis McConnell.

He was the son of a studious, progressive-leaning Methodist minister father and a studious, intensely devout, strong-willed Methodist mother. His father, I. H. McConnell, diligently studied the sermons of Horace Bushnell, Phillips Brooks, and James Martineau, and whenever possible he traveled to hear Henry Ward Beecher. I. H. McConnell conducted lengthy revivals while regretting that American Protestantism was dependent on revivals; his preaching focused on individual morality and salvation, sometimes with a strong word against racial injustice or demon rum. His wife, Nancy J. McConnell, was an old-style Wesleyan sanctificationist who spoke of "heart purity" as the Christian ideal; for reading fare she preferred the mystical writings of Madame Guyon and Fénelon. Francis McConnell was born in 1871 on his maternal grandfather's Ohio farm, shortly before his father was ordained to the ministry. At the age of nine he made his profession of faith with no special urging from his parents. Every Sunday morning after the sermon his father issued a low-keyed altar call; one Sunday young Francis walked forward to the altar rail and shook hands with his father. "That was all there was to it, as far as ceremony was concerned," he later recalled. "When we returned to the parsonage after the service, both Mother and Father told me they were glad for what I had done."[19]

McConnell grew up in a series of Ohio Methodist parsonages; during his father's seventeen years of ministry the family moved nine times, their longest stint in any parish three years. As a youth in the county-seat towns of northern Ohio, McConnell knew many Civil War veterans who regaled him with war stories. Years later, when the family moved to a parish in Indiana, he was stunned to discover the existence of Northerners who still resented Abraham Lincoln and the Emancipation Proclamation. In later life McConnell atttributed his social conscience to his father's abolitionist and temperance politics. At the age of seventeen he lost his father to a sudden attack of appendicitis; I. H. McConnell was forty-three. Returning to Ohio, Nancy McConnell put three sons through Ohio Wesleyan University and into the Methodist ministry; Francis, the first, graduated from Ohio Wesleyan in 1894 and enrolled at Boston University the following autumn.

In 1897 McConnell married Eva Thomas, received his S.T.B. degree, and was ordained to the ministry; two years later he completed his Ph.D. under Bowne. As a seminarian he admired Henry Sheldon and Hinckley Mitchell, who brought his inherited evangelical progressivism up to date. As a graduate student he benefited from Bowne's judgment that a pastor can make use of only so much philosophy. When he asked McConnell if he planned to become a professional philosopher or a pastor, Bowne advised his student not to sharpen his philosophical sword any further. Too much philosophy can ruin a pastor, he cautioned; moreover, McConnell still had crucial educational gaps to fill, especially in economics and political theory. At Bowne's urging McConnell wrote his doctoral dissertation on the experientialist theory of knowledge of an obscure philosopher, Shadworth Hodgson; otherwise he concentrated on economics and political theory. His acquired knowledge of social science served him well when he set out to make Bowne's philosophy make sense to churchpeople.[20]

McConnell gave eight years to parish ministry, pastoring congregations in Ipswich, Massachusetts, and Brooklyn, New York, then accepted the presidency of DePauw University in 1908; his books started flowing before he entered academe. In *The Diviner Immanence* (1906) he observed that the most absorbing theme in contemporary theology was the idea of divine immanence. McConnell affirmed the modern emphasis on God's nearness. "There is and can be no place for mere stuff in the universe," he asserted. Bowne taught that time and space are only phenomenally real, not metaphysically real; McConnell reasoned that because space and time are merely forms of the mind's knowing, with no substantial reality in themselves, it followed that "we are not far from the Creative Mind either in space or in time." He worried, however, that modern theologians often confused two kinds of immanence in explicating the theme of the divine nearness, and thereby made modern theology vulnerable to the charge of pantheism, a charge that McConnell was anxious to refute. He told Knudson that "some kind of antidote is needed to the vast amount of nonsense which is being uttered today about the immanence of God."[21]

The kind of nearness that has to do with physical contact or physical communication is the province of science and philosophy, he proposed, but there is also such a thing as spiritual nearness. Good theology has to be intimately related to science and philosophy, for the findings of science and philosophy concerning the lower forms of nearness are critically determinative for theology. McConnell's prime example was Darwinism; good theological thinking after Darwin was necessarily very different from the best theological thinking that preceded Darwinism. But theology has its own ultimate object in a higher form of nearness, he argued, which is the immanence of soul. To McConnell, spiritual nearness was "the nearness of mutual understanding, of reciprocal interest, of sympathetic cooperation, of shared burden-bearing, of fellow-feeling, of good comradeship." *The Diviner Immanence* proposed that "in the spirit which vital Christianity breathes, we have given us a diviner nearness, a deeper immanence, than merely scientific and philosophical labor can establish, though the lower nearness may be gloriously preparatory and introductory to the higher."[22]

The Victorian devotion to the religion of higher things remained firmly in place for Bowne's disciples. McConnell gave several pages to the vicious, predatory side of nature, but this theme strengthened his insistence that the lower forms of immanence are not enough. We know God not merely through God's creation, but as ethical Redeemer and loving Spirit. The prominence of neo-Hegelian idealism in turn-of-the-century Anglo-American and Continental philosophy strengthened his conviction that Christian theology should tie itself to Bowne's personalistic idealism. "Nature is not stuff but thought," he explained; rightly understood, nature is nothing of itself; nature has no more capacity to stand on its own than thought has any capacity to exist apart from a thinker. God doesn't have to break through anything to get to us, for God is the Mind behind all reality and the spiritual source of our spirits. McConnell urged that this idealistic standpoint offered a winning strategy for modern theology: "In this conception we are steeped by the abundance of present preaching and in the abundance we rightfully rejoice."[23]

The Diviner Immanence popularized several of Bowne's favorite themes. If metaphysical idealism is correct in holding that the material world is the immediate expression of God's thought and will, McConnell argued, and if space is simply the form under which the will of God works, then idealistically based theologies provide for greater space in reality, not less. Just as a novelist might imagine six different story worlds, so can God; the difference is that God is the spiritual power who can will such imaginings into actual expression. When God energizes God's mental creations into reality, there is no reason why these different world systems cannot jostle and collide with each other: "Philosophical idealism bids us clear ourselves of the prejudice that there must be a self-existent, independent space in which this would take place." With a gentler touch than his teacher, McConnell assured that Christianity is superior to other religions as a bearer of God's truth; with Bowne's logic and moral feeling he asserted that other religions surely reflect the divine light to various lesser degrees. "The higher nearness can come about only as we get entirely away from all suggestion of patronizing the believer in another religion, and from all hostile spirit toward his religion," he counseled. "We must be willing to concede the degree of truth in pagan belief, and from the similarities of paganism and Christianity to build a bridge for closer approach."[24]

McConnell allowed that from the standpoint of historical criticism, the Synoptic Gospels are more valuable than the Gospel of John. The fourth Gospel is late in its composition and highly interpretive in its theologizing. But historical criticism is a product of lower-immanence thinking, he cautioned. It is necessary to theology, but it belongs to a lower realm than the realm of spiritual communication. From the higher-immanence standpoint, the Gospel of John is higher than historical criticism and higher than the Synoptic Gospels, for it communicates the

Spirit of Christ. The actual subject matter of the Gospel is the spirit or mind of Christ, not the historicity of the Gospel events. It followed that the church's highest authority is the authority of its spiritual influence, not its possession of any ostensibly infallible power or text: "The day is gone when the Church can ask to be obeyed because of the infallibility of Popes, or Councils, or because of the possession of an inerrant guide of any kind. The day is just dawning, however, when the Church, by giving herself to the development of the highest spiritual and ethical life, can win for herself in all relationships to the world such queenly power over the wills of men as she has never before known." *The Diviner Immanence* was short on social gospel arguments, but McConnell assured that he believed the gospel is necessarily social. The spiritual power that the modern world needs is "the spirit of holy love," he declared. In the spirit of a God who holds near to all people, including those who spurn God's grace, the church is called to express God's Spirit-to-spirit care for all the world's souls.[25]

This rendering of the progressive gospel gained a hearing in the Methodist Episcopal Church at the height of the social gospel ascendancy. In 1908 McConnell was called to the presidency of DePauw University, a Methodist insitution in Greencastle, Indiana, formerly named Indiana Asbury University. For four years he cultivated DePauw's connections to Indiana towns, expanded the university's faculty, wrote a weekly column for the *Sunday School Journal,* and urged audiences that the demand for absolute certainty in religion is not a religious motive. "Religion is preeminently a matter of life, and in life absolute infallibility plays small part," he urged. In 1912 the General Conference of the Methodist Episcopal Church, meeting in Minneapolis, elected McConnell, then forty years old, to the episcopacy on its twenty-first ballot. Though his ecclesiastical assignment took him further away from Boston—McConnell first assumed responsibility for Colorado, Wyoming, Utah, New Mexico, and Mexico—the personalist school gained much from his subsequent writings and public prominence.[26]

THE RELIGION OF PERSONALITY: EDGAR S. BRIGHTMAN

Edgar S. Brightman was closer to the mold of his teacher. Brilliant, deeply pious, and thoroughly academic, he surpassed even Bowne in his reverence for logic, and he gave more time to students. Born in 1884 in Holbrook, Massachusetts, where his father was a Methodist pastor, Brightman later described his father as a warm-hearted personality and a theological conservative whose ethical conception of the fatherhood of God "preserved him from practical illiberalism." His mother was the family's deep thinker, a fact that undoubtedly influenced his pioneering support for female doctoral students. "My mother, who was highly endowed, read the best books, and started teaching me French and botany at an early age." Brightman disappointed neither of his parents. As a youth he devoured Bible commentaries, works on ancient history, and realistic novels, especially Dickens. He wrote poetry and took long walks on the seashore, indulging a mild romanticist countercurrent to his rationalism. Theologically he grew up very conservative, insisting that Darwinism must be wrong. Brightman later recalled that "somehow I gradually outgrew that stage without any perceptible crisis or violent wrench with the past." He became a former theological conservative, but never a former Methodist.[27]

Educated at Brown University, where he received "as good an education as America afforded at that time," Brightman concentrated on philosophy, Greek, the theory of evolution, and Robert Browning's poetry, in that order. His philosophical mentor at Brown, Alexander Meiklehohn, instilled in him a devotion to logic and classical learning. As a college student he mastered Greek, Latin, German, and French, giving special attention to Plato, Homer, the New Testament, Epictetus, Kant, and Schopenhauer. His thinking was shaped by Kant and Schopenhauer until he read Josiah Royce, who turned him into a neo-Hegelian idealist for three years; Brightman's neo-Hegelian phase ended during his graduate school days at Brown, when William James's *Pragmatism* swept him away. But James was not the answer, either; shortly before Brightman completed his master's degree in philosophy, in 1908, he discovered that a proposition can be perfectly useful and perfectly wrong. He dropped pragmatism and enrolled at Boston University School of Theology; though he was officially a Bachelor of Divinity student, he found his reward in Bowne's philosophy classroom.[28]

Brightman got to Boston just in time to find his master thinker. Enthralled by Bowne's scintillating performances and convinced by his arguments, he later reflected, "My studies in Boston University under Bowne gave me a personalism which seemed to me to combine the truth that there was in Royce and James with a criticism of the errors of each." After Bowne's death in 1910 Brightman spent two years as a Jacob Sleeper Fellow in Germany. At Berlin he studied church history under Harnack, whom he greatly admired; at Marburg he studied under New Testament scholar Adolf Jülicher, neo-Kantian philosopher Paul Natorp, and Ritschlian theologian Wilhelm Herrmann. He forged a close friendship with the kindly Herrmann, who inquired about Bowne's philosophy and helped Brightman work out the argument of his dissertation on Ritschl's theory of religious knowledge. In 1912 Brightman completed his dissertation; in his conclusion he called for a theory of religious knowledge that corrected Ritschl's empiricism "by a personalism (of Professor Bowne's type) that recognizes the unity of the subject, and looks on the harmonious, consistent realization of the total personal life as the ultimate criterion of truth." Bowne's late-life acquaintance with Brightman was formative both for Brightman's intellectual career and for Bowne's intellectual legacy.[29]

Partly on the strength of Knudson's recommendation, Brightman landed his first academic position at Nebraska Wesleyan University, where for three years he taught an exhausting schedule of courses in psychology, philosophy, and Bible. In 1915 he joined the faculty of Wesleyan University, where he taught ethics and religion for four years and also became a popular lay preacher. In 1919, with another assist from Knudson, he returned to Boston University as professor of philosophy in the graduate school. For many years he was the only professor whose primary affiliation at the university was in the graduate school, though Brightman also taught at the College of Liberal Arts and the School of Theology. In 1925 he was named to the newly established Borden Parker Bowne Professorship of Philosophy.

Early in his Boston career he sought to make sense of the puzzling fact that Bowne-style personalism had little following in American philosophy or theology. In his time, Brightman observed, Bowne was a major figure who achieved "a position of unique prominence." Universally he was regarded as the most brilliant American Christian thinker of his generation; many also found him the most inspiring. "To anyone who has ever come into contact with Borden Parker Bowne, a reference to the unpopularity of personalism sounds strange and unreal," Brightman remarked. "For Bowne was one of those optimistic natures that carry with them an air of victory, a triumphant and infectious faith. They make their convictions popular." So why, Brightman asked, did Bowne's thinking have so little influence in the academy or the church less than a decade after his death?[30]

Brightman cautioned that appearances were somewhat deceiving, for contemporary theology and philosophy were deeply indebted to Bowne. In the 1870s the dominant currents of thought were the sensationalist empiricism of John Stuart Mill, the impersonal evolutionism of Herbert Spencer, and the impersonal absolute idealisms of various neo-Hegelians. All these philosophies rejected personal theism, Brightman recalled, but Bowne subjected each of them to withering criticism and made personal theism respectable again as a philosophical option. Moreover, contemporary philosophy was not lacking in theistic personalists more or less of Bowne's type. Among English philosophers, Brightman cited James Ward, W. R. Sorley, Hastings Rashdall, James Lindsay, and A. S. Pringle-Pattison; in Germany, Ernst Troeltsch and William Stern were theistic personalists; in the United States, Bowne's former students kept the personalist faith alive, as did idealist philosophers W. E. Hocking and Mary Whiton Calkins. Brightman overlooked University of California philosopher George Holmes Howison, who developed a teleological form of personalist philosophy in the early years of the twentieth century and was the first to claim the name "personal idealism" for his system. Brightman also refrained from naming Bowne's philosophical disciples, who included George Albert Coe (Teachers College), L. R. Eckardt (DePauw University), Ralph Tyler Flewelling (University of Southern California), H. C. Sanborn (Vanderbilt University), and G. A. Wilson (Syracuse University).[31]

Philosophically, personalism is the theory that personality is the primary metaphysical reality. Writing in the *Methodist Review,* Brightman defined the personalist doctrine religiously as "the thesis that the universe is a society of persons under the leadership of a Supreme Creative Person who gives meaning and immanent cooperation to all that is finite." The personalist option was alive in philosophy,

Brightman observed in 1921, but not thriving. He did not believe that World War I played much of a role in deflating the fortunes of personalist philosophy after Bowne's death. An intellectual to the core, Brightman, though allowing that temperamental and social factors were at work, emphasized the philosophical factors. The main problem was that personalism was being crowded out by competing worldviews, among them the Ritschlian pragmatism of the social gospel, which took no interest in metaphysical debates. The social gospelers called for a better social order, not a better philosophy. "Thus does their half-truth become the enemy of the truth," Brightman judged. "For much as we need a new social order, we need God more; if not, let us cease at once all talk of religion."[32]

Modern Christianity needed the social gospel, but it also needed to make God intelligible and credible, a job for the best religious philosophy Christianity could find. In an age seduced by bad worldviews, Brightman argued, modern Christianity needed to critique the reigning philosophies and provide an alternative. His list of regnant bad worldviews included the materialistic antipersonalisms of various modern atheisms, positivisms, and realisms. Another option was impersonal idealism, which often embraced the personalist insistence on the objectivity of value but rejected the personalist insistence on the metaphysical centrality of personality. Another group of thinkers made room for personal theism, but not on personalist grounds; Brightman had the Macintosh realists foremost in mind. He shook his head at the rise of a new realist school of theology; it was inevitable that some religious thinkers would try to buy off the zeitgeist by claiming that theology was an empirical science, but he would have saved them the trouble.[33]

The way forward in religious thinking was forthrightly to oppose all forms of positivist and empiricist materialism and all varieties of way-station idealism that failed to uphold personality as the really real. Brightman exhorted, "Personalistic philosophers should not allow themselves to be deterred by the social situation from expressing their position." He made a pitch for "productivity of philosophical scholarship," which was partly a self-exhortation. Brightman and most of Bowne's other disciples, by publishing very little thus far, were failing to keep personalistic idealism alive. The Borden Parker Bowne Professor urged that more philosophy in Bowne's style needed to be written and that pastors needed to read more philosophy in general, especially of Bowne's type. "The clergy should read more philosophy, and, if the suggestion be not too bold, come to think more philosophically," he declared. "This will result in more theological preaching, more interpretation of the fundamentals of religion in terms intelligible and helpful to our age." In the 1920s the Bownean personalists took this exhortation to heart.[34]

Brightman took for granted that Bowne deserved a school, though he was mindful of the problems of schools. Writing to personalist philosophers, he counseled that "we may as well frankly face the fact that the great work of Bowne is at once an inspiration and a problem." Bowne made permanent contributions to philosophy, Brightman believed, and he made them with inspiring conviction, but his prestige among many philosophers was "not great," and if his disciples were to extend his legacy "we must speak a language that they can understand and listen to with respect." Brightman steeled himself for the taunt of being a mere follower: "Anyone who is the follower of a master or of a tradition in philosophy will be conscious of the multitudes wagging their heads and crying, 'epigone, epigone.'" He replied that schools are the vehicles of progress in philosophy: "How can one survey the history [of philosophy] without seeing that it is no record of the individual insights of unique individuals, but the cooperative labor of free men not too free to learn from others?"[35]

The personalist school of Bowne, still struggling for birth, needed to be wary of the problems of schools, but it had perfect right "to be loyal to its own insights, to acknowledge, with pride and gratitude, its debt to Bowne, in short, to be a school." Brightman elaborated, "I do not see that we need apologize for having convictions, or for believing that Bowne's fundamental insights are a permanent contribution to philosophical opinion, related as they are to Berkeley and Leibniz, Kant and Lotze." While cautioning that "Bowne must not be erected into the St. Thomas of Methodism," he called for a self-conscious school of Bowne-style personalism that sustained an "open-minded temper" and that approached the problems of philosophy in new ways. "The relations of personalism to all contemporary movements of thought and life must be investigated, and vigorous polemic against all forms of impersonalism continued as need arises."[36] Brightman sought new personalist thinking on logic, epistemology, psychology, value theory, and the problems of society. He wanted personalists to emphasize the logical and epistemological "backbone" of philosophy, and, with a worried glance at Whitehead and Alexander, he urged his colleagues to avoid "the organic theory of internal relations advocated by speculative philosophers." Moreover, all social issues are germane to personalism, he believed: "For personalism, the whole problem of reality is a social problem; and every conflict in human relations involves our relations to that 'great *socius*' whom religion calls God." Any worthy notion of what society should be like "must be affected both by our theory of value and by our metaphysics, and hence, manifestly, by our religion."[37]

Brightman had reasons to be optimistic. Without citing what they were, he told readers of the *Methodist Review* that there were "numerous encouraging signs, which lead us to expect a renaissance of personalistic philosophy in the coming years." His own academic appointment was one of them, along with the books that he planned to write; Brightman poured out four books in the mid-1920s. From the beginning he attracted able students, notably Georgia Harkness. In 1922 he told Harkness that his introduction to philosophy course had an enrollment of 125 students, his ethics course had seventy-two students, his child was a year old, and he had lost his maid: "Take it all in all, I am busy."[38] Another sign of a personalist renewal was the recent establishment of a quarterly journal, *The Personalist*, in 1922, which published Brightman's calls for a movement-conscious personalist school. Founded and edited by Bowne disciple Ralph Tyler Flewelling, who anchored a network of personalist thinkers in California that included George Holmes Howison and John Wright Buckham, *The Personalist* featured sophisticated philosophical articles and a warm Methodist spirit. Flewelling called Bowne "our master," his editorial column was addressed "To the Gentle Personalist," and he offered the following creed for the journal and movement: "I believe in personality as the power of self-consciousness and self-direction. I believe in personality as the World-ground, the ever-creative source of all things, immanent yet transcendent. I believe in personality as the fundamental reality of life, man's highest possession, the source of all creativity, the perfect realization of which is his supreme goal. I believe that human personality is fully realized only as it comprehends and gives itself to the will of the Infinite Personality, or God, 'in whom we live, and move, and have our being.'"[39] Early contributors to the journal included John Wright Buckham, Frank Wilbur Collier, James Main Dixon, J. E. Turner, Virginia Taylor McCormick, Knudson, and Brightman; for fifty-nine years *The Personalist* kept Bowne-style personalism alive as a philosophical and religious option.[40]

Another sign was McConnell's rising eminence as a church leader and popular Christian writer. As a church leader he played active leadership roles in the Federal Council of Churches, the Methodist Federation for Social Service, the Methodist Board of Missions, and the Interchurch World Movement. For six years he presided over Methodist conferences in Mexico and subsequently toured extensively in China and India; during his many years in New York he chaired, for fifteen years, the Old Age Pension Association of New York/Social Security Association of New York, working closely with Governor Franklin D. Roosevelt to obtain pension legislation; in 1919 he led a church committee that investigated the national steel strike of that year; by 1929, when McConnell was president of the Federal Council of Churches, he was introduced by Rabbi Stephen S. Wise to former Democratic presidential candidate Al Smith as "the Protestant pope."[41]

Meanwhile, McConnell published a stream of books that reached a broad audience on theological and social topics. *The Increase of Faith* (1912) made a case for the compatibility of modernity and the Christian spirit, assuring that "there is nothing in the scientific spirit prohibitive of theistic or Christian belief."[42] *The Essentials of Methodism* (1916) interpreted Methodism as a religion that emphasizes conversion, entire sanctification, the witness of the Spirit, and the kingdom-building social mission of the church. "Religion has its deepest seat in the settled purpose to do right," McConnell urged.[43] *Understanding the Scriptures* (1917) thematized the Bible as the book of life, humanity, God, Christ, and the cross. Commenting on the recent scholarly emphasis on the apocalyptic consciousness of Jesus and the early church, McConnell argued that apocalyptic was the unavoidable cultural form of Jesus' teaching, not its content: "Jesus could not have lived when he did without making apocalyptic terms the vehicle for his doctrines. We have come to see that the manner of the coming of the kingdom of Jesus is not so important as the character of that kingdom."[44] *Democratic Christianity* (1919) linked the causes of modern democracy and Christian ethics, arguing that even the idea of God should be democratized. While cautioning against absolutist tendencies in socialism, McConnell advocated a reform-oriented progressive politics, praised the British Labour Party, and criticized the predatory spirit of capitalism.[45] Showing a more avuncular mood, *The Preacher and the People* (1922) told Beecher-like stories about the art of preaching.[46] In the form of a Sunday school textbook, *Christian Citizenship* (1922) made a case for a cooperativist social gospel approach to nationalism, the state, education, labor/capital issues, and other social concerns.[47]

McConnell's next book, *Living Together* (1923), pondered the same social questions as *Christian Citizenship* at a higher level of argument, while adding a belated word about the problem of race. The latter problem was essentially a problem of the dominant culture's infantilization and degradation of an oppressed people, he believed, observing that it was customary in American society to refer to American blacks as children. American popular culture depicted African Americans, at best, as childishly inept, weak-minded, and lazy; white Americans preferred black entertainers who reinforced this stereotype. "Years ago multitudes of men were inclined to treat the Negro in kindly manner if he would acquiesce in being a slave," McConnell remarked. "Today many of us would be glad to treat the Negro kindly if he would be content to remain a child. It is the stride out toward manhood which disturbs us. The rising tide of color is a good sign if it means, as it largely does, that the races which have been looked upon as being non-adult are insisting upon being taken seriously."[48]

McConnell was acutely conscious of his role in adding to Bowne's legacy. He occasionally noted that Bowne had little or no sympathy for the underclass and failed to appreciate "the degree of reality that attaches to institutions as such."[49] By failing to recognize that social structures consist of more than the individual personalities that create them, Bowne failed to account for the impact of social structures for good or ill on persons. Bowne had a social concience of sorts, but it was highly selective and tended to be conservative. In McConnell's writings the Boston school effected its first blend of Bowne-style personalism and the social gospel. McConnell pressed hard on the social meaning of Christianity without shying away from the metaphysical aspects of personalism. Starting with Bowne's thesis that self-consciousness is the ultimate unit of the real, he embraced Bowne's claims that creative evolution is a process of personal will, that personality is an ethical concept, and that ethical life finds its center and fulfillment in a religious relation to the divine. Following Bowne, he insisted that the impersonal world is not independent; the impersonal world serves the personal. McConnell gave an early verdict on the question of God's finiteness, an issue that eventually divided Brightman and Knudson. In his book *Is God Limited?* (1924), McConnell argued that while it is correct to say that God is self-limited for the sake of human freedom and for the sake of the moral exercise of God's power, these judgments do not provide a warrant for speaking of God as a finite entity. "If we are to reach final peace in our thought of God, we shall have to bind God and men together as parts of one vast organism," he believed.[50] In his sermonizing and formal writing alike he spoke of God as ethical Mind or personal Spirit. "I think of God as

Mind, not because I see specific marks of design in the world but because I find the world intelligible at all."[51]

With a lighter touch than his Boston-school colleagues, McConnell explained to popular audiences what it means to claim that nature is a direct manifestation of the divine will or that time and space are mental forms. "So far as we can see time is inherent in the nature of mental process itself," he observed. "It cannot be built up out of anything else. Any attempt to explain it assumes it at the outset." Persistently he sought to make his teacher's religious philosophy make sense to ordinary Christians, while fulfilling the ecclesiastical and social roles of a major church leader. *Is God Limited?* began with a characteristic half-apology: "I regret the metaphysical nature of some of my discussion, though I do not see how metaphysical questions can be handled without metaphysical discussion. The most confirmed metaphysicians—and the most harmful—are those who disavow metaphysics."[52] That was a trademark sentiment of what became the personalist school.

KNUDSON AND THE PHILOSOPHY OF PERSONALISM

Brightman's prediction of a personalist renaissance was partly self-fulfilling; his books were on the way. It also coincided with Knudson's liberation from Old Testament studies; that was the key breakthrough for personalism as a theological movement. On occasion Brightman noted that Bowne struggled to clear a path between philosophers who found him too religious and theologians who found him too philosophical. Like Bowne, Brightman advocated personalist theory as a philosopher, but he could not be the movement's theologian; this was the burden that Knudson belatedly assumed. Upon gaining a theological position, he launched his theological career with an assessment of the field as he found it. Knudson's *Present Tendencies in Religious Thought* (1924) made it clear that personalist theology as he conceived it belonged to the tradition of Schleiermacher and Ritschl; with Schleiermacher he affirmed that theology must be a scientific explication of the Christian experience or the Christian consciousness; with Ritschl he affirmed that the Christian experience of revelation is both the ground and norm of Christian truth.[53]

Knudson gave no quarter to conservative claims that he had to choose between the liberal tradition and John Wesley. He countered that liberal theology as a whole amounts to a logical, if inadequate, development of the experience-based empirical principle on which the Wesleyan tradition rests. In good liberal theology, he explained, as in Methodism, experience serves an apologetic function and a normative one. Experience is the wellspring of religious claims and the basis on which Christians rightly defend their claims. Repeating the maxim of his teacher, he urged that personality (interpreted experience) is the key to reality and that life (experience) is the test of truth. The human sources of all knowledge are fundamentally defined by the fact that they have experiences which they instinctively try to understand. For many years, while Bowne elaborated his system of personalist idealism, he debated what name he should give to it. In his early work, as Rufus Burrow Jr. has shown, Bowne stressed the objective idealist thesis that there is an objective order outside the self that experiencing subjects find, not create. In his middle career, approximately 1896–1904, Bowne called himself a transcendental empiricist, emphasizing that mind is the explanation of experience that itself cannot be explained. By 1904, having moved to a thoroughgoing emphasis on the priority of the self over the categories of thought, Bowne probably would have called himself a personal idealist except for the fact that George Holmes Howison had already claimed this name for his position. Thus Bowne settled on the term "personalism" and argued that the transcendental categories of thought are revealed in the experience of a self; they do not create or determine the self's experience.[54]

Knudson embraced Bowne's insistence on the priority of experience, but in a way that recalled Bowne's earlier name for his system, transcendental empiricism. This unusual pairing of terms pointed to something in the logic of personalist idealism that Knudson persistently stressed. Personalism was empirical in its focus on experience, but it was transcendental in its contention that that which explains everything else (personality) cannot be explained. Knudson's theological appropriation of Bowne's system gave a central place to the idea of the religious apriori that heightened the transcendental character of personalist idealism.

His centerpiece work of personalist philosophy and apologetics was *The Philosophy of Personalism* (1927). He dedicated the book to McConnell, "a distinguished representative of the personalistic philosophy and a wise and courageous leader of the progressive forces in the religious thought and life of America," and noted that McConnell's biography of Bowne was nearly finished and that personalism was gaining renewed esteem as a philosophical option. Knudson placed Bowne's philosophy in historical perspective, meticulously explaining the relation of Bowne's system to rival philosophies and to other conceptions of personalism. Bowne possessed keen insights into the history of philosophy, but he showed little historical sense, rarely cited the arguments of past thinkers when he expounded or defended his theories, and was not generous with contemporaries. He was fond of remarking that the important philosophers "have seldom been men learned in the bibliography of the science, but men who grappled with the problems themselves."[55] *The Philosophy of Personalism* was written in a very different spirit. It was a movement work, anxious to establish Bowne's place in the history of philosophy; it thematized Bowne's relation to the history of philosophy; paid careful attention to definitions, historical antecedents, and various fine points that Bowne didn't bother with; and defined the school that it called for.[56]

Modern theology was in a bad way, Knudson believed. Compared to the "intellectual depth and power" that theological liberalism possessed at the height of the Ritschlian movement, the current scene was dreadfully depressing. Theologians were confused about the fundamentals of their worldview and inclined to chase after pathetic fads: "Much of current theology as well as philosophy has run into the shallows." Especially pathetic, he argued, was the fact that "not a little of the advanced theological thinking of the day seems to be linking itself up with a crude realism, dualism, pragmatism, or positivism." The liberal theologians at Chicago and Yale were intellectually bankrupt, and the Barthians were worse yet. The result for theology was "a deplorable confusion of thought." Knudson urged that "nothing at present is more needed in the field of religious thought than a revival of metaphysical theology." Both theology and philosophy needed to regain the courage to struggle with metaphysical problems: "Clearer thought in this field will do much to save philosophy from shallowness and futility, and it will also help to remove many of the common objections to the higher beliefs and hopes of mankind."[57]

The personalist answer was very old and variously conceived. Knudson traced the origin of explicitly personalistic philosophy to Augustine, who professed that he desired to know God and the soul, "these and nothing more." Augustinian Christianity explicitly thematized the inklings of Greek philosophy and the Bible that the real things in life are personal souls and the personal God. In modern times, Knudson observed, the attempt to interpret reality in personal terms has taken a variety of philosophical forms. English neo-Hegelian J. M. E. McTaggart propounded an atheistic personalism; German neo-Hegelian William Stern espoused a pantheistic personalism; French idealist Charles Renouvier theorized a relativistic personalism; a host of absolute idealists including Edward Caird, Josiah Royce, A. E. Taylor, W. E. Hocking, and Mary W. Calkins ascribed personality to the Absolute; Bowne's contemporary George Holmes Howison conceived God as noncreative personality and human beings as noncreated, coeternal partners with God. Knudson carefully parsed the differences among these theories and explained that Bowne-style theistic personalism belonged to another category.[58]

The fundamental postulate of personalist thought is the reality of the self or soul or "I." A personalist can deny the existence of a personal God, but not the reality of a personal self. On this ground Knudson did not deny atheists or pantheists the right to the personalist name. One can be a personalist without believing in a personal God or any god at all, he allowed, but one cannot be a personalist and disbelieve in the reality of finite persons. At the same time, it made little sense to Knudson (or to Bowne and Brightman) to say that reality is personal without affirming the reality of a personal God. Knudson observed that he and Brightman had ample philosophical company in this view. His list of important personalists was similar to Brightman's; Knudson cited Arthur J. Balfour, A. S. Pringle-Pattison, J. Cook Wilson, Hastings Rashdall, James Ward, W. R. Sorley, C. C. J. Webb, and Rudolf Eucken. The intellectual affinity between Bowne and the Scotch Anglican idealist Pringle-Pattison was so close that Knudson sometimes quoted them interchangeably. Bowne and Pringle-Pattison similarly insisted that only personality is ontologically real. Humankind's personal agency is inexplicable, they acknowledged, yet it is also the surest datum that we possess and the only clue that we possess to the mystery of our existence. Thus Bowne's personalism was both empirical and transcendental. It held that the key to the problem of knowledge is their own experience (that which all subjects know directly), but it maintained that the personalist explanation cannot be explained.[59]

The philosophical lineage of theistic personalism was a mixed bag. Bowne's self-estimate was that he accepted half of Kant's system, but sharply rejected the rest; he appropriated some of Berkeley's immaterialism, but rejected his theory of knowledge; he largely agreed with Lotze's personalistic idealism, but transcended Lotze. Knudson judged that this estimate was nearly right. In his reading, the key philosophical sources of Bowne's position were Leibniz, Berkeley, Kant, and Lotze. From Leibniz he took his spiritual individualism and his theory of the soul as essentially active; from Berkeley he took his immaterialism; from Kant he took his theory of knowledge and his ethical conception of personality; from Lotze's synthesis of these sources he took the idea of his own synthesis.[60]

Against absolute idealism, Bowne-tradition personalism distinguished between thought and reality. Bowne was realistic enough to affirm that reality is something other and deeper than thought, Knudson explained, but against metaphysical realism, Bowne took an idealistic view of nature. The natural world has no independent reality of itself; nature is a phenomenal order constantly reproduced by a power or powers outside itself. Knudson emphasized that personalistic idealism is also voluntaristic rather than rationalistic. Bowne was a good Wesleyan on the freedom of the will. He viewed the will as a stronger force than reason and was fond of saying that life is deeper than logic. Personalism gives a prominent role to formal argumentation, Knudson assured, but it denies that reason alone can bridge the chasm between thought and reality. Faith alone can cross the Cartesian divide; in the final analysis all knowledge rests on faith.[61]

Personalism was nothing without its insistence on the metaphysical reality of the self. Knudson argued that it offers an essentially distinct alternative to Hume's dissolution of the self into a bundle of perceptions and to the pantheist reduction of the self to a phase of divine activity. Because personalist thinking centers so forcefully on its claim that the soul or self alone is ontologically real, however (or at least, in temporizing versions, that personality is the primary metaphysical reality), Knudson emphasized what he and Bowne did not mean when they referred to "the soul." They did not mean that the soul is a material substance (as in popular piety) or an immaterial substance (as in Plato) or a thinking substance (as in Descartes's identification of the soul with consciousness). They did not believe that the soul is any kind of substance at all. Ancient and medieval thought was predisposed to make the idea of substance more fundamental than that of cause, Knudson observed, but the tendency in modern philosophy is to regard activity as essential to being. Modern consciousness denies reality to forms of existence that lack the power of action. Thus Leibniz conceived the soul as the spiritual cause of material phenomena; Berkeley conceived it as the perceiving activity that creates ideas and the world of things; Kant theorized that the mind is creative, building up its world for itself by virtue of immanent principles or categories of thought, though Kant made no knowledge claims about the nature of the noumenal self that lies beyond the bounds of sense.[62]

Here as elsewhere, Kant was the personalists' hero and goat. For centuries philosophers took for granted that human subjects receive impressions from without, Knudson reflected. The schools of philosophy differed greatly over the nature of the external stimulus in sense experience, but they agreed that in the realm of reason, human subjects either read off whatever is implicit in sense experience or they bring to consciousness whatever is innate in the mind. Sense perception was linked to a realistic view of the external world. Berkeley cracked this link by showing that human perceptions do not necessarily refer to metaphysically existing objects, but even Berkeley assumed that sense experience is produced outside the human mind. "It was Kant who first made the individual mind a determining factor in the manufacture of experience," Knudson observed. "So long as sense-experience was accepted as something epistemologically ultimate, as something coordinate with or independent of thought, reason and the higher spiritual interests of men were left with an insecure title. They had on their flank an unsubdued and ambitious foe."[63]

The personalists exalted Kant for dethroning the things of sense, as well as for asserting that persons are moral ends in themselves. If sensations are thought products that lack any definite character until they are fashioned into being by the creative powers of mind, then the things of sense have no claim to primacy in human life and thought. Bowne told his classes that this insight of Kant's was his "great contribution to philosophy, and it remains, in spite of all criticism, a permanent possession of reflective thought." Knudson concurred that because of Kant's critical achievement, rationality and the higher spiritual interests need not fear "the aggression of sense." The higher things were securely enthroned in Kant's critical idealism.[64]

But there was also the bad Kant who marred his own magnificent achievement by ruling out any knowledge of transcendental "things-in-themselves" in his system, including knowledge of human souls. On this theme Knudson liked Union Seminary religious philosopher Eugene Lyman, who noted that Kant couldn't get along without a knowable soul and thus he replaced it with poor substitutes. Kant called these replacements the empirical ego, which is bound by causation; and the transcendental unity of apperception, which is a logical point of reference; and the ego as a thing-in-itself, which is unknowable; and the ego as a transcendental ideal, which is the goal of knowledge; and the moral ego, which posits its own freedom. In the name of epistemological rigor and modesty, Kant thus ended up with five egos, which Lyman called "a real bedevilment of the situation." Knudson nodded in agreement. The bad half of Kant—the half that Bowne rejected—was a terrible confusion. Unfortunately this half was deeply insinuated in liberal Protestant thought. The Ritschlian school and other liberals made broadsides against metaphysical reasoning that even Kant would not have endorsed.[65]

Following Lotze and Bowne, Knudson called for a liberal Protestantism that dared to assert the reality of the soul as a knowable first principle, though not as a substance. The soul that is known to consciousness is the conscious soul, he argued. The nature of the only soul that is revealed to us is revealed in conscious experience. Descartes was right to identify the soul with consciousness; the personalists cherished Descartes for contending that the existence of the soul is immediate and certain, while that of matter is an uncertain inference. On the other hand, Descartes's absolute dualism of body and soul was impossible. He viewed the body as an automaton and the soul as a purely thinking substance. The personalists countered that the knowing agent and the agent's activity are one. Following Lotze and Bowne, who interpreted reality in terms of self-consciousness, Knudson argued that there is "no consciousness without a subject, no thought without a thinker, no activity without an agent." The soul bears the "stamp of reality" by its consciousness of its unity and self-identity. Knudson concluded, "The true activistic theory of the self finds the reality of the soul in self-consciousness and self-direction, and says with Lotze that when it is in a state of complete unconsciousness and complete passivity 'the soul is not.'"[66]

Knudson's personalism was not as dualistic as Cartesian philosophy or classical theism, but it remained dualistic in its affirmation of the soul and the soul's "certain independence . . . objective to God himself." More schematically and clearly than Bowne, he presented personalism as an epistemologically dualist philosophy that affirms the dualism of idea and object, the creative activity of mind, the trustworthiness of reason, and the primacy of practical reason. With Kant he maintained that the categories of thought (being, causality, identity) are the preconditions of experience that make experience possible; they cannot be imported into the mind from without. Against Kant he insisted that if the categories of thought do not apply to things-in-themselves, then these things cannot be affirmed at all. This theme brought Knudson closer to Hegel than he acknowledged, but the Bowneans agreed on Kant's greatness as the theorist of the creativity of mind and the moral absoluteness of the person, as well as the futility of Kant's dichotomy between knowable phenomena and unknowable things-in-themselves.[67]

Along the line of this dichotomy, Kant distinguished sharply between knowledge and faith, a dichotomy that the mainstream of liberal Protestantism eagerly accepted. The personalists countered that in real life the line of distinction between knowledge and faith is not nearly so sharp. Bowne showed that knowledge is not limited to the phenomenal world, that theoretical reason always employs faith assumptions of its own, that theoretical reason cannot completely dispense with metaphysical categories, that science is not value free, that purpose is constitutive in thought, and that the idea of a good to be attained is constitutive in purpose. Persistently Knudson portrayed Bowne-style personalism as a third way that keeps its balance between the claims of faith and reason, freedom and divine sovereignty, traditional theology and pantheist theology, epistemological realism and absolute idealism, agnostic dualism and epistemological monism, pragmatic relativism and intellectualistic absolutism, and metaphysical monism and pluralism. He affirmed, with Leibniz, the principle of individuality and the spirit of Leibniz's claim that reality consists of uncounted "windowless monads." Leibniz argued that there are many substances, not one, and that every true substance is a unique and unitary being—a monad—that has no windows. Each monad acts by virtue of its own character and inner forces. The personalists liked Leibniz's monadology, though not the part about windowlessness, and they loved his puzzlement that anyone might question the existence of the soul and yet claim to know anything. Between the devouring concrete universalism of Hegel and the devouring abstract universalism of Spinoza, Knudson took his place with Leibniz. By his understanding of it, and for the sake of the school and movement that he sought to build, he defined personalism as a form of idealism "which gives equal recognition to both the pluralistic and monistic aspects of experience and which finds in the conscious unity, identity, and free activity of personality the key to the nature of reality and the solution of the ultimate problems of philosophy."[68]

Knudson's movement apologia ended with a chapter titled "Militant Personalism." He and Brightman both admired Bowne's intellectual militance, but Knudson had considerably more partisan spirit than Brightman. Brightman played up his differences with Bowne and the disagreements among various personalists and was irked when students asked for the party line on philosophical issues. Unlike Knudson, who appreciated how difficult it must have been for Bowne to sustain a philosophical career while serving as dean of the Graduate School, Brightman tended to belabor Bowne's shortcomings. He often noted, and clearly regretted, that Bowne's writings were frequently sarcastic, that Bowne ignored his philosophical colleagues, rarely quoted other thinkers except for polemical purposes, never joined the American Philosophical Association, and did not contribute to philosophical journals, and that his writings were pedagogical rather than technical. On occasion Brightman speculated about what his own position would be if he were not a personalist—he judged that he would probably opt for Ralph Barton Perry's analytic realism—but Knudson could not imagine himself as anything but a personalist. He embraced the role of a school and movement builder, and he wrote to make converts. He had ample zeal for what he called "the polemic aspects of the subject." It was imperative to him to build a personalist theological school not only because personalist theory solved perennial problems of philosophy, but because modern theology needed it so desperately.[69]

Knudson rarely mentioned the Chicago school without blasting its "amazing superficiality." It was amazing to him that the Chicago schoolers found humanistic naturalism profound. He struggled equally to imagine how the Barthians could be serious; his most generous description of the Barthian-dialectical-neo-orthodox movement was "sophisticated irrationalism." Macintosh's theological realism struck him as a nearly serious offshoot of the Chicago school, but Knudson judged that Macintosh's project was a product of "the picturing type of mind" and contradictory as well. The realist position is one in which neither faith nor reason can rest, he argued. The idea of spatial substance is contradictory, as is the idea of impersonal substance, and so reason is forced to transcend them. Faith has the same problem in a realist epistemology because from the standpoint of faith the impersonal can have no intrinsic worth: "Its value is purely instrumental, and since it is such, no impersonal thing can be self-existent, for self-existence carries with it the idea of existence for self, and this implies intrinsic value." Materialism is a conquering aggressor, Knudson warned; theologians who embrace it or make bargains with it are accomplices in the killing of God and the soul. The only way to prevent the conquering tyranny of the things of sense is to deny them true ontological reality.[70]

Knudson gave little place to Hegel in the personalist story—Hegel's idealism was insufficiently personal—but he granted immortal credit to Hegel for his insistence that the real is the rational and the rational is the real. "Whatever is irrational is unreal and impossible," Knudson contended. "Only as being is shaped by the categories of thought can it be given an intelligible content." This was his word of judgment on Barthians who wrapped themselves in paradoxes, and on realist and naturalist theologians who sold out their spiritual primacy over material things, and on social gospelers who failed to uphold the metaphysical claims of faith. Knudson warned that none of these strategies would persuade modern people to take religion seriously. He cited Gerald Birney Smith as the kind of theologian who believed that he could make religion more congenial to the secular consciousness by dwelling in the "intellectual twilight." Knudson countered that only the "noonday brightness of personalistic theism" was worth taking seriously.[71]

He gave short shrift to critiques of personalism. To those who objected that personalist theory was too systematic, rationalized, and sharply defined, Knudson argued that serious philosophical thinking is systematic, rationalized, and sharply defined. There is no tenable or even intelligible middle ground to be claimed between a mechanistic and a personalist worldview, he admonished, echoing Bowne's main theme. To critics like William James and Ralph Barton Perry, who argued that personalism was a concoction of compromises between rival systems with no strong center of its own, Knudson replied that personalism was, indeed, a mediating philosophy and that its spirit of synthesizing reconciliation was one of its virtues. To those who denied that personality is metaphysically real—usually on the ground that the "self" is a composite with no metaphysical glue that binds together its states of consciousness—Knudson replied that the human eye does not see itself, either, and yet without the eye nothing can be seen. The same thing is true of the self; to say that the self is real is not to claim that it manifests itself to consciousness as a distinct object, he argued; it is to say that the self is a special kind of object, different from the things of sense, which is given immediately in experience. We cannot escape this experience; we assume its existence even when we try to analyze it away. When pressed on the point that consciousness cannot be any definite thing, Bowne often replied: "Of course I cannot be unconsciously conscious or consciously unconscious; I cannot conceive of being both dead and alive at the same time." Knudson reached for a similar clincher, inspired by Augustine, whenever he was pressed on the question: it would be impossible to deny the existence of a self if a self did not exist to make the denial.[72]

The Philosophy of Personalism established the existence of a personalist school and its genealogy. Shortly before the book was published, the School of Theology at Boston University lost its dean, James A. Beebe, who accepted the presidency of Allegheny College; Boston University president Daniel L. Marsh offered the deanship to Knudson, who balked. His theological scholarship had just begun; the personalist movement needed him. But Marsh assured him that he would be given ample administrative assistance and that his scholarly productivity would not suffer from accepting the position. Knudson must have realized that becoming the dean of a major Methodist seminary would be a boon to his movement ambitions. He accepted the post at 72 Mt. Vernon Street—locals called the seminary "72"—and was promptly congratulated by Beebe, who confided that he didn't want to be a college president, "drudging away at campaigns for money." Implicitly Beebe told Knudson his reason for stepping down: "You are 'the big man' at '72'—the very cornerstone of our house. If anything should happen to you, I should expect the house to collapse." Beebe had resigned because he was not the one who could lift the School of Theology to top-tier status.[73]

Explicitly he explained himself to faculty colleague Earl B. Marlatt, who told Beebe that he didn't know whether to congratulate him or kick him. Beebe told Marlatt to congratulate the School of Theology: "I am leaving it to make room for a scholar, as well as an administrator, who can give it academic rating above its leading rivals." Marlatt agreed that Knudson was the one who could make the seminary a first rank institution; he and Knudson were close friends. At the same time he told Knudson that he worried about the potential personal effects of his promotion. Deaning might dissipate his otherworldly charm, "the air of elsewhere that hovers over you like a halo. I should miss that." But Knudson thrived in his new position. For nearly thirteen years he guided and strengthened the School of Theology with his customary thoroughness. On his watch the seminary's reputation rose nearly to the level of Union and Chicago. Under his intellectual influence and personable leadership two generations of American Methodist preachers learned to speak the language of religious personalism, keeping alive a vital stream of progressive theological discourse during a period when liberalism lost its movement glow.[74]

THEORIZING PERSONALITY:
BRIGHTMAN AND THE TRUTH OF RELIGION

Knudson was the Boston School's theologian and party leader; Brightman was emphatically neither. The two were close friends and intellectual allies, "continuously and intimately related through the past 44 years," as Brightman put it in

1952, renowned among colleagues and students for their enormous energy and disciplined productivity. Knudson maintained a grueling schedule of administrative tasks, teaching, and scholarship that nearly ruined his health in the mid-1930s. Aided by constantly updated index cards, Brightman faithfully corresponded with a staggering list of friends and former students; his precise appointment walks were legendary among students. He assumed leadership roles in several professional associations while continually expanding his range of intellectual interests. Knudson was the more approachable personality. Friends and students alike called him "Knoody," though some spelled it "Knudie." Brightman was courtly, dauntingly brilliant, and usually serious, though he possessed a sharp sense of humor. Even behind his back students didn't call him Edgar. Both were logical drillmasters in the classroom. Though Knudson made friends more readily, both were greatly respected by their students. Knudson inherited the essentials of his position from Bowne and expounded this position philosophically and theologically for the rest of his career. He added one major plank to the personalist platform—religious apriorism—but his creative contributions to personalism were in the areas of philosophical cartography and theological application, not philosophical rethinking.[75]

Brightman was a different kind of thinker. He prized his intellectual independence and insisted that he wrote on religious subjects strictly as a philosopher of religion, never as a theologian. He began his career as a down-the-line disciple of Bowne's, but in mid-career, while still revering his teacher, he became a more independent disciple. In his early career Brightman propounded the essential principles of Bowne's personalistic theism and idealism, while showing signs of his high regard for Hegel. Then he broke with Bowne's classical theism on the doctrine of divine omnipotence; shortly afterward he rejected Bowne's idealistic doctrine of divine nontemporality; soon after he decided that Bowne's theory of personality was short on psychological facts. For many years, troubled that Bowne's theory of the self still smacked of substantialist metaphysical glue, he worked on his own theory of personality; Brightman's last name for it was the "shining present."[76]

The fact that Brightman was more inclined than Knudson to range outside the boundaries of Bowne's system was a strength of the Boston school. Brightman reduced the party-line feeling of Boston personalism. On his account personalists vigorously debated the finitude of God, whether time has an effect on God, whether personalists should be temporalists, and what it means to make conscious experience the point of departure for one's philosophy. In a characteristically direct assertion, Brightman took the position that " a personalist should be a temporalist, a believer in the metaphysical reality of personal duration." Bowne's eternalism notwithstanding, Brightman reasoned, personality is active, free, and purposive. These qualities all require time, "and the time of their realization is both real and important." On this issue Brightman readily found personalist allies; Ralph Tyler Flewelling was one. On the other hand, on the issue that made him a big name by academic standards, he had to make allies among his students; Bowne's disciples blanched at Brightman's theorizing on God's inner conflicts. Brightman never tired of reminding theological readers that he was not a theologian; at the same time he enjoyed the comradeship of theologians who took a liberal view of their discipline "with no dogmatic or traditionalistic presuppositions lurking around the corner."[77]

In the 1920s Brightman wrote four books that strengthened the personalist cause and established his standing in the field. *Introduction to Philosophy* (1925) became a widely used textbook; *Immortality in Post-Kantian Idealism* (1925) surveyed beliefs about the immortality of the soul in neo-Hegelian and personalist philosophy; *Religious Values* (1925) interpeted the role of values in religious experience, arguing that values are conscious experiences of persons that have no meaning apart from consciousness; *A Philosophy of Ideals* (1928) contended that experience and nature are ideal systems that derive their existence and meaning from their embodiment of ideals. Brightman pressed the latter argument against a dominant current of realist and pragmatist philosophies. Idealists agree with realists and pragmatists that ideals are useful in human experience, he argued, but idealists reject the notion that ideals are merely socially useful inventions that humans construct in a coldly indifferent cosmos. From the standpoint of philosophical idealism, ideals reveal the very structure of the real world that indwells and transcends humanity.[78]

Brightman never doubted that ideals disclose the structure of the real; in his early career this conviction caused him to take a light pass at the problem of evil. In *Religious Values* he asserted that "the deepest reality is good." The problem of evil is filled with "seemingly irreducible mysteries," Brightman allowed, but the same thing is true of other quandaries. The problem of evil is like the problems of freedom, error, the experience of value, and the relation between mind and body. It has "unexplained facts" that need the demystifying attention of modern philosophy and science.[79] The problem of natural evil was more troublesome to his idealism than the existence of moral evil; Brightman took a page from Leibniz to explain how natural evils can exist in a good world. *Introduction to Philosophy* explained that natural evils are aspects of the best possible world. Even those evils that seem completely fruitless must play some role in God's work of creating a cocreative community of moral agents, Brightman reasoned. Just as there are natural events that science has not yet brought "within the province of causal law," there are natural evils in the world for which we do not understand God's moral purpose. Greater understanding of the way the world works will yield greater understanding of the moral functionality of natural evil.[80] Brightman's early writings thus epitomized the kind of liberal progressivism that failed to take moral and natural evil very seriously. He betrayed no feeling that the terrible evils of the world are not really analogous to the problem of the relation of mind and body. His concern was to uphold an idealistic religious view of the world that relegated the tragic realities of life to a folder marked "unsolved problems."

But Brightman's own experiences caused him to feel the tragedy of life more deeply than his books conveyed. As a child he was struck in the eye with a stick by a playmate; for the rest of his life he had almost no vision in this eye. In his youth he witnessed the moral and emotional disintegration of a man who committed terrible deeds after he lost his sanity. A few years later an acquaintance destroyed his nervous system in a swimming accident. During his Sleeper Fellow years in Germany Brightman met a cultured, high-spirited, ardently democratic German, Fräulein Charlotte Hülsen, whom he married in 1912. His wife embraced her new life in Nebraska, and she gave birth to a son, Howard Hülsen Brightman, in 1914, but the same year she contracted a facial cancer and the next year died a torturous death. (Brightman later had two children with his second wife, Irma Fall.) During World War I he taught military psychology and other war-related courses as an R.O.T.C. captain and instructor at Wesleyan University; he also censored German newspapers for the U.S. Department of Justice. He later recalled that the war seemed "peculiarly tragic" to him because it damaged his special affection for Germany; after the war he became a pacifist and sharply regretted that he aided the war effort as a military officer and academic.[81]

Brightman's early books repressed the tragic aspects of these experiences. He was determined to be the kind of idealist who lived in his head. To change his view about anything, he had to find his way through books and arguments. But the tragedies that he observed and experienced gnawed at him, and he puzzled over the problem of evil: How could he believe in God and idealism and take seriously the reality of evil? In the late 1920s he read several books on evolutionary science, especially Edmund Noble's *Purposive Evolution,* which moved him to rethink his concept of God.[82]

Armed with logical exactitude and the coherence criterion of truth, he fixated on the theodicy question: Is the existence of an omnipotent and omnibenevolent God the best hypothesis that one can make in the light of empirical evidence? Brightman later recalled that for many years his commitment to Bowne's metaphysical position and his deeper background in Royce's neo-Hegelian absolutism turned him away from scientific theory and research: "The teaching that science is merely phenomenal left me with a feeling of the exalted superiority of purely metaphysical knowledge and the relative unimportance of science." His renewed interest in evolutionary science heightened his personal doubts about the credibility of classical theism. Together these influences drove Brightman to confront the existence of what he called "surd" evils in creation and history. Evolutionary science presents a grim picture of surd evils, he reflected—evils that serve no good purpose. He was committed to the notion that God is good; what he could not figure was how the evolutionary picture of a world pervaded by meaningless evil could be reconciled with the classical view of God as all-good *and* all-powerful. Methodically he moved to the judgment that God's omnibenevolence can be defended only by giving up the notion of divine omnipotence. His early writings on this theme were not credible, and neither was classical theism. *The Problem of God* (1930) was Brightman's breakout book. "Few beliefs are more absurd than the belief that man's present ideas about God are incapable of improvement," he declared. Until Brightman turned to it, the theory of a finite God was identified with marginally Christian thinkers like William James and H. G. Wells; *The Problem of God* considerably boosted its mainstream Christian status.[83]

The personalist line on this subject was exemplified by McConnell's *Is God Limited?* which Brightman treated gingerly. Brightman acknowledged that he gained a great deal from McConnell's book, though he disagreed with its conclusion. Aside from his patronizing jibes that James and Wells lacked metaphysical acuity, McConnell's line was a model of idealistic modesty and chastened liberal realism. He argued that God is limited by virtue of being morally good, creating a material universe, and allowing freedom to self-conscious subjects. Every theology "limits" God in some way, he observed; the abstract theologies of Absolute Being produced by scholastic orthodoxy were no exception. The pertinent question is not whether God has limitations but how these limitations should be conceived. McConnell noted that some theologies impose limitations on God from without; the "finite God" theisms of James and Wells made notable examples. Other theologies recognize limitations in God that are self-willed or that inhere in the divine nature. The latter model of divine limitation is perfectly legitimate and necessary in Christian theology, McConnell argued, but the former model, of limitations on God from without, has to be resisted: "What the Christian consciousness demands is a God not dependent on anything else."[84]

Calling for a "full-orbed conception of a responsible God," McConnell sympathized with the moral concerns of the finite-God theorists, and he credited them with a stronger realism about evil than liberal theology had managed in many years. "For twenty-five years preceding the outbreak of the Great War popular theological thinking had run to a shallow doctrine of divine immanence which overlooked all the grim facts of our world," he conceded in 1924. Liberal Christian optimism failed to address the specters of overpopulation and environmental degradation, for example: "For unwillingness to face facts the generation just preceding the Great War is perhaps without a peer in the history of human thinking. We all glided along on a swiftly increasing current, unmindful that the current was bearing us to the abyss. The skies were overhead, the grass was beautiful on the banks, the birds were singing gaily. God was in all things. Why worry?"[85]

McConnell called for a different kind of theological progressivism. "We may as well face the truth that we live in a grim universe," he admonished. Human suffering is out of proportion with sin; most of the world's people suffer terribly from deprivation and oppression. Moreover, he noted, suffering in the animal world is equally grotesque, yet here there is no possibility of a moral utilization of pain. "There does seem to be some inherent fatality in the world of things around us which makes more pain than we can see any use for," McConnell acknowledged. He did not claim to understand it theologically. He took a brief pass at Leibniz's theodicy explanation—even an infinite Creator has to work with the limitations that are inherent in a finite system—but he did not claim that this theory explains or satisfies very much. "No solution of this mystery has ever been offered except those that add to our sense of woe," he admitted. "There is no explanation in terms of our present knowledge. We hate desperately to say that the Divine Creator is back of all this pain because he must be, but does it make it any easier for us to say that this pain exists because he prefers it?"[86]

There is no good answer to the problem, he believed, but some answers are worse than others. The kind of answer that gives up the notion of a responsible God is worse than the kind that struggles with the infinite and eternal God of Christian faith. In his closing pages McConnell argued that the God of Christianity suffers pain along with and for the sake of suffering existence. "Religious thought today is not so deeply engrossed with the divinity of Christ as formerly," he observed. "The preoccupation today is with the divinity of God himself, using the word in the Christly sense." Modern theology asks whether God is like Christ, not whether Christ is like God. This is the right question, McConnell believed: "If God is like Christ, then the suffering of the cross gives us a hint of the suffering of God." Only a suffering God with a "wealth of divine feeling" can save us. McConnell urged that the spiritual and ethical qualities of God are of greater consequence for religion than God's metaphysical qualities. He was prepared to accept a redefinition of God's omnipotence, but he warned against theologies that relieve God of moral responsibility or of fellow-suffering feeling: "If there are limitations which God assumes, they are assumed in the spirit of Christ. If there are limitations which seem essential to the Divine Life, they are essential because of the moral nature of the Christlike God."[87]

This argument was more realistic about evil and more adventuresome theologically than Brightman's early idealism. Three years after he published *Is God Limited?* McConnell expanded on his conclusion that the only compelling answer to the problem of evil is the God whose self-sacrificing, fellow-suffering character is disclosed through the life and death of Christ. *The Christlike God* (1927) declared that "the only relief is in a Christlike God whom we can trust but whom we cannot now understand." Though he sympathized with the moral feelings of those who resorted to the idea of a finite God, McConnell counseled that this strategy was a loser: "Limit the divine power to whatever extent we please, we cannot go far enough to get the relief we seek."[88]

This was exactly the counsel that Brightman rejected. Upon fixing his attention on the reality of morally useless evil, Brightman studied McConnell's work and appropriated some of his arguments, especially his theme that God is constrained by certain inner limitations. While leaving aside McConnell's theological claims about Christ and "Christly" experience, he embraced McConnell's provocative defense of patripassionism. The notion that God feels the pain of the world and suffers the world's agonies was partly legitimatized in American Christianity by McConnell's ecclesiastical status. But Brightman rejected McConnell's counsel not to seek relief by breaking with classical theism. Brightman resolved that defending God's goodness was more important than saving classical theism. McConnell backed away from the conclusion that God is actually finite; Brightman announced that he was seeing the matter through: "The view which I have come to hold is that of a God who is creative, supreme, and personal, yet is genuinely limited within his own nature by 'Given' experiences eternally present, which his will does not create, but which his will can control, no matter how refractory they may be."[89]

Brightman pressed four arguments toward the verdict that God is a conflicted finite being: First, that evolution is stunningly wasteful and violent; second, that God's nature as a conscious being and God's granting of free will to human beings set limits to God's will; third, that God's nature is not merely goodness but also dialectical struggle, characterized by the same dynamic of assertion and negation that pervades all reality; fourth, that God is perfect in will, but not in achievement. These arguments melded into a single thesis: Given the facts that we possess about the suffering-causing evils of the world that far exceed moral guilt or moral use, we must revise the classical view of either God's goodness or God's power. *The Problem of God* argued plainly for the latter. Since God is loving and good, Brightman contended, God would eliminate the evils that persons are not responsible for if God were able to do so, but God is evidently not able to do so. A nonrational "Given" in God's consciousness apparently thwarts God's capacity to achieve the divine purpose. God attains goodness only after a struggle with "Given" limiting factors that inhere in the divine being. "It is not a question of the kind of God we should like to have," Brightman admonished. "It is a question of the kind of God required by the facts." He denied that the finite God of the facts was not worthy of being worshiped: "If the worshiper confronts a being who is at once the supreme good and the supreme power in the universe, and if that being in the long run can find a meaning in every situation, a good beyond every evil, a value for every phase of The Given, then the worshiper has all that his experience could justify him in hoping for, even if he has to grant that his God is not omnipotent."[90]

Determined to explain the existence of evils that a good God did not create or will, and taking for granted that God's goodness cannot be compromised without falling into atheism, Brightman resorted to the idea of a God whose power is limited by coeternal nonrational elements within the divine being that oppose God's rational divine will. God is limited by "Given" factors in God's nature that God did not create. Brightman accepted McConnell's sanction against outside limitations on God, but he pressed the thesis of inner limitation to the point of positing a disabling conflict within God's being. Boldly he told mainline Christians not to fear the notion that God is finite, though he later preferred the formulation that God is a finite-infinite Being. The power of God's will is limited, he taught, but God is infinite in time, goodness, and love.

The Problem of God was better timed and more provocatively argued than *Is God Limited?* Brightman caught the mood of an American audience that no longer believed the world was getting better. When the Religious Book Club chose his book, and not Knudson's *The Doctrine of God* (1930), as its feature book, Brightman consoled Knudson that *The Doctrine of God* was better, but *The Problem of God* was cheaper and more accessible.[91] Later he enthused to Knudson that "the Boston boys and their wives are all reading *The Problem of God* and are becoming infected with finitude!"[92] Numerous reviewers were less enthralled with the book, some chiding that Brightman's God seemed to be cowered by the Given. In the *Harvard Theological Review*, Andrew Banning expressed a common concern that Brightman's God-limiting concept of the Given could "at some future time develop a new emergent aspect which will either fundamentally alter the nature of God or confront him with situations for which his principles will prove inadequate."[93]

Closer to home, *The Personalist* blasted Brightman's concept of the Given as the kind of solution that only made the problem worse. Flewelling wrote that, "greatly as it would please us to agree with our Personalistic colleague," he could not abide Brightman's claim that God lacks full power over evil. Brightman posited that there are restrictions in God's nature that God did not create and which limit God's control over evil; at the same time, anxious to affirm that he was still talking about the Christian God, Brightman assured that God bears moral responsibility for control of the Given. Flewelling countered that this was a conjuring trick that purchased nothing but deeper confusion. Are the restrictions within God's nature according to God's will, he asked? Are these restrictions determining? If God is self-limited, then God must be held morally responsible for the defeat and obstruction of God's will. If God is not self-limited, then the Given is a power beyond God's control that controls God. "The Given is either his servant, and an undesirable one, or his Frankenstein to destroy him," Flewelling protested. "We cannot get around this dilemma by any subterfuge of language."[94]

The Problem of God raised the question of metaphysical dualism. Like Bowne, Brightman was epistemologically dualistic; he also claimed to uphold Bowne's beliefs in the existence of a sovereign Creator and the unity of the World-Ground. He denied that his theory was actually guilty of metaphysical dualism, since it is possible for a finite person—especially the Supreme Person—to experience various inner tensions as a complex unity. But Brightman's notion of a duality within the divine consciousness drove personalist theism to the edge of metaphysical dualism, as he recognized. In *The Finding of God* (1931) he affirmed that this edge was where modern theists needed to take their stand; the pertinent choice was between his near-dualism and the old God-and-Satan dualism: "I think we must choose between accepting an eternal malicious Satan and an eternal nonmalicious but problematic resisting force that produces a tension and a drag within the divine nature." Since the old view of divine sovereignty is out and the old God-and-Satan dualism is equally repugnant and incredible, Brightman reasoned, modern religious thinkers were best advised to stop holding out for the God of classical theism. Some model of a finite God is the only morally acceptable solution, and at least his model preserved other attributes of divine infinity.[95]

Brightman's theory of the Given became a signature theme. His subsequent writings elaborated that the Given within God's experience consists of various uncreated laws of reason, such as logic and mathematical relations, as well as various impulses and desires, the experiences of pain and suffering, the forms of space and time, "and whatever in God is the source of 'surd' evil." In a novel emphasis for the genre, his textbook on the philosophy of religion devoted sixty-four pages to the problems of evil, theistic absolutism, and theistic finitism before asking, for thirty-five pages, "Is God Finite?" Brightman answered that God's will is finite "in a definite sense." God is absolute in the sense of being the ultimate source of creation, he reasoned, and God is infinite in the sense that God has no beginning or end and is not limited by anything external to Godself. At the same time, he argued, God is definitely limited by the Given, which is eternal within the experience of God and which is not a product of will or created activity. The theory of God's Given-finitude might not be the truth, Brightman allowed, but it is surely "an advance toward the truth."[96]

Though controversial in church circles, Brightman was increasingly viewed as some kind of religious leader, not merely as a philosopher of religion. He wrote books on spiritual experience and the search for God, he was an active church member, and he treasured his opportunities to train future pastors and theologians. He and Knudson agreed to disagree about God's inner conflicts, but it pleased Brightman greatly that Knudson otherwise commended *The Problem of God*. For forty years he and Knudson read each other's manuscripts, praised each other extravagantly, and usually offered only small points of criticism or correction. Though Brightman's theorizing on God's finitude was rejected, usually respectfully, by other personalists as well, he acquired strong personalist defenders on this subject, notably Peter A. Bertocci, Walter G. Muelder, and, with qualifications, S. Paul Schilling. Persistently Brightman urged that logical coherence is the sole criterion of truth, that religious experience furnishes data for truth about religion, and that all truth is hypothetical. There is no such thing as a good theology that is not rigorously logical, he insisted, yet logic is no substitute for experience. Brightman hated Bowne's slogan that "life is more than logic." He wished that Bowne had perceived the potentially disastrous effects of this maxim on students and readers. The maxim gained no stature for Brightman after he learned that Lotze and James often invoked it too. Aside from the superfluous sense in which it is true that playing baseball or negotiating a peace treaty is more than a question of being logical, he allowed, Bowne's saying was terribly misleading: it implied that there is something about actual experience which should cause people to accept beliefs that are not logically consistent.[97]

Brightman and Knudson persistently warred against this inference. "There is nothing about life which makes it desirable to have bad reasons for believing truths, or which allows us to believe any proposition without reason," Brightman insisted. It grieved him that theologians in the Barthian-dialectical school were practically making paradox a criterion of truth. He despised sloppy reasoning and disdained intellectual fads: "My interest is in religion as truth, not in religion as bandwagon." Brightman ruefully noted that even his philosophical hero sold out to a bandwagon. To his mind, Hegel was "the richest, most fertile, and profoundest mind in the history of philosophy." Yet Hegel absolutized the Prussian state of his time as the fulfillment of the dialectical ideal; his dialectic marched to his own society and stopped. "If he had adhered to his principle that only the rational is truly real, he would have marched beyond his present," Brightman judged.[98]

Brightman's rationalism was aggressive, and, he believed, unyielding; yet he cherished spiritual sincerity with equal fervor. His attraction to personalist philosophy had much to do with the fact that it affirmed his rationalism and his spirituality, though he always insisted that he was a personalist on the basis of its truth claims alone. He honored religious experience wherever he found it. His principle that religious experience furnishes the data for truth about religion opened his thinking to non-Christian traditions. Though he wrote very little about non-Christian religions, he studied the classic texts of Western and Eastern mysticism, claimed special kinships with Jews, Buddhists, and Muslims, and in his later years he was a close friend of Swami Akhilananda, whose spiritual practices he followed. "I have no sympathy with the idea that experience of God is confined to Christians," Brightman declared. "That view seems both pettily provincial and crudely intellectualistic." He judged that the Wesleyan Holiness sects were probably richer in genuine experience of God than many of his cultured colleagues and that sincere atheists were probably closer to God than the indifferent half-believers in various mainline churches. "Any consciousness of the presence of God is religious experience," he believed. "It makes no difference whether it is conventional or unconventional; a stereotyped 'conversion' experience or a brief blissful vision on the mountain top. If we are aware in any way of the presence of the Divine, we are having a religious experience." In *The Spiritual Life* (1942) he urged that spirit is power: "It changes the weak and dispirited consciousness into strong and energetic will. Longing for the spirit is longing for power."[99]

Brightman felt spiritually linked to all who devoted themselves to a superhuman order of reality and value. His spiritual ecumenism did not extend to those who took a nonmetaphysical view of religion. Henry Nelson Wieman was a respected friend, but Brightman could not abide the naturalistic humanists at Chicago. He had warm relationships with various kinds of idealists, but he shook his head at the MacTaggart atheists. It offended him when nonbelievers appropriated the name of religion. He doubted that the cause of religion would find so many ostensible allies among humanists and idealistic atheists "were it not for the fact that filthy lucre is available in theological schools and churches for those who are reputed to be religious." Brightman protested that if one has no faith in an objective source of value, then "one has given up religion, and it is only verbalism to deny this fact."[100]

Though he was often interpreted as believing otherwise, Brightman did not believe that the cause of religion stands or falls with the cause of personalistic metaphysics. He had no doubt that religion would survive if personalism was disproved, and he claimed to embrace personalism only because it seemed to be true, not because it supports religion. All truth is hypothetical, he argued, and personalist philosophy is simply the best explanation of the facts. In addition it carries the advantage of converging with religion on the truth that the personal is real and the real is personal. With distinctive persistence, intellectual acuity, and influence, Brightman pressed the question of what it means to say that personality is the key to reality.

He distinguished personalism from skepticism, which denies that there is a key to reality; from dogmatism, which appeals to outside authority; from appeals to subpersonal principles like matter or energy, which cannot account for the phenomenon of consciousness; and from the kind of superpersonal principles featured in mystical theology, which are too vague and undefinable to explain anything. He defined personalism as the view that personality is the principle that unites and explains everything else in life. Emphatically Brightman objected to the common impression that personalists identify the real with the human. The personalist personality is no more confined to the individual human self than the ego of Fichte's idealism is to be identified with Johann Gottlieb Fichte, he insisted. In personalist thinking, the real is always a complex of selves or an episode in the experience of a cosmic self. "Personalists are not talking primarily about human selves," Brightman explained. "They are talking about the objective structure of things, external to man's mind."[101]

Speaking in a general way, personalists agreed in defining a personality as a self-conscious unity of self-experience; a person is a conscious unity. Brightman cautioned that this does not mean that personality should be identified with reflective self-consciousness: "It is any consciousness of any kind experienced as belonging together in one unitary whole in the unique way which we mean when we say, 'This experience is mine.'" All experiences are self-experiences, but only occasionally do we reflect on being a self. In the grammar of personalism, to say that the self is a conscious unity excludes any sort of union with anything that is not the self's consciousness. Put differently, Brightman argued, the self has a body, but the self is not a body, "not even in part." It is not a part or process of the body. Brightman had enough interest in his body to follow an exercise regime of swimming and walking, but he wanted no part of his body to be identified with him. Whatever one remembers to be part of the unity of one's consciousness is part of oneself, he reasoned; whatever does not fall within the unity of one's consciousness is not part of oneself.[102]

This argument notwithstanding, Brightman was sensitive to the hazard of over-analytical distinctions. For example, Bowne distinguished between the agent (the agent as the self) and the agent's acts (which are products of the self). Various idealists similarly distinguished between the "I" and "me." Brightman countered that nothing real is gained by these distinctions. It is enough to say that the agent, the I, is the present unity of consciousness as now experienced: "If 'I' (vs. 'me') is substance it is to be rejected as unintelligible and functionless; if it is not substance but self-consciousness, then it is merely a name for 'me' or a phase of 'me.'"[103]

Skeptics question how one can know that there is such a thing as a person. Brightman gave Knudson's Augustinian-Cartesian answer, that in his immediate experience he found that he is such a being: "I find myself; I do not invent myself. I am experience." Credible claims to knowledge require more than immediate experience, he acknowledged, for knowledge entails understanding, relation, and interpretation. Experience contains immediacy (the presence of feelings, relations within the given) and references beyond immediacy (memories, things, relations beyond the given). Immediate experience as such is not knowledge, yet no person has any knowledge that was not immediate experience at some point. All knowing is mediated by immediate experience; it becomes knowledge by virtue of its coherence and adequacy. The claim that one experiences a self in immediate experience is an inference that, to be credible, must be based on coherent and adequate knowledge. Immediate experience is potentially rational, Brightman reflected, but self-knowledge requires reason. Through memory and anticipation, the self experienced in immediacy links itself to a past self and a future self, while reason judges the claims of both memory and anticipation. Thus, as a subjective fact, the self is self-known as a rationally remembered and anticipated unity of consciousness.[104]

But the self is more than a subjective fact. Brightman's disembodied personality only seemed Cartesian, for he emphasized that the self is not merely a unit of reflective self-experience; it is always interacting with something that is not itself; it can be known from within and from without. One can learn a great deal about one's self by learning about one's body, he acknowledged, or by learning about one's behavior or about the familial, geographical, and sociopolitical conditions of one's life. Introspection is a teacher, but so is empirical observation. Both are necessary to the making of a self. Brightman noted that personalist philosophy shared a good deal of ground with psychology in making this claim; on the other hand, the metaphysical reality named "personality" is prior to and more than the self studied in psychology. It is the presupposition and agent of all science and experience. Every science discloses something about the powers of personality in the course of investigating its aspect of the world, and personalist philosophy is obliged to be consistent with the empirical facts discovered by the various scientific disciplines. But philosophy has its own tasks and trajectory, Brightman emphasized, which are metaphysical; philosophy provides a view of the whole of experience by criticizing, unifying, and supplementing science. It presses certain questions distinctively, such as the criterion and nature of value, and it theorizes certain facts distinctively, such as the unity of personality.

Psychology does not ask whether personality is the key to reality; personalist philosophy asks the question and affirms that personality is cosmomorphic, not anthropomorphic. Space is found in human experience, Brightman noted, yet everyone agrees that space is cosmomorphic. Similarly, everyone attributes cosmomorphic status to time and mathematics; Plato taught that God geometrizes. Brightman pressed the personalist question: "If space and time and mathematics are regarded as characterizing the whole physical universe beyond man, without being condemned as purely subjective or anthropomorphic merely because they are found in man, is it not possible that the principle of personality is likewise a universal and cosmic principle found in man?" Critics of personalism charged that Lotze and Bowne interpreted the universe in personal terms, making God in their own image. Brightman countered, "Yet is it not at least equally possible that God made man in his own image, and that man is therefore theomorphic, cosmomorphic? To deny any clues to objective reality within man is to deny all science and all objective knowledge."[105]

Bowne-school personalists claimed that personality is such a clue. Brightman observed that if this claim has any validity at all, the implications are enormous: "If it is a clue at all, it is a first principle more fundamental than space or time or mathematics, for space and time and mathematics presuppose and require personality in order to be or be experienced." The personalist claim is not that the universe is a copy of the self in the mirror or the self portrayed in psychology textbooks; in personalist theory the real is a complex of selves. "Yet on the other hand," Brightman reflected, "it is equally certain that the universe must be such as to include and explain you and me, with all of our idiosyncracies; and a philosophy which omits from its data any of the facts of individual personality is just as uncritical and arbitrary as a philosophy which identifies my present tastes and preferences with the eternal purpose of the universe."[106]

For Brightman, as for Bowne and Knudson, personality was the unifying principle, its certainty secured by the fact that the reality of everything else depends upon it. Without personality, Brightman argued, space, time, and mathematics would be meaningless, and the great cosmomorphic truths would disintegrate into shards of vanishing experience. And if this much is certain, is there not sufficient reason to believe that personality is a more fundamental clue to objective reality than space, time, and number? Personality does not require space, but space, time, and number are attributes of personality. Brightman waxed nearly poetic in describing the kind of unifying principle that personalism affirms. It was a vision of the kingdom come: "Remove desire for victory in war, but leave desire for the highest and best; remove the particular local environment of this or that man's experience, but leave the power to interact with any environment; remove the memories of this man's particular weaknesses and sins, but leave memory as the unifying power binding past and present; remove petty and selfish purposes, but leave purpose as the movement of reality into the future; remove the traits of my partly-integrated personality, but leave the experience of the unity of consciousness as indivisible wholeness."[107]

In *Philosophy of Personalism* Knudson identified the basic traits of personality as conscious unity (individuality), identity (consciousness), and free activity (will); later he added a fourth characteristic, self-control. Brightman, in language a bit different, distinguished among the form of personality (the laws of reason), the content of personality (the brute facts of experience), and the activity of personality (its power of will to make choices and direct consciousness). The differences between these accounts were mostly semantic, however; Brightman and Knudson, with essentially the same understanding of personality, both excluded the body from their definition of personality, on the ground that the body cannot be present in consciousness. Brightman believed that by excluding the body from the idea of personality, he and Knudson showed their seriousness about purging all anthropomorphic elements from this idea; those who charged that personalism was anthropomorphic didn't know what they were talking about.[108]

Brightman and Knudson did not convince all their disciples to divorce consciousness from embodiment; otherwise their theorizing on personality defined the credo of the Boston school. For all of his modifications of Bownean idealism, Brightman was no less thoroughgoing in his idealism than Bowne and Knudson. For them, spirit and matter were aspects of a single unitary process, the process of divine will. Personalism is not the assertion of the superiority of mind over matter, they argued; that would be a form of dualism. Rather, personalist idealism is the assertion that nothing truly impersonal exists; the supposed problem of "mind and matter" is a misunderstanding of the spiritual significance of matter. A stone appears to be impersonal, Brightman explained, and it assuredly has no personality of its own, but from the standpoint of personalist idealism, even a stone is part of the conscious activity of the divine person. So-called matter is "nothing but the energizing of the will of the cosmic person." The supposed relation of mind and matter is actually a relation of spirit and spirit; in Brightman's words, "For the idealistic personalist, the whole of nature, as revealed in our sense experience, is truly what Berkeley called it, a divine language, which symbolizes to our minds the purpose and the reason of the divine mind."[109]

The seed of a nature-valorizing philosophy of nature was there, though the second-generation personalists did not develop it; if the natural world was merely phenomenally real, not metaphysically real, it was not quite worth their time. Brightman and Knudson fully shared that provincialism, though Brightman differed from Knudson in emphasizing that personality is a complex whole. To Brightman, the unified and unifying nature of the self was the key to the self's importance. A personality is a complex whole in which form, content, and activity are united inseparably, he argued. Brightman's signature essay on this theme, "Personality as a Metaphysical Principle," achieved a kind of canonical status in the field, though he continued to rethink what it meant. That restless rethinking marked another difference from Knudson.

PERSONALISM AS THEOLOGY: KNUDSON AND THE RELIGIOUS A PRIORI

Albert Knudson had a keen sense of living in dismal times, at least theologically. Though liberalism conquered the field of theology during his lifetime, he took little satisfaction from its professional success; he took it as a personal mission to rescue liberal theology from shallow reasoning and cultural fads. By 1927 he was a man in a hurry. Institutionally he had begun to build the kind of seminary that progressive Methodism needed; philosophically he had made his case for the personalist school; now he needed to provide the school's theology. His sense of urgency was fueled by his sense of the crisis of theology and of his own late start. His first volume of constructive theology, *The Doctrine of God*, appeared in 1930. Immediately Knudson diagnosed the crisis of theology: modern theology wins little respect in modern thought because modern thought is antiauthoritarian and antimetaphysical. To Knudson these were very different kinds of problems; he embraced the modern rejection of authority religion but regarded the second problem as a prejudice that had to be resisted.[110]

Knudson quickly disposed of the first problem. "Authoritarianism belongs to the past. Progressive Protestant theology has set it aside," he announced. The first problem, a hangover from Christianity's long authoritarian past, had no future. Implicitly, progressive Protestant theology simply needed to get out the word that it bowed to no external authority. The second problem was more disturbing. Throughout his career Bowne fought against philosophies that gave primacy to the things of sense, but Bowne lived at a time when neo-Hegelians still ruled the field of philosophy. Knudson's *Philosophy of Personalism* celebrated its connection to the broad currents of modern idealist philosophy, especially the stream of Lotze and Bowne. But *The Doctrine of God* conceded on its first page that an antimetaphysical temper ruled contemporary philosophy and culture. Modern thinkers looked down on theology because they presumed that theology is authoritarian and metaphysical. Many theologians dealt with the second problem in the same way they dealt with the first, by cutting loose from metaphysical claims.

Knudson countered that no theology worthy of the name gives up the claim to metaphysical truth. "Metaphysics has to do with ultimate reality; it has to do with what 'God' stands for in religion," he admonished. Some theologians expounded the biblical doctrine of God without grounding their thinking in a philosophical worldview; they retained the metaphysical contents of religious speech without providing methodological warrants for their claims. Others abandoned all metaphysical claims for theology. Knudson judged that the former strategy was pitifully superficial and the second strategy amounted to theological suicide. Theology cannot renounce metaphysics "without ceasing to be theology," he insisted. Modern theologians needed to struggle for a different kind of modernity; the new schools of liberal theology would never save theology. "Most of the crudities and vagaries of current popular and so-called 'scientific' theology are due to a lack of metaphysical insight," he declared. "To eschew metaphysics in the field of theology is to fall back into a shallow ecclesiastical or sense dogmatism."[111]

Knudson's conception of theology was straightforwardly rationalistic. He defined theology as "the systematic exposition and rational justification of the intellectual content of religion." His method of exposition was that of the normative sciences, which examined the relevant data of Christian experience and history; his method of justification eschewed all appeals to external authority, resting on the claims of reason and critically interpreted experience. Knudson shook his head at Barth's condemnation of natural theology. He never tired of blasting Barth's "irrational" insistence that theology must be carried out as the explication of self-authenticating revelation. Knudson's theology had his own version of a self-authenticating religious basis, however; he called it "the religious apriori." Bowne occasionally gave a glancing nod to this idea, but Knudson featured the religious apriori throughout his theological career.[112]

Bowne's version of this idea owed more to William James's *Varieties of Religious Experience* than to liberal theology. In the opening sentence of his book *Theism*, Bowne declared that humankind is religious, "however it came about." A few pages later he made a single-sentence aside that took a position on how religion came about: "We must assume that religion is founded in human nature as one of its essential needs and constitutional tendencies." Knudson's version of this idea linked him to Schleiermacher, Ernst Troeltsch, and Rudolf Otto. In a 1922 festschrift honoring Bowne's memory, he made four claims about the religious a priori. The fourth was that it was "the only logical position" for religious believers to take; the other three were straight from Schleiermacher. To say that there is such a thing as a religious a priori is not to claim that religion is an isolated phenomenon, he observed, for religion always "stands in a structural relation to life or reason as a whole." Religious experience is not derivative of anything else, but is "something fundamental and irreducible, as much so as the intellectual, moral, and aesthetic interests of men." Knudson's third claim for the religious a priori was that it "rests upon as sure a basis as does either science or ethics."[113]

These were the founding claims of Schleiermacher's *Speeches on Religion* (1799), which he developed in his dogmatics. The idea of a religious a priori did heavy work in Knudson's dogmatics as well, where it was connected to Otto's idea of an objectively numinous dimension of religious experience. Knudson argued that because religion always involves a personal attitude toward an objective realm of values, it is never purely subjective and its subjectivity is complex. The first essential element of religion is a trustful dependence on a higher power; Schleiermacher called this element the feeling of absolute dependence, Otto a creature-feeling religious awe. The second element is a longing for redemption, which has a more specific object than the feeling of trustful dependence or awe. To long for redemption is to look to the goal of life, not to ordinary experiences, Knudson observed, and to look with hope based upon faith in a supernatural power. The third essential aspect of religious experience is its implicit alliance with a moral ideal.[114]

Knudson appealed to the religious a priori to explain the difference between mere longing for redemption and the true religious longing that arises only through faith. Faith is not merely an inference, a product of unsatisfied desire, or the end of an argument, he contended. From the standpoint of faith, Julius Kaftan argued that religion is desire; from the standpoint of disbelief, Ludwig Feuerbach pressed a similar theory about the nature of religion. Knudson countered that faith is something deeper, more immediate and more encompassing than inferential reasoning or desire: "It is rooted in elementary experience and in the very structure of reason. There is such a thing as a religious apriori, and there is such a thing as a 'numinous' experience, a direct awareness of the Divine, both of which antedate the inference from human defeat to supernatural aid." While acknowledging that desire plays an important role in religious experience, he argued that religion derives from and concerns itself with something greater than the valid or invalid objectification of desire. Knudson agreed with Otto that religion and morality are linked by an a priori bond. Religion is about trustful dependence, the faithful longing for life abundant and salvation, and a sense of moral obligation to God and humanity. It is an experience of the divine that finds its ground in an ought-philosophy, not a wish-philosophy.[115]

Schleiermacher conceived the feeling of absolute dependence as "a universal element of life" that deserved to replace the proofs of God's existence as the cornerstone of Christian dogmatics. While allowing that Schleiermacher may have slightly exaggerated the apologetic value of the religious a priori, Knudson embraced his dictum that religious experience is structural in human nature and self-standing alongside science and ethics. Religion is self-authenticating, Schleiermacher argued; it does not need to be validated by science, morality, or history. Knudson agreed that religion has its own source and goal: "Religion is as independent, as ultimate and as irreducible as any other factor or element of our mental nature, and hence it may be regarded as verifying itself."[116]

From Otto, Knudson appropriated the idea of an irrational a priori; from Troeltsch he took the idea of linking the religious a priori to the Kantian theory of the categories. Troeltsch viewed religion as belonging to reason, though his conception of rationality was broader than theoretical reason. For Troeltsch, reason was equivalent to the theoretical, practical, and aesthetic endeavors of the human spirit. In Troeltsch's usage, Knudson noted, the religious a priori is formal in character—like the Kantian categories—and manifests itself only in and through experience. Religious experience presupposes a religious a priori, but this immanent principle has no independent existence. It is the condition of religious consciousness, not a separate factor within religious consciousness.[117]

Otto's version of the religious a priori elaborated the distinction between a rational and an irrational a priori. In Otto's theorizing, the rational religious a priori manifests itself in the attributes that religious people assign to God, such as God's absoluteness, personality, and goodness. The irrational a priori manifests itself in the numinous feeling of awe that people experience in the presence of God. Otto believed that the rational and irrational aspects of religion both have their wellsprings in the hidden depths of the spirit; moreover, he theorized that the numinous feeling and the conception of divine goodness are bound together in an inward union that has its own a priori character. According to Otto, the a priori bond between the rational and irrational aspects of religious experience shows forth when the religious spirit instinctively ratifies the moral character of God. In support of Otto's theory Knudson cited the response of Hebrew religion to the moral judgments of the prophets, though Knudson's deeper concern was always the apologetic use of the religious a priori. "The main truth . . . is that of the autonomous validity of our religious nature," he asserted. "Religion is as structural in reason or in our total personality as are science, art, and morality, and may, therefore, be regarded as equally permanent and equally trustworthy. As these other interests justify themselves, so also do religion and the belief in God."[118]

This was a both/and strategy. Hegelian theologies took their stand on meta-physical reason; the school of Schleiermacher claimed that religious experience is its own self-authenticating ground. Knudson said yes to both. Faith and reason belong together, he insisted: "There is no reason without a measure of faith, and there is no self-consistent reason without more or less of religious faith. On the other hand, there is no faith without some reason, and there certainly is no self-consistent faith without a very considerable admixture of reason." Though he fol-lowed Bowne in sharply distinguishing between phenomenal and metaphysical reality, Knudson contended that knowledge is not a dual kingdom in which rea-son and faith hold separate rule over independent spheres: "It is a monarchy gov-erned by rational faith or believing reason." In some instances the rational factor needs to be dominant, he reasoned; in other instances the believing factor needs to hold sway. "But the two cannot be completely separated. Only an illicit abstraction can divorce them."[119]

He had immense faith in the power of metaphysical reason to rationalize and defend Christianity, but he saw no reason to carry out this project without an immunized basis of faith on his side. The religious a priori not only provides a secure basis of faith, Knudson reasoned; it also provides an apologetic model for speaking about and securing the objectivity of values, the reality of the ideal, and the moral necessity of religion: "At bottom they all amount to about the same thing." The religious apriori includes a sense of "ought" that we cannot escape. Knudson followed Kant on the absoluteness of the moral law: "Duty stands above us with a sway we cannot break. This is an ultmate fact which each must recog-nize for himself and one which, when recognized, justifies itself." The value of a merely subjective law of right is merely practical and aesthetic, Knudson argued; the moral law is the ground of an objective belief only if it is absolute. The "ought" of moral obligation must come from "the larger realm of reality," not merely from one's ego or society, if it is to be morally serious. The morally seri-ous meaning of "I must" is that the nature of things commands me to do some-thing. "This assumption is implicit in the sense of duty, and it is this fact that gives to duty its absolute character," Knudson remarked. There is no moral law if the moral law is not absolute; but if there is a moral law, then the universe has a moral character.[120]

Knudson's Schleiermacherian argument for a religious a priori and his Kant-ian argument for the absoluteness of moral law were variations of the same argu-ment. Kant upheld the absoluteness of the moral law and the moral necessity of religion; Bowne spoke of an implicit faith in the reality of an ideal; Schleierma-cher, Troeltsch, and Otto described a prereflective experience of the divine. All were variations on the same logic of the a priori. Value judgments are meaning-less without an objective reference, Knudson observed; to affirm a value is to affirm an objective order that has value. When we appeal to moral or ideal values, the objectivity of these values is implied in their very conception. Our moral values would not be values if there were no existence that corresponded to them. Valuation implies objectification. The logic of the religious a priori thus grounded not only Knudson's claims for a God relation, but also his claims for the moral character of reality. It established that religion is self-standing and self-authenticating, that the idealizing process inherent in religion is structural in human reason, and that practical reason contains an inner logic that leads to religious faith. We cannot rationally deny value to reality, Knudson urged, for rationality begins with an implicit faith in ideals: "We may describe this faith as an objectification of our ideals or as a religious apriori, but however described, it is an ultimate fact of our nature, a kind of moral necessity." On this necessity he based his case for the reality of religion and the goodness of God.[121]

THE FOURFOLD RULE OF FAITH AND THE CHRISTLIKE GOD

Knudson was a devoted Methodist, though, like Bowne, he believed that Methodist theology could become modern only by starting over. He loved to quote John Wesley on the centrality of religious experience, but he quoted very selectively, and on other subjects he rarely quoted Wesley at all. For reasons that he plainly expressed, he ignored the major theologians of the Methodist tradition. Commenting on the work of his major theological predecessors—English Methodists Richard Watson and William Burt Pope, and American Methodists Miner Raymond and John Miley—he allowed that they did "creditable work" in systematizing traditional Methodist doctrine: "But they were not creative thinkers, they introduced no new theological method, they were guided by no new organizing principle, they gave no new direction to theological thought." Therefore they had little relevance for the work of modern theology: "They reflected for the most part the authoritarian standpoint of the current traditional evangelicalism."[122]

What Knudson did claim from the Methodist tradition was Wesley's emphasis on religious experience, free will, the personal and moral character of God, and, without identifying it as a specifically Wesleyan notion, the belief that theological affirmations should be based on four distinct sources of witness and information. A generation after Knudson propounded a decidedly liberal version, Methodist theologian Albert C. Outler named it "the Wesleyan Quadrilateral."[123]

The idea of the Wesleyan Quadrilateral is that Wesley initiated an approach to theology that appealed to the authority of Scripture, church tradition, reason, and Christian experience. Knudson's version of this idea helped Methodist thinkers resist the fundamentalist ascendancy of the 1920s; some who adopted it were more interested in accounting for the distinctive Wesleyan emphasis on sanctification. In its tradition-specific form, the argument for a fourfold rule is that Wesley, an Anglican priest, practiced an approach to theology that added Christian experience as an operative religious authority to the traditional Anglican triad of Scripture, tradition, and reason. Wesley believed that all knowledge begins with experience and that the Christian experience of "full salvation" is a material source of theology. One of his favorite expressions was that "the Spirit of God directly witnesses to my spirit."[124]

Outler later elaborated an influential argument about the legacy of Wesleyan theology that confirmed much of Knudson's feeling about it. Outler contended that none of Wesley's theological disciples construed the Christian faith with Wesley's theology-refiguring emphasis on the testimony of the Holy Spirit as an inward impression on the soul. The fathers of Methodist theology turned Wesleyan teaching into a traditional dogmatism, systematizing Wesley's belief in the infallibility of Scripture in a way that was not true to Wesley's spirit and practice. Many of their theological offspring were outright biblicists who laid the groundwork for what became Methodist fundamentalism. The theologians of twentieth-century mainline Methodism thus fastened on the idea that good Wesleyan theology tests all doctrine by the authority of Scripture, tradition, reason, and experience; at least implicitly, they argued, the Wesleyan approach to theology is modern.[125]

Knudson played a key role in establishing this rendering of the Wesleyan approach to theology, though he did not describe it as distinctively Wesleyan, and as a liberal he did not speak of Scripture or tradition as authorities for theology. "The question as to the sources of theology was in the past bound up with the idea of an infallible revelation made through a divinely inspired book or church or both," he observed. "This idea we no longer hold. We do not believe in either biblical or ecclesiastical infallibility." To his mind the concepts of inspiration and infallibility were inseparably linked, and infallibility belonged to the authoritarian past. He dismissed the idea of qualifying or reinterpreting infallibilty, and he took no interest in saving a doctrine of divine inspiration that did not claim infallibility. Though he allowed in a half-sentence aside that "much might be said in favor of the unique inspiration" of Scripture, his dogmatics said nothing else on this topic. For Knudson, these were premodern concerns. He gave only a few sentences to the question of how Scripture functions in theology. Carefully avoiding the word "authority," he described the Bible as the church's normative source of information about the founding events of Christianity. The Bible holds a preeminent status among the church's sources of information because it is the only place where we learn of God's revelation "through Jewish and early Christian history."[126]

The function of church tradition in theology got even briefer mention in his dogmatics. Two sentences handled theology's second source of information. Knudson noted that the creeds and confessions of the churches are part of the church's Christian self-understanding. To know what Christianity is, he asserted, "we must take into account not only the teaching of Scripture, but the whole history of the Christian Church." In the next sentence he expanded the meaning of tradition as a theological source, urging that "tradition" should not mean the Christian tradition only: "We need to extend our inquiries so as to take in the religious life and beliefs of men in general. Only against the background of other religions and in relation to them can Christianity be fully understood." It followed that in addition to drawing upon the disciplines of biblical exegesis and

Christian history, the theologian also needs to be informed by modern psychology of religion, the history of religions, and philosophy of religion.[127]

Knudson devoted considerably greater attention to the roles of reason and experience as sources of theology. Persistently he argued that a modern theology must be a theology of reason and experience that is informed by the witness of Scripture and the history of religion. "The characteristic thing in Protestantism is not its belief in the inspiration of the Bible, but its belief in the inspiration of the individual," he contended. The authoritarian churches of the Reformation spoke of the *testimonium spiritus* as the ultimate ground for accepting the biblical revelation; in Knudson's rendering modern Protestantism reclaimed and exalted this notion as the "power of appeal to the individual soul." He asserted that the Bible—"particularly the New Testament"—is the main source of information for theology, while the church, the natural reason, and Christian experience supplement the Bible as regulative sources. Thus, at least formally, he explicitly endorsed the four components of what was later called the Wesleyan Quadrilateral, though Outler and other advocates of the Wesleyan Quadrilateral usually claimed to recover Wesley's neglected method of approaching theology. Knudson made no such claim. He emphasized the divide between the premodern acceptance of external authority and the modern break from external authority. His aim was progress, not recovery. He sought to modernize the Wesleyan tradition, perhaps in Wesley's spirit, but not on his authority.[128]

Knudson cherished Wesley chiefly as a forerunner to Schleiermacher; the greatness of Wesley lay in his high regard for religious experience, Knudson argued, which planted the seed of modern theology. "The 'implicit' theology of Methodism is to be found in its emphasis on religious experience," he asserted. "According to Wesley the only genuine religion is experienced religion." Knudson took pride in the fact that Wesley's emphasis on experience "led to a large degree of liberality in doctrinal matters." More importantly, the Wesleyan emphasis on experience contained the germ of the modern empirical approach to theology. Knudson explained: "Conditions favorable to the development of this germ did not exist in early Methodism. But Wesley did much to prepare the way in the Anglo-Saxon world for the modern empirical theology associated with the names of Schleiermacher and Ritschl."[129] His favorite Wesley proof text was that experience is "the strongest of all arguments . . . and the most infallible of all proofs."[130] In his dogmatic theology no less than in his apologetics, Knudson proposed to explain what it means to take reason-tested experience seriously in theology.

The appeal of Bowne-Knudson style personalism in mainstream Methodism was greatly enhanced by its defense of the divine personality of Jesus and God. Knudson blasted various theologies to his left for shrinking the New Testament Christ and abandoning the personal-supernatural God of Christianity. Though he railed against neo-orthodoxy for its irrationalism and its refusal to accept "that in our day theology must be anthropocentric in its starting point," he was equally rough on the kind of historicism that stripped the New Testament Christ down to a liberal picture of the historical Jesus. Christianity was not founded on the

person or religion of a nondivine historical Jesus, he insisted. The liberal historicist dichotomy between the religion *of* Jesus and the religion *about* Jesus was
wholly misleading, because it treated the Christian religion about a divine Jesus
as a degenerate offshoot of Jesus's own gospel. Knudson admonished that Christianity was founded on the impression of divinity made by the personality *of* Jesus
on his disciples; there is no Christianity apart from this double impression: "The
disciples saw in Jesus and his work not simply a human quest after God, but a
divine quest after man. They beheld in him not merely the perfect sanctity of a
man, but the gracious advent of Deity. They heard in the message of his life and
death not only the voice of man, but the voice of God." The New Testament is
pervaded by this double impression, Knudson urged. Modern theology cannot
reduce it to something simpler without destroying the irreducible basis of Christianity. The notion that modern theology must do so is a naturalistic prejudice,
not a rational necessity.[131]

Knudson was equally opposed to the liberal drift away from classical theism.
Naturalistic theologies appalled him. Chicago-school naturalism treated nature
as metaphysically real and, at most, it viewed God as real only in a secondary
sense as a part or product of nature. By defining God as a law or process, the
Chicago schoolers attributed reality to God only in the sense that a law or social
process is real. Knudson countered that the real God of Christianity is a supernatural Person who is metaphysically absolute and ethically perfect. The personalist affirmation of the metaphysical God of Christianity corrects one key aspect
of classical theism, he allowed. Classical theism had a vague concept of personality and thus played up the reality of personality *in* God. Personalist theism was
informed by the modern understanding of a person as an individual center of
self-consciousness and by the demands of modern science for a unitary world
ground; thus it emphasized the personality *of* God. Human personality is not a
mirror of God's inner life, Knudson acknowledged; it is a symbol of God's personality. The divine personality transcends our comprehension—"what that life
is we cannot fully understand"—but something indispensably important to
Christian faith is secured in the affirmation that God's personality is something
like our own. To say that God is personal is to ascribe intelligence and freedom
to God. Without intelligence and freedom, God cannot be good; and if God is
not personal, there is no possibility of personal communion with God.[132]

To Knudson the reality of divine personality was the key to everything else,
and everything was at stake in the question of divine omnipotence. God cannot
be morally perfect if God is not omnipotent, he insisted, for absolute goodness
presupposes and requires absolute power. Knudson reasoned that God accepted
the conditions under which evil occurs because these conditions make divine and
human creativity possible. Respectfully he jousted with his best friend on this
subject. Brightman theorized that while God is perfectly good and rational in
Godself, there is a recalcitrant factor in God's being that frustrates the realization
of God's highest values. This endless struggle in God's nature makes God less than
omnipotent, though not less than absolutely good. Knudson liked Brightman's

metaphysical case for the idea of sacrificial love and was intrigued by the idea of moral struggle in God. But he rejected Brightman's picture of a dualism in the divine consciousness, which Knudson found intellectually wrong and religiously disastrous: "Two fundamental motives lie back of religion and of metaphysical philosophy. One is the need of a supreme good and the other the need of an ultimate unity. These two needs can find complete satisfaction only in an omnipotent Being who is able to reduce all multiplicity to unity and able to subdue all resisting forces to his own holy will." It is not enough to claim that God has good intentions, Knudson admonished; it was not even enough to say that God is the most powerful being in the universe. Perfect unity and perfect goodness require an all-powerful unitive ground. Brightman settled for perfect goodness of intention, "but what religion needs is an absolute objective goodness and this cannot exist even as an object of hope without an omnipotent will."[133]

On the doctine of the divine Trinity, Knudson preferred McConnell's "Christlike God" over the Nicene Creed. Like the early Unitarians, he emphasized the Christlike personality of God, but he was not tempted by Unitarianism. He liked the vitalistic and relational values of orthodox Trinitarianism; at the same time he found grave difficulties in its Neoplatonist categories. The church fathers had a vague concept of personality; they flirted with tritheism in defining the Father, Son, and Holy Spirit as persons; they made a weak case for the personality of the Holy Spirit; with their Neoplatonist realism, they subordinated personality to essence; and they two-sidedly identified the divine element in Christ with the Logos and the ego of Jesus. The crucial word "person" is hopelessly problematic in Nicene Christianity, Knudson noted; usually it is closely linked to the Greek *hypostasis,* which denotes a mode of being somewhere between a person and an attribute. Moreover, modern people do not believe in the distinct Logos imagined by Greek philosophy; modern theology affirms the existence of divine reason, he assured, but not as something detachable from the divine personality. Knudson preferred Schleiermacher on the divinity of Christ; what made Jesus different from other people was "the constant potency of His God-consciousness, which was a veritable existence of God in Him."[134]

The Trinity was a dilemma for modern theology; Knudson saw three viable options. The first was to affirm the Trinity as a symbol of the richness of God without claiming to know the inner structure of God's being. Classical theology claimed to know that God has one essence, two processions, three persons, four relations, and five notions. Knudson urged that even a metaphysically oriented modern theology has to be more modest: "We do not know what hypostatic distinctions there are, if any, in the Divine Being, nor what their relations to each other are, but we are confident that we come nearest the truth when we think of God as Father, Son, and Holy Spirit. These are symbolic terms that express the inexhaustible richness of the divine nature; and it is chiefly because of this fact that the church has clung so tenaciously to them and to the Trinitarian doctrine in which they have been embodied."[135]

The second option was a modified Sabellianism. The old Sabellian theology was not wrong for teaching a Trinity of manifestation, Knudson reasoned; it was wrong only for failing to bring the Trinity of manifestation into direct relation with God's essential nature. There *is* no Trinity of manifestation if it has no relation to a Trinity of essence. Put differently, the modalist doctrine of the Trinity associated with Sabellianism is compatible with, and necessarily related to, the idea of an immanent Trinity. Knudson argued that God's inner trinity of essence and God's triune manifestation as Father, Son, and Spirit belong together: "We learn the Trinity of essence from the Trinity of manifestation, and the Trinity of manifestation derives its religious significance from the Trinity of essence." The modified Sabellian option was to affirm that the terms Father, Son, and Spirit correlate with God's essential nature without claiming to know how they are distinct or related in God's inner being. Knudson noted that the systematic theology of his teacher, Henry C. Sheldon, offered a worthy example of this option.[136]

The third option was McConnell's emphasis on the Christlikeness of God. With all of its problems, McConnell observed, the doctrine of the Trinity has remained impressively vital in Christian thought and practice. Something must explain its persistence in Christian life over the centuries. McConnell judged that this something is the ethical conception of God that the doctrine conveys. The idea of the Trinity does not merely make a place for Christ in God's life "in the sense of granting him divine honors," he observed. Rather, the key to the Trinity is that it carries "the Christ-spirit into the Divine," or put differently, it reveals the divine "as throughout Christlike." The early Christians came to think of God differently by virtue of what they saw in Christ, McConnell explained. Christ made the impression of godliness upon them, which changed their image of godliness. The early Christians came to believe that the life which they saw in Christ was God's own life. "They were willing to follow that life even into their theories about the inner constitution of divinity," McConnell remarked. "Moral unity has weighed more than metaphysical unity."[137]

Without taking leave of the symbolic and modified Sabellian options, Knudson embraced McConnell's position. The key to the Trinity is the affirmation of the Christlikeness of God, he contended: "If this conception of God is granted, we have the heart of the Trinitarian doctrine and for practical purposes need nothing more." Christians believe that God loves the world with self-sacrificial love because they have seen God in Christ. Christ is the "express image" of the eternal for Christians. "In this conception we have the basis of all that is distinctive in the teaching of the New Testament and of the church concerning the divine grace," Knudson affirmed, downgrading the Holy Spirit. McConnell argued elsewhere that the early theologians of the Trinity recognized that the Father and Son could not be vitally united if each were the object of the other's eternal gaze: "So they made the forthgoing of the Spirit a mighty enterprise in which each was alike implicated. The fellowship of Father and Son was a fellowship in the Spirit, in the sending forth of the Spirit and in the ongoings of the Spirit."[138]

McConnell conceded that the third factor could have been a common ideal interest; it did not have to be a person. Knudson seized on this admission. There is nothing in either the idea of love or of self-consciousness "that warrants the ascription of personality to the Spirit," he declared. At best, the Holy Spirit had secondary significance for Knudson. The idea of the Trinity is a symbolic way of dramatizing the divine love, he reasoned. The symbolism of triunity undoubtedly has a practical value in appealing to the imagination. It was even to be expected that theologians would continue to write weighty tomes on God's triune self-relation. "But whatever value, practical or theoretical, it may have, it should not be forgotten that as an expression of the divine love it does not stand in its own right, but is dependent on faith in the Christlikeness of God." For similar reasons, Schleiermacher consigned his discussion of the Trinity to an appendix.[139]

From Bowne, Knudson took his epistemology, metaphysics, personalistic supernaturalism, and voluntarism; on ethical topics he fashioned his own moderate version of the social gospel; for most of the rest he leaned on Schleiermacher. His Christology was straight from Schleiermacher, as was his apriorist theory of religion, though Bowne could be quoted to the same effect on both subjects. On the subjects of sin and redemption he was a straightforward moral-influence atonement theorist, just like his heroes, though Knudson was distinctively emphatic that there is no sin apart from free-willed moral choice. In *The Doctrine of Redemption* (1933) he defined sin as "a defective attitude toward God, toward other people, and toward our true selves, for which we are accountable in God's sight." Knudson traced the origin of sin to humankind's power of self-determination: "Original sin in its traditional form is a fiction, and so are all theories that seek to explain its origin by a catastrophic act either in time or out of it. There is no such thing as inherited guilt or an inherited moral depravity."[140]

Freedom is essential to moral responsibility, and without free-willed moral choice and responsibility, there is no guilt for sin. Evil becomes moral "only when it is freely wrought." That is, evil becomes sin only when sin could have been avoided; "necessary sin" is not sin at all.[141] Knudson was fond of Wesley's saying that sin is a voluntary transgression of a known law, though he later qualified "this freedomistic definition" by affirming F. R. Tennant's principle that sin is moral imperfection for which a moral agent is accountable in God's sight. By its very nature, Knudson argued, sin is hostile to the divine will "and can therefore have had no place in the original divine plan for mankind." Sin is not a means to an end, even a hypothetical divine end: "The only responsibility that God has for sin is that he made it possible by the creation of free human beings."[142]

Knudson allowed that nonvoluntarist theologies have some scriptural passages on their side, but he argued that most of Scripture takes for granted that freely chosen moral blameworthiness is the essence of sin. The same judgment applied to atonement theory. While acknowledging that each of the objective atonement theories has a few scriptural proof texts, Knudson argued that the moral-influence theory of atonement is as long-standing as any theory in Christian history and has a preponderance of the relevant scriptural data on its side.[143]

Knudson's attention to objective atonement theories made him unusual among theological liberals of his generation. Objective atonement theory had been dead for long enough in modern theology that most of his theological colleagues gave it passing notice. In Knudson's telling the heroes of this story were Schleiermacher, Ritschl, and Horace Bushnell, who swept the house of theology clean of "impersonal" renderings of Christ's saving work. He described the ransom theory of atonement (prevalent in post-Nicene Christianity and conceiving of Christ's death as a ransom paid to Satan), and the satisfaction theory (formulated in the eleventh century by Anselm and conceiving of Christ's death as a sacrificial satisfaction of God's righteous honor and wrath), and the penal theory (a revision of satisfaction theory and conceiving of Christ's death as a retributive punishment that vicariously paid to God the full penalty due for sin), and the government theory (formulated in the seventeenth century by Hugh Grotius and conceiving of Christ's death as a penal example that demonstrated God's rectoral abhorrence of sin). These theories took various positions on the nature of Christ's atoning work, Knudson observed, but they held in common an impersonal view of the problem at issue. All of them pictured God as hampered or controlled in God's relation to human beings by nonpersonal factors.[144]

The essential problem with this picture was that God does not act like a loving, personal, omnipotent Father: "He bargains with Satan by offering a ransom for man's release. Or he provides a satisfaction for the dishonor that he has suffered as a kind of civil or ecclesiastical Potentate. Or he conducts himself as a heartless Judge requiring that the full penalty of sin be borne by an innocent Person before there can be any forgiveness of sins. Or he deals with men as a Ruler guided purely by considerations of public policy." All these theories portray God as something considerably less than a free and loving personality, Knudson observed. Aside from the ransom theory, which is crudely dualistic, the other theories limit God's free personality, by God's righteous honor, abstract justice, or the exigencies of effective government. Moreover, they wrongly treat merit and guilt as alienable from personality: the satisfaction theory proposes that one person's merit can be transferred to another; the penal theory represents guilt in the same way; all three of the objective postransom theories give a similar view of punishment or suffering. "The basal error in all the objective theories of the atonement is that they tend to treat persons as things," Knudson judged. He countered that ethical merit and sin are serious and personal; these realities cannot be detached from the persons to whom they belong. An innocent person can suffer because of the sins of others, Knudson allowed, "but he cannot justly be *punished* for their sins; nor can he acquire merit that may be transferred to others." Each person's character is necessarily one's own; that is the ethical personalist view that deserves to be called Christian.[145]

The ransom theory supposed that Satan is the chief obstacle to the redemption of humankind; the other objective theories pictured something in God's nature as the chief obstacle to salvation. Knudson observed that moral-influence theory conceives the problem of salvation very differently. It draws more from the ethical and intuitional understanding of salvation taught by the Johannine literature and implied in most of Paul's writing than from Paul's occasional legalistic and substitutionary images. Developed by Irenaeus, Origen, and Gregory of

Nazianzus in the early church and formulated as an independent theory by Abelard in the twelfth century, the moral-influence theory asserts that the chief obstacle to salvation is in the nature and moral choices of human beings, not in the nature or designs of God or Satan. The human problem is that people turn away from God and choose to live in sinful ways, Knudson argued. The problem was never that God was alienated from the world, or that some change in God's nature or will is necessary. God's essential nature is love; there was never anything in God's nature that stood in the way of humankind's redemption. It followed that the barrier to salvation can be removed only from the place in which it actually exists, which is the spiritual nature of human beings. Atonement theory has a single appropriate concern: the question of how human beings can be delivered from the egotism that causes them to live in sinful alienation from God's way. The problem of salvation is how human beings can be reconciled to God, not how God can be assuaged to love human beings.[146]

Abelard taught that Christ died on Calvary "that he might illuminate the world by his wisdom and excite it to the love of himself." Knudson agreed that this is the meaning and value of Christ's atonement; the death of Christ was "purely and simply a revelation of the divine love," he insisted. For Abelard, there was no difference between the meaning of Christ's incarnation and the meaning of his sacrificial death. Both were outpourings of self-giving love that sought to awaken feelings of gratitude and answering love in human souls, as well as a response of ethical conformity to God's will. Christ died to exert his moral and spiritual influence on sinful human hearts. It is true that this rendering of the meaning of Calvary makes the atonement of Christ subjective, Knudson acknowledged, but that is appropriate, for the problem is subjective. The problem is every individual's subjective alienation from God. Following Bowne, Knudson maintained that the problem is objective in only one sense. Bowne argued that the objective theories of atonement are insufficiently objective in the one sense of the problem that is objective, namely, "that sin itself can never be treated as a matter of indifference and that its forgiveness can never be a subject of arbitrary volition." Because God is moral to the core of God's being, Knudson explained, God must deal with sin and its forgiveness in a moral way. An atonement that does not address and remedy the sinful human heart is not saving: "There was no vicarous punishment. Sacrificial love is the key to all that Christ did for us on the cross."[147]

Knudson rarely had a good word for Shailer Mathews, but his version of the social gospel was much like Mathews's and he liked Mathews's *The Atonement and the Social Process,* which confirmed his suspicion that the historic theories of atonement were projections of feudal, monarchial, and other social patterns. Briefly he addressed the lack of transcendental necessity in moral-influence atonement theory. If Jesus did not have to die to ransom humankind from Satan, or satisfy God's honor, or pay God's penalty for sin, or uphold God's rectoral administration of the world, wasn't his martyrdom irrational, akin to suicide? Knudson replied that the death of Christ required no transcendental necessity to have revelational value. The value of Christ's sacrifice on the cross was inherent in Christ's offering of it, he argued, "in so far as the spirit of Jesus was a reflection of the divine character." The mission of Jesus was to establish the kingdom of God. In the act of sacrificing his life for the kingdom ideal, Jesus revealed both his love for humankind and his personal holiness. Because the fullness of God dwelt uniquely in Christ, Jesus's sacrifice on Calvary also revealed the love and righteousness of God. "The event itself was a mirror of the heart of God," Knudson asserted. "No backlying necessity of a ransom or a satisfaction or a vicarious punishment or a penal example was required in order to transform it into a manifestation of the divine grace." God's grace was manifest in the crucifixion itself and revealed in Christ's sacrificial spirit, "and back of that we do not need to go."[148]

Knudson generally avoided specifically Methodist arguments and references, but he made occasional exceptions when he discussed Christian experience. In *The Validity of Religious Experience* he appealed to Wesley several times on the theme of the centrality of religious experience; in *The Doctrine of Redemption* he sought to clarify what was not permanent in the Methodist doctrine of sanctification. Early Methodism vigorously preached the simultaneity of or close relation between the experiences of justification and sanctification, and claimed that full salvation is attainable in this life. Affirming this heritage, Olin Curtis claimed that Wesley's teaching had nearly the same epochal significance for the doctrine of holiness as Luther's theology for the doctrine of justification by faith and Athanasius's theology for the doctrine of the incarnation. Knudson corrected his teacher and most of the Wesleyan heritage on these points. Wesley's teaching on holiness was not to be compared to the ecumenical significance of Luther's and Athanasius's theologies, he declared: "It was a theological provincialism, and has been gradually losing its importance. We are no longer concerned, as the Methodist Fathers were, with the question as to whether sanctification is an instantaneous experience and the question as to whether entire sanctification is attainable in this life."[149]

Early Methodism was a needed spiritual rebellion against a lethargic Anglican church. In the eighteenth and early nineteenth centuries, Knudson explained, the Methodist founders laid claim to "a higher type of Christian experience" by appealing to Wesley's doctrine of sanctification. Knudson asserted that the idea of sanctification was still needed in modern Christianity, but he counseled that it could not mean the same thing to modern people that it meant to Wesley: "Today the whole subject is viewed in a different light." Modern Christianity believes in ethical sanctification, not in mystical sanctification, he explained; it speaks the kingdom-building language of the social gospel, not the individualistic soul language of Protestant pietism.[150] Knudson was not as keenly devoted to social causes as McConnell, but he embraced McConnell's social gospel claim that "entire sanctification" encompasses personal and social salvation. McConnell explained that the social gospel sought to sanctify modern society by the Christian spirit, not to impose a new Christendom on modern society. Knudson agreed that modern Christianity was right to place its hope on the transformation of society by the persuasive power of the Christian spirit. The social gospel rightly proclaims that the individual *and* society must be saved from sin, regenerated, and made new, he affirmed: "The conversion of individuals here and there will not suffice. Society itself must be converted, inwardly and outwardly transformed, so that it may be a fit home for the children of God. Nothing short of this will satisfy either the secular or the religious mood of our day." This is what it meant to speak of sanctification in the age that made Christianity modern.[151]

THE DIVINE GOOD
AND THE SPIRIT OF THE AGE

The personalists were in tune with the socioethical idealism of their age. Though McConnell and Brightman were stronger social gospelers than Knudson, all of the Boston personalists had strong ethical concerns, and several were pacifists or near-pacifists. McConnell exemplified the social gospel ideal of religion as personal and social salvation; Knudson strongly affirmed that ethical meaning is constitutive of the Christian personalist understanding of the gospel; Brightman supported a variety of antiwar and civil liberties organizations, and his theory of moral laws shaped the ethical thinking of personalist colleagues Walter Muelder and L. Harold DeWolf, who further developed personalist thinking on value theory and social ethics. In the spirit of Hegel, Brightman identified three types of moral laws—formal, axiological, and personalistic—and argued that a serious moral theory must be universalistic. At the same time, against Hegel's presumption that Hegelianism marked the culmination of philosophical development, Brightman contended that moral science must be progressive in a continually open-ended sense: its laws or principles must be open to criticism and modification from various standpoints.

Brightman's value theory contained eleven principles that subdivided into two formal laws, six axiological laws, and three personalistic laws. Moving from the abstract to the concrete, and in a progressive fashion that made each law dependent on and inclusive of the laws that preceded it, he began with the two formal laws: logical coherence (that all persons ought to will logically) and autonomy (that only rationally derived, self-imposed moral laws are imperative). Of his axiological laws, the law of value was that all persons ought to choose self-consistent and coherent values; the law of consequences was that the foreseeable consequences of an act must always be considered; the law of best possible was that all persons ought to will the best possible values in every situation; the law of specification was about developing the values that are specifically relevant to particular situations; the law of most inclusive end was about living in a way that realizes the widest possible range of value; and the law of ideal control was about controlling one's consequence-regarding empirical values by ideal values. Brightman conceived the personalistic laws as the highest of the moral laws and as foundational for all moral existence. The law of individualism was about realizing in one's own experience the maximum value of which one is capable in harmony with moral law; the law of altruism stated that all persons ought to respect other persons as moral ends-in-themselves and cooperate with others in the realization of shared values; the law of the ideal of personality stated that all persons ought to be guided by their ideal conception of personality as an individual and social reality, in harmony with the other moral laws.

This theory of "moral science" played a significant role in the thinking of third- and fourth-generation Boston personalism, but it had little impact in Brightman's time. His book *Moral Laws* attracted slight attention outside the circle of his disciples, who urged that it was wrongly overlooked. While teaching Brightman's scheme to his ethics classes in the 1950s and 1960s, DeWolf added explicit communitarian principles to the theory that mediated norm conflicts between Brightman's principles of individuality and community; one of his students who deeply absorbed and employed aspects of Brightman's theory was Martin Luther King Jr. At the same time, Muelder embraced Brightman's moral theory and DeWolf's classroom additions to it in his writings, arguing that Brightman's unfortunately neglected work took account of contextual factors while offering a needed universalistic antidote to contextualist moral theory. Values are real, Brightman and his disciples argued, yet their existence is intelligible only on personalist grounds; matter cannot be the cause of values any more than matter can be the cause of mind. Personality is the ground of the real, an intrinsic value, and the ground of the most intelligible and life-giving social ethic. Put differently, personality is valuable in itself apart from being a means to any end, and if personality did not exist, neither would any other values exist.[152]

The latter sentiment was classically liberal, and rarely disputed among theological progressives as a sentiment, but the personalists convinced few progressives outside their school to invest as much importance as they did in the Lotze-Bowne-Brightman theories of personality. Their long lists of universal moral laws made them seem quaint to many theologians, and their fixation on the golden key of personality isolated them within American theology and philosophy, which gravitated toward nonspeculative philosophies such as pragmatism, empiricism, language analysis, and existentialism. Though the conceptuality of personalist idealism was vigorously theistic, cosmic, and social-ethical, it was often caricatured as a philosophy of individualistic projection; though Brightman left room in his moral theory for the relativity of context, his preoccupation with universal laws was alienating to a contextualist-turning generation of theologians; though the Boston personalists formally rejected the idea of a dualistic bifurcation between persons and nature, their mind-centered idealism was weak on the moral and metaphysical importance of embodiment, nature, and environmental concern. Brightman and Knudson divorced consciousness from embodiment, and neither of them thematized the dignity of nature. These weaknesses were magnified by the rise of Whiteheadian process theology, which offered an organicist, panpsychic, holistic alternative to the personalist school's blend of Cartesian dualism and Kantian-Hegelian idealism. In the 1940s the theological followers of Whitehead and Charles Hartshorne became a serious rival to Boston personalism in the competition for philosophically minded Christian influence; in the 1950s they became the stronger party.

The second generation of Bownean personalists built an impressive theological school but did not change the direction of the theological field. They kept predicting that the field was about to turn in their direction, but it never did. To Knudson it was a point of pride that personalistic theology was "rooted in one of the great streams of idealistic thought," but critics often repeated William James's objection that this was exactly the problem with personalism: it was a patchwork of idealisms, not an original philosophy. A later dean of the Boston University School of Theology, Robert Neville, emphasized this point in explaining why, in his view, personalism lacked persuasive force and staying power. Instead of analyzing the underlying implications of modernity in the original manner of James, Heidegger, Husserl, Wittgenstein, or Whitehead, Neville argued, the Bownean personalists reassembled the most attractive parts of an expiring German idealism. By implication, they might have done better by at least remaining up to date in their borrowings, but Knudson saw nothing worth appropriating in what he called "the popular naturalistic, skeptical, and so called empirical philosophies of the day." To his mind, personalism was a richly founded challenge to the shallowness of contemporary thought and a call for a new basis of religious life and thought. "These philosophies seem to me superficial, self-contradictory, and devoid of positive religious value," Knudson reflected. "The attempt to graft religion upon them is in my opinion wasted energy. I do not see that anything is gained by trying to grow grapes on thorns or figs on thistles."[153]

Against the presumption that naturalism is philosophically objective and disinterested and that full-blooded theism inevitably smacks of religious prejudice, Knudson countered that life is the source of every philosophy. Naturalism is not objective, he argued, nor is it an exception to the "strife of vital human interests" in philosophy: "Every fundamental interest produces its own philosophy, and so it must be with religion also. It must have its own congenial philosophy, and this philosophy must be metaphysical. The present anti-metaphysical tendency in religious thought seems to me pathological, and is, I believe, destined to disappear along with the general intellectual depression through which we are passing."[154]

Compared to the depressed generation that ruled the field of theology in the 1930s, the 1890s world of his youth seemed like a golden age of spirited possibility, and Knudson longed to see another age of its kind in his lifetime. While Brightman called for wider forms of interreligious dialogue and a new philosophy of world religions, Knudson deepened the Kantian basis of his religious apriorism. While Brightman continued to revise the metaphysical commitments that he took from Bowne and Hegel, Knudson contended that Bowne had already solved the perennial problems of philosophy. Brightman's idea of a philosophy of world religions was based on a "metaphysical ideal" that he contasted to the "dogmatic ideal" of authoritarian religion. His metaphysical ideal located religious authority in God alone, "a God who not merely tolerates differences of opinion, but also uses those differences as a means of bringing his followers nearer to him, and nearer to one another." Essentially it was the view that all God concepts and religions are fallible symbols and forms of a single transcendental reality. While allowing that this vision was unlikely to effect anything more than a very modest agreement among contemporary churches and religions, Brightman urged that it promoted "a method of growth toward harmony and a more generous view of divine purpose."[155]

Often he pressed on sensitive points that many liberal religious thinkers took for granted without addressing. If modern Christians do not believe that Jesus is the only way to salvation, he asserted, they should say so openly: "Many readers may feel that it is trifling to deal so painfully with literalistic views which no modernist believes. But modernists have often failed to be convincing because they have failed to face the most difficult points in the old view; and anyone who supposes that the battle is won for modernism either in Christendom at large or in the United States must base his supposition on his preferences rather than on the actual facts."[156] In *The Future of Christianity* (1937), Brightman looked forward to a Christian church that recognized Buddhism, Hinduism, Confucianism, and Islam as fully valid ways to God.[157] Meanwhile he taught himself Spanish in order to communicate with Latin American philosophers. "Most persons who undertake to write about Latin America have at least been there," he reflected in 1946. "I have the rare distinction of never having set foot south of the Rio Grande." Yet Brightman wrote valuable articles in his later life about trends in Latin American philosophy, all the while self-teasing that "it takes a good deal to jar a man out of provincialism."[158]

The pride of his later life was his metaphysical system, on which he completed thirteen chapters before his death in 1953, and which his disciple Peter Bertocci later published under the title *Person and Reality.* With Schopenhauer, Brightman believed that metaphysics is one of humankind's deepest needs; with Hegel he believed that metaphysics is the Holy of Holies of any civilization; with Hegel he proclaimed that truth is the whole. His empirical-personalistic method conformed to logical norms while standing before the court of experience. Brightman argued that the key test of any hypothesis is whether it makes systematic coherence out of experience. Throughout his career he followed Bowne and Descartes in making conscious experience his point of departure, but he rejected Bowne's soul-language. Bowne's theorizing on consciousness presumed that the self is something like a continuous substance. Brightman straightforwardly disbelieved in a substantive self; his idea of personality did not require one to believe that the "that" which experiences is identical with its experiences. In his *Philosophy of Religion* Brightman coined the term "situation-experienced" to designate the complex personal unity within which sensing, willing, feeling, desiring, remembering, and reasoning take place; sometimes he referred to it as the "datum-self." In his final, unfinished work he called it "a shining present."[159]

The term is a figurative abstraction, he cautioned; the shining present does not shine literally, nor does "present" have a single literal meaning. As Hegel emphasized, every now is a was that can never be again. Shining presents are "perishing occasions," Brightman theorized, using Whitehead's phrase; they are innumerably various and lacking any continuous substance: "Yet they contain messages from the past as well as traces of unremembered events and interactions with contemporary reality." Shining presents are interactions registered partly as sensations and partly, like Whitehead's prehensions of causal efficacy, "as other feelings of the action of reality on us." They look to the future with yearnings and plans, and every shining present has inner experiences, "regardless of its 'outer' relations—experiences of confusion and clarity, disorder and order, aimlessness and purpose, hate and love." A shining present is whatever a person is at the present moment, Brightman explained: "Wherever there is any awareness or feeling of any kind, there is a shining present." It is a conscious awareness, a "situation-experienced" always to be distinguished from any situation-believed-in.[160]

Brightman moved as far as he could from the language or suggestion of a substantive soul without giving up Bowne's view that conscious experience is the starting point of philosophy and the key to reality. He referred unsolvable transcendental questions about the ground of the unstable self to a category marked "illuminating absent." The shining present undoubtedly depends for its existence on something besides itself, he allowed, but to call this ground its substantive "soul" is not to give an answer that explains anything. The unity and continuity of experience do need to be explained, but "the soul" is not an explanation. For if the soul is a transcendent, unchanging, unity-continuity substance, it cannot account for the uncountable succession of temporal shining presents. The shining present is crammed with clues, signs, messages, effects, and the like that it did not create. It can understand these pieces of evidence, Brightman reasoned, only if it perceives its mind as "a receiving station for messages from beyond." It can interpret these messages in whatever way it prefers, "but it can know nothing about its own past or future, about other minds or nature or God, except on the basis of interpretation of the evidence now at hand." The shining present is all that we have; thus, the only source of evidence that we have for God is immediate experience.[161]

Brightman died before he wrote his chapters on the problem of God and the nature of divine reality, but Bertocci completed the book by inserting excerpts from Brightman's previous writings. He made a heavy draft on Brightman's theorizing about God's omnitemporality and conflicted will. Against Bowne's claim that time has no ontological reality, Brightman judged that Bowne's eternalism was a hangover from Platonist Christianity. In his view, personalists needed to be temporalists because freedom, activity, and purpose all require time. Though Brightman believed that God is never less than a person ontologically, he emphatically disbelieved that God is supertemporally eternal. *Person and Reality* featured Brightman's essay on the temporality of God, in which he stressed that change and activity are "the essence of the real." Nothing real is static, he observed: "The real endures; the real changes; the real grows. God is the real or at least the most significant part of the real." Reason establishes that the changes in experience conform to law, Brightman allowed, and it finds evidence of eternal form "which the changes never violate," but God is not an abstraction. God is a concrete living reality, "an ever enduring creator." God's traits have such names as energy, creative process, concentration, integration, and will. Put differently, God is not a timeless being; God's existence "is an eternally changing present." These arguments had a significant future in American liberal theology, but mostly under the influence of a rival theological school. Brightman's version of personalistic theism had much in common with what came to be called process theology.[162]

In the early 1920s he became acquainted with young philosopher Charles Hartshorne, who was then a graduate student at Harvard and already a panpsychic panentheist, but not yet a Whiteheadian. In 1928 Hartshorne began his long career as a Whiteheadian philosopher at the University of Chicago; five years later he and Brightman began to explore the relation between their temporalist metaphysical worldviews. Hartshorne's first book appeared in 1934; the same year he remarked in a letter to Brightman that "I have been aware for some time that we are not far apart in theology, since reading *The Problem of God,* in fact." Quickly the two philosophers got down to differences. Hartshorne objected to Brightman's belief that other selves are merely inferred by each center of self-consciousness. "Literal participation in each other's being is about my strongest belief," Hartshorne explained. "Are we not parts of each other, members of one another?" For him, as for Whitehead, souls or selves literally overlapped, "and some cement is needed to bind them together, and what binds them must itself overlap." Brightman replied that whenever he tried to make sense of the idea of a literal participation in other selves, he always found himself "landed in contradiction, in epistemological chaos, and in unfaithfulness to experience." His idea of God was similar to the views of Whitehead and Hartshorne, but this fact did not overturn his belief that each person is defined by an immediate experience that characterizes that person alone. We experience only ourselves directly, he cautioned; everything else is inferred.[163]

Hartshorne argued that other persons can be inferred from one's existence by the impression that they are necessary to one's existence; Brightman replied that this argument surrendered empirical and psychological evidence too completely to a logical claim. A flower is nourished by its soil, he analogized, but the flower is not the same as the soil. While Hartshorne repeatedly protested against Brightman's "absolute" bifurcation of experience and its object, Brightman insisted on a "sharp distinction between my actual self and its causes." Just as philosophy must not identify a cause with its effect, he argued, philosophy must protect the integrity of the only direct experience that is given to any knower; if two beings participate in each other's being, they are not two beings. Hartshorne reasoned that if a self is directly aware of the sun, the sun becomes a part of the self. To Brightman this argument exposed the irreducible impasse between his epistemological dualism and Hartshorne's monism: "For me, I am directly aware only of my own experience. What we (confusedly) call direct awareness of the sun is really a direct awareness of myself-as-believing-in-sun, or as referring-to-sun. No part of me is any part either of the sun or of God."[164]

This negation—that no part of individual selves is any part of God—struck at the core of Hartshorne's Whiteheadian organicist system. In his book *Man's Vision of God* (1941) Hartshorne argued that because all individuals are part of God, God's being includes all the beliefs that individuals hold. Brightman replied that, in that case, God must believe many absurd and contradictory things. His letters to Hartshorne and his review of *Man's Vision of God* objected that Hartshorne's panpsychism was not necessary to the kind of Epicurean-temporalist theism that they shared and that Hartshorne's dismissive remarks about pacifism were ungenerous and wrong. On pacifism they agreed to disagree; Brightman opposed war on moral and pragmatic grounds, though not quite as an absolute pacifist. On the question whether God is best conceived on a panpsychic model as cosmic mind, Hartshorne countered that embracing false beliefs within one's being and believing falsely are not the same thing—"no more the same than to embrace smallness as property of a part and to be small as a whole." To have a belief as part of oneself is not necessarily to believe the belief, he insisted.[165]

Back and forth they debated the logic of parts and wholes. Hartshorne argued that just as a small line can be part of a large surface without causing any contradiction between the line's smallness and the surface's largeness, a large mind may contain a small mind without accepting the smaller mind's false beliefs. Brightman replied that this is picture thinking; a true theory of mind cannot be based on the model of space relations. Hartshorne justly protested that Brightman failed to recognize the difference between pantheism and panentheism when he called Hartshorne a pantheist; Brightman stuck to his personalist denial that God's being contains beliefs that God does not hold. The basis of his system was the personalist claim that the mind is a complex *unity* of consciousness. In the name of organic relatedness and wholeness, the Whiteheadian system shredded this basis, at least from Brightman's standpoint. Brightman insisted that no individual mind contains acts that are not acts of that mind: "I do not agree that a part of a mind can perform an act which the whole mind does not perform, for the simple reason that I experience mind and its action as an indivisible, although complex, whole." He worried that Whiteheadian metaphysics ended up with an impersonal God as a consequence of breaking apart the unity of immediate experience: "If God contains my act as mine, but not as his, then my act is not his act in any personal sense, and the verb 'contain' is being used in an impersonal sense." The complex unity of consciousness is preserved only by epistemological dualism, he admonished: "I cannot believe that God's knowledge of me is ontologically identical with my actual being for myself."[166]

Despite its language of wholeness, interrelation, and organic process, Whiteheadian organicism was fragmenting, at least to Brightman. He protested that organicist panentheism broke down both the distinction between self and world that secures the self's unity and the distinction between God and world. The essence of a person is one's shining present, Brightman contended. Hartshorne replied that while he was not any part of Jane Austen, Jane Austen was certainly part of him. Moreover, he and Jane Austen were both parts of God as God presently exists, "but not as he once was and as he might have been now." Brightman shuddered at the Whiteheadian notion that consciousness includes Jane Austen, the sun, one's nervous system, someone else's nervous system, and other objects of consciousness. He and Hartshorne respected each other immensely, and for the most part they greatly enjoyed their dialogues; Hartshorne remarked in 1943 that "we deserve some sort of medal for keeping this up. Philosophers are not long in patience with each other usually." Brightman welcomed the Whiteheadian organicists as fellow Christian metaphysical liberals who propounded a temporalist view of divine reality. Against the vogue of neo-Thomist scholasticism promoted by Chicago president Robert Maynard Hutchins and the naturalistic humanism that otherwise prevailed at the Divinity School, Brightman welcomed the variations of "new metaphysics" that Hartshorne and Wieman pioneered at the University of Chicago. But Wieman drifted away from Christian theism, and Brightman worried that the Whiteheadian approach was almost equally mistaken. He wearied of Hartshorne's verbose assurances that panpsychic panentheism is not pantheism; sometimes his agitation poked through. "If I have not discussed the question of pantheism from your premises, it is because I cannot see the intelligibility of your premise," he snapped in 1942. "I am not at all satisfied with the state of our discussion!"[167]

Brightman shook his head at the prospect of a Whiteheadian theological school; a strong dose of organicist monism was not what modern theology or philosophy needed. Knudson paid less attention to the beginnings of process theology. On a metaphysical level he preferred to parry with absolute idealists, though he found a declining number of them in the "intellectual depression" of his generation; he admitted to Brightman that he did not keep up with philosophical trends as Brightman did.[168] In his militant-apologetic mode Knudson fixated on Barthians and humanists, whom he saw as reverse images of each other. "The Humanistic philosophy, as expounded by Dewey and his followers, is an inconsistent compound of naturalism and agnosticism," he declared. "Its exponents are very certain that there is no God and that the naturalistic world view is correct; but they do not as a rule offer a rational justification of their impersonal metaphysics. They simply assume it." In this they resembled the Barthians. The humanists rejected God and affirmed modern culture, while the Barthians affirmed a transcendent God and rejected modern culture and divine immanence, but both perspectives fed on philosophical skepticism: "Here Barth is in accord with the naturalistic Humanist. He denies that there is any way of justifying the Christian religion by an appeal to experience, to reason, or to utility."[169]

The Barthians were masters of dialectical spinning and obfuscation, Knudson complained: "All is left in mystery and in general intellectual befuddlement."

Barth's recent work was less cryptic than his early theology, Knudson allowed in 1935, but it remained essentially irrational, "and no amount of paradoxical hocus-pocus can remove the intellectual scandal involved in such a position." The challenge of modern Christianity is to theorize and live out a rational, healthy, socially transforming understanding of the gospel faith, he exhorted. The human mind cannot tolerate paradoxes indefinitely: "It insists on having a rational theology or none at all." Allowing himself an appeal to denominational pride, Knudson added that the Barthian movement's Calvinism was reactionary in another respect. It repudiated the entire core of distinctive Methodist themes: "There is no 'universal redemption,' no freedom of the will in the Arminian sense, no 'sanctification' in the Wesleyan conception of it as an actual triumph over the principle of sin, and no 'Social Gospel' such as we today preach. All of these beliefs are discarded as out of harmony with the Reformation theology." The Barthians derided sanctification and social salvation, and they took no interest in missions. To the extent that the Barthian movement gained power in the church, Knudson warned, the church would become strange, otherworldly, and socially useless.[170]

The earliest name for the Barthian movement was "crisis theology." Knudson judged that Barth and his followers caused much of the church's real crisis; one of his favorite maxims explained why: "A theology which feeds on philosophical skepticism will perish thereby." If one begins with philosophical skepticism, Knudson admonished, it doesn't matter which direction one chooses: "We may with Barth draw an authoritarian conclusion or we may with the American Humanist draw a naturalistic conclusion. The end will be the same in either case. Our metaphysical skepticism will undermine both our authoritarian and our humanistic faith." Modern theology was seriously ill from having fed on philosophical skepticism and social cynicism.[171] Knudson allowed that Paul Tillich's dialectical spinning was less irrational than Barth's, but only by degree. "I think Tillich's *Systematic Theology* has been overadvertised," he told Brightman. "It is not in my opinion a great and creative work." Modern theology could not be cured of its disease until Christian thinkers battled for the hearts and minds of jaded modern skeptics with a rationally grounded theism.[172]

That was the cause to which Knudson devoted his career and life. Exhausted from overwork, he gave up the dean's office in 1938 at the age of 65, but continued to teach on a full-time basis until 1943.[173] In 1948 he was saddened by the death of his wife, who endured chronic illness and invalidity for many years. Like his friend Brightman, Knudson poured out books and articles to the end of his days. *The Validity of Religious Experience* (1937) strengthened the Kantian basis of his appeal to a religious a priori; having written works on apologetics and dogmatics, *The Principles of Christian Ethics* (1943) fulfilled his ambition of becoming a "complete theologian"; *The Philosophy of War and Peace* (1947) offered a postwar analysis of various strategies for world peace; *Basic Issues in Christian Thought* (1950) summarized his religious views for a general audience.

Knudson's ethical writings steered a cautiously moderate path on most sociopolitical issues of the day, with progressive leanings. *The Principles of Christian*

Ethics cautioned that Christianity endorses no specific political ideology or economic doctrine; that the church's chief work in the sociopolitical arena is moral and spiritual, not political and technical; to the extent that the church involves itself in public policy matters, it should advocate principles, not plans and programs. The principles that Knudson emphasized in the socioeconomic arena were the personality of all human beings, the concept of wealth as a trust, and the concept of ownership as stewardship. While treading lightly on arguments for capitalism and socialism, he counseled that the best approach was to split the differences between them. "We need the capitalistic emphasis on free enterprise, on individual responsibility, and on adequate incentive for creative work," he urged. "But we need also the socialistic emphasis on cooperation, on social responsibility, and on ethical rather than financial incentives to social service." Thus he favored "a gradual socializing of the present system" in the direction of a reformed capitalism. Profit-sharing schemes and other forms of labor-management cooperation made sense to him. The key point was not whether America ended up with "a modified form of capitalism or a modified form of socialism," he believed; what was important was the preservation of the signature values of each system.[174]

Knudson's thinking on the ethics of war and the state was a bit stodgy for his school by the 1940s, though he shared the liberal Christian concern with finding alternatives to war. In *The Philosophy of War and Peace* (1947), he took a moderately conservative position on the ethics of international politics. Knudson acknowledged that the West's regnant powers were often oppressive and expansionist in their drive to dominate foreign peoples, exploit resources, and control markets. At the same time he contended that there is such a thing as good imperialism, pointing to the emergence of a "more benevolent and progressive type of colonial or imperial rule that has been developing during the past half century or more." Good imperialism is linked with democracy and freedom, he explained; it is "energetic and expansive, but not despotic," emphasizing consent and cooperation while eschewing domination. Knudson boasted that Anglo-Saxon cultures tend to be less racist than Teutonic cultures, though he allowed that Josiah Strong and other American celebrants of the early Progressive era were flaming in their "national self-glorification" and racialist chauvinism.

While sympathizing with the "rising tide of resentment on the part of the colored and so-called backward peoples the world over," he admonished that simple antiimperialism is too simple. "Many of the subject peoples are not ready for self-government," Knudson insisted. "They still need a long period of tutelage." He believed that the major Western powers still had a "civilizing mission to perform" in vast parts of the world such as the African continent; in 1947 Knudson did not see the postcolonial postwar world that was already dawning. Like Bowne, only more so, he lacked an appropriate sense of moral outrage at the existence of racism; later personalists felt compelled to censure Knudson for giving a poor representation of personalist moral values on this point, though he did criticize expressions of racial prejudice that occurred during debates over the union of the Methodist churches. Having identified personalist philosophy with the view that slaves and children are not persons—because they lack the requisite degree of intellectual and moral development—Knudson was in a poor position to defend the full humanity of America's descendants of slaves, and he took only occasional passes at doing so. Fortunately his school felt the immorality of racism more deeply. Personalist ethicist Rufus Burrow Jr. blasted Knudson for "nuthead thinking" on race and imperialism—"he must have fallen out of a tree"—and remarked that while he respected Knudson's role in creating a personalist school, he distrusted Knudson for his racism.[175]

Knudson showed a stronger sense of moral urgency on the war problem. Outlining eight strategies for attaining world peace, he favored mediation and arbitration approaches, a United Nations–model world organization, and voluntary cooperation as policy options, but his deeper hope lay in the cultivation of Kantian-Christian ideals of moral responsibility and peaceableness. What was needed was an international peace movement that practiced and appealed to reason, conscience, and faith, he urged. Without these qualities, no peace-oriented policy could succeed, but with enough devotion to the Kantian precepts of right and duty, Kant's ideal of perpetual peace was attainable. The warless vision of Kantian world federalism was a realistic hope in the new world order of 1947. Knudson did not believe that disarmament was a prudent moral option; at the same time he insisted that armaments could not secure perpetual peace. The goal was to create the social, cultural, and political conditions that made disarmament a moral possibility. "There must be a profound faith in world peace as the divinely appointed goal of human history," he exhorted; conversely, the world needed an equally profound faith in God's guidance of history and nature toward this end, "as Immanuel Kant expounded and justified."[176]

THE RELIGIOUS A PRIORI
AND THE PERSONALIST LEGACY

Knudson loved to tell the story of his conversion to personalist philosophy and the beginnings of American-school personalism. "It would be difficult to describe the effect which Bowne's exposition of this truth had upon those who heard him," he recalled in 1924. "It proved to them a veritable gospel, a deliverance from intellectual bondage. Their spirit was released from the leaden weight of a crude realism or materialism or pantheism. What the doctrine of justification by faith meant to Luther's religious life, that did a personalistic metaphysics mean to their intellectual life. It wrought for them their intellectual redemption."[177] Near the end of his life he confirmed that this recollection was a description of his own experience. He added that he still shared its confidence and enthusiasm "as fully today as I did then." On his good days the later Knudson tried to believe as fully as he did in 1924 that Bowne-style personalistic theology might renew modern theology as a whole; on other days he was at least grateful that Bowne's system and personal influence immunized the Boston schoolers from the "strange and perverted type of thought" that prevailed "in some influential theological circles." By his reckoning, Bowne's personalistic metaphysic was "a powerful bulwark of the Christian faith."[178] Knudson ended his career hoping that the best days of American Christian personalism were yet to come. His influence in American Methodism was immense; near the end of his life he casually remarked to Brightman that four of his students had been elected as bishops in the past month. When he and Brightman retired, they had the satisfaction of knowing that their work would be carried on by an able school of disciples that included philosopher Peter Bertocci, philosopher and theologian L. Harold DeWolf, philosopher John H. Lavely, ethicist Walter G. Muelder, and theologian S. Paul Schilling. Significantly, all of these thinkers were primarily disciples of Brightman and only secondarily, at most, of Knudson. The third generation personalists rightly judged that Brightman was the greater thinker and figure.[179]

The personalists built a significant school, but not a movement. In the philosophy of religion they achieved a prominent standing through the influence of Bowne and Brightman, though not as dominantly as Knudson supposed. In the field of theology they sustained one of the major streams of American liberal Christianity against an ascending neo-orthodox and neoliberal reaction, but they never achieved much influence outside the Methodist church. Knudson invested great hope in the claim that personalist ideas were prevailing in the philosophy of religion. For centuries the Platonist tradition in its various streams dominated Western philosophy of religion, he observed. Platonism had its virtues as a philosophical partner to Christianity, but its metaphysical substantialism and metaphysical universalism were seriously problematic, and it featured strong tendencies toward intellectualism and metaphysical dualism.[180]

It was the personalist tradition that supplanted the latter defects in modern philosophy, Knudson argued, especially in the philosophy of religion. The most salutary aspects of modern philosophy were its personalistic aspects, especially as theorized by Leibniz, Berkeley, Kant, Lotze, and Bowne; Brightman always added Hegel to this list of intellectual heroes. Thanks to the influence of its explicitly personalistic thinkers, modern philosophy as a whole was individualistic, voluntarist, dynamic, and idealistic. "The process has been carried out with varying degrees of thoroughness, and in large part has probably been half conscious rather than deliberate and systematic," Knudson reflected, neglecting to note that idealism was a fading star in philosophy. "The change has gone steadily forward; and slowly but surely progressive theological thought has been adjusting itself to the change."[181]

This was the mode of persuasion that he preferred. Modern culture was making progress, and personalism was the cause and name of its progress in the field of ideas; the future of modern theology therefore rightly belonged to Christian personalism. A movement person to the end, Knudson was willing to define personalism broadly enough to include realist-leaning theists like Georgia Harkness in the movement. "The realistic-idealistic debate does not necessarily have a decisive bearing on one's conception of ultimate reality," he reasoned. "One may be a personalistic theist and yet be a naive realist in one's view of the external world." Harkness worried that idealist epistemologies offer a shaky basis for affirming the reality of moral truths; Knudson countered that idealism "furnishes material for a profounder and more convincing apologetic" than any form of realism. Yet he allowed that personalism in the broad sense does not exclude a realist epistemology or cosmology: "All it insists on is a personal world-ground or a personal creator of the world."[182]

The apologetic function of theology was consuming for him; even his dogmatic and ethical writings were loaded with apologetics. The other story that Knudson loved to tell was the tale of how Kant saved reason for the sciences and morality; he loved this story because he identified with its apologetic moral. Just as Kant rescued reason from a barbaric empiricist skepticism on the one hand and a stifling uncritical dogmatism on the other, Knudson proposed to save religion from the same twin enemies. Though he blasted the Barthians unmercifully for basing their theological affirmations on a self-authenticating revelation, he had his own version of a self-authenticating religious basis, the theory of the religious a priori that he borrowed from Schleiermacher and Otto. Knudson believed that his appropriation of this theory rescued religion from skepticism and dogmatism in the same way that Kant saved reason; just as Kant theorized that there are principles immanent in the mind that make experience possible, the doctrine of the religious a priori posited that religion is woven into the structure of the human mind. Like the Kantian categories, the religious a priori explained the possibility of experience (in this case, religious experience), but like the Kantian categories, it resisted all attempts to explain the explanation.

The religious a priori made religion underivable and therefore self-authenticating. Knudson urged that religion bears an autonomous validity that transcends any type of pragmatic or historical validity that might be claimed for it. This does not mean that religious thinkers should reject the pragmatic method, he admonished; Knudson was sensitive to the suggestion that Bowne was more pragmatic and less rationalistic than the Bownean school.[183] He affirmed and employed pragmatic tests. "Apriorism does not, then, reject the pragmatic method in religious argumentation," Knudson asserted. "It accepts and utilizes it, but at the same time supplements it in a significant way by providing it with a more substantial philosophical underpinning." Jamesian pragmatism was true enough, and certainly valuable "so far as it goes, but it does not go far enough."[184]

Knudson proposed to go as far for the self-authenticating integrity of religion as Kant went for the a priori validity of reason. "Religion today is confronted with a double danger," he warned. These dangers were familiar to Kant, though the names and slogans had changed; Knudson cited the "religion is illusion" nihilists and the Barthians as examples. Against these twin perils he issued the apologetic version of his credo:

> To meet this double peril, one coming from theological irrationalism
> and the other from philosophical naturalism, a philosophy is needed
> which makes it clear that religion is something wrought into the very
> texture of human reason, that it is not a transitory or illusory phase
> of the social life of man but is woven into the very warp and woof of
> the human mind, so that it stands in its own right and is a perma-
> nent and essential constituent of human nature. Such a philosophy
> the doctrine of a religious apriori seeks to present. It contends for the
> rationality and inevitability of faith, and in doing so carries on a
> twofold polemic. One is directed against a destructive relativism and
> the other against a blind authoritarianism. As against these two ten-
> dencies in modern thought the religious apriorist maintains that reli-
> gion is grounded as deeply and ineradicably in the human spirit as
> are science, morality, and art.[185]

Knudson's single novelty cast a large shadow over his theological school. The case for a religious a priori gained a few stray sentences in Bowne's writings. In Knudson's work it became the apologetic hope of modern theology, interpreted from a personalist standpoint. He chided Brightman for refusing to affirm it, telling Brightman that his position "fits in very well with my religious apriorism, except where you are dealing with the subject by name!"[186] The second-generation founders of the Boston personalist school did not succeed in building the field-transforming movement that Knudson hoped and wrote for, but they did create an impressive theological school.

In 1953, all three of the major second-generation founders died, Brightman in February, McConnell and Knudson in August. In the closing chapters of his autobiography, published the year before his death, McConnell offered a warm recollection of stories about international conferences that he had attended, famous people that he had met, and being a bishop. On the intellectual front he singled out Knudson, Brightman, and Flewelling for praise, and lauded Muelder's performance as dean of the School of Theology. Then the mood shifted, if only for a moment: "As I look back over the years, at first glance I see large reason for pessimism as to the prospects of religion in such a world as ours. There is much reason for discouragement, if not of despair." The American Civil War divided America into two nations for half a century, he recalled, "the Spanish-American War threw the nation into an imperialistic whirlpool in con-tradiction to its own ideals, the First World War started out to make the world safe for democracy, but left democracy for a time sadly damaged both in quan-tity and quality, and the Second World War was in self-defense against social madness—like that of communism today."[187]

On the surface, McConnell allowed, "and even quite a distance below the sur-face," this was a terrible picture: "All these conflicts have had a dreadful effect upon even the temper of the churches. The worst product is the appearance in our schools of professional pessimists who find no good in anything unless it declares that there is no good." The neo-orthodox-neoliberal ascendancy in American Protestantism distressed McConnell nearly as much as it troubled

Knudson and Brightman. McConnell and Reinhold Niebuhr were friends dating back to Niebuhr's social gospel days, and McConnell tried to believe that the Niebuhr of recent years knew what he was talking about—"Barth has not thought as far as Niebuhr," McConnell assured—but it bothered him greatly that the Niebuhrians were twisting the faith into a kind of self-fulfilling cynicism. It was hard to believe that the social gospel had come to this. In fact, McConnell didn't believe it.[188]

"I have been through all this, and it sums up a bad total, but it is really not the total," he contended. The professional pessimists didn't see the big picture. They failed to recognize that "the churches have been at work through all these years," constantly making progress in education, outreach, and evangelism. The pessimists failed to recognize that rural life had been transformed over the past half-century, "and the churches have discovered the change." Some of the pessimists reminded McConnell of the stereotypical cranky Methodist at church conferences who was always warning of huge membership losses if the church didn't find a way to silence its radicals. McConnell told them to stop being so cranky: "Methodism is striving as never before toward a radicalism at least of the type that searches for the roots of things." The second-generation founders kept the faith that the best was yet to come for the Methodist church and American Christianity.[189]

6.
Practical Divinity

Harry Emerson Fosdick, Rufus Jones,
Georgia Harkness, Benjamin E. Mays,
and the Authority of Spiritual Experience

The major theorists of American liberal theology during its field-dominating phase were academic theologians. They were also white, male, and usually one step removed from the every-week preaching demands of pastors. But a field-dominating theological movement also needs practical and spiritual interpreters, preachers, and popularizers, and the leading seminaries of American liberal Protestantism during the liberal era attained their standing by producing both kinds of religious thinkers. Union Theological Seminary boasted William Adams Brown and Eugene Lyman, but it was also the academic home of preacher and religious interpreter Harry Emerson Fosdick. Boston University built a theological school on the personalist metaphysics of Bowne, Knudson, and Brightman, but one of its protégés, Georgia Harkness, reached a wider audience as a spiritual writer and theologian. The University of Chicago Divinity School advocated a liberal empiricist approach to religion and thus inspired one of its protégés, African American educator Benjamin E. Mays, to interpret the religious experience of black Americans in the course of becoming an important civil rights leader. At Harvard University, the idealist mysticism of philosopher William Ernest Hocking was a formative influence on Henry Nelson Wieman and Charles Hartshorne, who studied under Hocking; but earlier, before Hocking joined the Harvard faculty,

Harvard's philosophy department influenced Rufus M. Jones, who became the liberal theology movement's leading interpreter of mystical experience.

For most of the nineteenth century the leading theologians of American liberal Protestantism were pastors. In the twentieth century even its leading interpreters and popularizers were academics. Fosdick taught for nearly forty years at Union while doubling as a Sunday preacher; Harkness became the first female theologian to teach at an American seminary and the first female member of the American Theological Society; Mays trained two generations of Morehouse College undergraduates and played a leading role in the Federal Council of Churches; Jones taught philosophy at Haverford College for forty-one years and founded the Wider Quaker Fellowship. The theology of American liberal Christianity was theorized by the likes of Brown, Mathews, and Knudson, but none of them came close to Fosdick as a shaper of American religion, and for many churchpeople it was the liberal movement's trailblazing female and African American thinkers who represented progressive theology at its best. In similar ways Fosdick, Harkness, Mays, and Jones sought to make spiritual sense of liberal theology for ordinary people; in different ways they taught the authority of religious experience and the way of Christ for modern times.

BECOMING HARRY EMERSON FOSDICK

In a crowded field that included liberal church leaders George Buttrick, Henry Sloane Coffin, and G. Bromley Oxnam, Fosdick towered above other pastors and theologians as the symbol of American liberal Protestantism. He was born in 1878 in Buffalo, New York, where his father was a high school teacher and principal. Fosdick's parents were civic-minded, warm-spirited, temperamentally democratic, and religiously evangelical; they also suffered from depression, especially his mother. Harry was the family's first child. When he was three years old, his infant sister died of diphtheria; two years later his mother gave birth to twins; when Harry was seven years old, his mother suffered a severe nervous breakdown. For months she could barely lift her head from the pillow. While continuing to teach in the Buffalo school system, Fosdick's father coped with the family's difficult circumstances by moving to Westfield in the Chautauqua hills, where the children were divided between their grandparents.

Young Harry fretted about his mother's emotional health and his own salvation. Religiously zealous and, by his later estimation, "morbidly conscientious," he listened to Dwight L. Moody's revival preaching, which inspired him, and to local revival preaching, which leaned more heavily on threats of hellfire. "I vividly recall weeping at night for fear of going to hell, with my mystified and baffled mother trying to comfort me," Fosdick remembered in later life. "Once, when I was nine years old, my father found me so pale that he thought me ill." The latter incident was a case of fear sickness; Fosdick feared that he had committed the unpardonable sin. His father assured him that everyone has sacrilegious thoughts;

the trick was to keep them from making nests in one's hair. Throughout his life Fosdick described his parents with unequivocal affection and admiration, never hinting that, aside from their depression, they may have contributed to his emotional turmoil. He gratefully recalled that they were the kind of nurturing and deeply religious Victorians who trained their children to obey their own cultivated moral truths. Frank Fosdick was friendly, self-sacrificing, and light-hearted, in his son's portrait "a companion and chum"; Annie Weaver Fosdick was a model of evangelical piety and rectitude from whom Harry gained his assurance that the inner moral truths correspond to an everlasting and universal moral order.[1]

In 1894 the Fosdicks returned to Buffalo, where Frank Fosdick assumed the position of high school annex principal. The following year Harry enrolled at Colgate University in Hamilton, New York, where he came of age. He loved the freedom of college life, sailed through courses at the top of his class, and gave the appearance of a cocksure fraternity socializer: "I recall no disquieting premonitions of the explosion that was to follow." As a freshman he converted to believing in evolution and began to hone his extraordinary speaking skills. Debating tournaments and speaking contests were plentiful in late-Victorian academe, and often highly remunerative; Fosdick won a succession of them during his college years, and thus paid off much of his tuition. Having come from near-poverty, he talked his way through college. By the end of his freshman year the college yearbook staff had him pegged; they described him as "Himself his world and his own God."[2]

Fosdick's buoyant exuberance crashed in the spring of 1896, when his father suffered a nervous breakdown. Frank Fosdick had struggled to keep his family together for years. His wife's health was delicate, and though he made a small salary, he financially supported his in-laws and his father. Returning to a devastated family at the end of his freshman year, Harry dropped out of college and for a year clerked in a bookstore, reading voraciously on the side while his father recuperated. Grieving over his family situation, and feeling isolated, Fosdick had several mystical experiences. His early-youth conversion experience had occurred after his mother suffered a nervous breakdown; now his sense of belonging to God deepened with his father's emotional collapse. At the same time his doctrinal worldview unraveled. Like many evangelicals, he had accommodated evolutionary theory by reasoning that the biblical days of creation referred to geological eras, but this stopgap offered no relief from other problems of biblical science and history. The first problem that engaged Fosdick's attention was the crudeness of the Samson stories in 1 Samuel; why should he believe these stories if he gave no credence to the tales of Hercules? It stunned him to reflect that he did not need to believe anything simply because it was in the Bible. Truth was an open field, to be discovered by exploration and research; no belief could be settled by a proof text.

In that frame of mind he read Andrew White's *History of the Warfare of Science with Theology in Christendom,* which demolished Fosdick's aspiration to orthodoxy. "I devoured it," he later recalled. "It seemed to me unanswerable.

Here were the facts, shocking facts about the way the assumed infallibility of the Scriptures had impeded research, deepened and prolonged obscurantism, fed the mania of persecution, and held up the progress of mankind. I no longer believed the old stuff I had been taught. Moreover, I no longer merely doubted it. I rose in indignant revolt against it."[3]

He returned to college in that mood. Because religion had been the center of his life, his intellectual awakening shook him profoundly: "When my religion was disturbed, I was disturbed from the ground up." For the next two years he struggled to decide whether he believed anything. Morally he remained his mother's son, but he told his mother that "mentally I'm going to clear God out of the universe and start over to see what I can find." Fosdick's skeptical phase was brief; he was not a good candidate for atheism or agnosticism, but he was thoroughly disabused of traditional orthodoxy. He later reflected that for him the choice was not between orthodox and liberal religion, but between progressive religion and no religion. In his junior year he read John Fiske's books on evolutionary theism, which impressed him greatly; he also made the acquaintance of William Newton Clarke, who taught at Colgate Seminary. "Clarke was my guide, philosopher and friend," Fosdick later recalled, explaining elsewhere: "Long before I knew him as a loyal personal friend, he was a powerful influence in my life. Here was an honest man, saying what he really thought, defying the obscurantism of old opinions and daring to phrase the Christian faith in the categories of modern thinking. Every time he walked across the campus he was a living argument that it could be done."[4]

Fosdick viewed Clarke's *Outline of Christian Theology* (1898) as proof that Christianity could accommodate modern knowledge; he absorbed Clarke's teaching that theological categories must change with the times and that the divinity of Jesus consisted in his unique spiritual consciousness.[5] In 1898 he had no idea whether Clarke's textbook stood a chance of gaining acceptance in the mainline churches; more personally, he couldn't imagine that any denomination would be willing to accept him as a minister: "But I did not care. I wanted to make a contribution to the spiritual life of my generation. I said that to myself again and again. That was all I felt sure about. If I prepared myself to make a spiritual contribution to my generation, somewhere a door would open—with that faith I headed toward the ministry."[6]

Fosdick reasoned that it should be possible to preach what one actually sees and experiences. College lasted a year too long for him. His success had come easily, he was thoroughly full of himself, he filled university publications with obnoxious put-downs of his classmates, and he was anxious to begin the next phase of his life. He later attributed his youthful conceit to the fact that he had things too much his own way. As a junior he won an oratorical contest with a shamelessly jingoistic speech on Teddy Roosevelt's Rough Riders; for years afterward this speech was a staple of American high school declamation contests. "All this was not good for what ailed me," Fosdick later allowed. "Fewer winnings and more defeats would have been salutary."[7]

He entered divinity school in 1900 at Colgate Seminary, where he embraced Clarke's theology. "It was the water of life," he later recalled. "All the best meanings of personal religion could be mine again without the crucifixion of the intellect—this assurance he brought me and it was music in my ears." Clarke encouraged his students to think for themselves. On one occasion they challenged his attempt to make sense of the Trinity. "Well, gentlemen," he confessed, "sometimes when I read that passage over I think I have said something—and sometimes I don't." Fosdick, who never tired in later life of acknowledging his personal and intellectual debt to Clarke, called Clarke his "spiritual godfather" and observed that without Clarke's influence and encouragement he would not have entered the ministry. But Fosdick gave only a year to Colgate Seminary; he learned enough at Colgate to realize that, aside from Clarke, Colgate was an intellectual backwater. He wanted the best theological education that he could find in the United States; upon considering the matter carefully, he opted for the combined resources of Union Theological Seminary and Columbia University. On his way to New York City he became engaged to Florence Whitney, courting her in bookish countryside Victorian style. In New York he studied philosophy with Nicholas Murray Butler at Columbia, began his theological studies at Union, and landed a job at Mariners' Temple in the Bowery, where he worked at a mission for street people.[8]

He was not well suited for dealing with drunks and street toughs. The squalor of the Bowery repelled him, especially its "raw filth, poverty and degradation," and he made a poor impression on his audience. Emotionally he began to crack. "I never had been nervously tough," he later allowed. Fosdick's jarring experiences at the mission made it difficult for him to study, and for the first time in his life he was competing with students who matched his academic ability, in courses that taxed his ability. Though he later insisted that he was thrilled to be at Union—"the most exhilarating opportunity I had ever had"—he became tense and depressed. He lost the ability to sleep, and rapidly his symptoms multiplied: blurred vision, stomach spasms, pervasive fatigue, suicidal thoughts.[9]

Hoping to recover in the company of his fiancée, he fled to Worcester, Massachusetts, but his depression only deepened. He seemed to be losing his mind. Fosdick felt that he was spiraling into darkness and was helpless to stop it. He retreated to his family in Buffalo, where his anxiety worsened. "The harder I struggled, the worse I was," he later recalled. "It was what I did the struggling with that was sick. I, who had thought myself strong, found myself beaten, unable to cope not only with outward circumstances but even with myself." Only a few months after he left Buffalo in triumph, he returned "a humiliated nervous wreck." One day he decided that he couldn't stand any more of it; Fosdick held a razor to his throat with the apparent intention of killing himself, but his father intervened.[10]

Early in 1902 he entered the Gleason Sanitarium in Elmira, New York, which specialized in "nervous diseases." For four months Fosdick underwent hydropathy treatments and began to feel slightly better. At home he had worried about the feelings and problems of his family; in the sanitarium he let go of worrying about people's feelings. Afterward his fiancée's father paid for six weeks of convalescence in England, where Fosdick began sleeping again. His life turned a corner at Stratford-on-Avon, and the worst was behind him. At the time cases like his were called neurasthenia, which Robert Moats Miller justly calls a fashionable catchall diagnosis; more precisely, Fosdick seems to have suffered a severe case of neurotic reactive depression. He had the symptoms of depressive anxiety—insomnia, melancholia, gastrointestinal problems, blurred vision, loss of control, nervous tension, obsessive anxieties, suicidal impulses—but he didn't experience the confusion of thought that marks psychotic illness.[11]

His illness was undoubtedly neurotic. It was not a late-Victorian crisis of faith; Fosdick had already negotiated his religious crisis. Neither was it caused by astigmatism or faulty stomach nerves, as he occasionally claimed in later life. His mother suffered numerous nervous breakdowns, his father experienced at least one, and he probably inherited a genetic predisposition for depression. Most likely, the triggers were his jarring experiences in the Bowery and his academic anxieties at Union. Fosdick had been gently nurtured in Victorian Christian ideals, had always graduated first in his class, and cherished his ability to inspire audiences with his oratory. The crudeness of Bowery existence shocked him; his inability to inspire the people he met there was deflating; at Union he worried that top-of-the-class academic excellence was out of reach for him. In later life he repeatedly acknowledged that his emotional breakdown was the formative experience for the kind of ministry that he practiced. He preached knowing sermons about gently raised middle-class youth who cracked emotionally because they were afraid to fail. Fosdick learned how to pray during his emotional breakdown, reaching out to God as the power beyond himself who could save him from himself; through the practice of prayer he learned the art of spiritual receptivity and hospitality. A dozen years later he wrote in his classic meditation on prayer that "prayer is the soul of religion" and that failure in prayer "is the loss of religion itself in its inward and dynamic aspect of fellowship with the Eternal." For the rest of his life he openly recalled that "I wrote my most influential book, *The Meaning of Prayer*, because I had a nervous breakdown."[12]

Slowly he regained his emotional health while resuming his seminary studies. Fosdick studied English Bible and Christian social ethics under Thomas Hall, theology under William Adams Brown, Old Testament under Francis Brown, New Testament under James Everett Frame, church history under Arthur C. McGiffert, and practical theology and philosophy of religion under George William Knox. McGiffert was his favorite; he skipped haughty Charles Briggs; Knox warned him against the liberal impulse to baptize evolution and modern culture. Owing to the pedagogical influence of Butler, Fosdick adopted the Platonist belief in an eternal world of ideas and values. He also embraced Borden Parker Bowne's emphasis on the metaphysical primacy of personality; a bit later, William James's *Varieties of Religious Experience* (1902) convinced him that the way forward in religious thought was to blend James's pragmatism with Bowne's personalist idealism. In 1904 Fosdick graduated at the top of his class; though blessed with an inquisitive mind, he knew that he lacked the mind of a scholar. "Creative scholarship would not have been my forte," he later reflected. "My vocation was to be an interpreter in modern, popular, understandable terms, of the best that I could find in the Christian tradition." William Newton Clarke told friends that Fosdick was destined to become America's greatest preacher. Chastened by his harrowing experience, and enlightened by the best seminary education that he could find, Fosdick set out to fulfill his mentor's prophecy.[13]

He was slow to find his pulpit voice. Union gave little homiletical instruction, and upon beginning his pastoral career, Fosdick learned that contest oratory and preaching are not the same thing. For eleven years he served his first pastorate at the First Baptist Church of Montclair, New Jersey; early in his ministry he rented a phoneless room in a downtown bank, where he secluded himself for four hours of study and writing every weekday morning. Fosdick was a good pastor in the full sense of the term; he attended to pastoral tasks, involved himself in Montclair civic affairs, and became a stylish preacher, but he zealously guarded his study time. Unfailingly he gave priority to the crafting of his sermons; at the same time he refashioned his sermons into brief devotional and apologetic books that made him famous. His first book, *The Second Mile* (1908), was a fifty-two-page meditation on a sentence from the Sermon on the Mount. Refashioned from a summer conference sermon at Northfield, Massachusetts, this slender volume expounded with distinctly American flourishes on the teaching of Jesus that it is a vice not to give more than is requested in all walks of life. "Until willingness overflows obligation, men fight as conscripts instead of following the flag as patriots," Fosdick wrote. The success of this book was an augur of his future; invitations to speak at college chapels poured in from across the country; *The Second Mile*, reprinted over twenty-five times, was eventually condensed by *The Reader's Digest* and remained in print for more than fifty years.[14]

Fosdick got a foothold in academe in the same year that he began to make a name for himself. Union Theological Seminary hired him in 1908 to teach Baptist polity as a part-time lecturer. In 1911 he was promoted to instructor of homiletics; four years later he resigned from First Baptist Church of Montclair to become the first Morris K. Jesup Professor of Practical Theology at Union. Teaching was never enough for him, however. During World War I he turned war-boosting into a second job; in 1918, after three of New York City's historic Presbyterian churches merged to form the Madison Square Presbyterian Church, Fosdick doubled as an every-week Baptist preacher in a Presbyterian pulpit. In the meantime he published the mostly devotional works that made him famous: *The Assurance of Immortality* (1913), *The Manhood of the Master* (1913), *The Meaning of Prayer* (1915), *The Meaning of Faith* (1917), and *The Meaning of Service* (1920).[15]

All these books were rooted in his preaching, which Fosdick based on personal spiritual concerns. Crucial to his effectiveness as a preacher and popular religious writer was his perception, as he tartly put it, that modern people do not go to church to discover what happened to the Jebusites. Fosdick dispensed with the expository method of preaching during the early years of his ministry at Montclair; he later explained: "To start with a passage from Moses, Jeremiah, Paul or John and spend the first half of the sermon or more on its historic explanation and exposition, presupposed the assumption that the congregation came to church that morning primarily concerned about the meaning of those ancient texts. That certainly was not what my congregation in Montclair was bothered about." He tried his hand at topical preaching, but Fosdick was sensitive to the spiritual limitations of preaching as social or political commentary; the good preacher is not called to punditry, he judged. If people do not come to church to learn about the Jebusites, neither do they come for a Sunday rehash of the same issues on which they hear opinions throughout the week; people come to church because they have personal spiritual concerns. Fosdick reflected that throughout the week, pastors deal with these concerns while carrying out their pastoral tasks of counseling and making personal calls. Why not make these personal concerns the subject matter of Sunday preaching? To Fosdick, the point was not to dispense with the scriptural witness, but to make sense of the religious experiences described in Scripture by reflecting on the ways that modern people seek religious meaning.[16]

His early books accented the devotional and apologetic aspects of this project. *The Manhood of the Master* offered study-guide meditations on the character of Jesus, describing Jesus' qualities of magnanimity, sincerity, self-restraint, indignation, loyalty, fearlessness, affection, and the like. *The Assurance of Immortality* built up to its title by reasoning that the issue of mortality is a universal religious concern and that the immortality of souls cannot be ruled out as a possibility; the *assurance* of immortality is a phenomenon of faith, he argued. If God is real and good, then it is unreasonable not to believe in the immortality of the soul; the question of immortality is a subset of the question of God. In his closing pages Fosdick suggested that people of faith should face death in the same way that Columbus faced his first voyage from the shores of Spain: "What lies across the sea, he cannot tell; his special expectations all may be mistaken; but his insight into the clear meanings of present facts may persuade him beyond doubt that the sea has another shore. Such confident faith, so founded upon reasonable grounds, shall be turned to sight, when, for all the dismay of the unbelieving, the hope of the seers is rewarded by the vision of a new continent."[17]

His "meaning" trilogy reached an enormous audience. *The Meaning of Prayer,* which was published during the last year of his Montclair ministry, was organized as a daily study book on the naturalness of prayer, the nature of prayer as communion with God, the experience of unanswered prayer, and the problem of desire in prayer. *The Meaning of Faith* was a wartime reader, more apologetic than devotional in thrust, but organized in the same study-book format as *The Meaning of Prayer,* with daily readings, commentaries, and prayers. Thousands of American and British soldiers carried one or both of these slender volumes into battle; Fosdick told them that faith is reasonable and saving, that God is "the Spiritual Presence who calls us in ideals," and that God is "the Spirit of Righteousness in human life whose victories we see in every moral gain."[18] *The Meaning of*

Service made it clearer than his previous books that Fosdick was a social gospeler. On his opening page he allied himself with Walter Rauschenbusch and declared that "one of mankind's most insistent needs is the interpretation of religion in terms of service and the attachment of religion's enormous driving power to the tasks of service." The meaning of justice in 1920, he asserted, was that American whites needed to see what the world looked like from the perspectives of American blacks, and that Americans needed to empathize with the standpoints of the British, French, Italians, Japanese, and Chinese, and that capitalists needed to view their enterprises from the perspectives of their wage-laborers. Because others are oppressed, Fosdick urged, the spirit of justice calls privileged Christians "to attack the organized injustice of our social and economic order."[19]

At first separately, and later together in a one-volume edition, Fosdick's "meaning" volumes sold millions of copies and were translated into more than fifty languages. By 1920 he was a major figure in liberal theology; by 1930 he would have been the movement's most influential advocate even if he had written nothing else. The devotional accent of his early work helped him become an effective movement leader in the modernist/fundamentalist church battles of the 1920s. Fosdick's trilogy acquainted more Americans with modern theology and converted more of them to it than any other work. The key influences on his rendering of the modern meaning of Christianity were Clarke, Bowne, Rauschenbusch, and Quaker mystic Rufus Jones, whose book *Social Law in the Spiritual World* (1904) made a great impression on Fosdick at the onset of his ministry. He later recalled that he found in this book what William James called "a religion of veracity rooted in spiritual inwardness"; elsewhere he recalled that Jones's book "opened the door to a new era in my thought and life."[20]

RUFUS M. JONES AND THE LIBERAL QUAKER SPIRIT

The idea that progressive Christianity could be strengthened by a mystical approach to religion was a novel notion at the turn of the century. James's *Varieties of Religious Experience* made this notion respectable; in 1904 Catholic modernist Friedrich von Hügel's *Mystical Element of Religion* gave ballast to the largely counter-Protestant idea that mystical religion can be healthy, creative, and progressive. The apostle of mysticism in American liberal Protestantism was Rufus Jones. Georgia Harkness called Jones "America's greatest exponent of mysticism." Many years after they became friends, Fosdick called Jones "a uniquely radiant personality" whose life and writings disclosed the inner light of the Spirit to thousands. Long before Jones learned that his approach to religion was mystical and progressive, he imbibed the deeply mystical and selectively progressive religion of his rural Quaker family.[21]

Jones was born in 1863 in the farming village of South China, Maine; on both sides his forbears had belonged to the Society of Friends for generations. One of his ancestors who came to Massachusetts from Wales in 1690 was named Thankful; one of his great-grandmothers was named Peace, as was the beloved maiden aunt whom he idolized. Rufus Jones grew up in an intensely Quaker family that consisted of his parents Mary Hoxie Jones and Edwin Jones, two siblings, a paternal grandmother who bore eleven children and smoked a long clay pipe, and his Aunt Peace. He was raised by three strong-willed women and an emotionally distant father. In book after book after he became a religious writer, he lauded his Aunt Peace as the ideal of a radiantly Spirit-filled soul: "She had an 'opening' such as often came to her, for she was gifted with prophetic vision." Though he was never christened in a church, Jones recalled, "I was sprinkled from morning till night with the dew of religion. We never ate a meal which did not begin with a hush of thanksgiving; we never began a day without 'a family gathering' at which mother read a chapter of the Bible, after which there would follow a weighty silence." In 1945 Theodore Dreiser lifted this passage and two others from Jones's memoir in his fictional rendering of Quaker life, *The Bulwark*; unfortunately Dreiser failed to evoke the significance of the silence. Jones's books described it repeatedly: "These silences, during which all the children of our family were hushed with a kind of awe, were very important features of my spiritual development. There was work inside and outside the house waiting to be done, and yet we sat there hushed and quiet, doing nothing. I very quickly discovered that something *real* was taking place."[22]

The Jones home was morally and spiritually earnest, but not oppressively pious, so that Rufus never yearned to break free from it. He later recalled that he was "always reckoned among the religious boys of the school," but he played and stormed about like most children. Throughout his life he had a mercurial temperament. Characteristically he urged that "boys are much deeper, much better, than even their *mothers* know, and down below what they show and what they say, is a center of life which never is wholly silent." On his own initiative, supported by the women in his life, he enrolled in the Quaker boarding school of Providence, Rhode Island, and was subsequently admitted to Haverford College. At tiny Haverford, which boasted eighty students, he majored in philosophy, served in the YMCA, and made two related discoveries. The first was that the essays of Ralph Waldo Emerson spoke to him deeply; Jones discovered the word "mysticism" while studying Emerson and later recalled that reading Emerson's essay on the oversoul was "an epoch moment" of his life. The second discovery was that his family's religion and its founder, George Fox, belonged to a great spiritual tradition of mystical faith. In his youth Jones conceived the Society of Friends as a tiny Protestant sect, like most sects preoccupied with dogma and narrow conventions; under the influence of Emerson and Haverford professor Pliny E. Chase, he realized that he had overidentified his religion with its orthodox defenders. George Fox was not a proponent of forensic dogma or formalism, he judged; from its beginning in the sixteenth century, the Society of Friends was meant to be a catalyzing religious movement of a mystical type, emphasizing that which is spiritually real, living, and useful. Fox was the inaugurator of what Jones later called "a fresh movement essentially aiming to realize a universal religion of the Spirit."[23]

This conception of the essence of Quakerism was the seed of his ample spiritual and intellectual lifework. Jones taught for a year at a Quaker boarding school, took a German sabbatical at the universities of Heidelberg and Strasbourg, and consulted at Strasbourg with the eminent scholar of German mysticism Karl Schmidt. For several years he taught at the Providence Friends School (his alma mater) and at Oak Grove Seminary, before taking a deeper plunge into the cross-currents of Quaker factionalism. Quaker factions in the United States revolved around two sets of controversies. The bitter Hicksite-Orthodox schism of 1827 divided the liberal Hicksites from a tradition-guarding "remnant," especially in Philadelphia, New York, and Maryland. The second schism, the Wilbur-Gurney Separation of 1845, mostly affected the Orthodox group; it pitted the followers of Joseph John Gurney, a charismatic English evangelical, against the followers of John Wilbur, who resisted the preaching of Reformed-oriented evangelical doctrines about the Bible and salvation in the Society of Friends. Jones plunged into the politics of his tradition in 1893 by accepting the editorship of the Gurneyite journal, *The Friends Review*; immediately he announced that he opposed factionalism and would shill for no party interest. The mystical essence of the Society of Friends should be enough to define who is a Quaker, he argued. He walked a tightrope in the name of finding the common mind of the Society of Friends. The true spirit of the Quaker way was not compatible with an arid dogmatism or traditionalism, he argued; on the other hand, it was compatible with employing a paid pastor. From his editorial travels in Ohio and Indiana he judged that the "hireling Quaker minister" had come to stay.[24]

Persistently he contended that religions of external authority are soul-deadening: "The moment a religion becomes only a system of thought or a crystalized truth, its service to the world is over, it can no longer feed living souls, for it offers only a stone where bread is asked." True religion always begins with a manifestation, he counseled, "a revelation of God and the soul's answer to it." Whenever it calcifies into an orthodoxy, religion becomes "a dangerous hindrance to the advance of truth and a menace to a free access of the individual soul to its living God." The way of true religion is the way of spiritual immediacy and practical authentication; it asks only to be tested by direct experience. Genuinely Quaker Christianity "is not a theory, not a plan, not a scheme, but a dynamic force," Jones contended. We are called to test the beauty and power of God's Spirit in this world: "Here is our sphere, here is our arena." He took a page from Bowne-school apologetics, enthusing that the idealist core of Quaker Christianity was in tune with modern philosophical idealism: "Quakerism builds upon this demonstration of the Spirit, and in so doing, it is in harmony with all the great leaders of modern philosophy, notably, Descartes, Kant, Fichte, and Hegel, all of whom build their systems on the immediate testimony of self-consciousness." He urged American Quakers not to fear biblical criticism and other forms of modern thought: "It is a part of our business to demonstrate that modern thought and scholarly research do not undermine religion and that Christianity is not outdated and superseded."[25]

Under his influence *The Friends Review* merged with its chief rival, *The Christian Worker,* to form a new paper, *The American Friend,* edited by Jones. By the time that he fulfilled his long-delayed plan to study at Harvard University, Jones was a major figure in the small world of the Society of Friends; his editorials inspired a cottage industry of criticism and support. Collecting his editorials for a book titled *Practical Christianity* (1899), he made his first splash beyond Quaker circles. Just before he entered Harvard in 1900, Jones wrote his next book, *A Dynamic Faith* (1901), which set forth a programmatic statement of belief. It argued that the essence of true religion is love, that love is necessarily relational, that salvation is the transformation of one's life to a good end, and that revelation is a continuous process: "Deep calls unto deep; the deep in God calls to the deep in man, and they know each other." He undoubtedly hoped to discuss these claims with William James at Harvard, but James took a sabbatical in 1900–1901; upon learning that James was at work on his Gifford Lectures on religious experience, Jones arranged to meet with him. He later recalled, "It was always amazing the way this busy man welcomed a young quester and gave himself to him as though his main purpose in life was to help somebody get his feet upon the sun-road to truth. He saw more capacities in a person than the person himself did." Though he never accepted James's radical empiricism, and though he later decided that his early books were overinfluenced by James's emphasis on the subconscious irrationality of the self, Jones greatly admired James and confessed an "immense debt" to him.[26]

At Harvard Jones settled for George Herbert Palmer's courses on ethics and idealism, George Santayana's lectures on Greek philosophy, and Josiah Royce's lectures on metaphysics. Palmer had no taste for mysticism, but his ethical idealism appealed to Jones. Santayana would have laughed at Jones's belief in the beauty of moral fervor, but Jones caught the mystical spirit in Santayana's evocative excursuses on Platonism. He found his reward in Royce's expressively overflowing lectures on metaphysical idealism; except for its consuming monism, which came perilously close to a pantheist identification of God with the world, Jones fervently admired Royce's neo-Hegelian idealism. Throughout his theological career Jones carefully negotiated between what he called "a defeative dualism of a two-world theory" and an equally mistaken pantheism that negates God's capacity of transcendence. His was not the kind of mysticism that blurred all moral distinctions by naming everything "God." Jones appreciated that one of the few things that Royce and James had in common was a respect for mysticism as a pathway to reality; Royce was an especially keen interpreter of Meister Eckhart's mystical theology.[27]

While soaking himself in philosophy lectures and books, Jones gave numerous lectures to local groups, especially Quakers; throughout New England, Quakers attended lectures more fervently than any other group, and Boston-area Quakers were determined not to squander his presence. In February 1901 his fame inspired a remarkable invitation: Haverford College offered an endowed chair in philosophy, created specifically for him. At the time Jones was a widower with a young son, and his doctorate was only half finished. He weighed the prospect of making a permanent home at his college alma mater, gratefully accepted the position, and began his long career as a philosophy professor. The first book that he wrote upon taking his new position was *A Boy's Religion from Memory* (1902), a tender memoir of Jones's early life that William James cherished. His next book was *Social Law in the Spiritual World*.[28]

The title was a variation on Henry Drummond's *Natural Law in the Spiritual World*, an apologetic classic of 1884 that offered a modern Christian response to the challenge of the natural sciences, especially geology and biology. Jones proposed to respond to the challenge of the social sciences, especially psychology. He challenged the materialistic bias of the social sciences by appealing to the idealism of Kant, Hegel, and the English neo-Hegelian school of T. H. Green, John Caird, and Edward Caird. With Kant he argued that it is futile to look for God through logic or empirical reasoning; against Kant he argued that the existence of conscience depends on the existence of God, not the other way around. We must look for things where they belong, he urged. We do not look through a microscope to find love, sympathy, goodness, or patience, because these realities are "facts of personal life" that belong in the realm of spirit. Similarly, in looking for God "we must include under the knowledge-process our entire capacity for dealing with reality." God must be sought where God *could* be found, not in the things of logic or matter, but in the spiritual realm: "We must go at once where spirit manifests itself." Since God is not less personal than we are, all attempts to find God apart from the personal life are doomed to fail.[29]

There is a door that opens to the Holy of Holies, Jones assured. Science cannot open the door, but the door is accessible to every conscious person, for the only way into the spiritual realm is through the personal life: "The true path is through personality. The search must *begin* in our own bosom: Who am I? What do I live by? What does personality involve? How am I related to my fellows and to nature? What does my sense of worth imply? What do I mean by goodness? Can I draw any finite circle about 'myself'? Do I have any dealings with 'a Beyond'? These are questions which take us into regions where microscope and telescope do not avail, but the full answer to them would bring us to *that which is.*"[30] Because these are the crucial religious questions, Jones reasoned, the social sciences are more directly pertinent for religious understanding than the natural sciences. Society is an essential condition of self-consciousness and personality. There can be no self without many selves; self-consciousness is a possibility for each self only in a world in which self-consciousness already exists. Because personality necessarily involves interrelation at every stage of its development, religious thinking must be informed by social scientific understandings of the social influences upon personality.[31]

But social science is valuable only to a point, he cautioned, for the formative role of the social influence is limited. It is not creative and does not confer personality. Personality is an achievement that must be forged and won within society, Jones acknowledged, but it must be won by something that is more elemental to the self than its embodiment or its process of socialization. Personality can be won only by a self's will to be; until this personal force asserts itself, society can do nothing whatsoever to make a person. A self is created by its struggle to attain something personal that is not yet one's own. "There must be presented to consciousness a better state of existence than has yet been realized," Jones explained. "It must appeal to consciousness, furthermore, as a condition which would satisfy if it were put in the place of the actual present state." The ideals of consciousness propel and direct; they pass into life, making a self what it becomes. Jones played up the difference between conscious change and natural change. All changes in life are caused by forces acting from behind, he observed. Tides are moved from without by the moon; plants develop from without by forces of nature; even the self is shaped by subconscious forces and the socializing process. But the difference between changes caused from without as effects of empirically predictable causes and the kind of change produced by self-conscious idealization is "one of the widest chasms in the world." For Jones, as for the personalists, the homeland of religion was on the personal side of that chasm.[32]

Religion and theology either begin with personal experience, or they have no real starting point at all. Jones asserted that his understanding of God was grounded "in the Person of Christ and in the truth which His first interpreters declared as facts of their own experience." At the same time he cautioned that nobody else's experience can be a substitute for one's own: "The truth for me must be the truth I know, not the truth which I hear reported as once known by men of an earlier day." The more that we comprehend that God is essentially self-revealing, he taught, "the less is it possible for us to stop *satisfied* with a record." The more that we comprehend the meaning of God's revelation in Christ, "the more compulsion we feel to possess the experience which flowered into these immortal documents." Revelation is not a thing that believers come to possess; rather, it is the flame that kindles seekers to pursue their quest for God's presence and grace.[33]

Social Law in the Spiritual World was short on Christology; in several of Jones's subsequent books he explained why all his books were short on Christology. The important thing is not to believe a correct theory about Jesus, he argued, but to experience the divine presence that Jesus experienced profoundly; repeatedly he enrolled the liberal Jesus as an advocate and ideal of spiritual living. In *The World Within* (1918), he defined the best meaning of orthodoxy as "any way that makes a soul Christlike" and struck a therapeutic note in describing the inner life of Jesus: "Christ is always concerned to quiet strained nerves, to allay fear, to remove prejudice and suspicion, fret and worry, strain and anxiety. But he also goes farther. He regards health of body and buoyancy of spirit as the true normal condition of life, and he called men to a way of living which produced these results." *New Studies in Mystical Religion* (1927) put the theological point more baldly. "We argue endlessly in the Rabbinical manner about His theory of the Kingdom of God," Jones lamented. "As soon as we begin to use the eyes of our heart, we see that whatever else it may be, the Kingdom of God is the kind of life

He was living here among men. It is a new experience of God as Father—not a new theory of the Fatherhood of God."[34]

Much of his writing chronicled the history of mysticism and various aspects of Quaker history.[35] Repeatedly Jones cautioned against ascetical types of mysticism, arguing for the kind of worldly, affirmative, personalistic mysticism practiced by the Quakers; he wrote little about Quaker pacifism or social issues of any kind—his consuming interest in personal religion nearly always won out when he picked up a pen—though he had a strong social conscience. In 1917 he played a principal role in founding the American Friends Service Committee. As a Quaker pacifist, Jones was prohibited by conscience from taking part in the American war effort, but he yearned to give aid to victims and casualties of the war and to show his loyalty to the United States. The solution that he and other Quakers worked out during World War I was the American Friends Service Committee, which served as a bureau of the Civilian Department of the American Red Cross. Under Jones's leadership the committee organized relief missions in Europe; after the war it fed hundreds of thousands of starving German children; from 1917 until his death in 1948 Jones served as chair or honorary chair of this social outreach vehicle. In the early 1930s he also founded an international association named the Wider Quaker Fellowship. Loosely modeled on the Third Order Franciscans, this fellowship consisted of Quaker fellow travelers from a variety of religious and activist backgrounds who sought an opportunity to be affiliated with the Friends without officially joining them. Vida Scudder was an early member. In later life Jones often marveled that he could remember when Quakers were excommunicated for owning a piano or marrying out of Meeting. Often when he addressed Quaker meetings, he was introduced by such petitions as "Dear Lord, protect us in thy mercy from the false things we are about to hear." For American Friends, he was the symbol and chief advocate of reconceiving the Quaker way as an open-ended universal religion of spirit.[36]

He could be quoted either way on the question whether Quakerism should be Christian. Jones was deeply Christian in his inspiration and ethic; he unfailingly professed that he regarded Jesus as "the most complete revelation that has come to the world." But his theology opened the door to a religion of spirit that dispensed with this confession, for it was the spiritual *life* of Jesus that he idealized, and he never claimed that one needed to believe anything in particular about Jesus to know God fully.[37] For him the touchstone was always the experience of divinity that produces caregiving moral fruit; Jesus was an exemplar of this spiritual ideal. Jones never tired of asserting that moral and spiritual blessedness inhere in the experience of the divine presence. The prize is the glory of going on from grace to higher glory, he taught: "Mercy is a cumulative trait of the soul. The peacemaker grows Godlike until he is recognized as possessing a divine pedigree. Purity of heart adds to itself an increasing capacity to see the invisible and to correspond with the environment that enswathes the soul." In its "richest types," he declared in *Pathways to the Reality of God* (1931), religion is a vital and life-giving correspondence with reality: "It heightens the whole value of life and it seems like the most complete form of life-adjustment that man knows." Against Freudian psychology, he insisted that the idealizing tendency in human beings is at least as fundamental and ineradicable as the instinctual drives. Even if our Freudian desires were to be fulfilled, we would not know what it is that we live by: "There is a divine push, a Godward striving, a divine *urge,* revealed in the central nucleus of my being. The instinctive 'urges' explain only a fraction of me and a minor fraction at that."[38]

While courting his first wife, Sallie Coutant, who died of a respiratory illness in 1899, Jones confessed that he loved the Society of Friends and believed that the good part of the Society would triumph over the repressed and authoritarian part. Many years later, while courting his second wife, Elizabeth Cadbury, he characteristically proclaimed that there is nothing more beautiful in the world "than a soul all aglow with the fire of resolve to be *good* at all costs and hazards."[39] These sentiments took him a long way with his mainline Protestant audience. Fosdick studied and quoted Jones for the rest of his career; he savored Jones's stories and analogies, loved Jones's liberal Christian explication of the inner light and his unitive progressivism in church politics, and appreciated that Jones's theism kept a carefully personalistic balance between transcendence and immanence. In his early career Fosdick increasingly thought of himself as a Quaker fellow traveler; in his mid-career he and Jones became close friends. Aptly Fosdick noted that while Jones wrote profusely about the spiritual life, he wrote almost nothing about social issues, preferring to *do* things in the social arena. Fosdick admired the sentiment without quite agreeing with it. More instructive to him was the fact that Jones was a spellbinding speaker; even though very short on eloquence and oratorical flourishes, he held and inspired his audiences by his quality of spiritual intimacy. Fosdick explained, "He was natural, genuine, direct, human. He spoke from experience. He possessed the spiritual vitality he pled for, and he shared it." That was how Fosdick hoped to be remembered.[40]

THE MEANING OF PERSONAL RELIGION
AND THE ETHICS OF WAR

Fosdick's conversion to fellow-traveling Quakerism was theological before it was ethical and political. Like Walter Rauschenbusch, he later debated whether he should convert from the Baptist church to the Society of Friends, but in his early career he was no pacifist. *The Second Mile* commended the ideals of heroism and courage; *The Manhood of the Master* assured readers that Jesus epitomized these ideals; *The Assurance of Immortality* cautioned that the absolute essence of a person is one's immortal soul, not one's mortal body. The early Fosdick viewed the ethics of New Testament Christianity and true patriotism as variations on the same ethic of self-sacrificing love and courage. When World War I broke out in 1914, he spurned the social gospelers for striving to keep out of the war. His Anglophilism and excitability went into overdrive; faced with a Teutonic assault on the nation and culture of Shakespeare, Tennyson, and Milton, Fosdick leaped to the cause of American intervention, where he found very little liberal Protestant company. He preached across the country on "Things Worth Fighting For," blasting President Wilson for being "too proud to fight"; in 1916 he blasted Republican presidential candidate Charles Evans Hughes for failing to promise that he would take America into the war. When Wilson finally intervened in 1917, Fosdick joined Lyman Abbott, Henry Churchill King, and Shailer Mathews in the cause of generating moral enthusiasm for the war. Across the country he gave stirring nationalistic addresses that made the case for the moral imperative of winning the war. Later he preached to the troops in France and was deeply honored when an officer told him that he was worth a battalion.[41]

"There is no hope for the world with an autocratic, military Germany triumphant," Fosdick declared in 1917. *"We must win the war."* At the same time he cautioned against demonizing America's enemies: "Though we fight we must not hate. We are Christians. We know when we think of it that had we been born in Germany, there is not one chance in a million that we would be doing other than the Germans do." He could say, with Walt Whitman, "God damn the wars—all wars. God damn every war. God damn 'em! God damn 'em!" He could even admit that modern war had lost the gallantry of the armored knights who fought by the rules of chivalry: "War now is dropping bombs from aeroplanes and killing women and children in their beds; it is shooting, by telephonic orders, at an unseen place miles away and slaughtering invisible men; it is murdering innocent travelers on merchant ships with torpedoes from unknown submarines; it is launching clouds of poisoned gas and slaying men with their own breath."[42]

But none of this stopped Fosdick from equating the cause of Christ and the cause of American victory in the next breath; he refuted Christian pacifism by observing that Jesus "did not directly face our modern questions about war; they were not his problem." The moral problem of war is different for modern Christians, he reasoned, because modern Christians have the moral responsibility of repelling tyrants and invaders. In the manner of a revival sermon he built up to a story about a French mother who lost two of her sons in the war. The woman's youngest son had fled to Canada, and she wrote to him that his brothers had been killed in the service of their country. Your country needs you, the mother wrote, and if you do not return immediately to your homeland, do not ever return. Fosdick provided the moral of the story: "Multitudes are living in that spirit today. He must have a callous soul who can pass through times like these and hear a voice, whose call a man must answer, or else lose his soul. Your country needs *you.* The Kingdom of God on earth needs you. The Cause of Christ is hard bestead and righteousness is having a heavy battle in the earth—they need *you.*"[43]

On behalf of the YMCA, Fosdick spent four months at war camps in Britain, France, and Belgium, giving speeches and sermons; his reports in American magazines idealized the American doughboys and came very close to demonizing America's German enemies. In 1918 he preached a sermon that conveyed his wartime inner feeling. "We never were so excited about anything in our whole lives as we have been about this war, we never felt the deeps within us, the passion for sacrifice, as during this war," he exulted. Some things are intolerable, he admonished, "and the man who will not say so, and fight, cannot save his soul. Sin is to be crushed by militant righteousness." For those who squirmed at the singing of militaristic hymns, he had no sympathy: "A person who is so delicate that he cannot feel a thrill of pride and love for militant righteousness is too delicate for this world."[44]

Fosdick's war-boosting manifesto, *The Challenge of the Present Crisis,* quickly sold more than 200,000 copies and heightened his stature as a Protestant leader. Upon returning from the war camps in Europe, he assumed the position of Preaching Minister at New York's First Presbyterian Church, where he preached week after week about the war. Repeatedly he puzzled over the moral meaning of the war. During his speaking tours in the war camps he was shocked by tales of German brutality and shuddered to think that modern, civilized people could be so depraved. Though he apparently believed that only the Germans committed atrocities, Fosdick spent enough time in the war camps to realize that even the doughboys he idealized in print were very short on Christian morals. By 1919 he was already expressing chagrin about his enthusiasm for the war. America fought in a just cause, he still maintained, but that cause was betrayed by the Treaty of Versailles, which shredded Wilson's Fourteen Points and contained the seeds of future wars. From the pulpit Fosdick called his congregation to support politicians who favored American membership in the League of Nations.[45]

Typically, even his sharpest U-turn reflected a mainstream trend in American liberal Protestantism. In the early 1920s many liberal Protestants who had endorsed American intervention in 1917 had second thoughts about the moral and political justification of war. Some of them reeled from disillusioning experiences at the front; some were chastened by the war's bad ending at Versailles; both experiences cut Fosdick deeply. His sermons inched toward outright pacifism. In 1921 he preached a widely reprinted sermon, "Shall We End War?" that sought to create public support for a naval disarmament conference. Fosdick argued that war no longer stood for any kind of gallantry or glory, no longer produced public virtues, was no longer restrained by its costs or its methods of killing, and no longer shielded civilian populations from attack. The following year he joined pacifists Kirby Page and John Nevin Sayre in organizing an interdenominational church group that called for Christian resistance to militarism; the group's statement, drafted by Fosdick, was titled "The Churches' Plea Against War and the War System." Signed by 150 Protestant and Catholic leaders, this statement was the first ecumenical antiwar declaration of its kind in the United States.[46]

In 1923 Fosdick announced that he was finished with the war business. For many years he had consented to the necessity of war, he recalled; he had even believed that war could be righteous. Thus, when World War I broke out, he had felt that it was too late to claim an antiwar conscience; he had to show the courage of his convictions. Fosdick vowed, "For my part, I never will be caught that way again." On Christian grounds he embraced the Gandhian strategy of nonviolent resistance to evil. "War is the most colossal and ruinous social sin that afflicts mankind today . . . it is utterly and irremediably unchristian," he declared. "The war system means everything which Jesus did not mean and means nothing that he did mean. . . . It is a more blatant denial of every Christian doctrine about God and man than all the theoretical atheists on earth could ever devise." To take seriously the command to follow Christ is to see that war is the greatest evil that human beings commit against Christ: "The quarrels between fundamentalists and liberals, high churchmen, broad churchmen, and low churchmen, are tithing mint, anise, and cummin if the church does not deal with this supreme moral issue of our time: Christ against war."[47]

For the rest of his life Fosdick assailed war and the warmaking system. "I have watched them coming gassed from the front-line trenches," he preached. "I have seen the long, long hospital trains filled with their mutilated bodies. I have heard the cries of the crazed and the prayers of those who wanted to die and could not, and I remember the maimed and ruined men for whom the war is not yet over." He repented of the "atrocious" sermons and speeches that he gave on behalf of state-sanctioned killing: "I too was a gullible fool and thought that modern war could somehow make the world safe for democracy. They sent men like me to explain to the army the high meanings of war and, by every argument we could command, to strengthen their morale."[48]

Repeatedly he urged that to avert future wars, nations had to surrender some of their national sovereignty. Although Fosdick's pacifism was essentially moral, it was also political and internationalist; American isolationism held no allure for him. Like other liberal pacifists between the world wars, he viewed nonviolent activism essentially as an internationalist alternative to nationalism. Nationalism was the breeding ground of chauvinism and militarism; Fosdick dreamed of an effective world federalism that disarmed and transformed the clash of nations. Next to the title page of his later books his publisher always listed all of his books, with one exception; at his request, *The Challenge of the Present Crisis* was never listed, because Fosdick was ashamed of it. "I was never more sincere in my life than when I wrote it, but I was wrong," he explained. The message of that book "was not the business of a Christian minister to be saying."[49]

The memories of his war-camp sermons haunted him: "We went out to the army and explained to these valiant men what a resplendent future they were preparing for their children by their heroic sacrifice." He confessed that sometimes he didn't want to believe in immortality; Fosdick didn't want to meet the boys he had cheered to their deaths. Famously, in 1933, he pledged to the Unknown Soldier never to do it again: "We can have this monstrous thing or we can have Christ, but we cannot have both. O my country, stay out of war! Cooperate with the nations in every movement that has any hope for peace; enter the World Court, support the League of Nations, contend undiscourageably for disarmament, but set your face steadfastly and forever against being drawn into another war. O church of Christ, stay out of war! Withdraw from every alliance that maintains or encourages it."[50] In the early 1930s America's mainline Protestant churches pledged to do exactly that.

PREACHING THE RELIGION OF PERSONALITY

Fosdick's only radical cause was his pacifism, and for much of his career, even pacifism was a mainstream Protestant sentiment. He made more enemies as a theological liberal than as an antiwar activist. Though he epitomized the pacifist liberal Christianity that Reinhold Niebuhr repudiated in the 1930s, Fosdick remained on reasonably good terms with Niebuhr and other Christian realists; his legendary congeniality served him well in his dealings with Niebuhrians. But his factional role in the modernist-fundamentalist blowout of the 1920s made him a lightning rod of controversy, though he claimed that he sought to keep the blowout from occurring. In 1922 Fosdick's Cole Lectures at Vanderbilt, published as *Christianity and Progress,* offered a timely summary of his theological outlook; the same year he preached an explosive sermon, "Will the Fundamentalists Win?" that triggered the climactic phase of the modernist-fundamentalist struggle for the churches. Both offerings proved to be loaded with lightning-rod material, though to his mind both were models of peaceable, irenic, mainstream Protestantism.

In *Christianity and Progress* he identified the cause of Christian ethics with the cause of social progress; at the same time he argued that progressives often underestimated the power of human sin, relied too heavily on politics and "social palliatives" to solve the world's problems, and showed a radical disrespect for the wisdom of the past. Fosdick was a not a progress ideologue. The predatory spirit of capitalism was alien to him, but so was the collectivist ideologial spirit of socialism. John D. Rockefeller Jr. was his dear friend, as were many of Rockefeller's capitalist friends, but Fosdick openly agreed with Rauschenbusch that American capitalism was the most unregenerate sector of American life. His view of the class struggle was exactly the universalist liberal moralism of appealing to goodwill and ignoring class stuctures that Niebuhr later ridiculed, though Niebuhr picked on the likes of Shailer Mathews, not Fosdick, when he did so. Fosdick lauded the attitude of "single tax" populist Henry George, who denied that he was a friend of working people or a friend of capitalists. George was for persons simply as persons; so was Fosdick. He believed in the universal power of reason and the latent good faith in every person: "Until we can get that larger loyalty into the hearts of men, all the committees on earth cannot solve our industrial problems."[51]

Though conceding that progress never takes place in a straight line, Fosdick read the Bible essentially as a testimony to progressive revelation in a progressing world; his chief works of biblical scholarship, *The Modern Use of the Bible* (1924) and *A Guide to Understanding the Bible* (1938), argued that the principle of progressive revelation is the key to the Bible's unity and meaning.[52] In *Christianity and Progress* he made the case concisely: "From Sinai to Calvary—was ever a record of progressive revelation more plain or more convincing?" Scripture began with Yahweh in a thunderstorm and ended with Christ saying, "God is Spirit." It began with a tribal deity leading warriors to battle and ended with the admonition that God is love. It began with an enemy-hating monarch who commanded the slaying of the Amalekites and ended with Christ commanding love of enemies and acts of mercy toward persecuters. The biblical revelation is not a pool but a river, Fosdick urged: "The riverbed in which this stream of thought flows is stable and secure; the whole development is controlled by man's abiding spiritual need of God and God's unceasing search for man."[53]

His writings were short on counterexamples. To Fosdick the essence of the New Testament was the Person and Spirit of Jesus, especially the love theme of Jesus, which trumped the New Testament's inferior nonprogressive material. He allowed that much of Christian history is more difficult to read as a narrative of progress. "Priestly Christianity" was the same oxymoron for him that it was for Rauschenbusch and Mathews; he also shared their rejection of the monarchical concept of God that supported priestly Christianity. "The idea that God must be approached by stated ceremonies came directly from thinking of God in terms of a human monarch," Fosdick observed. His own images of divine reality were drawn from the progressive portions of Scripture and the poetry of Tennyson, Coleridge, and Wordsworth. Tennyson professed that in the meeting of divine and human spirit, God comes closer to human beings than their own breathing; Coleridge exulted in the vast ever-acting energy of God in nature; Wordsworth called God's dwelling the light of setting suns; Fosdick affirmed that the world is charged with God's shining glory. In his rendering, the idea of God as a creative, loving, personal power informed the most developed forms of religion and fueled the most worthy alternative worldview to fundamentalism and secularism. Liberal theology remained the true third way between authority religion and godlessness and stood for progress, which it understood to be the ideal, though not always the reality. Fosdick noted that Europe and America were "on a far lower moral level" in 1922 than they were before the war; the mission of modern Christianity was to stand for social progress and progressive revelation, not give in to the kingdom's setbacks.[54]

Henry Ward Beecher was fond of saying that a text is like a small gate that provides access to an open field and that, unfortunately, most ministers spend all their time swinging on the gate; Fosdick applied this image to the relation of personal religion and the social gospel. He observed that many pastors come to their vocation through the gate of personal religion and then swing on that gate exclusively, while others enter the ministry through the gate of social concern and swing exclusively upon it. "We are both wrong," he admonished. "These are two gates into the same city, and it is the city of our God. The authentic Christian gospel is both personal and social." The great aim of the gospel is the redemption of personality, Fosdick explained; thus the Christ-following church must always be dedicated to personal and social salvation alike, for the inner and outward burdens of human beings are always linked.[55]

Rufus Jones loved Emerson and William James for their insistence that secondhand religion is someone else's truth; Fosdick loved Emerson, James, and Jones for the same reason. "The one vital thing in religion is first-hand, personal experience," he preached. "Religion is the most intimate, inward, incommunicable fellowship of the human soul." There is a role for authority in true religion, he allowed, but there is no role for belief-dictating external authority. External authority takes the place of human perception; it compels believers to consent to what it sees. Genuine authority is empowering, like a good teacher of literature, Fosdick reasoned, who opens the eyes of readers to literary beauty and complexity. Genuine authority enables seekers to appreciate the wisdom of the past and the revelations of God's seers: "That is the only use of authority in a vital realm. It can lead us up to the threshold of a great experience where we must enter, each man for himself, and that service to the spiritual life is the Bible's inestimable gift."[56]

His clear-eyed preaching on this theme contributed mightily to his reputation among fundamentalists as the symbol and leader of modernizing apostasy in the churches; one fateful sermon lit the fuse of the modernist-fundamentalist explosion. "Shall the Fundamentalists Win?" decried the rise of an essentially reactionary movement in modern Protestantism and raised the specter of a fundamentalist rout. Fosdick acknowledged that theological conservatism and theological fundamentalism were not exactly the same thing; all fundamentalists are conservative, he explained, but not all conservatives are fundamentalist. The best conservatives have a liberal spirit, "but the Fundamentalist program is essentially illiberal and intolerant." It repudiated the "great mass of new knowledge" that modern people possess about the physical universe, the history of the world, and the history of religions. It insisted that all Christians are required to believe unbelievable things about the inerrancy of Scripture, the virginal conception of Christ and the second coming of Christ. Fosdick plainly disavowed these beliefs. He noted that the ancient world routinely accounted for great personalities by attributing miraculous births to them; in fact, among the great founders of religions, only Moses, Confucius, and Muhammad are not ascribed a miraculous birth. Moreover, Fosdick observed, every idea in the Koran that modern Christians dislike is contained in the Bible. The Bible takes patriarchal polygamy and slavery for granted; in its cruder sections it pictures God as an Oriental monarch; vast portions of Scripture approve of violence and other forms of coercion against unbelievers. The difference is that in the Bible these elements are superseded by a love ethic of reverence for personality: "revelation is progressive." God becomes a compassionate father, patriarchy and slavery are increasingly undermined by the Bible's increasing regard for personality, Christ commands love of enemies. The ancient world had no concept of progressive development, Fosdick allowed, and neither did contemporary fundamentalists, but this concept is the key to the true meaning of Christianity.[57]

Fosdick lamented that so many Christians insisted on trying to believe unbelievable things, but to him the worst thing about fundamentalism was that it denied to all nonfundamentalists the right to the Christian name. "The

Fundamentalists propose to drive out from the Christian churches all the conse-crated souls who do not agree with their theory of inspiration," he warned. "What immeasurable folly!" He conceded that fundamentalists did not have a monop-oly on intolerance. In church politics Fosdick was a moderate; he sought to pre-vent denominational schisms between modernists and fundamentalists. In the mid-1920s he took flak from church radicals who denounced him for trying to hold the churches together. Unitarian leader Alfred Dieffenbach declared that while he could respect a consistent Roman Catholic or fundamentalist, he could not respect Fosdick, who wanted to be a liberal without facing up to the eccle-sial implications of modernist criticism. Attacks of this kind were personally wounding to Fosdick; even thirty years later he still recalled them vividly.[58]

Fosdick found it especially hard to take criticism from his left; at the same time, he tended to magnify the significance of radical criticism to reinforce his moder-ate self-image. In 1922 the unity of the church was not equally threatened by radicals and conservatives. The party of the schismatic left was small, centered edi-torially at the Unitarian *Christian Register,* and had little influence. By contrast, the fundamentalist side was large and deeply rooted in the mainline denomina-tions. To Fosdick and other liberals, the reactionary intolerance of fundamental-ism was a church-threatening matter. Against this threat he pleaded "the cause of magnanimity and liberality and tolerance of spirit." Modernists and fundamen-talists were bound to disagree, he counseled; for that matter, fundamentalists were bound to disagree with all nonfundamentalists, but these disagreements did not justify splitting the churches. The fundamentalists and church radicals who pressed for a deck-clearing schism were both wrong; what was needed was a spirit of tolerance and cooperation that allowed different theologies to coexist within the existing denominations.[59]

"Shall the Fundamentalists Win?" was ostensibly a call for broad-church civil-ity, but its effect was dramatically divisive; it inflamed fundamentalists, nerved wishy-washy liberals for battle, and caused many pastors to choose sides. Fosdick bewailed that "the Fundamentalists are giving us one of the worst exhibitions of intolerance that the churches of this country have ever seen." With these words he settled the question of who was to be the lightning rod of the antifundamen-talist cause. With his consent a liberal Presbyterian publicist, Ivy Lee, distributed the sermon throughout the country, which sparked a firestorm in the northern Baptist and northern Presbyterian churches, which were deeply split between their fundamentalist and liberal-moderate sides. Though Fosdick lacked the par-tisan temperament of a factional leader, the infuriated fundamentalist reaction to his sermon lifted him to factional-leader status. He later recalled that "if ever a sermon failed to achieve its object, mine did." His sermon was a plea for good-will, he explained, "but what came of it was an explosion of ill will, for over two years making headline news of a controversy that went the limit of truculence." The fact that he preached his liberal Baptist opinions in a Presbyterian pulpit gave special offense to conservative Presbyterians, who maneuvered to expel him from his Presbyterian pulpit.[60]

As a member of a noncreedal denomination, Fosdick was protected from losing his ordination or facing a heresy trial. A coalition of Presbyterians led by William Jennings Bryan demanded that he had to become a Presbyterian or resign his position; while Bryan maneuvered at General Assembly to have Fosdick removed from First Presbyterian Church, Presbyterian fundamentalist J. Gresham Machen blasted him for demeaning the beliefs and feelings of orthodox Protestants. Quoting from Fosdick's controversial sermon, Machen observed in *Christianity and Liberalism* (1923): "They speak with disgust of those who believe 'that the blood of our Lord, shed in a substitutionary death, placates an alienated Diety and makes possible welcome for the returning sinner.'" Machen's rebuttal was deeply personal: "Against the doctrine of the Cross they use every weapon of caricature and vilification. Thus they pour out their scorn upon a thing so holy and so precious that in the presence of it the Christian heart melts in gratitude too deep for words. It never seems to occur to modern liberals that in deriding the Christian doctrine of the Cross, they are trampling upon human hearts."[61]

The liberal rhetoric of love, compassion, and goodwill was galling to fundamentalists for that reason. For all their claims to moral sensitivity, the Fosdickian liberals seemed to dismiss long-cherished Christian doctrines and the spiritual feelings of fundamentalists with apparent contempt. Chief among them was the biblical picture of a six-day creation; though some fundamentalists, such as Machen, did not embrace anti-evolutionary creationism as an orthodox cause, many fundamentalists made it the superbadge of orthodoxy in the early 1920s. Bryan was prominent among them, and during the same period that he pressed for Fosdick's removal from First Presbyterian Church, he defended the Tennessee state law forbidding the teaching of evolution in its public schools. Shortly before the famous Scopes trial of 1925 in Dayton, Tennessee, Fosdick blasted Bryan's position as a "gross injustice to the Bible." By then Bryan held the upper hand in his campaign to make Fosdick convert to Presbyterianism (and face heresy charges) or resign his Presbyterian pulpit. After two years of intense legal maneuvering to save his position at First Presbyterian, Fosdick gave up and resigned in 1925; he was not a Presbyterian and he had no intention of enduring a Presbyterian heresy trial. His case received enormous publicity, which drew overflow crowds to his church. "They call me a heretic," he observed in his farewell sermon. "Well, I am a heretic if conventional orthodoxy is the standard. I should be ashamed to live in this century and not be a heretic."[62]

Despite such appearances of success, however, the fundamentalists were not winning. Between 1920 and 1925 fundamentalists had gained impressive influence and movement energy, threatening to gain control of several denominations. After the Scopes trial, however, the fortunes of their movement swiftly deteriorated. Fundamentalists lost battle after battle in the late 1920s, failing to capture a single denomination. In response they gave up on the dominant culture and built their own vast network of independent ministries, parachurch organizations, and fundamentalist denominations. Bryan was humiliated at the Scopes trial, which was devastating to the movement's ambitions and public image;

Machen resigned from Princeton Seminary in 1928 after a bitterly contested reorganization relegated the seminary's fundamentalists to minority status; modernist forces gained decisive control of the northern Baptist and northern Presbyterian churches; and in 1925 Fosdick was lured by Rockefeller to the Park Avenue Baptist Church, which served as an ample way station while Rockefeller built a spectacular Gothic cathedral for Fosdick in Morningside Heights.[63]

Fosdick never doubted that fundamentalist evangelicalism had been thoroughly routed from mainstream American Christianity. In "Shall the Fundamentalists Win?" he asserted that fundamentalism was destined to fail; in his memoir he dismissed the controversy as an "ephemeral" episode, "despite the noise it made." Though he enjoyed the fame that he earned apart from the fundamentalist controversy, Fosdick professed that he could have done without his antifundamentalist notoriety, repeatedly bemoaning the fact that the issues in dispute were trivial and that it embarrassed him to have to combat such a woefully outdated theology. His ascending fame raised the demands on his time throughout the 1920s, which forced him to cut back on his teaching commitments at Union Seminary. Fosdick's core curriculum consisted of courses titled "Sermon Outlines," "Brief Sermons," and "The Use of the Bible in Modern Preaching." In 1927, a year after Henry Sloane Coffin replaced an emotionally exhausted Arthur C. McGiffert as Union Seminary president, Fosdick told Coffin that he appreciated the seminary's generosity "in allowing me to try the experiment" of combining a pastoral and academic career. A year later he reminded Coffin that while his teaching load was down to "only a few hours," his course on biblical preaching enrolled nearly two hundred students. The following year he graciously gave up his seminary pension while bargaining to keep his faculty apartment; "My time and energy at the disposal of the seminary are likely to grow less rather than more," he informed Coffin. In 1931, while continuing to teach at Union, Fosdick became the first pastor of interdenominational Riverside Church, where he increasingly defined good religion in explicitly therapeutic terms.[64]

Fosdick's widely circulated Riverside sermons translated traditional Christian language into a religious language of health, aesthetic appreciation, and mutual care. Having come to the ministry through the gate of personal religion, he emphasized the religion of personal faith and virtue. Though he occasionally spoke a critical word about capitalism, he epitomized the postwar social gospelism that pushed hard for pacifism, emphasized a "spirit of Jesus" personal religion, and downplayed the class struggle. His sermons and essays played up the personal basis of social religion and the spiritual kinship of religion and art; repeatedly Fosdick affirmed that good religion is an art that upholds, cultivates, and nourishes human personality. In *Adventurous Religion* (1926), he declared that Christianity is an adventure that begins with daring, not with religious beliefs: "No one is asking you just now to believe them. Start where you are and follow what you do see."[65] *As I See Religion* (1932) declared that Christianity is denied wherever personality is cramped, fettered, or abused; he contended that the churches should preach the religion of personality "instead of remaining what too largely they are—societies for the propagation of an outgrown mythology." *The Power to See It Through* (1935) capsulized his message: "Let me tell you my philosophy. I can put it in a few words. Everyone who follows this ministry will recognize it. All my thinking starts from and comes back to it. Here it is: *the key to the understanding of all life is the value of personality.*"[66]

Christianity is true and superior to other religions as the religion of personality, Fosdick argued; Jesus is distinctive in the history of religion precisely as the champion of personality: "He thought of personality as the central fact in the universe and used it as the medium of interpretation for all other facts." To say that Jesus is divine is to affirm that God should be symbolized "by the best personal life we know."[67] Wherever goodness, beauty, truth, and love exist, Fosdick contended, the divine is present. Human beings are divine to the extent that they embody and mobilize these qualities; Jesus was uniquely divine because he embodied them fully. Fosdick's anchor was William Newton Clarke's principle that "the divinity of Jesus is the divinity of his spiritual life."[68] Divinity is not a supernatural reality, but rather the perfection of immanent love that every person is capable of mobilizing. Christianity is the truest religion because it valorizes personality uniquely; by this criterion Buddhism rated poorly as a religion, because it despairs of personality. "Christianity is aggressive and spiritually militant," Fosdick declared. "It believes in personality, its infinite possibility, its permanent continuance, its ultimate victory."[69]

It followed that sin is the victory of bad social influences and bodily impulses over the instincts of a higher self; long after the passing of the Victorian age, Fosdick remained a quintessentially liberal Victorian. Good religion brings people to an awareness of their better nature and mobilizes their capacity to live out of it, he preached. This is the best hope of every individual, of the church, and of the world. Fosdick's ecclesiology and his social ethic were extensions of his personal faith. He reasoned that the church is rightly a moral community that cultivates good religion, "the point of incandescence where, regardless of denominationalism or theology, the Christian life of the community bursts into flame." The mission of the church is to redeem the world by nourishing the development of personality.[70]

It was crucially important to Fosdick to express and defend religion in a way that did not conflict with modern science; at the same time he resisted the science-aspiring empiricism of Mathews, Macintosh, and Wieman. The appropriate language of religion is that of art, he insisted, not the language or method of science: if Jesus had used the scientific jargon of his time, his sayings would have been quickly forgotten. Instead, Jesus speaks to all ages, because he used the language of beauty, which alone is timeless and universal. Fosdick observed that the armies and empires of ancient Greece are fallen; even Greek science is wholly outdated; but the Greek language and representations of beauty are assured of permanence. Having survived a nervous breakdown, he took for granted that religion must nourish emotional health. Having struggled to find a faith he could live with, he was keenly attuned to the spiritual and intellectual needs of educated, upwardly mobile, mostly white Americans who yearned for religious meaning in their lives, though he also had a significant following among black-church pastors. In a society dominated by science and economics, Americans yearned especially for beauty; religion is worthless if it is not beautiful, Fosdick assured. Americans were "hoodwinked and hypnotized" by the dominant myth that all truth must be subsumed under the category of science; Fosdick countered that art, music, poetry, love, and religion can never be confined to the limits of science, for these creations and expressions of the human spirit belong to the realm of beauty.[71]

"There is no excuse for the expensive horror of hundreds of our churches with the amphitheatrical arrangement, sloping floors, high platforms, with a man on a red plush chair as the center of attention, a speaker's desk in front of him and painted organ pipes behind," he protested. Such churches are fit for droning sermons on doctrine and duty, but not for worship. Of the three realms of spiritual virtue—truth, goodness, and beauty—Protestantism was strong on the first two, he allowed, but it was dreadfully lacking on the third. It took pride in its ugly churches and its barren worship services, making a virtue of "aesthetic starvation." Fosdick exhorted that only beautiful worship is worth producing, "for beauty subdues, integrates, and unifies the soul, washes the spirit clean, and sends one out with a vision of the Divine, not simply believed in but made vivid. We are discovering once more that nothing in human life, least of all religion, is ever right until it is beautiful."[72]

He cautioned that religion-as-art does not dispense with truth claims. Great art is not simply beautiful, he reasoned; it also tells the truth, and good religion tells the truth in the same way. Neither art nor religion is merely subjective, for both are convinced "that no one can know the whole of reality without seeing what the artist sees." The territory of religion is the realm of spirit, personality, and beauty, which religion shares with art; Fosdick's sermonizing on this theme linked him to the romanticist tradition of Channing, Bushnell, Beecher, and Munger. He had minimal sympathy with his generation's complaint that Schleiermacherian romanticism is too subjective. Fosdick countered that nothing is deeper in liberal Christianity than spiritual feeling; religion must respect science in its sphere, but religion must not aspire to be like science. His favored authorities on this theme were English poets (especially Coleridge, Wordsworth, Tennyson, and Browning) and the trinity of American liberal religious philosophers: Emerson, James, and Bowne. All were quoted as advocates of experiential religious immediacy. His personal notebooks contained forty pages of quotes from Emerson and twenty-one pages from James.[73]

Fosdick had little taste for academic theology, mainly because it provided little grist for his sermonizing, and the ascendance of Barthian theology reinforced this predisposition. He had a passing acquaintance with Barth's early writings and his brief *Dogmatics in Outline,* but there is no evidence that he ever explored Barth's *Church Dogmatics.* Theologically he leaned on Bowne, Clarke, Rauschenbusch, and Jones, taking little heed of non-Americans, especially Germans; in biblical studies he also favored British and American scholars, notably James Moffatt and Edgar Goodspeed. His favorite reading matter was biography; Fosdick read hundreds of biographies, quoted them extensively in his sermons, and filled twenty-seven notebook pages with quotes from his favorite American, Abraham Lincoln. Aside from its value as source material for sermons, he loved biography because it provides contact with the world's most interesting subject—personality—in the pleasant space of one's own study. "When folks are incarnate at our elbows, treading on our toes, competing with us in business and upsetting our hopes in politics, they can be decidedly unpleasant," he explained. But the same people can be fascinating to read about: "Biography offers human contact in its most amiable form."[74]

Week after week, Fosdick celebrated the amiable virtues of modern culture from the pulpit, but he warned that modern culture also has a scientistic dark side. Repeatedly he warned against the exaltation of science over other modes of knowing. Science ideologized—scientism—was reductionist and imperialist, desacralizing everything that it touched, stripping human selves of their spiritual connections to the past, their communities, and the cosmos. Scientism reduced life to dead matter and blind energy and it could not account for the life of spirit or the existence of moral value. This was the genius of religion in Fosdick's rendering; religion was the royal road to the world of spirit behind the veil of appearances. It rejected the scientistic dogma that mystery must give way to facts. Science cannot explain the meaning of anything, while religion is the "appreciation of life's meaning as a whole." Fosdick explained that religion has the same relation to scientific facts that a poet's vision has to the ether waves of a sunset or a mother's love has to the measurements of her growing son: "It clothes them with radiant meanings. It perceives in them eternal worth and significance. It lifts the ponderous world to its ear as we lift a seashell, and hears mysterious messages of hope and peace. It is evaluation in its most exalted and comprehensive exercise." The genuine mystery of life expressed in religion is not even touched after science has finished its work.[75]

ON BEING AN EMOTIONALLY HEALTHY PERSON

Though he maintained essentially the same conception of good religion throughout his career, Fosdick's advocacy of it went through three phases: his early preaching and writings were mostly devotional; in the 1920s he focused on the fundamentalist crisis, the relationship between personal and social religion, and the relationship between science and religion; in the 1930s and for the rest of his career he gave top priority to the therapeutic function of religion. Though his early sermons were widely distributed in various forms and he was quick to capitalize on the advent of religious broadcasting in the early 1920s, his first volume of collected sermons, *The Hope of the World*, was not published until 1933. In a typical entry, "Making the Best of a Bad Mess," Fosdick argued that a good life must be created, not found or given. In a companion sermon, "The Service of Religious Faith to Mental Health," he declared that the root of holiness is the desire to be whole, wholesome, and physically and emotionally healthy.[76] The religion of positive thinking found a national audience through these sermons. In 1924 Fosdick began to broadcast his sermons at RCA's radio station WJZ; by 1927 he was the every-Sunday star of NBC's "National Vespers," the flagship of Protestant broadcasting, which gained him an enormous national following. For nineteen years he presented shortened versions of his Sunday sermons on the afternoon National Vespers program, which was sponsored by the Federal Council of Churches; admirers called him the dean of radio preachers. By the time that Fosdick published *The Hope of the World,* he was known to an audience that may have averaged two million listeners per week. The success of his first sermon collection led to nine additional volumes, to which he gave such titles as *Successful Christian Living, Living Under Tension,* and *On Being Fit to Live With.*[77]

Sunday after Sunday he crafted earnest, accessible, humane sermons that made millions feel that he was speaking to them directly; often he declared, "I want some decisions made here today." Fosdick sprinkled his sermons with inspiring stories about famous overcomers—Abraham Lincoln, Helen Keller, and Florence Nightingale were among his favorites—and he employed some of his trademark quotations more than a dozen times. Tennyson's "Be loyal to the royal in thyself" was a typical favorite. Always direct and flowing, always long on moral high-mindedness and conversational intimacy, his sermons set the standard for positive-thinking motivational speaking. His anecdotes casually reflected his personal world of country clubs, servants, summer resorts, and stock options, to which much of his audience aspired. For thousands of pastors he was the lodestar preacher of his generation; often he was introduced to clerical audiences as "the one whose sermons you often preach." Fosdick was unfailingly gracious, with no hint of chastisement, to those who confessed that they recycled his sermons. He never tired of exhorting his listeners to overcome their personal obstacles in the manner of Keller, Nightingale, and Jesus. Often he settled for a soothing effect in a high-minded way. His debut in the literature of self-help, *Twelve Tests of Character* (1923), set his perspective apart from what he called "the popular books about success"; it is not enough to "grit our teeth" and strive for success, he counseled, for success is often cheap and vulgar. Many who are admired for their success have no taste at all for "real music" or beautiful worship or great literature or the "benedictions of a pure heart." Fosdick called for a higher standard of success: "You can always tell a man's quality by noting the things to which he is alive." To appreciate something truly great is to enrich oneself spiritually, which is the highest success.[78]

He could be gritty in describing human sin, though not by a Pauline standard; Fosdick once declared that Paul's descriptions of human perversity were too graphic to read in church. He could be whimsical on occasion and freely admitted to various changes of mind, but Fosdick was almost never ironic; his earnest liberal moralism was allergic to irony, and he indulged paradox only as much as necessary. Fosdick allowed that Calvary was somehow both sublime and horrible at the same time; one of his Palm Sunday sermons was titled "The Cross, an Amazing Paradox."[79] The inspirational power of vicarious sacrifice was one of his chief themes, though he played down its paradoxical aspects; he preached that the "prodigious lifting power" of self-sacrifice is "the most impressive fact in the moral world." Helen Keller's teacher, Anne Sullivan (whom he called Mrs. Macy), was a favorite example: "Helen Keller was a world figure, known by every one. Still in the background was this magician, this self-effacing teacher, putting her life into another's and liberating it. It is one of the most amazing stories in the human record. . . . Once more vicarious sacrifice works its miracle." Fosdick called this ideal "the gospel of Christ . . . of which I am not ashamed." In his personal bearing, his carefully chosen examples, and his theology, he assured a liberalizing Protestant majority that late-Victorian morality and culture still defined the Christian ideal.[80]

In virtually every way he reflected and symbolized the sensibility of mainstream liberal Protestantism, which took a therapeutic turn partly under his influence. Fosdick often recalled, ruefully, that seminarians of his generation received no training in pastoral counseling or psychology of religion; as a young pastor he schooled himself in the early psychology-of-religion literature, especially William James's *Varieties of Religious Experience* (1902), Edwin Starbuck's *The Psychology of Religion* (1906), Edward Scribner Ames's *The Psychology of Religious Experience* (1910), and George A. Coe's *The Psychology of Religion* (1916).[81] In the mid-1920s he supported various efforts to turn pastoral counseling into a serious academic field, which bore fruit with the formation of the Council for the Clinical Training of Theological Students in 1930. Subsequent offshoots of the clinical movement in theology included the Institute for Pastoral Care, the Association for Clinical Pastoral Education, and the Academy of Religion and Mental Health, all of which Fosdick supported.

With the social gospelers, Fosdick bemoaned the increasing narcissism of American society in the 1920s, but against certain social gospelers he insisted that the clinical turn in American Protestantism was one of its better features. Social gospeler Justin Wroe Nixon was a critic of the liberal Protestant resort to therapeutic religion, as he saw it; he longed for the prewar days when the social gospelers preached the kingdom of God, envisioned a cooperative economic commonwealth, and knew nothing of the difference between neurosis and psychosis. He noted that many tired progressives found psychiatry to be as pleasant an escape "from the problems of real life as was premillennialism in its palmiest days." Fosdick winced and defended himself; he had an answer for those who told him, as he put it, to "stop fussing about yourself; stop taking your own spiritual temperature; get away from yourself."[82]

His answer was that emotional pain is just as real and disabling as social injustice. The Nixon-type social gospelers possessed a kernel of gospel truth, Fosdick allowed, but their blasts against the clinical movement in theology were insensitive to the life situations of emotionally vulnerable and hurting people. During his ministry at First Presbyterian Church, Fosdick grew dissatisfied with his star-performer arrangement. It wasn't enough to preach stirring sermons on Sundays; he wanted to connect with his parishioners on a more personal level. As an experiment he devoted a few hours each week to pastoral counseling. Soon the demand for his counsel overwhelmed the time that he allotted for it, and Fosdick realized he had found his calling. He loved clinical work, though he soon realized that he lacked the requisite knowledge for dealing with hard cases. His early involvement in the clinical theology movement was partly for self-education; he took informal clinical training from a psychiatrist friend, Thomas W. Salmon, and supported the nascent movement to create formal organizations and seminary programs in pastoral counseling. He traded on his own experiences of depressive anxiety, often assuring clients that he knew exactly how they felt; depressed people usually feel much worse than they really are, he told them. During his years at Riverside Church he ranked pastoral counseling as his top ministerial priority and described his style of preaching as "pastoral counseling on a group scale." The care of the self is part of the work of social religion, Fosdick argued; he analogized that when a flood devastates a river valley, two duties prevail: to serve the common good and to keep oneself from drowning: "It is worth emphasizing: the more difficult the social situation, the greater the need of strongly nurtured inner lives."[83]

The authorial culmination of his therapeutic turn was his bestselling book *On Being a Real Person* (1943). Fosdick summarized what he had learned in twenty years of pastoral counseling. The book was light on psychological theory, though he occasionally quoted Gordon Allport, Karen Horney, J. A. Hadfield, and William James.[84] In the manner of his sermons he featured anecdotes and citations drawn from British and American literature, especially poetry, literary commentary, and biography. Many of his insights about depression and anxiety were derived from personal experience, both inner and clinical. Though he favored the theme of overcoming adversity through moral will and positive thinking, Fosdick knew from his clinical experience that trying hard is sometimes the worst therapy; in neurasthenic patients victimized by shock or chronic fatigue, he observed, the object of good therapy is to get the patient to let go of willful effort. Fosdick's advice to depressed patients was humanistic and vaguely religious, like the kind of humanistic psychology later developed by Union Seminary graduates Rollo May and Carl Rogers. He counseled that a certain degree of depression should be taken for granted, since low moods are inevitable for almost everyone; that people should identify themselves with their better moods, not their low periods; that people should examine themselves when they are depressed, not blame their outward circumstances; that depressed people must remember to be kind and good-spirited toward others; that in any situation, depressed people must look for the possibilities instead of giving in to negative thinking; and that some tasks are too important to be evaded, not matter how depressed one might feel.[85]

"Look for the possibilities" was a Fosdick mantra; one of his favorite words was "undiscourageable." His sermons surveyed a wide range of personal and social problems, but always in a way that accented the solutions a good spirit could contribute to them. *On Being a Real Person* counseled that "despondency is chronically associated with negative thinking." No depressing situation into which people fall is entirely homogeneous, he advised: "We ourselves make our situations seem like that by our selective attention, our absorbed concern with their depressing elements." Fosdick liked Booker T. Washington's praise of "the advantage of disadvantages." When people find themselves in oppressive circumstances, Fosdick urged, they need to call upon the power of inner moral will, but they also need insight, "the capacity positively to see the possibilities for good still resident in the situation." Repeatedly he preached the practical use of faith in identifying the possibilities for good. Faith is not something that we *get* from divine intervention or personal effort, he contended, but a constitutive aspect of human psychology. Everyone has faith in something; the question is whether one will invest his or her faith in one kind of religion or another, or one kind of politics or another, or one kind of worldview or another: "If a man says he will have no faith, then the policy of no-faith is what he has faith in."[86]

LIBERAL THEOLOGY AS CHASTENED MODERNISM

To a vast audience Fosdick preached that faith is an inherent power in human nature and that the lovingly sacrificial way of Christ defines the ideal of good faith. Routinely he was identified by liberals and conservatives alike as the symbol of a triumphant modernizing culture religion that reduced Jesus to a moral exemplar. The image of Fosdick as the archetypal modernizer was never quite right, however. His sermonizing was laced with biblical themes, he unfailingly claimed to be centered in the gospel picture of Jesus and the gospel message of salvation, and in the mid-1930s he began to counsel that the modernizing phase of liberal theology had run its course. Fosdick recognized that Reinhold Niebuhr's scathing attacks on liberal Christianity hit a cultural nerve. He grasped that the liberal language of progress and idealism seemed like sentimental mush in the Depression era of collapsing economies and political turmoil.

Responding to the crisis of liberalism, liberal stalwarts like Brown, Mathews, Macintosh, Knudson, and J. S. Bixler vigorously defended their tradition in the 1930s and 1940s.[87] Fosdick joined them in defending the necessity of liberal theology, scholarship, and personal religion. Recalling that as a child he was terrified of going to hell, he wanted no part of a church or theology that terrified children. In his view the modernization of Christianity was the best thing that ever happened to Christianity, and he could never demean the achievements of liberal Protestantism as Niebuhr did; his gratitude to the liberal movement was too great for that.

But Niebuhr's scorching attack on liberal moralism struck him hard. In 1927, a year before Niebuhr assumed his faculty position at Union Seminary, Niebuhr wrote a cutting put-down of Fosdick's *Adventurous Religion*. While granting that

Fosdick had done good work in fighting off the fundamentalist insurgency, he chided that Fosdick's religion was middle class and not very adventurous. Like liberal Protestantism itself, Niebuhr pronounced, Fosdick failed to challenge "the fundamental immoralities of modern civilization, its immoral nationalism, its lust for power, and its accentuated greed." The following year the two Union professors met for the first time at Riverside Church, where Niebuhr preached as Fosdick's guest; Niebuhr later recalled, "I was naturally embarrassed to find myself on the faculty with an eminent man, whom I had treated with little grace." Fosdick concurred, "He was a good deal embarrassed at the thought of running into me as a fellow member of the Faculty." After the service Fosdick took Niebuhr into his study and quietly remarked, without mentioning Niebuhr's attack upon him, that each generation has only one battle in its system. Fosdick's generation had fought off the fundamentalist insurgency; now they had to trust Niebuhr's generation to fight the church's next battle.[88]

Niebuhr's embarrassment deepened; confronted by Fosdick's geniality and humility, Niebuhr felt the rashness of his attack upon him. In subsequent years he praised Fosdick as a singularly gracious figure, and when he blasted liberal theology, he named Shailer Mathews or Charles Clayton Morrison, not Fosdick; often he dispensed with names altogether. Meanwhile Fosdick struggled to come to terms with Niebuhrian criticism. Niebuhr's neo-Marxist politics repelled him, and he had no taste for Niebuhr's paradox-spinning dialecticism in theology, but he respected Niebuhr greatly and took to heart the Niebuhrian charge that liberal theology overaccommodated Christianity to modern culture. In his review of *Adventurous Religion,* Niebuhr observed that Fosdick's idea of adventure was like that of the knights of chivalry: "It develops within the limits of the age and does not challenge the age itself." By 1935 Fosdick believed that liberals needed to admit that the Barthians and Niebuhrians were right on that score. His widely noted sermon, "The Church Must Go beyond Modernism," exhorted that modernism was too limited to be enshrined as an object of faith. Fosdick reflected that from 1880 to 1930 American liberal theology was necessarily preoccupied with the intellectual problems of accommodating modern science and historical criticism. During his seminary days, he recalled, students and professors defined themselves theologically on the basis of their positions on these issues; as a modernist project, liberal theology necessarily prized rationality over imagination.[89]

But religion is wider and deeper than rationality, Fosdick cautioned. Good religion is about heart knowledge, conscience, and imagination, not merely about intellectual credibility; moreover, the issues that defined liberal theology for decades were no longer absorbing. The modernists had prevailed on the issues over which they fought. They fought off a fundamentalist insurgency only to find that their victory sealed the demise of liberal theology. For the past half-century liberal theology had been fueled by its modernism, Fosdick explained, but the modernizing phase of the movement's struggle to reinvent Christianity was over. Critics like Niebuhr took liberal gains for granted. Mainline seminary classrooms no longer buzzed over doctrinal issues; the question for Depression-era Protestantism was not whether liberal theology was legitimate, but whether it was relevant to the social crisis and cultural mood of the present time.

Fosdick urged that liberal theology had to regain its relevance: "The classrooms in the seminary where the atmosphere grows tense today concern Christian ethics and the towering question whether Christ has a moral challenge that can shake this contemporary culture to its foundations and save us from our deadly personal and social sins." Liberal theology was mainly about adjustment and accommodation to the modern world; even the social gospelers were essentially accommodationists, though Fosdick sometimes made an exception for Rauschenbusch. In the social circumstances of the 1930s, this predisposition made liberal theology seem "trivial and out of date," he judged: "Our modern world, as a whole, cries out not so much for souls intellectually adjusted to it as for souls morally maladjusted to it, not most of all for accommodators and adjusters but for intellectual and ethical challengers."[90]

Niebuhr's crack that Fosdick had nothing to say about the immorality of nationalism was nonsense; Fosdick seized the mantle of prophecy on issues pertaining to nationalism and militarism, albeit not to Niebuhr's later liking. Otherwise Niebuhr hit the mark; by temperament and conviction, and by virtue of his social standing, Fosdick was not well suited to challenge the dominant order. His therapeutic turn and his friendships with Rockefeller and other powerful backers muffled his voice on social justice issues; yet he was sufficiently chastened by the crisis of liberal theology to call for an end to the liberal religion of culture. Liberal theology made a religion out of Paul's maxim in 1 Corinthians to "become all things to all people" (1 Cor. 9:22), but Fosdick urged that Paul's command in 2 Corinthians not to be "mismatched with unbelievers" (2 Cor. 6:14) was more relevant to the moment: "Church of Christ, take that to yourself now! Stop this endeavor to harmonize yourself with modern culture and customs as though they were a standard and criterion." Liberal theology promoted a religion of "inevitable progress" and "lush optimism," he proclaimed. Rightly it supported scientific advances, social welfare policies, the spread of democracy, the increase of humanitarianism, and evolutionary theory; unfortunately it was overimpressed by these advances: "So many hopeful and promising things were afoot that two whole generations were fairly bewitched into thinking that every day in every way man was growing better and better."[91]

He insisted that a more chastened liberalism was possible. Traditional liberal rhetoric about the fatherhood of God, the brotherhood of man, the leadership of Christ, salvation by character, and the inexorable progress of humankind had become an embarrassment, he observed: "Well, if that is the whole creed, this is a lovely world with nothing here to dread at all." But Depression-era Americans knew for a certainty that progress had stopped; their world was filled with insecurity and dreadful deprivations, and the mannered ideals of Victorian moralism were alien to them. Fosdick sought to speak to their reality: "My soul, what a world, which the gentle modernism of my younger ministry, with its kindly sentiments and limitless optimism, does not fit at all! We must go beyond that." He acknowledged that in speaking to Christian minds "powerfully affected by modernism," he was also speaking to himself: "Come out of these intellectual cubicles and sentimental retreats which we built by adapting Christian faith to an optimistic era. Underline this: *Sin is real.* Personal and social sin is as terribly real as our forefathers said it was, no matter how we change their way of saying so." Liberal theology could not return to the orthodox way of saying it, Fosdick assured, but had to confess again that sin leads to personal and social damnation. In dark times, real faith is like a Rembrandt portrait. It must shine from the dark background of fearful apprehension. While insisting that liberal Christianity remained the religion of wholesome moral character, Fosdick cautioned that character must be forged "against the terrific down-drag of an antagonistic world." Liberal theology could no longer make progress by keeping up with modern culture.[92]

FEMINIZING A MALE TRADITION:
GEORGIA HARKNESS

Only a chastened liberalism had a future in 1930, as the liberals who refused to trim their idealistic moralism became echoes of a bygone era. Those who cut their theological teeth on social gospel idealism had to rethink the basis of their progressivism. The first woman to crash the ranks of American professional theologians was a prominent example. Georgia Harkness was a liberal of Fosdick's evangelical personalist type whose theological career began in the early 1920s. By virtue of her professional training she was more deeply rooted than Fosdick in personalist philosophy; by virtue of her age, she was more deeply affected than Fosdick by the shifting cultural tides of the Depression era. In her early career she identified herself as a progressive idealist and Boston school personalist; in her later career she made her renown as a realist-leaning popular theologian and self-identified "chastened liberal"; throughout her career she upheld the ethic of Christian pacifism and championed the rights of women in church and society.

Born in 1891, she was the youngest of four children of J. Warren and Lillie Harkness of Harkness, New York. Six of her father's eight great-grandparents were Quakers, and the hamlet of Harkness—"four corners with some houses clustered about"—was named in honor of her grandfather Nehemiah Harkness. Her father was a prosperous farmer, community leader, Sunday school teacher, and Ben Franklinesque wise man who influenced her deeply. Both of her parents were devout Methodists, though short on familial displays of piety; a family maid taught her to pray. "There was a Scotch-Irish taciturnity in our background which made us hesitate to say much about what lay deepest in us," Harkness later recalled. In her youth the village featured a general store, a sawmill, and a butter factory. Harkness later recalled that the sawmill subsequently burned and the butter factory was shipped away "to some mysterious place known as 'the city.'" She loved to tell the story of her paternal great-grandparents, whose marriage in 1802 got Daniel Harkness expelled from the Society of Friends. Daniel's wife Abigail, who was a non-Quaker, affronted local Quakers by "appearing out of plainness." They called her "the woman in the red coat." Georgia Harkness cherished her Quaker heritage and the independence of her great-grandparents; in later life she thought of herself as the woman in the red coat.[93]

She was schooled in a one-room schoolhouse that doubled as the community's Methodist church—"we were guileless of any issues as to the separation of Church and State, and nobody objected." Like many children exposed to revival preaching in what was still called the "burned-over district," Harkness yearned for a definitive conversion experience. Every winter she attended revival services and came forward to be saved, but none of her conversions survived summer vacation, and at the age of nine or ten she went through an atheist period. Her requests to join the church began at the age of seven; seven years later Lillie Harkness judged that she was finally old enough. By then her parents were puzzling over how best to support their intellectually gifted youngest child. For the rest of her life Georgia Harkness remained a member of the Harkness Methodist congregation and the Troy, New York, Methodist Conference. Her resolve to be a theologian of the people—"to speak in plain language to common folk," as she later put it—was rooted in her deep sense of connection to her rural family and friends. "I have no better friends anywhere on earth," she reflected in the 1950s. "These *were* and *are* my roots—and for these roots I humbly thank God."[94]

A precocious student, she started high school at the age of twelve and passed the New York Regents exams at fourteen. For the sake of her social adjustment she stayed in high school for an extra two and a half years—"nobody thought I was then old enough to go to college"—and took her last extra year of high school on her own volition, "perhaps through timidity." In 1908 she won a competitive scholarship to Cornell University, which proved to be a socially dismal place for her. Being female excluded her from many campus organizations; being "shy, green, and countrified" made her an outcast. On the day that Harkness left for college, she had never been more than twenty miles from home. "To be plunged abruptly into a big, sophisticated, urban university was a radical change," she later recalled. "My clothes were queer; I had no social graces; and I did not come within gun-shot of being asked to join a sorority." Though she later judged that "Cornell University was not the right place for me, academically or personally," Harkness excelled in languages, philosophy, and the social sciences. Her introduction to philosophy under James Edwin Creighton was a formative experience. A speculative idealist, Creighton taught that the experience of the knower is the primary subject of philosophy. "Philosophy must bake some bread," he told his students; "it must, like the other sciences, minister to human life." Harkeness's training in Creighton's personalist-leaning idealism prepared her for an unexpected career.[95]

As a woman she judged that two career choices were open to her: teaching and foreign missions. Harkness had long assumed that she would be a teacher, though her chief social outlets at Cornell turned her toward mission work. She was active in the Student Christian Association (affiliated with the Young Women's Christian Association) and the Student Volunteer Movement. The latter organization, founded by John Mott in 1888, sought to supply denominational mission boards with enough missionary volunteers to evangelize the world for Christ. Harkness signed the SVM pledge to become a foreign missionary; the student movement was the available outlet for her idealism. In 1912 she graduated from Cornell but cooled on mission work, partly because she wanted to be close to her parents. For six years she puzzled about what she should do with her education; she taught languages for two years at a high school in Schuylerville, New York, until school officials asked for her resignation. Harkness lacked the maturity and classroom skills to handle difficult students—"they were too much for me." A second classroom assignment in Scotia, New York, was not as rough, but she still disliked public school teaching. She could no longer imagine herself as a foreign missionary, and the door was closing on her second option. The only thing she really liked about teaching was the relative proximity that it afforded to her parents. Her life turned a corner when she learned that a new profession was opening to women, in the field of religious education. Harkness seized this option as a life raft, and in 1918 she enrolled at the Boston University School of Religious Education and Social Service to obtain a master's degree in religious education and arts; the following year Edgar S. Brightman arrived at Boston University.[96]

Founded at the same time that public controversy began to stir in American cities over what were called "the new immigrants," the School of Religious Education and Social Service was in its second year of operation in 1918. The old immigrants had come to the United States mostly from northern and western Europe; the new immigrants came from places like Austria-Hungary, Russia, Italy, Romania, Turkey, and Greece. Under the tutelage of former YMCA official George W. Tupper, sociologist Charles E. Carroll, and school founder and dean Walter Scott Athearn, Harkness adjusted to the dizzying pace of urban life at the very moment that northern cities were transformed by the new immigrants and by the continuing "Great Migration" of African Americans from the South. With a sense of moral urgency, her teachers maintained that the problem of assimilating and Christianizing the new Americans was American Christianity's central postwar challenge. Americans should not fear the new immigrants, they urged; xenophobia is immoral and counterproductive. Tupper emphasized that assimilation is a generative process; just because the new immigrants were from southern and eastern Europe did not mean that they needed to shed their accustomed ways of living, he contended. The assimilationist ideal was to blend the cultures of the old and new worlds, not to erase what remained of the old world in the new. According to Harkness's teachers, the school of Christian personalist idealism pioneered by Borden Parker Bowne was an indispensable aid to this cause, offering the best theoretical basis for conceptualizing and inculcating America's democratic ideals.[97]

Harkness absorbed these ideas and claimed them for herself. Under Tupper's guidance she wrote a master's thesis titled "The Church and the Immigrant" that was published in 1920. In the book's introduction, Tupper explained that Harkness sought to help young social gospelers think clearly about the immigration issue. Many young people inspired by the social gospel wanted to help their foreign-born neighbors, he observed, but they "realized their helplessness as they invaded this great unknown realm where Old World backgrounds, race psychology and myriad languages loomed large." Harkness was one of them. Her first book proclaimed that the racially charged immigration issue was a central social gospel issue and that the social gospel was necessarily about personal and social regeneration. "The program of the church for racial progress must aim to minister to every side of the immigrant's nature," she asserted. "Giving material aid, relieving bodily ills, supplying a right environment—all are activities worth doing in themselves. But a deeper purpose must underlie our work. Social service cannot be fully successful unless through it we develop the higher spiritual values. Our ultimate goal must be the more abundant life which Christ came to bring to man. We must minister to the souls of men."[98]

Harkness took her first course from Brightman in 1919; she later recalled that his "kindling mind" held her spellbound. Brightman's lectures on the philosophy of religion were dazzling, difficult, and inspiring; they inspired her ambition to become a religious philosopher. She later recalled that "beyond question [it was] the most stirring and illuminating course I ever took." Boldly she approached Brightman about the possibility of enrolling in the doctoral program; her boldness may have been aided by the fact that she was only seven years younger than he. She dismissed the option of applying to the School of Theology's Bachelor of Divinity program. Brightman was her model, and women were denied full membership privileges in the Methodist Episcopal Church anyway. In Harkness's later recollection, Brightman praised her preparation and intelligence while questioning her stamina; she assured him that she had no lack of resilience; Brightman remembered the conversation differently. In either case, he practiced his belief that graduate education should be open to women, and in the early 1920s he served as faculty mentor to three female doctoral students.[99]

Harkness's program consisted essentially of his curriculum in philosophy of religion, practical ethics, epistemology, and metaphysics; she took seven of her doctoral courses with Brightman and two with Knudson. She later recalled that her commitment to theological liberalism was "deepened and clarified" by her doctoral studies: "I had already become familiar with the historical approach to the Bible and the general assumptions of liberal thought."[100] The correspondence phase of her relationship with Brightman began after Harkness completed her doctoral qualifying exams in 1921. He counseled her to write a dissertation on the religious philosophy of Oxford neo-Hegelian T. H. Green and she agreed; he urged her to dig into Kant and Hegel and she did; most of the time he corrected her mistakes on philosophical method.[101] Over the next twenty-five years they exchanged more than two hundred letters. Unfailingly their letters were friendly and mutually admiring. Harkness changed her early salutations from "My dear Dr. Brightman" to "Dear Dr. Brightman" after he persisted in writing "Dear Miss

Harkness," or, after she finished her doctorate, "Dear Dr. Harkness." She was forty-nine years old before "Dear Georgia" and "Dear Edgar" became possible for him. Long after she completed her doctorate, Harkness peppered him with questions: What were the best books on metaphysics? Did Nikolai Hartmann believe in the League of Nations? What was Gestalt psychology?[102]

Brightman's replies were gracious, detailed, and professorial. He praised her clear mind and marveled at her productivity; he paid attention to style as well as substance. On one occasion he scolded her against referring to Rufus Jones as "Jones," for Rufus Jones was not in a category with Cicero, Kant, and Hegel. Despite their formality, Brightman and Harkness quickly established a deeper level of personal interchange than was typical of either of them. He admitted to her that he had problems communicating with some of his students; she told him gently that he tended to assume that his students shared his brilliance. In 1922 he helped her attain a faculty position at Elmira College, a women's college in upstate central New York. A few weeks after she began teaching at Elmira, Brightman raised the question whether he should now address her as "Professor Harkness"; she shied away from saying yes, and Brightman continued with "Dr. Harkness"; even his woman-respecting mind could not quite manage to address a woman as "Professor." Faithfully he recommended her for fellowships and better academic positions through the years. "She is not only a scholar of a high type, but also a woman of broad culture and human interests," Brightman told one administrator. To another he allowed that "the only defect of her mind of which I am conscious is a certain narrowness of range; yet this is a source of intensity of work." Harkness completed her 399-page dissertation in 1923. Her commitment to Brightman-style personalistic idealism deepened in the course of expositing Green's religious philosophy. Like the Boston personalists, Green affirmed the idealist belief that God's eternal self-consciousness reproduces itself in human consciousness; he also affirmed that faith and the moral life are as intimately linked as religion and metaphysics. Though she cautioned that Green vacillated between theism and pantheism, and that he overemphasized the immanent Christ at the expense of the historical Jesus, Harkness read him essentially as a valuable precursor of the personalist school. She carved two articles out of her dissertation, gave up the idea of turning it into a publishable book, and plunged into the novel work of being a woman philosophy professor.[103]

Harkness made a splash at Elmira almost immediately; appalled at her tiny classes, she galvanized a curriculum reform movement that made philosophy a required subject. In 1924 she triumphantly reported to Brightman that "our pernicious former system is now defunct"; there would be no more philosophy classes of three or four students.[104] At the same time she spoke out as an advocate of the rights of women in the Methodist Episcopal Church; it was simply wrong to deny women the rights and responsibilities held by men, she argued in the *Christian Advocate*. The church was lagging behind American society in recognizing the rights of women: "Practically every avenue of leadership today is open to women save in the Church, and there she must content herself either with rendering volunteer service or working in a subordinate capacity." Harkness argued that because women are equal to men in ability, women should be equal to men in opportunity. It is wrong to refuse the full rights of ordination to women just because they are women, she admonished, adding that she did not press this claim as "an ultra-feminist." The issue was a question of elementary fairness and progressive feeling, not radical ideology. It was time to apply the democratizing logic of the kingdom ethic to the rights of women: "We wonder if the advancement of the Kingdom is not more important than the maintenance of an ancient prejudice."[105]

Having turned aside from a ministerial track in her seminary days, Harkness still advised young women not to pursue the Bachelor of Divinity degree with the expectation of being accepted as ministers. Yet her mind was changing on the practicality of preparing for ministry. Increasingly, theologically educated women like herself were being asked to give guest sermons, and in 1922 she had taken the next step of attaining a local preacher's license in the Methodist Episcopal Church. Guest sermonizing did not require a local preaching license, and Methodist Episcopal women were not excluded from local licenses; moreover, women were not excluded from being ordained to deacon's and elder's orders. They were excluded from the right to be received as full members of a Methodist Episcopal Conference, which brought with it a guaranteed church appointment. Women could be ordained to the ministry, but the question was whether they should bear the same rights of membership and guaranteed appointment that male ministers possessed. Harkness gave her voice to the cause of gaining this right for female ministers; at the same time she decided to champion the cause as a Methodist minister. In 1927 she was ordained to the Methodist Episcopal ministry, and for the next forty years she played a leading role in advocating the rights of women in the successive denominations of the Methodist Episcopal, Methodist, and United Methodist churches.[106]

Her other major social commitment was the cause of abolishing war. Harkness came to pacifism by a route and a specific experience that were typical of liberal Protestant leaders of her generation. The route was the generational experience of postwar disillusionment that she shared with Fosdick, Brightman, Vida Scudder, D. C. Macintosh, Charles Clayton Morrison, and Reinhold Niebuhr. The specific experience was her participation in "the Sherwood Eddy party" that she shared with Morrison and Niebuhr. Sherwood Eddy was the International Secretary of the YMCA and founding chairman of the Fellowship for a Christian Social Order (FCSO), which was closely affiliated with the pacifist Fellowship of Reconciliation. For many years he was the YMCA's chief evangelist in Asia; during the war he and his personal secretary, young Disciples of Christ pastor Kirby Page, organized YMCA missions at Allied war camps. The latter experience turned both men into pacifist Christian socialists, and they committed themselves to the transformation of the industrial capitalist system that produced World War I. In 1921 they founded the FCSO as a vehicle of their idealistic social vision.[107]

Eddy's novel idea was the progressivist travel tour. Instead of taking American tour groups to the usual European landmarks and watering holes, each summer he and Eddy took approximately ninety ministers, educators, social workers and activists to a series of conferences and sightseeing activities that they organized in cooperation with European political leaders, trade unions, and activist groups. Formally it was called "the American Seminar"; the American participants called it "the Sherwood Eddy party." In addition to its American Seminar the FCSO sponsored domestic conferences, retreats, summer outings, and special programs. Eddy and Page were straightforward about their purpose: to advance the cooperative and nonviolent way of Christ as an alternative to traditional power politics. The American Seminar program was specifically designed to foster cooperative international understanding and peace. From 1921 to 1939 the FCSO summer tours exercised an important influence over the dreams and self-understanding of American Christian leaders.[108]

Harkness's Eddy party departed for England on June 28, 1924. The group contained several Protestant clerics who had begun to make names for themselves: Evanston Methodist pastor Ernest Fremont Tittle, *Christian Century* editor Charles Clayton Morrison, Methodist Federation for Social Service leader Harry F. Ward, and Detroit Evangelical pastor Reinhold Niebuhr. Harkness explained to Brightman that Niebuhr was the brother of Hulda Niebuhr, Harkness's classmate in religious education at Boston University; thirty years later Harkness recalled, "I believe that Niebuhr-then was nearer to the truth than Niebuhr-now." From Glasgow to Berlin to Geneva to Paris, with many stops in between, the Americans heard two or three lectures per day for nearly two months. They met government officials, party leaders, and activists throughout Europe; they were admonished by many speakers that German aggression was not the sole cause of the war; and they got a vivid picture of the postwar hostility between France and Germany. Harkness told Brightman that it disturbed her "to find so much war bitterness and mutual misunderstanding, with the feeling in both countries that though war has done no good, there is no way out except more wars." The group visited the battlefields of Rheims and witnessed the terrible effects of the wartime hunger blockade against Germany. For Harkness, the blockade marked a turning point. She told Brightman that she felt more sympathy for the Germans than for the French, because the Germans were starved by the hunger blockade and oppressed by the unjust Versailles Treaty. In Germany she decided that she was finished with making moral allowances for war; and became "a pacifist, I think, forevermore."[109]

Haunted by the undersized and sickly German children whom she met, Harkness warned against blaming Germany entirely for the war.[110] "We had better blame economic imperialism, secret diplomacy, and the whole war system," she admonished in the *Christian Advocate*. "The sufferings of France may yet bring a blessing to the world if they teach us not to hate our enemies, but to hate war—and to blend all our energies toward banishing it from the earth." Unlike Niebuhr and Eddy, who turned away from pacifism in the 1930s, Harkness remained a principled antiwar activist for the rest of her life. In 1939 she reflected that her reasons were both pragmatic and theological: "War destroys every value for which Christianity stands, and to oppose war by more war is only to deepen the morass into which humanity has fallen." She did not believe that evil is entirely avoidable, but she did believe that fighting never secures peace: "I believe that life is inevitably a sphere of conflict and that our choices are not often to be made between good and evil, but between alternative evils. I believe that in all of life's dark areas the triumph which shines through tragedy comes not with the sword which our Lord rejected, but with the cross toward which he walked."[111]

PHILOSOPHICAL IDEALS
AND THE WAY OF THE CROSS

Harkness's early books were few, a bit late in starting, and firmly in the mold of her mentor and friend. She was too busy to give herself to scholarship; she spoke constantly to church and civic groups, which generated a steady stream of topical articles but not the reflective books that she wanted to write. Ruefully she remarked to Brightman that they both worked too much, "resulting in a rather excitable state of nervous tension." She seemed to need to be constantly active. She also had early misgivings about the personalist school, which may have given her pause about writing in her field; as early as 1925 Harkness expressed to Brightman her concern that the spirit of Boston personalism was overly dogmatic and cocksure: "It is anti-behavioristic, anti-deterministic, anti-Deweyite, anti-Columbian, anti-everything-not-personalistic." The following week she added that she had never heard Brightman admit that he was wrong about anything; this was before Brightman began to challenge various aspects of Bowne's system and substantially revised his own position. Brightman replied that being obstinate was a trait that he and Harkness shared.[112]

The following year, "feeling some stuffiness in the Elmira atmosphere," Harkness took a semester's leave of absence at Harvard, where she studied under William Ernest Hocking and Alfred North Whitehead and graded papers for Hocking. With Hocking's strong support she tried to get a teaching position at Radcliffe, but she and Hocking were rebuffed, on the grounds that only Harvard professors could teach at Radcliffe, and only men could be Harvard professors. In 1928 Harkness applied for a Sterling Fellowship for a year of postgraduate study at Yale University. She wanted to broaden her intellectual base beyond the personalistic categories of her graduate training. In Brightman's otherwise highly complimentary recommendation, which he sent to her, he made an offhand reference to Harkness's "lack of feminine charm." Harkness assured Brightman that she knew what he meant, and she wasn't offended; she had a large body, she was physically awkward, and she was often uncomfortable in social relationships with men. But she asked him to excise the statement because it could be read "as suggesting freakishness, or at least a conspicuous masculinity of dress or manner."[113]

Undoubtedly she was deeply hurt by Brightman's remark. She also feared that the statement might eliminate her as a candidate for the fellowship. "I wonder whether you realize the extent to which a woman with a Ph.D. must, among other obstacles, contend against the tradition that female Ph.D.'s are so 'intellectual' that they are freakish and sloppy," Harkness explained. "A degree of queerness that would be overlooked in a man is unforgivable in a woman—when both are contending for the same prize." Brightman's reply was superficially apologetic and essentially clueless. He was sorry for his "thoughtlessness"— especially in letting her see the remark—but he refused to retract the statement, ostensibly on the ground that he lacked a second application form. His blunder would have to stand, he counseled; meanwhile he betrayed no recognition that his remark was a ripe piece of sexism. Edgar Brightman would never have referred to the sex appeal of a male candidate, though Harkness did win the Sterling Fellowship.[114]

Harkness's close and trusting relationship to Brightman survived this incident, though she let on to family members that his remark was hurtful to her. In 1929 she made her first bid for standing in her field with a book that reflected his profound influence on her work. She explained at the outset of *Conflicts in Religious Thought* that her book was a popularized version of the philosophy of religion taught by Brightman and Hocking; after six years of trying to help Brightman and Hocking make sense to college students, Harkness provided access with a textbook of her own. The book made personalist arguments for God's existence, offered a personalist account of human and divine personality, and gave a decidedly pre-1930 rendering of Brightman's progressivist idealism. "Little by little, man has moved forward in the direction of the supremacy of the spiritual over the carnal," she asserted. "In spite of temporary eddies in human progress, such as the World War and its after-effects, a long look over the past reveals a tremendous advance from the ideals and standards of former days." Harkness saw no point in cleaning up the doctrine of original sin. Children are neither moral nor immoral, she reasoned. Because they are incapable of moral choice, they are essentially nonmoral beings: "The doctrine of 'original sin' is fast disappearing— and the sooner it disappears, the better for theology and human sympathy." Because it was a work of religious philosophy, not theology, *Conflicts in Religious Thought* gave short shrift to the figure of Christ, yet Harkness ended on a reverential note: "We live in a mind-like universe, a universe of long purposes, a universe that is sheer mystery without an Infinite Mind and an Infinite Purpose. The religious experience of humanity bears witness that it has seen God, and seeing has lived anew."[115]

Increasingly she resisted the constraints of writing as a religious philosopher. In 1935, while studying as a postgraduate scholar at Union Theological Seminary, she labored over a companion volume to *Conflicts in Religious Thought* that crossed into the territory of theology. When Harkness wrote *The Resources of Religion*, she was attending five Reinhold Niebuhr lectures per week, and the book contained numerous signs of Niebuhr's lengthening shadow over liberal theol-

ogy. In a judgment that signaled her forthcoming turn from philosophical idealism, she praised the realist aspect of the Barth-Niebuhr movement in theology.
"Karl Barth has had a potent and very constructive influence on many persons
who do not go with him to the point of affirming man's utter helplessness and
God's complete 'otherness,'" she observed. She found a similar realism in
Niebuhr, who told his classes, in her report, "that the world is more evil and tragic
than most liberals have supposed." Harkness appreciated that the new antiliber-
alism in theology was not a reactionary throwback; Barth and Niebuhr were not
going back to the old orthodoxy. She allowed that the realist aspect of dialectical
theology was a welcome tonic for modern Christianity: "The realism which is
ringing through current theology, demanding that we face the fact of sin and look
to a transcendent God rather than to human science for power to overcome it, is
an element of very great hope." Yet she also believed that in the past decade "we
have moved an amazing distance toward a warless world."[116]

Harkness's concessions to an ascending neo-orthodoxy and neoliberalism were
selective. Like Fosdick she enthused that the growing pacifist sentiment in liberal
Protestantism was a growth in the spirit of Jesus; she never accepted Niebuhr's
view that liberal pacifism was a chief symptom of what was wrong with liberal
Christianity. Like Fosdick she also disliked Barth's and Niebuhr's stigmatizing
attacks on the liberal tradition, which were unappreciative, ungenerous, and most
importantly to her, strangely unreal. Niebuhr and American theologian Walter
Marshall Horton proclaimed that liberal theology was dying the death it
deserved, Harkness observed, yet they took liberal gains for granted. *The
Resources of Religion* highlighted the real-life problem with this attitude, which
was that liberalism still did not exist "in the hinterlands where dwell the rank-
and-file Christians." Harkness never forgot that she came from the hinterlands
and was of them, and she feared that a triumphant neo-orthodoxy could be disastrous for the large regions of American Christianity that had never entered the
modern age. "Until the liberalization of religious thought which has been going
on in Europe and America for the past seventy-five years reaches such churches
as these, it is premature to hold funeral obsequies," she admonished. By her reckoning the "luminous figure" of modern Christianity was Fosdick. Harkness
exhorted that Fosdick's brand of theology surely had "more to offer the world"
than the old orthodoxy. In Fosdickian tones she called for a renewed liberal Christianity that was chastened by neo-orthodox criticism. Barthian revelationism was
too narrow; the Word becomes flesh and dwells among us in our common life,
she asserted, and through such experiences we ourselves become incarnations of
the Word.[117]

Brightman liked the "clear, incisive and compact style" of *The Resources of
Religion*; and also its spiritual fire. His worry was that Harkness was losing her
intellectual coherence. The book lacked any formal or substantive unity, he
judged; in her quest to accommodate many positions, Harkness ended up all over
the place.[118] Brightman liked her next book *The Recovery of Ideals,* much more,
except the chapter that he hated, which convinced him that she was abandoning

the idealist core of personalist philosophy. Harkness wrote *The Recovery of Ideals* (1937) fresh from her year of studying under Niebuhr and Paul Tillich. In her new book, addressed to "the lost generation" of disillusioned college graduates who found themselves pumping gasoline and waiting tables for a living, she called for a recovery of moral and spiritual idealism. The present economic depression was a terrible thing, she allowed, but "the most serious aspect of current affairs is not an economic depression but a depression in morale." Harkness warned that the latter kind of depression is the kind that destroys civilizations. Correctly understood, religion is essentially idealistic, for "religion means fundamentally faith in a meaningful existence." *The Recovery of Ideals* proposed that the way to recover the faith of true religion in a depressed age is to recognize "that a meaningful existence implies *wholeness*—the integration of life about a center with radii extending in proper balance to every aspect of life." Correctly understood, philosophy enables people to think consistently about the meaning of life as a whole. That was Harkness's project.[119]

She was not a philosophical pragmatist, she assured; because she believed that philosophy has to deal with all that is, she believed that philosophy and theology must not stop short of metaphysical theorizing. Yet she proposed that it was the pragmatists who correctly determined the proper end of philosophical inquiry; an idea is worth pursuing if it makes a practical difference. "My philosophy is based frankly on the assumption that morals and religion are man's most important interests," Harkness wrote. "I believe this to be true because life itself is more inescapable than anything else save death, and morals and religion make a supreme difference in living. There is nothing more important than the questions of the standards by which to live in our inevitable living and the supports, if any, by which to be sustained in the innermost areas of personality." Unlike Brightman, she loved Bowne's maxim that life is more than logic; it expressed her thesis that the two most important interests in human life are morals and religion.[120]

All human beings are doomed by their nature to struggle with egocentric impulses and profoundly disturbing emotions, Harkness acknowledged: "Yet at the same time we are blessed by our human nature with the capacity to generate ideals by which to escape, in part, from our sin and limitation." These ideals are concepts of what ought to be. They are not illusions. They come to us with revelatory potency, yet we make them: "The road to the emotional inception and galvanizing of ideals is through incarnation in life—a process achieved through prayer, through the redemptive power of suffering, through many other channels among which personal example and personal participation in vital action are indispensable." Harkness appreciated the irony that the most important things in life are the things that are least yielding of objective certainty. The road to religious knowledge is slippery and difficult, she acknowledged; by her lights, the best road was a "synoptic approach" that starts from empirical foundations and leads into a supernaturalist metaphysic.[121]

Thus far she was a good personalist in the tradition of Bowne, Knudson, and Brightman. On the nature of divine reality, she stayed in the mainstream of that tradition up to the point where Brightman broke from it. Harkness broke from it too, but in a different way from Brightman. In good personalist fashion she argued that God is not a force, a person, nature itself, or a process. She distinguished between the personalistic understanding of God as divine mind and the anthropomorphic projection of God as a superhuman person. Wieman's process divinity was interesting to her, but she judged that Wieman's God possessed "no more-than-human power" to make the social ideals of religion operative. There was also the spiritual problem that nobody prays to an interaction or to a process of growth. Harkness proposed that God is better conceived as organizing mind, as the source and goal of ideals, as the cosmic companion, and as the poet of the universe. As organizing mind, God is the interacting ground of the universe's order; as the source and goal of ideals, God is the cosmic ground of true goodness; as the cosmic companion, God is the Whiteheadian "climax of creativity" who suffers with us and makes us feel that we are not alone; as the poet of the universe, God is the creative and meaning-conferring maker of heaven and earth.[122]

Increasingly she appropriated Whiteheadian and Tillichian themes, though usually in ways that complemented her grounding in Brightman's idealism. The issue that evoked her declaration of independence from personalist idealism was the same issue that evoked Brightman's novel revisionism, the problem of God and evil. Harkness observed that the "usual liberal" tack is to emphasize God's voluntary self-limitation in the creation of a world of human freedom and natural law. To his credit, Brightman faced up to the fact that divine self-limitation is only one piece of the answer. It does not account for the immense suffering and wastefulness in human and animal existence. Brightman's theory of a recalcitrant Given within the nature of God took the problem more seriously, Harkness judged, but at the price of placing "a sort of stigma upon God." Brightman solved the theodicy problem by sacrificing the notion of God as an all-perfect object of devotion and trust. Harkness argued that he would have done better by giving up the either/or of personalist metaphysics. Brightman was right to theorize that some recalcitrant X-factor is the root of the theodicy problem, but his commitment to personalist metaphysics gave him only two choices about the source of recalcitrance. From a personalist standpoint the entire recalcitrant X-factor has to be placed either within human persons or the divine person, because personalist theory maintains that only personality is metaphysically real.[123]

This marked her point of departure. Harkness no longer believed that only God and human persons are real. "I was reared in the personalistic tradition," she reflected, and she still affirmed most of the personalistic credo, but not its metaphysical premise: "My present view comes closer to a form of theistic realism. I now see no valid sense in which it is possible to say that only persons are metaphysically real." It is true that only persons are reflectively conscious or have rational apprehension of the world, she allowed. Persons are the only beings who act freely, initiate intelligent activity, and are governed by ideals. But none of this proves that anything which lacks such powers lacks metaphysical reality, she argued. Events are real, living and inanimate things are real, and eternal forms

are real. Events and things have a reality that depends on total sets of circumstances, not merely upon the circumstances of reflective subjects of consciousness. And if the world external to consciousness is metaphysically real, Harkness
contended, then the recalcitrant X-factor may come from something besides God
and human beings. It may be a "given" in the divine nature and the structure of
the universe that certain things happen which God does not will. God may be
limited by the circumstances of a really existing world.[124]

To Harkness, the religious philosophy in *The Recovery of Ideals* had the same
relation to personalist idealism that she advocated toward liberal theology. It was
essentially right, but needed to be chastened by the real world. Harkness assured
that she still believed that only ideals are saving. Her closing chapter proclaimed
that she believed in a continuing incarnation ("symbol of the eternal union of
God with man"), and a continuing cross ("symbol of the eternal union of love
with suffering"), and a continuing resurrection ("symbol of the eternal union of
tragedy with triumph"), and a continuing ascension ("symbol of the union of
temporal with eternal values"). The language of progressive spiritual idealism was
still her grammar, but Christian idealism had to make firmer contact with the
real world if it was to be redemptive in the world.[125]

Brightman agreed with the latter sentiment. He liked most of her argument
and her centering of thought around ideals. What he didn't like was her realist
chapter on nature and God, which he criticized mostly on performative grounds:
"I therefore condemn the chapter as overtechnical, insufficiently developed for the
technical reader, irrelevant and confusing to the nontechnical reader, helpful only
to one trying to escape from personalistic metaphysics, while retaining its values
and its philosophy of religion." Harkness's neo-Cartesianism was "too facile" as a
critique of his theory of the limited God, Brightman judged, though otherwise he
liked her analysis. "You may have all the realism you can think (I, alas, can't grasp
your thought); but having that Other, that X, which limits God, then if God is
conscious and knows the X and contends against it, there must appear a Given
within the divine experience, exactly as on my view." Brightman had one ultimate
God, "in God," while Harkness had two ultimate Givens, "one in X and one in
God's knowledge of and reaction against X." He professed not to begrudge her "an
irrelevant and luxious X or two" if she found comfort in them.[126]

Harkness probably felt a bit of relief that Brightman didn't write her off or
condemn the substance of her realist turn; at the same time she realized that his
first response skirted the key issue. He attacked her discussion of realism on style
points while claiming that he didn't take personally her abandonment of personalist idealism. Harkness pressed him to clear the air between them: "It seems
to me the term 'metaphysically real' is ambiguous, and whether physical nature
is, or is not, metaphysically real depends on the meaning you attach to this term."
She recalled that in her graduate school days she had "an awful time" with the
personalist theory of nature until she finally grasped that the reality of physical
nature is not denied if one regards it as produced by the continuous activity of
God. However, Harkness remarked, "I cannot for the life of me see why the eter-

nal activity of God is not just as 'metaphysically real' as God is. What I do is just as real as I am." It is true that the things that one does are not independently real, she allowed. The things that one does are only derivatively real; they have no ultimate causation. But why should the definition of metaphysical reality have to include ultimate causation?[127]

As for being some kind of dualistic neo-Cartesian realist, Harkness begged off from knowing how to describe herself. Epistemologically she stressed the interrelatedness of the constituent reals. She might be a pluralist, she allowed, but if so, she was the kind of pluralist who was rooted in a metaphysical and ethical monism. As for realism and idealism, she no longer knew what to say: "I really don't know whether I am a realist or idealist, for I have never heard my realist friends talk about physical nature enough to know what they think about it." Increasingly she asked herself what Reinhold Niebuhr or Yale theologian Robert Calhoun would say, not what Brightman would say.[128]

This time Brightman was characteristically direct in reply. Harkness did not understand the personalist view that she rejected. The "real joker" in the problem of nature is not the distinction between God's metaphysical being and God's eternal activity, he observed; personalist theory agrees that God's eternal activity is just as real as God. Unlike soul substance theories, there is no basis in personalist theory for distinguishing between God and God's activity; personalist theory conceives the being of God as consisting precisely of God's conscious activity; God is God's consciousness. The idea that the world contains some kind or level of metaphysical activity that is distinct from God's being is a deist or dualistic creationist belief, Brightman observed. Personalist idealism has nothing to do with this notion. In personalist theory the space-time order is part of God's experience, and the concept of creation applies only to nondivine personalities. Brightman reflected that in her graduate school days, Harkness apparently accepted the personalistic idea of nature "only on the hypothesis that God's activity would be illusory unless it produced something other than his activity, such as 'events, things, and eternal forms.'" This assumption is dualistic, he cautioned. Genuine personalism is something quite different. It holds that everything that is apparently not a person (such as events and things) is *really* some experience or aspect of a person. "I confess I am not wholly clear where you stand," Brightman remarked. He could see that she was turning against personalistic idealism, but he wasn't sure that she had ever grasped the real thing.[129]

Harkness conceded her unclarity without retreating from her realist-leaning shift in position. She had never shaken the feeling that there is something inherently unreal about metaphysical idealism, and this feeling deepened as the field of theology turned overwhelmingly realist. Yale liberalism was realist, especially as advocated by Macintosh and Calhoun; the Chicago schoolers were realists of various kinds; the Niebuhrians practically made realism a God term. Ironically, *The Recovery of Ideals* marked Harkness's formal departure from her idealist philosophical background. She remained close friends with Brightman, who worked out his own theological revisions in the 1930s, and she continued to incorporate much of the ontic idealism of personalist metaphysics into her position, but her position was increasingly defined by its evangelical liberalism, not by her training in the Boston school. "With the personalists I regard nature as the eternal activity of God," she remarked in 1938. "But I do not equate it with an aspect of God's consciousness. Both human and physical nature are the product of God's creative will, and in both there is an interweaving of what Tillich calls freedom and fate." Her sense of intellectual independence was strengthed by four sabbatical leaves at Harvard, Yale, and Union. At Harvard in 1926 she studied under Hocking and Whitehead; at Yale in 1928–29 she worked with Macintosh, Calhoun, and Roland Bainton; at Union in 1935 and 1936–37 she studied under Niebuhr, Tillich, and Eugene Lyman. Each of these experiences strengthened her sense of belonging to a wider tradition of modern theology than the school tradition of her Boston teachers—especially her sabbaticals at Union, where she basked in the seminary's intellectual energy and welcoming friendliness.[130]

During the same years Harkness poured out a flood of articles on the ecumenical movement, trends in biblical interpretation, the practice of prayer, the cause of women's ordination, the struggle for world peace, varieties of pacifism, and similar topics. She attended the Oxford Conference on Church, Community, and State in 1937 and the Madras Conference of the International Missionary Council in 1938. In all of her denominational and ecumenical activities she symbolized and spoke for the importance of opening church leadership positions to women. In 1933 she was the only female invited to join the Yale-centered Younger Theologians Group, and in 1937 she became the first woman to be elected to the American Theological Society. Her colleagues in the Younger Theologians Group included Edwin E. Aubrey, John Bennett, J. Seelye Bixler, Robert L. Calhoun, Walter Marshall Horton, Benjamin E. Mays, Reinhold Niebuhr, H. Richard Niebuhr, Wilhelm Pauck, Douglas Steere, Paul Tillich, Henry Pitney Van Dusen, and Gregory Vlastos. The group met twice a year to vigorously discuss each other's papers (often on the challenge of naturalistic humanism) and changed its name in the late 1930s to the Theological Discussion Group as a concession to the aging process.

Harkness enjoyed her increasing prominence in theology, thrived on her high-powered academic connections, and used both to promote her causes. Repeatedly she and Brightman puzzled over her failure to land a higher prestige academic position; the feeling that she was stuck at Elmira frustrated her greatly in the 1930s. Though she increasingly complained of fatigue, Harkness maintained an exhausting speaking schedule, in 1938 giving so many speeches that she spared Brightman her usual catalogue of them. In later life she recalled of her participation in the Oxford Conference: "I made a four-minute speech on the place of women in the church which caused quite a stir, and being cabled under the Atlantic in an AP dispatch, gave me a good deal of publicity at home. This would not be worth mentioning except that it precipitated so many invitations to speak here and there that I ran myself ragged in the attempt to keep up my school work and accept even a few of them."[131]

She ran herself ragged seeking to promote her causes and career ambitions. Asked by the *Christian Century* in 1939 to describe the drift of her recent thinking, Harkness reflected that she was becoming more of a theologian, less of a philosopher, more Christ-centered, more biblically oriented, more interested in mysticism and worship, and more church-minded. She had started writing poetry and had become "a peripatetic evangelist, speaking often on personal religious living." After she had spent fifteen years at Elmira College, her keenly desired call to a prestigious institution had come in 1937, with her appointment at Mt. Holyoke College; three years later she moved to the Garrett Biblical Institute. Theologically she was still a liberal, Harkness reported in 1939, "unrepentant and unashamed," but she recognized that liberalism needed to change: "We were in danger of selling out to science as the only approach to truth, of trusting too hopefully in man's power to remake his world, of forgetting the profound fact of sin and the redeeming power of divine grace, of finding our chief evidence of God in cosmology, art or human personality, to the clouding of the clearer light of the incarnation." Theological liberalism lost its gospel center even when it claimed to be evangelical: "Liberalism needed to see in the Bible something more than a collection of moral adages and a compendium of great literature. It needed to see in Christ something more than a great figure living sacrificially and dying for his convictions. It needed to be recalled to the meaning of the cross and the power of the resurrection."[132]

Liberal theology was making these correctives, she assured. Her own thinking increasingly absorbed them. "With many others in America I have profited from the currents coming out of continental Europe and too superficially called Barthian," Harkness observed. "These have come to me through books, but more through the forceful personalities of Reinhold Niebuhr and Paul Tillich—men with whom I do not agree very far but by whom I am stirred to rethink my faith." More than ever she cherished the gains of the liberal tradition and the spirit of free inquiry that liberalism bequeathed to theology. Harkness declared, "I believe in the essential greatness of man, in a Christian social gospel which calls us to action as co-workers with God in the redemptive process, in a Kingdom which will come in this world by growth as Christians accept responsibility in the spirit of the cross." Unlike Barth and Niebuhr, she did not find the central locus of Christianity in Paul's theology. The liberal tradition had chosen well in focusing on the incarnation of God in the Jesus of the Gospels.[133]

Liberal Protestantism was customarily short on ecclesiology, but Harkness exemplified a generational countertrend fueled by the ecumenical movement and the civilizational crisis of the 1930s. Like many liberals who played active roles in the ecumenical movement, she increasingly cherished the church as the custodian of the gospel and seedbed of its growth. Like Vida Scudder, her pacifist idealism gave her special reason to invest hope in the world-embracing work of the church. Harkness remarked that "pacifist though I am, I find great vigor in the phrase, 'the church militant,' and I see growing evidence of its reality." At the Oxford Conference "the body of Christ" became more than a worn-out phrase to her; it became a symbol and literal bearer of the world's hope while the world's great powers prepared for war. Harkness's pacifist idealism and her hope for the church were profoundly linked. She found herself saying Scudder-like things about the importance of the church: "Because it is a supra-national fellowship, it is the only truly international organism. When almost everything else trembles it is least shaken of all our major institutions. Into a world of strife and gloom it brings brotherhood and light. Both because of its foundations and its mission, the gates of hell cannot prevail against it. The Christian can be confident that whatever the outcome of the present turmoil, the church will survive and will go forward 'with the cross of Jesus going on before.'"[134]

Harkness's 1939 account of her recent history and her vision for modern Christianity prefigured almost exactly the kind of theology that she wrote for the rest of her life. Aside from its reticence about her abiding commitment to women's rights—her thinking on this subject hadn't changed in recent years— her testimonial identified the keystones of her later theology. What she did not fully explain was what happened to make her invest her hope in a renewed evangelical liberalism. In her telling she was prodded by Niebuhr and Tillich and inspired by her involvement in the ecumenical movement; what she could not disclose in 1939 was a deeper personal struggle that made her confront the spiritual thinness of her faith.

In 1929 her mother Lillie Harkness died after years of battling diabetes, "a release from suffering for a patient soul." Harkness was lovingly devoted to her mother, but she was fonder and more proud of her father. In later life she reflected, "Having spoken at such length of my father, I should say something of my mother. There is much less to say. Due to a fall and ensuing illness, she did not go to school beyond the eighth grade. She married my father at the age of eighteen and adapted her life to his." The only negative word that Harkness ever wrote about her father was that he took his wife for granted; Warren Harkness failed to praise Lillie as much as he should have. Georgia Harkness may have belatedly realized that the same thing was true of herself. In 1937, shortly before she left Elmira College, she lost her beloved father as well. Warren Harkness was the major influence and loving presence in her life. "I have never been privileged to know a more serene, quietly content, 'well-adjusted' personality, or one who, within the sphere to which his influence reached, was a more useful one," she later recalled. She nursed him through the last weeks of his life, and in his last hour Warren Harkness asked his daughter how many books she had written. She told him seven. He replied, "I think they must be good books. Wise men say they are. But I wish you would write more about Jesus Christ."[135]

Harkness later recalled that those words burned into her soul, marking "a definite turn in my writing and thinking toward a more Christ-centered approach to religious truth." Her father helped her recover the incarnate living source of her ideals. In the years of her bereavement and lonely exhaustion she resolved to write more about Jesus Christ. Harkness's frenetic performing had taken a mounting toll on her emotional and physical strength. Over the years she complained to Brightman of various ailments: anemia, frazzled nerves, sacroiliac problems, hypothyroidism, feeling "drained dry." Only a person of immense physical energy could have withstood the speaking and writing schedule that she maintained on top of full-time teaching. Often she admitted that she only appeared to have immense energy; she kept telling Brightman that she lacked his enormous capacity for work, yet she sustained a complex of professional and intellectual commitments that was equal to Brightman's.[136]

The numerous insults and passive-aggressive slights that she endured as a champion of women's rights and antimilitarism added significantly to her emotional burden. At academic, civic, and ecclesiastical gatherings throughout her career Harkness put up with male colleagues who suggested, often covertly, that she did not belong in their company. Knowingly she told the Oxford Conference that "it is a matter of grave concern that in many instances, the energy and intelligence of able women are being drained away from the Church." The same year she observed in the *Christian Century* that it was extremely difficult for "the trained woman" to secure placement or win professional recognition in supposedly up-to-date American Christianity: "It is a paradoxical fact that the Christian gospel has done more than any other agency for the emancipation of women; yet the church itself is the most impregnable stronghold of male dominance. It is this fact more than any other which makes women of intelligence and ability restive, and skeptical of the church as the most effective channel for their effort." She held no brief against chivalry, Harkness assured, "but paternalism often parades unrecognized under the cloak of chivalry."[137]

The loss of her father cut her deeply, leaving a void that nearly swallowed her in the early 1940s. Though she dated several men during her twenties and thirties, Harkness's only serious romantic relationship during this period occurred during her Yale sabbatical in 1928–29. It was apparently with Yale church historian Kenneth Scott Latourette, but according to Rosemary Skinner Keller, the relationship broke off because Harkness and Latourette could not reconcile marriage with their Christian callings and careers. Harkness later expressed thanks to God for being delivered from her "abortive love affair."[138] In 1940 she struggled not to show the draining emotional effects of her physical fatigue, the loss of her father, and her fear of another world war. She wrote a stream of spirited articles that called American Christians to condemn Hitler's treatment of Jews and his military aggression. Echoing Esther 4:14, Harkness urged Methodist women not to keep silent "at such a time as this." Insistently she claimed that antiwar liberal Christianity had much to say to a world at war: "We have something to say to a world that needs many things, but above all else needs prayer, prophetic utterance, and incisive Christian action." The church has been building the kingdom precisely to meet the crisis of this day, she proclaimed.[139]

In public her voice was outspokenly prophetic; in private she zigged and zagged between exuberance and exhaustion. Harkness's appointments at Mt. Holyoke and Garrett were gratifying to her, but she struggled with depression and a variety of physical ailments. Often she compared herself to the woman in

Mark 5:26 who suffered at the hands of many physicians, in 1941 recounting to a mailing list of friends: "During the past two years I have been prescribed for by three general practice physicians, three orthopedists, two gland specialists, two psychiatrists, a consulting psychologist, two osteopaths, a naprapath, a physio-therapist, a chiropodist, an oculist, two dentists, and a neurologist. All are experts and supposedly the best of their kind in the vicinity." She assured her friends that better days were coming soon, but instead she lapsed into deeper depression, insomnia, and physical distress. In 1943 she begged out of teaching her classes, explaining to Garrett president Horace Greeley Smith that she suffered from streptococcus infection, glandular imbalance, nervous exhaustion, insomnia, too much work, and emotional conflicts. She was humiliated at having to cancel speaking engagements, disgusted at doing a mediocre job of teaching, frustrated at not being able to pursue research, and ashamed at drowning in her private drama while the world was at war. Her private drama amounted to a spiritual defeat, she judged: "I feel as if my personality were disintegrating, and instead of being able to live and work with enthusiasm and zest as I once did, I endure exis-tence. And this is no way for a Christian to be!"[140]

THE DARK NIGHT AND THE LIFE OF FAITH

Harkness anguished that she fell into darkness at the very moment that the world plunged into war. She admired Fosdick for continuing to speak against warmaking while America fought against Japan and Germany, but Fosdick was sixty-five years old in 1943 and was known to be near retirement. His opposition to America's military intervention was indulged by parishioners and observors beyond his expectation. These were the years when Harkness yearned to be at the forefront of a church campaign to keep the candle of faith burning in a war-ravaged world. She did as much as she could, giving what she called "a pacifist ecumenical witness" in alliance with Fosdick, George Buttrick, Robert Calhoun, Halford Luccock, Charles Clayton Morrison, Kirby Page, Ernest Fremont Tittle, and other Christian antiwar leaders. She exhorted that words such as "appeaser" and "war-monger" had no place in the church's fellowship and that the church needed to keep its fellowship unbroken between pacifists and nonpacifists. But Harkness was consumed by her personal struggle. In 1942 she published an arti-cle in the *Christian Century* titled "If I Make My Bed in Hell"; three years later this article was republished as the first chapter of her book *The Dark Night of the Soul*. Though she was remarkably open to friends and employers in describing her ailments, even Harkness could not bring herself to admit that her current work was autobiographical.[141]

The book opened with a word of thanks to her beloved pastor, pacifist social gospeler Ernest Fremont Tittle, and to Verna Miller, who had become her friend and housemate. Tittle facilitated the friendship, perceiving that Harkness was depressed, awkward in social situations, and in need of in-house companionship. Miller was a member of his congregation and an administrative secretary; Tittle reasoned that her friendly sociability could be a saving tonic for Harkness. His intuition was perceptive and fortunate; for the rest of her life Harkness shared her home and a close friendship with Miller. Miller typed her manuscripts, managed her affairs, helped her get well, and devoted her own life to Harkness's.[142]

The Dark Night of the Soul is the title of an important spiritual work by the sixteenth-century Spanish mystic John of the Cross. Harkness observed that it is also the reality of "spiritual desolation, loneliness, frustration, and despair" of those who lose their sense of the living presence of God; she deftly described the experience without explaining how she came to know so much about it. The dark night is not the experience of praying in vain to have some ailment or hurtful situation taken away, she reflected. It is "the more subtle and terrible torment of sheer inability to find power in God to bear the pain or meet the situation." The dark night is the terror of godforsakenness that haunts certain sensitive souls: "Irritable, depressed, unable to sleep, and tormented by physical pains that may strike anywhere in the body, they do not understand themselves." Victims of the dark night experience searing humiliation and despair, she observed; they feel that they have already lost their religion and are now losing their minds.[143]

This was Harkness's condition when she began writing the book. Describing her experience was part of her therapy; she later recalled that she wrote *The Dark Night of the Soul* "as an alternative to having a nervous breakdown." In her therapy and her book she drew heavily upon the spiritual classic *The Practice of the Presence of God,* by seventeenth-century Flemish quietist Brother Lawrence. By the time that she wrote about the experience of "joy for mourning" in her book's closing pages, she was ready to dispense some hard-won advice about how to overcome depression. "To overcome depression, one must do what can be done to locate and correct its causes," she counseled. Most of us know how to live better than we actually live, and in almost every instance something can be done to make life better. At the same time, part of the work of learning how to live better is to accept one's limitations and the various sources of pain that cannot be helped. Harkness exhorted that to secure release from debilitating emotional pain, one must look beyond oneself; Christian faith and action are "the supreme corrective" to the depression and nervous fretting of the dark night: "For depression is primarily a form of introversion—of turning one's gaze inward in abnormal self-concern." To get rid of depression is to recover a true perspective on what is important, how much self-concern is healthy, and how one should live as a child of God. Victims of the dark night lose the meaning of life, but Christianity imparts meaning to life: "A living faith that is centered in the God revealed in Christ takes our chaotic, disorganized selves, with their crude jumble of pleasures and pains, and knits them together into a steadiness and joy that can endure anything with God. The meaning of the cross is that sin can be forgiven, pain overcome, by the victory of God."[144]

For most of her career Harkness sought her fulfillment through career achievement. She filled her calendar with speaking engagements, wrote for publication every morning, fretted for years about being stuck at Elmira College, and broke the male monopoly of American theology. Her frustration at not landing a more prestigious teaching position caused her to work harder to get one, which made her feel guilty when her teaching performance slacked off. Lacking close friends aside from Brightman and her father, she compensated by vesting more and more of herself in career achievements. For years she believed that she would be happy if she won a job at a more prestigious institution; when success finally came, her joy was short-lived. Harkness's tenure at Mt. Holyoke was brief and disappointing, and she didn't receive the position that she expected and wanted at Garrett Biblical Institute; the title that Garrett awarded her in 1939—Professor of Applied Theology—was created for her. Harkness believed that she was being groomed to succeed Harris Franklin Rall as the seminary's professor of theology and confided to Brightman that while seminary president Horace Greeley Smith had not explicitly declared that she would be Rall's successor, "I think this is what it amounts to." "It" was her appointment to teach practical theology at a seminary where the systematic theologian was seventy years old.[145]

Rall was a respected theologian whose books espoused a Ritschlian version of the Methodist social gospel; Harkness wanted very much to be his successor, and it is undoubtedly not coincidental that she fell into darkness during the months following her realization that she would not be named to his position. Already drained from emotional distress, overwork, and assorted physical ailments, she took it personally when Smith judged that she was not the right person to hold the seminary's newly established Henry Pfeiffer Chair in Systematic Theology. Smith probably felt that he had already gone perilously far simply by appointing a woman to a seminary position in theology. Because the Pfeiffer professorship was an endowed chair and was in systematic theology, Smith and Harkness both regarded it as the ultimate prize at Garrett. Smith was wrong in believing that Harkness was not worthy of the Pfeiffer chair, but her later career would not have been possible had she not made her peace with being a practical theologian rather than a systematic theologian. In the 1950s she claimed never to have sensed "the slightest shadow of discrimination in the two seminaries where I have taught."[146]

Harkness survived her harrowing emotional trauma by leaning upon the gospel truths of spiritual death and new birth in Jesus Christ. In this experience she found her calling for the days that remained to her: to explicate the essential meaning of gospel-centered liberal Christianity, which, for her, always included the causes of peace, women's rights, and racial justice. In the late 1940s she published a trilogy on the meaning and living of Christianity: *Understanding the Christian Faith* (1947), an overview of Christian belief and practice; *Prayer and the Common Life* (1948), a manual on the purpose and methods of prayer; and *The Gospel and Our World* (1949), a description of the state of the church and the gospel in current American Christianity. Like all of her later books, they were written for a lay audience, though Harkness cautioned that she wrote "for the *lay*, not the *lame*, mind." Without apology she pitched her later writings at the prose level of the *Saturday Evening Post:* "In the churches it is the layman, not the theologian in the seminary or even the minister, who is the ultimate consumer for whom churches exist," she explained. "What goes out from the pulpit or press must somehow get to the layman if the common people, who hear Jesus gladly, are to hear his message in our time."[147]

Understanding the Christian Faith centered on the meaning and experience of Christ's salvation. Without rejecting them altogether, Harkness kept her distance from objectivist atonement theories; without embracing it altogether, she gave a more positive account of moral-influence theory. Her hedge in both cases was crucial to her argument, for Harkness contended that Christ's death on Calvary was more than a moral example of sacrificial love. If Jesus died simply out of fidelity to his morally exemplary convictions, she argued, then the death of Jesus is no more significant religiously than the death of Socrates. Harkness countered that "the view that is truest may be called the *redemptive* or *evangelical* doctrine." Bowne's incarnationalist experientialism was her idea of a good evangelical rendering of Christ's salvation. For her as for Bowne, Christian salvation centered in the incarnation of Christ and in human experience. It proclaimed that in Christ we see the nature and find the power of God for salvation. The cross is the perfect pattern of suffering love, Harkness argued; but more than that, it is the symbol of God's own eternal self-giving for the sake of undeserving human beings. Divine love meets and conquers human sin at Calvary; Harkness taught that this is the center of Christianity, from which comes new power for living. Christians are followers of the suffering and triumphant God revealed in Christ.[148]

She worried that Roman Catholicism and fundamentalist Protestantism, both authority-based religions, were overtaking liberal Protestantism as vital religious movements. They censured the historical-critical approach to Scripture, believed in literal inspiration, and rejected the progressive view of revelation; they also seemed to have greater spiritual power than postwar American liberal Protestantism. Harkness laid much of the blame on innocuous liberal preachers: "So many seem mainly to preach inoffensive moral injunctions, and apparently pride themselves on keeping their congregations from discovering that in the seminary they acquired any new ideas!" Liberal Protestantism could die of blandness, she warned. She loved Fosdick's teaching that the Bible contains "abiding truth in changing categories" and urged her students to preach like Fosdick, who proclaimed that Christianity holds abiding spiritual truths through its relative and changing cultural forms. The Protestant mainstream was increasingly broad and shallow, she observed, but a river does not have to be shallow to be broad: "It is from God's life-giving, never-failing sources that liberalism, in so far as it is authentic, draws its truth and power. It must therefore recover and increase its urgency and evangelistic passion—in short, its depth—if it is to mediate God's truth and power to an age in desperate need."[149]

Her conviction that laypeople need competent guidance through the entire field of theology, Christian philosophy, biblical scholarship, ethics, and spirituality gave her plenty of work to do in her later years. Mostly she wrote brief guides to basic topics pertaining to Christian belief, such as *Toward Understanding the Bible* (1952) and *What Christians Believe* (1965).[150] A more ambitious work, *Foundations of Christian Knowledge* (1955) argued for a synthesis of faith and reason in Christian experience and defended the liberal tradition against neo-orthodox criticism. Harkness adopted Anglican Archbishop William Temple's distinction between revealed truth and the revelation of God in Christian experience; Temple taught that while it is correct to speak of "truths of revelation" that express correct thinking about revelation, there is no such thing as revealed truth. Revelation consists in the coincidence of event and appreciation, the interaction of the structural dynamic process and the human mind that occurs as appreciative event under the guidance of God. Harkness urged that this way of conceiving revelation ensures a proper place for both faith and reason in Christian experience. Faith makes possible the coincidence of event and appreciation; reason gives critical attention to the truths that may be drawn from the experience of revelation.[151]

William Temple was her kind of liberal. He belonged to the liberal tradition but conceived liberal theology at its best as belonging to the historic mainstream of Christian orthodoxy. Harkness insisted that the liberal tradition was never as de-Christianized as the Barthians and Niebuhrians routinely claimed; none of the great liberal theologians or pastoral leaders denied that human beings are sinful and in need of saving help from God, or actually believed in automatic progress or denied transcendent holiness to God's nature. Harkness called the roll of great American liberals: "This was never the liberalism of Washington Gladden, Walter Rauschenbusch, Borden P. Bowne, William Adams Brown, Albert C. Knudson, Harry Emerson Fosdick, Ernest Fremont Tittle, Harris Franklin Rall, Henry Sloane Coffin, or any of the other great liberal leaders of the late nineteenth or first half of the twentieth centuries. What these men and thousands of ministers trained under their influence have done was to find God *both* in the Bible and in the world accessible to philosophy and science; to see man *both* as child of God, of infinite worth, and as sinner in need of individual and social salvation; to find God as Creator, Redeemer, and Father *both* above and beyond this world and within it in nature and the currents of human history."[152]

The liberal tradition had its weaknesses, she allowed, but its dual character was not a weakness, and it was mistaken only in what it left unstressed. The liberal tradition was deeply concerned with applying the moral teaching of Jesus to a violent and unjust world and thus did not say enough about Christ's salvation; it sought to counteract the otherworldliness and crude apocalypticism of the fundamentalist movement and thus obscured the eschatological aspect of kingdom faith; it sought to heal the breach between religion and modern science and thus capitulated too far to secular naturalism in speaking about miracles and divine providence; it faced up to historical critical analysis of the Bible but sometimes treated the Bible as merely one source among others. These underemphases got liberal theology into trouble, Harkness allowed, but there was a way out of trouble that did not reproduce the one-sided polemics of neo-orthodoxy. This was to renew and insist upon the "both-and" character of liberal theology. Liberal Christianity is a religion of faith *and* reason. Harkness lamented that liberal theology was a victim of its success; its keynotes were taught at seminaries throughout the country, even by "those neoorthodox leaders who inveigh against it." To her, the latter fact spoke loudly about the future of theology. There was room for a better theological liberalism, but there was no compelling alternative to it.[153]

With spiritual zeal she called on liberal Protestantism to renew and defend itself. To her renewal always meant, first, renewal in personal spirituality. Harkness embraced Rufus Jones's distinction between negative and affirmative mysticism. The *via negativa* is ascetical and hierarchical, she observed, following Jones. It emphasizes the inscrutable otherness of God and the need to strip off all personal and social entanglements that get in the way of experiencing the beatific vision of God. It climbs the classical ascetic ladder of perfection by the way of purification, illumination, and union, and it underwrites a spiritual worldview of ineffability and passivity. With Jones, Harkness preferred a mysticism of affirmative communion over the ascetical union ideal of negative mysticism. The affirmative type is more wholesome and theologically sound, she urged, and it is "exemplified at its best by Rufus Jones himself." Harkness judged that most Quaker mysticism is affirmative, and so is the best tradition of liberal Protestant and Catholic piety: "It is simply a heightened sense of the need and possibility of communion with God in prayer." At its core it is the faithful practice of a personal devotional life; in virtually the same words as Jones, she described affirmative mysticism as the practice of immediate and intimate consciousness of the divine presence.[154]

"This kind of mysticism never assumes that even momentarily God and man become one, save in unity of will and purpose," she cautioned. It finds God within the soul of the self, and the souls of other selves, and the glory of God that fills the world, but it does not conflate God with the world or human souls. The divine presence is always "the Beyond that is within." Affirmative mysticism affirms the transcendence of God, but not in the ways of classical mysticism or recent neo-orthodoxy. Classical mysticism produced a spirituality of negation and esoteric knowledge; Barthian neo-orthodoxy denied what George Fox called "that of God in every man." Harkness countered that wholesome, personalistic, affirmative mysticism is a piety of radiance and illumination. Modern Christianity desperately needed the language and practice of devotion to renew itself. She worried that in the name of leaving Catholic asceticism behind, her tradition was losing its soul.[155]

Light-heartedly, she sometimes claimed that she had "the most important job in the world" because she taught theology at the flagship Methodist seminary. If the world was to be saved, Harkness reasoned, it had to be saved under the influence of the church, and the strongest part of world Christianity was in the United States. Moreover, the Methodist church was the key religious body in the United States, and Garrett was the largest Methodist seminary. Moreover, theology was the heart of a seminary curriculum, and applied theology was the place where theology came to bear on the needs of the world. This made her position the most important job in the world.[156]

Harkness kept that spirit to the end of her days, ending her career in the warmer climes of Berkeley, California, at the Pacific School of Religion. The glorious vistas of the San Francisco Bay caused her to "tear up my roots in Evanston" and become a Californian. "I came to Berkeley; I saw; it conquered," she later explained. From the beginning of her career in 1922 to its end in 1961 she remained, at heart, a teacher of religious education and a faithful mainstream Methodist. She championed the cause of women in the Methodist church, wrote hymns that expressed her social commitments and her experiences of grace, and taught hundreds of seminarians how to teach the faith to laypeople. Though she thought of herself as having somewhat outgrown her personalist background, her friends and successors at Boston University rightly persisted in claiming her. Inviting her to contribute to a festschrift for Knudson in 1941, Brightman assured that "you don't have to be an I-am-a-personalist to write for the book." Harkness contributed a grateful tribute to Knudson on the relation of divine sovereignty and human freedom.[157]

Her last generation of students found her something of a paradox. Harkness dared to be boring in the classroom, lecturing in cold, rote, neatly outlined propositions from which she never deviated. Students usually found her dry and aloof at first, but with time many of them discovered the warm and compassionate religious educator who loved the church and her students. Many of her former students fully appreciated her vocation only after they began their own careers as religious educators; Harkness modeled for them the kind of teaching that they conducted in their parishes. To some she offered a model of the Christ-follower as Christian pacifist, though during the Korean War Harkness cautiously allowed that under certain circumstances it might be justifiable for the United Nations to conduct international police actions. To a greater number of students and readers, she was the symbol of the right of women to play leading roles in Christian parishes and academic institutions.[158]

In 1948 Harkness took part in the founding convention of the World Council of Churches. Speaking at the conference's section on the Life and World of Women in the Churches, she argued for the equality of men and women in the church, whereupon she met Karl Barth for the first time. Barth took the floor, claimed that Harkness was completely wrong, and explained that Scripture teaches that man is the head of woman. Harkness cited Galatians 3:28 for support; Barth countered with Ephesians 5. His performance got poor reviews, and the following year a friend asked him if he remembered meeting a woman theologian from the United States. Barth retorted, "Remember me not of that woman!" Georgia Harkness was hardly a radical feminist; she believed that inclusive language is unnecessary and that women's equal rights are best secured under a single mainstream theology that represents all persons. But her feminism was far too radical for Karl Barth.[159]

BENJAMIN E. MAYS
AND THE THEOLOGY OF RACIAL JUSTICE

Feminist theology was barely a glimmer in the eye of Harkness, who lived just long enough to witness the birth of theologies that make gender a fundamental category of analysis. Benjamin Elijah Mays was a similar kind of trailblazer and forerunner as an advocate of racial justice. Like Harkness he was theologically and politically liberal, not a radical; and he had little concept of what came to be called black theology. Unlike Harkness, he spent only select parts of his career working in white institutions among white male colleagues, and he spent even less of his career working as a professional academic theologian. Benjamin E. Mays was a pathbreaking African American religious thinker who pushed the liberal Protestant establishment of his time to deal with racial injustice and who helped to make black theology possible. More importantly, he was a giant figure in the field of black education who gave two generations of African American students, including Martin Luther King Jr. and Howard Thurman, a model of dignified antiracist rebellion.

Mays was born in the town of Ninety Six, South Carolina, in 1894, one year before the constitutional convention of South Carolina stripped blacks of the right to vote and two years before the U.S. Supreme Court ruled that racial segregation was legal. Until 1946, when Georgia's white primary system was declared unconstitutional, he was completely disenfranchised. His earliest childhood memory was of watching his father bow down to a South Carolina lynch mob associated with the infamous Phoenix Riot in 1898. His father, S. Hezekiah Mays, was born into slavery in 1856; his mother, Louvenia Carter Mays, was born in 1862 during the Civil War. As a child Hezekiah Mays was fed by his slavemaster's wife from a plantation trough; he drank milk with his hands. He was taught to read, illegally, by his slavemaster's son, and thus could pass the gift of literacy to his eight children. Hezekiah and Louvenia Mays were cotton farmers who owned their own mules and usually rented forty or sixty acres. Of their eight children, only two of whom were schooled beyond the fifth grade, Benjamin was the baby. Louvenia Mays was a devout Baptist who encouraged her gifted youngest child to get as much education as possible, but her husband disapproved of formal schooling, and he was both kindly and abusive to her. Sometimes he beat her after getting drunk. At an early age, "repelled and disgusted by my father's indulgence in these habits," Benjamin Mays vowed never to smoke, chew tobacco, or drink alcohol; he also vowed to get as much education as possible.[160]

He was schooled in a world of shrinking opportunity; across the South in the 1890s blacks lost their Reconstructionist positions in politics and the courts, the ballot was taken away, segregation was enacted into law, lynching was widespread, and the courts routinely took the word of whites over blacks. The prevailing rule in Mays's home was "Stay out of trouble with white people!" Mays later recalled that black people often got into trouble no matter how they acted; those who cringed and kowtowed took just as many beatings as those who kept their dignity: "Hundreds of innocent Negroes were insulted, cheated, beaten, even lynched for the sole reason that they had incurred the displeasure of some white man." White newspapers routinely described lychings as paybacks for alleged sexual offenses by black males against white women. As a youth Mays lived in constant fear of being lynched: "The white press deliberately created the myth that lynching was necessary to protect white womanhood." While he cringed at the servility that many blacks displayed toward whites, he avoided white people assiduously, and accepted his mother's otherworldly Baptist religion. He had no friendships with whites; such a thing was unthinkable to him. Many nights he trembled in his bed as white mobs rampaged through his neighborhood. Mays grew up so deeply alienated from white Southerners that even in later life he was shocked when he received accolades from Southern white newspapers and civic groups.[161]

Like most black children in his area Mays attended school for only four months per year, in order to help his father in the cotton and tobacco fields. At the age of seventeen he enrolled at State College, a black institution in Orangeburg, South Carolina, where he was placed in the eighth grade. The experience of being taught by African American graduates of Benedict College, Lincoln University, Fisk University, and Oberlin College was life-changing for him. It gave him models of educational achievement and heightened his determination to excel academically. During his third year of high school he broke free from his parents, refusing his father's call to return to the cotton fields, and thus was able to complete high school at the age of twenty-one. In later life he sorely regretted what he called the "lost years" of his youth. Enrolling at Virginia Union University in Richmond, Virginia, Mays befriended two professors who had graduated from Bates College in Lewiston, Maine. Mays told them of his ambition to study at a Northern college, "where I could compete with whites," and they helped him transfer to Bates.[162]

"I had the erroneous belief that the 'Yankee' was superior to the Southern white man," Mays later recalled. "So, I said to myself, 'I will go to New England and compete with the 'Yankee.'" Bates College was a breakthrough experience for him. He felt that he had entered a better world, one in which emancipating self-discoveries could occur. For the first time in his life he met white people who treated him as a human being. The college's handful of African American students helped him identify the local bigots, but there were only a few, and his classmates quickly stood up for him in the face of the only racist incident that he experienced. In this environment he excelled and flourished. Mays won the sophomore declamation prize, joined a host of student organizations, became one of two blacks on the football team, and made many white friends. By his senior year he was president of the Forum Club, the Phil-Hellenic Club, and the Debating Council; he represented Bates in the Northfield YMCA Conference; he was selected Class Day Orator by his classmates; and he graduated in 1920 with honors.[163]

His competitive achievements were personally transforming; at Bates he conquered the internalized sense of inferiority that his early socialization drilled into him. "One of my dreams came true at Bates," Mays later recalled. "Through competitive experience, I had finally dismissed from my mind for all time the myth of the inherent inferiority of all Negroes and the inherent superiority of all whites." He judged that only four of his classmates were academically superior to him, though the college delayed fifteen years his election to Phi Beta Kappa. His college experience similarly transformed his outlook on race relations; Mays was surprised and enriched by his friendships with white students and faculty: "This was a new experience for me. I was getting another view of the white man—a radically different view. They were not all my enemies." Though he emphasized that none of his white friends were southerners, "I had made many friends at Bates and my racial attitude was undergoing a tremendous change." For the rest of his life he expressed unyielding gratitude for "my three wonderful years" at Bates, and he returned to the campus on various occasions to see old friends and receive awards, one of which was the renaming of the college's highest honor as the Benjamin Elijah Mays Award. Mays reflected, "Bates College did not 'emancipate' me; it did the far greater service of making it possible for me to 'emancipate' myself, to accept with dignity my own worth as a free man."[164]

Bates religion professor Herbert H. Purinton advised Mays to apply for graduate studies at Newton Theological Seminary and the University of Chicago Divinity School, but a Newton admissions officer informed him that Newton did not admit black students. Purinton told Mays not to worry; Chicago was better anyway. Purinton and Chicago church historian Shirley Jackson Case were friends and former colleagues, and Mays had long dreamed of attending Chicago. One of his favorite high school teachers at State College, N. C. Nix, was a Divinity School alum and fervent booster. To Mays, Chicago was the school of choice for Baptists; it was the most prestigious of the Baptist-founded universities; he had a vague understanding that it was also extremely liberal. That did not faze him; Bates prepared him just enough for the Chicago approach to religion. In 1921, the same year that he was ordained to the Baptist ministry, Mays enrolled at the University of Chicago Divinity School.[165]

As a minister he served as an assistant to Lacey Kirk Williams, pastor of the historic Olivet Baptist Church in Chicago and president of the National Baptist Convention, U.S.A. As a student he readily adopted the sociohistorical approach to religion advocated by Shailer Mathews and Shirley Jackson Case. "Despite my extremely conservative background and orthodox religious upbringing, the ultramodern views of the University of Chicago scholars did not upset my faith," Mays later reflected. "What they taught made sense to me." To understand the Bible, he explained elsewhere, "you need to know the political, social and economic conditions of what was written." It made sense to him that all doctrines have a story, that religious thinking is rightly concerned with understanding the story behind the canonical narratives of Scripture, and that religious meanings are always layered within relative, culturally conditioned historical forms.[166]

Though he enjoyed his course work at Chicago, Mays's social existence was another matter. Jim Crow was pervasive in Chicago, in 1919 the city had exploded in race riots, and the Great Migration was on, during which huge numbers of African Americans migrated to Northern cities from the South. Mays arrived in Chicago two years after the race riots. He was chagrined to have to deal with white Southerners again, none of whom would eat at the same table with him. Some would relocate themselves two or three times to avoid having to sit near a black person. A smaller number of Northern white students behaved the same way. At Bates, Mays's professors always spoke to him when they saw him on campus or downtown; at Chicago he had two professors who never greeted him. He later recalled how the black students made a special point of greeting one of these professors profusely; they bowed and tipped their hats and called him by name, forcing him to acknowledge their existence: "Interesting and stimulating though the University of Chicago was, it was not quite the 'heaven' Professor Nix's fond recollection had painted—at least not with regard to racial discrimination." More self-consciously than at Bates, Mays developed the social skills that he needed to survive the different-looking but deeply entrenched racism of the North.[167]

He aspired to an academic career, but for the next fourteen years Mays was sidetracked by what he called "distracting temptations." The first was a teaching appointment at Morehouse College in Atlanta, which returned him to the humiliation of riding segregated train coaches, drinking from segregated fountains, and being addressed as "boy," all of which cut him deeper than ever. He later reflected that Southern culture appeared to stand for the proposition "*Anything* to be offensive." On the one hand, he despaired that the South seemed hopelessly devoid of democracy and Christianity; on the other hand, there were black institutions like Morehouse College, Spelman College, Atlanta University, and Morris Brown University that represented hope for a new day in the South. Morehouse president John Hope convinced him to stay on for three years, during which he pastored the Shiloh Baptist Church of Atlanta on the side. One of Mays's debate students in 1923 was young Howard Thurman, with whom he maintained a friendship of more than fifty years; the same year he tragically lost his young wife, Ellen Harvin Mays, who died from complications as a result of surgery. At Morehouse he met Mordecai Wyatt Johnson, who was then pastor of the First Baptist Church of Charleston, West Virginia; in a stirring chapel address, Johnson exhorted the Morehouse men that they were called to do God's work of building the kingdom. Many years later Mays recalled that Johnson moved him profoundly: "Surely God called Mordecai Wyatt Johnson to expound the social gospel in America and to make Howard University a truly great university."[168]

With the intention of completing his doctorate, Mays returned to Chicago in 1924, where white students still ran from blacks in the cafeteria, and most restaurants refused to serve blacks, and relations were no better between African Americans and Asian Americans. He studied Case's writings, took courses with Henry Nelson Wieman, Shailer Mathews, and Edwin Aubrey, and wrote a thesis titled "Pagan Survivals in Christianity" that bore the stamp of his teachers. Mays argued that Christianity's cultural environment was formative for the kind of religion that it became and that it absorbed numerous pagan thought forms and customs into its thinking and practices. "Those who deny it think that Christianity is too noble, too sacred to be associated with heathenism," he remarked. "They take the attitude that everything pagan is bad and should be rejected, and that everything Christian is good, and should be accepted." He countered that "traditional views of this kind do not conform with the facts, and are not in accord with sound reasoning."[169]

"Pagan Survivals in Christianity" identified Christian motifs that derived from or were influenced by pagan sources, including the miraculous birth of a god figure, which appears in Hindu, Buddhist, Chinese, Egyptian, Greek, and Roman sources, and the deification of a savior god, where Mays followed Case in emphasizing the Greek and Roman prototypes, and the death and resurrection of a savior god and the immortality of the soul, which has prototypes in Hellenistic mystery cults and philosophy. Without denying the formative role of Hebrew Scripture and tradition in Christianity, he argued that Christianity survived and flourished because it absorbed vital elements of its pagan background into a dynamic new religion—especially a philosophical conception of spiritual deity and the idea of immortality—and because it took advantage of the existence of a universal empire and a growing spirit of cosmopolitanism. To decipher the pagan aspects of Christianity is not to negate Christian faith, he cautioned; baptism has a heathen origin, but that does not make baptism less Christian or less valuable: "It simply means that Christianity was inevitably bound up with the environmental forces of the Roman world; that it is an evolutionary movement; and must be modified, as all movements are, by its environment."[170]

He was charting his own course. Mays's eighty-nine-page thesis made a heavy draft on Chicago school liberalism, but Chicago liberalism was alien and threatening to the church-based culture of African American higher education. It had gained barely a toehold in black colleges through a handful of academics. With full awareness of the cultural variables, Mays followed the facts as he saw them. He approached his intellectual work with the same moral and intellectual conviction with which he resisted racial prejudice. Throughout his career he spoke in declarative phrases: "it is crystal clear," "the truth is," and especially "the fact is." He had little taste and no time for equivocation or ironical spinning. Except for an occasional resort to wry sarcasm, his articles and speeches had no laugh lines. Dignity, wisdom, moral seriousness, passion for justice—these were his trademarks. By his lights there were always important moral and factual truths that needed to be faced and expressed. Persistently, seemingly without tiring, he admonished throughout his life that servility to ignorance, prejudice, or injustice of any kind is never to be tolerated. He was fond of saying that no person is free who backs away from the truth.[171]

A second detour took him to South Carolina State College in 1925; the following year he married a teacher and social worker, Sadie Gray, whom he had known at the University of Chicago. In 1926 they moved to Tampa, Florida, where he served as executive secretary of the Tampa Urban League and she worked for the Tampa Family Service Association. Mays burned with frustration at the temporizing demands of Urban League work in a segregated state. His position allowed him to work for the rights of area blacks, but at the same time it made him a semiofficial liaison between black and white Tampa. He felt the contradiction deeply. Inwardly he seethed against the evils of segregation while working to reform it. He scored a few small victories and headed back to Atlanta in 1928, this time to serve as National Student Secretary of the YMCA.[172]

But working for the YMCA was a lot like working for the Urban League. The YMCA had an impressive record of cultivating black Christian leaders such as Ralph W. Bullock, William Craver, J. H. McGrew, James Moreland, and Channing Tobias; it also had an abysmal record of upholding segregation. Throughout the South and most of the North the YMCA and YWCA were rigidly segregated. Mays later reflected that "the sky would have fallen, the world collapsed" if the YMCA had sent a black representative to a white college. Having benefited from generally positive contacts with the YMCA during his high school and college years, he appreciated that the YMCA and YWCA were the only national organizations that spoke meaningfully to the needs of black students; no other organization offered programs and conferences to cultivate black leaders. But he fumed with resentment at his employer's cowardly racial politics: "Surely the leadership of the YMCA must have felt a furtive blush of shame to label their segregated God 'Christian!'"[173]

In 1930 Mays took another detour from his academic goal, which seemed to be slipping out of reach. Accepting an offer from the Rockefeller-funded Institute of Social and Religious Research, he conducted a sociological study of black churches in the United States. For fourteen months Mays and Christian Methodist Episcopal minister Joseph W. Nicholson collected data on 609 black churches in twelve urban areas and another 185 churches in rural areas. Aside from Carter G. Woodson's *History of the Negro Church* (1921) and two earlier studies produced by the Institute of Social and Religious Research—W. A. Daniel's *The Education of Negro Ministers* (1925) and C. Luther Fry's *The U.S. Looks at Its Churches* (1930)—they had the field to themselves. In 1933 Mays and Nicholson published their findings under the title *The Negro's Church*.[174]

They called their book "a rather dark picture." African American Christianity was born in a "strange and somewhat hostile environment," they observed. Spawned by slavery, racism, and African American necessity, the independent black church tradition was founded at Silver Bluff, South Carolina, in 1773. Mays and Nicholson moved quickly to the contemporary scene, showing in grim detail that most black churches were poorly financed and deeply in debt, that most black neighborhoods had too many churches, that most black ministers were poorly trained academically, and that the prevailing theology of the black church, "except in rare instances, is static, non-progressive, and fails to challenge the loyalty of many of the most critically-minded Negroes."[175]

Mays never doubted that enlightened leadership was the key to black advancement; *The Negro's Church* insisted that the black church needed educated pastors and an educated theology more than anything else. Eighty percent of the ministers in current black churches did not hold a college degree, over ninety percent of the ministers in rural areas had not advanced beyond high school, and less than one fourth of the black ministers in urban areas held a seminary degree. The authors judged that the undereducated minister was usually a preacher, but not a real pastor, and what he preached was an emotional religion of otherworldly salvation: "The Negro churchgoer has been consistently reminded of the otherworldly aspect of religion and life." By their count, more than three-fourths of the sermons in urban churches were "other-worldly and unpracticable," and less than one-fourth were constructive. In the rural areas, black preaching was nearly always otherworldly. Mays and Nicholson provided extensive excerpts of typical black preaching, which they criticized for its lack of rationality, and commented dryly: "It is hardly possible that fifty-four sermons, with fifty-four different texts, could all logically end on the idea of heaven." A higher standard of discourse was sorely needed, they urged: "It is a conviction of the writers that preachers often underestimate the intelligence of their audience and fail to give men and women of little formal training credit for being able to appreciate and follow a logical, constructive discourse. It is a further conviction that ministers frequently try to hide their own nakedness, their lack of preparation, when they resort to a type of preaching that seems to be designed to 'shout' the people."[176]

Pointedly they allowed that "it could hardly have been otherwise"; the grotesque repression of black Americans throughout American history produced impoverished black churches that clung mainly to the hope of heaven. But Mays and Nicholson ended their work on a hopeful and appreciative note. The shortcomings of the black churches had to be faced, but not at the cost of ignoring or denigrating their virtues, for the black churches were culturally and emotionally indispensable to African American life. They helped an oppressed people cope with oppression; they offered emotional consolation and spiritual hope; they functioned as all-purpose community centers; uniquely in black culture, they were owned and controlled by African Americans; most importantly, they offered a saving source of recognition and affirmation to downtrodden individuals. "The Negro church has been the training school that has given the masses of the race opportunity to develop," the authors remarked. "The opportunity found in the Negro church to be recognized, and to be 'somebody,' has stimulated pride and preserved the self-respect of many Negroes who would have been entirely beaten down by life, possibly completely submerged." In the everyday world most American blacks were made to feel that their lives counted for nothing. "But in the church on X street, *she* is Mrs. Johnson, the Church Clerk; and *he* is Mr. Jones, the Chairman of the Deacon Board."[177]

And there was one thing more, which Mays and Nicholson modestly mentioned in their closing pages: the black church was a genuinely democratic fellowship. It was one of the few institutions in American society that welcomed people of all races. It treated whites and Asian Americans with respect, and it opened its pulpits to visiting white ministers even though they as African Americans were not welcome in white churches and their pastors were not invited to speak in white churches. The authors remarked, "The Negro church generally preaches love and tolerance toward all races and abides by these ideals in its practice."[178]

The Negro's Church filled a gaping sociological and religious need. It had no rival in its time, and for thirty-five years it ruled the field of black church studies. The book's argument was influenced by the theorizing of prominent University of Chicago sociologist Robert Ezra Park, who before he moved to Chicago worked with Booker T. Washington. In turn, the field-shaping influence of *The Negro's Church* enhanced Park's standing as an intepreter of the African American situation. Park taught that oppressed people need effective organizations to resist and overcome the social structures of domination that govern their lives. He believed that the black churches were too dependent on emotional appeals and spontaneity to provide the kind of leadership for social change that was needed. His alliance with Booker T. Washington gave him unusual moral authority among black academics, and Mays believed that Park was essentially correct. *The Negro's Church* launched a Parkian-influenced field of study—the sociology of black religion—that was subsequently developed at a higher level of methodological rigor by sociologists E. Franklin Frazier and Charles Johnson.[179]

The Negro's Church also led directly to the idea of Mays's major scholarly work. His research for the book heightened his resolve to complete his doctorate. In 1932 he returned to Chicago, completed his course work (mostly under Henry Nelson Wieman and Edwin Aubrey), and wrote a dissertation titled *The Negro's God as Reflected in His Literature.* "The aim of the author is to tell America what the Negro thinks of God," Mays declared. Until recently few white Americans had cared what blacks thought about anything, but Mays observed with an air of puzzlement that his project was a novel one, "strange as it may seem." His interpretation rested on two sets of distinctions and a three-epoch scheme. The first era began in 1760, with the poetry of Jupiter Hammon and ended with the end of the Civil War; the second era was the Reconstructionist, pre–World War I period of 1865 to 1914; the third era was the past generation of American history. Shaping Mays's argument were two distinctions: between "classical" and "mass" literature and between "constructive" and "compensatory" views of God and religion.[180]

In this interpretive scheme, "classical" literature consisted of novels, poetry, slave narratives, formal speeches, biography, academic discourses, and the like, while "mass" literature included African American sermons, Sunday school literature, and the spirituals. Mays's second distinction was even more weighted with his personal convinctions, though he claimed for it "a high degree of objectivity." He described "compensatory" religion as partial, anthropomorphic, vengeful, highly emotional, supernaturalist, and virtually defined by its "shallow pragmatism," while "constructive" religion was oriented to the struggle for social emancipation and justice. In some forms, constructive religion was universal in scope "but inclusive of the needs of the Negro"; in other forms it was concerned primarily with the social and economic needs of African Americans; but in either case it emphasized that African Americans are entitled to the same rights as other groups.[181]

The Negro's God was an exercise in Park-style sociology of knowledge. Like his Divinity School teachers, Mays believed that the social scientific approach to religion is the best way to understand religion and the best way to help religion build a better society. His thesis was that all ideas of God are constructs produced by particular social circumstances. Before the Civil War, African Americans generally conceived God as being involved in their struggle for emancipation. During Reconstruction and the post-Reconstructionist aftermath of the 1896 *Plessy* decision, black writers and composers conceived God as being involved in their continuing struggle against segregation. In the generation after World War I, the focus of black God language shifted to the experience of disillusionment after the Great Migration led to new forms of social misery in America's northern urban centers. Mays's own social situation pervaded the text, sometimes explicitly. He was loyal to the black church, but made clear that he was not entirely of it; he appreciated the survival ministry of traditional black evangelicalism, but warned that it stood in the way of successful black assimilation into American society. He sprinkled the book with recollections of his own background in Southern compensatory religion, which reminded the reader that he straddled the two worlds.[182]

For Mays, the spirituals belonged almost entirely to the compensatory category. They emphasized miracles, the spectacular, consolation, and the consoling belief that God punishes the wicked. He remarked: "In the midst of the most stifling circumstances, this belief in God has given the Negro masses emotional poise and balance; it has enabled them to cling on to life though poor, miserable, and dying, looking to God and expecting Him, through miraculous and spectacular means, to deliver them from their plight. The idea has made Negroes feel good; it has made life endurable for them; and it has caused them to go to church on Sunday and shout and sing and pray." Compensatory religion is good therapy, he acknowledged from experience; it is also a mixed blessing: "This idea of God had telling effects upon the Negroes in my home community. It kept them submissive, humble, and obedient. It enabled them to keep on keeping on. And it is still effective in 1937."[183]

Mays allowed that some of the spirituals broke through to another kind of religion. "Go Down, Moses" was a chief example, as were "Oh, Freedom" and "No More, No More, No More Auction Block for Me." These hymns of African American Christianity rebelled against oppression without seeking relief in a heavenly afterlife. They reflected the African American practice of correlating American and Egyptian slavery; American blacks were God's suffering people in America just as the Hebrews suffered as slaves in Egypt. Mays gave a similar accounting of black preaching before and just after Reconstruction, most of which fell into the compensatory category, with notable exceptions that he quoted generously. Presbyterian pastor Highland Garnet and African Methodist Episcopal bishop Daniel A. Payne were prominent among the exceptions. In his account, classical black American literature before Reconstruction represented something of an antidote to the heavily otherworldly character of black religion. Black writers such as Frances Ellen Watkins Harper and Frederick Douglass took their ideas of God from black religion, but they were selective in doing so, emphasizing that God is just, that God is love, and that God takes the side of the righteous and oppressed.[184]

The Negro's God covered more material than its binary distinctions could handle. On the whole, Mays found that between Reconstruction and World War I black religion was mainly compensatory, while classical literature leaned toward constructive action, but he devoted ample space to countercurrents on both sides, and his categories often blurred to the point of seeming arbitrary. He relegated preachers as a class to the "mass" category, ignored the irony that some "mass" literature was as profound and sublime as anything in the "classical" category, and treated prophetic ministers as exceptions to the "mass" disinterest in social gospel religion. At the same time, he importantly emphasized that even the most otherworldly forms of traditional black religion were not detached from the struggles of African Americans against slavery, segregation, and discrimination. Compensatory religion represented one kind of response to the conditions of oppression. It enabled a degraded people to survive their mistreatment, kept alive the true values of the gospel in a situation of domination and repression, and proclaimed hope for a new day under the shadow of God's hand.

The great disillusionment that followed the Great Migration spawned two crosscurrents of reaction, in his accounting. The first trend was the development of an African American social gospel. While cautioning that the masses resisted prophetic religion, Mays noted that some black pastors interpreted God and salvation along social gospel lines. Black social gospelers such as American Methodist Episcopal Zion bishop Alexander Walters preached a theology of social salvation and resisted a rising tide of disillusioned otherworldly religion. The second development was that contemporary black writers in the "classical" tradition were dropping God altogether.[185]

To illustrate the trend that he liked, Mays recycled a long section from *The Negro's Church* that quoted an unnamed African American pastor on the meaning of "thy kingdom come." American Christians routinely prayed, "Thy Kingdom come," the pastor remarked, but they didn't really want the kingdom to come at all, for the kingdom has to do with emancipating and lifting up the condition of the oppressed. If the kingdom were to come to America, America would have to get rid of its selfish economic system, and its "prostituted conception of nationalism," and its "distorted notion of race superiority." The minister built up to a sweeping conclusion: "If this kind of Kingdom should come to the earth, no race would want to keep another race down. Our military forces would not be in Nicaragua; they would not be in Haiti. We would gladly help the Philippines to independence and without condescension and without patronage. India would be free and Africa would not be exploited. All forms of segregation and discrimination such as those that exist in the United States in the expenditure of public funds, in travel, in politics, and those that operate against us in social and economic areas would all disappear if the Kingdom of God should come."[186]

That was Mays's kind of religion, which wedded the race consciousness of African American Christianity to the progressive politics and religion of the social gospel, with a decidedly anti-imperialist edge. By the time he published *The Negro's God* in 1938, he was dean of the School of Religion at Howard University; he had attended the World Conference of the YMCA in Mysore, India, in 1937; and he had met Mohandas Gandhi. He and Gandhi discussed the philosophy and tactics of nonviolent resistence to oppression and the politics of the caste system; they agreed that oppressed people throughout the world needed to make connections with and support each other. A few weeks later, the headmaster of a school for Indian "untouchables" introduced Mays as an untouchable from the United States who had proven how far a person can rise despite being a member of a despised class. Mays was stunned and insulted by this introduction; it took him weeks to absorb that the label applied to him almost exactly. He had been treated for most of his life as a member of an impossibly contemptible class.[187]

Meanwhile it worried him greatly that black American intellectuals were turning against God. Young postwar poets such as Countee Cullen and Langston Hughes insisted that blacks needed to give up the God illusion; eminent poet James Weldon Johnson and cultural critic George Schuyler gave up the God idea for themselves, while allowing that God was still compensatory for poor blacks; Mays judged that W. E. B. DuBois appeared to be some kind of deist. For Hughes, he noted, communism had become a substitute faith—a novel development in African American history, for blacks had always sustained their faith in God, no matter how much they suffered. Mays explained the phenomenon as a distinctive form of disillusionment. Until World War I, American blacks had believed as fervently as white progressives that the world was getting better; America's gains toward greater democracy and equality were promising for black progress. Then the march of progress and hope stopped cold. The war that was fought for noble ideals ended with the betrayal of those ideals. American blacks returned from serving their country in the war and were told to go back to their servile station in life; they migrated to Northern cities and were treated despicably, while the Ku Klux Klan staged a comeback. Under these circumstances, Mays observed, "it is not surprising to find frustration, doubt, cynicism, and denial of God's existence in the writings of Negroes during this post-war period."[188]

MAYS AS EDUCATOR AND PUBLIC THEOLOGIAN

This picture of the state of black America set Mays's professional agenda, which he pursued as an academic administrator, church leader, and public theologian, not as a scholar. *The Negro's God* was his last scholarly book. Responding to a plea from Mordecai Johnson, Mays joined Howard's faculty as dean of the School of Religion. In 1926 Johnson had become the first black president of Howard, which operated under the U.S. Department of the Interior as a federally owned university. White and black critics alike charged that no black president could get sufficient appropriations from Southern politicians to keep the university operating. Mays later recalled of his move to Howard: "I am basically a 'race' man. I believe in the black man's ability, and my heart leaps with joy when a Negro performs well in my field. For me it was imperative that the first Negro president of Howard University be an unqualified and triumphant success." In that mood he joined an all-star collection of black academics that included sociologist of religion E. Franklin Frazier and chapel dean Howard Thurman.[189]

Mays gave six years to Howard University, where he built up the School of Religion's faculty, curriculum, library, and enrollment, and during which he became a leader in the world ecumenical movement. In 1937 he took part in the Oxford Conference on Church, Community, and State; three years later he accepted the presidency of Morehouse College, which he served for twenty-seven years; in 1944 he was elected vice president of the Federal Council of the Churches of Christ in America. The latter position made him an important figure in world ecumenical affairs and brought him a windfall of honors and publicity, all of which cast a welcome spotlight on Morehouse. The year after Mays was elected Federal Council of Churches vice president, American colleges and universities began to shower him with honorary doctorates; he took special delight in those from Howard University and Bates College.[190]

With a regal dignity that became legendary at Morehouse, he improved the college's fiscal condition and raised its educational standards. Morehouse was at a low point when he arrived. The college was founded in 1867 in the basement of the Springfield Baptist Church of Augusta, Georgia, with a student body of thirty-eight illiterate adult ex-slaves. When Mays arrived in 1940, the school had barely any endowment, ran yearly budget deficits, and was rapidly deteriorating into a junior college; it also attracted noisy protests from church conservatives, who were appalled that the Morehouse presidency went to a University of Chicago liberal. Mays raised the college's endowment only slightly during his long tenure at Morehouse, but he put its fiscal house in order and considerably raised its level of academic distinction. Students tagged him "Buck Benny" for his fiscal discipline. Every Tuesday morning he spoke in chapel, usually on moral responsibility and the good society, often warning that African Americans were in danger of "forsaking and even belittling" the religious faith that sustained their ancestors. Theologically he preached a gospel-centered version of liberal religion. "Christian light reveals a spiritual and ethical order which governs nature and human relationships," he affirmed. "But Christian light is not enough. We need the power of God unto salvation."[191]

From 1944 to 1948, one of the Morehouse students who absorbed his chapel sermons was Martin Luther King Jr.; often they talked together after chapel, Mays later recalled, and a deep friendship developed between them, "strengthened by visits in his home and by fairly frequent informal chats on the campus and in my office." Mays and King usually agreed about religion and politics, but King often had a probing question to ask and sometimes dared to disagree. For the rest of his life, King called Mays his spiritual mentor, "one of the great influences in my life." *Ebony* magazine editor and former Morehouse student Lerone Bennett Jr. called Mays "the last of the great schoolmasters." Under his commanding leadership Morehouse College became a national treasure.[192]

Mays's career as a public theologian flowed out of his work as a chapel-speaking college president and his leadership roles in the Federal Council of Churches and the World Council of Churches. In 1948 he took part in the First Assembly of the World Council of Churches as a delegate from the black National Baptist Convention, U.S.A., and from 1948 to 1954 he served on the Central Committee of the World Council of Churches, which organized the council's Second Assembly in Evanston, Illinois, in 1954. In 1952 Mays admonished that racial discrimination was the original sin of America and remained America's greatest evil: "Segregation on the basis of color or race is a wicked thing because it penalizes a person for being what God has made him and for conditions over which he has no control. Of all the sins, this is the greatest." He dismissed the claim that segregation could not be abolished by legislation. "Segregation was established by legislation; it can be abolished by legislation. If men can legislate evil they can and they should legislate good. The Christian must choose the weapons that he will use to advance the Kingdom of God."[193]

Persistently Mays contended that race should not matter and that complete integration is the only morally worthy goal for a Christian to pursue. The Bible recognizes religious and cultural distinctions, he allowed, but it gives no sanction whatsoever to racial discrimination. Early Christianity wrestled with the exclusionary import of Jewish law for Christians, but the early church's debates over Judaizing had nothing to do with discrimination on the basis of race, and ultimately the universalist character of Jesus's message prevailed in early Christian practice: "From the beginning of his teaching, Jesus proclaimed a religion that was super-racial, super-national, super-cultural, and super-class. To deny the universalism in the gospel of Christ is to deny the very genius of the movement." This genius is symbolized in Christian Scripture by the founding of the church at Pentecost, when people of fifteen nations drew together out of love for Jesus: "It is crystal clear that the Christian community began in what one might call an amalgamation of the spirit."[194]

Before the modern era, Mays pointedly emphasized, Christianity never claimed that Christ belongs to some races more than others. That betrayal belongs exclusively to modern Christianity. He put it provocatively in his speech to the Second Assembly of the World Council of Churches in 1954: "It is the modern church that again crucifies the body of Christ on a racial cross. Race and color did not count in the early existence of the Protestant church. It was when modern Western imperialism began to explore and exploit the colored peoples of Africa, Asia and America that the beginning of segregation and discrimination based on color and race was initiated. It was then that color was associated with 'inferiority' and white with 'superiority.'"[195]

Mays took pride in the World Council of Churches' condemnations of racial prejudice, and he took special pride in his leadership of the Federal (later

National) Council of Churches. At its 1946 meeting in Columbus, Ohio, the Federal Council declared that it "hereby renounces the pattern of segregation in race relations as unnecessary and undesirable and a violation of the gospel of love and human brotherhood. Having taken this action, the Federal Council requests its constituent communions to do likewise."[196] But it galled Mays that the statements of church leaders had little effect. His chief theme during the early civil rights movement was that the power of courage was lacking in American life. American Christianity at the elite level issued declarations against racial injustice, but aside from a smattering of northern congregations, little change took place at the local level. White ministers who did rebel against segregation were often fired, and thus, not many of them did. Many black pastors also feared that they might lose power if America eliminated segregation. Mays told both groups to stop cowering in fear; not to resist racial exclusivism was to be complicit in its evil. "Segregation is the great scandal in the church, especially in the United States and South Africa. We have plenty of light on the subject, but like Pilate of old we lack the power to act on the light we have." In America, as in South Africa, "social custom makes cowards of most Christians and I fear of the majority of ministers."[197]

Like Rauschenbusch, Mays employed the terms "Christianizing" and "democratizing" interchangeably; a generation after Rauschenbusch's death, Mays believed that the language of democratizing Christianization was exactly appropriate for America's social and cultural situation. What American society needed was to replace its modicum of Christianity and democracy with the real things. Like Rauschenbusch, whom he greatly admired, Mays insisted that profound social changes can occur over the course of a single generation: "If Germany through brutal means can build a kingdom of evil in one decade and if Russia, through brutal processes, can construct a new order in two decades, we can democratize and Christianize America in one generation."[198]

Martin Luther King Jr. and Howard Thurman shared their teacher's faith that at least a profoundly democratizing transformation, if not a Christianization, of American society was possible. Mays took pride in their contributions to the civil rights movement of the 1950s and 1960s. The surge of Christian activism that fueled the movement was heartwarming to him in his later years, though only to a point: he had worked for the moral awakening of American black and white Christianity, but the white churches never mounted a serious effort to eradicate segregation. "The church leaders did not have the faith nor the courage to initiate a program to desegregate society," Mays lamented. "The Supreme Court had to do it." Even after the Supreme Court outlawed "separate but equal" segregation in American education, white church leaders lacked the moral courage to actively support the court's decision. A precious opportunity for American Christianity was lost: "We ministers dragged our feet and the politicians took over."[199]

Soberly he warned black audiences that the end of segregation would not bring the end of their special suffering. White America will not make any allowance for three centuries of slavery and one century of segregation, he warned in 1964. Neither would white America make any allowance for impoverished black families or the inferior schools that blacks attended for decades: "The only comment you will hear will be, 'Negroes are not qualified. They fail the test.'" Mays told black students to steel themselves for new forms of humiliation: "You are now required to compete in the open market with those who have been in more favorable circumstances than you for several centuries. Our inadequacies will be printed in the press, flashed over the radio, and screened on television. Nobody will explain the reason for our shortcomings." He advised the students not to curse the past (that was useless) or look for people to accuse (that would not change their circumstances); the only solution was to become the best and most productive people that they were capable of becoming: "We must read more and socialize less, study more and frolic less, do more research and play less, write books and articles and become recognized in our respective fields." Under crippling conditions, American blacks were doing remarkably well, he judged, "but not well enough to pass."[200]

That was his schoolmaster voice. In the same year, however, Mays spoke in a sunny, almost lyrical voice about the integrated church that was surely coming: "The process of desegregation will continue; it cannot be stopped. So the churches will have no choice; they will follow. Powerful laymen, supporting their minister in his desire to live as well as preach the gospel, will free his hands. The guilt that besets the minister's conscience because he preaches what he cannot practice will be washed away, and there will be peace in his soul." That was just the beginning; real integration was the payoff: "Within his heart every church member will feel better, for his conscience will no longer trouble him. Negroes will worship in and join white churches. White people will worship in and join Negro churches. How many? It doesn't matter! God's people will be free to worship God anywhere they choose." In the South, Mays envisioned, black ministers would be invited to speak to white Christians, just as white pastors had long been welcome to preach in black churches. Some congregations would have black and white copastors. "In that day Negro and white Christians will worship together, sing together, pray together, share each other's joys and sorrows. And none shall be afraid. We will then know that our greatest fears are fears of things that never happen. And God will bless us."[201]

In 1968, after Martin Luther King Jr. was assassinated, King's friend and theology professor at Boston University, L. Harold DeWolf, gave the eulogy at his funeral at Ebenezer Baptist Church in Atlanta. Afterward fifty thousand people marched five miles in a funeral procession from Ebenezer Church to Morehouse College, in oppressive heat, where a second funeral service was held. The eulogy at the second service was given by Mays: "He died striving to desegregate and integrate America, to the end that this great nation of ours, born in revolution and blood, conceived in liberty and dedicated to the proposition that all men are created free and equal, will truly become the lighthouse of freedom where none will be denied because his skin is black and none favored because his eyes are blue;

where our nation will be militarily strong but perpetually at peace, economically secure but just, learned but wise, where the poorest—the garbage collectors—will have bread enough and to spare, where no one will be poorly housed, each educated up to his capacity, and where the richest will understand the meaning of empathy. *This* was his dream, and the end toward which he strove." This was the dream that King took to heart at Morehouse College chapel.[202]

THE WANING OF LIBERAL THEOLOGY

The theologians of Mays's generation could feel the liberal era slipping away. Fosdick, Jones, Harkness, and Mays came into the movement during its ascendancy; all of them lived to see its decline. They resisted taking a defensive posture when their theological tradition was roundly attacked, yet none of them ever quite imagined that there might be a genuine alternative to the liberal tradition. All of them upheld the gains of biblical criticism; all were anxious not to conflict with modern science; all of them cherished the progressive values of the social gospel, especially the principle of equal opportunity for all individuals. All of them therefore believed in the liberal integrationist ideal of racial justice, though Mays was the only one who gave highest priority to this commitment. All of them were peace activists and advocates of Gandhian nonviolent resistance to oppression, though they accepted the necessity of the police power of the state. Along with Mordecai Johnson and several others, Mays was one of the black leaders whose commitment to Gandhian nonviolent resistance influenced Martin Luther King Jr.[203] The liberal theologians were so deeply defined by these liberal values of intellectual freedom, individual rights, equality, and peace that it was difficult for them to absorb the seriousness of the neo-orthodox and neoliberal challenge to liberal theology. For the whites it was equally difficult to absorb that the typical liberal response to racial injustice was superficial and often patronizing.

For Mays the problem with the kind of theological liberalism that built the Federal Council of Churches was not that it embraced any illusory beliefs; the problem was that it lacked the moral courage and conviction of its beliefs. Liberal theologians and church leaders were adept at taking over seminaries and building networks of religious elites; in the 1940s and 1950s some of them became fairly good at making formal statements against racial discrimination. But they were pitifully ineffective at challenging the racism of everyday America. On the whole, the theological leaders of American liberal Christianity gave low priority to the battle against racism. They rarely treated the issue with the kind of passion they devoted to peace or intellectual freedom, and their own rhetoric was often casually racist. Harkness was better than most on racial discrimination, yet she wrote very little about it. Fosdick publicly addressed the issue more often, yet his racial attitude typified the problem of American liberal Protestantism.

It was a point of pride to Fosdick that his family inherited Civil War Republicanism, that his home was filled with pro-Blaine, anti-Cleveland political discussion in his youth, and that expressions of racial prejudice were anathema in his home. Throughout his career he sprinkled his sermons with condemnations of racial prejudice and discrimination, and his sermons were highly esteemed by Mays, Howard Thurman, Martin Luther King Jr., and other black leaders. On various occasions Fosdick asserted that racism is a denial of the Christian God, because it denies God's universal fatherhood, and that Jesus made a hero of the Good Samaritan, who came from a despised race. From the pulpit he denounced the five thousand lynchings that occurred in America between 1890 and 1940, "a large percentage of them Negroes and many of them under circumstances—tortured alive, burned alive—that beggar description." He quoted Mays approvingly on the evils of discrimination and recounted Mays's story of his reaction to being called an untouchable in India.[204]

Yet Fosdick also sprinkled his sermons and conversation with "funny" stories that were either attributed to "colored folks" or which implicitly made them the butt of his so-called humor. He was especially fond of dialect humor. He censured racial discrimination as immoral and anti-Christian, but admonished that it was a plain fact of history that the races are not equal. Some races have produced great civilizations and others are culturally backward, he explained. From the pulpit he put it more precisely in 1920: "You put the Anglo-Saxon people almost anywhere on earth, and before long they will be running the government. The African people after unimpeded tenure of a whole continent for unnumbered ages have never, unaided, been able to establish a settled government. There is no use in blinking our eyes to these plain facts." In the name of combating racism he pictured what a leading white racist of the 1920s, Lothrop Stoddard, would be like if he had grown up in Africa: "You know well that Lothrop Stoddard would grow up a cannibal, that he would be afraid of ghosts and believe in witch doctors, that he would marry ten wives if he could possibly gain money enough to buy them, that he would eat meat raw, and be petrified with fright the first time he saw an automobile, if he should ever see one." In his later career Fosdick toned down his imaginings about what he called "darkest Africa," but he never budged from his absolute disapproval of racial intermarriage. When pressed on the subject, he noted that most African Americans disapproved of intermarriage as well. In his long career he never performed a racially mixed wedding. He viewed the intermarriage issue as a red herring raised by racists who wanted to keep segregation in place. On the whole Fosdick's ministry aided the cause of desegregation and racial progress, but not nearly as much as it could have, and always with a whiff of white supremacy.[205]

Mays became intimately acquainted with the phenomenon of white liberal fecklessness toward racism during his years of service in the ecumenical movement. Repeatedly he had to prod the World Council of Churches to strengthen its declarations against racial preduice; not until 1946 did the Federal Council of Churches, under his prodding, come out against racial segregation. Unfailingly he attributed the weakness of liberal Protestantism's stand against racism to a failure of moral courage, which *was* the main problem. There was also the problem, however, that despite its gains in church membership, mid-century liberal Protestantism was a declining force in American society. Mays assumed a strong church with a vast public influence. He took for granted that liberal Christianity was a powerful force that needed to become courageous, repeatedly claiming that America would rapidly abolish segregation if its ministers took a stand against it. This factually challenged belief functioned for him like what he elsewhere called compensatory religion.

Mays made the strongest indictment of liberal Christianity as a form of practice; Harkness and Fosdick went the farthest in trying to head off neo-orthodox criticism; Jones called for a "new liberalism" that essentially repackaged the old one. His pass at theological reconsideration was titled *Re-thinking Religious Liberalism.* "It is just now a bad moment for liberals," he observed in 1935. "It is the open season for hunting and trapping all types of them." Jones noted that Reinhold Niebuhr "and other leaders of radical thought" were blasting liberalism for being soft and mushy: "They want something hard to bite on." The Niebuhrians and Barthians preferred apocalyptic prophecy and the dialectics of crisis theology to the sentimental idealism of liberal theology. Jones counseled that their noisy demands were not to be ignored: "There is a loud cry today for realism and the liberal must heed it."[206]

Jones's strategy for heeding the cry for realism was to give up the Enlightenment rationalism that still lurked around the edges of liberal theology. Liberalism is not fundamentally a body of ideas, he proposed: "Liberalism is first of all a spirit, an attitude, a state of mind." It is not a liberal impulse to swear fidelity to a worldview or system of thought. Liberal religion is open religion, he argued; it is the kind of faith that keeps itself vital by staying in fresh contact with the central stream of life. The liberal faith, rightly understood, has two commitments. Liberal religion is loyal to the unending pursuit of truth wherever that pursuit may need to go, and it is faithful to "the enlarging vision of the soul." Put differently, Jones's liberal mysticism was good religion that took a pass on much of the battling currently taking place in theology. It conceived true religion as "a way of letting the unseen order break through into revelation."[207] His last book explained that life is a laboratory of the Spirit in which deep calls unto deep and life answers to life: "The soul of man is still oracular. The God Who is Spirit is still, as always, a revealing God, and man, who is essentially Spirit, is a recipient of tidings from beyond."[208]

This was the idealist mystical music that Fosdick and Harkness loved, but they were mainline Protestants. The battling was unavoidable for them. Harkness devoted four sabbaticals to rethinking her acquired personalist liberalism; her theology adopted realist and evangelical elements as she confronted the theological crisis of her generation and the personal crisis of her soul's dark night. On the life-and-death question of how liberal Christianity should accommodate the onslaught of neo-orthodox criticism, the bellwether figure, as usual, was Fosdick. Always he began with Jones's theme that he was not dogmatic about anything, even liberalism; all theological trends are relative and partial, he cautioned.

Liberal theology is the most open theological perspective, which is why he was a liberal, and the best kind of liberal theology appropriates the best insights of other perspectives.

But because liberalism was unfairly attacked for decades, and because Fosdick was often the lightning rod for these attacks, he rose to its defense. It was often claimed, but falsely, he observed, that mainstream liberals of his type believed in inevitable social progress. Neither did they believe that sin is mere ignorance or that the kingdom of God can be completed in history by the moral efforts of human beings. Fosdick quoted himself from *Christianity and Progress* to support these denials. Another staple of neo-orthodoxy was that liberal theology reduced the gospel to the ethics of Jesus; Fosdick quoted himself from *As I See Religion* to prove otherwise. He added that he never knew an evangelical liberal of his kind who reduced the gospel to the ethics of Jesus. On the other hand, it was true that liberal theology overly accommodated the gospel to modern culture, just as he had argued in "The Church Must Go beyond Modernism." And some theologians overemphasized divine immanence, even though he had warned against emphasizing God's subjective presence in human souls to the point of losing sight of God's presence anywhere else. And many liberal theologians were too rationalistic to show any feeling for the unfathomable mystery of life, though Fosdick reminded that he had emphasized the mystery theme throughout his ministry.[209]

Liberal theology and neo-orthodoxy had much to learn from each other, he proposed: "Liberalism cannot remain as it was fifty years ago; neo-orthodoxy cannot remain as it is today; there will be a synthesis." But the diplomatic appearance of this formulation was not quite what he meant. Fosdick had a definite idea about how the theologies of liberalism and neo-orthodoxy should be related. Neo-orthodox theology had much wisdom and insight to offer, he allowed, but the Barthian school was not a good place to come from. It was a good thing when liberals gained corrective insights from their neo-orthodox critics, but it was not a good thing when seminarians started out as Barthians without passing through liberalism. Fosdick got his fill of the latter phenomenon during his last decade at Union Seminary. He reported that in the course of listening to student sermons, he became adept at distinguishing "between students who had come into their neo-orthodoxy through liberalism—as Reinhold Niebuhr did—and those who had taken their first plunge into theology under neo-orthodox auspices." The self-critical liberals learned a great deal from Barth, Niebuhr, and Emil Brunner, he recalled; they took their stand on the progressive gospel faith without accommodating the gospel to cultural fads. But the Barthian students were unbearable; their obnoxious dogmatism made Fosdick ill: "In a few cases especially I never had heard at Union such homiletical arrogance, such take-it-or-leave-it assumption of theological finality, such cancellation of the life and words of the historic Jesus by the substitution of a dogmatic Christ."[210]

Fosdick scrounged for some nice things to say about Barth. He noted that Barth was more interesting and provocative than his followers, that Barth played a brave role in the German Confessing Church's resistance to Nazi-accommodating

"German Christianity," and that Barth's *Dogmatics in Outline* said some sensible things about the role of reason in theology. But Karl Barth exposed the limit of Fosdick's famous geniality. Fosdick's spirit could not accommodate the dogmatic spirit of Barthianism. In his *Epistle to the Romans,* Barth proclaimed that "faith takes reason by the throat and strangles the beast." Fosdick shook his head: "Why does Barth say things like this?" It bothered him greatly that Barth's "inadequate and irritating" books were reshaping the field of theology, and he didn't like the effect that he saw in the classroom. Pointedly he remarked that the distinguishing mark of the liberal tradition is its tolerance, inclusiveness, and open-mindedness. This was the spirit that created good theology. Near the end of his career at Union Seminary, Fosdick told his faculty colleagues that while every liberal theologian needed to learn something from neo-orthodoxy, the only good neo-orthodoxy was the kind that grew out of and sustained its blood relation with theological liberalism. Though he often sounded otherwise, Reinhold Niebuhr believed the same thing.[211]

7.
Revolt of the Neoliberals
Reinhold Niebuhr, John C. Bennett, Paul Tillich,
and the Dialectics of Transcendence

The Niebuhrian turn in American theology is overloaded with irony. Vehemently it was a revolt against American liberal Protestantism. Keen on irony and paradox, and thriving on crisis, it traded the liberal language of process, moral progress, and evolutionary idealism for the orthodox-sounding language of sin, redemption, tragedy, and transcendence. In the course of ending the reign of liberalism in American theology, the Niebuhrian revolt made "liberal" a sneer word among theologians. Yet Reinhold Niebuhr belonged to the liberal tradition that he attacked. Many of his disciples strayed into forms of neo-orthodox theology and political neoconservatism that repudiated their roots in the social gospel, but he did not, nor did his closest disciple and professional colleague, John C. Bennett. Niebuhr's governing intellectual assumptions were liberal; he had few affinities with Karl Barth or the Barthian movement in theology, and he never doubted the social gospel assumption that Christians have a social mission to secure the just ordering of the world. In a significant sense Niebuhr and his German expatriate colleague Paul Tillich do not belong to the tradition of American theological liberalism—they insisted as much for over thirty years—yet the past seventy-five years of this tradition are inexplicable without them. Though they never used the word "neoliberal," this term fits them better than any other.

Though they blasted liberal theology repeatedly and contributed mightily to its eclipse, their thinking always belonged essentially to it, and they, along with Bennett, contributed greatly to its refashioning.

The crowning Niebuhrian irony is that Niebuhr claimed not to be a theologian; a preacher, social activist, and religious social ethicist, he had little formal training in theology and even less taste for formal theologizing. The wellspring of his power was his driving concern to influence the course of American social and foreign policy from the standpoint of a realistic Christian ethic. Yet he was also a profound theologian who theorized the transcendence of God's mode of being over the contingent, temporal, transient, and fallen being of all creatures. By mid-century his influence over American Protestantism was enormous, though declining in relation to that of his colleague and friend, Paul Tillich, who towered over American theology in the 1950s and early 1960s. When Tillich referred to liberal theology, he fixed in mind the Ritschlian school and its social gospel, historicist, and humanist offshoots. American liberal theology would be much easier to account for if it consisted only of these schools of thought; the real thing is more complex and includes, with great irony, the major theologians of twentieth-century America, Niebuhr and Tillich.

BECOMING REINHOLD NIEBUHR

Niebuhr's relation to theological liberalism was ironic and conflicted nearly throughout his life. Born in Wright City, Missouri, in 1892, he was the son of a German Evangelical Synod pastor, Gustav Niebuhr, who emigrated to the United States from Germany at the age of eighteen in 1881. The German Evangelical Synod of North America was a product of the 1817 union of the Reformed and Lutheran churches of Prussia, and Gustav Niebuhr was a vigorous, opinionated, high-minded church leader who read Harnack and Schleiermacher, voted for Teddy Roosevelt, and studied the Bible in Hebrew and Greek. His essentially pietist faith combined liberal and evangelical commitments. Gustav believed in intellectual freedom and opposed the scholastic dogmatism of orthodox theology, but bitterly opposed liberal modernists who discounted the New Testament miracles. He was deeply committed to the Evangelical Synod but spurned the cultural and confessional provincialism that prevailed in much of his denomination. Despite the fact that many German Americans viewed temperance as an Anglo-Saxon plot against German culture, Gustav strongly supported the temperance movement; he also took an ecumenical view toward other Protestant denominations. Socialism was anathema to him, and feminism horrified him; at the same time he urged that the federal government was morally obliged to restrain the excesses of capitalism and that the church had a social mission to promote a good society.

Gustav and Lydia Niebuhr had five children; the oldest was a girl, Hulda; the oldest boy, Walter, was a bit rebellious; a second boy died in infancy; the fourth child—Karl Paul Reinhold Niebuhr—was Gustav's favorite. From an early age Reinhold warmed to his father and tried to be like him. He was exuberant but disciplined, opinionated and spontaneous but cooperative. Gustav caught a reflection of himself in his fourth child. He joked and confided with young Reinhold, who took for granted that he would become a minister like his father: "My father was the most interesting man in our community." In later life Reinhold was shocked to discover that his younger brother, Yale theologian Helmut Richard Niebuhr, carried bitter memories of their father. To outgoing Reinhold, Gustav was a compelling, friendly, and exemplary model: "I have only pleasant memories of my father and the sense of partnership he established with an adolescent boy."

To introverted Helmut he was coldly disapproving and tyrannical. Gustav Niebuhr had little use for his youngest child, who shared little of his own spirit; meanwhile he told Hulda to forget about college, since higher education was not meant to be wasted on girls. Gustav demanded that Hulda be like her mother, whose life as a pastor's wife and helper was a seamless web of domestic and parish tasks. Upon graduating from high school, Hulda took up a succession of parish commitments, just like Lydia Niebuhr; but after her father died unexpectedly in 1913, at the age of fifty, she resumed her education and eventually became a seminary professor.[1]

Reinhold Niebuhr was not impressively educated, aside from the theology and Greek that he learned from his father. At the age of fourteen, in the ninth grade, he took his last science and math classes; the following year he entered the German Synod's "pro-seminary" program at unaccredited Elmhurst College, fifteen miles west of Chicago, which amounted to a second-rate boarding school. Elmhurst was a weak version of the German gymnasium; it ignored the sciences and modern history, and its pass at Latin and English was pitiful. Niebuhr rankled at the school's incompetence and later recalled, a bit blandly, that "the little college had no more than junior college status in my day, and I was not interested in any academic disciplines." As a student he organized a protest against the school's Latin and English teachers, which did not endear him to the faculty—especially after Niebuhr's father intervened and the Latin and English teachers were fired. In 1910 Niebuhr enrolled at his father's alma mater, Eden Theological Seminary, which proved to be more of the same, aside from the fatherly influence of Samuel Press. Press, the first native-born member of the Eden faculty and the first who spoke English as his first language, was a learned, irenic scholar, who later served for many years as Eden's president. As a consequence of his living in a half-English, half-German environment, Niebuhr's English and German were both inadequate. Under Press's influence he imagined the possibility of a ministry that transcended the social and cultural confines of the midwest German Synod; he also found his first surrogate father.[2]

Gustav Niebuhr judged that his favored son needed to be trained at a thoroughly American university, preferably one that approximated German university standards of teaching and scholarship. In April 1913, five months before Reinhold enrolled at Yale Divinity School as a third-year Bachelor of Divinity student, Gustav died unexpectedly. The funeral lasted all afternoon, Samuel Press gave a memorial address, and for five months Reinhold assumed his father's pastoral chores at St. John's Church of Lincoln, Illinois. For many years afterward he felt that he was completing his father's life and work. From the beginning of his preaching career, his sermons were marked by an emphasis on the sin of self-ishness and the paradoxical character of Christianity and life. In Niebuhr's rendering, Matthew 10:39 expressed "the paradox of all life: that self-preservation means self-destruction and self-destruction means self-preservation." Only the person who gives up one's life can be saved, he preached; the essential problem of every human life is every person's captivity to selfishness, and the solution to it is love and self-sacrifice: "The image of God that is still within us will never be satisfied until it is satisfied by the principle that made it—love." Niebuhr confessed that he did not understand the doctrines of the divinity of Christ, the two natures of Christ, the Trinity of God, and the communion of the Spirit, and "maybe you don't either." But everyone can understand "the moral and social program of Christ," he observed; on the basis of this affirmation he proposed to preach Christ as the solution to the problem of every human life.[3]

Niebuhr acutely realized that he had no chance of being admitted to Union Theological Seminary and was a beneficiary of Yale's relaxed admission standards. He gained admission to Yale Divinity School (then called the Yale School of Religion) only because it was in a rebounding and expanding phase after twenty years of stagnation. In biblical studies, Yale had attracted some distinguished scholars in the 1880s and 1890s, notably William Rainey Harper before he founded the University of Chicago; Old Testament scholar Edward L. Curtis, who joined the faculty in 1891; biblical theologian Frank C. Porter, who assumed the Winkley Chair of Biblical Theology in 1891; and New Testament scholar Benjamin W. Bacon, who joined the faculty in 1896. Despite this breakthrough in the biblical field, however, Yale continued to resist modern theology, the social gospel, and the ecumenical approach to theological education. It clung to its identity as the seminary of a moderately conservative and declining Congregationalism. As a consequence, class enrollments dropped sharply throughout the 1890s, and by 1906, Yale's nadir, the entering Bachelor of Divinity class was down to thirteen men. But that year the faculty replaced its core curriculum with an elective system and added new courses on contemporary issues; the following year the Divinity School declared its independence from the Congregational church; in 1909 Douglas Clyde Macintosh joined the faculty; and in 1911 the school appointed a therapeutically oriented theological liberal, Charles Reynolds Brown, as its dean.[4]

Niebuhr's reaction to Yale was typically conflicted. Though grateful to be there and humbled by the learning of his teachers and classmates, he reported to Press that he learned more from his private reading than from classes. He resolved to "cast my lot with the English" but worried that he was forgetting how to speak German. His dominant feeling was humiliation; "I feel all the time like a mongrel among thoroughbreds and that's what I am," he told Press. It galled him to realize that the culprit was his denominational background: "The more I see how highly scholarship is prized in other denominations the more the penny-wise attitude of our church makes me sore. But what we need more than several special students is a *college* education for all of our students. The more I look at the thing the more I see that I have been cheated out of a college education. Elmhurst is little more than a high school." His teenage years had been wasted intellectually, he judged; he especially lacked a decent training in English, philosophy, ethics, and science. It made him "boil" to realize that his denomination substituted piety for critical scholarship, and he was finished with "this half-way business" of speaking neither English nor German very well. He had enormous gaps to fill if he was to become "a voice in our church."[5]

For the most part, Yale represented what he wanted; the school was too mannered and uppity for his taste—the only professor that Niebuhr really liked was Macintosh, another outsider—but educationally and theologically, Yale had the goods that he was seeking. Niebuhr enthused that relations between the Divinity School and the rest of the university were closer at Yale than anywhere else, with the possible exception of Chicago: "Being thus in the very heart of one of America's greatest centers of learning gives one opportunities that are impossible in any isolated seminary." In his judgment, the Divinity School combined scholarship and spirituality "about as ideally as this can be done"; he especially appreciated Brown, "the biggest spiritual force in Yale," who had a good rapport with students and who knew how to speak to their personal struggles. Theologically, Niebuhr observed, conservatives often charged that Yale was Unitarian, but this made sense only if "Unitarian" and "liberal" meant the same thing: "The general tendency of all larger American universities is of course in the general direction of unitarianism. But if this be unitarianism we may give all liberal theology that name, especially German liberal theology." He reported that the German cast of the new theology taught at Yale was very pronounced: "In the classes one hears nothing but German names referred to: Holtzman, Weizsaecker, Weinel, Gunkel, Weiss, Deissman, Dobschuetz and all of the rest of the tribe are constantly passing in review."[6]

On this count Niebuhr observed that his family background was fortuitous. Though he lacked the training and degrees of his classmates, at least he could read German, while most of them couldn't. Niebuhr's teachers included Macintosh, biblical scholars Benjamin Bacon and Frank Porter, church historian Williston Walker, ethicist Hershey Sneath, and homiletics professor Henry Tweedy; in his view, the best teachers among them were Bacon, Porter, and Macintosh. To his understanding, Yale was committed to the liberal, German, history-of-religions approach to religion, and so was he. In this approach, Niebuhr explained, "the Bible vanishes as any supernatural authority and Christianity is forced to compete with all religions upon a common basis." There is such a thing as biblical truth, he reasoned, but the content of this truth can only be established by the best reason and highest spiritual interests of modern people.[7]

Under Macintosh's guidance he read William James, wrote a Bachelor of Divinity thesis on the pragmatic validity of religious knowledge, and appealed to human personality as a privileged realm of spirit not subject to the laws of nature. Niebuhr was slow to notice Walter Rauschenbusch; his two years at Yale were absorbed with the problems of personal belief. With an eye on graduate school and an academic career, he took four courses in the college's philosophy department, but he earned mediocre grades and lost both his enthusiasm for philosophy and his eligibility for a graduate degree. Macintosh's epistemological typologizing confirmed for Niebuhr that academe was not for him; in later life he recalled: "This professor meant a lot to me, but I found his courses boring." Elsewhere he recalled with typically puckish humor: "The more I threw myself into these philosophical studies, the more I got bored with all the schools of epistemology that had to be charted—the realists, the idealists, the logical idealists, the psychological idealists, the psychological logical idealists, and the other different kinds of idealists and realists. Frankly, the other side of me came out in the desire for relevance rather than scholarship." Not so frankly, Niebuhr neglected to explain that his grades disqualified him for doctoral study. His last paper for Macintosh, on the Pauline doctrine of immortality, argued that Paul's concern was the persistence of the individual personality. At the last minute in June 1915, apparently at Macintosh's urging, Yale surprised Niebuhr by awarding him a Master of Arts degree, but he was finished with graduate education. His two years of Americanizing higher education would have to do.[8]

A few weeks after he graduated from Yale, Niebuhr discovered that his older brother Walter, who had supported the Niebuhr family since Gustav's death, was financially ruined, so that the responsibility of being the family's breadwinner passed to Reinhold. He confessed to Press that the prospect of entering the ministry as a liberal was unsettling to him: "I am a good deal worried that my liberalism will not at all be liked in our church and will jeopardize any influence which I might in time have won in our church." At the same time, though he craved influence, he could see no alternative to being theologically liberal: "One would have to go to Princeton to escape it."[9] Niebuhr wanted for his first pastorate a progressive, Americanized, reasonably well-paying church; instead he was sent by synod President-General John Baltzer to a Germanic mission parish on the northwest edge of Detroit, Bethel Evangelical Church.

This assignment was deflating; after two years of freedom and stimulation, his life had suddenly turned into a web of unwelcome responsibilities. The Bethel pastorate paid a poor salary, Niebuhr had never had a romantic relationship of any kind, now his mother was living with him, he may have had to help with his older brother's debts, and he didn't want to live in Detroit, where the synod ministers impressed him as a "nest of reaction." He groused that "the ministry is the only profession in which you can make a virtue of ignorance," for the German Synod pastors of Detroit represented exactly "the imbecile standpatism" that he loathed. They clung to the German language and a discredited orthodoxy, and in 1915 they abetted a wave of pro-German nationalism in reaction to wartime anti-German sentiments that were spreading throughout the United States. "The German propaganda is so hysterical among many of our ministers that largely by default I am getting to be a violent American patriot," he told Press. "There is no real interest in the welfare of this country and no genuine American patriotism. . . . To be very candid with you I do not feel at all at home in our church."[10]

Niebuhr's first social cause was to make German-American Protestantism unabashedly American. While his mother conducted Bethel Church's daily business, including the Sunday school program and choir, he wrote a barrage of articles on church reform. While Bethel Church accepted his requests for English hymnals and a weekly English service, Niebuhr clashed repeatedly with local clerical leaders and brooded that pro-German provincialism was prevailing in the synod. His first article for a national magazine, published in the *Atlantic* in July 1916, was titled "The Failure of German-Americanism." Niebuhr argued that German culture at its best was liberal, cosmopolitan, and forward-looking in its politics and religion, but German-American Protestantism typically represented German culture at its worst: conservative, provincial, and stodgy. Americans had good reason to resent the lack of American patriotism recently displayed by German-Americans, he implied. German-Americans needed to become "less indifferent to the ideals and principles of this nation." If they became better Americans, Niebuhr insisted, German-Americans would find that they embraced what was best in their culture of origin.[11]

Unfortunately the less enlightened aspects of German culture were prevailing in both contexts; Americans were justified in disliking German militarism, Niebuhr believed, and German-Americans were wrong not to identify with the United States. From the pulpit he accented the positive; on the synod's seventy-fifth anniversary in 1915 he praised the distinctive seriousness and thoroughness of German culture, remarking that German-American Christianity was highly intelligent and active on this account, if not "always as intelligent and active as in the Old World." What was needed was a German-American Christianity that gave its best to its adopted country, he urged: "What could be more natural than to use our unique strengths for the good of our nation and to work for the victory of God's kingdom as an expression of gratitude for being allowed to grow in accordance with our individuality? If we want to do it as a church, we must also lead genuinely Christian lives as individuals, sympathetic to our country."[12]

Niebuhr was sensitive to the problem of repetition, though he overused the technique of dialectical pairing. "Now that I have preached about a dozen sermons I find I am repeating myself," he reflected in 1915. "A different text simply means a different pretext for saying the same thing over again."[13] From the beginning of his career, he invoked the Homeric legend of Scylla and Charybdis, the two great cliffs containing sea monsters between which Ulysses charted his course: "There is a Scylla and Charybdis in almost every undertaking, two opposite dangers, two extremes, between which one must sail and both of which one must avoid if the undertaking is to be successful." Even the gymnastic altar calls of evangelist Billy Sunday evoked a "yes and no" from Niebuhr, who judged that Sunday's popular revivals contained "a peculiar mixture of good and evil." Though Sunday was often ridiculed for his anti-intellectualism, fundamentalism, and showboating histrionics, Niebuhr admonished that he rightly emphasized the "fundamental paradox of Christian faith" that God is both righteous and merciful; if Sunday overplayed the theme of divine wrath, at least his God remained capable of righteous judgment, unlike the sentimentalized deity of liberal Christianity.[14]

Niebuhr worried that liberal theology was too tender-minded, and he envied the freedom and national renown of Sunday, who was not bound to a local congregation or even a denomination. Like Gustav Niebuhr, Reinhold entered the ministry "with a few thoughts and a tremendous urge to express myself."[15] He felt constrained by his position and denominational ties, though his mother freed him to write attention-getting articles. He wanted to speak to multitudes, but as a minister he was confined to members of his denomination, and his denomination was puny: "Perhaps if I belonged to a larger denomination this wouldn't irk me so much," Niebuhr ruminated. "I suffer from an inferiority complex because of the very numerical weakness of my denomination."[16]

His deliverance came shortly after Woodrow Wilson declared war against Germany. The Evangelical Synod established a War Welfare Commission to organize pastoral services for its soldiers, and Niebuhr was appointed executive secretary. Synod President-General Baltzer wanted him to operate out of St. Louis, but Niebuhr worried that his mother's emotional health depended on her work and security in Detroit. Lydia Niebuhr suffered from depression and anxiety attacks; she needed to be needed at Bethel Church. Thus, instead of moving to St. Louis, Niebuhr preached on most Sundays and spent the rest of each week on the road, touring military training camps in several states. His sister Hulda moved to Detroit to help their mother manage Bethel Church, and his brother Helmut— a graduate student at Washington University—substituted on Sundays when Niebuhr could not attend. Though the traveling was often exhausting, Niebuhr exulted in his opportunities to tour the country, influence denominational politics, and meet with officials of the Federal Council of Churches. He pressed his Evangelical colleagues to believe in the war they were training to enter or at least to act like they believed in the goodness of their country. "When I talk to the boys I make much of the Wilsonian program as against the kind of diplomacy which brought on the war," he observed. He blanched at witnessing a bayonet practice, "yet I cannot bring myself to associate with the pacifists. Perhaps if I were not of German blood I could." If he had not needed to prove his Americanism, he might have chosen pacifism. Niebuhr realized that this was not a noble reason to reject the pacifist option—"that may be cowardly"—but he reasoned that "a new nation has a right to be pretty sensitive about its unity. Some of the good old Germans have a hard time hiding a sentiment which borders very closely on hatred for this nation." For him the real-world choice was between being a good American and romanticizing the Kaiser: "And the Kaiser is certainly nothing to me. I'll certainly feel better on the side of Wilson than on the side of the Kaiser."[17]

The fact that he was not actually *in* the war proved increasingly troubling to him. When Niebuhr told Baltzer that he wanted to become a military chaplain, Bultzer replied that the War Welfare work was too valuable to give up; the war ended before Niebuhr had a chance to wear a military uniform. Gradually Baltzer became a father figure to him, like Samuel Press and like several others afterward, all of whom supported Niebuhr personally, opened doors for him professionally, and gave him models of social Christian leadership. During the war he and Baltzer were consumed with the problem of securing German-American loyalty as a means of victory; Niebuhr urged that a victory aided by American intervention would make possible a new world order based on reconciliation, democracy, free trade, and the League of Nations. The Paris Peace Conference rudely punctured his belief that the war was a means to achieve Wilsonian democratic ideals; before the conference ended, Niebuhr judged that it was a disaster for the cause of a just world order: "Wilson is a typical son of the manse. He believes too much in words." The war victors let Wilson cover their deeds with fine words, he observed, but the deeds were vengeful and wrong. While clinging to the hope that Wilson's democratic faith might still prevail—"words have certain meanings of which it is hard to rob them, and ideas may create reality in time"—Niebuhr worried that liberalism was fatally flawed as a means to create a just world order. He declared in the *New Republic* that liberal idealism "lacks the spirit of enthusiasm, not to say fanaticism, which is so necessary to move the world out of its beaten tracks. [It] is too intellectual and too little emotional to be an efficient force in history." The Versailles Treaty showed the weakness of the liberal alternative to the old order: "We need something less circumspect than liberalism to save the world."[18]

That sentiment eventually made Niebuhr famous, though he still assumed that the purpose of good politics is to save the world. Bethel Church grew tremendously in the early 1920s, feeding off the skyrocketing growth of Henry Ford's Detroit, despite Niebuhr's continued absences. Not coincidentally, the church also voted to worship exclusively in the English language. Americanization was the wave of the future in the Evangelical Synod, and Niebuhr was its apostle. He became a star attraction on the college and church conference lecture circuit, which attracted new members to his congregation. Niebuhr combined a highly charged intellectual message on an expanding variety of social themes with a constantly animated, whirling, gesticulating style of speaking. In 1922 he caught the attention of Charles Clayton Morrison, who was looking for someone to keep the *Christian Century* interesting while Morrison concentrated on the peace issue. Niebuhr became Morrison's fire hydrant of political and religious opinions, honing his distinctively dialectical, aggressive, ironic writing style in a profusion of *Century* editorials, articles, and reviews. Though Morrison paid him only for unsigned editorials, Niebuhr's were never hard to pick out, and Morrison could never get enough of them. "Just send them in," he urged in 1923, "and as many as possible, and as often as possible. You have the right touch."[19]

Morrison became another one of Niebuhr's father figures, as did Detroit Episcopal bishop Charles Williams, who pushed Niebuhr toward democratic socialism, and Sherwood Eddy, who founded (with Kirby Page) the Fellowship for a Christian Social Order in 1921. In 1922 Niebuhr and Williams founded a

Detroit branch of the FCSO that was strongly prolabor, though not explicitly socialist. At Williams's urging, Niebuhr for the first time studied Rauschenbusch's writings, which disabused him of the impression that Rauschenbusch's socialism was dangerously utopian. In 1923 Williams died of a heart attack, leaving a stunned Niebuhr with the sense that he was called to complete his mentor's work. "Nowhere have I seen a personality more luminous with the Christ spirit than in this bishop who was also a prophet," he wrote in his diary. "Here was a man who knew how to interpret the Christian religion so that it meant something in terms of an industrial civilization." To Williams's diocese he wrote, "Your diocese has lost a great bishop, but the church universal has lost infinitely more, it has lost a prophet who had the courage to challenge the complacency of a very self-righteous civilization." The conviction hardened in Niebuhr that being a good American had nothing to do with overlooking America's social evils, especially its class divisions.[20]

In 1923 he took the same Sherwood Eddy tour that Georgia Harkness joined. Niebuhr was predisposed to the convicting effect that the tour had upon Harkness and him. Before he left, he wrote in his diary, "Gradually the whole horrible truth about the war is being revealed. Every new book destroys some further illusion." The war had little to do with battling for or against democratic ideals, he believed; it was simply a struggle for power and economic advantage between two grasping alliances of states. In Europe Niebuhr heard terrible stories about France's mistreatment of Germans in the occupied Ruhr valley, which deepened his resentment of France's punitive attitude toward his ancestral homeland. Upon visiting the Ruhr, in the company of Kirby Page and Episcopal priest Will Scarlett, to see its condition for himself, he witnessed what he called "the closest thing to hell I have ever seen." For three days Niebuhr listened to blood-curdling stories about atrocities and sexual assaults committed by the occupying French forces; he saw severely malnourished German children at the Red Cross centers and families separated by barbed wire. The atrocity stories, atmosphere of hate, and starving children drove him across a line. "This, then, is the glorious issue for which the war was fought!" he bitterly observed. Niebuhr dreamed of sending "every sentimental spellbinder of war days" to the Ruhr and made a resolution: "This is as good a time as any to make up my mind that I am done with the war business. . . . I am done with this business. I hope I can make that resolution stick." He no longer felt pressed to prove his Americanism, and he had lost his other reasons for not being a pacifist; thus he vowed "to try to be a disciple of Christ, rather than a mere Christian, in all human relations and experiment with the potency of trust and love much more than I have in the past."[21]

For nearly ten years he struggled to keep this resolution, all the while objecting that his pacifist colleagues in the FCSO and the Fellowship of Reconciliation were naive and idealistic. Reporting on "the great affliction" in the Ruhr, Niebuhr judged that France's brutal occupation represented the consummation of its "dreams of vengeance." Never an isolationist, he urged that America needed to use its diplomatic leverage to prevent the complete collapse of European civilization. The hopes of Europe rested on England and the United States, because they were the only Western powers not consumed with revenge, "but England is practically powerless because America has withdrawn from European affairs and has left the continent to the tender mercies of French chauvinism." Throughout the 1920s, later as the national executive council chair of the Fellowship of Reconciliation, Niebuhr argued for an aggressively internationalist foreign policy while fearing, as he wrote in the *Christian Century,* that "the principle of nonresistance is too ideal for a sinful human world."[22]

He struggled to be a pacifist while doubting that pacifism always served the end of justice; in the 1920s he moved more gradually, and with much deeper certainty, toward an explicitly socialist politics. "There is no Christian basis to modern industry," Niebuhr wrote in 1923. "It is based upon a purely naturalistic conception of life and cynically defies every spiritual appreciation of human beings. Christianity has had nothing to do with the organization of industrial civilization. It ought therefore to have no pride in it." He was not quite ready to come out for socialism; the examples of Rauschenbusch and Vida Scudder notwithstanding, it was still uncommon for liberal social gospelers to explicitly endorse socialist politics and economics. But Eddy and Page were socialists, the FCSO was socialist in all but name, and in the mid-1920s Niebuhr spent much of his time touring the country as the FCSO's traveling secretary. Increasingly he chided the kind of Christians who "enjoyed their theological liberalism" but were terrified "of even the mildest economic and political heresy."[23] In 1926 he charged that Henry Ford's reputation as a good employer was a product of self-deception and relentless self-promotion, like that of American capitalism. Ford was both naive and cunning, Niebuhr wrote in the *Christian Century;* he actually believed that as long as he paid the generous wages for which he was famous—which Niebuhr showed he was, in fact, no longer paying—his workers didn't need unemployment insurance, old-age pensions, and disability compensation. Sarcastically Niebuhr pronounced that Henry Ford was a perfect symbol of American civilization; elsewhere he remarked, "What a civilization this is! Naive gentlemen with a genius for mechanics suddenly become the arbiters over the lives and fortunes of hundreds of thousands." By 1928 Niebuhr was voting for Socialist presidential candidate Norman Thomas; the following year he joined the Socialist Party.[24]

Niebuhr's socialist turn caused his first public rift with Morrison. Though Morrison was also a sharp critic of Henry Ford, he steered away from broadsides against American capitalism and concentrated on two issues: peace and temperance. For Morrison, the presidential election of 1928 came down to a choice between what he saw as the foreign policy imperialism and antilabor politics of President Herbert Hoover and the Catholic anti-Prohibitionism of Democratic candidate Al Smith. On the ground that temperance was a trump in the political and cultural circumstances of the moment (and because he regarded traditional Catholicism as un-American in its opposition to democracy and the separation of church and state), Morrison chose Hoover. To Morrison, antimilitarism and temperance were the heart of the social gospel, and in 1928, temperance was in trouble. To give up on Prohibition was to give up the social gospel project of morally transforming American society. Though Smith's politics were otherwise closer than Hoover's to the social agenda of liberal Protestantism, Smith seemed to care nothing about the politics of moral community. As a Catholic he dealt with the politically delicate problem of religion by adopting a secular, instrumentalist approach to politics that ignored religious concerns. That approach would never create a good society, the *Christian Century* editorialized.[25]

Niebuhr did not support Smith, either, and as late as October 1927 he declared that Smith's "hopelessly wet" opposition to Prohibition was beyond the pale for those who cared about the moral character of America. He could not support a candidate who proposed to weaken the Volstead Act and repeal the eighteenth amendment. Smith had no appreciation of "puritan virtues and values," Niebuhr complained, which made democrats like himself politically homeless. But when the election season arrived, Niebuhr criticized Morrison for making temperance the holy grail of American politics. While assuring that he still supported Prohibition, Niebuhr urged that if Prohibition could be saved only by swallowing Hoover's right-wing economic policies and imperialist adventures in Latin America, then Prohibition had to be sacrificed. As usual, liberal Protestantism was too moralistic. To be truly progressive, liberal Protestantism had to give higher priority to economic justice than to moral purity. For those who were too timid to vote Socialist, the only morally defensible choice was Smith—a claim that made no moral or logical sense at all to Morrison. This disagreement foreshadowed the break between the liberalism of the postwar social gospel and what came to be called Christian realism.[26]

Throughout the 1920s Niebuhr filled the *Christian Century* with calls for a "robust" faith in human possibilities while warning that all "immediate evidences" contradicted this faith. Modern civilization needed a fusion of reason and religiously inspired good will, he argued; at the same time, liberal Christianity grievously overestimated human virtue. In his first book, *Does Civilization Need Religion?* (1927), Niebuhr collected his favorite variations on this doubleminded theme, arguing that religion was "dying in modern civilization" because it came into conflict with a triumphant modern science and because it failed to apply its ethical and social resources to solve "the moral problems of modern civilization." The answer to the first problem, yet to be completed, was the victory of the liberal reconceptualization of theology. The second problem was his subject. Christian idealism was the key to the answer, Niebuhr assured, but modern Christian idealism had to change, beginning with its relinquishment of nationalism and greed: "If Christian idealists are to make religion socially effective they will be forced to detach themselves from the dominant secular desires of the nations as well as from the greed of economic groups." Any religious idealism that did not forcefully advocate "the equalization of living standards" stood convicted of "insincerity and moral confusion."[27]

Echoing Ernst Troeltsch, Niebuhr instructed that Christianity is the fate of Western civilization: "Spiritual idealisms of other cultures and societies may aid it in reclaiming its own highest resources; and any universal religion capable of inspiring an ultimately unified world culture may borrow from other religions. But the task of redeeming Western society rests in a peculiar sense upon Christianity." Niebuhr did not claim to know if there was still time to save Western civilization from moral bankruptcy; what he did know was that modern society could not be saved without the inspiring and culture-forming influence of a renewed Christian idealism: "Civilization may be beyond moral redemption; but if it is to be redeemed a religiously inspired moral idealism must aid in the task." The ideal of ethical freedom is implicit in human character, he asserted, "and awakened personalities will seek to realize that ideal." *Does Civilization Need Religion?* was half-filled with the language of crisis, collapsing civilizations, and human fallibility, yet Niebuhr assured that old-style, idealistic, spirit-over-nature liberal Christianity was still the answer: "It is the virtue of a vital religious idealism that it lifts life above the level of nature and makes the development of an ethical personality the ultimate goal of human existence." The work of religion was to advance the ideal realm of personality in the face of impersonal social and natural forces.[28]

Does Civilization Need Religion? was written mostly in 1924 and 1925; by the time it was published in 1927, Niebuhr's politics had moved further left. Increasingly he resolved the contradiction between his warnings of civilizational crisis and his optimistic idealism by appealing to a hard-edged socialism; to his delight, the book brought a windfall of lecture invitations and new choices. For several years, while Niebuhr kept a foot in the door at Bethel Church, his mentors jockeyed to gain his full-time services. He spoke occasionally for the Evangelical Synod but disappointed Baltzer by seeking a larger stage. He wrote profusely for Morrison but turned down his requests to join the *Christian Century* as a full-time associate. He spoke frequently for the FCSO but backed out of an Eddy-Page proposal to join the evangelism team of Henry P. Van Dusen and Samuel Shoemaker. In 1927 Niebuhr was offered an academic position at Boston University, where his sister Hulda taught Christian education; he politely declined but told Eddy and other friends that he could be tempted to teach at the right seminary.

Eddy and Page promptly put together a New York package: half-time as an editor at Page's journal, *The World Tomorrow,* and half-time as a teacher of social ethics at Union Theological Seminary. Because Union had no funds for a new position, Eddy promised Union president Henry Sloane Coffin that he would pay Niebuhr's entire salary for the first year. Coffin, then in his second year as Union's president, surmised that Niebuhr might attract ministerial students to the seminary; he believed that during Arthur McGiffert's presidency, Union placed too much emphasis on graduate research at the expense of training students for the ministry. Except for socialist Harry F. Ward, Union's professors were less excited than Coffin at the prospect of having Niebuhr as a colleague. They worried about his lack of academic credentials, which could create the appearance of lowered academic standards; many of Union's starched-collar faculty were also put off by his excited pulpit behavior, rough manners, and Midwestern twang. Coffin countered that since Niebuhr's position would cost Union nothing, the seminary had little to lose by approving the appointment; that argument barely prevailed, as the faculty approved Niebuhr's appointment by a single vote. In later life the circumstances of his appointment were too embarrassing for him to remember correctly, and Niebuhr would claim that the faculty called him "to a Chair of Christian Ethics."[29]

CHRISTIAN REALISM AS SOCIALIST FAITH

Niebuhr moved to New York in 1928, accompanied by his mother, and immediately attracted an excited following of students at Union. His mother, who apparently pleaded with him to remain in Detroit, lost her partnership with him in the Lord's work, and thus felt abandoned; his students exulted that Niebuhr's engaging personality and brash, electric, opinionated lectures made politics and religion come alive. Students overflowed his classroom and crowded around him in the cafeteria and hallways; to them he was a catalyzing figure who opened Union Seminary to the outside world. To the reserved, scholarly Scots who dominated Union's senior faculty, he was hard to take. Theologically Union was steeped in the social gospel, and William Adams Brown was a major figure in international Christian ecumenism, but the Union faculty was short on figures who addressed secular society. Senior faculty members such as Brown, church historian James Moffatt, and biblical theologian Ernest Findlay Scott shuddered at Niebuhr's wild generalizations, his radical friends, his unrefined manners, and the fact that students called him "Reinie." Brown lamented that Niebuhr was heading down the same socialist path that Brown's former star student at Union, Norman Thomas, had taken on his exit from the ministry. The tremendous student reaction to Niebuhr, however, and the fact that Yale Divinity School tried to steal him in 1929, convinced Coffin that Niebuhr was indispensable to Union; he countered Yale's offer by appointing Niebuhr to the Dodge Professorship in Applied Christianity. Niebuhr felt the irony of his academic success; in later life he confessed that ten years passed before he did not feel like a fraud in the classroom.

Upon arriving at Union he plunged immediately into the crosscurrents of New York radical politics. Niebuhr's editorial position at the Christian pacifist-socialist *World Tomorrow* gave him a base of intellectual influence, including access to intellectuals and activist leaders such as John Dewey, Norman Thomas, John Haynes Holmes, and Edmund Chaffee. He joined the leftist New York Teachers' Union, Paul Douglas's League for Independent Political Action, and Norman Thomas's League for Industrial Democracy. After Thomas received an embarrassing 267,000 votes in the 1928 election, Niebuhr joined the Socialist Party. The rise of Thomas, a former Presbyterian minister and Rauschenbusch social gospeler, to the top of the Socialist Party allowed Niebuhr and other Christian progressives to join the party, which was no longer dominated by the anticlerical types that Rauschenbusch avoided. The onset of the Great Depression confirmed Niebuhr's fears about the crisis of capitalist civilization. In 1930, along with Eddy, Page, and social ethicist John C. Bennett, he cofounded the radical Fellowship of Socialist Christians, which became Niebuhr's primary organizational outlet. Other members included Christian socialists Roswell Barnes, Buell Gallagher, Francis Henson, and Frank Wilson, and shortly afterward, Paul Tillich and Eduard Heimann. The rising figures of a new theological generation stopped using euphemisms for socialism and called for the abolition of private industrial property.[30]

Niebuhr believed that his radical turn took him well beyond the boundaries of liberal Christianity. For years he had preached an idealistic religion of pacifism, political reform, and liberal theology while complaining that liberal Christianity was too soft to confront the evils of the world. He called for moral efforts to redeem American society while warning that moral idealism had little power. In the early 1930s, these awkwardly mixed feelings and the terrible human wreckage of the Great Depression drove him to a sterner creed. In his experience liberal Christianity was overwhelmingly bourgeois, moralistic, enamored with modern progress, and overtrusting in its hope for a community of love. Typically it reduced politics to moral striving and religion to moral striving and personal faith. Fosdick added aesthetic appeals and Mathews appealed to the authority of science, but these were poor substitutes for the prophetic Christianity that was needed. The seeds of this critique of liberal Christianity were scattered throughout Niebuhr's early writings, but in the early years of the Great Depression he came to the verdict that even his socialist friends who remained pacifists or idealists were part of the problem. Many of them were stunned to find the core of their faith dismissed in Niebuhr's frosty jeremiad, *Moral Man and Immoral Society.* With the publication of this socioethical and political blockbuster in 1932, old-style American liberal theology was dethroned.

In 1932 Niebuhr ran for Congress on the Socialist Party ticket and told New Yorkers that only socialism could save Western civilization. He warned readers of *Harper's* magazine that "it will be practically impossible to secure social change in America without the use of very considerable violence."[31] *Moral Man and Immoral Society* was published a month after Niebuhr won only 4 percent of the vote. In the book he drew back from his posturing about "considerable violence," but he repudiated any kind of progressive politics that failed to recognize that politics is about struggling for power. His tone was icy, aggressive, and eerily omniscient, ridiculing the moral idealism of liberal Christianity and marking the end of his calls to build the kingdom of God. Niebuhr argued that while individuals are occasionally capable of self-transcending virtue or altruism, human groups never willingly subordinate their interests to the interests of others. Morality belongs to the individual sphere of action; individuals occasionally act out of self-disregarding compassion or love, Niebuhr allowed, but groups never overcome the power of self-interest and collective egotism that sustains their existence. The liberal Christian attempt to moralize society was therefore not only futile but stupid.[32]

With this book, "stupid" became Niebuhr's favorite epithet. He argued that because liberal idealists failed to recognize the brutal character of human groups and the resistance of all groups to moral suasion, they were always driven to "unrealistic and confused political thought." Secular liberals like John Dewey appealed to reason, and Christian liberals typically appealed to love in their struggles for a just society, but both strategies were hopelessly inadequate. In their practical effects, both strategies were maddeningly stupid. *Moral Man and Immoral Society* seethed with Niebuhr's anger at the human ravages of the Depression and his frustration at America's aversion to socialism. The book embraced a Christian variant of Marxism, which provided an explanation for the impending collapse of bourgeois civilization and an antidote to the pious moralism of liberal Christianity. "The full maturity of American capitalism will inevitably be followed by the emergence of the American Marxian proletarian," Niebuhr predicted. "Marxian socialism is a true enough interpretation of what the industrial worker feels about society and history, to have become the accepted social and political philosophy of all self-conscious and politically intelligent industrial workers."[33]

Like Christianity at its best, Marxism was both realistic and utopian; it had a tragic view of history that was tempered by its hope for the transformation of history. Niebuhr lectured that liberal Christianity needed to regain the realistic Christian sense of the tragedy of life: "The perennial tragedy of human history is that those who cultivate the spiritual elements usually do so by divorcing themselves from or misunderstanding the problems of collective man, where the brutal elements are most obvious. These problems remain unsolved, and force clashes with force, with nothing to mitigate the brutalities or eliminate the futilities of the social struggle." The historical sweep of human life will always reflect the predatory world of nature, Niebuhr admonished. For that reason he gave up his vow to follow Jesus as a pacifist, citing Augustine's dictum that to the end of history "the peace of the world must be gained by strife." For the sake of justice *and* peace, modern Christianity was obliged to renounce its sentimental idealism: "If the mind and the spirit of man does not attempt the impossible, if it does not seek to conquer or to eliminate nature but tries only to make the forces of nature the servants of the human spirit and the instruments of the moral ideal, a progressively higher justice and more stable peace can be achieved."[34]

Liberal Protestant leaders howled that Niebuhr ignored the teachings of Jesus, he had no theology of the church or the kingdom, and his faith in God's socially regenerative power was nonexistent. Norman Thomas and John Haynes Holmes both lambasted Niebuhr's "defeatism," while Yale theologian Robert Calhoun, Union theologian Henry Van Dusen, and World Student Christian Federation leader Francis Pickens Miller all complained that Niebuhr's theology relinquished any notion of a socially transformative presence of God in history. Stunned by Niebuhr's aggressive sarcasm against Christian moralism, Charles Gilkey, dean of the chapel at the University of Chicago, declared to his family that "Reinie's gone crazy."[35] Most important to Niebuhr, the *Christian Century* mourned that "pessimism can speak no gloomier word." Morrison assigned the book for review to Niebuhr's friend, Chicago pastor Theodore C. Hume, who declared that "to call the book fully Christian in tone is to travesty the heart of Jesus' message to the world." *Moral Man and Immoral Society* contained a "tonic rigor" in its broadside against the social meliorism of liberal Christianity, Hume acknowledged, but the book quickly took on a "darker hue of cynicism" that eventually hardened to "unrelieved pessimism." Hume shook his head at Niebuhr's pronouncement that the religion of Rufus Jones offered nothing of value to modern Christians who sought to discern the social meaning of their faith. He chided Niebuhr for offering "a fainter sprinkling of theology than might have been expected from a professor of Christian ethics." He worried that Niebuhr's pessimism made him a spiritual bedfellow of religious conservatives; in the meantime, Hume declared, many of Niebuhr's true friends "are still bold enough to believe in the potency of the Christian 'good news,' for society as well as for man's inner life."[36]

ATTACKING LIBERAL THEOLOGY: NIEBUHR, IDEALISM, AND MYTH

The impassioned liberal outcry against his book heightened Niebuhr's sense of alienation from liberal Protestantism and gave him plenty of grist for his attacks upon it; he aggressively defended his position, especially on the sensitive point of his personal faith. "My conclusions are not in accord with liberal Christianity," he acknowledged. "I believe that liberalism has sentimentalized the message of Jesus beyond all recognition. But I fail to see why that should make my book unchristian in tone. I am trying honestly to find the relevance between the message of Jesus and the problems of our day. I may be mistaken in my conclusions, but my conclusions have no unchristian motive or purpose." It was true that his emphasis on human sinfulness made him sound like a conservative, he allowed, but that was only because liberal Protestantism had forsaken its biblical and classical roots on this subject: "I hold it to be the chief sin of liberalism that it has given selfish man an entirely too good opinion of himself." Liberal theology was wrong in its politics and its theology for this reason. Politically it was too comfortable in its moralistic middle-class idealism; theologically it was too humanistic: "In general my position has developed theologically to the right and politically to the left of modern liberal Protestantism. If such a position seems unduly cynical and pessimistic to the American mind my own feeling is that this judgment is due to the fact that the American mind is still pretty deeply immersed in the sentimentalities of a dying culture."[37]

That *Moral Man and Immoral Society* attacked liberal Christianity from the socialist political left was clear enough to Niebuhr's critics. That he was turning into some kind of theological conservative was a more ambiguous proposition. Theological liberals were inclined to protest that he gave comfort to conservatives, but their strongest charge was that Niebuhr's thinking had little or no faith in divine power of any kind. Niebuhr's eagerness to affirm his kinship to orthodoxy was fueled by the religious criticisms that he received from liberals and influenced by the penetrating criticism that he received from his brother Helmut.

His brother's critique was loaded with familial weight. In 1931, Helmut Richard Niebuhr had accepted a theology position at Yale Divinity School and started going by his "American" middle name; the same year Reinhold suddenly ended his longtime bachelor status by marrying a visiting English fellow at Union, Ursula Keppel-Compton, deeply wounding Lydia Niebuhr.

In a rare moment of unconflicted celebration, Richard rejoiced at his brother's marriage and offered to take responsibility for their mother; the following year the two brothers squared off, in the only public disagreement of their careers, over the moral responsibility of American Christians to respond to the Japanese invasion of Manchuria. Should American Christians call for an economic embargo against Japan, despite the possibility that such a response might lead to war? In the *Christian Century,* Richard made a Christian non-interventionist case for "the grace of doing nothing," arguing that God has God's own plans for history, and it is not the calling of Christians to make history come out right. Reinhold replied that justice is the highest attainable ideal in the sphere of social and political relations, and Christians are called to secure justice; there is no grace to be found in doing nothing. Responding to this reply, Richard disclaimed any interest in "demolishing my opponent's position—which our thirty years' war has shown me to be impossible."[38]

For many years Richard had competed with his brother, assisted him, and looked up to him; outside the public eye, the two regularly scrutinized each other's work. Repeatedly they had argued about Japan before allowing their disagreement to be aired in public. Richard clung to a pacifist understanding of the way of Jesus, but not for liberal reasons. Theologically he shared more with the rising Barthian movement (though not in method or Christology) than with the liberal tradition. In January 1933, amid the liberal outcry against *Moral Man and Immoral Society,* he seized the chance to dislodge Reinhold from his essentially liberal perspective.[39]

"I have no defense of idealism to offer. I hate it with all my heart as an expression of our original sin," Richard wrote. The problem was that for all the critical pounding that he took from liberal idealists, Reinhold was still an idealist in his thinking about human nature and religion. With regard to the virtue of "moral man," for example, Richard pointedly asked him to consider the phenomenon of brotherly love: "I hate to look at my brotherly love for you to see how it is compounded with personal pride." First there was the pride of basking in Reinhold's reflected glory, which was painfully mixed, in Richard's experience, with the selfish pride of "trying to stand on my own feet, trying to live up to you, being jealous of you . . . enough to make one vomit." Richard reasoned that if he could love Reinhold despite the layerings of evil pride and jealousy that pervaded their relationship, "it isn't because any ideal or will to love prevails over my putrid instinct and desire, but because something else which is not my will was at work long before I had a will or an ideal." The moral gift that human beings possess is a gift of judging right and wrong, not a gift of goodness, he explained. All morally reflective people know that they are bad. Therefore Richard rejected his brother's claim that individual selves are morally superior to the groups to which they belong: "The apparently more decent behavior of men in face-to-face relationships is not due at all to any element of reason or of moral idealism, any inclination of the will, but to the fact that there is more coercion, more enlightened self-interest (because the relations are more easily seen) and more possibility of identifying ourselves with the other man and loving ourselves in him or her." Richard did not deny the existence of ideals; he denied that ideals are effective in influencing human action.[40]

More important was the fact that Reinhold still conceived religion in thoroughly liberal terms. "You think of religion as a power—dangerous sometimes, helpful sometimes," Richard observed. "That's liberal. For religion itself religion is no power, but that to which religion is directed, God." Besides preserving the liberal notion of the self as a rational agent possessed of a nature-transcending spiritual power of goodwill, Reinhold preserved the liberal idea that religion is saving and transformative. Richard countered, "I think the liberal religion is thoroughly bad. It is a first-aid to hypocrisy. It is the exaltation of goodwill, moral idealism. It worships the God whose qualities are 'the human qualities raised to the nth degree,' and I don't expect as much help from this religion as you do. It is sentimental and romantic. Has it ever struck you that you read religion through the mystics and ascetics? You scarcely think of Paul, Augustine, Luther, Calvin. You're speaking of humanistic religion so far as I can see. You come close to breaking with it at times but you don't quite do it."

Though Reinhold was the one who emulated and had been favored by their father, implicitly Richard admonished Reinhold that their family's faith was the evangelical religion of Paul, Augustine, Luther, and Calvin. For Reinhold, as for liberal Christianity, religion was an energizing power that served human needs and dictated human responsibilities. Richard exhorted him to break away from this human-centered moralization of Christianity. "I agree wholly with you on the amorality of violence and nonviolence," he allowed. "A pacifism based on the immorality of violence hasn't a leg to stand on. But I do think that an activism which stresses immediate results is the cancer of our modern life." Reinhold's fixation on political issues and his frenetic chasing after causes were spiritually dessicating. "We want to be saviors of civilization and simply bring down new destruction," Richard admonished. "You are about ready to break with that activism. I think I discern that."[41]

Richard Niebuhr was wrong about his brother's break from activist religion. Liberal Christianity took for granted that religion is supposed to be a power for social good, and so did Reinhold Niebuhr. For Reinhold, as for the liberal tradition, religion was a human construct, grounded in human moral and religious strivings, that was made possible by humanity's unique capacities for transcendence, good, and evil. To the extent that he reflected at all upon nature beyond human nature, he regarded the natural world as the servant of human need and gratification. Reinhold could never embrace a religion that refused to save civilization; for him the liberal, specifically Troeltschian or social gospel view of religion as energy for the social struggle was a core assumption. He could never say, and must have felt chastised at being told, that activism is the cancer of modern life. His realistic turn was a critique of the way that the social gospelers went about trying to save and transform civilization, not a rejection of the social gospel project. For all the criticism that he took from liberal social gospelers, Reinhold could never turn away from the cause of creating a just world order.

But Richard may have perceived that his brother was newly open to their evangelical roots, which differed from the evangelical stream of liberal theology. Evangelical liberalism fixated on the religion of Jesus and the social meaning of the kingdom ideal; while censuring Reinhold for writing as though Paul and Calvin never existed, Richard may have surmised, correctly, that his brother was ready to reclaim at least part of their family's classical Lutheran-Calvinist heritage. In the closing pages of his next book, *Reflections on the End of an Era,* Reinhold invoked the themes of divine providence and grace in a way that reassured Morrison and Union colleague Henry Van Dusen, who had worried that Niebuhr was losing his faith. Throughout the 1930s his writings became increasingly religious and theological, invoking the classical themes of divine transcendence, grace, providence, judgment, and justification by grace through faith. At the end of the decade Niebuhr reflected that "even while imagining myself to be preaching the Gospel, I had really experimented with many modern alternatives to Christian faith, until one by one they proved unavailing."[42]

Niebuhr's polemical relation to liberal Protestantism heightened as a consequence of this theological turn and his deepening political radicalism. In *Reflections on the End of an Era,* his most explicitly Marxist work, he declared that liberal Christianity was too soft to provide or endorse the emancipatory alternative that was needed. Reformists like Shailer Mathews and Franklin D. Roosevelt were kidding themselves; there was no third way between capitalism and socialism. Modern technology made intranational cooperation and international reciprocity absolutely necessary, but capitalism made justice and cooperation impossible. The ravages of capitalist injustice could not be removed by moral effort, because injustice, exploitation, and imperialism were not mere by-products of capitalist modernization; they were constitutive in the structure of capitalism itself. Niebuhr declared, "If Christianity is to survive this era of social disintegration and social rebuilding, and is not to be absorbed in or annihilated by the secularized religion of Marxism it must come to terms with the insights of Marxist mythology." Though he allowed that Marxism was naive and utopian in its own way—Niebuhr never bought the Marxist dream of a stateless communism—he insisted that Marx's theory of the class struggle and his critique of the capitalist modes of production and distribution were more valuable than all the preachings of moral reformers.[43]

Niebuhr's next book blasted liberal Christianity from the religious side. In *An Interpretation of Christian Ethics* (1935), he charged that "liberal Christian literature abounds in the monotonous reiteration of the pious hope that people might be good and loving." Shailer Mathews was a favorite target. Niebuhr ridiculed

Mathews's "strikingly naive" idealism, which called Christians to be "champions of the underprivileged" without giving moral sanction to the underprivileged themselves to fight for their interests. For Niebuhr, Mathews's idealism epitomized the moralistic stupidity of the liberal approach to politics, and his myth-dispensing modernism typified what was wrong with liberal theology. Niebuhr argued that the basic defect of liberal theology was its mistaken approach to Christian myth. In effect, he judged, liberal theology amounted to a reverse fundamentalism. Liberal theology rightly contended that the myths of the Bible are myths, but liberal theologians like Mathews spoiled this recognition and reduced Christianity to superficial bromides by failing to appropriate the religious meaning of Christian myth. Traditional orthodoxy was hopelessly wrong because it insisted on taking Christian myths literally, Niebuhr explained; liberal theology was equally wrong because it refused to take Christian myths seriously: "It is the genius of true myth to suggest the dimension of depth in reality and to point to a realm of essence which transcends the surface of history, on which the cause-effect sequences, discovered and analyzed by science, occur."[44]

His thinking about religious myth was crucially influenced by Paul Tillich, who fled Nazi Germany in 1933 and, on Niebuhr's initiative, joined Niebuhr at Union Theological Seminary. Tillich's approach to the problem was formulated in the 1920s, only a few years after he barely survived four years of duty as a German chaplain in World War I. The colossal brutality and evil of the war drove him to two nervous breakdowns and influenced his subsequent preoccupation with the mythic nature of religion. He argued that myth is a symbolic expression of the relation of human beings to that which concerns them ultimately, not merely a prescientific explanation of events in the world; myth is the essential mode of encounter with the sacred. It is the language of faith, which, as the "universal category of the religious as such," cannot be eliminated without negating faith. Against the liberal attempt to replace the language of myth with a nonmythical religious symbolism or discourse, Tillich countered that myth is an essential element in all cultural and intellectual endeavor, and, in its "broken" form, the key to whatever is true in religion.[45]

Tillich and Niebuhr subsequently developed this theory of the mythic nature of religion and its accompanying concept of religion as the dimension of depth in life. For Niebuhr, as for Tillich, religious myth pointed to "the ultimate ground of existence and its ultimate fulfillment." Myth is a product of human spirituality that symbolically expresses human experiences of sacred power or presence in the natural realm, Niebuhr argued. If taken literally, the Christian myths of divine creation, the fall of humankind, and the double nature of Christ are absurd; but if taken as myths, they are religiously deep in meaning. The myth of the fall was his bellwether example. Orthodox Christianity makes absurd claims about the fall as an historical event, he noted, but at least orthodoxy takes with utter seriousness the biblical notion that human nature is thoroughly corrupted by sin. On this count, traditional orthodoxy tended to be more profound, religiously, than liberal Christianity, which failed to take seriously the defining myths of Christianity. Having dispensed with a literalistic reading of the fall, for example, liberal Christianity degenerated into a culture religion that substituted the Enlightenment myths of progress and human perfectibility for the biblical idea of human fallenness.[46]

In the scriptural story of the fall, Adam and Eve brought sin into a sinless world by defying the command of a jealous God not to eat the fruit of the tree of knowledge. In liberal Christianity, Niebuhr observed, the effort to overcome literalism, anthropomorphism, and supernaturalism produced a theology that reduced the meaning of this story to an expression of the fears of primitive people toward higher powers. Having repudiated a mistaken appropriation of religious myth, liberal Christianity typically proceeded to discard the myth of the fall altogether. But the religious truth of the fall is precisely what is crucially lacking in liberal Christianity, Niebuhr argued. The biblical image of a jealous creator is not a dispensable anthropomorphism but a mythical depiction of the human situation; the root of human evil is the prideful human pretension of being God. As creatures made in the image of God, human beings possess capacities for self-transcendence that enable them to become aware of their finite existence in distinction from, though constitutive with, God's infinite existence. The same awareness moves human beings, however, to attempt to overcome their finiteness by becoming infinite, like God. This was Adam's sin. Fundamentally, evil is always a good that imagines itself to be better than it is. Evil is driven by egotism, which is always wrapped in self-deceit and deceit of others. Thus the biblical myth of the fall is not a dispensable relic of primitive fear and superstition, Niebuhr reasoned, "but a revelation of a tragic reality of life." The truth of the myth is attested to by every page of human history.[47]

Niebuhr affirmed that he was seeking to refurbish the classical doctrine of original sin, though not in any of its classical forms. Rightly understood, he contended, the myth of original sin is not an account of the literal origin of evil or a theory of biologically transmitted evil; Augustine's notion that original sin is transmitted through lust in the act of procreation is self-defeating, because it destroys the basis for moral responsibility that Christian morality requires.[48] If original sin is an inherited corruption, human beings lack the freedom to choose not to sin and thus cannot be held morally responsible for being in sin. For Niebuhr, the true meaning of original sin was existential, not biological. Its reality is attested by history, but original sin itself is not historical. Just as the myth of the fall is a description of the nature of evil rather than account of the origin of evil, so the reality of original sin is an inevitable fact of human existence but not an inherited corruption of existence. The human capacity for self-transcendence makes original sin inevitable; though it has no history, original sin is a reality "in every moment of existence." Niebuhr concentrated his reoriented religious thinking on this paradoxical truism; his major theological work, *The Nature and Destiny of Man,* was based upon it: sin is an inevitable existential corruption for which human beings are morally responsible.[49]

An Interpretation of Christian Ethics thus delineated Niebuhr's relation to theological liberalism and conservatism, his understanding of religious myth, and his theory of original sin, but all of this was prolegomena to the book's crucial delineative exercise. For years his friends, critics, and brother Richard challenged him to spell out his relation to the faith and teaching of Jesus. In 1934, Niebuhr resigned from the Fellowship of Reconciliation, dramatically declaring that Christian pacifism was too consumed with its own sense of virtue to make gains toward justice. "Recognizing, as liberal Christianity does not, that the world of politics is full of demonic forces, we have chosen on the whole to support the devil of vengeance against the devil of hypocrisy," he announced. He chose to support Marxist vengeance, knowing there was a devil in it, rather than choose the devil of hypocrisy and thereby avoid conflict and preserve the status quo. Those who tried to avoid any traffic with devils simply made themselves accomplices to injustice and potential accomplices to genocide, he judged; moral purity was an illusion.[50]

These were political arguments, however; they did not challenge the religious claims of Christian pacifists like Fosdick, Harkness, Scudder, Page, John Haynes Holmes, Walter Russell Bowie, Edmund Chaffee, Richard Roberts, and John Nevin Sayre. These Christian leaders appealed primarily to the nonviolent way of Jesus as the normative way of Christian discipleship. Niebuhr surmised that most mainline church members probably did not share the pacifism of their leaders, but in the mid-1930s, virtually all of America's mainline Protestant churches officially declared that they would never support another war. Between 1934 and 1936, "the war business" was unequivocally renounced by the Disciples of Christ, the Episcopal Church, the Northern Baptist Convention, the General Council of Congregational and Christian Churches, both of the major Presbyterian churches, and both of the major Methodist Episcopal churches. Niebuhr's break from Christian pacifism thus occurred at the moment of its strongest influence in American life, which explains some of the immense influence that he later achieved in American Protestantism. The specter of American Christendom actually embracing pacifism was alarming to him. His resignation from the Fellowship of Reconciliation spelled out his political reasons for renouncing pacifism, but he knew that for him to seriously challenge the pacifistic ethos of American liberal Protestantism, he had to challenge its prevailing understanding of the teaching and way of Jesus.

A fateful rejoinder by Holmes pressed this point home to Niebuhr in a very personal way. A prominent Unitarian pacifist, John Haynes Holmes was appalled by Niebuhr's recent religious and political turn, especially his Marxist revolutionism. *Reflections on the End of an Era* exhausted his patience with Niebuhr; from his standpoint, the book was not even slightly Christian. Lashing back at Niebuhr's attacks on liberal Christianity, Holmes repudiated Niebuhr's "growing dogmatism of temper, his flat repudiation of idealism, his cynical contempt for the morally minded, his pessimistic abandonment of the world to its own unregenerate devices, and his desperate flight to the unrealities of theological illusion." Then Holmes got nasty; it offended him that Niebuhr dismissed the faith of Jesus while laying claim to the Christian name. Holmes declared: "It is clear enough that Jesus' serene trust in human nature, his stern acclaim of the moral law, his utter reliance upon spiritual forces, his sunny optimism, his radiant passion, would all have seemed a little ridiculous to Niebuhr. The latter would not have opposed the Man of Galilee, but he certainly would have despised him. And with what relief he would have turned to the 'cynical and realistic' Pilate. Pilate as the man of the hour!"[51]

This attack deeply offended Niebuhr, for Holmes was ridiculing his claim to a personal relationship with Christ. After Niebuhr protested Holmes's "monstrous" unfairness, Holmes insisted that he remained Niebuhr's friend. His criticisms were motivated as much by friendship and pastoral concern as by his religious and social commitments, he explained; he was merely seeking to minister to Niebuhr's "distintegration, confusion, and breakdown." Niebuhr's recent writings displayed "a tragic instance of intellectual and spiritual bankruptcy" that Holmes, as a friend, offered to name correctly.[52]

Niebuhr told his real friends that he despised Holmes, but the episode was clarifying to him; it confirmed that he had to explain what he did not believe about the teaching or way of Jesus. He did not believe it was socially relevant. On one crucial point, he allowed, Christian liberals like Mathews grasped the true character of Jesus's teaching. Mathews argued that Jesus's teaching was not about getting justice, but about giving it. Mathews's mistake was to claim that a relevant social ethic could be derived from Jesus's ethic of love perfectionism. Niebuhr asserted his alternative starkly; in later years he admitted that it was too stark: "The ethic of Jesus does not deal at all with the immediate moral problem of every human life—the problem of attempting some kind of armistice between various contending factions and forces. It has nothing to say about the relativities of politics and economics, nor of the necessary balances of power which exist and must exist in even the most intimate social relationships."[53]

The teachings of Jesus are counsels of perfection, not prescriptions for social order or justice, Niebuhr argued. They have nothing to say about how a good society should be organized and lack any horizontal point of reference and any hint of prudential calculation. The points of reference in Jesus's teaching are always vertical, defining the moral ideal for individuals in their relationship to God. Jesus called his followers to forgive because God forgives; he called them to love their enemies because God's love is impartial. He did not teach that enmity can be transmuted into friendship by returning evil with love. He did not teach his followers that it was their mission to redeem the world through their care or moral effort. These Gandhian admonitions were being read into the teaching of Jesus by liberal Christianity. The ethic of Jesus is an ethic of love perfectionism, Niebuhr admonished. It is socially relevant as a reminder that there is such a thing as a true moral ideal that judges all forms of social order or rule. But as a perfectionistic ideal, it offers no guidance on how to hold the world in check until the coming of the kingdom. It offers no direct guidance whatsoever on the central problem of politics, which is the problem of justice.

The problem of justice is always the problem of how to gain, sustain, and defend a relative balance of power. "The very essence of politics is the achievment of justice through equilibria of power," Niebuhr argued. "A balance of power is not conflict; but a tension between opposing forces underlies it. Where there is tension there is potential conflict, and where there is conflict there is potential violence." The justice-making work of politics therefore cannot disavow all resorts to violence; this is the fact that liberal Christianity cannot swallow, Niebuhr observed. Liberal Christian leaders persisted in the illusion that a fully Christianized society would not require coercive violence. Mathews was his favorite example, though Niebuhr did not note the irony that Mathews was not an absolute pacifist. Niebuhr incredulously observed that Mathews had apparently learned nothing since the high tide of the social gospel. He was still contrasting the gospel ethic of cooperation, peace, and love to the politics of revolutionary coercion; he was still claiming that Christianity is committed to a "moral process" of regeneration and not to any economic philosophy. Niebuhr acidly summarized the liberal gospel of Mathews and his kin: "Christianity, in other words, is interpreted as the preaching of a moral ideal, which men do not follow, but which they ought to."[54]

NIEBUHRIAN DELINEATIONS: WALTER MARSHALL HORTON AND JOHN C. BENNETT

Liberal idealism was no match for the civilizational crisis of the Great Depression or the cynical evils of fascism. Niebuhr became a towering figure in American life on the basis of that claim, first as a neo-Marxist opponent of the New Deal, then as a liberal Democat who made his peace with the legacy of Roosevelt's reformism.[55] Despite its initial drubbing in the liberal Christian press, the reputation of *Moral Man and Immoral Society* rose throughout the 1930s as the rise of Nazi fascism made Niebuhr's dark vision seem prophetic. For a younger theological generation that no longer believed the world was getting better, *Moral Man and Immoral Society* marked a turning point; the age of religious idealism had passed, and with it had passed the politics of moral community. While old-style liberals attacked Niebuhr's realist turn as a betrayal of Christianity, chastened younger liberals like John C. Bennett declared that Niebuhr defined reality for a new generation. "The most important fact about contemporary American theology is the disintegration of liberalism," Bennett announced in 1933. A half-generation after it happened in Europe, Protestantism in America witnessed the collapse of its fondest liberal dreams. The liberal language of process, ideals, cooperation, personality, and progress lost its credibility and currency, and while Niebuhr took key liberal assumptions and gains for granted, he and his followers believed they were forging a new path.[56]

Walter Marshall Horton caught and reflected the mood perfectly. A liberal 1920 graduate of Union Theological Seminary, where his teachers were William Adams Brown, Eugene Lyman, Arthur C. McGiffert, Harry F. Ward, and George Albert Coe, Horton taught theology at Oberlin College in the 1930s and wrote a series of influential books on current theological trends.[57] Like Bennett and Fosdick, he distinguished between the Barthians and Niebuhrians who came to their perspective from a liberal background and the increasing number of younger thinkers who started out as Barthians or Niebuhrians; the latter group made him nervous, especially the Barthians. Like Bennett, he argued that the distinctively liberal approach to theology was dead but that much of what the liberal tradition had stood for "must not be allowed to die." In his books the Niebuhrian turn acquired its first sense of feeling like a movement. "I sense a great groundswell of new life in the general 'realistic' tendency of our times, which I believe is capable of furnishing the guiding principles of the new theology that is required," Horton declared in 1934. "I am convinced that the disease of our civilization is deep-rooted, and only radical measures can hope to cure it; but I find in traditional Christianity a deep-going diagnosis of our human predicament and a vast reservoir of divine power and wisdom, without which no program of social change can possibly succeed."[58]

Horton believed that Niebuhr's socialistic neo-orthodoxy was showing the way in theology: "With Reinhold Niebuhr, I find that the attempt to face the exigencies of our times is driving me 'politically to the left, theologically to the right'—thus bringing me into simultaneous relations of sympathy with Christian orthodoxy on the one hand and with social radicalism on the other." He was sensitive to the danger of a cynical liberal-bashing overreaction that cast aside the genuine gains of liberal theology: "*Realpolitik* is an ugly word which will tax all of Reinhold Niebuhr's powers to Christianize! I propose, therefore, that we make it our business, before quitting the camp of liberalism for the camp of realism, to make a fair appraisal of the liberal theology, with a view to carrying over and incorporating into our realistic theology whatever genuine values may be rescued from the wreck, while at the same time candidly recognizing the illusions and shortcomings which have brought the liberal cause to disaster." Fosdick's dictum remained true for Horton: If he had to choose between the old orthodoxy and no religion at all, he would choose to live without religion. Because he saw nothing of this spirit in Karl Barth, Horton believed that Barth's theology offered little constructive guidance to Americans; the slogan of the Barthian movement was "back to Calvin," he noted, but Americans were liberated too recently from Calvinism to be nostalgic for it: "To us, Barthianism seems as wide of the mark on one side as humanism is on the other." In Horton's reading, the Barthian approach adopted a crude realism with respect to humanity and an unreal idealism with respect to God. Thus the new theological departure that was needed would not be Barthian, at least not in the United States.[59]

Though he was repeatedly lumped with Barth for decades afterward as a leading neo-orthodox theologian, Niebuhr took the same view throughout his career. While praising Barth for reintroducing "the note of tragedy in religion," Niebuhr judged in 1928 that Barth's revelational dogmatism amounted to "a new kind of fundamentalism or an old kind of orthodoxy." Barth replaced the liberal Jesus with a dogmatic "Christ-idea," Niebuhr observed. And how was one to know that this Christ idea was absolute and not every bit as subjective as the historical Jesus of liberal theology? "We do not know," Niebuhr answered. "That is simply dogmatically stated. The proof that is offered is the proof of human need." In the Barthian scheme, according to Niebuhr, only the absolute Christ idea could save sinners from a cursed existence that conceived ideals beyond attainments and which lived simultaneously in time and eternity. To accept this absolute was to experience justification by faith. "Here we have the whole pathos of this kind of abstruse theological thought," Niebuhr admonished. "In order to escape the relativism of a theology which is based upon and corrected by biology, psychology, social science, philosophy and every other field of knowledge, we accept a theology which has no way of authenticating itself except by the fact that it meets a human need. This is a sorry victory. Relativism may be defeated but at the price of a new and more terrifying subjectivism."[60]

Two years later, while traveling in Germany, Niebuhr tried to debate a group of Barthians and gave up. "A positivism which stands above reason is not debatable so what's the use?" he wrote to John Bennett. "It is really hopeless to argue with Barthians." The experience confirmed to Niebuhr that his own premises were liberal. The Barthians renounced, and he affirmed, the spiritual authority of reason and experience. Armed with a neo-Reformationist doctrine of the Word of God, the Barthians retreated to the Reformationist way of revelation and faith alone, while Niebuhr believed that faith and salvation are intimately connected to contemporary moral, social, and spiritual experience. Theologically, he judged, Barthianism was a sophisticated form of otherworldliness; ethically it produced a Lutheranlike quietism; theologically and ethically it amounted to "sanctified futilitarianism."[61] Niebuhr admired Barth's resistance to German Christianity after Hitler took power in 1933, but he never stopped thinking of Barthian theology as essentially a dogmatic retreat from the real world and the intellectual problems of modern Christian belief. No religious relief was to be looked for in a theology that so hopelessly renounced its liberal origins.

That is what Niebuhr believed, though it took John Bennett, a more temperate spirit than his, to define the proper relationship between Niebuhr's movement and the liberal tradition. Niebuhr railed against liberal theology for twenty-five years and then regretted that he gave so much of his spirit and career to polemics; his friend and comrade John Bennett expressed for both of them the ways that they remained theologians of the liberal tradition. John C. Bennett earned his divinity and master's degrees at Union Seminary in 1926 and 1927 and forged a close friendship and intellectual partnership with Niebuhr shortly after Niebuhr arrived in New York; he later recalled that for his generation there were two guides to the necessary remaking of theology: "Reinhold Niebuhr and the catastrophic history of the period."[62] Bennett taught at Auburn Theological Seminary and the Pacific School of Religion before returning to Union in 1943 as the Dodge Professor of Applied Christianity. A prolific scholar, some of his books rivaled Niebuhr's as texts that shaped and defined the Niebuhrian realist movement in Christian ethics, especially *Social Salvation* (1935) and *Christian Realism* (1952).

For decades he and Niebuhr collaborated on numerous movement-building theological projects, including the major conferences of the world ecumenical movement, various activist organizations, and the management of *Christianity & Crisis* magazine. In 1955 Bennett was appointed faculty dean of Union Seminary; two years later he was appointed the Reinhold Niebuhr Professor of Social Ethics; and in 1963 he assumed Union's presidency, which he held until 1970.[63]

Bennett's early reading of the disintegration and enduring legacy of liberal theology was characteristically discerning. He judged in 1933 that in the sense of being a coherent structure of belief and practice, liberal theology was breaking apart, but this did not mean that all the pieces of the shattered liberal system were discredited. Bennett considered four pieces crucial to the kind of theology worth advocating. The first was the fact that the liberal tradition was "a cleansing force" in modern Christian history: "It has removed a great deal of excess baggage, especially all that went with biblical literalism. It has taken the emphasis off doctrine and ecclesiasticism and put it on those things which are most essential for the Christian life." Bennett and Niebuhr remained straightforward liberals in maintaining that Christianity is a life, not a doctrine, by which they meant primarily the spiritual and ethical life of the individual, not the life of the church.

Bennett's second point, closely related to the first, was that though ultimate authority in religion must be God or the Truth, from the standpoint of the seeker of religious truth, "the ultimate authority in religion must rest with the insight of the individual." The liberal appeal to the privileged authority of individual reason and experience cannot be overthrown without doing immense harm to modern Christianity: "Any attempt to override the insight of the individual by appealing to obedience to any external authority leads to unreality in religion, breaks up the unity of the personality, and destroys the right relation to God as the God of truth."[64] This was the keystone to which Niebuhr and Bennett firmly adhered, despite their words of judgment against the liberal tradition: liberal theology was and is fundamentally defined by the privileged authority that it gives to individual reason and experience.

Bennett observed that as a consequence of its fidelity to the authority of reason and experience, liberal theology stripped away much of the church's mythology about Jesus and gained a clearer grasp of the Jesus of history; this was the third major contribution of liberal theology. The liberal quest of the historical Jesus had its problems, Bennett allowed—it sometimes produced "a thin and over-pragmatic interpretation of Christianity"—but overall the liberal emphasis on the Jesus of history strengthened the intellectual integrity of modern Christianity and aided its spiritual health: "There has been a wholesome simplification of Christianity as a result of the liberal criticism of tradition." Bennett contrasted this enduring liberal achievement to the obfuscating Christologies of the Barthian movement, in which theologians dismissed the historical Jesus as an unknowable enigma while appealing to the eternal Christ of faith. This strategy was a loser for modern theology and Christianity, he judged: "We have here a flat contradiction of the Christian belief in the incarnation usually in the name of a reassertion of it. It is only in the human life of Jesus, in his personality and his teaching that the word is revealed to men in its fulness."[65]

Bennett argued that liberal theology was not wrong to play up the doctrine of the incarnation; here again, he felt closer to the liberal tradition than to Barth. Instead of drawing a line and placing the divine on the other side of everything that is human, he urged, it is better "to give full weight to the values which are present in humanity as our clue to those aspects of God which are most important for our lives." The Barthian movement dismissed the historical Jesus while making the Christ of faith an isolated figure set apart from humanity; to Bennett's reckoning, the liberal strategy of viewing Jesus as the highest revelation of God was a better idea. Liberal scholarship may have yielded mistaken pictures of the historical Jesus, "but the reaction against the historical Jesus is sure to have worse results in the long run."

The fourth major contribution of liberal theology to the new theology followed from the third. Liberal Christianity was a religion of continuity between God and humankind, grace and nature, revelation and natural religion, faith and reason, and Christianity and other religions. Bennett and Niebuhr censured liberal Protestantism for exaggerating the immanence of God and the continuities of the sacred and profane orders, but Niebuhr, and, even more, Bennett, also believed that the Barthian movement went too far in emphasizing the themes of transcendence and discontinuity. They wanted no part of the Barthian assertion of a radical discontinuity between revelation and reason. "It is at this point that the attack from the Barthian theologians seems to me to be most unsound," Bennett remarked. "Revelation which is purely arbitrary, which is beyond rational defense, which has nothing to do with the experiences of God which come to men in mere religion or in secular idealism is itself a precarious foundation for faith and it excludes too many of us from any approach to faith which is possible for us." The new theology must be open to revelation, he assured, but it must also be guided by reason and common experience. *Sola scriptura* is too limiting: "The roots of faith are many and various, and I can't believe that any theology is the sounder for beginning its task by cutting away all but one."[66]

If the new theology remained so deeply liberal, what was distinctive to it that cut against the grain of the liberal tradition? Bennett mentioned Niebuhr's realistic view of human nature, his sense of humanity's dependent relationship on a transcendent God, his socialist belief in the self-destructiveness of capitalism, and the hope of a Christian movement that spoke "a decisive word to the spiritual confusion of the world." All these themes had a history within liberal theology, Bennett allowed, but recent liberal theology had little to say about human evil and the systemic evils of capitalism, and as a structure of themes the Niebuhrian theology amounted to a new departure in American religion. "The great contribution of Reinhold Niebuhr's much criticized book, *Moral Man and Immoral Society,* is that it challenges in an inescapable way our illusions about men in society," Bennett declared. Much of the social gospel was unsalvageable after Niebuhr's attack upon it; moreover, "Niebuhr is also important because through him more effectively than through any one else the European criticism of liberalism is being mediated to American Christianity, and the dose is mild enough to be taken without too much risk of complications." Niebuhr was the American Barth, but unlike Barth he was grounded in the real world. Bennett promised: "We will never again be even tempted to substitute humanity for God. We will look elsewhere than to enthusiasm for a social goal for our dynamic. We will be forced by our experience to find a deeper basis for living in faith in a God who transcends history."[67]

Against the Chicago school belief that God is another name for the world process, the American Niebuhrians insisted that God is transcendent, personal, and really active; against the Barthian belief that Christianity is the religion of God's self-revelation, Bennett cautioned that "there must be searching to put us in the place where we can recognize God's revelation." Beginning in the 1930s and expanding into the 1950s, the Niebuhrian movement grew to a position of dominating influence and prestige in American theology, though always in a way that Bennett found a bit unsettling. Undiscriminating dismissals of the liberal tradition were commonplace; many of Niebuhr's followers adopted his polemical slogans and exaggerations, especially that liberals "didn't believe in sin." Repeatedly Bennett objected to this caricature; in 1939 he protested that he did not recognize the theological liberalism of his youth in "most of the tirades against theological liberalism which have become the commonplaces of current discussion." Fosdick's distinction was true to Bennett's experience; many of those who became Barthians or Niebuhrians in the 1930s and '40s lacked the requisite grounding in liberal theology that Niebuhr himself took for granted. In the early 1960s Bennett vigorously criticized Paul Ramsey and other right-leaning Niebuhrians on this count; in 1939 he urged: "I still believe that we cannot afford to depart far from the spirit and the method of liberalism. As for the conclusions of liberals ten years ago, they must be modified but not entirely rejected."[68]

Persistently Bennett defended the liberal convictions that modern Christianity's idea of God must not be cut loose from its highest moral standards, that God is not honored by being restricted to one channel of revelation, and that the teaching and figure of the historical Jesus are crucial to Christianity. At the same time he upheld Niebuhr's conviction of the tragic dialectic of sin through all existence. Niebuhr taught that the good never fully prevails over evil because good and evil are always bound up with each other. Every act of altruism has a selfish aspect, he reasoned, the destructive "death instinct" in human beings often serves the life impulse (as when people kill to defend themselves, their loved ones, or their civilization), and democratic gains increase the possibilities for greater numbers of people to do evil things. Thus the possibilities for evil expand with the possibilities for good. Christians are morally obliged to struggle for gains toward social justice and fellowship, yet every movement that engenders greater democracy, equality, freedom, or community engenders new opportunities to create tyranny, squalor, and anarchy. Bennett put it poignantly: "The sense that there is no social choice, especially in international relations, which is not intolerably evil, is the thing that haunts me constantly."[69]

NIEBUHRIAN DIALECTICS: HUMAN NATURE, DIVINE TRANSCENDENCE, AND POWER POLITICS

Niebuhr and Bennett struggled mightily in the late 1930s with lesser-evil quandaries. Though he made his fame as a blistering critic of liberal Christian idealism and pacifism, even Niebuhr was slow to concede the necessity of Franklin Roosevelt's rearmament campaign against fascism. In 1937, while continuing to blast Roosevelt for propping up the capitalist system, he condemned Roosevelt's naval buildup as a "sinister" evil, declaring that "this Roosevelt navalism must be resisted at all costs."[70] The following year he lamented that Roosevelt's billion-dollar defense budget "cries to heaven as the worst piece of militarism in modern history." Modern history included the specter of an armed and menacing Nazi tyranny; did Niebuhr mean that Roosevelt's military buildup was more evil than Hitler's? Until the Munich crisis, Niebuhr made exactly that claim; he shared enough of the liberal Christian resistance to war to make hysterical charges about the evil of countering the Nazi threat. Roosevelt's response to fascist militarism, Niebuhr urged, was "the most unjustified piece of military expansion in a world full of such madness." The best way to avoid war was not to prepare for one; collective security was the realistic alternative to war; Niebuhr wanted the United States to enact neutrality legislation and voluntarily support sanctions imposed by the League of Nations.[71]

But in 1939, Hitler demonstrated his disregard for international law and his determination to conquer Europe. The German army invaded Czechoslovakia in March 1939, having obtained the Sudetenland through the Munich appeasement pact of 1938; on September 1 Germany invaded Poland and rebuffed an ultimatum from Britain and France to withdraw; on September 3 Britain and France formally declared war against Germany. Niebuhr bitterly judged that the Munich accords whetted Hitler's appetite for conquest and fed his contempt for international law. "Munich represented a tremendous shift in the balance of power in Europe," he observed. "It reduced France to impotence . . . it opened the gates to a German expansion in the whole of Europe." In 1940 he confessed that Roosevelt "anticipated the perils in which we now stand more clearly than anyone else." Though Roosevelt was often too cunning for America's good, Niebuhr believed, his reelection in 1940 was imperative for America and the world; it was time to prepare for war against an intolerable tyranny.[72]

Niebuhr wrote the first part of his theological magnum opus during the fateful months that he faced up to the inevitability of World War II. His Gifford Lectures, titled *The Nature and Destiny of Man*, were delivered at Edinburgh in the spring and fall of 1939. In April his friend German theologian Dietrich Bonhoeffer told him that German army sources were whispering about a September invasion of Poland; in October, while Niebuhr lectured on human destiny, German planes bombed an Edinburgh naval base a few miles away. Niebuhr fretted that his abstract theological lectures were sadly irrelevant in the crisis of the moment, but for the most part he kept to the high road. For three afternoons per week he lectured on "man's most vexing problem," the problem of how human beings should think of themselves. Reinterpreting classical Christian teaching, *The Nature and Destiny of Man* asserted that biblically rooted Christianity possessed distinctive spiritual, moral, and intellectual resources to help modern people think about themselves and their world. These resources were desperately needed in a world plagued by various kinds of cynical militarism and nihilism, on the one hand, and a variety of naive idealisms on the other hand. "The fateful consequence in contemporary political life of Hobbes's cynicism and Nietzsche's nihilism are everywhere apparent," he admonished. Only Christianity had the resources to save Europe from fascist barbarism, but it had to be a Christianity that believed in the Christian doctrine of sin.[73]

Niebuhr always thought in terms of a dialectic between one hand and another. In *The Nature and Destiny of Man* one hand was the cluster of views that variously derived from the view of humankind promoted in the Greco-Roman world of classical antiquity; the other hand was what Niebuhr called the biblical view. The classical view, represented by Platonist, Aristotelian, and Stoic conceptions of human nature, emphasized the primacy and uniqueness of human rationality; human beings are unique within nature because they are spiritual beings gifted with the capacity for self-reflective thought and reason. The biblical view emphasized the unity of a human self as a created and finite existence in both body and spirit, Niebuhr argued. It is dialectical in its insistence on the essential relation of body and soul, and it opposes the idealistic notion that mind is essentially good or eternal, as well as the romantic notion that the good is to be sought in humanity's "natural" state of embodiment.

In Niebuhr's reading, classical Christianity represented a series of attempts to synthesize the views of Scripture and classical antiquity, most importantly in the theologies of Augustine and Aquinas. Modern culture represented, and began with, the destruction of the classical Christian synthesis, as the artists and philosophers of the Renaissance dispensed with the biblical elements and the preachers and theologians of the Reformation dispensed with the elements of classical antiquity. Niebuhr interpreted modern liberal Protestantism as an attempt to reunite the Greco-Roman and biblical worldviews, but this project was doomed to failure, especially after modern thought adopted a naturalistic interpretation of human nature and destiny. Even in their premodern forms, Niebuhr observed, the worldviews of biblical Christianity and classical antiquity had little in common; with the modern turn to naturalism, the classical view of humanity's spiritual nature was negated as well. Modern people believe in a naturalized version of the Greco-Roman view of themselves. Niebuhr urged that it was precisely the poverty and triumph of this "modernized classical view of man" that made modern life so confused and nihilistic. In *The Nature and Destiny of Man* he made an argument for the recovery of the biblical and Reformationist view of the self, though, unlike the Barthians, Niebuhr contended that the freedom-cherishing humanism of the Renaissance had a role to play in realizing the fullness of biblical religion.[74]

Liberal Christianity came in for a vigorous drubbing. The liberal impulse in theology is humanistic, deeply indebted to modern culture, and therefore religiously superficial, Niebuhr judged; liberal Christianity "makes the central message of the gospel, dealing with sin, grace, forgiveness and justification, seem totally irrelevant." In order to maintain some point of contact with traditional Christianity, he remarked, liberal Christians generally affirmed "that Jesus was a very, very, very good man." But this credo raised the unsettling question: What if a better person should appear? Would modern Christians be obliged to transfer their loyalties? Niebuhr admonished: "These moderns do not understand that they cannot transcend the relativities of history by the number of superlatives which they add to their moral estimate of Jesus." In their ultimate freedom and self-transcendence, he argued, human beings stand beyond time and nature. Therefore they cannot find a true religious norm "short of the nature of ultimate reality."[75]

He scolded liberal Christianity for selling out the deep mythical meanings of Christian teaching. Albrecht Ritschl, "the most authoritative exponent of modern liberal Christianity," taught that the gospel offers salvation from the contradiction of finiteness and freedom. This problem underlies all religion, Niebuhr allowed, but the gospel subordinates the problem of finiteness to the problem of sin. Biblical religion seeks redemption from sin, which is the disruption of the harmony of creation by human pride and will to power. Liberals typically rejected the Pauline doctrine that the righteousness of Christ is imputed to the repentant sinner, who does not possess righteousness except by faith. To liberals, the doctrine of imputed righteousness was unacceptably non-moral; Niebuhr countered that this doctrine rightly "recognizes the sinful corruption in every human life on every level of goodness." Sin is rebellion against God, and divine forgiveness is "a form of love which is beyond good and evil."[76]

Niebuhr's idea of "biblical religion" was thus essentially Reformationist in its language and content, though in his second volume he made room for what he called "a Renaissance version of the answer to the cultural problem." The Barthians simply returned to the self-authenticating revelation of the Reformers and told modern people to like it or lump it, Niebuhr judged. Barth's impact on theology was solely negative and confined to the church, and it "defied what was true in Renaissance culture too completely to be able to challenge what was false in it." The Renaissance was not wrong to cherish intellectual freedom and personal experience, Niebuhr believed. On issues pertaining to religious authority and the sources of theology, he preferred the real-world, heterogeneous humanism of the Renaissance to the cramped Reformationist principle of *sola scriptura*. He also leaned toward Renaissance humanism on the relation of thought and grace.[77]

His thinking on the latter issue was deeply influenced by Tillich. In *The Interpretation of History* (1936), Tillich argued that there is a type of thought that transcends all conditioned and finite thought and which proves its transcendence by its realization of the finiteness of thought. Subjective thinking can never reach the unconditioned truth, Tillich reasoned, but this judgment is itself independent of its forms of expression: "It is the judgment which constitutes truth as truth." The ultimate self-transcendence of the human spirit is revealed in the self's capacity to understand its own finiteness. Niebuhr embraced this argument as a formulation of the problem of finiteness. The root of sinful rebellion against God is the refusal to admit finiteness. This refusal is sinful because the human spirit has the capacity to recognize its finiteness; when the self refuses out of its sinful pride to recognize its finiteness, its self-glorification can be broken only by the convicting gift of grace. Christianity is a religion of redemption and grace, Niebuhr and Tillich affirmed, not a religion of the universality of spirit. It is not about the realization of self-transcendence as universal spirit, as in philosophical and Christian idealism; Christianity is about the redemptive shattering of the ego's sense of self-sufficiency.[78]

Niebuhrian neoliberalism, usually called neo-orthodoxy, was a religion of the dialectic of divine transcendence and relation. For Niebuhr, transcendence referred to the divine realm beyond all finite experience; to the principle or ground of reality, meaning, judgment, and hope; and to the capacity of the human spirit to transcend itself and relate to God. God is beyond society, history, and the highest ideals of existence, Niebuhr argued, yet God is also intimately related to the world. The human spirit finds a home and grasps something of the stature of its freedom in God's transcendence, yet the self also finds in the divine transcendence the limit of the self's freedom, the judgment spoken against it, and the mercy that makes judgment bearable. Langdon Gilkey aptly observes that "the dialectical ontological presence of God as absolute and yet related—one of Niebuhr's many 'paradoxes'—forms the necessary presupposition for all of his theology." Epistemologically, Niebuhr posited a divine ground of meaning and coherence beyond all finite notions of meaning and coherence; ontologically, he asserted the transcendence of God's being over all contingent and temporal being while affirming that God is continually present to God's creation in the workings of providence, the history of judgment, the grace of renewal, and the stirrings of individual moral conscience. "Insofar as man transcends the temporal process he can discern many things in life and history by tracing various coherences, sequences, causalities and occurrences through which the events of history are ordered," Niebuhr observed in *Faith and History.* "But insofar as man is himself in the temporal process which he seeks to comprehend, every sequence and realm of coherence points to a more final source of meaning than man is able to comprehend rationally."[79]

These were the dominant themes of the Niebuhrian "neo-orthodoxy" that overtook American theology in the 1930s and 1940s. Though Niebuhr was never neo-orthodox in the manner of American Barthians and many Niebuhrians, he effected a transformation of American theological consciousness. His emphasis on sin and tragedy was chastening to liberals such as Fosdick, Harkness, and

Brightman; his whirling dialecticism proved overpowering even to many liberals, such as Gregory Vlastos, who worried that Niebuhr practically made paradox a criterion of truth. Reviewing *The Nature and Destiny of Man*, Vlastos marveled and winced at Niebuhr's "high record for being at home in the paradoxical, the ultra-rational, the irrational." He tried to resist Niebuhr's intellectual power, but confessed, "We read his books with affectionate wonder, like the ideas of our other self, but a self endowed with volcanic energy, capable of out-thinking and out-talking our ordinary self ten times to one."[80]

Niebuhr later recalled that his turn against a regnant liberal idealism was the key to his career: "When I came here [to Union], this was absolutely a paradise of Social Gospel liberalism." Elsewhere he reflected: "It was in full swing when I arrived at the seminary in 1928. The Social Gospel was creative in redeeming American Protestantism from an arid Calvinistic or pietistic individualism. But it was defective in identifying the Christian faith with a mild socialism and a less mild pacifism all encased in an overall utopianism." Tillich observed that Niebuhr transformed the American theological scene with the same suddenness and force that Barth upended liberal German theology after World War I. Having played a role in the Barthian revolt against the Ritschlian and Troeltschian schools in Germany, Tillich arrived in New York just in time to witness a similar transformation: "When I remember what happened here, it was similarly astonishing. When I came [to America in 1933], everybody asked only one question— whatever was discussed theologically—namely the question, 'What do you think about pacifism?'" As a newcomer to America and not a pacifist, Tillich hesitated to address the question. Niebuhr changed the question by transforming the social climate of American theology, Tillich observed: "This disappeared after Reinie made his tremendous attack. I believe it was absolutely necessary, and I tried to support him as much as I could in my lectures and early writings, but he was the man who changed the climate in an almost sudden way."[81]

NIEBUHRIAN REALISM, WORLD WAR II, AND THE COLD WAR

Niebuhr's climactic blast against the pacifist idealism of American liberal Christianity took place between the outbreak of World War II in September 1939 and America's entry into the war in December 1941. He worried that the democracies seemed "almost defenseless against the concentrated fury which the totalitarian powers are unleashing."[82] He judged that Roosevelt grasped the reality of the fascist threat to democratic civilization, but that most Americans did not, especially American church leaders. He condemned the "burst of hysterical self-righteousness which now consumes the energies of the American churches."[83] Morrison especially offended him. After supporting Roosevelt in 1936, the *Christian Century* opposed his reelection in 1940, charging that Roosevelt was an American-style fascist who played to the working class and militarized a peaceable nation. In

May 1940 Morrison claimed that it was not too late for America to broker an armistice; the following month he claimed that it was too late for America to affect the course of the war by intervening against Hitler; repeatedly he held out for neutrality and called for efforts to slow down Roosevelt's march toward war. In the December 10, 1941, issue that went to press just before Japan attacked Pearl Harbor, the *Christian Century* insisted: "Every national interest and every moral obligation to civilization dictates that this country shall keep out of the insanity of a war which is in no sense America's war."[84]

Morrison's pacifism was practical, not absolute, which infuriated Niebuhr all the more. The *Christian Century* apparently believed that Christians are virtuous to the extent that they avoid all involvement in conflict, he observed. Against this predisposition, Niebuhr proclaimed in the *Century* that America was obliged to "prevent the triumph of an intolerable tyranny":

> Most of our pacifism springs from an unholy compound of gospel perfectionism and bourgeois utopianism, the latter having had its rise in eighteenth-century rationalism. This kind of pacifism is not content with martyrdom and with political irresponsibility. It is always fashioning political alternatives to the tragic business of resisting tyranny and establishing justice by coercion. However it twists and turns, this alternative is revealed upon close inspection to be nothing more than capitulation to tyranny. Now capitulation to tyranny in the name of non-resistant perfection may be very noble for the individual. But it becomes rather ignoble when the idealist suggests that others besides himself shall be sold into slavery and shall groan under the tyrant's heel.

In the name of social gospel idealism, the *Christian Century* was advocating connivance with tyranny and preaching that slavery is better than war; Niebuhr countered that a genuinely moral American Christianity must fight Nazi fascism, "lest we deliver the last ramparts of civilization into the hands of the new barbarians."[85]

To a "very, very sick" civilization, liberal Protestantism preached weakness and purity; Niebuhr acidly observed that it was a dogma of American Christianity "that any kind of peace is better than war." He countered that no morally worthy peace could be brokered with a Nazi regime that was fed by genocidal ambitions and a "pagan religion of tribal self-glorification." To their shame, he admonished, Americans were trying to ignore that the Nazi government intended to abolish Christianity, that it defied all universal standards of justice and moral law, that it "threatens the Jewish race with annihilation and visits a maniacal fury upon these unhappy people which goes far beyond the ordinary race prejudice which is the common sin of all nations and races," that it explicitly vowed to subject all other races of Europe "into slavery to the 'master' race," that it sought "a monopoly of military violence" and colonizing imperial force throughout Europe, and that it was already destroying and enslaving Poland and Czechoslovakia.[86]

The appeasing moralism of America's dominant liberal culture was making the world safe for this fascist nightmare, Niebuhr admonished: "It imagines that there is no conflict of interest which cannot be adjudicated. It does not understand what it means to meet a resolute foe who is intent upon either your annihilation or enslavement." He warned that America would pay dearly for its self-deception and cowardice if Hitler conquered Europe and then invaded South America, where the Nazis could easily erect a colonized slave economy. As "an American of pure German stock," he pleaded with Americans to recognize that fighting Germany was more tolerable than submitting to it, and he pointedly denied that his thinking was swayed by his well-known affection for England: "I thought Britain was much too slow in understanding or challenging the peril which nazi imperialism presented to both our common civilization and the vital interests of Britain." In his darker moods Niebuhr fretted that American democracy did not deserve to survive: "The fact is that moralistic illusions of our liberal culture have been so great and its will-to-power has been so seriously enervated by a confused pacifism, in which Christian perfectionism and bourgeois love of ease have been curiously compounded, that our democratic world does not really deserve to survive."[87]

Since the *Christian Century* epitomized what was wrong with American Protestantism, Niebuhr resolved to create an alternative to it. Mainline Protestantism needed a journal that renounced the prevailing liberal Christian sentiment that anything is better than war. Niebuhr already had one journal, the Fellowship of Socialist Christians' magazine *Christianity and Society* (which was named *Radical Religion* until 1940), but he understood that this outlet was too politicized and socialistic to get a hearing among most pastors and church leaders. In February 1941, therefore, he launched *Christianity & Crisis* as an antidote to the *Century's* isolationism, enlisting the support of liberal Christian friends who agreed that the *Century's* isolationism had become an embarrassment to mainline Protestantism; these friends included Bennett, Sherwood Eddy, Francis McConnell, William Adams Brown, Will Scarlett, Henry Sloane Coffin, Henry Van Dusen, and John R. Mott. The format of *Christianity & Crisis* was cloned after the *Century*, but its editorial line spoke the Christian realist language of tragic necessities, group interests, power politics, lesser evils, and internationalism. Niebuhr and Bennett plunged into the day-to-day business of creating a realignment in American liberal Protestantism; at the same time, Niebuhr took a large step toward the liberal mainstream of the Democratic Party by assuming the leadership of a national labor-socialist organization called the Union for Democratic Action (UDA).

He was just as concerned about isolationist trends in American secular politics, especially American Progressivism, as about parallel developments in the churches. The Union Seminary liberals who supported *Christianity & Crisis*—especially Coffin, Brown, and Van Dusen—were chastened about war and idealism, but they could never rub elbows with Niebuhr's friends in the trade union and socialist movements. The Union liberals represented one segment of the progressive interventionist movement that he envisioned; Niebuhr conceived the UDA as the key to the other part. Ultimately he wanted to build a national farmer-labor party, but that goal was out of reach in 1941. Under Niebuhr's leadership, the UDA enlisted intellectuals, political activists, and major union leaders Lewis Corey, Murray Gross, George Counts, and A. Phillip Randolph into a common struggle for justice and democracy; the group's core consisted of New York social democrats and Marxists who were disgusted by the Socialist Party's isolationism. At Niebuhr's insistence, the UDA renounced the traditional socialist denigration of religion, excluded Communists from membership, and exhorted Americans to face up to the necessity of joining the war against fascism. A generation of left-wing activists and intellectuals found their way into the Democratic Party establishment by this route; in 1947 Niebuhr folded the UDA into a new organization dominated by establishment liberals, the Americans for Democratic Action.

Much of Niebuhr's subsequent work and influence, which I have analyzed elsewhere, belongs more to the field of Christian social ethics than to the field of theological interpretation and criticism. Though he blasted liberal Christians as naively sentimental and idealistic "children of light" in his 1944 essay on the meaning of democracy, *The Children of Light and the Children of Darkness,* for the most part Niebuhr scaled back his attacks on liberal theology after America entered the war.[88] After Japan attacked Pearl Harbor, the *Christian Century* editorialized, "We, too, must accept the war. We see no other way at the moment but the bloody way of slaughter and immeasurable sacrifice. Our government has taken a stand. It is our government." Though Morrison still believed that Roosevelt should have kept America from becoming entangled in the war and should have brokered "an adjustment in the Pacific," he accepted that the American government had chosen "the way of unimaginable cost and of doubtful morality." All Americans were implicated in the acts of their government, he counseled: "Those who approved and encouraged the policy which has brought us to this tragic hour and those who have resisted this policy whether on moral or prudential grounds are one people. . . . We stand with our country. We cannot do otherwise."[89]

For Niebuhr, the war was strictly a lesser-evil affair; he did not believe in just wars, and he worried that "the stupid children of light" would not content themselves with fighting merely to thwart a greater evil. The United States had barely entered the war against Japan when Niebuhr began to complain that American Christianity's prowar pronouncements were nearly as insufferable as its earlier isolationism. "Many of the sermons which now justify the war will be as hard to bear as the previous ones which proved it was our 'Christian' duty to stay out," he cautioned. The purpose of the war was to stop fascism, not to create a new international order in which war would be abolished.[90] His important wartime work, *The Children of Light and the Children of Darkness,* expounded a realist-leaning dialectic of idealism and realism, arguing that America needed to find a moral balance between the cynical amorality of the fascist and Stalinist "children of darkness" and the sentimental idealism of the modern liberal "children of light."

Niebuhr believed that Stalinist-style Soviet communism was nearly as evil as Nazi fascism, though he downplayed this judgment while America and Russia were linked as wartime allies. In 1939 he wrote in the *Christian Century* that he felt "genuinely sorry for my friends who seem to be under a spiritual necessity to deny obvious facts about Russian tyranny." In the same year he told Bennett and other friends that the tyrannical evil of Soviet communism was "almost, though not quite" as bad as that of Nazi Germany. Niebuhr muddled the latter judgment in the wartime *Children of Light and the Children of Darkness*, but as soon as the war was over he pointed a harsh light on Soviet brutality. Like the Nazis, he charged, the Stalinist children of darkness were wise because they grasped the power of self-interest, and they were evil because they recognized no law beyond themselves. Conversely, the children of light were virtuous because they recognized the existence of a moral law beyond their own will, but they were dangerously foolish in their underestimation of the power of self-will. "The excessively optimistic estimates of human nature and human history with which the democratic credo has been historically associated are a source of peril to democratic society," Niebuhr warned. *The Children of Light and the Children of Darkness* thrashed Adam Smith, Thomas Jefferson, and John Dewey as theorists of the liberal illusion of social harmony, but Niebuhr made only glancing references to the sentimental idealism of liberal Christianity. By 1944, there was much less of it to condemn; the Protestant mainstream spoke increasingly like Niebuhr, while in his politics, he became comfortable in the liberal mainstream of the Democratic Party.[91]

In 1947 the Fellowship of Socialist Christians changed its name to Frontier Fellowship, reflecting Niebuhr's acceptance of welfare-state capitalism and the politics of anticommunist "Vital Center" liberalism; four years later Niebuhr changed the group's name to the even more innocuous Christian Action. He was testy with those, including the *Christian Century*, who worried that his politics were veering toward a middle-of-the-road conformism. Niebuhr countered that the middle ground did not have to be a "dead center," for throughout the world, the struggle for the middle ground was a fight for democracy. This fight necessarily included a long-term battle against the spread of communism, he insisted, for "we are fated as a generation to live in the insecurity which this universal evil of communism creates for our world."[92]

In the early 1950s, while America convulsed over McCarthyism and FBI agents dug for incriminating details about Niebuhr's radical past, he provided much of the ideological scaffolding for the "containment" strategy of Cold War liberalism. Niebuhr portrayed the Communist creed as a perverted religion and the Communist movement as a devouring totalitarian monolith committed to world domination. He warned that communism, though tactically flexible, was inherently fanatical, "with its simple distinctions between exploited and exploiter, its too-simple conception of the class structure of society, its too-simple derivation of all social evil from the institution of property, and its consequent division of every nation and of the whole world into friends and enemies 'of the people.'" Traditional realpolitik failed to grasp the "noxious demonry" of this predatory movement, Niebuhr admonished, for Soviet communism was not merely "the old Russian imperialism in a new form." At the same time, in the name of realism, he counseled against a crusading hot war. America's battle against communism needed to walk a fine, patient, vigilant line between treating the Soviet state as a geopolitical great power rival and as a Nazi-like enemy that had to be frontally attacked. Communism was morally utopian, he argued, not morally cynical like Nazi fascism, but this fact made communism more threatening to the cause of democratic civilization than fascism had ever been, because communism made a universalist appeal to the disinherited masses of the Third World.[93]

Niebuhr explained that in power politics, a perverted moralism is always more dangerous than explicit evil. The moral utopianism of the Communist movement gave it greater drawing power than the Nazi movement ever possessed. For this reason communism was capable of creating greater and longer-lasting evils in the world than fascism. "We are embattled with a foe who embodies all the evils of a demonic religion," Niebuhr admonished. "We will probably be at sword's point with this foe for generations to come." Repeatedly he counseled that the best analogy for the Communist threat to the West was not the Third Reich, but the rise of militant Islam in the high Middle Ages: "Moslem power was consolidated in the Middle Ages and threatened the whole of Christendom much as Communist power threatens Western civilization today." Just as militant Islam brandished a quasiuniversalist ideology that transcended nationalism while being rooted in the Arab world, the Communist movement wielded a pseudo universalist creed that served Russian imperialist ambitions. Moreover, the Islamic conception of a necessary holy war against all infidels was "analogous to the Communist conception of the inevitable conflict between capitalism and Communism."[94]

Niebuhr pressed this religiously objectionable analogy as an argument for a realist anticommunism; his implication that militant Islam was a demonic religion gave him no pause. The mistakes of the crusaders needed to be taken into account in figuring out how to fight communism, he urged; precisely because communism was a demonic religion, anticommunist containment was not a job for idealogues or religious crusaders. Like the Islamic power of the Middle Ages, the Communist movement was deeply entrenched, threatening, and ideologically driven; like the Islamic power, it was much more likely to disintegrate from its inner contradictions and corruptions than from external force by its enemies. Niebuhr recalled that the sultan of Turkey was ultimately unable to sustain his double role as spiritual leader of the Islamic world and head of the Turkish state; he reasoned that Stalin had essentially the same double role "in the world of communist religion."[95]

Like his friend, the diplomatic historian and ambassador George Kennan, Niebuhr believed that communism was unsustainable as a combined form of political rule and creedal faith; it promised a universal utopia while practicing a tyrannical politics of repression, conspiracy, and moral squalor. Sooner or later, the Soviet state would disintegrate under the pressure of its internal contradictions, though Niebuhr assumed that this process of disintegration would take several generations. He instructed, "If we fully understand the deep springs which feed the illusions of this religion, the nature of the social resentments which nourish them and the realities of life which must ultimately refute them, we might acquire the necessary patience to wait out the long run of history while we take such measures as are necessary to combat the more immediate perils." For Niebuhr and Kennan, the purpose of containment strategy was to keep enough diplomatic and military pressure on the Soviet Union to accelerate the implosion of the Soviet state. Soviet communism was an evil, conspiratorial, universalist religion that would eventually self-destruct if the West maintained a self-respecting and patient strategy of containment.[96]

Niebuhr's later thinking about communism took various twists and turns in response to world events; he stopped predicting the eventual disintegration of communism, and protested that the politics of American anticommunism was distorted by hard-liners who overmilitarized and overideologized the strategy of containment. Many of the latter Cold Warriors called themselves Niebuhrians, a fact that caused Niebuhr much dismay in his later years, especially after he came out against America's war in Vietnam. In the 1960s, Niebuhr's failing health left it to Bennett to sort out the disagreements among Niebuhrians and make a case for a prudent anticommunism. A decade earlier, while he struggled against poor health to retain his influence in American Christianity and politics, Niebuhr's view of America's domestic situation was more approving, with one exception. In 1952 he enthused: "We have equilibrated power. We have attained a certain equilibrium in economic society itself by setting organized power against organized power. When that did not suffice we used the more broadly based political power to redress disproportions and disbalances in economic society." Welfare-state capitalism was attaining as much of the democratic socialist ideal of social justice as appeared to be attainable, he believed. By creating a system of countervailing labor, capitalist, and governmental power, American civilization had vindicated the dreams of the social gospelers and progressives without resorting to (much) economic nationalization.[97]

While he cautioned that the struggle for social justice is never finished, Niebuhr's realism thus became, in the 1950s, a form of apologetics for the American status quo. In 1952 he suffered a stroke that paralyzed much of his left side and left him depressed, physically drained, and unable to speak without slurring his words. Niebuhr coped bravely with his limitation, marshaled his physical resources, regained much of his ability to write and perform, and concentrated on the politics of anticommunism, all with the indispensable aid of his wife Ursula, who taught religious studies at Barnard College. He taught at Union Seminary until 1960 and wept openly at his retirement dinner, feeling deeply the loss of a vital bond. At his retirement dinner the creation of an endowed Reinhold Niebuhr Professorship of Social Ethics was announced. Contributors to the endowment included W. H. Auden, Sherwood Eddy, T. S. Eliot, Hubert Humphrey, Walter Lippmann, Jacques Maritain, Adlai Stevenson, Norman Thomas, Paul Tillich, and Arnold Toynbee, and the first occupant of the Niebuhr chair was John Bennett. Befitting his basically approving view of post–World War II American society, Niebuhr spoke little about economic justice in his later career and only a little more about the one significant exception to his claim that America was essentially just.

This exception was America's racial prejudice and segregation. Niebuhr never gave racial injustice the high importance that he gave to pacifism in his early career, socioeconomic equality in his middle career, and antifascism and anticommunism in his later career, but throughout his career he wrote occasional articles opposing racial discrimination. His sensitivity to the tangled hypocrisy of moral pride was especially keen in this area; he observed that a white Protestant who apologizes to American blacks or Jews for the sins of white America will often win moral points for humility and contrition, but the confession is always dictated by pride and thus carries a whiff of hypocrisy. For the penitent's confession is almost never meant to be taken at face value; what the "humble" confession communicates is that the penitent is morally superior to his or her group. It also troubled Niebuhr that, in his experience, victims of racial discrimination rarely confessed their own short-comings, though he allowed that this phenomenon could be a defensive reaction to the insincerity of white Americans' contrition for racism.[98]

These concerns contributed to Niebuhr's failure to oppose racism with the same energy that he gave to economic and foreign policy, but he did repeatedly criticize the ravages of racial discrimination in American religion and society. With particular feeling he admonished that racism always ignores the conditioned character of one's life and culture and that it feeds on the false pretense that one's color, creed, or culture represent the final good. "This is a pathetic and dangerous fallacy, but it is one in which almost all men are involved in varying degrees," he wrote in 1948. Racial bigotry cannot be cured by social engineering, Niebuhr judged, though government policies to prohibit racial discrimination and promote racial justice are necessary. The problem of racial bigotry is ultimately a spiritual issue: "The mitigation of racial and cultural pride is finally a religious problem in the sense that each man, and each race and culture, must become religiously aware of the sin of self-worship, which is the final form of human evil and of which racial self-worship is the most vivid example." Racism is like every other form of evil in its egotistical presumption, he reasoned: "Religious humility, as well as rational enlightenment, must contribute to the elimination of this terrible evil of racial pride."[99]

Niebuhr believed that his country was correcting its worst problem in the 1950s. The problems of liberty and equality are more difficult than Americans typically realized, he observed in 1957, but America had already solved these problems "beyond the dreams of any European nation"—except for racial discrimination: "We failed catastrophically only on one point—in our relation to the Negro race." Quickly he assured that the American tragedy of racism was "on the way of being resolved," however. The U.S. Supreme Court recognized equality as a criterion of justice, and in its 1954 decision that barred racial discrimination in public schools, Niebuhr believed, the court redeemed the promise of

America for black Americans: "At last the seeming sentimentality of the preamble of our Declaration of Independence—the declaration that 'all men are created equal'—has assumed political reality and relevance." Having believed during his early career that England was the best country of all, in his later career he inclined to the proud conclusion that his own country had become the model of the modern liberal democratic idea.[100]

NIEBUHR AND THEOLOGICAL LIBERALISM

In the 1940s and early 1950s Niebuhr scaled down his attacks on liberal theology, but he took nothing back. On the occasions that he warmed to the subject, as in a *Journal of Religion* article of 1951, he still blasted liberal Christianity for its purported simplemindedness, moralism, idealism, and sentimentality. In his characterization, liberal Christianity reduced creation to an evolutionary concept, God to the process of evolution, sin to a "provisional inertia of impulses," and Christ to a symbol of history.[101]

In 1956, however, liberal theologian Daniel Day Williams pressed Niebuhr to account for this characterization. "What liberalism is he looking at?" Williams asked. "Hegel cannot be reduced to these dimensions. Neither can Rauschenbusch." Niebuhr described Ritschl and his own teacher, D. C. Macintosh, as representative liberals, Williams noted, but nothing in Niebuhr's descriptions applied to Ritschl or Macintosh; neither did his account describe Union Seminary religious philosopher Eugene Lyman or Yale theologian Robert Calhoun, nor such eminent liberal philosophers as Josiah Royce or William Ernest Hocking. But these were major liberal religious thinkers, Williams objected; in a subsequent discussion, he added Henry Nelson Wieman to the list of good and important liberal thinkers. Niebuhr specialized in demolishing a caricature; he never confronted liberal Protestantism at its best. The simplistic utopians that he skewered were extremists or lightweights or both. "Profound liberalism always regards the struggle with evil as meaningful in itself," Williams admonished. "Some liberalism, it is true, found meaning in history only by believing in a complete victory over evil in time, the building of the Kingdom of God on earth. But the more realistic element in the liberal spirit was not so concerned about complete triumph. Can we not believe in an actual redemptive working of God in history without falling into the utopianism which Niebuhr rightly exposes and rejects?"[102]

This argument was an example of the polemical gerrymandering that it criticized. Williams did not recognize his own liberalism in the idealistic Progressivism that Niebuhr attacked, and he rightly objected that liberal Christianity was a richer tapestry than Niebuhr acknowledged. Niebuhr gave an "exaggerated statement to what he regards as the essential tendency and outcome of all liberal faith," Williams observed. To seal his own victory, however, Williams dismissed Niebuhr's polemical targets as thinkers unworthy of attention. He claimed that

Niebuhr ignored the important figures while ridiculing "the extreme views of a few theologians." But Mathews and Fosdick were major figures, Shirley Jackson Case and Gerald Birney Smith were important theologians, Morrison was hardly a minor figure, and Francis McConnell and G. Bromley Oxnam were eminent bishops. Niebuhr blasted them all, though he later eased up on Fosdick out of friendship. McConnell was another friend, but Niebuhr pronounced that McConnell's writings revealed "the final bankruptcy of the liberal Christian approach to politics." His attacks on secular liberalism repeatedly focused on its star proponent, John Dewey. Of the four recent American theologians on Williams's list, only Macintosh compared to Mathews in influence or stature, and none of them had anywhere near the impact on the making of liberal Protestantism that Fosdick and Morrison exerted. Royce and Hocking were philosophers, and aside from Rauschenbusch, the American religious thinkers that Williams cited—Macintosh, Calhoun, Lyman, and Wieman—were curious choices, except (in three cases) for their personal relation to Niebuhr. Macintosh was Niebuhr's fondly regarded teacher; Calhoun, who published very little, had clashed with Niebuhr over Niebuhr's scholarly deficiencies; Lyman was Niebuhr's colleague at Union who, having begun his career as a Ritschlian liberal and pragmatist, had gradually moved toward a liberal philosophical realism that emphasized intuition as a source of objective truth; Wieman was a later add-on (by Williams) whose naturalism Niebuhr abhorred. This was hardly an intimidating list, intellectually, but it did make the point that there was such a thing as liberal realism, and Williams's argument got to Niebuhr personally.[103]

In years past he undoubtedly would have replied to Williams that he took on a pervasive religious and cultural disposition while liberal academics like Macintosh and Calhoun wrote more cautiously for each other. But by the mid-1950s, Niebuhr no longer wanted this fight. He disliked being lumped with neo-orthodoxy and he had never been a Barthian. He admired Royce and Hocking and respected Williams. If they were liberals, so was he. In the past year Russell Kirk's recent book *The Conservative Mind* had caused Niebuhr to clarify his relationship to liberalism and conservatism. Niebuhr's tragic view of human nature and his praise for Edmund Burke had caused many observers to judge that he was becoming a conservative; Kirk's enlistment of Burke as an apologist for inequality and conformity forced Niebuhr to explain why he was not a conservative. He distinguished between Kirk's traditional conservatism, which defended hierarchy, inequality, and undemocratic authority, and traditional liberalism, which was committed to social justice but lacked a realistic understanding of the realities of sin, power, and interest. His own perspective, Niebuhr explained, was a realistic liberalism that grasped the limiting reality of human egotism while pushing for the fullest possible attainment of democracy and distributive justice.[104]

Williams's challenge drove Niebuhr to further clarify his position. "When Professor Williams names names I am embarrassed," he admitted. Niebuhr conceded that his repeated characterizations of modern liberalism were too sweeping and categorical, that he overidentified liberalism with certain currents in American politics and philosophy (especially Deweyan philosophy), and that he overgeneralized the connection between liberalism and historical optimism. Though he disputed Williams's suggestion that Wieman was one of the good liberal theologians, Niebuhr conceded that there was such a thing as good, realistic liberal theology. On the whole, the Ritschlian school exemplified this possibility, as did Hocking and Williams. "I did define liberalism too consistently in terms of its American versions," he remarked, explaining that this was why he ignored the Ritschlian school, which was "a theological offshoot of Kantian philosophy."[105] In Niebuhr's usage, "liberalism" was a faith that trusted in the virtue of rational individuals and the fact of historical progress. It was an especially American faith; in 1936 he vividly explained that liberals believed "that injustice is caused by ignorance and will yield to education and greater intelligence," that Western civilization was gradually becoming more moral, that individual morality is the guarantee of justice in society, that goodness and knowledge can overcome the social power of greed, that all problems can be solved by appeals to "love, justice, good will, and brotherhood," and that "wars are stupid and can therefore be caused only by people who are more stupid than those who recognize the stupidity of war."[106]

But in the late 1950s Niebuhr began to allow that his attacks on liberal "blindness" and "stupidity" applied chiefly to the Deweyan stream of secular liberalism and the more spiritually uprooted forms of social gospel Christianity. Liberal Christianity was a richer, more diverse, and more realistic tradition than his attacks upon it claimed, he acknowledged. By the 1950s he was beginning to regret that he had given comfort to reactionary attacks on liberal Protestantism; in later life he had similar misgivings about neoconservative Niebuhrians.[107] His own thinking, after all, was nothing if not a type of liberal Christianity. He took for granted that religion is a humanly constructed power for social good; that a passionate commitment to social justice is the heart of good politics; that religion is made possible by humanity's unique capacities for good, transcendence, and evil; that Christian Scripture and teaching are pervaded by myth; that the Christian doctrines of the deity and resurrection of Christ are religious myths; and that, while reason and experience must be subjected to criticism, they are nonetheless the tests of religious truth.

He had never meant to bolster any kind of illiberalism, dogmatism, or conservatism in politics or religion, though his writings were frequently invoked for these purposes. He had never been theologically neo-orthodox, he reflected in 1960, and with the decline of the kind of liberalism that viewed the world entirely through its idealism, it was time to say so: "When I find neo-orthodoxy turning into a sterile orthodoxy or a new Scholasticism, I find that I am a liberal at heart, and that many of my broadsides against liberalism were indiscriminate." In politics and religion alike he believed in a chastened liberal empiricism: "On the whole I regret the polemical animus of my theological and political activities and am now inclined to become much more empirical, judging each situation and movement in terms of its actual fruits." Elsewhere he explained that as a youthful product of the social gospel, he had been predisposed to approach theology as a polemical enterprise, which he lived to regret: "There is no need for polemics today, and there was no need for them when I wrote. My polemics were of an impatient young man who had certain things to say and wanted to get them said clearly and forcefully."[108]

Niebuhr's last writings commended Christian realism in a cooler voice. He disavowed the "rather violent, and sometimes extravagant" assaults on religious and political liberalism that filled his major works. Against conservative Niebuhr-quoters he insisted that "a realist conception of human nature should be made the servant of an ethic of progressive justice and should not be made into a bastion of conservatism, particularly a conservatism which defends unjust privileges." Sadly he judged that America's peculiar weakness for utopianism had led the Johnson administration to its "fantastic involvement in Southeast Asia." Against the aggressively militarized and ideological version of anticommunist "containment" that created a fiasco in Vietnam, Niebuhr argued for a chastened realism in foreign policy, though his opposition to the war in Vietnam did not redeem Christian realism in the eyes of a radical-turning generation of younger theologians. Liberationist critics charged that Christian realism was part of the problem.[109]

From a liberationist standpoint, Niebuhrian realism was part of the problem because it viewed the world from the standpoint of American political and economic interests. In his prime, Niebuhr advised government officials, appeared on the cover of *Time* magazine, attracted a large following of religious and secular admirers, and dominated his field to the point where, as Protestant ethicist Alan Geyer observed, he seemed "an omnipresent figure in theology and ethics." In his last years he lost his field-dominating stature in Christian ethics as critics charged that his realism was an American ideology that served the interests of American power. Latin American liberationist Rubem Alves aptly summarized the liberationist charge: "Realism is functional to the system, contributes to its preservation and gives it ideological and theological justification." By the time that Niebuhr died in 1971, liberation theologians of various kinds had given ample notice that the reign of Christian realism was over in Christian ethics.[110]

Niebuhr's stature among the giants of modern theology was anomalous. He created an approach to Christian ethics that dominated its field in his time and remains a major theoretical option and tradition in the field, but he rarely defined his terms with precision or gave attention to methodological problems, and his ethical thinking was very short on a theory of justice or a positive vision of a good society. Bennett remarked of the latter problem: "I think you get at Niebuhr negatively so much better than you do positively. That's the reason that there's lack of vision in a way, lack of a positive vision. It's the criticism of inequality that's more obvious than the actual vision of what an equal world would be like."[111] Niebuhr interpreters Dennis McCann and Karen Lebacqz emphasize the dispositional character of his ethic, arguing that Niebuhr's conceptions of liberty, order, and equality as principles of justice were never systematized clearly enough to yield criteria for distinguishing between moral and immoral uses of power. Other interpreters, notably James Gustafson, Robin W. Lovin, Harlan Beckley, and Merle Longwood, counter that Niebuhr's ethical thinking contains, at least implicitly, the elements of a workable theory of justice, though none of them disputes that Niebuhr's ethic was highly dispositional and intuitive.[112]

For Niebuhr, justice was a relational term that has no meaning apart from the provisional meaning given to it through its dependence on love. He conceived the rules of justice as "applications of the law of love," which do not have any independence from the law of love; justice is an application of the law of love to the sociopolitical sphere, he argued, and love is the motivating energy of the struggle for justice. The struggle for justice is regulated by such middle axioms as freedom, equality, and order (or balance of power), but the concrete meaning of justice in any given situation cannot be taken directly from these principles; the meaning of justice can be determined only in the interaction of love and situation, through the mediation of the principles of freedom, equality, and order. When pressed by one of his conservative disciples, Paul Ramsey, to ground these principles in a modern version of natural law theory, Niebuhr replied that while he believed "in an 'essential' nature of man," he did not believe that there was any formulation of this essential nature that escaped the ambiguities and biases of historical relativity. Debates over the extent of Niebuhr's anthropological essentialism, historical relativism, and ethical dispositionalism still preoccupy a significant wing of the field of Christian ethics, thirty years after Niebuhr's death.[113]

The deeper irony of Niebuhr's stature among the giants of modern theology is that he refused the responsibilities and title of a theologian. His thinking was theologically profound and not lacking in systematic coherence, yet he was keenly aware that he lacked the training and temperament of a professional theologian. With powerful religious force he urged Christians to take seriously the "permanently valid" myths of Christianity as living symbolizations of Christian experience; he interpreted the cross, religiously, as the means by which God establishes God's mercy and judgment on human sin and, ethically, as the ultimate symbol of the importance and unattainability of the law of love; and he described Easter faith as "the very genius of the Christian idea of the historical." Niebuhr's theology of the cross combined elements of the Anselmic idea of atonement as a dialectic of divine justice and divine mercy with an overriding Abelardian doctrine of the spiritual effect of Christ's sacrifice. The cross of Christ symbolizes God's work of taking the suffering of the world onto God's self, he affirmed: "The message of the Son of God who dies upon the cross, of a God who transcends history and is yet in history, who condemns and judges sin and yet suffers with and for the sinner, this message is the truth about life." Similarly he interpreted the idea of the resurrection as a symbol "from our present existence to express concepts of a completion of life which transcends our present existence." Niebuhr explained that the idea of bodily resurrection "can of course not be literally true, but neither is any other idea of fulfillment literally true." The biblical idea of the resurrection of the body is no less rational than the idea of the immortality of the soul, and

the biblical idea affirms the unity of body and soul. The Easter faith is that neither life nor death can separate us from the love of the God revealed in Christ.[114]

Though he emphasized the unity of body and soul as a mystery of faith, however, Niebuhr was much clearer about his belief in the reality of eternal life than
about the nature or importance of Christ's resurrection. In *Beyond Tragedy,* he
declared that the "whole genius of the Christian Faith" is expressed in the affirmation of the Apostles' Creed, "I believe in the resurrection of the body." In *The
Nature and Destiny of Man* he called for "a second measure of restraint in expressing the Christian hope" and interpreted the entire subject of the resurrection as an
issue about the historical and eternal relation of body and soul. In a private reflection in 1967 later published by the *Christian Century,* Niebuhr affirmed that he
believed "in both the immortality and the mortality of persons," explaining that
the individual person, "though mortal, is given, by self-transcendent freedom, the
key to immortality." Individuals enter "the mystery of immortality" through their
personal relation to God, Niebuhr wrote. At the same time, while affirming the
profound religious significance of the myth of Christ's resurrection, Niebuhr was
elusive about its meaning or nature. "There are very few theologians today who
believe the Resurrection actually happened," he observed, clearly siding with the
majority: "There is a progressive retrogression in the New Testament. I mean, there
are more and more details about Christ's appearance." In reply to Catholic theologian Gustave Weigel, who accused him of abandoning orthodox Christian
teaching, Niebuhr declared with a whiff of incredulity, "I do not know how it is
possible to believe in anything pertaining to God and eternity 'literally.'" Niebuhr
reasoned that Christian myths can be permanently valid symbols, but he failed to
explain how. Exactly how should modern Christians understand the mythical
character of Christian teaching? What is the nature of a myth or symbol? What
kind of reality lies behind the symbols of the incarnation and resurrection? Are
they merely regulative principles in the Kantian sense? Do they have a more substantive reality? Is the resurrection more symbolic than the religious truth symbolized in the cross? Throughout his career Niebuhr waved off such questions; he
was a social ethicist, he explained, not a theologian: "I have never been very competent in the nice points of pure theology; and I must confess that I have not been
sufficiently interested heretofore to acquire the competence." By his reckoning,
Niebuhr reflected "the strong pragmatic interest of American Christianity." He left
it to "the stricter sects of theologians in Europe" to define and systematize the
meaning of Christian language and thought; in American seminaries, as Tillich
sadly discovered in the 1930s, theology was a handmaiden of social ethics.[115]

Tillich was foremost among the European theologians to whom Niebuhr and
other Americans looked for guidance, though Niebuhr and Tillich always had
important theological differences. At the outset of his contribution to Niebuhr's
festschrift, Tillich teased that the problem with writing an article about Niebuhr's
epistemology was that he didn't have one: "Niebuhr does not ask, 'How can I
know?'; he starts knowing. And he does not ask afterward, 'How could I know?',
but leaves the convincing power of his thought without epistemological support."

Tillich judged that because Niebuhr failed to distinguish between calculating reason and the classical *logos* idea of reason as divine mind or structure, he sold short the establishing role of reason in theology. Reason is more than the arguing reason of the calculative type, he admonished; *logos*-reason is divine and creative, not merely calculative; it unites divine power with meaning. Tillich further judged that Niebuhr shortchanged the role of reason in theology because he dispensed with the Hellenic mode of thought exclusively in favor of historical Hebraic thinking.[116]

Niebuhr countered that he regarded Hebraic and Hellenistic thinking as equally necessary and did not denigrate classical rationalism. With Greek philosophy, he accepted that God is divine mind and that human beings owe their unique spiritual personality to the power of the divine *logos* within them. "But the self has a freedom which cannot be equated with this reason; and God has freedom beyond the rational structure," Niebuhr asserted. He did not reject the Hellenistic (and Tillichian) idea of God as the power of being; what he rejected was the Hellenistic (and ostensibly Tillichian) project of fitting the divine mystery of being into a rational system. While affirming that calculative reason cannot attain knowledge of God, Tillich developed an ontological theology from the *logos* idea of reason. Niebuhr replied that ontological categories cannot do justice to the freedom of God or the human self and that reason cannot establish or prove the knowledge of God's forgiving love in the drama of Christ's life, death, and resurrection. Faith is validated in critically interpreted experience, he believed, but it is not established by "purely rational arguments." Anticipating Tillich's stock rejoinder, Niebuhr declared: "If it is 'supernaturalistic' to affirm that faith discerns the key to specific meaning above the categories of philosophy, ontological or epistemological, then I must plead guilty of being a supernaturalist. The whole of the Bible is an exposition of this kind of supernaturalism. If we are embarrassed by this and try to interpret Biblical religion in other terms, we end in changing the very character of the Christian faith."[117]

For all that he shared theologically with Tillich, Niebuhr worried that Tillich relinquished the biblical character of Christian faith; for all that he shared theologically with Niebuhr, Tillich could never plead guilty to being any kind of supernaturalist. Tillich was fond of telling philosophers, "Of course I would have no interest in God if I did not consider him part of myself." That was exactly the romantic idealism that Niebuhr believed had ruined liberal theology; for thirty years he and Tillich formed a conflicted partnership while refashioning the field of American theology.[118]

PAUL TILLICH, GERMAN IDEALISM, AND THE GERMAN CATASTROPHE

Tillich was forty-seven years old when he fled Nazi Germany in 1933 and began a new life in the United States. His thinking was already fully formed; he knew next to nothing about American theology; he dreaded that American culture was provincial and superficial; he told Wilhelm Pauck and other friends that leaving cultured Germany for the United States was a kind of death for him. Though he was grateful to the United States and Union Theological Seminary for rescuing him from likely harm by the Nazi regime, he doubted that he could continue his theological and philosophical work anywhere outside Germany, and he found American academe especially unpromising. American philosophy was pragmatic and empiricist; American theology seemed undeveloped at best; American students bantered with professors practically as equals, a phenomenon that shocked Tillich at first. Yet it was in the United States that he won astounding academic and public renown as a theologian. Tillich became an American citizen but never an American theologian; he made his home and his fame in the United States after he could have returned to Germany, but he remained very much a German philosopher. In the 1950s he dominated American theology without quite belonging to it.[119]

For Tillich, modern German philosophy was homeland, as well as the pinnacle of philosophical and religious thought. His love of German philosophical idealism survived his traumatizing experience as an Army chaplain during World War I. The son of a Lutheran pastor and parish superintendent, he earned his doctorate in philosophy in 1910 at the University of Breslau, where he wrote a dissertation on Schelling's philosophy of nature, and his licentiate in theology in 1912 at the University of Halle, where he studied under postliberal gadfly Martin Kähler. Tillich's attraction to Schelling was rooted in his lifelong nature romanticism and his cultivated affinity for the poetry of Goethe, Hölderlin, Novalis, and Rilke. Schelling's transcendental idealism expressed and confirmed Tillich's feeling of nature as the finite expression of the infinite ground of all things. For two years Tillich served as a pastor in the Evangelical Church of the Prussian Union—Niebuhr's ancestral church—before entering an unfortunate first marriage on September 28, 1914; three days later he volunteered to serve his country at war.[120]

Though his philosophical sophistication precluded what Tillich later called the "nice God" of conventional religion, in other respects he was a sheltered academic—ignorant and naive about politics, clueless about the class struggle, sexually repressed, and eager to serve king and fatherland. He had never dealt with working-class people, and he watched many of them lose their faith; their assumption that the church was on the side of the ruling class struck him deeply. At the western front he endured four years of bayonet charges, battle fatigue, and nervous waiting, the disfigurement and death of friends, mass graves, and two nervous breakdowns. The battle of Champagne in 1915 marked a turning point: Tillich ministered all night to the wounded and dying as they were brought in, "many of them my close friends. All that horrible, long night I walked along the rows of dying men, and much of my German classical philosophy broke down that night." It seemed to him that the world was ending; when a friend sent him a picture of herself sitting on a lawn, clothed in a white dress, Tillich wrote to her that it was inconceivable to him that something like that still existed. In the French forest, while reading Nietzsche's *Thus Spoke Zarathustra*, he experienced a rare emotional lift; Nietzsche's ecstatic affirmation of life and his searing assault on Christian morality were intoxicating to the depressed chaplain; Tillich later recalled that he entered the forest a dreaming innocent and emerged from it a wild man.[121]

The only kind of theology that deserved to be written after the war, he believed, had to address the "abyss" in human existence that the war revealed. Tillich judged that Schelling, whom he still cherished, had seen the terrible void in life, but Schelling was obliged by his romantic idealism to cover up the abyss. Tillich later remarked, "The experience of the four years of war tore this chasm open for me and for my entire generation to such an extent, that it was impossible ever to cover it up." At the Spandau military base in Berlin, he witnessed the final disintegration of the kaiser's government in 1918. While Germany abolished the monarchy and inaugurated a republic, Tillich developed a keen interest in politics, stopped going to church, and developed friendships with a wide circle of Berlin intellectuals and bohemians. He began his academic career in 1919 at the University of Berlin, still dressed in his army grays and Iron Cross. In his first lecture he opined that Ernst Troeltsch's *Social Teachings of the Christian Churches* would become a classic text; later that year, in a speech to the Kant Society of Berlin, he developed a signature argument that religion is the substance of culture and culture is the form of religion. The following year he joined a band of religious socialists in Berlin, half of whom were Jews, and developed some of the key ideas of his theological system.[122]

These ideas included Tillich's later-famous concepts of kairos, religious socialism, and the demonic, his theory of the mythical essence of religion, and his dialectic of heteronomy and autonomy. He advocated democratic "religious socialism" as the best option for postwar Germany, arguing that Germany needed an emancipatory socialist revolution that broke the power of the capitalist class while recovering a premodern sense of the sacred. His hope for a democratic socialist transformation of Europe was linked to his belief in Germany's "kairotic" postwar potential. *Kairos* in Greek is literally the "right time," distinguished from formal time, *chronos*; in Tillich's appropriation, the term implied a regenerative transformation of consciousness. The *kairos* was the rare historical moment when the eternal, which is ethically normative, breaks into the ambiguous relativity of existence and creates something new. Tillich believed that Germany's humiliation and defeat in war contained kairotic potential, when bold new directions were suddenly possible. Modern bourgeois culture was corrupt, discredited, and spiritually deracinated, he argued, but the socialisms of the social democratic and Marxist movements were products of the spiritually bankrupt modern culture that these movements opposed. What was needed was an emancipatory religious socialism that synthesized and transcended the "heteronomous" consciousness of the premodern, authoritarian, theocratic past and the "autonomous" consciousness of the modern, individualistic, bourgeois present. The socialist movement perceived the kairos, Tillich believed, but it did not grasp the *kairos* in its spiritual depth. Religious socialism "strives to be more radical, more revolutionary, than socialism, because it wishes to reveal the crisis from the viewpoint of the unconditional. It wishes to make socialism conscious of the present kairos."[123]

This hope of kairotic liberation was rooted in Tillich's experience of personal transformation. In postwar Berlin he cultivated interests in art, literature, psychoanalysis, and politics; immersed himself in the culture of bohemian cafés and dance clubs; and indulged himself sexually, even after remarrying. He thrived on his new friendships and interests, sexual and otherwise, and rationalized that he could not fulfill his intellectual potential if he did not satisfy himself erotically, though he never completely threw off feelings of guilt about his promiscuity. In 1924 he wrote in *Blätter für Religiösen Sozialismus*, "I have come to know the Bohème; I went through the war; I got involved in politics; I became fascinated by the art of painting, and, in the course of this winter, with greatest passion by music." His second wife, Hannah Gottschow, shared his sexual lifestyle during their years in Germany, though not after they were exiled to America. Tillich was sexually promiscuous for most of the rest of his life, a fact that, after they moved to America, Hannah Tillich bitterly regretted and he assiduously kept secret.[124]

Following a career move to Marburg in 1924 and just before he transferred to the Institute of Technology at Dresden, Tillich published *The Religious Situation* (1926), which criticized the despiritualizing and commodifying logic of capitalism. Invoking Max Weber's concept of the "spirit of capitalism," he charged that under capitalism "there is no trace of self-transcendence, of the hallowing of existence." Capitalism relentlessly sells as many commodities as possible to as many consumers as possible, Tillich lamented, and thus it "seeks to arouse and to satisfy ever increasing demands without raising the question as to the meaning of the process which claims the service of all the spiritual and physical human abilities." *The Religious Situation* proposed that a "faithful realist" revolt against bourgeois civilization (*gläubiger realismus*) was occuring in contemporary European art, philosophy, and science. In various ways the expressionist and postexpressionist movements in painting, the Nietzschean and Bergsonian philosophies of life, the Freudian discovery of the unconscious, and the Einsteinian revolution in physics were all characterized by a fundamental openness to "the Unconditioned," he claimed; the Unconditioned was Tillich's God term. By his reckoning, the most significant currents in modern intellectual life were revolting against the spiritless materialism of the bourgeoisie, but the churches were lagging behind, still trying to work out terms of peace with bourgeois civilization. His alternative was a union of the religious substance of mysticism, exemplified in Rudolf Otto's *The Idea of the Holy*, and the transformationist social radicalism of Jewish and Christian prophecy.[125]

Tillich recognized the prophetic spirit in Barth's dialecticism but warned that if the postwar political crisis of Europe were to pass, Barthian theology was likely to turn into a sophisticated form of otherworldliness. What was needed was the theonomous spirit of religious socialism, which restored the "religious symbols of eternity" to the center of society in prophetic new forms.[126] Though he and Barth were allies of sorts in the dialectical theology movement of the 1920s, and

Tillich praised Barth's withering assaults on modern religious and cultural idolatry, he judged that Barth's dialectic of transcendence was insufficiently dialectical. In essence, Barth offered the God of Pauline supernaturalism as the answer to modern religious needs. The Barthian prescription spoke powerfully to many people, Tillich allowed, but it amounted to a one-sided supernaturalism that was neither credible nor even cognizant of its religious elements. Despite his polemics against religion, Barth's religion of faith was still religion; it presupposed creation and grace but did not speak of these religious realities dialectically. Tillich countered that nature and grace are knowable only as realities made known paradoxically *everywhere*, "in nature and spirit, in culture and religion."[127]

Barth replied that Tillich's God, the Unconditioned, was a "frosty monster" that smacked of Schleiermacher and Hegel, not Martin Luther. He rejected Tillich's "broad, general steamroller of faith and revelation, which, when I read Tillich, I cannot help seeing affecting everything and nothing as it rolls over houses, men, and beasts as if it were self-evident that everywhere, everywhere, judgment and grace reigned, that everything, simply everything, is drawn into the strife and peace of the 'positive paradox.'" For Barth, modern theology could be saved only by recovering its Reformationist character as the explication of a Spirit-illuminated, self-authenticating revelation. Tillich countered that theologians must be philosophers of culture as well as theologians if they have any ambition to make sense: "Revelation is revelation to me in my concrete situation, in my historical reality."[128]

In 1929, at the age of forty-three, Tillich was named professor of philosophy at the University of Frankfurt, a position that he relished. For four years he exulted in Frankfurt's academic stature, his sophisticated new friends, and the large following of students that he attracted, who appreciated his generous, sympathetic teaching style. Tillich thrived on personal interactions with his students, colleagues, and women of every sort, and he was open to a fault, treating even Nazi students with respect. His first doctoral student, Theodor Adorno, affectionately nicknamed him "Pacidius" for his pacific temperament. Shortly after Tillich arrived at Frankfurt, he helped engineer a faculty position for Max Horkheimer, who became director of the neo-Marxist *Institut für Sozialforschung,* later famed as the Frankfurt School. The Frankfurt School critical theorists were more inclined to theory than practical political engagement, and theoretically most of them were socialists positioned between the compromised revisionism of the German Social Democratic Party and the antidemocratic collectivism of the Communists. They included Leo Lowenthal, Friedrich Pollock, Adolph Löwe, Karl Mannheim, Kurt Riezler, Karl Mennicke, Adorno, and Horkheimer; in the company of these Hegelianized Marxists, several of whom were Jews, Tillich found a home.[129]

He was slow to take the Nazis seriously as a political force, mainly because they disgusted him. Tillich was not completely oblivious to political reality; in 1929, though he disdained the Social Democrats for selling out socialism, he held his nose and joined the Social Democratic party, mostly in response to the ascendancy of the Nazi and Communist movements. Yet his friends noted a persistent child-like optimism in him, especially when he warmed to political themes; as late as June 1932, he refused to believe that cultured Germany would turn to the thuggish National Socialists. Tillich was shocked into reality in July, when he witnessed a savage attack upon Jewish and leftist students at Frankfurt by Nazi students and storm troopers; he dragged the students to safety and, in his capacity as dean of the philosophical faculty, made an enraged speech that demanded the expulsion of the Nazi students. Later that summer his belated sense of catastrophe moved him to write *The Socialist Decision,* in which he warned against a German stampede toward fascism and a second world war. Like the various fascist movements in Europe, Tillich acknowledged, religious socialism was critical of modernity and affirmed, in some form, the religious values of certain myths of origin, but true socialism was the antithesis of National Socialism, because true socialism included the prophetic ethos of Protestantism and the humanistic values of the Enlightenment and nineteenth-century liberalism. Tillich called for a fascist-opposing political union of the middle class and the proletariat: "The salvation of European society from a return to barbarism lies in the hands of socialism."[130]

In October 1932, while Tillich was completing *The Socialist Decision,* he attended one of Hitler's rallies, which he found terrifying and repugnant; his wife later recalled that he saw the demon in Hitler's eyes. The experience moved Tillich to finish his book, but Hitler was appointed chancellor over a coalition government in January 1933, while the book was in production; the March elections gave Hitler a solid majority and on March 21 he was granted dictatorial powers. Tillich's imaginary coalition of proletarians and middle-class Christians chose fascism, and *The Socialist Decision,* printed too late to leave the warehouse, was among the first books to be condemned by the Third Reich. On April 13 Tillich was declared an enemy of the state, along with Berthold Brecht, Ernst Cassirer, Albert Einstein, Thomas Mann, Bruno Walter, and Tillich's Jewish colleagues Horkheimer, Löwe, and Riezler. Though Tillich often described himself as the first non-Jew to be suspended as a state enemy, in fact there were several other non-Jewish academics on the same list, including theologian Günther Dehn and Frankfurt Schooler Karl Mennicke.[131]

In May 1933, Columbia University was one of many American universities that offered refuge to suspended German academics. Union Seminary president Henry Sloane Coffin attended a planning meeting at Columbia under the assumption that the deposed German professors were all Jews, but upon learning about Tillich, he volunteered to create a position for him on two conditions: Tillich had to be able to teach in English, and Columbia had to give him a joint appointment in the philosophy department. Coffin knew hardly anything about Tillich; aside from H. Richard Niebuhr, who had translated *The Religious Situation,* few Americans did. While Coffin acquainted himself with Tillich's writings, Reinhold Niebuhr secured information about his personal circumstances, including the nature of Hitler's hostility toward him. Niebuhr and Coffin became Tillich's advocates on the Union faculty, which, at the depth of the Depression, accepted a 5 percent pay reduction to fund Tillich's stipend. Niebuhr made the offer to Tillich, who balked before accepting; for years afterward he identified with Abraham, often quoting Genesis 12:1: "Now the Lord said to Abram, 'Go from your country and your kindred and your father's house to the land that I will show you.'" He also routinely described Niebuhr as "my savior."[132]

TILLICH IN AMERICA:
THEOLOGY IN EXILE

For years Tillich struggled with the English language, finding it easy to read, but hard to understand and extremely difficult to speak. He never became more than a passable English speaker. He was comforted in New York by the presence of Adorno and Horkheimer at Columbia, Heimann and Löwe at the New School for Social Research, and other emigrés from Nazi Germany, many of whom he helped find work and accommodations. He was slow to bond with his new country. Tillich taught at Union for four years before receiving tenure and another three before he was made a full professor; by then he was only eleven years from the normal retirement age of sixty-five. He had little interest in American theology, though he enjoyed personal interactions with American theologians; he would have preferred a university position in philosophy as opposed to teaching in a seminary, but his rootage in German idealism had little place in American philosophy; though he had kindly relations with his Union colleagues, some of them doubted that he should be teaching future ministers; though he loved the bustle and internationalism of New York City, he missed Germany desperately. At first he pleaded for his academic reinstatement in Germany, telling the German government that "as the theoretician of Religious Socialism I have fought throughout the years against the dogmatic Marxism of the German labor movement, and thereby I have supplied a number of concepts to the National Socialist theoreticians." This pathetic boast was true—Nazi theologian Emanuel Hirsch appropriated Tillich's language and arguments—but fortunately, Tillich soon stopped taking credit for his former friend Hirsch.[133]

Even at the height of his socialist movement fervor in the 1920s, Tillich was never an ideologue. In 1922 he distinguished between the obligations and limits of religious engagement in political life, arguing that religious people are obliged to struggle for particular social ends while recognizing their own interpretive fallibility and the transcendent mystery that religion ultimately represents. In 1934 he protested that Hirsch distorted religious socialism by discarding Tillich's distinction between the *obligatum religiosum* and the *reservatum religiosum*. Hirsch reworked the Tillichian concepts of the *kairos,* the demonic, the boundary, the myths of origin, and the religious interpretation of history to support his conflation of Christian and Nazi faith. He perverted the idea of the *kairos,* Tillich observed, "into a sacerdotal-sacramental consecration of a current event." Against Hirsch's claim that the ascendancy of Nazi fascism represented the fulfillment of

Christian faith and hope, Tillich countered that the chief vocation of a theologian in a social movement is to uphold the integrity of religion against all ideological and utopian enthusiasms: "Your book shows me that you have neither seen it nor fulfilled it."[134]

Though he joined Niebuhr's Fellowship of Socialist Christians, for the most part Tillich kept a low profile politically. He didn't understand American politics, he was eager to get along with his American hosts, he felt the futility of being a socialist in a country without a socialist tradition, and he took seriously the *reservatum religiosum*. In 1936 he sought to introduce himself to Americans by explaining his personal history and chief concepts; more precisely, in a revealing fashion that he never quite repeated, he described himself through his concepts. *The Interpretation of History* opened with an autobiographical essay in which Tillich presented himself as a thoroughly dialectical creature standing "on the boundary" between various logical and historical options. "It has been my fate, in almost every direction, to stand between alternative possibilities of existence, to be completely at home in neither, to take no definitive stand against either." Temperamentally he combined the meditative, melancholic, guilt-ridden respect for authority of his east German father and the zestful, democratic, "sensuous concreteness" of his west German mother; similarly he combined nature romanticism and love of cities, a bourgeois sense of duty and an antibourgeois bohemianism, a rationalist devotion to the real and a romanticist devotion to the play of imagination, and a belief in the necessity of theory and practice.[135]

Tillich allowed that he was "marked out for theory, and not for practical activity." But in the life of religious faith, he observed, theory has to mean more than philosophical contemplation: "In religious truth the stake is one's very existence and the question is to be or not to be. Religious truth is existential truth, and to that extent it cannot be separated from practice." Explicating his dialectic of heteronomy/autonomy, Tillich placed Barth squarely on the side of authoritarianism and himself in the tradition of liberal theology. The Barthian theology played a prophetic role in the German Confessional church's resistance to fascism, he acknowledged, "but it created at the same time a new heteronomy, an anti-autonomous and anti-humanistic feeling, which I must regard as an abnegation of the Protestant principle." For Tillich, the "Protestant principle" was the constitutively Protestant commitment to the spirit of criticism; it followed for him that the most authentically Protestant theologies belonged to the liberal tradition, although he was critical of the Ritschlian school. "It was and is impossible for me to associate myself with the all too-common criticism of 'liberal thinking,'" he declared. "I would rather be accused of being 'liberalistic' myself, than aid in discounting the great and truly human element in the liberal idea."[136]

Tillich's opposition to Ritschlian liberalism centered on the two convictions that he took from his theological teacher, Martin Kähler. The first was that the central doctrine of Christianity is the Pauline-Lutheran doctrine of justification; the second was that the foundation of Christian belief is not the Jesus of history discovered by historical criticism, but the biblical picture of Christ. These convictions placed Tillich in the orbit of the dialectical theology movement, despite his opposition to what he called Barth's "new Supranaturalism." The upshot of the Pauline-Lutheran doctrine of justification is that no human belief, claim, or work has any saving value, he argued; the doctrine of justification radically relativizes all orthodoxies, while affirming that the burden of human sin is overcome by the paradoxical judgment that the sinner is just before God. Like Kähler, Tillich spurned the liberal tendency to dissolve the paradox of justification into moral categories; he further embraced Kähler's judgment that the center of Christianity is not the constantly changing picture of the historical Jesus produced by historical criticism, but rather the picture of Christ that thrives in human experience and is preached by the Christian church. Tillich failed to note that both of these arguments could be made on Ritschlian grounds; his protest was against the tendency of Ritschlian school theology to moralize the gospel and cling to the shifting tides of historical criticism. For Tillich, liberal criticism was the glory of liberal theology, but liberal dogmatics tended to be religiously shallow.[137]

Before World War I, he believed that Schelling's Christian philosophy of existence and his interpretation of history as the history of salvation showed how the disciplines of theology and philosophy should be united. After the war Tillich still found more "theonomous philosophy" in Schelling than in any other thinker, but he judged that Schelling played down the experience of the void. Tillich's experience of the abyss in existence effected the only intellectual turn that he ever made. "The World War in my own experience was the catastrophe of idealistic thinking in general," he remarked; for philosophy to be true and real, it had to speak to the existential realities of estrangement, despair, the void, the demonic, and death. For Tillich, the models were Nietzsche and Martin Heidegger; in 1924 he and Heidegger were colleagues at Marburg, a quaint university town sixty miles north of Frankfurt. Hannah Tillich later recalled that she and her husband hated Marburg, where "everything seemed coarse and unbearable" to them, including the food, the muddled Hessian accent, the claustrophobic encircling hills, the cultural provincialism, and the sexually repressive atmosphere. Tillich also dreaded the fact that most of his students at Marburg were Barthians. Though he had no personal relationship at Marburg with Heidegger or even Rudolf Bultmann (his only friends there were Rudolf Otto and historian of religions Friedrich Spiegelberg), Tillich's Marburg experience was redeemed by the impact of Heidegger's developing thinking.[138]

Heidegger was then conceiving his early masterwork *Being and Time*, which blended existential analysis with the phenomenological method of his teacher, Edmund Husserl. He described human beings as the unique type of being through whom Being (the primordial ground) presents itself to be known. Tillich was fascinated by Heidegger's vivid theorizing of the "thrown" character of human "being-there" *(Dasein)* and the perils that attend the self's coming-to-awareness of its arbitrarily given ("thrown") existence. Heidegger's description of the choice between "authentic" and "inauthentic" existence impressed Tillich and Bultmann as a powerful, modern, existential way of expressing the truths of

Pauline theology. In Heidegger's account, the inauthentic self falls into anxiety, or it replaces its first (infantile) totalized form of life with a substitute, or it gives up caring ("fallenness"). The authentic self faces up to one's nothingness and becomes a caretaking "being-toward-death" by changing the form of one's totalized givenness. Authentic existence, Heidegger argued, is the way of death-accepting moral courage and care for the world.[139]

Though Heidegger was an atheist, Tillich emphasized the Christian wellspring of his thinking. Much of Heidegger's ostensibly original language derived from the sermon literature of German pietism, Tillich noted: "By its explanation of human existence it establishes a doctrine of man, though unintentionally, which is both the doctrine of human freedom and human finiteness." Heideggerian philosophy did not include the theological answer to the problem of existence or offer a philosophical version of this answer, Tillich cautioned. That would be idealism, not existentialism: "However, the philosophy of existence asks the question in a new and radical manner." This was the value of existential analysis for Tillich's developing system; it clarified and developed the ontological problem to which faith and theology are the answer. Every theology presupposes some philosophical account of reality, Tillich insisted; the critical philosophical task of the theologian is to identify and work with the best constellation of philosophical descriptions that one can find. Tillich's philosophical canon gave central place to Schelling and Heidegger, while affirming that "the boundary line between philosophy and theology is the center of my thought and work."[140]

Several of his dialectics were variations on the theonomous dialectic of religious socialism. On the dialectic of church and society, Tillich claimed that the church "has always been my home in spite of all criticism," though he rarely attended church if he wasn't preaching, and he had to be urged, at first, to attend Union's chapel services. Closer to the center of his life and thinking, he clarified his understanding of the religious substance of culture and the cultural form of religion; in religion the substance is designated, he explained, and this substance is ultimate concern, "the unconditioned source and abyss of meaning." In culture the form is designated, and it has a conditioned meaning. The unconditioned meaning of religion, its substance, is perceptible only indirectly, through forms that bear the limits of historical and cultural relativity. The substance of Tillich's personal religion was Lutheran, he affirmed, and his politics were democratic socialist, which created an especially tensive pairing in his life. On his account, Lutheran religion emphasized the fallen condition of existence, the illusions of utopian thinking, the reality of the demonic in personal and social existence, an appreciation of the mythical aspects of religion, "and a repudiation of Puritan legality in individual and social life." By this criterion, Tillich counted himself a good Lutheran, but he was also a good socialist. With a Niebuhrian flourish he observed that his religion and politics made sense as a unity only if there was such a thing as nonutopian socialism: "The Kingdom of God can never become an immanent reality, and the absolute can never be realized in space and time. Every Utopianism must end with a metaphysical disappointment."[141]

Another Tillichian dialectic involved idealism and Marxism. German idealism was bread and life to Tillich, beginning with Kant's demonstration that the possibility of theoretical knowledge cannot be explained by pointing to the realm of things: "I nurtured German idealism, and I do not believe that I can ever unlearn what I learned there." Epistemologically he was an idealist without equivocation: "I am an idealist if idealism means the assertion of the identity of thinking and being as the principle of truth." The crucial insight that Tillich took from Marx, however, was that all systems of thought, including metaphysical idealism, have an ideological character. Tillich shunned the utopian, economistic, materialist, and atheist aspects of Marxism, but Marx's ideology critique was chastening to him; it taught him that every vision and concept of harmony is untrue under the conditions of the class struggle. For Marx, truth was found in the interest of the exploited class that becomes conscious of itself as the force that overcomes the class struggle. This paradoxical idea is intelligible from a Christian standpoint, Tillich observed: that the greatest possibility of obtaining a truth not tainted by ideology occurs at the point of despair, "of the broadest self-alienation of human essence." Elsewhere, Tillich called it the human border-situation that linked "the Protestant principle and the proletarian situation."[142]

His last dialectic was the personal one between home and alien land. It was his fate to carry on his work in an alien country, Tillich reflected, but like "every real fate," his situation was a sign of freedom. The boundary between Germany and the United States was not merely the external boundary of nature or history but also the border of two inner forces, "two possibilities of human existence." Like Abraham, who left his homeland for the sake of a promise that he did not comprehend in faithfulness to a God who transcended nation and cult, Tillich left his country out of faithfulness to a transcendent promise. He was driven to do so by the "demonic" self-destructiveness of European nationalism, of which Nazi fascism was the worst example. Nationalism throughout Europe was a tragic and destructive evil, Tillich reflected, but this judgment did not convert him to pacifism. For one thing, many pacifists had an "effeminate character" that repelled him; other pacifists displayed a self-righteous "pharisaic taint" that repelled him equally; in any case, pacifists had no answer to the problem of how to restrain "the trespassers of peace." In the mid-1930s Tillich came to the conviction that the United States stood for a better idea than either nationalistic will to power or the pacifist abdication of power politics. America represented the possibility of the unity of humankind under a single democratic republic. While noting that a "large gap" existed between the American ideal and American reality, Tillich enthused that America united "the representatives of all nations and races." As a nation of nations, America was developing into "a symbol for the highest possibility of history—Mankind." Increasingly he appreciated the American achievement and its promise: "I feel grateful that in the life of this new continent, on which I am allowed to live through the hospitality of this country, an ideal is suggested which is similar to the picture of the unity of mankind in contrast to the self-destruction of Europe."[143]

The Interpretation of History attracted little notice in 1936 apart from quietly negative responses at Union Seminary, where it confirmed local suspicions that Tillich was a religious philosopher in the traditions of Neoplatonism and German idealism, with neo-Marxist and existentialist twists, rather than a Christian theologian. The book was written in German and rather poorly translated, which did not encourage American readers to struggle with Tillich's concepts. Near the end of his autobiographical section Tillich confessed that he was "very uncertain" whether he would be able to formulate his system in a foreign country. He feared that the goal of giving his philosophy a definitive form had been put out of reach by his wrenching dislocation from Germany and his struggle with the English language. In 1966, after Tillich's storied career at Union, Harvard, and the University of Chicago had made him famous beyond his dreams, and a year after he died, a revised edition of the autobiographical section of *The Interpretation of History* was published in recognition that it represented the best available introduction to his thought.[144]

In 1937 Tillich made a key breakthrough, receiving an appointment at Union as Associate Professor of Philosophical Theology. This appointment gave him a new home and confirmed his self-conception as a "triboro bridge" (the name of a bridge about two miles from Union) of systematic theology, philosophy, and history. Increasingly he wrote English-language articles for American journals and overcame his fear that he could be a theologian only in Germany.[145] Though he never read much American theology or philosophy, he acquainted himself with American philosophical trends through his active involvement in the New York–centered Philosophy Club, which included Carl Hempel, Sidney Hook, Ernest Nagel, J. Robert Oppenheimer, John H. Randall Jr., John E. Smith, Paul Weiss, and John Wild; the friendship of Randall was especially important to him during his New York years. For information on American theological trends, Tillich relied on his membership in the Theological Discussion Group, the Yale-centered body founded by Henry P. Van Dusen, to which Reinhold Niebuhr, Bennett, Calhoun, Harkness, H. Richard Niebuhr, and approximately thirty others belonged. One episode from his participation in the Philosophy Club, recalled by Randall, entered the Tillich lore. On one occasion, after Tillich read a paper on existential philosophy, British analytic philosopher G. E. Moore rose to complain: "Now really, Mr. Tillich, I don't think I have been able to understand a single sentence of your paper. Won't you please try to state one sentence or even one word, that I can understand?" Tillich took such Anglo-American complaints graciously; friends and critics alike remarked on his gentle, peaceable, agreeable manner. Though Coffin often fretted that Tillich's theology was semi-Christian, he judged that Tillich had "a devout spirit and a very tender heart."[146]

In contexts that called for plain speech and strong conviction, however, Tillich was capable of making his beliefs perfectly clear. In later life he wrote several academic best-sellers; in 1942, two years after he became an American citizen, the U.S. Office of War Information invited him to write weekly radio addresses for the Voice of America for broadcast into Germany. Beginning at an Allied low point in the war and concluding just before D-Day 1944, Tillich wrote 112 speeches, each of which began with the salutation, "My German friends!" Passionately he called for the defeat of fascism and the federation of Europe; repeatedly he condemned the Nazi annihilation of the Jews. His first address declared that "the Jews are the people of history, the people of the prophetic, future-judging spirit" and that the blood of the Jews was "upon us and our children." In December 1942 he began to give detailed descriptions of the death trains and the machine-gun executions of Jews: "Today they are being hauled away to mass death by German hangmen, by those who are trash and the disgrace of the German people, and you are standing by! Can you stand by any longer, German officers, when you still have a sword to use and an honor to lose? . . . Do you know that the cattle cars that roll through the German cities with this burden of wretchedness are bolted up for days; that no bread and water is let in, no dying or dead are let out; and that at the end of the journey, frequently over half of the deportees are lying dead on the ice-cold floor of the car? And you want to be spectators of that, German clergy, you who are praying for German victory?"[147]

Bitterly he pronounced that the hope of a unified Europe led by Germany had been forfeited by the spectacular evil of the Nazi torturers and executioners: "I believe that National Socialism was the outbreak and the concentration of nearly all that was diseased within the German soul. Long have these poisons accumulated within it." At Advent he warned: "You can't have it both ways. Whoever follows National Socialism must persecute the child in the manger." To describe the moral backwardness of contemporary German life, he reached for terms like "pre-human," judging that Germans needed to be reborn into the human race: "Two thousand years of German education out of barbarity into humanity have been taken back. The chivalry of the Middle Ages toward the enemy is forgotten, but the cruelty of the Middle Ages has arisen again and has brutalized the hearts and trampled all nobility underfoot. The humanity of the classical age of Germans is being made contemptuous, but the warlike instincts of the German past have become intensified beyond all boundaries." The Nazi regime was based on "the desire for human degradation, abuse, and elimination of the enemy," Tillich declared: "National Socialism is brutality coupled with lust for revenge and a deep inner weakness." With a hopeful spirit he assured: "Everything that is creative in the German people demands a return to the human race. . . . For all nations—but particularly for Germany, the country of Middle Europe—everything will depend on the fact that the national remains subordinated to the human race as a whole."[148]

In the latter months of the war Tillich chaired a national German émigré organization, the Council for a Democratic Germany, that advocated a disarmed Germany without economic or political dismemberment; it was a bruising experience that turned out to be his last serious venture in American politics. Members of the council fiercely debated the group's exclusion of Communists, among other disagreements, and Tillich was blacklisted by the U.S. Army, which interpreted his chairmanship of the council as proof that he was pro-German and pro-Communist. Both charges were false, but this episode and the postwar atmosphere of American politics in general convinced Tillich to keep his distance from the political scene. In 1948 he returned to Germany, gave numerous lectures, and was warmly received, as long as he stayed off the topic of German guilt. Tillich was disturbed by the self-pity of his German friends and their refusal to think of themselves as guilty for the fate of the Jews; he reasoned that their feeling of guilt was so great that they were forced to repress it. His reunions included an unexpectedly jovial conversation with Barth (in Basel) and a poignant meeting with Hirsch, who was blind, impoverished, bitter, and unapologetic. Offered teaching positions at various German universities, Tillich carefully considered each one but returned to the United States. He no longer worried that he could not write theology outside Germany. A collection of his articles, *The Protestant Era,* was published to great acclaim in 1948, as was a collection of his sermons, *The Shaking of the Foundations.* To a friend Tillich wrote, "Harvest time is here; indeed I am now gathering in my harvest!"[149]

A remarkable group of intellectual laborers helped him gather his harvest. Though Tillich attracted few theological disciples in the narrow sense of the term (he advised only a small number of doctoral students in his American career, few of whom devoted themselves to refining his system), he attracted extraordinary helpers and advocates. One was historical theologian Wilhelm Pauck, also a German émigré, who befriended and advised Tillich, helping him adapt to American ways; another was American Unitarian theologian James Luther Adams, who served as a translator, editor, friend, and adviser. With Pauck's assistance, Adams made *The Protestant Era* a breakthrough work, carefully selecting, translating, and editing Tillich's best German and American essays; *The Protestant Era* described the work of theology as mediation between the mystery *(theos)* and the understanding *(logos).* Tillich acknowledged that to approach this task in an Anglo-Saxon culture required him to take seriously the interdependence of theory and practice, and that to write theology in English required him to clarify the "mystical vagueness" of his German vocabulary and thought. Without Pauck, Adams, and the assistants who worked on his *Systematic Theology*—John Dillenberger, Cornelius Loew, Albert T. Mollegen, and Clark Williamson—Tillich could not have produced it. Lacking extraordinary assistance, he would not have become a major figure in modern theology. Though Tillich always acknowledged the work of his associates, he never showed that he realized how unusual it was.[150]

His belated start on his systematic theology began during the same period that he gave up on the *kairos* and accentuated his psychological interests. Tillich no longer believed that he was living in the right time for creative action in the social sphere; America had no socialist tradition to speak of, postwar American politics was consumed by shows of anticommunist militance, and he despaired of believing that transformative social change was possible. His sermons, articles, and formal theology increasingly gave to existential and psychological concerns the privileged place that he previously had given to politics. In the 1940s he took an active part in the New York Psychology Group, which included anthropologist

Ruth Benedict, psychologists Erich Fromm and Rollo May, and theologians Seward Hiltner and David E. Roberts. In the subsequent decade, much of Tillich's dominating theological influence was due to his supportive and energizing impact on the burgeoning field of pastoral counseling. He spoke at conferences of psychoanalytic societies and institutes, succeeded Fosdick as a popular preacher of psychologized sermons, and in 1950, while working on his systematic theology, gave the enormously successful Terry Lectures at Yale on the meaning of anxiety and courage. Published as *The Courage to Be,* a year after the first volume of his *Systematic Theology* appeared, Tillich's Terry Lectures expressed the core of his religious thinking in a form that spoke to a wide audience and thus amplified the impact of his theological system.[151]

The Courage to Be analyzed the phenomenon of modern anxiety as a symptom of the modern loss of meaning in life. Courage is an ethical reality rooted in the structure of being, Tillich argued. It is ethical as a human act and value, and it is ontological as the universal and essential self-affirmation of one's being. To understand the ethical phenomenon of courage, one must consider its ontological basis. The courage to be is the ethical act in which human beings affirm their own being despite the experiences of anxiety and meaninglessness that contradict their essential self-affirmation.[152]

Crucial to the book's generative influence in the fields of theology and pastoral counseling was its discussion of the relation between existential and pathological anxiety. Existential anxiety is constitutively human, Tillich contended; it cannot be removed, even by courage, because existential anxiety is awareness of the reality of nonbeing, the void. In essence, existential anxiety is a symptom of humanity's universal estrangement, and neurotic anxiety is the failure to cope with existential anxiety. Tillich distinguished three responses to the threat of nonbeing perceived in existential anxiety. In the despairing response, the self gives in to an overpowering aggressor and gives up on life; in the neurotic response, the pathologically anxious self takes a shortcut to self-affirmation by settling for an unreal world of shrunken and often imaginary goods; in the courageous response, the self fights off the paralyzing aggression of the void by accepting the reality of nonbeing and affirming one's life in spite of it. Courage is redemptive in its willingness and capacity to take the anxiety of nonbeing into itself and live with spirit.

His description of pathological anxiety as a neurotic reaction to existential anxiety had disciplinary implications. Psychiatrists and psychotherapists are skilled in dealing with pathological anxiety, Tillich observed, but they lack the resources of theologians and philosophers in seeking to understand the varieties of existential anxiety in which all forms of neurotic pathology are rooted. Even the psychiatrist who insists that anxiety is always pathological has to explain the universality of finitude, doubt, and guilt, and therefore has to admit the possibility of an illness in human nature. "This is why more and more representatives of medicine generally and psychotherapy specifically ask for the cooperation with the philosophers and theologians," Tillich observed. "And it is why through this cooperation a practice of 'counseling' has developed." Pathological anxiety is a medical problem, but existential anxiety is "an object of priestly help." To fulfill its own theoretical and practical functions, medically oriented psychology needed a better understanding of the human problem, "and it cannot have a doctrine of man without the permanent cooperation of all those faculties whose central object is man."[153]

Tillich's thematization of anxiety and courage was a variation on the early thinking of Heidegger, whom Tillich described as an apostle of a despairing form of courage. The early Heidegger was a master phenomenologist of anxiety, finitude, nonbeing, guilt, and care, while, more recently, French existentialist Jean-Paul Sartre took the existential viewpoint to its extreme conclusion, that aside from the sense in which one's essence is one's existence, human beings have no essential nature at all. The early Heidegger was saved from pure existentialism by his mystical concept of being, Tillich noted, but for both Heidegger and Sartre, existential philosophy stood for a despairing ethic of courage in a modern world that has no meanings. Tillich's argument for a more positive, religious form of courage rested on the reality of faith, which he defined as "the state of being grasped by the power of being-itself." The courage to care and flourish in spite of existential anxiety is an experience of faith, he argued, and faith must be understood through the phenomenon of the courage to be.[154]

Tillich's favorite and most famous sermon, "You Are Accepted," which was published in *The Shaking of the Foundations,* asserted that the essence of being a religious person is the acceptance of the fact that one is accepted. In *The Courage to Be* Tillich spelled out the theology behind this claim. The power of courage is the power of being that is effective in every act of courage, he reasoned, and faith is the experience of this courage to be, which has a paradoxical character. Just as being itself transcends every finite being infinitely, God transcends every individual self unconditionally. There is an infinite chasm between God and every self, but faith bridges this gap by accepting the fact that despite the existence of the chasm, the power of being is present. The one who is separated from God is nonetheless accepted. Just as courage is saving in its acceptance of estrangement and nonbeing, faith is saving in its acceptance of acceptance. Faith accepts in spite of separation, "and out of the 'in spite of' of faith the 'in spite of' of courage is born." Tillich cautioned that faith is not an opinion about something uncertain; it is the existential acceptance of something that transcends the world of ordinary experience described by secular existentialism: "It is the state of being grasped by the power of being which transcends everything that is and in which everything that is participates."[155]

The Courage to Be ended with a religiously Nietzschean flourish; Tillich sympathized with the Nietzschean atheism of existential philosophy because he believed that the God described by Nietzsche had to be killed. The God of theism is a being, not being itself, he explained. As a being, and thus an object of thought, the God of traditional theism is bound to the structural dichotomy of subject and object. God is an object for human subjects, and human beings are objects for God as a subject. This is precisely the world picture that Nietzsche rightly repudiated, Tillich argued: "For God as a subject makes me into an object which is nothing more than an object. He deprives me of my subjectivity because he is all-powerful and all-knowing. I revolt and try to make him into an object, but the revolt fails and becomes desperate. God appears as the invincible tyrant, the being in contrast with whom all other beings are without freedom and subjectivity." If God is a being among other beings, God inevitably becomes the enemy of freedom and subjectivity: "This is the God Nietzsche said had to be killed because nobody can tolerate being made into a mere object of absolute knowledge and absolute control."[156]

The God of theism is not the divine ground of the courage to be, but its enemy, Tillich concluded. The anxiety of meaningless and nonbeing can be taken into the courage to be only if the divine power of being transcends the God of theism. From Christian mysticism Tillich took the idea of a "God above God," while cautioning that mysticism pursues the God beyond theism by leaving the world of finite values and meanings behind. Thus mysticism waves off the problem of meaninglessness. Tillich countered that the genuine hope of salvation comes to life within this world of struggling and caring after the God of theism has been buried: "The courage to be is rooted in the God who appears when God has disappeared in the anxiety of doubt."[157]

The Courage to Be gave Tillich his first taste of celebrity outside the realms of academe and church. The book spoke to many readers who appreciated its affirmation of doubt and its nonchurchly atmosphere. Though his writings had always substituted philosophical language for traditional religious terms, Tillich's therapeutic turn appealed to a growing audience of middle-class readers that would not have read a treatise on religious socialism. Though many of his colleagues at Union were alarmed by his semi-Nietzschean pronouncements, the book's skillful synthesis of philosophy, depth psychology, and theology offered a model of cultural theology to many pastors. His popularity among students at Union soared to Niebuhrian heights, and Tillich made time to counsel many students about their struggles with anxiety and depression. His sermons were widely quoted, and, increasingly, he took pride in his effective preaching.

Meanwhile the chief fruit of his harvest, the first volume of his systematic theology, lifted his name above all contemporary American theologians. Tillich's *Systematic Theology* is one of the major works of twentieth-century systematics, ranking with Barth's *Church Dogmatics* and Karl Rahner's *Foundations of the Christian Faith*. Though it was too independent and Germanic to belong to the tradition of American theology, for mid-century American liberal theologians it towered above everything else in the field. American Ritschlians, social gospelers, evangelical liberals, religious humanists, personalists, mystics, Whiteheadians, Chicago school empiricists, and liberal Niebuhrians often paid little attention to each other in the 1950s, but none ignored Tillich. As they carried out the task of reinterpreting their theological positions in the 1950s and 1960s, nearly all of them drew upon Tillich's fund of concepts and arguments.

METHOD, BEING, EXISTENCE,
AND THE NEW BEING: TILLICH'S SYSTEM

For fifteen years after he arrived in the United States, Tillich expressed his desire to begin what he called the "real work" of his life, while lamenting his various interruptions, his supposed lack of an American audience, and his very real problems with organization. He was incapable of managing administrative tasks, especially anything having to do with academic credits or curriculum, and he had related problems with intellectual execution. Though he always thought and taught systematically, relating each problem in theology to all other problems, for twenty-five years Tillich struggled and failed to begin his masterwork. His pedagogical style was informally organized around lists of propositions, on which he tended to expound with few notes. After World War II, at what proved to be perfect timing for Tillich's career and influence, his graduate assistant John Dillenberger helped get him started. Using a self-taught shorthand, Dillenberger took down everything that Tillich said in his lectures and then dictated the notes to a typist immediately after class; these notes comprised the first draft of Tillich's *Systematic Theology*. For years he and Dillenberger labored over the manuscript of volume one, with substantial assistance from Union graduate assistant Cornelius Loew and Virginia Theological Seminary ethicist Albert T. Mollegen. After Tillich moved to Harvard in 1955, where he and Dillenberger were colleagues, Dillenberger performed the same preparatory and editorial work for Tillich on the second volume of his systematics; in 1962, after Tillich moved to the University of Chicago, his assistant Clark Williamson conducted similar labor on volume three, though Tillich arrived in Chicago with a completed first draft.[158]

In *Systematic Theology* Tillich offered a method of correlation between the existential questions raised in the modern cultural situation and the answers contained in the symbols of the Christian message. Christianity has true answers to the questions raised by modern inquiry, Tillich affirmed, but the agenda for theology is shaped by human questioning and striving, not by the answers. Because relevance is important, and because theology is inherently contextual, the work of theology must begin with an analysis of the human situation. It is not credible for any theologian to claim to speak out of faith and revelation alone, he insisted, for every theologian belongs not only to the theological circle of faith, but also to the cultural environment of one's time: "Every theologian is committed and alienated; he is always in faith *and* in doubt; he is inside *and* outside the theological circle. Sometimes the one side prevails, sometimes the other; and he is never certain which side really prevails." Tillich assured that the ultimate concern of the theologian is the theological answer, but no formulation of the answer is infallibly correct or culturally unconditioned. Religion is ultimate concern, and ultimate concern is unconditional, "independent of any conditions of character, desire, or circumstance." To absolutize something that is merely relative and conditional is idolatrous; in his view, most bad theology was "demonic" in precisely this sense. Good theology gives itself only to the unconditioned, he argued; put differently, the object and first formal criterion of theology is that which concerns us ultimately: "Only those propositions are theological which deal with their object in so far as it can become a matter of ultimate concern for me."[159]

And what is the appropriate content of ultimate concern? Tillich answered: "Our ultimate concern is that which determines our being or not-being. Only those statements are theological which deal with their object in so far as it can become a matter of being or not-being for us." This was his second formal criterion of theology: nothing can be an appropriate ultimate concern that does not possess the power of threatening or saving one's being. Tillich cautioned that "being" does not refer to existence in time and space, for existence is constantly threatened and saved by things and events that fall short of the status of ultimacy. In his language, "being" meant the "whole of human reality, the structure, the meaning, and the aim of existence." True religion is about cosmic meaning, the saving of the whole that is threatened. It is unconditionally concerned about that which conditions human existence beyond all the conditions that are in and around human beings.[160]

In the same way that Schleiermacher described true religion before making an argument for Christianity as the best example of true religion, Tillich thus described the twofold criterion of good theology before making an argument for Christianity as the best theological answer. Christian theology is like other theologies, he observed; it is *logos* of *theos*, a rational interpretation of religious rituals, symbols, and myths, but Christian theology makes a claim to being the theology because it is founded on the claim that the Logos entered history in and through the life of a human being, Jesus. The essential Christian affirmation is that the divine logos, the mind of God, was uniquely revealed in the event of Jesus as the Christ. Christianity is distinctively concrete and universal, Tillich explained: it makes a claim about Jesus that is more concrete than any mystical vision or metaphysical principle, yet no vision or principle is as universal as the logos, "which itself is the principle of universality." In comparison to the logos, everything else is particular, including the "half-God" Arian theology that nearly captured Christianity in the fourth century. Implicitly Tillich judged that the church of Athanasian orthodoxy was right to condemn Arianism, because Arian theology sold short the universality and the concreteness of the Johannine confession that the Word became flesh and dwelt among us.[161]

Tillich recognized four sources of theology—the Bible, church history, the history of religions, and culture—while dissenting from the liberal convention of conceiving personal experience as a theological source. Schleiermacher derived the entire content of Christianity from the religious consciousness of the Christian; other varieties of liberal theology and pietism spoke of personal experience as one of the sources of theology; Tillich countered that experience is the medium through which the sources of theology speak to religious thinkers. Theologians experience the power of their sources before analyzing them. Experience is receptive, not productive, for the productive power of experience is limited to the transformation of what is given to it. True reception intends only reception; if it intends something else, such as transformation, it falsifies that which is received. Though the event of Jesus as the Christ is infinite in its meaning, Tillich acknowledged, it remains the singular, defining event of Christianity and is thus the criterion of religious experience. Experience is a vehicle for theology, not a norm or independent source, for the event of Jesus as the Christ is given to experience, not derived from it. Tillich allowed that if a univocal unity existed between the (regenerated) human spirit and the divine Spirit, it would be possible to conceive experience as an independent source of theology, but on this point he remained a good Lutheran. The unity of the human and divine spirits is an enthusiast mistake and a modern conceit, he admonished; even the saint is also a sinner. Revelation may occur through modern saints, as it occurred through the prophets and apostles, but revelation always comes *to* the saints and against their nature, not from them: "Insight into the human situation destroys every theology which makes experience an independent source instead of a dependent medium of systematic theology."[162]

Crucial to the character and influence of Tillich's theology was his thematization of myth and symbolism. Throughout his career he insisted that myth is an essential component of human life and thought, not a disposable form of religious expression, and that symbols convey the mythical truths of religion. Myths are not merely prescientific explanations of events in the world, he argued; they are constellations of symbols that express humanity's relation to that which concerns human beings ultimately. Though science is antimythical in its study of objects, even science is myth-creative in its conceptual theorizing. Science makes sense of the world of things by making use of concepts (such as "evolution") that are transcendent to things. By its nature, myth (like science) seeks to unify creation, or at least make it intelligible, under a single conceptuality; the key to myth is its unifying impulse, Tillich argued, yet ironically, myth is true only in its broken form. To the mythical consciousness, the transcendent realm is perfectly knowable, and the workings of the natural world are readily explainable. Pure unbroken myth is always a history of the gods. With the rise of Hebrew monotheism, the mythical unity of religion and science began to break apart. God was transcendent; his name was not to be spoken; he lived even if his nation died. Human consciousness of the relativity of knowledge in the transcendent realm and the natural world made each realm more independent.[163]

But Tillich urged that the desacralization of the world does not negate the necessity of true myth; rather, the breaking of mythical consciousness allows the true character of myth to come forth as an aspect of thought. Even in its broken state, the mythical imagination still seeks to find the hidden wholeness of reality; in this meaning-seeking drive to reunify the world, broken myth has its primary value for theology, Tillich theorized. The world of things described by science is related to its unconditioned ground; the unconditioned transcendent is interpreted from the viewpoint of modern knowledge; the unifying impulse of religion is restored in the mythical symbol. Put differently, science becomes myth-creative out of its need to theorize that which transcends the world of things; theology accepts the authority of science regarding knowledge of the natural world; and theology relates all such knowledge to the religious transcendent. In its drive to unify these fields of experience, myth participates in and points to the unconditioned: "The thing referred to in the mythical symbol is the unconditioned transcendent, the source of both existence and meaning, which transcends being-in-itself as well as being-for-us."[164]

Because symbolism is the language of faith, myth is intrinsic to every act of faith. Tillich cautioned that this does not make it beyond criticism. He took for granted that all mythical speech must be demythologized by modern knowledge before it can be useful to theology. The religious ultimate transcends space and time, but myth expresses its stories of the divine into the framework of space and time; it even negates the ultimacy of the divine by dividing the divine into multiple figures. Demythologizing is valuable as a program that breaks religious myth and deliteralizes it. Though he complained that the term is "negative and artificial," Tillich allowed that demythologizing performs an important function "if it points to the necessity of recognizing a symbol as a symbol and a myth as a myth." But demythologizing is terribly wrong as a program of myth-negation, he asserted. It silences the experience of the Holy and deprives religion of its language. It fails to understand that myth and symbol are ever-present forms of human consciousness. One can replace a myth by another myth, but myth itself is constitutive to the spiritual life.[165]

It followed for Tillich that Christian symbols and myths should not be criticized for being symbols and myths; they are subject to criticism on the basis of their power to express the spiritual realities in which they participate and to which they point. Religious symbols are different from signs inasmuch as symbols participate in the reality to which they point, he argued. Symbols and signs both point beyond themselves to something else, but symbols participate in the meaning and power of the reality for which they stand. They open up the deepest dimension of the human soul and reality, which is the ultimate power of being, and radiate the power of being and meaning of that for which they stand. They are true to the extent that they express the inner necessity that a symbol carries for consciousness. That is, a religious symbol is true to the degree that it reaches its Unconditioned referent. "The only criterion that is at all relevant is this: that the Unconditioned is clearly grasped in its Unconditionedness," Tillich argued. "A symbol that does not meet this requirement and that elevates a conditioned thing to the dignity of the Unconditioned, even if it should not be false, is demonic." To worship anything less than the Unconditioned transcendent is to commit idolatry.[166]

This theory of religious symbolism pervaded the first volume of Tillich's *Systematic Theology*, which argued that all God language is symbolic except for the assertion that God is being itself; in his second volume Tillich disavowed the exception. Moreover, his discussion of the reality of God centered on his thematization of idolatry and the religion of Unconditioned transcendence. Conceiving

God as the ground and power of being itself, Tillich reasoned that God is not subject to the ontological structure of being because God is the ground and power that determines the structure of everything that has being. In volume one he claimed that the statement, "God is being-itself," is direct, conceptual, and therefore nonsymbolic; in volume two he allowed that even "being-itself" is a symbol that points beyond itself. In both cases he curiously failed to acknowledge that the only nonsymbolic statements that one can make about God are negative statements (e.g., "God is not a man" and "God does not exist"), but in both volumes, Tillich's emphasis on the symbolic nature of religious language effected a field-shaping influence in theology and religious studies. Religious symbols are true in a double sense, he argued; they *have* truth and they *are* true. They bear truth to the extent that they are adequate to the revelation that they express, and they are true as expressions of a true revelation. They are also double-edged: religious symbols are directed toward the infinite, which they symbolize, but they are also directed toward the finite, through which they symbolize the infinite.[167]

Tillich conceived theology as the interpretation of religious symbols according to theological principles and methods. For example, the doctrine of creation is a symbolic description of the relation between God and the world, not a story about a prehistoric event. As a theological answer to an existential question, the doctrine of creation is the correlate to the question of finitude, teaching that the meaning of human finitude is creatureliness and that divine creativity is correlated with creatureliness. It affirms that God as the ground of being eternally creates Godself as the one whose life is identical with creation. Because the divine life is essentially creative, Tillich argued, all three modes of time must be employed to symbolize God's past, present, and future creativity. God's originating creativity has created the world; God's sustaining creativity is creative in the present moment; God's directive creativity will creatively fulfill God's *telos*. Tillich's system thus subsumed the themes of the preservation of the world and divine providence under the doctrine of the divine creativity. Without explaining what would *not* be an act of God according to this interpetation, he conceived divine providence as the permanent activity of God through which God directs everything toward its fulfillment, always working through the freedom and integrity of creatures.[168]

Systematic Theology, volume one, was immediately recognized as a major event in theology, notwithstanding numerous complaints that its language was too abstract and formal. Daniel Day Williams worried that Tillich's Hegelian understanding of divine reality precluded the possibility of saying anything particular about the divine character, but he lauded the publication of Tillich's system as "an event of great importance not only throughout the theological world but wherever there is serious discussion about the meaning of life." He praised Tillich's "extraordinary power to speak to contemporary culture in its own terms" and concluded that "Tillich's theology is one of the high peaks in the whole range of Christian thought." H. Richard Niebuhr judged that while volume one was too difficult, abstract, and ontological, it was also "a great voyage of discovery into a rich and deep, an inclusive and yet elaborated vision and understanding of human life in the presence of the mystery of God." Yale philosopher Theodore M. Greene declared that Tillich was "the most enlightening and therapeutic theologian of our time," while T. S. Eliot, who read the book twice, told Tillich that he considered it a great work. Reinhold Niebuhr predicted that Tillich's first volume would become "a landmark in the history of modern theology" because it rigorously addressed the problems of modern culture and religious doubt and because it appreciated the limits of reason "in penetrating to the ultimate mystery or in comprehending the mystery of human existence." Among American theological works of the middle decades, only Niebuhr's *Nature and Destiny of Man* came close to *Systematic Theology* in field-dominating influence, and in 1951, while Niebuhr was losing his robust health and vitality, Tillich was just entering his glory years.[169]

Tillich's first volume of systematics opened a floodgate of honors and lecture invitations through which he expanded his influence. The inaugural volume of a heralded series of festschrifts titled "The Library of Living Theology" was devoted to Tillich's thought in 1952, the same year that he published *The Courage to Be.* In that year he also delivered the Firth Lectures at the University of Nottingham, which argued for the unity of love, power, and justice at the level of their ontological meanings; these lectures were published in 1954. In 1955, the year that Tillich retired from Union Theological Seminary and accepted an appointment as University Professor at Harvard University, he published another sermon collection, *The New Being,* and another lecture collection, *Biblical Religion and the Search for Ultimate Reality.* The latter work defended his positive interpretation of religion and his dialectic of theology and philosophy, arguing that the symbols of biblical religion lead by their logic and dynamism toward the philosophical quest for being.[170]

Biblical Religion and the Search for Ultimate Reality contended that there is a structural identity between the symbols of biblical religion and the being language of ontology insofar as both address the problem of faith and doubt. Both languages stand on the boundary line between being and nonbeing, Tillich argued; moreover, the biblical symbols of creation, the *logos* of Jesus Christ, and the eschaton both imply and require an ontology. What does it mean to say that the world was created by the Word out of nothing? Or that the universal *logos* was present in Jesus as the Christ? Or that history is going somewhere? Tillich observed that every religious answer to these questions employs an ontology, and every philosophy is rooted in the existential problems of faith and doubt. Though he rarely replied to critics, *Biblical Religion and the Search for Ultimate Reality* contained at least the suggestion of a critical reply to those who complained about too much ontology in his system: "If one starts to think about the meaning of biblical symbols, one is already in the midst of ontological problems."[171]

By the mid-1950s Tillich was highly skilled at condensing the essence of his theological system into popular essays. His most successful venture in this genre, published during the same year (1957) as his keenly anticipated second volume of systematics, was titled *Dynamics of Faith*. This book explained his theory of religious symbolism to a mass audience and reflected on the intellectual, emotional, and volitional dimensions of faith, spurning the Barthian insistence that faith is not a human possibility. For Tillich, to understand faith as a human possibility did not preclude its conception as a gift of the Holy Spirit, since God always works through human freedom. Faith is religious, Tillich observed, yet it transcends religion; it is universal, yet it is also concrete; it is infinitely variable, yet it is always the same: "Faith is an essential possibility of man, and therefore its existence is necessary and universal." To a vast popular audience, *Dynamics of Faith* made sense of faith; to many readers, the book also served as a gentle warm-up for the demanding prose of *Systematic Theology,* volume two.[172]

Originally delivered in Aberdeen as two series of Gifford Lectures in 1953 and 1954, Tillich's second volume of systematics was subtitled *Existence and the Christ.* Before giving both sets of lectures, he lectured extensively across Europe and thus was ill and exhausted both times by the time that he arrived in Aberdeen. His Aberdeen experience was dismal on other counts, a rarity in his years of fame. Though Tillich's second series ended on a warm note, most of the time his audiences averaged less than twenty listeners, and the reserved Scots gave little sign of appreciating his Christology. The latter reaction was an omen; Tillich's Christology had fundamental flaws, and it never gained the influence of his theories of ultimate concern or religious language. For some of his disciples, however, notably Albert T. Mollegen and Langdon Gilkey, his interpretation of Christ, existence, and the New Being was the center and highlight of his system.[173]

Tillich emphatically regarded volume two as the center of his system. Volume one interpreted God as the symbol of living, personal, creative, loving, fatherly, Triune, and providential being; volume two addressed the question that ended volume one: How does God reveal Godself in the personal order of existence? Employing what he called "a half-way demythologization" of the biblical myth of the fall, Tillich argued that the story of the fall is a symbol of the universal human condition, not a story about a prehistorical event. To eliminate the connotation of "once upon a time" from the fall story, he described it as the "transition from essence to existence." This translation takes demythologizing only half-way, he acknowledged, for while it replaces mythological figures with abstract concepts, it still speaks about the divine in temporal terms; theology requires a fair amount of demythologization, but complete demythologization would be the death of theology and religion. In Tillich's rendering, the biblical myth of the fall symbolized the human realization that sin is not created and that the transition from essence to existence is a fact of experience, "the actual in every fact." Human beings exist, and their world exists with them; this is the original fact: "It means that the transition from essence to existence is a universal quality of finite being. It is not an event of the past; for it ontologically precedes everything that happens in time and space." The fall symbolizes the conditions of existence, which are manifest in every person's growth into actualization and guilt.[174]

Appropriating a Hegelian term, Tillich theorized that the state of every person's existence is one of "estrangement" from the ground of being, other beings, and one's own being. He favored the term "estrangement" for its abstract conceptual independence from the history of Christian sin language and because it implies that one belongs essentially to that from which one is unfortunately separated. At the same time, Tillich allowed that the word "estrangement" cannot be employed as a perfect substitute for sin. The word "sin" carries too much classical and liturgical weight to be replaceable, he judged; more importantly, it effectively points to the moral truth that every human being bears some personal responsibility for his or her existential estrangement, unbelief, hubris, and concupiscence. Every expression of estrangement or sin contradicts the essential being of human beings. Tillich observed that evil is parasitic on the good, just as nonbeing is dependent on being and death is dependent on life. Even the nihilating corruption of life toward nothingness has structures: "It 'aims' at chaos; but, as long as chaos is not attained, destruction must follow the structures of wholeness; and if chaos is attained, both structure and destruction have vanished."[175]

Tillich often startled his classes by announcing that he believed in the demonic; World War I convinced him of the reality of destructive powers of being that militate against the flourishing of life. At the same time, he believed that the question of salvation can be asked only if salvation is already at work; the despairing soul does not ask how one might be saved from the creation-reversing powers of the demonic; just as the search for truth presupposes the existence of truth, the quest for the New Being presupposes the reality of salvation. Salvation requires searching for it, and thus already believing in it, Tillich argued, but its realization is never a human achievement. Any religion that teaches self-salvation derives both religion and salvation from estranged humanity; true salvation is a revelatory deliverance, an experience of saving power. Tillich called it the manifestation of the New Being; his famous sermon "The New Being" declared that Christianity is the proclamation of a new reality, "the New Being, the New state of things." In his rendering, the quest for the New Being was universal; it appears in all religions, and wherever it appears, it reveals and claims the reality of saving power. As the religion of divine-human unity in Jesus as the Christ, Tillich argued, Christianity is the consummate religion of New Being, though he left open the possiblity of divine manifestations in other dimensions or periods of being.[176]

Emphatically he rejected the claim that Christian faith rests upon a core of objective or professed historical events. There is no faith without risk, he allowed, but the risk of faith is existential; it concerns the totality of our being, not the acceptance of uncertain historical claims. The basis of faith cannot be a certain degree of probability that Jesus really lived or that the essentials of the gospel story are historically accurate: "Is it not destructive for the Christian faith if the nonexistence of Jesus can somehow be made probable, no matter how low the degree of probability?" Neither is the historical foundation of Christianity proven by the historical power of Christianity. Tillich countered that faith is able to guarantee only its own foundation, which is the revelation of the New Being that conquers estrangement and makes faith possible. Historical matters pertaining to Jesus of Nazareth lie outside the experience of the faithful person, but faith is able to guarantee the reality of that which has created faith in the first place, because the existence of faith is identical with the experienced reality of the New Being. Faith is the immediate evidence of the experience of salvation, not the end of an argument: "No historical criticism can question the immediate awareness of those who find themselves transformed into the state of faith." While theology must be informed and chastened by historical criticism, the foundation of Christian faith can be neither given nor taken away by it. Tillich analogized that just as Augustine and Descartes refuted radical skepticism by pointing to the immediacy of a self-consciousness that proves itself by its participation in being, the experience of faith is the only proof that Christianity is based on something real and true.[177]

This argument could be pressed along liberal lines—the Herrmannian wing of the Ritschlian school did so, as did Knudson—but Tillich took it to the "neo-orthodox" extreme that Bennett criticized. His Christology was a very liberal example of the neo-orthodox strategy of making orthodox-sounding claims about Christ while relativizing the historical Jesus. Christian faith guarantees a new life of saved New Being, he argued, but it cannot guarantee that Jesus of Nazareth is the agent of this transformation. Though the founder of Christianity was probably named Jesus, we cannot be certain of it. For Christianity, the crucial fact is that the New Being was and is actual in this figure who is called the Christ, regardless of the probability that we have his name right. Tillich did not go as far as Kierkegaard, who claimed that it is enough to say that in the years 1–30 God sent his son. The newness of the New Being is empty if it is not grounded more concretely in history than this, Tillich allowed. Following Kähler's example he resorted to the "picture" of Jesus preserved by the community of the faithful and affirmed that there must have been a concrete being who created the picture in the minds and experience of the early church. The early Christian community was concretely powered by the picture of the Christ from whom this community took its name, Tillich reasoned. No particular part of this picture can be verified with certainty, but it is beyond any doubt that through this picture, many people have experienced and been transformed by the power of the New Being. Faith guarantees only the appearance of the reality that has created the New Being. The picture of Jesus as the Christ concretely mediated the transforming power of salvation to the early Christians, and it continues to mediate the power of the New Being to faithful people around the world.[178]

Without adopting the special language of philosophical personalism, Tillich adopted the personalist claim that the potentialities of being are fully actualized only in the lives of persons. Only a person confronts a world to which he or she simultaneously belongs, and only a person has freedom, the structure of rationality, and the unlimited power of self-transcendence; therefore the New Being can appear only in a person. Tillich's account of the appearance of the New Being in Christ distinguished between the symbolic framing of the picture of Jesus in the New Testament and the experiential substance in which the power of the

New Being is manifested. For example, he argued, the differences between the Synoptic and Johannine Christs are matters of symbolic framing, not substance. The symbol of Christ as the "Son of Man" correlates with the Synoptic eschatological frame; the symbol "Messiah" plays up the healing and preaching activities of Jesus; the symbols "Son of God" and "Logos" correlate with the Johannine frame.

The New Testament describes the appearance of the New Being in Christ through a variety of interpretive frameworks, Tillich argued, but the substance in which the power of the New Being is manifested remains the same in all of them. It shines through the unity of Christ's being with God, and through the majesty and serenity of Christ in sustaining this unity despite being persecuted by a sinful world, and through the actualization of God's self-surrendering love in the sacrificial and self-surrendering love of Christ. For Tillich, this threefold manifestation of the New Being in the Gospel picture of Christ was the heart of Christianity. Against the Harnackian, personalist, and modernist critics of hellenized Christianity, he admonished that the church fathers used the best concepts at their disposal. These concepts may have been inadequate, but it is unfair to criticize the church fathers for employing them. In Christology, Tillich preferred the Johannine Logos-frame to its alternatives, but he urged that the frame is ultimately a secondary matter. Nothing in the New Testament diminishes the saving power of the manifestation of New Being; the experience of that reality is the center of Christianity.[179]

Tillich's theology conceived the story of Jesus's resurrection as connected to the center of Christianity only in its interdependence with the symbol of the cross. The cross symbolizes Christ's conquering of the death of existential estrangement and the resurrection symbolizes the new life of the one who subjected himself to the death of existential estrangement. In the New Testament, Tillich allowed, the cross and resurrection are both viewed as symbols and events, and the objectivity of the resurrection is affirmed; from a critical standpoint, however, the cross and resurrection are quite different kinds of events. The cross was a public episode like many executions of its kind, while the resurrection is shrouded in mystery. Tillich judged that the cross and resurrection should be viewed as both symbols and events, but differently, because the cross is primarily an event, while the resurrection is primarily a symbol. His account of the factual aspect of the resurrection rejected the physical, spiritualistic, and psychological theories before advancing his own "restitution" theory.

The physical theory is presupposed in the empty tomb stories of the Gospels, in which resurrection is identified with the absence of a physical body. This theory is a primitive rationalization of the resurrection event, Tillich judged; it was unknown to the church of Paul's time and raises absurd questions—such as, what happened to the molecules of Jesus's corpse?—that quickly give rise to blasphemy. The spiritualistic theory interprets the resurrection appearances as manifestations of the soul of Jesus to his followers. This theory fits into a doctrine of the immortality of the soul, Tillich noted, but it does not do justice to the New Testament faith in the factual reality of Christ's resurrection, which is symbolized as the reappearance of Christ's total personality, including his embodiment. The psychological theory turns the factual aspect of the resurrection into an inner event in the minds of Jesus's followers. This explanation undoubtedly gets part of the factual problem right, Tillich surmised; for example, the story of Paul's conversion has a strongly psychological bent. But on the whole, the psychological theory does not account for the reality of the event of Christ's resurrection that the New Testament symbol of resurrection presupposes.

The nature of the reality of the event is the key question. The resurrection of Christ is not about the revival of an individual man or the reappearance of his spirit or even the spiritual experiences of his grieving followers, Tillich argued. It is about the overcoming of estrangement by the New Being and the overcoming of the disappearance of the New Being; the followers of Jesus beheld in him the power of New Being, but to their profound shock and grief he was suddenly consigned to the past by his death on Calvary, which threw into question the enduring reality of New Being: "In this tension something unique happened. In an ecstatic experience the concrete picture of Jesus of Nazareth became indissolubly united with the reality of the New Being." The disciples had convicting experiences of the presence of Jesus in their own continuing experiences of New Being. Jesus was present wherever the New Being was present. His death did not push him into the past or negate the presence of New Being. He was present again as spiritual presence, not as a revived body or illuminated soul. In effect, Tillich's restitution theory offered a reformulation of the psychological theory that comported with his Logos Christology. In this theory, the factual aspect of the resurrection of Christ was the restitution of the unity of the New Being and its bearer, Jesus of Nazareth: "The Resurrection is the restitution of Jesus as the Christ, a restitution which is rooted in the personal unity between Jesus and God and in the impact of this unity on the minds of the apostles."[180]

Though he claimed that the apostle Paul's non-literalism supported his side of the argument, Tillich distinguished between his (and Paul's) theory and Christian faith. Like all theories of the resurrection event, he counseled, restitution theory belongs to the realm of probability, not to the certainty of faith. Faith provides the certainty that the savior-figure pictured in the New Testament was the bearer of the New Being and that Jesus is present in the ongoing salvation of the world. Theology tries to explain why the death of Jesus did not separate the picture of Jesus from the New Being.

Tillich believed that these arguments formed the crux of his theology, but his theory of the New Being achieved far less influence than his theories of religion, ultimate concern, myth, symbol, divine reality, and cultural correlation. Numerous critics objected that he subsumed the biblical picture of Christ under the category of believing reception, so that faith became its own object; Tillich made various statements to this effect, but he also asserted that some degree of historicity is necessary to Christian faith and that the disciples did not *create* the biblical picture of Christ. The more discerning critics of his position thus charged that he tried to have it both ways. Tillich claimed that the biblical picture has a factual core in the life of Jesus and that historical criticism has no bearing on faith. He claimed historicity while refusing the risk of historicity. Theologian James C. Livingston protested, "The theologian must be willing to open his christological claims to the kind of historical investigation in which the continuity between Jesus and the kerygma is once again being tested." Theologian David Kelsey blasted the same contradiction: "Historical claims are made about revelatory events. The events are analyzed in ontological terms. Then the claims about the events are justified on ontological grounds, when what was needed was independent support on historical grounds."[181]

Tillich's second volume gave ballast to the vocal contention of theological conservatives that he was not a Christian. Theologian Kenneth Hamilton, Tillich's most discerning conservative critic, argued that his system amounted to an inverted Platonism; in a rare gesture, Tillich responded to Hamilton in the opening paragraph of volume two, claiming that Hamilton didn't comprehend the necessity of systematic thinking in theology.[182] Neo-personalist theologian Nels F. S. Ferré bolstered conservative criticism of Tillich by claiming that "in intellectual honesty a person is Christian or Tillichian, but he cannot be both." Ferré explained that Tillich's absolute was the idea of divine infinity, the Unconditioned that cannot become finite or conditioned without becoming a source of idolatry. Tillich believed in transcendent meaning, but not in a transcendent realm, Ferré observed; he believed in the expression of God's mind in nature and history as the Logos, but not in the incarnation of the divine nature in Jesus Christ. In Ferré's reading, everything that was wrong with Tillich's Christology flowed from his understanding of God as unconditioned Being. Tillich taught that the Ultimate cannot become incarnate without contradiction and blasphemy; Ferré countered that "either his ultimate is wrong or the Christian faith is false." Tillich replaced the Supreme Being idea of God with the idea of Being itself that cannot be limited by being conditioned; Ferré agreed that Western metaphysics was wrong to define divine being in terms of substance, but protested that Tillich threw out the personal God of Christian faith: "He actually did not believe in the Christian God who raises the dead and who works personally in human history."[183]

Numerous critics embraced Ferré's claim that Tillich employed dialectics to obscure his heterodoxy. In his later career Tillich worried that his theology attracted increasing criticism of this kind. Yet he remained on friendly terms with Ferré and other critics while pleading for more generous readings of his system; it wounded Tillich when people suggested that Ferré was his enemy. At Harvard's reception for Tillich on his seventieth birthday, Tillich rushed across the room to greet Ferré, threw his arms around him and exclaimed, "I am glad you came; people say we are enemies!" For his part, Ferré professed that he loved Tillich for his warm and kindly spirit; he also exaggerated only slightly in declaring that for many years Tillich's prestige was so great that it was "professional suicide" to openly reject his theology.[184]

TOWARD A THEOLOGY OF RELIGIONS

In his last years Tillich traveled widely and was showered with honorary degrees, medals, and media praise. He loved his seven years at Harvard, where he was welcomed by old friends James Luther Adams, John Dillenberger, and Paul Lehmann, and where he welcomed his liberation from the churchlike atmosphere of seminary life; Tillich prided himself on never going to church at Harvard. Mindful that he owed his renown to Union Seminary, he graciously asserted on various occasions that Union would always be home to him. In 1959 he made the cover of *Time* magazine, which editorialized, "Though Harvard's University Professor Paul Tillich is a rarefied philosopher and theologian, speaking and writing in a language he had to learn at the age of forty-seven, in a country noted for its impatience with theology, he has come to be regarded by the U.S. as its foremost Protestant thinker." Tillich basked in the freedom and prestige of his appointment as a university professor, in which he was not bound to any particular school or department, and his courses were highly popular with undergraduates. For a time he occupied a huge office in Harvard's Semitic Museum that he proudly described as "big enough for dancing"; later he moved to the top floor of Widener Library. On one occasion he confessed to Lehmann that he felt guilty about his royal treatment at Harvard, but Lehmann responded that the treatment merely reflected his greatness. Tillich's reply gave voice to the inner doubts that were known to his friends: "In ten years, no one will be interested in my theology any more."[185]

Nearly every weekend during his Harvard years he spoke to large audiences for sizable fees across the country, usually speaking on some aspect of the theology of culture, often depth psychology and the fine arts. He also traveled to parts of the world that he had not seen before: Greece and Mexico in 1956, Japan in 1960, and in 1963, a year after he moved to the University of Chicago, Egypt and Israel. Mexico made little impression on him, but he was overwhelmed by the temples of Greece. A visit to the Parthenon convinced Tillich that the pagan gods were real creative forces; after visiting the Erechtheion, a classic-style temple on the acropolis at Athens, he wrote to a friend, "Some revisions of my theology are now unavoidable. I should write 'On the Reality of the Pagan gods.' Nothing can be compared with the unity of landscape and architecture in Greece."[186]

His trip to Japan, which took place during the time that he worked on his sprawling third volume of systematics, made a similarly deep impression. Tillich later confessed that for many years he experienced inner torment over a friend's question: Why was the Eastern world missing from his religious and political thought? Upon being invited to lecture in Tokyo and Kyoto, the force of this question overcame his fear that he was too old to make such a trip. Greeted with great friendliness and courtesy that captivated him thoroughly, Tillich lectured for eight weeks on theology, culture, and the philosophy of religion, met with Christian leaders, took tours of museums and Buddhist rock gardens, and had stimulating discussions with Shinto and Buddhist scholars and priests. He was fascinated by Buddhist mysticism, which reminded him of his favorite aspects of Christian mysticism, and by Zen Buddhist painting, which reminded him of Schelling's concept of essentialization. Shortly after returning to the United States from Japan, he began to tell friends that the highest priority for theology was to overcome Western provincialism.[187]

Often Tillich added that he wished he could start his theological work over again, though the third volume of his *Systematic Theology* was nearly completed. Volume three, a rambling excursus on "Life and the Spirit" and "History and the Kingdom of God," was an anticlimax, Tillich knew; he confessed on the first page that his system was "fragmentary and often inadequate and questionable." Like the rest of his system, volume three was thoroughly apologetic in the twofold Schleiermacherian mode of relating Christianity to secular culture and defending true religion against its cultured despisers. It insisted that "a theology which does not deal seriously with the criticism of religion by secular thought and some particular forms of secular faith, such as liberal humanism, nationalism, and socialism, would be 'a-*kairos*'—missing the demand of the historical moment." Tillich acknowledged that the present historical moment demanded another kind of theological analysis, however—one that fell outside the apologetic framework of his system. Though he had not supported the establishment of the Center for the Study of World Religions at Harvard Divinity School, in the early 1960s he began to argue that interreligious dialogue was crucial to the work and progress of modern theology. Volume three expressed this conviction in the form of an imperative for all future theological work: "I must say that a Christian theology which is not able to enter into a creative dialogue with the theological thought of other religions misses a world-historical occasion and remains provincial."[188]

Tillich barely made a beginning in the theology of world religions, but his last years were absorbed by the need to overcome provincialism in theology. In 1961 he delivered the Bampton Lectures at Columbia University on the topic "Christianity and the Encounter of World Religions." The following year he moved to the University of Chicago as the Nuveen Professor of Theology, where he taught joint seminars with religious historian Mircea Eliade on the history and future of religion. His idea of how interreligious dialogue should proceed centered on four rules; his idea of a Christian theology of religions centered on three substantive arguments. The rules were that each participant in an interreligious dialogue must respect the value of the other's religious conviction, that each must be able to represent her own religious perspective with conviction, that each must presuppose the existence of a common ground that makes dialogue and conflict possible, and that each must be open to criticism of one's own religious perspective. Tillich did not claim that all religions are fundamentally alike; his own experiments in interreligious dialogue accentuated various differences. He emphasized that Buddhism contains nothing like the social, political, and personalistic symbol of the kingdom of God, and thus there is no analogy in Buddhism for the liberal, democratic, and socialist offshoots of Christianity. Buddhism has a strong sense of compassion, but no will to transform social structures; it is about salvation from reality, not transformation of reality. Tillich cautioned that this does not mean that dialogue between Christianity and Buddhism is pointless; for one thing, history itself forces Buddhists to take history more seriously; for another, many points of commonality exist. But the purpose of dialogue, for him, was not merely to claim or look for commonalities.[189]

His sketch of a theology of religions began with the claim, adapted from his thematizations of idolatry, the Unconditioned, and ultimate concern, that Christianity must be conceived as a faith that transcends religion and nonreligion, not as one religion among others. Tillich's second substantive idea held out for the superiority of the Hegelian principle of dialectical participation (that things and the universe are nonidentical but united by participation) over the Eastern principle of identity (that things and the universe are one), though he allowed that the Eastern principle of identity (especially in Japanese Buddhism) sustained a superior sense of the religious significance of nature. His third idea was that Eastern wisdom, like every form of wisdom, belongs to the self-manifestations of the logos; therefore if Christ is rightly to be called the incarnation of the logos, all forms of Eastern wisdom must be included in the interpretation of Jesus as the Christ.[190]

Tillich favored the logos idea because of its universality. In his reading, the early church was saved from turning Christ into the property of a factional party by the strength of Johannine theology, which identified Christ with the universal principle of divine self-manifestation. The church fathers asserted that the logos is present in all religions and cultures, and Tillich argued that only after the rise of Islam in the seventh century did Christianity begin to think of itself as one (embattled) religion among others. Christianity became fanatically exclusive, lost its universalistic self-confidence, and thereby lost its inclusiveness as a religion of Spirit. Tillich's favorite pre–nineteenth century Christian thinkers—Nicholas of Cusa, Erasmus, Zwingli, Faustus Socinus, Jacob Boehme, Locke, Kant—held in common a rejection of medieval exclusivism. In his telling, these thinkers renewed the universalism of early Christianity, and from them came the Enlightenment project of judging all religions by the same rational criterion. The Enlightenment faith in reason gave birth to the philosophy of religion, in which Christianity was subsumed under the universal concept of religion.[191]

This story has the appearance of recovery and progress, Tillich observed, but Enlightenment religion produced a faulty kind of universality. The type of Christian universalism that informed eighteenth- and nineteenth-century philosophers of religion led straight to humanist relativism, in which Christianity became merely the exemplar of the species religion. This was a dead end, despite the great names associated with it: Kant, Schleiermacher, Hegel, Schelling, and Troeltsch. The giants of liberal theology subsumed Christianity under the concept of religion, construing Christianity as the best realization of religion, but their concept of religion was itself a Christian-humanist construction of their own making. Tillich noted that Troeltsch was sensitive to the problem of the circularity of liberal Christianity, and thus he gave up the claim to universality. Troeltsch settled for what he called "Europeism," the claim that Christianity is the ideal religion for Western civilization. Instead of contesting the religions of the East or ranking Christianity above them (outside the West), Troeltsch advocated a "cross-fertilization" strategy of cultural exchange and dialogue.[192]

Tillich did not claim that he had developed a better way than the strategy of liberal theology, but he believed that he had made a beginning. What is needed is a nonparochial understanding of religion and a conception of Christianity that transcends religion and nonreligion, he argued. Liberal theology tried to find a home for religion in moral reason (Kant), religious feeling (Schleiermacher), metaphysical knowledge (Hegel), and the community of faith (Ritschl), but the best home for religion is everywhere. Throughout his career Tillich persistently argued that religion is the dimension of depth in all the functions of humanity's spiritual life; it should not be reduced to one function of the human spirit. The Bible pictures no temples in the kingdom, for in the fulfillment of the kingdom God shall be all in all. It followed that the way forward in theology is not to relinquish one's religious tradition for the sake of a universal concept that is not universal and is merely a concept: "The way is to penetrate into the depth of one's own religion, in devotion, thought and action. In the depth of every living religion there is a point at which the religion itself loses its importance, and that to which it points breaks through its particularity, elevating it to spiritual freedom and with it to a vision of the spiritual presence in other expressions of the ultimate meaning of man's existence."[193]

Universally, if the Holy is experienced, three movements or elements are present. Tillich employed a familiar dialectic to describe them. The founding element is the experience of the Holy within the finite, which he variously called the sacramental basis of religions or, within Christianity, the "Catholic substance." Universally, in everything that exists, the Holy appears in a special way. The second element is the critical check against idolatry, the "demonization of the sacramental," which can take the form of mysticism or, in modern Christianity, the Protestant principle. Mysticism and the Protestant principle are judgments against the absolutization of all concrete expressions of the Ultimate; in Tillich's words, "the Holy as the Ultimate lies beyond any of its embodiments." The embodiments of the Holy are needed, but they are merely secondary to the Ultimate itself. The third constitutive aspect of the experience of the Holy is the ethical or prophetic element. Justice is a universal principle that transcends every particular religion, Tillich argued, and the denial of justice in the name of the Holy is always demonic; religion without justice becomes a party to evil, while religion without the sacramental and mystical-critical elements becomes moralistic and eventually secular.[194]

Tillich's idea of a theology of religions thus rephrased his original theology of religious socialism. In 1965, near the end of his life, in his last public appearance, he offered a typically Tillichian name for the unity of the three elements: "the religion of the concrete spirit." The history of religions has an inner aim, he proposed, and this aim is to become the sacramental-mystical-prophetic religion of the concrete spirit. The entire history of religions has been and continues to be a struggle to realize the religion of the concrete spirit, which is the fight of the Unconditioned against religion within religion. Tillich recalled Harnack's observation that Christianity embraces everything within the history of religions; this remark contained a germ of truth, Tillich judged, but Harnack failed to follow it through. He failed to see that the truth of his observation called for a more positive relationship between Christianity and the history of religions. Instead, Harnack settled for the bourgeois moralism of the Ritschlian school, in his case with a high-bourgeois flavor. Tillich's last word was a plea for a universalism of concrete spirit: "The universality of a religious statement does not lie in an all-embracing abstraction which would destroy religion as such but in the depths of every concrete religion. Above all, it lies in the openness to spiritual freedom both from one's own foundation and for one's foundation."[195]

Eliade later recalled that when he and Tillich began their joint seminar, he was under the impression that Tillich was in the process of working out a new theology of religions. Tillich's frequent statements about starting over undoubtedly contributed to this impression. But Eliade soon realized that Tillich was still working on his original project. He had spent his entire academic career formulating a theological system, and in his last years he tried to renew the system as a way of thinking about the history of religions. Eliade recalled that in Tillich's early career, he appropriated existentialism before it became fashionable; later, he developed a religious valorization of nature and life that anticipated the popularity of Catholic evolutionist Teilhard de Chardin; in his last years, he reconceptualized his theology of ultimate concern in anticipation of a major theological shift toward the problems of religious pluralism. Tillich thus remained "an innovator and a precursor" to the end of his life, launching "another renewal of his thought" that showed the way in theology for a succeeding generation. For these reasons Eliade expected Tillich's commanding influence in theology to climb to new heights: "It is probable that Tillich's influence will prove to be more powerful and stimulating after his death."[196]

LEGACY OF THE NIEBUHR AND TILLICH GENERATION

Eliade predicted that Tillich's influence would grow; Tillich feared that his theology would be forgotten soon after his death. Neither was correct, but Tillich's premonition came closer to the truth. Tillich's mixture of ontology, German idealism, existentialism, and depth psychology did not wear well in the generation that gave birth to "death of God" theology and liberation theology. In his later life he realized that "spirit" was a cleaner and more inclusive category for his theological project than the ontological category of "being," but by then, aside from sections of his third volume of systematics and his final lectures, it was too late to rethink his system. In the 1970s his religious socialist essays of the 1920s retained a fresher feeling than much of the psychologized ontological theology of his American career.

More importantly, Tillich's enormous influence during his lifetime had much to do with the distinctive generational role that he played in a declining Protestant Christendom. Like Niebuhr, he benefited greatly from the existence of an American institutional and media establishment that still cared what leading Protestant theologians were thinking. Like Niebuhr, he was a star on the college chapel circuit just before it ended, and his fame was enhanced by the interest of *Time* magazine and other mass-circulation outlets. Tillich's glory years coincided with the post–World War II generational boom in church attendance and activity that sustained the cultural importance of theology. At the same time he filled a distinctively important role as a religious guide to thousands of postchurch readers, just before the steep declines in mainline American Protestant membership and participation began in the 1960s. University of Chicago Divinity School historian and dean Jerald C. Brauer aptly observed that Tillich spoke to people on the borderline of religion, "people who were outside the church but leaning toward it." After Tillich's death, Brauer expected his influence to grow, because increasingly theologians and ordinary church members found themselves on the borderline of religion: "The people who are on the borderline are growing in number everywhere. They are the people for whom Tillich's theology is really made, so Tillich now has more to say than ever."[197]

Tillich's ministry to the religious feelings of postchurch people began during his chaplaincy in World War I; near the end of his life he recalled: "If I used Biblical language to the soldiers, it meant nothing to them—they were about to die, and yet the Bible had nothing to say to them. I preached sermons, therefore, that never used any of the language of the Bible. They were a little mystical, a little poetical, and also had a touch of common sense, and they had an effect." His popular later writings used a similar strategy to great effect. Tillich believed that modern churches were required to "find a new function, they must take on new meaning. If there is no religion of any kind, the void is filled by quasi-religion, whether it's science or Fascism." And what about secularists like British philosopher Bertrand Russell, who claimed to feel no need for religion of any kind? "They deceive themselves," he contended. "There are certain people who just can't see the color green, and one can't argue with them. Russell would be one of them."[198]

For many academics who organized or reorganized college or university departments of religion in the 1950s and 1960s, Tillich's conception of religion as the ground and depth of humanity's spiritual life was enormously important. It provided the basis on which many departments of religion and religious studies reconceptualized their teaching of religion as an academic discipline. In seminaries the immense prestige of Tillich's thinking and person lifted the prestige of theology as a whole, setting a standard that no American theologian came near in the succeeding half-century. Brauer noted that Tillich was taken seriously by a wider audience of religious and nonreligious readers than any other theologian of his time: "His books were read by countless thousands, impossible demands were made on him as a lecturer, his concepts were commonplace at cocktail parties, he was quoted and interviewed constantly by all media of mass communication, and he was listened to gladly by students, which was for him a great source of joy." A few months before his death Tillich lectured at Berkeley with almost no advance publicity, and seven thousand students turned out to hear him.[199]

In his later life he found it impossible to resist the exaggerated praise that was showered on him continually. Tillich's friends described him as peaceable, kindly, gentle, and unpretentious, with a strong sensual magnetism, yet the same friends admitted that in later years he fell for his image. Pauck reports: "At times he was strangely inflexible and omniscient in manner; he sometimes assumed the pose of the 'famous man' glancing Narcissus-like at his own image." Journalist Ved Mehta caught a similar impression of him near the end of Tillich's life; Tillich assured Mehta that the influence of his thought reverberated throughout the world except for England. But he was also sensitive to the burden and ambiguity of his renown. Tillich lamented to Mehta, "I have so many pressures on me. If you only knew the pressures! My letters have been growing each year—sometimes there are twenty-five or thirty a day. I reply to all of them. I use this office and my secretary only for writing letters. It's the agape in me. If I had been born in Tibet, I would have retired twenty years ago. It would not have been my role to answer letters." In 1963 Tillich was the featured speaker at *Time* magazine's fortieth-anniversary party. Addressing a glittering audience of cover-story celebrities like himself, he gave a Niebuhr-like lecture on the ambiguity of achievement, cautioning that the human condition is an "inseparable mixture of good and evil, of creative and destructive forces, both individual and social." American society, for example, was remarkably free and democratic, but it was also mindlessly commercialized, fixated on material expansion, and lacking in spiritual depth; Tillich exhorted the *Time* achievers to "fight against being absorbed by the culture as another cultural good." Like all of his best sermons, this one was addressed to himself.[200]

His keen sense of the ambiguity of his success had a deeper personal wellspring. Tillich lived with the fear of being exposed for his sexual promiscuity. He knew very well that such a disclosure could destroy his carefully cultivated reputation as a spiritual figure; for years his secretaries puzzled over the fact that he never let them answer a telephone for him, he spoke German over the phone whenever he could, and he never shook the feeling of being watched constantly. Eight years after his death, his promiscuity was exposed by Hannah Tillich, which greatly damaged his reputation in church and seminary circles. Having inherited his collected writings, unpublished papers, love letters, and photographs of his lovers, Hannah Tillich wrote that she was strongly tempted "to place between the sacred pages of his highly esteemed lifework those obscene signs of the real life that he had transformed into the gold of abstraction—King Midas of the spirit."[201] Tillich's psychoanalyst friend and former student Rollo May followed with a defensive memoir, explaining that Tillich liked only "good" pornography, that he was not a sexual predator (women flocked to him), and that if he had lived into the 1970s, his promiscuity would not have been controversial: "He was perhaps three decades ahead of his time." Reinhold Niebuhr took a different view. His personal friendship with Tillich cooled in the 1940s, partly because he was appalled by Tillich's sexual morality, especially by an advance that Tillich reportedly made toward one of Niebuhr's female students.[202]

For the most part Niebuhr kept his misgivings about Tillich out of print. In 1952 he identified Barth as "the Tertullian of our day" and Tillich as "the Origen of our period." Tillich peaceably replied that Origen was a great philosopher, while letting pass the fact that Niebuhr tagged him with the name of a heretic.[203] In 1956, after Tillich lauded Picasso's *Guernica* as a Protestant masterpiece, Niebuhr exploded that there is nothing Protestant about art that sees the world as totally disjointed and tragic with no hope of redemption; Tillich calmly replied that Christians should welcome modern art, not fear it. Niebuhr openly distrusted Tillich's aestheticism, his reliance on ontological speculation, and what he called "this Neo-platonic side to him, a mystical side." For his part, Tillich thought that Ernest Jones's description of Freud applied to Niebuhr: a man possessed by powerful instincts and overpowering repressions; Tillich found it a sad description. Union Seminary abounded with stories that illustrated the contrast between Tillich's aes-thetic sensuality and Niebuhr's hard-charging moralism. On one occasion Tillich tried to interest Niebuhr in the flowers blossoming in the seminary courtyard; Niebuhr rushed past him, pronouncing that "they were there last year, too."[204]

On several private occasions Niebuhr apparently had sharp words with Tillich over what Niebuhr delicately called, in public, Tillich's "otherworldly" morality. "Morality has always been an issue with us," Niebuhr told an interviewer in 1965. "We've been debating it ever since he came to this country." In 1963 Tillich ded-icated a slender book on the relativity of ethical reason, *Morality and Beyond,* to Niebuhr, who was mortified: "Doing that was a scandal. I was embarrassed by the dedication, since morality has always been a point with us." In Niebuhr's telling, his longtime alliance with Tillich was based on their socialist politics: "We were both social radicals, and we both thought that the world depression and the Second World War were going to end the bourgeois order." After the war, Niebuhr implied, Tillich was more interested in the Metropolitan Opera than the struggle for social justice.[205]

Thus there were significant causes of personal tension between them, but the friction between them should not be overestimated. For the most part, Tillich and Niebuhr sustained a genuine and mutually respectful friendship, and their students detected little or no sign of tension in their relationship. Together they towered over American theology in the 1940s and 1950s, but in different ways and not at the same time. Niebuhr's influence correlated with the world-historical crises of the Depression, World War II, and the early years of the Cold War; Tillich spoke to an affluent postwar society that worried about the spiritual basis of its worldly success and personal anxieties. Niebuhr's closest friends were liberal-realist Christians, especially Will Scarlett and John Bennett; Tillich had cordial relations with his seminary colleagues, but his close friends were non-church intellectuals such as salon hostess Ruth Nanda Anshen and her husband Ralph Brodsky. Niebuhr and Tillich were both theological neoliberals who shared similar reasons for attacking the liberal tradition and who inspired new forms of liberal theology by their criticism. Near the end of Tillich's life, Union Seminary ethicist Roger Shinn aptly used Tillich's words in *The Protestant Era* to predict that he would be remembered not so much for the achievement of his impressive system as for his anticipation of "a new form of Christianity, to be expected and prepared for, not yet to be named."[206]

Though he spent his career calling for an unnamed new liberalism, Tillich thought of himself as steering a third way in religious thought between supernaturalism and atheistic naturalism, like the liberal tradition as a whole. He never tired of admonishing Barthians and conservatives that religious symbols are not stones thrown from heaven; at the same time he abhorred the desacralizing thrust of modern naturalism and rationalism. His method of correlation was designed to mediate the conflict between these modes of thinking. Tillich judged that much of the liberal tradition in theology conceded too much to the religiously enervating forces of modern naturalism, rationalism, and humanism; at the same time he contended that the greatest achievement of liberal theology "has to be defended with great religious, ethical and scientific passion; namely, the right and duty of philological-historical criticism of the biblical literature without any condition except integrity of research and scientific honesty."[207]

From his graduate school days onward, Tillich took for granted the superiority of liberal scholarship, especially the historical-critical theological scholarship emanating from the Ritschlian school and its offshoot, the history-of-religions school. But philosophically, he judged, Ritschlian liberalism was an escape theology. It secured a safe harbor for theology in the ethical personality of practical reason and declared a truce with scientific naturalism. It ceded the entire world to a triumphant naturalism except in the realm of values. It disavowed Christian claims to metaphysical knowledge and reduced the Christ of faith to its image of the historical Jesus. Tillich set himself against the religiously enervating reductionism of this strategy before he went off to war; during the war he found other reasons to oppose it. The Ritschlian liberals underestimated the demonic dimension of human existence, he judged, and their substantive value-theorizing valorized the ideals of bourgeois society. They reduced the ecstatic and paradoxical aspects of Christianity to an ethical faith in progress and turned religiosity into a function of humanness. In Germany the Ritschlian school and liberal theology were practically synonymous during Tillich's formative years, which made him averse to calling himself a liberal theologian of any kind. He later recalled that by the mid-1920s "real liberalism was dead or transmuted" in Germany; he never stopped thinking of "real liberalism" as the Ritschlian school and its historicist, social gospel, and humanist offshoots.[208]

But Tillich never stopped thinking of himself as belonging to the theological tradition of Schleiermacher, Schelling, and Hegel, and his beliefs about the metaphysical basis of Christian belief and the nihilating reality of individual and social evil were shared, in different ways, by such liberals of his time as Alfred North Whitehead, William E. Hocking, Edgar S. Brightman, Albert Knudson, and Daniel Day Williams. The latter thinkers were rarely cited in Tillich's books, though he remained remarkably open in personal discussion with colleagues and students throughout his career; his American career was about translating his thinking to a new audience, not forging alliances with Anglo-American traditions or movements. On occasion he explained that his spiritual father was Schleiermacher, his intellectual father was Schelling, and his grandfather on both sides was the German mystic Jacob Boehme.[209]

Though deeply dependent on his German sources, Tillich seemed remarkably independent in the American context, which was a source of his immense intellectual authority during his American career. Though aloof from American theological liberalism, he contributed more to its standing and revision than any other thinker between 1945 and 1965. The Tillichian language of ultimate concern, religious symbolism, and the God beyond God pervaded the writings of his disciples, entered popular culture, and influenced established liberal schools that operated from different premises. His correlationist theology of culture, which pursued theological dialogues with depth psychology, the fine arts, politics, and philosophy, helped to create entire subfields in theology. His early writings on religious socialism were scrutinized in the 1970s and 1980s for their relevance to liberation theology. His blend of existential, psychological, and phenomenological motifs built bridges to numerous disciplines and shaped the constructive theologies of many religious thinkers, notably Langdon Gilkey and Robert Scharlemann.[210]

Gilkey later recalled that when he began his theological career in the early 1950s, he assumed that he would spend his career working out the finer points of the systems of his teachers, Tillich and Niebuhr. Many of his friends had similar plans. "We saw ourselves a generation of 'scholastics' whose function would be to work out in greater detail the firm theological principles already forged for us," Gilkey explained. "We knew from our teachers what theology was, what its principles and starting point were, how to go about it."[211]

Gilkey thought of his teachers and himself as neo-orthodox theologians. The better versions of neo-orthodoxy comprised the genuine third way in theology that liberalism had failed to represent, he believed. Good neo-orthodoxy synthesized the better aspects of the liberal tradition with the Reformationist principles of divine transcendence, divine revelation, and the sinfulness of humankind. To the extent that he felt required to choose between Tillich and Niebuhr, Gilkey leaned toward Niebuhr, but for the most part he felt confident about his ability and that of his generational colleagues to synthesize the Tillichian and Niebuhrian systems. He assumed there was such a thing as a neo-orthodox alternative to liberal theology and that his teachers had bequeathed it to him. One of the turning points of twentieth-century theology occurred in the early 1960s, when Gilkey came to the confusing and troublesome conclusion that, in fact, his teachers belonged to the liberal tradition of Schleiermacher, Hegel, and Troeltsch, and so did he.[212]

8.
Modern Gospels

H. Richard Niebuhr, Henry P. Van Dusen,
Howard Thurman, and the Liberal Era
in American Theology

The liberal era in American theology evoked extraordinary criticism, much of it deserved, but the most influential critiques were highly exaggerated. The prize example belonged to H. Richard Niebuhr: "A God without wrath brought men without sin into a kingdom without judgment through the ministrations of a Christ without a cross." This scathing epitaph would not have been immortalized by frequent quotation if it had not struck at least part of its target. The American tradition of theological liberalism produced its share of argument and preaching that sentimentalized the divine nature, reduced divine reality to immanent process, underestimated the force of sin and evil, and overestimated the goodness of reason and modern culture. Liberal theology contained enough of the faults that the Niebuhrs and many others attributed to it that it made an easy target for polemical assault. From 1900 to 1914 the movement abounded with buoyant certainties and outward-reaching social programs; from 1915 to 1931 it trimmed its social sails and debated alternative theological frameworks; from 1932 onward it reeled from devastating criticism by its own disillusioned offspring.[1]

But the Niebuhrian characterization of liberal theology was a polemical exaggeration, as Reinhold Niebuhr subsequently confessed. Both Niebuhrs unfairly equated the entire liberal tradition with its most idealistic and immanentalist versions. The Niebuhrs claimed that liberals did not believe in human sinfulness, but in fact, liberal thinkers often spoke powerfully about the ravages of evil, as in William Newton Clarke's emphasis on sin as badness, William Adams Brown's similar emphasis on the willful choice of moral evil, Walter Rauschenbusch's thematization of the "kingdom of evil," Harry Emerson Fosdick's sermonizing against personal and social sin, and Edgar S. Brightman's theorizing on evil and divine finitude. The Niebuhrs claimed that liberals had no theology of the cross, but in fact, liberal thinkers often spoke movingly about the moral and spiritual meaning of the cross, especially Clarke, Vida Scudder, Georgia Harkness, and Albert C. Knudson. Virtually all liberal thinkers rejected the language of depravity and original sin that the Niebuhrs sought to reclaim in the 1930s, and there were significant differences between the ways that liberals and Reinhold Niebuhr thought about sin, but the difference was not that liberals like Clarke, Brown, Rauschenbusch, Harkness, and Henry Nelson Wieman did not believe in sin. Similarly, the liberal theologians repudiated the objectivist theories of atonement that conceived Christ's sacrifice on Calvary as a means of satisfying God's wrath or righteousness or rectoral honor, but it was not fair to claim that they preached a Christ without a cross.

American liberal theology became a movement in the 1880s under the leadership of Henry Ward Beecher, Theodore Munger, Newman Smyth, Washington Gladden, Borden Parker Bowne, Charles A. Briggs, and George Gordon. It made a smooth transition to power in the movement's second generation, partly because it attracted assuring and responsible leaders such as William Adams Brown, Henry Churchill King, Walter Rauschenbusch, Harry Emerson Fosdick, Shailer Mathews, Edward Scribner Ames, Douglas Clyde Macintosh, Rufus Jones, and Albert C. Knudson. At the high tide of the social gospel, liberals believed that Schleiermacherian romanticism and Ritschlian historicism could be combined, that historical criticism yielded the liberal-like Jesus of history, and that the kingdom of God is advanced by evolution, faithful living, and social progress. In its strongest religious forms liberal Protestantism lived off these convictions into the 1930s, usually fortified by the ethical and spiritual religion of personality. In its second generation the movement produced two epochal religious figures—Rauschenbusch and Fosdick—and a host of accomplished, constructive theologians and church leaders. All of them prized personal piety and the regenerative mission of the church; even the movement's most notorious freethinker, George Burman Foster, was a person of tender piety. Partly under Foster's influence, Mathews boasted that at Chicago "the religious spirit is deepening, and the amount of religious work done by our students is very gratifying."[2]

CATHOLIC MODERNISM
AND THE BOUNDARIES OF ECUMENISM

Emphatically the early-twentieth-century liberals were Protestants who held little hope of a wider ecumenism in their lifetime. In the late nineteenth and early twentieth centuries, Newman Smyth and Charles A. Briggs heralded the apparent beginnings of a theologically modernist movement in the Roman Catholic church, which was led, intellectually, by English theologian George Tyrrell and French theologians Alfred Loisy and Maurice Blondel. In the United States, a few American priests tried to create an American Catholic modernism. Chief among them were University of Notre Dame chemistry and physics professor and Holy Cross priest John A. Zahm, who was a popular speaker on the Catholic summer-school circuit in the mid-1890s; Paulist priest William L. Sullivan, who tried to goad American Catholic clergy into taking a stand against the Vatican's authoritarianism; and a handful of Sulpician priests at St. Joseph's Seminary in Yonkers (Dunwoodie), New York, led by seminary president James Francis Driscoll, who published a short-lived Catholic modernist journal titled the *New York Review*.[3]

European and American Catholic modernism imagined a Roman Catholic church that used modern methods to revise and defend Catholic teaching, but this idea was repudiated in the papal condemnations of Americanism and modernism. In *Testem benevolentiae* (1899), Pope Leo XIII censured Americanism by name; in *Lamentabili Sane* (1907), Pius X condemned the historical critical approach to Scripture and sixty-four related modernist ideas; in *Pascendi Dominici Gregis* (1907), Pius X described modernism as the synthesis of all heresies; in 1910, the Vatican instituted an antimodernist oath for all Catholic clergy and theology professors. The beginnings of a theologically modernizing movement in American Catholicism were crushed by these condemnations. Zahm was forced to disavow his book *Evolution and Dogma,* in which he argued for the compatibility of Catholic teaching and Darwinian evolution. Sullivan lauded the modernist spirit of liberty, blasted the Vatican's repression of intellectual and spiritual freedom, and renounced the Catholic church. In a hopeful spirit, Driscoll and coeditor Francis Patrick Duffy, along with colleagues Francis Ernest Charles Gigot, Gabriel Oussani, John Brady, and Joseph Bruneau, founded the *New York Review,* which published articles by Tyrrell, Sullivan, French Protestant Paul Sabatier, American Paulist Joseph McSorley, Catholic University professor James J. Fox, and many others. Gigot established the group's general line on biblical criticism, which adhered closely to Loisy's moderate formulations.[4]

The Dunwoodie brand of modernism was very mild by liberal Protestant standards; Driscoll's and Gigot's model Catholic modernist was John Henry Newman. As they explained, Newman took an historical approach to apologetics and supported the intellectual freedom of natural and social scientists; otherwise he was robustly orthodox. To the Dunwoodie reformers, the Catholic church's regnant neoscholastic Thomism had outlived its usefulness; Newman's historically oriented apologetics was the best alternative, though Fox made a case for the medieval apologetics of John Duns Scotus. Scotus taught that the will is superior to intellect and that reason is limited in apprehending metaphysical reality; implicitly, Fox assured that good modernist theology was classically rooted, not alien or new. In either case, the *New York Review* reformers agreed that the church's official Thomism was no longer credible. Forging a strong alliance and friendship with Briggs, who asserted that biblical criticism did not undermine the doctrine of the immaculate conception of Mary, the Dunwoodie reformers called for a more biblically oriented, historical theology. The deductivist intellectualism and scholastic certainties of Vatican Catholicism were unreal in a generation that possessed the tools of historical criticism. Good theology accepted the modern natural and social sciences and used historical criticism as an apologetic weapon to defend Catholic teaching.[5]

But this strategy had no short-term future in Catholic teaching. The keystone of modernist theology, even in its mildest Catholic forms, was intellectual freedom, especially the right to interpret Scripture and church tradition with historical-critical tools. The *New York Review* straightforwardly defended biblical criticism as an aid to faith; just as plainly, *Pascendi Dominici Gregis* condemned textual and higher criticism as forms of disbelief. For several months the Dunwoodie reformers pretended that the anathemas of *Lamentabili* and *Pascendi* applied only to liberal and radical modernists, not to loyal Catholics like themselves. They took comfort in Friedrich von Hügel's assurance that the Vatican was appealing to scholars on scholarly matters, not making dogmatic decrees. The Catholic modernists assured themselves that the Vatican did not mean to censure modern science, the higher critical approach to the Synoptic problem, or Newman's developmental theory of doctrine; it sought only to censure disbelief and issue a scholarly appeal that welcomed differing positions.

Reality caught up with St. Joseph's Seminary in 1908. The church's Apostolic Delegate to the United States, Archbishop Diomede Falconio, noted that the *New York Review* was a forum for exactly the modernist ideas condemned in *Lamentabili* and *Pascendi*. Shortly afterward, Driscoll was dispatched to an obscure parish in Manhattan, coeditor Duffy and managing editor John Brady were assigned to parishes in the Bronx and Brooklyn, a neoscholastic curriculum was reinstated at the seminary, and the *New York Review* folded after three years of publication. Gigot and Gabriel Oussani remained at their teaching posts, but gave up their ambitions to cutting-edge scholarship. The Vatican crushed the wellsprings of Catholic modernism and regained neoscholastic uniformity at all Catholic institutions, which froze the development of Catholic doctrine for two generations. American Catholicism produced progressive social thinkers, notably John A. Ryan, and a handful of scholars who pressed the edge of permissible criticism, but the spirit and methods of modern scholarship on matters pertaining to faith were disallowed. For two generations, while priests and theologians took the antimodernist oath, American Catholicism played no role in the development of liberal theology except as a lamented specter.[6]

The Protestant theologians who dominated American liberal theology during the liberal era experienced the Catholic church as alien. Routinely they dismissed Roman Catholic theology as backward, undemocratic, and authoritarian; few of them made anti-Catholicism an important theme in their work, but those who did simply elaborated the liberal dismissal. Walter Rauschenbusch and Charles Clayton Morrison were prominent examples. To Rauschenbusch, Catholicism was the historical root of the problem of antiprogressive Christianity, because the

Catholic Church hellenized the kingdom-building teaching of Christ and offered itself as a substitute for the kingdom; if the modern church was to recover the prophetic social gospel of Jesus, it had to overcome the ecclesiastical neopaganism and illiberalism of the Catholic church. Rauschenbusch took for granted that Catholicism was too marginalized in liberal, democratic, Protestant America to threaten the American way of life, but thirty years after Rauschenbusch's death, Morrison warned in the *Christian Century* that times had changed. In his view, Catholicism was still the reactionary monolith that Rauschenbusch portrayed, but the Catholic church was making enormous gains in American society. Morrison worried that misguided Protestant ecumenists were smoothing the way to a Catholic subversion of the American idea: "They allow to other faiths a parity with their own and, by invoking what I think is a false conception of tolerance, thus reduce all faiths to a common denominator."[7]

Morrison was a strong ecumenist, but to him and the *Christian Century,* good ecumenism was about Protestant unity, not common-denominator Christianity. He was ready to dispense with a great deal of the Protestant heritage for the sake of Protestant unity; modern Protestantism needed to disavow the doctrinal edifices that separated its various denominations from each other, he urged, for all intra-Protestant sectarianism was a product of historical egotism and factionalism. The Protestant churches' disagreements over salvation, the sacraments, and church polity were not worth the divisions that they created in the Christian body. In Morrison's view, the only basis that modern Christianity needed and the only principle that could sustain the unity of Protestant Christendom was the sovereign authority of Christ: "Everything else—I say it sweepingly—*everything else*—Bible, creed, sacraments, tradition, 'ancient order of things'—is divisive, sectarian, hopeless, when it is held without being referred to Christ for his judgment upon it." The Protestant fetish of *sola scriptura* belonged to the category of everything else, he affirmed, because this was precisely the principle that fueled the sectarian mentality of Protestantism. Every Protestant denomination prized its particular interpretation of the Bible, which *became* the Bible for that denomination: "Thus Protestantism has proliferated an astonishing litter of miniature papal infallibilities, each based upon the essential principle in the papacy against which Protestantism had revolted."[8]

The kind of ecumenism that Morrison wanted was militantly Protestant, prepared to relinquish Protestant denominational heritages, and firmly anti-Catholic. For Morrison, it was an illusion that Protestants and Catholics shared a common spiritual fellowship, and he worried that many ecumenical leaders were indulging this illusion. Every serious religion is fired by a competitive missionary spirit, he countered. Liberal Protestantism would not thrive, and perhaps not even survive, if it did not begin to speak the language of competition and conversion, and thus take itself more seriously than its ecumenical leaders: "Protestantism cannot cooperate ecclesiastically with a dictatorship. It must make a clear-cut decision to accept its task of winning America to Christ without any illusion that it has a collaborator in Roman Catholicism."[9]

A more hopeful view of the Catholic church's ecumenical potential was taken by William Adams Brown, Georgia Harkness, Vida Scudder, and John C. Bennett. Though he took for granted the superiority of Protestant Christianity, Brown pursued ecumenical dialogues with Catholic prelates and theologians; Harkness pointedly cautioned Protestant readers that some Catholic congregations had more democratic spirit than many Protestant congregations; Scudder urged that Protestants had much to learn from Catholic spirituality and that liberal Protestant leaders needed to tone down their anti-Catholicism. By later standards, the early ecumenical movement made very modest gains in Protestant-Catholic reconciliation. Both sides were quick to assert the necessity of their basic presuppositions, and liberal Protestant theologians gave short shrift to Catholic theology. In the 1930s, while Karl Barth treated Catholic theology as his most significant rival, no leading American Protestant theologian bothered to interrogate Catholic Thomism as a serious theological option; even those who pressed the cause of church unity typically felt little spiritual kinship with the Christianity of the Roman church. As usual, Fosdick expressed the ruling feeling of the liberal theologians: "I do not believe in Christianity. I believe in the spirit of Christ, not in this vast snowball which has been gathering size and momentum for twenty centuries, and which has been gathering much rot as well as pure snow. Ninety percent of it is pagan."[10]

Anglican liberals such as Scudder and W. Norman Pittenger pressed for a more generous reading of the Catholic tradition. Scudder loved the spiritual practices and liturgies of Roman Catholicism, and her spirituality was nourished by the writings of Catholic saints. She counseled that Protestantism needed the Catholic sacramentalist understanding of the church as the body of Christ as a corrective to Protestant individualism; the social gospel will not flourish in churches that perpetuate a bootstrap theory of salvation in their theology and worship, she warned. Scudder's Anglo-Catholicism reduced the narrowly Protestant feeling of the *Christian Century* and other social gospel outlets, while Pittenger advised Protestants in 1943 that there were contemporary Catholic theologians worth reading and that Catholic theology increasingly relinquished the mechanical understanding of the church that prevailed in official Catholic neoscholasticism. Among Catholic religious thinkers, Pittenger recommended German theologians Karl Adam and Romano Guardini, French philosopher Jacques Maritain, and French theologian Henri de Lubac. Though he found no American Catholic theologians to recommend, he counseled that American Catholicism was not lacking in undercurrents of new life.[11]

One of America's leading ecumenists, John C. Bennett, symbolized the ambiguous, but increasingly positive, relationship between American Protestantism and Catholicism. Bennett played major roles in the 1937 Oxford Conference, the 1948 founding convention of the World Council of Churches (WCC) at Amsterdam, and the WCC assemblies at Evanston (1954), New Delhi (1961), and Uppsala (1968), as well as the WCC-sponsored World Conference on Church and Society (1966) in Geneva. For more than twenty years he exemplified the cautiously respectful, but generally superior attitude toward Catholicism that Protestant ecumenical leaders took for granted. In the late 1950s, however, to Bennett's surprise, the writings of Jacques Maritain and American Jesuit John Courtney Murray convinced him that there was such a thing as modern, prodemocratic, Catholic social theory. In 1958 Bennett became the first American Protestant leader to support public financial aid for Catholic parochial schools, reasoning that it was unfair for Catholics to bear a "double burden of expense" for education. Well before the reforms of Vatican II engendered a new spirit of fellowship between American Catholics and Protestants, Bennett became a major proponent of Catholic-Protestant dialogue and cooperative ministry, and after Vatican II he pressed for concrete gains in ecumenical recognition. Like Vida Scudder, he lauded the Catholic church's distinctive capacity to organize and sustain organic, religiously vital communities; as president of Union Theological Seminary he made an ecumenically precedent-setting appointment, naming Catholic moral theologian Bernard Häring to the Harry Emerson Fosdick Visiting Professorship; in his lectures and writings he lauded Maritain and Murray for developing theories of democracy and religious freedom that drew upon distinctively Roman Catholic sources.[12]

While appreciative Catholic universities showered him with honorary doctorates, Bennett's writings on Protestant-Catholic dialogue became increasingly friendly and familiar, nearly devoid of the edgy defensiveness and superior unease that had marked liberal Protestant rhetoric about Catholicism for decades. Yet in his later career Bennett recalled that he had come very late to a friendly view of the Catholic church. "So long as I assumed that my church, the church to which I looked for inspiration and guidance, was limited to worldwide Protestantism, my church was sadly truncated," he reflected. "This was actually true of me until the late 1950s, and I doubt if I was exceptionally bigoted in such matters." Bennett understood very well that his early view was entirely typical of his group and tradition; it was his conversion to a wider ecumenism that made him exceptional in the years before Vatican II. His friend and colleague Reinhold Niebuhr made the same ecumenical pilgrimage during this period, for the same reasons. "In the past, I had a typical Protestant polemical attitude against Catholicism," Niebuhr reflected in 1966. "Now I realize that the mystery of life and the mystery of human history are so great that the Catholic approach is a valid one and might well be more valid than our approach. I don't say that my ambivalence about this is dishonest. I simply say that this is the insight of old age against the polemical attitude of youth."[13]

LIBERAL THEOLOGY AS A FIRST WAY

In a key sense, the theologians of the liberal era were too successful for their tradition; through their work liberal theology became identified with the social optimism, evolutionism, and immanentalist God language of the social gospel. Though some liberals, especially Macintosh and Wieman, sought to expunge liberal theology of its romanticist and historicist subjectivism, they failed to persuade most of the field, and they belonged to the social gospel generation more than they dissented from it. The conception of liberal theology as a handmaiden of the progressive social gospel has been so influential that today, more than eighty years after Rauschenbusch's death, it remains the predominant way of describing liberal theology.

Daniel Day Williams's definition of liberal theology, offered in 1949, is typical: "By 'liberal theology' I mean the movement in modern Protestantism which during the nineteenth century tried to bring Christian thought into organic unity with the evolutionary world view, the movements for social reconstruction, and the expectations of 'a better world' which dominated the general mind. It is that form of Christian faith in which a prophetic-progressive philosophy of history culminates in the expectation of the coming of the Kingdom of God on earth." As I argued in the first volume of this work, Williams's definition appropriately emphasized the evolutionist orientation, social gospel ethos, and social optimism that characterized liberal Protestant theology during the Progressive era. Like much of the secondary literature in the field, however, Williams overidentified the liberal tradition with factors that were peculiar to its period of dominance. His definition excluded Kant, Schleiermacher, Coleridge, Theodore Parker, Horace Bushnell, and all other pre-Darwinian thinkers who gave little or no importance to the evolutionary worldview. It identified liberal theology with dated beliefs about the Christianizing moral progress of Western civilization and the postmillenial hope of a literal kingdom of God on earth. Moreover, it made no reference to historical criticism or related forms of intellectual inquiry, or to the values and authority of individual reason and experience.[14]

It must have occurred to Williams that he was promoting a definition of liberal theology that excluded liberals like himself; he criticized Reinhold Niebuhr and others when they characterized liberal theology as optimistic idealism. Yet the force of the Progressive era model of liberal theology was so great that Williams continued to recycle it, even as he protested that the liberal tradition was not lacking in chastened, realistic analysis. He also used this definition to support his argument for a "new theology" beyond the old liberalism and the neo-orthodox reaction. Several years later, in an otherwise schematically-perceptive interpretation, *American Theology in the Liberal Tradition,* Lloyd Averill based his analysis explicitly on Williams's definition.[15]

Having begun as a third way in theology between a regnant orthodoxy and a threatening "infidelism" and atheistic rationalism, liberal theology became a new orthodoxy in the social gospel generation. It was the language of a dominant first way; Edward Scribner Ames aptly titled his book on liberal theology *The New Orthodoxy.* After World War I and the Great Depression eviscerated the optimistic Victorian moralism and progressivism that fueled liberal theology at its height, however, the liberal tradition was saddled with the optimism of its days of enthusiasm. Reinhold Niebuhr and a host of others assiduously reinforced the identification of liberal theology with sentimental progressivism, and not even the protests and course-corrections of Fosdick and Wieman could alter the prevailing concept of liberal Christianity.

But liberal theology had an ample history in the United States before the Progressive era, and because it did not reduce to moralistic idealism and immanentalism, it endured as an important theological tradition after the Progressive era. Central to liberal theology was (and is) the idea of a third way between authority-based orthodoxies and secularizing unbelief. Other modern theologies of a neo-confessionalist or neo-orthodox type also claimed to represent a third way in theology, but they upheld the principle of external authority in religion, usually by appealing to a neo-Reformationist principle of the paradoxical unity of Word and Spirit. Liberal theology was a clearly and coherently different way in theology. It rejected external authority as the basis of religious belief and affirmed the authority of reason and religious experience; it accepted Scripture, doctrines, and creeds as authoritative only as they were received as authoritative in human experience. Not coincidentally, it was within New England Congregationalism, which combined advanced education and low-church polity, that these Enlightenment-individualist ideas first took root in the American Protestantism, but by the early twentieth century liberal theology existed in every mainline Protestant denomination.

Both of the movement's epochal figures, Rauschenbusch and Fosdick, were Baptists, as were Mathews, Foster, Macintosh, and Gerald Birney Smith; having produced Washington Gladden, Theodore Munger, Newman Smyth, and George Gordon, American Congregationalism did not give as much theological leadership to the next generation, but its theologians included Henry Churchill King, Robert L. Calhoun, and Eugene Lyman; the emergence of theologically progressive currents in the Presbyterian, Episcopal, and Society of Friends communions were represented respectively by Brown, Scudder, and Jones; Ames and Morrison represented the small Disciples tradition; through the work of Borden Parker Bowne, George Albert Coe, Georgia Harkness, Albert Knudson, Daniel Day Williams, Francis McConnell, Harris Franklin Rall, Harry F. Ward, G. Bromley Oxnam, F. Ernest Tittle, and many others, the Methodist church became a major player in the movement. Against an ascending neo-orthodox movement and in the name of modernizing the Methodist tradition, Knudson negotiated his denominational heritage in a way that was typical of liberal theology.

The liberals of the Progressive era knew that they were liberals and that liberalism marked a sharp turn in Christian thought. They saw themselves as good Baptists, good Methodists, and the like, but most of them did not pretend that they were merely recovering earlier ideals obscured by post-Reformation developments; modernity was something new, and so, therefore, was liberal theology. Knudson employed the Bible and tradition as sources of theology, and he emphasized the interlinked authority of reason and religious experience for theology. Thus, at least formally, he endorsed the four components of what was later called the Wesleyan Quadrilateral, but he did not invoke the authority of Scripture, tradition, reason, and experience in the manner of John Wesley, nor did he claim to do so, unlike Albert Outler and other mid-twentieth-century theorists of the Wesleyan Quadrilateral.

Knudson plainly rejected the concepts of infallibility and external authority in religion; he conceived tradition as the entire history of religions; and he interpreted Christian experience essentially as religious feeling. By contrast, Wesley accepted the Bible and church tradition as external authorities for theology. Though he left room for incidental errors in the Bible, Wesley believed in scriptural inspiration and infallibility, strongly asserting that Scripture is infallible for its saving purpose when its faithful reading is illuminated by the Holy Spirit. Though he judged that the Greek Fathers understood the gospel better than the Latin Fathers, Wesley believed that the Christian tradition alone was authoritative for theology, and he lacked any concept of tradition as the history of religions. His appeal to experience was also different from Knudson's; for Wesley, the specific experience that constituted an authoritative source of information for Christian belief was the Christian's experience of the inward assurance of God's grace. He conceived experience as a soteriological category, not as Schleiermacher's "feeling as such." To Wesley, Christian experience was the sense of being led by the Holy Spirit into salvation, which he often described, following Galatians 5:6, as faith working through love.[16]

Knudson's Methodism was formative, deeply felt, and ironic. He spent his life in Methodist institutions and published his books exclusively with Methodist houses, yet his writing was pitched to a transdenominational liberal audience. Most of his books rarely quoted or even referred to Wesley, and he dismissed the major theologians of the Methodist tradition. Sadly he repeated Bowne's appraisal of Methodist theologian Randolph Foster's six-volume dogmatics: "The pathetic thing about them was that they were obsolete before they came from the press." With Bowne, he vowed that Methodist theology had to start over, making Methodism modern. "The Methodist theologians from Watson to Miley and Foster were authoritarian rationalists," Knudson explained with typical directness. "They based the Christian faith on the divine authority of Scripture, and this authority they believed could be established by purely rational considerations." On both counts Methodism needed to make a new beginning by affirming its natural connection to the liberal tradition. Knudson identified with the tradition of Kant, Schleiermacher, Hegel, Troeltsch, Otto, Lotze, and Bowne, yet his considerable impact on American theology occurred almost entirely in the parishes and academic institutions of the Methodist church. Unlike Bowne, and also unlike Rauschenbusch and Fosdick, Knudson had little influence outside his own denomination, but like them, he strongly asserted that Christian theology had no future worth struggling for if it did not make a clean break from authority religion.[17]

GOSPEL BASIS, MODERNIST BASIS

The latter sentiment was shared by liberals who asserted the relevance of gospel norms for modern theology and liberals who argued for a more thoroughgoing modernism in theology. The distinction between "evangelical" and "modernist" liberalism is problematic, important, and long established in the primary and secondary literature of American liberal theology. The problematic aspects of the distinction are unfortunately ignored in much of the secondary literature in the field, which overworks the distinction.[18] Every American liberal theologian of the twentieth century was a modernist; all of them accommodated Christian beliefs and practices to modern knowledge and culture; all of them opposed the premodern privileging of revelation over reason and the sacred realm over the secular. Liberal theologians as a class believed that the Christian gospel and modern knowledge fit together.

But the evangelical/modernist distinction marks an important division in the field, even if one wishes that American liberals had selected different labels for their differences. In his influential book *The Modernist Impulse in American Protestantism,* William R. Hutchison dispenses altogether with the distinction, noting that every liberal Protestant theologian of the Progressive era appealed to gospel norms. He observes that Mathews explicitly identified theological modernists as evangelicals who accepted Christ as divine revelation. But contrary to Hutchison, Mathews makes a good example of the value of the evangelical/modernist distinction. Mathews made his claim, quoted by Hutchison, about the evangelical basis of modernism in 1924, in a book that expressed the last gasp of his evangelical phase; *The Faith of Modernism* was a transitional work. Mathews was the last of the Chicago theologians to think of himself as an evangelical, but his books after 1924 were models of Chicago-style naturalistic empiricism, in which a social-scientific language of immanent process trumped the biblical language of sin, redemption, and transcendence, and God was identified with the process of history. The evangelical/modernist distinction is potentially misleading, yet the idea behind it does identify something worth naming. It refers to the difference between those liberals who insisted that modern Christianity has no message of deliverance if it cannot lay claim to the actual spirit and picture of Jesus and those liberals who accentuated the sociohistorical chasm between ancient and modern Christianity. It names, awkwardly, the difference between claiming that God transcends history and claiming that God is the reality of historical process.[19]

The modernist liberals argued that reason and experience must be followed wherever they lead and that historical criticism cannot be counted upon to confirm the liberal picture of Jesus. The evangelical liberals countered that liberal Christianity at its best remains faithfully committed to gospel norms and that modern knowledge, rightly understood, does not conflict with the social gospel construal of the spirit or picture of Jesus. The differences between these broad theological tendencies sometimes blurred at the borderline; the most gospel-oriented modernist, Macintosh, could sound like an evangelical liberal when he preached the gospel of moral optimism. Yet Macintosh clearly expounded the "modernist" principle that no historical claim pertaining to Jesus (or anyone else) is necessary to Christianity. The Christian ideas of God and goodness are true whether or not Jesus lived at all, he asserted: "All that has been said of the reasonableness and truth of Christianity is demonstrably valid, whether we have any

Christology or not, and whatever we may or may not believe about the historic Jesus. It would still be valid if it should turn out that Jesus was essentially different from what has been commonly believed, or even that he was not truly historical at all." Ironically, in the name of practicing thoroughgoing historical criticism, the more thoroughgoing modernists thus protected their religious claims from historical refutation by cutting loose from any historical basis, and when Wieman came to the University of Chicago, the historicist orientation of Chicago theology was quickly overturned. What mattered was empirical truth; history just got in the way. The American descendants of Harnack and Herrmann refused to go that far. The differences between the evangelical/transcendental and the modernist/naturalistic streams of liberal theology are too significant not to delineate; even Hutchison allows that the distinction between modernist and evangelical liberalism may have some value as a judgment about the theological consequences of different kinds of liberal advocacy.[20]

The Gospel-centered liberals tended to be more discriminating than the Chicago schoolers in sifting the wheat and chaff of Barthian theology, conceding that they had lessons to learn from Barth, Brunner, and the school of neo-orthodoxy. Fosdick, Harkness, and Coffin took seriously the Barthian attacks on the dilution of Christianity in liberal theology; under Barthian influence, Brown's later books emphasized divine transcendence and the experience of revelation; more grudgingly, even Knudson allowed that the Barthian revolution capitalized on the religious deficiencies of liberal Protestantism. These theologians viewed themselves, after making chastened corrections, as an integrative antidote to Barth's one-sided supernaturalism and Wieman's religious naturalism. The first- and second-generation Chicago theologians, on the other hand, found much less to learn from neo-orthodoxy. To them the Barthian ascendancy was a nearly unqualified disaster for theology and Christianity. It denigrated reason and experience in the name of a phantom revelation. It turned the search for truth on its head and reversed two centuries of theological progress.

These differing reactions made sense for the most part, though not without irony. The evangelical liberals and Barthians made competing claims to gospel truth, and thus shared enough common ground to make interrogation fruitful, while the Chicago theologians and other religious naturalists felt deeply alienated from the spirit and ideas of the dialectical theology movement. Yet on the question of the founding capacity of historical reason, the historicism of the early Chicago school gave way to an ahistorical skepticism that was closer to Barth than to evangelical liberalism. While rejecting Barth's constructive dialectics, Macintosh approximated Barth's skepticism in disclaiming any historical basis of Christian truth, and Wieman dismissed historical investigation as unhelpful to the search for truth. Thirty years of Chicago historicism had yielded little fruit for the real work of theology, in his view. Insistently, and sometimes indignantly, as in Knudson's case, the gospel-centered liberals countered that skepticism cannot yield a healthy theology. They objected that Barthianism and thoroughgoing naturalism were extreme positions that fed on epistemological and historical skepticism. They could relate to Mathews's early work, which focused on gospel religion and Christian history, but the ahistorical naturalistic empiricism of the later Chicago school was alien to them.

The differences between the "evangelical" and "modernist" streams of the liberal theology movement thus were significant, but the movement's commonalities were more significant and defining. One way or another, liberal theology always took its stand on the verdicts of modern knowledge and experience without bowing to external authority claims. Liberals of all kinds decried the Barthian ascendancy as biblicist, dogmatic, authoritarian, provincial, and irrational. They accepted the naturalistic premises of modern historiography and the modernist valorization of objective knowledge. They specialized in cultural accommodation and religious progressivism. Every liberal theologian sought to bring Christian claims into line with beliefs derived from modern critical consciousness, and thus every liberal theologian from Schleiermacher to Macintosh took for granted that the authority of reason makes the mythical aspects of Christianity problematic for modern theology.

MYTH AND REASON; GOOD AND EVIL

Somehow, liberals agreed, the mythical parts of Christianity had to be overcome. The myths of the Bible were an offense to reason, and something of an embarrassment. The eighteenth- and nineteenth-century liberal theologians who first took seriously the problem of Christian myth took for granted that myth belongs to a primitive stage of consciousness. Their early-twentieth-century American descendants carried on the liberal project of adapting Christianity to an Enlightened myth-negating consciousness. Part of what it meant to make theology modern and progressive was to advance theology beyond the pictorial, prescientific language of myth. Most American liberals followed the Harnackian strategy of interpreting the mythical aspects of Christianity as marginal and dispensable; a few appropriated the Hegelian argument that the pictorial explanations and images of myth, which belong to the lifeworld of precritical religion, must be refashioned hermeneutically into philosophical concepts. In both cases, theology had to dispense with the mythical aspects of Christianity in order to speak the rational language of truth. Theology was required to replace mythical symbolism with the concepts and images of a purportedly nonmythical symbolism such as the Hegelian philosophy of Absolute Spirit or the social scientific language of process.[21]

The possibility of a different liberal view of myth was introduced by Paul Tillich in the 1920s and adopted by Reinhold Niebuhr in the 1930s. As a corrective to the desacralized rationalism of liberal theology, Tillich contended that myth is the essential language of religion. Modern theology was digging its own grave by repudiating the mythical impulse, he warned; the rationalist denigration of mythical consciousness that liberal theology took for granted stripped the world of sacredness and theology of its natural language. Tillich and Niebuhr conceived the mythical impulse as essentially unitive; the fundamental character and value of myth is that it seeks to find the hidden wholeness of reality. They assured that modern consciousness has a crucial role to play in recovering the spiritual truths that myths contain. Myths are true only in broken form, they explained; even in a broken state, the mythical imagination still seeks the unity of things, but the unitive symbolism of myth is true only insofar as it is understood to be mythical. Without rational understanding, the myths of Christianity are falsifying and regressive; understood critically as myths, mythical symbols uniquely participate in and point to the unconditioned ground of experience.

To Niebuhr, the challenge of getting myth right exposed the fundamental faults of conservative and liberal Christianity. Conservative forms of Christianity were wrong because they took Christian myths literally, he explained; conservatives failed to acknowledge that Christian myths are myths. Theological liberalism made the opposite mistake; having grasped that Christian myths are myths, liberals refused to take them seriously. So-called American neo-orthodoxy drew much of its considerable spiritual power from the Niebuhrian and Tillichian contention that religious myths should be taken seriously, but not literally. As long as Niebuhr and Tillich were perceived as opponents of liberal theology, liberal theologians were slow to adopt the neo-orthodox language of mythical symbolism. Niebuhr's concept of "true myth" was alien to the rationalist and historicist wellsprings of a declining liberal movement. But Niebuhr, and especially Tillich, influenced a subsequent generation of theologians to speak the language of mythical symbolism and remythologizing. Some were Tillich and Niebuhr protégés, such as Langdon Gilkey and F. W. Dillistone, who renegotiated their relationships to the liberal tradition. While theologians such as John B. Cobb Jr. and Schubert Ogden continued to uphold the liberal-rationalist denigration of mythical consciousness, others such as Bernard E. Meland, Daniel Day Williams, Sallie McFague, and David Tracy advanced the myth-creative approach as a liberal option. On this key issue as on others related to it, Niebuhr and Tillich inspired new forms of liberal theology through their criticism and constructive theorizing.[22]

A key related issue was the conception and status of reason in modern theology. Even in its romanticist forms, liberal theology always prized its claim to rational credibility and coherence; this concern was practically consuming in personalist and Hegelian theologies. More importantly, liberal theology preached that rationality is an instrument of redemption. Through the training and exercise of reason, human beings are liberated from ignorance, backwardness, selfishness, provincialism, and aggression. In the wake of World War I and its disillusionment, Tillich and Niebuhr dared to criticize the exalted status of reason in modern theology. Tillich's dialectic of sacramentalism and rationalism was driven by his critique of rationalist autonomy. Repeatedly he cautioned that reason is not necessarily good or objective; this theme made appearances in Niebuhr's early writing, and in *Moral Man and Immoral Society* Niebuhr featured it. The argument of his title, that groups are inevitably selfish and hypocritical, kindled an immediate controversy in American liberal Protestantism, but the book's more important argument was that reason is inherently ambiguous.

On the one hand, Niebuhr argued, reason is the principle and means of creativity in human life; people grasp the existence of a good that is larger than their private interests through the exercise of reason. On the other hand, reason is the principle and means by which people rationalize and defend their selfish interests; reason is the servant of interest. Liberal theology taught that power is inherently corrupt and that rational goodwill is the answer to society's problems. Niebuhr countered that people do not cease to be dishonest after their dishonesty has been self-discovered or revealed by others: "Whenever men hold unequal power in society, they will strive to maintain it. They will use whatever means are convenient to that end and will seek to justify them by the most plausible arguments they are able to devise." On this theme, *Moral Man and Immoral Society* coined one of Niebuhr's most famous epigrams: "The will to power uses reason as kings use courtiers and chaplains, to add grace to their enterprise." Unrelentingly Niebuhr admonished that reason rationalizes and expands the predatory impulses of nature. Far from delivering humankind from the smallness and immorality of selfish ends, reason defends the gains of individuals and their groups, creates more advanced means of destruction, and rationalizes the use of advanced weaponry. The predatory instincts of animals are sated by a full stomach, but human lusts are refueled by the imaginative capacities of reason: "He will not be satisfied until the universal objectives which the imagination envisages are attained."[23]

The human problem is not the fact that we have not fulfilled our highest ideals, Niebuhr argued; it is not even our predatory animal nature, as liberalism claimed. The problem is humanity itself—our moralism and pride—our insistence on thinking more highly of ourselves, more highly of our intelligence, of our achievements, morality, and ideals, than we should. Human nature at its best offends against God because it engenders self-love and idolatry. Hubris is always the primary form of human sin, and salvation must therefore mean deliverance from egocentrism. Christianity delivers isolated selves from their pride and self-absorption by defeating their self-will. Christian salvation is not about reaching for ideals, but about deliverance from egocentrism, moralism, and self-righteousness.

This chastening message was very hard, though not impossible, for liberals to swallow; their favorite countercharge was that Niebuhr was a pessimist. Just as liberals exaggerated the connection between Niebuhrian pessimism and conservative reaction, Niebuhr exaggerated the perfectionistic idealism of liberal theology; hardly any liberal theologians matched the picture of moralistic sentimentality and naïveté that Niebuhr repeatedly ridiculed in his writings. There were no prominent liberal theologians who did not believe in sin or interpreted sin merely as ignorance, though Niebuhr implied that they were legion. Yet Niebuhr's powerful doctrine of sin and his emphasis upon it cut against the grain of even the most realistic liberal theologies. Among leading liberal theologians, Rauschenbusch came closest to Niebuhr's understanding of the inevitability of personal and social evil and the limitations of middle-class idealism. Rauschenbusch in *Theology for the Social Gospel* devoted separate chapters to the consciousness of sin, the fall of humanity, the nature of sin, the transmission of sin, the superpersonal forces of evil, and the kingdom of evil. His concept of the kingdom of evil presented a stronger sense of the organic socio-historical inheritance of evil than Niebuhr's existential interpretation of original sin, and his various writings on the class struggle could have been written by Niebuhr during his Marxist phase. Rauschenbusch admonished that "we must not blink the fact that idealists alone have never carried through any great social change." The struggle for any great truth "must depend on the class which makes that truth its own and fights for it." On these issues, Rauschenbusch was closer to Niebuhr than to the moralistic liberal idealism that Niebuhr blasted.[24]

But even Rauschenbusch was typically liberal in conceiving the social gospel as a struggle between the "forces of righteousness" and the forces of ignorance and sin. Though he emphasized the annihilating power of the kingdom of evil, Rauschenbusch never doubted that the kingdom of God is a stronger force, not only beyond, but also within history. Though he emphasized that the kingdom of evil is solidaristic and accumulative, and though he recognized that the kingdom of evil afflicts all human hearts and all social orders, he persisted, like his movement, in a straightforward ethical dualism. To his understanding, the divine kingdom was prefigured in the life of the church as the body of Christ and as a sign of true community. Rauschenbusch assumed that the reign of God will never be fully realized in history; at the same time he assumed that the church's vocation is to work at building the divine kingdom. The church will never build a perfect social order, he allowed, yet the church is obliged to strive for as much of the kingdom ideal as is attainable; the only way to find out how much of the ideal is attainable is to struggle for the whole thing in faith. The kingdom will never be fully disclosed in history, "but every approximation to it is worthwhile."[25]

That was the essential theology and ethic of the social gospel. Like all the social gospelers, Rauschenbusch conceived evil as an enemy that can be impeded and even defeated by the good. The social imperative of the social gospel was that Christians are to regenerate the social order through moral, political, and spiritual efforts that diminish the force of evil in the world. Rauschenbusch straightforwardly identified certain social structures as regenerate and others as unregenerate. He described the struggle for social justice as a fight between the "forces of righteousness" and the "forces of evil," and he urged that regenerated social institutions can have redeeming effects on individuals.

This was precisely the mind-set that Niebuhr attacked. The problem was not merely that liberals had a weak sense of evil or were naive about politics; sometimes they had a strong sense of evil and a fairly realistic grasp of politics. In either case, the problem was their simplistic ethical dualism. In *Moral Man and Immoral Society* Niebuhr launched a ferocious attack on the social gospel faith that democratized collectivities can have redeeming effects on individuals; later Niebuhr decided that the notion of "moral man" was a social gospel illusion, too. His alternative was a dialectic of sin. Good and evil are not merely opposing forces, Niebuhr reasoned; they are inevitably mixed together in human nature and history.

Sigmund Freud helped Niebuhr find the root of his realism. Niebuhr judged that the popularity of Freudian psychology owed much to its conception of a death instinct that competes with eros for control over self and society. To disillusioned intellectuals who no longer believed in the Enlightenment myth of human progress, Freud's account of the struggle between eros and death marked a compelling advance over rationalistic psychologies. Freud envisioned the work of eros as binding together "single individuals, then families, then tribes, races, nations, into one great unity, that of humanity." In his view, culture and civilization were products of the work of eros, which competes in every individual, group, and society with the death instinct, the annihilating power that destroys culture and civilization. To Freud, this struggle of the human species for existence was the essential clue to the meaning and evolution of culture; it explained, for example, the meaning of religion: "And it is this battle of Titans that our nurses and governesses try to compose with their lullaby song of Heaven."[26]

Niebuhr appreciated Freud's realism about the tragic aspects of human nature and society. He allowed that Freudian psychology marked an advance in the modern secular attempt to confront the reality of evil. He remarked that Freudian psychology had the virtue "of calling attention to the dynamic character of evil in the world." But he gave short shrift to Freud's understanding of evil: "These supposedly profound words, which pretentiously offer a clue to the meaning of 'the evolution of culture,' throw little light on the actual human situation." Freud posited an inner conflict between a distinct death impulse and a distinct life impulse, but Niebuhr countered that only psychopaths act out of a pure love of destruction. For most people, and for all animals, the death instinct serves the life impulse. People attack and kill to save their own lives and the lives of their loved ones, and to protect the communities and social orders created by eros. The death instinct is real, Niebuhr reasoned, but not Freud's dualistic understanding of it.[27]

Freudian psychology and the Rauschenbuschian social gospel had the same problem; they viewed the forces of creativity and destruction as distinct. Niebuhr admonished that the death instinct is more than a destructive power that competes with and struggles against the life impulse, for the powers of creativity and destruction are inextricably bound up with each other. Morally, evil is always constitutive in the good. No human act, no matter how loving, altruistic, or seemingly innocent, is devoid of egotism. Purity of any kind is an illusion. It is not enough to see that evil is real or that evil competes in every soul and society with the good. A truly realistic dialectic must view the powers of creativity and destruction not as forces held in tension, but as a dialectic of interpenetration. Good and evil are always part of each other.

Niebuhr conceded that his view of the interpenetration of good and evil was bound to seem "morbidly pessimistic to moderns." The chief implication of his view for politics was that any gain toward a good end simultaneously engenders new opportunities for evil. Every movement that creates greater democracy, equality, freedom, or community also creates new opportunities for tyranny, squalor, or anarchy, and every effort to make the public sphere more humane heightens the possibility of producing unintended evil consequences. Democratic gains increase the possibilities for greater numbers of people to do evil things. It followed, for Niebuhr, that reformist and revolutionary movements are most dangerous when they are oblivious to the harmful possibilities they create. He knew very well how this advice sounded to his progressive friends: "The conclusion most abhorrent to the modern mood is that the possibilities of evil grow with the possibilities of good, and that human history is therefore not so much a chronicle of the progressive victory of the good over evil, of cosmos over chaos, as the story of an ever-increasing cosmos, creating ever-increasing possiblities of chaos."[28]

Niebuhr's distinctive neoliberal realism was rooted in his dialectic of sin, which insisted that all human behavior is infected with self-interest, that reason is the servant of interest, and that groups are synergistically more self-regarding than individuals. Persistently he admonished that realism about sin does not impede the cause of social justice; rather, realism about sin is the truth-telling virtue that makes genuine gains toward justice possible and copes with the unanticipated consequences of reform movements. The life-giving impulse within human beings makes democracy possible; the life-destroying impulse within human beings makes democracy necessary. Democracy is most valuable and important as the best political brake that we possess on human greed, will to power, and destructiveness, Niebuhr taught, including the destructiveness that inheres in the life impulse.

This message was too morbid and depressing for liberal theologians and secular progressives alike, as Niebuhr keenly understood. Like the Niebuhrian-Tillichian rendering of Christian myth, his dialectic of sin had to wait to be recognized as a possibility for liberal theology. In later life, even as he was making his peace with liberal theology and his place within it, Niebuhr recalled that for many years he was "falsely accused of being a reactionary" by secular critics who sneered at his Christian faith. It was instructive to him that the Deweyan liberals and socialists who mocked his "reactionary" commitment to Christianity never derided the Christianity of the social gospelers: "But it must be remembered that the proponents of the Social Gospel were not under suspicion, because they did not believe in 'sin'; and they had in any case a faith which did not differ too grievously from the main outlines of the 'American dream.'" Niebuhr carried that bitter remembrance to the end of his days. One reason that he attacked liberal Protestantism so stridently was that the social gospelers got exemptions from secular criticism that were not granted to him.[29]

SPIRIT, NATURE, AND MANNERS

In the 1930s liberal Christian leaders shook their heads at Niebuhr's "pessimism" and Marxist radicalism; not coincidentally, they also shuddered at his manners. As guardians of the civilizing higher things, every liberal Protestant of the Progressive era preached the late-Victorian religion of personality. Religion was about the triumph of spirit and the higher things over the bestial impulses of nature. Though the Chicago theologians repudiated the typical spirit/nature dualism of liberal theology in the name of naturalistic empiricism, that did not stop them from preaching that salvation is the realization of personality and ideals. More revealingly yet, even Niebuhr preached the religion of personality, first with the stock metaphors of liberal theology, and later in the language of a gritty, realistic, dialectical neo-Augustinianism.

In *The Nature and Destiny of Man* Niebuhr analyzed the complex interrelations of vitality and form in the human self, which he pictured as a conflicted blend of animal nature and supra-animal spirit. In both its animal nature and supra-animal spirit, he theorized, the human self possesses vitality (energy, creativity, freedom) and form (rational and moral order), but only in the higher self's freedom of spirit does the self transcend the organic givens of life. Throughout his many years of attacking liberal theology for its sentimental idealism, Niebuhr's premises about religion and theology remained thoroughly liberal. In his early career, while trying to be a good Christian pacifist, he bristled at the cultivated softness of his comrades. He worried that Christian pacifists were passive, feminized, and morally precious. Historian Richard Wightman Fox aptly observes that "what annoyed him most of all about liberal Protestantism was its effeminate, namby-pamby faith in goodness and love."[30]

From Niebuhr's perspective, liberal Protestant leaders were decorous and prized their gentility; their aggression was usually of the passive variety, they were personally demanding and needy, and they devoted inordinate time to small talk. Fox exaggerates Niebuhr's difficulties in making friends—Niebuhr forged close friendships with John Bennett, Will Scarlett, Sherwood Eddy, and June Bingham—but it is true, as Fox emphasizes, that Niebuhr's friends often found him too busy saving the world to take time for friendship. Niebuhr's persona was vigorously masculine and aggressive long before he dumped the pacifist movement. After he joined the faculty at Union Seminary, he was anxious to prove that he belonged at the seminary intellectually, but he made little attempt to adopt the seminary's mannerly decorum. Union Seminary epitomized the liberal Protestant culture of "niceness." Faculty leaders did not believe that polite manners were incidental or optional; they argued that niceness was intrinsic to liberalism. Liberals were polite, courteous, soft-spoken, self-effacing, sensitive toward the feelings of others, especially respectful toward elders, and devoted to the higher things. In the 1930s liberal leaders worried that liberal theology, liberal politics, and liberal manners were all going down together.

Union Seminary president Henry Sloane Coffin was a champion of liberal gentility and protested against the savaging of liberalism by fundamentalists and social radicals. Though fundamentalists and social radicals were profoundly different, Coffin allowed, both groups lacked any scruples about fighting fairly, and thus they were "twins in faith, in temper, and in method. Both hate and despise liberalism." The liberal faith is tolerant and genial, Coffin explained, but fundamentalists and social radicals were intolerant and abusive toward anyone who disagreed with them. They specialized in imputing sinister motives to liberals: "Fundamentalists think liberals are hugging secret sins; social radicals consider them economically conditioned, and class-bound." Equally important, they also derided liberal manners: "Both are contemptuous of the courtesies of which liberalism makes much. Both have atrocious manners. Fundamentalists consider amenities the veneer of pagans, and social radicals deem them the fopperies of the long outmoded gentleman—graces of the defunct aristocrat prized by the imitative bourgeois." For Coffin it followed, logically and in fact, that fundamentalists and social radicals openly despised the liberal devotion to fair play: "Both give no quarter in battle. Their gods are jealous gods, and liberals are their Canaanites to be exterminated."[31]

This warning was published at the height of Niebuhr's neo-Marxist screeds against "modern liberal culture." Coffin kept a wary eye on his star professor, who assured him that he was trying to hold off his Communist-leaning colleague Harry F. Ward and a left flank of truly radical students. With a dreadful sense that the worst was yet to come, Coffin counseled that "liberalism's sons may be in for a Golgotha in this generation." World War I was a time of crucifixion for the liberal faith, and "another and more awful struggle with these deadly foes may be ahead." Liberals needed to wake up to the fact that they were in a fight for survival, but they had to fight as liberals, not like their enemies. They had to keep the liberal faith alive as a means and an end, Coffin declared: "To this end were they born, and for this cause are they in the world, to bear witness to the truth. The issue is with Him who standing within the shadow keepeth watch above His own."[32]

Repeatedly the liberal theologians vowed not to be nostalgic for the glory days before the war, only to break the vow within a few sentences. For all their illusions, they saw clearly that their preferred world of moral idealism and Christianized modernity was ending. To them, the world had stopped getting better after Europe went to war, and it never returned to the path of ethical and social progress. The America of Harding and Coolidge repelled them. In 1925 Fosdick protested that "the lawlessness of the American people is appalling." Self-expression was running amok; America was becoming a country of self-indulgent consumers and narcissists. In poetry, he observed, the new cult of self-expression yielded free verse; in music it spawned jazz; in art it produced cubism; in ethics it created the morality of "do as you please." Instead of calling people to a higher way of life, artists and intellectuals were telling Americans to let themselves go: "Snap your fingers at morals. Assert your liberty. Let yourself go. Multitudes are thinking that and multitudes are living that." Fosdick countered that "let yourself go" is an idiotic mockery of the good; to be found, the good must be surrendered to: "Give yourself to the highest you know and you will have all the thrills of self-expression and at the same time the cleanliness and the self-respect of a controlled life. And lo, the highest you know will give yourself back to you twice over."[33]

Liberal Protestants paid a steep price for their moralizing successes. Female suffrage and Prohibition were both enacted in 1920, the latter with great resentment, and Americans wearied of liberal Protestant exhortations to Christianize America and the world. Faced with a less welcome cultural environment, many social gospelers settled for peace movements and psychotherapy, while a few tried to rekindle Rauschenbuschian economic democracy. Social gospeler Justin Wroe Nixon judged that World War I exhausted Americans' willingness to cooperate for the common good: "They were tired of 'service.' They sought to forget the war and Europe. They wanted to have their fling." Though social gospel thinking still dominated the mainline Protestant seminaries, Nixon observed, the self-indulgent consumerism of the 1920s put the social gospelers out of a job in the social sphere. In its glory days the social gospel lived off the idealism of the young, but 1920s youth had no idealism; in Nixon's telling, they "exchanged the bondage of laws for that of impulses." Nixon called them to throw off their self-absorption and the misspent years of their youth, "the years of the tired radicals and the peace of exhaustion, the years when the pilgrimage of man meant little journeys from the stock ticker to the golf course and back to the bridge game and the highball."[34]

Nixon wanted a renewal of Rauschenbuschian Christian socialism, but most of the social gospel movement had never been economically radical, and even Rauschenbusch, like other Baptist leaders, was a good friend of John D. Rockefeller. The succeeding generation of Baptist leaders was equally close to the succeeding Rockefeller. Believing that their movement deserved its establishment status and was needed to guide American society into righteousness, the liberal Protestants gave political priority to the peace and temperance issues and kept on good terms with their capitalist benefactors. The relationship between Fosdick and John D. Rockefeller Jr. was especially close and symbolic; Rockefeller treasured Fosdick's preaching and national influence, though occasionally Fosdick disturbed him with a critical word about American capitalism. On one occasion Rockefeller wrote to him, "As you know, all my life I have sought to stand between labor and capital, trying to sympathize with and understand the point of view of each, and seeking to modify the extreme attitude of each and to bring them into cooperation. If I had sided with labor against capital, I would have lost all the influence of my position with capital. If I had sided with capital against labor, there would have been no hope of my being of service to labor. This middle ground of sympathy with both . . . has been the position which I have sought to occupy." Rockefeller insisted that his business practices were entirely ethical and his Colorado coalmines were the best in the state. It disturbed him when Fosdick criticized business leaders, he explained, not because they couldn't take criticism, but because Fosdick risked the impression of unfairness: "I covet so much the preserving of your powerful influence with all classes of men that I am particularly sensitive to anything which may even to a minute degree lessen that influence."[35]

Fosdick did not question his powerful friend's absurd self-image as a mediator between labor and capital; in many of his interactions with Rockefeller, polite manners and self-interested tact prevailed over truthful speaking. As always, he was grateful for Rockefeller's solicitude for his influence, though he cautioned Rockefeller that he also risked losing influence if he said nothing about economic justice. If he criticized business leaders, he reflected, he risked alienating the wealthy members of his church, though in fact, "I say far more critical things about my own realm, the ecclesiastical, than I ever dream of saying about the industrial realm." On the other hand, "I am very occasionally criticized for being severe on some industrial question but I am constantly and bitterly criticized because, being in a powerful church with powerful men, I do not (or they think I do not) deal so frankly with the industrial problems." Fosdick felt the scorn of Niebuhr-quoting socialists, even after he and Niebuhr became friendly colleagues. He had no doubt about how a liberal Christian leader should react to cultural degeneration, but, like much of his movement, he struggled to find his balance on matters pertaining to economic justice. Generally he supported the mixed-economy progressivism of fellow liberals Francis McConnell and Albert Knudson, and he unfailingly affirmed that liberal Christian leaders needed to address concrete socioeconomic problems, but he was constrained against doing so by self-interest, proximity, manners, and the crisis of liberalism itself.[36]

A later exchange with Rockefeller illustrated how part of this story turned out. In 1944 Rockefeller became belatedly alarmed about radical trends at Union Seminary. He asked Fosdick what Union was planning to do about communist fellow traveller Harry F. Ward, socialist Reinhold Niebuhr, and whatever other radicals it employed on its faculty. Fosdick replied that Ward retired from Union's faculty "two or three years ago, and we see nothing of him here." He reported that Niebuhr was "another breed altogether, definitely anti-communist," though still some kind of socialist. "He is certainly a liberal on economic and social questions. I suppose that to call him a conservative type of socialist would describe him as well as anything, and he is interested in this campaign to help reelect President Roosevelt." But this was not what really mattered about Niebuhr, Fosdick urged. Niebuhr was a wonderful person and colleague; that was what mattered. If Rockefeller knew Niebuhr and his family, he would stop worrying about Niebuhr: "He is a vigorous, provocative, stimulating personality, honest and forthright, and in his religious thinking he is so concerned about conserving the values in our Christian tradition that he is often called neo-orthodox. One often disagrees with him in detail, but always loves and admires him."[37]

Fosdick reported that Rockefeller's third question was the easiest to answer. "There was a time a few years ago during the depression when economic radicalism did flourish at the Seminary, not however so much among the Faculty as among the students," Fosdick wrote. "That has completely faded out. I have never seen so thoroughgoing a change in a few years as has happened in that regard in the tone of the student-sermons I have to listen to."[38] Union students gave up on democratic socialism before Niebuhr did, in Fosdick's perception, but by 1948, Niebuhr was a mainstream Democrat who pleaded "never mind" regarding his earlier economic positions. Having blasted the New Deal for years as a typical example of liberal reformism, cowardice, stupidity, and futility,

Niebuhr decided, with no loss of personal influence, that the liberals had been right after all about economic policy. On this issue, liberal Protestants found post-war mid-century America a more congenial place than the turbulent 1930s.

The liberal theologians were soft on capitalism, as Niebuhr had previously charged; they believed that middle-class idealism was a better alternative to cap-italism than the socialist ideology of Rauschenbusch, Scudder, and early Niebuhrian realism. For all the pounding that they took for being mere liberals in politics, however, mainstream social gospelers like Mathews and McConnell made more sense than most of their critics. They stood for cooperation, individ-ualism, democracy, and reform while fashionable ideologues of the political right and left promoted antiliberal collectivisms. Like Washington Gladden in the founding social gospel generation, they denounced the predatory ethos and imperialism of the capitalist system while worrying that socialism was too grandiose, bureaucratic, and potentially authoritarian. In the 1930s they advo-cated agricultural relief, unemployment insurance, public works projects, a pen-sion system, slum clearance, a more progressive income tax, expansion of the cooperative sector, and nationalization of select monopolies. Repeatedly McConnell and the Boston personalists made the case for a generally social democratic approach to politics; less concretely, but with a similar spirit, Math-ews judged that the creative period of capitalism had long passed and that the good society required a political economy that promoted cooperation and com-munity. The ideologies of the 1930s are long discredited, but the reformist coop-erativism that the social gospelers advocated is still a credible and authentically progressive politics.

KEEPING THE FAITH: HENRY P. VAN DUSEN AND THE SCHOOLS OF LIBERAL THEOLOGY

Three main schools of thought kept the liberal theology movement alive in the mid-century decades of its waning, in addition to a mystical stream of think-ing and practice that won a smaller following. The movement's situation was never as dire as its defensive and sorrowful literature suggested, for the dominant theologies of the time—those of Niebuhr and Tillich—were forms of (neo)lib-eral thinking. Yet for those who consciously sought to be champions of an ongo-ing American liberal tradition that claimed its ties to Horace Bushnell, Henry Ward Beecher, Theodore Munger, Washington Gladden, Borden Parker Bowne, Walter Rauschenbusch, Shailer Mathews, and Rufus Jones, little comfort was taken in the prominence of Niebuhr and Tillich. They were too prominently implicated in the humiliation of liberal theology. Aside from its mystical expres-sions, American liberal theology of the old kind survived the 1940s and 1950s mainly in three forms: a variegated evangelical liberalism that remained strongly represented at Union Seminary; the mostly evangelical school of personalist the-ology centered at Boston University; and the school of naturalistic empirical theology centered at the University of Chicago, which took a Whiteheadian turn in the 1940s. Liberal pacifism was usually an evangelical, personalist, or mystical phenomenon, owing to the idealism of these traditions, but all of the liberal schools produced antiwar activists as well as nonpacifists influenced by Niebuhr and World War II. By mid-century all three of the dominant schools gave the appearance of persistence and continuity at the institutions where they were centered, but each had serious identity issues to negotiate.

At Chicago the historicist empiricism of Mathews, Case, and Smith gave way to the ahistorical process empiricism of Wieman, which gave way in the 1940s to the Whiteheadian process metaphysics of Charles Hartshorne, Bernard M. Loomer, Daniel Day Williams, and more ambivalently, Bernard Meland. Chicago theology entered a third major phase under the influence of Loomer (who served as dean of the Divinity School and the Federated Theological Faculty from 1945 to 1954), Meland (who joined the Chicago faculty in 1945), Hartshorne (who taught in Chicago's philosophy department and Divinity School), and Williams (who taught at Chicago Theological Seminary and the Federated Theological Faculty). Though he wrote very little, Loomer's embrace of Whiteheadian philosophy set into motion a crucial theological turn at Chicago, one that replaced Wieman's flat instrumentalism with a commitment to process metaphysics and, in Meland's case, a strong interest in myth, spiritual culture, and faith. Invoking William James's distinction between "knowledge of" (knowledge by acquaintance) and "knowledge about" (knowledge by description), Meland pressed beyond Wieman's narrow empiricism, arguing that theology must pursue the "internal track of meaning" that issues from knowledge by acquaintance. There is a feeling dimension of "knowledge of" that bears internal meanings that cannot be stated scientifically, Meland proposed. The key problem of liberal theology in a postliberal context is how to articulate the witness of faith, which he described as "an enduring mythos of the culture." Under Meland's influence especially, Chicago theology sought to overcome the coldness and sterility of its earlier empiricisms by studying myth, faith, and ritual as vehicles of knowledge by acquaintance. Under the influence, especially, of Loomer and Hartshorne, it also became the theological center of Whiteheadian process thought.[39]

This theological turn breathed new life and creativity into the Chicago school, though it offended some of Wieman's protégés, who believed that phase two was cut short. One of them, prominent humanist pastor Duncan Littlefair, later lamented that the Chicago school lost its nerve in the mid-1940s. "Meland and Loomer were my friends, but they ruined the Chicago school of theology," he contended. "Here we had a breakthrough in theology, a major new school in the making. Wieman showed how you could take a thoroughly naturalistic approach to theology, one that dropped all the garbage about 'revelation' and the supernatural, and they refused to keep it going. The direction that Meland and Loomer took was worthless. Theology stopped making progress after Wieman left Chicago, and it hasn't made any progress since then." In his later career, Wieman strongly influenced a succeeding group of religious thinkers, including Larry Axel, Emmanuel

Goldsmith, Cedric Heppler, William Minor, Howard Parsons, Creighton Peden, and Marvin Shaw. But most Chicago schoolers perceived that Wieman's post-Christian empiricism was a dead end for theology, and even Wieman's followers were usually more sympathetic than Littlefair to the Chicago school's third generation. Wieman's approach was too permeated by a laboratory atmosphere to sustain the liberal tradition. Wieman noted the problem, if not the reason for it, near the end of his career: "After more than forty years of search and study, writing and speaking, I find that I have made no headway whatsover in winning acceptance for my undertaking and my thoughts. Rather, the opposite tendency has been increasingly manifest. I am ignored by religious, educational, philosophical, and all other groups where a problem and a search like mine is supposed to find entry. Reviews and other notice of my writings are increasingly hostile and fewer in number. No important secular journal that discusses current books ever takes any notice of mine. A new book by me sells less widely now than some did in the past. None of the enthusiasm is shown that once arose in some circles. Many who once supported me have turned away into indifference or hostility. The surest way to reduce an audience to the minimum is to announce me as the speaker."[40]

Wieman's frankness attracted more readers than this confession implied, but the crucial problem with his position was identified by Smith just before Wieman's Chicago career began, and just after Smith had come to think such thoughts. If modern theology restricts itself to narrowly empirical formulations, Smith observed, reviewing Wieman's recent book, "will it not mean the disappearance of religious significance?" Smith's protégé, Meland, took this question very seriously in the 1940s, and took Chicago theology in a religiometaphysical direction that valorized the roots of theology in myth and sacred mystery. In addition, Loomer launched a theological movement by arguing that Whiteheadian metaphysics is the system that best conceptualizes and expresses the Chicago school belief that God is the concrete reality of historical process. In his later career, Loomer argued that Chicago theism leads logically to the verdict that God is morally ambiguous. Chicago empiricism in its third phase produced an impressive school of process theologians, but it had to effect a significant shift in orientation to do so.[41]

Mid-century Boston personalism faced a different kind of identity crisis. The basic theory of personalist idealism was reaffirmed, but the movement's giant figures came to the end of their days. The successors of Knudson, McConnell, and Brightman faced a different situation from that confronted by the successors of Mathews, Ames, and Wieman. Meland and Loomer felt keenly the need to modify Chicago empiricism in fundamental ways, but the third-generation Boston personalists felt no such need. Moreover, the theorists of the first and second phases of Chicago theology were highly respected figures, but they were not revered as spiritual leaders in the ways that American Methodists treasured Knudson, McConnell, and Brightman.

The third generation of Boston personalists had the advantage and disadvantage of succeeding legendary figures whose accomplishments were viewed as being worthy of preservation. As a consequence, they inherited and sustained a highly systematized and coherent liberal school. In its third generation, the personalist approach was restated and defended by philosophers Peter Bertocci and John Lavely, theologians L. Harold DeWolf and S. Paul Schilling, and social ethicist and School of Theology dean Walter Muelder. These religious thinkers sharpened and expanded the tradition they received, strengthened their school's socioethical voice, widened the social and epistemological theory of its mind-centered idealism, and passed the theology and philosophy of idealist personalism to a fourth generation. They also sustained their tradition's deep and comprehensive commitment to the personalist metaphysical theory of personality, which was both the strength of Boston personalism in its third generation and the cause of its limited appeal, as well as a contributing factor to its subsequent decline.[42]

The biggest name in mid-century American Christianity—Fosdick—was proud to call himself an evangelical liberal, as were theological leaders Coffin, Brown, Morrison, Harkness, Harris Franklin Rall, and Henry Pitney Van Dusen. As Roosevelt Professor of Systematic Theology at Union Seminary from 1926 to 1963, and as seminary president from 1945 to 1963, Van Dusen sustained the Union tradition of movement-conscious, gospel-centered liberalism championed by Union presidents Coffin and Arthur C. McGiffert. His writings vigorously defended the evangelical character of liberal theology and charted the progress of modern Protestant ecumenism and world missions. Van Dusen was fond of saying that evangelical liberalism was the most christocentric tradition in the history of Christian thought; like many gospel-centered liberals, he disputed that there was any other kind of authentically liberal theology.

With typical directness he insisted that humanistic naturalism was the chief opponent of liberal theology, not a possible version of it, and that "at the heart of Evangelical Liberalism stands Jesus Christ." Van Dusen allowed that some evangelical liberals took "Jesus Christ" to mean their own picture of the historical Jesus, and for others it meant the spiritual presence of the living Christ. He countered that there was such a thing as normative evangelical liberalism, for which "*the Jesus of History* and *the Living Christ* are a single organic, indissoluble personal reality*.*" The singular reality of Jesus Christ is defined in the life, teaching, work, spirit, and faith of the historical Jesus, Van Dusen explained, and it is known in spiritual power in the living Christ: "The main point is, Liberal Theology in every one of its authentic expressions has been *through and through Christocentric.*" More than that, liberal theology revered and followed Jesus Christ with a singularity of faithfulness that was distinctive in Christian history: "Indeed, the contention may be advanced that Evangelical Liberalism is the *first* thoroughly and consistently Christocentric theology."[43]

Van Dusen's theological heroes were familiar and recent: Harnack, Herrmann, Clarke, Brown, and Fosdick. He conceded that liberal Protestantism often invoked a Christ of its imagination and that modern Protestantism was littered with alternatives to the Christ of Brown and Fosdick. But liberal Protestantism was strongest when it held fast to the lordship and teaching of Jesus Christ, he urged. There was no worthy alternative to gospel-centered faithfulness: "If Liberal Theology holds validity, it is precisely because its interpretation of Jesus Christ is most fully adequate, most true to authentic Christian Faith." Liberals could not afford to give up the evangelical claim to a recovered orthodoxy or the belief in a personal transcendent God or the claim to continuity with historic Christianity. Their mission was to overthrow authority religion without reducing Christianity to culture religion or moralism.[44]

With echoes of Herrmann and Clarke, Van Dusen called liberal Protestantism to hold fast to "the mind and especially the faith of Jesus." Neo-orthodoxy put the transcendent and ineffable mystery of God at the center; Van Dusen replied that genuine liberal theology put the face of Christ at the center. It kept faith with Paul's appeal to "the light of the gospel of the glory of Christ, who is the image of God" (2 Cor. 4:6). It centered on the claim that Christ is the agent of Christianity's life-transforming influence, the inspirer of its prophetic outreach, the basis of its only worthwhile unity, and the one who reveals God. The gospel portraits through which Christians attain their picture of Christ are flawed, he allowed, but through these imperfect records "Jesus ever afresh lays constraint upon his Movement in the world, holding it more or less true to his mind and faith, and impelling it to new advances for fulfillment of his purposes."[45]

From its Enlightenment Progressivist heritage, liberal theology derived its devotion to truth, its deference to science, its typical agnosticism about metaphysical reason, its emphasis on the continuity between reason and revelation, and its spirit of tolerance and gentility. From its evangelical background, liberal theology inherited its emphases on the authority of Christian experience, the centrality of Jesus Christ, the principle of continuity with the historic faith of Christianity, and the missionary commitment to personal and social salvation. The leaders of mainstream American liberal theology theorized these commitments by drawing upon their backgrounds in American evangelical religion and their training in Ritschlian theology. Ritschl rested his entire system on the experience of reconciliation through Christ; Harnack taught that the essence of Christianity is "Jesus Christ and his Gospel"; Herrmann insisted that evangelical liberalism brought the Protestant Reformation to completion; the social gospel idea of social salvation was championed by Ritschlians and Bushnellians. These themes passed directly into the theologies of Brown, McGiffert, King, Rauschenbusch, Coffin, and the early Mathews, and in the 1930s Coffin and Van Dusen were not shy about distinguishing "authentic" liberal theology from kinds that centered upon modern philosophies. For nearly forty years Van Dusen spoke for the majority stream of the liberal theology movement that pointedly reminded liberals of their evangelical heritage. He objected sharply to the Chicago school's emphasis on the sociohistorical gap between modern and premodern Christianities. Evangelical liberalism was also modern, he protested, but it remained "fully within the stream of historic Christian development . . . in striking contrast to other branches of the liberal movement which did not maintain their center of reference within the Church."[46]

Gospel-centered liberals defended their right to this continuity claim against strong criticism from right and left. From the right, conservatives protested that "evangelical" liberalism discarded the doctrines of biblical infallibility and authority, substitutionary atonement, and salvation through Christ alone; from the left, modernists and religious radicals countered that the evangelical liberal desire for continuity betrayed intellectual confusion and a weakness of moral courage. At the same time, Barthians and Niebuhrians condemned liberal theology from right *and* left, objecting that liberals believed in middle-class idealism, not the convention-blasting Word of God. Because their training prepared them for disputes with conservatives and radicals, the gospel-centered liberals were well suited to take criticism from their right and left flanks. The task of mediating between overbelief and nonbelief was characteristic of liberal theology as a whole, and especially of its gospel-centered tradition; liberal theology began as a third-way phenomenon and it remained one long after it lost its field-dominating status.

What proved harder for liberal theologians to take was the loud criticism they received from Barthian and Niebuhrian beneficiaries of the liberal tradition. These critical blasts annoyed modernist and evangelical liberals alike. Mathews complained that religious thinkers rarely capitalized on experience: "Instead of learning how to use parental experience to avoid duplicating parental mistakes a new generation apparently wishes to recapitulate foolishness before making new moral adventures." The spirit of neo-orthodoxy repulsed Matthews: "I cannot believe that such a mood is either healthy or conducive to religious faith. It is more akin to the eschatology of a subject Jewish people and savors too much of defeatism and distrust of intelligently implemented love. One might almost describe it as premillenarian liberalism." Having witnessed and aided the development of a liberal theological establishment in his lifetime, he shook his head at the rise of a theological generation that exalted crisis, pessimism, otherworldliness, and power over love, process, science, and cooperation.[47]

Van Dusen struck a similar note of generational disappointment, though Barthian biblicism was less deeply alien to him, and in his case, it was his own generation that proved disappointing. "Those who are the children of the liberal movement should guard themselves against the familiar vices of the younger generation—unfairness and ingratitude toward their parentage," he counseled. From his perspective as a liberal Niebuhrian, John C. Bennett similarly judged that there was an adolescent quality to the currently routine attacks on liberalism. Each generation typically criticizes its predecessors beyond all fairness, while exaggerating the novelty of its own wisdom, Bennett observed. The Niebuhrian upsurge was a case in point; it routinely caricatured the liberal tradition because the Niebuhrians were determined to replace the liberal establishment.[48]

On occasion the liberals struck back in a way that wounded Niebuhr personally. Robert L. Calhoun's blistering critique of the first volume of *The Nature and Destiny of Man* was a showcase example. Calhoun and Niebuhr knew each other from the Younger Theologians Group (by then renamed the Theological Discussion Group), but Calhoun broke from the spirit of niceness that prevailed at group meetings, charging that Niebuhr lacked professional competence. *The Nature and Destiny of Man* was a brilliant expression of Niebuhr's private vision, he judged, but as a work of scholarship it failed miserably. It completely abandoned the scholar's duty to weigh evidence with care and precision, and it swiftly divided authors into sheep and goats: "Swiftness is the word always." In Calhoun's description, Niebuhr treated the sheep as geniuses and the goats as worthless. Always he mined the Christian tradition selectively to dramatize his personal vision: the prophets were better than the Wisdom literature, Hebrew religion was better than Hellenism, Paul was better than the Synoptic Gospels, the Reformation was better than the Renaissance, and so on.[49]

Calhoun assured that he respected Niebuhr's personal struggle and intellectual brilliance. He affirmed that good theology often comes directly from a theologian's personal struggle. In Niebuhr's case, he explained, the "real ground" of the argument was not scholarship "but what has happened to him as a struggling self." What Calhoun did not respect was that Niebuhr distorted history to make his case. *The Nature and Destiny of Man,* he charged, was hurried, rash, one-sided, and careless with nuances and detail. "He does not understand 'classical thought,' a chief villain throughout the book, and many of his references to it make painful reading," Calhoun observed. "The statements about Greek philosophy are especially bad, a jumble of oddments in which ignorance and carelessness are not concealed by a confident style." Niebuhr wrote shooting-gallery nonsense about classicism and the Renaissance, he oversimplified idealism and romanticism to refute them as well, he made a mess of Hellenistic Christianity, he showed gross ignorance of science and philosophy, and despite his consuming concern with personality and the nature of the self, he completely ignored personalist philosophy, "a major alternative view." As a work of historical scholarship, Calhoun judged, Niebuhr's book put "the whole history of Christian thought into false perspective." In other words, "it seems not unfair to judge that on its historical side this book cannot be taken seriously."[50]

This attack offended Niebuhr, who smelled ideological revenge; the liberal-pacifist Calhoun was out to cut him down to size. Calhoun replied that his judgments were strictly professional: "Your account of Christian and secular thought shows clearly that at various points you have lacked either time, equipment, or inclination to study the relevant data." Calhoun, who knew the data, never wrote a major work; on the other hand, his occasional writings revealed a capacity for introspective insight that Niebuhr wholly lacked. Niebuhr's few attempts at writing about himself were superficial and lifeless, and he may have resented Calhoun's judgment that the valuable parts of his work were projections of his inner struggle. More importantly, Calhoun's judgments on his scholarly competence wounded him deeply, yet on both counts Niebuhr must have realized that Calhoun was right. Niebuhr's shrewd descriptions of attention-seeking pride and power lust obviously drew on personal experience, and he lacked the temperament and training of a scholar. At the same time he couldn't plead guilty to Cal-

houn's indictment of his scholarship, especially since it came from a liberal pacifist with a superior attitude.[51]

The Nature and Destiny of Man, volume two, contained Niebuhr's reply to
Calhoun's charges. He toned down his shooting-gallery atmosphere, enlisted his
wife Ursula and Henry Sloane Coffin to smooth his writing style, and criticized
Barthians and the Reformers for one-sidedly disdaining Renaissance humanism.
Calhoun and Bennett noticed the differences; though Calhoun noted that volume two contained "a fair number of historical problems," he welcomed
Niebuhr's warm words for the Renaissance as evidence that he still belonged to
the liberal tradition. Volume two was a blend of liberal Protestantism and sophisticated Paulinism, Calhoun judged, "not an expression of 'neo-orthodoxy.'" Bennett similarly rejoiced that Niebuhr clearly rejected the "errors of Luther and
Calvin, Barth and Brunner." Niebuhr replied to Bennett that he was heartened
to receive better reviews, though it had always been wrong to associate him with
Continental neo-orthodox theologians: "I have never thought of myself in their
category. I think when it comes to the crux I belong to the liberal tradition more
than to theirs. Whenever I read them or argue with them, Brunner for instance,
I always feel that they are trying to fit life into a dogmatic mold and that they
have hard and fast Biblical presuppositions which I do not share."[52]

That put the matter as clearly as Niebuhr ever expressed it. His thinking was
firmly liberal in the sense of its resistance to any dogmatic mold, and, his beliefs
about Christ, miracles, salvation, and eternal life were conventionally liberal. At
the same time, liberals such as Harkness, Fosdick, Coffin, Wieman, Brightman,
Meland, and Van Dusen variously allowed that their tradition needed to selectively accommodate Niebuhrian criticism. Fosdick's 1935 sermon against har-
monizing Christ with modern culture was repeatedly cited as a turning point for
liberal theology; Van Dusen declared that the cultural religion that Fosdick
renounced was a dead letter in liberal theology: "That outlook is now definitely
discredited. Criticism has proven its premises invalid. The passage of events has
branded its expectations absurd. It must be discarded."[53]

Other liberal beliefs came under searching self-criticism in the mid-century
decades of liberal theology's fall from favor. The liberal principle of loyalty to
truth rather than tradition was a bulwark against authority religion, but liberals
increasingly worried that it had the effect of taking theology away from ordinary people. Only privileged academics could do theology if it was defined as
the pursuit of intellectual truth in the field of religion. To mitigate the academic ethos of Chicago theology, Bernard Meland initiated a turn toward the
feeling side of religion and the practical aspects of Christian life and worship;
more than their teachers, the third-generation Boston personalists emphasized
practical issues in ecclesiology, worship, Methodist history, and personal and
social ethics; more pointedly yet, Van Dusen exhorted Christian thinkers to
remember that the highest good in human life is not truth, but love expressed
in spiritual personality.[54]

Another weakness of liberal theology was the epistemological dualism that it inherited from Kant and Ritschl. The Ritschlian strategy gave up any claim to metaphysical knowledge of transcendental realities and accepted a bifurcated disjunction of realms between scientific theoretical reason and moral-religious practical reason. This strategy delivered theological liberalism from the orthodox dualism of nature and supernature, and it bought liberal theology a needed respite from the conflict between science and religion, but at the price of a crippling metaphysical agnosticism and epistemological dualism. The Boston personalists and Chicago empiricists strongly maintained that this price was not worth paying. There is only one world, they countered; religion must stake its claim to truth as part of the only universe that exists. Theology had to take the risk of making metaphysical truth claims, as the personalists did, or it had to take the empirical realist option of making theology as scientific as possible. Both of these constructive alternatives had limited appeal. Though personalist language was widely appropriated in liberal theology, the distinctive metaphysical theory of personalist idealism attracted few advocates outside the Methodist denomination; and by 1945, Macintosh had few followers and the Chicago schoolers realized that Wieman-style empiricism was religiously wanting. The third generation personalists stuck with their metaphysical theory, while revising some of its weak points, and the third generation Chicago school opted for a metaphysical theory that claimed a basis in the "new physics" of quantum mechanics and relativity theory. Meanhile, most evangelical liberals stuck with the Ritschlian strategy, but not with their former confidence. Increasingly they worried that their neo-Kantian dualism was not a viable solution to religion-and-science problems; Van Dusen allowed that the Ritschlian school's epistemological dualism was its most questionable feature.

A related problem area was the liberal appeal to Christian experience. What exactly did this mean? Was it a reference to a specifically *Christian* experience, as in John Wesley, or a Schleiermacherian appeal to "religious feeling as such," in which Christian experience became the highest example of religious feeling? If the former, how did liberals negotiate the reality of different kinds of Christian experience, and how did they justify their exclusion of other religious traditions? If the latter, is Christianity an example of a universal religious experience? Is there such a thing as universal religious experience? And in either case, how could such a subjective and variable category as "Christian experience" carry the immense weight that liberal theologies assigned to it? In cases where Christians give different accounts of religious experience, Gerald Birney Smith pointedly asked, "How shall we determine whose experience is reliable?" In his later career Smith worried that by relying so heavily on appeals to experience, liberal theology opened the door to being refuted or explained away by psychological research.

The liberal appeal to experience was formulated by early-nineteenth-century theologians who took for granted the training of modern Christians in Christian Scripture and piety. Schleiermacher, Channing, and Bushnell presupposed their audiences' backgrounds in forms of orthodox and pietist religion, and the next generation of liberals traded on the existence of liberal Christianity. Virtually all of the liberal leaders of the social gospel era were raised in homes that featured family devotions, Bible reading, personal prayer, and Sunday observance. They continued these spiritual practices in their own lives, but in raising their children, many of them considerably cut back on family devotions and Bible study. Langdon Gilkey, whose father was a classic example of this trend, observes that liberal leaders like Fosdick, Mathews, and Charles Gilkey were products of a Protestant spiritual culture that began to wither in the next generation. Gilky recalls that at the funeral of his mother, Geraldine Gilkey, Fosdick recited Scripture passages for half an hour from memory; Gilkey remarks: "My generation of neo-liberals studied the Bible, but Fosdick's generation read it every day and knew it line by line. No wonder they would talk so easily of 'Christian experience.' My generation hardly had a clue as to what it meant!"[55]

"Christian experience" was a bedrock for the social gospel liberals, but it became more problematic to the succeeding generation, which had less "Christian experience" in its background and faced a more secularized and diverse culture. Mid-century liberals asked: What becomes of the authority of Christian experience for those who have little of it? And what about those who lack any background in Christianity? The latter question was barely raised by the social gospel generation; it was raised provocatively by Tillich, whose enormous influence rested largely on his capacity to speak to a religiously unmoored audience; the question became unavoidable to liberal theologians in the second half of the twentieth century.

A similar problem attached to the evangelical liberal claim of continuity with historic Christianity. Fosdick provided the often-repeated liberal slogan on this subject: "Abiding experiences in changing categories." This slogan became less assuring to liberals after liberalism lost its field-dominating authority, however. Van Dusen judged that Fosdick provided merely "a temporary resting point" for a reeling and puzzled liberal generation. Theological categories are not supposed to be representations of mere subjective experiences, he admonished; they are supposed to represent objective realities. Liberal Christianity was in crisis because of modern secular doubt about the existence of fundamental religious realities, not because modern secularists questioned the worthiness of liberal Christian experiences. Van Dusen urged that this was why the evangelical liberal claim to historic Christian continuity was vitally important. Continuity matters if it claims fundamental continuity in what it means for Christianity to be true; if the truth claims are always changing, no other continuity is worth very much. Liberal theology had two problems that transcended all others, he judged. The first was the prevailing public mood of pessimism and disillusionment that cast the old liberal theology out of favor. The second was that liberal Protestantism was deficient at transmitting its truth claims from generation to generation, and thus it was not good at passing its faith to its children.[56]

Van Dusen blamed much of the latter problem on the spiritual and ecclesiological thinness of Protestantism as a whole, especially liberal Protestantism.

Liberal Protestant piety was individualistic, its conception of experience was therefore subjective, and it generally took for granted a low-church ecclesiology. Its
focus was the individual way of Jesus, as in "Jesus and his gospel." Liberal Protestants such as Bennett and Harkness, through their participation in the ecumenical movement, discovered new feelings for the church as the corporate body of
Christ, but for the most part American liberal Protestantism was low on catholic
feeling and liturgical sensibility. Van Dusen suggested that under these circumstances, if Roman Catholicism ever modernized, it would find a large audience for
its ministrations in the United States. The popularity of Friedrich von Hügel's
writings on mysticism showed that many people were hungry for the spirituality
of the Catholic church, though not in the Catholic church as it presently existed.
Liberal Protestantism needed to develop new forms of spiritual awareness, cate-
chesis, and communal practice, Van Dusen counseled, for the individual seeker
can absorb the meaning of Christianity "only as his life is guided, nurtured, chastened and redeemed within the community of his fellows." Throughout his career
as a theologian, church leader, and seminary president, Van Dusen tracked the
progress of liberal Protestant world missions and ecumenism. Though his writings
never lacked a critical edge, they projected an upbeat spirit, often in the form of
a progress report.[57]

H. Richard Niebuhr delivered a different kind of report in *The Kingdom of
God in America* (1937), judging that liberal Protestantism was caught in an
inevitably degenerative process. In Niebuhr's description, liberal theology was the
child of a merger between nineteenth-century romantic liberalism and evangelicalism. Romantic liberalism was evolutionary, progressive, immanentalist, and
idealistic, while evangelicalism was revolutionary, sin-conscious, and conversion-
oriented. According to Niebuhr, the key to the story of liberal theology was that
while liberal theologians usually claimed to maintain a balance between their tradition's romantic and evangelical elements, in fact they continually whittled away
their evangelical inheritance. The light of the gospel faith died quickly in the Unitarian church, where William Ellery Channing's blend of romantic and evangelical themes was overwhelmed by Emersonian transcendentalism and Theodore
Parker's semi-Christian theology of Absolute Religion.

In mainline Protestantism a similar process was unfolding a bit more deliberately. Horace Bushnell was the Channing figure who held his romantic liberalism in tension with his emphasis on the necessity of regeneration and "his
constant struggling with the problem of atonement." In Niebuhr's telling, the
Bushnellians quickly went to work on Bushnell's evangelicalism, as Washington
Gladden reinterpreted his hero's theology of sovereignty and salvation to fit the
modern mind. "So the process went on," Niebuhr remarked. "It was not God
who ruled, but religion ruled a little, and religion needed God for its support."
The last figure that he named was Rauschenbusch, since the others that Niebuhr
might have named were still alive in 1937; still, he spared no sarcasm or disdain
in describing their work:

Whatever memory of the gospel of rebirth had been conserved by early romanticism, the later liberalism increasingly identified human values with the divine, proclaimed the glad tidings of progress and hallowed man's moral efforts though they led to civil, international and class war. As youth traveled daily "farther from the east" the splendid vision of the transalpine good, of the kingdom beyond, faded into the light of a common day. The coming kingdom of late liberalism, like the heaven of a senile orthodoxy, came to be a place not of liberty and glory but of material delights, the modern counterparts of those pleasures which it had laughed to scorn when it spoke of ancient superstitions. For the golden harps of the saints it substituted radios, for angelic wings concrete highways and high-powered cars, and heavenly rest was now called leisure. But it was all the same old pattern; only the symbols had changed.[58]

The Kingdom of God in America stoked every party's agenda. Evangelical liberals quoted it to naturalistic modernists and themselves as a prophetic warning; modernists argued that Richard Niebuhr showed the futility of splitting the difference between the modern mind and the old religion; Niebuhrians took its closing pages as a manifesto for a new third way in theology. Richard Niebuhr urged that the church is not supposed to adjust its faith to the changing, relative, temporal aspects of modern civilization. It is supposed to adjust itself, amid the changing aspects of modern civilization, to the eternal. The church should respond to the crisis of the world in the church, not the other way around.

Yet even Richard Niebuhr was closer to the liberal tradition than he liked or claimed. He "hated" liberal Protestantism, which was "thoroughly bad" in its moralism and idealism, and, unlike his brother, he never apologized for his attacks upon it, yet his constructive theology took liberal premises for granted. Richard Niebuhr did not establish or defend his arguments with appeals to external authority; he assumed the liberal historical-critical account of scriptural development and was deeply influenced by Troeltschian historicism; his Christology, to the extent that he had one, was liberal; he emphasized the reality of historical and cultural relativity; and his value theory and persistent concern with faith and culture were quintessentially liberal preoccupations. Niebuhr conceived his "radical monotheism" and his perspectival theory of revelation as a third way, theologically, between Barth and Troeltsch, but this third way tilted toward liberalism, not Barth's neo-biblicist dogmatics. His theory of revelation was not a dialectic of scriptural Word and Word of the Spirit within the confessional circle of the church, as in Barth; for Richard Niebuhr, the event of revelation was about the disclosure of God as a valued reality that creates a basis for practical reasoning about God and the world.

"Revelation means for us that part of our inner history which illuminates the rest of it and which is itself intelligible," he asserted. Revelation is a type of experience; it is like reading a single luminous sentence that makes sense of an entire difficult book. To be a Christian, Niebuhr reasoned, is to participate in a particular history and story of faith that, like all good stories, has (at least) one special occasion. In Christianity, he observed, the special occasion "is called Jesus Christ," through whom the power and righteousness of God are revealed. For those who live within the inner history of the ongoing, corporate story of Christ, the event of Christ bears revelatory meaning that makes all of life intelligible. That is, the revelatory event yields concepts that give intelligibility to the world as a whole: "Revelation means this intelligible event which makes all other events intelligible." Niebuhr argued that the Christian heart finds its reason in Christian revelation, and the kind of reason that correlates with revelation is personal, valuing, Kantian practical reason, "the reason of a self" as opposed to scientific reason: "The conflict of practical reason is with practical irrationality as pure reason is at war with irrationality in the head and not with reason in the heart." In other words, "when we use revelation as the basis of our reasoning we seek to conquer the evil imaginations of the heart and not the adequate images of an observing mind."[59]

That was straight out of the liberal playbook, but Richard Niebuhr believed that liberalism no longer preached about "the evil imaginations of the heart" or "the religion of rebirth," and he loathed liberal sentimentality and idealism. Liberal Protestantism gave him much to oppose; at the same time, he was wrong to claim that evangelical liberalism no longer existed, for Clarke, Brown, Knudson, Harkness, Van Dusen, and numerous others retained more of the evangelical gospel-theology than he did. The liberal era was not lacking in theological leaders who held together the evangelical and modernist sources of liberal theology. Moreover, the trajectory of Richard Niebuhr's thinking carried into mainline liberal Protestantism; neo-orthodoxy was shortlived in American theology, and most of Richard Niebuhr's protégés were neoliberals in the tradition of the Niebuhrs, Tillich, and Bennett.

Meanwhile a host of stubborn thinkers kept alive an assortment of evangelical, personalist, naturalistic-modernist, and mystical theologies that belonged without equivocation to the liberal tradition of old. They identified with Fosdick's self-description; for them it was either liberal religion or no religion at all; whatever its problems, they believed in the liberal faith of reasonableness, openness, modernity, and the social gospel. The "mystery X" dialectical revelationism of neo-orthodoxy was alien to them; they stuck with the historical Jesus and the complementarity of reason and revelation, or at least for the Wieman naturalists, reason and faith. Calhoun described them, and himself, as liberals who were "bandaged but unbowed." Having begun his theological career as a Macintosh-style modernizer, Calhoun surprised himself by crossing to the evangelical side, explaining that "I have been driven, willy-nilly, to recognize that theology cannot get on without special revelations." He even came to believe that good theology needs "creeds, theological tradition, and the Christian church." He cautioned, however, that all intelligent liberals understood that every appeal to special revelation has to be checked by historical criticism, rationality, and the general experience of humankind. This was why he had to remain "some obstinate sort of liberal." Liberals were the only ones who made sense; the Barthians attacked liberal theology for being subjective, but the really subjective theologians were the Barthians, who appealed solely to the authority of a nonobjective Word. Calhoun countered, "I see no way in which theology can get on without history, philosophy and common sense."[60]

The social arena proved to be more chastening to liberals, but even here, most of them remained essentially unbowed about the idealistic nature of good religion. In the 1920s and 1930s they scaled back the socioeconomic ambitions of the social gospel but vowed to abolish war. Even decidedly nonpacifist liberals like Mathews and Knudson were dedicated peace activists in the 1930s. In the 1940s World War II separated the absolute pacifists from other liberals, but there were many more liberal theologians who remained pacifists than during the previous war, and most of them were not stigmatized as Rauschenbusch was. Calhoun's trajectory was typical in several ways. He supported America's intervention in World War I, was bitterly disillusioned by the vengeance of the war's victors, and became a pacifist. After the bottom fell out of the Coolidge bull market he stopped believing that economic justice was primarily a question of individual honesty and good will. "Mea culpa," he later reflected. "It took three years of growing disillusionment and anxiety to cure me of that particular blindness." Two years before America entered World War II, Calhoun called for "a much larger minority than there was in 1914 to resist the inevitable war hysteria, the orthodox dehumanizing of the enemy, and the making of another nationalistic peace." After America entered the war, he joined Fosdick, Harkness, Rufus Jones, George Buttrick, Ernest Fremont Tittle, Halford Luccock, Howard Thurman, and other liberal pacifists in sustaining that minority.[61]

The liberals of the post–World War I generation cut back on their hopes for a cooperative commonwealth, but not on the moral necessity of ideals. They persisted in their belief that power politics is no cure for the ills of humanity and that working toward a moral ideal is the only way to discover how much of it is attainable. Most of them accepted America's intervention in World War II, but generally they did not recycle the Wilsonian rhetoric of the previous war about saving the world for democracy. The Depression-era liberals were too chastened by experience to idealize the war as something more than a tragic necessity, and they were too determined to remain idealists to do so. To them it was second nature to equate good religion with moral ideals and the religion of Jesus; even the cooler-blooded Chicago empiricists argued this way when they sermonized. The liberal theologians thought of themselves as stubborn idealists who held out for the common good and the ideals of modern Christianity.

This self-conception compounded their difficulty in perceiving their complicity in America's sins. Liberal Protestantism preached that racism is evil, but its resistance to the evil of American segregation was pitifully tepid, as Martin Luther King Jr. frequently observed. On related issues liberal Protestant leaders were impervious to the existence of wrongdoing. Liberal theologians and church leaders in the 1950s had barely any sensitivity to their society's discrimination against women, and they tended to see cultural pluralism as a threat to the common good. The

Christian Century hammered on the latter theme in the 1950s, worrying about the erosion of Protestant authority in America. *Christian Century* stalwarts Charles Clayton Morrison, Luther Wiegle, William Bower, and F. Ernest Johnson described their country as a redeemer nation, the nation with the soul of a church. If they did not define and represent America's hope of a democratic, faithful, and freedom-cherishing common faith, who would? They feared that the increasing pluralization and secularization of America was destroying its soul. In the 1950s, the *Christian Century* editorialized repeatedly that in the name of protecting the rights of Catholics, atheists, and other minorities, American lawmakers were infringing the majority's right to maintain a common American Protestant faith. To the liberal Protestants, it was a civic and moral duty for the public schools to tell the story of the American experiment in a way that highlighted its Protestant character and renewed America's religiously grounded virtues.[62]

Protestant leaders had a conscience about their country's racial injustice, and they welcomed Benjamin E. Mays to the highest ranks of their organizations, but they were careful, as Mays lamented, not to step far out of line with the dominant culture and system of a segregated society. Feminism broke into the consciousness of theology during this period only minimally; without Georgia Harkness it barely would have existed. Liberal theology supported Protestant ecumenism, but it had a strained relationship with Catholic and Orthodox forms of Christianity, and it gave low priority to dialogues with traditions outside Christianity. It continued to speak a language of freedom, equality, peaceableness, and community, but nearly always from a white, male, status-conscious, middle-class perspective. When it preached on the parable of the Good Samaritan, it identified with the Samaritan, not the victim on the road.

Liberal theology was not exclusively male or white, however. In the pathbreaking career and work of Georgia Harkness, American liberal theology broke out of its male mold; in the careers of a critical group of African American social gospelers, the social idealism of American liberal Christianity was embraced and transfigured. Many of the founders of the American civil rights movement were figures from black church backgrounds who were trained, academically, in liberal theology and who took to heart the social gospel ethic of freedom, equality, peaceableness, and community. In their work the middle-class idealism of the social gospel was reinterpreted from the perspectives of an oppressed class of Americans. These proponents of a black social gospel included Benjamin Mays, Mordecai Wyatt Johnson, William Stewart Nelson, Frank T. Wilson, and Howard Thurman. To them the social gospel movement had barely begun; what was needed was an American Christianity that took seriously its own best preaching and ethics on behalf of equal opportunity, racial integration, and peace. They took little interest in theological trends that obscured or relativized these goals. They were preachers, movement leaders, and institution builders, not academic theologians. The most promising religious thinker among them, Thurman, gave up his academic career to launch a model ministry of inclusion. He called American Christianity to its best religious vision and in several ways exemplified it.

HOWARD THURMAN: THE RELIGION OF JESUS, THE MYSTIC WAY, AND THE DISINHERITED

Howard Thurman was a product of the Southern black church and a class-mate of Martin Luther King Sr., became a social gospeler, a Quaker-influenced mystic and pacifist, a pathbreaking advocate and practitioner of racial integration, an adviser to civil rights movement leaders, a professor, a pastor, a chapel dean, a prolific author, and a spiritual influence on Martin Luther King Jr.

He was born in 1899 to Saul and Alice Thurman in the Waycross section of Daytona, Florida. His father, who laid track for the Florida East Coast Railroad, died of pneumonia when Thurman was seven years old. Alice Thurman, pious and highly reticent, supported her three children by cooking and cleaning for white people; meanwhile Thurman was raised mainly by his maternal grandmother Nancy, a former slave who lived until the Civil War on a plantation near Madison, Florida. From his grandmother, Thurman learned of the persecution suffered by American slaves and of their deep religious faith. One of his regular chores was to read the Bible to her. Though illiterate, his grandmother knew the Bible well and was especially fond of the devotional Psalms, Isaiah, and the Gospels. Pointedly she never asked him to read from Paul's epistles, except 1 Corinthians 13; in later years she explained to Thurman that during her youth the slavemasters regularly recited Paul's statements about slavery to the slaves and that she had vowed to herself that if freedom ever came to her, she would have no further dealings with the apostle Paul.[63]

In his youth Thurman had no positive contacts with white people and no idea that such a thing was possible. The entire state of Florida had only three public high schools for black children, and local politics in the Daytona Beach area was controlled by the Ku Klux Klan. He later recalled, "There are few things more devastating than to have it burned into you that you do not count and that no provisions are made for the literal protection of your person. The threat of violence is ever present, and there is no way to determine precisely when it may come crushing down upon you."[64] In his experience, the only white people who treated blacks like fellow human beings were the rich Northern families who wintered in Daytona, especially the Rockefellers and Gambles. Thurman grew up Baptist and later recalled, with gratitude, that the preachers of his youth were manuscript sermonizers, not "whoopers." Aided by financial assistance from James Gamble, a part-owner of the Procter and Gamble Company, he attended the Florida Baptist Academy in Jacksonville, graduating in 1919 as class valedictorian. Thurman's valedictory status earned him a scholarship to Morehouse College, where he won literary prizes, studied voraciously in politics, economics, literature, and philosophy, starred on Benjamin Mays's debating team, avoided white people, and in 1923 graduated at the top of his class.[65]

At Morehouse, college president John Hope always addressed Thurman and his classmates as "young gentlemen"; this sign of respect was enormously important to Thurman's faltering ego, and those of his classmates, in the severely repressive atmosphere of Atlanta. He later recalled: "Lynchings, burnings, unspeakable cruelties were the fundamentals of existence for black people. Our physical lives were of little value. Any encounter with a white person was inherently dangerous and frequently fatal." At the age of twenty-four he was eager to see if the North was much different, and if he could compete with whites in a Northern seminary, as Mays had. Thurman applied to Newton Theological Seminary, as Mays had, but was told that Newton still did not admit blacks. He applied to Rochester Theological Seminary and received a letter of congratulation; Rochester had a policy of admitting two black students per year. Thurman's experience at Rochester was like Mays's at Bates College; his intellectual ability was affirmed, and he discovered the possibility of friendly relations with white people. The novel experience of being treated by white people as a friend and Christian brother expanded his moral horizon; at Rochester it occurred to him for the first time "that my magnetic field of ethical awareness applied to other than my own people."[66]

His first pastorate was at Mount Zion Baptist Church in Oberlin, Ohio, where, newly married to Kate Kelly Thurman, he sought at first to educate his congregation about modern theology and biblical scholarship. Thurman's personal piety had a mystical quality, however, and during his two years in Oberlin he increasingly fed his spiritual hunger by practicing contemplative prayer and meditation. This spiritual turn changed his life and ministry. He later recalled that when he first began to cultivate the mystical stirrings of his spirit, he thought that he was responding to a personal hunger that had no connection to the needs of his parishioners, "but as I began to acquiesce to the demands of the spirit within, I found no need to differentiate human need, theirs and my own. I became more and more a part of the life of my people and discovered that at last I was able to pray in public as if I were alone in the quiet of my own room. The door between their questing spirits and my own became a swinging door." The feeling deepened in him that he was called to help people feel their spiritual unity in the love of God; at the same time he was uneasy about giving himself to a form of spirituality in which he had little training. One day, while making an early exit from a church convention, he purchased a copy of Rufus Jones's *Finding the Trail of Life*, sat on the church steps, and read the book in one sitting. Thurman was enthralled; he had found his spiritual mentor: "When I finished I knew that if this man were alive, I wanted to study with him."[67]

Thurman wrote to Jones, made arrangements for a semester of personal study with him, sent his wife and newborn daughter to live with his wife's parents, resigned from the Oberlin church, and decided against graduate school. A semester with Rufus Jones would be his graduate school: "I sensed somehow that if I were to devote full time to the requirements of a doctoral program, academic strictures would gradually usurp the energy I wanted so desperately to nourish the inner regions of my spirit." In the winter and spring of 1929 he was Jones's daily companion, attending his lectures, participating in a special seminar for area philosophy professors on Meister Eckhart—"exciting and stimulating beyond anything I had known before"—and taking part in Quaker meetings. "These were seminal times," he later recalled. "Rufus was utterly informal and his discussions ranged over the broad expanse of his thought and experience." Gently, never with any urging, Jones invited Thurman to a life of mystically inspired faith, teaching, ministry, and social activism.[68]

In all but one respect, Thurman found his model in Jones. "My study at Haverford was a crucial experience, a watershed from which flowed much of the thought and endeavor to which I was to commit the rest of my working life," he later recalled; yet it puzzled him that they never talked about race. Jones spoke passionately about war, nationalism, poverty, world hunger, and peacemaking, but his attitude about race seemed to be that it should not matter and therefore was not worth discussing. During their months together, to his great surprise, Thurman caught something of this attitude: "I felt that somehow he transcended race; I did so, too, temporarily." It was a new experience for Thurman, and a relief, not to have to think about being black in America. But later he wondered about Jones's apparent racial blindness. Was it really possible to disregard race in racist America? And even if Jones truly ignored race, how could he ignore its ethical importance? Why did he not assign the same importance to racial justice that he gave to antiwar activism? To Thurman, for the rest of his life, this aspect of Jones's witness remained an enigma. He sprinkled his writings with quotes from Jones, and he treasured Jones's gift of sharing his spiritual experience in a personal way that caused no embarrassment—Thurman possessed the same gift in abundance—but he could never ignore the reality and ethical importance of race.[69]

In 1929 Thurman accepted a joint faculty position at Morehouse and Spelman colleges, where he taught for three years, lost his wife to a tragic illness, and, at Spelman, taught a course on the idea of self-worth that focused on the life of Jesus. Thurman did not yet think of himself as approaching Jesus's life from the distinct standpoint of oppressed people, yet "the racial climate was so oppressive and affected us all so intimately that analogies between His life as a Jew in a Roman world and our own were obvious." This course led eventually to his signature book, *Jesus and the Disinherited*. Thurman's courses at Morehouse and Spelman centered on personal questions, such as "How can we immunize ourselves against the destructive aspects of the environment? How manage the carking fear of the white man's power and not be defeated by our own rage and hatred?" In 1932 he married a national YWCA traveling secretary, Sue Bailey, and embraced Mordecai Johnson's vision of a community of black scholars at Howard University, accepting an appointment at Howard's School of Religion. Three years later, while Thurman toured India as a member of the World Student Christian Federation's Delegation of Friendship, he was appointed dean of Rankin Chapel at Howard.[70]

His Student Christian Federation goodwill tour, which was cosponsored by the American YMCA and YWCA, marked another personal turning point. Thurman and his wife were sensitive to the appearance of being missionaries for a racist American Christianity. Repeatedly they assured their Indian audiences that they were nothing of the kind and that their critical views of American Christianity were supported by the Student Christian Federation. Repeatedly they were challenged to explain how this could be so. What were they doing in India? How could they speak on behalf of American Christianity? If Christianity had legitimized the enslavement of blacks in America, and if Christianity was powerless to abolish racial oppression in America, how could Thurman speak for Christianity in India? One interrogator put it bluntly: "I think that an intelligent young Negro such as yourself, here in our country on behalf of a Christian enterprise, is a traitor to all of the darker peoples of the earth. How can you account for yourself being in this unfortunate and humiliating position?"[71]

Thurman responded with his version of the gospel, which centered on the religion of Jesus. He had no interest in bolstering a declining institutional Christianity or making converts to it, he assured. He was not a soul-saving evangelist in the tradition of famed missionary E. Stanley Jones, who had heralded Thurman's arrival in India. Thurman had come to India in a spirit of friendship and sharing, seeking to be true to the spirit of Jesus as he understood it. "I think the religion of Jesus in its true genius offers a promising way to work through the conflicts of a disordered world," he explained. "I make a careful distinction between Christianity and the religion of Jesus. My judgment about slavery and racial prejudice relative to Christianity is far more devastating than yours could ever be." In his view, the peaceable religion of Jesus was a "creative solution to the pressing problem of survival" for oppressed people in the ancient and modern worlds. On the other hand, imperial Christianity was an instrument of oppression. The spirit of Jesus "is on the side of freedom, liberty, and justice for all people, black, white, red, yellow, saint, sinner, rich, or poor," he affirmed. Near the end of his tour Thurman met with Gandhi, who welcomed him as a soul mate and asked him to sing the spiritual, "Were You There When They Crucified My Lord?"[72]

To Thurman the religion of Jesus and the inward presence of God's illuminating Spirit were enough; though inclined to emphasize his positive religion, he believed that organized Christianity misrepresented Jesus and thus betrayed the hope of the disinherited. To Thurman, Jesus was the exemplar and medium of God's love and sustaining spiritual power. In 1944 he gave up the security of a tenured position at Howard to launch an interracial, nondenominational church in San Francisco, the Church for the Fellowship of All Peoples; one of the church's founding financial supporters was Eleanor Roosevelt. Five years later he published *Jesus and the Disinherited,* declaring that "for years it has been a part of my own quest so to understand the religion of Jesus that interest in his way of life could be developed and sustained by intelligent men and women who were at the same time deeply victimized by the Christian Church's betrayal of his faith." Thurman had little interest in formal theology and no interest at all in theological orthodoxy. In *Jesus and the Disinherited* he stated bluntly, "I belong to a generation that finds very little that is meaningful or intelligent in the teachings of the Church concerning Jesus Christ." For example, Thurman explained, traditional atonement theory is not saving for oppressed people: "The underprivileged everywhere have long since abandoned any hope that this type of salvation deals with the crucial issues by which their days are turned into despair without consolation."[73]

Yet the spirit of Jesus was precious to him, "so perfect a flower from the brooding spirit of God." Persistently, firmly, with prophetic passion, often in a lyrical voice, Thurman preached that Christianity is true as the religion of Jesus and the claiming of God's inward spiritual presence. In his view, the blending of the ethical and spiritual in true Christianity was intrinsic to its character. Speaking self-consciously as an African American in racially segregated America, he emphasized the ethic of "love your enemies" and, thus, the ethical and spiritual imperative for black people of finding a way to love their white oppressors: "The religion of Jesus says to the disinherited, 'Love your enemy. Take the initiative in seeking ways by which you can have the experience of a common sharing of mutual worth and value. It may be hazardous, but you must do it.'" It could be done if black Americans viewed whites as belonging to a common humanity, he contended, though the way of Jesus does not amount to a form of pretending: "The fact that a particular individual is white, and therefore may be regarded in some over-all sense as the racial enemy, must be faced; and opportunity must be provided, found, or created for freeing such an individual from his 'white necessity.'" Hatred met by hatred will never free the oppressor from his or her bondage to sin, he taught; only the enemy-loving spirit exemplified by Jesus can do that.[74]

Thurman looked hate in the eye. He noted that hate burns hotter at some times than others, but "in season and out of season," oppressed people are always intimately acquainted with hate as its victims. As a pacifist he emphasized that hatred is always "in season" during wartime. Hate becomes respectable as an effect of the psychology and propaganda of war, he observed, "even though it has to masquerade often under the guise of patriotism." After America entered World War II, Thurman noticed that expressions of racial hostility and rudeness toward black Americans and other nonwhite groups suddenly increased, "especially in trains and other public conveyances." Shortly after Japan attacked Pearl Harbor, a Chicago taxi driver exclaimed to him, "Who do they think they are? Those little yellow dogs think they can do that to white men and get away with it!" The cabdriver's uninhibited language was revealing to Thurman, who reasoned that war hatred eliminates the social sanctions that comparatively civilized societies apply to the expression of common race hatred. Racism is commonplace "in season and out of season," he reflected, but war gives social license and even a patina of respectability to racist feelings that would otherwise stay beneath the surface.[75]

At the same time he emphasized the emotional damage that racism and other forms of oppression inflict on their victims. Near the end of her life, Thurman's mother came to San Francisco to live with him. The Church for the Fellowship of All Peoples was bewildering to her; she could not fathom and did not like its race-mixing; she trusted her son and tried to be gracious to his guests, but it greatly disturbed her to have to deal with white people in his home and church. In her last days, confined to Stanford Hospital, she begged Thurman to take her

home. She was terrified at being surrounded by "Buckra," as she called white people: "The first chance they get, you don't know what they will do to you. I'm scared
to go to sleep at night, and you just have to take me out of this place."[76] Thurman took his mother to his home to die in peace. Elsewhere he reflected that vic-
timization often yields harsher forms of emotional reaction. While seated in a Jim
Crow car at a railway station in Texas, he overheard a teenaged black girl fanta-
size about two younger white girls who were skating toward the train. The black
girl told a friend that she would love to see the white girls fall and splatter their
brains across the pavement. Thurman shivered with sadness and fright: "I looked
at them. Through what torture chambers had they come—torture chambers that
had so attacked the grounds of humaneness in them that there was nothing capable of calling forth any appreciation or understanding of white persons?"[77]

Thurman believed in the moral power and political necessity of self-
disregarding action, expounding this theme in exactly the manner that Reinhold
Niebuhr wrote off as socially impossible. Without replying to Niebuhr, Thurman
took for granted that preaching unselfishness and preaching the gospel were the
same thing. On this theme he liked Anglican moral theologian Kenneth Kirk
who defined selfishness as a "lack of due regard for the well-being of others" and
unselfishness as the payment of due concern for the well-being of others. It followed for Kirk and Thurman that unselfish service to others is the only kind that
is redeeming or serves any morally worthy cause. Thurman elaborated: "Disinterested service is a kind of service in which the person served is not a means to
some end in which he does not share and participate directly." The religion of
Jesus calls people not to base their actions toward others on their personal or
material interests, he taught. More than that, the religion of Jesus calls people
actively to relieve human suffering and build structures of social justice so that
all people may be freed from the shackles of hatred, torment, oppression, and
selfishness. "It is in this latter sense that we come upon the mandatory *raison
d'être* of the mystic's interest in social change and in social action," Thurman
reflected. Mysticism is about the realization that all life is one. On the basis of his
mystical experience of the unity of all things, Thurman preached that human
beings are meant to participate in the transformation of all being into the summum bonum, the vision of God: "The mystic is forced to deal with social relations because, in his effort to achieve the good, he finds that he must be responsive
to human need by which he is surrounded, particularly the kind of human need
in which sufferers are victims of circumstances over which, as individuals, they
have no control."[78]

In the phrases of mystical diction Thurman taught that while some people
come to God through nature and others find their way to God through the witness of Spirit-filled people, whoever seeks God "with all of his heart will someday on his way meet Jesus." The religion of Jesus is the way of true religion, he
preached; it is the way of living in God's presence "with renewed minds and chastened spirits." This was Thurman's persistent concern, "to focus the mind and
the heart upon God as the Eternal Source and Goal of Life." For him, everything

rested upon the existence and recognition of the Spirit of God as "the unifying principle of all life." The mission of the church is to be an exemplar of Spirit-filled community and build the kingdom of God. To know the inner presence of God's Spirit is to know one's spiritual unity with all creatures and creation, as Jesus showed: "To be in unity with the Spirit is to be in unity with one's fellows." It followed that alienation from other people is alienation from God's Spirit. "When I have lost harmony with another, my whole life is thrown out of tune," Thurman reflected. "For the sake of my unity with God, I keep working on my relations with my fellows. This is ever the insistence of all ethical religions."[79]

In 1953 he moved to Boston University, where he finished his ministerial and academic career as dean of Marsh Chapel and Professor of Spiritual Disciplines, and where he befriended doctoral student Martin Luther King Jr. Throughout his career his favorite religious thinker was Rufus Jones, who showed the way; with Jones, Thurman held out for the religious and ethical primacy of the mystical vision of spiritual unity, the superiority of life-embracing, affirmative mysticism over life-denying, ascetical, negative mysticism, and the ethical practices of pacifist peacemaking and nonviolent resistance to injustice. Like Jones he insisted that all forms of violence, oppression, and prejudice offend against the divine good. Above all, he repeated Jones's maxim that the best kind of prayer is prayed out of sheer love and enjoyment of God. Thurman and Jones were prophets of what Thurman called "the overflowing of the heart as an act of grace toward God." To awaken to the unitive divine presence within is to be held in graceful adoration, he confessed: "It is the sheer joy in thanksgiving that God is God and the soul is privileged and blessed with the overwhelming consciousness of this." Remarking on Jones's influence over his life, Thurman recalled, "He gave to me confidence in the insight that the religion of the inner life could deal with the empirical experience of man without retreating from the demands of such experience."[80]

In Thurman's lyrical mysticism, one of the most durable forms of the liberal faith survived the liberal and neoliberal eras of American theology. Like Jones, Scudder, Fosdick, and Harkness, Thurman contended that true religion is grounded in the mystical experience of God's unitive presence and that it makes no compromise with violence or oppression. Repeatedly he proclaimed that religious truth is never conferred by authority, for religions are true only to the extent that they teach and practice universal love. For him, Jesus was the singular expression and exemplar of God's saving love. While Niebuhrians used the word "perfectionist" as an epithet, Thurman held fast to the perfectionist principle that the essence of true religion is the experience and practice of divine love; it is natural to hate and fight one's enemies, he taught, but true religion is a call to transformed existence: "The insistence here is that the individual is enjoined to move from the natural impulse to the level of deliberate intent. One has to bring to the center of his focus a desire to love even one's enemy."[81]

In Thurman's case, however, the white, middle-class, idealist milieu of liberal Christianity that Niebuhr skewered was both affirmed and transcended. Niebuhr's ridicule of moral and religious idealism was completely alien to Thurman, even though Thurman knew the ravages of hatred and violence far more intimately than Niebuhr. From his acquaintance with exclusion he offered an example of radically inclusive religion. Just as he made no compromise with violence, Thurman conceded no exceptions to the universality of the good. The hope of the disinherited is to be included in the flourishing of democracy and the saving work of God's Spirit, he taught. If moral truth is not universal, it is neither moral nor true; while coping with their oppression, the disinherited of the world needed to claim their rights without reproducing the world's mendacity and hatred. Thurman's belief in the unitive reality of God's Spirit sustained his belief that the good will prevail: "The disinherited will know for themselves that there is a Spirit at work in life and in the hearts of men which is committed to overcoming the world. It is universal, knowing no age, no race, no culture, and no condition of men."[82]

These words inspired and sustained Martin Luther King Jr. during the many years that he struggled to abolish racial apartheid in the United States. King and Thurman were not close associates, but the two men sustained a mutually appreciative friendship; just as King drew upon Fosdick's sermons, he reportedly carried a copy of *Jesus and the Disinherited* on his travels, and his sermons drew on Thurman's insights. Progressive American Christianity has no greater legacy than that.

Notes

Introduction

1. Henry Churchill King, *Reconstruction in Theology* (New York: Macmillan Co., 1901), v.
2. Charles A. Briggs, "The Scope of Theology and Its Place in the University," *American Journal of Theology* 1 (Jan. 1897): 38–70, quote, 38.
3. See Gary Dorrien, *The Making of American Liberal Theology: Imagining Progressive Religion, 1805–1900* (Louisville, Ky.: Westminster John Knox Press, 2001), xix–xxi.
4. See Ralph Tyler Flewelling, *Personalism and the Problems of Philosophy: An Appreciation of the Work of Borden Parker Bowne* (New York: Methodist Book Concern, 1915); Flewelling, *The Person, or the Significance of Man* (Los Angeles: Ward Ritchie Press, 1952); John Wright Buckham, *Personality and the Christian Ideal* (Boston: Pilgrim Press, 1909); Buckham, *Religion as Experience* (New York: Abingdon Press, 1922); Buckham, *Christianity and Personality* (New York: Round Table Press, 1936).
5. Kenneth Cauthen, *The Impact of American Religious Liberalism* (New York: Harper & Row, 1962); see Cauthen, "A Call for a New Modernism," *American Journal of Theology and Philosophy* 13 (Jan. 1992): 3–24.
6. William R. Hutchison, *The Modernist Impulse in American Protestantism* (Durham: Duke University Press, 1992), 7–9; Francis Schüssler Fiorenza, "Theological Liberalism: An Unfinished Challenge," *Harvard Divinity Bulletin* 28 (1998): 9–12; see Levi Leonard Paine, *A Critical History of the Evolution of Trinitarianism and Its Outcome in the New Christology* (New York: Houghton Mifflin Co., 1900); Paine, *The Ethnic Trinities and their Relations to the Christian Trinity: A Chapter in the Comparative History of Religions* (Boston: Houghton Mifflin Co., 1901); Frank Hugh Foster, *The Modern Movement in American Theology: Sketches in the History of American Protestant Thought from the Civil War to the World War* (Freeport, N.Y.: Books for Libraries, 1939); Foster, "The Theology of the New Rationalism," *American Journal of Theology* (1909): 407–419.
7. Gerald Birney Smith, "The Task and Method of Systematic Theology," *The American Journal of Theology* 14 (Apr. 1910): 215–33; Daniel Sommer Robinson, *The God of the Liberal Christian: A Study of Social Theology and the New Theism as Conflicting Schools of Progressive Religious Thought* (New York: D. Appleton, 1926), quote, 220–21. Notwithstanding James's pragmatism and radical empiricism, Robinson placed him decidedly on the side of the idealistic theists because his idea of a finite God was "really only a halfway stage in the development of the new theist conception," quote, 123.
8. William Dean, *American Religious Empiricism* (Albany: State University of New York Press, 1986), 5–12.
9. See Newman Smyth, *Passing Protestantism and the Coming Catholicism* (New York: Charles Scribner's Sons, 1908), 40–131; Shailer Mathews, *The Faith of Modernism* (New York: Macmillan Co., 1924; reprint, New York: AMS Press, 1969); Charles Harvey

Arnold, "The Terminology of American Religious Liberalism, 1876–1939," *American Journal of Theology and Philosophy* 1 (May 1980): 45–59.

10. Lloyd Averill, *American Theology in the Liberal Tradition* (Philadelphia: Westminster Press, 1967), 100; Cauthen, *The Impact of American Religious Liberalism*, 29.

11. Theodore Parker, *A Discourse of Matters Pertaining to Religion*, 4th ed. (New York: G. P. Putnam's Sons, 1877), 449, 465; Octavius Brooks Frothingham, *The Religion of Humanity* (New York: David G. Francis, 1873); Frothingham, *Recollections and Impressions, 1822–1890* (New York: G. P. Putnam's Sons, 1891).

12. See Ferdinand Christian Baur, *Die christliche Gnosis, oder die christliche Religions-Philosophie in ihrer geschichtlichen Entwicklung* (Tübingen: C. F. Osiander, 1835); Baur, *Vorlesungen über neutestamentliche Theologie*, ed. Ferdinand Friedrich Baur (Leipzig: Fues's Verlag, 1864); Peter C. Hodgson, *The Formation of Historical Theology: A Study of Ferdinand Christian Baur* (New York: Harper & Row, 1966).

13. David Friedrich Strauss, *The Life of Jesus Critically Examined*, trans. George Eliot, ed. Peter C. Hodgson (Ramsey, N.J.: Sigler Press, 1994); Strauss, *Die christliche Glaubenslehre in ihrer geschichtlichen Entwicklung und im Kampfe mit der modernen Wissenschaft dargestellt*, 2 vols. (Tübingen: C. F. Osiander, 1840–41).

14. See Ernst Troeltsch, "Historical and Dogmatic Method in Theology" (1898), trans. Ephraim Fischoff, and "The Dogmatics of the History-of-Religions School" (1913), both reprinted in Troeltsch, *Religion in History*, ed. James Luther Adams (Minneapolis: Fortress Press, 1991), 11–32, 87–108; Troeltsch, *Die Absolutheit der Christentums und die Religionsgeschichte* (Tübingen: J. C. B. Mohr-Paul Siebeck, 1902, reprint 1912; Joachim Wach, "Introduction: The Meaning and Task of the History of Religions (*Religionswissenschaft*)," in *The History of Religions: Essays on the Problem of Understanding*, ed. Joseph M. Kitagawa (Chicago: University of Chicago Press, 1967).

15. Gustav Ecke, *Die theologische Schule Albrecht Ritschls und die Evangelische Kirche der Gegenwart* (Berlin: Reuther & Reichard, 1897). See Johannes Rathje, *Die Welt des freien Protestantismus: Ein Beitrag zur deutsch-evangelischen Geistesgeschichte, dargestellt an Leben und Werk von Martin Rade* (Stuttgart: Ehrenfried Klotz Verlag, 1952), 102–3.

16. See R. J. Campbell, *The New Theology* (London: George Bell & Sons, 1907); Josiah Royce, *The Conception of God* (Berkeley: Philosophical Union, 1895); Royce, *The Problem of Christianity* (New York: Macmillan Co., 1913); Charles Gore, *The New Theology and the Old Religion* (London: John Murray, 1907). Campbell later adopted a more mainstream liberal Catholic perspective and re-entered the Church of England. On Hegel's historical conservatism, see David Friedrich Strauss, *Streitschriften zur Verteidigung Meiner Schrift über das Leben Jesu und zur Charakteristik der gegenwärtigen Theologie*, vol. 3 (Tübingen: C. F. Osiander, 1841), 60–94.

17. See Johannes Weiss, *The History of Primitive Christianity*, 2 vols., trans. and ed. Frederick C. Grant (New York: Wilson-Erickson, 1937); Weiss, *Jesus' Proclamation of the Kingdom of God* (1892), trans. D. Larrimore Holland and Richard H. Hiers (Philadelphia: Fortress Press, 1971); Albert Schweitzer, *The Quest of the Historical Jesus: A Critical Study of Its Progress from Reimarus to Wrede* (1906), trans. W. Montgomery (New York: Macmillan Co., 1968); Adolf von Harnack, "Fifteen Questions to the Despisers of Scientific Theology," and Karl Barth, "Fifteen Answers to Professor Adolf von Harnack" (1923), in *Adolf von Harnack: Liberal Theology at Its Height*, ed. Martin Rumscheidt (Minneapolis: Fortress Press, 1991), 85–91.

18. See Charles Clayton Morrison, *What Is Christianity?* (Chicago: Willett, Clark & Co., 1940); Justin Wroe Nixon, *The Moral Crisis in Christianity* (New York: Harper & Brothers, 1931); Henry Pitney Van Dusen, "The Significance of Jesus Christ," in *Liberal Theology: An Appraisal*, ed. David E. Roberts and Henry Pitney Van Dusen (New York: Charles Scribner's Sons, 1942), 205–22; Albert C. Knudson, *The Doctrine of Redemption* (Nashville: Abingdon Press, 1933); Eugene William Lyman, *The Meaning and Truth of Religion* (New York: Charles Scribner's Sons, 1933).

Chapter 1. Creating a New Mainstream

1. See Robert T. Handy, *A History of Union Theological Seminary in New York* (New York: Columbia University Press, 1987), 95–120; Henry Sloane Coffin, *A Half Century of*

Union Theological Seminary, 1896–1945 (New York: Charles Scribner's Sons, 1954), 21–57.

2. See Arthur C. McGiffert, *A History of Christianity in the Apostolic Age* (New York: Charles Scribner's Sons, 1897); Coffin, *A Half Century of Union Theological Seminary, 1896–1945,* 34–40.

3. The Williams Adams Brown Collection at Burke Library, Union Theological Seminary, New York, New York, contains three large boxes of Brown family letters; see William Adams Brown, *A Teacher and His Times: A Story of Two Worlds* (New York: Charles Scribner's Sons, 1940), 3–7, 11–13, 21–23, 26–30; Handy, *A History of Union Theological Seminary in New York,* 34, 52, 102, 112, 115–16.

4. Brown, *A Teacher and His Times,* 11–12, 29–30, 44–49. Brown's impersonal account of his father was at least partly a case of upper-class Victorian reticence. In his book *The Christian Hope* he referred to an unnamed acquaintance who was "tender in sympathy," humble, and well liked by numerous friends: "He was a man who had schooled himself by unremitting discipline to a loyalty to duty which shrank from no sacrifice." A family friend, Chauncey Goodrich, later informed Samuel McCrea Cavert that Brown was describing his father in this passage; see Samuel McCrea Cavert, "William Adams Brown: Servant of the Church of Christ," *The Church through Half a Century: Essays in Honor of William Adams Brown,* ed. Samuel McCrea Cavert and Henry Pitney Van Dusen (New York: Charles Scribner's Sons, 1936), 8.

5. Brown, *A Teacher and His Times,* 72–74, quote, 74. See Henry Drummond, *Natural Law in the Spiritual World* (reprint, 1898; New York: A. L. Burt Co., 1883); Drummond, *The Lowell Lectures on the Ascent of Man* (London: Hodder & Stoughton, 1899).

6. Brown, *A Teacher and His Times,* 68.

7. Ibid., 76, 78–79; see William Graham Sumner, *Earth-Hunger and Other Essays* (New Haven, Conn.: Yale University Press, 1913); Sumner, *The Challenge of Facts and Other Essays* (New Haven, Conn.: Yale University Press, 1914); Sumner, *Social Darwinism: Selected Essays of William Graham Sumner* (Englewood Cliffs, N.J.: Prentice-Hall, 1963).

8. Agnes von Zahn-Harnack, *Adolf von Harnack* (Berlin: Walter de Gruyter & Co., 1936, 2d ed. 1951), quote, 64; see Adolf von Harnack, *History of Dogma,* 7 vols., 3d German ed., trans. Neil Buchanan (Eugene, Ore.: Wipf & Stock Publishers, 1997); Harnack, *Das apostolische Glaubensbekenntnis* (Berlin: Haack, 1892); *Adolf von Harnack: Liberal Theology at Its Height,* ed. Martin Rumscheidt (Minneapolis: Fortress Press, 1991).

9. On Ritschl's life and career, see Otto Ritschl, *Albrecht Ritschls Leben,* 2 vols. (Freiburg: J. C. B. Mohr, 1892, 1896); Albert Temple Swing, *The Theology of Albrecht Ritschl,* trans. Alice Mead Swing (New York: Longmans, Green & Co., 1901), 10–22; Rolf Schafer, *Ritschl* (Tübingen: J. C. B. Mohr, 1968).

10. Albrecht Ritschl, *The Christian Doctrine of Justification and Reconciliation* (1874), ed. H. R. Hackintosh and A. B. Macaulay (Edinburgh: T. & T. Clark, 1902), 205; see Ritschl, "Theology and Metaphysics," reprinted in Ritschl, *Three Essays,* trans. and ed. Philip Hefner (Philadelphia: Fortress Press, 1972), 149–218; Immanuel Kant, *Critique of Pure Reason* (1787), trans. Norman Kemp Smith (London: Macmillan Press, 1973); Kant, *Religion within the Limits of Reason Alone* (1793), trans. Theodore M. Greene and Hoyt H. Hudson (Chicago: Open Court Publishing Co., 1934).

11. Ritschl, *The Christian Doctrine of Justification and Reconciliation,* 3. This section adapts material from Gary Dorrien, *The Word as True Myth: Interpreting Modern Theology* (Louisville, Ky.: Westminster John Knox Press, 1997), 46–58.

12. Ritschl, *The Christian Doctrine of Justification and Reconciliation,* 8–13; see Ritschl, "Instruction in the Christian Religion," *Three Essays,* 229–40.

13. On Herrmann's relation to Ritschl, see Gary Dorrien, *The Barthian Revolt in Modern Theology: Theology without Weapons* (Louisville: Westminster John Knox Press, 1999), 15–27.

14. Adolf von Harnack, *What Is Christianity?* trans. Thomas Bailey Saunders (1900; reprint, Philadelphia: Fortress Press, 1986), 8, 11.

15. Ibid., 11; von Zahn-Harnack, *Adolf von Harnack,* 130–33; see Wilhelm Pauck, "The Significance of Adolf von Harnack among Church Historians," *Union Theological Seminary Quarterly Review,* Special Issue (Jan. 1954): 13–24; G. Wayne Glick, *The Reality*

of Christianity: A Study of Adolf von Harnack as Historian and Theologian (New York: Harper & Row, 1967).

16. Brown, *A Teacher and His Times*, 84, 87.

17. Ibid., 83, 90–91. Harnack publicly renounced the invasion of Belgium after the war.

18. Handy, *A History of Union Theological Seminary in New York*, 98–99; Brown, *A Teacher and His Times*, 102–3; Cavert, "William Adams Brown: Servant of the Church of Christ," 13–14. Brown's memoir has to be used carefully; aside from mauling quite a few names, he occasionally misremembered key episodes. In the present case, he claimed that Stearns accepted Union's theology position, but then "almost immediately" took sick and died, like van Dyke and Worcester. In fact, Stearns rejected Union's offer; the following year, he gave a widely noted address to the International Congregational Council in London on trends in American theology; and in 1892 he published an important book on Henry Boynton Smith. See Stearns, *Henry Boynton Smith*; Lewis F. Stearns, "The Present Direction of Theological Thought in the Congregational Churches of the United States," in *Present-Day Theology: A Popular Discussion of Leading Doctrines of the Christian Faith* (New York: Charles Scribner's Sons, 1893), 533–36.

19. Brown, *A Teacher and His Times*, 103–5; see I. A. Dorner, *A System of Christian Doctrine*, I: 17–184.

20. Brown, *A Teacher and His Times*, 105–6.

21. William Adams Brown, *Christ the Vitalizing Principle of Christian Theology* (New York: W. C. Martin, 1898), 3–21, quotes, 19–20; see Wilhelm Herrmann, *The Communion of the Christian with God: Described on the Basis of Luther's Statements*, trans. of fourth German edition (1903) by J. Sandys Stanyon (New York: G. P. Putnam's Sons; reprint, Philadelphia: Fortress Press, 1971), 15–17, 59–61, 71–78.

22. Ibid., 23; "natural language" quote in Brown, *A Teacher and His Times*, 106.

23. William Adams Brown, "An American Theologian," in *William Newton Clarke: A Biography, with Additional Sketches by His Friends and Colleagues*, ed. Emily A. Clark (New York: Charles Scribner's Sons, 1916), 201–10; William Newton Clarke to William Adams Brown, 21 Dec. 1893, ibid., 202; Clarke to Brown, 26 Sept. 1896, ibid., 202.

24. William Newton Clarke, *Sixty Years with the Bible: A Record of Experience* (New York: Charles Scribner's Sons, 1909), quotes, 3, 4.

25. Ibid., 14–21, 185, 188–92, quotes, 14, 15; see Clark, ed., *William Newton Clarke: A Biography*, 6–15.

26. Clarke, *Sixty Years with the Bible*, 33–42, quotes, 40; see Clark, ed., *William Newton Clarke: A Biography*, 20–21.

27. Clarke, *Sixty Years with the Bible*, 87–109, quote, 106–7; see Clark, ed., *William Newton Clarke: A Biography*, 24–61.

28. Clark, ed., *William Newton Clarke: A Biography*, 44–45; Clarke, *Sixty Years with the Bible*, 110; see Horace Bushnell, *The Vicarious Sacrifice: Grounded in Principles of Universal Obligation* (New York: Charles Scribner & Co., 1866).

29. Clark, ed., *William Newton Clarke: A Biography*, 45; Clarke, *Sixty Years with the Bible*, quote, 115; on Bushnell's later atonement theology, see Gary Dorrien, *The Making of American Liberal Theology: Imagining Progressive Religion, 1805–1900* (Louisville, Ky.: Westminster John Knox Press, 2001), 163–72.

30. William Newton Clarke, *Commentary on the Gospel of Mark* (Philadelphia: American Baptist Publication Society, 1881); Clarke, *Sixty Years with the Bible*, 129–40, quotes, 133, 139; Clark, ed., *William Newton Clarke: A Biography*, 54.

31. Clarke, *Sixty Years with the Bible*, 172–76, quote, 176.

32. Ibid., 176–92, quotes, 178, 188.

33. Ibid., 193; Clark, ed., *William Newton Clarke: A Biography*, 64. Dodge died on 5 January 1890; Clarke replaced him immediately, and was named Professor of Theology at Hamilton's commencement.

34. Clarke, *Sixty Years with the Bible*, 194–95.

35. Brown, *A Teacher and His Times*, 107–9, quote, 107.

36. William Newton Clarke, *An Outline of Christian Theology* (New York: Charles Scribner's Sons, 1898; 15th ed., 1906), quotes, 20–21.

37. Ibid., 12–47, quotes, 21, 39, 41.

38. Ibid., 37–40, quotes, 39.

39. Ibid., 39.
40. Ibid., 63–102, quotes, 66, 73, 89; see William Newton Clarke, *The Christian Doctrine of God* (New York: Charles Scribner's Sons, 1909), 56–107.
41. Clarke, *An Outline of Christian Theology,* 215–45, quote, 235.
42. Ibid., 258–59.
43. Ibid., 263–308, quotes, 279, 274.
44. Ibid., 286–308, quote, 300.
45. Ibid., 315–47, quotes, 320, 343.
46. Ibid., 354–62, quotes, 354, 356.
47. Ibid., 444.
48. Edward G. Andrews to William Newton Clarke, 27 March 1899, reprinted in Clark, ed., *William Newton Clarke: A Biography,* 70–71; William Newton Clarke, *What Shall We Think of Christianity?* (New York: Charles Scribner's Sons, 1899); Douglas Clyde Macintosh, "Professor Clarke at Yale," in Clark, ed., *William Newton Clarke: A Biography,* 257; William Newton Clarke, *The Use of the Scriptures in Theology* (New York: Charles Scribner's Sons, 1906), 19.
49. William Newton Clarke, *The Christian Doctrine of God* (New York: Charles Scribner's Sons, 1909), 5.
50. William Newton Clarke, *The Ideal of Jesus* (New York: Charles Scribner's Sons, 1911), quotes, 312, 317.
51. Clarke, ed., *William Newton Clarke: A Biography,* quotes, 102, v.
52. Walter Rauschenbusch to Emily A. Clark, undated, ibid., 124–25; Macintosh, "Professor Clarke at Yale," 257; Henry H. Peabody, "An Appreciation," in Clark, ed., *William Newton Clarke: A Biography,* 179; Fosdick remembrance, cited in Clark, ed., *William Newton Clarke: A Biography,* 119.
53. William Adams Brown, "The 'Theology' of William Newton Clarke," *Harvard Theological Review* 3 (Apr. 1910); reprinted in Clark, ed., *William Newton Clarke: A Biography,* 185–200, quotes, 186.
54. Macintosh, "Professor Clarke at Yale," 258; Brown, "An American Theologian," 203–8; Clarke, *Sixty Years with the Bible,* quote, 210.
55. William Newton Clarke to William Adams Brown, 22 April 1897, cited in Brown, "An American Theologian," 203; see George Cross, "As Theologian," in Clark, ed., *William Newton Clarke: A Biography,* 228–56; Claude L. Howe Jr., *The Theology of William Newton Clarke* (New York: Arno Press, 1980).
56. William Adams Brown, *The Essence of Christianity: A Study in the History of Definition* (New York: Charles Scribner's Sons, 1906, 1st ed., 1902), 231–33.
57. See G. W. F. Hegel, *Phenomenology of Spirit,* trans. A. V. Miller (Oxford: Clarendon Press, 1977); Hegel, *Lectures on the Philosophy of Religion,* 3 vols., trans. from 2d ed. by E. B. Speirs and J. Burdon Sanderson (New York: Humanities Press, 1974).
58. See Philipp K. Marheineke, *Die Grundlehren der christlichen Dogmatik als Wissenschaft* (Berlin: Verlag von Duncker und Homblot, 1827); Karl Rosenkranz, *Encyklopädie der theologischen Wissenschaften* (Halle: C. A. Schwetschke und Sohn, 1831); Karl Daub, *Die dogmatische Theologie jetziger: Zeit oder die Selbstsucht in der Wissenschaft des Glaubens und ihrer Artikel* (Heidelberg: J. C. B. Mohr, 1833); Carl Friedrich Göschel, *Von den Bewissen für die Unsterblichkeit der menschlichen Serk im Lichte der spekulativen Philosophie* (Berlin: Verlag von Duncker und Humblot, 1835); Brown, *The Essence of Christianity,* 186–222. On the tridimensional structure of Hegel's dialectic, see Dieter Henrich, "Formen der Negation in Hegels Logic," in *Seminar: Dialektik in der Philosophie Hegels,* ed. Rolf-Peter Horstmann (Frankfurt: Suhrkamp Taschenbuch Verlag, 1978), 213–29; for Hegel's critique of Göschel's hypostatization of divine reality, see G. W. F. Hegel, *Berliner Schriften, 1818–1831,* ed. J. Hoffmeister (Hamburg: Verlag von Felix Meiner, 1956), 324–29.
59. For his denial that he was a strict Hegelian in any sense, see F. C. Baur, *Ausgewählte Werke in Einzelausgaben,* ed. Klaus Scholder, 5 vols. (Stuttgart: Friedrich Fromann Verlag, 1963–75), 1:313. See Baur, *Die christliche Gnosis, oder die christliche Religions-Philosophie in ihrer geschichtlichen Entwicklung* (Tübingen: C. F. Osiander, 1835); A. E. Biedermann, *Christliche Dogmatik,* 2 vols. (Berlin: Verlag von Georg Reimer, 1884–85); David Friedrich Strauss, *Die christliche Glaubenslehre in ihrer geschichtlichen Entwicklung*

und im Kampfe mit der modernen Wissenschaft dargestellt, 2 vols. (Tübingen: C. F. Osiander, 1840–41); on the relation of Baur and Strauss to Hegelianism and Christian myth interpretation, see Dorrien, *The Word as True Myth*, 25–47.

60. See Carl Immanuel Nitsch, *System der christlichen Lehre* (Bonn: Adolph Marcus, 1829; 6th ed., 1851); Willibald Beyschlag, *Neutestamentliche Theologie*, 2 vols. (Halle: E. Strien, 1891; 2d ed., 1895); Johannes von Hofmann, *Theologische Ethik* (Nördlingen: C. H. Beck, 1878); Johann Peter Lange, *Christliche Dogmatik*, 3 vols. (Heidelberg: K. Winter, 1849–52); Carl Ullmann, *Historisch oder Mythisch? Beiträge zur Beantwortung der gegenwärtigen Lebensfrage der Theologie* (Hamburg: Perthes, 1838); Richard Rothe, *Theologische Ethik*, 3 vols. (Wittenberg: Zimmermann, 1845–48); Rothe, *Dogmatik: Aus dessen handschriftlichen Nachlasse herausgegeben von Dr. D. Schenkel*, 2 vols. (Heidelberg: J. C. B. Mohr, 1870); Christian Hermann Weisse, *Die evangelische Geschichte kritisch und philosophisch bearbeitet*, 2 vols. (Leipzig: Breitkopf & Härtel, 1838); Brown, *The Essence of Christianity*, 217–19. On Dorner, see Jorg Rothermundt, *Personale Synthese: Isaak August Dorners dogmatische Methode* (Göttingen: Vandenhoeck & Ruprecht, 1968).

61. Brown, *The Essence of Christianity*, 225, 227.

62. Ibid., 225–26.

63. Ibid., 228, 231; see Ritschl, "Theology and Metaphysics," 151–61, 187–212; Wilhelm Herrmann, *Die Metaphysik in der Theologie* (Halle: Max Niemeyer, 1876).

64. Brown, *The Essence of Christianity*, 234–35, 238; see Ritschl, *The Christian Doctrine of Justification and Reconciliation*, 1–11.

65. Ritschl, *The Christian Doctrine of Justification and Reconciliation*, 8, 196–98; Brown, *The Essence of Christianity*, 239–40.

66. Ritschl, *The Christian Doctrine of Justification and Reconciliation*, 11–12; see Albrecht Ritschl, "Instruction in the Christian Religion," *Three Essays*, 232–40.

67. Ritschl, *The Christian Doctrine of Justification and Reconciliation*, 13, 20–21; see Ritschl, "Theology and Metaphysics," 149–217.

68. Brown, *The Essence of Christianity*, 242–50; Ritschl, *The Christian Doctrine of Justification and Reconciliation*, 9–10, 29–30, 473; Friedrich Schleiermacher, *The Christian Faith*, ed. H. R. Mackintosh and J. S. Stewart (Edinburgh: T. & T. Clark, 1989, 2d German ed., 1830), 62.

69. See Harnack, *What Is Christianity?* 10–17, 55.

70. See Adolf Harnack, *Lehrbuch der Dogmengeschichte*, 3 vols. (Tübingen: J. C. B. Mohr, 1886–89); Wilhelm Herrmann, *Die Religion im Verhältnis zum Welterkennen und zur Sittlichkeit* (Halle: Max Niemeyer, 1879); Max Wilhelm T. Reischle, *Christliche Glaubenslehre in Leitsätzen für eine akademische Vorlesung*, 2d ed. (Halle: Max Niemeyer, 1902); Reischle, *Die Frage nach dem Wesen der Religion Grundlegung zu einer Methodologie der Religionsphilosophie* (Freiburg: J. C. B. Mohr, 1889); W. Bornemann, *Unterricht im Christentum* (3d ed., Göttingen: Vandenhoeck & Ruprecht, 1893); Wilhelm Bender, *Friedrich Schleiermacher und die Frage nach dem Wesen der Religion* (Bonn: Eduard Weber's Verlag, 1877); Otto Ritschl, *Dogmengeschichte des Protestantismus*, 4 vols. (Leipzig: J. C. Hinrichs, 1908–27); Johannes Weiss, *Die Nachfolge Christi und die Predigt der Gegenwart* (Göttingen: Vandenhoeck & Ruprecht, 1895); Theodor Häring, *Zur Versöhnungslehre, eine dogmatische Untersuchung* (Göttingen: Vandenhoeck & Ruprecht, 1893); Martin Rade, *Die Wahrheit der christlichen Religion* (Tübingen: J. C. B. Mohr, 1900); Ferdinand Kattenbusch, *Von Schleiermacher zu Ritschl: Zur Orientierung über den gegenwärtigen Stand der Dogmatik* (Giessen: Ricker, 1892); Friedrich Loofs, *Leitfaden zum Studium der Dogmengeschichte* (Halle: M. Niemeyer, 1889); Julius Kaftan, *Dogmatik* (Freiburg: J. C. B. Mohr, 1897); Ernst Troeltsch, *Geschichte und Metaphysik* (Freiburg: J. C. B. Mohr, 1888); Brown, *The Essence of Christianity*, 267.

71. Harnack, *What Is Christianity?* 20–21, 23–30, 149–50; 160–64.

72. Brown, *The Essence of Christianity*, 280, 293; Martin Kähler, *The So-called Historical Jesus and the Historic Biblical Christ*, trans. Carl E. Braaten (Philadelphia: Fortress Press, 1988), 46, 57; see Kähler, *Dogmatische Zeitfragen: Angewandte Dogmen*, 2 vols. (2d ed., Leipzig: A. Deichert, 1908).

73. Kähler, *The So-Called Historical Jesus and the Historic Biblical Christ*, 63–66, quote, 66.

74. See Carl E. Braaten, "Martin Kähler on the Historic Biblical Christ," *The Historical Jesus and the Kerygmatic Christ: Essays on the New Quest of the Historical Jesus*, ed. Carl E.

Braaten and Roy A. Harrisville (New York: Abingdon Press, 1964), 94–99. Barth remarked that Kähler's critique of the historical Jesus quest "cannot be overpraised." See Karl Barth, *Church Dogmatics: The Doctrine of the Word of God,* vol. 1, bk. 2, trans. G. T. Thomson and Harold Knight (Edinburgh: T. & T. Clark, 1956), 64–65.

75. Brown, *The Essence of Christianity,* 279.
76. Ibid., 297–300.
77. Ibid., 291, 309.
78. Review of Brown, *The Essence of Christianity,* from the *Church Economist,* 1903, in Brown family album, 1893–1903, Series 1, Box 2, William Adams Brown Collection, Burke Library, Union Theological Seminary; see William Adams Brown, *Modern Theology and the Preaching of the Gospel* (New York: Charles Scribner's Sons, 1914); Brown, *The Creative Experience* (New York: Charles Scribner's Sons, 1923); Brown, *The Quiet Hour* (New York: Association Press, 1926); Brown, *The Life of Prayer in a World of Science* (New York: Charles Scribner's Sons and Association Press, 1926); Brown, *God at Work: A Study of the Supernatural* (New York: Charles Scribner's Sons, 1933); Brown, *Finding God in a New World* (New York: Harper & Brothers, 1935).
79. William Adams Brown, *The Christian Hope: A Study of the Doctrine of Immortality* (New York: Charles Scribner's Sons, 1912); Brown, *Beliefs That Matter: A Theology for Laymen* (New York: Charles Scribner's Sons, 1928); Brown, *Pathways to Certainty* (New York: Charles Scribner's Sons, 1930); Brown, *Is Christianity Practicable?* (New York: Charles Scribner's Sons, 1916); Brown, *The Church in America* (New York: Macmillan Co., 1922); Brown, *Imperialistic Religion and the Religion of Democracy: A Study in Social Psychology* (New York: Charles Scribner's Sons, 1923); Brown, *The Church: Catholic and Protestant* (New York: Charles Scribner's Sons, 1935); Brown, *A Creed for Free Men: A Study of Loyalties* (New York: Charles Scribner's Sons, 1941); Brown, *A Teacher and His Times,* 110–190; Cavert, "William Adams Brown: Servant of the Church of Christ," 16–33.
80. Clarke, *An Outline of Christian Theology,* 165–81, quotes, 177.
81. William Adams Brown, *Christian Theology in Outline* (New York: Charles Scribner's Sons, 1906), 139–63, quotes, 161.
82. Ibid., 261–82, quote, 273–74.
83. Ibid., 271–77, quote, 275.
84. Ibid., 276.
85. Ibid., 270, 314.
86. Ibid., 314–15.
87. Otto Schmoller, *Die Lehre vom Reiche Gottes in den Schriften des Neuen Testaments* (Leiden: E. J. Brill, 1891); Ernst Issel, *Die Lehre vom Reich Gottes im Neuen Testament* (Leiden: E. J. Brill, 1891); Johannes Weiss, *Die Predigt Jesu von Reiche Gottes* (Göttingen: Vandenhoeck & Ruprecht, 1892).
88. Clarke, *An Outline of Christian Theology,* 433–48, quotes, 442, 443.
89. Brown, *Christian Theology in Outline,* 185; Harnack, *What Is Christianity?* 52–56.
90. William Adams Brown, *How to Think of Christ* (New York: Charles Scribner's Sons, 1945), 76–77.
91. See George M. Marsden, *Fundamentalism and American Culture: The Shaping of Twentieth-Century Evangelicalism, 1870–1925* (Oxford: Oxford University Press, 1980), 117–18; Gary Dorrien, *The Remaking of Evangelical Theology* (Louisville: Westminster John Knox Press, 1998), 15–16.
92. William Adams Brown, "The Old Theology and the New," *Harvard Theological Review* 4 (Jan. 1911): 13–17, 19.
93. William Adams Brown, "The Task and Method of Systematic Theology," *American Journal of Theology* 14 (April 1910): 205–15; Benjamin B. Warfield, same title and issue, 192–205; Gerald Birney Smith, same title and issue, 215–33.
94. Brown, *A Teacher and His Times,* 126–33, quotes, 130, 131; see Handy, *A History of Union Theological Seminary in New York,* 136.
95. Brown, *A Teacher and His Times,* 133.
96. Brown, "The Task and Method of Systematic Theology," 210.
97. Ibid., 210–11, 215.
98. Gerald Birney Smith, "Systematic Theology and Christian Ethics," *A Guide to the Study of the Christian Religion,* ed. Gerald Birney Smith (Chicago: University of Chicago Press,

1916), 483–577, quote, 500. Smith placed William Newton Clarke and Lewis Stearns in the same category.

99. Auguste Sabatier, *Religions of Authority and the Religion of the Spirit*, trans. Louise Seymour Houghton (New York: McClure, Philips & Co., 1904); see Sabatier, *Outlines of a Philosophy of Religion based on Psychology and History* (New York: James Pott & Co., 1910).

100. Gerald Birney Smith, "The Task and Method of Systematic Theology," 226.

101. William Adams Brown, "Is Our Protestantism Still Protestant?" *Harvard Theological Review* (January 1908); William Adams Brown, "Seeking Beliefs That Matter," *Contemporary American Theology: Theological Autobiographies*, 2d series, ed. Vergilius Ferm (New York: Round Table Press, 1933), 94–95.

102. William Adams Brown, *Pathways to Certainty* (New York: Charles Scribner's Sons, 1930), 251, 255.

103. Brown, "Seeking Beliefs That Matter," 98.

104. Ibid., 68.

105. William Adams Brown, "Intercession for Those for Whom We Are Working," Devotional Meeting Address, 1917, Series 3, Box 3, William Adams Brown Collection, Union Theological Seminary; see William Adams Brown, *The Church in America* (New York: Macmillan Co., 1922).

106. *The General War-Time Commission of the Churches. Its organization and its purpose* (New York: Federal Council of the Churches of Christ in America, 1917); Committee on the War and the Religious Outlook, *The Religion of American Men* (New York: Federal Council of the Churches of Christ in America, 1920); idem, *The Missionary Outlook in the Light of the War* (New York: Federal Council of the Churches of Christ in America, 1920); idem, *The Church and Industrial Reconstruction* (New York: Federal Council of the Churches of Christ in America, 1921); idem, *Christian Unity: Its Principles and Possibilities* (New York: Federal Council of the Churches of Christ in America, 1922).

107. See G. K. A. Bell, *The Kingship of Christ: The Story of the World Council of Churches* (London: Harmondsworth, 1954); William Adams Brown, *The Church: Catholic and Protestant* (New York: Charles Scribner's Sons, 1935); Brown, *The Church in America*; Samuel McCrea Cavert, "William Adams Brown: Servant of the Church of Christ," 27–33; Brown, *A Teacher and His Times*, 337–65; Brown, "Seeking Beliefs That Matter," 73–74.

108. Brown, "Seeking Beliefs That Matter," 91.

109. See Linda-Marie Deloff, "Charles Clayton Morrison: Shaping a Journal's Identity," in Linda-Marie Deloff, Martin E. Marty, Dean Peerman, and James M. Wall, *A Century of the Century* (Grand Rapids: Wm. B. Eerdmans Co., 1987), 3–16; Gary Dorrien, *Soul in Society: The Making and Renewal of Social Christianity* (Minneapolis: Fortress Press, 1995), 77–84.

110. John Barnard, *From Evangelicalism to Progressivism at Oberlin College, 1866–1917* (Columbus: Ohio State University Press, 1969); Donald M. Love, *Henry Churchill King of Oberlin* (New Haven: Yale University Press, 1956), 29–30; Foster, *The Modern Movement in American Theology*, 172.

111. King to Fairchild, January 20, 1883, Fairchild Papers, Oberlin College Library, cited in Love, *Henry Churchill King of Oberlin*, 35–36, see 2–42.

112. Love, *Henry Churchill King of Oberlin*, 62–76; see Foster, *The Modern Movement in American Theology*, 172–73; Hermann Lotze, *Grundzüge der Religionsphilosophie* (Leipzig: G. Hirzel, 1884); Lotze, *Metaphysik* (Leipzig: F. Meiner, 1912).

113. Henry Churchill King, *Reconstruction in Theology* (New York: Macmillan Company, 1901), v, 2–4, 12.

114. Ibid., 35, 54–55, 91, 122, 151–55, 176–77.

115. Ibid., 186–87. On Herrmann's deepening existentialism, see Gary Dorrien, *The Barthian Revolt in Modern Theology: Theology without Weapons* (Louisville: Westminster John Knox Press, 1999), 168–73.

116. King, *Reconstruction in Theology*, 187–95; see Adolf von Harnack, *Christianity and History*, trans. Thomas Bailey Saunders (London: A. & C. Black, 1896), 47; Wilhelm Herrmann, *Der Verkehr des Christen mit Gott* (2d ed., Stuttgart: Cotta, 1892), 97.

117. "Golden words" quote in Henry Churchill King, *Theology and the Social Consciousness: A Study of the Relations of the Social Consciousness to Theology* (New York: Hodder &

Stoughton, 1902), 199. See Wilhelm Herrmann, *Gesammelte Aufsätze*, ed. F. W. Schmidt (Tübingen: J. C. B. Mohr, 1923); Herrmann, *Schriften zur Grundlegung der Theologie*, 2 vols., ed. Peter Fischer-Appelt (Munich: Chr. Kaiser Verlag, 1966, 1967).

118. King, *Reconstruction in Theology*, 196; King, *Theology and the Social Consciousness*, 1; see Walter Rauschenbusch, *Christianity and the Social Crisis* (New York: Hodder & Stoughton, 1907).

119. King, *Theology and the Social Consciousness*, ix, 6. See Albrecht Ritschl, *The Christian Doctrine of Justification and Reconciliation*, ed. H. R. Mackintosh and A. B. Macaulay (Edinburgh: T. & T. Clark, 1902), 205.

120. King, *Theology and the Social Consciousness*, 17, 22.

121. Borden Parker Bowne, *Theory of Thought and Knowledge* (New York: American Book Co., 1897), 91, 111; King, *Theology and the Social Consciousness*, 43–44.

122. King, *Theology and the Social Consciousness*, 44, 86–87.

123. Ibid., 93–94, 103, 108.

124. Eulogy excerpted in Love, *Henry Churchill King of Oberlin*, 93.

125. Henry Churchill King, *The Moral and Religious Challenge of Our Times* (New York: Macmillan Co., 1911); 312–13; Herbert Croly, *The Promise of American Life* (1st ed., 1909; reprint, Boston: Northeastern University Press, 1989), 454.

126. King, *The Moral and Religious Challenge of Our Times*, 1, 9, 348–49.

127. See ibid., 189–234, 350–84; Love, *Henry Churchill King of Oberlin*, 190–208.

128. Love, *Henry Churchill King of Oberlin*, 209–23, quote, 221; see Inter-allied Commission on Mandates in Turkey, American Section, *Report of American Section of Inter-allied Commission of Mandates in Turkey: An Official United States Government Report* (New York: Editor & Publisher Co., 1922), v. 55, no. 27, 2d section.

129. Love, *Henry Churchill King of Oberlin*, 223, 224–26, 232; see Walter Marshall Horton, *Theism and the Scientific Spirit* (New York: Harper & Brothers, 1933); Horton, *Realistic Theology* (New York: Harper & Brothers, 1934); Horton, *Christian Theology: An Ecumenical Approach* (New York: Harper & Brothers, 1955).

130. See Frank Hugh Foster, "The Theology of the New Rationalism," *American Journal of Theology* (1909), 407–19; Foster, "The Christology of a Modern Rationalist," *American Journal of Theology* (1911): 587–614; Foster, *The Modern Movement in American Theology*, 186–87.

Chapter 2. Thy Kingdom Come

1. August Rauschenbusch, *Leben und Wirken von August Rauschenbusch*, completed and edited by Walter Rauschenbusch (Cassel: J. G. Oncken, 1901), 15–97; Dores Robinson Sharpe, *Walter Rauschenbusch* (New York: Macmillan Co., 1942), 20–22.

2. *Leben und Wirken von August Rauschenbusch*, 130–84; Walter Rauschenbusch, "Augustus Rauschenbusch, D.D.," *Baptist Home Missions Monthly* (Sept. 1898): 323–24; see Paul M. Minus, *Walter Rauschenbusch: American Reformer* (New York: Macmillan Co., 1988), 2–4.

3. The charge of alcoholism was made by Dores Robinson Sharpe, *Walter Rauschenbusch*, 42. A Baptist pastor and longtime executive secretary of the Cleveland Baptist Association, Sharpe was Walter Rauschenbusch's private secretary for many years and a close friend. August Rauschenbusch to Maria Ehrhardt, 24 July 1873, Archives, North American Baptist Conference, Sioux Falls, South Dakota; cited in Minus, *Walter Rauschenbusch*, 14–15.

4. Strong quoted in *Autobiography of Augustus Hopkins Strong*, ed. Crerar Douglas (Valley Forge, Pa.: Judson Press, 1981), 231; Walter Rauschenbusch to August Rauschenbusch, 15 Oct. 1882, Box 34, Rauschenbusch Family Collection, American Baptist–Samuel Colgate Historical Library, Rochester, N.Y.

5. Walter Rauschenbusch to D. C. Vandercook, 23 Feb. 1917, Box 32, Rauschenbusch Family Collection.

6. Walter Rauschenbusch, "The Kingdom of God," 2 Jan. 1913 address at the Cleveland YMCA, excerpts reprinted in *Cleveland's Young Men* 27 (9 Jan. 1913); reported in *Rochester Democrat and Chronicle* (25 Jan. 1913); excerpts reprinted in Robert T. Handy, ed., *The Social Gospel in America, 1870–1920: Gladden, Ely, Rauschenbusch* (New York:

Oxford University Press, 1966), 264–67; conversion quote and "ran with a gang" recollection, 264.

7. Rauschenbusch, "The Kingdom of God," 1913 YMCA address, excerpt reprinted in Handy, ed., *The Social Gospel in America,* 264–65.

8. Walter Rauschenbusch to Munson Ford, 19 Mar. 1882, Box 23, Rauschenbusch Family Collection.

9. Walter Rauschenbusch to Munson Ford, 18 Mar. 1883, Box 23, Rauschenbusch Family Collection.

10. "Scholarly awe" quote in Mitchell Brunk, "Walter Rauschenbusch," *Adult Leader* (Oct. 1934), cited in Minus, 36; "breezy and geniusy," Walter Rauschenbusch to Munson Ford, 28 Feb. 1884, Box 23, Rauschenbusch Family Collection; see Sharpe, *Walter Rauschenbusch,* 40–52.

11. Augustus Hopkins Strong, *Lectures on Theology* (Rochester: E. R. Andrews, 1876); Strong, *Systematic Theology: A Compendium and Commonplace Book Designed for the Use of Theological Students* (Rochester: E. R. Andrews, 1886; 7th ed., New York: A. C. Armstrong & Son, 1902); see Grant Wacker, *Augustus H. Strong and the Dilemma of Historical Consciousness* (Macon, Ga.: Mercer University Press, 1985).

12. Walter Rauschenbusch, "The Bushnellian Theory of the Atonement," 17 Nov. 1885, Box 14, Rauschenbusch Family Collection; closing quote, Rauschenbusch's undated, handwritten cover note to this section of his collected materials.

13. "I began," "awake in their hearts," and "no longer my fond hope," Walter Rauschenbusch to Munson Ford, 31 Dec. 1884, Box 23; "I fear the sing-song" and "marching army," Rauschenbusch to Ford, 14 June 1884, Box 23, Rauschenbusch Family Collection.

14. "Just beginning to believe," Walter Rauschenbusch to Munson Ford, 30 May 1885, Box 23, Rauschenbusch Family Collection; "on the whole," Rauschenbusch to Ford, 31 Dec. 1884; "hard work for God" and "ought to follow Jesus Christ," Rauschenbusch, "The Kingdom of God," 1913 YMCA address, excerpts reprinted in Handy, ed., *The Social Gospel in America,* 265; see Sharpe, *Walter Rauschenbusch,* 52–57.

15. "He kept me at school," Rauschenbusch to Vandercook, 23 Feb. 1917; "I am struggling," Walter Rauschenbusch to Munson Ford, 20 Feb. 1886, Box 23, Rauschenbusch Family Collection; Walter Rauschenbusch to Caroline Rauschenbusch, 24 Sept. 1886, North American Baptist Conference Archives, cited in Minus, *Walter Rauschenbusch,* 53.

16. "There are many," Walter Rauschenbusch to Munson Ford, 30 June 1886, Box 23, Rauschenbusch Family Collection; "My idea," Walter Rauschenbusch, "Genesis of 'Christianity and the Social Crisis,'" *Rochester Theological Seminary Bulletin: The Record* (Nov. 1918), 51; Walter Rauschenbusch, Sermon Notebook 2, 1886, Box 150, Rauschenbusch Family Collection.

17. Sharpe attributed Rauschenbusch's hearing problems to a relapse from the Russian grippe in the winter of 1888; Sharpe, *Walter Rauschenbusch,* 65–66.

18. Walter Rauschenbusch to Lina Döring, 14 July 1886, 14 December 1886, North American Baptist Conference Archives; Minus, *Walter Rauschenbusch,* 54; August Rauschenbusch, *Leben und Wirken von August Rauschenbusch,* iii–v.

19. See Walter Rauschenbusch, with Ira D. Sankey, *Neue Lieder.* Authorized translation of *Gospel Hymns Number 5* (New York: Bigelow & Main, 1889); Rauschenbusch and Sankey, *Evangeliums-Lieder 2* (New York: Bigelow & Main, 1894); Rauschenbusch and Sankey, *Evangeliums-Lieder 1 und 2* (New York: Bigelow & Main, 1897).

20. Rauschenbusch, "The Kingdom of God," 1913 YMCA address, excerpts reprinted in Handy, ed., *The Social Gospel in America,* 266.

21. Rauschenbusch, "Genesis of 'Christianity and the Social Crisis,'" "no idea" and "didn't fit" quotes, 51; Walter Rauschenbusch to Maria Döring, 14 Jan. 1887, North American Baptist Conference Archives, cited in Minus, *Walter Rauschenbusch,* 60.

22. "Children's funerals" in Rauschenbusch, "The Kingdom of God," Cleveland YMCA address, 265–66; "implored me almost" and "all our inherited ideas" in Walter Rauschenbusch, *Christianizing the Social Order* (New York: Macmillan, 1912), 92; "I went ahead" in Rauschenbusch, "Genesis of 'Christianity and the Social Crisis,'" 51.

23. Henry George, *Progress and Poverty* (New York: Robert Schalkenbach Foundation, 1879, reprint 1955); Fred Nicklason, "Henry George, Social Gospeller," *American Quarterly*

22 (1970): 649–64; James Dombrowski, *The Early Days of Christian Socialism in America* (New York: Columbia University Press, 1936), 35–49.

24. "The time will probably come," Walter Rauschenbusch to "Madame," 16 Feb. 1897, Box 23, Rauschenbusch Family Papers; Rauschenbusch, *Christianizing the Social Order,* 91–92, "I owe" quote, 394; see Stephen Bell, *Rebel, Priest, and Prophet: A Biography of Dr. Edward McGlynn* (New York: Devin-Adair, 1937), 33–38. Rauschenbusch may have served as a ward captain in George's campaign, though solid documentation is lacking thus far; see Minus, *Walter Rauschenbusch,* 209, n.26.

25. See John R. Everett, *Religion in Economics: A Study of John Bates Clark, Richard T. Ely, Simon N. Patten* (New York: King's Crown Press, 1946); Charles H. Hopkins, *The Rise of the Social Gospel in American Protestantism, 1865–1915* (New Haven: Yale University Press, 1940), 113–17, 175–76, 194–95; Robert T. Handy, ed., "Richard T. Ely: An Introduction," in *The Social Gospel in America,* 173–75; Dombrowski, *The Early Days of Christian Socialism in America,* 50–59.

26. Richard T. Ely, *The Past and the Present of Political Economy* (Baltimore: Johns Hopkins University Press, 1884); Ely, *Introduction to Political Economy* (New York: Chautauqua Press, 1889); Ely, *Ground under Our Feet: An Autobiography* (New York: Macmillan Co., 1938), 140.

27. Richard T. Ely, *The Labor Movement in America* (New York: Macmillan Co., 1886), quotes, 311, 313; Ely, *Studies in the Evolution of Industrial Society* (New York: Macmillan, 1911); Ely, *Problems of To-Day* (New York: T. Y. Crowell, 1890); Ely, *Political Economy, Political Science and Sociology* (Chicago: University Association, 1898); Ely, *Social Aspects of Christianity, and Other Essays* (London: W. Reeves, 1897). The latter book contains the 1888 lecture heard by Rauschenbusch. Closing quote in Walter Rauschenbusch, "Noch einmal die sociale Frage," *Der Sendbote* (28 Jan. 1891), cited in Minus, *Walter Rauschenbusch,* 64.

28. Walter Rauschenbusch, "Henry George: My First Paper on the Social Question," December 1887, cited in Sharpe, *Walter Rauschenbusch,* 80; this paper has been lost. Rauschenbusch, "Beneath the Glitter," *Christian Inquirer* (2 Aug. 1888); quoted in Sharpe, *Walter Rauschenbusch,* 81–82.

29. See Leighton Williams, "The Brotherhood of the Kingdom and Its Work," Brotherhood Leaflet No. 10; reprinted in *The Kingdom* 1 (Aug. 1907): no pagination; Williams, "The Reign of the New Humanity," *The Kingdom* 1 (Dec. 1907); E. F. Merriam, "The Brotherhood of the Kingdom," *The Watchman* (13 Aug. 1908); Nathaniel Schmidt to Walter Rauschenbusch, 18 Apr. 1889, Box 23, Rauschenbusch Family Collection; Minus, *Walter Rauschenbusch,* 57–58.

30. "Compelled to stop," Rauschenbusch, "The Kingdom of God," 1913 Cleveland YMCA Lecture, reported in *Rochester Democrat and Chronicle* (25 Jan. 1913); "We desire to make," editorial, *For the Right* 1 (Nov. 1889); see Sharpe, *Walter Rauschenbusch,* 86–87. The most representative example that we possess of Rauschenbusch's "dangerous book" is the text that Max L. Stackhouse discovered, reconstructed, and published under the title *The Righteousness of the Kingdom* (Nashville: Abingdon Press, 1968; reprint, Lewiston, N.Y.: Edwin Mellen Press, 1999). The precise history of the manuscript is unknown; Schmidt evidently held onto it for lengthy periods of time, and Rauschenbusch continued to work on it in the early 1890s. For the history of the text, see editor's introduction, *The Righteousness of the Kingdom,* 14–18. Elizabeth Post may have been the sister of Louis Freeland Post, a journalist and social reformer who was a prominent supporter of Henry George.

31. "Declaration of Principles of the Society of Christian Socialism," *The Dawn* 1 (15 May 1889): 3; editorial, "Declaration of Principles of the Christian Socialist Society of New York City," *For the Right* (Apr. 1890); see Walter Rauschenbusch, "Some Words about Socialism in America," *For the Right* 1 (Apr. 1890); Dombrowski, *The Early Days of Christian Socialism in America,* 96–107; William Dwight Porter Bliss, *A Handbook of Socialism* (New York: S. Sonnenschein, C. Scribners, 1895); Christopher L. Webber, "William Dwight Porter Bliss (1856–1926): Priest and Socialist," *Historical Magazine of the Protestant Episcopal Church* 28 (Mar. 1959): 9–39; Richard B. Dressner, "William Dwight Porter Bliss's Christian Socialism," *Church History* 47 (Mar. 1978): 66–82. Bliss's periodical *The Dawn* was published from 1889 to 1896.

32. Walter Rauschenbusch, "Good Men and Good Government," *For the Right* 2 (Aug. 1890).

33. "Foresight" quote in Walter Rauschenbusch, "Municipal Socialism," *The Voice* (3 Sept. 1891); see Emma Rauschenbusch Clough, *A Study of Mary Wollstonecraft and the Rights of Woman* (London: Longmans, Green & Co., 1898); Peter d'A. Jones, *The Christian Socialist Revival, 1877–1914* (Princeton: Princeton University Press, 1968), 41–42; Minus, *Walter Rauschenbusch,* 71–72.

34. Rauschenbusch, *The Righteousness of the Kingdom,* 233–34.

35. Leighton Williams to Walter Rauschenbusch, 3 July 1891, Box 23, Rauschenbusch Family Collection; Minus, *Walter Rauschenbusch,* 75–79; editor's introduction, *The Righteousness of the Kingdom,* 17–20.

36. Rauschenbusch, *The Righteousness of the Kingdom,* quotes, 79, 87; see Rauschenbusch, "Noch einmal die sociale Frage," *Der Sendbote.*

37. Rauschenbusch, "The Kingdom of God," 1913 Cleveland YMCA lecture, excerpts reprinted in Handy, ed., *The Social Gospel in America,* 267.

38. Ibid., 267.

39. *Annual Report of the Baptist Congress, 1892,* quote, 127; Leighton Williams, *The Baptist Position: Its Experimental Basis* (New York: E. Scott & Co., 1892), 4–5, 13–15; see Leighton Williams, "The Brotherhood of the Kingdom and Its Work," *The Kingdom* (Aug. 1907); Winthrop S. Hudson, ed., *Walter Rauschenbusch: Selected Writings* (New York: Paulist Press, 1984), 21–24; Minus, *Walter Rauschenbusch,* 83–84; Vernon Parker Bodein, *The Social Gospel of Walter Rauschenbusch and Its Relation to Religious Education,* Yale Studies in Religious Education, 16 (New Haven: Yale University Press, 1944), 22–24; Sharpe, *Walter Rauschenbusch,* 116–17.

40. "Spirit and Aims of the Brotherhood of the Kingdom," Preamble to the Constituting Document of the Brotherhood of the Kingdom; this statement was reproduced as a frontispiece to all annual reports of the Brotherhood of the Kingdom. See Williams, "The Brotherhood of the Kingdom and Its Work"; Mitchell Bronk, "An Adventure in the Kingdom of God," *Crozer Quarterly* (Jan. 1937), 21–28; C. Howard Hopkins, "Walter Rauschenbusch and the Brotherhood of the Kingdom," *Church History* 7 (June 1938): 138–56.

41. Brotherhood aims described in Brotherhood of the Kingdom letter from Walter Rauschenbusch, corresponding secretary, undated, Box 23, Rauschenbusch Family Collection; Walter Rauschenbusch, "The Brotherhood of the Kingdom," Brotherhood Leaflet No. 2, 1893, reprinted in Hudson, ed., *Walter Rauschenbusch: Selected Writings,* 74–76, quotes, 74, 75.

42. Walter Rauschenbusch, "The Kingdom of God," Brotherhood Leaflet No. 4, 1894; reprinted in Hudson, ed., *Walter Rauschenbusch: Selected Writings,* 76–79.

43. Ibid., quote, 78.

44. Walter Rauschenbusch, "A Conquering Idea," *The Examiner* (31 July 1892), reprinted in Hudson, ed., *Walter Rauschenbusch: Selected Writings,* 71–74, quotes, 72.

45. Ibid., quotes, 72, 73–74; Walter Rauschenbusch, "Our Attitude Toward Millenarianism," *The Examiner* (24 Sept. and 1 Oct. 1896), reprinted in Hudson, ed., *Walter Rauschenbusch: Selected Writings,* 79–94; see Rauschenbusch, "Some Words about Socialism in America," 3.

46. Rauschenbusch, "The Kingdom of God," Brotherhood Leaflet No. 4, 76–78, "sum of all" quote, 78; Walter Rauschenbusch, "The Ideals of Social Reformers," *American Journal of Sociology* 2 (July 1896): 202–19; reprinted in Handy, ed., *The Social Gospel in America,* 274–89, closing quotes, 275, 282.

47. Walter Rauschenbusch, class letter [to Rochester Seminary class of 1886], 1893, Box 153, Rauschenbusch Family Collection.

48. Sharpe, *Walter Rauschenbusch,* 104–10, quote, 107; Rauschenbusch, "The Kingdom of God," 1913 Cleveland YMCA lecture, 266; Minus, *Walter Rauschenbusch,* 100; Frederic M. Hudson, "The Reign of the New Humanity," Ph.D. diss., Columbia University, 1968, 190–203.

49. See James M. Berquist, "German-America in the 1890s: Illusions and Realities," in *Germans in America: Aspects of German-American Relations in the Nineteenth Century,* ed. Allen McCormick (New York: Brooklyn College Press, 1983); Lawrence B. Davis,

Immigrants, Baptists, and the Protestant Mind in America (Urbana, Ill.: University of Illinois Press, 1973).

50. *Annual Report of the Baptist Congress,* 1888, "for I believe" quote, 87; Walter Rauschenbusch (unsigned), "What Shall We Do with the Germans?" (pamphlet, 1895); see Minus, *Walter Rauschenbusch,* 105; John R. Aiken, "Walter Rauschenbusch and Education for Reform," *Church History* 36 (Dec. 1967): 459–60.

51. Walter Rauschenbusch (unsigned), "The German Seminary in Rochester" (pamphlet, 1897), Box 47, Rauschenbusch Family Collection; Walter Rauschenbusch, "The Contribution of Germany to the National Life of America," Commencement address, Fiftieth Anniversary of the Rochester Theological Seminary German Department, Box 92, Rauschenbusch Family Collection, quoted in *Rochester Democrat and Chronicle* (8 May 1902). Sharpe devoted a single one-sentence aside to this issue, with no hint of controversy or racism; see Sharpe, *Walter Rauschenbusch,* 367.

52. Walter Rauschenbusch, "England and Germany," *The Watchman* 8 (16 Nov. 1899): 9–11; reprinted in Handy, ed., *The Social Gospel in America,* 300–307; "Wherever Germany goes" quotes, 306; Rauschenbusch, Thanksgiving Sermon, 1898, *Rochester Post-Express* (25 Nov. 1898); see Rauschenbusch, "Shall I Join an English Church?" *Der Jugend Herold* (July 1896), 147.

53. Pauline Rauschenbusch to Walter Rauschenbusch, 4 Aug. 1902, Box 35, Rauschenbusch Family Collection; Minus, *Walter Rauschenbusch,* 117–18, Pauline Rauschenbusch and Augustus Strong statements quoted, 117; Sharpe, *Walter Rauschenbusch,* 177–78.

54. Walter Rauschenbusch, *Christianity and the Social Crisis* (New York: Macmillan, 1907; reprint, Louisville, Ky.: Westminster John Knox Press, 1991), xxxvii; citations of Harnack on 95, 112, 129, 130, 132, 156, 191, 298.

55. See Wacker, *Augustus Hopkins Strong and the Dilemma of Historical Consciousness,* 73–137; *Autobiography of Augustus Hopkins Strong,* 340; *Annual Report, New York Baptist Union for Ministerial Education, 1906,* 42; Minus, *Walter Rauschenbusch,* 139, 145; Walter Rauschenbusch, "Impressions of Germany" (8 Oct. 1908, lecture manuscript), Box 21, Rauschenbusch Family Collection.

56. Rauschenbusch, *Christianity and the Social Crisis,* xxxviii.

57. Ibid., 3–43, quotes, 3, 11, 26, 42–43. Rauschenbusch's main scholarly source on prophetic religion was G. A. Smith, *The Book of the Twelve Prophets* (New York: Hodder & Stoughton, 1898).

58. Rauschenbusch, *Christianity and the Social Crisis,* quotes, 47, 48, 63.

59. Ibid., 54–71, quote, 63.

60. Ibid., quotes, 62, 63; citations of Mathews's *The Messianic Hope in the New Testament* on 56, 108; and Weiss's *Biblical Theology of the New Testament,* 104.

61. Rauschenbusch, *Christianity and the Social Crisis,* quotes, 64, 65.

62. Ibid., quotes, 152, 153, 160.

63. Ibid., quotes, 162, 168.

64. Ibid., quotes, 170, 174, 181–82, 91.

65. Walter Rauschenbusch, "Dogmatic and Practical Socialism," *Rochester Democrat and Chronicle* (25 Feb. 1901), reprinted in Handy, ed., *The Social Gospel in America,* 308–22; Rauschenbusch, *Christianity and the Social Crisis,* quote, 285.

66. Rauschenbusch, *Christianity and the Social Crisis,* quote, 240.

67. Ibid., quotes, 237.

68. Ibid., quotes, 195, 204, 205, 271. See *Fabian Essays in Socialism,* ed. G. Bernard Shaw (1889; reprint, New York: Doubleday & Co., 1967); G. D. H. Cole, *Guild Socialism Restated* (London: L. Parsons, 1920).

69. Rauschenbusch, *Christianity and the Social Crisis,* quote, 341.

70. Ibid., quotes, 397, 398.

71. Ibid., quotes, 400, 401.

72. Ibid., quotes, 401, 410–11.

73. Ibid., 420, 421.

74. See Washington Gladden, *Applied Christianity: Moral Aspects of Social Questions* (Boston: Houghton, Mifflin & Co., 1889); Josiah Strong, *Our Country, Its Possible Future, and Its Present Crisis* (New York: American Home Missionary Society, 1886; revised ed., New

York: Baker & Taylor, 1891; reprint, Cambridge: Harvard University Press, 1963); George D. Herron, *The Larger Christ* (Chicago: Fleming H. Revell Co., 1891); Shailer Mathews, *The Social Teaching of Jesus: An Essay in Christian Sociology* (New York: Macmillan, 1897); Francis Greenwood Peabody, *Jesus Christ and the Social Question* (New York: Macmillan, 1900).

75. "If the church" quote, Rauschenbusch, *Christianity and the Social Crisis,* 339; "an expression of," Rauschenbusch, "Genesis of 'Christianity and the Social Crisis,'" 53; Albion W. Small, review of *Christianity and the Social Crisis,* by Walter Rauschenbusch, *Unity* (12 Dec. 1907); Minus, *Walter Rauschenbusch,* 162–63; see George Herron, *The Christian State* (New York: T. Y. Crowell, 1895); Herron, *Woodrow Wilson and the World's Peace* (New York: Kennerly, 1917); Herron, *Germanism and the American Crusade* (New York: Kennerley, 1918); Herron, *The Defeat in the Victory* (London: Palmer, 1921).

76. Augustus Hopkins Strong to Walter Rauschenbusch, 27 June 1907, Box 92, Rauschenbusch Family Collection; Walter Rauschenbusch to Augustus Hopkins Strong, 25 Apr. 1911, Box 93. King's address was titled, "The Contribution of Modern Science to the Ideal Interests"; Mathews spoke on "The Theological Seminary as a School of Religious Efficiency"; see Minus, *Walter Rauschenbusch,* 142–43, 161; Leroy Moore Jr., "The Rise of American Religious Liberalism at the Rochester Theological Seminary, 1872–1928," Ph.D. diss., Claremont Graduate School, 1966.

77. See Samuel McCrea Cavert, *The American Churches in the Ecumenical Movement, 1900–1968* (New York: Association Press, 1968); Charles Howard Hopkins, *History of the YMCA in North America* (New York: Association Press, 1951); Grace H. Wilson, *The Religious and Philosophical Works of the YWCA* (New York: Teachers College Press, 1933); Henry J. Pratt, *The Liberalization of American Protestantism: A Case Study in Complex Organizations* (Detroit: Wayne State University Press, 1972); Sidney E. Mead, *The Lively Experiment: The Shaping of Christianity in America* (New York: Harper & Row, 1963), 177–83; Martin E. Marty, *Righteous Empire: The Protestant Experience in America* (New York: Dial Press, 1970), 206–9; Frank Mason North to Walter Rauschenbusch, 3 Aug. 1908, Box 25, Rauschenbusch Family Collection; *The Social Creed of the Churches,* ed. Harry F. Ward (Cincinnati: Eaton & Maine, 1912).

78. Walter Rauschenbusch, *For God and the People: Prayers of the Social Awakening* (Boston: Pilgrim Press, 1910), 45, 126.

79. Josiah Strong to Walter Rauschenbusch, 30 Dec. 1910, Box 25, Rauschenbusch Family Collection; see Walter Rauschenbusch, *Unto Me* (Boston: Pilgrim Press, 1912); Rauschenbusch, *Dare We Be Christians?* (Boston: Pilgrim Press, 1914). Most of *Christianizing the Social Order* was delivered as the Earl Lectures at Pacific Theological Seminary in Berkeley, California, in April 1910, and the Merrick Lectures at Ohio Wesleyan University in Delaware, Ohio, in April 1911.

80. Rauschenbusch, *Christianizing the Social Order,* quote, vii.

81. Ibid., quotes, viii, 9.

82. Ibid., 48–60, quotes, 49, 58, 56. Rauschenbusch singled out I. M. Haldemann, a New York minister and prominent premillennial fundamentalist, who condemned *Christianity and the Social Crisis* as sub-Christian; see I. M. Haldemann, *Professor Rauschenbusch's 'Christianity and the Social Crisis'* (New York: Charles C. Cook, n.d.), booklet. Haldemann was pastor of First Baptist Church in New York City; his pamphlets were widely distributed.

83. Rauschenbusch, *Christianizing the Social Order,* quotes, 85, 89–90.

84. Ibid., quotes, 90, 121.

85. Ibid., 123–25, quote, 125.

86. Ibid., 124–25, quotes, 125.

87. Ibid., 125–30, quote, 125.

88. Ibid., 130–38, quotes, 131, 135. Janet Fishburn's early work claimed that Rauschenbusch opposed female suffrage and that he "abhorred feminism because it was potentially destructive of family and society." See Janet Forsythe Fishburn, *The Fatherhood of God and the Victorian Family: The Social Gospel in America* (Philadelphia: Fortress Press, 1981), 124. Martin E. Marty, among others, has repeated Fishburn's claims; see Martin E. Marty, *Modern American Religion,* Volume 1: *The Irony of It All, 1893–1919* (Chicago: University of Chicago Press, 1986), 292. Fishburn's excellent recent work is more care-

ful and discriminating on this subject. She allows that Rauschenbusch supported the movement for women's rights, while emphasizing that he persistently championed the late-Victorian ideal of the mother-nurtured family. Janet Forsythe Fishburn, "Walter Rauschenbusch and 'The Women Movement': A Gender Analysis," unpublished paper delivered at the 1999 Social Gospel Conference, Colgate Rochester Divinity School/Crozer Theological Seminary, 18 Mar. 1999.

89. Rauschenbusch, *Christianity and the Social Crisis,* quotes, 279, 276; see Walter Rauschenbusch, "Some Moral Aspects of the 'Woman Movement,'" *Biblical World* 42 (Oct. 1913): 195–98; Walter Rauschenbusch, "What About the Woman?" Box 20, Rauschenbusch Family Papers; Peter Gabriel Filene, *Him Her Self: Sex Roles in Modern America* (New York: Harcourt Brace Jovanovich, 1974), 23–29; Fishburn, *The Fatherhood of God and the Victorian Family,* 120–27; Fishburn, "Walter Rauschenbusch and 'The Women Movement': A Gender Analysis"; Susan Curtis, *A Consuming Faith: The Social Gospel and Modern American Culture* (Baltimore: Johns Hopkins University Press, 1991), 107–8, 112.

90. Rauschenbusch, *Christianizing the Social Order,* 137–55, quotes, 139, 141, 152, 153.

91. Ibid., quotes, 156, 157, 158.

92. Daniel Bell, *The Cultural Contradictions of Capitalism* (New York: Basic Books, 1976); Rauschenbusch, *Christianizing the Social Order,* quote, 212; see Gary Dorrien, *The Neoconservative Mind: Politics, Culture, and the War of Ideology* (Philadelphia: Temple University Press, 1993), 226–28.

93. Rauschenbusch, *Christianizing the Social Order,* 311–23, quotes, 317.

94. Ibid., quotes, 311, 313, 314.

95. Ibid., 341–43, 352–56, quotes, 343, 353.

96. Ibid., quote, 361.

97. John Stuart Mill, *Principles of Political Economy,* 2 vols. (New York: Appleton & Co., 1884), 2:357–59; Rauschenbusch, *Christianizing the Social Order,* 356–71; Walter Rauschenbusch, "Christian Socialism," *A Dictionary of Religion and Ethics,* ed. Shailer Mathews and Gerald Birney Smith (New York: Macmillan Co., 1923), 90–91.

98. Rauschenbusch, *Christianizing the Social Order,* quotes, 369, 437.

99. Ibid., quotes, 367–68, 329.

100. Walter Rauschenbusch to Francis G. Peabody, 14 Dec. 1912, Box 26, Rauschenbusch Family Collection.

101. Rauschenbusch, *Christianizing the Social Order,* 458–66, quotes, 433, 464–65.

102. "Compressed anxiety," Walter Rauschenbusch to John Wright Buckham, 24 Dec. 1912, Box 26, Rauschenbusch Family Collection.

103. Walter Rauschenbusch, Address to Religious Citizenship League, 30 Jan. 1914; Rauschenbusch, "The Contribution of Germany to the National Life of America," Box 92; Rauschenbusch, *For God and the People,* 109; Walter Rauschenbusch to Hilmar Rauschenbusch, 23 Sept. 1914, Box 37, Rauschenbusch Family Collection; Minus, *Walter Rauschenbusch,* 177–78.

104. Rauschenbusch, *Christianizing the Social Order,* 366, "ablest ruler" quote, 334; Rauschenbusch, *For God and the People,* "ever the pride" quote, 109; Walter Rauschenbusch to *The Congregationalist,* 24 Sept. 1914.

105. "My cradle" quote, Rauschenbusch, "The Contribution of Germany to the National Life of America," Box 92; "I was stunned," Walter Rauschenbusch to "a Friend," 7 Mar. 1917, Box 32, Rauschenbusch Family Collection; Walter Rauschenbusch, "Be Fair to Germany: A Plea for Open-mindedness," *The Congregationalist,* 15 Oct. 1914.

106. "Methodists Do Not Want to Hear Pro-German Divine," *Regina Morning Leader* (5 Nov. 1914).

107. Rauschenbusch to "A Friend," 7 Mar. 1917.

108. Walter Rauschenbusch to John S. Phillips, 16 May 1917, Box 32, Rauschenbusch Family Collection.

109. W. A. P. Faunce to Walter Rauschenbusch, 22 Jan. 1917, Box 32; Walter Rauschenbusch to W. A. P. Faunce, 11 Feb. 1917, Box 32, Rauschenbusch Family Collection.

110. Walter Rauschenbusch to Washington Gladden, 17 Jan. 1917, Box 32, Rauschenbusch Family Collection; Walter Rauschenbusch to Algernon Crapsey, open letter published in *Rochester Herald,* 23 Aug. 1915; Rauschenbusch to Dores Robinson Sharpe, 21 Apr.

1916; Minus, *Walter Rauschenbusch,* 179–82; Sharpe, *Walter Rauschenbusch,* 378–79. Rauschenbusch was one of Crapsey's few defenders when he was tried a decade earlier for heresy; his letter to Crapsey in 1915 was a reply to a quite formal letter in which Crapsey questioned the soundness of his ideology and theology.

111. Walter Rauschenbusch, *The Social Principles of Jesus* (New York: Association Press, 1916), quotes, 196–97.

112. Walter Rauschenbusch, *A Theology for the Social Gospel* (New York: Macmillan, 1917; reprint, Louisville, Ky.: Westminster John Knox Press, 1997), 4. This section adapts material from Gary Dorrien, *Soul in Society: The Making and Renewal of Social Christianity* (Minneapolis: Fortress Press, 1993), 52–54, and Dorrien, *Reconstructing the Common Good: Theology and the Social Order* (Maryknoll, N.Y.: Orbis Books, 1992), 38–40.

113. Rauschenbusch, *A Theology for the Social Gospel,* 4.

114. Ibid., 7–30, quotes, 279, 25, 24.

115. Ibid., 31–37, quotes, 33, 34; Rauschenbusch, *Christianity and the Social Crisis,* 158.

116. Rauschenbusch, *A Theology for the Social Gospel,* 45–68, quotes, 53, 59, 60.

117. Albrecht Ritschl, *Die christliche Lehre von der Rechtfertigung und Versöhnung* I (4th ed.: Bonn: A. Marcus und Webers Verlag, 1903), 496, 555–56; Friedrich Schleiermacher, *The Christian Faith,* ed. H. R. Mackintosh and J. S. Stewart (2d German ed., 1830; English trans., Edinburgh: T. & T. Clark, 1928), 287–89, quote 288; Rauschenbusch, *A Theology for the Social Gospel,* 92–94.

118. Rauschenbusch, *A Theology for the Social Gospel,* 79.

119. Ibid., 81–92, quotes, 81–82, 86, 87.

120. Ibid., 159–87, quotes, 165, 174, 175.

121. Ibid., quotes, 178, 179.

122. Ibid., 74–75, quote, 74; Rauschenbusch's statement responded to President Wilson's 2 Apr. 1917 address to Congress. On Rochester Seminary's response to the war effort, see *Annual Report, New York Baptist Union for Ministerial Education,* 1917, 32, 37; Minus, *Walter Rauschenbusch,* 183.

123. Gerald Birney Smith, *American Journal of Theology* 22 (Oct. 1918): 583; Charles Clayton Morrison, *The Christian Century* (14 Feb. 1918); James Bishop Thomas, *The Social Preparation* (July 1918), 23; Augustus Hopkins Strong to Walter Rauschenbusch, 28 Dec. 1917, Box 31, Rauschenbusch Family Collection; Minus, *Walter Rauschenbusch,* 187–88.

124. Walter Rauschenbusch to William B. Riley, 24 Mar. 1914, Box 28, Rauschenbusch Family Collection; see Minus, *Walter Rauschenbusch,* 190; William Vance Trollinger Jr., *God's Empire: William Bell Riley and Midwestern Fundamentalism* (Madison, Wis.: University of Wisconsin Press, 1990).

125. L. Hamman to John R. Williams, 28 May 1918, Box 93; Hamman to Williams, 3 June 1918, Box 93; "I have overworked," Walter Rauschenbusch to Herbert White, 18 Jan. 1918, Box 32; Walter Rauschenbusch to Clarence A. Barbour, 25 Feb. 1918, Box 32; Walter Rauschenbusch, "Instructions in Case of My Death," 31 Mar. 1918, Box 87, Rauschenbusch Family Collection.

126. Walter Rauschenbusch to Cornelius Woelfkin, first draft, 25 Apr. 1918; published version, 1 May 1918; Rochester Seminary press release version subtitled "ALWAYS AN AMERICAN," 11 July 1918, Box 91, Rauschenbusch Family Collection.

127. Sharpe, *Walter Rauschenbusch,* 388–92; Clarence A. Barbour to Walter Rauschenbusch, 23 May 1918, Box 91; Cornelius Woelfkin to Walter Rauschenbusch, 1 May 1918, Box 91, Rauschenbusch Family Collection. Woelfkin replied: "I think in my own soul I understood your position all along."

128. Walter Rauschenbusch to Lemuel Call Barnes, 10 May 1918, Box 32, Rauschenbusch Family Collection.

129. Walter Rauschenbusch, "God," Spring 1918; Pauline Rauschenbusch retitled this poem "The Little Gate to God" and circulated it widely; among other places it was published in the *Rochester Theological Seminary Bulletin* (Nov. 1918), 38–40, and by the Federal Council of Churches.

130. Walter Rauschenbusch to W. G. Ballantine, 4 Feb. 1918, Box 93, Rauschenbusch Family Collection; see Sharpe, *Walter Rauschenbusch,* 453; Curtis, *A Consuming Faith,* 114.

131. See Shailer Mathews, *The Faith of Modernism* (New York: Macmillan Co., 1924); Charles S. Macfarland, *Across the Years* (New York: Macmillan Co., 1936); Harry Emerson Fosdick, *Christianity and Progress* (New York: Fleming H. Revell Co., 1922); Justin Wroe Nixon, *The Moral Crisis in Christianity* (New York: Harper & Brothers, 1931); Francis J. McConnell, *Democratic Christianity* (New York: Macmillan Co., 1919).

132. See Dorrien, *Soul in Society*, 54–90.

133. Vida Dutton Scudder, *On Journey* (New York: E. P. Dutton & Co., 1937), 15–30, quote, 30. Aside from Theresa Corcoran's monograph in the Twayne's United States Author Series, the secondary literature on Scudder is very slight. See Theresa Corcoran, *Vida Dutton Scudder* (Boston: Twayne Publishers, 1982); Corcoran, "Vida Dutton Scudder: The Progressive Years," Ph.D. diss., Georgetown University, 1973; Arthur Mann, *Yankee Reformers in an Urban Age* (Cambridge: Harvard University Press, 1954), 217–28; Peter J. Frederick, "Vida Dutton Scudder: The Professor as Social Activist," *New England Quarterly* 43 (Sept. 1970): 407–33; Nan Bauer Maglin, "Vida to Florence: 'Comrade and Companion,'" *Frontiers* 4 (Fall 1979): 13–20; Susan Hill Lindley, *"You Have Stept Out of Your Place": A History of Women and Religion in America* (Louisville, Ky.: Westminster John Knox Press, 1996), 138–41.

134. Scudder, *On Journey*, 33–53.

135. Ibid., 57–74, quotes, 59, 68.

136. Ibid., quotes, 72.

137. Vida Scudder, "Recollections of Ruskin," The Contributor's Club, *Atlantic Monthly* 85 (April 1900): 568–71, quote, 568; Derrick Leon, *Ruskin the Great Victorian* (London: Routledge & Kegan Paul, 1969), 500–509, 540–44; see John Ruskin, *Fors Clavigera*, 4 vols. (New York: J. Wiley & Sons, 1871); Ruskin, *Praeterita* (New York: J. Wiley & Sons, 1886); Scudder, *On Journey*, 78–79; Joan Abse, *John Ruskin, the Passionate Moralist* (New York: Alfred Knopf, 1982); J. D. Hunt, *The Wider Sea: A Life of John Ruskin* (New York: Viking Press, 1982); Roger B. Stein, *Ruskin and Aesthetic Thought in America, 1840–1900* (Cambridge: Harvard University Press, 1967).

138. "Gently put," "could art flourish," and "eagerness and reverence" quotes, Scudder, "Recollections of Ruskin," 569–71; "something within me" quote, Scudder, *On Journey*, 84; see John Ruskin, *Unto This Last* (New York: J. Wiley & Sons, 1866; reprint, New York: Viking Penguin, 1986); Ruskin, *The Ethics of the Dust* (New York: John W. Lovell Co., 1885).

139. Scudder, *On Journey*, 84–85.

140. Ibid., 77–96, "it was at Oxford" quote, 78, "I always needed," 90; Vida Scudder, "The Socialism of Christ," *The Dawn* 3 (18 Dec. 1890): 3–4.

141. Vida D. Scudder, "Socialism and Spiritual Progress—A Speculation," Address to the Society of Christian Socialists, Boston, Mar. 1891; published in *The Andover Review* 16 (July–Dec., 1891): 49–67, quotes, 49, 53; see Edward Bellamy, *Looking Backward, 2000–1887* (New York: Regent Press, 1887).

142. Scudder, "Socialism and Spiritual Progress—A Speculation," quotes, 58, 61, 62.

143. Vida D. Scudder, "The Place of College Settlements," *Andover Review* 18 (Oct. 1892): 339–50, quotes, 345, 347, 349–50; see Scudder, "The College Settlement in New York City," *The Dawn* 2 (Oct. 1890): 230–33; Scudder, "College Settlements," *Holy Cross Magazine* 5 (Jan. 1894): 37–38; Scudder, "College Settlements and Religion," *The Congregationalist* 80 (2 May 1895): 682; Scudder, "The College Settlements Movement," *Smith College Monthly* (May 1900), 447–54; Scudder, "College Settlements and College Women," *Outlook* 70 (19 Apr. 1902): 973–76; Jane Addams, *Philanthropy and Social Progress* (New York: Thomas Y. Crowell & Co., 1893), 1–26.

144. Scudder, "The College Settlements Movement," 447; Scudder, *On Journey*, 110–11, 140–46.

145. See Vida D. Scudder, "The Effect of the Scientific Temper on Modern Poetry," *Andover Review* 8 (Sept. 1887): 225–46; Scudder, "A Shadow of Gold," *Overland Monthly* (Oct. 1887), 380–89; Scudder, "The Poetry of Matthew Arnold," *Andover Review* 10 (Sept. 1888): 232–49; Scudder, "The Curate's Afterthought," *The Christian Union* 39 (17 Jan. 1889): 74–75; Scudder, "Womanhood and Modern Poetry," *Poet Lore* 1 (15 Oct. 1889): 449–65; Scudder, "A Comparative Study of Wordsworth's 'Michael,' Tennyson's 'Enoch Arden,' Browning's 'Andrea del Sarto,'" *Poet Lore* 3 (16 Feb. 1891): 87–93; Scudder,

"Two Italian Poets," *Wellesley Magazine* 3 (12 Jan. 1895): 185–88; Scudder, "Arnold as an Abiding Force," *The Dial* 27 (16 Dec. 1899): 481–82; Scudder, "A Hidden Weakness in Our Democracy," *Atlantic Monthly* 89 (May 1902): 638–44; Scudder, "Democracy and Education," *Atlantic Monthly* 89 (June 1902): 816–22; Scudder, "Democracy and the Church," *Atlantic Monthly* 90 (Oct. 1902): 521–27.

146. *Introduction to the Writings of John Ruskin,* The Students' Series of English Classics, ed. Vida Scudder (Boston: Leach, Shewell & Sanborn, 1890), 11–18, "best results," 18.

147. Vida D. Scudder, *The Life of the Spirit in the Modern English Poets* (Boston: Houghton Mifflin Co., 1895), quotes, 327, 342.

148. Vida D. Scudder, *Social Ideals in English Letters* (Boston: Houghton, Mifflin & Co., 1898), quotes, 275; see Matthew Arnold, *Literature and Dogma* (New York: Macmillan Co., 1902); Thomas Carlyle, *Collected Works: The Centenary Edition of the Works of Thomas Carlyle,* 30 vols. (London: Chapman & Hall, 1896–99).

149. Scudder, *On Journey,* quotes, 127–28, 130, 131.

150. Vida D. Scudder, "Ill-Gotten Gifts to Colleges," *Atlantic Monthly* 86 (Nov. 1890): 679; Horace Scudder to Vida Scudder, 1 May 1900, Scudder Papers, Wellesley College Archives; Caro Lloyd, *Henry Demarest Lloyd: A Biography,* 2 vols. (New York: G. P. Putnam, 1912), 1: 308; Scudder, *On Journey,* 181–82. Scudder published a fictionalized account of this episode in Scudder, *A Listener in Babel: Being a Series of Imaginary Conversations* (Boston: Houghton, Mifflin & Co., 1903), 185–209. See Henry Demarest Lloyd, *Wealth against Commonwealth* (New York: Harper & Brothers, 1894).

151. "Hated" her salary discussion, Scudder, *On Journey,* 178; Vida Scudder to Ellen Pendleton (president of Wellesley Board of Trustees), 15 Mar. 1912, Scudder Papers, Wellesley College Archives; see Vida D. Scudder, *Saint Catherine of Siena as Seen in Her Letters* (London: J. M. Dent & Co., 1905).

152. Vida Scudder to Walter Rauschenbusch, 9 Oct. 1912, Box 93, Rauschenbusch Family Collection.

153. "Miss Scudder's Criticized Speech: Just What She Said at a Citizen's Meeting in Lawrence," *The Boston Common* (9 Mar. 1912), 6–7; editorial, *Boston Evening Transcript* (5 Mar. 1912); Vida Scudder to Walter Rauschenbusch, 21 Sept. 1912, Box 93, Rauschenbusch Family Collection; see Theresa Corcoran, "Vida Dutton Scudder and the Lawrence Textile Strike of 1912," *Essex Institute Historical Collections* 125 (July 1979): 183–95; Corcoran, *Vida Dutton Scudder,* 55–56; Scudder, *On Journey,* 184–90.

154. Scudder to Rauschenbusch, 21 Sept. 1912; see Vida D. Scudder, "Why Join the Party?" *The Intercollegiate Socialist* 2 (Oct.-Nov. 1913): 5–7.

155. Vida D. Scudder to Walter Rauschenbusch, 8 Aug. 1911, Box 93, Rauschenbusch Family Collection.

156. Scudder to Rauschenbusch, 21 Sept. 1912.

157. Vida D. Scudder, "The Social Conscience of the Future," reply to H. W. Inkpin, *The Hibbert Journal* 8 (Oct. 1909): 190–92, quote, 191; see Scudder, "The Social Conscience of the Future: I," *The Hibbert Journal* 7 (Jan. 1909): 314–22; Scudder, "The Social Conscience of the Future: Part II," *The Hibbert Journal* 7 (Apr. 1909): 578–95; Scudder, "For Justice' Sake," *The Survey* 28 (16 Apr. 1912): 76–79.

158. Vida D. Scudder, "Christianity in the Socialist State," *The Hibbert Journal* 8 (Apr. 1910): 562–81, quote, 567.

159. Ibid., quotes, 568–69; see Scudder, "Religion and Socialism," *Harvard Theological Review* 3 (Apr. 1910): 230–47; Scudder, "Socialism as the Basis of Religious Unity," *The Unity of Life: Proceedings and Papers of the National Federation of Religious Liberals Held in New York, April 26–28, 1911,* ed. Henry W. Wilbur (Philadelphia: National Federation of Religious Liberals, 1911); Scudder, "Why Doesn't the Church Turn Socialist?" *The Coming Nation* (29 Mar. 1913), 9–10.

160. Vida D. Scutter, *Socialism and Character* (Boston: Houghton Mifflin Co., 1912), quotes, vi, 4, 15, 5–6; *An Introduction to the Writings of John Ruskin,* 155, see 140.

161. Scudder, *Socialism and Character,* 23–50, quotes, 38, 42, 46, 55.

162. Ibid., quotes, 279, 145.

163. Ibid., 163–73, quotes, 167, 171; Herbert Croly, *The Promise of American Life* (1909; reprint, Boston: Northeastern University Press, 1989), 210–11.

164. Scudder, *Socialism and Character,* 400.

165. Scudder, *On Journey*, quote, 191.
166. Ibid., 278–82, quote, 279; Vida D. Scudder, "Some Signs of Hope," *The Intercollegiate Socialist* 3 (Apr.–May 1915): 6–8; see Scudder, *The Church and the Hour: Reflections of a Socialist Churchwoman* (New York: E. P. Dutton & Co., 1917), especially "Introduction," 1–39, "The Alleged Failure of the Church to Meet the Social Emergency," 40–73, and "Two Letters to *The Masses*," 95–102.
167. Scudder, *On Journey*, quotes, 286, 280; see Theresa Corcoran, "Vida Dutton Scudder: The Impact of World War I on the Radical Woman Professor," *Anglican Theological Review* (spring 1975), 164–181.
168. Vida D. Scudder, "The Doubting Pacifist," *The Yale Review* 6 (July 1917): 738–51; reprinted in Scudder, *The Privilege of Age: Essays Secular and Spiritual* (New York: E. P. Dutton & Co., 1939), 153–67, quotes, 157–58.
169. "Yearly my respect" quote, Scudder, *On Journey*, 235; "confident of the justice" quote, Scudder, "The Doubting Pacifist," 167.
170. Mark G. Toulouse, "Progress and 'relapse': The *Century* and World War I," *The Christian Century* 117 (8 Mar. 2000): 260–62; Linda-Marie Delloff, "The *Century* in Transition, 1916–1922," *A Century of the Century*, eds. Linda-Marie Delloff, Martin E. Marty, Dean Peerman, James M. Wall (Grand Rapids: Wm. B. Eerdmans Co., 1984), 17–26.
171. See Dorrien, *Soul in Society*, 54–58; Paul A Carter, *The Decline and Revival of the Social Gospel: Social and Political Liberalism in American Protestant Churches, 1920–1940* (Ithaca, N.Y.: Cornell University Press, 1954), 17–45; Frederick Lewis Allen, *Only Yesterday: An Informal History of the 1920's* (New York: Harper & Row, 1931; Perennial Classics edition, New York: HarperCollins Publishers, 2000), 13–38; Robert T. Handy, *A Christian America: Protestant Hopes and Historical Realities* (New York: Oxford University Press, 1984), 159–79.
172. Scudder, *On Journey*, 212–13.
173. Vida D. Scudder, *Social Teachings of the Christian Year: Lectures Delivered at the Cambridge Conference, 1918* (New York: E. P. Dutton & Co., 1921), 5–6.
174. Ibid., quotes vi, 11.
175. Vida D. Scudder, "Is the Christian Church Christian?" *The Christian Century* 38 (7 Apr. 1921): 11–14, quotes on League of Industrial Democracy, 13; Scudder, "Property and Creative Joy," *The Christian Century* 39 (9 Nov. 1922): 1392–94, "simple compunction" quotes, 1393.
176. Scudder, *On Journey*, quotes, 300, 301, 302.
177. Vida D. Scudder, "Can the Church Be Saved?" *The Christian Century* 48 (21 Jan. 1931): 82–85, "the support" quote, 83; "My attitude" quotes, Scudder, *On Journey*, 302, 303. See Scudder, "The Christian Way Out," *The Witness* 16 (25 Feb. 1932): 4–5; Scudder, "Christian Conflicts," *Christendom* 4 (Mar. 1934): 12–23.
178. Vida D. Scudder, "The Anglo-Catholic Movement in the Next Century: Its Social Outlook," *The Living Church* 90 (17 Nov. 1934), 589–91, quotes, 589; Reinhold Niebuhr, *Moral Man and Immoral Society: A Study in Ethics and Politics* (New York: Charles Scribner's Sons, 1932).
179. Scudder, "The Anglo-Catholic Movement in the Next Century," quotes, 589, 590; see Scudder, "The Christian Way Out," 5.
180. Scudder, "The Anglo-Catholic Movement in the Next Century," quotes, 590.
181. Vida D. Scudder, "Foemen Vassals: A Pacifist Apologia," *The Protestant* 4 (Oct.–Nov. 1941): 45–54, quotes, 51; see Scudder, *On Journey*, 337–38; Scudder, *The Christian Attitude toward Private Property* (Milwaukee: Morehouse Publishing Co., 1934); Scudder, *My Quest for Reality* (Wellesley: Privately published, 1952), 78–84.
182. Walter Rauschenbusch, "The Belated Races and the Social Problems," *Methodist Review* 40 (Apr. 1914): 258.
183. Rauschenbusch, *Christianizing the Social Order*, 60; Rauschenbusch, *Dare We Be Christians?* 31–32, 58–59. "The Belated Races and the Social Problems" was Rauschenbusch's most extensive treatment of racial injustice as a social issue. On the role of the social gospel movement in America's struggle for racial justice, see Ralph E. Luker, *The Social Gospel in Black and White: American Racial Reform, 1885–1912* (Chapel Hill: University of North Carolina Press, 1991); and Ronald C. White Jr., *Liberty and Justice for All: Racial Reform and the Social Gospel (1877–1925)* (New York: Harper & Row, 1990).

184. Scudder, *On Journey,* quotes, 141, 143.
185. Charles Clayton Morrison, *The Social Gospel and the Christian Cultus* (New York: Harper & Bros., 1933), 13, 15.
186. Ibid., 4–5. This section adapts material from Dorrien, *Soul in Society,* 77–84.
187. Morrison, *The Social Gospel and the Christian Cultus,* 5.
188. Ibid., 5–6.
189. Ibid., 17–20, quote, 20.
190. For a similar account on this theme, see Reinhold Niebuhr, "The Radical Minister and His Church," *Radical Religion* 2 (Winter 1936): 25–27.
191. Morrison, *The Social Gospel and the Christian Cultus,* 44.
192. Ibid., quotes, 44, 101.
193. Ibid., 101–2; see Charles Clayton Morrison, *Can Protestantism Win America?* (New York: Harper & Bros., 1948); Dorrien, *Soul in Society,* 221–28.
194. Morrison, *The Social Gospel and the Christian Cultus,* 243–51.

Chapter 3. Post-Ritschlian Religion

1. Richard J. Storr, *Harper's University: The Beginnings* (Chicago: University of Chicago Press, 1966), 18–20; see Thomas W. Goodspeed, *William Rainey Harper* (Chicago: University of Chicago Press, 1928).
2. Floyd W. Reeves, et al., *University Extension Services* (Chicago: University of Chicago Press, 1933), 129–37; see Joseph E. Gould, *The Chautauqua Movement: An Episode in the Continuing American Revolution* (New York: State University of New York Press, 1961).
3. Charles Harvey Arnold, *Near the Edge of Battle: A Short History of the Divinity School and the "Chicago School of Theology," 1866–1966* (Chicago: Divinity School Association, 1966), 6–8; Storr, *Harper's University,* 15–16.
4. Storr, *Harper's University,* 35–85; Arnold, *Near the Edge of Battle,* 8–10; James P. Wind, *The Bible and the University* (Atlanta: Scholars Press, 1987), 147–61, quote, 178; George M. Marsden, *The Soul of the American University: From Protestant Establishment to Established Nonbelief* (New York: Oxford University Press, 1994), 239–50; see Thomas W. Goodspeed, *A History of the University of Chicago, Founded by John D. Rockefeller, The First Quarter Century (1891–1916)* (Chicago: University of Chicago Press, 1916); Goodspeed, *Ernest DeWitt Burton: A Biographical Sketch* (Chicago: University of Chicago Press, 1926).
5. Charles W. Eliot, "On the Education of Ministers," *Princeton Review* (May 1883), 340–56.
6. Ibid., 349–54. See W. Clark Gilpin, *A Preface to Theology* (Chicago: University of Chicago Press, 1996), 83–85.
7. William Rainey Harper, "The University and Democracy," *The Trend in Higher Education* (Chicago: University of Chicago Press, 1905), 11–12.
8. William Rainey Harper, "Shall the Theological Curriculum Be Modified, and How?" *American Journal of Theology* 3 (Jan. 1899): 45–66, quote, 47.
9. See Arnold, *Near the Edge of Battle,* 9–11; The Decennial Publications of the University of Chicago, *The President's Report* (Chicago: University of Chicago Press, 1903), 156–210; Perry Stackhouse, *Chicago and the Baptists* (Chicago: University of Chicago Press, 1933).
10. "Editorial Announcement," *The American Journal of Theology* 1 (Jan. 1897): v. Harper told Foster's friend C. E. Haworth that he was the "greatest living thinker in his line"; funeral oration by C. E. Haworth for George Burman Foster quoted in *The Huntington (W. Va.) Herald-Dispatch* (30 Nov. 1919); copy in President's Papers, 1889–1925: William Rainey Harper Papers, the University of Chicago Library, Department of Special Collections, Box 34, Folder 2; see Edgar A. Towne, "A 'Singleminded' Theologian: George Burman Foster at Chicago," I, *Foundations* 20 (1977): 36; William Rainey Harper, *Religion and the Higher Life* (Chicago: University of Chicago Press, 1904).
11. On Foster's early life, see Hjalmar W. Johnson, "The Religious Thought of George B. Foster," (Ph.D. diss., Yale University, 1931), 114–49; James H. Tufts, "George Burman Foster," *University Record* 5 (Apr. 1919): 180–85; William Wallace Fenn, "George Bur-

man Foster," *University Record* 5 (Apr. 1919): 172–85; Harvey Arnold, "The Death of God—'06," *Foundations* 10 (Oct.–Dec. 1967): 331–53; Hjalmar W. Johnson, "George Burman Foster," *Encyclopedia of Religion*, ed. Vergilius Ferm (New York: Philosophical Library, 1945), 286–97; Larry E. Axel, "Conflict and Censure: The Religious Odyssey of George Burman Foster," in *Alone Together: Studies in the History of Liberal Religion*, ed. Peter Iver Kaufman and Spencer Lavan (Boston: Beacon Press, 1978), 92. On Foster's Rochester Seminary days, see letters from O. J. White, J. C. Burkett, W. C. Taylor, D. T. Denman, G. W. Hicks, and J. L. McCutcheon to Hjalmar W. Johnson, "The Religious Thought of George B. Foster," 230–37. See Augustus Hopkins Strong, *Systematic Theology*, one-vol. ed. (1907, reprint, Philadelphia: Judson Press, 1954).

12. See George Burman Foster, "Kaftan's Dogmatik," *The American Journal of Theology* 2 (Oct. 1898): 802–27; Towne, "A 'Singleminded' Theologian: George Burman Foster at Chicago," I, 38–43; Alan Gragg, *George Burman Foster: Religious Humanist* (Danville, Va.: Association of Baptist Professors of Religion, 1978), 37–38; Hjalmar W. Johnson, "George Burman Foster," *An Encyclopedia of Religion*, 286–87; Storr, *Harper's University*, 49.

13. Mrs. L. G. Hoover, "A Timeless Life," *West Virginia Review* 6 (Feb. 1929): 158; Gragg, *George Burman Foster: Religious Humanist*, 2; Shailer Mathews, *New Faith for Old: An Autobiography* (New York: Macmillan Co., 1936), quote, 69.

14. *Twenty-Seventh Annual Session of the Baptist Congress* (Chicago: University of Chicago Press, 1909), 106; George Burman Foster, "The Theological Training for the Times," *Biblical World* 9 (Jan. 1897): 24–25.

15. George Burman Foster, "The Influence of the Life and Teaching of Jesus on the Doctrine of God," *Biblical World* 40 (May 1898): 306–18, quote, 310; see Foster, "The Doctrine of the Incarnation, by Robert L. Ottley," *Biblical World* 8 (Dec. 1896): 510.

16. "An Explanation by Dr. Foster," *The Standard* 51 (24 Oct. 1903): 204; see Foster, "Some Modern Estimates of Jesus," *The American Journal of Theology* 9 (Apr. 1905): 334–35; "G. B. Foster to Donald D. Maclaurin," *Standard* 56 (3 July 1909): 1339.

17. George Burman Foster, *Christianity in Its Modern Expression*, ed. Douglas Clyde Macintosh (New York: Macmillan Co., 1921), 31. This posthumously published work was the manuscript of Foster's lectures on dogmatics at the University of Chicago Divinity School in 1905.

18. George Burman Foster, *The Finality of the Christian Religion* (Chicago: University of Chicago Press, 1906), 494.

19. Extemporary remarks of George Burman Foster, quoted in *Sixteenth Annual Session of the Baptist Congress for the Discussion of Current Questions* (New York: Baptist Congress Publishing Co., 1898), 49, 76, 173; see Gragg, *George Burman Foster: Religious Humanist*, 13–14.

20. "So far from" quote, "An Explanation by Dr. Foster," 204; "immanent values" quote, Foster, *Christianity in Its Modern Expression*, 32.

21. J. V. Read to Eri Baker Hulbert, 9 June 1897, University of Chicago Library, Department of Special Collections, Divinity School Correspondence, Office of the Dean's Records, 1890–1942, Box 6, Folder 6; "the religious spirit," Shailer Mathews to Simon P. Cole, September 1900, Box 6, Folder 2; Robert M. Rabb to Shailer Mathews, 11 Jan. 1900, Divinity School Correspondence, Box 6, Folder 6; Shailer Mathews to George Burman Foster, 22 Jan. 1900, Divinity School Correspondence, Box 6, Folder 9.

22. Shailer Mathews to J. Spencer Dickerson, 26 Mar. 1910, Divinity School Correspondence, Box 6, Folder 9; "generally awaited," Bernard E. Meland, "Reflections on the Early Chicago School of Modernism," *American Journal of Theology and Philosophy* 5 (Jan. 1984): 1–12, quote, 7; William Rainey Harper to Eri Baker Hulbert, 3 October 1903, William Rainey Harper Papers, Box 5, Folder 6.

23. George Burman Foster to William Rainey Harper, 5 Sept. 1902, William Rainey Harper Papers, Box 34, Folder 2; William Rainey Harper to Mr. and Mrs. John R. Stetson, 29 Feb. 1904, William Rainey Harper Papers, Box 34, Folder 2. I agree with Edgar A. Towne, against C. Harvey Arnold, that Harper's letter to the Stetsons was a pitch for a philosophy of religion position for Foster. Harper's friends politely turned down his request for financial help, citing legal problems at the university. See John R. Stetson to William Rainer Harper, 12 Mar. 1904, ibid., Box 18, Folder 16; Towne, "A 'Singleminded'

Theologian: George Burman Foster at Chicago," 51–53; C. Harvey Arnold, *God before You and behind You: The Hyde Park Union Church through a Century, 1874–1974* (Chicago: Hyde Park Union Church, 1974), 161.

24. George Burman Foster to William Rainey Harper, 14 Dec. 1904, William Rainey Harper Papers, Box 34, Folder 2. Characteristically, Mathews told this story in a way that smoothed out its rough edges: "President Harper would not consent to dismiss Professor Foster but as there was a vacancy in the department of Systematic Theology he determined to appoint a man who would represent a different type of theology. He finally came to the conclusion that I should be transferred from the department of New Testament to that of theology. I agreed to accept the transfer under certain conditions. When those conditions were known Professor Foster immediately wrote me a courteous letter in which he said he planned to ask to be transferred from the department of Systematic Theology to that of Comparative Religion. This was accomplished and he became thus a member of the faculty of Arts and Literature" (Mathews, *New Faith for Old*, 69).

25. William Rainey Harper to George Burman Foster, 14 Dec. 1904, William Rainey Harper Papers, Box 34, Folder 2; George Burman Foster and Mary Lyon Foster to William Rainey Harper, 15 Feb. 1905, Box 7, Folder 19; see Towne, "A 'Singleminded' Theologian: George Burman Foster at Chicago," I, 54.

26. Mathews, *New Faith for Old*, 68.

27. "The Foster Incident," *Standard* 53 (24 Feb. 1906): 764; "Ministers' Meeting," *Standard* 53 (10 Mar. 1906): 841–42; Johnston Myers, "About That Protest," *Standard* 53 (24 Mar. 1906): 894; "Dr. George B. Foster Replies to His Critics," *Standard* 53 (14 Apr. 1906): 894–97; "Replies to Professor Foster," *Literary Digest* 32 (14 Apr. 1906): 573–75; F. J. Gurney, "The Foster Matter—Per Contra," *Standard* 53 (14 Apr. 1906): 989; Arnold, "The Death of God—'06," 333; William R. Hutchison, *The Modernist Impulse in American Protestantism* (Durham, N.C.: Duke University Press, 1992), 215–18; Nolan R. Best to Shailer Mathews, 30 Nov. 1907, Divinity School Correspondence, Box 6, Folder 1; "assail Christianity" quoted in John Horsch, *Modern Religious Liberalism: The Destructiveness and Irrationality of Modernist Theology* (1st ed., 1921; 3d ed., Chicago: Bible Institute Colportage Association, 1938), 277; Foster quote in Mathews, *New Faith for Old*, 68.

28. Foster, *The Finality of the Christian Religion*, 6–7, 21.

29. Ibid., 9, 16. See Auguste Sabatier, *Religions of Authority and the Religion of the Spirit*, trans. Louise Seymour Houghton (New York: McClure, Phillips & Co., 1904); Sabatier, *Outlines of a Philosophy of Religion Based on Psychology and History* (New York: James Pott & Co., 1910).

30. Foster, *The Finality of the Christian Religion*, 18, xii–xiii; see David Friedrich Strauss, *The Old Faith and the New*, trans. Mathilde Blind (New York: Henry Holt, 1873), 9.

31. Foster, *The Finality of the Christian Religion*, 87.

32. Ibid., 128–32, 137, 142.

33. Ibid., 136–37.

34. Ibid., 184; see Borden Parker Bowne, *Theory of Thought and Knowledge* (New York: American Book Co., 1897); Bowne, *Theism* (New York: American Book Co., 1902).

35. Foster, *The Finality of the Christian Religion*, 184–85.

36. Hermann Lotze, *Microcosmus: An Essay Concerning Man and His Relation to the World*, 2 vols., trans. Elizabeth Hamilton and Emily E. C. Jones (Edinburgh: T. & T. Clark, 1888), I:xvi; Foster, *The Finality of the Christian Religion*, 227, 232, 211.

37. Shailer Mathews, *The Social Teaching of Jesus: An Essay in Christian Sociology* (reprint, 1910; New York: Macmillan, 1897), reprint, 1910, 54; Mathews, *The Messianic Hope in the New Testament* (Chicago: University of Chicago Press, 1905), 81–85; see Willibald Beyschlag, *Leben Jesu*, 2 vols. (Halle: E. Strien, 1885); Beyschlag, *Neutestamentliche Theologie*, 2 vols. (Halle: E. Strien, 1891); Otto Schmoller, *Die Lehre vom Reiche Gottes in den Schriften des Neuen Testaments* (Leiden: E. J. Brill, 1891); Ernst Issel, *Die Lehre vom Reiche Gottes im Neuen Testament* (Leiden: E. J. Brill, 1891); Johannes Weiss, *Die Predigt Jesu von Reiche Gottes* (Göttingen: Vandenhoeck & Ruprecht, 1892); Frederick C. Grant, "Ethics and Eschatology in the Teachings of Jesus," *Journal of Religion* 22 (Oct. 1942): 358–59.

38. Foster, *The Finality of the Christian Religion*, 249.

39. Ibid., 249–50, 414–15.

40. Ibid., 260.
41. Ibid., 273–75.
42. Ibid., 403–4.
43. Ibid., 396–99.
44. Ibid., 187.
45. Ibid., 480–81.
46. Ibid., 481, closing quote, 405.
47. Ibid., 185–86.
48. George Burman Foster, "Pragmatism and Knowledge," *American Journal of Theology* 11 (Oct. 1907): 591–96, quote, 591; Foster, *The Finality of the Christian Religion*, 177; see Tufts, "George Burman Foster," 182; Hutchison, *The Modernist Impulse in American Protestantism*, 218. Foster mentioned in the preface to the second edition of *The Finality of the Christian Religion* (1909) that the new situation in philosophy compelled him to rewrite his projected companion volume.
49. George Burman Foster, *The Function of Religion in Man's Struggle for Existence* (Chicago: University of Chicago Press, 1909), xi, 79–84.
50. Ibid., 84, 86, 57, 88.
51. Ibid., 90–91, 100–102, 108–9.
52. Ibid., 205, 225–38, quote, 142–43.
53. Ibid., 108, 216.
54. See Darnell Rucker, *The Chicago Pragmatists* (Minneapolis: University of Minnesota Press, 1969), 3–56, 107–31; Katherine C. Mayhew and Anna C. Edwards, *The Dewey School* (New York: D. Appleton-Century, 1936); James Hayden Tufts, "Ethical Value," *Journal of Philosophy, Psychology, and Scientific Methods* 5 (10 Sept. 1908): 517–22; John Dewey and James Hayden Tufts, *Ethics* (New York: Henry Holt, 1908); Tufts, "George Burman Foster," *University Record* 5 (Apr. 1919): 180–85.
55. Edward Scribner Ames, *The Psychology of Religious Experience* (Boston: Houghton Mifflin, 1910); see Ames, "Theology from the Standpoint of Functional Psychology," *American Journal of Theology* 10 (Apr. 1906): 221–38; Ames, *Beyond Theology: The Autobiography of Edward Scribner Ames*, ed. Van Meter Ames (Chicago: University of Chicago Press, 1959); Irving King, *The Differentiation of the Religious Consciousness* (New York: Macmillan Co., 1905); Frederick G. Henke, *The Psychology of Ritualism* (Chicago: University of Chicago Press, 1910); Henke, "Advantages Accruing from the Functional View of Religion," *Biblical World* 40 (Dec. 1912): 366–73.
56. On the Chicago tradition of theological empiricism, see Bernard E. Meland, "The Empirical Tradition in Theology at Chicago," *The Future of Empirical Theology*, ed. Bernard E. Meland (Chicago: University of Chicago Press, 1969), 1–62; Daniel Day Williams, "Tradition and Experience in American Theology," in *The Shaping of American Religion*, ed. James Ward Smith and A. Leland Jamison (Princeton: Princeton University Press, 1961), 443–95; William J. Hynes, *Shirley Jackson Case and the Chicago School: The Socio-Historical Method* (Chico, Calif.: Scholars Press, 1981); Arnold, *Near the Edge of Battle*; Randolph Crump Miller, *The American Spirit in Theology* (Philadelphia: United Church Press, 1974), 19–139.
57. See "The Case of Professor Foster," *Standard* 56 (19 June 1909): 1280; "Some Foster Correspondence," *Standard* 56 (3 July 1909): 1339; "The Battle of the Jargons," *Outlook* 92 (3 July 1909): 530; "Fostering Peace," *Standard* 56 (24 July 1909): 1416; Edgar A. Towne, "A 'Singleminded' Theologian: George Burman Foster at Chicago," II, *Foundations* 20 (1977): 168–70; Myers quoted in Towne, 167, from article in *The Chicago Socialist*, 14 June 1909; Arnold, "The Death of God—'06," 334–35; Ernest R. Sandeen, *The Roots of Fundamentalism: British and American Millenarianism 1800–1930* (Chicago: University of Chicago Press, 1970), 19.
58. Lyman Stewart to A. C. Dixon, 24 July 1915, cited in Sandeen, *Roots of Fundamentalism*, 188–89.
59. "G. B. Foster to Donald D. MacLaurin," 1339; see citation and discussion in Towne, "A 'Singleminded' Theologian: George Burman Foster at Chicago," II, 170.
60. Harry Pratt Judson to Ernest Dewitt Burton, 4 Aug. 1909, President's Papers, Box 42, Folder 15; Towne, "A 'Singleminded' Theologian: George Burman Foster at Chicago," II, 170.

61. George Burman Foster, "Concerning the Religious Basis of Ethics," *American Journal of Theology* 12 (Apr. 1908): 211–30, quotes, 219, 226–27.

62. Mathews, *New Faith for Old*, 69.

63. George Burman Foster, "A Homely Meditation, without Subtlety, on the Tragedy of the Steamship Titanic," *Chicago Sunday Tribune* 52, no. 16 (21 Apr. 1912): 4.

64. Foster to Macintosh, 1 July 1912, reprinted in Douglas Clyde Macintosh, *The Problem of Religious Knowledge* (New York: Harper & Brothers, 1940), 106; see Douglas Clyde Macintosh, *The Problem of Knowledge* (New York: Macmillan Co., 1915); Macintosh, *Theology as an Empirical Science* (New York: Macmillan Co., 1919).

65. George Burman Foster, "What Are the Basic Principles of Modern Theology?" in *Proceedings of the Baptist Congress at Ithaca, New York, 1912*, 30 (Chicago: University of Chicago Press, 1912), 10–21, 66–68, 99–101; Macintosh's 1911 dissertation at the University of Chicago was titled *The Reaction against Metaphysics in Theology*. Excerpts from both works reprinted in Macintosh, *The Problem of Religious Knowledge*, 107–8.

66. George Burman Foster, "The Contribution of Critical Scholarship to Ministerial Efficiency," in *A Guide to the Study of the Christian Religion*, ed. Gerald Birney Smith (Chicago: University of Chicago Press, 1916), 729–51, quotes, 739, 742; closing quote in Macintosh, *The Problem of Religious Knowledge*, 110.

67. Student notes of 1917 and 1918 published in Macintosh, *The Problem of Religious Knowledge*, 112–13; George Burman Foster, *Friedrich Nietzsche*, ed. Curtis Reese (New York: Macmillan Co., 1931), 211.

68. Student notes cited in Macintosh, *The Problem of Religious Knowledge*, 114.

69. George Burman Foster, "Revealed Religion," reprinted in Johnson, "The Religious Thought of George B. Foster," 754.

70. George Burman Foster to Edward Scribner Ames, 9 Oct. 1918, reprinted in Johnson, "The Religious Thought of George B. Foster," 645; and Macintosh, *The Problem of Religious Knowledge*, 114.

71. George Burman Foster, review of *The New Orthodoxy*, by Edward Scribner Ames, *Christian Century* 35 (24 Oct. 1918): 17–18. Foster read most of this review to his class on 20 June 1918.

72. William Wallace Fenn, "Professor Foster as a Theologian," *University Record* 5 (Apr. 1919): 177; J. M. Powis Smith, "Professor Foster as a Man," *University Record* 5 (Apr. 1919): 173; Douglas Clyde Macintosh, "Editor's Preface," in George Burman Foster, *Christianity in its Modern Expression*, ed. Douglas Clyde Macintosh (New York: Macmillan Co., 1921), vi.; Arnold, "The Death of God—'06," 349.

73. Clarence Darrow to Hjalmar Johnson, 1 Feb. 1931, reprinted in Johnson, "The Religious Thought of George B. Foster," 651; closing quote in J. V. Nash, "A Twentieth Century Emancipator," *Open Court* 36 (June 1922): 328; see Towne, "A 'Singleminded' Theologian: George Burman Foster at Chicago," 172; Arnold, "The Death of God—'06," 347–49.

74. Douglas Clyde Macintosh, "Toward a New Untraditional Orthodoxy," in *Contemporary American Theology: Theological Autobiographies*, two vols., ed. Vergilius Ferm (New York: Round Table Press, 1932), 277–319, quotes, 311.

75. Ibid., 310; the lectures volume was *Christianity in its Modern Expression*. See Bernard E. Meland, "The Empirical Tradition in Theology at Chicago," 1–62, in *The Empirical Theology of Henry Nelson Wieman*, ed. Robert W. Bretall (New York: Macmillan Co., 1963).

76. See Towne, "A 'Singleminded' Theologian: George Burman Foster at Chicago," I–II; Towne, "Introduction to George Burman Foster," in *The Chicago School of Theology— Pioneers in Religious Inquiry*, ed. W. Creighton Peden and Jerome A. Stone (Lewiston, N.Y.: Edwin Mellen Press, 1996), 1:3–5; Arnold, *Near the Edge of Battle*, 28–35; Axel, "Conflict and Censure: The Religious Odyssey of George Burman Foster," 91–101; Gragg, *George Burman Foster: Religious Humanist*, 59–66; W. Creighton Peden, "The Radical Tradition: Paine and Foster," *American Journal of Theology and Philosophy* 5 (Jan. 1984): 28–32; Peden, *The Chicago School: Voices in Liberal Religious Thought* (Bristol, Ind.: Wyndham Hall Press, 1987), 24–43.

77. Clarence Darrow to Hjalmar Johnson, 25 Feb. 1931, reprinted in Johnson, "The Religious Thought of George B. Foster," 651.

78. Macintosh, *The Problem of Religious Knowledge*, 112, 114–15; Fenn quote, 115.

79. Ibid., 115; see Fenn, "Professor Foster as a Theologian," 177–80.

80. Shailer Mathews, "Theology as Group Belief," in *Contemporary American Theology: Theological Autobiographies*, 2d series, ed. Vergilius Ferm (New York: Round Table Press, 1933), quotes, 163–64; Mathews, *New Faith for Old*, 1–14. For secondary literature on Mathews's life, see Robert Eldon Mathews, "Shailer Mathews: A Biographical Note," in *The Process of Religion: Essays in Honor of Dean Shailer Mathews*, ed. Miles H. Krumbine (New York: Macmillan Co., 1933), 3–14; *Shailer Mathews: Selections from the Memorial Service Held in Joseph Bond Chapel*, ed. Edwin Aubrey (Chicago: University of Chicago Press, 1941); Robert Wesley Clark, "The Contribution of Shailer Mathews to the Social Movement in American Protestantism," Ph.D. diss. (Southern Baptist Seminary, New Orleans, La., 1960); Bernard Meland, "Shailer Mathews," in *Dictionary of American Biography*, supp. III: 1941–1945, ed. Edward T. James (New York: Scribner's, 1973), 514–16.

81. Mathews, "Theology as Group Belief," 164–65; see Mathews, *New Faith for Old*, 15–23; Theo Suranye-Unger, "Economic Thought: The Historical School," *International Encyclopedia of the Social Sciences*, ed. David L. Sills (New York: Macmillan Co., 1968), 4: 454–57.

82. Mathews, *New Faith for Old*, 25–26, 28; see Mathews, "Theology as Group Belief," 165–66.

83. Mathews, *New Faith for Old*, 32–33, 39–43; Mathews, "Theology as Group Belief," 166–67, quote, 167; closing quote, Mathews, *New Faith for Old*, 42; see Kenneth Smith and Leonard Sweet, "Shailer Mathews: A Chapter in the Social Gospel Movement," *Foundations* 19 (1976): 227–29.

84. Mathews, *New Faith for Old*, 43–44; see Charles F. Thwing, *The American and the German University* (New York: Macmillan Co., 1928).

85. See Richard T. Ely, *The Labor Movement in America* (New York: 1886); Ely, *Social Aspects of Christianity, and Other Essays* (New York: 1889); Ely, *Outlines of Economics* (New York: 1893); Ely, "The Past and the Present of Political Economy," *Johns Hopkins University Studies in Historical and Political Science* 2 (1884): 64–67.

86. Mathews, *New Faith for Old*, 45–46, 49, quote, 45.

87. Ibid., 50–51; Mathews, "Theology as Group Belief," 167.

88. Mathews, *New Faith for Old*, 50–51.

89. Shailer Mathews, "Christian Sociology," *American Journal of Sociology* 1 (1895–96): 69–78, 94, 182, 359–60, 457–72, 604–17, 771–84; Mathews, "Christian Sociology," *American Journal of Sociology* 2 (1896–97): 108–17, 274–87, 416–32. On Mathews's early thinking, see William D. Lindsey, *Shailer Mathews's Lives of Jesus: The Search for a Theological Foundation for the Social Gospel* (Albany, N.Y.: State University of New York Press, 1997), 35–47; Peden, *The Chicago School: Voices in Liberal Religious Thought*, 12–13; Peden, "Shailer Mathews," *Makers of Christian Theology in America*, eds. Mark G. Toulouse and James O. Duke (Nashville: Abingdon Press, 1997), 392–94; Leslie A. Muray, "Introduction to Mathews," *The Chicago School of Theology—Pioneers in Religious Inquiry*, I, 119–21; Kenneth Cauthen, *The Impact of American Religious Liberalism* (New York: Harper & Row, 1962), 147–48; Arnold, *Near the Edge of Battle*, 35–38.

90. Mathews, *The Social Teaching of Jesus*, 8, 40.

91. Ibid., 40–43, quote, 40.

92. Ibid., 40–53, quote, 52.

93. Ibid., 54–61, 115–31, 199–201, quotes, 130, 201.

94. See Charles M. Sheldon, *In His Steps* (1st ed. 1896; reprint, Grand Rapids: Zondervan, 1967); Shailer Mathews, *Jesus on Social Institutions* (New York: Macmillan Co., 1928; reprint, Philadelphia: Fortress Press, 1971). *In His Steps* has sold over 60 million copies.

95. Gustav Ecke, *Die theologische Schule Albrecht Ritschls und die Evangelische Kirche der Gegenwart* (Berlin: Reuther & Reichard, 1897), 74–78; see Johannes Rathje, *Die Welt des freien Protestantismus: Ein Beitrag zur deutsch-evangelischen Geistesgeschichte, dargestellt an Leben und Werk von Martin Rade* (Stuttgart: Ehrenfried Klotz Verlag, 1952), 102–3; George Rupp, *Culture-Protestantism: German Liberal Theology at the Turn of the Twentieth Century* (Atlanta: Scholars Press, 1977), 15–55.

96. See Mathews, *The Social Teaching of Jesus*, 47; Lindsey, *Shailer Mathews's Lives of Jesus*, 101.

97. Shailer Mathews, "The Social Teaching of Paul, 1: The Social Content of Early Messianism," *Biblical World* 19 (1902): 34–46; "2: The Social Content of Messianism in New Testament Times," 113–21; "3: The Apocalyptic Messianism of the Pharisees," 178–89; Mathews, "The Gospel and the Modern Man," *Christendom* 1 (1903): 300–302, 352–53, 399–401, 446–49, 489–91, 537–39, quotes, 352, 537; see Lindsey, *Shailer Mathews's Lives of Jesus,* 131–32.

98. Shailer Mathews, *The Messianic Hope in the New Testament* (Chicago: University of Chicago Press, 1905), 68.

99. Ibid., 69.

100. Ibid., closing quote, 82; "broke utterly," 108.

101. Ibid., 320; see Albert Schweitzer, *The Quest of the Historical Jesus: A Critical Study of Its Progress from Reimarus to Wrede,* trans. W. Montgomery (New York: Macmillan Co., 1910).

102. For a collection of his editorials for *World Today,* see Shailer Mathews, *The Making of To-Morrow: Interpretations of the World To-Day* (New York: Eaton & Mains, 1913).

103. See Shirley Jackson Case, "Education in Liberalism," *Contemporary American Theology: Theological Autobiographies,* vol. 1, ed. Vergilius Ferm (New York: Round Table Press, 1932), 107–25; Hynes, *Shirley Jackson Case and the Chicago School: The Socio-Historical Method.*

104. See *The Woman's Citizen's Library: A Systematic Course of Reading in Preparation for the Larger Citizenship,* 12 vols., ed. Shailer Mathews (Chicago: Civics Society, 1913–14); for his accounts of his prewar civic and institutional service, see Mathews, *New Faith for Old,* 75–80, 106–18, 152–70.

105. "We don't read," Meland, "Reflections on the Early Chicago School of Modernism," quote, 9; "at once critical," Mathews, *The Messianic Hope in the New Testament,* 321; see Shailer Mathews, *The French Revolution—A Sketch* (New York: Longmans, Green & Co., 1901).

106. See Shailer Mathews, *The Church and the Changing Order* (New York: Macmillan Co., 1909), 92, 115; Mathews, *The Social Gospel* (Philadelphia: American Baptist Publishing Society, 1909), 19–22; Mathews, *The Individual and the Social Gospel* (New York: Missionary Education Movement of the United States and Canada, 1914), 20, 59, 62, 81–82; Mathews, "The Social Optimism of Faith in a Divine Jesus," *Biblical World* 43 (1914): 154; for a good discussion of this issue, see Lindsey, *Shailer Mathews's Lives of Jesus,* 150–51.

107. Shailer Mathews, "The Kingdom of God," *Biblical World* 35 (1910): 420–427; Mathews, *The Church and the Changing Order,* 16–18, 49–57, 81–90.

108. Mathews, *The Church and the Changing Order,* quotes, 178, 89.

109. Shailer Mathews, "The Struggle between the Natural and Spiritual Order as Described in the Gospel of John," *Biblical World* 42 (1913): 31–32; Mathews, "A Positive Method for an Evangelical Theology," *American Journal of Theology* 13 (1909): 43; Mathews, review of *Christianizing the Social Order,* by Walter Rauschenbusch, *Biblical World* 41 (1916): 138; Henry Churchill King to Shailer Mathews, 3 Dec. 1906, Divinity School Correspondence, Box 6, Folder 9; Shailer Mathews to Henry Churchill King, 5 Dec. 1906, Divinity School Correspondence, Box 6, Folder 9; see Lindsey, *Shailer Mathews's Lives of Jesus,* 144.

110. Mathews, Review of *Christianizing the Social Order,* 138–39; Mathews, *New Faith for Old,* quote, 289; see Mathews, *The Making of To-Morrow,* 90–105.

111. "If we refuse," Mathews to Dickerson, 26 Mar. 1910; Mathews, *The Church and the Changing Order,* 171–72, 173, 175.

112. Shailer Mathews, *The Social Gospel* (New York: Macmillan Co., 1910), 11–13.

113. Ibid., 121–22.

114. Mathews, *The Individual and the Social Gospel,* 68.

115. Shailer Mathews, *The Gospel and the Modern Man* (New York: Macmillan Co., 1910), 111–12.

116. Shirley Jackson Case, "The Religious Meaning of the Past," *Journal of Religion* 4 (1924): 586.

117. Mathews, "The Historical Study of Religion," in *A Guide to the Study of the Christian*

Religion, 21–79, quotes, 32; Shirley Jackson Case, "The Study of Early Christianity," ibid., 241–326, quote, 244.

118. Case, "Education in Liberalism," quotes, 114, 117.

119. Shirley Jackson Case, *The Social Origins of Christianity* (Chicago: University of Chicago Press, 1923), 79–116; Case, "The Rise of Christian Messianism," in *Studies in Early Christianity,* ed. Shirley Jackson Case (New York: The Century, 1928), 313–32; Case, *Jesus through the Centuries* (Chicago: University of Chicago Press, 1932); Case, *The Evolution of Early Christianity: A Genetic Study of First-Century Christianity in Relation to Its Religious Environment* (Chicago: University of Chicago Press, 1914); Case, *Christianity in a Changing World* (New York: Harper & Brothers, 1941), quote, 40; see William J. Hynes, "Introduction to Shirley Jackson Case," in *The Chicago School of Theology,* I.

120. Shailer Mathews, "Theology and the Social Mind," *Biblical World* 46 (Oct. 1915): 204–48, quotes, 240, 242; see Lester Ward, *Dynamic Sociology.* Mathews and Albion Small were fervent admirers of Ward's book.

121. Mathews, "Theology and the Social Mind," 243. For his subsequent elaborations of this argument, see Mathews, "The Historical Study of Religion," *A Guide to the Study of the Christian Religion,* 21–79; Mathews, *The Spiritual Interpretation of History* (Cambridge: Harvard University Press, 1916); and Mathews, "Theology from the Point of View of Social Psychology," *Journal of Religion* 3 (July 1923): 337–51.

122. Mathews, "Theology and the Social Mind," quotes, 243.

123. Ibid., 244, 245.

124. Ibid., 246–48, quotes, 247, 248.

125. Mathews, *The Individual and the Social Gospel,* 70.

126. Ibid., 66–67.

127. Mathews, "Theology as Group Belief," quote, 175–76; see Mathews, *New Faith for Old,* 196–206.

128. See Hutchison, *The Modernist Impulse in American Protestantism,* 238–39.

129. Mathews, *New Faith for Old,* 207–8.

130. Shailer Mathews, *Patriotism and Religion* (New York: Macmillan Co., 1918), 4, 39. This section adapts material from Gary Dorrien, *Soul in Society: The Making and Renewal of Social Christianity* (Minneapolis: Fortress Press, 1995), 56–57. On Barth and German "war experience" theology, see Dorrien, *The Barthian Revolt in Modern Theology: Theology without Weapons* (Louisville, Ky.: Westminster John Knox, 2000), 36–42.

131. Mathews, *Patriotism and Religion,* 75–76, 136–46.

132. Mathews, *New Faith for Old,* 206–7, quotes, 207.

133. Mathews, "Theology as Group Belief," quote, 176; for a more extensive discussion, see Dorrien, *Soul in Society,* 57–60.

134. Shailer Mathews, *Will Christ Come Again?* (Chicago: American Institute of Sacred Literature, 1917); Shirley Jackson Case, *The Truth about the Book of Revelation* (Chicago: American Institute of Sacred Literature, 1917); see Case, *The Millennial Hope: A Phase of War-Time Thinking* (Chicago: University of Chicago Press, 1918).

135. I. M. Haldeman, *Professor Shailer Mathews' Burlesque on the Second Coming of Our Lord* (New York: Privately printed, n.d.); Horsch, *Modern Religious Liberalism: The Destructiveness and Irrationality of Modern Theology,* 266–78; see Shailer Mathews, "Why I Believe in the Deity of Christ," *Standard* 66 (1919): 630–31; Mathews, "How Science Helps Our Faith," *Baptist* 3 (1922): 1108–9.

136. See Harry Emerson Fosdick, "Shall the Fundamentalists Win?" in *American Protestant Thought: The Liberal Era,* ed. William R. Hutchison (New York: Harper & Row, 1968), 170–81; J. Gresham Machen, *Christianity and Liberalism* (New York: Macmillan Co., 1923). The term "fundamentalist" was coined by Baptist conservative Curtis Lee Laws in 1920 as a signifier for the traditionalist Christian movement associated with the famous twelve-volume series, *The Fundamentals.* See R. A. Torrey, A. C. Dixon, et al., *The Fundamentals: A Testimony to the Truth,* 4 vols. (1917; reprint, Grand Rapids: Baker Book House, 1993).

137. Shailer Mathews, *The Faith of Modernism* (New York: Macmillan Co., 1924; reprint, New York: AMS Press, 1969), 5.

138. Ibid., 10.
139. Ibid., 13, closing quote, 16.
140. Ibid., 22, 34; see Mathews, *The Church and the Changing Order,* 177–79.
141. Mathews, *The Faith of Modernism,* 23, 35.
142. Ibid., 144–46, quote, 35.
143. Ibid., 180.
144. Mathews, *The Making of To-Morrow,* "social evolution" quote, 109; see Bernard E. Meland, "Some Unresolved Issues in Theology," *Journal of Religion* 24 (Oct. 1944): 234–37.
145. Mathews, *Jesus on Social Institutions,* 148; Shirley Jackson Case, *Jesus: A New Biography* (Chicago: University of Chicago Press, 1927), quote, 110.
146. Shailer Mathews, "Introduction," in *Contributions of Science to Religion,* ed. Shailer Mathews et al. (New York: D. Appleton & Co., 1924), 11.
147. Mathews, "Introduction," "The Evolution of Religion," "Scientific Method and Religion," "Science Justifies the Religious Life," and "Science Gives Content to Religious Thought," in *Contributions of Science to Religion,* 1–13, 351–77, 378–90, 391–402, 403–22; quotes, 11, 403.
148. Shailer Mathews, *The Atonement and the Social Process* (New York: Macmillan Co., 1930), 9.
149. Ibid., 193.
150. Ibid., 193–94, 205.
151. Shailer Mathews, *The Growth of the Idea of God* (New York: Macmillan Co., 1931), 3–4.
152. Ibid., 11, 214.
153. Ibid., 215, 218–19.
154. Ibid., 219–28, quotes, 219, 226, 228.
155. Shailer Mathews, *Is God Emeritus?* (New York: Macmillan Co., 1940), 19–38, quotes, 27, 34.
156. Mathews, *The Growth of the Idea of God,* 232.
157. Mathews, *Is God Emeritus?* 90, 92.
158. Shailer Mathews, "Unrepentant Liberalism," *American Scholar* 7 (July 1938): 296–308, quotes, 296.
159. Ibid., quote, 298; see Shailer Mathews, *Creative Christianity* (Nashville: Cokesbury Press, 1935), 7.
160. Mathews, "Unrepentant Liberalism," quotes, 301.
161. Ibid., quote, 302; Mathews, *New Faith for Old,* closing quote, 219.
162. Mathews, *New Faith for Old,* 296.
163. See Bernard E. Meland, "Introduction: The Empirical Tradition in Theology at Chicago," in *The Future of Empirical Theology,* 1–62; Randolph Crump Miller, *The American Spirit in Theology* (Philadelphia: United Church Press, 1974).

Chapter 4. In the Spirit of William James

1. William James, *Pragmatism: A New Name for Some Old Ways of Thinking and The Meaning of Truth* (1st ed., 1907; reprint, Cambridge: Harvard University Press, 1978), 27–44, 95–113, "attitude of looking" quote, 32; "carefully posited," 272; closing quote, 97; see Charles Sanders Peirce, "The Fixation of Belief," *Popular Science Monthly* 12 (Nov. 1877): 1–15; reprinted in Peirce, *Charles S. Peirce: Selected Writings,* ed. Philip P. Wiener (New York: Dover Publications, 1958), 91–112; see Peirce, "How to Make Our Ideas Clear," ibid., 113–36.
2. William James, *Essays in Radical Empiricism* (New York: Longmans, Green & Co., 1912), 95; on the relation between James and Peirce, see Christopher Hookway, "Logical Principles and Philosophical Attitudes: Peirce's Response to James's Pragmatism," *The Cambridge Companion to William James,* ed. Ruth Putnam (Cambridge: Cambridge University Press, 1997), 145–65; though Hookway overstates the antirealist aspects of James's pragmatism. For a corrective reading that emphasizes James's "natural realism," without denying the antirealist aspects, see Hilary Putnam, *The Revival of Pragmatism: New Essays on Social Thought, Law, and Culture* (Durham, N.C.: Duke University Press, 1998), 37–53.

3. James, *Essays in Radical Empiricism*, 100–116, quote, 107.
4. Ibid., 42.
5. William James, *Some Problems of Philosophy: A Beginning of an Introduction to Philosophy* (New York: Longmans, Green & Co., 1911), 35–44; see James, *Pragmatism: A New Name for Some Old Ways of Thinking*, 9–26.
6. William James, *The Will to Believe and Other Essays in Popular Philosophy* (New York: Longmans, Green & Co., 1897), vii–viii.
7. James, *The Meaning of Truth*, 172.
8. Ibid., 172–73; see James, *Essays in Radical Empiricism*, 36, 41–61; F. H. Bradley, *Appearance and Reality: A Metaphysical Essay* (Oxford: Oxford University Press, 1893); Bradley, *Essays on Truth and Reality* (Oxford: Oxford University Press, 1914); John M. E. McTaggart, *Studies in the Hegelian Dialectic* (1896; reprint, New York: Russell & Russell, 1964); Josiah Royce, *The Religious Aspect of Philosophy: A Critique of the Bases of Conduct and of Faith* (Boston: Houghton, Mifflin Co., 1885); Royce, *The World and the Individual*, 2 vols. (New York: Macmillan Co., 1899, 1901); Royce, *The Spirit of Modern Philosophy* (Boston: Houghton Mifflin Co., 1892).
9. James, *The Will to Believe and Other Essays in Popular Philosophy*, 25; see W. K. Clifford, "The Ethics of Belief," *Contemporary Review* 29 (1876–77): 289–309, reprinted in Clifford, *Lectures and Essays*, 2 vols., ed. Stephen and Frederick Pollock (London: Macmillan Co., 1879), 182–86; David A. Hollinger, "James, Clifford, and the Scientific Conscience," in *The Cambridge Companion to William James*, 69–83; Gail Kennedy, "Pragmatism, Pragmaticism, and the Will to Believe—A Reconsideration," *Journal of Philosophy* 55 (July 1958): 578–88; Richard M. Gale, "William James and the Ethics of Belief," *American Philosophical Quarterly* 17 (1980): 1–14.
10. James, *The Will to Believe and Other Essays in Popular Philosophy*, quotes, 20, 97; see Ralph Barton Perry, *In the Spirit of William James* (New Haven: Yale University Press, 1938), 170–208; Patrick K. Dooley, "The Nature of Belief: The Proper Context for James' 'The Will to Believe,'" *Transactions of the Charles S. Peirce Society* 8 (summer 1972): 141–51; Robert J. O'Connell, S.J., *William James on the Courage to Believe* (New York: Fordham University Press, 1997). O'Connell dissects the relation between James's "will to believe" and Pascal's "wager" and contends that James's argument works primarily to validate select overbeliefs.
11. William James, *The Varieties of Religious Experience* (New York: Longmans, Green & Co., 1902), quotes, 45, 46; for critiques of James's shortcomings regarding the social nature of Christianity and religion, Nicholas Lash, *Easter in Ordinary: Reflections of Human Experience and the Knowledge of God* (Charlottesville: University Press of Virginia, 1988), 52–58; Charles Taylor, "Transformations in Religious Experience: The William James Lecture," *Harvard Divinity Bulletin* 28, no. 4 (1999): 18–20; Stanley Hauerwas, *With the Grain of the Universe: The Church's Witness and Natural Theology* (Grand Rapids: Brazos Press, 2001), 65–81.
12. James, *The Varieties of Religious Experience*, 136–48; see Ralph Barton Perry, *The Thought and Character of William James*, (Boston: Little, Brown, 1935; reprint, Cambridge: Harvard University Press, 1948), 325–26; 359–60; Linda Simon, *Genuine Reality: A Life of William James* (New York: Harcourt, Brace & Co., 1998), 309–13; Louis Menand, "William James and the Case of the Epileptic Patient," *New York Review of Books* 45 (17 Dec. 1998): 81–93; Richard R. Niebuhr, "William James on Religious Experience," in *The Cambridge Companion to William James*, 214–36.
13. James, *Pragmatism: A New Name for Some Old Ways of Thinking*, 13.
14. See Richard M. Gale, *The Divided Self of William James* (New York: Cambridge University Press, 1999).
15. James, *The Varieties of Religious Experience*, 406–7.
16. Ibid., 407–8.
17. Ibid., 415.
18. James to Peabody quoted in Perry, *The Thought and Character of William James*, 259; William James, *A Pluralistic Universe* (New York: Longmans, Green & Co., 1909), "page upon page," 25–26.
19. James, *The Varieties of Religious Experience*, 370.
20. James, *Essays in Radical Empiricism*, 194.

21. George Santayana, *Character and Opinion in the United States* (New York: Charles Scribner's Sons, 1920), 77; see Linda Simon, *William James Remembered* (Lincoln, Neb.: University of Nebraska Press, 1996), 89–105.

22. William James to James Leuba, 1914, cited in Perry, *The Thought and Character of William James,* 266.

23. William James to George A. Gordon, 24 Jan. 1907, reprinted in George A. Gordon, *My Education and Religion: An Autobiography* (Boston: Houghton Mifflin Co., 1925), 198–99; see James to Gordon, 31 Oct. 1909, ibid., 199–200; George A. Gordon, *The Christ of To-Day* (Boston: Houghton, Mifflin & Co., 1899); Gordon, *The New Epoch for Faith* (Boston: Houghton, Mifflin & Co., 1902); Gordon, *Religion and Miracle* (Boston: Houghton Mifflin Co., 1909). James commended the latter book especially.

24. James, *A Pluralistic Universe,* quotes, 313, 253, 314.

25. Edward Scribner Ames, *Beyond Theology: The Autobiography of Edward Scribner Ames,* ed. Van Meter Ames (Chicago: University of Chicago Press, 1959), 1–27, quote, 21; Ames, "Theory in Practice," *Contemporary American Theology: Theological Autobiographies,* 2d series, ed. Vergilius Ferm (New York: Round Table Press, 1933), 1–2; see Creighton Peden, *The Chicago School: Voices in Liberal Religious Thought* (Bristol, Ind.: Wyndham Hall Press, 1987), 57–71.

26. Ames, *Beyond Theology,* 27–35, "this revolutionary conception," 28; Ames, "Theory in Practice," closing quote, 3; see Otto Pfleiderer, *The Philosophy of Religion on the Basis of Its History,* 3 vols., trans. Allan Menzies (London: Williams & Norgate, 1888).

27. Ames, *Beyond Theology,* quote, 37.

28. Ibid., 38–40; see Arthur Schopenhauer, *The World as Will and Representation,* 2 vols., trans. E. F. J. Payne (New York: Dover Publications, 1966); Schopenhauer, *Philosophical Writings,* ed. Wolfgang Schirmacher (New York: Continuum, 1994); Schopenhauer, *Essays and Aphorisms,* trans. R. J. Hollingdale (London: Penguin Books, 1970).

29. Ames, *Beyond Theology,* 37–38, quote, 57–58; see William James, *The Principles of Psychology,* 2 vols. (New York: Henry Holt, 1890; Harvard Edition, Cambridge: Harvard University Press, 1981, 1983).

30. Ames, "Theory in Practice," 4; Ames, *Beyond Theology,* 42–47; see John Locke, *The Reasonableness of Christianity,* ed. George W. Ewing (Washington, D.C.: Regnery Gateway, 1965); Robert Richardson, *Memoirs of Alexander Campbell, Embracing a View of the Origin, Progress, and Principles of the Religious Reformation Which He Advocated,* 2 vols. (Philadelphia: J. B. Lippincott, 1868, 1870); R. F. West, *Alexander Campbell and Natural Religion* (New Haven: Yale University Press, 1948).

31. See Linda-Marie Delloff, "Charles Clayton Morrison: Shaping a Journal's Identity," in *A Century of The Century,* Linda-Marie Deloff, Martin E. Marty, Dean Peerman, James M. Wall (Grand Rapids: Wm. B. Eerdmans Co., 1987), 3–16; Mark Toulouse, "The Origins of the *Christian Century,* 1884–1914," *Christian Century* 117 (26 Jan. 2000): 80–83.

32. Ames, "Theory in Practice," quote, 5.

33. Edward Scribner Ames, *The Psychology of Religious Experience* (Boston: Houghton Mifflin Co., 1910), 15–29, 303–37; see George A. Coe, *The Psychology of Religion* (Chicago: University of Chicago Press, 1916); Coe, *Education in Religion and Morals* (Chicago: Revell, 1909); Coe, *A Social Theory of Religious Education* (New York: Charles Scribner's Sons, 1917); J. R. Angell, A. W. Moore, and others, *Studies from the Psychological Laboratory* (Chicago: University of Chicago Press, 1896); Edwin D. Starbuck, *The Psychology of Religion: An Empirical Study of the Growth of Religious Consciousness* (New York: Charles Scribner's Sons, 1906).

34. Ames, *The Psychology of Religious Experience,* 7–29, quote, 21.

35. James on free will quoted in Perry, *The Thought and Character of William James,* 121; Ames, *The Psychology of Religious Experience,* quotes, 318, 319.

36. John Dewey, "The Theory of Emotion," *The Psychological Review* 1 (Nov. 1894): 553–69; discussion in Ames, *The Psychology of Religious Experience,* 326–37.

37. Edward Scribner Ames, *The Divinity of Christ* (Chicago: Bethany Press, 1911), 3–21, quotes, 3, 18.

38. Ibid., quotes, 27–28, 28–29.

39. Ibid., quotes, 31, 32–33.

40. Ibid., quotes, 39, 50.
41. Edward Scribner Ames, *The New Orthodoxy* (2d ed., Chicago: University of Chicago Press, 1925), v–vi, xvi–xvii, quote, vi.
42. Edward Scribner Ames, *Religion* (New York: Henry Holt & Co., 1929), 29–33, quotes, 29, 32, 33.
43. Ibid., 149–62, quotes, 154, 155; see Jerome A. Stone, *The Minimalist Vision of Transcendence: A Naturalist Philosophy of Religion* (Albany, N.Y.: State University of New York Press, 1992), 53–54.
44. Ames, *Religion*, 151–59, quotes, 153, 153–54; "atheism" quote in Charles Harvey Arnold, *Near the Edge of Battle: A Short History of the Divinity School and the "Chicago School of Theology" 1866–1966* (Chicago: Divinity School Association, 1966), 57.
45. Ames, *Religion*, 176–77; James H. Leuba, *A Psychological Study of Religion: Its Origin, Function, and Future* (New York: Macmillan Co., 1912), 10; see Leuba, *The Psychology of Religious Mysticism* (New York: Harcourt, Brace & Co., 1925).
46. Ames, *The New Orthodoxy*, 102.
47. Ames, *Religion*, 185.
48. Ames, "Theory in Practice," 10.
49. Edward Scribner Ames, "Radical Protestantism," in *Varieties of American Religion: The Goal of Religion as Interpreted by Representative Exponents of Seventeen Distinctive Types of Religious Thought*, ed. Charles Samuel Braden (Chicago: Willett, Clark & Co., 1936), 63–75, quotes, 65.
50. Ibid., quotes, 66–67.
51. Ibid., quotes, 68–69, 69, 70.
52. Ibid., 73.
53. Douglas Clyde Macintosh, "Toward a New Untraditional Orthodoxy," *Contemporary American Theology: Theological Autobiographies*, I, ed. Vergilius Ferm (New York: Round Table Press, 1932), 277–83, quotes, 282, 283.
54. Douglas Clyde Macintosh, *Personal Religion* (New York: Charles Scribner's Sons, 1942), 315.
55. Macintosh, "Toward a New Untraditional Orthodoxy," 283–90.
56. Ibid., 288, 292–94, quote, 294.
57. Ibid., 295–97; see Douglas Clyde Macintosh, *The Pilgrimage of Faith in the World of Modern Thought: Stephanos Nirmalendu Ghosh Lectures, 1927–28* (Calcutta, India: University of Calcutta Press, 1931), 39–56, 74–126. In the form of a description of the pilgrimage of modern thought, this book contains a veiled description of Macintosh's philosophical journey.
58. Macintosh, "Toward a New Untraditional Orthodoxy," 297–98; Macintosh, *The Pilgrimage of Faith in the World of Modern Thought*, 127–54; 155–79.
59. Douglas Clyde Macintosh, "The Reaction against Metaphysics in Theology," Ph.D. diss., University of Chicago, 1911, 1–86; see Macintosh, "Toward a New Untraditional Orthodoxy," 299–300; Macintosh, *The Pilgrimage of Faith in a World of Modern Thought*, 230–65.
60. Douglas Clyde Macintosh, "Personal Idealism, Pragmatism, and the New Realism," *American Journal of Theology* 14 (Oct. 1910): 650–56, quote, 656.
61. Macintosh, "Toward a New Untraditional Orthodoxy," 302–3, quote, 303; Douglas Clyde Macintosh, "Hocking's Philosophy of Religion: an Empirical Development of Absolutism," *Philosophical Review* 23 (Jan. 1914): 27–47; Macintosh, "The Religious Philosophy of W. E. Hocking," *Yale Divinity Quarterly* 10 (Jan. 1914): 73–78.
62. Macintosh to Foster, 7 May 1912, cited in Macintosh, "Toward a New Untraditional Orthodoxy," 304.
63. Douglas Clyde Macintosh, "Is 'Realistic Epistemological Monism' Inadmissible?" *Journal of Philosophy* (18 Dec. 1913); see Edwin B. Holt, Walter T. Marvin, William P. Montague, Ralph Barton Perry, Walter B. Pitkin, Edward G. Spaulding, *The New Realism: Cooperative Studies in Philosophy* (New York: Macmillan Co., 1912); Durant Drake, Arthur O. Lovejoy, James Bissett Pratt, Arthur Kenyon Rogers, George Santayana, Roy Wood Sellars, Charles A. Strong, *Essays in Critical Realism: A Co-operative Study of the Problem of Knowledge* (New York: Macmillan Co., 1920); Arthur O. Lovejoy, *Bergson and Romantic Evolutionism* (Berkeley, Calif.: University of California Press, 1914);

Ralph Barton Perry, *Present Philosophical Tendencies: A Critical Survey of Naturalism, Idealism, Pragmatism and Realism Together with a Synopsis of the Philosophy of William James* (1st edition, 1912; reprint, New York: Longmans, Green, 1919).

64. Douglas Clyde Macintosh, *The Problem of Knowledge* (New York: Macmillan Co., 1915), 13–309.

65. Ibid., 310–11.

66. Douglas Clyde Macintosh, "Experimental Realism in Religion," in *Religious Realism*, ed. Douglas Clyde Macintosh (New York: Macmillan Co., 1931), 307–409, quote, 361; see Macintosh, *The Reasonableness of Christianity* (New York: Charles Scribner's Sons, 1926), 161–216.

67. Macintosh, *The Problem of Knowledge*, 336–50, quotes, 349–350; see Peter A. Bertocci, "Macintosh's Theory of Natural Knowledge," *Journal of Religion* 23 (July 1943): 91–103; James Alfred Martin Jr., *Empirical Philosophies of Religion: With Special Reference to Boodin, Brightman, Hocking, Macintosh, and Wieman* (New York: King's Crown Press, 1945), 67–69.

68. Editor's Preface, *Religious Realism*, vi.

69. Douglas Clyde Macintosh, *Theology as an Empirical Science* (New York: Macmillan Co., 1919), 2–3, quote, 3.

70. Ibid., 11.

71. Macintosh, "Toward a New Untraditional Orthodoxy," 307. Parts of this section are adapted from Gary Dorrien, *The Word as True Myth: Interpreting Modern Theology* (Louisville, Ky.: Westminster John Knox Press, 1997), 66–70.

72. Macintosh, *Theology as an Empirical Science*, 15–19, quotes, 18, 19.

73. Ibid., 19–21, quote, 21.

74. Macintosh, *The Problem of Knowledge*, 422–34; Macintosh, *Theology as an Empirical Science*, 22–24.

75. Macintosh, *Theology as an Empirical Science*, 25, 45.

76. Ibid., 29; see Macintosh, "Experimental Realism in Religion," 383–95.

77. Macintosh, *Theology as an Empirical Science*, quotes, 26, 103.

78. Douglas Clyde Macintosh, *The Problem of Religious Knowledge* (New York: Harper & Brothers, 1940), 163.

79. Macintosh, *Theology as an Empirical Science*, 140–56, quote, 42; see Macintosh, *The Problem of Religious Knowledge*, 170–75, 188–213.

80. Macintosh, "Experimental Realism in Religion," 378; Macintosh, editor's preface, *Religious Realism*, vi.

81. Macintosh, *The Reasonableness of Christianity*, 46.

82. Ibid., quotes, 48, 50; on the relation of Macintosh's empiricism to his moral optimism, see Randolph Crump Miller, "Professor Macintosh and Empirical Theology," *Personalist* 21 (Jan. 1940): 39–40; and Miller, *The American Spirit in Theology* (Philadelphia: United Church Press, 1974), 108–9.

83. Macintosh, "Toward a New Untraditional Orthodoxy," 311; see Macintosh, *The Reasonableness of Christianity*, 136; George Burman Foster, *Christianity in Its Modern Expression* (1921), 8, 156–58.

84. Macintosh, *The Reasonableness of Christianity*, 137, 138.

85. Henry Nelson Wieman, Douglas Clyde Macintosh, Max Carl Otto, *Is There a God? A Conversation* (Chicago: Willett, Clark & Co., 1952), 21–29, 131–41, quote, 140.

86. Macintosh, *The Problem of Religious Knowledge*, 163–213; Macintosh, "Experimental Realism in Religion," 307–409; Macintosh, *The Reasonableness of Christianity*, 217–44; see Rudolf Otto, *The Idea of the Holy: An Inquiry into the Non-Rational Factor in the Idea of the Divine and its Relation to the Rational*, trans. John W. Harvey (1st German ed., 1917; 5th English ed., London: Oxford University Press, 1928), 5–30.

87. Macintosh, *The Problem of Religious Knowledge*, quotes, 165; see Macintosh, *The Reasonableness of Christianity*, 236–42; Macintosh, Preface to *Religious Realism*, vi; Martin, *Empirical Philosophies of Religion*, 72–75; Peter A. Bertocci, "An Analysis of Macintosh's Theory of Religious Knowledge," *Journal of Religion* 24 (Jan. 1944): 42–45.

88. Macintosh, *The Reasonableness of Christianity*, 17–25.

89. Macintosh, "Toward a New Untraditional Orthodoxy," quotes, 312; Macintosh,

"Experimental Realism in Religion," 385–409; Macintosh, *The Problem of Religious Knowledge*, 368–69.

90. Martin, *Empirical Philosophies of Religion*, 82.

91. Macintosh, "Toward a New Untraditional Orthodoxy," 312–13.

92. See Julius Seelye Bixler, *Religion for Free Minds* (New York: Harper & Brothers, 1939); Bixler, *Conversations with an Unrepentant Liberal* (New Haven, Conn.: Yale University Press, 1946); Robert Lowry Calhoun, *God and the Common Life* (New York: Charles Scribner's Sons, 1935); H. Richard Niebuhr, *The Kingdom of God in America* (New York: Harper & Row, 1937); Filmer Stuart C. Northrop, *The Meeting of East and West* (New York: Macmillan Co., 1946).

93. Julius Seelye Bixler, "Can Religion Become Empirical?" Robert L. Calhoun, "The Semi-Detached Knower: A Note on Radical Empiricism," Helmut Richard Niebuhr, "Value Theory and Theology," Reinhold Niebuhr, "The Truth in Myths," Filmer S. C. Northrop, "The New Scientific and Metaphysical Basis for Epistemological Theory," and George F. Thomas, "A Reasoned Faith," in *The Nature of Religious Experience: Essays in Honor of Douglas Clyde Macintosh*, ed. Julius Seelye Bixler, Robert Lowry Calhoun, and Helmut Richard Niebuhr (New York: Harper & Brothers, 1937), 68–92, 156–82, 93–116, 117–35, 183–200, 44–67; Douglas Clyde Macintosh, *Social Religion* (New York: Charles Scribner's Sons, 1939), 133–91. In 1929, the federal court in New Haven, Connecticut, denied U.S. citizenship to Macintosh because Macintosh declared that he could not pledge in advance to fight in an unjust war. While acknowledging Macintosh's high moral character, the judge asserted that "if men of his views are admitted, when the powder begins to burn and the bullets to fly, no one will fight." This decision was unanimously reversed by the circuit court of appeals, but it was upheld by a five-to-four decision of the Supreme Court in a celebrated legal case. Macintosh retired from Yale in 1942 and died in 1948. See Jerome Davis, "If Not Dr. Macintosh, Who?" *Christian Century* 50 (8 Mar. 1933): 322–24.

94. See Bertocci, "An Analysis of Macintosh's Theory of Religious Knowledge," 53; James C. Livingston, *Modern Christian Thought* (New York: Macmillan, 1971), 428; Martin, *Empirical Philosophies of Religion*, 84–86; Daniel D. Williams, "Tradition and Experience in American Theology," in *The Shaping of American Religion*, eds. James Ward Smith and A. Leland Jamison (Princeton, N.J.: Princeton University Press, 1961), 468–71; Miller, *The American Spirit in Theology*, 112–14; Roland H. Bainton, *Yale and the Ministry* (New York: Harper & Row, 1957), Niebuhr and Macintosh quotes, 227. Howison's words were, "Yes, but not one of them teaches the truth." The former students that he had in mind included American philosophers Arthur O. Lovejoy, Sidney Mezes, and C. M. Bakewell; see W. H. Werkmeister, *A History of Philosophical Ideas in America* (New York: Ronald Press, 1949), 57; James McLachlan, "George Holmes Howison: The Conception of God Debate and the Beginnings of Personal Idealism," *Personalist Forum* 11 (spring 1995): 2.

95. Wieman, Macintosh, and Otto, *Is There a God?* 131–41, quote, 141; see Randolph Crump Miller, *The Language Gap and God* (Philadelphia: Pilgrim Press, 1970); Miller, *The American Spirit in Theology*.

96. Macintosh, *The Problem of Religious Knowledge*, 164–75, quotes, 165, 175.

97. Wieman, Macintosh, and Otto, *Is There a God?* 11–19, 24–25, 249–54, quotes, 21, 24, 251; for overviews of Macintosh's intellectual career, see Herbert R. Reinelt, "D. C. Macintosh," in *A Handbook of Christian Theologians*, ed. Martin E. Marty and Dean G. Peerman, enlarged ed. (Nashville: Abingdon Press, 1984), 212–32; Kenneth C. Cauthen, *The Impact of American Religious Liberalism* (New York: Harper & Row, 1962), 169–87; Wieman and Meland, *American Philosophies of Religion*, 159–62.

98. See Larry L. Greenfield, "Gerald Birney Smith: Introduction," in *The Chicago School of Theology—Pioneers in Religious Inquiry*, 2 vols., ed. W. Creighton Peden and Jerome A. Stone (Lewiston, N.Y.: Edwin Mellen Press, 1996), 186–90; Peden, *The Chicago School: Voices in Liberal Religious Thought*, 44–55.

99. Gerald Birney Smith, *Social Idealism and the Changing Theology: A Study of the Ethical Aspects of Christian Doctrine* (New York: Macmillan Co., 1913); Smith, "Systematic Theology and Christian Ethics," in *A Guide to the Study of the Christian Religion*, ed. Gerald Birney Smith (Chicago: University of Chicago Press, 1916), 483–577, quote, 501.

100. Gerald Birney Smith, "The Task and Method of Systematic Theology," *American Journal of Theology* 14 (Apr. 1910): 220–33, quotes, 220, 230.

101. "Derives his religious life," Gerald Birney Smith, "What is Christianity?" review of *What Is Christianity?* by Adolf Harnack, *The Fundamental Truths of the Christian Religion,* by Reinhold Seeberg, and *The Gospel and the Modern Man,* by Shailer Mathews, *Biblical World* 44 (Nov. 1914): 341–49, quotes, 348; "how reluctant," Smith, "Theology and Religious Experience," *Biblical World* 40 (Aug. 1912): 97–108, quote, 108; "the norm," Smith, "Theology and Scientific Method," *Biblical World* 40 (Oct. 1912): 236–47, quote, 247.

102. Smith, "Systematic Theology and Christian Ethics," quotes, 491, 492, 494; see Gerald Birney Smith, "The Function of a Critical Theology," *Biblical World* 40 (Nov. 1912): 307–17; Smith, "Theology and the Doctrine of Evolution," *Biblical World* 45 (Jan. 1915): 37–44; Smith, "Making Christianity Safe for Democracy," *Biblical World* 53 (Jan. 1919): 3–13.

103. Meland, "Introduction: The Empirical Tradition in Theology at Chicago," 25. See Gerald Birney Smith, "A Quarter-Century of Theological Thinking in America," *Journal of Religion* 5 (Nov. 1925): 576–94; Smith, "What Does Biblical Criticism Contribute to the Modern Preacher?" *Journal of Religion* 5 (Mar. 1925): 178–86; Gerald Birney Smith, *The Principles of Christian Living* (Chicago: University of Chicago Press, 1924); Ernest Dewitt Burton, John Merlin Powis Smith, and Gerald Birney Smith, *Biblical Ideas of the Atonement: Their History and Significance* (Chicago: University of Chicago Press, 1909).

104. Gerald Birney Smith, "An Overlooked Factor in the Adjustment between Religion and Science," *Journal of Religion* 7 (July 1927): 337–59, quotes, 341, 352; see Smith, "Traditional Religion in a Scientific World," *Journal of Religion* 8 (July 1928): 487–90; Delwin Brown, "The Fall of '26: Gerald Birney Smith and the Collapse of Socio-Historical Theology," *American Journal of Theology and Philosophy* 2 (Sept. 1990): 183–201; Leonard I. Sweet, "The University of Chicago Revisited: The Modernization of Theology, 1890–1940," *Foundations* 22 (1979): 331; Martin Bulmer, *The Chicago School of Sociology* (Chicago: University of Chicago Press, 1984), 35–45; Robert Faris, *Chicago Sociology: 1920–1932* (Chicago: University of Chicago Press, 1967), 103.

105. Gerald Birney Smith, "Science and Religion," review of *Landmarks in the Struggle between Science and Religion,* by James Y. Simpson, and *Religious Experience and Scientific Method,* by Henry Nelson Wieman, *Journal of Religion* 6 (Nov. 1926): 637–40, quote, 640.

106. Meland, "Introduction: The Empirical Tradition in Theology at Chicago," 25; Gerald Birney Smith, *Current Christian Thinking* (Chicago: University of Chicago Press, 1928), 142.

107. Gerald Birney Smith, "Theological Thinking in America," in *Religious Thought in the Last Quarter-Century,* ed. Gerald Birney Smith (Chicago: University of Chicago Press, 1927), 95–115, quote, 111; Smith, *Current Christian Thinking,* quotes, 142, 143.

108. Smith, *Current Christian Thinking,* 143.

109. Ibid., quotes, 144, 169, 170.

110. Bernard E. Meland, *The Realities of Faith: The Revolution in Cultural Forms* (New York: Oxford University Press, 1962), 109–11, quotes, 109, 110; see Arnold, *Near the Edge of Battle,* 65; Meland, "A Long Look at the Divinity School and Its Present Crisis," *Criterion* 1 (summer 1962): 24–25.

111. Henry Nelson Wieman, "The Confessions of a Religious Seeker," *American Journal of Theology and Philosophy* 12 (May and Sept. 1991): 67–119, quotes, 83, 84; Wieman, "Theocentric Religion," in *Contemporary American Theology: Theological Autobiographies,* I, 339–52.

112. "It always seemed," and "the fascination," Wieman, "The Confessions of a Religious Seeker," 82, 87; "great light," Wieman, "Theocentric Religion," 344; see Wieman, in "Intellectual Autobiography of Henry Nelson Wieman," in *The Empirical Theology of Henry Nelson Wieman,* ed. Robert W. Bretall (New York: Macmillan Co., 1963), 3–18.

113. See Henry Nelson Wieman, "A Criticism of Coordination as Criterion of Moral Value," *Journal of Philosophy* 14 (17 Sept. 1917): 533–42; Wieman, "Personal and Impersonal Groups," *Ethics* 31 (July 1921): 381–93; Wieman, "Knowledge of Other Minds," *Journal of Philosophy* 19 (26 Oct. 1922): 605–11; Wieman, "Experience, Mind, and Concept," *Journal of Philosophy* 21 (29 Oct. 1924): 561–72; Wieman, "How Do We Know

God?" *Journal of Religion* 5 (Mar. 1925): 113–29; Wieman, "Objectives Versus Ideals," *Ethics* 35 (Apr. 1925): 296–307.

114. Samuel Alexander, *Space, Time, and Deity,* 2 vols. (New York: Macmillan Co., 1920); C. Lloyd Morgan, *Emergent Evolution* (New York: Henry Holt, 1923); Alfred North Whitehead, *Inquiry into the Principles of Natural Knowledge* (Cambridge: Cambridge University Press, 1919); Whitehead, *The Concept of Nature* (Cambridge: Cambridge University Press, 1920); Whitehead, *The Principle of Relativity* (Cambridge: Cambridge University Press, 1922); Whitehead, *Science and the Modern World* (New York: Macmillan Co., 1925); Meland, *The Realities of Faith,* quote, 111; see Henry Nelson Wieman, "Two Views of Whitehead," review of *Religion in the Making,* by Alfred North Whitehead, *New Republic* 11 (16 Feb. 1927): 361–62; Wieman, "Religion Redefined," review of *Religion in the Making,* by Alfred North Whitehead, *Journal of Religion* 7 (July 1927): 487–90. In *The New Republic,* Wieman expounded Whitehead's thinking enthusiastically, in opposition to Dickinson S. Miller, who charged that Whitehead was deliberately and unnecessarily obscure (Wieman, "Two Views of Whitehead," 362).

115. Meland, "A Long Look at the Divinity School and Its Present Crisis," quotes, 25; Wieman, "The Confessions of a Religious Seeker," quotes, 104, 105.

116. Henry Nelson Wieman, *Religious Experience and Scientific Method* (New York: Macmillan Co., 1926), 5–7, 9–16, quotes, 5, 9.

117. Ibid., 21–47.

118. Ibid., 5–59, quotes, 48, 50, 5, 38, 148; Wieman, "Two Views of Whitehead," 362; Wieman, "Religion Redefined," 489–490.

119. Henry Nelson Wieman, *The Wrestle of Religion with Truth* (New York: Macmillan Co., 1928), quotes, vi, vii; on Wieman's youth and vocational decision, see Wieman, "Theocentric Religion," 339–43, quote, 340; quotes on the Bible, Wieman, "The Confessions of a Religious Seeker," 78.

120. Wieman, *The Wrestle of Religion with Truth,* 1–7, 28–31, quote, 3; Wieman, "Two Views of Whitehead," 362; Alfred North Whitehead, *Religion in the Making* (New York: Macmillan Co., 1927), 16–17.

121. Wieman, *The Wrestle of Religion with Truth,* 3–7; Wieman, "Two Views of Whitehead," 362.

122. Wieman, *The Wrestle of Religion with Truth,* 179–90, quote, 182; Whitehead, *Religion in the Making,* 88–105, 149–60.

123. Wieman, *The Wrestle of Religion with Truth,* 191–97; see Wieman, "Religion Redefined," 488–89.

124. Alfred North Whitehead, *Process and Reality: An Essay in Cosmology* (New York: Macmillan Co., 1929), 519–33; see Whitehead, *Modes of Thought* (1938; reprint, New York: Free Press, 1966).

125. Wieman, *The Wrestle of Religion with Truth,* 191–97, 198–212; Wieman, "Two Views of Whitehead," 361–62; Wieman, "Religion Redefined," 488–90.

126. Henry Nelson Wieman, "A Philosophy of Religion," review of *Process and Reality: An Essay in Cosmology,* by Alfred North Whitehead, *Journal of Religion* 10 (Jan. 1930): 137–39; Wieman, "Theocentric Religion," 345–46.

127. Wieman, "Theocentric Religion," 346.

128. Ibid., 346; see Henry Nelson Wieman, "A Philosophy of Religion"; Wieman, "God and Value," in *Religious Realism,* ed. Douglas Clyde Macintosh, 155–58, 174–75.

129. Wieman, "Theocentric Religion," 346–47.

130. Ibid., 348–49.

131. Ibid., 349–51, quote, 350. On divine personality, see Henry Nelson Wieman, *The Issues of Life* (New York: Abingdon Press, 1930), 209–37; Wieman, "God and Value," 171–76; Wieman, Macintosh and Otto, *Is There a God?* 15–19; Wieman and Walter Marshall Horton, *The Growth of Religion* (Chicago: Willett, Clark & Co., 1938), 359–65; for a later elaboration of his view that events are the fundamentally constitutive reality, see Henry Nelson Wieman, *The Directive in History* (Boston: Beacon Press, 1949), 18–21.

132. Wieman, *The Issues of Life,* 227–30; Wieman, Macintosh, and Otto, *Is There a God?* 11–12.

133. Wieman, "God and Value," quotes, 155; Henry Nelson Wieman and Regina Westcott-Wieman, *Normative Psychology of Religion* (New York: Thomas Y. Crowell Co., 1935), 43–62.

134. Wieman, Macintosh, and Otto, *Is There a God?* quotes, 12, 13; Henry Nelson Wieman, "God Is More Than We Can Think," *Christendom* 1 (spring 1936): 433.

135. Wieman, Macintosh, and Otto, *Is There a God?* 17–18, quote, 48; see 165–66, 205–7; Wieman and Westcott-Wieman, *Normative Psychology of Religion*, 137–38; Wieman, *The Directive in History*, 19–21.

136. John Dewey, *The Quest for Certainty* (New York: Minton, Balch, 1929); Dewey, *A Common Faith* (New Haven: Yale University Press, 1934); Dewey, *Individualism Old and New* (New York: Minton, Balch & Co., 1930), quote, 70; Wieman, Macintosh, and Otto, *Is There a God?* 164–65.

137. John Dewey, "A God or The God?: Review of *Is There a God? A Conversation,*" by Henry Nelson Wieman, Douglas Clyde Macintosh, and Max Carl Otto, *Christian Century* 50 (8 Feb. 1933): 193–96, quotes, 195.

138. Ibid., quote, 195.

139. Ibid, quotes, 195, 196.

140. "Mr. Wieman and Mr. Macintosh 'Converse' with Mr. Dewey," *Christian Century* 50 (1 Mar. 1933), 299–302, quotes, 299, 300.

141. Ibid., 300; see "Dr. Dewey Replies," *Christian Century* 50 (22 Mar. 1933): 394–95; editorial, "Dewey and Wieman," *Christian Century* 50 (5 April 1933): 448–49; "Mr. Wieman Replies to Mr. Dewey," *Christian Century* 50 (5 Apr. 1933): 466–67. Dewey and Wieman had no personal relationship to speak of—they met only once—but Wieman sustained a deep admiration for Dewey's work for the rest of his career; see Henry Nelson Wieman, *Intellectual Foundation of Faith* (New York: Philosophical Library, 1961), 30–57.

142. See Wieman and Westcott-Wieman, *Normative Psychology of Religion*; Henry Nelson Wieman and Bernard Eugene Meland, *American Philosophies of Religion* (Chicago: Willett, Clark & Co., 1936); Wieman and Horton, *The Growth of Religion*.

143. Henry Nelson Wieman, *Now We Must Choose* (New York: Macmillan Co., 1941), quotes, 1–2.

144. See Henry Nelson Wieman, *Methods of Private Religious Living* (New York: Macmillan Co., 1929); Wieman and Wieman-Westcott, *Normative Psychology of Religion*, 210–27; Henry Nelson Wieman, "Keep Our Country Out of This War," *Christian Century* 56 (27 Sept. 1939): 1162–64; Wieman, *Now We Must Choose*; Wieman, "Democracy and Language," *Ethics* 52 (Jan. 1942): 216–21; Wieman, *The Directive in History*; Brown, "The Fall of '26: Gerald Birney Smith and the Collapse of Socio-Historical Theology," 195–96.

145. Wieman and Horton, *American Philosophies of Religion*, 295–305, quote, 297.

146. Henry Nelson Wieman, *The Source of Human Good* (Carbondale, Ill.: Southern Illinois University Press, 1946), 272.

147. Ibid., 27–43, quotes, 40, 41.

148. Ibid., 268–76, quotes, 268, 273.

149. Henry Nelson Wieman, "Neo-Orthodoxy and Contemporary Religious Reaction," in *Religious Liberals Reply*, ed. Wieman, Arthur E. Murphy, Gardner Williams, Jay William Hudson, M. C. Otto, James Bissett Pratt, Roy Wood Sellers (Boston: Beacon Press, 1947), 3–15, quotes, 4–5.

150. Henry Nelson Wieman, *Man's Ultimate Commitment* (Carbondale, Ill.: Southern Illinois University Press, 1958), 12; see Marvin C. Shaw, "Assessing Wieman's Contribution: The Theistic Stance without the Supernatural God," *American Journal of Theology and Philosophy* 20 (Sept. 1999): 241–57.

151. Wieman, "Reply to Weigel," in *The Empirical Theology of Henry Nelson Wieman*, ed. Robert W. Bretall, 355.

152. Wieman, *Man's Ultimate Commitment*, 12.

153. Wieman, "Neo-Orthodoxy and Contemporary Religious Reaction," 3–4.

154. Wieman, "The Confessions of a Religious Seeker," quotes on Dewey, 102; Wieman, "Intellectual Autobiography of Henry Nelson Wieman," "what operates," 4.

155. Wieman, *Man's Ultimate Commitment*, 174.

156. Wieman, "Reply to Miller," in *The Empirical Theology of Henry Nelson Wieman*, 43; "Reply to Burtt," ibid., 388.

157. Wieman, *Man's Ultimate Commitment*, 12.
158. Henry Nelson Wieman, "Some Blind Spots Removed," *Christian Century* 56 (27 Jan. 1939): quotes, 117–18.
159. Wieman, "Intellectual Autobiography of Henry Nelson Wieman," 4; for a perceptive reading of Wieman on this point, see Marvin C. Shaw, *Nature's Grace: Essays on H. N. Wieman's Finite Theism* (New York: Peter Lang, 1995), 60–61; and Shaw, "Assessing Wieman's Contribution: The Theistic Stance without the Supernatural God," 255–56.
160. Wieman, "Intellectual Autobiography of Henry Nelson Wieman," 4–5; see Wieman, *Intellectual Foundation of Faith*, 30–57.
161. See Wieman, *The Source of Human Good*, 87–93; Wieman, *Intellectual Foundation of Faith*, 118–20.
162. Wieman, *Intellectual Foundation of Faith*, 1–14, on Dewey, 30–57; quotes, 2, 7. For works that favor the term "creative communication," see Wieman, *The Source of Human Good*, and Henry Nelson Wieman, "The Promise of Protestantism—Whither and Whether," in *The Protestant Credo*, ed. Vergilius Ferm (New York: Philosophical Library, 1953), 163–87. On Dewey and religion, Wieman's last book reflected, "I do not think that Dewey would call himself a Christian except in the sense of inheriting the Christian tradition like all the rest of us. So far as I know he never belonged to any church nor attended church. He signed the Humanist Manifesto which was a declaration of faith by a group denying that there is any God in the traditional and popular form of that belief. Yet in the little book on *A Common Faith* which is the one book Dewey wrote on religion, he professed belief in God as interpreted by him. But as we shall see, his reference to God is very ambiguous; and in his most explicit statements about the divine presence, I do not think any one, or hardly any one, would accept what he says about God as being acceptable" (Wieman, *Intellectual Foundation of Faith*, 37).
163. Wieman, *Intellectual Foundation of Faith*, 6–7; see Meland, "Introduction: The Empirical Tradition in Theology at Chicago," 36; Robert L. Calhoun, "God As More Than Mind," *Christendom* 1 (winter 1936): 341; Miller, *The American Spirit in Theology*, 94–95; Shaw, "Assessing Wieman's Contribution: The Theistic Stance without the Supernatural God," 252–53; Nancy Frankenberry, *Religion and Radical Empiricism* (Albany, N.Y.: State University of New York Press, 1987), 122–29.
164. Shaw, "Assessing Wieman's Contribution: The Theistic Stance without the Supernatural God," 257. Shaw's source is Edward Hobbs; Pauck told this story at a meeting of the New Testament Club of the Divinity School in the late 1940s.
165. Bernard Eugene Meland, "The Root and Form of Wieman's Thought," in *The Empirical Theology of Henry Nelson Wieman*, 44–68, quote, 57; Daniel Day Williams, "Wieman as a Christian Theologian," ibid., 73–96, quote, 77; "Wieman is my Barth" quote in Meland, "A Long Look at the Divinity School and Its Present Crisis," 25; see Meland, "Introduction: The Empirical Tradition in Theology at Chicago," 33–37; Williams, "Tradition and Experience in American Theology," 466–68.
166. Meland, "The Root and Form of Wieman's Thought," 60–68; Williams, "Wieman as a Christian Theologian," 90–96.
167. William Dean, *American Religious Empiricism* (Albany, N.Y.: State University of New York Press, 1986); Dean, "Empiricism and God," in *Empirical Theology: A Handbook*, ed. Randolph Crump Miller (Birmingham, Ala.: Religious Education Press, 1992), 107–28; Dean, *History Making History: The New Historicism in American Religious Thought* (Albany, N.Y.: State University of New York Press, 1988), 45–73; Frankenberry, *Religion and Radical Empiricism*, 113–29, 189–92; Brown, "The Fall of '26: Gerald Birney Smith and the Collapse of Socio-Historical Theology," 198–201, quote, 201.
168. Robert L. Calhoun, "How Shall We Think of God?" *Christendom* 1 (summer 1936): 594–97, quote, 595–96; see Calhoun, "God As More Than Mind," 340–43; Calhoun, "The Power of God and the Wisdom of God," *Christendom* 2 (winter 1937): 44–47.
169. Williams, "Wieman as a Christian Theologian," quotes, 90–91, 93; see Bernard E. Meland, "The Chicago School of Theology," in *Twentieth Century Encyclopedia of Religious Knowledge: An Extension of the New Schaff-Herzog Encyclopedia of Religious Knowledge*, ed. Lefferts A. Loetscher (Grand Rapids: Baker Book House, 1955), 232–33; Meland, "A Time of Reckoning—An Editorial," *Journal of Religion* 29 (Jan. 1949): 1–4.

170. John B. Cobb Jr., *Living Options in Protestant Theology: A Survey of Methods* (Philadelphia: Westminster Press, 1962), 91–119, 312–23.

Chapter 5. The Real Is the Personal

1. Albert Cornelius Knudson, "A Personalistic Approach to Theology," in *Contemporary American Theology: Theological Autobiographies* I, ed. Vergilius Ferm (New York: Round Table Press, 1932), quotes, 219; Elmer A. Leslie, "Albert Cornelius Knudson, the Man," in *Personalism in Theology: A Symposium in Honor of Albert Cornelius Knudson*, ed. Edgar Sheffield Brightman (Boston: Boston University Press, 1943), 1–4; Elmer A. Leslie, "Albert Cornelius Knudson: An Intimate View," *Personalist* 35 (Oct. 1954): 357–68.

2. Knudson, "A Personalistic Approach to Theology," quotes, 220–21; Leslie, "Albert Cornelius Knudson, the Man," 4–5; Josiah Royce, *The Spirit of Modern Philosophy* (Boston: Houghton Mifflin Co., 1892); Edward Caird, *The Evolution of Religion,* 2 vols. (Glasgow: Maclehose & Son, 1893).

3. Knudson, "A Personalistic Approach to Theology," quote, 221.

4. Henry C. Sheldon, *System of Christian Doctrine* (Cincinnati: Methodist Book Concern, 1903); Olin A. Curtis, *The Christian Faith Personally Given in a System of Doctrine* (1905; reprint, Grand Rapids: Kregel Publications, 1956); Albert C. Knudson, "Henry Clay Sheldon," *Methodist Review* 107 (Mar. 1925): 175; on "modified orthodoxy" see William H. Bernhardt, "The Influence of Borden Parker Bowne upon Theological Thought in the Methodist Episcopal Church," Ph.D. diss., University of Chicago, 1928, 15–17.

5. Knudson, "A Personalistic Approach to Theology," quote, 222; Leslie, "Albert Cornelius Knudson, the Man," 6–7; S. Paul Schilling, "Albert Cornelius Knudson: Person and Theologian," in *The Boston Personalist Tradition in Philosophy, Social Ethics, and Theology*, ed. Paul Deats and Carol Robb (Macon, Ga.: Mercer University Press, 1986), 81.

6. "To an almost" and "on the most," Albert C. Knudson, "Bowne As Teacher and Author," *Personalist* 1 (July 1920): 5–14, quotes, 5, 7; Brightman quotes in Edgar S. Brightman, "Bowne: Eternalist or Temporalist," *Personalist* 28 (summer 1947): 257–65, quotes, 257; "Here at last," Knudson, "A Personalistic Approach to Theology," 223.

7. Knudson, "Bowne As Teacher and Author," quotes, 7. 8.

8. Knudson, "A Personalistic Approach to Theology," quote, 223. On Bowne, see Gary Dorrien, *The Making of American Liberal Theology: Imagining Progressive Religion* (Louisville, Ky.: Westminster John Knox Press, 2001), 371–92; Peter A. Bertocci, "Borden Parker Bowne and His Personalistic Theistic Idealism," in *The Boston Personalist Tradition in Philosophy, Social Ethics, and Theology,* 55–80.

9. "It brought me," Knudson, "A Personalistic Approach to Theology," 223; "He saw distinctly," Knudson, "Bowne as Teacher and Author," 6; "It was his" and "I have felt," quoted in Leslie, "Albert Cornelius Knudson, The Man," 8.

10. Jannette E. Newhall, "Edgar Sheffield Brightman: A Biographical Sketch," *Philosophical Forum* 12 (1954): 12. Brightman told Newhall, his longtime assistant and colleague, that he had three encounters with Bowne during his two years of studying under him. In the first Bowne gave him a one-word answer to a question; in the second Bowne gave him a terse one-sentence answer; in the third, after Brightman won the university's Jacob Sleeper Fellowship, Bowne told Brightman that he was hearing good things about him. See Schilling, "Albert Cornelius Knudson: Person and Theologian," 81–82; Leslie, "Albert Cornelius Knudson, The Man," 8–9; Knudson, "A Personalistic Approach to Theology," 223–24.

11. Hinckley G. Mitchell to Albert C. Knudson, 17 Nov. 1905, Albert C. Knudson Papers, Boston University School of Theology Archives, Mugar Library, Boston University.

12. Hinckley G. Mitchell to Albert C. Knudson, 8 Feb. 1906, Albert C. Knudson Papers. In his letter of 16 Jan. 1906 to Mitchell, Knudson apparently expressed his concerns about Mitchell's plans. This letter is lost, but Mitchell refers to these concerns in his February 8 letter.

13. Albert C. Knudson, *The Old Testament Problem* (Cincinnati: Jennings and Graham, 1908), quote, 52; Knudson, "The Evolution of Modern Bible Study," *Methodist Review* 93 (Nov. 1911): 899–910.

14. Albert C. Knudson, *The Beacon Lights of Prophecy* (New York: Methodist Book Concern, 1914); Knudson, *The Religious Teaching of the Old Testament* (New York: Abingdon-Cokesbury Press, 1918); Knudson, *The Prophetic Movement in Israel* (New York: Methodist Book Concern, 1921), quotes, 124, 137. Knudson's friend and colleague historical theologian George Croft Cell believed that Knudson's style of teaching was more appropriate for seminarians than Mitchell's; Cell to Knudson, 22 Jan. 1907, Albert C. Knudson Papers.

15. Leslie, "Albert Cornelius Knudson, the Man," 10–11, quotes, 11.

16. Albert C. Knudson to George Croft Cell, 22 Apr. 1910, Albert C. Knudson Papers.

17. Knudson, "A Personalistic Approach to Theology," quote, 224; Leslie, "Albert Cornelius Knudson, the Man," 12; George A. Gordon, *The Witness to Immortality* (Boston: Houghton, Mifflin and Co., 1893); Gordon, *Through Man to God* (Boston: Houghton, Mifflin and Co., 1906); Gordon, *Ultimate Conceptions of Faith* (Boston: Houghton, Mifflin and Co., 1902); John Wright Buckham, *Personality and the Christian Idea* (Boston: Pilgrim Press, 1909); Buckham, *Mysticism and Modern Life* (New York: Abingdon Press, 1915); Buckham, *Religion as Experience* (New York: Abingdon Press, 1922); Buckham, *Christianity and Personality* (New York: Round Table Press, 1936); Ralph Tyler Flewelling, *Personalism and the Problems of Philosophy: An Appreciation of the Work of Borden Parker Bowne* (New York: Methodist Book Concern, 1915).

18. Francis J. McConnell, "Bowne and Personalism," in *Personalism in Theology: A Symposium in Honor of Albert Cornelius Knudson*, 21–39, quote, 34; McConnell, "Bowne in American Ethical Progress," *Personalist* 27 (summer 1947): 237–46; Albert C. Knudson, "Bowne in American Theological Education," *Personalist* 27 (summer 1947): 247–56. Harry F. Ward, *Poverty and Wealth: From the Viewpoint of the Kingdom of God* (New York: Methodist Book Concern, 1915); Ward, *The New Social Order* (New York: Macmillan, 1919); Ward, *In Place of Profit* (New York: Scribner's, 1933); Ward, *The Soviet Spirit* (New York: International Publishers, 1944); Ward, ed., *The Social Ministry* (New York: Eaton & Mains, 1910); George Albert Coe, *The Religion of a Mature Mind* (Chicago: Fleming H. Revell, 1902); Coe, *Education in Religion and Morals* (New York: Fleming H. Revell, 1904); Coe, *The Psychology of Religion* (Chicago: University of Chicago Press, 1916); Coe, *A Social Theory of Religious Education* (New York: Charles Scribner's Sons, 1917); Harris Franklin Rall, *A Working Faith* (New York: Abingdon Press, 1914); Rall, *A Faith for Today* (New York: Abingdon Press, 1936); Rall, *Christianity: An Inquiry into its Nature and Truth* (New York: Charles Scribner's Sons, 1941); J. Neal Hughley, *Trends in Protestant Social Idealism* (New York: King's Crown Press, 1948); *Theology and Modern Life: Essays in Honor of Harris Franklin Rall*, ed. Paul Arthur Schilpp (Chicago: Willett, Clark & Co., 1940); Walter G. Muelder, *Methodism and Society in the Twentieth Century* (New York: Abingdon Press, 1961); Robert T. Handy, *A History of Union Theological Seminary in New York* (New York: Columbia University Press, 1987); Stephen A. Schmidt, *A History of the Religious Education Association* (Birmingham, AL: Religious Education Press, 1983).

19. Francis J. McConnell, *By the Way: An Autobiography* (New York: Abingdon-Cokesbury Press, 1952), 11–40, quote, 36; Earl Kent Brown, "Liberal in the Land," in *Ohio Biography Series*, ed. Earl Kent Brown (North Canton, Ohio: Bicentennial Commission of the East Ohio Annual Conference of the United Methodist Church, 1984), 71–88.

20. McConnell, *By the Way*, 23–94; see McConnell, "Bowne and Personalism," in *Personalism in Theology: A Symposium in Honor of Albert Cornelius Knudson*, 21–39; McConnell, *Borden Parker Bowne: His Life and Philosophy* (New York: Abingdon Press, 1929).

21. Francis J. McConnell, *The Diviner Immanence* (New York: Methodist Book Concern, 1906), quote, 11; Francis J. McConnell to Albert C. Knudson, 4 Jan. 1907, Albert C. Knudson Papers.

22. McConnell, *The Diviner Immanence*, quotes, 15, 17.

23. Ibid., quotes, 18.

24. Ibid., quotes, 59, 131–32.

25. McConnell, *The Diviner Immanence*, 86–91, 114–37, quotes, 124–25, 125.

26. Francis J. McConnell, *Religious Certainty* (New York: Eaton & Mains, 1910), quote, 6; McConnell, *Christian Focus: A Series of College Sermons* (Cincinnati: Jennings & Graham; New York: Eaton & Mains, 1911); McConnell, *By the Way*, 105–43; see Carroll

D. W. Hildebrand, "Bishop McConnell—Personalist," *Personalist* 35 (Oct. 1954): 380–88.

27. Edgar Sheffield Brightman, "Religion As Truth," in *Contemporary American Theology: Theological Autobiographies*, I, quotes, 55, 56; Newhall, "Edgar Sheffield Brightman: A Biographical Sketch," 9–21.

28. Brightman, "Religion As Truth," quote, 56.

29. "My studies" quote, ibid., 57; Brightman, "The Criterion of Religious Truth in the Theology of Albrecht Ritschl," Ph.D. diss., Boston University, 1912, quote, 106; Newhall, "Edgar Sheffield Brightman: A Biographical Sketch," 12–13.

30. Edgar S. Brightman, "The Unpopularity of Personalism," *Methodist Review* 104 (Jan. 1921): 9–28, quotes, 9, 10; see Edgar S. Brightman, "Personalism and the Influence of Bowne," *Personalist* 8 (Jan. 1927), 25–32.

31. See James Ward, *Naturalism and Agnosticism* (London: A. & C. Black, 1906); W. R. Sorley, *Moral Values and the Idea of God* (Cambridge: Cambridge University Press, 1918); Hastings Rashdall, *Philosophy and Religion* (London: Duckworth, 1910); A. S. [Andrew Seth] Pringle-Pattison, *Hegelianism and Personality* (1887; reprint, New York: Burt Franklin, 1971); William Ernst Hocking, *The Meaning of God in Human Experience: A Philosophic Study of Religion* (New Haven, Conn.: Yale University Press, 1912); Mary Whiton Calkins, *The Persistent Problems of Philosophy* (3d ed., New York: Macmillan, 1912); George Holmes Howison, *The Limits of Evolution, and Other Essays Illustrating the Metaphysical Theory of Personal Idealism* (New York: Macmillan, 1901; 2d, enlarged ed., 1904). Brightman later offered an extensive list of personalists in his contribution, "Personalism," to *A History of Philosophical Systems*, ed. Vergilius Ferm (New York: Philosophical Library, 1950), 344.

32. Brightman, "The Unpopularity of Personalism," quotes, 12, 13; Brightman, "Why Is Personalism Unpopular?" *Methodist Review* 104 (July 1921): 524–35.

33. Brightman, "The Unpopularity of Personalism," 12–23.

34. Brightman, "Why Is Personalism Unpopular?" quotes, 534, 535.

35. Edgar S. Brightman, "The Tasks Confronting a Personalistic Philosophy, Part 1," *Personalist* 2 (July 1921): 162–71, quotes, 162, 164; see [Ralph Tyler Flewelling], "Why a School of Philosophy?" *Personalist* 10 (July 1929): 157–61.

36. Brightman, "The Tasks Confronting a Personalistic Philosophy, Part 1," quotes, 164–65.

37. Edgar S. Brightman, "The Tasks Confronting a Personalistic Philosophy, Part 2," *Personalist* 2 (Oct. 1921): 254–66, quotes, 257, 263.

38. "Numerous encouraging signs," Brightman, "Why is Personalism Unpopular?" 534; Edgar S. Brightman to Georgia Harkness, 4 Oct. 1922, Edgar S. Brightman Collection, Department of Special Collections, Boston University.

39. Personalist Creed, [Ralph Tyler Flewelling], "To the Gentle Personalist," *The Personalist* 2 (Apr. 1921): 72; see Flewelling, "Can Civilization Become Christian?" *Personalist* 1 (Apr. 1920): 7–17; Flewelling, "Self-Limitation, Freedom and Democracy," *Personalist* 1 (July 1920): 40–48; Flewelling, "Lingering Prussian Ghosts," *Personalist* 1 (Oct. 1920): 5–13; "The Pseudo-Science in Psycho-Analysis," *Personalist* 2 (Jan. 1921): 25–34; Flewelling, "Dogma in Science, Religion, and Life," *Personalist* 2 (Apr. 1921): 106–11; Flewelling, "This Thing Called Personalism," *Personalist* 28 (summer 1947): 229–36; *George Holmes Howison, Philosopher and Teacher: A Selection from His Writings with a Biographical Sketch*, eds. John Wright Buckham and George Malcolm Stratton (Berkeley, Calif.: University of California Press, 1934); Buckham, *Personality and the Christian Ideal* (Boston: Pilgrim Press, 1909).

40. John Wright Buckham, "A Group of American Idealists," *Personalist* 1 (Apr. 1920): 18–31; Buckham, "Three Centuries of Pilgrim Theology," *Personalist* 2 (Jan. 1921): 16–24; Frank Wilbur Collier, "Personalism: A Vital Philosophy," *Personalist* 1 (Apr. 1920): 34–43; James Main Dixon, "The Common Thread in French and English Culture," *Personalist* 1 (Apr. 1920): 44–53; J. E. Turner, "Webb's Gifford Lectures on Personality," *Personalist* 2 (July 1921): 172–81; Virginia Taylor McCormick, "Let us Talk of Flecker," *Personalist* 3 (Apr. 1922): 85–94; McCormick, "Ibsen's Portraiture of Women," *Personalist* 3 (July 1922): 157–69; Albert C. Knudson, "The Social Gospel and Theology," *Personalist* 5 (Apr. 1924): 102–14; Edgar S. Brightman, "The Use of the

Word Personalism," *Personalist* 3 (Oct. 1922): 254–59; see Ralph Tyler Flewelling, "Studies in Personalism," *Personalist* 31 (summer 1950): 229–44; Flewelling, "Studies in American Personalism," *Personalist* 31 (autumn 1950): 341–51; Wilbur Long, "Thirty Five Years in Retrospect," *Personalist* 35 (July 1954): 229–37.

41. McConnell, *By the Way*, 127–223; Paul Deats, "Bishop Francis J. McConnell and Social Justice," in *The Boston Personalist Tradition in Philosophy, Social Ethics, and Theology*, 148–49; Walter G. Muelder, *Methodism and Society in the Twentieth Century* (New York: Abingdon Press, 1961), 96–103.

42. Francis J. McConnell, *The Increase of Faith: Some Present-Day Aids to Belief* (New York: Eaton & Mains; Cincinnati: Jennings & Graham, 1912), quote, 17.

43. Francis J. McConnell, *The Essentials of Methodism* (New York: Methodist Book Concern, 1916), quote, 51.

44. Francis J. McConnell, *Understanding the Scriptures* (New York: Methodist Book Concern, 1917), quote, 26.

45. Francis J. McConnell, *Democratic Christianity* (New York: Macmillan Co., 1919), on socialism, 49–51.

46. Francis J. McConnell, *The Preacher and the People* (New York: Abingdon Press, 1922).

47. Francis J. McConnell, *Christian Citizenship: An Elective Course for Young People* (New York: Methodist Book Concern, 1922).

48. Francis J. McConnell, *Living Together: Studies in the Ministry of Reconciliation* (New York: Abingdon Press, 1923), quotes, 217, 218.

49. Francis J. McConnell, "Bowne and the Social Questions," *Studies in Philosophy and Theology: By Former Students of Borden Parker Bowne*, ed. E. C. Wilm (New York: Abingdon Press, 1922), 128–43, quote, 135; McConnell, "Bowne and Personalism," 33–34.

50. Francis J. McConnell, *Is God Limited?* (New York: Abingdon Press, 1924), quote, 291.

51. Francis J. McConnell, "The Eternal Spirit," in *My Idea of God: A Symposium of Faith*, ed. Joseph Fort Newton (Boston: Little, Brown, 1926), quote, 253.

52. McConnell, *Is God Limited?* quotes, 45, 11.

53. Albert C. Knudson, *Present Tendencies in Religious Thought* (New York: Abingdon Press, 1924), 132–250.

54. Rufus Burrow Jr., *Personalism: A Critical Introduction* (St. Louis, Mo.: Chalice Press, 1999), 27–31; Burrow Jr., "Authorship: The Personalism of George Holmes Howison and Borden Parker Bowne," *Personalist Forum* 13 (Fall 1997), 287–303; see Albert C. Knudson, "Bowne As Teacher and Author," *Personalist* 1 (July 1920): 5–14; Howison, *The Limits of Evolution, and Other Essays Illustrating the Metaphysical Theory of Personal Idealism*.

55. Borden Parker Bowne, *Personalism* (Boston: Houghton Mifflin Co., 1908), 16–17.

56. Albert C. Knudson, *The Philosophy of Personalism: A Study in the Metaphysics of Religion* (New York: Abingdon Press, 1927), quote, 5; see Francis J. McConnell, *Borden Parker Bowne: His Life and Philosophy* (New York: Abingdon Press, 1929). Knudson's decision to thematize Bowne's relation to the history of philosophy was probably influenced by George Croft Cell's disapproving view of Bowne's deficiencies in this area. Before either of them joined the Boston University faculty, Cell warned Knudson that Bowne's historical scholarship was not to be trusted. He gave a detailed list of Bowne's misrepresentations of Kant under the categories (1) doubtful, (2) inaccurate, (3) misleading, and (4) wrong. In Cell's reading, (3) and (4) predominated; he remarked, "This is a pretty serious charge, I know." George Croft Cell to Albert C. Knudson, 5 July 1905, Albert C. Knudson Papers.

57. Knudson, *The Philosophy of Personalism*, quotes, 13, 14.

58. See J. M. E. McTaggart, *Studies in the Hegelian Dialectic* (reprint 1964; New York: Russell & Russell, 1896); William Stern, *Psychologie der Veränderungsauffassung* (Breslau: Preuss & Jünger, 1906); Charles Renouvier, *Manuel républicaine de l'homme et du citoyen* (Paris: A. Colin, 1904); Josiah Royce, *The Religious Aspect of Philosophy* (Boston: Houghton, Mifflin & Co., 1885); W. E. Hocking, *The Meaning of God in Human Experience* (New Haven, Conn.: Yale University Press, 1912); Howison, *The Limits of Evolution, and Other Essays Illustrating the Metaphysical Theory of Personal Idealism*, 2d ed., 421–25. On Howison, Bowne, and the origins of personalist idealism, see John Wright Buckham, *Christianity and Personality* (New York: Round Table Press, 1936),

38; Burrow Jr., *Personalism: A Critical Introduction*, 54–66; Burrow Jr., "Authorship: The Personalism of George Holmes Howison and Borden Parker Bowne," 287–303; James McLachlan, "George Holmes Howison: The Conception of God Debate and the Beginnings of Personal Idealism," *Personalist Forum* 11 (spring 1995): 1–16.

59. A. S. Pringle-Pattison, *Hegelianism and Personality,* 214–30; Pringle-Pattison, *The Idea of God in the Light of Recent Philosophy* (New York: Oxford University Press, 1917), 342–417; see Arthur J. Balfour, *Theism and Thought: A Study in Familiar Beliefs* (London: Hodder & Stoughton, 1923); Balfour, *Theism and Humanism* (New York: Hodder & Stoughton, 1915); Balfour, *The Foundations of Belief* (London: Longmans, Green, 1894; J. Cook Wilson, *Statement and Inference,* 2 vols. (Oxford: Clarendon Press, 1900); James Ward, *The Realm of Ends; or, Pluralism and Theism* (Cambridge: Cambridge University Press, 1900); Hastings Rashdall, *The Christian Faith* (New York: E. P. Dutton, 1922); Sorley, *Moral Values and the Idea of God;* C. C. J. Webb, *God and Personality* (London: Allen & Unwin, 1920); Webb, *Divine Personality and Human Life* (Aberdeen: University of Aberdeen, 1920).

60. Borden P. Bowne to Mrs. K. M. Bowne, 31 May 1909, reprinted in K. M. Bowne, "An Intimate Portrait of Bowne," *Personalist* 2 (Jan. 1921): 10; Knudson, *The Philosophy of Personalism,* 62; see Hermann Lotze, *Microcosmos: An Essay Concerning Man and His Relation to the World,* 2 vols., trans. Elizabeth Hamilton and Emily E. C. Jones (Edinburgh: T. & T. Clark, 1888); Lotze, *Grundzüge der Religionsphilosophie* (Leipzig: G. Hirzel, 1884); Lotze, *Metaphysik* (Leipzig: F. Meiner, 1912); Lotze, *Logik* (Leipzig: Weidmann'sche Buchhandlung, 1843); Lotze, *Grundzüge der Ästhetik* (Leipzig: S. Hirzel, 1884).

61. Knudson, *The Philosophy of Personalism,* 62–67.

62. Ibid., 67–75.

63. Ibid., quotes, 131; see George Berkeley, *A Treatise Concerning the Principles of Human Knowledge* (1710; Open Court edition, LaSalle, Ill.: Open Court, 1986).

64. Bowne, *Personalism,* 56; Knudson, *The Philosophy of Personalism,* 130–34, quote, 131.

65. Knudson, *The Philosophy of Personalism,* 72–74; Eugene W. Lyman, "The Place of Intuition in Religious Experience and Its Validity as Knowledge," *Journal of Religion* 9 (Mar. 1924): 113–32, 128–29. See Eugene Lyman, *The Meaning and Truth of Religion* (New York: Charles Scribner's Sons, 1933).

66. Knudson, *The Philosophy of Personalism,* 73–74, 141–42, quote, 74.

67. Ibid., 89–167, quote, 99.

68. Borden Parker Bowne, *Theory of Thought and Knowledge* (New York: Harper & Brothers, 1897); Bowne, *Kant and Spencer: A Critical Exposition* (Boston: Houghton Mifflin Co., 1912); Gottfried Wilhelm Leibniz, *Discourse on Metaphysics; Correspondence with Arnauld; Monadology,* trans. George Montgomery (LaSalle, Ill.: Open Court, 1988); Knudson, *The Philosophy of Personalism,* 158–62, 216–18, 185–88, quote, 87.

69. Knudson, *The Philosophy of Personalism,* 336–434, "polemical aspects," 336; Brightman, "Personalism and the Influence of Bowne," 31–32; Brightman, "Religion As Truth," 58; L. Harold DeWolf, "Albert Cornelius Knudson: As Philosopher," *Personalist* 35 (Oct. 1954): 366–67.

70. S. Paul Schilling, "Albert Cornelius Knudson: Person and Theologian," "amazing superficiality," 83; Albert Cornelius Knudson, *Basic Issues in Christian Thought* (New York: Abingdon-Cokesbury Press, 1950), "sophisticated irrationalism," 113; Knudson, *The Philosophy of Personalism,* "its value," 375.

71. G. W. F. Hegel, *Philosophy of Right,* trans. T. M. Knox (1821; English trans., Oxford: Clarendon Press, 1952, 10); Knox's rendering is "What is rational is actual and what is actual is rational"; Knudson, *The Philosophy of Personalism,* quote, 384, 422; Gerald Birney Smith, "Is Theism Essential to Religion?" *Journal of Religion* 5 (July 1925): 356–77.

72. Knudson, *The Philosophy of Personalism,* 418–25; Bowne quoted in James T. Carlyon, "Bowne in the Classroom," *Personalist* 28 (summer 1947): 266–72, quote, 271; William James, *Pragmatism: A New Name for Some Old Ways of Thinking* (Cambridge: Harvard University Press, 1907), 18; Ralph Barton Perry, *The Present Conflict of Ideals* (New York: Longmans, Green, 1918), 202, 218.

73. James A. Beebe to Albert C. Knudson, July 15, 1925, Albert C. Knudson Papers.

74. Beebe quoted by Marlatt, Earl B. Marlatt to Albert C. Knudson, 5 Feb. 1926, Albert C. Knudson Papers; see Leslie, "Albert Cornelius Knudson, the Man," 13; Leslie, "Albert

Cornelius Knudson: An Intimate View," 360; Schilling, "Albert Cornelius Knudson: Person and Theologian," 82.

75. Edgar S. Brightman to Albert C. Knudson, 26 Dec. 1952, Edgar S. Brightman Collection. See Paul E. Johnson, "Brightman's Contribution to Personalism," *Personalist* 35 (Jan. 1954): 60–61; Peter A. Bertocci, "The Personalism of Edgar S. Brightman and Ultimate Reality," *Ultimate Reality and Meaning* 6 (Mar. 1983): 32–50; Schilling, "Albert Cornelius Knudson: Person and Theologian," 85; Leslie, "Albert Cornelius Knudson, the Man," 13–14.

76. Brightman, "Bowne: Eternalist or Temporalist," 257–65; Brightman's theory of the "shining present" was published in his unfinished *Metaphysics* as Brightman, *Person and Reality*, ed. Peter A. Bertocci (New York: Ronald Press, 1958).

77. Brightman, "Bowne: Eternalist or Temporalist," quotes, 258; Ralph Tyler Flewelling, *Bergson and Personal Realism* (New York: Abingdon Press, 1920), 230; "with no dogmatic," Brightman, "Religion as Truth," 53; see Peter A. Bertocci and M. Alicia Corea, "Edgar Shieffield Brightman: Through His Students' Eyes," *Philosophical Forum* 12 (1954): 53–67; Daniel Callahan, "Human Experience and God: Brightman's Personalistic Theism," in *American Philosophy and the Future: Essays for a New Generation*, ed. Michael Novak (New York: Charles Scribner's Sons, 1968), 219–46; Robert Gillies, "A Little Known American," *Expository Times* 97 (Aug. 1986): 323–28.

78. Edgar S. Brightman, *An Introduction to Philosophy* (New York: Henry Holt & Co., 1925); Brightman, *Immortality in Post-Kantian Idealism* (Cambridge: Harvard University Press, 1925); Brightman, *Religious Values* (New York: Abingdon Press, 1925); Brightman, *A Philosophy of Ideals* (New York: Henry Holt & Co., 1928).

79. Brightman, *Religious Values*, quotes, 134.

80. Brightman, *An Introduction to Philosophy*, 332–33.

81. Newhall, "Edgar Sheffield Brightman: A Biographical Sketch," 14–15, 18; Brightman, "Religion as Truth," quote, 75.

82. Edgar S. Brightman, *The Problem of God* (New York: Abingdon Press, 1930), 10; Edmund Noble, *Purposive Evolution: The Link between Science and Religion* (New York: H. Holt & Co., 1926).

83. Brightman, "Religion as Truth," 56–57, "the teaching" quote, 57; Brightman, *The Problem of God*, "few beliefs" quote, 9–10; H. G. Wells, *God the Invisible King* (New York: Cassell, 1917); see Rannie Belle Baker, *The Concept of a Limited God* (Washington, D.C.: Shenandoah Publishing House, 1934).

84. McConnell, *Is God Limited?* 15–44, quote, 17.

85. Ibid., 56–67, 132–34, quotes, 133, 61; Brightman, *The Problem of God*, 10–11.

86. McConnell, *Is God Limited?* 56–67, quotes, 62, 63.

87. Ibid., quotes, 288, 289, 295, 296.

88. Francis J. McConnell, *The Christlike God: A Survey of the Divine Attributes from the Christian Point of View* (New York: Abingdon Press, 1927), quotes, 88, 89; see McConnell, *The Just Weight and Other Chapel Addresses* (New York: Abingdon Press, 1925), 40–45.

89. Brightman, *The Problem of God*, 10.

90. Ibid., quotes, 107–38, 166–93, quotes, 137–38, 187.

91. Edgar S. Brightman to Albert C. Knudson, 11 Sept. 1930, Albert C. Knudson Papers.

92. Edgar S. Brightman to Albert C. Knudson, 10 Oct. 1930, Albert C. Knudson Papers.

93. "Finite-Infinite God," in Edgar S. Brightman, *Personality and Religion* (New York: Abingdon Press, 1934), 71–100; Andrew Banning, "Professor Brightman's Theory of a Limited God," *Harvard Theological Review* 27 (July 1934): 145–68, quote, 168; James John McLarney, *The Theism of Edgar Sheffield Brightman* (Washington, D.C.: Catholic University of America, 1936), 134–48; Arthur Carl Piepkorn, "The Finite-Infinite God of Edgar Sheffield Brightman," *Concordia Theological Monthly* 25 (Jan. 1954): 28–53; Ted B. Clark, "The Doctrine of a Finite God," *Review and Expositor* 52 (Jan. 1955): 21–43; Joseph J. Labaj, *An Exposition of the Problem of Evil and Its Solution in the Writings of Edgar Sheffield Brightman* (Rome: Pontificia Universitas Gregoriana, 1964).

94. Ralph Tyler Flewelling, "Notes and Discussions: The Problem of God," *Personalist* 11 (Oct. 1930): 275–79, quotes, 275, 276.

95. Edgar S. Brightman, *The Finding of God* (New York: Abingdon Press, 1931), 166–93,

quote, 186; see David Ray Griffin, *God, Power, and Evil: A Process Theodicy* (Philadelphia: Westminster Press, 1976), 250.

96. Edgar S. Brightman, *A Philosophy of Religion* (New York: Prentice-Hall, 1940), 240–304, 305–41, description of the Given, 336–37, quotes, 337, 341; see Brightman, *Person and Reality: An Introduction to Metaphysics,* 338–42.

97. Brightman, *The Finding of God*; Brightman, *The Spiritual Life* (New York: Abingdon-Cokesbury Press, 1942); Peter A. Bertocci, *Introduction to the Philosophy of Religion* (New York: Prentice-Hall, 1953), 436–37; Bertocci, "The Personalism of Edgar S. Brightman and Ultimate Reality," 40–44; S. Paul Schilling, *God and Human Anguish* (Nashville: Abingdon Press, 1977), 242–43; Brightman, "Religion As Truth," 58–80; see Rufus Burrow Jr., "The Personalistic Theism of Edgar S. Brightman," *Encounter* 53 (spring 1992): 165–82.

98. Brightman, "Religion As Truth," quotes, 59, 66, 67.

99. "I have no sympathy," ibid., 63; "any consciousness of," Brightman, *The Finding of God,* 94; "it changes the weak," Brightman, *The Spiritual Life,* 23; Muelder, "Edgar S. Brightman: Person and Moral Philosopher," 106.

100. Brightman, "Religion As Truth," 72.

101. Edgar S. Brightman, "Personality As a Metaphysical Principle," in *Personalism in Theology: A Symposium in Honor of Albert Cornelius Knudson,* 40–63, quote, 43.

102. Ibid., quotes, 44, 45.

103. Ibid., quotes, 45.

104. Ibid., 45–46, quote, 45.

105. Ibid., 46–54, quotes, 53, 54; see Edgar S. Brightman, "What Is Personality?" *The Personalist* 20 (spring 1939): 129–38.

106. Brightman, "Personality As a Metaphysical Principle," quotes, 54.

107. Ibid., quotes, 55–56.

108. Knudson, *The Philosophy of Personalism,* 87; Albert C. Knudson, *The Doctrine of God* (New York: Abingdon-Cokesbury Press, 1930), 311; Brightman, "Personality As a Metaphysical Principle," 56–57.

109. Edgar S. Brightman, *Is God a Person?* (New York: Association Press, 1932), quotes, 4–5, 14.

110. Knudson, *The Doctrine of God,* 15.

111. Ibid., 15–16; see Albert C. Knudson, "The Theology of Crisis," in *Report of the Sixth Biennial Meeting of the Conference of Theological Seminaries in the United States and Canada Bulletin* 6 (28 Sept. 1928): 52–77.

112. Knudson, *The Doctrine of God,* quote, 19; see Albert C. Knudson, "Humanism and Barthianism," *Religion in Life* 4 (winter 1935): 22–31; Knudson, "The Theology of Crisis," 52–77.

113. Borden Parker Bowne, *Theism* (New York: American Book Concern, 1902), quotes, 1, 9; Albert C. Knudson, "Religious Apriorism," in *Studies in Philosophy and Theology: By Former Students of Borden Parker Bowne,* ed. E. C. Wilm (New York: Abingdon Press, 1922), 93–127, quotes, 126.

114. Friedrich Schleiermacher, *The Christian Faith,* ed. H. R. Mackintosh and J. S. Stewart (1830; English edition, Edinburgh: T. & T. Clark, 1928), 12–18; Rudolf Otto, *The Idea of the Holy: An Inquiry into the Non-Rational Factor in the Idea of the Divine and its Relation to the Actual,* trans. John W. Harvey (London: Oxford University Press, 1928); Knudson, *The Doctrine of God,* 45–47.

115. Knudson, *The Doctrine of God,* 46–49, quotes, 46; Julius Kaftan, *Das Wesen der christlichen Religion* (Basel: C. Detloff, 1888); Ludwig Feuerbach, *The Essence of Christianity,* trans. George Eliot (New York: Harper & Row, 1957).

116. Schleiermacher, *The Christian Faith,* 133–37, "a universal element," 133; Friedrich Schleiermacher, *On Religion: Addresses in Response to Its Cultured Critics,* trans. Terrence N. Tice (1799; English ed., Richmond, Va.: John Knox Press, 1969), 77–95; Knudson, *The Doctrine of God,* 222–23.

117. Knudson, *The Doctrine of God,* 223–24; Ernst Troeltsch, *Gesammelte Schriften* (Aalen: Scientia, 1925), 805–36.

118. Knudson, *The Doctrine of God,* 224–25; Otto, *The Idea of the Holy,* 116–20, 140–46.

119. Knudson, *The Doctrine of God,* 67–85, 125–45, quotes, 84–85.

120. Ibid., 354–60, quotes, 358–59.
121. Ibid., quotes, 359–60.
122. Albert C. Knudson, "Methodism," in *An Encyclopedia of Religion*, ed. Vergilius Ferm (New York: Philosophical Library, 1945), 488; see Richard Watson, *Theological Institutes* (New York: Emory and Waugh, 1831); William Burt Pope, *Compendium of Christian Theology; Being Analytical Outlines of a Course of Theological Study, Biblical, Dogmatic, Historical*, 3 vols. (New York: Phillips & Hunt, 1880); Miner Raymond, *Systematic Theology*, 3 vols. (New York: Nelson & Phillips, 1877); John Miley, *Systematic Theology*, 2 vols. (New York: Hunt & Eaton, 1893).
123. See *The Wesleyan Theological Heritage: Essays of Albert C. Outler*, ed. Thomas C. Oden and Leicester R. Longden (Grand Rapids: Zondervan Publishing House, 1991), 21–37, 39–54, 97–110, 111–24.
124. Wesley, "The Witness of the Spirit," I, i, 7.
125. See *The Wesleyan Theological Heritage: Essays of Albert C. Outler*, 35–36.
126. Knudson, *The Doctrine of God*, 174–76, quote, 174.
127. Ibid., 175.
128. Ibid., quotes, 183, 187.
129. Knudson, "Methodism," 488.
130. Quoted in Albert C. Knudson, *The Validity of Religious Experience* (New York: Abingdon Press, 1937), 21.
131. Knudson, *The Doctrine of God*, quotes, 191–92, 180.
132. Ibid., 203–41, 285–324, quote, 300.
133. Ibid., quotes, 273, 274.
134. Ibid., 370–428; Schleiermacher, *The Christian Faith*, quote, 385; see Knudson, *Basic Issues in Christian Thought*, 122–41.
135. Knudson, *The Doctrine of God*, 422–24, quote, 424.
136. Ibid., 425–26, quote, 425; see Sheldon, *System of Christian Doctrine*, 227; Knudson *Basic Issues in Christian Thought*, 85–86.
137. McConnell, *The Christlike God*, 70.
138. Knudson, *The Doctrine of God*, quotes, 426–28; McConnell, *Living Together*, 28–30, quote, 29.
139. Knudson, *The Doctrine of God*, 418, 427–28.
140. Albert C. Knudson, *The Doctrine of Redemption* (New York: Abingdon-Cokesbury Press, 1933), 222–70, quotes, 266, 257.
141. Ibid., 223–49, quote, 233.
142. Knudson, *Basic Issues in Christian Thought*, 87–121, quotes, 119, 120; see F. R. Tennant, *The Concept of Sin* (Cambridge: Cambridge University Press, 1912), 45.
143. Knudson, *The Doctrine of Redemption*, 334–87.
144. Ibid., 334–66.
145. Ibid., 366–69, quotes, 366, 368, 369.
146. Ibid., 369–72.
147. Ibid., 370–76, quotes, 371, 376; quote from Abelard, 371; Borden Parker Bowne, *Studies in Christianity* (Boston: Houghton Mifflin Co., 1909), quote, 154; see Dorrien, *The Making of American Liberal Theology: Imagining Progressive Religion*, 385–87; Hastings Rashdall, *The Idea of Atonement in Christian Theology* (London: Macmillan Co., 1919), 357–62, 435–64.
148. Shailer Mathews, *The Atonement and the Social Process* (New York: Macmillan Co., 1930); Knudson, *The Doctrine of Redemption*, 377.
149. Curtis, *The Christian Faith Personally Given in a System of Doctrine*, 373; Knudson, *The Doctrine of Redemption*, 388–432, quote, 412.
150. Knudson, *The Doctrine of Redemption*, quotes, 412, 413.
151. Albert C. Knudson, "The Social Gospel and Theology," *Personalist* 5 (Apr. 1924): 102–14, quote, 109; McConnell, *Christian Citizenship*, 9; see Knudson, *The Principles of Christian Ethics* (New York: Abingdon-Cokesbury Press, 1943), 135–75.
152. Edgar S. Brightman, *Moral Laws* (New York: Abingdon Press, 1933); Brightman, *Persons and Values* (Boston: Boston University Press, 1952); Brightman, *Nature and Values* (New York: Abingdon-Cokesbury Press, 1945); Brightman, "A Personalistic View of Human Nature," *Religion in Life* 14 (spring 1945): 216–27; Knudson, *The Principles of*

Christian Ethics, 236–304; Walter G. Muelder, "Communitarian Dimensions of the Moral Laws," in *The Boston Personalist Tradition,* 240–44; Muelder, *Moral Law in Christian Social Ethics* (Richmond, Va.: John Knox Press, 1966); L. Harold DeWolf, *Responsible Freedom: Guidelines to Christian Action* (New York: Harper & Row, 1971).

153. Robert Neville, review of *The Boston Personalist Tradition in Theology,* ed. Paul Deats and Carol Robb, *Personalist Forum* 5 (spring 1989): 62–63; Knudson, "A Personalistic Approach to Theology," 240.

154. Knudson, "A Personalistic Approach to Theology," 240.

155. Edgar S. Brightman, "The Church, the Truth, and Society," in *Theology and Modern Life: Essays in Honor of Harris Franklin Rall,* ed. Paul A. Schilpp (Chicago: Willett, Clark & Co., 1940), 253–62, quotes, 262; see Amos Yong, "From Pietism to Pluralism: Boston Personalism and the Liberal Era in American Methodist Theology, 1876–1953," M.A. thesis, Portland State University, Portland, Ore.., 1995, 115–16.

156. Brightman, *The Finding of God,* 40.

157. Edgar S. Brightman, *The Future of Christianity* (New York: Abingdon Press, 1937), 80.

158. Edgar S. Brightman, "South of the Rio Grande," *Religion in Life* 15 (spring 1946): 191–201, quotes, 191; Brightman, "Personalism in Latin America," *The Personalist* 24 (spring 1943): 147–62.

159. Arthur S. Schopenhauer, *The World As Will and Idea,* 2 vols. (London: Routledge & Kegan Paul, 1906), 2: 359–95; G. W. F. Hegel, *Science of Logic,* trans. Johnson and Struthers (New York: Macmillan Co., 1929), 34; Brightman, *Person and Reality,* 13–14, 34–38; Bertocci, "The Personalism of Edgar S. Brightman and Ultimate Reality," 33; Brightman, *A Philosophy of Religion,* 347–49.

160. Brightman, *Person and Reality,* 46–48, quotes, 46.

161. Ibid., 46–54, quotes, 51; see Bertocci, "The Personalism of Edgar S. Brightman and Ultimate Reality," 34.

162. Brightman, "Bowne: Eternalist or Temporalist," 258–60, 264–65; Brightman, *Person and Reality,* 300–42, quotes, 323; Brightman, "A Temporalist View of God," *Journal of Religion* 12 (1932): 545–55; Bertocci, "The Personalism of Edgar S. Brightman and Ultimate Reality," 41.

163. Charles Hartshorne to Edgar S. Brightman, 18 Oct. 1934; Edgar S. Brightman to Charles Hartshorne, 10 Dec. 1934, Edgar S. Brightman Papers. Two major studies of the Brightman-Hartshorne correspondence have been published. The first, by Robert A. Gillies, contains extensive excerpts of the letters; more recently Randall E. Auxier and Mark Y. A. Davies have published the entire correspondence. See "The Brightman-Hartshorne Correspondence, 1934–1944," ed. Robert A. Gillies, *Process Studies* 17 (spring 1988): 9–18; and *Hartshorne and Brightman on God, Process, and Persons: The Correspondence, 1922–1945,* ed. Randall E. Auxier and Mark Y. A. Davies (Nashville: Vanderbilt University Press, 2001).

164. Edgar S. Brightman to Charles Hartshorne, 10 Dec. 1934; Hartshorne to Brightman, 10 Feb. 1935; Brightman to Hartshorne, 30 Jan. 1938; Hartshorne to Brightman, 22 Dec. 1938; Hartshorne to Brightman, 8 May 1939; Brightman to Hartshorne, 12 May 1939, Edgar S. Brightman Papers.

165. Charles Hartshorne, *Man's Vision of God* (Chicago: Willett, Clark & Co., 1941); Edgar S. Brightman, review of *Man's Vision of God,* by Charles Hartshorne, *Journal of Religion* 22 (Jan. 1942): 96–99; Charles Hartshorne to Edgar S. Brightman, 22 Jan. 1942; "no more the same," Hartshorne to Brightman, 23 Sept. 1942; Brightman to Hartshorne, 25 Sept. 1942, Edgar S. Brightman Papers. Gillies mistakenly identifies the Hartshorne book as *Moral Values and the Idea of God* (14); Auxier and Davies reprint excerpts of this book, 35–40.

166. Edgar S. Brightman to Charles Hartshorne, 31 Oct. 1942; Hartshorne to Brightman, 9 Nov. 1942; "I do not agree" and "If God contains," Brightman to Hartshorne, 31 Jan. 1943; "I cannot believe," Brightman to Hartshorne," 18 Sept. 1942; in the latter letter Brightman also defended his pacifism on pragmatic grounds; Edgar S. Brightman Papers.

167. "But not as he," Charles Hartshorne to Edgar S. Brightman, 13 Jan. 1944; "some sort of medal," Hartshorne to Brightman, 5 June 1943; "If I have not," Brightman to Hartshorne, 31 Oct. 1942, Edgar S. Brightman Papers.

168. Albert C. Knudson to Edgar S. Brightman, 5 May 1952, Edgar S. Brightman Papers.
169. Albert C. Knudson, "Humanism and Barthianism," *Religion and Life* 4 (winter 1935): 22–31, quotes, 25, 29.
170. Ibid., quotes, 29, 30.
171. Ibid., quotes, 31.
172. Albert C. Knudson to Edgar S. Brightman, 19 Dec. 1951, Edgar S. Brightman Papers.
173. Daniel L. Marsh to Albert C. Knudson, 26 Apr. 1938; Marsh to Knudson, 19 Aug. 1938; Albert C. Knudson Papers.
174. Knudson, *The Principles of Christian Ethics*, 262–80, quotes, 280.
175. Albert C. Knudson, *The Philosophy of War and Peace* (New York: Abingdon-Cokesbury Press, 1947), quotes, 82, 87, 90; Rufus Burrow Jr. to author, 22 May 2002, Burrow quote; see Knudson, *The Philosophy of Personalism*, 83; Paul Deats, "Introduction to Boston Personalism," in *The Boston Personalist Tradition in Philosophy, Social Ethics, and Theology*, 11; Burrow, *Personalism: A Critical Introduction*, 107–8; Schilling, "Albert Cornelius Knudson: Person and Theologian," in *The Boston Personalist Tradition in Philosophy, Social Ethics, and Theology*, 102–3.
176. Knudson, *The Philosophy of War and Peace*, 113–210, quote, 208.
177. Knudson, *Present Tendencies in Religious Thought*, 226–27; cited in Knudson, *Basic Issues in Christian Thought*, 45.
178. Knudson, Basic Issues in *Christian Thought*, quotes, 45.
179. Albert C. Knudson to Edgar S. Brightman, 20 July 1952, Edgar S. Brightman Papers; see Peter A. Bertocci, *Free Will, Responsibility, and Grace* (New York: Abingdon Press, 1957); Bertocci, *The Person God Is* (London: Allen & Unwin, 1970); L. Harold DeWolf, *A Theology of the Living Church* (New York: Harper & Brothers, 1953); DeWolf, *The Religious Revolt against Reason* (New York: Harper & Brothers, 1949); John H. Lavely, "Personalism Then and Now and Perhaps Hereafter," *Personalist Forum* 4 (fall 1988): 21–41; Walter G. Muelder, *Foundations of the Responsible Society* (New York: Abingdon Press, 1960); *Toward a Discipline of Social Ethics: Essays in Honor of Walter George Muelder*, ed. Paul K. Deats Jr. (Boston: Boston University Press, 1972); S. Paul Schilling, *God in an Age of Atheism* (New York: Abingdon Press, 1969).
180. Albert C. Knudson, "Personalism and Theology," *Personalist* 20 (summer 1939): 256–66; see Frederick Ferré, "Boston Personalism," *Religion and Philosophy in the United States of America* 1 (Essen: Verlag Die Blaue Eule, 1987), 197–211.
181. Knudson, "Personalism and Theology," quotes, 258–59.
182. Ibid., quotes, 257.
183. The strongest case for emphasizing the pragmatist aspects of Bowne's philosophy was made by Edward T. Ramsdell, "The Religious Pragmatism of Borden Parker Bowne (1847–1910)," *Personalist* 15 (Oct. 1934): 305–14. Ramsdell charged that "conservative students of his philosophy have, in general, underestimated the importance of the pragmatic elements by subsuming them under his rationalism," 305. See Ramsdell, "Pragmatism and Rationalism in the Philosophy of Borden Parker Bowne," *Personalist* 16 (Jan. 1935): 23–35; Ramsdell, "The Sources of Bowne's Pragmatism," *Personalist* 16 (spring 1935): 132–41.
184. Knudson, *The Validity of Religious Experience*, quotes, 170.
185. Ibid., 173–74.
186. Albert C. Knudson to Edgar S. Brightman, 25 Jan. 1940, Edgar S. Brightman Papers.
187. McConnell, *By the Way*, 224–69, quote, 266.
188. Ibid., quotes, 266, 254.
189. Ibid., quotes, 267, 268.

Chapter 6. Practical Divinity

1. Harry Emerson Fosdick, *The Living of These Days: An Autobiography* (New York: Harper & Brothers, 1956), 1–36, quotes, 35, 36; see Robert Moats Miller, *Harry Emerson Fosdick: Preacher, Pastor, Prophet* (New York: Oxford University Press, 1985), 3–20.
2. Fosdick, *The Living of These Days*, quote, 49; Miller, *Harry Emerson Fosdick*, yearbook quote, 34.
3. Fosdick, *The Living of These Days*, quote, 52.

4. Ibid., quotes, 53, 54, 55; "Clarke was my guide," Harry Emerson Fosdick to Rev. C. A. Roberts, 14 Feb. 1958, Harry Emerson Fosdick Collection, Series 2A, Box 8, Burke Library, Union Theological Seminary.

5. William Newton Clarke, *An Outline of Christian Theology* (1898; 15th ed., New York: Charles Scribner's Sons, 1906).

6. Fosdick, *The Living of These Days*, 57.

7. Ibid., 59, 60.

8. Ibid., quotes, 65, 66.

9. Ibid., quotes, 70, 71, 72.

10. Ibid., 75.

11. Ibid., 75; Miller, *Harry Emerson Fosdick*, 44–45.

12. Harry Emerson Fosdick, *The Meaning of Prayer* (Philadelphia: American Baptist Publication Society, 1915), quotes, xi; closing quote, Harry Emerson Fosdick to Dorothy A. Brockhoff, 14 Feb. 1958, Series 2A, Box 2, Harry Emerson Fosdick Collection.

13. Fosdick, *The Living of These Days*, 71–79, quote, 78; Miller, *Harry Emerson Fosdick*, 45–54.

14. Harry Emerson Fosdick, *The Second Mile* (New York: Association Press, 1908), quote, 24; see Miller, *Harry Emerson Fosdick*, 68; Fosdick, *The Living of These Days*, 87–88.

15. Harry Emerson Fosdick, *The Assurance of Immortality* (New York: Macmillan Co., 1913); Fosdick, *The Manhood of the Master* (New York: Association Press, 1913); Fosdick, *The Meaning of Faith* (New York: Association Press, 1917); Fosdick, *The Meaning of Service* (New York: Association Press, 1920).

16. Fosdick, *The Living of These Days*, quotes, 92, 93.

17. Fosdick, *The Assurance of Immortality*, quote, 140–41.

18. Fosdick, *The Meaning of Faith*, quotes, 101.

19. Fosdick, *The Meaning of Service*, quotes, 1, 104.

20. Rufus M. Jones, *Social Law in the Spiritual World: Studies in Human and Divine Inter-Relationship* (Philadelphia: J. C. Winston Co., 1904); "Religion of veracity," Fosdick, *The Living of These Days*, 110; "opened the door," *Rufus Jones Speaks to Our Time: An Anthology*, ed. Harry Emerson Fosdick (New York: Macmillan Co., 1951), v.

21. Georgia Harkness, *Foundations of Christian Knowledge* (New York: Abingdon Press, 1955), 130; Fosdick, *Rufus Jones Speaks to Our Time*, v; see Friedrich von Hügel, *The Mystical Element of Religion* (1904; 2d ed., London: J. M. Dent, 1923).

22. Rufus M. Jones, *Finding the Trail of Life* (New York: Macmillan, 1931), quotes, 20, 21; Elizabeth Gray Vining, *Friend of Life: The Biography of Rufus M. Jones* (Philadelphia: J. B. Lippincott, 1958), 17–22; see David Hinshaw, *Rufus Jones, Master Quaker* (New York: Putnam, 1951); Theodore Dreiser, *The Bulwark* (Garden City, N.Y.: Doubleday, 1946). Jones judged that *The Bulwark* "never gets inside of this Quaker family or of a Quaker meeting, and his characters remain too much like constructed frames for presenting the author's theories," quoted in Vining, *Friend of Life*, 29.

23. Jones, *Finding the Trail of Life*, quotes 146, 130; Rufus M. Jones, "Why I Enroll with the Mystics," in *Contemporary Theology: Theological Autobiographies*, ed. Vergilius Ferm (New York: Round Table Press, 1932), 1:191–215, closing quote, 195; see Jones, *The Story of George Fox* (New York: Macmillan, 1919); Jones, *George Fox, Seeker and Friend* (New York: Harper & Brothers, 1930).

24. Jones, "Why I Enroll with the Mystics," 195–96; Vining, *Friend of Life*, 53–65; Rufus M. Jones, *Practical Christianity* (Philadelphia: John C. Winston, 1899), 162–71, 179–206; see Jones, *Quakerism and the Simple Life* (London: Headley Brothers, 1906); Jones, *Quakerism: A Religion of Life* (London: Headley Brothers, 1908).

25. Jones, *Practical Christianity*, quotes, 188–89, 194, 199, 196, 200.

26. Rufus M. Jones, *A Dynamic Faith* (London: Headley Brothers, 1901), "deep calls unto deep," 31; Jones, "Why I Enroll with the Mystics," quote, 196.

27. Jones, "Why I Enroll with the Mystics," 196–98, 211; Vining, *Friend of Life*, 85–90; Josiah Royce, *Studies of Good and Evil: A Series of Essays upon the Problems of Philosophy and of Life* (New York: D. Appleton, 1898).

28. See Rufus M. Jones, *A Boy's Religion from Memory* (Philadelphia: Ferris & Leach, 1902). Jones's *Finding the Trail of Life*, cited above, was an expanded revision of this memoir.

29. Jones, *Social Law in the Spiritual World*, 30–44, quotes, 43–44.

30. Ibid., 44.
31. Ibid., 49–85.
32. Ibid., 69–73, quotes, 70, 71.
33. Ibid., 30–31.
34. Rufus M. Jones, *The World Within* (New York: Macmillan, 1918), quotes, 131, 147; Jones, *New Studies in Mystical Religion* (New York: Macmillan, 1927), quote, 121–22; see Jones, *The Life of Christ* (Chicago: American Library Association, 1926).
35. See Rufus M. Jones, *Some Exponents of Mystical Religion* (New York: Abingdon Press, 1930); Jones, *The Faith and Practice of the Quakers* (London: Methuen, 1927); Jones, *The Later Periods of Quakerism*, 2 vols. (London: Macmillan, 1921).
36. Rufus M. Jones, *A Service of Love in War-Time: American Friends' Relief Work in Europe, 1917–1919* (New York: Macmillan, 1920).
37. Rufus M. Jones, "How Shall We Think of Christ?" in *Religious Foundations*, ed. Rufus M. Jones (New York: Macmillan, 1923), 15–29, quote, 21.
38. Rufus M. Jones, *Pathways to the Reality of God* (New York: Macmillan, 1931), quotes, 17, 187, 215.
39. Quoted in Vining, *Friend of Life*, 62, 24.
40. Fosdick, *Rufus Jones Speaks to Our Time*, xii.
41. Fosdick, *The Living of These Days*, 120–31; Harry Emerson Fosdick, "I Will Not Bless War!" *Christian Century* 58 (22 Jan. 1941), 115; Fosdick, "The Trenches and the Church at Home," *Atlantic Monthly* (Jan. 1919).
42. Harry Emerson Fosdick, *The Challenge of the Present Crisis* (New York: George H. Doran Co., 1917), quotes, 52, 53, 63, 61–62.
43. Ibid., quotes, 27, 99.
44. Harry Emerson Fosdick, untitled sermon, 28 Nov. 1918, cited in Miller, *Harry Emerson Fosdick*, 78; Fosdick, "Then Our Boys Came!" *American Magazine* (Dec. 1918); Fosdick, "A 'Y' Canteen Next to No Man's Land," *Independent* (9 Nov. 1918).
45. Harry Emerson Fosdick, Christmas sermon of 1919, cited in Miller, *Harry Emerson Fosdick*, 89.
46. Harry Emerson Fosdick, Kirby Page, William P. Merrill, "The Churches' Plea Against War and the War System," 1922, Swarthmore College Peace Collection, cited in Miller, *Harry Emerson Fosdick*, 496–97.
47. Harry Emerson Fosdick, introduction to Kirby Page, *War: Its Causes, Consequences, and Cure* (New York: George H. Doran, 1923), n.p. [quotes, i, iii].
48. Harry Emerson Fosdick, "The Unknown Soldier," Armistice Day sermon, 1933, reprinted in Fosdick, *Riverside Sermons* (New York: Harper & Brothers, 1958), quotes, 352, 343–344.
49. Fosdick, *The Living of These Days*, 121.
50. Fosdick, "The Unknown Soldier," 351.
51. Harry Emerson Fosdick, *Christianity and Progress* (New York: Fleming H. Revell Co., 1922), 113–19, 167–206, quote, 119; see Henry George, *Progress and Poverty* (New York: Robert Schalkenbach Foundation, 1879, reprint 1955).
52. Harry Emerson Fosdick, *The Modern Use of the Bible* (New York: Macmillan Co., 1924); Fosdick, *A Guide to Understanding the Bible: The Development of Ideas within the Old and New Testaments* (New York: Harper & Brothers, 1938).
53. Fosdick, *Christianity and Progress*, 208–13, quotes, 209, 212. This section adapts material from Dorrien, *Soul in Society: The Making and Renewal of Social Christianity* (Minneapolis: Fortress Press, 1995), 64–65.
54. Fosdick, *Christianity and Progress*, 225–30, quotes, 219, 106.
55. Ibid., 123–24, quotes, 123.
56. Ibid., 159–63, quotes, 160, 161; see Harry Emerson Fosdick, *What Is Vital in Religion: Sermons on Contemporary Christian Problems* (New York: Harper & Brothers, 1955).
57. Harry Emerson Fosdick, "Shall the Fundamentalists Win?" *Christian Work* 112 (10 June 1922): 716–22; reprinted in *American Protestant Thought: The Liberal Era*, ed. William R. Hutchison (New York: Harper & Row, 1968), 170–82, quotes, 172, 176.
58. Fosdick, "Shall the Fundamentalists Win?" quote, 181; Dieffenbach quoted in the *New York Times*, 29 Nov. 1924; cited in Fosdick, *The Living of These Days*, 166.
59. Fosdick, "Shall the Fundamentalists Win?" quote, 173.

60. Ibid., quote, 179; Fosdick, *The Living of These Days*, "if ever" quote, 145.
61. J. Gresham Machen, *Christianity and Liberalism* (New York: Macmillan Co., 1923), 120; Fosdick, "Shall the Fundamenalists Win?" 173.
62. Harry Emerson Fosdick, "Evolution and Mr. Bryan," *New York Times* (12 Mar. 1925); Fosdick, *The Living of These Days*, heretic quote, 176.
63. See George M. Marsden, *Fundamentalism and American Culture: The Shaping of Twentieth-Century Evangelicalism 1870–1925* (Oxford: Oxford University Press, 1980); Joel A. Carpenter, *Revive Us Again: The Reawakening of American Fundamentalism* (New York: Oxford University Press, 1997); Gary Dorrien, *The Remaking of Evangelical Theology* (Louisville: Westminster John Knox Press, 1998).
64. Harry Emerson Fosdick to Henry Sloane Coffin, 27 Apr. 1927; Fosdick to Coffin, 10 May 1928; Fosdick to Coffin, 27 May 1929, Harry Emerson Fosdick Collection, Series 2A, Box 2; Fosdick, *The Living of These Days*, 164; Fosdick, "Shall the Fundamentalists Win?" 179, 181.
65. Harry Emerson Fosdick, *Adventurous Religion and Other Essays* (New York: Harper & Brothers, 1926), 11.
66. Harry Emerson Fosdick, *As I See Religion* (New York: Grosset & Dunlap, 1932), 51; Fosdick, *The Power to See It Through* (New York: Harper & Brothers, 1935), 35.
67. Fosdick, *As I See Religion*, quotes, 41, 42, 58.
68. Harry Emerson Fosdick, *The Hope of the World* (New York: Harper & Brothers, 1933), 103.
69. Fosdick, *As I See Religion*, 62.
70. Fosdick, *Christianity and Progress*, quote, 233–34.
71. Fosdick, *As I See Religion*, 119–59.
72. Ibid., quotes, 135, 136.
73 Ibid., quote, 141; see Miller, *Harry Emerson Fosdick*, 353–67.
74. Harry Emerson Fosdick, "Blessed Be Biography," *Ladies' Home Journal* 41 (Apr. 1924): 18, 113–14, quotes, 18.
75. Fosdick, *Adventurous Religion and Other Essays*, quotes, 175–76.
76. Harry Emerson Fosdick, *The Hope of the World: Twenty-Five Sermons on Christianity Today* (New York: Harper & Brothers, 1933), 49–58, 117–25.
77. Harry Emerson Fosdick, *Successful Christian Living: Sermons on Christianity Today* (New York: Harper & Brothers), 1937; Fosdick, *Living under Tension: Sermons on Christianity Today* (New York: Harper & Brothers, 1941); *On Being Fit to Live With: Sermons on Post-War Christianity* (New York: Harper & Brothers, 1946).
78. Harry Emerson Fosdick, *Twelve Tests of Character* (New York: Association Press, 1923), 57, 58.
79. Fosdick, *Successful Christian Living*, reference to Paul, 82; Fosdick, *Living Under Tension*, Palm Sunday sermon, 233–42.
80. Fosdick, *Successful Christian Living*, 79–82, quotes, 80, 81; see *Harry Emerson Fosdick's Art of Preaching: An Anthology*, ed. Lionel Crocker (Springfield, Ill.: Charles C. Thomas, 1971).
81. William James, *The Varieties of Religious Experience* (New York: Longmans, Green & Co., 1902); Edwin D. Starbuck, *The Psychology of Religion: An Empirical Study of the Growth of Religious Consciousness* (New York: Charles Scribner's Sons, 1906); Edward Scribner Ames, *The Psychology of Religious Experience* (Boston: Houghton Mifflin Co., 1910); George A. Coe, *The Psychology of Religion* (Chicago: University of Chicago Press, 1916).
82. Justin Wroe Nixon, *The Moral Crisis in Christianity* (New York: Harper & Row, 1931), 32–33; Fosdick, *Successful Christian Living*, 9.
83. Fosdick, *Successful Christian Living*, quote, 9; on "preaching as group counseling," see Fosdick, *The Living of These Days*, 214–15; Fosdick, "Personal Counseling and Preaching," *Pastoral Psychology* 3 (Mar. 1952), reprinted in *Harry Emerson Fosdick's Art of Preaching*, 51–57; Edmund Holt Linn, *Preaching as Counseling: The Unique Method of Harry Emerson Fosdick* (Valley Forge, Pa.: Judson Press, 1966).
84. Gordon W. Allport, *Personality: A Psychological Interpretation* (London: Constable, 1938); Karen Horney, *The Neurotic Personality of Our Time* (New York: W. W. Norton, 1937); J. A. Hadfield, *Psychology and Morals: An Analysis of Character* (London: Methuen, 1936); Hadfield, *Psychology and Modern Problems* (New York: Longmans, 1936). As always, Fosdick cited James's *Varieties of Religious Experience*.

85. Harry Emerson Fosdick, *On Being a Real Person* (New York: Harper & Brothers, 1943), 188–209; see Rollo May, *Existential Psychology* (New York: McGraw Hill, 1969); Carl Rogers, *Dealing with Psychological Tensions* (Indianapolis: Bobbs-Merrill, 1965); Rogers, *Carl Rogers—Dialogues: Conversations with Martin Buber, Paul Tillich, B. F. Skinner, Gregory Bateson, Michael Polanyi, Rollo May, and Others* (London: Constable, 1990).

86. Fosdick, *On Being a Real Person*, quotes, 200, 202, 240.

87. See Julius Seelye Bixler, *Religion for Free Minds* (New York: Harper & Brothers, 1939); Bixler, *Conversations with an Unrepentant Liberal* (New Haven, Conn.: Yale University Press, 1946).

88. Reinhold Niebuhr, "How Adventurous Is Dr. Fosdick?" *Christian Century* 44 (6 Jan. 1927): 17–18; Reinhold Niebuhr, "The Significance of Dr. Fosdick in American Religious Thought," *Union Seminary Quarterly Review* 8 (May 1953): 3–6, quote, 5; Harry Emerson Fosdick to D. B. Robertson, 17 Mar. 1959, Harry Emerson Fosdick Collection, Series 2A, Box 8.

89. Fosdick, *Successful Christian Living*, 153–64.

90. Ibid., quotes, 156.

91. Ibid., 156–57, quotes 157.

92. Ibid., quotes, 158, 159.

93. Georgia Harkness, "Days of My Years," unpublished autobiographical sketch written for the Pacific Coast Theological Group (1950s), Georgia Harkness Collection, The United Library, Garrett-Evangelical Theological Seminary/Seabury-Western Seminary, 1–4, 9; "taciturnity" quote in Georgia Harkness, *Grace Abounding* (New York: Abingdon Press, 1963), 26.

94. Harkness, "Days of My Years," 3, 8–11. See Harkness, *Grace Abounding*, which gives brief reflections on various periods of her life; Rosemary Skinner Keller, *Georgia Harkness: For Such a Time As This* (Nashville: Abingdon Press, 1992); Keller, "Georgia Harkness—Theologian of the People: Evangelical Liberal and Social Prophet," in *Spirituality and Social Responsibility: Vocational Vision of Women in the United Methodist Tradition,* ed. Rosemary Skinner Keller (Nashville: Abingdon Press, 1993), 205–29; Margaret Frakes, "Theology Is Her Province," *Christian Century* 69 (15 Mar. 1939): 348–51; Helen Johnson, "Georgia Harkness: She Made Theology Understandable," *United Methodists Today* 1 (Oct. 1974): 55–58. Keller gives a detailed account of Harkness's family background and early life, 33–78.

95. Harkness, "Days of My Years," 12, 15; Keller, *Georgia Harkness*, 79–87. See James Edwin Creighton, *Studies in Speculative Philosophy* (New York: Macmillan Co, 1925); Patricia A. Graham, "Expansion and Exclusion: A History of Women in American Higher Education," *Signs* 3 (summer 1978): 759–87; Roberta Frankfort, *Collegiate Women: Domesticity and Career in Turn-of-the-Century America* (New York: New York University Press, 1977).

96. Harkness, "Days of My Years," 14, 16–18; see Galen M. Fisher, *John R. Mott: Architect of Co-operation and Unity* (New York: Association Press, 1952); C. Howard Hopkins, *John R. Mott* (Grand Rapids: Eerdmans, 1979).

97. Walter Scott Athearn, *An Adventure in Religious Education: The Story of a Decade of Experimentation in the Collegiate and Professional Training of Christian Workers* (New York: Century Co., 1930); Athearn, *Character Building in a Democracy* (New York: Macmillan Co., 1925); George W. Tupper, "The Church and New Americans," *Department of Social and Public Service,* Service Series 32 (Boston: Unitarian Association, n.d.), 1–14; Charles Carroll, *The Community Survey in Relation to Church Efficiency* (New York: Association Press, 1915); Keller, Georgia Harkness, 102–9; Alan M. Kraut, *The Huddled Masses: The Immigrant in American Society, 1880–1921* (Arlington Heights, Ill.: Harlan Davidson, 1982).

98. Georgia Harkness, *The Church and the Immigrant* (New York: George H. Doran Co., 1921), Tupper quote, vii–viii; Harkness quote, 100–101; see discussion in Keller, *Georgia Harkness*, 108–11.

99. Harkness, "Days of My Years," "beyond question," 18; Georgia Harkness to Edgar S. Brightman, 24 Jan. 1937, Edgar S. Brightman Papers, Mugar Library, Boston University. Harkness wrote, "Do you remember when I asked you in the spring of 1920 whether I should go on [to] get a Ph.D. you spoke doubtfully on the score that I lacked

physical rigor and gave up on things too easily?" Brightman scrawled in the margin that he did not remember the conversation that way. His other female doctoral students in the early 1920s were Mildred Cranston and Pearl Winans.

100. Harkness, "Days of My Years," 19.
101. Edgar S. Brightman to Georgia Harkness, 17 Aug. 1921; Harkness to Brightman, 22 Aug. 1921; Brightman to Harkness, 28 Aug. 1921; Harkness to Brightman, 10 Sept. 1921; Brightman to Harkness, 14 Oct. 1921; Harkness to Brightman, 24 Oct. 1921; Brightman to Harkness, 17 June 1922; Harkness to Brightman, 9 Jan. 1925; Harkness to Brightman, 20 June 1934; Edgar S. Brightman Papers. Brightman let pass Harkness's simplistic rendering of Hegelian dialectic.
102. Edgar S. Brightman to Georgia Harkness, 9 Mar. 1925; Brightman to Harkness, 20 Nov. 1925; Harkness to Brightman, 24 Nov. 1925; Edgar S. Brightman Papers.
103. Edgar S. Brightman to Georgia Harkness, [?] Oct. 1922; "Jones" letter, Brightman to Harkness, 26 Dec. 1936; "high type," Brightman to Bernice V. Brown, 2 Feb. 1926; "only defect," Brightman to Agnes L. Rogers, 7 Jan. 1925; Edgar S. Brightman Papers. Georgia Harkness, "T. H. Green As a Philosopher of Religion," *Personalist* (July 1924): 172–78; Harkness, "Robert Elsmere and Thomas Hill Green," *Personalist* (Apr. 1926), 115–19; Harkness, "The Relations between Philosophy of Religion and Ethics in the Thought of T. H. Green," (Boston University, Ph.D. diss., 1923). The official manuscript of her dissertation is missing from the library of Boston University.
104. Georgia Harkness to Edgar S. Brightman, 2 May 1924.
105. Georgia Harkness, "The Ministry As a Vocation for Women," *Christian Advocate* (10 Apr. 1924), 454–55.
106. See discussion in Keller, *Georgia Harkness: For Such a Time as This*, 136.
107. Sherwood Eddy, *Eighty Adventurous Years: An Autobiography* (New York: Harper & Brothers, 1955), 127–28; *Kirby Page, Social Evangelist: The Autobiography of a Twentieth-Century Prophet for Peace*, ed. Harold E. Fey (Nyack, N.Y.: Fellowship Press, 1975), 99–100.
108. Robert Moats Miller, *American Protestantism and Social Issues* (Chapel Hill, N.C.: University of North Carolina Press, 1958), 46, 251; Eddy, *Eighty Adventurous Years: An Autobiography*, 127–28; *Kirby Page, Social Evangelist*, 99–100; Sherwood Eddy, *What Shall We Do about War?* (New York: Eddy & Page, 1935); Harkness, *Grace Abounding*, 131–32; Keller, *Georgia Harkness: For Such a Time As This*, 137–38; Richard Wightman Fox, *Reinhold Niebuhr: A Biography* (New York: Pantheon Books, 1985), 75–76.
109. "Niebuhr-then" quote, Harkness, "Days of My Years," 21; remaining quotes in Georgia Harkness to Edgar S. Brightman, 21 Sept. 1924, Edgar S. Brightman Papers.
110. Georgia Harkness, "Germany's Place in the Shadow," *Christian Advocate* (22 Jan. 1925), 111.
111. Georgia Harkness, "What the War Has Done to France," *Christian Advocate* (19 Feb. 1925), "we had better" quotes, 243; Harkness, "A Spiritual Pilgrimage," *Christian Century* 56 (15 Mar. 1939), "war destroys" and "I believe" quotes, 350; see Keller, *Georgia Harkness: For Such a Time As This*, 142–43.
112. "Resulting" quote, Georgia Harkness to Edgar S. Brightman, 24 Nov. 1925; "anti" quote, Harkness to Brightman, 8 Nov. 1925; Harkness to Brightman, 15 Nov. 1925; Brightman to Harkness, 20 Nov. 1925, Edgar S. Brightman Papers.
113. "Feeling some stuffiness," Harkness, "Days of My Years," 21; Georgia Harkness to Edgar S. Brightman, 27 Jan. 1928.
114. Georgia Harkness to Edgar S. Brightman, 27 Jan. 1928; Brightman to Harkness, 29 Jan. 1928; see Keller, *Georgia Harkness: For Such a Time As This*, 152–55.
115. Georgia Harkness, *Conflicts in Religious Thought* (New York: Henry Holt & Co., 1929), quotes, 131, 221, 317. Fifteen years after Harkness died, her niece Peg Overholt told Rosemary Skinner Keller that she knew about the man whose recommendation for Harkness reported "that she was completely without sex appeal" (Keller, *Georgia Harkness: For Such a Time As This*, 155).
116. Georgia Harkness, *The Resources of Religion* (New York: Henry Holt & Co., 1936), quotes, 97, 98.
117. Ibid., quotes, 93, 97, closing argument 209.

118. Edgar S. Brightman to Georgia Harkness, 8 Dec. 1935; Edgar S. Brightman Papers.
119. Georgia Harkness, *The Recovery of Ideals* (New York: Charles Scribner's Sons, 1937), quotes, 3, 30.
120. Ibid., 78–82, quote, 80–81.
121. Ibid., 93–103, quotes, 101, 102.
122. Ibid., 135–58; see Alfred North Whitehead, *Process and Reality: An Essay in Cosmology* (New York: Macmillan Co., 1929), 532.
123. Harkness, *The Recovery of Ideals,* 158–63, quotes, 162.
124. Ibid., 162–82, quotes, 165, 166.
125. Ibid., 215–22, quotes, 221, 222.
126. Edgar S. Brightman to Georgia Harkness, 26 Nov. 1936; Edgar S. Brightman Papers.
127. Georgia Harkness to Edgar S. Brightman, 19 Feb. 1938; Edgar S. Brightman Papers.
128. Ibid.
129. Edgar S. Brightman to Georgia Harkness, 27 Feb. 1938; Edgar S. Brightman Papers.
130. Georgia Harkness to Edgar S. Brightman, 20 Nov. 1935; Harkness to Brightman, 20 Nov. 1936; Edgar S. Brightman Papers; Georgia Harkness, "The Abyss and the Given," *Christendom* 3 (autumn 1938), quote, 519–20; see Martha Lynne Scott, "The Theology and Social Thought of Georgia Harkness," Ph.D. diss., Northwestern University, joint Garrett-Evangelical Theological Seminary/Northwestern University program, 1984; Diane E. S. Carpenter, "Georgia Harkness's Distinctive Personalistic Synthesis," Ph.D. diss., Boston University Graduate School, 1988.
131. Samuel McCrea Cavert, "The Younger Theologians," *Religion in Life* 4 (autumn 1936): 520–31; Georgia Harkness to Edgar S. Brightman, 28 Oct. 1938, Edgar S. Brightman Papers; Harkness, "Days of My Years," quote, 24.
132. Harkness, "A Spiritual Pilgrimage," 349; for examples of her verse, see Georgia Harkness, *Holy Flame* (Boston: B. Humphries, 1935); Harkness, *The Glory of God: Poems and Prayers for Devotional Use* (New York: Abingdon-Cokesbury, 1943); Harkness, *Be Still and Know* (New York: Abingdon, 1953).
133. Harkness, "A Spiritual Pilgrimage," 349.
134. Ibid., 349.
135. Harkness, "Days of My Years," 5, 7, 22–23, quotes 7, 23; see Harkness, *Grace Abounding,* 24–26.
136. Harkness, "Days of My Years," quote, 23; Georgia Harkness to Edgar S. Brightman, 10 Sept. 1931; Harkness to Brightman, 30 Oct. 1939; Edgar S. Brightman Papers.
137. "Remarks of Dr. Georgia Harkness at the Oxford Conference," Summer 1937, Harkness Collection, Garrett-Evangelical Theological Seminary; Harkness, "Women and the Church, *Christian Century* (2 June 1937), 708.
138. Keller, *Georgia Harkness: For Such a Time As This,* 162–63; Harkness, "Days of My Years," 21; Rosemary Skinner Keller, "'When the Subject Is Female': The Impact of Gender on Revisioning American Religious History," in *Religious Diversity and American Religious History: Studies in Traditions and Cultures,* ed. Walter H. Conser Jr. and Sumner B. Twiss (Athens, Ga.: University of Georgia Press, 1997), 111.
139. Georgia Harkness, "For Such a Time As This," *Christian Advocate* (18 July 1940), 686; see Harkness, *The Faith by Which the Church Lives* (New York: Abingdon Press, 1940).
140. Georgia Harkness, Christmas Letter to Friends, "Just Before Christmas, 1941," Edgar S. Brightman Papers; Georgia Harkness to Horace Greeley Smith, 17 Apr. 1943, Harkness Collection, Garrett-Evangelical Theological Seminary; see Keller, *Georgia Harkness: For Such a Time As This,* 219–20.
141. Georgia Harkness, "A Pacifist Ecumenical Witness," *Christian Century* 58 (July 2, 1941), 859–860; see Harry Emerson Fosdick, "I Will Not Bless War!" *Christian Century* 58 (22 Jan. 1941), 115–18; Harkness, "The Christian's Dilemma," *Christian Century* 58 (6 Aug. 1941), 977–79.
142. Keller, *Georgia Harkness: For Such a Time As This,* 232–35.
143. Georgia Harkness, *The Dark Night of the Soul* (New York: Abingdon-Cokesbury Press, 1945), quotes, 9, 15, 20.
144. "Alternative" quote, Harkness, "Days of My Years," 26; Harkness, *The Dark Night of the Soul,* 168–84, quotes, 171, 175, 179.
145. Georgia Harkness to Edgar S. Brightman, 10 July 1939, Edgar S. Brightman Papers. See

Harris Franklin Rall, *Der Leibnizsche Substanzbegriff* (Halle: Ehrhardt Karras, 1899; Rall, *The Teachings of Jesus* (New York: Abingdon Press, 1918); Rall, *The Meaning of God* (Nashville: Cokesbury Press, 1926).

146. Georgia Harkness to Edgar S. Brightman, 17 Aug. 1939; Harkness to Brightman, 13 May 1942, Edgar S. Brightman Papers. This episode is extensively discussed in Keller, *Georgia Harkness: For Such a Time As This,* 236–44. "Never to have sensed," Harkness, "Days of My Years," 26.

147. Georgia Harkness, *Understanding the Christian Faith* (New York: Abingdon Press, 1947), quotes, 13, 9; Harkness, *Prayer and the Common Life* (New York: Abingdon Press, 1948); Harkness, *The Gospel and Our World* (New York: Abingdon Press, 1949).

148. Harkness, *Understanding the Christian Faith,* 66–85, quote, 83.

149. Harkness, *The Gospel and Our World,* 41–58, quotes, 53, 58; Harkness, *Understanding the Christian Faith,* 31; see Fosdick, *The Modern Use of the Bible,* 97–130.

150. Georgia Harkness, *Toward Understanding the Bible* (Cincinnati: Women's Division of Christian Service, Board of Missions and Church Extension, Methodist Church, 1952); Harkness, *What Christians Believe* (Nashville: Abingdon Press, 1965).

151. Harkness, *Foundations of Christian Knowledge,* 73–94; William Temple, *Nature, Man, and God* (London: Macmillan Co., 1934), 312–22.

152. Harkness, *Foundations of Christian Knowledge,* 98.

153. Ibid., quote, 100.

154. Ibid., 130–35.

155. Ibid., 131–35, quotes, 133, 135.

156. Murray Leiffer and Dorothy Leiffer, *Enter the Old Portals: Reminiscences: Fifty Years on a Seminary Campus* (Evanston, Ill.: Garrett-Evangelical Theological Seminary, 1987), 66; Keller, *Georgia Harkness: For Such a Time As This,* 251.

157. "I came," Harkness, "Days of My Years," 29; Edgar S. Brightman to Georgia Harkness, 7 Mar. 1941, Edgar S. Brightman Papers; Harkness, "Divine Sovereignty and Human Freedom," in *Personalism in Theology: A Symposium in Honor of Albert Cornelius Knudson,* ed. Edgar S. Brightman (Boston: Boston University Press, 1943), 136–51. Two of Harkness's best known hymns were "This Is My Song" and "Hope of the World," in *United Methodist Hymnal* (Nashville: United Methodist Publishing House, 1989), 437, 178. "Hope of the World" won the Hymn Society of America's contest for a new hymn in 1954 in recognition of the Evanston Assembly of the World Council of Churches. See Deborah Carlton Loftis, "The Hymns of Georgia Harkness," master's thesis, Southern Baptist Theological Seminary, 1977. On Harkness's place in the Boston personalist school, see Dianne Carpenter and Rolaine Franz, "Georgia Harkness As a Personalist Theologian," in *The Boston Personalist Tradition in Philosophy, Social Ethics, and Theology,* ed. Paul Deats and Carol Robb (Macon, Ga.: Mercer University Press, 1986), 159–85.

158. Harkness, *Grace Abounding,* 132; see Marianne H. Micks, "Georgia Harkness: Chastened Liberal," *Theology Today* 53 (Oct. 1996): 311–19; Keller, "'When the Subject Is Female': The Impact of Gender on Revisioning American Religious History," 122–25; Mary Elizabeth Mullino Moore, "To Search and to Witness: Theological Agenda of Georgia Harkness," *Quarterly Review* 13 (fall 1993): 3–23.

159. Harkness, "Days of My Years," 28.

160. Benjamin E. Mays, *Born to Rebel* (New York: Charles Scribner's Sons, 1971), vii, 1–14, quote, 10; see Benjamin E. Mays, "Why I Believe There Is a God," in *Why I Believe There Is a God: Sixteen Essays by Negro Clergymen,* ed. Howard Thurman (Chicago: Johnson Publishing Co., 1965), 3–4. According to local legend, the town of Ninety Six, N.C. got its name from an event during the Revolutionary War; the town was ninety-six miles from the Old Star Fort in North Carolina, which was then occupied by the British.

161. Mays, *Born to Rebel,* 22–34, quotes, 23, 27, 34; see Benjamin E. Mays, *Disturbed about Man* (Richmond, Va.: John Knox Press, 1969), 91.

162. Mays, *Born to Rebel,* 35–63, quotes, 38, 40; "where I could compete," Benjamin E. Mays, "Why I Went to Bates," *Bates College Bulletin* (Jan. 1966), n.p.

163. "I had the erroneous," Mays, "Why I Went to Bates," n.p.; Mays, *Born to Rebel,* 54–61, quotes, 55; see William Anthony, *Bates College and Its Background: A Review of Origins and Causes* (Philadelphia: Judson Press, 1936); Donald W. Harward, "Benjamin Mays

and Bates College," *Walking Integrity: Benjamin Elijah Mays, Mentor to Generations*, ed. Lawrence Edward Carter Sr. (Atlanta: Scholars Press, 1996), 477–79.

164. Mays, *Born to Rebel*, quotes, 55, 60.

165. Ibid., 160–61; Randal M. Jelks, "Mays's Academic Formation, 1917–1936," in *Walking Integrity: Benjamin Elijah Mays, Mentor to Martin Luther King Jr.*, 121–22; Charles H. Arnold, *Near the Edge of Battle: A Short History of the Divinity School and the "Chicago School of Theology," 1866–1966* (Chicago: Divinity School Association, 1966), 27.

166. "Despite my extremely," Mays, *Born to Rebel*, 65; "you need to know," Mays interview with J. Oscar McCloud, Jan. 1982, quoted in Jelks, "Mays's Academic Formation, 1917–1936," 119.

167. Mays, *Born to Rebel*, quote, 65; see Allan H. Spear, *Black Chicago: The Making of a Negro Ghetto, 1890–1920* (Chicago: University of Chicago Press, 1967), 22–23, 129–50; Carter, "The Life of Benjamin Elijah Mays," in *Walking Integrity: Benjamin Elijah Mays, Mentor to Martin Luther King Jr.*, 2–3.

168. Mays, *Born to Rebel*, 66–98, quotes, 80, 89–90; closing quote, Benjamin Elijah Mays, eulogy for Mordecai Wyatt Johnson, cited in Carter, "The Life of Benjamin Elijah Mays," 3.

169. Benjamin E. Mays, "Pagan Survivals in Christianity" (master's thesis, University of Chicago Divinity School, 1925), 1; see Shirley Jackson Case, *The Evolution of Christianity: A Genetic Study of First-Century Christianity in Relation to Its Religious Environment* (Chicago: University of Chicago Press, 1914); Case, *The Social Origins of Christianity* (Chicago: University of Chicago Press, 1923); Arnold, *Near the Edge of Battle*, 27.

170. Mays, "Pagan Survivals in Christianity," 19–41, quote, 89.

171. Benjamin E. Mays, *Quotable Quotes of Benjamin E. Mays* (New York: Vantage Press, 1983), 18–19.

172. Mays, *Born to Rebel*, 99–124; Carter, "The Life of Benjamin Elijah Mays," 4–5; Maceo Crenshaw Daily Jr., "Benjamin E. Mays on Aspects of Black History: Booker T. Washington, W. E. B. DuBois, Mordecai Johnson, Emmett Jay Scott, and Howard University," in *Walking Integrity: Benjamin Elijah Mays, Mentor to Generations*, 333–46.

173. Mays, *Born to Rebel*, quotes, 125, 127.

174. Carter G. Woodson, *The History of the Negro Church* (Washington, D.C.: Associated Publishers, 1921); W. A. Daniel, *The Education of Negro Ministers* (New York: Institute of Social and Religious Research, 1925); C. Luther Fry, *The U.S. Looks at Its Churches* (New York: Institute of Social and Religious Research, 1930).

175. Benjamin E. Mays and Joseph W. Nicholson, *The Negro's Church* (New York: Institute of Social and Religious Research, 1933), quotes, 3, 278; see Benjamin E. Mays, "Christianity in a Changing World," *National Education Outlook among Negroes* (Dec. 1937), 18–21.

176. Mays and Nicholson, *The Negro's Church*, 16–19, 38–93, quotes, 17, 85, 91; see Benjamin E. Mays, "The Negro Church in American Life," *Christendom* 5 (summer 1940): 387–89.

177. Mays and Nicholson, *The Negro's Church*, 278–92, quotes, 281; see Benjamin E. Mays, "The American Negro and the Christian Church," *Journal of Negro Education* 8 (July 1939): 530–38.

178. Ibid., 288–89.

179. See Booker T. Washington and Robert E. Park, *The Man Farthest Down: A Record of Observation in Europe* (1912; reprint, New Brunswick, N.J.: Transaction, 1984); Dorothy Ross, *The Origins of American Social Science* (Cambridge: Cambridge University Press, 1991), 357–61, 438–40; Jelks, "Mays's Academic Formation," 123–24. For a critique of Park's argument and influence, see Aldon D. Morris, *Origins of the Civil Rights Movement: Black Communities Organizing for Change* (New York: Free Press, 1984).

180. Benjamin E. Mays, *The Negro's God As Reflected in His Literature* (1938, reprint, New York: Atheneum, 1968), preface, n.p.

181. Ibid., 1–15, quotes, preface, 14, 15.

182. Ibid., preface, n.p.

183. Ibid., quotes, 25, 26.

184. Ibid., 19–53, 97–127.

185. Ibid., 65–161.

186. Ibid., 78–79; cited from Mays and Nicholson, *The Negro's Church*, 64–65.

187. Mays, *Born to Rebel*, 149–61.

188. Mays, *The Negro's God*, 218–44; see Countee Cullen, *Color* (New York: Harper & Brothers, 1925), 3, 20–21, 39–40; Cullen, *The Black Christ* (New York: Harper & Brothers, 1929), 77–85; W. E. B. DuBois, *Dark Water* (New York: Harcourt, Brace & Howe, 1920), 25, 275–276; James Weldon Johnson, *Along This Way* (New York: Viking Press, 1933), 414, 431.

189. Mays, *Born to Rebel*, 139–48, quote, 141; Walter Dyson, *Howard University, the Capstone of Negro Education—A History 1867–1940* (Washington, D.C.: The Graduate School, Howard University, 1941), 172–77; Miles Mark Fisher IV, "The Howard Years," in *Walking Integrity: Benjamin Elijah Mays, Mentor to Martin Luther King Jr.*, 131–51.

190. Mays, *Born to Rebel*, 252; see Benjamin E. Mays, "The Second Assembly of the World Council of Churches," *Journal of Religious Thought* 10 (spring–summer 1953): 144–48. Mays received twenty-eight honorary doctorates between 1945 and 1970.

191. Benjamin E. Mays, "Have You Forgotten God?" *Our World* (Nov. 1952), 40–41, "forsaking and even," 40; "Christian light reveals," Mays, *Quotable Quotes of Benjamin E. Mays*, 18–19.

192. Mays, *Born to Rebel*, quote, 265; Martin Luther King Jr., *Stride Toward Freedom: The Montgomery Story* (New York: Harper & Brothers, 1958), quote, 145; Lerone Bennett Jr., "The Last of the Great Schoolmasters," *Walking Integrity: Benjamin Elijah Mays, Mentor to Martin Luther King Jr.*, 333–40; see Freddie C. Colston, "Mays As Mentor to King"; Barbara Sue K. Levinson, "Mays's Educational Philosophy"; Doris Levy Gavins, "Mays's Commencement Addresses"; Noel E. Burtenshaw, "Seeds of Revolution: Mays in Morehouse Chapel"; Derek Joseph Rovaris, "Mays's Leadership at Morehouse College," *Walking Integrity: Benjamin Elijah Mays, Mentor to Martin Luther King Jr.*, 197–214, 215–31, 289–324, 341–44, 353–76.

193. Benjamin E. Mays, "The Christian in Race Relations," Henry B. Wright Lecture, Yale University Divinity School, 16 Apr. 1952, reprinted in *Rhetoric of Racial Revolt*, ed. Roy L. Hill (Denver: Golden Bell Press, 1964), quotes, 127–28, 135.

194. Benjamin E. Mays, "Christianity and Race," *Pulpit* 25 (May 1954): 11–12.

195. Benjamin E. Mays, "The Church and Racial Tensions," *Christian Century* 71 (8 Sept. 1954): 1068.

196. Federal Council text reprinted in Mays, *Born to Rebel*, 253.

197. Mays, "The Christian in Race Relations," 123–25; Mays, "Christianity and Race," 13; see Benjamin B. Mays, "The South's Racial Policy," *Presbyterian Outlook* 132 (6 Nov. 1950): 2–6; Mays, "The Church Will Be Challenged at Evanston," *Christianity and Crisis* 14 (9 Aug. 1954): 106; David M. Reimers, *White Protestantism and the Negro* (New York: Oxford University Press, 1965); David W. Wills, "An Enduring Distance: Black Americans and the Establishment," in *Between the Times: The Travail of the Protestant Establishment in America, 1900–1960*, ed. William R. Hutchison (Cambridge: Cambridge University Press, 1989), 168–92.

198. Benjamin B. Mays, "Democratizing and Christianizing America in This Generation," *Journal of Negro Education* 14 (fall 1945): 527–34, quotes, 528; see *A Rauschenbusch Reader: The Kingdom of God and the Social Gospel*, ed. Benjamin E. Mays (New York: Harper, 1957).

199. Benjamin E. Mays, *Seeking to Be Christian in Race Relations* (New York: Friendship Press, 1957; rev. ed., 1964), 75.

200. Benjamin E. Mays, "Desegregate and Integrate to What End?" Founder's Day Speech, Livingstone College, Salisbury, N.C., February 11, 1964, reprinted in *The Negro Speaks: The Rhetoric of Contemporary Black Leaders*, ed. Jamye Coleman Williams and McDonald Williams (New York: Noble & Noble, 1970), 89–98, quotes, 95, 96.

201. Mays, *Seeking to Be Christian in Race Relations*, 79.

202. Benjamin E. Mays, "Eulogy of Dr. Martin Luther King Jr.," Atlanta, Ga., 6 Apr. 1968, *Pan-African Journal* 1 (spring and summer, 1968): 83–85, quote, 83.

203. See Mays, *Seeking to Be Christian in Race Relations*, 83.

204. Fosdick, *The Living of These Days,* 24–25; Harry Emerson Fosdick, *A Great Time to Be Alive: Sermons on Christianity in Wartime* (New York: Harper & Brothers, 1944), 148–49, 214; Keith D. Miller, *Voice of Deliverance: The Language of Martin Luther King Jr., and Its Sources* (New York: Free Press, 1992; reprint, Athens, Ga.: University of Georgia Press, 1998), 45–62.

205. For a thorough discussion of this issue, see Miller, *Harry Emerson Fosdick,* 449–63, quotes, 452–53.

206. Rufus M. Jones, *Re-thinking Religious Liberalism* (Boston: Beacon Press, 1935), quotes, 3, 4, 5.

207. Ibid., quotes, 6, 7, 23; see Jones, *The Radiant Life* (New York: Macmillan, 1944).

208. Rufus M. Jones, *A Call to What Is Vital* (New York: Macmillan, 1948), 27–28.

209. Fosdick, *The Living of These Days,* 229–56; see Fosdick, *What Is Vital in Religion* (New York: Harper & Brothers, 1955), 75–88.

210. Fosdick, *The Living of These Days,* quotes, 266, 247.

211. Ibid., 257–66, quotes, 257; see Karl Barth, *Dogmatics in Outline* (New York: Philosophical Library, 1947).

Chapter 7. Revolt of the Neoliberals

1. Reinhold Niebuhr, *The Reminiscences of Reinhold Niebuhr* (New York: Columbia University, Columbia Oral History Research Office, 1953), 14 Feb. 1953 interview with Harlan B. Phillips, 1–9, quotes, 1, 3; see Carl E. Schneider, *The German Church on the American Frontier* (St. Louis: Eden Publishing House, 1939); William G. Chrystal, *A Father's Mantle: The Legacy of Gustav Niebuhr* (New York: Pilgrim Press, 1982), 3–13; Richard Wightman Fox, *Reinhold Niebuhr: A Biography* (Ithaca, N.Y.: Cornell University Press, 1996), 3–12. *The Reminiscences of Reinhold Niebuhr* is a transcript of tape-recorded interviews conducted by the Oral History Research Office at Columbia University. The single "regret" about Gustav Niebuhr that Reinhold Niebuhr expressed was that his father opposed higher education for Hulda. Niebuhr emphasized that his father was much less patriarchal in his family relations than most German immigrant fathers, however; *The Reminiscences of Reinhold Niebuhr,* 5–7.

2. Reinhold Niebuhr, "Intellectual Autobiography of Reinhold Niebuhr," *Reinhold Niebuhr: His Religious, Social, and Political Thought,* ed. Charles W. Kegley and Robert W. Bretall (New York: Macmillan, 1956), 3–23, quote, 3; *Young Reinhold Niebuhr: His Early Writings, 1911–1931,* ed. William D. Chrystal (St. Louis: Eden Publishing House, 1977), 27–29; Fox, *Reinhold Niebuhr,* 13; see Reinhold Niebuhr, "Religion: Revival and Education" (1913), *Young Reinhold Niebuhr,* 46–52; Walter Brueggemann, *Ethos and Ecumenism, An Evangelical Blend: A History of Eden Theological Seminary, 1925–1975* (St. Louis: Eden Publishing House, 1975), 1–7.

3. Niebuhr, *Reminiscences of Reinhold Niebuhr,* 14 Feb. 1953 interview with Harlan B. Phillips, 6; 26 Feb. 1953 interview with Phillips, 11; Reinhold Niebuhr, Union Service Sermon, 17 Aug. 1913, Reinhold Niebuhr Papers, Library of Congress, 1–6; Fox, *Reinhold Niebuhr,* 22–23.

4. Niebuhr, *Reminiscences of Reinhold Niebuhr,* 26 Feb. 1953 interview with Harlan B. Phillips, 12–18; Roland Bainton, *Yale and the Ministry* (New York: Harper & Row, 1957), 198–211; Charles Reynolds Brown, *The Social Message of the Modern Pulpit* (New York: Scribner's, 1906).

5. Reinhold Niebuhr to Samuel D. Press, 3 Mar. 1914, Reinhold Niebuhr Papers.

6. Reinhold Niebuhr, "Yale—Eden," *Keryx* (Dec. 1914), reprinted in *Young Reinhold Niebuhr,* 53–58, quotes, 54, 55.

7. Ibid., 56, 57; see Benjamin W. Bacon, *Jesus the Son of God* (New York: Henry Holt, 1930); Bacon, "Enter the Higher Criticism," *Contemporary American Theology: Theological Autobiographies,* 2 vols., ed. Vergilius Ferm (New York: Round Table Press, 1932), 1: 1–50.

8. "This professor meant," Patrick R. Granfield, O.S.B., "Interview with Reinhold Niebuhr," *Commonweal* (16 Dec. 1966), reprinted in Granfield, *Theologians at Work* (New York: Macmillan, 1967), 51–68, quote, 65; "the more I threw," Niebuhr,

Reminiscences of Reinhold Niebuhr, 26 Feb. 1953 interview with Phillips, quote, 16; Reinhold Niebuhr, "The Validity and Certainty of Religious Knowledge," B.D. thesis, Yale Divinity School, 1914, Reinhold Niebuhr Papers; Niebuhr, "The Contribution of Christianity to the Doctrine of Immortality," master's thesis, Yale University, 1915, Yale University Library; see Niebuhr, "Yale—Eden," 57; Fox, *Reinhold Niebuhr,* 34–38.

9. Reinhold Niebuhr to Samuel D. Press, 1 July 1915, Reinhold Niebuhr Papers.

10. Quotes in Reinhold Niebuhr to Samuel D. Press, 3 Nov. 1915, Reinhold Niebuhr Papers; "virtue of ignorance" quote in Reinhold Niebuhr, *Leaves from the Notebook of a Tamed Cynic* (1st ed., 1929, New York: Meridian Books, 7th printing, 1966), 30; see Fox, *Reinhold Niebuhr,* 41–43.

11. Reinhold Niebuhr, "The Failure of German-Americanism," *Atlantic* (July 1916), 16–18.

12. Reinhold Niebuhr, "An Anniversary Sermon," 15 Oct. 1915, *Young Reinhold Niebuhr,* 59–63, quotes, 61, 63.

13. Niebuhr, *Leaves from the Notebook of a Tamed Cynic,* 22.

14. Reinhold Niebuhr, "The Scylla and Charybdis of Teaching," *Evangelical Teacher* (May 1916), reprinted in *Young Reinhold Niebuhr,* 74–78; Reinhold Niebuhr, "Billy Sunday—His Preachments and His Methods," *Detroit Saturday Night* (14 Oct. 1916), 3.

15. Reinhold Niebuhr to Will Scarlett, 23 June 1960, Reinhold Niebuhr Papers.

16. Niebuhr, *Leaves from the Notebook of a Tamed Cynic,* 26.

17. Ibid., 32–33; see Reinhold Niebuhr, "A Message from Reinhold Niebuhr, *Keryx* (Oct. 1918), reprinted in *Young Reinhold Niebuhr,* 95–100.

18. "Typical son" and "words have certain" quotes, Niebuhr, *Leaves from the Notebook of a Tamed Cynic,* 40, 41; "spirit of enthusiasm" and "Less circumspect," Reinhold Niebuhr, letter to the editor, "The Twilight of Liberalism," *The New Republic* (14 June 1919), 218.

19. "Just send them in," quoted in Charles C. Brown, *Niebuhr and His Age: Reinhold Niebuhr's Prophetic Role in the Twentieth Century* (Philadelphia: Trinity Press, 1992), 25.

20. "Nowhere have I seen," Niebuhr, *Leaves from the Notebook of a Tamed Cynic,* 93; Williams died in February 1923, but this entry was mistakenly published under the heading "1924"; "your diocese has lost," quoted in Fox, *Reinhold Niebuhr,* 76.

21. Niebuhr, *Leaves from the Notebook of a Tamed Cynic,* quotes, 61, 67, 68, 69; Reinhold Niebuhr, "A Trip through the Ruhr," *Evangelical Herald* (9 Aug. 1923), reprinted in *Young Reinhold Niebuhr,* 124–27.

22. "Great affliction" and "dreams of vengeance," Niebuhr, "A Trip through the Ruhr," 128; "practically powerless," Reinhold Niebuhr, "Germany in Despair," *Evangelical Herald* (13 Sept. 1923), reprinted in *Young Reinhold Niebuhr,* 128–31, quote, 130; "too ideal," Reinhold Niebuhr, "Wanted: A Christian Morality," *Christian Century* 40 (15 Feb. 1923): 202; see Niebuhr, "The Despair of Europe," *Evangelical Herald* (20 Sept., 1923); and Niebuhr, "America and Europe," *Evangelical Herald* (1 Nov. 1923); Niebuhr, "The Dawn in Europe," *Evangelical Herald* (7 Aug. 1924); Niebuhr, "Is Europe on the Way to Peace?" *Evangelical Herald* (25 Sept. 1924), reprinted in *Young Reinhold Niebuhr,* 132–36, 141–44, 151–53, 157–59.

23. "No Christian basis," Niebuhr, "Wanted: A Christian Morality," 202; "economic and political heresy," Niebuhr, *Leaves from the Notebook of a Tamed Cynic,* 83.

24. Reinhold Niebuhr, "Henry Ford and Industrial Autocracy," *Christian Century* 43 (4 Nov. 1926): 1354; Niebuhr, "How Philanthropic Is Henry Ford?" *Christian Century* 43 (9 Dec. 1926): 1516–17; "What a civilization," Niebuhr, *Leaves from the Notebook of a Tamed Cynic,* 181; see *Reminiscences of Reinhold Niebuhr,* 28 Feb. 1953 interview with Harlan B. Phillips, 21–39.

25. Editorial, "Independents and the Election," *Christian Century* 45 (13 Sept. 1928): 1098.

26. Reinhold Niebuhr, "Puritan and Democrat," *Christian Century* 44 (20 Oct. 1927): 1224; Niebuhr, "Governor Smith's Liberalism," *Christian Century* 45 (13 Sept. 1928): 1107–08; see Reinhold Niebuhr, "Protestantism and Prohibition," *New Republic* (24 Oct. 1928): 266–67.

27. Reinhold Niebuhr, *Does Civilization Need Religion?: A Study in the Social Resources and Limitations of Religion in Modern Life* (New York: Macmillan, 1927), quotes, 220, 229, 231.

28. Ibid., quotes, 235, 238–39.

29. Fox, *Reinhold Niebuhr,* 105–6; Morgan Phelps Noyes, *Henry Sloane Coffin: The Man and His Ministry* (New York: Scribner, 1964), 192; Brown, *Niebuhr and His Age,* 34; Niebuhr, "Intellectual Autobiography of Reinhold Niebuhr," quote, 8.

30. See Reinhold Niebuhr, "Why We Need a New Economic Order," *World Tomorrow* 11 (Oct. 1928): 397–98; Niebuhr, "Anglo-Saxon Protestant Domination," *World Tomorrow* 11 (Nov. 1928): 438–39.

31. Reinhold Niebuhr, "Catastrophe or Social Control?" *Harper's* 165 (June 1932): 118.

32. Reinhold Niebuhr, *Moral Man and Immoral Society: A Study in Ethics and Politics* (1932; reprint, New York: Charles Scribner's Sons, 1947). This section adapts material from Dorrien, *Soul in Society: The Making and Renewal of Social Christianity* (Minneapolis: Fortress Press, 1995), 91–161.

33. Niebuhr, *Moral Man and Immoral Society,* quotes, xx, 144.

34. Ibid., 256.

35. Norman Thomas, review of *Moral Man and Immoral Society,* by Reinhold Niebuhr, *The World Tomorrow* 15 (14 Dec. 1932): 565, 567; John Haynes Holmes, review of ibid., *Herald Tribune Books* (8 Jan. 1933), 13; Charles Gilkey quoted in Langdon Gilkey, "Reinhold Niebuhr as Political Theologian," in *Reinhold Niebuhr and the Issues of Our Time,* ed. Richard Harries (Grand Rapids: Eerdmans, 1986), 182; see Fox, *Reinhold Niebuhr,* 142–43. Gilkey recalled that his father later changed his estimate of Niebuhr's book.

36. Theodore C. Hume, "Prophet of Disillusion," *Christian Century* 50 (4 Jan. 1933): 18–19.

37. Reinhold Niebuhr, "Dr. Niebuhr's Position," *Christian Century* 50 (18 Jan. 1933): 91–92.

38. H. Richard Niebuhr, "The Grace of Doing Nothing," *Christian Century* 49 (23 Mar. 1932): 379; Reinhold Niebuhr, "Must We Do Nothing?" *Christian Century* 49 (30 Mar. 1932): 416–17; H. Richard Niebuhr, "The Only Way into the Kingdom of God," *Christian Century* 49 (6 Apr. 1932): 447; see [Reinhold Niebuhr,] "The League and Japan," *World Tomorrow* 15 (Mar. 1932): 4; *Remembering Reinhold Niebuhr: Letters of Reinhold and Ursula M. Niebuhr,* ed. Ursula M. Niebuhr (San Francisco: HarperSanFrancisco, 1991),

39. See H. Richard Niebuhr, *The Social Sources of Denominationalism* (New York: Henry Holt, 1929); H. Richard Niebuhr, *The Kingdom of God in America* (New York: Harper & Row, 1937).

40. H. Richard Niebuhr to Reinhold Niebuhr, n.d. [mid-Jan. 1933], Reinhold Niebuhr Papers; Fox, *Reinhold Niebuhr,* 144–45.

41. Theodore C. Hume, "Prophet of Disillusion," review of *Moral Man and Immoral Society,* by Reinhold Niebuhr, *Christian Century* 50 (4 Jan. 1933), 18–19.

42. Reinhold Niebuhr, "Dr. Niebuhr's Position," *Christian Century* 50 (18 Jan. 1933), 91–92. See Niebuhr, "Ten Years That Shook My World," *Christian Century* 56 (26 Apr. 1939): 546.

43. Reinhold Niebuhr, *Reflections on the End of an Era* (New York: Scribner's, 1934), quote, 135; see Niebuhr, "After Capitalism—What?" *World Tomorrow* 16 (1 Mar. 1933), 203–4; Niebuhr, "Is Religion Counter-Revolutionary?" *Radical Religion* 1 (autumn 1935): 14–20.

44. Reinhold Niebuhr, *An Interpretation of Christian Ethics* (1935; reprint, San Francisco: Harper & Row, 1963), quotes, 105, 108, 7.

45. Paul Tillich, *Religionsphilosophie, in Lehrbuch der Philosophie,* ed. M. Dessoir (Berlin: Ullstein, 1925), reprinted in Tillich, *What Is Religion?* trans. James Luther Adams (New York: Harper & Row, 1969), 101–5.

46. Niebuhr, *An Interpretation of Christian Ethics,* 7.

47. Ibid., 54; see Reinhold Niebuhr, *The Nature and Destiny of Man: A Christian Interpretation,* 2 vols. (New York: Charles Scribner's Sons, 1941, 1949), 1:265–80. This section adapts material from Dorrien, *Soul in Society,* 96–97.

48. Niebuhr, *An Interpretation of Christian Ethics,* 55; Reinhold Niebuhr, *Faith and History: A Comparison of Christian and Modern Views of History* (New York: Charles Scribner's Sons, 1949), 120–23; Niebuhr, *The Self and the Dramas of History* (New York: Charles Scribner's Sons, 1955), 12–19.

49. See Niebuhr, *The Nature and Destiny of Man*, 1:178–86.
50. Reinhold Niebuhr, "Why I Leave the F.O.R.," *Christian Century* 51 (3 Jan. 1934); reprinted in Reinhold Niebuhr, *Love and Justice: Selections from the Shorter Writings of Reinhold Niebuhr*, ed. D. B. Robertson (1957; reprint, Louisville, Ky.: Westminster John Knox, 1992), 254–59.
51. John Haynes Holmes, "Reinhold Niebuhr's Philosophy of Despair," *Herald Tribune Books* (18 Mar. 1934), 7.
52. Fox, *Reinhold Niebuhr*, 153.
53. Niebuhr, *An Interpretation of Christian Ethics*, 23, 105.
54. Ibid., 106–7, 116.
55. On the development of Niebuhr's political philosophy, see Dorrien, *Soul in Society*, 106–61.
56. John C. Bennett, "After Liberalism—What?" *Christian Century* 50 (8 Nov. 1933): 1403.
57. Walter Marshall Horton, "Rough Sketch of a Half Formed Mind," in *Contemporary American Theology: Theological Autobiographies*, 1:161–88; Horton, *Theism and the Modern Mood* (New York: Harper & Brothers, 1930); Horton, *Theism and the Scientific Spirit* (New York: Harper & Brothers, 1933).
58. Walter Marshall Horton, *Realistic Theology* (New York: Harper & Brothers, 1934), ix–x.
59. Ibid., quotes, ix, 15, 37.
60. Reinhold Niebuhr, "Barth—Apostle of the Absolute," *Christian Century* 45 (13 Dec. 1928): 1523–24.
61. Reinhold Niebuhr to John C. Bennett, 10 June and 20 July 1930; cited in Fox, *Reinhold Niebuhr*, 123.
62. John C. Bennett, "How My Mind Has Changed," *Christian Century* 76 (23 Dec. 1959), 1500; see Reinhold Niebuhr, "John Coleman Bennett: Theologian, Churchman, and Educator," in *Theology and Church in Times of Change: Essays in Honor of John Coleman Bennett*, ed. Edward LeRoy Long Jr. and Robert T. Handy (Philadelphia: Westminster Press, 1970), 234–35.
63. John C. Bennett, *Social Salvation: A Religious Approach to the Problems of Social Change* (New York: Charles Scribner's Sons, 1935); Bennett, *Christian Realism* (New York: Charles Scribner's Sons, 1952). For discussions of Bennett's social ethics, see Dorrien, *Soul in Society*, 164–86; David Smith, *The Achievement of John C. Bennett* (New York: Herder & Herder, 1970); Robert Lee, *The Promise of Bennett* (Philadelphia: J. P. Lippincott, 1969).
64. Bennett, "After Liberalism—What?" 1403.
65. Ibid., 1403–4.
66. Ibid., 1404.
67. Ibid., 1404–5.
68. John C. Bennett, "A Changed Liberal—But Still a Liberal," *Christian Century* 56 (8 Feb. 1939), 179–81, quotes, 179; see John C. Bennett, "A Critique of Paul Ramsey," *Christianity and Crisis* 27 (30 Oct. 1967), 247–50; Bennett, "How My Mind Has Changed," 1501–2.
69. Bennett, "A Changed Liberal—But Still a Liberal," quote, 179; Niebuhr, *An Interpretation of Christian Ethics*, 59–60.
70. Reinhold Niebuhr, "Brief Comments," *Radical Religion* 3 (winter 1937): 7.
71. Reinhold Niebuhr, "Brief Comments," *Radical Religion* (spring 1938): 7.
72. Reinhold Niebuhr, "The London Times and the Crisis," *Radical Religion* 4 (winter 1938–39): 32; Niebuhr, "Willkie and Roosevelt," *Christianity and Society* 5 (fall 1940): "anticipated" quote, 5.
73. Niebuhr, *The Nature and Destiny of Man*, 1:25; see Fox, *Reinhold Niebuhr*, 187–91.
74. Niebuhr, *The Nature and Destiny of Man*, quote, 1:5.
75. Ibid., 1:145, 146.
76. Ibid., "the most," 178; "recognizes" and "a form of," 2:104.
77. Ibid., quote, 1:159.
78. Paul Tillich, *The Interpretation of History* (New York: Charles Scribner's Sons, 1936), 169–71; Niebuhr, *The Nature and Destiny of Man*, 1:217–18.
79. Niebuhr, *Nature and Destiny of Man*, 1:126–27; Langdon Gilkey, *On Niebuhr: A Theological Study* (Chicago: University of Chicago Press, 2001), 16–28, quote, 19; Rein-

hold Niebuhr, *Faith and History: A Comparison of Christian and Modern Views of History* (New York: Charles Scribner's Sons, 1949), 49.

80. Gregory Vlastos, "Sin and Anxiety in Niebuhr's Religion," *Christian Century* 58 (1 Oct. 1941): 1202–4.

81. Reinhold Niebuhr, "Professor's Column," *Union Seminary Tower* (May 1960), "when I came here," 3, cited in Brown, *Niebuhr and His Age,* 37; Ronald H. Stone, *Professor Reinhold Niebuhr: A Mentor to the Twentieth Century* (Louisville, Ky.: Westminster John Knox Press, 1992), "it was in," 84; Paul Tillich, "Sin and Grace in the Theology of Reinhold Niebuhr," in *Reinhold Niebuhr: A Prophetic Voice in Our Time,* ed. Harold R. Landon (Greenwich, Conn.: Seabury Press, 1962), 32–33.

82. Reinhold Niebuhr, *Christianity and Power Politics* (New York: Charles Scribner's Sons, 1940), 71.

83. Reinhold Niebuhr, "Christian Moralism in America," *Radical Religion* 5 (1940): 16–17; see Niebuhr, "An Open Letter," *Christianity and Society* 5 (summer 1940): 30–33.

84. [Charles C. Morrison], "No Third Term!" *Christian Century* 57 (16 Oct. 1940): 1273; [Charles C. Morrison], "Defending Democracy," *Christian Century* 57 (5 June 1940); [Charles C. Morrison], "Why We Differ," *Christian Century* 58 (10 Dec. 1941): 1534–38, quote, 1538; see [Charles C. Morrison], "The Neutrality Act Is Discarded," *Christian Century* 58 (26 Nov. 1941): 1459; Morrison, *The Christian and the War* (Chicago: Willett, Clark & Co., 1942).

85. Reinhold Niebuhr, "To Prevent the Triumph of an Intolerable Tyranny," *Christian Century* 57 (18 Dec. 1940): 1580; see Niebuhr, "Editorial Notes," *Christianity and Society* 5 (spring 1940): 10.

86. Niebuhr, *Christianity and Power Politics,* 44, 68; Niebuhr, "To Prevent the Triumph of an Intolerable Tyranny," 1579; different versions of the same statements.

87. Reinhold Niebuhr, "Notes," *Christianity and Society* 5 (autumn 1940): 12–13; "pure German stock" and "I thought Britain," Niebuhr, "To Prevent the Triumph of an Intolerable Tyranny," 1579; "moralistic illusions," Niebuhr, *Christianity and Power Politics,* 47.

88. See Reinhold Niebuhr, *The Children of Light and the Children of Darkness: A Vindication of Democracy and a Critique of Its Traditional Defense* (New York: Charles Scribner's Sons, 1944); Dorrien, *Soul in Society,* 116–61.

89. [Charles C. Morrison], "An Unnecessary Necessity," *Christian Century* 58 (17 Dec. 1941): 1565–67, quotes, 1565.

90. Reinhold Niebuhr, "Editorial Notes," *Christianity and Society* 7 (winter 1941–42): quote, 9.

91. "Genuinely sorry," Reinhold Niebuhr, "Ten Years That Shook My World," *Christian Century* 56 (26 Apr. 1939): 542–46, quote, 543; "Almost, though not quite," Niebuhr quoted in John C. Bennett, "Tillich and the 'Fellowship of Socialist Christians,'" *North American Paul Tillich Society Newsletter* 16 (Oct. 1990): 3; "excessively optimistic," Niebuhr, *The Children of Light and the Children of Darkness,* x; see Niebuhr, *Christian Realism and Political Problems* (New York: Charles Scribner's Sons, 1953), 33–42; Donald Meyer, *The Protestant Search for Political Realism, 1919–1941* (2d ed.: Middletown, Conn: Wesleyan University Press, 1988).

92. Reinhold Niebuhr, "Frontier Fellowship," *Christianity and Society* 13 (autumn 1948): 4; Niebuhr and others, "Christian Action Statement of Purpose," *Christianity and Crisis* 11 (1 Oct. 1951), 126; Niebuhr, "Superfluous Advice," *Christianity and Society* 17 (winter 1951–52): 4–5; Niebuhr, *Christian Realism and Political Problems,* "we are fated," 33; see Niebuhr, "The Organization of the Liberal Movement," *Christianity and Society* 12 (spring 1947): 8–10.

93. Reinhold Niebuhr, "The Change in Russia," *New Leader* 38 (3 Oct. 1955): "with its simple distinctions," 18–19; Niebuhr, "Communism and the Protestant Clergy," *Look* 17 (17 Nov. 1953), 37; Niebuhr, *Christian Realism and Political Problems,* "noxious demony," and "old Russian imperialism," 34.

94. Niebuhr, "The Peril of Complacency in Our Nation," *Christianity and Crisis* 14 (8 Feb. 1954): "we are embattled," 1; Niebuhr, "The Change in Russia," quotes on Islamic analogy, 18–19.

95. Reinhold Niebuhr, *The Irony of American History* (New York: Charles Scribner's Sons, 1952), 128.

96. X [George F. Kennan], "The Sources of Soviet Conduct," *Foreign Affairs* 25 (July 1947): 579–80; Niebuhr, *The Irony of American History,* "if we fully," 129.

97. On Christian realism and the politics of anticommunism in the 1950s and 1960s, see Dorrien, *Soul in Society,* 128–39, 173–81; Niebuhr, *The Irony of American History,* quote, 101; for Niebuhr's early declarations against the war in Vietnam, see Reinhold Niebuhr, "The Peace Offensive," *Christianity and Crisis* 25 (24 Jan. 1966), 301; Niebuhr, "Escalation Objective," *New York Times* (14 Mar. 1967); Niebuhr, foreword to *Martin Luther King Jr., John C. Bennett, Henry Steele Commager, and Abraham Heschel Speak on the War in Vietnam* (New York: Clergy and Laymen Concerned about Vietnam, 1967), 3.

98. Reinhold Niebuhr, "The Confession of a Tired Radical," *Christian Century* 45 (30 Aug. 1928), reprinted in *Love and Justice: Selections from the Shorter Writings of Reinhold Niebuhr,* ed. D. B. Robertson (Philadelphia: Westminster Press, 1957), 120–24.

99. Reinhold Niebuhr, "The Sin of Racial Prejudice," *The Messenger* 13 (3 Feb. 1948): quote, 6; reprinted in *A Reinhold Niebuhr Reader: Selected Essays, Articles, and Book Reviews,* ed. Charles C. Brown (Philadelphia: Trinity Press International, 1992), 70–71; see Niebuhr, "Christian Faith and the Race Problem," *Christianity and Society* (spring 1945); and Niebuhr, "The Race Problem," *Christianity and Society* (summer 1942), reprinted in *Love and Justice,* 125–32.

100. Reinhold Niebuhr, *Pious and Secular America* (New York: Charles Scribner's Sons, 1958), 76.

101. Reinhold Niebuhr, "Coherence, Incoherence, and Christian Faith," *Journal of Religion* 31 (July 1951): 162.

102. Daniel Day Williams, "Niebuhr and Liberalism," *Reinhold Niebuhr: His Religious, Social, and Political Thought,* 194–213, quotes, 196–97, 207. This section adapts material from Dorrien, *Soul in Society,* 141–42.

103. Williams, "Niebuhr and Liberalism," quotes, 197; Niebuhr, *An Interpretation of Christian Ethics,* "final bankruptcy," 110; see Eugene W. Lyman, *Theology and Human Problems* (New York: Charles Scribner's Sons, 1910); Lyman, *The Experience of God in Modern Life* (New York: Charles Scribner's Sons, 1918); Lyman, *The Meaning and Truth of Religion* (New York: Charles Scribner's Sons, 1933).

104. Russell Kirk, *The Conservative Mind: From Burke to Eliot* (Chicago: Henry Regnery, 1953); Reinhold Niebuhr, "Liberalism and Conservatism," *Christianity and Society* 20 (winter 1954–55): 3–4.

105. Reinhold Niebuhr, "Reply to Interpretation and Criticism," in *Reinhold Niebuhr: His Religious, Social, and Political Thought,* 441–42.

106. Reinhold Niebuhr, "The Blindness of Liberalism," *Radical Religion* 1 (autumn 1936): 4.

107. For accounts of the ideological breakup of Niebuhrian Christian realism and Niebuhr's relation to the neoconservative movement, see Dorrien, *Soul in Society,* 128–43, 162–81, 189–94, 205–7; Gary Dorrien, *The Neoconservative Mind: Politics, Culture, and the War of Ideology* (Philadelphia: Temple University Press, 1993), 219–22.

108. Reinhold Niebuhr, "The Quality of Our Lives," *Christian Century* 77 (11 May 1960): quotes, 568; "there is no need" quote, Granfield, *Theologians at Work,* 55.

109. Reinhold Niebuhr, *Man's Nature and His Communities: Essays on the Dynamics and Enigmas of Man's Personal and Social Existence* (New York: Charles Scribner's Sons, 1965), quotes, 21, 25; "fantastic involvement" quote, Granfield, *Theologians at Work,* 54–55.

110. Alan Geyer, quoted in symposium on "Christian Realism: Retrospect and Prospect," *Christianity and Crisis* 28 (5 Aug. 1968): 178; Rubem A. Alves, "Christian Realism: Ideology of the Establishment," *Christianity and Crisis* 33 (17 Sept. 1973): 176; see M. M. Thomas, "A Third World View of Christian Realism," *Christianity and Crisis* 46 (3 Feb. 1986): 8–12.

111. Bennett quote, 1961 colloquium discussion, *Reinhold Niebuhr: A Prophetic Voice in Our Time,* 92–93.

112. Dennis P. McCann, *Christian Realism and Liberation Theology: Practical Theologies in Creative Conflice* (Maryknoll, N.Y.: Orbis Books, 1980), 80–93, 103; Karen Lebacqz, *Six Theories of Justice* (Minneapolis: Augsburg Press, 1986), 83–99; James Gustafson, "Theology in the Service of Ethics: An Interpretation of Reinhold Niebuhr's Theological Ethics," in *Reinhold Niebuhr and the Issues of Our Time,* 24–45; Robin W. Lovin,

Reinhold Niebuhr and Christian Realism (Cambridge: Cambridge University Press, 1995), 198–234; Harlan Beckley, *Passion for Justice: Retrieving the Legacies of Walter Rauschenbusch, John A. Ryan, and Reinhold Niebuhr* (Louisville, Ky.: Westminster John Knox Press, 1992), 312–43; Merle Longwood, "Niebuhr and a Theory of Justice," *Dialog* 14 (fall 1975): 253–62.

113. Paul Ramsey, "Love and Law," in *Reinhold Niebuhr: His Religious, Social, and Political Thought*, 80–123; Niebuhr, "Reply to Interpetation and Criticism," quotes, 435.

114. Reinhold Niebuhr, *Beyond Tragedy: Essays on the Christian Interpretation of History* (New York: Charles Scribner's Sons, 1937), quotes 20–21, 290; Niebuhr, *The Nature and Destiny of Man*, 2:55–99, 2:294–95.

115. Niebuhr, *Beyond Tragedy*, quote, 290; Niebuhr, *The Nature and Destiny of Man*, 2:294–298, quote, 298; Ved Mehta, *The New Theologian* (New York: Harper & Row, 1965), "there are very" quote, 39; Gustave Weigel, "Authority in Theology," *Reinhold Niebuhr: His Religious, Social, and Political Thought*, 368–77; Niebuhr, "Reply to Interpretation and Criticism," reply to Weigel, 446; Emil Brunner, "Some Remarks on Reinhold Niebuhr's Work as a Christian Thinker," in *Reinhold Niebuhr: His Religious, Social, and Political Thought*, 28–33; Niebuhr, "Intellectual Autobiography of Reinhold Niebuhr," 3.

116. Paul Tillich, "Reinhold Niebuhr's Doctrine of Knowledge," in *Reinhold Niebuhr: His Religious, Social, and Political Thought*, 36–43, quote, 36.

117. Niebuhr, "Reply to Interpretation and Criticism," 432–33.

118. Quoted in John Herman Randall Jr., "The Philosophical Legacy of Paul Tillich," in *The Intellectual Legacy of Paul Tillich*, ed. James R. Lyons (Detroit: Wayne State University Press, 1969), 22.

119. Wilhelm and Marion Pauck, *Paul Tillich: His Life and Thought* (San Francisco: Harper & Row, 1989, 139–62; Paul Tillich, *Theology of Culture*, ed. Robert C. Kimball (New York: Oxford University Press, 1959), 159; see Tillich, *My Search for Absolutes* (New York: Simon & Schuster, 1967), 46–50.

120. Paul Tillich, "Die religionsgeschichtliche Konstruktion in Schellings positiver Philosophie, ihre Voraussetzungen und Prinzipien," (doctoral dissertation, University of Breslau, 1910); Tillich's dissertation for the licentiate of theology was published under the title *Der Begriff des Uebernatürlichen, sein dialektischer Charakter und das Prinzip der Identität, dargestellt an der supranaturalistischen Theologie vor Schleiermacher* (Königsberg: Madrasch, 1915); see Friedrich W. J. Schelling, *Vorlesungen über die Methode des academischen Studium* (Stuttgart: J. G. Cotta, 1830); Schelling, *System of Transcendental Idealism*, trans. Peter Heath (Charlottesville, Va.: University of Virginia, 1993).

121. Paul Tillich, *The New Being* (New York: Charles Scribner's Sons, 1955), "nice God," 52; [cover story, no byline], "To Be or Not to Be," *Time* 73 (16 Mar. 1959): "many of them" quote, 47; Pauck and Pauck, *Paul Tillich*, 40–41, 51; Tillich, "Autobiographical Reflections of Paul Tillich," in *The Theology of Paul Tillich*, ed. Charles W. Kegley and Robert W. Bretall (New York: Macmillan, 1952), 12; Tillich, *My Search for Absolutes*, 39; Tillich, *On the Boundary: An Autobiographical Sketch* (New York: Charles Scribner's Sons, 1966), 52. The latter text is a revision of Tillich's first autobiographical sketch, published in *The Interpretation of History*, 3–73.

122. Tillich, *The Interpretation of History*, quote, 35; for extensive discussions of Tillich's early religious socialism, see Gary Dorrien, *Reconstructing the Common Good: Theology and the Social Order* (Maryknoll, N.Y.: Orbis Books, 1990), 48–76; Ronald H. Stone, *Paul Tillich's Radical Social Thought* (Atlanta: John Knox Press, 1980); Eduard Heimann, "Tillich's Doctrine of Religious Socialism," in *The Theology of Paul Tillich*, ed. Charles W. Kegley and Robert W. Bretall (New York: Macmillan, 1952), 312–25.

123. Paul Tillich, "Kairos," *Die Tat* 14 (Aug. 1922): 330–50; Tillich, *Masse und Geist* (Berlin: Verlag der Arbeitsgemeinschaft, 1922); Tillich, *Das System der Wissenschaften nach Gegenständen und Methoden* (Göttingen: Vandenhoeck & Ruprecht, 1923); Tillich, *The Interpretation of History*, 123–75; Tillich, *The Protestant Era*, trans. and ed. James Luther Adams (London: Nisbet & Co., 1951), quote, 57; Tillich, *Political Expectation*, ed. James Luther Adams, trans. James Luther Adams and Victor Nuovo (New York: Harper & Row, 1971), 58–88.

124. Paul Tillich, "Die religiöse und philosophische Weiterbildung des Sozialismus," *Blätter für religiösen Sozialismus* 5 (May 1924), 18; Pauck and Pauck, 79–93, citation, 83; Hannah Tillich, *From Time to Time* (New York: Stein and Day, 1973).

125. Paul Tillich, *Die religiöse Lage der Gegenwart* (Berlin: Ullstein, 1926); English edition, *The Religious Situation*, trans. H. Richard Niebuhr (New York: Henry Holt, 1932), quotes, 47–48.

126. Ibid., "religious symbols of eternity," 216.

127. Paul Tillich, "Kritisches und positives Paradox: eine Aufeinandersetzung mit Karl Barth und Friedrich Gogarten," *Theologische Blätter* 2 (Nov. 1923), 263–69; English edition, "Critical and Positive Paradox: A Discussion with Karl Barth and Friedrich Gogarten," in *The Beginnings of Dialectic Theology*, ed. James M. Robinson, trans. Louis De Grazia and Keith R. Crim (Richmond: John Knox Press, 1968), 133–41.

128. Karl Barth, "The Paradoxical Nature of the 'Positive Paradox': Answers and Questions to Paul Tillich," in *The Beginnings of Dialectic Theology*, 142–54; Paul Tillich, *Religiöse Verwirklichung* (Berlin: Furche Verlag, 1929); chapter "Realism and Faith," reprinted in Tillich, *The Protestant Era*, 74–92, quote, 91.

129. See Max Horkheimer and Theodor W. Adorno, *Dialektik der Aufklärung* (New York: Social Studies Association, 1944); *The Essential Frankfurt School Reader*, ed. Andrew Arato and Eike Gebhardt (New York: Continuum, 1982); Martin Jay, *The Dialectical Imagination: A History of the Frankfurt School and the Institute of Social Research, 1923–1950* (Boston: Little, Brown & Co., 1973).

130. Paul Tillich, *Die sozialistische Entscheidung* (Potsdam: Alfred Protte, 1933); English edition, *The Socialist Decision*, trans. Franklin Sherman (New York: Harper & Row, 1977), 27–44, 47–65, 127–62, quote, 161.

131. See Fritz K. Ringer, *The Decline of the German Mandarins: The German Academic Community, 1890–1933* (Cambridge: Harvard University Press, 1972), 440; E. V. Hartshorne, *The German Universities and National Socialism* (Cambridge: Harvard University Press, 1937), 87, 100; Pauck and Pauck, *Paul Tillich*, 130–31.

132. Henry Sloane Coffin, *A Half Century of Union Theological Seminary, 1896–1945* (New York: Charles Scribner's Sons, 1954), 134–35.

133. Paul Tillich to the German Ministry for Science, Art, and Education, 20 Jan. 1934, reprinted in Pauck and Pauck, *Paul Tillich*, 148–50.

134. Paul Tillich, "Basic Principles of Religious Socialism" (1922), in *Political Expectation*, 58–88; Paul Tillich, "Open Letter to Emanuel Hirsch," 1 Oct. 1934, reprinted in *The Thought of Paul Tillich*, ed. James Luther Adams, Wilhelm Pauck, and Roger L. Shinn (New York: Harper & Row, 1985), 353–88, quotes, 363, 366; see Emanuel Hirsch, *Die gegenwärtige geistige Lage im Spiegel philosophischer und theologischer Besinnung: Akademische Vorlesungen zum Verständnis des deutschen Jahr 1933* (Göttingen: Vandenhoeck & Ruprecht, 1934).

135. Tillich, *The Interpretation of History*, 3–22, quote, 3.

136. Ibid., quotes, 17, 18, 26, 29.

137. Ibid., 31–35; see Martin Kähler, *Die Wissenschaft der christlichen Lehre* (Leipzig: A. Beichert, 1893); Kähler, *The So-Called Historical Jesus and the Historic, Biblical Christ*, trans. Carl E. Braaten (Philadelphia: Fortress Press, 1988); Kähler, *Dogmatische Zeitfragen: Angewandte Dogmen* (Leipzig: A. Deichert, 1908).

138. Tillich, *The Interpretation of History*, quote, 35; Hannah Tillich, *From Time to Time*, 115; Pauck and Pauck, *Paul Tillich*, 94–98.

139. Martin Heidegger, *Being and Time*, trans. John Macquarrie and Edward Robinson (New York: Harper & Row, 1962); see Heidegger, *The Basic Problems of Phenomenology*, trans. Albert Hofstadter (Bloomington, Ind.: Indiana University Press, 1988).

140. Tillich, *The Interpretation of History*, 39–40, quotes, 40; Tillich, *The Protestant Era*, 93–104, "boundary line" quote, 93; Tillich, *Theology of Culture*, 10–29, 112–26.

141. Tillich, *The Interpretation of History*, quotes, 41, 50, 54, 56.

142. Ibid., quotes, 60, 64; Paul Tillich, *Protestantisches Prinzip und proletarische Situation* (Bonn: Friedrich Cohen, 1931); Tillich, *The Protestant Era*, 237–59.

143. Tillich, *The Interpretation of History*, quotes, 67, 71, 72.

144. Ibid., quotes, 72, 73; Tillich, *On the Boundary: An Autobiographical Sketch*.

145. See Paul Tillich, "The Church and Communism," *Religion in Life* 6 (summer 1937): 347–57; Tillich, "Protestantism in the Present World-Situation," *American Journal of Sociology* 42 (Sept. 1937): 236–48; Tillich, "The Gospel and the State," *Crozer Quarterly* 15 (Oct. 1938): 251–61; Tillich, "The Meaning of Anti-Semitism," *Radical Religion* 4 (winter 1938): 34–36; Tillich, "The Conception of Man in Existential Philosophy," *Journal of Religion* 14 (July 1939): 201–15; Tillich, "The Religious Symbol," *Journal of Liberal Religion* 2 (summer 1940): 13–33.

146. Samuel McCrea Cavert, "The Younger Theologians," *Religion in Life* 4 (autumn 1936): 520–31; Randall, "The Philosophical Legacy of Paul Tillich," 21–51, Moore quote, 23; Coffin, *A Half Century of Union Theological Seminary, 1896–1945,* 135; see Pauck and Pauck, *Paul Tillich,* 183–88.

147. Paul Tillich, *Against the Third Reich: Paul Tillich's Wartime Radio Broadcasts into Nazi Germany,* ed. Ronald H. Stone and Matthew Lon Weaver, trans. Matthew Lon Weaver (Louisville, Ky.: Westminster John Knox Press, 1998), "The Question of the Jewish People," 31 Mar. 1942, quotes, 14, 16; "Dark Clouds Are Gathering," Dec. 1942, quotes, 89.

148. Ibid., "Where Hope Lies This Advent Season," 8 Dec. 1942, quote, 93; "The Fourth War Christmas," 15 Dec. 1942, quote, 98; "The Tenth Anniversary of Hitler's Regime," Feb. 1943, quote, 118; "The Germanic Legacy," 2 Mar. 1943, quote, 122; "Germany's Rebirth into the Human Race," 23 Mar. 1943, quotes, 134.

149. Pauck and Pauck, *Paul Tillich,* 201–19, "harvest time" quote, 219; Paul Tillich, *The Shaking of the Foundations* (New York: Charles Scribner's Sons, 1948).

150. Tillich, *The Protestant Era,* xxiv; Pauck and Pauck, *Paul Tillich,* 220–21, 235–37; Coffin, *A Half Century of Union Theological Seminary, 1896–1945,* 138. Adams's assiduous attempt to clarify Tillich's meanings convinced Tillich in the late 1930s that Adams understood his thought more thoroughly than he himself did. See James Luther Adams, *Paul Tillich's Philosophy of Culture, Science, and Religion* (New York: Harper & Row, 1965); Adams, "Tillich's Concept of the Protestant Era," in *The Protestant Era* (American edition, Chicago: University of Chicago Press, 1948), 273–316; Pauck and Pauck, *Paul Tillich,* 220–21.

151. See Paul Tillich, "Beyond Religious Socialism," *Christian Century* 66 (15 June 1949): 732–33; Seward Hiltner, "Tillich the Person," *Theology Today* 30 (1974): 383; Hiltner, "Pastoral Psychology—After Paul Tillich," *Pastoral Psychology* 19 (Feb. 1968): 5–6; Wayne E. Oates, "The Contribution of Paul Tillich to Pastoral Psychology," *Pastoral Psychology* 19 (Feb. 1968): 11–16; Don Browning, "Analogy, Symbol, and Pastoral Theology in Tillich's Thought," *Pastoral Psychology* 19 (Feb. 1968): 41–54; William R. Rogers, "Tillich and Depth Psychology," *The Thought of Paul Tillich,* 102–18; Peter Homans, "Toward a Psychology of Religion: By Way of Freud and Tillich," in *The Dialogue between Theology and Psychology,* ed. Peter Homans (Chicago: University of Chicago Press, 1968), 53–81; Earl A. Loomis, "The Psychiatric Legacy of Paul Tillich," in *The Intellectual Legacy of Paul Tillich,* 79–98.

152. Paul Tillich, *The Courage to Be* (New Haven: Yale University Press, 1952), 1–9, 32–70.

153. Ibid., quotes, 71, 77; see Ann Belford Ulanov, "The Anxiety of Being," *The Thought of Paul Tillich,* 119–36.

154. Tillich, *The Courage to Be,* 148–50, 139–40, 171–72, quote, 172.

155. Paul Tillich, *The Shaking of the Foundations* (New York: Charles Scribner's Sons, 1948), 153–63; Tillich, *The Courage to Be,* quotes, 172, 173.

156. Tillich, *The Courage to Be,* quotes, 184, 185.

157. Ibid., 186–90, quote, 190.

158. Pauck and Pauck, *Paul Tillich,* 235–36.

159. Paul Tillich, *Systematic Theology* (Chicago: University of Chicago Press, 1951), 1:8–13, 62, quotes, 10, 12.

160. Ibid., 1:14–15, quotes, 14.

161. Ibid., 1:16, 17–18, quote, 16.

162. Ibid., 1:40–46, quote, 46.

163. Paul Tillich, "Das religiöse symbol," *Blätter für deutsche Philosophie* 1 (1928); revised version, Tillich, "The Religious Symbol," *Journal of Liberal Religion* 2 (1940): 13–33; further revised version, Tillich, "The Religious Symbol," *Symbolism in Religion and Lit-*

erature, ed. Rollo May (New York: George Braziller, 1960), 75–98; Tillich, *Theology of Culture*, 36–38; this section adapts material from Dorrien, *The Word as True Myth*, 118–122.

164. Tillich, "The Religious Symbol," *Symbolism in Religion and Literature*, 87–89, quote, 89.

165. Paul Tillich, *Dynamics of Faith* (New York: Harper & Brothers, 1957), 48–54, quote, 50; Tillich, *Systematic Theology* (Chicago: University of Chicago Press, 1957), 2:152; Tillich, *Biblical Religion and the Search for Ultimate Reality* (Chicago: University of Chicago Press, 1955), 78–85.

166. Paul Tillich, "The Meaning and Justification of Religious Symbols," in *Religious Experience and Truth*, ed. Sidney Hook (New York: New York University Press, 1961), 4, 10; Tillich, "The Religious Symbol," quote, 91; Tillich, *Theology of Culture*, 53–67; Tillich, *Dynamics of Faith*, 53–54; Tillich, *Systematic Theology*, 2:152.

167. Tillich, *Systematic Theology*, 1:238–40; Tillich, *Systematic Theology*, 2:9.

168. Tillich, *Systematic Theology*, 1:252–70.

169. Daniel Day Williams, "High Peak of Theology," review of *Systematic Theology*, vol. 1, by Paul Tillich, *Christian Century* (1 Aug. 1951), 893; H. Richard Niebuhr, review of *Systematic Theology*, vol. 1, by Paul Tillich, *Journal of Religion* 46 (1966): 203, 205; Theodore M. Greene, "Paul Tillich and Our Secular Culture," *The Theology of Paul Tillich*, 50–66, quote, 50; T. S. Eliot to Paul Tillich, 22 Mar. 1954, cited in Pauck and Pauck, *Paul Tillich*, 237; Reinhold Niebuhr, "Biblical Thought and Ontological Speculation in Tillich's Theology," in *The Theology of Paul Tillich*, 216–27, quote, 217.

170. The festschrift was *The Theology of Paul Tillich*; see Paul Tillich, *Love, Power, and Justice: Ontological Analyses and Ethical Applications* (London: Oxford University Press, 1954); Tillich, *The New Being*.

171. Tillich, *Biblical Religion and the Search for Ultimate Reality*, quote, 83.

172. Tillich, *Dynamics of Faith*, quote, 126.

173. See Albert T. Mollegen, "Christology and Biblical Criticism in Tillich," *The Theology of Paul Tillich*, 230–45; Langdon Gilkey, "The New Being and Christology," in *The Thought of Paul Tillich*, 307–29; Gilkey, *Gilkey on Tillich* (New York: Crossroad, 1990); Pauck and Pauck, *Paul Tillich*, 240–42.

174. Tillich, *Systematic Theology*, 2:29–39, quotes, 29, 36.

175. Ibid., 2:44–75, quote, 60.

176. Tillich, *The Interpretation of History*, 77–122; Tillich, *Systematic Theology*, 2:62–96; Tillich, *The New Being*, 15–24, quote, 24.

177. Tillich, *Systematic Theology*, 2:113, 114; see Tillich, *The Interpretation of History*, 33–34.

178. Tillich, *Systematic Theology*, 2:114, 115.

179. Ibid., 2:120–145.

180. Ibid., 2:153–58, quotes, 157.

181. James C. Livingston, "Tillich's Christology and Historical Research," in Nels F. S. Ferré, Charles Hartshorne, John Dillenberger, James C. Livingston, and Joseph Haroutunian, *Paul Tillich: Retrospect and Future* (Nashville: Abingdon Press, 1966), 42–50, quote, 50; David H. Kelsey, *The Fabric of Paul Tillich's Theology* (New Haven, Conn.: Yale University Press, 1967), 89–126, quote, 101; for a similar critique, see D. Moody Smith, "The Historical Jesus in Paul Tillich's Christology," *Journal of Religion* 46 (Jan. 1966): 131–48.

182. Tillich, *Systematic Theology* 2:3; see Kenneth Hamilton, *The System and the Gospel: A Critique of Paul Tillich* (London: SCM Press, Ltd., 1964).

183. Nels F. S. Ferré, "Tillich and the Nature of Transcendence," in *Paul Tillich: Retrospect and Future*, 7–18, quotes, 8, 16; see Ferré, "Tillich's View of the Church," in *The Theology of Paul Tillich*, 248–65.

184. Ferré, "Tillich and the Nature of Transcendence," 18, 9.

185. "To Be or Not to Be," 46–52, quote, 46; Pauck and Pauck, *Paul Tillich*, "big enough" and "in ten years," 249.

186. Paul Tillich to Marion Hausner, undated, cited in Pauck and Pauck, *Paul Tillich*, 258.

187. Paul Tillich, "On the Boundary Line," *Christian Century* 77 (7 Dec. 1960), 1435–37; Pauck and Pauck, *Paul Tillich*, 258–61. Tillich noted that the friend who posed the question to him was someone "in whose political judgment I have an almost unlimited con-

fidence." This was probably Wilhelm Pauck, since Pauck was Tillich's lodestar on political matters.

188. Paul Tillich, *Systematic Theology* (Chicago: University of Chicago Press, 1963), quotes, 3:v, 6.

189. Paul Tillich, *Christianity and the Encounter of World Religions* (New York: Columbia University Press, 1963; reprint, Minneapolis: Fortress Press, 1994), 39–47.

190. Tillich, "On the Boundary Line," 1435–36.

191. Tillich, *Christianity and the Encounter of World Religions*, quote, 26.

192. Ibid., 23–32; see Ernst Troeltsch, *Die Absolutheit der Christentums und die Religionsgeschichte* (1902; reprint, Tübingen: J. C. B. Mohr [Paul Siebeck], 1912); Troeltsch, *Religion in History*, trans. James Luther Adams and Walter F. Bense (Minneapolis: Fortress Press, 1991).

193. Tillich, *Theology of Culture*, 3–9; Tillich, *Christianity and the Encounter of World Religions*, quote, 61–62.

194. Paul Tillich, "The Significance of the History of Religions for the Systematic Theologian," in *The Future of Religions*, ed. Jerald C. Brauer (New York: Harper & Row, 1966), 86–87, quote, 87; see Tillich, *The Protestant Era*, 238–40; Tillich, *Christianity and the Encounter of World Religions*, 20.

195. Tillich, "The Significance of the History of Religions for the Systematic Theologian," 80–94, quotes, 88, 94.

196. Mircea Eliade, "Paul Tillich and the History of Religions," in *The Future of Religions*, 31–36, quotes, 35.

197. Mehta, *The New Theologian*, Brauer quote, 43.

198. Ibid., Tillich quotes, 50, 51.

199. Jerald C. Brauer, "Paul Tillich's Impact on America," in *The Future of Religions*, 15–22, quote, 15.

200. Pauck and Pauck, *Paul Tillich*, "strangely inflexible," 275; Mehta, *The New Theologian*, 45–47, "so many pressures," 45; Paul Tillich, "The Ambiguity of Perfection," *Time* (17 May 1963), 69, cited in Pauck and Pauck, *Paul Tillich*, 273–74.

201. Hannah Tillich, *From Time to Time*, 169–243, quote, 241; see Pauck and Pauck, *Paul Tillich*, 165–66; Mehta, *The New Theologian*, 45.

202. Rollo May, *Paulus: Reminiscences of a Friendship* (New York: Harper & Row, 1973), 49–66, quote, 65; Fox, *Reinhold Niebuhr*, 257.

203. Reinhold Niebuhr, "Biblical Thought and Ontological Speculation in Tillich's Theology," *The Theology of Paul Tillich*, 217; Tillich, "Reply to Interpretation and Criticism," 338, 343.

204. Reinhold Niebuhr, "Editorial Notes," *Christianity and Crisis* (6 Feb. 1956), 2–3; Paul Tillich, letter to the editor, *Christianity and Crisis* (5 Mar. 1956), 24; Mehta, *The New Theologian*, "this Platonic side," 39; Fox, *Reinhold Niebuhr*, 257–59, closing quote, 257.

205. Mehta, *The New Theologian*, quotes, 39, 40; see Paul Tillich, *Morality and Beyond*, ed. Ruth Nanda Anshen (New York: Harper & Row, 1963).

206. Roger L. Shinn, "Paul Tillich as a Contemporary Theologian," in *The Intellectual Legacy of Paul Tillich*, 73; Tillich, *The Protestant Era*, xxii.

207. Tillich, "Beyond Religious Socialism," quote, 733; see Tillich, "The Significance of the History of Religions for the Systematic Theologian," 93.

208. Paul Tillich to Thomas Mann, 23 May 1943, reprinted in *The Intellectual Legacy of Paul Tillich*, 101–7, quote, 106.

209. Tillich's dictum about Schleiermacher, Schelling, and Boehme was apparently first expressed to Nels F. S. Ferré, Walter Muelder, and others at a gathering in Ferré's home; see Ferré, "Tillich and the Nature of Transcendence," 11; for a late example of his dialogical spirit, see *Ultimate Concern: Tillich in Dialogue*, ed. D. Mackenzie Brown (New York: Harper & Row, 1965).

210. See *Religion and Culture: Essays in Honor of Paul Tillich*, ed. Walter Leibrecht (New York: Harper & Brothers, 1959); Gilkey, *Gilkey on Tillich*; Robert P. Scharlemann, *Reflection and Doubt in the Theology of Paul Tillich* (New Haven, Conn.: Yale University Press, 1969); Wayne W. Mahan, *Tillich's System* (San Antonio, Tex.: Trinity University Press, 1974; Alexander J. McKelway, *The Systematic Theology of Paul Tillich: A Review and Analysis* (Richmond, Va.: John Knox Press, 1964); Adrian Thatcher, *The Ontology of*

Paul Tillich (Oxford: Oxford University Press, 1978); John R. Stumme, *Socialism in Theological Perspective: A Study of Paul Tillich, 1918–1933* (Missoula, Mont.: Scholars Press, 1978).

211. Langdon Gilkey, "Dissolution and Reconstruction in Theology," *Christian Century* 82 (5 Feb. 1965): 135.

212. See Langdon Gilkey, "Neo-Orthodoxy," in *A Handbook of Christian Theology: Definition Essays on Concepts and Movements of Thought in Contemporary Protestantism*, ed. Marvin Halverson and Arthur A. Cohen (Cleveland: World Publishing Co., 1958), 259; Gilkey, *How the Church Can Minister to the World without Losing Itself* (New York: Harper & Row, 1964), 105; Gilkey, *Maker of Heaven and Earth: A Study of the Christian Doctrine of Creation* (Garden City, N.Y.: Doubleday & Co., 1959); Gilkey, "Cosmology, Ontology, and the Travail of Biblical Language," *Journal of Religion* 41 (July 1961): 196–202.

Chapter 8. Modern Gospels

1. H. Richard Niebuhr, *The Kingdom of God in America* (New York: Harper & Brothers, 1937), 193; see H. Richard Niebuhr, *Christ and Culture* (New York: Harper & Brothers, 1951), 108–15.

2. Shailer Mathews to Simon P. Cole, Sept. 1900, University of Chicago Library, Department of Special Collections, Divinity School Correspondence, Office of the Dean's Records, 1890–1942, Box 6, Folder 2.

3. Newman Smyth, *Passing Protestantism and Coming Catholicism* (New York: Charles Scribner's Sons, 1908), 40–131; Charles C. Briggs, *Church Unity: Studies of Its Most Important Problems* (New York: Charles Scribner's Sons, 1909); George Tyrell, *Tradition and the Critical Spirit: Catholic Modernist Writings*, ed. James C. Livingston (Minneapolis: Fortress Press, 1991); Alfred F. Loisy, *The Gospel and the Church*, trans. Christopher Hume (New York: Charles Scribner's Sons, 1903); Loisy, *The Birth of the Christian Religion and The Origins of the New Testament*, single-volume edition, trans. L. P. Jacks (New Hyde Park, N.Y.: University Books, 1962); Maurice Blondel, *The Letter on Apologetics and History and Dogma*, trans. Alexander Dru and Illtyd Trethowan (New York: Rinehart and Winston, 1964).

4. Pope Pius X, *Lamentabili Sane*, 3 July 1907; Pius X, *Pascendi Dominici Gregis*, 8 Sept. 1907, *The Papal Encyclicals*, ed. Anne Freemantle (New York: New American Library, 1963), 202–7, 197–201; John A. Zahm, *Evolution and Dogma* (reprint, New York: Arno Press, 1978); William L. Sullivan, *Letters to His Holiness Pope Pius X* (Chicago: Open Court Publishing Co., 1910).

5. James F. Driscoll, S.S., "Recent Views on Biblical Inspiration," 1, *New York Review* 1 (June–July 1905): 48; Wilfrid Ward, "The Spirit of Newman's Apologetics," *New York Review* 1 (June–July 1905): 4–11; James J. Fox, D.D., "Scotus Redivivus," *New York Review* 1 (June–July 1905): 30–46; Francis E. Gigot, D.D., "The Higher Criticism of the Bible: Its Constructive Aspect," *New York Review* 2 (Nov.–Dec. 1906), 302–5; Gigot, "The Higher Criticism of the Bible: Its Relation to Tradition," *New York Review* 2 (Jan.–Feb. 1907): 442–44; R. Scott Appleby, *"Church and Age Unite!": The Modernist Impulse in American Catholicism* (Notre Dame, Ind.: University of Notre Dame Press, 1992), 117–67.

6. Appleby, *"Church and Age Unite!"* 163–67; John A. Ryan, *Distributive Justice: The Right and Wrong of Our Present Diistribution of Wealth* (New York: Macmillan, 1916); see Robert D. Cross, *The Emergence of Liberal Catholicism in America* (Cambridge: Harvard University Press, 1958); Gabriel Daly, *Transcendence and Immanence: A Study in Catholic Modernism and Integralism* (Oxford: Clarendon Press, 1980).

7. Walter Rauschenbusch, *Christianity and the Social Crisis* (New York: Macmillan Co., 1907), 177–86; Charles Clayton Morrison, *Can Protestantism Win America?* (New York: Harper & Brothers, 1948), quote, 1.

8. Morrison, *Can Protestantism Win America?*, quotes, 87, 93.

9. Ibid., 87.

10. William Adams Brown, *A Teacher and His Times: A Story of Two Worlds* (New York: Charles Scribner's Sons, 1940), 220–24, 232–40, 266–68, 360–62; Georgia Harkness,

The Faith by Which the Church Lives (New York: Abingdon Press, 1940), 124; Harry Emerson Fosdick, "The Future of the Church," address at Harvard University, 12 Dec. 1926, quoted in "Throngs at Harvard Stirred by Fosdick," *New York Times* (13 Dec. 1926).

11. Vida D. Scudder, "The Anglo-Catholic Movement in the Next Century: Its Social Outlook," *Living Church* 90 (17 Nov. 1934): 589–91; W. Norman Pittenger, "Changing Emphases in American Theology," *Religion in Life* 12 (summer 1943): 418–19.

12. John C. Bennett, *Christians and the State* (New York: Charles Scribner's Sons, 1958), 240–49; see editorial, "New Opportunity for Education," *Christianity and Crisis* 25 (8 Mar. 1965): 31; Bernard Häring, C.Ss.R., "Deossification of Theological Obstacles in View of Ecumenism," *Theology and Church in Times of Change: Essays in Honor of John Coleman Bennett*, ed. Edward LeRoy Long Jr. and Robert T. Handy (Philadelphia: Westminster Press, 1970), 35–69; Robert W. Lynn, "The Eclipse of a Public: Protestant Reflections on Religion and Public Education, 1940–1968," in *Theology and Church in Times of Change*, 193–211.

13. John C. Bennett, *The Radical Imperative: From Theology to Social Ethics* (Philadelphia: Westminster Press, 1975), quote, 91; Patrick R. Granfield, O.S.B., "An Interview with Reinhold Niebuhr," *Commonweal* (16 Dec. 1966), reprinted in Granfield, *Theologians at Work* (New York: Macmillan, 1967), 51–68, quote, 55.

14. Daniel Day Williams, *God's Grace and Man's Hope* (New York: Harper & Brothers, 1949), 22.

15. Lloyd J. Averill, *American Theology in the Liberal Tradition* (Philadelphia: Westminster Press, 1967), 22–26.

16. *The Wesleyan Heritage: Essays of Albert C. Outler*, ed. Thomas C. Oden and Leicester R. Longden (Grand Rapids: Zondervan Publishing House, 1991), 22–37, 160–73.

17. Albert C. Knudson, "Henry Clay Sheldon—Theologian," *Methodist Review* 108 (Mar. 1925): 175–92. Foster's dogmatics were completed in 1899.

18. See Kenneth Cauthen, *The Impact of American Religious Liberalism* (New York: Harper & Row, 1962); Averill, *American Theology in the Liberal Tradition*, 100–106.

19. See William R. Hutchison, *The Modernist Impulse in American Protestantism* (Durham, N.C.: Duke University Press, 1992), 7–9; Francis Schüssler Fiorenza, "Theological Liberalism: An Unfinished Challenge," *Harvard Divinity Bulletin* 28 (1998): 9–12.

20. Douglas C. Macintosh, *The Reasonableness of Christianity* (New York: Charles Scribner's Sons, 1928), 135–36.

21. For an extensive analysis of this subject, see Gary Dorrien, *The Word as True Myth: Interpreting Modern Theology* (Louisville, Ky.: Westminster John Knox Press, 1997).

22. See John B. Cobb Jr., "Christianity and Myth," *Journal of Bible and Religion* 33 (Oct. 1965): 316–17; Schubert M. Ogden, *The Reality of God and Other Essays* (New York: Harper & Row, 1966), 104–17; Langdon Gilkey, *Naming the Whirlwind: The Renewal of God-Language* (Indianapolis: Bobbs-Merrill Co., 1965); Bernard E. Meland, *Faith and Culture* (New York: Oxford University Press, 1953); F. W. Dillistone, *The Power of Symbols in Culture and Religion* (New York: Crossroad, 1986); David Tracy, *Blessed Rage for Order: The New Pluralism in Theology* (New York: Crossroad, 1975); Sallie McFague, *Models of God: Theology for an Ecological, Nuclear Age* (Philadelphia: Fortress Press, 1987).

23. Reinhold Niebuhr, *Moral Man and Immoral Society: A Study in Ethics and Politics* (New York: Charles Scribner's Sons, 1932), quotes, 34, 44.

24. Walter Rauschenbusch, *A Theology for the Social Gospel* (New York: Macmillan Co., 1917), 31–94; Rauschenbusch, *Christianity and the Social Crisis* (New York: Macmillan Co., 1907), quotes, 400–401.

25. Rauschenbusch, *Christianity and the Social Crisis*, 420–21; this section adapts material from Gary Dorrien, *Soul in Society: The Making and Renewal of Social Christianity* (Minneapolis: Fortress Press, 1995), 148–50.

26. Sigmund Freud, *Civilization and Its Discontents*, trans. James Strachey (1930; reprint, New York: W. W. Norton, 1961), 102–3; Reinhold Niebuhr, *An Interpretation of Christian Ethics* (New York: Charles Scribner's Sons, 1935), 59.

27. Niebuhr, *An Interpretation of Christian Ethics*, 59–60.

28. Ibid., 60.

29. Reinhold Niebuhr, "Intellectual Autobiography of Reinhold Niebuhr," in *Reinhold Niebuhr: His Religious, Social, and Political Thought,* ed. Charles W. Kegley and Robert W. Bretall (New York: Macmillan Co., 1956), quote, 13.

30. Richard Wightman Fox, "Niebuhr's World and Ours," in *Reinhold Niebuhr Today,* ed. Richard John Neuhaus (Grand Rapids: Wm. B. Eerdmans Co., 1989), quote, 8.

31. Henry Sloane Coffin, "Can Liberalism Survive?" *Religion in Life* 4 (spring 1935): 194–203, quotes, 199.

32. Ibid., 203; see Gaius Glenn Atkins, "Whither Liberalism?" *Religion in Life* 3 (summer 1934): 330–41.

33. Harry Emerson Fosdick, commencement speech, Rochester University, 15 June 1925, quoted in "Self Expression Cult Denounced by Dr. Fosdick," *New York Herald Tribune* (16 June 1925).

34. Justin Wroe Nixon, *The Moral Crisis of Christianity* (New York: Harper & Brothers, 1931), 20–21, 26, 189–90.

35. John D. Rockefeller Jr. to Harry Emerson Fosdick, 19 Dec. 1927, Harry Emerson Fosdick Collection, Series 2A, Box 8; see Rockefeller to Fosdick, 23 Nov. 1923; Rockefeller to Fosdick, 2 Feb. 1927; Fosdick to Rockefeller, 18 Feb. 1927; Fosdick Collection, Series 2A, Box 8.

36. Harry Emerson Fosdick to John D. Rockefeller Jr., 22 Dec. 1927, Harry Emerson Fosdick Collection, Series 2A, Box 8; see Albert C. Knudson, *The Principles of Christian Ethics* (New York: Abingdon-Cokesbury Press, 1943), 262–80; Walter G. Muelder, *Religion and Economic Responsibility* (New York: Charles Scribner's Sons, 1953).

37. Harry Emerson Fosdick to John D. Rockefeller Jr., 28 Sept. 1944, Harry Emerson Fosdick Collection, Series 2A, Box 8.

38. Ibid.

39. Bernard E. Meland, *Faith and Culture* (New York: Oxford University Press, 1953), "reconstructed liberalism," v; Meland, "The Root and Form of Wieman's Thought," in *The Empirical Theology of Henry Nelson Wieman,* ed. Robert W. Bretall (New York: Macmillan Co., 1963), 44–68, "internal track," 67; Meland, "Introduction: The Empirical Tradition in Theology at Chicago," in *The Future of Empirical Theology,* ed. Bernard E. Meland (Chicago: University of Chicago, 1969), 1–62, "enduring mythos," 49; see Meland, *Seeds of Redemption* (New York: Macmillan Co., 1947); Bernard M. Loomer, "Neo-Naturalism and Neo-Orthodoxy," *Journal of Religion* 28 (1948): 79–91; Loomer, "Christian Faith and Process Philosophy," *Journal of Religion* 29 (1949): 181–203.

40. Author's interview with Duncan Littlefair, 8 Aug. 2001; Wieman, "The Confessions of a Religious Seeker," 118; see Duncan Littlefair, "Logical Analysis of Concepts in Selected Systems of Theology," Ph.D. diss., University of Chicago Divinity School, June 1940. Littlefair pastored the Fountain Street Church in Grand Rapids, Michigan, for many years.

41. Gerald Birney Smith, "Science and Religion," review of *Landmarks in the Struggle between Science and Religion,* by James Y. Simpson, and *Religious Experience and Scientific Method,* by Henry Nelson Wieman, *Journal of Religion* 6 (Nov. 1926): 637–40, quote, 640; Bernard M. Loomer, "The Size of God," in *The Size of God: The Theology of Bernard Loomer in Context,* ed. William Dean and Larry E. Axel (Macon, Ga.: Mercer University Press, 1987), 43–51.

42. See Peter A. Bertocci, *Religion as Creative Insecurity* (New York: Association Press, 1958); L. Harold DeWolf, *The Religious Revolt against Reason* (New York: Harper & Brothers, 1949); S. Paul Schilling, *God in an Age of Atheism* (New York: Abingdon Press, 1969); Walter Muelder, *Foundations of the Responsible Society* (New York: Abingdon Press, 1959).

43. Henry P. Van Dusen, *The Vindication of Liberal Theology: A Tract for the Times* (New York: Charles Scribner's Sons, 1963), 41; see Arthur C. McGiffert, "The Future of Liberal Christianity in America," *Journal of Religion* 15 (Apr. 1935): 161–75.

44. Van Dusen, *The Vindication of Liberal Theology,* quote, 45; see Henry P. Van Dusen, *Spirit, Son, and Father: Christian Faith in the Light of the Holy Spirit* (New York: Charles Scribner's Sons, 1958), 106–15.

45. Van Dusen, *The Vindication of Liberal Theology,* 93–148, quotes, 115, 148; for an earlier version of this discussion, see Henry Pitney Van Dusen, "The Significance of Jesus Christ," *Liberal Theology: An Appraisal,* ed. David E. Roberts and Henry Pitney Van Dusen (New York: Charles Scribner's Sons, 1942), 205–22.

46. Henry P. Van Dusen, "A Half-Century of Liberal Theology," *Religion in Life* 5 (summer 1936): 336–53, quote, 346; see Henry Sloane Coffin, "The Scriptures," in *Liberal Theology: An Appraisal,* 223–37; Coffin, "Can Liberalism Survive?" 202–3.

47. Shailer Mathews, *New Faith for Old: An Autobiography* (New York: Macmillan Co., 1936), 219, 298.

48. Van Dusen, "A Half-Century of Liberal Theology," quote, 349; John C. Bennett, "The Social Interpretation of Christianity," in *The Church through Half a Century: Essays in Honor of William Adams Brown,* ed. Samuel Cavert and Henry P. Van Dusen (New York: Charles Scribner's Sons, 1936), 113.

49. Robert L. Calhoun, "A Symposium on Reinhold Niebuhr's *The Nature and Destiny of Man,*" *Christendom* 6 (autumn 1941): 573–76; Calhoun, review of *The Nature and Destiny of Man,* vol. 1, by Reinhold Niebuhr, *Journal of Religion* 21 (Oct. 1941): 473–80; see Henry P. Van Dusen, introduction to *The Christian Answer,* ed. Henry P. Van Dusen (New York: Charles Scribner's Sons), 1946, vii–xi; Samuel McCrea Cavert, "The Younger Theologians," *Religion in Life* 4 (autumn 1936): 520–31.

50. Calhoun, review of *The Nature and Destiny of Man,* vol. 1, by Reinhold Niebuhr, quotes, 475, 476, 477.

51. Robert L. Calhoun to Reinhold Niebuhr, 1 Nov. 1941, Reinhold Niebuhr Papers, Library of Congress; cited in Richard Wightman Fox, *Reinhold Niebuhr: A Biography* (Ithaca, N.Y.: Cornell University Press, 1996), 204; see Robert L. Calhoun, "A Liberal Bandaged but Unbowed," *Christian Century* (31 May 1939), 701–4.

52. Robert L. Calhoun, review of *The Nature and Destiny of Man,* vol. 2, by Reinhold Niebuhr, *Journal of Religion* 24 (Jan. 1944): 59–64, quotes, 59, 61; John C. Bennett, review of *The Nature and Destiny of Man,* vol. 2, *Union Review* 4 (Mar. 1943): 24–26; Reinhold Niebuhr to John C. Bennett, 13 Mar. 1943, Reinhold Niebuhr Papers; cited in Fox, *Reinhold Niebuhr,* 214.

53. Harry Emerson Fosdick, *Successful Christian Living: Sermons on Christianity Today* (New York: Harper & Brothers, 1937), 153–64; Van Dusen, "A Half-Century of Liberal Theology," 349.

54. See Bernard E. Meland, *The Reawakening of Christian Faith* (New York: Macmillan Co., 1949); Meland, *Modern Man's Worship* (New York: Harper & Brothers, 1934); Peter A. Bertocci, *The Human Venture in Sex, Love, and Marriage* (New York: Association Press, 1950); Bertocci, *Sex, Love, and the Person* (New York: Sheed & Ward, 1967); L. Harold DeWolf, *A Theology of the Living Church* (New York: Harper & Brothers, 1953).

55. Gerald Birney Smith, *Current Christian Thinking* (Chicago: University of Chicago Press, 1928), quote, 85; Langdon Gilkey to author, 27 May 2002..

56. Van Dusen, "A Half-Century of Liberal Theology," 351–52; see Van Dusen, *The Vindication of Liberal Theology,* 21–48; Henry P. Van Dusen, "The Sickness of Liberal Religion," *The World Tomorrow* (Aug. 1931).

57. Van Dusen, "A Half-Century of Liberal Theology," 351; see Friedrich von Hügel, *The Mystical Element of Religion* (London: J. M. Dent & Sons, 1923); Henry P. Van Dusen, *World Christianity: Yesterday, Today, and Tomorrow* (New York: Abingdon-Cokesbury Press, 1947); Van Dusen, "Christianity Today: An Eye-Witness Report," in *Christianity on the March,* ed. Henry P. Van Dusen (New York: Harper & Row, 1963), 67–104.

58. Niebuhr, *The Kingdom of God in America,* quotes, 195–96.

59. H. Richard Niebuhr, *The Meaning of Revelation* (New York: Macmillan, 1941), quotes, 93–94; see H. Richard Niebuhr, *Radical Monotheism and Western Culture, With Supplementary Essays* (New York: Harper Brothers, 1960; reprint, Louisville: Westminster John Knox Press, 1993); H. Richard Niebuhr, Wilhelm Pauck, and Francis P. Miller, *The Church against the World* (Chicago: Willett, Clark & Company, 1935), quote, 11; on American neo-orthodoxy, see Brevard S. Childs, *Biblical Theology in Crisis* (Philadelphia: Westminster Press, 1970); Gary Dorrien, *The Word as True Myth: Interpreting Modern Theology* (Louisville, Ky.: Westminster John Knox Press, 1997), 128–54.

60. Calhoun, "A Liberal Bandaged but Unbowed," 703.

61. Ibid., 702.

62. See *American Education and Religion,* ed. F. Ernest Johnson (New York: Institute for Religious and Social Studies, 1952); Morrison, *Can Protestantism Win America?* 87–89; Robert W. Lynn, "The Eclipse of a Public: Protestant Reflections on Religion and

Public Education, 1940–1968," *Theology and Church in Times of Change: Essays in Honor of John Coleman Bennett,* 198–200.

63. Howard Thurman, *Jesus and the Disinherited* (New York: Abingdon-Cokesbury Press, 1949; reprint, Boston: Beacon Press, 1996), 30–31.
64. Ibid., 39–40.
65. Howard Thurman, *With Head and Heart: The Autobiography of Howard Thurman* (New York: Harcourt Brace & Co., 1979), 3–34.
66. Ibid., quotes, 36, 51.
67. Ibid., quotes, 73, 74.
68. Ibid., 76.
69. Ibid., 77.
70. Ibid., quotes, 78–79, 81.
71. Ibid., 103–36, quote, 114.
72. Ibid., 116, 130–35, quote, 114.
73. Thurman, *Jesus and the Disinherited,* quotes, 29–30.
74. Ibid., quotes, 16, 100.
75. Ibid., 78.
76. Thurman, *With Head and Heart,* 155–56.
77. Thurman, *Jesus and the Disinherited,* 78–79.
78. Kenneth E. Kirk, *The Vision of God: The Christian Doctrine of the Summum Bonum* (New York: Longmans, Green, & Co., 1931), 451; Howard Thurman, *Deep Is the Hunger: Meditations for Apostles of Sensitiveness* (New York: Harper & Brothers, 1951), quotes, 44–45.
79. "With all of his heart" and "with renewed minds," Thurman, *Deep Is the Hunger,* 176, 177; "to focus the mind," Howard Thurman, *The Inward Journey* (New York: Harper & Brothers, 1961), 7; "the unifying principle" and succeeding quotes, Thurman, *Meditations of the Heart* (New York: Harper & Row, 1953), 120–21.
80. "The overflowing" and "it is the sheer joy," *A Strange Freedom: The Best of Howard Thurman on Religious Experience and Public Life,* ed. Walter Earl Fluker and Catherine Tumber (Boston: Beacon Press, 1998), 95; "he gave to me," Howard Thurman, *Mysticism and the Experience of Love* (Wallingford, Pa.: Pendle Hill Publications, 1961), 3.
81. Howard Thurman, *Footprints of a Dream: The Story of the Church for the Fellowship of All Peoples* (New York: Harper & Brothers, 1959), 144; Thurman, *Mysticism and the Experience of Love,* quote, 19.
82. Thurman, *Jesus and the Disinherited,* 108–9; see Howard Thurman, *The Search for Common Ground: An Inquiry into the Basis of Man's Experience of Community* (Richmond, Ind.: Friends United Press, 1986).

Index

17789612R00397

Made in the USA
Lexington, KY
29 September 2012